The Challenge of Democracy

Government in America

5th Edition

Kenneth Janda
Northwestern University

Jeffrey M. Berry
Tufts University

Jerry Goldman
Northwestern University

HOUGHTON MIFFLIN COMPANY
Boston   New York

Editor-in-Chief: Jean L. Woy
Senior Sponsoring Editor: Paul A. Smith
Senior Associate Editor: Melissa Mashburn
Senior Production/Design Coordinator: Carol Merrigan
Senior Manufacturing Coordinator: Priscilla Bailey
Marketing Associate: Amanda Rappaport

Cover Designer: Deborah Azerrad Savona
Cover photograph: Burton Pritzker
Preface photo: Ann Janda

Printed in the U.S.A.

Library of Congress Catalog Card Number: 96-76913

Student text ISBN: 0-395-83393-0
Examination text ISBN: 0-395-84386-3
 23456789-VH-00 99 98 97

TO: **Bessie Janda and in memory of John Janda**
Mae and Abe Berry
Esther Goldman and in memory of Louis Goldman

Brief Contents

Contents

Boxed Features

Features

Preface

As the United States approaches the end of the twentieth century, our thoughts naturally turn to the enormous changes that have taken place since we published the first edition of this textbook in 1987. In each edition that followed, we've chronicled these developments and tried to make sense of what is new and important in American politics.

Through the process of writing five editions, however, what we are most struck by is how enduring our original framework is. *The Challenge of Democracy* is built around two themes that remain as relevant today as they were when we first conceived of this project. The first is the clash among the values of freedom, order, and equality, while the second focuses on the tensions between pluralist and majoritarian visions of democracy. Knowledge of these conflicts enables citizens to recognize and analyze the difficult choices they face in politics.

Because we wanted to write a book that students would actually read, we sought to discuss politics—a complex subject—in a captivating and understandable way. American politics isn't dull, and its textbooks needn't be either. But equally important, we wanted to produce a book that students would credit for stimulating their thinking about politics. While offering all the essential information about American government and politics, we believed that what was most important was to give students a framework for analyzing politics that they could use long after their studies ended. Based on the reactions to our first four editions, we believe we succeeded in developing a lively book built on a framework that fulfills our goal of helping students analyze and interpret the political process in the United States.

Our framework travels well over time, and the past few years are no exception. After the Republicans' stunning victory in the 1994 congressional elections, they made a concerted effort to move the country toward majoritarian democracy. The party claimed that the voters gave them a mandate to proceed with their Contract with America. The Republican-led House of Representatives dominated the political news in the year after the election. The 1996 election was in large part a referendum on the Republicans' control of Congress and the two parties' differing views on the values of freedom, order, and equality.

Our framework also travels well over space—to other countries with a very different political heritage. At the time we devised our analytical themes, the Soviet Union (in Ronald Reagan's words) stood as the "evil empire." Now the U.S.S.R. stands no more, and the former communist countries in central and eastern Europe are engaged in the transition to democratic government and are dealing with alternative models of democracy. Little did we know that our book would become so widely used in teaching students in these countries about democratic politics. Houghton Mifflin has donated copies of earlier editions of our book to English-speaking faculty and students in Bulgaria, Croatia, the Czech Republic, Georgia, Hungary, Poland, Romania, Slovakia, and of course, Russia itself.

Moreover, the brief edition of our text has been translated into Hungarian and Georgian, and plans are under way for translation into Czech and other central and eastern European languages. We are pleased that *The Challenge of Democracy* will soon be available to many more students in these countries—students who are confronting the challenge of democracy in a time of political transition.

THEMATIC FRAMEWORK

As noted above, two themes run through our book. One deals with the conflict among values and the other with alternative models of democracy. In Chapter 1, we suggest that American politics often reflects conflicts between the values of freedom and order and between the values of freedom and equality. These value conflicts are prominent in contemporary American society, and they help to explain political controversy and consensus in earlier eras.

For instance, in Chapter 3 we argue that the Constitution was designed to promote order, and it virtually ignored issues of political and social equality. Equality was later served, however, by several amendments to the Constitution. In Chapter 15, "Order and Civil Liberties," and Chapter 16, "Equality and Civil Rights," we demonstrate that many of this nation's most controversial issues represent conflicts among individuals or groups who hold differing views on the values of freedom, order, and equality. Views on issues such as abortion are not just isolated opinions; they also reflect choices about the philosophy citizens want government to follow. Yet choosing among these values is difficult, sometimes excruciatingly so.

The second theme, introduced in Chapter 2, asks students to consider two competing models of democratic government. One way that government can make decisions is by means of **majoritarian** principles; that is, by taking the actions desired by a majority of citizens. For instance, in Chapter 20, "Global Policy," we discuss the impact of public opinion in making foreign policy. A contrasting model of government, **pluralism,** is built around the interaction of decision makers in government with groups concerned about issues that affect them. Pluralism is a focus of Chapter 17, "Policymaking," which discusses issue networks in the nation's capital.

These models are not mere abstractions; we use them to illustrate the dynamics of the American political system. In Chapter 12, "The Presidency," we discuss the problem of divided government. More often than not over the past forty years, the party that controlled the White House didn't control both houses of Congress. When these two branches of government are divided between the two parties, majoritarian government is difficult. As Bill Clinton found out during 1993 and 1994, even when the same party controls both branches, the majoritarian model is not always realized.

Throughout the book we stress that students must make their own choices among the competing values and models of government. Although the three of us hold diverse and strong opinions about which choices are best, we do not believe it is our role to tell students our own answers to the broad questions we pose. Instead, we want our readers to learn first hand that a democracy requires thoughtful choices. That is why we titled our book *The Challenge of Democracy.*

FEATURES OF THE FIFTH EDITION

The fifth edition maintains the basic structure of the previous edition while updating the political events of the past few years. We have also drawn on the latest research in political science to make sure that *The Challenge of Democracy* continues to represent the state of the art in our discipline.

To accommodate the major changes and new issues in politics that have occurred since the last edition, every chapter in the text has been thoroughly revised. One of the most significant changes we've made is in Chapter 1. Previous users of the book will notice that in our framework encompassing four different ideologies, we have replaced the term *populist* with *communitarian.* In contemporary usage, *populist* is used in many different ways and we worried that students might find it confusing that politicians of both the left and the right claim to be populists, while journalists, pundits, and social scientists all have their own definitions of what it means to be a populist. As explained in Chapter 1, *communitarian* more clearly evokes the political thinking underlying a preference for order and equality.

Chapter 6, "The Media," examines the landmark telecommunications deregulation law as well as the recent mega-mergers in the telecommunications industry that increasingly raise the issue of concentration of private ownership of media companies. In Chapter 9, "Nominations, Elections, and Campaigns" and Chapter 11, "Congress," the Contract with America is discussed in detail. We follow the Contract from the fall campaign of 1994 through the first one hundred days and then close our discussion by documenting the final outcome on all the Contract legislation (Table 11.1 and accompanying text). More broadly, throughout the book we focus on the Contract with America in the context of the majoritarian model of democracy. Full coverage of the 1996 presidential and congressional elections is offered in Chapters 9 and 11 and in Chapter 12, "The Presidency." In addition, Chapter 12 fully incorporates an analysis of the Clinton presidency. Chapter 18, "Economic Policymaking," reviews recent developments in the fight over balancing the federal budget, including passage of the line item veto and the defeat of the proposed balanced budget amendment to the Constitution. Chapter 19, "Domestic Policy," takes up the controversial welfare reform law. Will it really "end welfare as we know it"?

In this edition, we provide a new, close connection between the words in our text and external computer resources. The rich resources of the Internet are featured in several ways. Each chapter concludes with "World Wide Web Resources," a list of World Wide Web sites that includes the URL and a brief description of each site. Chapters also contain marginal notations at places in the text where a particular Internet resource will deepen students' understanding of text material. Moreover, there are marginal notations to the award-winning *IDEAlog* and *Crosstabs* computer programs that accompany the book as part of our teaching/learning package. The Fifth Edition will also herald *The Challenge of Democracy Web Site* <http://www.hmco.com/college/COD/home.html>, an important resource for faculty and student users of our text. Additionally, *The Challenge of Democracy, Fifth Edition,* is referenced in *PoliticsNow Classroom,* the premier educational Web site on the Internet for U.S. politics. (See below for more details regarding *The Challenge of Democracy Web Site* and *PoliticsNow Classroom.*) These advances keep *The Challenge of Democracy* at the leading edge of technology in studying American government.

As in previous editions, each chapter begins with a vignette. The purpose of each vignette is to draw students into the substance of that chapter, while suggesting one of the themes of the book. Chapters with new vignettes include: Chapter 4, "Federalism," where we look at Lousiana's minimum drinking age law; Chapter 7, "Participation and Voting," which begins with a vignette on the Viper Militia, asking students whether membership in a militia is a form of political participation; Chapter 8, "Political Parties," which opens with an account of the recent efforts of Ross Perot's Reform Party and considers the problems of a third party in a two-party system; Chapter 13, "The Bureaucracy," which uses the tragic story of the ValuJet crash as a means of introducing the subject of regulation, a primary focus of the chapter; and Chapter 15, "Order and Civil Liberties," which opens with the story of a University of Michigan student who put fictional accounts of his fantasies on the Internet and was expelled, arrested, and jailed. Was his freedom of speech abridged?

In the last edition we introduced a new series of features, "Politics in a Changing America," designed to illustrate changes over time in the political opportunity, participation, and status of groups such as women, African Americans, youth, Hispanics, and religious fundamentalists. These features allow us to highlight many controversial and complex issues in American society and we have continued them in this edition. Some of the original features have been kept and others updated. Many, however, are new to this edition, including features on Native-American gambling casinos, Hispanics in the electoral arena, assisted suicides, and same-sex marriages.

Through every edition of our book, we have believed that students can better evaluate how our political system works when they compare it with politics in other countries. Once again, each chapter has at least one boxed feature called "Compared with What?" that treats its topic in a comparative perspective. How much importance do citizens in other parts of the world place on freedom, order, and equality? Do American television reporters color the news with their commentary more than reporters do in other countries? How do crime rates differ around the world? What does health care spending buy in terms of life expectancy rates? Some of these features focus on a single country. Is Britain ready for a written constitution? What are interest groups like in Israel? Why did Indian political parties have such a difficult time forming a government after the most recent parliamentary elections?

Each chapter concludes with a brief summary, a list of key terms, a short list of recommended readings, and the World Wide Web Resources feature described above. At the end of the book, we have included the Declaration of Independence, the Articles of Confederation, an annotated copy of the Constitution, *Federalist* Nos. 10 and 51, a glossary of key terms, and some other valuable appendices.

THE TEACHING/LEARNING PACKAGE

When we began writing *The Challenge of Democracy*, we viewed the book as part of a tightly integrated set of instructional materials. We have worked closely with some very talented political scientists and with educational specialists at Houghton Mifflin to produce what we think is a superior set of ancillary materials to help both instructors and students.

For the Instructor: Innovative Teaching Tools

The *Instructor's Resource Manual*, written by the authors and carefully updated by Lori Brainard, provides teachers with material that relates directly to the thematic framework and organization of the book. The *Instructor's Resource Manual* includes learning objectives, chapter synopses, detailed lecture outlines (including a lecture format that encourages class participation), and ideas for class, small group, and individual projects and activities.

The *Test Item* bank, by Nicholas C. Strinkowski of Clark College, provides over 1,500 identification, multiple-choice, and essay questions.

Software ancillaries available to instructors include a *Computerized Test Bank* test generation program in Macintosh and IBM-compatible formats, containing all the items in the printed *Test Item* bank, and *Power Presentation Manager*, a tool to create customized classroom presentations.

A transparency package, containing thirty full-color overhead transparencies, is available to adopters of the book. Adopters may also receive the six videotapes from Houghton Mifflin's *Videotape Program in American Government*, written and produced by Ralph Baker and Joseph Losco of Ball State University, including a new 1996 campaign and election video. A corresponding video guide contains summaries and scripts of each tape, definitions of key terms, multiple-choice questions, and ideas for classroom activities.

A sixty-minute videodisc composed of archival footage on four topics—Campaigns and Elections, The Presidency, Civil Rights, and Watergate—is also available to adopters. The video segments range from half a minute to about three minutes. A video guide with shot descriptions and bar codes is packaged with the disc. Instructors will find the videodisc useful in designing multimedia lectures.

Instructors can request that their students receive a ten-week subscription to *Newsweek* for an additional $5.00 added to the base price of the text. *Newsweek*, a fresh, weekly source of contemporary political news and commentary, provides material for class discussion, papers, and projects.

The Challenge of Democracy Web Site <http://www.hmco.com/college/COD/home.html>, will allow all student and faculty users of the fifth edition to access a host of text-specific materials. *The Challenge of Democracy Web Site* will include chapter summaries, links to all Web sites mentioned in the text, downloadable versions of *IDEAlog*, and many additional resources. As major political events unfold, we will post information, report data, and provide interpretations for lectures and class discussion. The World Wide Web is transforming how we gather information and communicate ideas. We are committed to using new information technologies to assist users of our text in their search for current knowledge and information about American government and politics.

PoliticsNow Classroom, a state-of-the-art home page on the World Wide Web focusing on political news, issues, and figures, is created expressly for college classrooms and integrated with Houghton Mifflin American government textbooks. *PoliticsNow Classroom* includes links to relevant political news and commentary from *PoliticsNow* affiliates ABC News, the *National Journal, The Washington Post, Newsweek,* and the *Los Angeles Times.* It will also present students with on-line research opportunities, interactive "live" political events, conversations with political figures and scholars, and the most up-to-date analysis of political information available—all aimed at the needs of American government students. The *PoliticsNow Classroom* site is available at a modest subscription price for use with *The Challenge of Democracy.* For more information and details about subscription rates, please contact your Houghton Mifflin sales representative.

For the Student: Effective Learning Aids

The *Study Guide,* written by Melissa Butler of Wabash College, is designed to help students master *The Challenge of Democracy*'s content. The *Study Guide* provides chapter summaries, research topics and resources (both in print and on the World Wide Web), exercises in reading tables and graphs, sample multiple-choice exam questions, and advice on improving study skills, finding internships, and participating in American politics.

Crosstabs with Student Workbook for IBM or Macintosh, winner of a Distinguished Software Award from EDUCOM, allows students to crosstabulate survey data on the 1992 presidential election and the 1993–94 voting records of members of Congress in order to analyze voter attitudes and behavior. Marginal notes in the fifth edition of *The Challenge of Democracy* refer students to appropriate points in the text.

IDEAlog 3.0 (for DOS, MacOS, and Windows), winner of the 1992 Instructional Software Award from the American Political Science Association, is closely tied to the text's "value conflicts" theme. A Java version of *IDEAlog 3.0* can be found on our Web site <http://www.hmco.com/college/COD/home.html>. Students answer twenty questions dealing with the conflicts of freedom vs. order and freedom vs. equality. Their responses are then classified according to libertarian, conservative, liberal, or communitarian ideological tendencies. Marginal notes in the fifth edition of *The Challenge of Democracy* refer students to *IDEAlog* at appropriate points in the text.

The Houghton Mifflin Guide to the Internet for Political Science, Second Edition, written and updated in 1996 by Cecilia G. Manrique of the University of Wisconsin—La Crosse, is a brief introductory guide for students to political science resources on the Internet. The second edition of the *Guide to the Internet* includes information about conducting research on the World Wide Web and referencing Web sites in research papers. It is available to students for free with each new copy of *The Challenge of Democracy.*

We invite your questions, suggestions, and criticisms of the teaching/learning package and *The Challenge of Democracy*. You may contact us at our respective institutions, or, if you have access to an electronic mail service, you may contact us through our collective e-mail address <cod@nwu.edu>.

ACKNOWLEDGMENTS

All authors are indebted to others for inspiration and assistance in various forms; textbook authors are notoriously so. In producing this edition, we especially want to thank David Bishop, Northwestern University Librarian, and Stu Baker and Claire Dougherty of the library's New Media Center; Phyllis Siegel, Northwestern's American Studies Program; Peter S. Ginsberg, Esq.; Dave Dahl, Joe Germuska, Paul Hertz, Rich Barone, and Bob Taylor of Northwestern's Computing Center; and Mary Krosky and Diane Petersmarck of Northwestern's Political Science Department.

Our colleagues at Northwestern and Tufts are a constant source of citations, advice, and constructive criticism. Special thanks to colleagues T. H. Breen, James Oakes, James Campbell, Dennis Chong, and the late Herbert Jacob (Northwestern); and Richard Eichenberg, Jim Glaser, Don Klein, Tony Messina, Kent Portney, and Pearl Robinson (Tufts). Our research assistants were indispensable. We wish to thank Jasen Castillo, David Andrew, Rion Odenbach, Mara Johnston, Brian Fletcher, Dean Schloyer, and Steven Light (Northwestern); Joshua Goldman (University of Colorado at Boulder); Michael Devigne and Pam Slipakoff (Tufts); and Lori Brainard (Brandeis).

In the preparation of this edition we imposed on Tom Smith, National Opinion Research Center; James Johnson, University of Nebraska, Omaha; and Mario Brossard, *The Washington Post*. We gratefully acknowledge their help.

We're delighted to be able to thank Professor Revaz Gachechiladze of Tbilisi State University, who translated our book into Georgian by candlelight. He's one of the pioneers bringing democracy to Georgia. We are grateful to Philip Reeker of the United States Information Agency for arranging the Hungarian translation of our book, and to Martin Palous for negotiating its translation into the Czech language.

We all owe special thanks to Ted and Cora Ginsberg, whose research endowment helped launch several small investigations by our students that eventually found their way into this edition.

Once again in this edition we were lucky enough to have Melissa Butler contribute Chapter 20, "Global Policy." She is also the author of the excellent study guide that accompanies the text.

We have been fortunate to obtain the help of many outstanding political scientists across the country who provided us with critical reviews of our work as it has progressed through five separate editions. We found their comments enormously helpful, and we thank them for taking valuable time away from their own teaching and research to write their detailed reports. More specifically, our thanks go to:

The Authors (left to right):
Kenneth Janda, Jeffrey Berry,
Jerry Goldman

David Ahern
University of Dayton

James Anderson
Texas A&M University

Theodore Arrington
*University of North Carolina,
    Charlotte*

Denise Baer
Northeastern University

Linda L. M. Bennett
Wittenberg University

Stephen Earl Bennett
University of Cincinnati

Thad Beyle
*University of North Carolina,
    Chapel Hill*

Bruce Bimber
*University of California—
    Santa Barbara*

Michael Binford
Georgia State University

Bonnie Browne
Texas A&M University

Jeffrey L. Brudney
University of Georgia

J. Vincent Buck
*California State University,
    Fullerton*

Gregory A. Caldeira
University of Iowa

Robert Casier
Santa Barbara City College

James Chalmers
Wayne State University

John Chubb
Stanford University

Allan Cigler
University of Kansas

Stanley Clark
*California State University,
    Bakersfield*

Ronald Claunch
*Stephen F. Austin State
    University*

Guy C. Clifford
Bridgewater State College

Gary Copeland
University of Oklahoma

W. Douglas Costain
*University of Colorado at
    Boulder*

Cornelius P. Cotter
*University of Wisconsin,
    Milwaukee*

Christine L. Day
University of New Orleans

David A. Deese
Boston College

Victor D'Lugin
University of Florida

Art English
University of Arkansas

Henry Fearnley
College of Marin

Elizabeth Flores
Del Mar College

Patricia S. Florestano
University of Maryland

Steve Frank
St. Cloud State University

Mitchel Gerber
Hofstra University

Dorith Grant-Wisdom
Howard University

Paul Gronke
Duke University

Sara A. Grove
Shippensburg University

David J. Hadley
Wabash College

Kenneth Hayes
University of Maine

Ronald Hedlund
*University of Wisconsin,
    Milwaukee*

Richard Heil
Fort Hays State University

Beth Henschen
The Institute for Community and Regional Development, Eastern Michigan University

Marjorie Randon Hershey
Indiana University

Roberta Herzberg
Indiana University

Jack E. Holmes
Hope College

Peter Howse
American River College

Ronald J. Hrebenar
University of Utah

James B. Johnson
University of Nebraska at Omaha

William R. Keech
Carnegie Mellon University

Scott Keeter
Virginia Commonwealth University

Sarah W. Keidan
Oakland Community College (Michigan)

Beat Kernen
Southwest Missouri State University

Vance Krites
Indiana University of Pennsylvania

Clyde Kuhn
California State University, Sacramento

Jack Lampe
Southwest Texas Junior College

Joseph Losco
Ball State University

Philip Loy
Taylor University

Wayne McIntosh
University of Maryland

David Madlock
University of Memphis

Michael Maggiotto
University of South Carolina

Edward S. Malecki
California State University, Los Angeles

Michael Margolis
University of Cincinnati— McMicken College of Arts and Sciences

Thomas R. Marshall
University of Texas at Arlington

Steve J. Mazurana
University of Northern Colorado

Jim Morrow
Tulsa Junior College

William Mugleston
Mountain View College

David A. Nordquest
Pennsylvania State University, Erie

Bruce Odom
Trinity Valley Community College

Laura Katz Olson
Lehigh University

Bruce Oppenheimer
University of Houston

Richard Pacelle
Indiana University

William J. Parente
University of Scranton

Robert Pecorella
St. John's University

James Perkins
San Antonio College

Denny E. Pilant
Southwest Missouri State University

Curtis Reithel
University of Wisconsin, La Crosse

Chester D. Rhoan
Chabot College

Michael J. Rich
Emory University

Richard S. Rich
Virginia Tech

Ronald I. Rubin
Borough of Manhattan Community College, CUNY

Gilbert K. St. Clair
University of New Mexico

Barbara Salmore
Drew University

Todd M. Schaefer
Central Washington University

Denise Scheberle
University of Wisconsin—Green Bay

Paul R. Schulman
Mills College

William A. Schultze
San Diego State University

Thomas Sevener
Santa Rosa Junior College

Kenneth S. Sherrill
Hunter College

Sanford R. Silverburg
Catawba College

Mark Silverstein
Boston University

Robert J. Spitzer
SUNY Cortland

Candy Stevens Smith
Texarkana College

Charles Sohner
El Camino College

Dale Story
University of Texas, Arlington

Nicholas Strinkowski
Clark College

Neal Tate
University of North Texas

James A. Thurber
The American University

Eric M. Uslaner
University of Maryland

Charles E. Walcott
Virginia Tech

Thomas G. Walker
Emory University

Benjamin Walter
Vanderbilt University

Gary D. Wekkin
University of Central Arkansas

Jonathan West
University of Miami

John Winkle
University of Mississippi

Clifford Wirth
University of New Hampshire

Ann Wynia
North Hennepin Community College

Jerry L. Yeric
University of North Texas

Finally, we want to thank the many people at Houghton Mifflin who helped make this edition a reality. Jean Woy, now Vice President and Editor-in-Chief of History and Political Science, signed us to do the book. Jean suffered through the traumas of the first edition and played a critical role in developing the book in its subsequent editions. There's not enough room here to list all the different people at Houghton Mifflin who helped us with the four previous editions, but all we can say is you know who you are and how much we appreciate what you did for *The Challenge of Democracy*. For the fifth edition we were lucky enough to work with Paul Smith, Senior Sponsoring Editor for Political Science. He's given us the kind of support that all authors dream about. June Smith, Executive Vice President and Director of the College Division, has always let us know that *The Challenge of Democracy* is a priority for everyone at the publishing house. Others who made important contributions to the fifth edition are: Carol Merrigan, Senior Production/Design Coordinator; Mark Corsey, photo researcher; Bruce Crabtree, copyeditor; Janet Theurer, designer and art editor; and Patrice Rossi Calkin, illustrator.

It's obvious to us that Melissa Mashburn, Senior Associate Editor, was a saint in a previous life. She supervised this project with equal parts of skill, patience, and humor. She pored over the manuscript with the devotion of a dozen Talmudic scholars. Working on the "output" side of the project was Peggy J. Flanagan, our Project Editor, who pulled together text, photos, captions, tables, and graphs, and oversaw the actual physical production of the book. The proof of her effectiveness is the beauty of the pages that follow. We look forward to working with Melissa and Peggy on many editions to come. We only wish they could supervise the rest of our lives.

Our experience proves that authors, even experienced authors working on their fifth edition, can benefit from the suggestions and criticisms of a gifted staff of publishing experts. No publisher has a more capable group of dedicated professionals than Houghton Mifflin, and we have been fortunate to have their guidance over the past decade and the five editions of our text.

K.J., J.B., J.G.

I

Dilemmas of Democracy

chapter

1

Freedom, Order, or Equality?

SUPPOSE YOU ARE TERMINALLY ILL and suffer excruciating pain. Do you have a "right" to die in this country? Does the state (that is, the government) have the right—even the duty—to prevent you from committing suicide? How about preventing a doctor from helping a doomed and tormented patient commit suicide?

From 1990 to 1996, Dr. Jack Kevorkian, a retired Michigan pathologist, assisted in at least twenty-seven suicides involving gravely ill people.[1] Dr. Kevorkian had eluded conviction for murder because he was careful to let his patients trigger the lethal action. But in 1992, Michigan outlawed assisted suicide. Facing prosecution, Kevorkian said, "I have never cared about anything but the welfare of the patient in front of me. I don't care about the law."[2] Put on trial three times, he was acquitted by juries each time and continued his macabre mission.

In contrast to the government's position in Michigan, Oregon voters in 1994 passed a law that allowed doctor-assisted suicide. Test your own feelings about this controversial issue. On what basis would you decide whether the government's interest in protecting life outweighs an individual's freedom to end his or her life?

Which is better: to live under a government that allows individuals complete freedom to do whatever they please or to live under one that enforces strict law and order? Which is better: to allow businesses and private clubs to choose their customers and members or to pass laws that require them to admit and serve everyone, regardless of race or sex?

For many people, none of these alternatives is satisfactory. All pose difficult dilemmas. The dilemmas are tied to opposing philosophies that place different values on freedom, order, and equality.

This book explains American government and politics in light of these dilemmas. It does more than explain the workings of our government; it encourages you to think about what government should—and should not—do. And it judges the American government against democratic ideals, encouraging you to think about how government should make its decisions. As its title implies, *The Challenge of Democracy* argues that good government often involves difficult choices.

College students frequently say that American government and politics are hard to understand. In fact, many people voice the same complaint. Two-thirds of a national sample interviewed after the 1992 presidential election agreed with the statement "Politics and government seem so complicated that a person like me can't understand what's going on."[3]

● ● ● ● ● ● ● ● ● ● ●

I Now Pronounce You . . .

Gay couples renew their vows at Metropolitan Community Church in San Francisco in June 1996. Because few institutions have been more central to society than marriage between a man and a woman, same-sex marriages represent a threat to the social order. Liberals and conservatives usually divide sharply on this issue.

With this book, we hope to improve your understanding of "what's going on" by analyzing the norms, or values, that people use to judge political events. Our purpose is not to preach what people ought to favor in making policy decisions; it is to teach what values are at stake.

Teaching without preaching is not easy; no one can completely exclude personal values from political analysis. But our approach minimizes the problem by concentrating on the dilemmas that confront governments when they are forced to choose between important policies that threaten equally cherished values, such as freedom of speech and personal security.

Every government policy reflects a choice between conflicting values. We want you to understand this idea, to understand that all government policies reinforce certain values (norms) at the expense of others. We want you to interpret policy issues (for example, should assisted suicide go unpunished?) with an understanding of the fundamental values in question (freedom of action versus order and protection of life) and the broader political context (liberal or conservative politics).

By looking beyond the specifics to the underlying normative principles, you should be able to make more sense out of politics. Our framework for analysis does not encompass all the complexities of American government, but it should help your knowledge grow by improving your comprehension of political information. We begin by considering the basic purposes of government. In short, why do we need it?

THE PURPOSES OF GOVERNMENT

Most people do not like being told what to do. Fewer still like being coerced into acting a certain way. Yet every day, millions of American motorists dutifully drive on the right-hand side of the street and obediently stop at red lights. Every year, millions of U.S. citizens struggle to complete their income tax forms before midnight on April 15. In both examples, the coercive power of government is at work. If people do not like being controlled, why do they submit to it? In other words, why do we have government?

Government may be defined as the legitimate use of force—including imprisonment and execution—within specified geographic boundaries to control human behavior. All governments require their citizens to surrender some freedom as part of being governed. Although some governments minimize their infringements on personal freedom, no government has as a goal the maximization of personal freedom. Governments exist to control; *to govern* means "to control." Why do people surrender their freedom to this control? To obtain the benefits of government. Throughout history, government seems to have served two major purposes: maintaining order (preserving life and protecting property) and providing public goods. More recently, some governments have pursued a third purpose: promoting equality, which is more controversial.

Maintaining Order

Maintaining order is the oldest objective of government. *Order* in this context is rich with meaning. Let's start with "law and order." Maintaining order in this sense means establishing the rule of law to preserve life and protect property. To the seventeenth-century English philosopher Thomas Hobbes (1588–1679), preserving life was the most important function of government. In his classic philosophical treatise, *Leviathan* (1651), Hobbes described life without government as life in a "state of nature." Without rules, people would live as predators do, stealing and killing for their personal benefit. In Hobbes's classic phrase, life in a state of nature would be "solitary, poor, nasty, brutish, and short." He believed that a single ruler, or sovereign, must possess unquestioned authority to guarantee the safety of the weak, to protect them from the attacks of the strong. Hobbes named his all-powerful government Leviathan, after a biblical sea monster. He believed that complete obedience to Leviathan's strict laws was a small price to pay for the security of living in a civil society.

Most of us can only imagine what a state of nature would be like. We might think of the "Wild West" in the days before a good guy in a white hat rode into town and established law and order. But in some parts of the world, people actually live in a state of lawlessness today. It occurred in Somalia in 1992 after the central government collapsed and in Haiti in 1994 after the elected president had to flee. President George Bush sent U.S. troops into Somalia to restore a semblance of order and to prevent more starvation, and President Bill Clinton responded similarly in Haiti. Throughout history, authoritarian rulers have used people's fear of civil disorder to justify taking power. Ironically, the ruling group itself—whether monarchy, aristocracy, or political party—then became known as the *established order.*

Hobbes's conception of life in the cruel state of nature led him to view government primarily as a means of guaranteeing people's survival. Other theorists, taking survival for granted, believed that government protected order by preserving private property (goods and land owned by individuals). Foremost among them was John Locke (1632–1704), an English

Read Locke's work on-line:
`<hypermall.com/`
`LibertyOnline/Locke/index.`
`html>`

●●●●●●●●●●●●
Leviathan, Hobbes's All-Powerful Sovereign

This engraving is from the 1651 edition of Leviathan, *by Thomas Hobbes. It shows Hobbes's sovereign brandishing a sword in one hand and the scepter of justice in the other. He watches over an orderly town, made peaceful by his absolute authority. But note that the sovereign's body is composed of tiny images of his subjects. He exists only through them. Hobbes explains that such government power can be created only if people "confer all their power and strength upon one man, or upon one assembly of men, that may reduce all their wills, by plurality of voices, unto one will."*

Read Marx's work on-line:
`<www.shef.ac.uk/uni/
projects/gpp/Tapestry/
society/thecom1.html>`

philosopher. In *Two Treatises on Government* (1690), he wrote that the protection of life, liberty, and property was the basic objective of government. His thinking strongly influenced the Declaration of Independence; it is reflected in the Declaration's famous phrase identifying "Life, Liberty, and the Pursuit of Happiness" as "unalienable Rights" of citizens under government.

Not everyone believes that the protection of private property is a valid objective of government. The German philosopher Karl Marx (1818–1883) rejected the private ownership of property used in the production of goods or services. Marx's ideas form the basis of **communism**, a complex theory that gives ownership of all land and productive facilities to the people—in effect, to the government. In line with communist theory, the 1977 constitution of the former Soviet Union set forth the following principles of government ownership:

> State property, i.e., the common property of the Soviet people, is the principal form of socialist property. The land, its minerals, waters, and forests are the exclusive property of the state. The state owns the basic means of production in industry, construction, and agriculture; means of transport and communication; the banks; the property of state-run trade organizations and public utilities, and other state-run undertakings; most urban housing; and other property necessary for state purposes.[4]

Even after the Soviet Union collapsed and the Russians elected Boris Yeltsin as president, the Russian public was deeply split over changing the old communist-era constitution to permit the private ownership of land. Even outside the formerly communist societies, the extent to which government protects private property is a political issue that forms the basis of much ideological debate.

Providing Public Goods

After governments have established basic order, they can pursue other ends. Using their coercive powers, they can tax citizens to raise money to spend on **public goods,** which are benefits and services that are available to everyone—such as education, sanitation, and parks. Public goods benefit all citizens but are not likely to be produced by the voluntary acts of individuals. The government of ancient Rome, for example, built aqueducts to carry fresh water from the mountains to the city. Road building was another public good provided by the Roman government, which also used the roads to move its legions and to protect the established order.

Government action to provide public goods can be controversial. During President James Monroe's administration (1817–1825), many people thought that building the Cumberland Road (between Cumberland, Maryland, and Wheeling, West Virginia) was not a proper function of the national government, the Romans notwithstanding. Over time, the scope of government functions in the United States has expanded. During President Dwight Eisenhower's administration in the 1950s, the federal government outdid the Romans' noble road building. Despite his basic conservatism, Eisenhower launched the massive Interstate Highway System, at a cost of $27 billion (in 1950s dollars). Yet some government enterprises that have been common in other countries—running railroads, operating coal mines, generating electric power—are politically controversial or even unacceptable in the United States. People disagree about how far the government ought to go in using its power to tax to provide public goods and services and how much of that realm should be handled by private business for profit.

Promoting Equality

The promotion of equality has not always been a major objective of government. It has gained prominence only in this century, in the aftermath of industrialization and urbanization. Confronted by the paradox of poverty amid plenty, some political leaders in European nations pioneered extensive government programs to improve life for the poor. Under the emerging concept of the welfare state, government's role expanded to provide individuals with medical care, education, and a guaranteed income, "from cradle to grave." Sweden, Britain, and other nations adopted welfare programs aimed at reducing social inequalities. This relatively new purpose of government has been by far the most controversial. People often oppose taxation for public goods (building roads and schools, for example) because of its cost alone. On principle, they oppose more strongly taxation for government programs to promote economic and social equality.

The key issue here is government's role in redistributing income, taking from the wealthy to give to the poor. Charity (voluntary giving to the poor) has a strong basis in Western religious traditions; using the power of the state to support the poor does not. (In his nineteenth-century novels, Charles Dickens dramatized how government power was used to imprison the poor, not to support them.) Using the state to redistribute income was originally a radical idea, set forth by Marx as the ultimate principle of developed communism: "from each according to his ability, to

● ● ● ● ● ● ● ● ● ● ●

**Rosa Parks: She Sat
for Equality**

*Rosa Parks had just finished a
day's work as a seamstress
and was sitting in the front of
a bus in Montgomery,
Alabama, going home. A
white man claimed her seat,
which he could do according
to the law in December 1955.
When she refused to move and
was arrested, angry blacks,
led by Dr. Martin Luther King,
Jr., began a boycott of the
Montgomery bus company.*

each according to his needs."[5] This extreme has never been realized in any government, not even in communist states. But over time, taking from the rich to help the needy has become a legitimate function of most governments.

That function is not without controversy, however. Especially since the Great Depression of the 1930s, the government's role in redistributing income to promote economic equality has been a major source of policy debate in the United States. The Republicans in the 104th Congress, for example, opposed the Depression-era AFDC program (Aid to Families with Dependent Children) and looked kindly on a "flat" income tax, which favors people with higher incomes. On both issues, they were vigorously opposed by most Democrats in Congress.

Government can also promote social equality through policies that do not redistribute income. For example, it can regulate social behavior to enforce equality, as it did when the Texas Supreme Court cleared the way for homosexuals to serve in the Dallas police department in 1993. Policies that regulate social behavior, like those that redistribute income, inevitably clash with the value of personal freedom.

**A CONCEPTUAL
FRAMEWORK FOR
ANALYZING
GOVERNMENT**

Citizens have very different views of how vigorously they want government to maintain order, provide public goods, and promote equality. Of the three objectives, providing for public goods usually is less controversial than maintaining order or promoting equality. After all, government spending for highways, schools, and parks carries benefits for nearly every citizen. Moreover, services merely cost money. The cost of maintaining order and promoting equality is greater than money; it usually means a tradeoff in basic values.

To understand government and the political process, you must be able to recognize these tradeoffs and identify the basic values they entail. Just as people sit back from a wide-screen motion picture to gain perspective, to understand American government you need to take a broad view, a view much broader than that offered by examining specific political events. You need to use political concepts.

A concept is a generalized idea of a set of items or thoughts. It groups various events, objects, or qualities under a common classification or label. The framework that guides this book consists of five concepts that figure prominently in political analysis. We regard the five concepts as especially important to a broad understanding of American politics, and we use them repeatedly throughout the book. This framework will help you evaluate political events long after you have read this text.

The five concepts that we emphasize deal with the fundamental issues of what government tries to do and how it decides to do it. The concepts that relate to what government tries to do are order, freedom, and equality. All governments by definition value order; maintaining order is part of the meaning of government. Most governments at least claim to preserve individual freedom while they maintain order, although they vary widely in the extent to which they succeed. Few governments even profess to guarantee equality, and governments differ greatly in policies that pit equality against freedom. Our conceptual framework should help you evaluate the extent to which the United States pursues all three values through its government.

How government chooses the proper mix of order, freedom, and equality in its policymaking has to do with the process of choice. We evaluate the American governmental process using two models of democratic government: majoritarian and pluralist. Many governments profess to be democracies. Whether they are or are not depends on their (and our) meaning of the term. Even countries that Americans agree are democracies—for example, the United States and Britain—differ substantially in the type of democracy they practice. We can use our conceptual models of democratic government both to classify the type of democracy practiced in the United States and to evaluate the government's success in fulfilling that model.

The five concepts can be organized into two groups.

- Concepts that identify the values pursued by government:

  Freedom

  Order

  Equality

- Concepts that describe models of democratic government:

  Majoritarian democracy

  Pluralist democracy

The rest of this chapter examines freedom, order, and equality as conflicting values pursued by government. Chapter 2 discusses majoritarian democracy and pluralist democracy as alternative institutional models for implementing democratic government.

THE CONCEPTS OF FREEDOM, ORDER, AND EQUALITY

These three terms—*freedom, order,* and *equality*—have a range of connotations in American politics. Both *freedom* and *equality* are positive terms that politicians have learned to use to their own advantage. Consequently, freedom and equality mean different things to different people at different times, depending on the political context in which they are used. Order, on the other hand, has negative connotations for many people, for it symbolizes government intrusion in private lives. Except during periods of social strife, few politicians in Western democracies call openly for more order. Because all governments infringe on freedom, we examine that concept first.

Freedom

For the full text of Roosevelt's Four Freedoms speech: `<www.hicom.net/~oedipus/4free3.html>`

Freedom can be used in two major senses: freedom of and freedom from. President Franklin Delano Roosevelt used the word in both senses in a speech he made shortly before the United States entered World War II. He described four freedoms—freedom of religion, freedom of speech, freedom from fear, and freedom from want. The noted illustrator Norman Rockwell gave Americans a vision of these freedoms in a classic set of paintings published in the *Saturday Evening Post* (see Feature 1.1).

Freedom of is the absence of constraints on behavior; it means freedom *to* do something. In this sense, *freedom* is synonymous with *liberty*. Two of Rockwell's paintings—*Freedom of Worship* and *Freedom of Speech*—exemplify this type of freedom.

Freedom from is the message of the other paintings, *Freedom from Fear* and *Freedom from Want*. Here freedom suggests immunity from fear and want. In the modern political context, *freedom from* often symbolizes the fight against exploitation and oppression. The cry of the civil rights movement in the 1960s—"Freedom Now!"—conveyed this meaning. If you recognize that freedom in this sense means immunity from discrimination, you can see that it comes close to the concept of equality.[6] In this book, we avoid using *freedom of* to mean "freedom from"; for this sense, we simply use *equality*. When we use *freedom*, we mean "freedom of."

Order

When *order* is viewed in the narrow sense of preserving life and protecting property, most citizens would concede the importance of maintaining order and thereby grant the need for government. For example, "domestic Tranquility" (order) is cited in the preamble to the Constitution. However, when *order* is viewed in the broader sense of preserving the social order, people are more likely to argue that maintaining order is not a legitimate function of government (see Compared with What? 1.1). *Social order* refers to established patterns of authority in society and to traditional modes of behavior. It is the accepted way of doing things. The prevailing social order prescribes behavior in many different areas: how students should dress in school (neatly, no purple hair) and behave toward their teachers (respectfully); under what conditions people should have sexual relations (married, different sexes); what the press should not publish (sexually explicit photographs); and what the proper attitude toward religion

● compared with what?

1.1   The Importance of Order as a Political Value

Compared with citizens in other nations, Americans do not value maintaining order as much as others do. Surveys in the United States and in fifteen other countries asked respondents to select which of the following four national goals was the "most important in the long run":

● Maintaining order in the nation

● Giving the people more say in important government decisions

● Fighting rising prices

● Protecting freedom of speech

Just 28 percent of those surveyed in the United States chose "maintaining order." Only respondents in Belgium and Canada attached appreciably less importance to maintaining order. Compared with citizens in most other Western countries and Russia, Americans seem to want less government control of social behavior.

Source: World Values Survey, 1990–1991. The tabulation was provided by Professor Ronald F. Inglehart, University of Michigan.

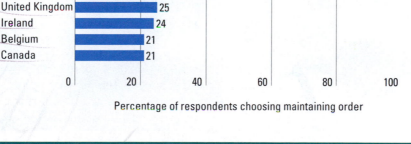

Country	Percentage
Norway	64
Russia	59
Denmark	59
Austria	41
Sweden	38
Germany	37
Japan	35
Spain	31
United States	28
France	28
Netherlands	27
Italy	27
United Kingdom	25
Ireland	24
Belgium	21
Canada	21

Percentage of respondents choosing maintaining order

and country should be (reverential). It is important to remember that the social order can change. Today, perfectly respectable men and women wear bathing suits that would have caused a scandal at the turn of the century.

A government can protect the established order by using its **police power**—its authority to safeguard residents' safety, health, welfare, and

1.1

The Four Freedoms

Norman Rockwell became famous in the 1940s for the humorous, homespun covers he painted for the *Saturday Evening Post*, a weekly magazine. Inspired by an address to Congress in which President Roosevelt outlined his goals for world civilization, Rockwell painted *The Four Freedoms*, which were reproduced in the *Post*. Their immense popularity led the government to print posters of the illustrations for the Treasury Department's war bond drive. The Office of War Information also reproduced *The Four Freedoms* and circulated the posters in schools, clubhouses, railroad stations, post offices, and other public buildings. Officials even had copies circulated on the European front to remind soldiers of the liberties for which they were fighting. It is said that no other paintings in the world have ever been reproduced or circulated in such vast numbers as *The Four Freedoms*.

Freedom of Speech

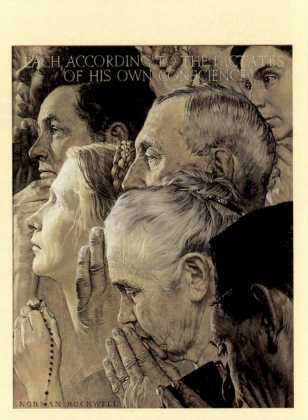

Freedom of Worship

Freedom from Fear   **Freedom from Want**

morals. The extent to which government should use this authority is a topic of ongoing debate in the United States and is constantly being redefined by the courts. In the 1980s, many states used their police powers to pass legislation that banned smoking in public places. In the 1990s, a hot issue is whether government should control the dissemination of pornography on the Internet. There are those who fear the evolution of a police state—a government that uses its power to regulate nearly all aspects of behavior. For example, South Africa under the former apartheid regime had laws governing intermarriage between blacks and whites and prescribing where an interracial married couple could live. It is no accident that the chief law enforcement officer in South Africa was called the minister of law and *order*.

Most governments are inherently conservative; they tend to resist social change. But some governments have as a primary objective the restructuring of the social order. Social change is most dramatic when a government is overthrown through force and replaced by a revolutionary government. Societies can also work to change social patterns more gradually through the legal process. Our use of the term *order* in this book includes all three aspects: preserving life, protecting property, and maintaining traditional patterns of social relationships.

● ● ● ● ● ● ● ● ● ● ●

A Woman's Place Is in the Sky

During World War II, women served in the military in "auxiliary" corps. The U.S. Army had the Women's Army Auxiliary Corps (shortened to WAC), and the Navy had the Women Appointed for Voluntary Emergency Service (WAVES). Women in these corps usually served in clerical and support units and were not trained for "men's work." In today's military, women often occupy traditionally male roles—such as helicopter pilots.

Equality

As with *freedom* and *order, equality* is used in different senses, to support different causes. **Political equality** in elections is easy to define: each citizen has one and only one vote. This basic concept is central to democratic theory—a subject explored at length in Chapter 2. But when some people advocate political equality, they mean more than one person, one vote. These people contend that an urban ghetto dweller and the chairman of the board of Microsoft are not politically equal, despite the fact that each has one vote. Through occupation or wealth, some citizens are more able than others to influence political decisions. For example, wealthy citizens can exert influence by advertising in the mass media or by contacting friends in high places. Lacking great wealth and political connections, most citizens do not have such influence. Thus, some analysts argue that equality in wealth, education, and status—that is, **social equality**—is necessary for true political equality.

There are two routes to achieving social equality: providing equal opportunities and ensuring equal outcomes. **Equality of opportunity** means that each person has the same chance to succeed in life. This idea is deeply ingrained in American culture. The Constitution prohibits titles of nobility and does not make owning property a requirement for holding public office. Public schools and libraries are free to all. For many people, the concept of social equality is satisfied just by offering equal opportunities for advancement—it is not essential that people actually end up being equal. For others, true social equality means nothing less than **equality of outcome.**[7] They believe that society must see to it that people are equal. According to this view, it is not enough that governments provide people with equal opportunities; they must also design policies that redistribute wealth and status so that economic and social equality are actually achieved. In education, equality of outcome has led to federal laws that require comparable funding for men's and women's college sports (see Politics in a Changing America 1.1). In business, equality of outcome has led to certain affirmative action programs to increase minority hiring and to the active recruitment of women, blacks, and Latinos to fill jobs. Equality of outcome has also produced federal laws that require employers to pay men and women equally for equal work. In recent years, the very concept of affirmative action has come under scrutiny. In 1996, for example, the University of California's Board of Regents ended its policy of using race and gender criteria in admitting students and hiring professors.

Some link equality of outcome with the concept of government-supported rights—the idea that every citizen is entitled to certain benefits of government, that government should guarantee its citizens adequate (if not equal) housing, employment, medical care, and income as a matter of right. If citizens are entitled to government benefits as a matter of right, government efforts to promote equality of outcome become legitimized.

Clearly, the concept of equality of outcome is quite different from that of equality of opportunity, and it requires a much greater degree of government activity. It also clashes more directly with the concept of freedom. By taking from one to give to another—which is necessary for the redistribution of income and status—the government clearly creates winners and losers. The winners may believe that justice has been served by the redistribution. The losers often feel strongly that their freedom to enjoy their income and status has suffered.

TWO DILEMMAS OF GOVERNMENT

The two major dilemmas facing American government in the 1990s stem from the oldest and the newest objectives of government—maintaining order and promoting equality. Both order and equality are important social values, but government cannot pursue either without sacrificing a third important value: individual freedom. The clash between freedom and order forms the original dilemma of government; the clash between freedom and equality forms the modern dilemma of government. Although the dilemmas are different, each involves trading some amount of freedom for another value.

The Original Dilemma: Freedom Versus Order

The conflict between freedom and order originates in the very meaning of government as the legitimate use of force to control human behavior. How much freedom must a citizen surrender to government? The dilemma has occupied philosophers for hundreds of years. In the eighteenth century, the French philosopher Jean Jacques Rousseau (1712–1778) wrote that the problem of devising a proper government "is to find a form of association which will defend and protect with the whole common force the person and goods of each associate, and in which each, while uniting himself with all, may still obey himself alone, and remain free as before."[8]

● politics in a changing america

1.1 The Attempt to Achieve Gender Equity in College Sports

Since the 1970s, the number of women's sports programs at American colleges and universities has risen steadily. This graph shows the growth in the number of men's programs in basketball and tennis and women's programs in basketball and volleyball (the sports with the largest numbers of programs for each sex) as a percentage of all member institutions of the National Collegiate Athletic Association (NCAA) since the mid-1950s. (Comparable data for women's sports begin in the mid-1960s.) The men's programs have held fairly steady over time but have declined slightly in recent years. The women's programs, however, jumped markedly after 1972 and increased somewhat thereafter. While some growth in women's programs may owe to voluntary acts by the institutions, a good deal of it can be attributed to the federal government's demand for equal treatment of the sexes under the 1972 civil rights law. Title IX of that law outlawed gender discrimination in any institution that receives federal funding.

As applied to sports, Title IX requires that men and women have (1) equal opportunities for participation, (2) equitable shares of athletic scholarships, and (3) equitable conditions for athletes in coaching, scheduling, equipment, recruiting, and facilities. Many institutions responded by increasing the number of sports programs for women, as shown here for basketball and volleyball. Nevertheless, inequities in sports programs for men and women have remained at virtually every participating institution, with men's sports getting most of the athletic scholarship funds and other spending. In large part this is because of men's football programs, which cost so much to run.

With more attention being focused on gender equity in college sports and with increasing numbers of investigations under Title IX by the Office of Civil Rights, institutions are responding by cutting men's sports (e.g., gymnastics) and adding more women's sports (e.g., soccer). Jack Weidenbach, the athletic director of the University of Michigan, said that the effect will inevitably be felt by cutting men's sports: "If you're going to have gender equity, you're going to have to take the money from some place, and the men are the only place left." In a changing America, enforcing social equality does have its costs—but it also carries rewards. Some observers at the 1996 Olympics credit the outstanding gold-medal performance of U.S. women's teams in basketball, soccer, softball, and track and field to government requirement of

The original purpose of government was to protect life and property, to make citizens safe from violence. How well is the American government doing today in providing law and order to its citizens? More than 40 percent of the respondents in a 1993 national survey said that they were afraid to walk alone at night within a mile of their home.[9] In another survey the same year, almost 15 percent said that they had been a victim of a violent crime.[10] Simply put, Americans view increasing crime as a serious issue and do not trust their government to protect them.

When the old communist governments still ruled in Eastern Europe, the climate of fear in urban America stood in stark contrast to the pervasive sense of personal safety in such cities as Moscow, Warsaw, and Prague. Then it was common to see old and young strolling late at night along the

equal athletic opportunities for women. Donna Lopiano, executive director of the Women's Sports Foundation, said, "There's no question it's a direct product of Title IX."

Sources: National Collegiate Athletic Association, The Sports and Recreational Programs of the Nation's Universities and Colleges, Report Number 7, 1956–87 (Mission, Kansas: NCAA, 1990); data for 1991–1992 were kindly provided by Todd Petr of the NCAA and taken from Ed Sherman, "Men vs. Women: It's a Brand New Ball Game," *Chicago Tribune,* 28 April 1993, p. 1; and Gene Wojciechowski and Andrew Gottesman, "Golden Era for Women: Atlanta Games a Tribute to 24-Year-Old Equality Law," *Chicago Tribune,* 4 August 1996, pp. 1, 16.

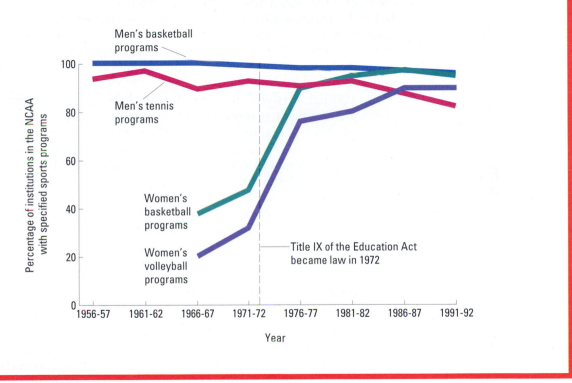

streets and in the parks of these communist cities. The formerly communist regimes gave their police great powers to control guns, monitor citizens' movements, and arrest and imprison suspicious people, which enabled them to do a better job of maintaining order. Communist governments deliberately chose order over freedom. But with the collapse of order under communism, things have changed in these countries. Since the fall of communism in 1989, all have experienced unprecedented crime waves, with total crimes virtually doubling by 1994 in Poland, Hungary, the Czech Republic, and Slovakia.[11] In 1993, more than two thousand residents of Russia's capital were asked, "Do you feel protected from criminal action in Moscow?" Only 7 percent said yes, and 86 percent said no.[12] Partially due to citizens' desire for more law and order, the Communist

Party won the most votes in the 1995 parliamentary elections, and the Communist candidate for Russian president forced Boris Yeltsin into a runoff election in 1996 before losing by a few percentage points.

The crisis over acquired immune deficiency syndrome (AIDS) adds a new twist to the dilemma of freedom versus order. Some health officials believe that AIDS, for which there is no known cure, is the greatest medical threat in the history of the United States. Over 501,000 cases of AIDS were reported to the Centers for Disease Control through late 1995. Of these, almost half were reported since 1993. Over 310,000 (62 percent) of these patients died.[13]

To combat the spread of the disease in the military, the Department of Defense began testing all applicants for the AIDS virus. Other government agencies have begun testing current employees. And some officials are calling for widespread mandatory testing within the private sector as well. Such programs are strongly opposed by those who believe they violate individual freedom. But those who are more afraid of the spread of AIDS than of an infringement on individual rights support aggressive government action to combat the disease.

The conflict between the values of freedom and order represents the original dilemma of government. In the abstract, people value both freedom and order; in real life, the two values inherently conflict. By definition, any policy that strengthens one value takes away from the other. The balance of freedom and order is an issue in enduring debates (whether to allow capital punishment) and contemporary challenges (how to deal with urban gang members who spray-paint walls; whether to allow art galleries to display sexually explicit photographs). And in a democracy, policy choices hinge on how much citizens value freedom and how much they value order.

The Modern Dilemma: Freedom Versus Equality

Popular opinion has it that freedom and equality go hand in hand. In reality, the two values usually clash when governments enact policies to promote social equality. Because social equality is a relatively recent government objective, deciding between policies that promote equality at the expense of freedom, and vice versa, is the modern dilemma of politics. Consider these examples:

- During the 1960s, Congress (through the Equal Pay Act) required employers to pay women and men the same rate for equal work. This means that some employers are forced to pay women more than they would if their compensation policies were based on their free choice.

- During the 1970s, the courts ordered the busing of schoolchildren to achieve a fair distribution of blacks and whites in public schools. This action was motivated by concern for educational equality, but it also impaired freedom of choice.

- During the 1980s, some states passed legislation that went beyond the idea of equal pay for equal work to the more radical notion of pay equity—equal pay for comparable work. Women had to be paid at a rate equal to men's even if they had different jobs, providing the women's jobs were of "comparable worth." For example, if the skills and responsibilities of a female nurse were found to be comparable to those of a male laboratory technician in the same hospital, the woman's salary and the man's salary would have to be the same.

- In the 1990s, Congress prohibited discrimination in employment, public services, and public accommodations on the basis of physical or mental disabilities. Under the 1990 Americans with Disabilities Act, businesses with twenty-five or more employees cannot pass over an otherwise qualified disabled person in employment or promotion, and new buses and trains have to be made accessible to them.

These examples illustrate the problem of using government power to promote equality. The clash between freedom and order is obvious, but the clash between freedom and equality is more subtle. Americans, who think of freedom and equality as complementary rather than conflicting values, often do not notice the clash. When forced to choose between the two, however, Americans are far more likely to choose freedom over equality than are people in other countries (see Compared with What? 1.2). The emphasis on equality over freedom was especially strong in the former Soviet Union, which guaranteed its citizens medical care, inexpensive housing, and other social services. Although the quality of the benefits was not much by Western standards, Soviet citizens experienced a sense of equality in shared deprivation. Indeed, there was such aversion to economic inequality that citizens' attitudes hindered economic development in a free market after the fall of the Soviet Union. In 1990, one Russian politician said, "The ideal of social justice here is that everybody should have nothing, not that entrepreneurs should prosper and spread the wealth."[14] Five years later, many Russians are looking back nostalgically at the olden days, as evidenced by the Communist Party's victory in the 1995 parliamentary elections. As the director of the Moscow Arts Theater explained, "People are longing for the lost paradise—the lost Communist paradise."[15]

The conflicts among freedom, order, and equality explain a great deal of the political conflict in the United States. The conflicts also underlie the ideologies that people use to structure their understanding of politics.

IDEOLOGY AND THE SCOPE OF GOVERNMENT

People hold different opinions about the merits of government policies. Sometimes their views are based on self-interest. For example, most senior citizens vociferously oppose increasing their personal contributions to Medicare, the government program that defrays medical costs for the elderly, preferring to have all citizens pay for their coverage. Policies also are judged according to individual values and beliefs. Some people hold an assortment of values and beliefs that produce contradictory opinions on government policies. Others organize their opinions into a **political ideology**—a consistent set of values and beliefs about the proper purpose and scope of government.

How far should government go to maintain order, provide public goods, and promote equality? In the United States (as in every other nation), citizens, scholars, and politicians have different answers. We can analyze

● compared with what?

1.2   The Importance of Freedom and Equality as Political Values

Compared with citizens' views of freedom and equality in fifteen other nations, Americans value freedom more than others do. Respondents in each country were asked which of the following statements came closer to their own opinion:

- "I find that both freedom and equality are important. But if I were to make up my mind for one or the other, I would consider personal freedom more important, that is, everyone can live in freedom and develop without hindrance."

- "Certainly both freedom and equality are important. But if I were to make up my mind for one of the two, I would consider

equality more important, that is, that nobody is underprivileged and that social class differences are not so strong."

Americans chose freedom by a ratio of nearly 3 to 1. No other nation showed such a strong preference for freedom, and citizens in four countries favored equality instead. When we look at this finding together with Americans' disdain for order (see Compared with What? 1.1), the importance of freedom as a political concept in the United States is clear.

Source: World Values Survey, 1990–1991. The tabulation was provided by Professor Ronald F. Inglehart, University of Michigan.

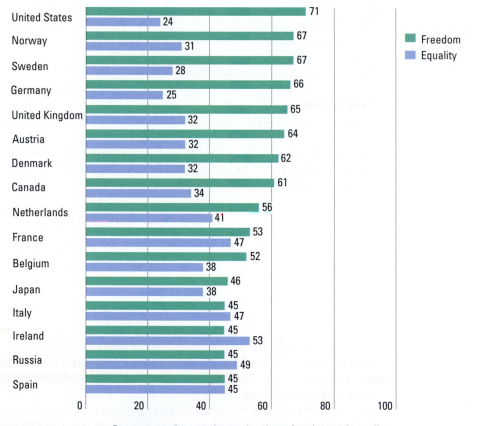

	Freedom	Equality
United States	71	24
Norway	67	31
Sweden	67	28
Germany	66	25
United Kingdom	65	32
Austria	64	32
Denmark	62	32
Canada	61	34
Netherlands	56	41
France	53	47
Belgium	52	38
Japan	46	38
Italy	45	47
Ireland	45	53
Russia	45	49
Spain	45	45

Percentage of respondents who chose freedom and equality

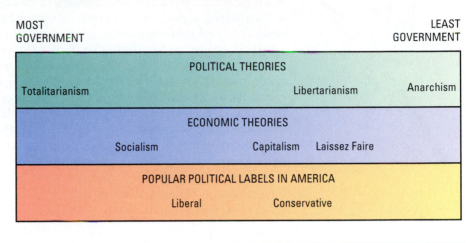

figure 1.1 ● Ideology and the Scope of Government

We can classify political ideologies according to the scope of action that people are willing to allow government in dealing with social and economic problems. In this chart, the three lines map out various philosophical positions along an underlying continuum ranging from "most" to "least" government. Notice that conventional politics in the United States spans only a narrow portion of the theoretical possibilities for government action.

In popular usage, liberals favor a greater scope of government; conservatives want a narrower scope. But over time, the traditional distinction has eroded and now oversimplifies the differences between liberals and conservatives. See Figure 1.2 for a more discriminating classification of liberals and conservatives.

their positions by referring to philosophies about the proper scope of government—the range of its permissible activities. Imagine a continuum. At one end is the belief that government should do everything; at the other is the belief that government should not exist. These extreme ideologies—from the most government to the least government—and those that fall in between are shown in Figure 1.1.

Totalitarianism

Totalitarianism is the belief that government should have unlimited power. A totalitarian government controls all sectors of society: business, labor, education, religion, sports, the arts. A true totalitarian favors a network of laws, rules, and regulations that guides every aspect of individual behavior. The object is to produce a perfect society serving some master plan for "the common good." Totalitarianism has reached its terrifying full potential only in literature and films (for example, George Orwell's *1984*), but several real societies have come perilously close to "perfection." One thinks of Germany under Hitler and the Soviet Union under Stalin. Not many people openly profess totalitarianism today, but the concept is useful because it anchors one side of our continuum.

Socialism

Whereas totalitarianism refers to government in general, **socialism pertains to government's role in the economy. Like communism, socialism is an economic system based on Marxist theory.** Under socialism (and communism), the scope of government extends to ownership or control of the basic industries that produce goods and services. These include communications, mining, heavy industry, transportation, and power. Although socialism favors a strong role for government in regulating private industry and directing the economy, it allows more room than communism does for private ownership of productive capacity.

Many Americans equate socialism with the communism practiced in the old closed societies of the Soviet Union and Eastern Europe. But there is a difference. Although communism in theory was supposed to result in a "withering away" of the state, communist governments in practice tended toward totalitarianism, controlling not just economic life but both political and social life through a dominant party organization. Some socialist governments, however, practice **democratic socialism.** They guarantee civil liberties (such as freedom of speech and freedom of religion) and allow their citizens to determine the extent of the government's activity through free elections and competitive political parties. Outside the United States, socialism is not universally viewed as inherently bad. In fact, the governments of Britain, Sweden, Germany, and France, among other democracies, have at times since World War II been avowedly socialist. More recently, the formerly communist regimes of Eastern Europe have abandoned the controlling role of government in their economies in favor of elements of capitalism.

Capitalism

Capitalism also relates to the government's role in the economy. In contrast to both socialism and communism, **capitalism** supports free enterprise—private businesses operating without government regulation. Some theorists, most notably economist Milton Friedman, argue that free enterprise is necessary for free politics.[16] This argument, that the economic system of capitalism is essential to democracy, contradicts the tenets of democratic socialism. Whether it is valid depends in part on our understanding of democracy, a subject discussed in Chapter 2.

The United States is decidedly a capitalist country, more so than Britain or most other Western nations. Despite the U.S. government's enormous budget, it owns or operates relatively few public enterprises. For example, railroads, airlines, and television stations are privately owned in the United States; these businesses are frequently owned by the government in other countries. But our government does extend its authority into the economic sphere, regulating private businesses and directing the overall economy. American liberals and conservatives both embrace capitalism, but they differ on the nature and amount of government intervention in the economy that is necessary or desirable.

Libertarianism

Libertarianism opposes all government action except what is necessary to protect life and property. **Libertarians** grudgingly recognize the necessity of government but believe that it should be as limited as possible. For example, libertarians grant the need for traffic laws to ensure safe and efficient automobile travel. But they oppose as a restriction on individual actions laws that set a minimum drinking age, and they even oppose laws outlawing marijuana and other drugs. Libertarians believe that social programs that provide food, clothing, and shelter are outside the proper scope of government. Helping the needy, they insist, should be a matter of individual choice. Libertarians also oppose government ownership of basic industries; in fact, they oppose any government intervention in the economy. This kind of economic policy is called **laissez faire**, a French phrase that means "let (people) do (as they please)." Such an extreme policy extends beyond the free enterprise advocated by most capitalists.

Libertarians are vocal advocates of hands-off government, in both the social and the economic sphere. Whereas those Americans who favor a broad scope of government action shun the description *socialist*, libertarians make no secret of their identity. The Libertarian Party ran candidates in every presidential election from 1972 through 1996. However, not one of these candidates won more than 1 million votes.

Do not confuse libertarians with liberals. The words are similar, but their meanings are quite different. *Libertarianism* draws on *liberty* as its root and means "absence of governmental constraint." In American political usage, *liberalism* evolved from the root word *liberal*. **Liberals** see a positive role for government in helping the disadvantaged. Over time, liberal has come to mean something closer to *generous*, in the sense that liberals (but not libertarians) support government spending on social programs. Libertarians find little benefit in any government social program.

Anarchism

Anarchism stands opposite totalitarianism on the political continuum. Anarchists oppose all government, in any form. As a political philosophy, anarchism values freedom above all else. Because all government involves some restriction on personal freedom (for example, forcing people to drive on one side of the road), a pure anarchist would object even to traffic laws. Like totalitarianism, anarchism is not a popular philosophy, but it does have adherents on the political fringes.

In July 1993, about ten thousand hippies and anarchists held a festival in a national forest in Alabama, continuing a decades-old tradition. In 1995, a group of anarchists in New York City sparked a melee that enabled neighbors to reclaim a local park from harassed authorities.[17] These minor events illustrate the fact that anarchists still exist. For our purposes, anarchism serves to anchor the right side of the government continuum and to indicate that libertarians are not as extreme in opposing government as is theoretically possible.

Liberals and Conservatives— The Narrow Middle

As shown in Figure 1.1, practical politics in the United States ranges over only the central portion of the continuum. The extreme positions—totalitarianism and anarchism—are rarely argued in public debate. And in this era of distrust of "big government," few American politicians would openly advocate socialism (although one did in 1990 and won election to Congress as an independent candidate). On the other hand, over one hundred people ran for Congress in 1994 as candidates of the Libertarian Party. Although none won, American libertarians are sufficiently vocal to be heard in the debate over the role of government.

Still, most of that debate is limited to a narrow range of political thought. On one side are people commonly called *liberals*; on the other are *conservatives.* In popular usage, liberals favor more government, conservatives less. This distinction is clear when the issue is government spending to provide public goods. Liberals favor generous government support for education, wildlife protection, public transportation, and a whole range of social programs. **Conservatives** want smaller government budgets and fewer government programs. They support free enterprise and argue against government job programs, regulation of business, and legislation of working conditions and wage rates.

But in other areas, liberal and conservative ideologies are less consistent. In theory, liberals favor government activism, yet they oppose government regulation of abortion. In theory, conservatives oppose government activism, yet they support government control of the publication of sexually explicit material. What's going on? Are American political attitudes hopelessly contradictory, or is something missing in our analysis of these ideologies today? Actually, something is missing. To understand the liberal and conservative stances on political issues, we have to look not only at the scope of government action but also at the purpose of government action. That is, to understand a political ideology, it is necessary to understand how it incorporates the values of freedom, order, and equality.

AMERICAN POLITICAL IDEOLOGIES AND THE PURPOSE OF GOVERNMENT

Much of American politics revolves around the two dilemmas just described: freedom versus order and freedom versus equality. The two dilemmas do not account for all political conflict, but they help us gain insight into the workings of politics and organize the seemingly chaotic world of political events, actors, and issues.

Liberals Versus Conservatives: The New Differences

Liberals and conservatives are different, but their differences no longer hinge on the narrow question of the government's role in providing public goods. Liberals still favor more government and conservatives less, but this is no longer the critical difference between them. Today, that difference stems from their attitudes toward the purpose of government. Conservatives support the original purpose of government—maintaining social order. They are willing to use the coercive power of the state to force citizens to be orderly. They favor firm police action, swift and severe punishment for criminals, and more laws regulating behavior. Conservatives would not stop with defining, preventing, and punishing crime, however. They tend to want to preserve traditional patterns of social relations—the domestic role of women and the importance of religion in school and family life, for example.

Liberals are less likely than conservatives to want to use government power to maintain order. In general, liberals are more tolerant of alternative lifestyles—for example, homosexual behavior. Liberals do not shy away from using government coercion, but they use it for a different purpose—to promote equality. They support laws that ensure equal treatment of homosexuals in employment, housing, and education; laws that

● ● ● ● ● ● ● ● ● ●

A Kiss Is but a Kiss

A city worker stares at a controversial poster on an elevated train station in Chicago. Part of a national AIDS awareness campaign, this advertisement was intended to show that AIDS is not transmitted through kissing. Public officials and clergy who tried to ban the ad found that they could not, because it was neither untruthful nor obscene: it simply conveyed unconventional images of a conventional act and was contrary to the established order.

require the busing of schoolchildren to achieve racial equality; laws that force private businesses to hire and promote women and members of minority groups; laws that require public transportation to provide equal access to the disabled; and laws that order cities and states to reapportion election districts so that minority voters can elect minority candidates to public office.

Conservatives do not oppose equality, but they do not value it to the extent of using the government's power to enforce equality. For liberals, the use of that power to promote equality is both valid and necessary.

A Two-Dimensional Classification of Ideologies

To classify liberal and conservative ideologies more accurately, we have to incorporate the values of freedom, order, and equality into the classification. We can do this using the model in Figure 1.2. It depicts the conflicting values along two separate dimensions, each anchored in maximum freedom at the lower left. One dimension extends horizontally from maximum freedom on the left to maximum order on the right. The other extends vertically from maximum freedom at the bottom to maximum equality at the top. Each box represents a different ideological type: libertarians, liberals, conservatives, and communitarians.*

---

*   The communitarian category was labeled "populist" in previous editions of this book. We have relabeled it for two reasons. First, we believe communitarian is more descriptive of the category. Second, we recognize that the term populist has been used increasingly to refer to the political styles of Ross Perot and Pat Buchanan. In this sense, a populist appeals to mass resentment against those in power. Given the debate over what "populist" really means, we have decided to use communitarian, a less familiar term with fewer connotations.[18]

1.2   ● Ideologies: A Two-Dimensional Framework

The four ideological types below are defined by the values they favor in resolving the two major dilemmas of government: how much freedom should be sacrificed in pursuit of order and equality, respectively? Test yourself by thinking about the values that are most important to you. Which box in the figure best represents your combination of values?

Equality

THE MODERN DILEMMA

Liberals

Favor: Government activities that promote equality, such as affirmative action programs to employ minorities and increased spending on public housing.

Oppose: Government actions that restrict individual liberties, such as banning sexually explicit movies or mandatory testing for AIDS.

Communitarians

Favor: Government activities that promote equality, such as affirmative action programs to employ minorities and increased spending on public housing.

Favor: Government actions that impose social order, such as banning sexually explicit movies or mandatory testing for AIDS.

Libertarians

Oppose: Government activities that interfere with the market, such as affirmative action programs to employ minorities and increased spending on public housing.

Oppose: Government actions that restrict individual liberties, such as banning sexually explicit movies or mandatory testing for AIDS.

Conservatives

Oppose: Government activities that interfere with the market, such as affirmative action programs to employ minorities and increased spending on public housing.

Favor: Government actions that impose social order, such as banning sexually explicit movies or mandatory testing for AIDS.

Freedom

Freedom ◄――――――――――――――――――――► Order

THE ORIGINAL DILEMMA

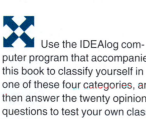

Use the IDEAlog computer program that accompanies this book to classify yourself in one of these four categories, and then answer the twenty opinion questions to test your own classification.

Libertarians value freedom more than order or equality. (We will use this term for people who have libertarian tendencies but may not accept the whole philosophy.) In practical terms, libertarians want minimal government intervention in both the economic and the social sphere. For example, they oppose affirmative action and laws that restrict transmission of sexually explicit material.

Liberals value freedom more than order but not more than equality. Liberals oppose laws that ban sexually explicit publications but support affirmative action. Conservatives value freedom more than equality but would restrict freedom to preserve social order. Conservatives oppose affirmative action but favor laws that restrict pornography.

Finally, we arrive at the ideological type positioned at the upper right in Figure 1.2. This group values both equality and order more than freedom. Its members support both affirmative action and laws that restrict pornography. We will call this new group *communitarians*. The *Oxford English Dictionary* (1989) defines a communitarian as "a member of a community formed to put into practice communistic or socialistic theories." The term is used more narrowly in contemporary politics, to reflect the philosophy of the Communitarian Network, a political movement founded by sociologist Amitai Etzioni.[19] This movement rejects both the liberal-conservative classification and the libertarian argument that "individuals should be left on their own to pursue their choices, rights, and self-interests."[20] Like liberals, Etzioni's communitarians believe that there is a role for government in helping the disadvantaged. Like conservatives, they believe that government should be used to promote moral values—preserving the family through more stringent divorce laws, protecting against AIDS through testing programs, and limiting the dissemination of pornography, for example.[21]

The Communitarian Network is not dedicated to big government, however. According to its platform, "The government should step in only to the extent that other social subsystems fail, rather than seek to replace them."[22] Nevertheless, in recognizing the collective nature of society, the Network's platform clearly distinguishes its philosophy from that of libertarianism:

> It has been argued by libertarians that responsibilities are a personal matter, that individuals are to judge which responsibilities they accept as theirs. As we see it, responsibilities are anchored in community. Reflecting the diverse moral voices of their citizens, responsive communities define what is expected of people; they educate their members to accept these values; and they praise them when they do and frown upon them when they do not.[23]

Although it clearly embraces the Communitarian Network's philosophy, our definition of communitarian (small "c") is broader and more in keeping with the dictionary definition. Thus **communitarians** favor government programs that promote both order and equality, in keeping with socialist theory.

By analyzing political ideologies on two dimensions rather than one, we can explain why people can seem to be liberal on one issue (favoring a broader scope of government action) and conservative on another (favoring less government action). The answer hinges on the purpose of a given government action: which value does it promote, order or equality? According to our typology, only libertarians and communitarians are consistent in their attitude toward the scope of government activity, whatever its purpose. Libertarians value freedom so highly that they oppose most government efforts to enforce either order or equality. Communitarians (in our usage) are inclined to trade freedom for both order and equality. Liberals and conservatives, on the other hand, favor or oppose government activity depending on its purpose. As you will learn in Chapter 5, large groups of Americans fall into each of the four ideological categories. Because Americans increasingly choose four different resolutions to the original and modern dilemmas of government, the simple labels of *liberal* and *conservative* no longer describe contemporary political ideologies as well as they did in the 1930s, 1940s, and 1950s.

SUMMARY

The challenge of democracy lies in making difficult choices—choices that inevitably bring important values into conflict. This chapter has outlined a normative framework for analyzing the policy choices that arise in the pursuit of the purposes of government.

The three major purposes of government are maintaining order, providing public goods, and promoting equality. In pursuing these objectives, every government infringes on individual freedom. But the degree of that infringement depends on the government's (and, by extension, its citizens') commitment to order and equality. What we have, then, are two dilemmas. The first—the original dilemma—centers on the conflict between freedom and order. The second—the modern dilemma—focuses on the conflict between freedom and equality.

Some people use political ideologies to help them resolve the conflicts that arise in political decision making. These ideologies define the scope and purpose of government. At opposite extremes of the continuum are totalitarianism, which supports government intervention in every aspect of society, and anarchism, which rejects government entirely. An important step back from totalitarianism is socialism. Democratic socialism, an economic system, favors government ownership of basic industries but preserves civil liberties. Capitalism, another economic system, promotes free enterprise. A significant step short of anarchism is libertarianism, which allows government to protect life and property but little else.

In the United States, the terms *liberal* and *conservative* are used to describe a narrow range toward the center of the political continuum. The usage is probably accurate when the scope of government action is being discussed. That is, liberals support a broader role for government than do conservatives. But when both the scope and the purpose of government are considered, a different, sharper distinction emerges. Conservatives may want less government but not at the price of maintaining order. In other words, they are willing to use the coercive power of government to impose social order. Liberals, too, are willing to use the coercive powers of government, but for a different purpose—promoting equality.

It is easier to understand the differences among libertarians, liberals, conservatives, and communitarians and their views on the scope of government if the values of freedom, order, and equality are incorporated into the description of their political ideologies. Libertarians choose freedom over both order and equality. Communitarians are willing to sacrifice freedom for both order and equality. Liberals value freedom more than order and equality more than freedom. Conservatives value order more than freedom and freedom more than equality.

The concepts of government objectives, values, and political ideologies appear repeatedly in this book as we determine who favors what government action and why. So far, we have said little about how government should make its decisions. In Chapter 2, we complete our normative framework for evaluating American politics by examining the nature of democratic theory. There, we introduce two key concepts for analyzing how democratic governments make decisions.

Key Terms

government	public goods	political equality	equality of outcome
order	freedom of	social equality	rights
communism	freedom from	equality of opportunity	totalitarianism

socialism	libertarianism	laissez faire	communitarians
democratic socialism	libertarians	anarchism	
capitalism	liberals	conservatives	

Selected Readings

Bock, Gisela, and Susan James (eds.). *Beyond Equality and Difference: Citizenship, Feminist Politics, and Female Subjectivity.* New York: Routledge, 1992. A collection of essays by women on the meaning of equality and its relationship to the differences between the sexes, with special reference to sexual politics.

Ebenstein, William, and Edwin Fogelman. *Today's Isms: Communism, Fascism, Capitalism, Socialism,* 10th ed. Englewood Cliffs, N.J.: Prentice-Hall, 1994. This standard source describes the history of the four major "isms" and relates each to developments in contemporary politics. It is concise, informative, and readable.

Etzioni, Amitai. *Rights and the Common Good: The Communitarian Perspective.* New York: St. Martin's Press, 1995. Reprints the Communitarian Network's platform and presents thirty essays on various aspects of the communitarian perspective.

Foley, Michael. *American Political Ideas: Traditions and Usages.* New York: St. Martin's Press, 1991. A foreigner's perspective on the major concepts in American political thought. It has chapters on freedom, equality, capitalism, liberalism, and conservatism, among other topics.

World Wide Web Resources

The World Wide Web (WWW) on the Internet has many sites with information relevant to studying American government and politics. Below are some that are particularly relevant to the ideological typology described in this chapter. The Uniform Resource Locator (URL) needed to find the site on the WWW is given within pointy brackets < >. Because these addresses may change over time, you may have to search the WWW by keywords to locate the site.

The Communitarian Network. This site "is a coalition of individuals and organizations who have come together to shore up the moral, social, and political environment. We are a nonsectarian, nonpartisan, nationwide association."
`<www.gwu.edu/~ccps/>`

Libertarian Student Clubs' WWW Network. This site "is a links and updates page for all the libertarian student clubs using the Web. This includes both student affiliates of the Libertarian Party and other student groups seeking to further the cause of libertarianism."
`<www.mit.edu:8001/activities/libertarians/lscwn.html>`

Lefties on the Web. "This page is for those of us who don't buy into Newt's New Right agenda, and who still believe there's a constructive role for government in America."
`<www.tiac.net/users/rafeb/>`

The Right Side of the Web. A creation of Jeff Donels, whose home page describes him as "Webmaster, member of the Militia of Northern Virginia AND digeratti wanna-be (even though WiReD hates me)," this site contains a melange of material dealing with conservative causes.
`<www.clark.net/pub/jeffd/index.html>`

Christian Coalition. "A grassroots citizen organization working on behalf of families who want to see less government intrusion in their lives and more family-friendly public policy."
`<cc.org/>`

chapter 2

Majoritarian or Pluralist Democracy?

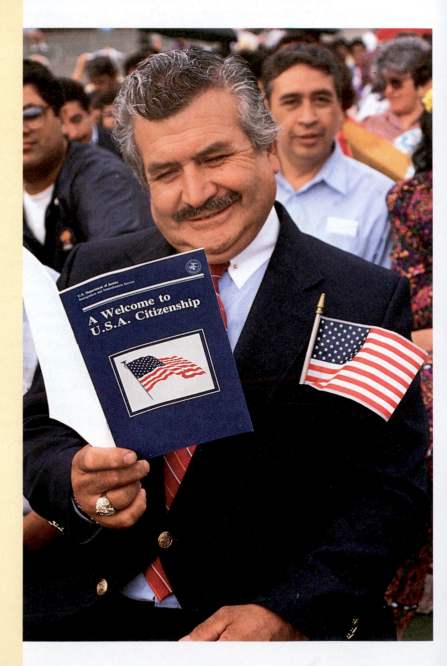

BRYL TAYLOR PHILLIPS CAME TO BEAR WITNESS. She sat in a back row while the Rules Committee prepared the legislation to send it to the floor. Holding a photograph in her hands, she turned to the stranger next to her and said, "This is Scott Phillips, my seventeen-year-old son." The congressmen at the front of the room droned on, quickly disposing of the procedural steps necessary before they could vote to send the bill on. She continued, "A classmate [of Scott's] bought an AK-47. . . . You could buy that gun at the time." She finished the story: "Semiautomatic. It held 50 rounds of ammunition. He took him in the woods. He shot him six times. One bullet severed his spinal cord. Then he shot him at his leisure."[1]

The Rules Committee finally voted and sent the bill on to the full House, where it passed 239 to 173. The legislation was designed to repeal the ban on assault weapons—guns like the one used in the murder of Scott Phillips. His mother, like many other Americans, was mystified at the House's March 1996 actions. Only a few years earlier, Congress had passed a *ban* on assault weapons. At the time, Congress appeared to be saying that there is no need for these weapons, which can kill so many in a matter of seconds. (Semiautomatics are military assault rifles; they can fire in very rapid succession.) What may seem most puzzling is that polls consistently show that Americans overwhelmingly support a ban on assault weapons. Why wasn't the House following the majority opinion? Isn't that what legislators in a democracy are supposed to do?

Critics of the House vote pointed to the National Rifle Association (NRA), which pushed hard for lifting the assault weapons ban. They noted that the NRA is a strong financial backer of legislators who oppose gun control. Those who voted against the prohibition on assault weapons received an average of $14,056 in NRA campaign contributions during the past decade. Supporters of the ban received just $659.[2] Advocates of the repeal scoff at the criticism. They believe the ban has been ineffective; criminals can still buy guns, and thus little has been accomplished to make America truly safer. As Representative Gerald Solomon (R.-NY) put it, "The way to stop crime is to put criminals in prison, not take away from law-abiding citizens the right to protect themselves."[3] For the NRA, the explanation was simple: members of the House voted the way they did because they realized that the ban infringed upon the Second Amendment's "right of the people to keep and bear arms."

The assault ban repeal died in the Senate, however. Seeing little public support for the repeal, Senate Majority Leader Bob Dole quickly indicated

31

Gunning for the NRA

Senator Dianne Feinstein (D.-CA) and Senator Paul Simon (D.-IL), who retired at the end of 1996, show off some of the hardware they're trying to keep off the street during a press conference publicizing their fight against a repeal of the assault weapons ban. The failure of Congress to repeal the ban after the Republican sweep in the 1994 election was a remarkable defeat for the National Rifle Association. With strong Republican majorities in both houses the NRA had high hopes for a repeal of what it regards as a gross infringement on citizens' constitutional right to keep and bear arms. Although still powerful, the NRA has clearly lost some of its influence. Legislators are not as fearful of the group and the NRA's membership has been declining.

 The initial vote on the decision to ban assault weapons is one of the variables in the Crosstabs program that accompanies this book. Find "Assault Weapons Ban" in the program and analyze the congressional vote.

that he wouldn't bring the bill up for a vote. Although he had earlier pledged his support for a repeal, Dole didn't want to have to explain his opposition to the ban during the fall presidential race.[4] The split between the House and the Senate reflects a dilemma that legislators often face: an interest group representing a small minority of the population comes to Congress to ask that it enact or defend some policy that the group's members favor. But what is good for that group may not be what is best for the public at large. Moreover, the majority may not be well mobilized, because it is apathetic about the issue, thus making it enticing for legislators to earn the gratitude of the interest group's followers, who are watching closely to see what Congress will do on that particular policy. Is it democratic for policymakers to favor an intense minority at the expense of a less-committed majority?

In Chapter 1 we discussed three basic values that underlie what government should do. In this chapter we examine how government should decide what to do. In particular, we set forth criteria for judging whether a government's decision-making process is democratic.

THE THEORY OF DEMOCRATIC GOVERNMENT

The origins of democratic theory lie in ancient Greek political thought. Greek philosophers classified governments according to the number of citizens involved in the process. Imagine a continuum running from rule by one person, through rule by a few, to rule by many.

Differing Paths to Democracy

After gaining its freedom from the Soviet Union, Lithuania made a smooth, peaceful transition to democracy. This woman takes advantage of her new rights to cast her election ballot in her neighborhood in Vilnius, the capital. The road to democracy has been much rockier in the former Yugoslavia. This rally for a Serbian radical party in Belgrade reflected the widespread ethnic hatred in the Balkans. Many Serbs dream of a greater Serbia and do not respect the political boundaries that have divided that area of the world into different countries. The support of the Serbs outside of Bosnia for the Serbs living there was critical in fueling the terrible war in Bosnia among Serbs, Muslims, and Croats. It may be some time before true democracy comes to that area of the world.

At one extreme is an **autocracy,** in which one individual has the power to make all important decisions. The concentration of power in the hands of one person (usually a monarch) was a more common form of government in earlier historical periods. Some countries are still ruled autocratically, such as Iraq under Saddam Hussein.

Oligarchy puts government power in the hands of an elite. At one time, the nobility or the major landowners commonly ruled as an aristocracy. Today, military leaders are often the rulers in countries governed by an oligarchy.

At the other extreme of the continuum is **democracy,** which means rule by the people. Most scholars believe that the United States, Britain, France, and other countries in Western Europe are genuine democracies. Others contend that these countries only appear to be democracies because they hold free elections but that they actually are run by wealthy business elites for their own benefit. Nevertheless, most people today agree that governments should be democratic.

The Meaning and Symbolism of Democracy

Americans have a simple answer to the question, "Who should govern?" It is, "The people." Unfortunately, this answer is too simple. It fails to define who *the people* are. Should we include young children? Recent immigrants? Illegal aliens? This answer also fails to tell us how the people should do the governing. Should they be assembled in a stadium? Vote by mail? Choose others to govern for them? We need to take a closer look at what "government by the people" really means.

The word *democracy* originated in Greek writings around the fifth century B.C. *Demos* referred to the common people, the masses; *kratos* meant "power." The ancient Greeks were afraid of democracy—rule by rank-and-file citizens. That fear is evident in the term *demagogue.* We use the term today to refer to a politician who appeals to and often deceives the masses by manipulating their emotions and prejudices.

Many centuries after the Greeks first defined democracy, the idea still carried the connotation of mob rule. When George Washington was president, opponents of a new political party disparagingly called it a *demo-cratic* party. No one would do that in politics today. In fact, the term has become so popular that the names of more than 20 percent of the world's political parties contain some variation of the word *democracy*.[5]

There are two major schools of thought about what constitutes democracy. The first believes democracy is a form of government. It emphasizes the procedures that enable the people to govern—meeting to discuss issues, voting in elections, running for public office. The second sees democracy in the substance of government policies, in freedom of religion and the provision for human needs. The procedural approach focuses on how decisions are made; the substantive approach is concerned with what government does.

The Procedural View of Democracy

Procedural democratic theory sets forth principles that describe how government should make decisions. The principles address three distinct questions:

1. *Who* should participate in decision making?

2. *How much* should each participant's vote count?

3. *How many* votes are needed to reach a decision?

According to procedural democratic theory, all adults should participate in government decision making; everyone within the boundaries of the political community should be allowed to vote. If some people, such as recent immigrants, are prohibited from participating, they are excluded only for practical or political reasons. The theory of democracy itself does not exclude any adults from participation. We refer to this principle as **universal participation.**

How much should each participant's vote count? According to procedural theory, all votes should be counted *equally*. This is the principle of **political equality.**

Note that universal participation and political equality are two distinct principles. It is not enough for everyone to participate in a decision; all votes must carry equal weight. President Abraham Lincoln reportedly once took a vote among his cabinet members and found that they all opposed his position on an issue. He summarized the vote and the decision this way: "Seven noes, one aye—the ayes have it."[6] Everyone participated, but Lincoln's vote counted more than all the others combined. (No one ever said that presidents have to run their cabinets democratically.)

Finally, how many votes are needed to reach a decision? Procedural theory prescribes that a group should decide to do what the majority of its participants (50 percent plus one person) wants to do. This principle is called **majority rule.** (If participants divide over more than two alternatives and none receives a simple majority, the principle usually defaults to *plurality rule*, under which the group does what most participants want.)

A Complication: Direct Versus Indirect Democracy

The three principles—universal participation, political equality, and majority rule—are widely recognized as necessary for democratic decision making. Small, simple societies can meet these principles with a direct or **participatory democracy,** in which all members of the group meet to make decisions, observing political equality and majority rule. The origins of participatory democracy go back to the Greek city-state, where the important decisions of government were made by the adult citizens meeting in an assembly. The people ruled themselves rather than having a small number of notables rule on their behalf. (In Athens, the people who were permitted to attend the assemblies did not include women, slaves, and those whose families had not lived there for generations. Thus, participation was not universal. Still, the Greek city-state represented a dramatic transformation in the theory of government.)[7]

Something close to participatory democracy is practiced in some New England villages, where rank-and-file citizens gather in a town meeting, often just once a year, to make key community decisions together. A town meeting is impractical in large cities, although there are some cities that have incorporated participatory democracy in their decision-making processes by instituting forms of neighborhood government. For example, in Birmingham, Alabama; Dayton, Ohio; Portland, Oregon; and St. Paul, Minnesota, each area of the city is governed by a neighborhood council. The neighborhood councils have authority over zoning and land use questions, and they usually control some funds for the development of projects within their boundaries. All adult residents of a neighborhood may participate in the neighborhood council meetings, and the larger city government respects their decisions.[8] In Chicago, the school system uses participatory democracy. Each school is primarily governed by a parents' council and not by the citywide school board.[9]

Philosopher Jean Jacques Rousseau contended that true democracy is impossible unless all citizens gather to make decisions and supervise the government. Rousseau said that decisions of government should embody the general will, and "will cannot be represented."[10] Yet in the United States and virtually all other democracies, participatory democracy is rare. Few cities have decentralized their governments and turned power over to their neighborhoods.

Participatory democracy is commonly rejected on the grounds that in large, complex societies we need professional, full-time government officials to study problems, formulate solutions, and administer programs. Also, the assumption is that relatively few people will take part in participatory government. This, in fact, turns out to be the case. In a study of neighborhood councils in the cities mentioned above, only 16.6 percent of residents took part in at least one meeting during a two-year period.[11] In other respects, participatory democracy works rather well on the neighborhood level. Yet even if participatory democracy is appropriate for neighborhoods or small villages, how could it work for the national government? We cannot all gather at the Capitol in Washington to decide defense policy.

The framers of the Constitution were convinced that participatory democracy on the national level was undesirable and instead instituted

representative democracy. In such a system, citizens participate in government by electing public officials to make decisions on their behalf. Elected officials are expected to represent the voters' views and interests—that is, to serve as the agents of the citizenry and to act for them.

Within the context of representative democracy, we adhere to the principles of universal participation, political equality, and majority rule to guarantee that elections are democratic. But what happens after the election? The elected representatives might not make the decisions the people would have made had they gathered for the same purpose. To account for this possibility in representative government, procedural theory provides a fourth decision-making principle: **responsiveness.** Elected representatives should respond to public opinion. This does not mean that legislators simply cast their ballots on the basis of whether the people back home want alternative A or alternative B. Issues are not usually so straightforward. Rather, responsiveness means following the general contours of public opinion in formulating complex pieces of legislation.[12]

By adding responsiveness to deal with the case of indirect democracy, we have four principles of procedural democracy:

- Universal participation
- Political equality
- Majority rule
- Government responsiveness to public opinion

The Substantive View of Democracy

According to procedural theory, the principle of responsiveness is absolute. The government should do what the majority wants, regardless of what that is. At first this seems a reasonable way to protect the rights of citizens in a representative democracy. But think for a minute. Christians are the vast majority of the U.S. population. Suppose that the Christian majority backs a constitutional amendment to require Bible reading in public schools, that the amendment is passed by Congress, and that it is ratified by the states. From a strictly procedural view, the action would be democratic. But what about freedom of religion? What about the rights of minorities? To limit the government's responsiveness to public opinion, we must look outside procedural democratic theory, to substantive democratic theory.

Substantive democratic theory focuses on the substance of government policies, not on the procedures followed in making those policies. It argues that in a democratic government, certain principles must be incorporated into government policies. Substantive theorists would reject a law that requires Bible reading in schools, because it would violate a substantive principle, freedom of religion. The core of our substantive principles of democracy is embedded in the Bill of Rights and other amendments to the Constitution.

In defining the principles that underlie democratic government—and the policies of that government—most substantive theorists agree on a

● ● ● ● ● ● ● ● ● ●

Is Housing a Right?

Some argue that a democratic government is one that promotes social and economic rights. There is little agreement in this country, however, concerning what qualifies as rights requiring substantive policy measures. This homeless man in Washington, D.C., has firm beliefs on one such issue.

basic criterion: government policies should guarantee civil liberties (freedom of behavior, such as freedom of religion and freedom of expression) and civil rights (powers or privileges that government may not arbitrarily deny to individuals, such as protection against discrimination in employment and housing). According to this standard, the claim that the United States is a democracy rests on its record in ensuring its citizens these liberties and rights. (We look at how good this record is in Chapters 15 and 16.)

Agreement among substantive theorists breaks down when the discussion moves from civil rights to social rights (adequate health care, quality education, decent housing) and economic rights (private property, steady employment). They disagree most sharply on whether a government must promote social equality in order to qualify as a democracy. For example, must a state guarantee unemployment benefits and adequate public housing to be called democratic? Some insist that policies that promote social equality are essential to democratic government.[13] Others restrict the requirements of substantive democracy to those policies that safeguard civil liberties and civil rights.

A theorist's political ideology tends to explain his or her position on what democracy really requires in substantive policies. Conservative theorists have a narrow view of the scope of democratic government and a narrow view of the social and economic rights guaranteed by that government. Liberal theorists believe that a democratic government should guarantee its citizens a much broader spectrum of social and economic rights. In later chapters, we review important social and economic policies that our government has actually followed over time. Keep in mind, however, that what the government has done in the past is not necessarily a correct guide to what a democratic government should do.

Procedural Democracy Versus Substantive Democracy

The problem with the substantive view of democracy is that it does not provide clear, precise criteria that allow us to determine whether a government is democratic. It is, in fact, open to unending arguments over which government policies are truly democratic. Substantive theorists are free to promote their pet values—separation of church and state, guaranteed employment, equal rights for women, whatever—under the guise of substantive democracy.

The procedural viewpoint also has a problem. Although it presents specific criteria for democratic government, those criteria can produce undesirable social policies, such as those that prey on minorities. This clashes with **minority rights**—the idea that all citizens are entitled to certain things that cannot be denied by the majority. Opinions proliferate on what those "certain things" are, but all would agree, for example, on freedom of religion. One way to protect minority rights is to limit the principle of majority rule—by requiring a two-thirds majority or some other extraordinary majority for decisions on certain subjects, for example. Another way is to put the issue in the Constitution, beyond the reach of majority rule.

The issue of prayer in school is a good example of the limits on majority rule. No matter how large, majorities in Congress cannot pass a law to permit organized prayer in public schools, because the Supreme Court has determined that the Constitution forbids such a law. The Constitution could be changed so that it no longer protects religious minorities, but amending the Constitution is a cumbersome process that involves extraordinary majorities. When limits such as these are put on the principle of majority rule, the minority often rules instead.

Clearly, then, procedural democracy and substantive democracy are not always compatible. In choosing one instead of the other, we are also choosing to focus on either procedures or policies. As authors of this text, we favor a compromise. On the whole, we favor the procedural conception of democracy, because it more closely approaches the classical definition of democracy—"government by the people." And procedural democracy is founded on clear, well-established rules for decision making. But the theory has a serious drawback: it allows a democratic government to enact policies that can violate the substantive principles of democracy. Thus, pure procedural democracy should be diluted so that minority rights and civil liberties are guaranteed as part of the structure of government. If the compromise seems familiar, it is: the approach has been used in the course of American history to balance legitimate minority and majority interests.

INSTITUTIONAL MODELS OF DEMOCRACY

A small group can agree to make democratic decisions directly by using the principles of universal participation, political equality, and majority rule. But even the smallest nations have too many citizens to permit participatory democracy at the national level. If nations want democracy, they must achieve it through some form of representative government, electing officials to make decisions. Even then, democratic government is not guaranteed. Governments must have a way to determine what the people want, as well as some way to translate those wants into decisions.

In other words, democratic government requires institutional mechanisms—established procedures and organizations—to translate public opinion into government policy (and thus be responsive). Elections, political parties, legislatures, and interest groups (which we discuss in later chapters) are all examples of institutional mechanisms in politics.

Some democratic theorists favor institutions that closely tie government decisions to the desires of the majority of citizens. If most citizens want laws banning the sale of pornography, the government should outlaw pornography. If citizens want more money spent on defense and less on social welfare (or vice versa), the government should act accordingly. For these theorists, the essence of democratic government is majority rule and responsiveness.

Other theorists place less importance on the principles of majority rule and responsiveness. They do not believe in relying heavily on mass opinion; instead, they favor institutions that allow groups of citizens to defend their interests in the public policymaking process. Health care is a good example. Everyone cares about it, but it is a complex problem with many competing issues at stake. What is critical here is to allow differing interests to participate, so that all sides have the opportunity to influence policies as they are developed.

Both schools hold a procedural view of democracy, but they differ in how they interpret "government by the people." We can summarize the theoretical positions by using two alternative models of democracy. As a model, each is a hypothetical plan, a blueprint for achieving democratic government through institutional mechanisms. The majoritarian model values participation by the people in general; the pluralist model values participation by the people in groups.

The Majoritarian Model of Democracy

The **majoritarian model of democracy** relies on our intuitive, elemental notion of what is fair. It interprets "government by the people" to mean government by the *majority* of the people. The majoritarian model tries to approximate the people's role in a direct democracy within the limitations of representative government. To force the government to respond to public opinion, the majoritarian model depends on several mechanisms that allow the people to participate directly.

The popular election of government officials is the primary mechanism for democratic government in the majoritarian model. Citizens are expected to control their representatives' behavior by choosing wisely in the first place and by reelecting or voting out public officials according to their performance. Elections fulfill the first three principles of procedural democratic theory: universal participation, political equality, and majority rule. The prospect of reelection and the threat of defeat at the polls are expected to motivate public officials to meet the fourth criterion: responsiveness.

Usually, we think of elections only as mechanisms for choosing among candidates for public office. Majoritarian theorists also see them as a means for deciding government policies. An election on a policy issue is called a *referendum.* When a policy question is put on the ballot by citizens circulating petitions and gathering a required minimum number of

● ● ● ● ● ● ● ● ● ● ● ● ●

Separating Church from State

In Ireland's 1937 Constitution, divorce and remarriage were forbidden. Since then the Roman Catholic Church hierarchy was successful in beating back all attempts to rescind the prohibition, including the defeat of a 1986 referendum that would have permitted divorce and remarriage. In 1995, however, supporters of divorce reform were able to get another national referendum put before the nation. A rancorous campaign ensued and emotions ran high on both sides. Pictured here is an anti-divorce reform rally in Dublin, but some pro-divorce reform supporters appeared to have shown up, too. Out of 1.6 million ballots cast, the referendum succeeded in overturning the constitutional prohibitions by just over 9100 votes.

Activists are harnessing electronic media in all forms to promote democratic movements worldwide.

`<www.auburn.edu/tann/>`

signatures, it is called an *initiative.* Twenty-one states allow their legislatures to put referenda before the voters and give their citizens the right to place initiatives on the ballot. Five other states provide for one mechanism or the other.[14]

Statewide initiatives and referenda have been used to decide a wide variety of important questions, many of which have national implications. In 1996 Californians voted on an initiative to ban affirmative action in all state programs. Even before this vote, public opinion in California led the governor and the regents of the University of California to take steps to reverse affirmative action programs (see Politics in a Changing America 2.1). The ballot question stimulated hard-fought and emotional campaigns by supporters and defenders of affirmative action. In the end, California voters passed the ban on affirmative action by 54 to 46 percent.

In the United States, no provisions exist for referenda at the federal level, although some countries do allow policy questions to be put before the public. In Ireland, divorce had been forbidden by the country's constitution. Ireland was the only country in Europe where divorce was illegal. In a 1995 referendum, however, Irish voters narrowly approved a constitutional change to permit divorce.[15]

Americans strongly favor instituting a system of national referenda. In a survey, 65 percent of those queried indicated that voters should have a direct say on some national issues. Only 25 percent felt that we should leave all policymaking decisions to our elected representatives.[16] The most fervent advocates of majoritarian democracy would like to see modern technology used to maximize the government's responsiveness to the majority. Some have proposed incorporating public opinion polls, first used regularly in the 1930s, in government decision making. More recently, some have suggested using computers for referenda. For instance, citizens could vote on an issue by inserting plastic identification cards in computer terminals installed in all homes.[17]

The majoritarian model contends that citizens can control their government if they have adequate mechanisms for popular participation. It also assumes that citizens are knowledgeable about government and politics, that they want to participate in the political process, and that they make rational decisions in voting for their elected representatives.

Critics contend that Americans are not knowledgeable enough for majoritarian democracy to work. They point to research that shows that only 22 percent of a national sample of voters said that they "followed what's going on" in government "most of the time." More (40 percent) said that they followed politics "only now and then" or "hardly at all."[18] Calls for enhancing majoritarian democracy through interactive electronic technology raises other concerns. Some believe that instead of quick and easy mass voting on public policy, what we need is more deliberation by citizens and their elected representatives. **Deliberative democracy** emphasizes reasoned and full debate by those who immerse themselves in the substance of public policy problems.[19]

Defenders of majoritarian democracy respond that while individual Americans may have only limited knowledge of or interest in government, the American public as a whole still has coherent and stable opinions on major policy questions. One study concludes that people "do not need large amounts of information to make rational voting choices."[20] Finally, some note that while the population today participates in only a limited way, Americans are actually interested in participating more. However, they need more attractive and accessible opportunities to get involved.[21]

An Alternative Model: Pluralist Democracy

For years, political scientists struggled valiantly to reconcile the majoritarian model of democracy with polls that showed widespread ignorance of politics among the American people. When only a little more than half of the adult population bothers to vote in presidential elections, our form of democracy seems to be "government by *some* of the people."

The 1950s saw the evolution of an alternative interpretation of democracy, one tailored to the limited knowledge and participation of the real electorate, not the ideal one. It was based on the concept of *pluralism*—that modern society consists of innumerable groups that share economic, religious, ethnic, or cultural interests. Often, people with similar interests organize formal groups: the Future Farmers of America, chambers of commerce, and the Rotary Club, for example. Many social groups have little contact with government, but occasionally they find themselves backing or opposing government policies. When an organized group seeks to influence government policy, it is called an **interest group.** Many interest groups regularly spend much time and money trying to influence government policy (see Chapter 10). Among them are the International Electrical Workers Union, the American Hospital Association, the Associated Milk Producers, the National Education Association (NEA), the National Association of Manufacturers, the National Organization for Women (NOW), and, of course, the NRA.

● ● ● ● ● ● ● ● ● ● ●

Why They Are Called
Lobbyists

At the national level, interest groups are usually represented by paid lobbyists. These people are called lobbyists because they often gather in the lobby outside congressional meeting rooms, positioned to contact senators and representatives coming and going. Here, lobbyists are waiting to help members of the House Ways and Means Committee understand the importance of their pet tax loopholes.

"Bowling Alone" by Robert Putnam explores the decline in voluntary associations and its implications for American democracy:
`<muse.jhu.edu/journals/journal_of_democracy/v006/putnam.html>`

The **pluralist model of democracy** interprets "government by the people" to mean government by people operating through competing interest groups. According to this model, democracy exists when many (plural) organizations operate separately from the government, press their interests on the government, and even challenge the government.[22] Compared with majoritarian thinking, pluralist theory shifts the focus of democratic government from the mass electorate to organized groups. The criterion for democratic government changes from responsiveness to mass public opinion to responsiveness to organized groups of citizens.

The two major mechanisms in a pluralist democracy are interest groups and a decentralized structure of government that provides ready access to public officials and that is open to hearing the groups' arguments for or against government policies. In a centralized structure, decisions are made at one point, the top of the hierarchy. The few decision makers at the top are too busy to hear the claims of competing interest groups or to consider those claims in making their decisions. But a decentralized, complex government structure offers the access and openness necessary for pluralist democracy. For pluralists, the ideal system is one that divides government authority among numerous institutions with overlapping authority. Under such a system, competing interest groups have alternative points of access for presenting and arguing their claims.

Our Constitution approaches the pluralist ideal in the way it divides authority among the branches of government. When the National Association for the Advancement of Colored People (NAACP) could not get Congress to outlaw segregated schools in the South, it turned to the federal court system, which did what Congress would not. According to the ideal of pluralist democracy, if all opposing interests are allowed to organize, and if the system can be kept open so that all substantial claims are heard, the decision will serve the diverse needs of a pluralist society.

Although many scholars have contributed to the model, pluralist democracy is most closely identified with political scientist Robert Dahl. According to Dahl, the fundamental axiom of pluralist democracy is that "instead of a single center of sovereign power there must be multiple centers of power, none of which is or can be wholly sovereign."[23] Some watchwords of pluralist democracy, therefore, are *divided authority*, *decentralization*, and *open access*.

The Majoritarian Model Versus the Pluralist Model

In majoritarian democracy, the mass public—not interest groups—controls government actions. The citizenry must therefore have some knowledge of government and be willing to participate in the electoral process. Majoritarian democracy relies on electoral mechanisms that harness the power of the majority to make decisions. Conclusive elections and a centralized structure of government are mechanisms that aid majority rule. Cohesive political parties with well-defined programs also contribute to majoritarian democracy, because they offer voters a clear way to distinguish alternative sets of policies.

Pluralism does not demand much knowledge from citizens in general. It requires specialized knowledge only from groups of citizens, in particular their leaders. In contrast to majoritarian democracy, pluralist democracy seeks to limit majority action so that interest groups can be heard. It relies on strong interest groups and a decentralized government structure—mechanisms that interfere with majority rule, thereby protecting minority interests. We could even say that pluralism allows minorities to rule.

An Undemocratic Model: Elite Theory

If pluralist democracy allows minorities to rule, how does it differ from elite theory—the view that a small group (a minority) makes most important government decisions? According to elite theory, important government decisions are made by an identifiable and stable minority that shares certain characteristics, usually vast wealth and business connections.[24] Elite theory argues that these few individuals wield power in America because they control its key financial, communications, industrial, and government institutions. Their power derives from the vast wealth of America's largest corporations and the perceived importance of the continuing success of those corporations to the growth of the economy. An inner circle of top corporate leaders not only provides effective advocates for individual companies and for the interests of capitalism in general but also supplies people for top government jobs—from which they can further promote their interests.[25]

According to elite theory, the United States is not a democracy but an oligarchy. Although the voters appear to control the government through elections, elite theorists argue that the powerful few in society manage to define the issues and to constrain the outcomes of government decisions to suit their own interests. Clearly, elite theory describes a government that operates in an undemocratic fashion.

The Power Elite?

This picture symbolizes the underlying notion of elite theory—that government is driven by wealth. In truth, wealthy people usually do have more influence in the government than do people of ordinary means. Critics of elite theory, however, point out that it is difficult to demonstrate that an identifiable ruling elite usually sticks together and gets its way in government policy.

Elite theory appeals to many people, especially those who believe that wealth dominates politics. The theory also provides plausible explanations for specific political decisions. Why, over the years, has the tax code included so many loopholes that favor the wealthy? The answer, claim adherents of elite theory, is that the policymakers never really change—they are all cut from the same cloth. Even when a liberal Democrat is in the White House, many of the president's top economic policymakers will likely be people drawn from Wall Street or other financial institutions.

Political scientists have conducted numerous studies designed to test the validity of elite theory. One study, sympathetic to elite theory, tried to identify the power elite in America by defining the elite positions in the corporate, public interest, and government sectors of society. The author found 7,314 people who fit his definition of the national elite.[26] Although the figure represents only a tiny fraction of the nation's population, 7,314 seems to be too many rulers to provide coherent and coordinated leadership of government and society. Common sense suggests that a group this size is going to experience considerable disagreement.

Many studies have looked at individual cities to see whether a clearly identified elite rules across different issue areas. One influential study of New Haven, Connecticut, demonstrated that different groups won on different issues. No power elite could be found in that city.[27] Yet other studies, such as one on Atlanta, Georgia, show the dominance of a downtown business elite. This group may not be a power elite that controls a broad range of important decisions across policy areas, but it nevertheless is consistently the most influential group affecting the key economic development decisions that are crucial to the future of the city.[28]

It is surely easier for an elite to exist on the local level than on the national level, where far more well-organized interest groups compete directly against one another on different policies. A recent study of national politics examined four broad issue areas and tried to assess whether an elite coordinated and influenced government decision making. By tracking the interaction of representatives of hundreds of groups, the authors determined that there was no elite that coordinated lobbying across the four issue areas. Their evidence supports a critical part of the pluralist argument: each issue area has a separate set of organizations that influence government.[29]

Although not all studies come to the same conclusion, the preponderance of available evidence documenting government decisions on many different issues does not generally support elite theory—at least in the sense that an identifiable ruling elite usually gets its way. Not surprising, elite theorists reject this view. They argue that studies of decisions made on individual issues do not adequately test the influence of the power elite. Rather, they contend that much of the elite's power comes from its ability to keep things off the political agenda. That is, its power derives from its ability to keep people from questioning fundamental assumptions about American capitalism.[30]

Consequently, elite theory remains part of the debate about the nature of American government and is forcefully argued by some severe critics of our political system.[31] Although we do not believe that the scholarly evidence supports elite theory, we do recognize that contemporary American pluralism favors some segments of society over others. The poor are chronically unorganized and are not well represented by interest groups. On the other hand, business is very well represented in the political system. As many interest group scholars who reject the elitist theory have documented, business is better represented than any other sector of the public.[32] Thus, one can endorse pluralist democracy as a more accurate description than elitism in American politics without believing that all groups are equally well represented.

Elite Theory Versus Pluralist Theory

The key difference between elite and pluralist theory lies in the durability of the ruling minority. In contrast to elite theory, pluralist theory does not define government conflict in terms of a minority versus the majority; instead, it sees many different interests vying with one another in each policy area. In the management of national forests, for example, many interest groups—logging companies, recreational campers, environmentalists—have joined the political competition. They press their various viewpoints on government through representatives who are well informed about how relevant issues affect group members. According to elite theory, the financial resources of big logging companies ought to win out over the arguments of campers and environmentalists, but this does not always happen.[33]

politics in a changing america

2.1

The University of California Rethinks Affirmative Action

Affirmative action to help minority groups is a clear manifestation of pluralist government. Pluralist democracies try to satisfy the demands of different groups by establishing public policies tailored to fit their particular needs. Affirmative action can give ethnic and racial minorities preferential treatment in such areas as hiring and college admissions. Because such preferences typically come at the expense of the majority in this country (whites), affirmative action is highly controversial. The policies are justified, however, on the ground that they are intended to overcome the effects of systemic discrimination against minority groups in the past. But what is the justification if affirmative action helps some minority groups but works against *other* minority groups?

Such may be the case at the University of California at Berkeley. Admission to the state university system's flagship campus at Berkeley is highly coveted. Because it is one of the finest research universities in the world, gaining acceptance to the school is difficult, with more than 20,000 applicants competing for about 3,500 freshman slots each year. Quite simply, Berkeley has many more fully qualified applicants than it has room for. In a recent year, one-fifth of the applicants who were rejected had near-perfect grade point averages.

As do virtually all colleges and universities, Berkeley pursues diversity in its student body. This should not be hard to do in California, where the population is a diverse mix of ethnic groups, and whites will be a minority sometime around the year 2000. Yet, achieving diversity is difficult at Berkeley, because blacks and Hispanics meet the academic requirements for admission at much lower rates than do whites and Asian Americans. Only 6 percent of Hispanic and 4 percent of black high school graduates meet the university's standard entrance requirements. By comparison, 16 percent of whites and 26 percent

of Asian Americans meet the minimum requirements. In terms of the state's population, however, Asians are just 9 percent of all California residents, while 7 percent are black and 26 percent are Hispanic. Asian Americans have been especially critical of affirmative action at Berkeley and the other state university campuses, claiming that many Asian applicants are being kept out because admissions are based on additional criteria besides merit (grades and SAT scores).

Merit, however, is difficult to define in such simple terms. For those blacks and Hispanics who grew up in poverty, went to poor schools, and had little exposure to life outside their neighborhood, should merit be judged on the basis of grades and SAT scores alone? If applicants have had to overcome significant obstacles—and by no means do all black and Hispanic applicants come from disadvantaged backgrounds—should that not be taken into account by college admissions officers? If two runners are racing and one has a clear lane but the other must leap a series of hurdles, how do you measure who does better?

After years of controversy over the admissions policy at California's universities, majoritarian sentiment overcame pluralist politics. Polls in California showed clear public dislike of affirmative action, and in 1995 the university's board of regents voted to ban racial preferences in hiring, contracting, and admissions at all nine campuses. The charge against affirmative action was led by Ward Connerly, an African American member of the board of regents who said, "What we're doing is inequitable. We are relying on race and ethnicity not as one of many factors but as a dominant factor to the exclusion of all others." Berkeley chancellor Chang-Lin Tien has passionately defended affirmative action, arguing that it creates "the best educational atmosphere for all students."

The regents adopted a new policy that, in its own way, still encourages diversity in admissions. New admissions guidelines call for half of those admitted to be selected on the basis of academic merit alone. For the other half, additional factors would be used in judging whether applicants meet the minimum academic standards of the university. These additional criteria are designed to help students who have faced adverse circumstances growing up, have had to work, have shown unusual determination, or come from "difficult family situations." How these new admissions standards will affect the racial and eth-nic composition of the university remains to be seen. On the surface, however, this new policy appears not so much to do away with affirmative action but to redefine it so that it places more emphasis on social class and less on race and ethnicity.

Source: Data on 1994 enrollment and projections based on merit are from Sarah Lubman, "Campuses Mull Admissions Without Affirmative Action," *Wall Street Journal,* May 1995, p. B1.

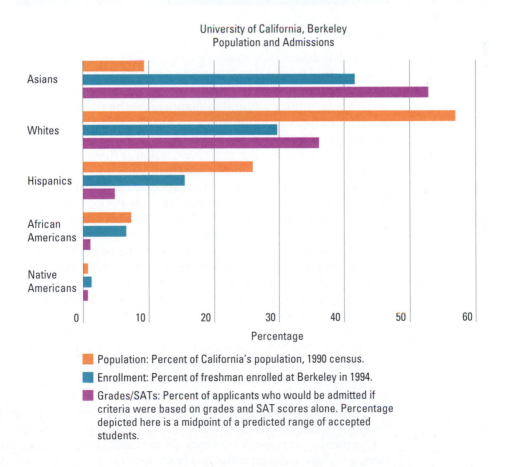

University of California, Berkeley Population and Admissions

Percentage

■ Population: Percent of California's population, 1990 census.

■ Enrollment: Percent of freshman enrolled at Berkeley in 1994.

■ Grades/SATs: Percent of applicants who would be admitted if criteria were based on grades and SAT scores alone. Percentage depicted here is a midpoint of a predicted range of accepted students.

Christian Democracy

Fundamentalist Christians have successfully organized and become a significant force in American politics. The Christian Coalition, allied with the Reverend Pat Robertson, plays a central leadership role in mobilizing Christian conservatives and getting them involved in the political process. Critics charge that this group is trying to impose its own religious views on the rest of society by advocating a substantive theory of democracy with fundamentalist Christian values at its core. The executive director of the Christian Coalition, Ralph Reed (pictured here), vehemently rejects this charge, arguing that the group is simply empowering its constituents, informing them about issues and opportunities to influence public policy.

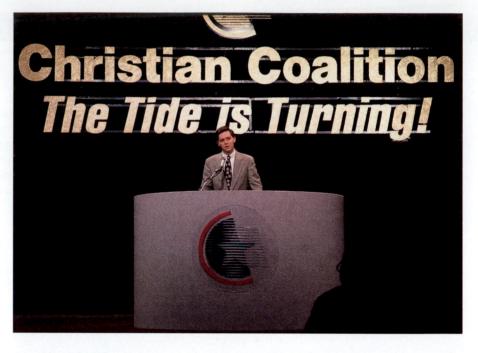

Pluralist democracy makes a virtue of the struggle between competing interests (see Politics in a Changing America 2.1). It argues for government that accommodates the struggle and channels the result into government action. According to pluralist democracy, the public is best served if the government structure provides access for different groups to press their claims in competition with one another. Note that pluralist democracy does not insist that all groups have equal influence on government decisions. In the political struggle, wealthy, well-organized groups have an inherent advantage over poorer, inadequately organized groups. In fact, unorganized segments of the population may not even get their concerns placed on the agenda for government consideration, which means that what government does not discuss (its "nondecisions") may be as significant as what it does discuss and decide. This is a critical weakness of pluralism, and critics relentlessly attack the theory because it appears to justify great disparities in levels of political organization and resources among different segments of society. Pluralists contend that so long as all groups are able to participate vigorously in the decision-making process, the process is democratic.

Another criticism of pluralism is that in contemporary America, interest group politics has gotten out of hand. The sharp rise in the number of groups active in Washington has made policymaking ever more complex, as literally hundreds of lobbies can be active on a single issue.[34] Some believe that the growth of interest group politics has contributed to "gridlock"—the failure of government to move one way or the other.[35]

Obviously, pluralist democracy differs from the classical, ideal conception, which is based on universal participation, political equality, and majority rule. But the pluralist reliance on access is compatible with contemporary thinking that democratic government should be open to groups that seek redress of grievances. The pluralist concept also fits the facts about the limited political knowledge of most American citizens. Clearly, pluralist democracy is worthy of being embraced as a rival to majoritarianism, the traditional model of procedural democracy.

DEMOCRACIES AROUND THE WORLD

We have proposed two models of democratic government. The majoritarian model conforms with classical democratic theory for a representative government. According to this model, democracy should be a form of government that features responsiveness to majority opinion. According to the pluralist model, a government is democratic if it allows minority interests to organize and press their claims on government freely.

No government actually achieves the high degree of responsiveness demanded by the majoritarian model. No government offers complete and equal access to the claims of all competing groups, as is required by an optimally democratic pluralist model. Still, some nations approach these ideals closely enough to be considered practicing democracies.

Establishing Democracies

Most countries are neither majoritarian nor pluralist; rather, most are governed in an authoritarian manner or are struggling to move out of an authoritarian tradition but are not yet true democracies. By a true democracy we mean countries that meet the criteria for a procedural democracy (universal participation, political equality, majority rule, and government responsiveness to public opinion) and have established substantive policies supporting such civil liberties as freedom of speech and freedom of association, which create the necessary conditions for the practice of democracy. Until recently, fewer than twenty countries fully met all the criteria necessary to be judged a true democracy.[36] What is encouraging, however, is that today the world is awash in countries that are trying to make a transition to democracy. In Africa alone, at least twenty countries are moving in some fashion toward a democratic form of government (see Compared with What? 2.1).[37] But **democratization is** a difficult process, and many efforts fail completely or succeed only in the short run and lapse into a form of authoritarianism.[38]

Russia is an example of a country struggling to make a transition to democracy. In September 1993 President Boris Yeltsin dissolved the Russian parliament because he was frustrated with its antagonism toward his programs. Some of his opponents barricaded themselves inside the White House (the Russian Parliament building), and tanks shelled the building to force these critics into surrendering. Later, rebels in Chechnya, a Russian province on the Caspian Sea, initiated an armed insurrection to try to force the government to grant them independence. The problematic shift to democracy and capitalism in Russia is, perhaps, best symbolized by the December 1995 parliamentary elections, in which the Communist Party did better than any other single political party.[39] Apparently, the rocky road to democracy has made many Russians yearn for the bad old days when Communist rule at least offered stability.

The political and economic instability that typically accompanies transitions to democracy makes new democratic governments vulnerable to

2.1   Democratization in Africa

The African continent is awash in democratizing countries. Although many newly democratizing nations in Africa have a long way to go to meet all the criteria of a true democracy, a number of long-standing authoritarian regimes have been replaced in recent years.

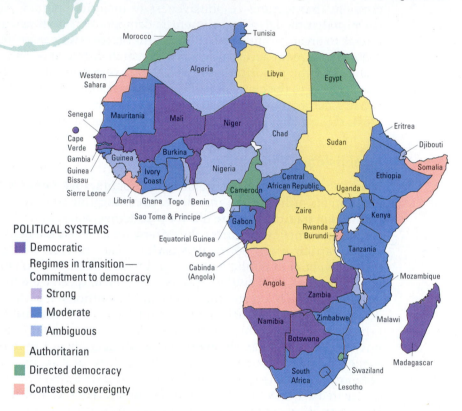

POLITICAL SYSTEMS

- ■ Democratic
- Regimes in transition—
Commitment to democracy
- ■ Strong
- ■ Moderate
- ■ Ambiguous
- ■ Authoritarian
- ■ Directed democracy
- ■ Contested sovereignty

Definitions.   For countries in transition to democracy, the commitment to democracy was evaluated in the following manner. *Strong:* "The strength of commitment is demonstrated by substantive incorporation of democratic processes, by devolution of power, and by gradual or wholesale abandonment of party monopolies." *Moderate:* "Measured, cautious and preliminary steps toward institutionalization or pluralism." *Ambiguous:* "Ruling elite's commitment to democracy is at best precarious, at worst a ruse, and at most times unclear."

Directed democracy: "A system in which formal institutions and practices of constitutional democracy are present. In practice, however, the extensive powers of the ruler, party, or regime severely limit contestation by individuals, organized groups, legislative assemblies, and the judiciary."

Contested sovereignty: In these countries there is a dispute over what group of people or institutions constitutes the government.

Source: Africa Demos, African Governance Program, The Carter Center, Emory University, July–August, 1993, pp. 1, 19. Used with permission.

attack by their opponents. The military will often revolt and take over the government on the ground that progress cannot occur until order is restored. As we noted in Chapter 1, all societies wrestle with the dilemma of choosing between freedom and order. The open political conflict that emerges in a new democracy may not be easily harnessed into a well-functioning government that tolerates opposition. Consequently, situations emerge, as in contemporary Russia, in which different factions within the government regard the opposition not as a legitimate part of a democratic political system but as a fundamental threat to the well-being (order) of the country.[40]

Despite such difficulties, strong forces are pushing authoritarian governments toward democratization. Nations find it difficult to succeed economically in today's world without establishing a market economy, but market economies (that is, capitalism) give people substantial freedoms. Thus, authoritarian rulers may see economic reforms as a threat to their regime. Yet, the electronic and communications revolution has made it more difficult for authoritarian countries to keep information about democracy and capitalism from their citizens. One scholar calls the global tendency toward a uniform type of government (democracy) and a uniform type of economy (capitalism) a movement toward a "McWorld." Nations are being pressed "into one commercially homogeneous global network: one McWorld tied together by technology, ecology, communications, and commerce."[41]

But the pressures against democratization are substantial. Ethnic and religious conflict is epidemic, and such conflict complicates efforts to democratize because antagonisms can run so deep that opposing groups do not want to grant political legitimacy to each other. As a result, ethnic and religious rivals are often more interested in achieving a form of government that oppresses their opponents (or, in their minds, maintains order) than in establishing a real democracy. Nowhere is this more apparent than in the new countries of the former Soviet Union and in parts of Eastern Europe. Once freedom came to the former Yugoslavia, the country split into a number of new nations. Their boundaries did not conform exactly with where various ethnic and religious groups live, and in Bosnia war soon broke out among Croats, Serbs, and Muslims.

Established democracies are not free of the destabilizing effects of religious and ethnic conflict, either. French-speaking Canadians have pushed for autonomy for Quebec, and India's democracy has been sorely tested by violence inspired by ethnic and religious rivalries. Democracies usually try to cope with such pressures with some form of pluralism so that different groups feel they are being treated fairly by their government. Indeed, majoritarian democracy can be risky where ethnic and religious rivalries endure, because a majority faction can use its votes to suppress minorities.

More common than democracies coping with the problem of minority rights, however, are situations in which ethnic and racial minorities are subject to authoritarian rule and are excluded from or discriminated against in the governmental process. One study found 230 minority groups at risk around the globe in the early 1990s. The countries that are home to these groups have failed to establish ways to protect them from the majority or from rival minorities.[42]

American Democracy: More Pluralist Than Majoritarian

Canadian folksinger Eileen McGann has her own take on democracy. If you've installed RealAudio on your computer, you can listen to her song at: `<oyez.at.nwu.edu/cases/COD>`

It is not idle speculation to ask what kind of democracy is practiced in the United States. The answer can help us understand why our government can be called democratic despite a low level of citizen participation in politics and despite government actions that sometimes run contrary to public opinion.

Throughout this book, we probe more deeply to determine how well the United States fits the two alternative models of democracy, majoritarian and pluralist. If our answer is not already apparent, it soon will be. We argue that the political system in the United States rates relatively low according to the majoritarian model of democracy but that it fulfills the pluralist model quite well. Yet, the pluralist model is far from a perfect representation of democracy. Its principal drawback is that it favors the well organized, and the poor are the least likely to be members of interest groups. As one advocate of majoritarian democracy once wrote, "The flaw in the pluralist heaven is that the heavenly chorus sings with a strong upper-class accent."[43]

Given the survey data that shows that the people's trust in American government has fallen over the years, it may seem that pluralist democracy is not serving us very well. Indeed, many Americans describe government and politicians in only the harshest terms. Radio talk show hosts like Rush Limbaugh and politicians themselves pile invective on top of insult when they talk about what's wrong with Washington. Yet in comparison to most other countries, people in the United States are actually more satisfied with their form of democracy (see Compared with What? 2.2). It's not at all clear that Americans would be more satisfied with another type of democracy. Surveys show that respondents in states that have instruments of majoritarian democracy such as initiatives or referenda are no more trusting than those who live in states lacking such devices.[44]

This evaluation of the pluralist nature of American democracy may not mean much to you now. But you will learn that the pluralist model makes the United States look far more democratic than the majoritarian model would. Eventually you will have to decide the answers to three questions: Is the pluralist model truly an adequate expression of democracy, or is it a perversion of classical ideals, designed to portray America as democratic when it is not? Does the majoritarian model result in a "better" type of democracy? If so, could new mechanisms of government be devised to produce a desirable mix of majority rule and minority rights? These questions should play in the back of your mind as you read more about the workings of American government in meeting the challenge of democracy.

SUMMARY

Is the United States a democracy? Most scholars believe that it is. But what kind of democracy is it? The answer depends on the definition of *democracy*. Some believe democracy is procedural; they define democracy as a form of government in which the people govern through certain institutional mechanisms. Others hold to substantive theory, claiming that a government is democratic if its policies promote civil liberties and rights.

compared with what?

2.2   Americans: Happy Campers Compared to the Rest of the World

When the Gallup Poll asked residents of sixteen countries, "How satisfied are you with the way democracy works in your country—are you very satisfied, somewhat satisfied, neither satisfied nor dissatisfied, somewhat dissatisfied, or very dissatisfied?" the results indicated that Americans are relatively satisfied with their government. Americans are full of complaints about the political process, of course, but it appears that the French, the Japanese, the Hungarians, the Mexicans, and just about everyone else outside the United States have even more to complain about.

Source: The Gallup Organization International Newsletter, June 1995, via http://gallup.com.

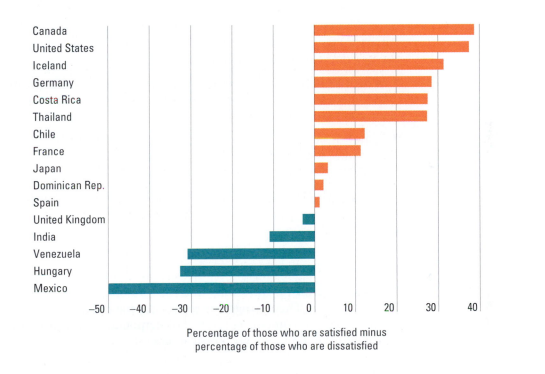

Percentage of those who are satisfied minus percentage of those who are dissatisfied

In this book, we emphasize the procedural concept of democracy, distinguishing between direct (participatory) and indirect (representative) democracy. In a participatory democracy, all citizens gather to govern themselves according to the principles of universal participation, political equality, and majority rule. In an indirect democracy, the citizens elect representatives to govern for them. If a representative government is elected mostly in accordance with the three principles just listed and also is usually responsive to public opinion, it qualifies as a democracy.

Procedural democratic theory has produced rival institutional models of democratic government. The classical majoritarian model—which depends on majority votes in elections—assumes that people are knowledgeable about government, that they want to participate in the political process, and that they carefully and rationally choose among candidates. But surveys of public opinion and behavior, and voter turnout, show that this is not the case for most Americans. The pluralist model of democracy—which depends on interest group interaction with government—was devised to accommodate these findings. It argues that democracy in a complex society requires only that government allow private interests to organize and to press their competing claims openly in the political arena. It differs from elite theory—the belief that America is run by a small group of powerful individuals—by arguing that different minorities win on different issues.

In Chapter 1 we talked about three political values—freedom, order, and equality. Here we have described two models of democracy—majoritarian and pluralist. The five concepts are critical to an understanding of American government. The values discussed in the last chapter underlie the two questions with which the text began:

- Which is better: to live under a government that allows individuals complete freedom to do whatever they please or to live under one that enforces strict law and order?

- Which is better: to allow businesses and private clubs to choose their customers and members or to pass laws that require them to admit and serve everyone, regardless of race or sex?

The models of democracy described in this chapter lead to another question:

- Which is better: a government that is highly responsive to public opinion on all matters, or one that responds deliberately to organized groups that argue their cases effectively?

These are enduring questions, and the framers of the Constitution dealt with them, too. Their struggle is the appropriate place to begin our analysis of how these competing models of democracy have animated the debate about the nature of our political process.

Key Terms

autocracy	majority rule	majoritarian model of	pluralist model of
oligarchy	participatory democracy	democracy	democracy
democracy	representative democracy	deliberative democracy	elite theory
procedural democratic	responsiveness	interest group	democratization
theory	substantive democratic		
universal participation	theory		
political equality	minority rights		

Selected Readings

Berry, Jeffrey M., Kent E. Portney, and Ken Thomson. *The Rebirth of Urban Democracy*. Washington, D.C.: Brookings Institution, 1993. An examination of neighborhood government in five American cities. The authors conclude that participatory democracy on the local level is a feasible and desirable alternative.

Clawson, Dan, Alan Neustadtl, and Denise Scott. *Money Talks*. New York: Basic Books, 1992. Using data on campaign contributions, the three authors make an elitist interpretation of the American political process.

Dahl, Robert A. *Democracy and Its Critics*. New Haven, Conn.: Yale University Press, 1989. The nation's leading expert on pluralist theory examines the basic foundations of democracy. Dahl defends democracy against a variety of criticisms that have focused on its shortcomings.

Grossman, Lawrence K. *The Electronic Republic*. New York: Viking, 1995. The author argues that whether we like it or not, high tech is pushing us toward electronic democracy.

Huntington, Samuel P. *The Third Wave*. Norman: University of Oklahoma Press, 1991. A historical and comparative analysis of the democratization process, with a particular focus on the worldwide movement toward democracy that began in 1974.

World Wide Web Resources

Democracy in Action.   Help promote greater involvement of citizens in governing, get information about political behavior, and learn about the practice of democratic systems in various countries.

`<www.gbar.dtu.dk/~itsjg/macpherson.html>`

Impact On Line.   This is an on-line public interest organization that seeks to "plug you into the existing conduits for making positive change." In addition to providing access to other public interest groups (both conservative and liberal), you can learn about current issues and volunteer opportunities in your community and you can exchange views with other concerned citizens.

`<www.impactonline.org/>`

Direct Democracy Center.   Find out current definitions and interpretations of *democracy* and *republic*. Discuss the issue of whether we have democracy in America. Get suggestions for recommended readings on these issues and links to other like-minded Web sites. This organization recommends direct democracy through interactive voting on the Internet.

`<www.primenet.com/%7Econduit/>`

p a r t

II

Foundations of American Government

The Constitution

Computer Enhanced Image

This image of the Bill of Rights has been electronically enhanced by a special digital computer system. The process used is similar to the ones developed by NASA scientists for satellite image enhancement.

The purpose of this "false color" technique is to bring out details that are hard to see or are invisible to the unaided eye. The same approach that enables scientists to view satellite pictures to evaluate the effects of pollution on our natural resources can allow conservators to assess the condition of the document.

The recent introduction of very powerful computers has allowed electronic image processing to gain inroads in the fields of medicine, aerospace, television and publishing. The image you see here is believed to be among the first to use these techniques to observe and monitor the condition of a historic document on tour.

THE MIDNIGHT BURGLARS made a small mistake. They left a piece of tape over the latch they had tripped to enter the Watergate office and apartment complex in Washington, D.C. But a security guard found their tampering and called the police, who surprised the burglars in the offices of the Democratic National Committee at 2:30 A.M. The arrests of the five men—four Cuban exiles and a former CIA agent—in the early hours of June 17, 1972, triggered a constitutional struggle that eventually involved the president of the United States, the Congress, and the Supreme Court.

The arrests took place a month before the 1972 Democratic National Convention. Investigative reporting by Carl Bernstein and Bob Woodward of the *Washington Post*, and a simultaneous criminal investigation by Assistant U.S. Attorney Earl J. Silbert and his staff, uncovered a link between the Watergate burglary and the forthcoming election.[1] The burglars were carrying the telephone number of another former CIA agent, who was working in the White House. At a news conference on June 22, President Richard Nixon said, "The White House has had no involvement whatsoever in this particular incident."[2]

At its convention in July, the Democratic party nominated Senator George McGovern of South Dakota to oppose Nixon in the presidential election. McGovern tried to make the break-in at the Democratic headquarters a campaign issue, but the voters either did not understand or did not care. In November 1972, Richard Nixon was reelected president of the United States, winning forty-nine of fifty states in one of the largest electoral landslides in American history. Only then did the Watergate story unfold completely.

Two months later, seven men answered in court for the break-in. They included the five burglars and two men closely connected with the president: E. Howard Hunt (a former CIA agent and White House consultant) and G. Gordon Liddy (counsel to the Committee to Re-Elect the President, or CREEP). The burglars entered guilty pleas. Hunt and Liddy were convicted by a jury. The Senate launched its own investigation of the matter. It set up the Select Committee on Presidential Campaign Activities, chaired by a self-styled constitutional authority, Democratic senator Sam Ervin of North Carolina.

A stunned nation watched the televised proceedings and learned that the president had secretly tape-recorded all of his conversations in the White House. The Ervin committee asked for the tapes. Nixon refused to produce them, citing the separation of powers between the legislative and the executive branches and claiming that "executive privilege" allowed him to withhold information from Congress.

Nixon also resisted subpoenas demanding the White House tapes. Ordered by a federal court to deliver specific tapes, Nixon proposed a compromise: he would release written summaries of the taped conversations. Archibald Cox, the special prosecutor appointed by the attorney general to investigate Watergate and offenses arising from the 1972 presidential election, rejected the compromise. Nixon retaliated with the "Saturday night massacre," in which Attorney General Elliot L. Richardson and his deputy resigned, Cox was fired, and the special prosecutor's office was abolished.

The ensuing furor forced Nixon to appoint another special prosecutor, Leon Jaworski, who eventually brought indictments against Nixon's closest aides. Nixon himself was named as an unindicted co-conspirator. Both the special prosecutor and the defendants wanted the White House tapes, but Nixon continued to resist. Finally, on July 24, 1974, the Supreme Court ruled that the president had to hand over the tapes. At almost the same time, the House Judiciary Committee voted to recommend to the full House that Nixon be impeached for, or charged with, three offenses: violating his oath of office to faithfully uphold the laws, misusing and abusing executive authority and the resources of executive agencies, and defying congressional subpoenas.

The Judiciary Committee vote was decisive but far from unanimous. On August 5, however, the committee and the country finally learned the contents of the tapes released under the Supreme Court order. They revealed that Nixon had been aware of a cover-up on June 23, 1972, just six days after the break-in. He ordered the FBI, "Don't go any further in this case, period!"[3] Now even the eleven Republican members of the House Judiciary Committee, who had opposed impeachment on the first vote, were ready to vote against Nixon.

Faced with the collapse of his support and likely impeachment by the full House, Nixon resigned the presidency on August 9, 1974. Vice President Gerald Ford, the only unelected vice president, became the first unelected president of the United States. A month later, acting within his constitutional powers, Ford granted private citizen Richard Nixon an unconditional pardon for all crimes that he may have committed. Others were not so fortunate. Three members of the Nixon cabinet (two attorneys general and a secretary of commerce) were convicted and sentenced for their crimes in the Watergate affair. Nixon's White House chief of staff, H. R. Haldeman, and domestic affairs adviser, John Ehrlichman, were convicted of conspiracy, obstruction of justice, and perjury. Other officials were tried, and most were convicted, on related charges.[4]

In 1992, twenty years after the break-in and cover-up, the release of additional White House tapes tended to support Nixon's claim that he was unaware of the break-in plan.[5] Ironically, the tapes were from the set that clearly implicated Nixon in the cover-up and conspiracy that led to his resignation from office.

The Watergate affair posed one of the most serious challenges to the constitutional order of modern American government. The incident ultimately developed into a struggle over the rule of law, between the president on the one hand and Congress and the courts on the other. In the end, the constitutional principle separating power among the executive, leg-

The Supreme Court heard oral argument in the Watergate case on July 8, 1974, and reached its decision on July 24, 1974. Listen to these materials on the WWW.
`<oyez.at.nwu.edu/cases/73-1766>`
(You must first install the RealAudio Player `<www.realaudio.com>`)

• • • • • • • • • •

Witness in the Spotlight

John Dean served as special counsel to President Richard Nixon. Dean testified before the Senate Select Committee on Presidential Campaign Activities, created in 1973 to investigate events surrounding Watergate. Dean's claim of a presidential cover-up was later verified by secret tape recordings Nixon had unsuccessfully sought to protect from release.

islative, and judicial branches prevented the president from controlling the Watergate investigation. The principle of checks and balances allowed Congress to threaten Nixon with impeachment. The belief that Nixon had violated the Constitution finally prompted members of his own party to support impeachment, leading the president to resign.

Nixon resigned the presidency a little more than a year and a half into his second term. In 1992, 70 percent of Americans still viewed Nixon's actions as having warranted his resignation.[6] In some countries, an irregular change in government leadership provides an opportunity for a palace coup, an armed revolution, or a military dictatorship. But here, significantly, no political violence erupted after Nixon's resignation; in fact, none was expected. Constitutional order in the United States had been put to a test, and it passed with high honors.

This chapter poses several questions about the Constitution. How did it evolve? What form did it take? What values does it reflect? How can it be altered? And which model of democracy—majoritarian or pluralist—does it fit best?

THE REVOLUTIONARY ROOTS OF THE CONSTITUTION

The Constitution is just 4,300 words long. But those 4,300 words define the basic structure of our national government. A comprehensive document, the Constitution divides the government into three branches and describes the powers of those branches, their relationships, and the interaction between the government and the governed. The Constitution makes itself the supreme law of the land and binds every government official to support it.

Most Americans revere the Constitution as political scripture. To charge that a political action is unconstitutional is akin to claiming that it is unholy. And so the Constitution has taken on symbolic value that strengthens its authority as the basis of American government. Strong belief in the Constitution has led many politicians to abandon party for principle when constitutional issues are at stake. The power and symbolic value of the Constitution were forcefully demonstrated in the Watergate affair.

The U.S. Constitution, written in 1787 for an agricultural society huddled along the coast of a wild new land, now guides the political life of a massive urban society in the postnuclear age. The stability of the Constitution—and of the political system it created—is all the more remarkable because the Constitution itself was rooted in revolution.

The historian Samuel Eliot Morison observed that "the American Revolution was not fought to obtain freedom, but to preserve the liberties that Americans already had as colonials."[7] The U.S. Constitution was designed to prevent anarchy by forging a union of states. To understand the values embedded in the Constitution, we must understand its historical roots. They lie in colonial America, in the revolt against British rule, and in the failure of the Articles of Confederation that governed the new nation after the Revolution.

Freedom in Colonial America

Although they were British subjects, American colonists in the eighteenth century enjoyed a degree of freedom denied most people in the world. In Europe, ancient customs and the relics of feudalism restricted private property, compelled support for established religions, and restricted access to trades and professions. In America, landowners could control and transfer their property at will. In America, there were no compulsory payments to support an established church. In America, there was no ceiling on wages, as there was in most European countries, and no guilds of exclusive professional associations. In America, colonists enjoyed almost complete freedom of speech, press, and assembly.[8]

By 1763, Britain and the colonies had reached a compromise between imperial control and colonial self-government. America's foreign affairs and overseas trade were controlled by the king and Parliament, the British legislature; the rest was left to colonial rule. But the cost of administering the colonies was substantial. The colonists needed protection from the French and their American Indian allies during the Seven Years' War (1756–1763), which was an expensive undertaking. Because Americans benefited the most from that protection, their English countrymen argued, Americans should bear the cost.

When brushing up on American history, it helps to have a time line handy. <lcweb2.loc.gov/ammem/ bdsds/timeline.html>

The Road to Revolution

The British believed that taxing the colonies was the obvious way to meet the costs of administering the colonies. The colonists did not agree. They especially did not want to be taxed by a distant government in which they had no representation. Nevertheless, a series of taxes (including a tax on all printed matter) was imposed on the colonies by the Crown. In each instance, public opposition was widespread and immediate.

A group of citizens—merchants, lawyers, prosperous traders—created an intercolonial association called the Sons of Liberty. This group de-

● ● ● ● ● ● ● ● ● ●

Toppling Tyrants: Then and Now

A statue of George III (left) stood for years at the tip of Manhattan. On July 9, 1776, citizens responded to the news of the Declaration of Independence by toppling the statue. It was melted down and converted into musket balls. A statue of V. I. Lenin, (right) leader of the Russian Revolution and first head of the Soviet Union, stood for years in Valmiera, Latvia. When the Soviet Union started to unravel in 1990, delighted citizens removed the statue. It was melted down and perhaps converted into refrigerator parts.

stroyed taxed items (identified by special stamps) and forced the official stamp distributors to resign. In October 1765, residents of Charleston, South Carolina, celebrated the forced resignation of the colony's stamp distributor by displaying a British flag with the word *Liberty* sewn across it. (They were horrified when a few months later local slaves paraded through the streets calling for "Liberty!"[9])

Women resisted the hated taxes by joining together in symbolic and practical displays of patriotism. A group of young women calling themselves the Daughters of Liberty met in public to spin homespun cloth and encourage the elimination of British cloth from colonial markets. They consumed American food and drank local herbal tea as symbols of their opposition.[10]

On the night of December 16, 1773, a group of colonists reacted to a British duty on tea by organizing the Boston Tea Party. A mob boarded three ships and emptied 342 chests of that valuable substance into Boston Harbor. The act of defiance and destruction could not be ignored. "The die is now cast," wrote George III. "The Colonies must either submit or triumph."[11] In an attempt to reassert British control over its recalcitrant colonists, Parliament passed the Coercive (or "Intolerable") Acts (1774). One act imposed a blockade on Boston until the tea was paid for; another gave royal governors the power to quarter British soldiers in private American homes. The taxation issue became secondary; more important was the conflict between British demands for order and American demands for liberty. The Virginia and Massachusetts assemblies summoned a continental congress, an assembly that would speak and act for the people of all the colonies.

All the colonies except Georgia sent representatives to the First Continental Congress, which met in Philadelphia in September 1774. The objective was to restore harmony between Great Britain and the American colonies. In an effort at unity, all colonies were given the same voting power—one vote each. A leader, called the president, was elected. (The terms *president* and *congress* in American government trace their origins to the First Continental Congress.) In October, the delegates adopted a statement of rights and principles; many of these later found their way into the Declaration of Independence and the Constitution. For example, the congress claimed a right "to life, liberty, and property" and a right "peaceably to assemble, consider of their grievances, and petition the king." Then the congress adjourned, planning to reconvene in May 1775.

Revolutionary Action

By early 1775, however, a movement that the colonists themselves were calling a revolution had already begun. Colonists in Massachusetts were fighting the British at Concord and Lexington. Delegates to the Second Continental Congress, meeting in May, faced a dilemma: should they prepare for war or should they try to reconcile with Britain? As conditions deteriorated, the Second Continental Congress remained in session to serve as the government of the colony-states.

On June 7, 1776, the Virginia delegation called on the Continental Congress to resolve "that these United Colonies are, and of right ought to be, free and Independent States, that they are absolved from all allegiance to the British Crown, and that all political connection between them and the State of Great Britain is, and ought to be, totally dissolved." The congress debated but did not immediately adopt the resolution. A committee of five men was appointed to prepare a proclamation expressing the colonies' reasons for declaring independence.

The Declaration of Independence

Thomas Jefferson, a young farmer and lawyer from Virginia, was a member of the committee. Because Jefferson had a way with words, he drafted the proclamation. Jefferson's document—the **Declaration of Independence**— was modestly revised by the committee and then further edited by the congress. It remains a cherished statement of our heritage, expressing simply, clearly, and rationally the many arguments for separation from Great Britain.

The principles underlying the declaration were rooted in the writings of the English philosopher John Locke and had been expressed many times by speakers in the congress and the colonial assemblies. Locke argued that people have God-given, or natural, rights that are inalienable—that is, they cannot be taken away by any government. According to Locke, all legitimate political authority exists to preserve these natural rights and is based on the consent of those who are governed. The idea of consent is derived from **social contract theory**, which states that the people agree to establish rulers for certain purposes, but they have the right to resist or remove rulers who violate those purposes.[12]

The Library of Congress has mounted a WWW exhibit on the drafting of the Declaration of Independence. You can see Jefferson's rough first draft. `<lcweb.loc.gov/exhibits/declara/declara4.html>`

Jefferson used similar arguments in the Declaration of Independence. His simple yet impassioned statement of faith in democracy resonates to this day: "We hold these truths to be self-evident, that all men are created equal, that they are endowed by their Creator with certain unalienable rights, that among these are life, liberty, and the pursuit of happiness."

The First Continental Congress had declared in 1774 that the colonists were entitled to "life, liberty, and property." Jefferson reformulated these objectives as "life, liberty, and the pursuit of happiness." Furthermore, he continued:

That to secure these rights, governments are instituted among men, deriving their just powers from the consent of the governed. That whenever any form of government becomes destructive of these ends, it is the right of the people to alter or to abolish it, and to institute new government,

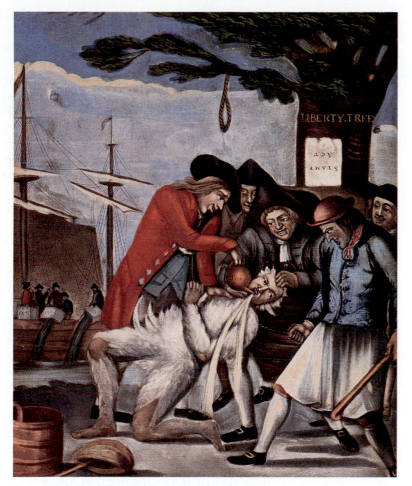

Uniquely American Protest

Americans protested the Tea Act (1773) by holding the Boston Tea Party (see background, left) and by using a unique form of painful punishment—tarring and feathering—on the tax collector (see Stamp Act upside-down on the Liberty Tree). An early treatise on the subject offered the following instructions: "First, strip a person naked, then heat the tar until it is thin, and pour upon the naked flesh, or rub it over with a tar brush. After which, sprinkle decently upon the tar, whilst it is yet warm, as many feathers as will stick to it."

laying its foundation on such principles, and organizing its power in such form, as to them shall seem most likely to effect their safety and happiness.

He went on to list the many deliberate acts of the king that had exceeded the legitimate role of government. The last item on Jefferson's original draft of the Declaration was the king's support of the slave trade. Although Jefferson did not condemn slavery, he denounced the king for enslaving a people, engaging in the slave trade, and proposing that the slaves be freed in order to attack their masters. When South Carolina and Georgia—two states with an interest in continuing the wretched practice—objected, Jefferson and the committee dropped the offending paragraph. Finally, Jefferson declared that the colonies were "Free and Independent States," with no political connection to Great Britain.

The major premise of the Declaration of Independence is that the people have a right to revolt if they determine that their government is denying them their legitimate rights. The long list of the king's actions was evidence of such denial. So the people had the right to rebel, to form a new government. On July 2, 1776, the Second Continental Congress finally voted for independence. The vote was by state, and the motion carried,

11 to 0. (Rhode Island was not present, and the New York delegation, lacking instructions, did not cast its yea vote until July 15.) Two days later, on July 4, the Declaration of Independence was approved, with few changes. A number of representatives insisted on removing language they thought would incite the colonists. But in the end, Jefferson's compelling words were left almost exactly as he had written them.

By August, fifty-five revolutionaries had signed the Declaration of Independence, pledging "our lives, our fortunes and our sacred honor" in support of their rebellion against the world's most powerful nation. This was no empty pledge: an act of rebellion was treason. Had they lost the Revolutionary War, the signers would have faced a gruesome fate. The punishment for treason was hanging and drawing and quartering—the victim was first hanged until half-dead from strangulation, then disemboweled, and finally cut into four pieces while still alive. We celebrate the Fourth of July with fireworks and flag waving, parades and picnics. We sometimes forget that the Revolution was a matter of life and death.

The war imposed an agonizing choice on colonial Catholics, who were treated with intolerance by the overwhelmingly Protestant population. No other religious group found the choice so difficult. Catholics could either join the revolutionaries, who were opposed to Catholicism, or remain loyal to England and risk new hostility and persecution. But Catholics were few in number, perhaps twenty-five thousand at the time of independence (or 1 percent of the population). Anti-Catholic revolutionaries recognized that if Catholics opposed independence in Maryland and Pennsylvania, where their numbers were greatest, victory might be jeopardized. Furthermore, enlisting the support of Catholic France for the cause of independence would be difficult in the face of strong opposition from colonial Catholics. So the revolutionaries wooed Catholics to their cause.[13]

The War of Independence lasted far longer than anyone expected. It began in a moment of confusion, when a shot rang out as British soldiers approached the town of Lexington, Massachusetts, on April 19, 1775. The end came six and a half years later with Lord Cornwallis's surrender of his six-thousand-man army at Yorktown, Virginia, on October 19, 1781. It was a costly war: a greater percentage of the population died or was wounded during the Revolution than in any other U.S. conflict except the Civil War.[14]

With hindsight, of course, we can see that the British were engaged in an arduous and perhaps hopeless conflict. America was simply too vast to subdue without imposing total military rule. Britain also had to transport men and supplies over the enormous distance of the Atlantic Ocean. Finally, although the Americans had neither paid troops nor professional soldiers, they were fighting for a cause—the defense of their liberty. The British never understood the power of this fighting faith.

FROM REVOLUTION TO CONFEDERATION

By declaring their independence from England, the colonists left themselves without any real central government. So the revolutionaries proclaimed the creation of a **republic.** Strictly speaking, a republic is a government without a monarch, but the term had come to mean a gov-

Voting for Independence

The Second Continental Congress voted for independence on July 2, 1776. John Adams of Massachusetts viewed the day "as the most memorable epocha [significant event] in the history of America." In this painting by John Trumbull, the drafting committee presents the Declaration of Independence to the patriots who would later sign it. The committee, grouped in front of the desk, consisted of (from left to right) Adams, Roger Sherman (Conn.), Robert Livingston (N.Y.), Thomas Jefferson (Va.), and Benjamin Franklin (Pa.).

ernment based on the consent of the governed, whose power is exercised by representatives who are responsible to them. A republic need not be a democracy, and this was fine with the founders; at that time, democracy was associated with mob rule and instability (see Chapter 2). The revolutionaries were less concerned with determining who would control their new government than with limiting its powers. They had revolted in the name of liberty, and now they wanted a government with strictly defined powers. To make sure they got one, they meant to define its structure and powers in writing.

The Articles of Confederation

Barely a week after the Declaration of Independence was signed, the Second Continental Congress received a committee report entitled "Articles of Confederation and Perpetual Union." A **confederation** is a loose association of independent states that agree to cooperate on specified matters. In a confederation, the states retain their sovereignty, which means that each has supreme power within its borders. The central government is weak; it can only coordinate, not control, the actions of its sovereign states. Consequently, the individual states are strong.

The congress debated the **Articles of Confederation,** the compact among the thirteen original colonies that established the first government of the United States, for more than a year. The Articles were adopted by the Continental Congress on November 15, 1777. They finally took effect on March 1, 1781, following approval by all thirteen states. For more than three years, then, Americans had fought a revolution without an effective government. Raising money, troops, and supplies for the war had daunted and exhausted the leadership.

The Articles jealously guarded state sovereignty; their provisions clearly reflected the delegates' fears that a strong central government would resemble British rule. Article II, for example, stated, "Each state retains its sovereignty, freedom, and independence, and every power, jurisdiction, and right, which is not by this Confederation expressly delegated to the United States, in Congress assembled."

Under the Articles, each state, regardless of its size, had one vote in the congress. Votes on financing the war and other important issues required the consent of at least nine of the thirteen states. The common danger—Britain—had forced the young republic to function under the Articles, but this first effort at government was inadequate to the task. The delegates had succeeded in crafting a national government that was largely powerless.

The Articles failed for at least four reasons. First, they did not give the national government the power to tax. As a result, the congress had to plead for money from the states to pay for the war and to carry on the affairs of the new nation. A government that cannot reliably raise revenue cannot expect to govern effectively. Second, the Articles made no provision for an independent leadership position to direct the government (the president was merely the presiding officer of the congress). The omission was deliberate—the colonists feared the reestablishment of a monarchy—but it left the nation without a leader. Third, the Articles did not allow the national government to regulate interstate and foreign commerce. (When John Adams proposed that the confederation enter into a commercial treaty with Britain after the war, he was asked, "Would you like one treaty or thirteen, Mr. Adams?")[15] Finally, the Articles could not be amended without the unanimous agreement of the congress and the assent of all the state legislatures; thus, each state had the power to veto any changes to the confederation.

The goal of the delegates who drew up the Articles of Confederation was to retain power in the states. This was consistent with republicanism, which viewed the remote power of a national government as a danger to liberty. In this sense alone, the Articles were a grand success. They completely hobbled the infant government.

Disorder Under the Confederation

Once the Revolution had ended and independence was a reality, it became clear that the national government had neither the economic nor the military power to function. Freed from wartime austerity, Americans rushed to purchase goods from abroad. The national government's efforts to restrict foreign imports were blocked by exporting states, which feared retaliation from their foreign customers. Debt mounted, and for many, bankruptcy followed.

The problem was particularly severe in Massachusetts, where high interest rates and high state taxes were forcing farmers into bankruptcy. In 1786, Daniel Shays, a Revolutionary War veteran, marched on a western Massachusetts courthouse with 1,500 supporters armed with barrel staves and pitchforks. They wanted to close the courthouse to prevent the foreclosure of farms by creditors. Later, they attacked an arsenal. Called Shays's Rebellion, the revolt against the established order continued into 1787. Massachusetts appealed to the confederation for help. Horrified by the threat of domestic upheaval, the congress approved a $530,000 requisition for the establishment of a national army. But the plan failed: every state except Virginia rejected the request for money. Finally, the governor of Massachusetts called out the militia and restored order.[16]

The rebellion demonstrated the impotence of the confederation and the urgent need to suppress insurrections and maintain domestic order. Proof to skeptics that Americans could not govern themselves, the rebellion alarmed all American leaders, with the exception of Jefferson. From Paris, where he was serving as American ambassador, he remarked, "A little rebellion now and then is a good thing; the tree of liberty must be refreshed from time to time with the blood of patriots and tyrants."[17]

FROM CONFEDERATION TO CONSTITUTION

Order, the original purpose of government, was breaking down under the Articles of Confederation. The "league of friendship" envisioned in the Articles was not enough to hold the nation together in peacetime.

Some states had taken halting steps toward encouraging a change in the national government. In 1785, Massachusetts asked the congress to revise the Articles of Confederation, but the congress took no action. In 1786, Virginia invited the states to attend a convention at Annapolis to explore revisions aimed at improving commercial regulation. The meeting was both a failure and a success. Only five states sent delegates, but they seized the opportunity to call for another meeting—with a far broader mission—in Philadelphia the next year. That convention would be charged with devising "such further provisions as shall appear . . . necessary to render the constitution of the Federal Government adequate to the exigencies of the Union." The congress later agreed to the convention but limited its mission to "the sole and express purpose of revising the Articles of Confederation."[18]

Shays's Rebellion lent a sense of urgency to the task before the Philadelphia convention. The congress's inability to confront the rebellion was evidence that a stronger national government was necessary to preserve order and property—to protect the states from internal as well as external dangers. "While the Declaration was directed against an excess of authority," observed Supreme Court Justice Robert H. Jackson some 150 years later, "the Constitution [that followed the Articles of Confederation] was directed against anarchy."[19]

Twelve of the thirteen states named a total of seventy-four delegates to convene in Philadelphia, the most important city in America, in May 1787. (Rhode Island, derisively renamed "Rogue Island" by a Boston newspaper, was the one exception. The state legislature sulkily rejected participating, because it feared a strong national government.) Fifty-five delegates eventually showed up at the statehouse in Philadelphia, but no more than thirty were present at any one time during that sweltering spring and summer. The framers were not demigods, but many historians believe that a like assembly will not be seen again. Highly educated, they typically were fluent in Latin and Greek. Products of the Enlightenment, they relied on classical liberalism for the Constitution's philosophical underpinnings.

● ● ● ● ● ● ● ● ● ● ● ●

Farmers' Protest Stirs Rebellion

Shays's Rebellion (1786–1787) became a symbol of the urgent need to maintain order. Here, farmers led by Daniel Shays close the courthouse to prevent farm foreclosures by creditors. The uprising demonstrated the military weakness of the confederation: the national government could not muster funds to fight the insurgents.

They were also veterans of the political intrigues of their states, and as such they were highly practical politicians who knew how to maneuver. Although well versed in ideas, they subscribed to the view expressed by one delegate that "experience must be our only guide, reason may mislead us."[20] Fearing for their fragile union, the delegates resolved to keep their proceedings secret.

The Constitutional Convention—at the time called the Federal Convention—officially opened on May 25. A year earlier, at Annapolis, five states had called for the convention to draft a new, stronger charter for the national government. The spirit of the Annapolis meeting seems to have pervaded the Constitutional Convention, although the delegates were authorized only to "revise" the Articles of Confederation. Within the first week, Edmund Randolph of Virginia had presented a long list of changes, suggested by fellow Virginian James Madison, that would replace the weak confederation of states with a powerful national government. The delegates unanimously agreed to debate Randolph's proposal, called the **Virginia Plan**. Almost immediately, then, they rejected the idea of amending the Articles of Confederation, working instead to create an entirely new constitution.

●●●●●●●●●●

James Madison, Father of the Constitution

Although he dismissed the accolade, Madison deserved it more than anyone else. As do most fathers, he exercised a powerful influence in debates (and was on the losing side of more than half of them).

The Virginia Plan

The Virginia Plan dominated the convention's deliberations for the rest of the summer, making several important proposals for a strong central government:

- That the powers of the government be divided among three separate branches: a **legislative branch,** for making laws; an **executive branch,** for enforcing laws; and a **judicial branch,** for interpreting laws.

- That the legislature consist of two houses. The first would be chosen by the people, the second by the members of the first house from among candidates nominated by the state legislatures.

- That each state's representation in the legislature be in proportion to the taxes it paid to the national government or in proportion to its free population.

- That an executive, consisting of an unspecified number of people, be selected by the legislature and serve for a single term.

- That the national judiciary include one or more supreme courts and other, lower courts, with judges appointed for life by the legislature.

- That the executive and a number of national judges serve as a council of revision, to approve or veto (disapprove) legislative acts. Their veto could be overridden by a vote of both houses of the legislature.

- That the scope of powers of all three branches be far greater than that assigned the national government by the Articles of Confederation, and that the legislature be empowered to override state laws.

By proposing a powerful national legislature that could override state laws, the Virginia Plan clearly advocated a new form of government. It was to have a mixed structure, with more authority over the states and new authority over the people.

Madison was a monumental force in the ensuing debate on the proposals. He kept records of the proceedings that reveal his frequent and brilliant participation and give us insight into his thinking about freedom, order, and equality.

For example, his proposal that senators serve a nine-year term reveals his thinking about equality. Madison foresaw an increase "of those who will labor under all the hardships of life, and secretly sigh for a more equal distribution of its blessings. These may in time outnumber those who are placed above the feelings of indigence."[21] Power, then, could flow into the hands of the numerous poor. The stability of the senate, however, with its nine-year terms and election by the state legislatures, would provide a barrier against the "sighs of the poor" for more equality. Although most delegates shared Madison's apprehension about equality, the nine-year term was voted down.

The Constitution that emerged from the convention bore only partial resemblance to the document Madison wanted to create. He endorsed seventy-one specific proposals, but he ended up on the losing side on forty of them.[22] And the parts of the Virginia Plan that were ultimately included in the Constitution were not adopted without challenge. Conflicts revolved primarily around the basis for representation in the legislature, the method of choosing legislators, and the structure of the executive branch.

The New Jersey Plan

When in 1787 it appeared that much of the Virginia Plan would be approved by the big states, the small states united in opposition. William Paterson of New Jersey introduced an alternative set of resolutions, written to preserve the spirit of the Articles of Confederation by amending rather than replacing them. The **New Jersey Plan** included the following proposals:

- That a single-chamber legislature have the power to raise revenue and regulate commerce.

- That the states have equal representation in the legislature and choose its members.

- That a multiperson executive be elected by the legislature, with powers similar to those proposed under the Virginia Plan but without the right to veto legislation.

- That a supreme tribunal be created, with a limited jurisdiction. (There was no provision for a system of national courts.)

- That the acts of the legislature be binding on the states—that is, that they be regarded as "the supreme law of the respective states," with the option of force to compel obedience.

The New Jersey Plan was defeated in the first major convention vote, 7–3. However, the small states had enough support to force a compromise on the issue of representation in the legislature. Table 3.1 compares the New Jersey Plan with the Virginia Plan.

The Great Compromise

The Virginia Plan provided for a two-chamber legislature, with representation in both chambers based on population. The idea of two chambers was never seriously challenged, but the idea of representation according to population stirred up heated and prolonged debate. The small states demanded equal representation for all states, but another vote rejected that concept for the House of Representatives. The debate continued. Finally, the Connecticut delegation moved that each state have an equal vote in the Senate. Still another poll showed that the delegations were equally divided on this proposal.

   A committee was created to resolve the deadlock. It consisted of one delegate from each state, chosen by secret ballot. After working straight through the Independence Day recess, the committee reported reaching the **Great Compromise** (sometimes called the Connecticut Compromise). Representation in the House of Representatives would be apportioned according to the population of each state. Initially, there would be fifty-six members. Revenue-raising acts would originate in the House. Most important, the states would be represented equally in the Senate, with two

table 3.1   ● **Major Differences Between the Virginia Plan and the New Jersey Plan**

Characteristic	Virginia Plan	New Jersey Plan
Legislature	Two chambers	One chamber
Legislative power	Derived from the people	Derived from the states
Executive	Unspecified size	More than one person
Decision rule	Majority	Extraordinary majority
State laws	Legislature can override	National law is supreme
Executive removal	By Congress	By a majority of the states
Courts	National judiciary	No provision for national judiciary
Ratification	By the people	By the states

senators each. Senators would be selected by their state legislatures, not directly by the people.

The delegates accepted the Great Compromise. The small states got their equal representation, the big states their proportional representation. The small states might dominate the Senate and the big states might control the House, but because all legislation had to be approved by both chambers, neither group would be able to dominate the other.

Compromise on the Presidency

Conflict replaced compromise when the delegates turned to the executive branch. They did agree on a one-person executive—a president—but they disagreed on how the executive would be selected and what the term of office would be. The delegates distrusted the people's judgment; some feared that popular election of the president would arouse public passions. Consequently, the delegates rejected the idea. At the same time, representatives of the small states feared that election by the legislature would allow the big states to control the executive.

Once again, a committee composed of one member from each participating state was chosen to find a compromise. That committee fashioned the cumbersome presidential election system we still use today, the *electoral college.* The college would consist of a group of electors chosen for the sole purpose of selecting the president and vice president. Each state legislature would choose a number of electors equal to the number of its representatives in Congress. Each elector would then vote for two people. The candidate with the most votes would become president, provided that the number of votes constituted a majority; the person with the next-greatest number of votes would become vice president. (The procedure was changed in 1804 by the Twelfth Amendment, which mandates separate votes for each office.) If no candidate won a majority, the House of Representatives would choose a president, with each state casting one vote.

The electoral college compromise eliminated the fear of a popular vote for president. At the same time, it satisfied the small states. If the electoral college failed to elect a president—which the delegates expected would happen—election by the House would give every state the same voice in the selection process.

Finally, the delegates agreed that the president's term of office should be four years and that the president should be eligible for reelection.

The delegates also realized that removing a president from office would be a serious political matter. For that reason, they involved both of the other two branches of government in the process. The House alone was empowered to charge a president with "Treason, Bribery, or other high Crimes and Misdemeanors" (Article II, Section 4), by a majority vote. The Senate was given the sole power to try the president on the House's charges. It could convict, and thus remove, a president only by a two-thirds vote (an extraordinary majority). And the chief justice of the United States was required to preside over the Senate trial.

THE FINAL PRODUCT

Once the delegates had resolved their major disagreements, they dispatched the remaining issues relatively quickly. A committee was then appointed to organize and write up the results of the proceedings. Twenty-three resolutions had been debated and approved by the convention; these were reorganized under seven articles in the draft constitution. The preamble, which was the last section to be drafted, begins with a phrase that would have been impossible to write when the convention opened. This single sentence contains four elements that form the foundation of the American political tradition.[23]

- *It creates a people:* "We the people of the United States" was a dramatic departure from a loose confederation of states.

- *It explains the reason for the Constitution:* "in order to form a more perfect Union" was an indirect way of saying that the first effort, the Articles of Confederation, had been inadequate.

- *It articulates goals:* "[to] establish Justice, insure domestic Tranquility, provide for the common defence, promote the general Welfare, and secure the Blessings of Liberty to ourselves and our Posterity"—in other words, the government exists to promote order and freedom.

- *It fashions a government:* "do ordain and establish this Constitution for the United States of America."

The Basic Principles

In creating the Constitution, the founders relied on four political principles—of which three were inspired by ideas that first sprouted on foreign soil—that together established a revolutionary new political order: republicanism, federalism, separation of powers, and checks and balances.

Republicanism. **Republicanism** is a form of government in which power resides in the people and is exercised by their elected representatives. The idea of republicanism may be traced to the Greek philosopher Aristotle

(384–322 B.C.), who advocated a constitution that combined principles of both democratic and oligarchic government. The framers were determined to avoid aristocracy (rule by a hereditary class), monarchy (rule by one person), and direct democracy (rule by the people). A republic was both new and daring: no people had ever been governed by a republic on so vast a scale.

The framers themselves were far from sure that their government could be sustained. They had no model of republican government to follow; moreover, republican government was thought to be suitable only for small territories, where the interests of the public would be obvious and where the government would be within the reach of every citizen. After the convention ended, Benjamin Franklin was asked what sort of government the new nation would have. "A republic," the old man replied, "if you can keep it."

Federalism. **Federalism** is the division of power between a central government and regional units. Citizens are thus subject to two different bodies of law. It stands between two competing government schemes. On the one side is unitary government, in which all power is vested in a central authority. On the other side stands confederation, a loose union of powerful states. In a confederation, the states surrender some power to a central government but retain the rest. The Articles of Confederation, as we have seen, divided power between loosely knit states and a weak central government. The Constitution also divides power between the states and a central government, but it confers substantial powers on a national government at the expense of the states.

According to the Constitution, the powers vested in the national and state governments are derived from the people, who remain the ultimate sovereigns. National and state governments can exercise their power over people and property within their spheres of authority. But at the same time, by participating in the electoral process or by amending their governing charters, the people can restrain both the national and the state governments if necessary to preserve liberty.

The Constitution lists the powers of the national government and the powers denied to the states. All other powers remain with the states. Generally speaking, the states are required to give up only the powers necessary to create an effective national government; the national government is limited in turn to the powers specified in the Constitution. Despite the specific lists, the Constitution does not clearly describe the spheres of authority within which the powers can be exercised. As we will discuss in Chapter 4, limits on the exercise of power by the national government and the states have evolved as a result of political and military conflicts; moreover, the limits have proved changeable.

Separation of Powers. **Separation of powers** is the assignment of the lawmaking, law-enforcing, and law-interpreting functions of government to independent legislative, executive, and judicial branches. This idea was formulated in a fragmentary way by John Locke and other thinkers, but its fullest exposition came from the French philosopher Charles-Louis de Secondat Montesquieu (1689–1755). Nationally, the lawmaking power resides in Congress, the law-enforcing power resides in the presidency, and

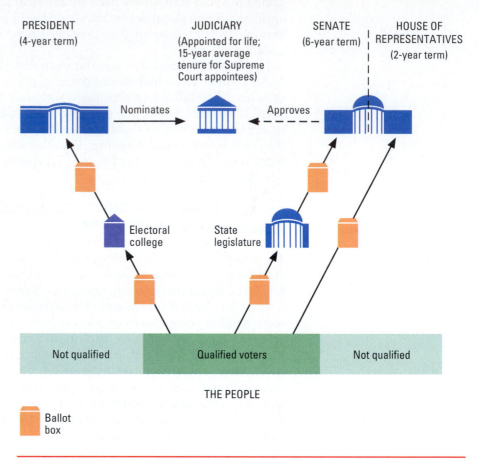

figure

3.1

● **The Constitution and the Electoral Process**

The framers were afraid of majority rule, and that fear is reflected in the electoral process for national office described in the Constitution. The people, speaking through the voters, participated directly only in the choice of their representatives in the House. The president and senators were elected indirectly, through the electoral college and state legislatures. (Direct election of senators did not become law until 1913, when the Seventeenth Amendment was ratified.) Judicial appointments are, and always have been, far removed from representative links to the people. Judges are nominated by the president and approved by the Senate.

PRESIDENT (4-year term)

JUDICIARY (Appointed for life; 15-year average tenure for Supreme Court appointees)

SENATE (6-year term)

HOUSE OF REPRESENTATIVES (2-year term)

Nominates

Approves

Electoral college

State legislature

Not qualified

Qualified voters

Not qualified

THE PEOPLE

Ballot box

the law-interpreting power resides in the courts. Service in one branch prohibits simultaneous service in the others. Separation of powers safeguards liberty by ensuring that all government power does not fall into the hands of a single person or group of people. But the framers' concern with protecting the liberty of the people did not extend to the election process. The Constitution constrained majority rule by limiting the direct influence of the people on that process (see Figure 3.1). In theory, separation of powers means that one branch cannot exercise the powers of the other branches. In practice, however, the separation is far from complete. One scholar has suggested that what we have instead is "separate institutions sharing powers."[24]

Checks and Balances.   The constitutional system of **checks and balances** is a means of giving each branch of government some scrutiny of and control over the other branches. Adapting the ideas of two Englishmen, the statesman Henry St. John Bolingbroke (1678–1751) and the jurist William Blackstone (1723–1780), the framers reasoned that checks and balances would prevent each branch from ignoring or overpowering the others.

When the Veto Pen Runs Dry

A president signals disapproval of legislation by writing the word veto *on it. Such ceremonies have become an art form, garnering much attention from the media. President Bill Clinton sought a special prop to signal his veto of the Republicans' balanced-budget bill on December 6, 1995. His veto instrument was the pen used by President Lyndon Johnson to sign the Medicare and Medicaid bills into law thirty years ago. This time, however, the pen ran out of ink, so an aid had to locate an inkwell for a refill.*

Separation of powers and checks and balances are two distinct principles, but both are necessary to ensure that one branch does not dominate the government. Separation of powers divides government responsibilities among the legislative, executive, and judicial branches; checks and balances prevent the exclusive exercise of those powers by any one of the three branches. For example, only Congress can enact laws. But the president (through the power of the veto) can cancel them, and the courts (by finding a law in violation of the Constitution) can nullify them. And the process goes on. In a "check on a check," Congress can override a president's veto by an extraordinary (two-thirds) majority in each chamber. Congress is also empowered to propose amendments to the Constitution, counteracting the courts' power to find a national law invalid. Figure 3.2 depicts the relationship between separation of powers and checks and balances.

The Articles of the Constitution

In addition to the preamble, the Constitution includes seven articles. The first three establish the separate branches of government and specify their internal operations and powers. The remaining four define the relationships among the states, explain the process of amendment, declare the supremacy of national law, and explain the procedure for ratifying the Constitution.

Article I: The Legislative Article. In structuring their new government, the framers began with the legislative branch, because they considered lawmaking the most important function of a republican government.

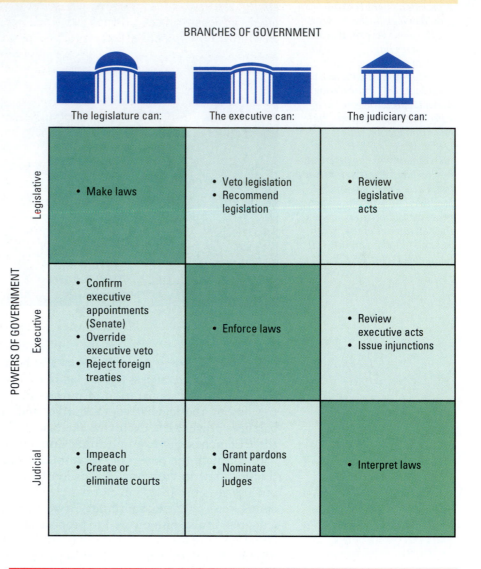

figure 3.2   ● Separation of Powers and Checks and Balances

Separation of powers is the assignment of lawmaking, law-enforcing, and law-interpreting functions to the legislative, executive, and judicial branches. The phenomenon is illustrated by the diagonal from upper left to lower right in the figure. Checks and balances give each branch some power over the other branches. For example, the executive branch possesses some legislative power, and the legislative branch possesses some executive power. These checks and balances are listed outside the diagonal.

BRANCHES OF GOVERNMENT

	The legislature can:	The executive can:	The judiciary can:
Legislative	• Make laws	• Veto legislation • Recommend legislation	• Review legislative acts
Executive	• Confirm executive appointments (Senate) • Override executive veto • Reject foreign treaties	• Enforce laws	• Review executive acts • Issue injunctions
Judicial	• Impeach • Create or eliminate courts	• Grant pardons • Nominate judges	• Interpret laws

POWERS OF GOVERNMENT

Article I is the most detailed and therefore the longest of all the articles. It defines the bicameral (two-chamber) character of Congress and describes the internal operating procedures of the House of Representatives and the Senate. Section 8 of Article I articulates the principle of **enumerated powers,** which means that Congress can exercise only the powers that the Constitution assigns to it. Eighteen powers are enumerated; the first seventeen are specific powers. For example, the third clause of Section 8 gives Congress the power to regulate interstate commerce. (One of the chief shortcomings of the Articles of Confederation was the lack of a means to cope with trade wars between the states. The solution was to vest control of interstate commerce in the national government.)

The last clause in Section 8, known as the **necessary and proper clause** (or the elastic clause), gives Congress the means to execute the enumerated powers (see the Appendix). This clause is the basis of Congress's **implied powers**—those powers that Congress needs to execute its enumerated powers. For example, the power to levy and collect taxes (clause 1) and the power to coin money and regulate its value (clause 5), when joined with the necessary and proper clause (clause 18), imply that Congress has the power to charter a bank. Otherwise, the national government would have no means of managing the money it collects through its power to tax. Implied powers clearly expand the enumerated powers conferred on Congress by the Constitution.

Article II: The Executive Article. Article II establishes the president's term of office, the procedure for electing the president through the electoral college, the qualifications for becoming president, and the president's duties and powers. The last include acting as commander in chief of the military; making treaties (which must be ratified by a two-thirds vote in the Senate); and appointing government officers, diplomats, and judges (again, with the advice and consent of the Senate).

The president also has legislative powers—part of the constitutional system of checks and balances. For example, the Constitution requires that the president periodically inform Congress of "the State of the Union" and of the policies and programs that the executive branch intends to advocate in the coming year. Today, this is done annually, in the president's State of the Union address. Under special circumstances, the president can also convene or adjourn Congress.

The duty to "take Care that the Laws be faithfully executed" in Section 3 has provided presidents with a reservoir of power. President Nixon tried to use this power when he refused to turn over the Watergate tapes despite a judicial subpoena in a criminal trial. He claimed broad executive privilege, an extension of the executive power implied in Article II. But the Supreme Court rejected his claim, arguing that it violated the separation of powers, because the decision to release or withhold information in a criminal trial is a judicial, not an executive, function.

Article III: The Judicial Article. The third article was left purposely vague. The Constitution established the Supreme Court as the highest court in the land. But beyond that, the framers were unable to agree on the need for a national judiciary or on its size, its composition, or the procedures it should follow. They left these issues to Congress, which resolved them by creating a system of federal (that is, national) courts, separate from the state courts.

Unless they are impeached, federal judges serve for life. They are appointed to indefinite terms "during good Behaviour," and their salaries cannot be reduced while they hold office. These stipulations reinforce the separation of powers; they see to it that judges are independent of the other branches and that they do not have to fear retribution for their exercise of judicial power.

Congress exercises a potential check on the judicial branch through its power to create (and eliminate) lower federal courts. Congress can also restrict the power of the federal courts to decide cases. And, as we have noted, the president appoints—with the advice and consent of the Senate—the justices of the Supreme Court and the judges of the lower federal courts.

Article III does not explicitly give the courts the power of **judicial review,** that is, the authority to invalidate congressional or presidential actions. That power has been inferred from the logic, structure, and theory of the Constitution.

The Remaining Articles.   The remaining four articles of the Constitution cover a lot of ground. Article IV requires that the judicial acts and criminal warrants of each state be honored in all other states and it forbids discrimination against citizens of one state by another state. This provision promotes equality; it keeps the states from treating outsiders differently than their own citizens. For example, say a justice of the peace in Hawaii marries John Doe and James Smith. (No state yet permits such unions, but Hawaii may soon act to grant them.) The couple move to California. John's employer provides health insurance for spouses, but under California law, legal marriages do not extend to persons of the same sex. Under the full faith and credit clause of Article IV, however, John's employer would have to cover James, and James would retain all other marriage-related rights, despite California's policy. Unless the states act to exempt same-sex marriages, they may be required to respect each other's judicial acts, including marriages. The origin of this clause can be traced to the Articles of Confederation.

Article IV also allows the addition of new states and stipulates that the national government will protect the states against foreign invasion and domestic violence.

Article V specifies the methods for amending (changing) the Constitution. We will have more to say about this shortly.

An important component of Article VI is the **supremacy clause,** which asserts that when they conflict with state or local laws, the Constitution, national laws, and treaties take precedence. The stipulation is vital to the operation of federalism. In keeping with the supremacy clause, Article VI also requires that all national and state officials, elected or appointed, take an oath to support the Constitution. The article also mandates that religion cannot be a prerequisite for holding government office.

Finally, Article VII describes the ratification process, stipulating that approval by conventions in nine states would be necessary for the Constitution to take effect.

The idea of a written constitution seems entirely natural to Americans today. But an unwritten constitution still rules Great Britain, at least for now (see Compared with What? 3.1).

The Framers' Motives

Some argue that the Constitution is essentially a conservative document written by wealthy men to advance their own interests. One distinguished historian who wrote in the early 1900s, Charles A. Beard, maintained that the delegates had much to gain from a strong national government.[25] Many held government securities dating from the Revolutionary War that had become practically worthless under the Articles of Confederation. A

compared with what?

3.1 Is Britain Ready for a Written Constitution?

Britain does not have a written constitution, a deliberate scheme of government formally adopted by the people and specifying special processes for its amendment. In Britain, no single document or law is known as "the constitution." Instead, Britain has an "unwritten constitution," an amalgam of important documents and laws passed by Parliament (the British legislature), court decisions, customs, and conventions. Britain's "constitution" has no existence apart from ordinary law. In contrast to the American system of government, in Britain the Parliament may change, amend, or abolish its fundamental laws and conventions at will. No special procedures or barriers must be overcome to enact such changes.

According to government leaders, Britain has done very well without a written constitution, thank you very much. Or at least that was the position of then prime minister Margaret Thatcher when she was presented with a proposal for a written constitution in 1989. Mrs. Thatcher observed that, despite Britain's lack of a bill of rights and an independent judiciary, "our present constitutional arrangements continue to serve us well.... Furthermore, the government does not feel that a written constitution in itself changes or guarantees anything."

The British people hold a different view. A 1995 nationwide poll revealed that three-fourths of British adults think it is time for a written constitution. Even more feel the need for a bill of rights. Seventeen years of Conservative government have brought privatization to full flower, but continuous Tory rule has also brought centralization of power in London at the expense of regional and local governments. The government has imposed more secrecy, and it has been associated with many scandals. These trends fuel the reformers' fire.

This should not be surprising to constitution watchers. Britain has a tradition of adherence to principles embodied in ancient legislative and monarchical acts, such as the Magna Carta (1215) and the Petition of Right (1628). But when push comes to shove, a majority in Parliament may do as it pleases, and no part of the British government is sufficiently independent to stand in its way.

The fear of central authority and the demand for a written bill of rights are familiar themes to students of the American constitution. Perhaps our experience with a written constitution will prove useful to our British "cousins," who appear anxious to improve on their unwritten rules.

Sources: Andrew Marr, *Ruling Britannia: The Failure and Future of British Democracy* (London: Michael Joseph, 1995); Will Hutton, *The State We're In* (London: Cape, 1995); Fred Barbash, "The Movement to Rule Britannia Differently," *The Washington Post,* 23 September 1995, p. A27.

strong national government would protect their property and pay off the nation's debts.

Beard's argument, that the Constitution was crafted to protect the economic interests of this small group of creditors, provoked a generation of historians to examine the existing financial records of the convention delegates. Their scholarship has largely discredited his once-popular view.[26] For example, it turns out that seven of the delegates who left the convention or refused to sign the Constitution held public securities worth more than twice the total of the holdings of the thirty-nine delegates who did sign. Moreover, the most influential delegates owned no securities. And only a few delegates appear to have directly benefited economically from the new government.[27] Still, there is little doubt about the general homogeneity of the delegates or about their concern for producing a stable economic order that would preserve and promote the interests of some more than others.

What did motivate the framers? Surely economic considerations were important, but they were not the major issues. The single most important factor leading to the Constitutional Convention was the inability of the national or state governments to maintain order under the loose structure of the Articles of Confederation. Certainly, order involved the protection of property, but the framers had a broader view of property than their portfolios of government securities. They wanted to protect their homes, their families, and their means of livelihood from impending anarchy.

Although they disagreed bitterly on the structure and mechanics of the national government, the framers agreed on the most vital issues. For example, three of the most crucial features of the Constitution—the power to tax, the necessary and proper clause, and the supremacy clause—were approved unanimously without debate; experience had taught the delegates that a strong national government was essential if the United States were to survive. The motivation to create order was so strong, in fact, that the framers were willing to draft clauses that protected the most undemocratic of all institutions—slavery.

The Slavery Issue

The institution of slavery was well ingrained in American life at the time of the Constitutional Convention, and slavery helped shape the Constitution, although it is mentioned nowhere by name in it. (According to the first national census in 1790, nearly 18 percent of the population—697,000 people—lived in slavery.) It is doubtful, in fact, that there would have been a Constitution if the delegates had had to resolve the slavery issue, for the southern states would have opposed a constitution that prohibited slavery. Opponents of slavery were in the minority, and they were willing to tolerate its continuation in the interest of forging a union, perhaps believing that the issue could be resolved another day.

The question of representation in the House of Representatives brought the slavery issue close to the surface of the debate at the Constitutional Convention, and it led to the Great Compromise. Representation in the House was to be based on population. But who counted in the population? States with large slave populations wanted all their inhabitants, slave and free, counted equally; states with few slaves wanted only the free population counted. The delegates agreed unanimously that in apportioning representation in the House and in assessing direct taxes, the population of each state was to be determined by adding "the whole Number of free Persons" and "three fifths of all other Persons" (Article I, Section 2). The phrase "all other Persons" is, of course, a substitute for "slaves."

The three-fifths formula had been used by the 1783 congress under the Articles of Confederation to allocate government costs among the states. The rule reflected the view that slaves were less efficient producers of

All Were Not Created Equal

This 1845 photograph of Isaac Jefferson, who had been one of Thomas Jefferson's slaves at Monticello, reminds us that the framers of the Constitution did not extend freedom and equality to all. Slavery was widely accepted as a social norm in the eighteenth century.

wealth than free people, not that slaves were three-fifths human and two-fifths personal property.[28]

The three-fifths clause gave states with large slave populations (the South) greater representation in Congress than states with small slave populations (the North). If all slaves had been included in the count, the slave states would have had 50 percent of the seats in the House. This outcome would have been unacceptable to the North. Had none of the slaves been counted, the slave states would have had 41 percent of House seats, which would have been unacceptable to the South. The three-fifths compromise left the South with 47 percent of the House seats, a sizable minority, but in all likelihood a losing one on slavery issues.[29] The overrepresentation resulting from the South's large slave populations translated into greater influence in selecting the president as well, because the electoral college was based on the size of the states' congressional delegations. The three-fifths clause also undertaxed states with large slave populations.

Another issue centered around the slave trade. Several southern delegates were uncompromising in their defense of the slave trade; other delegates favored prohibition. The delegates compromised, agreeing that the slave trade would not be ended before twenty years had elapsed (Article I, Section 9). Finally, the delegates agreed, without serious challenge, that fugitive slaves would be returned to their masters (Article IV, Section 2).

The experience of enslavement,
passage, arrival, and conditions
of life will be found at:
`<vi.uh.edu/pages/mintz/
primary.htm>`

In addressing these points, the framers in essence condoned slavery. Tens of thousands of Africans were forcibly taken from their homes and sold into bondage. Many died on the journey to this distant land, and those who survived were brutalized and treated as less than human. Clearly, slavery existed in stark opposition to the idea that all men are created equal. Although many slaveholders, including Jefferson and Madison, agonized over it, few made serious efforts to free their own slaves. Most Americans seemed indifferent to slavery and felt no embarrassment at the apparent contradiction between the Declaration of Independence and slavery. Do the framers deserve contempt for their toleration and perpetuation of slavery? The most prominent founders—George Washington, John Adams, and Thomas Jefferson—expected slavery to wither away. A leading colonial scholar has offered a defense of their inaction: the framers were simply unable to transcend altogether the limitations of the age in which they lived. Bear in mind that the colonial period was brutal and savage. While slavery was brutal and degrading, so was much of ordinary life in the colonial period.[30]

Nonetheless, the eradication of slavery proceeded gradually in certain states. Opposition to slavery on moral or religious ground was one reason. Economic forces—such as a shift in the North to agricultural production that was less labor-intensive—were a contributing factor, too. By 1787, Connecticut, Massachusetts, New Jersey, New York, Pennsylvania, Rhode Island, and Vermont had abolished slavery or provided for gradual emancipation. No southern states followed suit, although several enacted laws making it easier for masters to free their slaves. The slow but perceptible shift on the slavery issue in many states masked a volcanic force capable of destroying the Constitutional Convention and the Union.

SELLING THE CONSTITUTION

Nearly four months after the Constitutional Convention opened, the delegates convened for the last time, on September 17, 1787, to sign the final version of their handiwork. Because several delegates were unwilling to sign the document, the last paragraph was craftily worded to give the impression of unanimity: "Done in Convention by the Unanimous Consent of the States present."

Before it could take effect, the Constitution had to be ratified by a minimum of nine state conventions. The support of key states was crucial. In Pennsylvania, however, the legislature was slow to convene a ratifying convention. Pro-Constitution forces became so frustrated at this dawdling that they broke into a local boardinghouse and hauled two errant legislators through the streets to the statehouse so the assembly could schedule the convention.

The proponents of the new charter, who wanted a strong national government, called themselves Federalists. The opponents of the Constitution were quickly dubbed Antifederalists. They claimed, however, to be the true federalists, because they wanted to protect the states from the tyranny of a strong national government. Elbridge Gerry, a vocal Antifederalist, called his opponents "rats" (because they favored ratification) and maintained that he was an "antirat."[31] Such is the Alice-in-Wonderland character of political discourse. Whatever they were called, the viewpoints of these two groups formed the bases of the first American political parties.

The *Federalist* Papers

The press of the day became a battlefield of words, filled with extravagant praise or vituperative condemnation of the proposed constitution. Beginning in October 1787, an exceptional series of eighty-five newspaper articles defending the Constitution appeared under the title *The Federalist: A Commentary on the Constitution of the United States.* The essays bore the pen name Publius (for a Roman emperor and defender of the Republic, Publius Valerius, who was later known as Publicola); they were written primarily by James Madison and Alexander Hamilton, with some assistance from John Jay. Logically and calmly, Publius argued in favor of ratification. Reprinted extensively during the ratification battle, the *Federalist* papers remain the best single commentary we have on the meaning of the Constitution and the political theory it embodies.

Not to be outdone, the Antifederalists offered their own intellectual basis for rejecting the Constitution. In several essays, the most influential published under the pseudonyms Brutus and Federal Farmer, the Antifederalists attacked the centralization of power in a strong national government, claiming it would obliterate the states, violate the social contract of the Declaration of Independence, and destroy liberty in the process. They defended the status quo, maintaining that the Articles of Confederation established true federal principles.[32]

Of all the *Federalist* papers, the most magnificent and most frequently cited is *Federalist* No. 10, written by James Madison (see the Appendix). He argued that the proposed constitution was designed "to break and control the violence of faction." "By a faction," Madison wrote, "I understand a number of citizens, whether amounting to a majority or minority of the whole, who are united and actuated by some common impulse of passion, or of interest, adverse to the rights of other citizens, or to the permanent and aggregate interests of the community."

Madison was discussing what we described in Chapter 2 as *pluralism.* What Madison called factions are today called interest groups or even political parties. According to Madison, "The most common and durable source of factions has been the various and unequal distribution of property." Madison was concerned not with reducing inequalities of wealth (which he took for granted) but with controlling the seemingly inevitable conflict that stems from them. The Constitution, he argued, was well constructed for this purpose.

Through the mechanism of representation, wrote Madison, the Constitution would prevent a "tyranny of the majority" (mob rule). The government would not be controlled by the people directly but indirectly by their elected representatives. And those representatives would have the intelligence and the understanding to serve the larger interests of the nation. Moreover, the federal system would require that majorities form first within each state and then organize for effective action at the national level. This and the vastness of the country would make it unlikely that a majority would form that would "invade the rights of other citizens."

The purpose of *Federalist* No. 10 was to demonstrate that the proposed government was not likely to be dominated by any faction. Contrary to conventional wisdom, Madison argued, the key to mending the evils of factions is to have a large republic—the larger, the better. The more diverse the society, the less likely it is that an unjust majority can form. Madison certainly had no intention of creating a majoritarian democracy; his view of popular government was much more consistent with the model of pluralist democracy discussed in Chapter 2.

Madison pressed his argument from a different angle in *Federalist* No. 51 (see the Appendix). Asserting that "ambition must be made to counteract ambition," he argued that the separation of powers and checks and balances would control efforts at tyranny from any source. If power is distributed equally among the three branches, he argued, each branch will have the capacity to counteract the others. In Madison's words, "usurpations are guarded against by a division of the government into distinct and separate departments." Because legislative power tends to predominate in republican governments, legislative authority is divided between the Senate and the House of Representatives, which have different methods of election and terms of office. Additional protection arises from federalism, which divides power "between two distinct governments"—national and state—and subdivides "the portion allotted to each . . . among distinct and separate departments."

You can get a sense of the debates that raged between Federalists and Antifederalists at:
`<vi.uh.edu/pages/alhmat/ratdeb.html>`

The Antifederalists wanted additional separation of powers and additional checks and balances, which they maintained would eliminate the threat of tyranny entirely. The Federalists believed that such protections would make decisive national action virtually impossible. But to ensure ratification, they agreed to a compromise.

A Concession: The Bill of Rights

Despite the eloquence of the *Federalist* papers, many prominent citizens, including Thomas Jefferson, were unhappy that the Constitution did not list basic civil liberties—the individual freedoms guaranteed to citizens. The omission of a bill of rights was the chief obstacle to the adoption of the Constitution by the states. (Seven of the eleven state constitutions that were written in the first five years of independence included such a list.) The colonists had just rebelled against the British government to preserve their basic freedoms; why did the proposed Constitution not spell out those freedoms?

The answer was rooted in logic, not politics. Because the national government was limited to those powers that were granted to it and because no power was granted to abridge the people's liberties, a list of guaranteed freedoms was not necessary. In *Federalist* No. 84, Hamilton went even further, arguing that the addition of a bill of rights would be dangerous. To deny the exercise of a nonexistent power might lead to the exercise of a power that is not specifically denied. For example, to declare that the national government shall make no law abridging free speech might suggest that the national government could prohibit activities in unspecified areas (such as divorce), which are the states' domain. Because it is not possible to list all prohibited powers, wrote Hamilton, any attempt to provide a partial list would make the unlisted areas vulnerable to government abuse.

3.2   ● **The Bill of Rights**

The first ten amendments to the Constitution are known as the Bill of Rights. The following is a list of those amendments, grouped conceptually. For the actual order and wording of the Bill of Rights, see the Appendix.

Guarantees	Amendment
Guarantees for Participation in the Political Process	
No government abridgement of speech or press; no government abridgement of peaceable assembly; no government abridgement of petitioning government for redress.	1
Guarantees Respecting Personal Beliefs	
No government establishment of religion; no government prohibition of free religious exercise.	1
Guarantees of Personal Privacy	
Owners' consent necessary to quarter troops in private homes in peacetime; quartering during war must be lawful.	3
Government cannot engage in unreasonable searches and seizures; warrants to search and seize require probable cause.	4
No compulsion to testify against oneself in criminal cases.	5
Guarantees Against Government's Overreaching	
Serious crimes require a grand jury indictment; no repeated prosecution for the same offense; no loss of life, liberty, or property without due process; no taking of property for public use without just compensation.	5
Criminal defendants will have a speedy public trial by impartial local jury; defendants are informed of accusation; defendants may confront witnesses against them; defendants may use judicial process to obtain favorable witnesses; defendants may have legal assistance for their defense.	6
Civil lawsuits can be tried by juries if controversy exceeds $20; in jury trials, fact-finding is a jury function.	7
No excessive bail; no excessive fines; no cruel and unusual punishment.	8
Other Guarantees	
The people have the right to bear arms.	2
No government trespass on unspecified fundamental rights.	9
The states or the people retain all powers not delegated to the national government or denied to the states.	10

But logic was no match for fear. Many states agreed to ratify the Constitution only after George Washington suggested adding a list of guarantees through the amendment process. Well in excess of one hundred amendments were proposed by the states. These were eventually narrowed to twelve, which were approved by Congress and sent to the states. Ten became part of the Constitution in 1791, after securing the approval of the required three-fourths of the states. Collectively, the ten amendments are known as the **Bill of Rights.** They restrain the national government from tampering with fundamental rights and civil liberties and emphasize the limited character of the national government's power (see Table 3.2).

Ratification

The Constitution officially took effect upon its ratification by the ninth state, New Hampshire, on June 21, 1788. However, the success of the new government was not ensured until July 1788, by which time the Constitution was ratified by the key states of Virginia and New York after lengthy debate.

The reflection and deliberation that attended the creation and ratification of the Constitution signaled to the world that a new government could be launched peacefully. The French observer Alexis de Tocqueville (1805–1859) later wrote

> That which is new in the history of societies is to see a great people, warned by its lawgivers that the wheels of government are stopping, turn its attention on itself without haste or fear, sound the depth of the ill, and then wait for two years to find the remedy at leisure, and then finally, when the remedy has been indicated, submit to it voluntarily without its costing humanity a single tear or drop of blood.[33]

CONSTITUTIONAL CHANGE

The founders realized that the Constitution would have to be changed from time to time. To this end, they specified a formal amendment process—a process that was used almost immediately to add the Bill of Rights. With the passage of time, the Constitution has also been altered through judicial interpretation and changes in political practice.

The Formal Amendment Process

The amendment process has two stages, proposal and ratification; both are necessary for an amendment to become part of the Constitution. The Constitution provides two alternatives for completing each stage (see Figure 3.3). Amendments can be proposed by a two-thirds vote in both the House of Representatives and the Senate or by a national convention, summoned by Congress at the request of two-thirds of the state legislatures. All constitutional amendments to date have been proposed by the first method; the second has never been used.

A proposed amendment can be ratified by a vote of the legislatures of three-fourths of the states or by a vote of constitutional conventions held in three-fourths of the states. Congress chooses the method of ratification. It has used the state convention method only once, for the Twenty-first Amendment, which repealed the Eighteenth (prohibition of intoxicating liquors).

Note that the amendment process requires the exercise of **extraordinary majorities** (two-thirds and three-fourths). The framers purposely made it difficult to propose and ratify amendments (although nowhere near as difficult as under the Articles of Confederation). They wanted only the most significant issues to lead to constitutional change. Note, too, that the president plays no formal role in the process. Presidential approval is not required to amend the Constitution, although the president's political influence affects the success or failure of any amendment effort.

Calling a national convention to propose an amendment has never been tried, and the method raises several thorny questions. For example, the

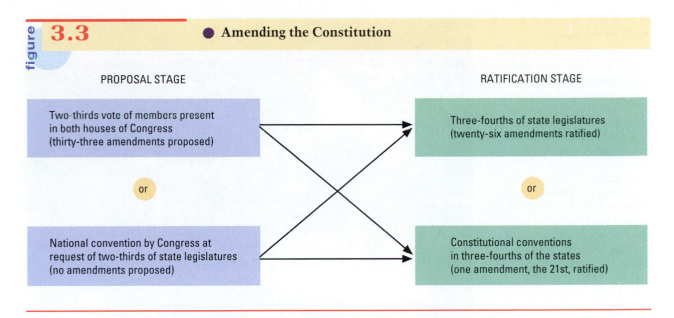

figure 3.3 ● **Amending the Constitution**

PROPOSAL STAGE

Two-thirds vote of members present in both houses of Congress (thirty-three amendments proposed)

or

National convention by Congress at request of two-thirds of state legislatures (no amendments proposed)

RATIFICATION STAGE

Three-fourths of state legislatures (twenty-six amendments ratified)

or

Constitutional conventions in three-fourths of the states (one amendment, the 21st, ratified)

There are two stages in amending the Constitution: proposal and ratification. Congress has no control over the proposal stage, but it prescribes the ratification method. Once a state has ratified an amendment, it cannot retract its action. However, a state may reject an amendment and then reconsider its decision.

Constitution does not specify the number of delegates who should attend, the method by which they should be chosen, or the rules for debating and voting on a proposed amendment. Confusion surrounding the convention process has precluded its use, leaving the amendment process in congressional hands.[34] The major issue is the limits, if any, on the business of the convention. Remember that the convention in Philadelphia in 1787, charged with revising the Articles of Confederation, drafted an entirely new charter. Would a national convention called to consider a particular amendment be within its bounds to rewrite the Constitution? No one really knows.

Most of the Constitution's twenty-seven amendments were adopted to reflect changes in political thinking. The first ten amendments (the Bill of Rights) were the price of ratification, but they have been fundamental to our system of government. The last seventeen amendments fall into three main categories: they make public policy, they correct deficiencies in the government's structure, or they promote equality (see Table 3.3). One attempt to make public policy through a constitutional amendment was disastrous. The Eighteenth Amendment (1919) prohibited the manufacture or sale of intoxicating beverages. Prohibition lasted fourteen years and was an utter failure. Gangsters began bootlegging liquor, people died from drinking homemade booze, and millions regularly broke the law by drinking anyway. Congress had to propose another amendment in 1933 to repeal the Eighteenth. The states ratified this amendment, the Twenty-first, in less than ten months, less time than it took to ratify the Fourteenth Amendment, guaranteeing citizenship, due process, and equal protection of the laws.

Roll Out the Barrels

The Eighteenth Amendment, which was ratified by the states in 1919, banned the manufacture, sale, or transportation of alcoholic beverages. The amendment was spurred by moral and social reform groups, such as the Women's Christian Temperance Union, founded by Evanston, Illinois, resident Frances Willard in 1874. The amendment proved to be an utter failure. People continued to drink, but their alcohol came from illegal sources.

Since 1787, about ten thousand constitutional amendments have been introduced; only a fraction have survived the proposal stage. Once an amendment has been approved by Congress, its chances for ratification are high. The Twenty-seventh Amendment, which prevents members of Congress from voting themselves immediate pay increases, was ratified in 1992. It had been submitted to the states in 1789 but languished in a political netherworld until 1982, when a University of Texas student, Gregory D. Watson, stumbled upon the proposed amendment while researching a paper. At that time, only eight states had ratified the amendment. Watson took up the cause, prompting renewed interest in the idea. In May 1992, ratification by the Michigan legislature provided the decisive vote, 203 years after congressional approval of the proposed amendment.[35] Only six amendments submitted to the states have failed to be ratified. Two such failures occurred in the 1980s: the Equal Rights Amendment (see Chapter 16) and full congressional representation for the District of Columbia.

Interpretation by the Courts

In *Marbury* v. *Madison* (1803), the Supreme Court declared that the courts have the power to nullify government acts that conflict with the Constitution. (We will elaborate on judicial review in Chapter 14.) The exercise of judicial review forces the courts to interpret the Constitution. In a way, this makes a lot of sense. The judiciary is the law-interpreting branch of the government; as the supreme law of the land, the Constitution is fair game for judicial interpretation. Judicial review is the courts' main check on the other branches of government. But in interpreting the Constitution, the courts cannot help but give new meaning to its provisions. This is why judicial interpretation is a principal form of constitutional change.

What guidelines should judges use in interpreting the Constitution? For one thing, they must realize that the usage and meaning of many words

table 3.3 ● **Constitutional Amendments: 11 Through 27**

No.	Proposed	Ratified	Intent	Subject
11	1794	1795	G	Prohibits an individual from suing a state in federal court without the state's consent.
12	1803	1804	G	Requires the electoral college to vote separately for president and vice president.
13	1865	1865	E	Prohibits slavery.
14	1866	1868	E	Gives citizenship to all persons born or naturalized in the United States (including former slaves); prevents states from depriving any person of "life, liberty, or property, without due process of law," and declares that no state shall deprive any person of "the equal protection of the laws."
15	1869	1870	E	Guarantees that citizens' right to vote cannot be denied "on account of race, color, or previous condition of servitude."
16	1909	1913	E	Gives Congress the power to collect an income tax.
17	1912	1913	E	Provides for popular election of senators, who were formerly elected by state legislatures.
18	1917	1919	P	Prohibits the making and selling of intoxicating liquors.
19	1919	1920	E	Guarantees that citizens' right to vote cannot be denied "on account of sex."
20	1932	1933	G	Changes the presidential inauguration from March 4 to January 20 and sets January 3 for the opening date of Congress.
21	1933	1933	P	Repeals the Eighteenth Amendment.
22	1947	1951	G	Limits a president to two terms.
23	1960	1961	E	Gives citizens of Washington, D.C., the right to vote for president.
24	1962	1964	E	Prohibits charging citizens a poll tax to vote in presidential or congressional elections.
25	1965	1967	G	Provides for succession in event of death, removal from office, incapacity, or resignation of the president or vice president.
26	1971	1971	E	Lowers the voting age to eighteen.
27	1789	1992	G	Bars immediate pay increases to members of Congress.

P Amendments legislating public policy
G Amendments correcting perceived deficiencies in government structure
E Amendments advancing equality

have changed during the past two hundred years. Judges must be careful to think about what the words meant at the time the Constitution was written. Some insist that they must also consider the original intent of the framers—not an easy task. Of course, there are records of the Constitutional Convention and of the debates surrounding ratification.

● politics in a changing america

3.1 What the Founders Did Not Say About Sexual Orientation

In a democracy, may a majority thwart efforts to adopt special government protections based on sexual orientation?

Survey evidence gathered in 1993 suggests that about 3 percent of American adults are homosexual or bisexual. Survey evidence also reveals that a majority of Americans look upon homosexuality with varying degrees of disfavor. But attitudes toward homosexuality have become somewhat more accepting. And the politics surrounding homosexuality have started to shift.

In 1992, fifty-three percent of Colorado voters approved a voter-initiated amendment to

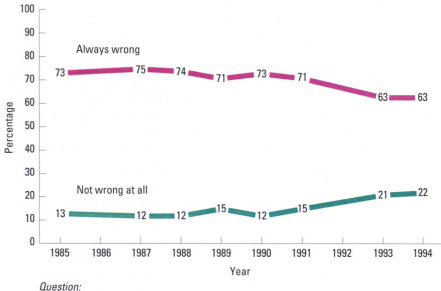

Question:
Do you think that sexual relations between two adults of the same sex is always wrong or not wrong at all?

But there are also many questions about the completeness and accuracy of those records, even Madison's detailed notes. And, at times, the framers were deliberately vague in writing the document. This may reflect lack of agreement on, or universal understanding of, certain provisions in the Constitution. Some scholars and judges maintain that the search for original meaning is hopeless and that contemporary notions of constitutional provisions must hold sway. Critics say that this approach comes perilously close to amending the Constitution as judges see fit, transforming law interpreters into lawmakers. Still other scholars and judges maintain that judges face the unavoidable challenge of balancing two-hundred-year-old constitutional principles against the demands of modern society.[36]

the state constitution. The amendment forbade state and local authorities to enact laws that would create any entitlement, minority preference, or legal basis for discrimination claims by homosexuals or bisexuals.

The amendment's immediate effect was to repeal state and local government laws and regulations that barred discrimination based on sexual orientation. Its ultimate effect would be to prohibit any government body from adopting similar or more protective policies in the future, short of constitutional amendment.

Several individuals and groups challenged Colorado's new amendment in court. They argued that the amendment "fences out" gay men, lesbians, and bisexuals from the political process, singling them out and prohibiting them from seeking favorable government action. Consequently, the amendment denies them equal participation in the political process.

The Colorado courts struck down the amendment on the novel ground that it violated a fundamental right of a group to participate equally in the political process. The final blow came in 1996.

The United States Supreme Court found a much narrower ground for decision. Speaking for a 6–3 majority in *Romer* v. *Evans*, Justice Anthony Kennedy held that the Colorado amendment violated the Fourteenth Amendment guarantee of equal protection. Kennedy declared that a state may not "deem a class of persons a stranger to its laws." Fencing off only one particularly unpopular group imposed "a special disability upon those persons alone."*

Colorado also lacked an adequate justification for its amendment. Courts require that laws have a rational basis. As a practical matter, rationality rests with the legislature. The passage of a law is usually sufficient proof that it is rational. The "rational basis" test sets a very low threshold for government to justify its actions. But in this case, the amendment failed to establish a rational link to a legitimate government purpose.

Antigay initiatives remain a conservative rallying point in many states, including Florida, Ohio, and Texas.

Sources: American Demographics, July 1993; *General Social Survey*, Feb. 1985–Jan. 1994; *Evans* v. *Romer*, 854 P. 2d 1270 (Colo. 1993); Ann Rovin and Louis Sahagun, "Colorado's Ban on Gay Rights Laws Is Voided," *Los Angeles Times*, 15 December 1993, p. A1. *Romer* v. *Evans* (docket no. 91-1039). Paul M. Barrett, "Court Rejects Ban on Laws Protecting Gays," *Wall Street Journal*, 21 May 1996, p. B1.

* You can find a copy of the Supreme Court opinion at <www.law.cornell.edu:80/supct/supct.may.1996.html>

Whatever the approach, judges run the risk of usurping policies established by the people's representatives (see Politics in a Changing America 3.1).

Political Practice

The Constitution is silent on many issues. It says nothing about political parties or the president's cabinet, for example, yet both have exercised considerable influence in American politics. Some constitutional provisions have fallen out of use. The electors in the electoral college, for example, were supposed to exercise their own judgment in voting for the president and vice president. Today, the electors function simply as a rubber stamp, validating the outcome of election contests in their states.

Meanwhile, political practice has altered the distribution of power without changes in the Constitution. The framers intended Congress to be the strongest branch of government. But the president has come to overshadow Congress. Presidents such as Abraham Lincoln and Franklin Roosevelt used their powers imaginatively to respond to national crises. And their actions paved the way for future presidents to further enlarge the powers of the office.

The framers could scarcely have imagined an urbanized nation of more than 265 million people stretching across a landmass some three thousand miles wide, reaching halfway over the Pacific Ocean, and stretching past the Arctic Circle. Never in their wildest nightmares could they have foreseen the destructiveness of nuclear weaponry or envisioned its effect on the power to declare war. The Constitution empowers Congress to consider and debate this momentous step. But with nuclear annihilation perhaps only minutes away, the legislative power to declare war must give way to the president's power to wage war as the nation's commander in chief. Strict adherence to the Constitution in such circumstances could destroy the nation's ability to protect itself.

AN EVALUATION OF THE CONSTITUTION

The U.S. Constitution is one of the world's most praised political documents. It is the oldest written national constitution and one of the most widely copied, sometimes word for word. It is also one of the shortest, consisting of about 4,300 words (not counting the amendments, which add 3,100 words). The brevity of the Constitution may be one of its greatest strengths. As we noted earlier, the framers simply laid out a structural framework for government; they did not describe relationships and powers in detail. For example, the Constitution gives Congress the power to regulate "Commerce . . . among the several States" but does not define interstate commerce. Such general wording allows interpretation in keeping with contemporary political, social, and technological developments. Air travel, for instance, unknown in 1787, now falls easily within Congress's power to regulate interstate commerce.

The generality of the U.S. Constitution stands in stark contrast to the specificity of most state constitutions. The constitution of California, for example, provides that "fruit and nut-bearing trees under the age of four years from the time of planting in orchard form and grapevines under the age of three years from the time of planting in vineyard form . . . shall be exempt from taxation" (Article XIII, Section 12). Because they are so specific, most state constitutions are much longer than the U.S. Constitution.

Freedom, Order, and Equality in the Constitution

The revolutionaries' first try at government was embodied in the Articles of Confederation. The result was a weak national government that leaned too much toward freedom at the expense of order. Deciding that the confederation was beyond correcting, the revolutionaries chose a new form of government—a *federal* government—that was strong enough to maintain order but not so strong that it could dominate the states or infringe on individual freedoms. In short, the Constitution provided a judicious balance between order and freedom. It paid virtually no attention to equality.

Consider social equality. The Constitution never mentioned the word *slavery*—a controversial issue even then. In fact, as we have seen, the Constitution implicitly condones slavery in the wording of several articles. Not until the ratification of the Thirteenth Amendment in 1865 was slavery prohibited.

The Constitution was designed long before social equality was ever even thought of as an objective of government. In fact, in *Federalist* No. 10, Madison held that protection of the "diversities in the faculties of men from which the rights of property originate" is "the first object of government." More than a century later, the Constitution was changed to incorporate a key device for the promotion of social equality—the income tax. The Sixteenth Amendment (1913) gave Congress the power to collect an income tax; it was proposed and ratified to replace a law that had been declared unconstitutional in an 1895 Supreme Court case. The income tax had long been seen as a means of putting into effect the concept of *progressive taxation,* in which the tax rate increases with income. The Sixteenth Amendment gave progressive taxation a constitutional basis.[37] Progressive taxation later helped promote social equality through the redistribution of income—that is, higher-income people are taxed at higher rates to help fund social programs that benefit low-income people.

Social equality itself has never been, and is not now, a prime *constitutional* value. The Constitution has been much more effective in securing order and freedom. A poll of Americans taken during the Constitution's bicentennial in 1987 reinforces this evaluation (see Figure 3.4). Nor did the Constitution take a stand on political equality. It left voting qualifications to the states, specifying only that people who could vote for "the most numerous Branch of the State Legislature" could also vote for representatives to Congress (Article I, Section 2). Most states at that time allowed only taxpaying or property-owning white males to vote. With few exceptions, blacks and women were universally excluded from voting. These inequalities have been rectified by several amendments (see Table 3.3).

Political equality expanded after the Civil War. The Fourteenth Amendment (adopted in 1868) guaranteed all persons, including blacks, citizenship. The Fifteenth Amendment (ratified in 1870) declared that "race, color, or previous condition of servitude" could not be used to deny citizens the right to vote. This did not automatically give blacks the vote; some states used other mechanisms to limit black enfranchisement. The Nineteenth Amendment (adopted in 1920) opened the way for women to vote by declaring that sex could not be used to deny citizens the right to vote. The Twenty-fourth Amendment (adopted in 1964) prohibited the poll tax (a tax that people had to pay to vote and that tended to disenfranchise poor blacks) in presidential and congressional elections. The Twenty-sixth Amendment (adopted in 1971) declared that age could not be used to deny citizens 18 years or older the right to vote. One other amendment expanded the Constitution's grant of political equality. The Twenty-third Amendment (adopted in 1961) allowed residents of Washington, D.C., who are not citizens of any state, to vote for president.

figure 3.4 ● "We the People" Evaluate the Constitution

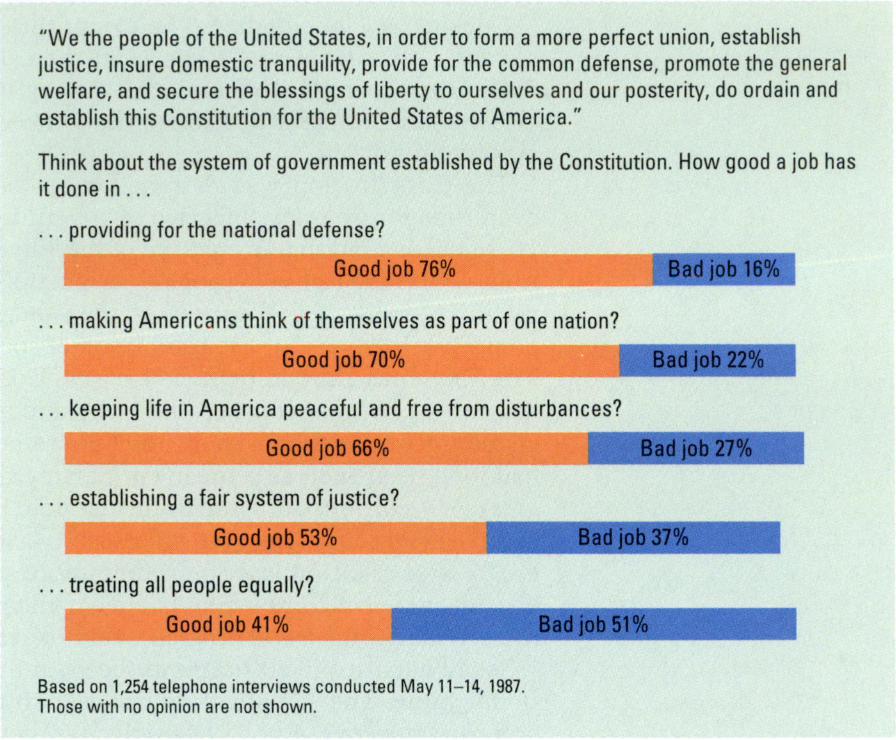

Two hundred years after the Constitutional Convention, a survey of Americans evaluated the nation's success at achieving the goals articulated in the preamble to the Constitution. According to the results, the Constitution has done a good job of forging one nation from separate states and securing an orderly and free society. Although equality was not an explicit goal in the preamble, the Constitution's success in treating all people equally received a relatively poor grade.
Source: *New York Times*, 26 May 1987, p. 10. Copyright © 1987 by the New York Times Company. Reprinted by permission.

"We the people of the United States, in order to form a more perfect union, establish justice, insure domestic tranquility, provide for the common defense, promote the general welfare, and secure the blessings of liberty to ourselves and our posterity, do ordain and establish this Constitution for the United States of America."

Think about the system of government established by the Constitution. How good a job has it done in . . .

. . . providing for the national defense?

| Good job 76% | Bad job 16% |

. . . making Americans think of themselves as part of one nation?

| Good job 70% | Bad job 22% |

. . . keeping life in America peaceful and free from disturbances?

| Good job 66% | Bad job 27% |

. . . establishing a fair system of justice?

| Good job 53% | Bad job 37% |

. . . treating all people equally?

| Good job 41% | Bad job 51% |

Based on 1,254 telephone interviews conducted May 11–14, 1987. Those with no opinion are not shown.

The Constitution and Models of Democracy

Think back to our discussion of the models of democracy in Chapter 2. Which model does the Constitution fit: pluralist or majoritarian? Actually, it is hard to imagine a government framework better suited to the pluralist model of democracy than the Constitution of the United States. It is also hard to imagine a document more at odds with the majoritarian model. Consider Madison's claim, in *Federalist* No. 10, that government inevitably involves conflicting factions. This concept coincides perfectly with pluralist theory (see Chapter 2). Then recall his description in *Federalist* No. 51 of the Constitution's ability to guard against concentration of power in the majority through separation of powers and checks and balances. This concept—avoiding a single center of government power that might fall under majority control—also fits perfectly with pluralist democracy.

The delegates to the Constitutional Convention intended to create a republic, a government based on majority consent; they did not intend to create a democracy, which rests on majority rule. They succeeded admirably in creating that republic. In doing so, they also produced a government that developed into a democracy—but a particular type of democracy. The framers neither wanted nor got a democracy that fit the majoritarian model. They may have wanted, and they certainly did create, a government that conforms to the pluralist model.

SUMMARY

The U.S. Constitution is more than an antique curiosity. Although more than two hundred years old, it governs the politics of a mighty modern nation. It still has the power to force from office a president who won reelection by a landslide. It still has the power to see the country through government crises.

The Constitution was the end product of a revolutionary movement aimed at preserving existing liberties. That movement began with the Declaration of Independence, which proclaimed that everyone is entitled to certain rights (among them, life, liberty, and the pursuit of happiness) and that government exists for the good of its citizens. When government denies those rights, the people have the right to rebel.

War with Britain was only part of the process of independence. A government was needed to replace the British monarchy. The Americans chose a republic and defined the structure of that republic in the Articles of Confederation. The Articles were a failure, however. Although they guaranteed the states the independence they coveted, they left the central government too weak to deal with disorder and insurrection.

The Constitution was the second attempt at limited government. It replaced a loose union of powerful states with a strong but still limited national government, incorporating four political principles: republicanism, federalism, separation of powers, and checks and balances. Republicanism is a form of government in which power resides in the people and is exercised by their elected representatives. Federalism is a division of power between the national government and the states. The federalism of the Constitution conferred substantial powers on the national government at the expense of the states. Separation of powers is a further division of the power of the national government into legislative (lawmaking), executive (law-enforcing), and judicial (law-interpreting) branches. Finally, the Constitution established a system of checks and balances, giving each branch some scrutiny of and control over the others.

When work began on ratification, a major stumbling block proved to be the failure of the Constitution to list the individual liberties the Americans had fought to protect. With the promise to add a bill of rights, the Constitution was ratified. The ten amendments guaranteed participation in the political process, respect for personal beliefs, and personal privacy. They also contained guarantees against government overreaching in criminal prosecutions. Over the years, the Constitution has evolved through the formal amendment process, through the exercise of judicial review, and through political practice.

The Constitution was designed to strike a balance between order and freedom. It was not designed to promote social equality; in fact, it had to be amended to redress inequality. The framers compromised on many issues, including slavery, to ensure the creation of a new and workable government. The framers did not set out to create a democracy. Faith in government by the people was virtually nonexistent two centuries ago.

Nevertheless, they produced a democratic form of government. That government, with its separation of powers and checks and balances, is remarkably well suited to the pluralist model of democracy. Simple majority rule, which lies at the heart of the majoritarian model, was precisely what the framers wanted to avoid.

The framers also wanted a balance between the powers of the national government and those of the states. The exact balance was a touchy issue, skirted by the delegates at the Constitutional Convention. Some seventy years later, a civil war was fought over that balance of power. That war and countless political battles before and since have demonstrated that the national government dominates the state governments in our political system. In Chapter 4, we will look at how a loose confederation of states has evolved into a "more perfect Union."

Key Terms

Declaration of Independence	legislative branch	separation of powers	implied powers
social contract theory	executive branch	checks and balances	judicial review
republic	judicial branch	enumerated powers	supremacy clause
confederation	New Jersey Plan	necessary and proper clause	Bill of Rights
Articles of Confederation	Great Compromise		extraordinary majorities
Virginia Plan	republicanism		
	federalism		

Selected Readings

Becker, Carl. *The Declaration of Independence: A Study in the History of Political Ideas.* New York: Alfred A. Knopf, 1942. A classic study of the theory and politics of the Declaration of Independence.

Bowen, Catherine Drinker. *Miracle at Philadelphia.* Boston: Atlantic–Little, Brown, 1966. An absorbing, well-written account of the events surrounding the Constitutional Convention.

Emery, Fred. *Watergate: The Corruption of American Politics and the Fall of Richard Nixon.* New York: Times Books, 1994. A compelling narrative of the greatest political scandal in our times.

Kammen, Michael. *A Machine That Would Go of Itself: The Constitution in American Culture.* New York: Alfred A. Knopf, 1986. A remarkable examination of the Constitution's cultural influence. The author argues that Americans' reverence for the Constitution is inconsistent with their ignorance of its content and meaning.

Norton, Mary Beth. *Liberty's Daughters.* Boston: Little, Brown, 1980. This book examines the role of women before, during, and after the American Revolution. Norton argues that the Revolution transformed gender roles and set women on a course toward equality.

Rakove, Jack N. *Original Meanings: Politics and Ideas in the Making of the Constitution.* New York: Alfred A. Knopf, 1996. The meaning, intention, and understanding of the U.S. Constitution from a historian's perspective.

Wood, Gordon S. *The Radicalism of the American Revolution.* New York: Alfred A. Knopf, 1992. Wood argues that the Revolution was not a conservative defense of American rights but a radical revolution that produced a free and democratic society far beyond what was envisioned by the founders.

World Wide Web Resources

The Charters of Freedom. View America's founding documents at the National Archives' virtual exhibit hall. Good graphics, especially of items never exhibited in public.

`<www.nara.gov/exhall/charters/charters.html>`

Comparing the World's Constitutions. English text and background materials for the world's constitutions. This site contains cross-references for quick comparison of constitutional provisions.

`<www.uni-hamburg.de/law/index.html>`

and mirrored at

`<www.law.cornell.edu/law/index.html>`

American History on the WWW. Take a quick refresher tour of American history from revolution to reconstruction through this rich WWW resource.

`<grid.let.rug.nl/~welling/usa>`

c h a p t e r

4

Federalism

THE LOCALS CALLED IT "our Blood Border." It was a stretch of flat country due east of Beaumont, Texas, down Interstate 10 to the Louisiana state line, where eighteen-year-olds could still drink legally. White crosses dotted the highway alongside the westbound lanes. In 1993, sixty-four westbound accidents marked by death or injury involved underage drinkers. (In the same period, a total of sixteen such accidents occurred in the eastbound lane.) The crosses were grim reminders of where Texas teenagers, driving home from bars across the Louisiana border, ran off the road, crashed, and died. Eighteen-year-olds could still drink alcoholic beverages in Louisiana, despite the fact that the minimum drinking age is twenty-one everywhere else in the country. July 1996 marked the last round, when the Louisiana Supreme Court brought the state in line with the rest of the nation.[1]

Our federal system of government explains both Louisiana's lonely stand and the drive toward uniformity. The Constitution divides power between the national and state governments. With only one sobering exception (Prohibition under the Eighteenth Amendment), regulating liquor sales and setting the minimum drinking age have always been the responsibilities of state governments. But over the years, the national government has found ways to extend its influence into areas that are well beyond those originally defined in the Constitution.

Back in 1981, twenty-nine states and the District of Columbia allowed people younger than twenty-one to purchase and consume some forms of alcoholic beverages. In 1984, however, an action taken in Washington, D.C., marked the beginning of the end of legalized drinking for those younger than twenty-one. Did Congress establish a national minimum drinking age? No, at least not directly. Congress simply added a provision to a highway bill. Under that provision, states would lose 5 percent of their federal highway funds in 1986 and 10 percent every year thereafter if they allowed the purchase or consumption of alcohol by those younger than twenty-one. States would have to change their own laws or risk losing federal funds. This was a roundabout method to achieve a national objective. If the national government wanted to set twenty-one as a national drinking age, why not act directly and pass legislation to do so? The plain fact is that the national government lacks the power to act directly in this area.

Mothers Against Drunk Driving is a nonprofit, grassroots organization with more than 400 chapters nationwide.
`<www.lifetimetv.com/ parenting/MADD/index.html>`

The national government became concerned about the drinking age because Mothers Against Drunk Driving (MADD) and other interest groups fought hard to increase public awareness of the dangers of driving drunk. These groups argued that a uniform drinking age of twenty-one would

● ● ● ● ● ● ● ● ● ● ●
Designated Drunk

A young New Orleans patron celebrated to excess in March 1996 when the Louisiana Supreme Court cleared the way for bars to serve liquor to teenagers despite national highway legislation aimed at a uniform minimum drinking age of 21. The court reversed its stand five months later.

reduce highway fatalities. The National Transportation Safety Board estimated that 1,250 lives could be saved each year by raising the drinking age. However, campaigning for change on a state-by-state basis would be slow and might even be dangerous. So long as some states allowed teenagers to drink, young people would be able to drive across state lines in order to drink legally. The borders between states would become bloody borders—it remained so in east Texas—strewn with victims of teenage drinking and driving.

Supporters of the legislation believed that the national government's responsibility to maintain order justified intervention. The lives and safety of people were at stake. Opponents of the plan argued that it constituted age discrimination and infringed on states' rights. They claimed the act was an unwarranted extension of national power, that it limited the freedom of the states and their citizens.

Despite the opposition, the bill passed handily and went to President Ronald Reagan for signing. Reagan had campaigned on a pledge to reduce the size and scope of the national government, and he strongly opposed replacing state standards with national ones. Where would he come out on this issue, which pitted order against freedom and national standards against state standards? Early on, he opposed the bill; later, he changed his position. At the signing ceremony, he said, "This problem is bigger than the individual states. It's a grave national problem, and it touches all our lives. With the problem so clear-cut and the proven solution at hand, we have no misgiving about this judicious use of federal power. I'm convinced that it will help persuade state legislators to act in the national interest."[2]

Listen to the arguments in *South
Dakota* v. *Dole.*
`<oyez.at.nwu.edu/cases/
86-260/>`

Several states took the matter to court, hoping to have the provision de-
clared unconstitutional under the Tenth and Twenty-first Amendments.
In June 1987, the Supreme Court reached a decision in *South Dakota* v.
Dole. The justices conceded that direct congressional control of the drinking age in the states would be unconstitutional. Nevertheless, the
Constitution does not bar the indirect achievement of such objectives.
The seven-justice majority argued that, far from being an infringement on
states' rights, the law was a "relatively mild encouragement to the States
to enact higher minimum drinking ages than they would otherwise
choose." After all, Chief Justice William H. Rehnquist wrote, the goal of
reducing drunk driving was "directly related to one of the main purposes
for which highway funds are expended—safe interstate travel."[3]

Rehnquist's words show how much the role of the national government
has changed since the Constitution was adopted. In the early part of the
nineteenth century, chief executives routinely vetoed bills authorizing
roads, canals, and other interstate improvements. They believed such
projects exceeded the constitutional authority of the national government.
Eventually, the national government used its authority over interstate
commerce to justify creating a role for itself in building roads (witness the
forty-three-thousand-mile interstate highway system). In 1996, the national government planned to spend more than $23 billion on cost-sharing
projects with the states for road research, planning, and construction.[4]

The Highway Act of 1984 (and its successor, the 1986 National
Minimum Drinking Age Act) shows how national and state governments
can interact. Congress did not challenge the constitutional power of the
states to regulate the minimum drinking age (under the Twenty-first
Amendment), but it used its own powers to tax and spend (Article I,
Section 8, clause 1) to encourage the states to implement a national standard. Lawmakers in Washington, D.C., believed that few states would pass
up highway funds to retain the power to set a minimum drinking age, and
they were right.

In 1986, Louisiana dutifully barred teenagers from buying alcohol in
order to retain its share of valuable highway funds. But a loophole in the
state law protected bar and store owners from prosecution for selling alcohol to teens. Without the threat of sanctions, sales of alcohol to teenagers
continued.

Local activists battled for nine years against the powerful state liquor
lobby and finally closed the loophole in 1995 with the passage of a provision imposing sanctions on retailers who sell alcoholic beverages to persons under the age of twenty-one. Then, in 1996, the Louisiana Supreme
Court tossed out both the 1986 and the 1995 laws, saying they amounted
to age discrimination barred by the state constitution. Since Louisiana
considers eighteen-year-olds adults, they cannot be stripped of any right
accorded other adults. According to Justice Catherine D. Kimball, the
state failed to prove that the twenty-one-and-older law "substantially fur-
thers the important government objective of improving highway safety."[5]
Shortly thereafter, the Clinton administration alerted Louisiana that it
would lose $17 million in federal highway funds if it did not comply with
the minimum drinking age of twenty-one set by Congress.

The court's 4–3 ruling outraged groups seeking tougher action against
drunk driving. They had secured the required legislative change only to be

● ● ● ● ● ● ● ● ● ●

Local Cops, National Cops

Local, state, and national governments share certain powers, such as law enforcement. Houston police officers enforce local criminal laws in a continuing campaign against illegal drugs (left). A SWAT team from the Federal Bureau of Investigation, the principal law-enforcement arm of the national government, arrives to quiet a riot at a federal penitentiary in Atlanta (right).

upended by the court. The state attorney general requested reargument—a final round—to persuade the judges to reconsider their initial decision. In the interim, a new judge was elected to replace a temporary appointment. Another judge from the original majority, who was up for reelection in the fall, switched sides. In July 1996, the Louisiana Supreme Court voted 5–2 in favor of the twenty-one-year-old drinking threshold. A beer industry representative remarked soberly afterward: "I give credit to MADD . . . and others who actively lobbied the court and put fear into those members who are seeking re-election."[6]

An important element of federalism was at work here: the respective sovereignty of national and state governments. (Sovereignty is the quality of being supreme in power or authority.) Congress acknowledged the sovereignty of the states by not legislating a national drinking age. And the states were willing to barter their sovereignty in this area in exchange for needed revenues. As long as this remains true, there are few areas where national power cannot reach.

Sovereignty also affects political leadership. A governor may not be the political equal of a president, but governors have their own sovereignty, apart from the national government. Consequently, presidents rarely command governors; they negotiate, even plead. For example, President John F. Kennedy negotiated repeatedly (and, it turned out, hopelessly) with Mississippi governor Ross Barnett to admit James Meredith as the first black student at the University of Mississippi. Kennedy lacked the power to order Barnett to admit Meredith. In the end, the U.S. Justice Department enforced a federal court order to secure Meredith's admission. Kennedy had to call out the National Guard to quell the rioting that followed.[7]

In this chapter, we examine American federalism in theory and in practice. Is the division of power between nation and states a matter of constitutional principle or practical politics? How does the balance of power between nation and states relate to the conflicts between freedom and order and between freedom and equality? Does federalism reflect the pluralist or the majoritarian model of democracy?

THEORIES OF FEDERALISM

The delegates who met in Philadelphia in 1787 were supposed to repair weaknesses in the Articles of Confederation. Instead, they tackled the problem of making one nation out of thirteen independent states by doing something much more radical. They wrote a new constitution and invented a new political form—federal government—that combined features of a confederacy with features of unitary government (see Chapter 3). Under the principle of **federalism,** two or more governments exercise power and authority over the same people and the same territory. For example, the governments of the United States and Pennsylvania share certain powers (the power to tax, for instance), but other powers belong exclusively to one or the other. As James Madison wrote in *Federalist* No. 10, "The federal Constitution forms a happy combination . . . the great and aggregate interests being referred to the national, and the local and particular to state governments." So the power to coin money belongs to the national government, but the power to grant divorces remains a state prerogative. By contrast, authority over state militias may sometimes belong to the national government and sometimes to the states. The history of American federalism reveals that it has not always been easy to draw a line between what is "great and aggregate" and what is "local and particular."*

Nevertheless, federalism offered a solution to the problem of diversity in America. Citizens feared that, without a federal system of government, they would be ruled by majorities from different regions with different interests and values. Federalism also provided a new political model. A leading scholar of federalism estimated in 1990 that 40 percent of the world's population live under a formal federal constitution, while another 30 percent live in polities that apply federal principles or practices without formal constitutional acknowledgment of their federalism.[8] Although federalism offers an approach that can unify diverse people into single nations, it also retains elements that can lead to national disunity. Canada is an example of a federal system coping with the possibility of the dissolution of its constituent parts (see Compared with What? 4.1).

REPRESENTATIONS OF AMERICAN FEDERALISM

The history of American federalism is full of attempts to capture its true meaning in an adjective or metaphor. By one reckoning, scholars have generated nearly five hundred ways to describe federalism.[9] Let us concentrate on two such representations: dual federalism and cooperative federalism.

Dual Federalism

The term **dual federalism** sums up a theory about the proper relationship between the national government and the states. The theory has four essential parts. First, the national government rules by enumerated powers

---

* *The phrase Americans commonly use to refer to their central government—federal government—muddies the waters even more. Technically speaking, we have a federal system of government, which includes both the national and state governments. To avoid confusion from here on, we use the term national government rather than federal government when we are talking about the central government.*

● compared with what?

4.1   The Perpetually Fragmenting Federation of Canada

Federalism tolerates the centrifugal forces (such as different languages and religions) that can sunder a nation and provides the centripetal forces that bind it (such as the powers to raise an army and control a national economy). But federalism is no guarantee that the forces of unity will always overcome those of disunity. Consider the example of Canada.

Canada is a federation of ten provinces. But the Canadian province of Quebec is different. Eighty percent of its population is French speaking; almost half speak little or no English. (The vast majority of Canadians outside Quebec speak only English.) Quebec has its own holidays, its own music videos, its own literature. By law, all signs must be in French. English is scarcely tolerated.

For decades, Canadians have struggled with the challenge of assimilating yet differentiating Quebec. When Canada drafted a new constitution in 1982, Quebec refused to sign it. Quebecers conditioned their union with the other provinces on a constitutional amendment that would recognize Quebec as a "distinct society" within the country. The amendment had to be approved by all ten provinces. It failed when two provinces refused to ratify the Quebec agreement by the June 1990 deadline.

In October 1992, Canadians rejected another constitutional solution to the Quebec question. The reforms aimed at recognizing Quebec's special status, electing the national senate, and providing self-government for native peoples. Québécois rejected the reforms because they did not go far enough; other provinces rejected the reforms because they went too far.

Repeated threats of secession reached a crescendo in October 1995 when Quebec's voters confronted the latest referendum on independence. The vote was the closest ever: 50.6 percent against independence and 49.4 percent in favor of it. Separatist leaders, taking hope from the substantial movement toward independence, planned for yet another referendum (or *neverendum*, a term coined by some English Canadian wags).

Canadians appeared doomed to endure continued wrangling over the structure of their nation. There is no assurance that they will be able to accommodate Quebec's determined demand for greater autonomy and official recognition of its distinctiveness. Perhaps this perpetual conflict has come to define Canada. While many would say that Canada would not be Canada without Quebec, many might also say that Canada would not be Canada without this perpetual conflict over Quebec's status.

---

only. Second, the national government has a limited set of constitutional purposes. Third, each government unit—nation and state—is sovereign within its sphere. And fourth, the relationship between nation and states is best characterized by tension rather than cooperation.[10]

Dual federalism portrays the states as powerful components of the federal system—in some ways, the equals of the national government. Under dual federalism, the functions and responsibilities of the national and state governments are theoretically different and practically separate from each other. Dual federalism sees the Constitution as a compact among sovereign states. Of primary importance in dual federalism are **states' rights,** a concept that reserves to the states all rights not specifically con-

Quebec Demonstration

Sources: Robert C. Vipond, "Seeing Canada Through the Referendum: Still a House Divided," *Publius* 23 (Summer 1993), p. 39; Clyde H. Farnsworth, "For Quebec, the Neverendum," *New York Times*, 5 November 1995, sect. 4, p. 3.

ferred on the national government by the Constitution. According to the theory of dual federalism, a rigid wall separates nation and states. After all, if the states created the nation, by implication they can set limits on the activities of the national government. Proponents of states' rights believe that the powers of the national government should be interpreted narrowly. Claims of states' rights often come from opponents of a given national government policy. Their argument is that the Constitution has not delegated to the national government the power to make such policy and that the power thus remains with the states or the people. They insist that despite the elastic clause, which gives Congress the **implied powers** needed to execute its enumerated powers (see Chapter 3), the activities of

Congress should be confined to the enumerated powers only. And they support their view by quoting the Tenth Amendment: "The powers not delegated to the United States by the Constitution, nor prohibited by it to the States, are reserved to the States respectively, or to the people."

Political scientists use a metaphor to describe dual federalism. They call it *layer-cake federalism;* the powers and functions of the national and state governments are as separate as the layers of a cake (see Figure 4.1). Each government is supreme in its own layer, its own sphere of action; the two layers are distinct, and the dimensions of each layer are fixed by the Constitution.

Dual federalism has been challenged on historical and other grounds. Some critics argue that if the national government is really a creation of the states, it is a creation of only thirteen states, those that ratified the Constitution. The other thirty-seven states were admitted after the national government came into being and were created by that government out of land it had acquired. Another challenge has to do with the ratification process. Remember, special conventions in the original thirteen states, not the states' legislatures, ratified the Constitution. Ratification, then, was an act of the people, not the states. Moreover, the preamble to the Constitution begins "We the People of the United States," not "We the States." The question of just where the people fit into the federal system is not handled well by dual federalism.

The concept of dual federalism, two levels of government operating on different tracks, each in control of its own activities, suited the American experience from 1789 to 1933. But the demands of the Great Depression gave birth to a new federal concept: cooperative federalism.

Cooperative Federalism

Cooperative federalism, a phrase coined in the 1930s, is a different theory of the relationship between the national and state governments. It acknowledges the increasing overlap between state and national functions and rejects the idea of separate spheres, or layers, for the states and the national government. Cooperative federalism includes three elements. First, national and state agencies typically undertake government functions jointly rather than exclusively. Second, nation and states routinely share power. And third, power is not concentrated at any government level or in any agency; the fragmentation of responsibilities gives people and groups access to many centers of influence.

The bakery metaphor used to describe this type of federalism is a marble cake. The national and state governments do not act in separate spheres; they are intermingled in vertical and diagonal strands and swirls. Their functions are mixed in the American federal system. Critical to cooperative federalism is an expansive view of the Constitution's supremacy clause (Article VI), which specifically subordinates state law to national law and charges every judge with disregarding state laws that are inconsistent with the Constitution, national laws, or treaties.

In contrast to dual federalism, cooperative federalism blurs the distinction between national and state powers. Some scholars argue that the layer-cake metaphor has never accurately described the American political structure.[11] The national and state governments have many common

figure

4.1 ● Metaphors for Federalism

The two views of federalism can be represented graphically.

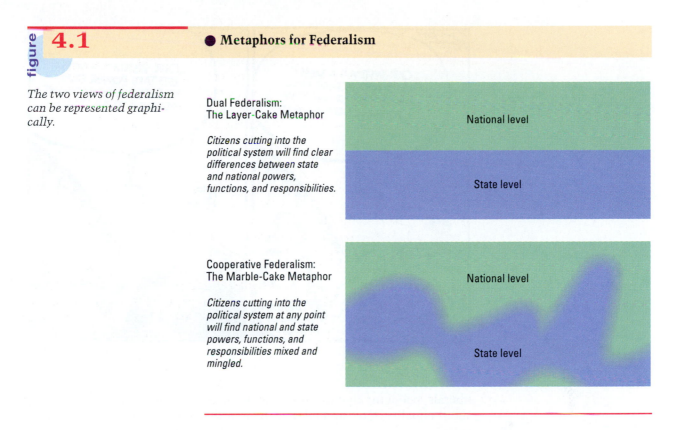

Dual Federalism:
The Layer-Cake Metaphor

Citizens cutting into the political system will find clear differences between state and national powers, functions, and responsibilities.

National level

State level

Cooperative Federalism:
The Marble-Cake Metaphor

Citizens cutting into the political system at any point will find national and state powers, functions, and responsibilities mixed and mingled.

National level

State level

objectives and have often cooperated to achieve them. In the nineteenth century, for example, cooperation, not separation, made it possible to develop transportation systems, such as canals, and to establish state land-grant colleges. The layer cake might be a good model of what dual federalists think the relationship between national and state governments *should* be, but it does not square with recent American history.

A critical difference between the theories of dual and cooperative federalism is the way they interpret two sections of the Constitution that set out the terms of the relationship between the national and state governments. Article I, Section 8, lists the enumerated powers of Congress, then concludes with the **elastic clause,** which gives Congress the power to "make all Laws which shall be necessary and proper for carrying into Execution the foregoing Powers" (see Chapter 3). The Tenth Amendment reserves for the states or the people powers not assigned to the national government or denied to the states by the Constitution. Dual federalism postulates an inflexible elastic clause and a capacious Tenth Amendment. Cooperative federalism postulates suppleness in the elastic clause and confines the Tenth Amendment to a self-evident, obvious truth. The widespread acceptance of cooperative federalism in the twentieth century contributed to an increasing centralization of power in the national government, often at the expense of the states. Today, the flow of power is drifting back to the states.

In their efforts to limit the scope of the national government, conservatives have given much credence to the layer-cake metaphor. In contrast,

liberals, believing that one function of the national government is to bring about equality, have argued that the marble-cake metaphor is more desirable.

Conservatives continue to argue that different states have different problems and resources and that returning control to state governments would thus actually promote diversity. States would be free to experiment with alternative ways to meet their problems. States would compete with one another. And people would be free to choose the state government they preferred by simply voting with their feet and moving to another state. This argument for flexibility may encourage behavior that conservatives lament, however; for example, poor people may gain marginally better welfare benefits by moving from one state to another.[12]

Conservatives also continue to maintain that the national government is too remote, too tied to special interests, and not responsive to the public at large. The national government overregulates, they add, and tries to promote too much uniformity. Moreover, the size and complexity of the federal system lead to waste and inefficiency. States, on the other hand, are closer to the people and better able to respond to specific local needs. If state governments were revitalized, individuals might believe that they could have a greater influence on decision making. The quality of political participation would improve. Furthermore, conservatives believe that shifting power to the states would help them achieve other parts of their political agenda. States would work harder to keep taxes down, they would not be willing to spend a lot of money on social welfare programs, and they would be less likely to pass stiff laws regulating businesses. The 1994 "Republican Revolution" brought a chorus of new conservative voices to Congress. It started a legislative wave that called explicitly for a return of power to the states.

What conservatives hope for, liberals fear. They remember that the states' rights model allowed extreme political and social inequalities and that it supported racism. Blacks and city dwellers were often left virtually unrepresented by white state legislators who disproportionately served rural interests. Liberals believe the states remain unwilling or unable to protect the rights or provide for the needs of their citizens, whether those citizens are consumers seeking protection from business interests, defendants requiring guarantees of due process of law, or poor people seeking a minimum standard of living.

These ideological conceptions of federalism reveal a simple truth. Federalism is not something written or implied in the Constitution; the Constitution is only the starting point in the debate. As one scholar observed, "To understand the condition of federalism, one needs to comprehend the functioning of the whole polity."[13]

THE DYNAMICS OF FEDERALISM

Although the Constitution establishes a kind of federalism, the actual balance of power between nation and states has always been more a matter of politics than of formal theory. A discussion of federalism, then, must do more than simply list the powers that the Constitution assigns the different levels of government. The balance of power has shifted substantially since President Madison agonized over the proper role the national government should play in funding roads. Today, that government has assumed functions never dreamed of in the nineteenth century.

Why has power shifted so dramatically from the states to the national government? The answer lies in historical circumstances, not debates over constitutional theory. By far the greatest test of states' rights arose when several southern states attempted to secede from the union. The threat of secession challenged the supremacy of the national government, a supremacy that Northern armies reestablished militarily in the nation's greatest bloodbath, the Civil War. But the Civil War by no means settled all the questions about relations between governments in the United States. Many more remained to be answered, and new issues keep cropping up.

Some changes in the balance of power were the product of constitutional amendments. Several amendments have had an enormous effect, either direct or indirect, on the shape of the federal system. For example, the due process and equal protection clauses of the Fourteenth Amendment (1868) and the Seventeenth Amendment's provision for the direct election of senators (1913) limited states' rights. The income tax mandated by the Sixteenth Amendment (1913) fueled the growth and strength of the national government in relation to the states.

Most of the national government's power has come to it through legislation and judicial interpretation. Let us examine these tools of political change.

Legislation and the Elastic Clause

The elastic clause of the Constitution gives Congress the power to make all laws that are "necessary and proper" to carry out its responsibilities. By using this power in combination with its enumerated powers, Congress has been able to increase the scope of the national government tremendously during the past two centuries. The greatest change has come about in times of crisis and national emergency—the Civil War, the Great Depression, the world wars. The role of the national government has also grown as it has responded to needs and demands that state and local governments were unwilling or unable to meet.

Legislation is one prod the national government has used to achieve goals at the state level. The Voting Rights Act of 1965 is a good example. Section 2 of Article I of the Constitution gives the states the power to specify qualifications for voting. But the Fifteenth Amendment (1870) provides that no person shall be denied the right to vote "on account of race, color, or previous condition of servitude." Before the Voting Rights Act, states could not specifically deny blacks the right to vote, but they could require that voters pass literacy tests or pay poll taxes, requirements that virtually disenfranchised blacks in many states. The Voting Rights Act was designed to correct this political inequality (see Chapter 16).

The act gives the national government the power to decide whether individuals are qualified to vote and requires that qualified individuals be allowed to vote in all elections, including primaries and national, state, and local elections. If denial of voting rights seems to be widespread, the act authorizes the appointment of national voting examiners to examine and register voters for *all* elections. By replacing state election officials with national examiners, the act clearly intrudes upon the political sovereignty of the states. The constitutional authority for the act rests on the second section of the Fifteenth Amendment, which gives Congress the power to enforce the amendment through "appropriate legislation."

Judicial Interpretation

The Voting Rights Act was not a unanimous hit. Its critics used the language of dual federalism to insist that the Constitution gives the states the power to determine voter qualifications. Its supporters claimed that the Fifteenth Amendment guarantee of voting rights takes precedence over states' rights and gives the national government new responsibilities.

The conflict was ultimately resolved by the Supreme Court, the umpire of the federal system. It upheld the Act as an appropriate congressional enforcement of the Fifteenth Amendment.[14] The Court settles disputes over the powers of the national and state governments by deciding whether the actions of either are unconstitutional (see Chapter 14). In the nineteenth and early twentieth centuries, the Supreme Court often decided in favor of the states. Then for nearly sixty years, from 1937 to 1995, the Court almost always supported the national government in contests involving the balance of power between nation and states. Today, a conservative majority on the Court has started to tip the balance back to the states.

Due Process and Reapportionment.   During Chief Justice Earl Warren's tenure (1953–1969), the Court used the Fourteenth Amendment to make the states subject to various provisions of the Bill of Rights, shifting power from the states to the national government. Court decisions seriously restricted the states' freedom to decide what constitutes due process of law within their jurisdictions. In the landmark *Miranda* decision, for example, the Court ordered that individuals apprehended by the police must be informed of their constitutional rights and that the arresting officer must preserve those rights.[15] The Supreme Court has set other minimum due process standards for criminal cases that the states have to meet. The standards provide equality before the law for individuals who are suspected of crimes, but critics argue that they hamper state governments in trying to maintain order.

A series of Supreme Court decisions concerning reapportionment—redrawing the boundaries of electoral districts—also eroded the power of the states in the early 1960s.[16] Until that time, states had set the boundaries of voting districts, but some had failed to adjust those boundaries to reflect shifts in population. As a result, small numbers of rural voters in certain areas were electing as many representatives as were large numbers of urban voters. The Court established a new standard of one person, one vote, which meant that voting districts must be apportioned on the basis of population to satisfy the equal protection clause of the Fourteenth Amendment. The new standard forced the states to redraw their districts and reapportion their legislatures.

In the due process and reapportionment cases, the Supreme Court was protecting individual rights and in the process championing political equality. But the Supreme Court is also part of the national government. When it defends the rights of an individual against a state, it also substitutes a national standard for the state standard that previously governed that relationship.

The Commerce Clause: Engine of National Power. The growth of national power has been advanced by the Supreme Court's interpretation of the Constitution's **commerce clause**. The third clause of Article I, Section 8, states that "Congress shall have Power . . . To regulate Commerce . . . among the several States." In early Court decisions, Chief Justice John Marshall (1801–1835) interpreted the word *commerce* broadly, to include virtually every form of commercial activity. The clause's grant of the power to regulate commerce to the national government substantially withdrew that power from the states. Later decisions by the Court attempted to restrict national power over commerce, but events such as the Great Depression necessitated its enlargement. One scholar has gone so far as to charge that the justices have toyed with the commerce clause, treating it like a shuttlecock volleyed back and forth by changing majorities.[17] A surprising volley in 1995 signaled a shift back to the states.

Though no longer in office, Republican presidents from Nixon to Bush can claim a role in the transfer of power from nation to states through the appointment of Supreme Court justices with a commitment to limits on national power. The shift toward the states became plain in 1995, when the Supreme Court rediscovered constitutional limits on Congress that had been dead and buried for nearly sixty years.

The Court's 5–4 ruling in *United States* v. *Lopez* held that Congress exceeded its authority under the commerce clause when it enacted a law in 1990 banning the possession of a gun in or near a school. Since the middle of the Great Depression, the Court had given Congress wide latitude to exercise legislative power by regulating interstate commerce. But a conservative majority, headed by Chief Justice William H. Rehnquist, concluded

Listen to the arguments in *United States* v. *Lopez.*
`<oyez.at.nwu.edu/cases/ 93-1260/>`

that having a gun in a school zone "has nothing to do with 'commerce' or any sort of economic enterprise, however broadly one might define those terms." Justices Sandra Day O'Connor, Antonin Scalia, Anthony Kennedy, and Clarence Thomas—all appointed by Reagan or Bush—joined in Rehnquist's opinion putting the brakes on congressional power.[18]

The Court's decision casts doubt on new and old congressional acts addressing a wide array of concerns, from domestic violence to laws protecting the safety of abortion clinic workers and patients. Whether the ruling will have wide or narrow consequences depends on its subsequent application and interpretation. At a minimum, however, the Court is still the umpire of the federal system.

The Eleventh Amendment: The Umpire Strikes Back.   In 1996, the umpire made another dramatic call curtailing congressional power in favor of the states. In a bitterly fought 5–4 ruling, the same five-justice majority bolstered state power by sharply curtailing the authority of Congress to subject states to lawsuits in federal courts. The ruling came in an obscure suit arising from a Seminole Indian tribe's dispute with Florida officials.[19]

A 1988 federal law allowed Indian tribes to sue a state in federal court if the state failed to negotiate in good faith over allowing gambling operations on tribal lands. Many federal laws have provisions that allow people hurt by state violations of such federal laws to sue in federal court. However, the Eleventh Amendment bars such courts from hearing cases in which a state is sued by citizens of another state or country.

The significance of the decision extends far beyond the particular facts; it affects whether individuals or groups can use the federal courts to force states to abide by a variety of national laws. In the majority opinion, the chief justice asserted that "the states, although a union, maintain certain attributes of sovereignty," including immunity from lawsuits. The decision means that the states will be less accountable to people who believe they have been wronged by a state government in connection with such diverse matters as water pollution and copyright infringement. Though the Indian tribes were losers in this lawsuit, they are big winners today thanks to certain principles of federalism that are sewn into the Constitution (see Politics in a Changing America 4.1).

Congress still has ample power to score for the national government. Money is the core of its power.

Grants-in-Aid

Since the 1960s, the national government's use of financial incentives has rivaled its use of legislation and judicial interpretation as a means of shaping relations with state governments. And state and local governments have increasingly looked to Washington for money. The principal method the national government uses to make money available to the states is grants-in-aid.

A **grant-in-aid** is money paid by one level of government to another level of government, to be spent for a specific purpose. Most grants-in-aid come with standards or requirements prescribed by Congress. Many are awarded

● ● ● ● ● ● ● ● ● ● ● ●

Indians' Deal

Native Americans have discovered a powerful source of revenue: casino gambling. Gambling activities on Indian land have thrived, thanks to the Indians' special status embodied in treaties, laws, and the Constitution. Americans spend well in excess of $300 billion a year on gambling (lotteries, casinos, bingo, parimutuals). While gambling brings enormous economic activity for some, it may also exact a high social cost for others—in ruined lives and organized crime that seem to follow in its step.

on a matching basis; that is, a recipient must make some contribution of its own, which is then matched by the national government. Grants-in-aid take two general forms: categorical grants and block grants.

Categorical grants target specific purposes, and restrictions on their use typically leave the recipient government relatively little discretion. Recipients today include state governments, local governments, and public and private nonprofit organizations. There are two kinds of categorical grants: formula grants and project grants. As their name implies, **formula grants** are distributed according to a particular formula, which specifies who is eligible for the grant and how much each eligible applicant will receive. The formulas used to distribute grant money vary from one grant to another. They may weigh such factors as state per capita income, number of school-age children, urban population, and number of families below the poverty line.

The latest figures reveal that the number of categorical grants has reached an all-time high. In 1993, for example, 159 of the 578 categorical grants offered by the national government were formula grants. The remaining 419 grants were **project grants**, grants awarded on the basis of competitive applications.[20] Comparing grants since 1989 reveals a shift in policy emphasis. New grants have focused on health (substance abuse and HIV-AIDS programs); natural resources and the environment (radon, asbestos, and toxic pollution); and education, training, and employment (for the disabled, the homeless, and the aged).

In contrast to categorical grants, Congress awards **block grants** for broad, general purposes. They allow recipient governments considerable freedom to decide how to allocate the money to individual programs. While a categorical grant promotes a specific activity—say, ethnic heritage studies—a block grant might be earmarked only for elementary, secondary, and vocational education. The state or local government receiving the block grant would then choose the specific educational programs to fund with it. The

politics in a changing america

4.1   "Thanks to Federalism, Some Native Americans Hit the Jackpot"

You could say a roll of the dice has delivered to Native Americans what a century of national policymaking failed to provide: economic development and an end to government handouts. But luck is not the ingredient moving many of the nation's 557 recognized tribes from dependence to independence; casino gambling is their savior.

Native Americans hold a special place under the American Constitution. Under one of the three constitutional provisions related to Indians, Congress has the power to "regulate Commerce . . . with the Indian tribes." Popular belief holds to the view that there are two sovereigns—the state and federal governments—in the United States. In fact, there is a third sovereign—the Indian tribes—operating within a limited but defined sphere.

In 1975, the Oneida reservation in New York sparked the Indian gambling phenomenon by testing the reach of its sovereignty. The Oneidas organized a bingo game to raise money for their fire department, a practice that many communities employ. But the Oneida prize money exceeded New York state limits. Under the American scheme of federalism, gambling laws are the states' concerns. The Oneidas claimed that New York's rules did not apply to them because they are an Indian nation. As such, their recognized right to sovereignty entitled them to run their own game and to offer prizes large enough to attract non-Indians, and their money, to places they otherwise might not visit.

Word spread quickly, and other tribes pushed their state's limits. The Seminoles started their own high-stakes bingo game in Florida. Local officials shut down both tribes' operations, but the Seminoles took state officials to court and won. More legal battles followed until 1987, when the Supreme Court effectively legalized gambling on reservations and sent state governments into retreat. Today, a state cannot ban gambling on Indian reservations unless it bans all forms of gambling for all its citizens. In addition, the Court affirmed the tribes' right to limited sovereignty. National and state governments cannot regulate activities on Indian reservations, and they cannot tax a tribe's profits or wealth.

Indians' tax-free status stacks the cards in their favor compared with their commercial competitors in places like Las Vegas and Atlantic City. Fearful that they would lose tax revenues siphoned off to Indian casinos, states pressured Congress to enact the 1988 Indian Gaming Regulatory Act.

The law gives states a substantial role in deciding how and where tribes can run casino-style gambling operations. State approval comes at a price: the government exacts fees since it cannot impose taxes. Tribes now must negotiate agreements, called compacts, with their states. Some states, like Florida, have resisted these negotiations in an effort to force a better deal for state government. The Seminole tribe sued Florida in federal court to secure the necessary compact. With

recipient might use some money to support ethnic heritage studies and some to fund consumer education programs. Or the recipient might choose to put all the money into consumer education programs and spend nothing on ethnic heritage studies. In 1975, there were only five block grants; by 1993, the number had grown to fifteen.

Grants-in-aid are a method of redistributing income. Money is collected by the national government from the taxpayers of all fifty states, then allocated to other citizens, supposedly for worthwhile social purposes.

some irony, this legal challenge provided the basis for the Supreme Court's latest volley in expanding states' rights *(Seminole Tribe of Florida* v. *Florida)*. The Seminoles were the nominal losers. The tribe can no longer sue Florida in a federal court. But it may seek approval from the executive branch, avoiding state government entirely. Their special status and limited sovereignty ensures that the tribe (like the house) always wins.

Many tribes have now ventured into casino gambling. The most successful is the Mashantucket Pequots of Connecticut, owner of the most profitable gambling enterprise in the country. Its Foxwoods Resort is said to be the largest casino in the world, serving forty-five thousand meals a day. The tribe has poured millions into the local Connecticut economy, serving as the economic engine of the community and its largest private employer.

Sources: Dennis McAuliffe, Jr., "For Many Indian Tribes, the Buffalo Are Back," *The Washington Post National Weekly Edition,* 18–24 March 1996, pp. 8–9; Kirk Johnson, "Connecticut Tribe to Invest Casino Profits in a Boatyard," *New York Times,* 4 May 1996, p. A1.

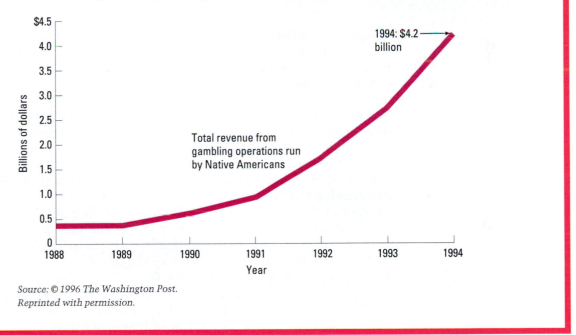

Total revenue from gambling operations run by Native Americans

1994: $4.2 billion

Source: © 1996 The Washington Post. Reprinted with permission.

Many grants have worked to reduce gross inequalities among states and their residents. But the formulas used to redistribute income are not impartial; they are highly political, established through a process of congressional horse trading.

Grant programs have grown by nearly two-thirds in constant-dollar terms, from $101 million in 1975 to $167 million in 1993 (using 1987 dollars). And more block grants are on the way from a Republican-led Congress eager to return more power to the states.

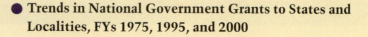

figure
4.2

● **Trends in National Government Grants to States and Localities, FYs 1975, 1995, and 2000**

National government grants to states and localities vary substantially. In 1975, education programs accounted for the biggest percentage of national government grants. In 1995, grants for health programs reached 42 percent of all national government spending to state and local governments. By 2000, health grants will approach half of all such national government spending.

Source: Budget of the United States Government, Analytical Perspectives FY 1997 (Washington, D.C.: U.S. Government Printing Office, 1996), p. 170.

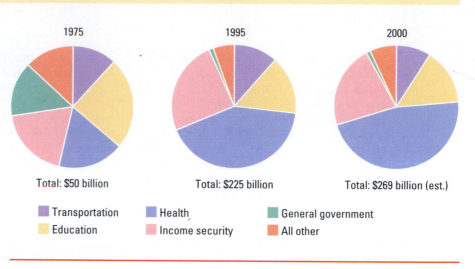

Significant shifts in the purposes of such grants occurred in the same period.[21] Figure 4.2 illustrates the distribution of grants to state and local government by policy area. Health was far more dominant in 1995 than it was in 1975; the opposite is true for transportation policy. The budget estimates for 2000 only accentuate this trend.

Whatever its form or purpose, grant money comes with strings attached. Some strings are there to ensure that the money is used for the purpose for which it was given; other regulations are designed to evaluate how well the grant is working. To this end, the national government may stipulate that recipients follow certain procedures. The national government may also attach restrictions designed to achieve some broad national goal not always closely related to the specific purpose of the grant. For example, as noted earlier, the Highway Act of 1984 reduced the funds available to states that allowed people younger than twenty-one to drink. Other grants prohibit discrimination in the activities they fund. States have been more than willing to accept the limitations. By 1988, for example, every state in the nation had approved legislation setting twenty-one as the minimum drinking age. (Recall that Louisiana did not *sanction* retailers who sold alcohol to underage drinkers.) The lure of financial aid has proved a powerful incentive for states to relinquish the freedom to set their own standards and to accept those set by the national government. In short, categorical grants clearly increase national power and decrease state power, and block grants increase state power and decrease national power.

THE DEVELOPING CONCEPT OF FEDERALISM

Federalism scholars have noted that each generation, faced with new problems, has had to work out its own version of federalism. Succeeding generations have used judicial and congressional power in varying degrees to shift the balance of power back and forth between the national and state governments.

McCulloch v. Maryland

Early in the nineteenth century, the nationalist interpretation of federalism prevailed over states' rights. In 1819, under Chief Justice John Marshall, the Supreme Court expanded the role of the national government in *McCulloch* v. *Maryland*. The Court was asked to decide whether Congress had the power to establish a national bank and, if so, whether states had the power to tax that bank. In a unanimous opinion written by Marshall, the Court conceded that Congress had only the powers conferred on it by the Constitution, which nowhere mentioned banks. However, Article I granted Congress the authority to enact all laws "necessary and proper" to the execution of Congress's enumerated powers. Marshall adopted a broad interpretation of this elastic clause: "Let the end be legitimate, let it be within the scope of the constitution, and all means which are appropriate, which are plainly adapted to that end, which are not prohibited, but consist with the letter and spirit of the constitution, are constitutional."

The Court clearly agreed that Congress had the power to charter a bank. But did the states (in this case, Maryland) have the power to tax the bank? Arguing that "the power to tax involves the power to destroy," Marshall insisted that states could not tax the national government, because the powers of the national government came not from the states but from the people. Marshall was embracing cooperative federalism, which sees a direct relationship between the people and the national government, with no need for the states to act as intermediaries. To assume that the states had the power to tax the national government would be to give them supremacy over the national government. In that case, Marshall wrote, "the declaration that the constitution, and the laws made in pursuance thereof, shall be the supreme law of the land is empty and unmeaning declamation."[22] The framers of the Constitution did not intend to create a meaningless document, he reasoned. Therefore, they must have meant to give the national government all the powers necessary to carry out its assigned functions, even if those powers are only implied.

States' Rights and Dual Federalism

Roger B. Taney became chief justice in 1836, and during his tenure (1836–1864) the balance of power began to shift back toward the states. The Taney Court imposed firm limits on the powers of the national government. As Taney saw it, the Constitution spoke "not only in the same words, but with the same meaning and intent with which it spoke when it came from the hands of its framers and was voted on and adopted by the people of the United States."[23] In the infamous *Dred Scott* decision (1857), for example, the Court decided that Congress had no power to prohibit slavery in the territories.

You can read a complete version of *McCulloch* v. *Maryland* here: <grid.let.rug.nl/~welling/usa/marshall/mar05.htm>

Made in the U.S.A.

Young boys working in a Georgia cotton mill around the turn of the century. The Supreme Court decided in 1918 that Congress had no power to limit child labor. According to the Court, that power belonged to the states, which resisted imposing limits for fear such legislation would drive businesses to other (less restrictive) states.

Many people assume that the Civil War was fought over slavery. It was not. The real issue was the character of the federal union, of federalism itself. At the time of the Civil War, economic and cultural differences between the Northern and Southern states were considerable. The Southern economy was based on labor-intensive agriculture, while mechanized manufacturing was developing in the North. Southerners' desire for cheap manufactured goods and cheap plantation labor led them to support both slavery and low tariffs on imports. Northerners, to protect their own economy, wanted high tariffs. When they sought national legislation that threatened Southern interests, Southerners invoked states' rights. They even introduced the theory of **nullification,** the idea that a state could declare a particular action of the national government null and void. The Civil War rendered the idea of nullification null and void, but it did not eliminate the tension between national and state power.

The New Deal and Its Consequences

The Great Depression placed dual federalism in repose. The problems of the Depression proved too extensive for either state governments or private businesses to handle. So the national government assumed a heavy share of responsibility for providing relief and pursuing economic recovery. Under the New Deal—President Franklin D. Roosevelt's response to the Depression—Congress enacted various emergency relief programs to stimulate economic activity and help the unemployed (see Chapter 19). Many measures required the cooperation of the national and state governments. For example, the national government offered money to support state relief efforts. However, to receive these funds, states were usually required to provide administrative supervision or to contribute some money of their own. Relief efforts were thus wrested from the hands of local bodies and centralized. Through the regulations it attached to funds, the national government extended its power and control over the states.[24]

At first, the Supreme Court's view of the Depression was different from that of the other branches of the national government. The justices believed the Depression was an accumulation of local problems, not a national problem demanding national action. In the Court's opinion, the whole structure of federalism was threatened when collections of local troubles were treated as one national problem.

In 1937, however, with no change in personnel, the Court began to alter its course. The Court upheld major New Deal measures. Perhaps the Court was responding to the 1936 election returns (Roosevelt had been re-elected in a landslide, and the Democrats commanded a substantial majority in Congress), which signified the voters' endorsement of the use of national policies to address national problems. Or perhaps the Court sought to defuse the President's threat to enlarge the Court with justices sympathetic to his views. ("The switch in time that saved nine," rhymed one observer.) In any event, the Court abandoned its effort to maintain a rigid boundary between national and state power. Only a few years earlier, the Supreme Court had based its thinking about federalism on a state-centered interpretation of the Tenth Amendment. But in 1941, Chief Justice Harlan Fiske Stone referred to the Tenth Amendment as "a truism that all is retained which has not been surrendered."[25] In short, the Court agreed that the layer cake had become stale and unpalatable.

Some call the New Deal era revolutionary. There is no doubt that the period was critical in reshaping federalism in the United States. The national and state governments had cooperated before, but the extent of nation-state interaction during Franklin Roosevelt's administration clearly made the marble-cake metaphor the most accurate description of American federalism. In addition, the size of the national government and its budget increased tremendously. But perhaps the most significant change was in the way Americans thought about their problems and the role of the national government in solving them. Difficulties that at one time had been seen as personal or local were now national problems, requiring national solutions. The general welfare, broadly defined, became a legitimate concern of the national government.

In other respects, however, the New Deal was not so revolutionary. For example, Congress did not claim any new powers to address the nation's economic problems. Congress simply used its constitutional powers to suit the circumstances.

The Civil Rights Revolution and the War on Poverty

During the 1950s and 1960s, the national government assumed the task of promoting social equality by combating racism and poverty (see Chapters 16 and 19). Both racism and poverty seemed impossible to solve at the state level.

Matters of race relations had generally been left to the states, which more or less ignored them, despite the constitutional amendments passed after the Civil War. When in 1896 the Supreme Court found no constitutional objection to a state policy of providing "separate but equal" facilities for whites and blacks,* the states were free to do as much—or as little—as they pleased about racial inequality.

In 1954, however, in *Brown* v. *Board of Education*, the Supreme Court decided that racially separate but objectively equal public schools were inherently unequal.[26] The decision put the national government in the position of ordering the desegregation of public schools. As the civil rights movement focused public attention on the problems of discrimination, Congress passed a momentous piece of legislation: the Civil Rights Act of 1964. Through this act, the national government outlawed racial discrimination in arenas of state regulation, employment, and public accommodations. The commerce clause served as a vital constitutional lever providing Congress with the power to act. The intervention by the national government was unprecedented. The act sharply limited invidiously discriminatory practices that had a substantial effect on interstate commerce. The enforcement of the nation's civil rights laws called for the assertion of national authority in schools, hospitals, restaurants, and other public facilities. The civil rights revolution established the national government as the principal guarantor of political and social equality.

In the 1960s, President Lyndon Johnson's War on Poverty generated an enormous amount of social legislation and a massive increase in the scope of the national government. In an attempt to provide equality of opportunity and improve the quality of life throughout the United States, the national government adopted a vast array of social legislation accompanied by monetary inducements. The funding included vastly increased aid to higher education, aid to elementary and secondary schools, school breakfasts and lunches, food stamps, and a huge number of economic development, public service, and employment-training projects. To administer the programs, government bureaucracies expanded at both the national and state level. In fact, during the 1960s and 1970s, state bureaucracies grew even faster than the national bureaucracy.

Johnson's recipe for marble-cake federalism included some new ingredients. Before 1960, nearly all intergovernmental assistance (that is, aid from one level of government to another) had flowed from the national government to state governments. But the War on Poverty frequently bypassed state government by offering direct aid to local governments and even to community groups.

As the expansion of the national government has become more widely accepted, the focus of the debate over federalism has changed. National, state, and local governments are no longer separate and distinct; they interact. The growth of government programs created a federal system that critics describe as overloaded and out of control. In keeping with the bakery metaphors often used to describe federalism, one writer suggested that layer-cake federalism and marble-cake federalism have given way to "fruitcake federalism"—a system that is dense and indestructible and offers lots of sweets for everyone.[27] The Advisory Commission on Intergovernmental Relations (ACIR), created by Congress to monitor the

---

* *In* Plessy v. Ferguson *(163 U.S. 537 [1896]), the Supreme Court upheld state-imposed racial segregation, ruling that separate facilities for blacks and whites could be maintained so long as they were "equal" (see Chapter 16).*

We'll Take Manhattan, The Bronx, and Staten Island, Too

The levels of government in the federal system are now intertwined. Here, Senators Alfonse D'Amato (left) and Daniel Patrick Moynihan (center) of New York discuss projected Medicaid cuts with New York Governor George Pataki (right).

federal system, concluded in 1980 that fruitcake federalism is not palatable; it just does not work. Since the 1960s, the commission said, relations between national and state governments had become "more pervasive, more intrusive, more unmanageable, more ineffective, more costly and, above all, more unaccountable."[28]

FROM NEW FEDERALISM TO NEW-AGE FEDERALISM

Like Freddie Kreuger in *Nightmare on Elm Street*, debates over federalism keep coming back. In the past quarter century, federalism has been dusted off and given some new uses. In 1969, Richard Nixon advocated giving more power to state and local governments. Nixon wanted to decentralize national policies. He called this the *New Federalism*. Today, Bill Clinton proposes that the national government act as guru, guiding and encouraging states to experiment with vexing problems. We call this *New-Age Federalism*.

An Evolving Federalism

Nixon's New Federalism called for combining and reformulating categorical grants into block grants. The shift had dramatic implications for federalism. Block grants were seen as a way to redress the imbalance of power between Washington and the states and localities. Conservatives in Washington wanted to return freedom to the states. New Federalism was nothing more than dual federalism in modern dress.

The perception that the federal system was bloated and out of control began to take hold. In 1976, Jimmy Carter campaigned for president as an outsider who promised to reduce the size and cost of the national government. And he did have some success. As Figure 4.3 shows, after 1978 national government aid to states and localities actually did begin to drop and then level off.

Ronald Reagan took office in 1981 charging that the federal system had been bent out of shape. Reagan promised a "new New Federalism" that

figure 4.3

● **The National Government's Contribution to State and Local Governments**

In 1960, the national government contributed less than 15 percent of total state and local spending. By 1978, the national government had nearly doubled its contribution to state and local government spending. By 1988, the national government's contribution had declined to about 18 percent. As the national government's spending remained static or declined, state and local government spending accelerated, especially for Medicaid, welfare, prisons, and education. (The slopes of the two figures here indicate the pace of spending change.)

Source: *The Budget for FY 1997: Historical Tables* (Washington, D.C.: U.S. Government Printing Office, 1996), Table 15.2, p. 257.

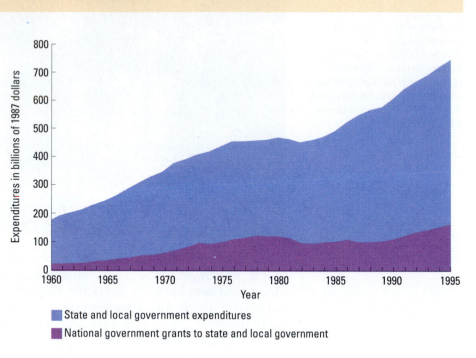

■ State and local government expenditures
■ National government grants to state and local government

would restore a proper constitutional relationship between the federal, state, and local governments. The national government, he said, treated "elected state and local officials as if they were nothing more than administrative agents for federal authority."[29]

Reagan's commitment to reduce both taxes and government spending meant he could not offer the incentive of new funding to make his version of New Federalism palatable. He did resurrect an element of Nixon's New Federalism, however, in his use of block grants. To build support for the plan, Reagan emphasized the freedom state officials would have in using their block grant money. State officials were enthusiastic about the prospect of having greater control over grant money; they were less enthusiastic when they realized that the amounts they received would be cut by approximately 25 percent. The share of state and local bills footed by the national government continued to fall (see Figure 4.3). In the mid-1970s, the national government contributed about 25 percent of state and local government spending. By 1990, its contribution had declined to below 20 percent. Bill Clinton's election to the presidency, coupled with Democratic control of Congress, affected spending patterns. By 1995, the national government's contribution to the states had edged back up to 22 percent.[30] The 1994 Republican congressional victory spelled stalemate for increased spending, however, especially when it implied greater control over the states.

Despite what some may say, money isn't everything. The national government's declining contributions to state coffers in the 1980s and the increased use of block grants in the 1990s did not necessarily imply reduced

●●●●●●●●●●●●●●

Bart Says, "Pay Up, Dudes!"

Californians urge their state legislators to provide more support for California's school system. In 1980, the national government shouldered more than 11 percent of public education costs. By 1991, that contribution had declined to approximately 8 percent. Because a 1 percent reduction in school aid equals nearly $3 billion, state governments are really feeling the pinch.

control over the states. Congress found other ways to restrict the states or require certain state actions, without spending money.

Preemption: The Instrument of Federalism

Before 1965, increased national power and diminished state power followed from the growth in categorical grant-in-aid programs—with their attached conditions—emanating from Washington, D.C. Since 1965, Congress has used its centralizing power in new fields and in novel ways.[31]

Preemption is the power of Congress to enact laws that have the national government assume total or partial responsibility for a state government function. When the national government shoulders a new government function, it restricts the discretionary power of the states. For example, under the Age Discrimination in Employment Act of 1967, the national government stripped the states of their power to establish a compulsory retirement age for their employees. Such a policy restricts the states' hiring practices, for everything from clerks to professors.

Mandates and Restraints.   Congressional preemption statutes infringe on state powers in two ways, through mandates and restraints. A **mandate** is a requirement that a state undertake an activity or provide a service, in keeping with minimum national standards. For example, in 1990, Congress mandated Medicaid coverage for all poor children. As a result, state Medicaid and welfare costs are expected to increase by about 66 percent (or $68 billion) from 1995 to 1999, at the same time that federal discretionary spending is expected to decline slightly. To pay for these mandates, state officials face stark choices: shift scarce resources by reducing or eliminating programs, or raise taxes.[32]

In contrast, a **restraint** forbids state government from exercising a certain power. Consider bus regulation, for example. To ensure bus service to small and remote communities, in the past some states would condition the issuance of bus franchises on bus operators' agreeing to serve such communities, even if the routes lost money. But in 1982, Congress passed the Bus Regulatory Reform Act, which forbade the states from imposing such conditions. Many states now provide subsidies to bus operators to ensure service to out-of-the-way areas.

Whether preemption takes the form of mandates or restraints, the result is additional costs for state and local government and interference with a fundamental government task: setting priorities. Furthermore, the national government is not obliged to pay for the costs it imposes. As preemption grew in the 1980s, the national government reduced spending in the form of grants to the states. For example, the 1988 Family Support Act required states to continue Medicaid coverage for a year to families who left welfare for jobs, but the states had to pick up the tab.

Despite a lack of resources, the national government seems no less determined to tell the states and local governments what to do. The national government has turned increasingly to mandates to control state and local activity without having to pay for it. Even presidential candidate Clinton commented from the stump in 1992 that the national government was "sticking it to all the states in the country and especially the poor states."[33]

Constraining Unfunded Mandates.   State and local government officials have long voiced strong objections to the national government's practice of imposing requirements on the states without providing the financial support needed to satisfy them. By 1992, more than 170 congressional acts had established partially or wholly unfunded mandates.[34]

The question of unfunded mandates rankles governors and mayors. For example, the Americans With Disabilities Act (1990) required all municipal golf courses to provide a spot for disabled golfers to get in and out of bunkers (sand traps). The regulations set precise gradations for all bunkers. The act also required reservation offices at golf courses to install telecommunications devices for the deaf. The legislation aimed to end discrimination and eliminate barriers that cordoned off the disabled from mainstream America. While these may be entirely laudable objectives, the national government did not foot the bill for the changes it mandated.[35] Municipalities already constrained by tight budgets were forced to fund these well-intentioned but expensive renovations.

One of the early results of the Republican-led 104th Congress was the Unfunded Mandates Relief Act of 1995. The legislation—adopted in the flurry of the first one hundred days—requires the Congressional Budget Office to prepare cost estimates of any proposed national legislation that would impose more than $50 million a year in costs on state and local governments or more than $100 million a year in costs on private business. It also requires a cost analysis of the impact of agency regulations on governments and private businesses. Congress can still pass along to the states the costs of the programs it mandates, but only after holding a separate vote specifically imposing a requirement on other governments without providing the money to carry it out. (The law does not apply to legislation protecting constitutional rights and civil rights or to anti-discrimination laws.)

To many state and local officials, the law seemed cosmetic, since it applied only to future mandates, not to unfunded mandates already in place. Republican governor John Engler of Michigan put the matter in perspective: "It's like a patient coming into an emergency room. The first step is you stop the hemorrhaging."[36]

The national government continues to support state and local governments. Yet spending pressures on state and local governments are enormous. The public demands better schools, harsher sentences for criminals (and more prisons to hold them), more and better day care for children and the elderly. The proportion of national government aid to states and local communities—either in the form of grants or in direct payments for the poor (Medicaid and welfare)—is at the same level in 1995 as it was in 1982, but its composition has changed substantially. Payments for the poor now take an increasing share of the national government's contribution to the states (see Chapter 19). And the trend is likely to continue. For the first time in decades, many state and local governments are raising taxes or adopting new ones to pay for public services that were once the shared responsibility of cooperative federalism.

OTHER GOVERNMENTS IN THE FEDERAL SYSTEM

We have concentrated in this chapter on the changing roles the national and state governments play in shaping the federal system. Although the Constitution explicitly recognizes only national and state governments, the American federal system has spawned a multitude of local governments as well. A 1992 census counted nearly eighty-seven thousand.[37]

Types of Local Governments

Americans are citizens of both a nation and a state, and they also come under the jurisdiction of various local government units. These units include **municipal governments,** the governments of cities and towns. Municipalities, in turn, are located in (or may contain or share boundaries with) counties, which are administered by **county governments.** (Sixteen states further subdivide countries into *townships* as units of government.) Most Americans also live in a **school district,** which is responsible for administering local elementary and secondary educational programs. They may also be served by one or more **special districts,** government units created to perform particular functions, typically when those functions—such as fire protection and water purification and distribution—spill across ordinary jurisdictional boundaries. Examples of special districts include the Port Authority of New York and New Jersey, the Chicago Sanitation District, and the Southeast Pennsylvania Transit Authority.

Local governments are created by state governments, either in their constitutions or through legislation. This means that their organization, powers, responsibilities, and effectiveness vary considerably from state to state. About forty states endow their cities with various forms of **home rule**—the right to enact and enforce legislation in certain administrative areas. Home rule gives cities a measure of self-government and freedom of

● ● ● ● ● ● ● ● ● ●

**Her Honor, the Mayor.
Hizzoner, the Mayor.**

A mayor is the elected chief executive and ceremonial officer of a city. In some modest-sized cities, mayors serve part-time. Many big-city mayors rise to national prominence, though no mayor has yet made the leap from city hall to the White House. These mayors are (clockwise, from top left): Sharon Sayles Belton of Minneapolis; Karen Lloreda of Dana Point, California; Kurt Schmoke of Baltimore; and Richard M. Daley of Chicago.

action. In contrast, county governments, which are the main units of local government in rural areas, tend to have little or no legislative power. Instead, county governments ordinarily serve as administrative units, performing the specific duties assigned to them under state law.

How can the ordinary citizen be expected to make sense of the maze of governments? And does the ordinary citizen really benefit from all the governments?

So Many Governments: Advantages and Disadvantages

In theory at least, one benefit of localizing government is that it brings government closer to the people; it gives them an opportunity to participate in the political process, to have a direct influence on policy. Localized government conjures visions of informed citizens deciding their own political fate—the traditional New England town meeting, repeated across the nation. From this perspective, overlapping governments appear compatible with a majoritarian view of democracy.

The reality is somewhat different, however. Studies have shown that people are much less likely to vote in local elections than national elections. In fact, voter turnout in local contests tends to be quite low (although the influence of individual votes is thus much greater). Furthermore, the fragmentation of powers, functions, and responsibilities among national, state, and local governments makes government as a whole seem complicated and hence incomprehensible and inaccessible to ordinary people. In addition, most people have little time to devote to public affairs, which can be very time-consuming. These factors tend to discourage individual citizens from pursuing politics and, in turn, enhance the influence of organized groups, which have the resources—time, money, and know-how—to sway policymaking (see Chapter 10). Instead of bringing government closer to the people and reinforcing majoritarian democracy, then, the system's enormous complexity tends to encourage pluralism.

One potential benefit of having many governments is that they enable the country to experiment with new policies on a small scale. New programs or solutions to problems can be tested in one city or state or in a few cities or states. Successful programs can then be adopted by other cities or states or by the nation as a whole. This fits President Clinton's brand of federalism. He views the states as "the laboratories of democracy." To this end, the Clinton administration has waived certain national welfare regulations for thirty-seven states so that they can experiment with innovative policies such as linking children's school attendance to their family's welfare benefits, restricting the time recipients are on welfare, and requiring recipients to take public service jobs while receiving government support.[38]

The large number of governments also makes it possible for government to respond to the diversity of conditions in different parts of the country. States and cities differ enormously in population, size, economic resources, climate, and other characteristics—the diverse elements that French political philosopher Montesquieu argued should be taken into account in formulating laws for a society. Smaller political units are better able to respond to particular local conditions and can generally do so more quickly than larger units. On the other hand, smaller units may not be able to muster the economic resources to meet some challenges.

Of course, the United States remains one nation no matter how many local governments there are. The question of how much diversity the nation should tolerate in the way different states treat their citizens is important. For example, thirty-six states impose the death penalty for capital crimes. Even the execution methods vary (lethal injection, electrocution, lethal gas, and hanging). Also important is the question of whether the national government (and, indirectly, the citizens of other states) should be called on to foot the bill for problems specific to a particular region. States turn to the national government for assistance to meet national disasters such as earthquakes and floods. States expect similar assistance when confronted with such social disasters as urban riots, crime, and poverty.

Throughout American history, the national government has used its funds for regional development, to equalize disparities in wealth and development among the states. The development of the Sunbelt (the southern and southwestern regions of the country), for example, has been and continues to be helped considerably by national policies and programs: the national government funded the Tennessee Valley Authority (TVA) electrification projects and western irrigation projects; national funding formulas designed to aid poorer areas of the country helped the Sunbelt enormously, particularly in the South; and national largesse in the form of huge defense contracts benefited California. Overall, the government has poured more money into the Sunbelt states than they have paid in taxes.

CONTEMPORARY FEDERALISM AND THE DILEMMAS OF DEMOCRACY

To what extent were conservative hopes and liberal fears realized as federalism developed from the 1980s to the 1990s? Neither were fully realized under the various renditions of federalism. Federalism of the Reagan-Bush variety was used as a tool for cutting the national budget by offering less money to the states. Contrary to the expectations of conservatives and liberals alike, however, states approved tax increases to pay for social services and education. In 1990 and 1991, thirty-seven states raised one or more major taxes (on income, sales, and motor fuels). Fewer states followed suit in 1992 and 1993, due in part to voter resistance and economic recovery.[39] To be sure, this was risky business for politicians. Raising taxes stirs voter ire; reducing vital services (such as education) also stirs voter ire. In an era when Washington has been less willing to enforce antitrust legislation, civil rights laws, and affirmative action plans, state governments have been more likely to do so. At a time when a conservative national government put little emphasis on the value of equality, state governments did more to embrace it.[40]

Conservatives thought that the value of freedom would be emphasized if more matters were left to the states. Traditionally, state governments were relatively small and lacked the wherewithal to limit large corporate interests, for example. But since the 1970s, state governments have changed. Their legislatures have become more professional. They meet regularly, and they maintain larger permanent staffs (see Figure 4.4). Governors have proved willing to support major programs to enhance the skills of their state's work force, to promote research and development, and to subsidize new industries. State governments have become big governments themselves. They are better able to tackle problems, and they are not afraid to use their power to promote equality.

To the surprise of liberals, who had originally looked to the national government to protect individuals by setting reasonable minimum standards for product safety, welfare payments, and employee benefits, states are now willing to set higher standards than the national government.

When Clinton came to the White House, liberals were delighted. His conservative predecessors Reagan and Bush had sought to reinstate layer-cake federalism and to dismantle the national government's welfare-state efforts to promote social and political equality. But Clinton's experience as a governor has created a strange brew when joined with the Democrats' liberal social welfare policies. Thus far, the Clinton administration has been silent on its brand of federalism; no coherent theory of federalism has emerged.[41] President Clinton is sympathetic to states burdened by new and costly mandates and restraints. On a few basic themes, liberals and conservatives are singing the same tune: smaller, more efficient government; less micromanagement by the national government; greater flexibility for state and local governments. But trying to pin down these concepts remains as challenging as nailing Jell-O to the wall.

 Use the CROSSTABS computer program that accompanies this book to analyze Americans' trust in the national government. You will find several variables in the "Voters" data set. Does trust in government vary by region or age, for example?

Does federalism have a future? A leading scholar contemplates the question.
<www.urban.org/PERIODCL/ pubsect/derthick.htm>

figure 4.4 ● **The Diversity of State Legislatures**

State legislatures across the country vary greatly in many respects, such as in the time that they meet and in the compensation given to their representatives. The National Conference of State Legislatures grouped them into three types based on their length of session, salaries, and staff sizes.

TYPES OF LEGISLATURES

TYPE 1 FULL TIME HIGH PAY LARGE STAFF	TYPE 2 IN-BETWEEN HYBRID	TYPE 3 PART TIME LOW PAY SMALL STAFF
California	Alabama	Arkansas
Illinois	Alaska	Georgia
Massachusetts	Arizona	Idaho
Michigan	Colorado	Indiana
New Jersey	Connecticut	Maine
New York	Delaware	Montana
Ohio	Florida	Nevada
Pennsylvania	Hawaii	New Hampshire
Wisconsin	Iowa	New Mexico
	Kansas	North Dakota
	Kentucky	Rhode Island
	Louisiana	South Dakota
	Maryland	Utah
	Minnesota	Vermont
	Mississippi	West Virginia
	Missouri	Wyoming
	Nebraska	
	North Carolina	
	Oklahoma	
	Oregon	
	South Carolina	
	Tennessee	
	Texas	
	Virginia	
	Washington	

LENGTH OF SESSION

Average number of months in session for two years (some legislatures meet every other year), 1990 to 1991, for each type of legislature. In that time, Congress met for 22 months.

LEGISLATOR COMPENSATION

Average compensation in 1991, including salaries and other reimbursements that are taxable. Congressional compensation averaged $125,100.

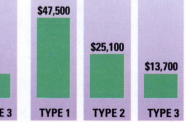

Source: Copyright © 1995 by The New York Times Co. Reprinted by permission.

Build It and It Will Flood

Melting snow in Minnesota and Wisconsin brought new flooding in 1996 to the people of Davenport, Iowa, who were devastated by record-breaking floods just three years before. Here, the mighty Mississippi filled John O'Donnell Stadium, home of the River Bandits, a minor league baseball team. Citizens had pitched in to sandbag the field, but to no avail. In disaster areas, the national government aids flood-ravaged states by allocating resources to rebuild or repair vital infrastructure, such as roads, water and sewage systems, and schools.

FEDERALISM AND PLURALISM

Our federal system of government was designed to allay citizens' fears that they might be ruled by a majority in a distant region with whom they did not necessarily agree or share interests. By recognizing the legitimacy of the states as political divisions, the federal system also recognizes the importance of diversity. The existence and cultivation of diverse interests are hallmarks of pluralism.

Each of the two competing theories of federalism supports pluralism, but in somewhat different ways. Dual federalism aims to decentralize government, to shift power to the states. It recognizes the importance of local rather than national standards and applauds the diversity of those standards. The variety allows the people, if not a direct voice in policymaking, at least a choice of policies under which to live.

In contrast, cooperative federalism is perfectly willing to override local standards for a national standard in the interests of promoting equality. Yet, this view of federalism also supports pluralist democracy. It is highly responsive to all manner of group pressures, including pressure at one level from groups unsuccessful at other levels. By blurring the lines of national and state responsibility, this type of federalism encourages petitioners to try their luck at whichever level of government offers them the best chance of success.

SUMMARY

The government framework outlined in the Constitution is the product of political compromise, an acknowledgment of the original thirteen states' fear of a powerful central government. The division of powers sketched in the Constitution was supposed to turn over "great and aggregate" matters to the national government, leaving "local and particular" concerns to the states. The Constitution does not explain, however, what is great and aggregate—and what is local and particular.

Federalism comes in many varieties. Two stand out, because they capture valuable differences between the original and modern vision of a national government. Dual, or layer-cake, federalism wants to retain power in the states and keep the levels of government separate. Cooperative, or marble-cake, federalism emphasizes the power of the national government and sees national and state government working together to solve national problems. In its own way, each view supports the pluralist model of democracy.

Over the years, the national government has used both its enumerated and its implied powers to become involved in virtually every area of human activity. The tools of political change include direct legislation, judicial interpretation, and grants-in-aid to states and localities. In the absence of financial incentives, the national government may use its preemption power, imposing mandates or restraints on the states without necessarily footing the cost.

As its influence grew, so did the national government. Major events, such as the Civil War and the Great Depression, mark major shifts in its growth in size and power. To alter its course, conservatives offered New Federalism and argued for cutting back on the size of the national government, reducing federal spending, and turning programs over to the states in order to solve the problem of unwieldy government. Liberals worried that in their haste to decentralize and cut back, conservatives would turn over important responsibilities to states that were unwilling or unable to assume them. Rather than being too responsive, government would become unresponsive. But neither happened in the 1980s. Congressional preemption forced states to meet national standards, with or without financial inducements. The states proved ready to tackle some major problems. More than this, they were prepared to fund many programs that promoted equality.

The debate over federalism has started to shift in the conservative direction as a result of two forces: the Republican congressional victory in 1994 and the formation of a slender but solid conservative majority on the Supreme Court. One truth emerges from this overview of federalism: the balance of power between the national and state governments will be settled by political means, not by theory.

Key Terms

federalism	commerce clause	nullification	school district
dual federalism	grant-in-aid	preemption	special district
states' rights	categorical grant	mandate	home rule
implied powers	formula grant	restraint	
cooperative federalism	project grant	municipal government	
elastic clause	block grant	county government	

Selected Readings

Beer, Samuel H. *To Make a Nation: The Rediscovery of American Federalism.* Cambridge, Mass.: Harvard University Press, 1993. A historical examination of federalism and nationalism in American political philosophy.

Berger, Raoul. *Federalism: The Founder's Design.* Norman: University of Oklahoma Press, 1987. Berger, a constitutional historian, argues that the states preceded the nation and that the states and the national government were meant to have mutually exclusive spheres of sovereignty.

Dye, Thomas R. *American Federalism: Competition Among Governments.* Lexington, Mass.: Lexington Books, 1990. Presents a theory of competitive federalism that encourages rivalry among states and local governments, to offer citizens the best array of public services at the lowest cost.

Peterson, Paul E. *The Price of Federalism.* Washington, D.C.: Brookings/A Twentieth Century Fund Book, 1995. Peterson argues that development projects such as roads and buildings are best left to state and local government and that redistributive policies such as welfare and social security are best left to the national government.

Rivlin, Alice. *Reviving the American Dream: The Economy, the States, and the Federal Government.* Washington, D.C.: Brookings Institution, 1992. A lucid examination of economic performance and government performance, resting on a reexamination of the division of responsibilities between the nation and the states.

Zimmerman, Joseph F. *Contemporary American Federalism: The Growth of National Power.* New York: Praeger, 1992. Argues that the expansion of preemption power has altered the allocation of power between nation and states.

World Wide Web Resources

The states have their own organization called The Council for State Government. One of its missions is to promote the sovereignty of the states and their role in the American federal system.

`<www.csg.org>`

Everything you always wanted to know about the states but were afraid to ask can be found at State-Search. This is a service of the National Association of State Information Resource Executives. It is designed to serve as a topical clearinghouse of state government information on the Internet.

`<www.state.ky.us/nasire/NASIREhome.html>`

If you want to be present for the Supreme Court oral arguments in all the leading federalism cases decided after 1955 and cited in this chapter, point your browser to "OYEZ. OYEZ. OYEZ.: A Supreme Court WWW Resource." You can listen from your computer using RealAudio.

`<oyez.at.nwu.edu/cases/subject-index.html>`

part

III

Linking People with Government

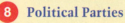

5

Public Opinion and Political Socialization

FRIDAYS ARE DIFFERENT in Saudi Arabia. After prayers, criminals are paraded in the streets, then punished publicly. Murderers are beheaded, adulterers are flogged, and thieves have their hands chopped off. The Saudi government wants its citizens to get the message: crime will not be tolerated. However, what constitutes a crime in Saudi Arabia may not be a crime in the United States. Members of the U.S. armed forces sent there in 1990 during the Persian Gulf crisis learned this when their mail was opened to keep out alcohol and sexually oriented magazines, both of which are illegal. It is also a crime for a woman to drive a car. Saudi Arabia, which claims the lowest crime rate in the world, is a country that greatly values order.

In contrast, the United States has one of the highest crime rates in the world. Its homicide rate, for example, is three to ten times that of most other Western countries. Although no one is proud of this record, our government would never consider beheading, flogging, or dismembering to lower the crime rate. First, the Eighth Amendment to the Constitution forbids "cruel and unusual" punishment. Second, public opinion would not tolerate such punishments.

However, the American public definitely is not squeamish about applying the death penalty (capital punishment) for certain crimes. The Gallup Organization has polled the nation on this issue for more than fifty years. Except in 1966, most respondents have consistently supported the death penalty for murder. In fact, public support for capital punishment has increased dramatically since the late 1960s. In 1995, seventy-seven percent of all respondents were in favor of the death penalty for murder, while only 13 percent opposed it.[1] Other research has shown that a substantial segment of the public favors the death penalty for attempting to assassinate the president (63 percent), for rape (51 percent), and for hijacking an airplane (49 percent).[2] In contrast to the United States, *all* Western European countries have eliminated capital punishment.

Government has been defined as the legitimate use of force to control human behavior. We can learn much about the role of public opinion in America by reviewing how we have punished violent criminals. During most of American history, government execution of people who threatened the social order was legal. In colonial times, capital punishment was imposed not just for murder but also for antisocial behavior—denying the "true" God, cursing one's parents, committing adultery, practicing witchcraft, or being a rebellious child, for example.[3] In the late 1700s, some writers, editors, and clergy argued for abolishing the death sentence. The

● ● ● ● ● ● ● ● ● ●

Women Should Be Heard and Not Seen

The culture of a nation shapes public attitudes and opinions. In Saudi Arabia, in accordance with that country's harsh interpretation of Islamic principles, women completely cover their heads and bodies when out in public. The Saudi culture also prohibits women from engaging in many activities (such as driving automobiles) typically enjoyed by women elsewhere.

campaign intensified in the 1840s, and a few states responded by eliminating capital punishment. Interest in the cause waned until 1890, when New York State adopted a new "scientific" technique, electrocution, as the instrument of death. By 1917, twelve states had passed laws against capital punishment. But the outbreak of World War I fed the public's fear of foreigners and radicals, leading to renewed support for the death penalty. Reacting to this shift in public opinion, four states restored it.

The security needs of World War II and postwar fears of Soviet communism fueled continued support for capital punishment. After anticommunist hysteria subsided in the late 1950s, public opposition to the death penalty increased. But public opinion was neither strong enough nor stable enough to force state legislatures to outlaw the death penalty. In keeping with the pluralist model of democracy, efforts to abolish the death penalty shifted from the legislative arena to the courts.

The opponents argued that the death penalty is cruel and unusual punishment and is therefore unconstitutional. Certainly, the public in the 1780s did not consider capital punishment either cruel or unusual. But nearly two hundred years later, opponents contended that execution by the state was cruel and unusual by contemporary standards. Their argument apparently had some effect on public opinion; in 1966, a plurality of respondents opposed the death penalty for the first (and only) time since the Gallup Organization began polling the public on the question of capital punishment.

The states responded to this shift in public opinion by reducing the number of executions, until they stopped completely in 1968 in anticipation of a Supreme Court decision. By then, however, public opinion had again reversed in favor of capital punishment. Nevertheless, in 1972, the Court ruled in a 5–4 decision that the death penalty as imposed by existing

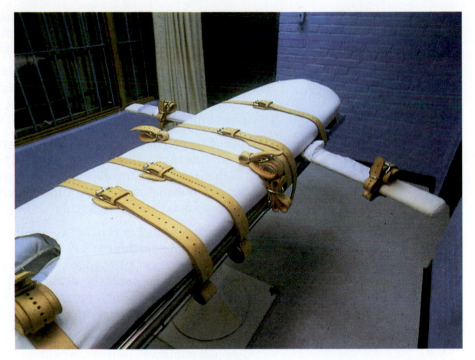

The Death Gurney

This grim-looking contraption at the prison in Huntsville, Texas, restrains a criminal condemned to death so that a lethal injection can be administered. It exemplifies the ultimate power that the government has to control behavior. Capital crimes may draw capital punishment.

state laws was unconstitutional.[4] The decision was not well received in many states, and thirty-five state legislatures passed new laws to get around the ruling. Meanwhile, as the nation's homicide rate increased, public approval of the death penalty jumped almost ten points and continued climbing.

In 1976, the Supreme Court changed its position and upheld three new state laws that let judges consider the defendant's record and the nature of the crime in deciding whether to impose a sentence of death.[5] The Court also rejected the argument that punishment by death in itself violates the Constitution, and it noted that public opinion favors the death penalty. Through the end of the 1970s, however, only three criminals were executed. Eventually, the states began to heed public concern about the crime rate. In 1995 alone, fifty-six murderers were executed, the highest number since 1957.[6]

Does the death penalty deter people from killing? A majority of the public thinks it does.[7] What do people think is the most humane method of execution? Opinion polls tell us that most people favor lethal injection (66 percent) over electrocution (10 percent). The gas chamber has more support (6 percent) than the old-fashioned firing squad or hanging (both 3 percent).[8] Presumably, no respondents regarded beheading as humane. Nevertheless, the public did not protest when the Saudis beheaded four countrymen who confessed to the 1995 bombing that killed five U.S. troops in Riyadh.

The history of public thinking on the death penalty reveals several characterics of public opinion:

1. *The public's attitudes toward a given government policy can vary over time, often dramatically.* Opinions about capital punishment

tend to fluctuate with threats to the social order. The public is more likely to favor capital punishment in times of war and when fear of foreign subversion and crime rates are high.

2. *Public opinion places boundaries on allowable types of public policy.* Chopping off a thief's hand is not acceptable to the American public (and surely not to courts interpreting the Constitution), but electrocuting a murderer is.

3. *If asked by pollsters, citizens are willing to register opinions on matters outside their expertise.* People clearly believe execution by lethal injection is more humane than electrocution, asphyxiation in a gas chamber, or hanging. But how can the public know enough about execution to make these judgments?

4. *Governments tend to respond to public opinion.* State laws for and against capital punishment have reflected swings in the public mood. The Supreme Court's 1972 decision against capital punishment came when public opinion on the death penalty was sharply divided; the Court's approval of capital punishment in 1976 coincided with a rise in public approval of the death penalty.

5. *The government sometimes does not do what the people want.* Although public opinion overwhelmingly favors the death penalty for murder, there were only fifty-six executions in 1995, but about twenty thousand murders.

The last two conclusions bear on our understanding of the majoritarian and pluralist models of democracy discussed in Chapter 2. Here, we probe more deeply into the nature, shape, depth, and formation of public opinion in a democratic government. What is the place of public opinion in a democracy? How do people acquire their opinions? What are the major lines of division in public opinion? How do individuals' ideology and knowledge affect their opinions? What is the relationship between public opinion and ideology?

PUBLIC OPINION AND THE MODELS OF DEMOCRACY

Public opinion is simply the collective attitude of the citizens on a given issue or question. Opinion polling, which involves interviewing a sample of citizens to estimate public opinion as a whole (see Feature 5.1), is such a common feature of contemporary life that we often forget it is a modern invention, dating only from the 1930s (see Figure 5.1). In fact, survey methodology did not become a powerful research tool until the advent of computers in the 1950s.

Before polling became an accepted part of the American scene, politicians, journalists, and everyone else could argue about what the people wanted, but no one really knew. Before the 1930s, observers of America had to guess at national opinion by analyzing newspaper stories, politicians' speeches, voting returns, and travelers' diaries. What if pollsters had been around when the colonists declared their independence from Britain in July 1776? We might have learned (as some historians estimate) that "40 percent of Americans supported the Revolution, 20 percent opposed it, and 40 percent tried to remain neutral."[9] When no one really knows what the people want, how can the national government be responsive to public

5.1

Sampling a Few, Predicting to Everyone

How can a pollster tell what the nation thinks by talking to only a few hundred people? The answer lies in the statistical theory of sampling. Briefly, the theory holds that a sample of individuals selected by chance from any population is "representative" of that population. This means that the traits of the individuals in the sample—their attitudes, beliefs, sociological characteristics, and physical features—reflect the traits of the whole population. Sampling theory does not claim that a sample exactly matches the population, only that it reflects the population with some predictable degree of accuracy.

Three factors determine the accuracy of a sample. The most important is how the sample is selected. For maximum accuracy, the individuals in the sample must be chosen randomly. *Randomly* does not mean "at whim," however; it means that every individual in the population has the same chance of being selected.

For a population as large and widespread as that of the United States, pollsters first divide the country into geographic regions. Then they randomly choose areas and sample individuals who live within those areas. This departure from strict random sampling does decrease the accuracy of polls, but only by a relatively small amount. Today, most polls conducted by the mass media are done by telephone, with computers randomly dialing numbers within predetermined calling areas. (Random dialing ensures that even people with unlisted numbers are called.)

The second factor that affects accuracy is the size of the sample. The larger the sample, the more accurately it represents the population. For example, a sample of four hundred randomly selected individuals is accurate to within six percentage points (plus or minus) 95 percent of the time. A sample of six hundred is accurate to within five percentage points. (Surprisingly, the proportion of the sample to the overall population has essentially no effect on the accuracy of most samples. A sample of, say, six hundred individuals will reflect the traits of a city, a state,

or even an entire nation with equal accuracy. Why this is so is better discussed in a course on statistics.)

The final factor that affects the accuracy of sampling is the amount of variation in the population. If there were no variation, every sample would reflect the population's characteristics with perfect accuracy. The greater the variation within the population, the greater is the chance that one random sample will be different from another.

The Gallup Poll and most other national opinion polls usually survey about 1,500 individuals and are accurate to within three percentage points 95 percent of the time. As shown in Figure 5.1, the predictions of the Gallup Poll for fourteen presidential elections since 1936 have deviated from the voting results by an average of only 2.2 percentage points. Even this small margin of error can mean an incorrect prediction in a close election. But for the purpose of estimating public opinion on political issues, a sampling error of three percentage points is acceptable.

Poll results can be wrong because of problems that have nothing to do with sampling theory. For example, question wording can bias the results. In surveys during the 1980s concerning aid to the Nicaraguan Contras fighting the Sandinista government, questions that mentioned President Reagan's name produced more support for increased aid by almost five percentage points.[*] Survey questions are also prone to random error, because interviewers are likely to obtain superficial responses from busy respondents who say anything, quickly, to get rid of them. Recently, some newspaper columnists have even urged readers to lie to pollsters outside voting booths, to confound election-night television predictions. But despite the potential for abuses or distortions, modern polling has told us a great deal about public opinion in America.

[*] Brad Lockerbie and Stephen A. Borrelli, "Question Wording and Public Support for Contra Aid, 1983–1986," *Public Opinion Quarterly 54* (Summer 1990), p. 200.

figure 5.1   ● **Gallup Poll Accuracy**

One of the nation's oldest polls was started by George Gallup in the 1930s. The accuracy of the Gallup Poll in predicting presidential elections over nearly fifty years is charted here. Although not always on the mark, its predictions have been fairly close to election results. The poll was most notably wrong in 1948, when it predicted that Thomas Dewey, the Republican candidate, would defeat the Democratic incumbent, Harry Truman, underestimating Truman's vote by 5.4 percentage points. In 1996, the Gallup Poll predicted that Bill Clinton would win 52 percent of the popular vote and he received 49 percent, which was within the poll's three point margin of error.

Source: *Gallup Report,* November 1992. Used by permission of The Gallup Poll.

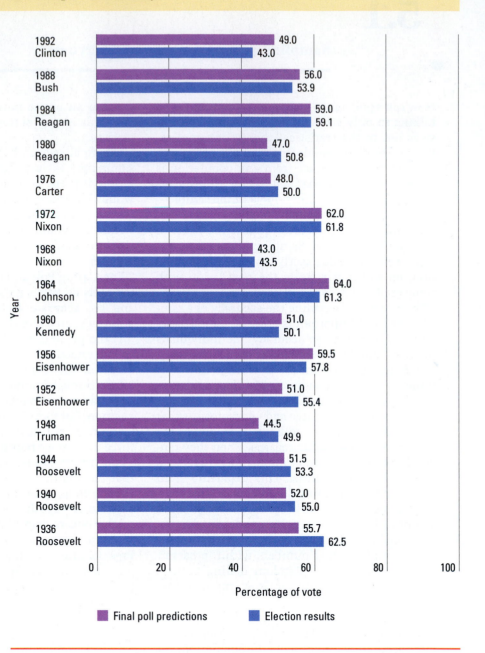

opinion? As we discussed in Chapter 3, the founders wanted to build public opinion into our government structure by allowing the direct election of representatives to the House and apportioning representation there according to population. The attitudes and actions of the House of Representatives, the framers thought, would reflect public opinion, especially on the crucial issues of taxes and government spending.

In practice, bills passed by a majority of elected representatives do not necessarily reflect the opinion of a majority of citizens. This would not

Stop the Presses! Oops, Too Late . . .

As the 1948 election drew near, few people gave President Harry Truman a chance to defeat his Republican opponent, Thomas E. Dewey. Polling was still new, and virtually all the early polls showed Dewey far ahead. Most organizations simply stopped polling weeks before the election. The Chicago Daily Tribune *believed the polls and proclaimed Dewey's victory before the votes were counted. Here, the victorious Truman triumphantly displays the most embarrassing headline in American politics. Later, it was revealed that the few polls taken closer to election day showed Truman catching up to Dewey. Clearly, polls estimate the vote only at the time they are taken.*

have bothered the framers, because they never intended to create a full democracy, a government completely responsive to majority opinion. Although they wanted to provide for some consideration of public opinion, they had little faith in the ability of the masses to make public policy.

The majoritarian and pluralist models of democracy differ greatly in their assumptions about the role of public opinion in democratic government. According to the classic majoritarian model, the government should do what a majority of the public wants. In contrast, pluralists argue that the public as a whole seldom demonstrates clear, consistent opinions on the day-to-day issues of government. At the same time, pluralists recognize that subgroups within the public do express opinions on specific matters—often and vigorously. The pluralist model requires that government institutions allow the free expression of opinions by these "minority publics." Democracy is at work when the opinions of many different publics clash openly and fairly over government policy.

Sampling methods and opinion polling have altered the debate about the majoritarian and pluralist models of democracy. One expert said, "Surveys produce just what democracy is supposed to produce—equal representation of all citizens."[10] Now that we know how often government policy runs against majority opinion, it becomes harder to defend the U.S. government as democratic under the majoritarian model. Even at a time when Americans overwhelmingly favored the death penalty for murderers, the Supreme Court decided that existing state laws applying capital punishment were unconstitutional. Even after the Court approved new state laws as constitutional, relatively few murderers were actually executed. Consider, too, the case of prayer in public schools. The Supreme Court has ruled that no state or local government can require the reading of the Lord's Prayer or Bible verses in public schools. Yet, surveys continually show that a clear majority of Americans (about 60 percent) do not agree with that ruling.[11] Because government policy sometimes runs against settled majority opinion, the majoritarian model is easily attacked as an inaccurate description of reality.

The two models of democracy make different assumptions about public opinion. The majoritarian model assumes that a majority of the people hold clear, consistent opinions on government policy. The pluralist model assumes that the public is often uninformed and ambivalent about specific issues, and opinion polls frequently support that claim. What are the bases of public opinion? What principles, if any, do people use to organize their beliefs and attitudes about politics? Exactly how do individuals form their political opinions? We will look for answers to these questions in this chapter. In later chapters, we assess the effect of public opinion on government policies. The results should help you make up your own mind about the viability of the majoritarian and pluralist models in a functioning democracy.

THE DISTRIBUTION OF PUBLIC OPINION

A government that tries to respond to public opinion soon learns that people seldom think alike. To understand and then act on the public's many attitudes and beliefs, government must pay attention to the way public opinion is distributed among the choices on a given issue. In particular, government must analyze the shape and the stability of that distribution.

Shape of the Distribution

The results of public opinion polls are often displayed in graphs such as those in Figure 5.2. The height of the columns indicates the percentage of those polled who gave each response, identified along the baseline. The shape of the opinion distribution depicts the pattern of all the responses when counted and plotted. The figure depicts three patterns of distribution— skewed, bimodal, and normal.

Figure 5.2a plots the percentages of respondents surveyed in 1995 who favored or opposed imposing the death penalty for a person convicted of murder. The most frequent response ("favor") is called the *mode*. The mode produces a prominent "hump" in this distribution. The relatively few respondents who didn't know or were opposed to the death penalty lie to one side, in its "tail." Such an asymmetrical distribution is called a **skewed distribution.**

Figure 5.2b plots responses to the question of whether homosexuality is a matter of choice.[12] These responses fall into a **bimodal distribution:** respondents chose two categories with nearly equal frequency, dividing almost evenly over whether being homosexual is a matter of choice or something that a person cannot change.

Figure 5.2c shows how respondents to a national survey in 1994 were distributed along a liberal-conservative continuum. Its shape resembles what statisticians call a **normal distribution**—a symmetrical, bell-shaped spread around a single mode. Here, the mode ("moderate") lies in the center. Progressively fewer people classified themselves in each category toward the liberal and conservative extremes.

5.2   ● Three Distributions of Opinion

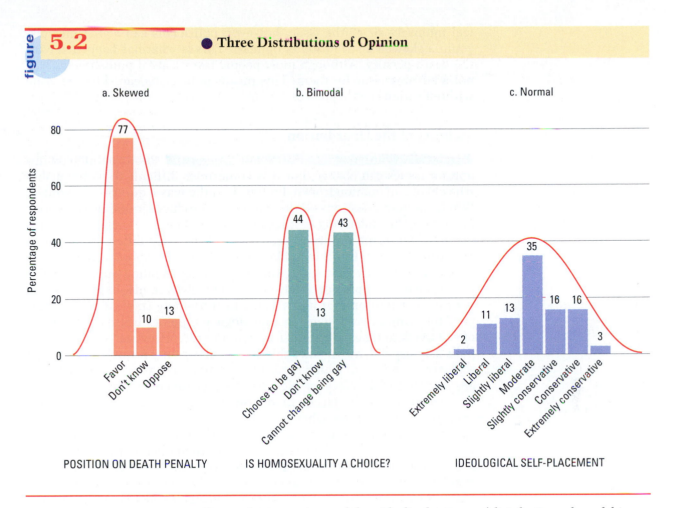

a. Skewed   b. Bimodal   c. Normal

POSITION ON DEATH PENALTY   IS HOMOSEXUALITY A CHOICE?   IDEOLOGICAL SELF-PLACEMENT

Here we have superimposed three idealized patterns of distribution—skewed, bimodal, and normal—on three actual distributions of responses to survey questions. Although the actual responses do not match the ideal shapes exactly, the match is close enough that we can describe the distribution of (a) thoughts on the death penalty as skewed, (b) opinions on the causes of homosexuality as bimodal, and (c) ideological attitudes as approximately normal.

Sources: (a) Gallup Organization, *Gallup Poll Monthly*, June 1995, p. 23. (b) 1993 *New York Times*/CBS News Poll that asked "Do you think being homosexual is something people choose to be, or do you think it is something they cannot change?"; Jeffrey Schmalz, "Poll Finds an Even Split on Homosexuality's Cause," *New York Times*, 5 March 1993, p. A11. (c) 1994 General Social Survey, National Opinion Research Center, cited in Harold W. Stanley and Richard G. Niemi (eds.), *Vital Statistics on American Politics* (Washington, D.C.: CQ Press, 1995), p. 150.

This site provides tables and graphs from the American National Election Studies (NES) for surveys conducted from 1952 through 1994. `<www.umich.edu/~nes/resourcs/nesguide/gd-index.htm>`

When public opinion is normally distributed on an issue, the public tends to support a moderate government policy on that issue. It will also tolerate policies that fall slightly to the left or the right, so long as they do not stray too far from the moderate center. In contrast, when opinion is sharply divided in a bimodal distribution—as over homosexuality—there is great potential for political conflict. A skewed distribution, on the other hand, indicates homogeneity of opinion. When consensus on an issue is overwhelming, those with the minority opinion risk social ostracism and even persecution if they persist in voicing their view. If the public does not feel intensely about the issue, however, politicians can sometimes discount a skewed distribution of opinion. This is what has happened with the death penalty. Although most people favor capital punishment, it is not a burning issue for them. This means politicians can skirt the issue without serious consequences.

Stability of the Distribution

A **stable distribution** shows little change over time. Public opinion on important issues can change, but it is sometimes difficult to distinguish a true change in opinion from a difference in the way a question is worded. When different questions on the same issue produce similar distributions of opinion, the underlying attitudes are stable. When the same question (or virtually the same question) produces significantly different responses over time, an actual shift in public opinion probably has occurred.

We have already discussed Americans' long-standing support of the death penalty. People's descriptions of themselves in ideological terms is another distribution that has remained surprisingly stable. Chapter 1 argued for using a two-dimensional ideological typology based on the trade-offs of freedom for equality and freedom for order. However, most opinion polls ask respondents to place themselves along only a single liberal-conservative dimension, which tends to force libertarians and communitarians into the middle category. Nevertheless, we find relatively little change in respondents' self-placement on the liberal-conservative continuum over time. Even in 1964, when liberal Lyndon Johnson won a landslide victory over conservative Barry Goldwater in the presidential election, more voters described themselves as conservative than liberal. Indeed, the ideological distribution of the public has been skewed toward conservatism in every presidential election year since 1964.[13] Despite all the talk about the nation's becoming conservative in recent years, the fact is that most people did not describe themselves as liberal at any time during the past thirty years. People's self-descriptions have shifted about 5 percentage points toward the right since 1964, but more people considered themselves conservative than liberal to begin with.

Sometimes changes occur within subgroups that are not reflected in overall public opinion. College students, for example, were far more liberal in the 1970s than today (see Politics in a Changing America 5.1). Moreover, public opinion in America is capable of massive change over time—even on issues that were once highly controversial. A good example is racially integrated schools. A national survey in 1942 asked whether "white and Negro students should go to the same schools or separate schools."[14] Only 30 percent of white respondents said that the students should attend schools together. When virtually the same question was asked in 1984 (substituting *black* for *Negro*), 90 percent of the white respondents endorsed integrated schools. Nevertheless, only 23 percent of the whites surveyed in 1984 were in favor of busing to achieve racial balance. And whites were more willing to bus their children to a school with a few blacks than to one that was mostly black.[15] So white opinion changed dramatically with regard to the *principle* of desegregated schools, but whites seemed divided on how that principle should be implemented.

In trying to explain how political opinions are formed and how they change, political scientists cite the process of political socialization, the influence of cultural factors, and the interplay of ideology and knowledge. In the next several sections, we examine how these elements combine to create and influence public opinion.

POLITICAL SOCIALIZATION

Public opinion is grounded in political values. People acquire their values through **political socialization,** a complex process through which individuals become aware of politics, learn political facts, and form political values. Think for a moment about your political socialization. What is your earliest memory of a president? When did you first learn about political parties? If you identify with a party, how did you decide to do so? If you do not, why don't you? Who was the first liberal you ever met? The first conservative? How did you first learn about nuclear bombs? About capitalism and communism?

Obviously, the paths to political awareness, knowledge, and values vary among individuals, but most people are exposed to the same sources of influence, or agents of socialization—especially from childhood through young adulthood. These influences are family, school, community, peers, and—of course—television.

The Agents of Early Socialization

Like psychologists, scholars of political socialization place great emphasis on early learning. Both groups point to two fundamental principles that characterize early learning:[16]

- *The primacy principle.* What is learned first is learned best.
- *The structuring principle.* What is learned first structures later learning.

Because most people learn first from their family, the family tends to be an important agent of early socialization. The extent of family influence—and of the influence of other socializing agents—depends on the extent of our exposure, communication, and receptivity to them.[17]

Family. In most cases, exposure, communication, and receptivity are highest in parent-child relationships, although parental influence has declined with the rise of single-parent families. Especially in two-parent homes, children learn a wide range of values—social, moral, religious, economic, and political—that help shape their opinions. It is not surprising, then, that most people link their earliest memories of politics with their family. Moreover, when parents are interested in politics and maintain a favorable home environment for studying public affairs, they influence their children to become more politically interested and informed.[18]

One of the most politically important things that many children learn from their parents is party identification. Party identification is learned in much the same way as religion. Children (very young children, anyway) imitate their parents. When parents share the same religion, children are almost always raised in that faith. When parents are of different religions, their children are more likely to follow one or the other than to adopt a third. Similarly, parental influence on party identification is greater when

● **politics in a changing america**

5.1   Are Students More Conservative Than Their Parents?

Do you remember filling out a questionnaire when you enrolled in college? If it asked about your political orientation, you may be represented in this graph. For about three decades, researchers at the University of California at Los Angeles have collected various data on entering freshmen, including asking them to characterize their political views as far left, liberal, middle-of-the-road, conservative, or far right. In contrast to Americans in general, who have shown little ideological change over time, college students described themselves as markedly more liberal in the early 1970s than they do now.

Sources: Alexander W. Astin, et al. *The American Freshman Twenty Year Trends, 1996–1985,* Los Angeles Higher Education Research Institute, Graduate School of Education, University of California, Los Angeles, 1987, 97; *The American Freshman National Norms for Fall 1986,* Los Angeles Higher Education Research Institute, Graduate School of Education, University of California, Los Angeles, 1986, 64; *Fall 1987* (1987), 61; *Fall 1988* (1988), 61; *Fall 1989* (1989), 57; *Fall 1990* (1990), 56; *Fall 1991* (1991), 26; *Fall 1992* (1992), 26; *Fall 1993* (1993), 25; *Fall 1994* (1994), 26; and *Fall 1995* (1995), 29. Figure "College Freshman-Idealogy" from Harold W. Stanley and Richard G. Niemi (eds.), *Vital Statistics on American Politics,* 1995, p. 151. Reprinted by permission.

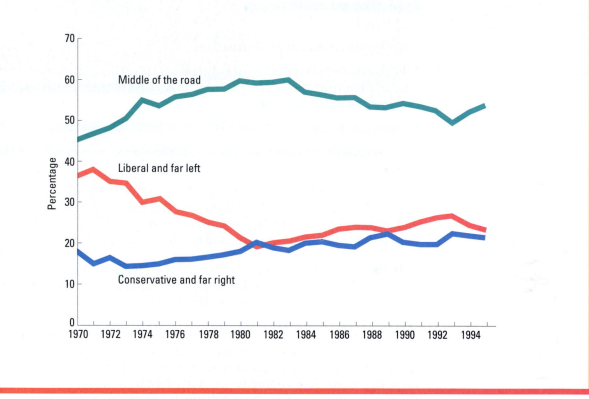

both parents strongly identify with the same party.[19] Overall, more than half of young American voters identify with the political party of their parents. Moreover, those who change their partisanship are more likely to shift from being partisan to independent or from independent to partisan than to convert from one party to the other.[20]

American Government 101

In 1996, Washington and Lee University enacted a "mock" primary of the Republican Party. It allowed students to learn about politics by taking roles of candidates and party activists and playing out the political event—sometimes with surprising results. A number of other universities sponsor mock conventions or legislatures or stage meetings of the United Nations. All of these efforts promote political socialization.

Two crucial differences between party identification and religion may explain why youngsters are socialized into a religion much more reliably than into a political party. The first is that most parents care a great deal more about their religion than about their politics. So they are more deliberate about exposing their children to religion. The second is that religious institutions recognize the value of socialization; they offer Sunday schools and other activities that reinforce parental guidance. American political parties, on the other hand, sponsor few activities to win the hearts of little Democrats and Republicans, which leaves children open to counterinfluences in their school and community.

School.   According to some researchers, schools have an influence on political learning that is equal to or greater than that of parents.[21] Here, however, we have to distinguish between elementary and secondary schools on the one hand and institutions of higher education on the other. Elementary schools prepare children in a number of ways to accept the social order. They introduce authority figures outside the family—the teacher, the principal, the police officer. They also teach the nation's slogans and symbols—the Pledge of Allegiance, the national anthem, national heroes and holidays. And they stress the norms of group behavior and democratic decision making (respecting the opinions of others, voting for class officers). In the process, they teach youngsters about the value of political equality.

Children do not always understand the meaning of the patriotic rituals and behaviors they learn in elementary school. In fact, much of this early learning—in the United States and elsewhere—is more indoctrination than education. By the end of the eighth grade, however, children begin to distinguish between political leaders and government institutions. They become more aware of collective institutions, such as Congress and elections, than younger children, who tend to focus on the president and other single figures of government authority.[22] In sum, most children emerge from elementary school with a sense of national pride and an idealized notion of American government.[23]

Although newer curricula in many secondary schools emphasize citizens' rights in addition to their responsibilities, high schools also attempt to build "good citizens." Field trips to the state legislature or the city council impress students with the majesty and power of government institutions. But secondary schools also offer more explicit political content in their curricula, including courses in recent U.S. history, civics, and American government. Better teachers challenge students to think critically about American government and politics; others limit themselves to teaching civic responsibilities. The end product is a greater awareness of the political process and of the most prominent participants in that process (see Figure 5.3).[24] Despite teachers' efforts to build children's trust in the political process, outside events can erode that trust as children grow up. For example, urban adolescents have been found to have a more cynical view of both the police and the president than nonurban youth.[25]

Political learning at the college level can be much like that in high school, or it can be quite different. The degree of difference is greater if professors (or the texts they use) encourage their students to question authority. Questioning dominant political values does not necessarily mean rejecting them. For example, this text encourages you to recognize that freedom and equality—two values idealized in our culture—often conflict. It also invites you to think of democracy in terms of competing institutional models, one of which challenges the idealized notion of democracy. These alternative perspectives are meant to teach you about American political values, not to subvert those values. College courses that are intended to stimulate critical thinking have the potential to introduce students to political ideas that are radically different from those they bring to class. Most high school courses do not. Still, specialists in socialization contend that taking particular courses in college has little effect on attitude change, which is more likely to come from sustained interactions with classmates who hold different views.[26]

Community and Peers.   Your community and your peers are different but usually overlapping groups. Your community is the people of all ages with whom you come in contact because they live or work near you. Peers are your friends, classmates, and coworkers. Usually they are your age and live or work within your community.

The makeup of a community has a lot to do with how the political opinions of its members are formed. Homogeneous communities—those whose members are similar in ethnicity, race, religion, or occupation—can exert strong pressures on both children and adults to conform to the dominant attitude. For example, if all your neighbors praise the candidates of

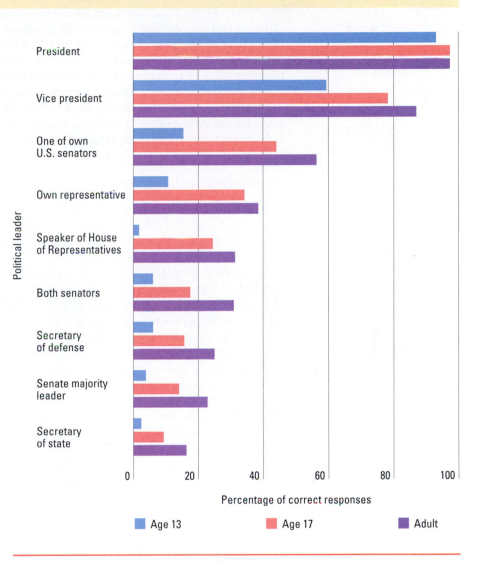

figure 5.3

● **Knowledge of Political Leaders, By Age Groups**

Do people actually learn any-thing about politics during high school? They seem to, according to a study that asked high school students aged thirteen and seventeen and as young adults for the last names of individuals holding the public offices listed here. (Respondents were not penalized for spelling errors.) The percentage of correct responses was consis-tently higher with increasing age, but the greatest increases occurred during the high school years, between ages thirteen and seventeen.

Source: Fred I. Greenstein, "What the President Means to Americans," in *Choosing the President,* ed. James D. Barber, p. 125. Copyright © 1974 The American Assembly. Reprinted with permission.

one party and criticize the candidates of the other, it is difficult to voice or even hold a dissenting opinion.[27] Communities made up of one ethnic group or religion may also voice negative attitudes about other groups. Although community socialization is usually reinforced in the schools, schools sometimes introduce students to ideas that run counter to com-munity values. (One example is sex education.)

For both children and adults, peer groups sometimes provide a defense against community pressures. Adolescent peer groups are particularly ef-fective protection against parental pressures. In adolescence, children rely on their peers to defend their dress and their lifestyle, not their politics. At the college level, however, peer group influence on political attitudes often grows substantially, sometimes fed by new information that clashes with parental beliefs. A classic study, of students at Bennington College in the 1930s, found that many became substantially more liberal than their affluent and conservative parents. Two follow-up studies twenty-five and fifty years later showed that most retained their liberal attitudes, in part because their spouses and friends (peers) supported their views.[28] Other evidence shows that the baby boomers who went to college during the late 1960s and became the affluent yuppies of the 1980s (perhaps your parents) became more liberal on social issues than their high school classmates who did not go to college. However, yuppies were about as conservative as nonyuppies on economic matters.[29]

Continuing Socialization

Political socialization continues throughout life. As parental and school influences wane in adulthood, peer groups (neighbors, coworkers, club members) assume a greater importance in promoting political awareness and developing political opinions.[30] Because adults usually learn about political events from the mass media—newspapers, magazines, television, and radio—the media emerge as socialization agents. The role of television is especially important: over 80 percent of adult Americans report regularly watching news on television.[31] (The mass media are so important in the political socialization of both children and adults that we devote a whole chapter—Chapter 6—to a discussion of their role.)

Regardless of how people learn about politics, they gain perspective on government as they grow older. They are apt to measure new candidates (and new ideas) against those they remember. Their values also change, increasingly reflecting their own self-interest. As voters age, for example, they begin to see more merit in government spending for Social Security than they did when they were younger. Finally, political education comes simply through exposure and familiarity. One example is voting, which people do with increasing regularity as they grow older—it becomes a habit.

SOCIAL GROUPS AND POLITICAL VALUES

No two people are influenced by precisely the same socialization agents in precisely the same way. Each individual experiences a unique process of political socialization and forms a unique set of political values. Still, people with similar backgrounds do share learning experiences; this means they tend to develop similar political opinions. In this section, we examine the ties between people's social background and their political values. In the process, we will examine the ties between background and values by looking at responses to two questions posed by the 1992 National Election Study, administered by the University of Michigan's Center for Political Studies. Many questions in the survey tap the freedom versus order or freedom versus equality dimensions. The two we chose serve to illustrate the analysis of ideological types.

The first question dealt with abortion. The interviewer said, "There has been some discussion about abortion during recent years. Which opinion

● ● ● ● ● ● ● ● ● ● ● ●
To Have and Have Not

Everyone feels uneasy at the sight of poverty in the presence of wealth. The question is, what should be done about poverty? Should the government step in to reduce income differences between the rich and the poor, perhaps by taxing the wealthy at higher rates and supplementing the income of the poor? Or should the government take no more from the wealthy than it does from the middle class (or even the lower class)?

on this page best agrees with your view? You can just tell me the number of the opinion you choose":

1. By law, abortion should never be permitted [10 percent agreed].
2. The law should permit abortion only in cases of rape, incest, or when the woman's life is in danger [28 percent].
3. The law should permit abortion for reasons other than rape, incest, or danger to the woman's life, but only after the need for the abortion has been clearly established [14 percent].
4. By law, a woman should be able to obtain an abortion as a matter of personal choice [47 percent].[32]

Those who chose the last category most clearly valued individual freedom over order imposed by government. Moreover, the pro-choice respondents did not view the issue as being restricted to freedom of choice in reproduction. Evidence shows that they also had concerns about broader issues of social order, such as the role of women and the legitimacy of alternative lifestyles.[33]

The second question posed by the 1992 National Election Study pertained to the role of government in guaranteeing employment:

Some people feel the government in Washington should see to it that every person has a job and a good standard of living. Suppose that these people are at one end of the scale....Others think the government should just let each person get ahead on his own. Suppose these people were at the other end....Where would you put yourself on this scale, or haven't you thought much about this?

Excluding those who "hadn't thought much" about this question, 30 percent of the respondents wanted government to provide every person with a living, and 22 percent were undecided. That left 48 percent who wanted the government to leave people alone to "get ahead" on their own. These respondents, who opposed government efforts to promote equality, apparently valued freedom over equality.

Overall, the responses to each of these questions were divided approximately equally. Somewhat less than half the respondents (47 percent) felt that government should not set restrictions on abortion, and nearly half (48 percent) thought the government should not guarantee everyone a job and a good standard of living. (To learn about public opinion on government guarantees of jobs in other countries, see Compared with What? 5.1.) However, sharp differences in attitudes emerged for both issues when the respondents were grouped by socioeconomic factors—education, income, region, race, religion, and sex. The differences are shown in Figure 5.4 as positive and negative deviations from the national average for each question. Bars that extend to the right identify groups that are more likely than most Americans to sacrifice freedom for a given value of government, either equality or order. Next, we examine the opinion patterns more closely for each socioeconomic group.

Education

Education increases people's awareness and understanding of political issues. Higher education also promotes tolerance of unpopular opinions and behavior and invites citizens to see issues in terms of civil rights and liberties. This result is clearly shown in the left-hand column of Figure 5.4, which shows that people with more education are more likely to view abortion as a matter of a woman's choice.[34] When confronted with a choice between personal freedom and social order, college-educated individuals tend to choose freedom.

With regard to the role of government in reducing income inequality, the right-hand column in Figure 5.4 shows that people with more education also tend to favor freedom over equality. The higher their level of education, the less likely respondents were to support government-guaranteed jobs and living standards. You might expect better-educated people to be humanitarian and to support government programs to help the needy. However, because educated people tend to be wealthier, they would be taxed more heavily for such government programs. Moreover, they may believe that it is unrealistic to expect government to make such economic guarantees.

Income

In many countries, differences in social class—based on social background and occupation—divide people in their politics.[35] In the United States, we have avoided the uglier aspects of class conflict, but here wealth some-

● compared with what?

5.1   Opinions on Government Provision of a Job

Compared with citizens of other industrial countries, Americans are much less likely to demand that the government guarantee employment. Respondents from twelve countries (including the former East Germany) were asked in 1991 whether they agreed or disagreed with this statement: "The government should provide a job for everyone who wants one." Not surprising, respondents in formerly communist countries still overwhelmingly considered this an appropriate role for government, but more than two-thirds of the respondents in Japan, West Germany, and the United Kingdom also felt that government should guarantee employment. Only in the United States were citizens equally divided on this issue.

Source: International Social Justice Project, a collaborative international research effort. The data for this chart, kindly provided by Antal Örkény at Eötvös Loránd University in Budapest, came from national surveys conducted in 1991 that were supported in whole or in part by the Institute for Social Research, University of Michigan; the Economic and Social Research Council (United Kingdom); the Deutsche Forschungsgemeinschaft; the Institute of Social Science, Chuo University (Japan); and the Dutch Ministry of Social Affairs.

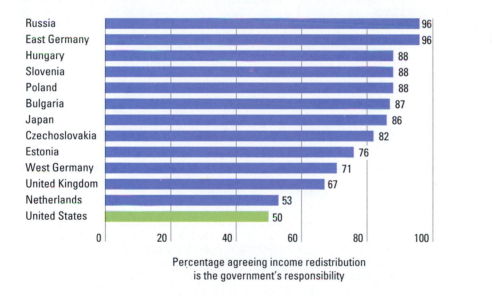

Percentage agreeing income redistribution is the government's responsibility

times substitutes for class. As Figure 5.4 shows, wealth is consistently linked to opinions favoring a limited government role in promoting order and equality. Those with a higher income are more likely to favor personal choice in abortion and to oppose government guarantees of employment and living conditions. For both issues, wealth and education have a similar effect on opinion: the groups with more education and higher income opt for freedom.

figure

5.4   ● Group Deviations from National Opinion on Two Questions

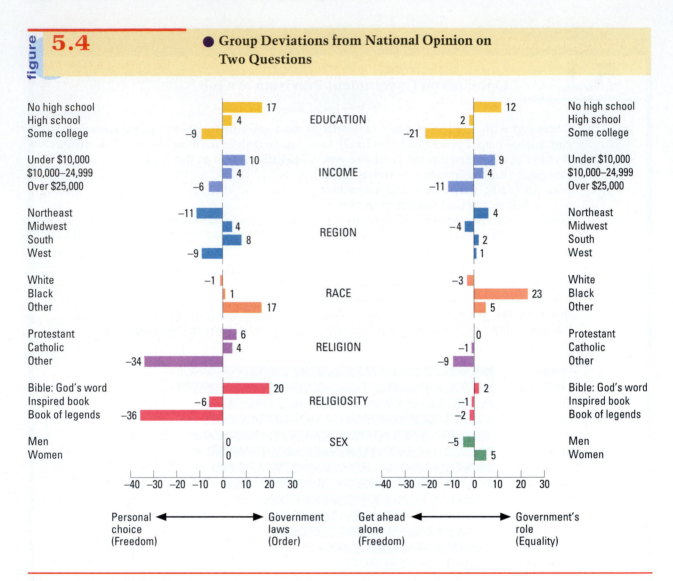

 Use the CROSSTABS computer program that accompanies this book to produce your own data tables. The program accesses responses to over fifty questions from the 1992 National Election Study, including the questions on abortion and on the government's guaranteeing employment. See how other social or political groups divide on these issues.

Two questions—one on abortion (representing the dilemma of freedom versus order) and the other on the government's role in guaranteeing employment (freedom versus equality)—were asked of a national sample in 1992. Public opinion for the nation as a whole was sharply divided on each question. These two graphs show how respondents in several social groups deviated from overall public opinion. The longer the bars next to each group, the more its respondents deviated from the expression of opinion for the entire sample. Bars that extend to the left show group opinions that deviate toward freedom. Bars that extend to the right show deviations away from freedom, toward order (part a) or equality (part b).

Source: Data from 1992 National Election Study, copyright © Center for Political Studies, University of Michigan. Reprinted with permission.

Region

Early in our country's history, regional differences were politically important—important enough to spark a civil war between the North and South. For nearly a hundred years after the Civil War, regional differences continued to affect American politics. The moneyed Northeast was thought to control the purse strings of capitalism. The Midwest was long regarded as the stronghold of isolationism in foreign affairs. The South was virtually a one-party region, almost completely Democratic. And the individualistic West pioneered its own mixture of progressive politics.

In the past, differences in wealth fed cultural differences between these regions. In recent decades, however, the movement of people and wealth away from the Northeast and Midwest to the Sunbelt states in the South and Southwest has equalized the per capita income of the various regions. One result of this equalization is that the formerly "solid South" is no longer solidly Democratic. In fact, the South has tended to vote for Republican presidential candidates since 1968.

Figure 5.4 shows more striking differences between the four major regions of the United States on social issues than on economic issues. Respondents in the Northeast and West were more likely to support personal choice than residents of the South, who were more likely to favor restricting abortion. People in the Midwest were somewhat more likely to oppose government efforts to equalize income than were people in the Northeast. Despite these differences, regional effects on public opinion are weaker than the effects of most other socioeconomic factors.

The "Old" and "New" Ethnicity: European Origin and Race

In the early twentieth century, the major ethnic minorities in America were composed of immigrants from Ireland, Italy, Germany, Poland, and other European countries who came to the United States in waves during the late 1800s and early 1900s. These immigrants entered a nation that had been founded by British settlers more than a hundred years earlier. They found themselves in a strange land, usually without money and unable to speak the language. Moreover, their religious backgrounds— mainly Catholic and Jewish—differed from that of the predominantly Protestant earlier settlers. Local politicians saw the newcomers, who were concentrated in low-status jobs in urban areas of the Northeast and Midwest, as a new source of votes and soon mobilized them politically. These urban ethnics and their descendants became part of the great coalition of Democratic voters that President Franklin Roosevelt forged in the 1930s. And for years after, the European ethnics supported liberal candidates and causes more strongly than the original Anglo-Saxon immigrants.[36] More recent studies of public opinion show the differences are disappearing.[37] But if this **"old" ethnicity,** based on European origin, is giving way to assimilation, a **"new" ethnicity,** based on race, is taking its place.

For many years after the Civil War, the issue of race in American politics was defined as "how the South should treat the Negro." The debate between North and South over this issue became a conflict between civil rights and states' rights—a conflict in which blacks were primarily objects, not participants. But with the rise of black consciousness and the grassroots civil rights movement in the late 1950s and 1960s, blacks secured genuine voting rights in the South and exercised those rights more vigorously in the North. Although they represented only about 12 percent of the total population, blacks made up sizable voting blocs in southern states and northern cities. Like the European ethnics before them, American blacks were courted for their votes; at long last, their opinions were politically important.

Blacks constitute the biggest racial minority in American politics but not the only significant one. Asians, American Indians (Native Americans), and other nonwhites account for another 5 percent of the population. People of Latin American origin are often called Latinos. If they speak Spanish (Haitians and Brazilians usually do not), they are also known as Hispanics. Hispanics are commonly but inaccurately regarded as a racial group, for they consist of both whites and nonwhites. Hispanics make up about 10 percent of the nation's population, but they constitute as much as 26 percent of the population in California and Texas and 38 percent in New Mexico.[38] Although they are politically strong in some communities, Hispanics (comprising groups as different as Cubans, Mexicans, Peruvians, and Puerto Ricans) have lagged behind blacks in mobilizing across the nation. However, Hispanics are being wooed by non-Hispanic candidates and are increasingly running for public office themselves.

Blacks and members of other minorities display somewhat similar political attitudes on questions pertaining to equality. The reasons are twofold.[39] First, racial minorities (excepting second-generation Asians) tend to have low **socioeconomic status,** a combination of education, occupation, status, and income. Second, all racial minorities have been targets of racial prejudice and discrimination and have benefited from government actions in support of equality. The right-hand column in Figure 5.4 clearly shows the effects of race on the freedom-equality issue. Blacks strongly favored government action to improve economic opportunity; other minorities also favored government action but to a lesser degree. On the abortion issue, however, blacks differed little from whites, whereas other minorities favored government restrictions.

Religion

Since the last major wave of European immigration in the 1930s and 1940s, the religious makeup of the United States has remained fairly stable. Today, almost 60 percent of the population are Protestant, about 25 percent are Catholic, only about 2 percent are Jewish, and about 15 percent deny any religious affiliation or choose some other faith.[40] For many years, analysts found strong and consistent differences in the political opinions of Protestants, Catholics, and Jews.[41] Protestants were more conservative than Catholics, and Catholics tended to be more conservative than Jews.

Some such differences have remained, especially on questions of freedom versus order (such as the abortion question), but they are less marked than one might expect. Protestants oppose personal choice on abortion slightly more than Catholics, despite the Pope's strong opposition to abortion. Nonreligious persons and non-Christians are much more likely to favor personal choice on abortion and are somewhat less inclined toward favoring government job guarantees.

Even greater differences on the order issue emerged when respondents to the 1992 National Election Study were classified by their "religiosity,"

● ● ● ● ● ● ● ● ● ● ●

Ethnicity in Elections

Irish Americans, Italian Americans, Polish Americans, and members of other ethnic groups have gained political power through elections for local offices. Margaret Chin followed tradition by running in the Democratic primary for the New York City Council in 1991 and 1993. Although she lost both times to the incumbent councilwoman, her contests raised the political consciousness of Chinese Americans in her district. Indeed, her 1991 campaign led to wider use of the Chinese language on ballots in New York districts with many voters of Chinese descent.

which was measured by their attitude toward the Bible. About 40 percent of the sample responded that it should be taken literally as the actual word of God. Almost 50 percent regarded it as a book inspired by God but not to be taken literally. The remaining 13 percent viewed it as an ancient book of fables, legends, history, and moral precepts recorded by humans. As Figure 5.4 indicates, religiosity has little effect on attitudes toward economic equality but a powerful influence on attitudes toward social order. Those who believed that the Bible is the word of God strongly favor more government action in regulating abortion. The minority, who do not think the Bible is inspired by God, is far more inclined to value freedom over order. This method of classifying respondents reveals that political opinions in the United States do differ sharply according to religious beliefs. A 1996 survey found that white Protestants divided almost equally between those who described themselves as "born-again" or "evangelical" Christians and those who did not. Moreover, 67 percent of these evangelical Protestants agreed that the Bible was the word of God, against less than a quarter of white mainline Protestants. The study concluded: "The conservatism of white evangelical Protestants is clearly the most powerful religious force in politics today."[42]

Gender

Differences in sex, which has become known as *gender* in American politics, are often related to political opinions, primarily on the issue of freedom versus equality. As shown in the right-hand column of Figure 5.4, women are more likely to favor government actions to promote equality. However, men and women usually differ less on issues of freedom versus order. Even on the abortion issue, women and men are equally likely to favor personal choice over government restrictions (see the column on the left in Figure 5.4). Still, on many issues of government policy, the "gender gap" in American politics is noticeable, with women more supportive than men of government spending for social programs.

FROM VALUES TO IDEOLOGY

We have just seen that differences in groups' responses to two survey questions reflect those groups, value choices between freedom and order and between freedom and equality. But to what degree do people's opinions on specific issues reflect their explicit political ideology (the set of values and beliefs they hold about the purpose and scope of government)? Political scientists generally agree that ideology influences public opinion on specific issues; they have much less consensus on the extent to which people explicitly think in ideological terms.[43] They also agree that the public's ideological thinking cannot be categorized adequately in conventional liberal-conservative terms.[44]

The Degree of Ideological Thinking in Public Opinion

In an early but important study of public opinion, respondents were asked to describe the parties and candidates in the 1956 election.[45] Only about 12 percent of the sample volunteered responses that contained ideological terms (such as *liberal, conservative,* and *capitalism*). Most respondents (42 percent) evaluated the parties and candidates in terms of "benefits to groups" (farmers, workers, or businesspeople, for example). Others (24 percent) spoke more generally about "the nature of the times" (for example, inflation, unemployment, and the threat of war). Finally, a good portion of the sample (22 percent) gave answers that contained no classifiable issue content. Other studies have found that the vast majority of the electorate is confused by ideological terms. Consider this response from a resident of the San Francisco Bay Area in 1972 to the question "What do the terms *liberal* and *conservative* mean to you?"

> Oh conservative. Liberal and conservative. Liberal and conservative. I haven't given it much thought. I wouldn't know. I don't know what those would mean! Liberal . . . liberal . . . liberal. And conservative. Well, if a person is liberal with their money they squander their money? Does it fall in that same category? If you're conservative you don't squander so much, you save a little, huh?[46]

A woman in Utica, New York, who participated in a separate in-depth study of how people think about politics, replied when asked if she had an idea about the meaning of *liberal* and *conservative,* "No. I read it. I read it in the paper. I read the editorials sometimes and sometimes it's just a little over my head. And I'd like to know more, but then I'll say why bother."[47]

Subsequent research found somewhat greater ideological awareness within the electorate, especially during the 1964 presidential contest between Lyndon Johnson, a Democrat and ardent liberal, and Barry Goldwater, a Republican who was then considered an archconservative.[48] But more recent research has questioned whether American voters have really changed in their ideological thinking.[49] The tendency to respond to questions by using ideological terms increases with increasing education, which helps people understand political issues and relate them to one another. People's personal political socialization experiences can also lead them to think ideologically. For example, children raised in strong union households may be taught to distrust private enterprise and to value collective action through government.

True ideologues hold a consistent set of values and beliefs about the purpose and scope of government, and they tend to evaluate candidates in ideological terms.[50] Some people respond to questions in ways that seem ideological but are not, because they do not understand the underlying principles. For example, most respondents dutifully comply when asked to place themselves somewhere on a liberal-conservative continuum. The result, as shown earlier in Figure 5.2, is an approximately normal distribution centering on "moderate," the modal category. But many people settle on moderate when they do not clearly understand the alternatives, because moderate is a safe choice. A study in 1992 gave respondents another choice—the statement "I haven't thought much about it"—which allowed them to avoid placing themselves on the liberal-conservative continuum. In this study, 25 percent of the respondents acknowledged that they had not thought much about ideology.[51] The extent of ideological thinking in America, then, is considerably less than it might seem from responses to questions that ask people to describe themselves as liberals or conservatives.[52]

The Quality of Ideological Thinking in Public Opinion

What people's ideological self-placement means in the 1990s also is not clear. At one time, the liberal-conservative continuum represented a single dimension: attitudes toward the scope of government activity. Liberals were in favor of more government action to provide public goods, and conservatives were in favor of less. This simple distinction is not as useful today. Many people who call themselves liberal no longer favor government activism in general, and many self-styled conservatives no longer oppose it in principle. As a result, many people have difficulty deciding whether they are liberal or conservative, while others confidently choose identical points on the continuum for entirely different reasons. People describe themselves as liberal or conservative because of the symbolic value of the terms as much as for reasons of ideology.[53]

Studies of the public's ideological thinking find that two themes run through people's minds when asked to describe liberals and conservatives.

People associate liberals with change and conservatives with tradition. The theme corresponds to the distinction between liberals and conservatives on the exercise of freedom and the maintenance of order.[54]

The other theme has to do with equality. The conflict between freedom and equality was at the heart of President Roosevelt's New Deal economic policies (social security, minimum wage legislation, farm price supports) in the 1930s. The policies expanded the interventionist role of the national government in order to promote greater economic equality, and attitudes toward government intervention in the economy served to distinguish liberals from conservatives for decades afterward.[55] Attitudes toward government interventionism still underlie opinions about domestic economic policies.[56] Liberals support intervention to promote economic equality; conservatives favor less government intervention and more individual freedom in economic activities.

In Chapter 1, we proposed an alternative ideological classification based on people's relative evaluations of freedom, order, and equality. We described liberals as people who believe that government should promote equality, even if some freedom is lost in the process, but who oppose surrendering freedom to government-imposed order. Conservatives do not oppose equality in and of itself but put a higher value on freedom than equality when the two conflict. Yet, conservatives are not above restricting freedom when threatened with the loss of order. So both groups value freedom, but one is more willing to trade freedom for equality, and the other is more inclined to trade freedom for order. If you have trouble thinking about these tradeoffs on a single dimension, you are in good company. The liberal-conservative continuum presented to survey respondents takes a two-dimensional concept and squeezes it into a one-dimensional format.[57]

Ideological Types in the United States

Our ideological typology in Chapter 1 (see Figure 1.2) classifies people as liberals if they favor freedom over order and equality over freedom. Conversely, conservatives favor freedom over equality and order over freedom. Libertarians favor freedom over both equality and order—the opposite of communitarians. By cross-tabulating people's answers to the two questions from the 1992 National Election Study about freedom versus order (abortion) and freedom versus equality (government job guarantees), we can classify respondents according to their ideological tendencies. As shown in Figure 5.5, people's responses to the two questions are virtually unrelated to each other—that is, the responses fall about equally within each of the quadrants. This finding indicates that people do not decide about government activity according to a one-dimensional ideological standard. Figure 5.5 also classifies the sample according to the two dimensions in our ideological typology. Using only two issues to classify people in an ideological framework leaves substantial room for error. Still, if the typology is worthwhile, the results should be meaningful, and they are.

It is striking that the ideological tendencies of the respondents in the 1992 sample depicted in Figure 5.5 are divided almost equally among the four categories of the typology. (Remember, however, that these cate-

figure

5.5   ● Respondents Classified by Ideological Tendencies

Two survey questions presented choices between freedom and order and between freedom and equality by asking respondents whether abortion should be a matter of personal choice or of government regulation and whether government should guarantee people a job and a good standard of living or people should get ahead on their own. (The questions are given verbatim on page 153.) People's responses to the questions showed no correlation, demonstrating that these value choices cannot be explained by a simple liberal-conservative continuum. Instead, their responses can be more usefully analyzed according to four different ideological types. (The one-point difference in the percentage of responses for the "Should government guarantee employment?" question from that given on page 154 is the result of losing a few cases when the questions were cross-tabulated.)

Source: 1992 National Election Study, Center for Political Studies, University of Michigan.

The self-test in our IDEAlog program asks your opinion on a woman's right to have an abortion and on government's role in insuring employment. How did you answer? Does our idealogical typing match your self-image?

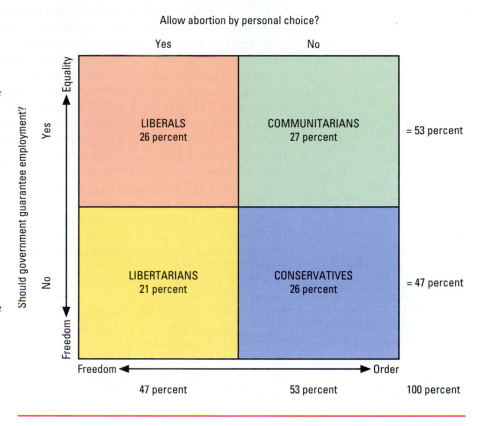

gories—like letter grades A, B, C, and D—are more rigid in the typology than in the respondents. Many would cluster toward the center of the figure if their attitudes were measured more sensitively.) The communitarian response pattern is the most common by a small margin and the libertarian the least common. The sample suggests that more than three-quarters of the electorate favor government action to promote order, increase equality, or both. The results resemble earlier findings by other researchers who conducted more exhaustive analyses involving more survey questions.[58]

Respondents who readily locate themselves on a single dimension running from liberal to conservative often go on to contradict their self-placement when answering questions about trading freedom for either order or equality.[59] A two-dimensional typology such as that in Figure 5.5 allows us to analyze responses more meaningfully.[60] Although a slight majority of the respondents to the 1992 survey (52 percent) expressed opinions that were either liberal (26 percent) or conservative (26 percent), almost as many expressed opinions that deviated from these familiar ideological types.

The ideological tendencies illustrate important differences between different social groups. Communitarians are prominent among minorities and among people with little education and low income, groups that tend to look favorably on the benefits of government in general. Libertarians are concentrated among people with more education and higher income, who tend to be suspicious of government interference in their lives. People in the southern states tend to be communitarians, those in the Midwest tend to be conservatives, and those in the Northeast are inclined to be liberals. Men are more likely to be conservative or libertarian than women, who tend to be liberal or communitarian.[61]

This more refined analysis of political ideology explains why even Americans who pay close attention to politics find it difficult to locate themselves on the liberal-conservative continuum. Their problem is that they are liberal on some issues and conservative on others. Forced to choose along just one dimension, they opt for the middle category, moderate. However, our analysis also indicates that many people who classify themselves as liberal or conservative do fit these two categories in our typology. There is value, then, in the liberal-conservative distinction, so long as we understand its limitations.

THE PROCESS OF FORMING POLITICAL OPINIONS

In 1996, nearly 500 people were brought together to discuss political issues. This site reports how their attitudes changed before and after a weekend of deliberation (very little).
`<www.pbs.org/results/ nicpoll.html>`

We have seen that people acquire their political values through socialization and that different social groups develop different sets of political values. We also have learned that some people, but only a minority, think about politics ideologically, holding a consistent set of political attitudes and beliefs. Now let us look at how people form opinions on a particular issue. In particular, how do those who are not ideologues—in other words, most citizens—form political opinions? Four factors—self-interest, political information, opinion schemas, and political leadership—play a part in the process.

Self-Interest

The **self-interest principle** states that people choose what benefits them personally.[62] The principle plays an obvious role in how people form opinions on government economic policies. Taxpayers tend to prefer low taxes to high taxes; farmers tend to favor candidates who promise them more support over those who promise them less. The self-interest principle also applies, but less clearly, to some government policies outside economics. Members of minority groups tend to see more personal advantage in government policies that promote social equality than do members of majority groups; teenage males are more likely to oppose compulsory military service than are older people of either sex. Group leaders often cue group members, telling them what policies they should support or oppose. (In the context of pluralist democracy, this often appears as grassroots support for or opposition to policies that affect only particular groups.[63])

For many government policies, however, the self-interest principle plays little or no role for the majority of citizens, because many issues directly affect relatively few people. Outlawing prostitution is one example;

doctor-assisted suicide is another. When moral issues are involved, people form opinions based on their underlying values.[64]

When moral issues are not in question and when individuals do not benefit directly from a policy, many people have trouble relating to the policy and forming an opinion about it. This tends to be true of the whole subject of foreign policy, which few people interpret in terms of personal benefits. Here, many people have no opinion, or their opinions are not firmly held and are apt to change quite easily, given almost any new information.

Political Information

In the United States today, education is compulsory (usually to age sixteen), and the literacy rate is relatively high. The country boasts an unparalleled network of colleges and universities, entered by two-thirds of all high school graduates. American citizens can obtain information from a variety of daily and weekly news publications. They can keep abreast of national and international affairs through nightly television news, which brings live coverage of world events via satellite from virtually everywhere in the world. Yet, the average American displays an astonishing lack of political knowledge.[65]

Citizens' knowledge of politics just after an election is low enough to make the basis of their vote questionable. In late 1995, for example, when the government was shut down while President Clinton and Congress were deadlocked over the budget, only 62 percent of a national sample correctly stated that the Republicans controlled the Senate, only 61 percent knew they controlled the House, and only 53 percent could name its Speaker, Newt Gingrich, who was in the news daily. Perhaps even more telling, only 34 percent could identify Bob Dole, who as Senate Majority Leader led the race for the Republican presidential nomination. Finally, a majority (54 percent) could not even guess the name of either of their U.S. senators.[66]

But Americans do not let lack of knowledge stop them from expressing their opinions. They readily offer opinions on issues ranging from capital punishment to nuclear power to the government's handling of the economy. When opinions are based on little knowledge, however, they change easily in the face of new information. The result is a high degree of instability in public opinion poll findings, depending on how questions are worded and on recent events that bear on the issue at hand. Nevertheless, some researchers hold that the *collective* opinion of the public—which balances off advocates' ignorance on both sides of an issue—can be interpreted as rational. Page and Shapiro analyzed the public's responses to 1,128 questions that were repeated in one or more surveys between 1935 and 1990.[67] They found that responses to more than half of the repeated policy questions "showed no significant change at all"—that is, they changed no more than six percentage points.[68] Moreover, Page and Shapiro concluded that when the public's collective opinion on public policy changes, it changes in "understandable, predictable ways."[69] Other scholars have contended that even collective public opinion may be misleading when the issues involve core beliefs (especially opposing beliefs) or when there is a sharp division in the quality of respondents' information (e.g., the opinions of upper-income respondents, who are usually more knowledgeable, can bias the survey results).[70]

The most thorough recent study of political knowledge was undertaken by Delli Carpini and Keeter.[71] In addition to conducting their own specialized surveys, they collected from existing surveys approximately 3,700 individual items that measured some type of factual knowledge about public affairs, and they focused on over 2,000 items that clearly dealt with political facts, such as knowledge of political institutions and processes, contemporary public figures, political groups, and policy issues. Despite evidence of citizens' ignorance of political facts, as discussed above, Delli Carpini and Keeter concluded that enough of the public is "reasonably well informed about politics . . . to meet high standards of good citizenship." They found, "Many of the basic institutions and procedures of government are known to half or more of the public, as are the relative positions of the parties on many major issues."[72]

Their analysis also found, however, that political knowledge is not randomly distributed within our society. "In particular, women, African Americans, the poor, and the young tend to be substantially less knowledgeable about politics than are men, whites, the affluent, and older citizens."[73] Education is the strongest single predictor of political knowledge, but other cultural or structural factors prevent women and blacks, for example, from developing the same levels of general political knowledge as white males.[74]

Researchers have not found any meaningful relationship between political sophistication and self-placement on the liberal-conservative scale. That is, people with equivalent knowledge of public affairs and levels of conceptualization are equally likely to call themselves liberals or conservatives.[75] Equal levels of political understanding, then, may produce quite different political views, as a result of individuals' unique patterns of political socialization.

Opinion Schemas

Even people who do not approach politics from the perspective of a full-blown ideology interpret political issues in terms of some preexisting mental structure. Psychologists refer to the packet of preexisting beliefs that people apply to a specific issue as an **opinion schema**—a network of organized knowledge and beliefs that guides the processing of information on a particular subject.[76] Figure 5.6 is a rendition of a partial opinion schema about Bill Clinton that might be held by a liberal Democrat. It suggests the wide range of attitudes and beliefs that affect people's thinking about political leaders and their policies. Our opinion schemas change as we acquire new information. A liberal embracing the opinion schema in Figure 5.6 would have been more disappointed in Clinton than a conservative Republican by Clinton's backing off on his pledge to admit gays into the military.

The schema concept gives us a more flexible tool for analyzing public opinion than the more rigid concept of ideology. The main value of schemas for understanding how opinions are formed is that they remind us that opinion questions trigger many different images, connections, and

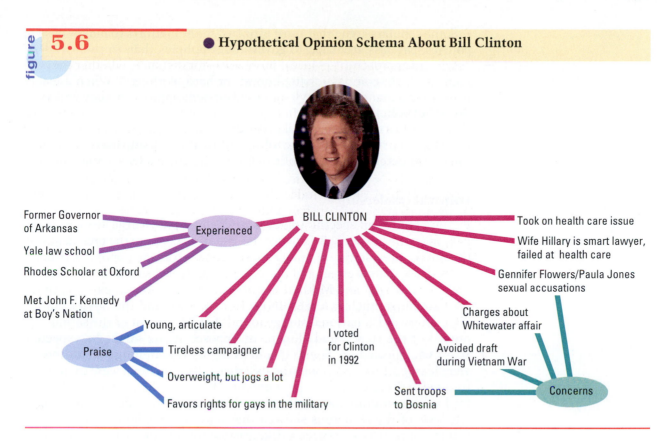

figure 5.6 ● **Hypothetical Opinion Schema About Bill Clinton**

People express opinions on issues, persons, or events according to preexisting attitudes and beliefs. Psychologists sometimes refer to this network of attitudes and beliefs, and their relationships, as an opinion schema. This is a hypothetical opinion schema that might be associated with Bill Clinton in the mind of a liberal Democrat who voted for Clinton in 1996.

values in the mind of each respondent. Given the complexity of the factors in individual opinion schemas, it is surprising that researchers find as many strong correlations as they do among individuals' social background, general values, and specific opinions. Opinion schemas can pertain to any political figure and to any subject—race, economics, or international relations, for example.[77] Often, people who have shared socializing experiences also share schema patterns. For instance, one study found that African Americans' views on the importance of race in determining one's chances in life could be analyzed according to five different schemas.[78]

Still, the more encompassing concept of ideology is hard to escape. Researchers have found that people's personal schemas tend to be organized in ways that parallel broader ideological categories. In other words, a conservative's opinion schema about Clinton may not differ factually from a liberal's, but it will differ considerably in its evaluation of those facts.[79] Clinton's co-opting of the Republican emphasis on a balanced budget, for example, might evoke anger in the conservative's schema but only resigned acceptance in the liberal's schema.

Some scholars argue that most citizens, in their efforts to make sense of politics, pay less attention to government policies than to their leaders' "style" in approaching political problems—for instance, whether they are seen as tough, compassionate, honest, or hard working.[80] When a leader behaves in a manner that style-oriented citizens approve of, they will view his or her policies favorably. In this way, citizens can relate the complexities of politics to their personal experiences. If many citizens view politics in terms of governing style, the role of political leadership becomes a more important determinant of public opinion than the leader's actual policies.

Political Leadership

Public opinion on specific issues is molded by political leaders, journalists, and policy experts. Because of the attention given to the presidency by the media, presidents are uniquely positioned to shape popular attitudes. Consider Ronald Reagan and the issue of nuclear disarmament. In 1987, President Reagan and Mikhail Gorbachev signed a treaty banning intermediate-range nuclear forces (INFs) from Europe and the Soviet Union. Soon afterward, a national survey found that 82 percent of the sample approved of the treaty, and 18 percent opposed it. As might be expected, those who viewed the Soviet Union as highly threatening ("hard-liners") were least enthusiastic about the INF treaty. Respondents were then asked to agree or disagree with this statement: "President Reagan is well known for his anticommunism, so if he thinks this is a good deal, it must be." Analysis of the responses showed that hard-liners who agreed with the statement were nearly twice as likely to approve of the treaty as those who were unmoved by Reagan's involvement. The researcher concluded that "a highly conciliatory move by a president known for long-standing opposition to just such an action" can override expected sources of opposition among the public.[81] The implication is that another president, such as Jimmy Carter or even George Bush—much less Bill Clinton the antiwar protester—could not have won over the hard-liners.

The ability of political leaders to influence public opinion has been enhanced enormously by the growth of the broadcast media, especially television.[82] The majoritarian model of democracy assumes that government officials respond to public opinion; but the evidence is substantial that this causal sequence is reversed, that public opinion responds to the actions of government officials.[83] If this is true, how much potential is there for public opinion to be manipulated by political leaders through the mass media? We examine the manipulative potential of the mass media in the next chapter.

SUMMARY   Public opinion does not rule in America. On most issues, it merely sets general boundaries for government policy. The shape of the distribution of opinion (skewed, bimodal, or normal) indicates how sharply the public is divided. Bimodal distributions harbor the greatest potential for political conflict. The stability of a distribution over time indicates how settled people are in their opinions. Because most Americans' ideological opinions are normally distributed around the moderate category and have been for decades, government policies can vary from left to right over time without provoking severe political conflict.

People form their values through the process of political socialization. The most important socialization agents in childhood and young adulthood are family, school, community, and peers. Members of the same social group tend to experience similar socialization processes and thus to adopt similar values. People in different social groups that hold different values often express vastly different opinions. Differences in education, race, and religion tend to produce sharper divisions of opinion today on questions of order and equality than do differences in income, region, or ethnicity.

Most people do not think about politics in ideological terms. When asked to do so by pollsters, however, they readily classify themselves along a liberal-conservative continuum. Many respondents choose the middle category, moderate, because the choice is safe. Many others choose it because they have liberal views on some issues and conservative views on others. Their political orientation is better captured by a two-dimensional framework that analyzes ideology according to the values of freedom, order, and equality. Responses to the survey questions we used to establish our ideological typology divide the American electorate almost equally among liberals, conservatives, libertarians, and communitarians. The quarter of the public that gave liberal responses—favoring government action to promote equality but not to impose order—was matched by an equal portion who gave the opposite, conservative responses. Similarly, the somewhat larger group of communitarians, who wanted government to impose both order and equality, was opposed by a smaller group of libertarians, who wanted government to do neither.

In addition to ideological orientation, many other factors enter the process of forming political opinions. When individuals stand to benefit or suffer from proposed government policies, they usually base their opinions of these policies on self-interest. When citizens lack information on which to base their opinions, they usually respond anyway, which leads to substantial fluctuations in poll results, depending on how questions are worded and intervening events. The various factors that impinge on the process of forming political opinions can be mapped out within an opinion schema, a network of beliefs and attitudes about a particular topic. The schema image helps us visualize the complex process of forming opinions. This process is not completely idiosyncratic, however: people tend to organize their schemas according to broader ideological thinking. In the absence of information, respondents are particularly susceptible to cues of support or opposition from political leaders, communicated through the mass media.

Which model of democracy, the majoritarian or the pluralist, is correct in its assumptions about public opinion? Sometimes, the public shows clear and settled opinions on government policy, conforming to the majoritarian model. However, public opinion is often not firmly grounded in knowledge and may be unstable on given issues. Moreover, powerful groups often divide on what they want government to do. The lack of consensus leaves politicians with a great deal of latitude in enacting specific policies, a finding that conforms to the pluralist model. Of course, politicians' actions are closely scrutinized by journalists reporting in the mass media. We turn to the effect on politics of this scrutiny in Chapter 6.

Key Terms

public opinion	normal distribution	"old" ethnicity	self-interest principle
skewed distribution	stable distribution	"new" ethnicity	opinion schema
bimodal distribution	political socialization	socioeconomic status	

Selected Readings

Delli Carpini, Michael X., and Scott Keeter. *What Americans Know About Politics and Why It Matters.* New Haven, Conn.: Yale University Press, 1996. A comprehensive review and analysis of the public's responses to thousands of factual questions about political processes and institutions, public figures, political parties and groups, and public policies.

Herbst, Susan. *Numbered Voices: How Opinion Polling Has Shaped American Politics.* Chicago: University of Chicago Press, 1993. Herbst explores the history of public opinion in the United States, illustrated with case studies. She argues that the use of opinion polls often narrows the political debate, slighting other, more important issues.

Mayer, William G. *The Changing American Mind: How and Why American Public Opinion Changed Between 1960 and 1988.* Ann Arbor: University of Michigan Press, 1992. The subtitle describes the book. Mayer finds that the public has become more liberal on some issues and more conservative on others. Most changes, he contends, are simply due to people's changing their minds after reflecting on the issues and the politics surrounding them.

Page, Benjamin I., and Robert Y. Shapiro. *The Rational Public.* Chicago: University of Chicago Press, 1992. Two experts in the field analyze more than one thousand poll questions on public policy that were repeated in identical form in at least two national surveys. After aggregating the individual responses and studying overall patterns of public opinion, they conclude that the public is indeed rational, demonstrating strong evidence for their claim.

Stimson, James A. *Public Opinion in America: Mood, Cycles, & Swings.* Boulder, Colo.: Westview, 1992. The result of a massive study of more than one thousand survey questions from 1956 to 1989, this book charts the drift of public opinion from liberal in the 1950s to conservative at the end of the 1970s and back toward liberal in the 1980s.

Traugott, Michael W., and Paul J. Lavrakas. *The Voter's Guide to Election Polls.* Chatham, N.J.: Chatham House, 1996. A guide for evaluating election polls, including sampling, interviewing, questionnaires, and data analysis. Done in a question-and-answer format.

World Wide Web Resources

National Opinion Research Center. NORC conducts the well-known "General Social Survey." This site describes some studies underway and discusses the statistics and methodology of survey research.

Pew Research Center for The People & The Press. "We are an independent opinion research group that studies attitudes toward the press, politics, and public policy issues. We are best known for regular national surveys that measure public attentiveness to major news stories, and for our polling that charts trends in values and fundamental political and social attitudes."

The Gallup Organization World Wide Web Server. George Gallup founded his polling organization in the United States in the 1930s, and the Gallup Poll is now an international institution. This site permits searching the *Gallup Newsletter Archives* for press releases of past surveys. You can also retrieve some results from the latest political polls.

`<www.gallup.com/index.html>`

   Roper Center for Public Opinion Research. Located at the University of Connecticut, this center was founded by Elmo Roper, a contemporary of George Gallup. This site offers a powerful question-retrieval system, but you will need access to the Lexis/Nexis subscription service to use it. Some colleges subscribe to that service.

`<www.lib.uconn.edu/RoperCenter/>`

chapter

6

The Media

● ● ● ● ● ● ● ● ● ● ●

IN OCTOBER 1993, the whole world watched the body of an American soldier being dragged through the streets of Mogadishu, Somalia. The unidentified soldier was killed in a disastrous attempt to capture General Farah Aidid, the Somali warlord wanted for his role in killing twenty-four U.N. troops stationed there to keep the peace among the warring factions. The grisly pictures of the American corpse flashed across a global satellite network, along with a television interview of another American soldier captured in the raid on Aidid's hideout. Viewers saw the bloody face and heard the fearful voice of Chief Warrant Officer Michael Durant, held prisoner somewhere in Mogadishu. Reacting to these images of death and injury in a faraway land, the American public clamored for the removal of U.S. soldiers from Somalia. Also moved by the television coverage, President Bill Clinton said, "I'm just not going to have those kids killed for nothing."[1] Revamping his policy on Somalia, he promised to remove U.S. troops in six months—and then he did so.

The public and the president were not the only ones who drew conclusions from the humiliating television images. Our friends abroad feared that the United States would lapse into isolationism and no longer play the role of superpower.[2] Our foes saw the United States as lacking the stomach for military confrontation, and they openly defied U.S. policies and taunted the American government. Later that October, when troops were sent to assist Haiti's return to democracy, armed supporters of the military government there prevented the U.S. ship from landing, threatening a repeat of our Somalia experience. Early the next month, the speaker of the Iranian parliament told an anti-American rally in Iran, "You saw the American soldier bound and dragged down the street. This is a sign of a United States humiliated and stuck in a quagmire."[3]

The political power of television, once largely limited to national audiences, now has a global range. Via satellite, Americans can watch the world—and the world can watch America. In the formerly communist country of Hungary, for example, viewers can now choose from several American TV news programs. Cable News Network (CNN) International broadcasts news twenty-four hours a day in Hungary and more than two hundred other countries. Citizens in Budapest can also watch the CBS "Evening News," ABC News's "Nightline" (both taped the previous night and broadcast every morning on Britain's Sky News channel), and the NBC "Nightly News" (rerun the next morning on Britain's Super Channel, owned by NBC).[4] In addition, from Budapest to Toyko and around the world,

As Seen on TV

In the fall of 1993, television viewers all over the world saw the battered face of Chief Warrant Officer Michael Durant, who was being held prisoner after a failed U.S. military raid on the headquarters of a local warlord in Mogadishu, Somalia. His captors forced Durant to appear on camera to pressure the United States to withdraw its forces from Somalia. The television image helped to accomplish just that.

citizens can connect their computers to the Internet and not only receive news but also exchange comments on U.S. politics. Before global television and the World Wide Web, the president and Congress had to deal only with news broadcasts in the United States. Now they must confront the international implications of the media and the information superhighway.

There is no doubt that the media affected American foreign policy in Somalia. After all, President George Bush had sent U.S. troops there in 1991 in response to heart-rending pictures of children starving during the civil war. Two years later, frightful pictures of killed and captured U.S. soldiers put pressure on President Clinton to pull them out. Decades earlier, the unfettered television coverage of the horrors of the Vietnam War contributed to antiwar sentiment and pressures for withdrawal. Having learned how images of war can sway public opinion, the military subsequently developed policies for controlling media coverage of combat zones. It used these policies in dealing with reporters during the Persian Gulf conflict of 1991.

When the ground war in Kuwait began, the Pentagon restricted news coverage, even suspending regular press briefings. To get around these restrictions, some journalists began traveling with Saudi and Egyptian forces to cover the war. Other journalists tried to operate on their own and were captured by Iraqi forces (but eventually released). Ultimately, the ground campaign was such a success that the military repealed its blackout to spread the good news. If the fighting had been fierce, the public would have been told less and told later. Many journalists claim that our government has infringed on freedom of the press during its last three international conflicts. Is this a cause for public concern, or does open press coverage of foreign conflicts unduly hamper the military's conduct of war and the pursuit of order?

Freedom of the press is essential to democratic government, but the news media also complicate the governing process. What is the nature of the media in America? Who uses the media, and what do they learn? Do the media promote or frustrate democratic ideals? Does freedom of the press conflict with the values of order or equality? What, if anything, should or can be done domestically about limiting the use of the Internet by hate groups? In this chapter, we describe the origin and growth of the media, assess their objectivity, and examine their influence on politics.

PEOPLE, GOVERNMENT, AND COMMUNICATIONS

"We never talk anymore" is a common lament of couples who are not getting along very well. In politics, too, citizens and their government need to communicate in order to get along well. *Communication* is the process of transmitting information from one individual or group to another. *Mass communication* is the process by which information is transmitted to large, heterogeneous, widely dispersed audiences. The term **mass media** refers to the means for communicating to these audiences. The mass media are commonly divided into two types:

- *Print media* communicate information through the publication of words and pictures on paper. Prime examples of print media are daily newspapers and popular magazines. Because books seldom have a large circulation relative to the general population, they are not typically classified as a mass medium.

- *Broadcast media* communicate information electronically, through sounds and images. Prime examples of broadcast media are radio and television.

Although telephones also transmit sounds and computer networks can transmit words, sounds, and images, both are usually used for more targeted communications and so are not typically included in the term *mass media*. Modern politics also utilize the *fax* (facsimile images sent by telephone) and computers linked over the *Internet*, however. We refer to these as *group media*, instead of mass media, and we consider them separately below.

Our focus here is on the role of the media in promoting communication from government to its citizens and from citizens to their government. In totalitarian governments, information flows more freely in one direction (from government to the people) than the other. In democratic governments, information must flow freely in both directions; a democratic government can respond to public opinion only if its citizens can make their opinions known. Moreover, the electorate can hold government officials accountable for their actions only if voters know what the government has done, is doing, and plans to do. Because the mass media (and increasingly the group media) provide the major channels for this two-way flow of information, they have the dual capability of reflecting and shaping our political views.

The media are not the only means of communication between citizens and government. As we discussed in Chapter 5, various agents of socialization (especially schools) function as "linkage mechanisms" that promote such communication. In the next four chapters we will discuss other mechanisms for communication: voting, political parties, campaigning in elections, and interest groups. Certain linkage mechanisms communicate better in one direction than in the other. Primary and secondary schools, for example, commonly instruct young citizens about government rules and symbols, whereas voting sends messages from citizens to government. Parties, campaigns, and interest groups foster communications in both directions. The media, however, are the only linkage mechanisms that *specialize* in communication.

Although this chapter concentrates on political uses of the four most prominent mass media—newspapers, magazines, radio, and television—political content can also be transmitted through other mass media, such as recordings and motion pictures. Rock acts such as Peter Gabriel and U2 often express political ideas in their music, as do rappers such as the late Tupac Shakur and Gangsta N.I.P.[5] Motion pictures often convey particularly intense political messages. The 1976 film *All the President's Men*, about the two *Washington Post* reporters who doggedly exposed the Watergate scandal, dramatized a seamy side of political life that contrasted sharply with an idealized view of the presidency. The powerful 1995 Oscar-winning drama *Dead Man Walking* explored issues surrounding the death penalty, from both sides—killer and victim.

THE DEVELOPMENT OF THE MASS MEDIA IN THE UNITED STATES

Although the record and film industries sometimes convey political messages, they are primarily in the business of entertainment. Our focus here is on mass media in the news industry—on print and broadcast journalism. The growth of the country, technological inventions, and shifting political attitudes about the scope of government—as well as trends in entertainment—have shaped the development of the news media in the United States.

Newspapers

Many newspapers have gone modern and gone "online." Editor and Publisher Online Newspapers will direct you to over 1,000 newspapers across the world that you can access through the Internet. <www.mediainfo.com/ephome/npaper/nphtm/online.htm>

When the Revolutionary War broke out in 1775, thirty-seven newspapers (all weeklies) were publishing in the colonies.[6] They had small circulations—they were not mass media but group media. The first newspapers were mainly political organs, financed by parties and advocating party causes. Newspapers did not move toward independent ownership and large circulations until the 1830s.

According to the 1880 census, 971 daily newspapers and 8,633 weekly newspapers and periodicals were then published in the United States. Most larger cities had many newspapers—New York had twenty-nine papers; Philadelphia, twenty-four; San Francisco, twenty-one; and Chicago, eighteen. Competition for readers grew fierce among the big-city dailies. Toward the latter part of the nineteenth century, imaginative publishers sought to win readers by entertaining them with photographs, comic strips, sports sections, advice to the lovelorn, and stories of sex and crime.

By the 1960s, under pressure from both radio and television, intense competition among big-city dailies had nearly disappeared. New York had only three papers left by 1969, and this pattern was repeated in every large city in the country. By 1993, only thirty-six U.S. towns or cities had two or more competing dailies under separate ownership.[7] The net result is that

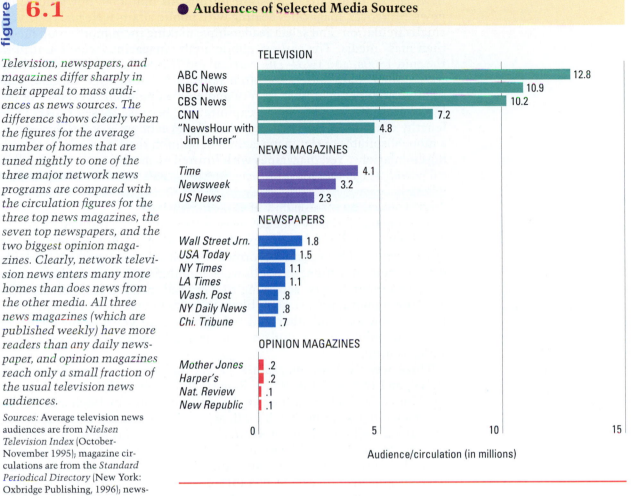

figure 6.1

● **Audiences of Selected Media Sources**

Television, newspapers, and magazines differ sharply in their appeal to mass audiences as news sources. The difference shows clearly when the figures for the average number of homes that are tuned nightly to one of the three major network news programs are compared with the circulation figures for the three top news magazines, the seven top newspapers, and the two biggest opinion magazines. Clearly, network television news enters many more homes than does news from the other media. All three news magazines (which are published weekly) have more readers than any daily newspaper, and opinion magazines reach only a small fraction of the usual television news audiences.

Sources: Average television news audiences are from *Nielsen Television Index* (October–November 1995); magazine circulations are from the *Standard Periodical Directory* (New York: Oxbridge Publishing, 1996); newspaper circulations are from the *Editor & Publisher International Yearbook* (New York: Editor & Publisher, 1995); NewsHour audience was obtained by telephone from the Public Broadcasting Service.

the number of newspapers per person has dropped about 33 percent since 1950.[8]

The daily paper with the biggest circulation in the mid-1990s (about 1.8 million copies) is the *Wall Street Journal*, which appeals to a national audience because of its extensive coverage of business news and close analysis of political news. *USA Today*, the only paper designed for national distribution, is second (1.6 million). The *New York Times*, which many journalists consider the best newspaper in the country, sells about a million copies, placing it third in circulation (see Figure 6.1).[9] In comparison, the weekly *National Enquirer*, which carries stories about people who return from the dead or marry aliens from outer space, sells about 2.5 million copies. Neither the *Times* nor the *Wall Street Journal* carries comic strips, which no doubt limits their mass appeal. They also print more political news and news analyses than most readers want to confront.

Magazines

Magazines differ from newspapers not only in the frequency of their publication but also in the nature of their coverage. Even news-oriented magazines cover the news in a more specialized manner than do daily newspapers. Many magazines are forums for opinions, not strictly for news. Moreover, magazines dealing with public affairs have had relatively small circulations and select readerships, making them more group media than mass media. The earliest public affairs magazines were founded in the mid-1800s, and two—*The Nation* and *Harper's*—are still publishing today. Such magazines were often politically influential, especially in framing arguments against slavery and later in publishing exposés of political corruption and business exploitation. Because these exposés were lengthy critiques of the existing political and economic order, they found a more hospitable outlet in magazines of opinion than in newspapers with big circulations. Yet, magazines with limited readerships can wield political power. Magazines may influence **attentive policy elites**—group leaders who follow news in specific areas—and thus influence mass opinion indirectly through a **two-step flow of communication.**

As scholars originally viewed the two-step flow, it conformed ideally to the pluralist model of democracy. Once group leaders (for instance, union or industry leaders) became informed of political developments, they informed their more numerous followers, mobilizing them to apply pressure on government. Today, according to a revised interpretation of the two-step flow, policy elites are more likely to influence public opinion (not just their "followers") and other leaders by airing their views in the media. In this view, public deliberation on issues is highly mediated by these professional communicators.[10]

Three weekly news magazines—*Time* (founded in 1923), *Newsweek* (1933), and *U.S. News & World Report* (1933)—enjoy big circulations in the United States (2.3 million to 4.1 million copies in 1995) and can be considered mass media. Their audience is tiny, however, compared with the fifteen million readers of *Reader's Digest*. In contrast to these mainstream, "capitalist" publications, a newer, "alternative" press is more critical of the prevailing power structure. Such periodicals as *Mother Jones* have spearheaded investigations into possible government malfeasance, such as the arms-for-hostages deal in the 1985 Iran-Contra affair.[11] As shown in Figure 6.1, *Mother Jones* has a bigger readership than mainstream opinion magazines such as the *National Review* and the *New Republic*.

Radio

Listen to two of the best daily public affairs programs in the nation—"Morning Edition" at the beginning of the day and "All Things Considered" during the afternoon. National Public Radio On-Line requires installation of the RealAudio player to hear the programs.

`<www.npr.org/>`

Regularly scheduled, continuous radio broadcasting began in 1920 on stations KDKA in Pittsburgh and WWJ in Detroit. Both stations claim to be the first commercial station, and both broadcast returns of the 1920 election of President Warren G. Harding. The first radio network, the National Broadcasting Company (NBC), was formed in 1926. Soon four networks were on the air, transforming radio into a national medium by linking thousands of local stations. Millions of Americans were able to hear President Franklin D. Roosevelt deliver his first "fireside chat" in 1933. However, the first coast-to-coast broadcast did not occur until 1937, when listeners were shocked by an eyewitness report of the explosion of the dirigible *Hindenburg* in New Jersey.

Because the public could sense reporters' personalities over radio in a way they could not in print, broadcast journalists quickly became house-

hold names. Edward R. Murrow, one of the most famous radio news personalities, broadcast news of the merger of Germany and Austria by short-wave radio from Vienna in 1938 and later gave stirring reports of German air raids on London during World War II. Today, radio is less salient for live coverage of events than for "talk radio," often criticized for polarizing politics by publicizing extreme views.[12]

Television

Experiments with television began in France in the early 1900s. By 1940, twenty-three television stations were operating in the United States, and—repeating radio's feat of twenty years earlier—two stations broadcast the returns of a presidential election, Roosevelt's 1940 reelection.[13] The onset of World War II paralyzed the development of television technology, but growth in the medium exploded after the war. By 1950, ninety-eight stations were covering the major population centers of the country, although only 9 percent of American households had television sets.

The first commercial color broadcast came in 1951, as did the first coast-to-coast broadcast—President Harry Truman's address to delegates at the Japanese peace treaty conference in San Francisco. That same year, Democratic senator Estes Kefauver of Tennessee called for public television coverage of his committee's investigation into organized crime. For weeks, people with television sets invited their neighbors to watch underworld crime figures answering questions before the camera. And Kefauver became one of the first politicians to benefit from television coverage. Previously unknown and representing a small state, he nevertheless won many of the 1952 Democratic presidential primaries and became the Democrats' vice-presidential candidate in 1956.

**Watching the President
on Television**

*Television revolutionized
presidential politics by allowing millions of voters to look
closely at the candidates'
faces and judge their personalities in the process. This close-
up of John Kennedy during a
debate with Richard Nixon in
the 1960 campaign showed
Kennedy to good advantage.
Close-ups of Nixon, on the
other hand, made him look as
though he needed a shave.
Kennedy won one of the closest elections in history; his
good looks on television may
have made the difference.*

By 1960, eighty-seven percent of U.S. households had television sets. By 1990, the United States had more than one thousand commercial and three hundred public television stations, and virtually every household (98 percent) had TV. Today, television claims by far the biggest news audience of all the mass media (see Figure 6.1). From television's beginnings, most stations were linked into networks founded by three of the four major radio networks. Many early anchormen of television network news programs came to the medium with names already made famous during their years of experience as radio broadcast journalists. But now that the news audience could actually see the broadcasters as well as hear them, news personalities (like Dan Rather and Peter Jennings) became instantly recognizable celebrities.

MODERN FORMS OF GROUP MEDIA

The revolution in electronics during the last quarter of the twentieth century produced two new technologies—the fax and the Internet—that have been readily adapted to politics. Neither are "mass" media that communicate with the general public, however. They are called **group media**—communications technologies used primarily within groups of people with common interests.

Facsimile Transmissions

Believe it or not, a technique for scanning an image to generate signals that could reproduce a facsimile (copy) of the image on electrochemical recording paper was invented in 1843. Eventually, the idea was adapted to the telephone, and by the early twentieth century it was used commercially by newspapers to transmit photographs, called Wirephotos. After World War II, the Japanese seized on the technology to transmit their complex written characters. They developed the modern "fax" machine in the 1970s and have maintained a virtual monopoly on its manufacture.

The fax machine has become standard communications equipment in practical politics. Campaign managers routinely communicate with campaign workers and media representatives via fax, and it is a major medium for communication among political officeholders in Washington.[14] Interest groups frequently rely on automated fax messages concerning issues before Congress—as many as ten thousand a night—sent automatically by computers to sympathizers across the country.[15] Increasingly, recipients of these faxes respond by faxing fervent messages of opposition or support to their congressional representatives, simulating a ground swell of public opinion—despite the fact that only 8 percent of U.S. homes had fax machines in 1995 (see High-Tech Lobbying, Chapter 10).[16]

The Internet

What we today call the Internet began in 1969 when, with support from the U.S. Defense Department's Advanced Research Projects Agency, computers at four universities were linked to form ARPANET. By 1972, thirty-seven universities were connected over ARPANET. Following the growth of other distinct computer networks (such as BITNET, designed for IBM mainframes), new communications standards worked out in 1983 allowed these networks to be interlinked, creating the Internet.[17]

In its early years, the Internet was used mainly to transmit messages, known as electronic mail, or *e-mail*, among researchers. In 1991, a group of European physicists devised a standardized system for encoding and transmitting a wide range of materials, including graphics and photographs, over the Internet, and the World Wide Web (WWW) was born. Now anyone on the Internet with a computer program called a "browser" can access Web "pages" from around the world. In January 1993 there were only fifty Web sites in existence.[18] Today there are many thousands of sites and millions of WWW users.

Like the fax, the Internet was soon utilized in political life. By 1995 there was enough political material on the Internet to fill a 375-page book, *Politics on the Net*.[19] The book's author, Bill Mann, classifies this material as "real news" reported by professionals, opinions and debates expressed by and involving citizens, publications by governments at all levels, and statements from political parties and other political organizations. More recently, the Internet has been proposed as a systematic means of registering citizens' opinions or votes. However, only 21 percent of respondents in a 1996 national survey said that they ever used a computer at work, school, or home to connect with other computers on the Internet, and only 3 percent ever obtained information on the presidential campaign from the Internet.[20] Of course, these percentages will grow over time.

PRIVATE OWNERSHIP OF THE MEDIA

In the United States, people take private ownership of the media for granted. Indeed, most Americans would regard government ownership of the media as an unacceptable threat to freedom that would interfere with the "marketplace of ideas" and result in one-way communication, from government to citizens. When the government controls the news flow, the people may have little chance to learn what the government is doing or to pressure it to behave differently. Certainly that was true in the former Soviet Union. China offers another illustration of how arbitrary government control of the media can be. The Chinese government permitted televised coverage of protests for democracy in Beijing's Tiananmen Square in 1989 and then harshly reimposed censorship overnight to smother the democracy movement. (Many dissidents used fax machines to send news of the government massacre to the outside world.) Private ownership of the media offers a more stable, continuing forum for government criticism.

In other Western democracies, the print media (both newspapers and magazines) are privately owned, but the broadcast media often are not. Before the 1980s, the government owned and operated the major broadcast media in most of these countries. Now, in Western Europe, government radio and television stations compete with private stations.[21] In the United States, except for about 300 public television stations (out of about 1,400) and 300 public radio stations (out of about 5,000), the broadcast media are privately owned.

The Consequences of Private Ownership

Just as the appearance of the newscaster became important for television viewers, so did the appearance of the news itself. Television's great advantage over radio—that it shows people and events—accounts for the influence of television news coverage. It also determines, to some extent, the news that television chooses to cover. In fact, private ownership of the mass media ensures that news is selected for its audience appeal.

Private ownership of both the print and broadcast media gives the news industry in America more political freedom than any other in the world, but it also makes the media more dependent on advertising revenues to cover their costs and make a profit. Because advertising rates are tied to audience size, the news operations of the mass media in America must appeal to the audiences they serve.

Of the seven hours or so that the average American spends watching television every day, only about ninety minutes are devoted to news or documentaries; the remainder goes to entertainment, movies, and sports.[22] More than 60 million copies of newspapers circulate daily, but more than 60 percent of their content is advertising.[23] For the space remaining, news must compete with fashion reports, comics, movie and restaurant reviews, and so on. Only a portion of newspaper space is devoted to news of any sort, and only a fraction of that news—excluding stories about fires, robberies, murder trials, and the like—can be classified as political. The news function of the mass media in the United States cannot be separated from the entertainment function. Entertainment increases audiences, which increases advertising revenues. The profit motive creates constant pressure to increase the ratio of entertainment news programs or to make the news itself more "entertaining."

You might think that a story's political significance, educational value, or broad social importance determines whether the media cover it. The sad truth is that most potential news stories are not judged by such grand criteria. The primary criterion of a story's **newsworthiness** is usually its audience appeal, which is judged according to its potential impact on readers or listeners, its degree of sensationalism (exemplified by violence, con-

6.2 ● **Local Television: No News Is Happy News**

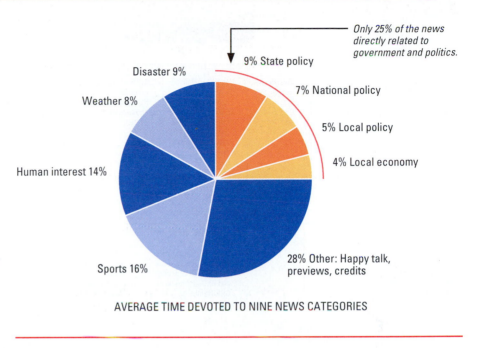

To determine the political content of local television news broadcasts, Robert Entman analyzed the content of local news on two television stations in Raleigh-Durham, North Carolina, during two full weeks in 1986. He found that reporting on local policy issues averaged less than two minutes per half-hour program. That amounts to about 250 words. The stations devoted more time to weather and twice as much time to sports. "Happy talk," previews of forthcoming programs, and credits accounted for the biggest portion of the half-hour programs. The total coverage of all substantive policy or political matters averaged about seven minutes per broadcast. Unfortunately, far more people regularly watch local than national news in the evening (77 percent to 60 percent).

Sources: Robert M. Entman, *Democracy Without Citizens* (New York: Oxford University Press, 1989), p. 111. Copyright © 1989 by Robert M. Entman. Used by permission of Oxford University Press, Inc. The stations were WRAL and WTVD in Raleigh-Durham, North Carolina. Also "Talk Radio," *American Enterprise,* September/October 1993, p. 96.

flict, disaster, or scandal), its treatment of familiar people or life situations, its close-to-home character, and its timeliness.[24]

The importance of audience appeal has led the news industry to calculate its audience carefully. (The bigger the audience, the higher the advertising rates.) The print media can easily determine the size of their circulations through sales figures, but the broadcast media must estimate their audience through various sampling techniques. Because both print and broadcast media might be tempted to inflate their estimated audience (to tell advertisers that they reach more people than they actually do), a separate industry has developed to rate audience size impartially. These ratings reports have resulted in a "ratings game," in which the media try to increase their ratings by adjusting the delivery or content of their news. Some local television stations favor "happy talk" on their news broadcasts—breezy on-the-air exchanges among announcers, reporters, sportscasters, and meteorologists. Other stations use the "eyewitness" approach, showing a preponderance of film footage with human interest, humorous, or violent content. Many stations combine the two, often pleasing viewers (most of whom watch local news more regularly than national news) but perhaps not informing them properly, as illustrated in Figure 6.2. Even the three mighty television networks have departed from their traditionally high journalistic standards, following their acquisition since 1986 by other corporations: Disney/Capital Cities acquired ABC, General Electric bought NBC, and Westinghouse absorbed CBS. All three major television networks are now cogs in mighty conglomerates with economic interests far broader than the news (see Figure 6.3).

From 1980 to 1990, ABC, CBS, and NBC suffered severe losses in their prime-time audience, dropping from nearly 90 to only 63 percent of all

6.3 ● Who Owns the News?

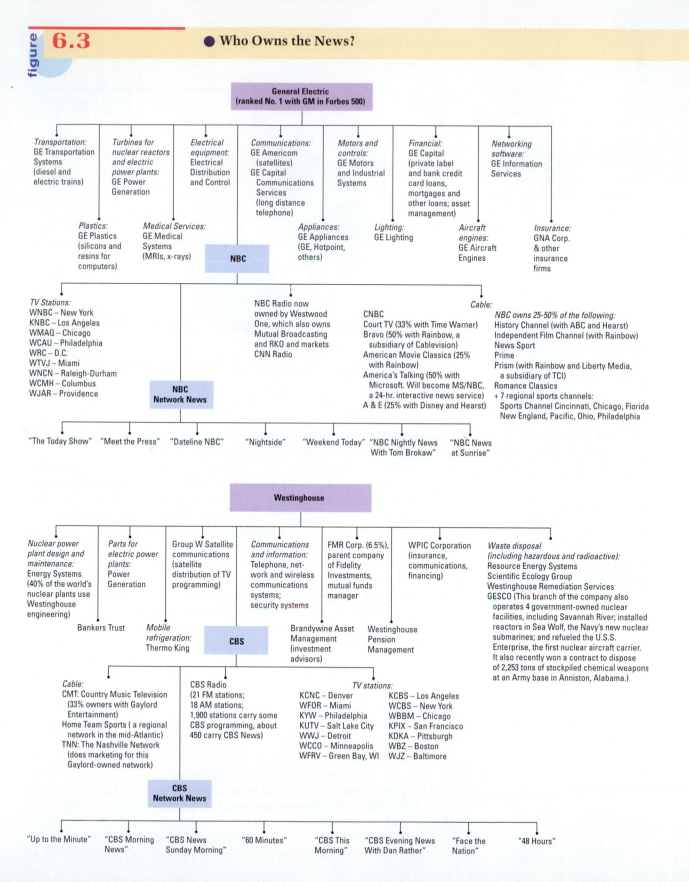

General Electric
(ranked No. 1 with GM in Forbes 500)

Transportation:
GE Transportation
Systems
(diesel and
electric trains)

*Turbines for
nuclear reactors
and electric
power plants:*
GE Power
Generation

*Electrical
equipment:*
Electrical
Distribution
and Control

Communications:
GE Americom
(satellites)
GE Capital
Communications
Services
(long distance
telephone)

*Motors and
controls:*
GE Motors
and Industrial
Systems

Financial:
GE Capital
(private label
and bank credit
card loans,
mortgages and
other loans; asset
management)

*Networking
software:*
GE Information
Services

Plastics:
GE Plastics
(silicons and
resins for
computers)

Medical Services:
GE Medical
Systems
(MRIs, x-rays)

NBC

Appliances:
GE Appliances
(GE, Hotpoint,
others)

Lighting:
GE Lighting

*Aircraft
engines:*
GE Aircraft
Engines

Insurance:
GNA Corp.
& other
insurance
firms

TV Stations:
WNBC – New York
KNBC – Los Angeles
WMAQ – Chicago
WCAU – Philadelphia
WRC – D.C.
WTVJ – Miami
WNCN – Raleigh-Durham
WCMH – Columbus
WJAR – Providence

NBC Radio now
owned by Westwood
One, which also owns
Mutual Broadcasting
and RKO and markets
CNN Radio

Cable:
CNBC
Court TV (33% with Time Warner)
Bravo (50% with Rainbow, a
    subsidiary of Cablevision)
American Movie Classics (25%
    with Rainbow)
America's Talking (50% with
    Microsoft. Will become MS/NBC,
    a 24-hr. interactive news service)
A & E (25% with Disney and Hearst)

NBC owns 25-50% of the following:
History Channel (with ABC and Hearst)
Independent Film Channel (with Rainbow)
News Sport
Prime
Prism (with Rainbow and Liberty Media,
    a subsidiary of TCI)
Romance Classics
+ 7 regional sports channels:
    Sports Channel Cincinnati, Chicago, Florida
    New England, Pacific, Ohio, Philadelphia

**NBC
Network News**

"The Today Show" "Meet the Press" "Dateline NBC" "Nightside" "Weekend Today" "NBC Nightly News
With Tom Brokaw" "NBC News
at Sunrise"

Westinghouse

*Nuclear power
plant design and
maintenance:*
Energy Systems
(40% of the world's
nuclear plants use
Westinghouse
engineering)

*Parts for
electric power
plants:*
Power
Generation

Group W Satellite
communications
(satellite
distribution of TV
programming)

*Communications
and information:*
Telephone, net-
work and wireless
communications
systems;
security systems

FMR Corp. (6.5%),
parent company
of Fidelity
Investments,
mutual funds
manager

WPIC Corporation
(insurance,
communications,
financing)

*Waste disposal
(including hazardous and radioactive):*
Resource Energy Systems
Scientific Ecology Group
Westinghouse Remediation Services
GESCO (This branch of the company also
operates 4 government-owned nuclear
facilities, including Savannah River; installed
reactors in Sea Wolf, the Navy's new nuclear
submarines; and refueled the U.S.S.
Enterprise, the first nuclear aircraft carrier.
It also recently won a contract to dispose
of 2,253 tons of stockpiled chemical weapons
at an Army base in Anniston, Alabama.)

Bankers Trust

*Mobile
refrigeration:*
Thermo King

CBS

Brandywine Asset
Management
(investment
advisors)

Westinghouse
Pension
Management

Cable:
CMT: Country Music Television
(33% owners with Gaylord
Entertainment)
Home Team Sports (a regional
network in the mid-Atlantic)
TNN: The Nashville Network
(does marketing for this
Gaylord-owned network)

CBS Radio
(21 FM stations;
18 AM stations;
1,900 stations carry some
CBS programming, about
450 carry CBS News)

TV stations:
KCNC – Denver
WFOR – Miami
KYW – Philadelphia
KUTV – Salt Lake City
WWJ – Detroit
WCCO – Minneapolis
WFRV – Green Bay, WI

KCBS – Los Angeles
WCBS – New York
WBBM – Chicago
KPIX – San Francisco
KDKA – Pittsburgh
WBZ – Boston
WJZ – Baltimore

**CBS
Network News**

"Up to the Minute" "CBS Morning
News" "CBS News
Sunday Morning" "60 Minutes" "CBS This
Morning" "CBS Evening News
With Dan Rather" "Face the
Nation" "48 Hours"

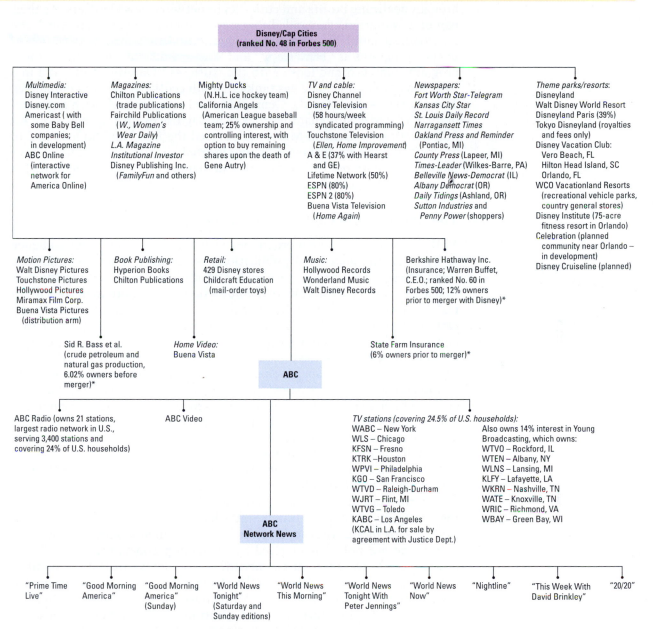

Disney/Cap Cities
(ranked No. 48 in Forbes 500)

Multimedia:
Disney Interactive
Disney.com
Americast (with
  some Baby Bell
  companies;
  in development)
ABC Online
  (interactive
  network for
  America Online)

Magazines:
Chilton Publications
  (trade publications)
Fairchild Publications
  (*W., Women's
  Wear Daily*)
*L.A. Magazine
Institutional Investor*
Disney Publishing Inc.
  (*FamilyFun* and others)

Mighty Ducks
  (N.H.L. ice hockey team)
California Angels
  (American League baseball
  team; 25% ownership and
  controlling interest, with
  option to buy remaining
  shares upon the death of
  Gene Autry)

TV and cable:
Disney Channel
Disney Television
  (58 hours/week
  syndicated programming)
Touchstone Television
  (*Ellen, Home Improvement*)
A & E (37% with Hearst
  and GE)
Lifetime Network (50%)
ESPN (80%)
ESPN 2 (80%)
Buena Vista Television
  (*Home Again*)

Newspapers:
*Fort Worth Star-Telegram
Kansas City Star
St. Louis Daily Record
Narragansett Times
Oakland Press and Reminder*
  (Pontiac, MI)
County Press (Lapeer, MI)
Times-Leader (Wilkes-Barre, PA)
Belleville News-Democrat (IL)
Albany Democrat (OR)
Daily Tidings (Ashland, OR)
Sutton Industries and
  Penny Power (shoppers)

Theme parks/resorts:
Disneyland
Walt Disney World Resort
Disneyland Paris (39%)
Tokyo Disneyland (royalties
  and fees only)
Disney Vacation Club:
  Vero Beach, FL
  Hilton Head Island, SC
  Orlando, FL
WCO Vacationland Resorts
  (recreational vehicle parks,
  country general stores)
Disney Institute (75-acre
  fitness resort in Orlando)
Celebration (planned
  community near Orlando –
  in development)
Disney Cruiseline (planned)

Motion Pictures:
Walt Disney Pictures
Touchstone Pictures
Hollywood Pictures
Miramax Film Corp.
Buena Vista Pictures
  (distribution arm)

Book Publishing:
Hyperion Books
Chilton Publications

Retail:
429 Disney stores
Childcraft Education
  (mail-order toys)

Music:
Hollywood Records
Wonderland Music
Walt Disney Records

Berkshire Hathaway Inc.
(Insurance; Warren Buffet,
C.E.O.; ranked No. 60 in
Forbes 500; 12% owners
prior to merger with Disney)*

Sid R. Bass et al.
(crude petroleum and
natural gas production,
6.02% owners before
merger)*

Home Video:
Buena Vista

State Farm Insurance
(6% owners prior to merger)*

ABC

ABC Radio (owns 21 stations,
largest radio network in U.S.,
serving 3,400 stations and
covering 24% of U.S. households)

ABC Video

TV stations (covering 24.5% of U.S. households):
WABC – New York
WLS – Chicago
KFSN – Fresno
KTRK –Houston
WPVI – Philadelphia
KGO – San Francisco
WTVD – Raleigh-Durham
WJRT – Flint, MI
WTVG – Toledo
KABC – Los Angeles
(KCAL in L.A. for sale by
agreement with Justice Dept.)

Also owns 14% interest in Young
Broadcasting, which owns:
WTVO – Rockford, IL
WTEN – Albany, NY
WLNS – Lansing, MI
KLFY – Lafayette, LA
WKRN – Nashville, TN
WATE – Knoxville, TN
WRIC – Richmond, VA
WBAY – Green Bay, WI

ABC
Network News

"Prime Time
Live"

"Good Morning
America"

"Good Morning
America"
(Sunday)

"World News
Tonight"
(Saturday and
Sunday editions)

"World News
This Morning"

"World News
Tonight With
Peter Jennings"

"World News
Now"

"Nightline"

"This Week With
David Brinkley"

"20/20"

* Ownership percentages are not finalized. Because 82% of stockholders opted for shares and not cash, Disney is still
working out with shareholders whether they will be paid in fractional shares or with partial cash payments.

After the passage of the Telecommunications Act of 1996, for the first time in its 130-year history, the liberal opinion magazine The Nation *published a centerfold. It depicted the three major news networks as segments of industrial and entertainment conglomerates. (The original drawing also included Time-Warner, which owns CNN, but it is omitted here for lack of space.) Mark Crispin Miller of Johns Hopkins University, who conceived the original diagram, suggests that "we are subjects of a national entertainment state" that produces our news. "Glance up from the bottom of each quarter of the chart, and see why, say, Tom Brokaw might find it difficult to introduce stories critical of nuclear power. Or why it is unlikely ABC News will ever again do an exposé of Disney's practices (as "PrimeTime Live" did in 1990)."*

Source: Mark Crispin Miller, "Free the Media," The Nation, 3 June 1996, pp. 10, 23–26. Reprinted with permission. Copyright © 1996

television viewers.[25] Increasingly, viewers have been watching cable stations or videotapes instead of network programs. Audience declines have brought declining profits and cutbacks in network news budgets. As their parent corporations demanded that news programs "pay their way," the networks succumbed to **infotainment**—mixing journalism with theater— in such programs as "Hard Copy" and "Inside Edition." Sometimes these programs play fast and loose with the truth, as "Dateline NBC" did in a 1992 broadcast on vehicle gas tanks that allegedly exploded in collisions. The program's staff rigged a General Motors pickup truck with an incendiary device to ensure that the truck would ignite in a filmed collision. An investigation by General Motors uncovered the fraud and forced NBC to apologize on the air. Instances of poor journalism and outright fraud have increased as network executives have demanded that television news become more profitable.

The Concentration of Private Ownership

Media owners can make more money either by increasing their audience or by acquiring additional publications or stations. There is a decided trend toward concentrated ownership of the media, increasing the risk that a few owners could control the news flow to promote their own political interests—much as political parties influenced the content of the earliest American newspapers. In fact, the number of *independent newspapers* has declined as newspaper chains (owners of two or more newspapers in different cities) have acquired more newspapers. Most of the more than one hundred newspaper chains in the United States today are small, owning fewer than ten papers.[26] Some are very big, however. The Gannett chain, which owns *USA Today,* with the second biggest circulation in the nation, also owns more than eighty newspapers in thirty-six states. Only about four hundred dailies are still independent; many of these papers are too small and unprofitable to invite acquisition.

At first glance, concentration of ownership does not seem to be a problem in the television industry. Although there are only three major networks, the networks usually do not own their affiliates. About half of all the communities in the United States have a choice of ten or more stations.[27] This figure suggests that the electronic media offer diverse viewpoints and are not characterized by ownership concentration. As with newspapers, however, chains sometimes own television stations in different cities, and ownership sometimes extends across different media. When it acquired CBS in 1995, Westinghouse owned TV stations in fourteen major cities and thirty-nine radio stations. In 1996, Westinghouse extended its media empire by purchasing Infinity Broadcasting, giving it a total of eighty-three AM and FM stations, many in the nation's largest markets.[28] Some people fear the concentration of media under a single owner, and government has addressed those fears by regulating media ownership, as well as various aspects of media operation.

GOVERNMENT REGULATION OF THE MEDIA

Although most of the mass media in the United States are privately owned, they do not operate free of government regulation. The broadcast media operate under more stringent regulations than the print media; initially this was because of technical aspects of broadcasting. In general, government regulation of the mass media addresses three aspects of their operation: technical considerations, ownership, and content.[29]

Technical and Ownership Regulations

In the early days of radio, stations that operated on similar frequencies in the same area often jammed each other's signals, and no one could broadcast clearly. At the broadcasters' insistence, Congress passed the Federal Radio Act (1927), which declared that the public owned the airwaves and private broadcasters could use them only by obtaining a license from the Federal Radio Commission. So, government regulation of broadcasting was not forced on the industry by socialist politicians; capitalist owners sought it to impose order on the use of the airwaves (thereby restricting others' freedom to enter broadcasting).

Seven years later, Congress passed the Federal Communications Act of 1934, a more sweeping law that regulated the broadcast and telephone industries for more than sixty years. It created the **Federal Communications Commission (FCC)**, which has five members (no more than three from the same political party) nominated by the president for terms of five years. The commissioners can be removed from office only through impeachment and conviction. Consequently, the FCC is considered an independent regulatory commission: it is insulated from political control by either the president or Congress. (We discuss independent regulatory commissions in Chapter 13.) Today, the FCC is charged with regulating interstate and international communications by radio, television, telephone, telegraph, cable, and satellite.

For six decades—as technological change made television commonplace and brought the invention of computers, fax machines, and satellite transmissions—the communications industry was regulated under the basic framework of the 1934 law that created the FCC. Pressured by businesses that wanted to exploit new electronic technologies, Congress, in a bipartisan effort, swept away most existing regulations in the Telecommunications Act of 1996. According to one member of Congress, the new act "breaks down the last remaining monopolies in the telephone and cable industries and makes possible an information revolution."[30] The *Wall Street Journal* said, "Let the telecom wars begin."[31]

The 1996 law relaxed or scrapped limitations on media ownership. For example, broadcasters were previously limited to owning only twelve TV stations and forty radio stations. Now there are no limits on the number of TV stations one company may own, just so long as their coverage doesn't extend beyond 35 percent of the market nationwide. The law set no national limits for radio ownership, and it relaxed local limits. In addition, it lifted rate regulations for cable systems, allowed cross-ownership of cable and telephone companies, and allowed local and long-distance telephone companies to compete with one another and to sell television services. As a result, the *Wall Street Journal* expected the rise of a few megacarriers that would provide all types of information and entertainment services by the twenty-first century.[32]

Although even those who wrote the law could not predict its long-range effect, the law quickly spurred even greater concentration of media ownership. US West (one of the regional "Baby Bell" telephone companies resulting from the breakup of AT&T) bought Continental Cablevision,

NYNEX (the New York and New England areas' telephone company) merged with Bell Atlantic, and Westinghouse purchased Affinity Broadcasting—all within weeks after the new law was approved. About the same time, a special issue of the opinion magazine *The Nation* warned of the dangers of "The National Entertainment State," in which the media would be under the control of a few conglomerates (see Figure 6.3).[33] In its defense, the industry argued that diversity among media news sources in America is great enough to provide citizens with a wide range of political ideas.

Regulation of Content

The First Amendment to the Constitution prohibits Congress from abridging the freedom of the press. Over time, *the press* has come to mean all the media, and the courts have decided many cases that define how far freedom of the press extends under the law. Chapter 15 discusses the most important of these cases, which are often quite complex. Although the courts have had difficulty defining obscenity, they have not included obscene expression under freedom of the press. In 1996, however, a federal court overturned an attempt to limit transmission of "indecent" (not obscene) material on the Internet, calling the attempt "profoundly repugnant to First Amendment principles."[34]

Usually the courts strike down government attempts to restrain the press from publishing or broadcasting the information, reports, or opinions it finds newsworthy. One notable exception concerns strategic information during wartime; the courts have supported censorship of information such as the sailing schedules of troop ships or the planned movements of troops in battle. Otherwise, they have recognized a strong constitutional case against press censorship. This stand has given the United States some of the freest, most vigorous news media in the world.

Because the broadcast media are licensed to use the public airwaves, they are subject to some additional regulation, beyond what is applied to the print media, of the content of their news coverage. The basis for the FCC's regulation of content lies in its charge to ensure that radio (and, later, television) stations would "serve the public interest, convenience, and necessity." The FCC has formulated two rules to promote the public interest concerning political matters. With its **equal opportunities rule**, the FCC requires any broadcast station that gives or sells time to a candidate for a public office to make an equal amount of time available under the same conditions to all other candidates for that office. The **reasonable access rule** requires that stations make their facilities available for the expression of conflicting views on issues by all responsible elements in the community.

The regulations seem unobjectionable to most people, but they have been at the heart of a controversy about the deregulation of the broadcast media. Note that neither of these regulations is imposed on the print media, which has no responsibility to give equal treatment to political candidates or to express conflicting views from all responsible elements of the community. In fact, one aspect of a free press is its ability to champion causes that it favors without having to argue the case for the other side. The broadcast media have traditionally been treated differently because they were licensed by the FCC to operate as semimonopolies.[35] With the rise of one-newspaper cities and towns, however, competition among television stations is greater than among newspapers in virtually every market area. Advocates of dropping all FCC content regulations argue that the broadcast media should be just as free as the print media to decide which candidates they endorse and which issues they support.

In 1987, under President Reagan, the FCC itself moved toward this view of unfettered freedom for broadcasters by repealing a third rule, the *fairness doctrine*, which had obligated broadcasters to provide fair coverage of all views on public issues. One media analyst noted that the FCC acted in the belief that competition between broadcasters, cable, radio, newspapers, and magazines would provide a vibrant marketplace of ideas. He feared, however, that the FCC had overestimated the public's demand for high-quality news and public affairs broadcasts. Without that demand, the media are unlikely to supply the news and public affairs coverage needed to sustain a genuine marketplace.[36]

In the United States, the mass media are in business to make money, which they do mainly by selling advertising. To sell advertising, they provide entertainment on a mass basis, which is their general function. We are more interested here in the five specific functions the mass media serve for the political system: *reporting* the news, *interpreting* the news, *influencing* citizens' opinions, *setting the agenda* for government action, and *socializing* citizens about politics.

REPORTING AND FOLLOWING THE NEWS

"News," for most journalists, is an important event that has happened within the past twenty-four hours. A presidential news conference or an explosion in the Capitol qualifies as news. And a national political convention certainly qualifies as news, although it may not justify the thousands of media representatives present at the 1996 party conventions. Who decides what is important? The media, of course. In this section, we discuss how the media cover political affairs, what they choose to report (what becomes "news"), who follows the news, and what they remember and learn from it.

Covering National Politics

All the major news media seek to cover political events with firsthand reports from journalists on the scene. Because so many significant political events occur in the nation's capital, Washington has by far the biggest press corps of any city in the world—over 6,000 accredited reporters: 2,100 from newspapers, 2,000 from periodicals, and 2,200 from radio and television.[37] Only a small portion of these reporters cover the presidency—only about seventy-five "regular" journalists are in the White House press corps.[38] Ever since 1902, when President Theodore Roosevelt first provided a special room in the White House for reporters, the press has had special access to the president. As recently as the Truman administration, reporters enjoyed informal personal relationships with the president. Today, the media's relationship with the president is mediated primarily through the Office of the Press Secretary.

To meet their daily deadlines, White House correspondents rely heavily on information they receive from the president's staff, each piece carefully crafted in an attempt to control the news report. The most frequent form is the news release—a prepared text distributed to reporters in the hope that they will use it verbatim. A daily news briefing at 11:30 A.M. enables reporters to question the press secretary about news releases and allows television correspondents time to prepare their stories and film for the evening newscast. A news conference involves questioning high-level officials in the executive branch—including the president, on occasion. News conferences appear to be freewheeling, but officials tend to carefully rehearse precise answers to anticipated questions.

Occasionally, information is given "on background," meaning the information can be quoted, but reporters cannot identify the source. A vague reference—"a senior official says"—is all right. (When he was secretary of state, Henry Kissinger himself was often the "senior official" quoted on foreign policy developments.) Information disclosed "off the record" cannot even be printed. Journalists who violate these well-known rules risk losing their welcome at the White House. In a sense, the press corps is captive to the White House, which feeds reporters the information they need to meet their deadlines and frames events so that they are covered on the evening news.[39] Beginning with the Nixon White House, press secretaries have obliged photographers with "photo opportunities," a few minutes to take pictures or shoot film, often of the president with a visiting dignitary or a winning sports team. The photographers can keep their editors supplied with visuals, and the press secretary ensures that the coverage is favorable by controlling the environment.

Most reporters in the Washington press corps are accredited to sit in the House and Senate press galleries, but only about four hundred cover Congress exclusively.[40] Most news about Congress comes from innumerable press releases issued by its 535 members and from an unending supply of congressional reports. A journalist, then, can report on Congress without inhabiting its press galleries.

Not so long ago, individual congressional committees allowed radio and television coverage of their proceedings only on special occasions—such as the Kefauver committee's investigation of organized crime in the 1950s and the Watergate investigation in the 1970s. Congress banned microphones and cameras from its chambers until 1979, when the House permitted live coverage (though it insisted on controlling the shots being televised). Nevertheless, televised broadcasts of the House were surprisingly successful, thanks to C-SPAN (the Cable Satellite Public Affairs Network), which feeds to 90 percent of the cable systems across the country and has a cultlike following among hundreds of thousands of regular viewers.[41] To share in the exposure, the Senate began television coverage in 1986. C-SPAN coverage of Congress has become important to professionals in government and politics in Washington—perhaps more so than to its small, devoted audience across the country. Even members of the Washington press corps watch C-SPAN.

In addition to these recognized sources of news, selected reporters occasionally benefit from leaks of information released by officials who are guaranteed anonymity. Officials may leak news to interfere with others' political plans or to float ideas ("trial balloons") past the public and other

•••••••••••

Feeding Time in the Press Room

President Clinton's press secretary, Mike McCurry, conducts a daily briefing for the White House press corps. Both print and broadcast journalists depend on getting the White House's views on the news to frame their reporting for the day.

political leaders to gauge their reactions. At times, one carefully placed leak can turn into a gusher of media coverage through "pack journalism"—the tendency of journalists to adopt similar viewpoints toward the news simply because they hang around together, exchanging information and defining the day's news with one another.

Presenting the News

Media executives, news editors, and prominent reporters function as **gatekeepers** in directing the news flow: they decide which events to report and how to handle the elements in those stories. Only a few individuals—no more than twenty-five at the average newspaper or news magazine and fifty at each of the major television networks—qualify as gatekeepers, defining the news for public consumption.[42] They are usually highly selective in choosing what goes through the gate.

The media cannot communicate everything about public affairs. There is neither space in newspapers or magazines nor time on television or radio to do so. Time limitations impose especially severe constraints on television news broadcasting. Each half-hour network news program devotes only about twenty minutes to the news. (The rest of the time is taken up by commercials, and there is even less news on local television; see Figure 6.2.) The average story lasts about one minute, and few stories run longer than two minutes. The typical script for an entire television news broadcast would fill less than two columns of one page of the *New York Times*.[43]

A parade of unconnected one-minute news stories, flashing across the television screen every night, would boggle the eyes and minds of viewers. To make the news understandable and to hold viewers' attention, television editors and producers carefully choose their lead story and group stories together by theme. The stories themselves concentrate on individuals, because individuals have personalities (political institutions do not—except for the presidency). A careful content analysis of a year's network news coverage of the president, Congress, and the Supreme Court found that the average television news program devotes seven and a half minutes to the president, compared with one minute for Congress and only half a minute for the Court.[44] Moreover, when television does cover Congress, it tries to personify the institution by focusing on prominent, quotable leaders, such as the Speaker of the House or the Senate majority leader. Such personification for the purpose of gaining audience appeal tends to distort the character of Congress, which harbors competing views among different powerfully placed members.

During elections, personification encourages **horse race journalism**, in which media coverage becomes a matter of "who's ahead in the polls, who's raising the most money, who's got TV ads and who's getting endorsed."[45] Stung by criticism of their 1988 coverage, the networks deliberately cut back on covering the horse race in 1992 and won praise for more emphasis on issues.[46] Nevertheless, American television still gives less attention to issues in its election coverage than television in other countries (see Compared with What? 6.1). Consequently, television presents U.S. elections as contests between individuals rather than as confrontations between parties and platforms.

Political campaigns lend themselves particularly well to media coverage, especially if the candidates create a **media event**—a situation that is too "newsworthy" to pass up. One tried-and-true method is to conduct a statewide walking campaign. Newspapers and television can take pictures of the candidate on the highway and conduct interviews with local folks who just spoke with the political hiker. (See Chapter 9 for further discussion of the media in political campaigns.) Television is particularly partial to events that have visual impact. Organized protests and fires, for example, "show well" on television, so television tends to cover them. Violent conflict of any kind, especially unfolding dramas that involve weapons, rate especially high in visual impact.

Where the Public Gets Its News

Until the early 1960s, most people reported getting more of their news from newspapers than from any other source. Television nudged out newspapers as the public's major source of news in the early 1960s. By the mid-1990s, nearly three-fourths of the public cited television as their main news source, compared with about two-fifths who named newspapers (some named both). Not only was television the public's most important source of news, but those polled rated television news as more trustworthy than newspaper news by a margin of 2 to 1.[47] But recent studies have found that fewer adults are regularly watching television news, particularly nightly network news (only 42 percent in 1996 versus 60 percent in 1993).[48] As found in the survey in Figure 6.4, more people by far watch local news than network news. Moreover, the survey found that believability of both the networks and their news anchors has eroded during the 1990s. Meanwhile, public readership of newspapers and evaluation of their credibility have not declined, and there has been no change in the radio news audience. So television may not be as dominant a news

6.1 Live (and Sometimes Colored): Election News on Television in Three Countries

Compared with television reporters in Britain and Germany, reporters in the United States are more likely to color campaign news through commentary before and after reporting a story. This finding comes from a cross-national study of television coverage of elections in the United States and Britain in 1992 and in Germany in 1990. Stories about the candidates' activities were coded by researchers according to reporters' comments in statements that preceded or followed film of the candidates' appearance. The comments were coded as "deflating," "straight or neutral," "mixed," or "reinforcing." Nearly one-quarter of all U.S. reporters' comments were deflating—nearly three times the incidence in Britain and more than ten times that in Germany. In fact, only about half the comments in the United States were straight or neutral, compared with more than two-thirds in Britain and nearly all in Germany.

Source: These data were calculated from Table 7 in Holli A. Semetko, "American Election News in Comparative Perspective," paper presented at the annual meeting of the American Political Science Association, Washington, D.C., September 1993.

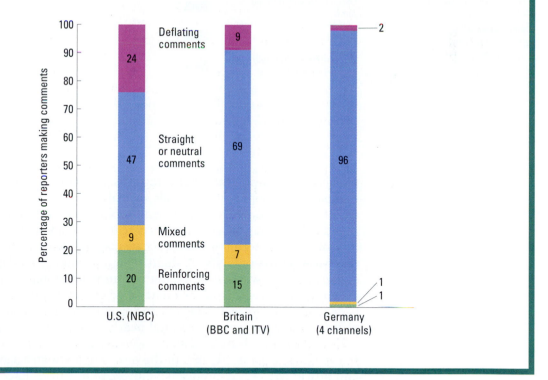

medium as it might seem, and we should inquire into the public's specific sources of news.

In one major study of American news media usage, based on nearly five thousand interviews during four months in 1990, 84 percent of respondents said that they had read or heard the prior day's news through print or broadcast media: newspaper, television, or radio.[49] The study further di-

figure 6.4 ● Regular Use of News Media by the Public

Here are the answers respondents gave in 1996 when asked whether they "regularly" read, watched, or listened to any of these news sources. Nearly three-fourths said they read a daily newspaper regularly—but perhaps only for sports, comics, or TV listings. To a separate question, more than 80 percent said they got "most" of their news about the presidential campaign from television. As for television news, many more people watch local than national news. The Public Broadcasting System's "NewsHour with Jim Lehrer"—arguably the best news program on television—ranks at the bottom of the entire list of twelve sources.

Source: Pew Research Center for The People & The Press, "TV News Viewership Declines," press release, 13 May 1996. National survey of 1,751 adults during April 19–25, 1996. The entries show the percent that "regularly" read, watch, or listen to each medium.

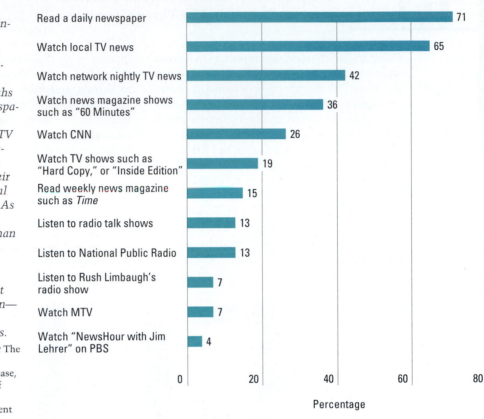

Read a daily newspaper — 71
Watch local TV news — 65
Watch network nightly TV news — 42
Watch news magazine shows such as "60 Minutes" — 36
Watch CNN — 26
Watch TV shows such as "Hard Copy," or "Inside Edition" — 19
Read weekly news magazine such as *Time* — 15
Listen to radio talk shows — 13
Listen to National Public Radio — 13
Listen to Rush Limbaugh's radio show — 7
Watch MTV — 7
Watch "NewsHour with Jim Lehrer" on PBS — 4

Percentage

vided the population into four categories, as Figure 6.5 illustrates. A small group of news sophisticates reads specialized opinion magazines and listens to news programs on National Public Radio or public television. A much bigger group of serious news consumers reads a weekly news magazine or a major metropolitan daily newspaper or watches Sunday morning interview shows or CNN. A slightly bigger group of moderate news consumers reads or watches news, but not from a national source. The smallest group, nonusers, do not regularly read or watch any news.

As one would expect, level of education is strongly related to these categories of news attentiveness, and nearly half the news sophisticates are college graduates. Figure 6.5 shows that age is also related to attentiveness to the news, with nearly half of the news sophisticates aged fifty or older and nearly half of the nonusers younger than thirty. Race bears no relationship to news attentiveness (nonwhites are as likely as whites to be news sophisticates),[50] but sex has a decided effect, with news sophisticates more likely to be male (56 percent) and nonusers to be female (60 percent). Researchers have attributed this finding and others on women's low interest in politics to what is taught at home and in school, saying that changes in girls' early learning experiences must occur before such gender differences evaporate.[51]

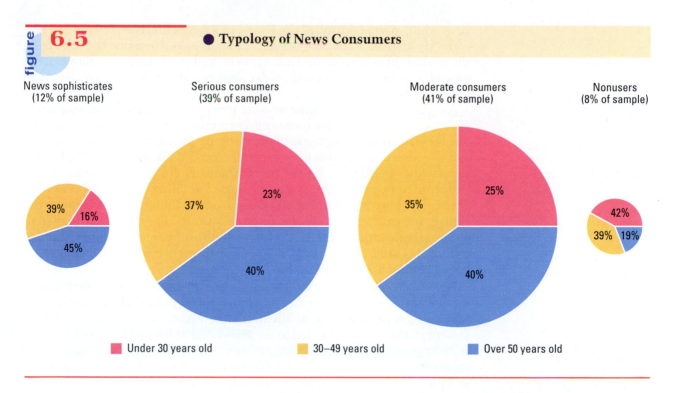

figure 6.5 ● **Typology of News Consumers**

News sophisticates (12% of sample)

Serious consumers (39% of sample)

Moderate consumers (41% of sample)

Nonusers (8% of sample)

■ Under 30 years old   ■ 30–49 years old   ■ Over 50 years old

In a major study of the American media, the Times-Mirror Center classified respondents according to the types of news sources they used regularly. News sophisticates regularly followed news programs on National Public Radio, public television's "MacNeil-Lehrer NewsHour" (now the "NewsHour with Jim Lehrer"), or read opinion magazines such as the Atlantic, Harpers, or the New Yorker. Serious consumers did not follow these sources but did read a news magazine or a major metropolitan daily newspaper, the Wall Street Journal, or USA Today, or watched Sunday morning interview shows or CNN. Moderate consumers read some other daily paper or watched or listened to news regularly. Nonusers followed no news source on a regular basis.

Surveys conducted from 1941 to 1975 showed that Americans younger than thirty followed news stories, such as Watergate and Vietnam, about as closely as their elders and knew almost as much about public affairs. But since then, they have been much less attentive, even to major developments. The opening of the Berlin Wall, ending the division between East and West Germany, was followed very closely by only 42 percent of those younger than thirty, compared with 58 percent of those older than fifty.

Leaders in the world of government, business, and higher education stand at the extreme end of news consumption. Virtually none of these leaders fails to follow the news, and from 40 to 60 percent report spending from one to two hours per day reading, listening to, or watching the news. In fact, from one-third to one-half say that they spend from two to five hours per day following the news.

Source: Times-Mirror Center for The People & The Press, press releases dated November 1989 and 28 June 1990. Used by permission.

What People Remember and Know

If, as surveys indicate, 84 percent of the public read or hear the news each day, and if nearly 75 percent regularly watch the news on television, how much political information do they absorb? By all accounts, not much. When a national sample was asked in the summer of 1992 (an election year) which party controlled the House of Representatives, fewer than half correctly identified the Democrats, but when asked to name the television show that Vice President Dan Quayle had criticized for glamorizing unwed motherhood several years before, two-thirds correctly said "Murphy Brown."[52]

As one would expect, those who are more attentive to the news answer more political knowledge questions correctly than those who are less attentive. Given the enormous improvements in television news coverage and the increasing reliance of the public on TV for news, we might also expect the public to know more than it did twenty years ago.[53] Unfortunately, that is not so. Similar surveys conducted in 1967 and 1987 asked respondents to name their state governor, their representative in the House, and the head of their local school district. Only 9 percent failed to name a single official in 1967, compared with 17 percent in 1987. The author of this study attributed the lower performance in 1987 to greater reliance on television for news.[54]

Numerous studies have found that those who rely on television for their news score lower on tests of knowledge about public affairs than those who rely on print media, as illustrated in Figure 6.6. Among media researchers, this finding has led to the **television hypothesis**—the belief that television is to blame for the low level of citizens' knowledge about public affairs.[55] This belief has a reasonable basis. We know that television tends to squeeze public policy issues into one-minute or, at most, two-minute fragments, which makes it difficult to explain candidates' positions. Television also tends to cast abstract issues in personal terms to generate the visual content that the medium needs.[56] Thus, viewers may become more adept at visually identifying the candidates and describing their personal habits than at outlining their positions on issues. Finally, because they are regulated by the FCC, the television networks are particularly concerned about being fair and equal in covering the candidates, and this may result in their failing to critique the candidates' positions. Newspapers, which are not regulated, enjoy more latitude in choosing which candidates to cover and how. Whatever the explanation, the technological wonders of television may have contributed little to citizens' knowledge of public affairs. Indeed, electronic journalism may work against the informed citizenry that democratic government requires.

Recent research has questioned the hypothesis that television is a poor medium for disseminating information on public affairs. Neuman, Just, and Crigler studied how citizens constructed political meaning from news gained from television, newspapers, and news magazines about five different issues prominent in 1987 and 1988: the 1987 stock market crash, AIDS, drugs, the Strategic Defense Initiative (SDI), and political change in South Africa.[57] Conceding that people who rely on television for news score lower on political knowledge tests than people who rely on print media, they argued that this was because those who knew more tended to select the print media in the first place. In a series of experiments that presented the same information via all three media, the researchers found that television was actually *more* successful in communicating abstract and distant political issues (SDI and South Africa), whereas the print media did better on the stock market crash, drugs, and AIDS.[58] The researchers also found that respondents learned differently from the media

figure

6.6   ● Reading Versus Watching the News

Study after study has demonstrated that people who rely on television for their news score lower on tests of knowledge of public affairs than those who rely on print media. This study, done in early 1993, yielded familiar results when respondents were asked, "How have you been getting most of your news about national and international issues?" Because such studies do not control for interest in the news, they do not necessarily mean that television communicates information poorly. But the better informed seem to prefer getting their news through the print media.

Source: The Times-Mirror Center for The People & The Press, Washington, D.C. Report dated 13 January 1993. Used with permission.

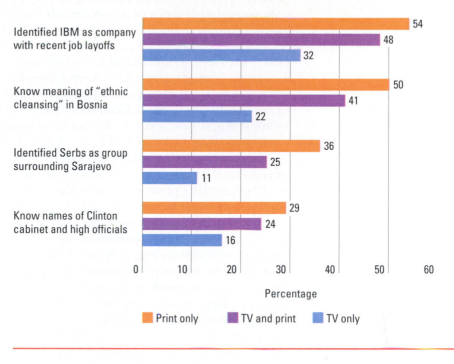

according to their cognitive skills, or ability to learn. People with high cognitive skills learned equally well from all three media, but those with average or low skills learned the most from television, and the least from newspapers.[59] The authors' key finding was that "television was more successful in communicating information about topics that were of low salience [significance] to the audience, while print media were superior in conveying information about topics that had high salience."[60] Despite their finding that television news has value for topics of low salience and for people with limited cognitive skills, the point remains that people with high cognitive skills prefer newspapers. Perhaps they are searching for something that other people aren't.

THE POLITICAL EFFECTS OF THE MEDIA

Virtually all citizens must rely on the mass media for their political news. This endows the media with enormous potential to affect politics. To what extent do the media live up to this potential? In this section, we probe the media's effects on public opinion, the nation's political agenda, and political socialization.

Influencing Public Opinion

Americans overwhelmingly believe that the media exert a strong influence on their political institutions, and nearly nine out of ten Americans believe that the media strongly influence public opinion.[61] However, measuring the extent of media influence on public opinion is difficult.[62]

Because few of us learn about political events except through the media, it could be argued that the media create public opinion simply by reporting events. Consider the dismantling of the Berlin Wall in 1989. Surely the photographs of joyous Berliners demolishing that symbol of oppression affected American public opinion about the reunification of Germany.

Studies of opinion change have found television coverage of particular events to have systematic, and in some cases dramatic, effects. In 1993, for example, Vice President Al Gore and Ross Perot held a "debate" about the North American Free Trade Agreement (NAFTA) on CNN's "Larry King Live." Contrary to Perot, Gore argued that NAFTA would create more jobs than it might cost. *USA Today* polled viewers before and after the debate and found those who favored NAFTA grew from 34 to 57 percent, with the main vote coming from the "undecideds."[63] Many commentators claimed that Gore's strong showing helped NAFTA pass Congress and become law.

Documenting general effects of the media on opinions about more general issues in the news is difficult. One study analyzed polls on eighty issues in foreign and domestic affairs at two points in time. For nearly half of these issues, public opinion changed over time by about six percentage points. The researchers compared these changes with policy positions taken by ten different sources of information, composed of commentators on television network news, including the president; members of the president's party; members of the opposition party; and members of interest groups. The authors found the news commentators to have the most dramatic effect—they could link a single commentary for or against an issue to a significant corresponding change in opinion (more than four percentage points).[64] A parallel study of the effects of newspapers on public opinion on fifty-one foreign and domestic issues found that a single story in a leading paper (the study used the *New York Times*) accounted for only two percentage points of opinion change toward the story's position, which fits with the public's lesser reliance on newspapers as a source of information.[65]

Setting the Political Agenda

Despite the media's potential for influencing public opinion, most scholars believe that the media's greatest influence on politics is found in their power to set the **political agenda**—a list of issues that people identify as needing government attention. Those who set the political agenda define which issues government decision makers should discuss and debate. Like the tree that falls in the forest without anyone hearing it, an issue that does not get on the political agenda will not have anyone in government working on it.

The mass media in the United States have traditionally played an influential role in defining the political agenda. Television, which brings pictures and sound into virtually every home, has an enormous potential for setting the political agenda. As a careful study designed to isolate and examine television's effects on public opinion concluded, "By attending to some problems and ignoring others, television news shapes the American public's political priorities."[66] Indeed, the further the viewer is removed from public affairs, "the stronger the agenda-setting power of television news."[67]

Today's newspapers also heighten the public's concern about particular social issues. Crime is a good example. Certain types of crime—particularly murder—are especially attractive to the media, which therefore tend to distort perceptions of the incidence of crime. A study of newspaper coverage of crime in nine cities found more attention given to violent crimes (murder, rape, and assault) than was justified by official police statistics. In addition, the study found that newspapers in recent years have given increased attention to political crimes—such as assassinations and kidnappings—and to violent crimes committed outside the metropolitan areas served by the papers.[68] In recent years, the overall U.S. crime rate has actually decreased, but one would never know it from the media.[69]

One study found varying correlations between media coverage and what the public sees as "the most important problem facing this country today," depending on the type of event. Crises such as the Vietnam War, racial unrest, and energy shortages drew extensive media coverage, and each additional news magazine story per month generated an almost one percentage point increase in citations of the event as an important problem. But public opinion was even more responsive to media coverage of recurring problems such as inflation and unemployment. Although these events received less extensive coverage, each magazine story tended to increase public concern by almost three percentage points.[70] What's more, evidence shows that television networks, at least, tend to give greater coverage to bad economic news (which is more dramatic) than to good economic news.[71] This tendency can have serious consequences for an incumbent president. (Ask George Bush, who had trouble convincing the public that the economy was good in 1992 and lost the presidency.)

The media's ability to influence public opinion by defining "the news" makes politicians eager to influence media coverage. Politicians attempt to affect not only public opinion but also the opinions of other political leaders.[72] The president receives a daily digest of news and opinion from many sources, and other top government leaders closely monitor the major national news sources. Even journalists work hard at following the news coverage in alternative sources. In a curious sense, the mass media have become a network for communicating among attentive elites, all trying to influence one another or to assess others' weaknesses and strengths. Suppose the White House is under pressure on some policy matter and is asked to send a representative to appear for fifteen minutes of intensive questioning on the "NewsHour with Jim Lehrer." The White House might comply as much to influence the thinking of other insiders (who faithfully watch the program) as to influence opinions among the relatively few news sophisticates in the public who watch public television. Criticisms of the president's policies, especially by members of his own party, embolden others to be critical in their comments to other media. In this way, opposition spreads and may eventually be reflected in public opinion.[73]

Socialization

The mass media act as important agents of political socialization, at least as influential as those described in Chapter 5.[74] Young people who rarely follow the news by choice nevertheless acquire political values through the entertainment function of the broadcast media. Years ago, children

Who Says 'Seeing is Believing'?

Not Sergeant Stacy Koon of the Los Angeles Police Department. Sgt. Koon was one of the four officers charged in the beating of black motorist, Rodney King, whom they stopped for a traffic violation. The blows were filmed by an amateur cameraman and viewed nationwide before the trial began. In court, Sgt. Koon argued that what most viewers saw as unrestrained brutality was actually controlled force. The jury apparently agreed, acquitting the officers of the charges. In response to the verdict, black neighborhoods in Los Angeles erupted in rioting and burning. Tried again on federal charges of depriving Rodney King of his civil rights, Sgt. Koon and a second officer were found guilty and sentenced to prison for two and a half years each.

learned from radio programs; now they learn from television. The average American child has watched about nineteen thousand hours of television by the end of high school.[75] What children learned from radio was quite different from what they are learning now, however. In the golden days of radio, youngsters listening to the popular radio drama "The Shadow" heard repeatedly that "crime does not pay . . . the *Shadow* knows!" In program after program—"Dragnet," "Junior G-Men," "Gangbusters"—the message never varied: criminals are bad; the police are good; criminals get caught and are severely punished for their crimes.

Needless to say, television today does not portray the criminal justice system in the same way, even in police dramas. Consider programs such as "Homicide" and "The X-Files," which have portrayed police and FBI agents as killers. Other series, such as "Law and Order" and even "NYPD Blue" sometimes portray a tainted criminal justice system and institutional corruption.[76] Perhaps years of television messages conveying distrust of law enforcement, disrespect for the criminal justice system, and violence shape impressionable youngsters. Certainly, one cannot easily argue that television's entertainment programs help prepare law-abiding citizens.

Some scholars argue that the most important effect of the mass media, particularly television, is to reinforce the hegemony, or dominance, of the existing culture and order. According to this argument, social control functions not through institutions of force (police, military, and prisons) but through social institutions, such as the media, that cause people to accept "the way things are."[77] By displaying the lifestyles of the rich and famous, for example, the media induce the public to accept the unlimited accumulation of private wealth. Similarly, the media socialize citizens to value "the American way," to be patriotic, to back their country, "right or wrong." Ironically, when former vice president Dan Quayle criticized "Murphy Brown" for undermining family values, he was really making a similar argument—that the media shape popular values through the cultural messages they convey.

So the media play contradictory roles in the process of political socialization. On one hand, they promote popular support for government by joining in the celebration of national holidays, heroes' birthdays, political anniversaries, and civic accomplishments. On the other hand, the media erode public confidence by publicizing citizens' grievances, airing investigative reports of official malfeasance, and even showing dramas about crooked cops.[78] Some critics contend that the media also give too much coverage to government opponents, especially to those who engage in unconventional opposition (see Chapter 7). However, strikes, sit-ins, violent confrontations, and hijackings draw large audiences and thus are newsworthy by the mass media's standards.

EVALUATING THE MEDIA IN GOVERNMENT

Are the media fair or biased in reporting the news? What contributions do the media make to democratic government? What effects do they have on the pursuit of freedom, order, and equality?

Is Reporting Biased?

News reports are presented as objective reality, yet critics of modern journalism contend that news is filtered through the ideological biases of the media owners and editors (the gatekeepers) and of the reporters themselves.

The argument that news reports are politically biased has two sides. On one hand, news reporters are criticized for tilting their stories in a liberal direction, promoting social equality and undercutting social order. On the other hand, wealthy and conservative media owners are suspected of preserving inequalities and reinforcing the existing order by serving a relentless round of entertainment that numbs the public's capacity for critical analysis. Let's evaluate these arguments, looking first at reporters.

Although the picture is far from clear, available evidence seems to confirm the charge of liberal leanings among reporters in the major news media. Studies of the voting behavior of hundreds of reporters and broadcasters show that they voted overwhelmingly for Democratic candidates in presidential elections from 1964 through 1980.[79] Moreover, a 1992 survey of 1,400 journalists found that 44 percent called themselves Democrats versus 16 percent who were Republicans.[80] But do reporters' personal opinions color news coverage?

A study of television coverage during the 1992 presidential campaign found that the candidates alternated in the spotlight before Labor Day. In the weeks before and during the Democratic convention, Clinton had 454 minutes on network news shows to Bush's 400. But between the Republican convention and Labor Day, Bush drew about 2.6 minutes per newscast versus Clinton's 1.6.[81] Of course, reporters can "spin" the news so that coverage is good or bad. As shown in Compared with What? 6.1, American reporters are far more likely to spin or slant the news than reporters in Britain or Germany. When Bush chose Texas to announce that he would sell fighter jets to Taiwan to save jobs, ABC's Brit Hume reported that Bush was using foreign policy to help his campaign in his home state. After Labor Day, the Times-Mirror Center for Media and Public Affairs analyzed all interviews about the candidates on the ABC, CBS, and NBC evening news broadcasts. It classified 69 percent of the comments about Bush as negative, compared with 63 percent about Clinton and only 54 percent about Perot.[82] Even 55 percent of the journalists interviewed during the campaign felt that press coverage had hurt Bush, while only 11 percent thought the coverage hurt Clinton. But most of the journalists felt that they were objectively reporting on Bush's record and the state of the economy.[83]

To some extent, working journalists in the national and local media are at odds with their own editors, who tend to be more conservative. This was demonstrated in a recent study of executives and reporters in national and local media (see Figure 6.7).[84] The editors, in their function as gatekeepers, tend to tone down reporters' liberal leanings by editing their stories or not placing them well in the medium. Also, newspapers are far more likely to endorse Republican than Democratic presidential candidates. This was certainly true in 1988, when newspapers favored George Bush over Michael Dukakis by nearly three to one.[85] Although 45 more papers endorsed Clinton than Bush in 1992 (with a combined circulation of 17.5 million for Clinton compared with 9.9 million for Bush), nearly two-thirds of the 884 papers surveyed—many of which had endorsed Bush before—declined to make an endorsement. (Only four papers endorsed Perot.)[86]

If media owners and their editors are indeed conservative supporters of the status quo, we might expect them to favor officeholders over challengers in elections, regardless of party. However, the evidence tends in the other direction. Let's compare 1980 (when Jimmy Carter, a liberal Democrat, was president and Ronald Reagan, a conservative Republican, was his challenger) with 1984 (when President Reagan faced Walter Mondale, a liberal Democrat). A comparison of television news in 1980 and 1984 found more negative coverage of the incumbent president both times.[87] The researcher concluded that virtually no *continuing* ideological or partisan bias exists on the evening news. Instead, what was seen as ideological or partisan bias in 1980 and 1984 was actually a bias against presidential *incumbents* and *front-runners* for the presidency.[88]

According to this reasoning, if journalists have any pronounced bias, it is against officeholding politicians. When an incumbent runs for reelection, journalists may feel a special responsibility to counteract his or her advantage by putting the opposite partisan spin on the news.[89] When Clinton became president, he began to feel the sting of media criticism. One study found that 73 percent of all evaluations of President Clinton by network news reporters were negative in 1993 and 1994—ironically, the same percentage of negative evaluations President Bush received during a comparable period.[90] Indeed, more than 65 percent of the public in 1995 felt that the press overdid Clinton's character problems, and the public gave the press only a "C" grade for its coverage of the Clinton administration.[91] Thus, whether the media coverage of campaigns is seen as pro-Democratic (and therefore liberal) or pro-Republican (and therefore conservative) depends on which party is in office at the time.

Of course, the media affect voting behavior simply by reporting the daily news, which publicizes officeholders throughout the year. Noncampaign news coverage leads to greater incumbent name recognition at election time, particularly for members of Congress (see Chapter 11). This coverage

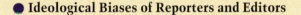

6.7 ● **Ideological Biases of Reporters and Editors**

Does the media have a liberal bias? That depends on whether you mean top executives or middle-level journalists—so says a 1995 study of 65 executives in the broadcast and print media (for example, presidents/CEOs, publishers, and general managers) and 252 journalists (such as political editors, senior producers, correspondents, and reporters). Both local- and national-level media executives tend to be more conservative than local and national journalists. Moreover, the executives resemble the public more in their ideological tendency. But the journalists match the public better in the spread of their ideological tendencies.

Source: The People, The Press, & Their Leaders (Washington, D.C.: Times-Mirror Center for The People and The Press, 1995. Computed from data on pp. 87 and 115. The national survey was taken in September 1994.

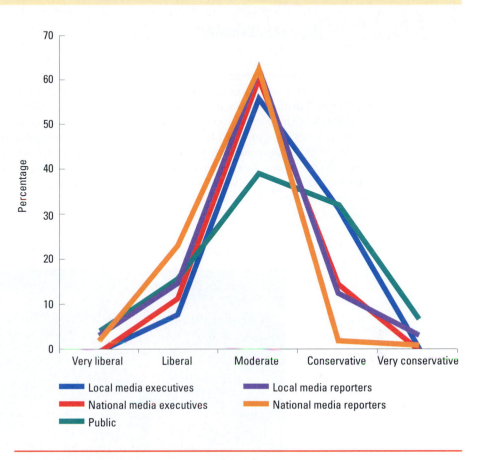

effect is independent of any bias in reporting on campaigns. Moreover, bias in reporting is not limited to election campaigns, and different media may reflect different biases on political issues. A study of stories on nuclear energy over a period of ten years found that reports in the *New York Times* were well balanced between pronuclear and antinuclear sources. In contrast, the major news magazines and television news programs tended to favor antinuclear sources and to slant their stories against nuclear energy.[92]

Contributions to Democracy

As noted earlier, in a democracy communication must move in two directions: from government to citizens and from citizens to government. In fact, political communication in the United States seldom goes directly from government to citizens without passing through the media. The point is important because, as just discussed, news reporters tend to be highly critical of politicians; they consider it their job to search for inaccuracies in fact and weaknesses in argument. Some observers have characterized the news media and the government as adversaries—each

● politics in a changing america

6.1   ¡Se habla Español!

Hispanics constitute the fastest-growing segment of the major minority groups in the United States. Although they accounted for only 9 percent of the population in the 1990 census, Hispanics are projected to rise to 21 percent by 2050.[1] At present, nearly half of all Hispanics do not speak English and another 40 percent understand English but prefer to communicate in Spanish.[2] In an effort to tap this expected market of over 30 million in the next century, advertisers increased their spending in Hispanic markets by nearly 30 percent from 1989 to 1993.[3] This increase in advertising revenues has sparked a growth in Spanish-language mass media in areas of the United States with heavy concentrations of Hispanics. This growth can be seen mainly in television and radio; Spanish-language newspapers have had problems.

Television: Two major networks—Univi-

sion and Telemundo—dominate Hispanic television. Univision, the larger of the two, claims an audience of nearly 25 million, which it reached through 37 broadcast and 670 cable affiliates in 1994.[6] In late 1992, the two networks spent some $16 million for the Nielsen rating service to provide authoritative measurement of Hispanic viewers, and the more credible rating information led to increased advertising. Univision relies more on foreign-produced Spanish-language entertainment programs, while Telemundo produces more domestic programming specifically designed for Hispanics in the United States. As yet, Hispanic television features relatively little news programming. A recent Ford Foundation study, however, reports that Hispanics are even more likely to get their news from television than the general U.S. population, for which television is already the most important news source.[7] So expect more news on Spanish-language television.

Radio: In several communities, Spanish floods the airwaves, sometimes beating English-language stations in Arbitron Company ratings. For example, these Hispanic stations have climbed to or near the top of their markets (rankings are in brackets): KXTN [1] in San Antonio, Texas; KLAX [1] in Los Angeles; WAQI [2] and WRTO [4] in Miami; KIWW [3], KGBT [4], and KKPS [7] in McAllen-Brownsville-Harlingen, Texas; XEMO [6] in San Diego North, California; and KLAX [9] in Anaheim-Santa Ana, California.[4] Although most of these stations feature entertainment in their programming, many also broadcast news, obtained from several networks: Cadena Radio Centro, UPI's Radio Noticias, the Spanish Information Service, and CNN's Radio Noticias. For example, CNN's Radio Noticias offers nearly six minutes of newscast at the top of each hour and separate regional reports for the eastern and western halves of the United States to some sixty stations in forty-three cities.[5]

Newspapers: The big story in Spanish-language newspapers is the battle between smaller Hispanic publishers, which have served local markets for years, and mainstream Anglo publishers seeking to enter the expanding Spanish-language market. Tito Duran, the president of the National Association of Hispanic Publishers, estimated the nationwide circulation of 329 Hispanic papers at about 10 million.[8] In the early 1990s, established metropolitan papers launched Spanish-language papers to compete for many of these readers. Examples included the Chicago Tribune Company, which started *Exito* in Miami and then published a sister paper in Chicago; the *Los Angeles Times' Nuestro Tiempo*; the *Fort-Worth Star-Telegram's La Estrella*; and the *Miami Herald's El Nuevo Herald*. But *Nuestro Tiempo* was closed, *La Estrella* was scaled back, and *El Nuevo Herald* cut its staff. The problem seems to be that advertising is following the audience away from Spanish-language newspapers to television and radio.[9]

1. Steve Coe, "Hispanic Broadcasting and Cable," *Broadcasting and Cable,* 15 November 1993, p. 40.
2. Jim Cooper, "Advertisers Rush into Growing Market," *Broadcasting and Cable,* 15 November 1993, p. 46.
3. Christy Fisher, "Hispanic Media See Siesta Ending," *Advertising Age,* 24 January 1994, p. S1.
4. Susan Taras, "Hispanic Radio Heats Up the Airwaves," *Advertising Age,* 24 January 1994, p. S8.
5. Peter Viles, "Spanish Radio News: Is There Room for Another Network?" *Broadcasting and Cable,* 15 November 1993, pp. 42–43.
6. Tim Jones, "New Vision Likely for Channel 66," *Chicago Tribune,* 14 March 1994, Section 4, p. 1.
7. Ibid., p. 2.
8. M. L. Stein, "Boast of Success," *Editor & Publisher,* 12 February 1994, p. 13.
9. Allen R. Myerson, "Newspapers Cut Spanish-Language Publications," *New York Times,* 16 October 1995, p. C7.

mistrusting the other, locked in competition for popular favor while try- ing to get the record straight. To the extent that this is true, the media serve both the majoritarian and the pluralist models of democracy well by improving the quality of information transmitted to the people about their government.

The mass media transmit information in the opposite direction by re- porting citizens' reactions to political events and government actions. The press has traditionally reflected public opinion (and often created it) in the process of defining the news and suggesting courses of government action. But the media's role in reflecting public opinion has become much more refined in the information age. Since the 1820s, newspapers conducted "straw polls" of dubious quality that matched their own partisan inclina- tions.[93] After commercial polls (such as the Gallup and Roper polls) were established in the 1930s, newspapers began to report more reliable read- ings of public opinion. By the 1960s, the media (both national and local) began to conduct their own surveys. In the 1970s, some news organiza- tions acquired their own survey research divisions. Occasionally, print and electronic media have joined forces to conduct major national sur- veys.

The media now have the tools to do a better job of reporting mass opin- ion than ever before, and they use those tools extensively, practicing "pre- cision journalism" with sophisticated data-collection and analysis techniques. The well-respected *New York Times*/CBS News Poll conducts surveys that are first aired on the "CBS Evening News" and then analyzed at length in the *Times*. After receiving heavy criticism for relying too heav- ily on polls in their election coverage, most major newspapers and the tele- vision networks cut down on reporting poll results in their election coverage in 1992. *USA Today* and CNN went the other way and reported a fresh poll every day from September 30 to the election.[94]

Citizens and journalists alike complain that heavy reliance on polls dur- ing election campaigns causes the media to emphasize the horse race and slights the discussion of issues.[95] But the media also use their polling ex- pertise for other purposes, such as gauging support for going to war against Iraq and for balancing the budget. Although polls sometimes create opin- ions just by asking questions, their net effect has been to generate more ac- curate knowledge of public opinion and to report that knowledge back to the public. Although widespread knowledge of public opinion does not guarantee government responsiveness to popular demands, such knowl- edge is necessary if government is to function according to the majoritar- ian model of democracy.

Effects on Freedom, Order, and Equality

The media in the United States have played an important role in advanc- ing equality, especially racial equality. Throughout the civil rights move- ment of the 1950s and 1960s, the media gave national coverage to conflict in the South as black children tried to attend white schools or civil rights workers were beaten and even killed in the effort to register black voters. Partly because of this media coverage, civil rights moved up on the politi- cal agenda, and coalitions formed in Congress to pass new laws promoting racial equality. Women's rights have also been advanced by the media, which have reported instances of blatant sexual discrimination exposed by groups working for sexual equality, such as the National Organization for Women (NOW). In general, the mass media offer spokespersons for any disadvantaged group an opportunity to state their case before a national audience and to work for a place on the political agenda.

Although the media are willing to encourage government action to promote equality at the cost of some personal freedom, they resist government attempts to infringe on freedom of the press to promote order. The media, far more than the public, believe freedom of the press is sacrosanct. For example, 98 percent of 2,703 journalists surveyed by the *Los Angeles Times* opposed allowing a government official to prevent the publication of a story the government claims to be inaccurate, compared with only 50 percent of the public. Whereas a majority of the public believes that certain types of news should never be published—exit polls saying who will win an election, secret documents dealing with national security issues, the names of CIA spies, photographs that invade people's privacy—journalists are more reluctant to draw the line anywhere.[96] Although reporters covering the Persian Gulf crisis chafed at the restrictions imposed by the military, a survey during the war found that 57 percent of the public thought that the military "should exert more control" over reporting.[97] Finally, more citizens favor curbing news reports about racial or ethnic insults than favor publicizing them.[98]

To protect their freedom, the media operate as an interest group along pluralist lines. They have an interest in being able to report whatever they wish, whenever they wish, which certainly erodes the government's efforts to maintain order. Three examples illustrate this point.

- The media's sensational coverage of airline hijackers and other terrorist activities gives terrorists exactly what they want, making it more difficult to reduce terrorist threats to order.

- The portrayal of brutal killings and rapes on television, often under the guise of entertainment, has produced "copycat" crimes admittedly committed "as seen on TV."

- The national publicity given to claims of syringes found in cans of Pepsi Cola in 1993 prompted similar tampering with other products.[99] Publicity given to the burning of black churches in 1996 raised fears of "copycat" arson.

Freedom of the press is a noble value and one that has been important to democratic government. But we should not ignore the fact that democracies sometimes pay a price for pursuing it without qualification.

SUMMARY

The mass media transmit information to large, heterogeneous, and widely dispersed audiences through print and broadcasts. The mass media in the United States are privately owned and in business to make money, which they do mainly by selling space or air time to advertisers. Both print and electronic media determine which events are newsworthy largely on the basis of audience appeal. The rise of mass-circulation newspapers in the 1830s produced a politically independent press in the United States. In their aggressive competition for readers, those newspapers often engaged in sensational reporting, a charge sometimes leveled at today's media.

The broadcast media operate under technical, ownership, and content regulations imposed by the government; these tend to promote more even-handed treatment of political contests on radio and television than in newspapers and news magazines. The main function of the mass media is entertainment, but the media also perform the political functions of re-porting news, interpreting news, influencing citizens' opinions, setting the political agenda, and socializing citizens about politics.

The major media maintain staffs of professional journalists in major cities around the world. Washington, D.C., hosts the biggest press corps in the world, but only a portion of those correspondents concentrate on the presidency. Because Congress is a more decentralized institution, it is cov-ered in a more decentralized manner. All professional journalists recog-nize rules for citing sources that guide their reporting. What actually gets reported in the media depends on the media's gatekeepers, the publishers and editors.

Although Americans today get more news from television than from newspapers, newspapers usually do a more thorough job of informing the public about politics. Despite heavy exposure to news in the print and electronic media, the ability of most people to retain much political infor-mation is shockingly low. The problem appears to be not with the media's ability to supply quality news coverage but with the lack of demand for it by the public. The media's most important effect on public opinion is in setting the country's political agenda. The role of the news media may be more important for affecting interactions among attentive policy elites than in influencing public opinion. The media play more subtle, contra-dictory roles in political socialization, both promoting and undermining certain political and cultural values.

Reporters from the national media tend to be more liberal than the pub-lic, as judged by their tendency to vote for Democratic candidates and by their own self-descriptions. Journalists' liberal leanings are checked some-what by the conservative inclinations of their editors and publishers. However, if the media systematically demonstrate any pronounced bias in their news reporting, it is a bias against incumbents and front-runners, re-gardless of their party, rather than a bias in favor of liberal Democrats.

From the standpoint of majoritarian democracy, one of the most impor-tant roles of the media is to facilitate communication from the people to the government through the reporting of public opinion polls. The media zealously defend the freedom of the press, even to the point of encouraging disorder by granting extensive publicity to violent protests, terrorist acts, and other threats to order.

Key Terms

mass media	newsworthiness	equal opportunities rule	media event
group media	infotainment	reasonable access rule	television hypothesis
attentive policy elites	Federal Communications	gatekeepers	political agenda
two-step flow of	Commission (FCC)	horse race journalism	
communication			

Selected Readings

Ansolabehere, Stephen, Roy Behr, and Shanto Iyengar. *The Media Game: American Politics in the Television Age.* New York: Macmillan, 1993. A recent text on media's influence in politics that explores how the media can filter, alter, distort, or even ignore what politicians have to say.

Lichter, S. Robert, and Richard E. Noyes. *Good Intentions Make Bad News: Why Americans Hate Campaign Journalism.* Lanham, Md.: Rowman & Littlefield, 1995. Argues that the "good intentions" of journalists to improve news coverage actually harms coverage. Contains numerous tables and graphs analyzing reporting content in the 1992 presidential campaign.

Kerbel, Matthew Robert. *Remote and Controlled: Media Politics in a Cynical Age.* Boulder, Colo.: Westview Press, 1995. A historical account of political journalism coverage that draws lessons for today.

Neuman, W. Russell, Marion R. Just, and Ann N. Crigler. *Common Knowledge: News and the Construction of Political Meaning.* Chicago: University of Chicago Press, 1992. Studies how people construct meaning from news they received on five topics in 1987: the stock market crash, drugs, racial politics in South Africa, the Strategic Defense Initiative, and AIDS.

Page, Benjamin I. *Who Deliberates: Mass Media in Modern Democracy.* Chicago: University of Chicago Press, 1996. Thoughtfully discusses and analyzes how the public "deliberates" through three specific case studies: the war with Iraq, the Los Angeles riots, and the failed nomination of Zoe Baird for Attorney General.

Rosenblum, Mort. *Who Stole the News?: Why We Can't Keep Up with What Happens in the World and What We Can Do About It.* New York: Wiley, 1993. Blames the American news media system for reporting less and less overseas news because of efforts to cut costs and increase profits.

World Wide Web Resources

ABC News Reports. This site offers some text files to view, but most of its news reports require the Real-Audio player so that you can listen to contemporary news, old news, Peter Jennings's commentary, and more. The software can be downloaded from the site and installed on your computer.

`<www.prognet.com/contentp/abc.html>`

CBS News. A general guide to the network's news operation. Contains the button UTTMlink—*CBS News Up-to-the-Minute Online:* "Here you'll find the latest on breaking news, Internet and CD-ROM developments as well as movie reviews, women's health reports, parenting and what's up in space and much more!"

`<www.cbs.com/news/>`

CNN Interactive. According to Scott Woelfel, editor in chief of CNN Interactive, "Our site will be rich with images, both still and moving. And the experience is made all the richer by the audio clips which we use to help tell the story as often as we can."

`<www.cnn.com/>`

NBC News—Inside NBC News. This site joins the news operation of NBC with the computer expertise of Microsoft. One innovative item for the 1996 campaign was its "Vox Box," which posed questions ("Disgusted with politics as usual?") and selected viewers' responses to report.

`<www.msnbc.com/>`

PBS Online. This site provides a gateway to various PBS progams, including a button to the "Online NewsHour," a page based on the comprehensive television evening news program hosted by Jim Lehrer. The page also covers stories in depth, usually involving interviews with key actors in politics.

`<www.pbs.org/>`

USA TODAY. The home page of this popular national newspaper provides buttons that take you to electronic versions of the paper's regular sections on news, opinion, features, sports, and so on.

`<www.usatoday.com/>`

Wall Street Journal Interactive. The *Journal* is the nation's largest-selling newspaper. Unlike the other sites mentioned here, this one requires a subscription. But if you like the *Journal,* you may find it worthwhile.

`<interactive2.wsj.com/>`

New York Times on the Web. Many people consider the nationally distributed *Times* to be as liberal as the *Wall Street Journal* is conservative. You don't have to subscribe, but you do have to register to use this service.

`<www.nytimes.com/>`

chapter 7

Participation and Voting

THEY SEEMED LIKE ORDINARY FOLKS. That's how their suburban neighbors regarded the ten men and two women arrested in Phoenix, Arizona, on July 1, 1996. One worked in a doughnut shop. Another worked for the telephone company. Others painted houses or sold office equipment.[1] One had even run for political office (unsuccessfully). But to the arresting federal agents, they were the Viper Militia, a small, secret paramilitary organization charged with plotting to destroy several public buildings. Indeed, the agents found the suspects' homes stocked with an arsenal of weapons—in addition to the 140 guns, there were hand grenades, rocket launchers, gas masks, silencers, and homemade bombs.[2]

Although it may represent the more extreme paramilitary groups in the United States today, the Viper Militia is but one of many active militia groups. About two hundred militia units exist in Arizona alone, and hundreds more operate throughout the nation. They communicate through group media: newsletters, faxes, and the Internet.[3] In fact, militia activity on the Internet has stimulated the growth of anti-militia sites on the World Wide Web. One of the most prominent is "The Militia Watchdog." This site warns that activity on the Internet underestimates the militia movement, which relies heavily on newsletters, faxes, and videotapes. Nevertheless, it lists scores of militia sites, including home pages for movements in ten states.[4]

Is involvement in a militia a form of political participation, or is it simply a form of recreation—playing war games in the woods? No doubt, some people are attracted to militias for fun and fellowship, but the militia movement also has a distinct political cast. It views the federal government as a threat to personal freedom. (This view of Washington was also held during the Reagan and Bush administration, when many militias were formed.) Militia members also see conspiracies against freedom coming from the United Nations (which they think is planning to invade the United States), the Council of Foreign Relations (an academically oriented institution that publishes *Foreign Affairs*, a respected journal on international politics), and the Trilateral Commission (a group headed by David Rockefeller, consisting of business, labor, academic, and media leaders from America, Europe, and Japan). These conspiracies are referenced in a militia movement Web site called "Restoring America." The militia movement is deadly serious in its pledges to defend its view of freedom. Its

Go to the home page of "the Militia Watchdog" for reports on the neo-militia movement.
`<www.sff.net/people/`
`pitman/militia.htm>`

There is little evidence of rational debate when pro-life and pro-choice demonstrators come into contact, as they did here outside an abortion clinic in Amherst, New York.

exaltation of weapons is apparent in the "Minuteman Prayer," seen on a militia Web site:

> God grant me the serenity to accept the things I cannot change; the courage to change the things I can; and the superior firepower to make the difference.[5]

Although most people think of political participation primarily in terms of voting, there are other forms of political activity that are more robust than voting. Have militia members exceeded the boundaries of political participation, or are they simply defending freedom, in the tradition of the minutemen of the American Revolution? How politically active are Americans in general? How do they compare with citizens of other countries? How much and what kind of participation is necessary to sustain the pluralist and majoritarian models of democracy?

In this chapter, we try to answer these and other important questions about popular participation in government. We begin by studying participation in democratic government, distinguishing between conventional and unconventional participation. Then we evaluate the nature and extent of both types of participation in American politics. Next, we study the expansion of voting rights and voting as the major mechanism for mass participation in politics. Finally, we examine the extent to which the various forms of political participation serve the values of freedom, equality, and order and the majoritarian and pluralist models of democracy.

DEMOCRACY AND POLITICAL PARTICIPATION

Government ought to be run by the people. That is the democratic ideal in a nutshell. But how much and what kind of citizen participation is necessary for democratic government? Neither political theorists nor politicians, neither idealists nor realists, can agree on an answer. Champions of

●●●●●●●●●●

Things Change

As a nineteen-year-old student at Cornell University, Tom Jones led an armed takeover of the administration building during campus protests, in the spring of 1969, against the Vietnam War and for black power. Now he is Thomas W. Jones, in his mid-forties and president and chief executive officer of TIAA-CREF, the college teachers' retirement fund, the world's biggest private pension fund ($115 billion). He is also a member of Cornell's board of trustees. He told the New York Times *that he "made the best decisions I could make under the circumstances, and I will not repudiate that twenty-five years later," but he does regret the incident for its potential for violence. Things change.*

direct democracy believe that if citizens do not participate directly in government affairs, making government decisions themselves, they should give up all pretense of living in a democracy. More practical observers contend that people can govern indirectly, through their elected representatives. And they maintain that choosing leaders through elections—formal procedures for voting—is the only workable approach to democracy in a large, complex nation.

Elections are a necessary condition of democracy, but they do not guarantee democratic government. Before the collapse of communism, the former Soviet Union regularly held elections in which more than 90 percent of the electorate turned out to vote, but the Soviet Union certainly did not function as a democracy, because there was only one party. Both the majoritarian and pluralist models of democracy rely on voting to varying degrees, but both models expect citizens to participate in politics in other ways. For example, they expect citizens to discuss politics, to form interest groups, to contact public officials, to campaign for political parties, to run for office, and even to protest government decisions.

We define **political participation** as "those actions of private citizens by which they seek to influence or to support government and politics."[6] This definition embraces both conventional and unconventional forms of political participation. In plain language, *conventional behavior* is behavior that is acceptable to the dominant culture in a given situation. Wearing a swimsuit at the beach is conventional; wearing one at a formal dance is not. Displaying campaign posters in front yards is conventional; spray-painting political slogans on buildings is not.

At times, figuring out whether a particular political act is conventional or unconventional is difficult. We find the following distinction useful in analyzing political participation:

- **Conventional participation** is relatively routine behavior that uses the established institutions of representative government, especially campaigning for candidates and voting in elections.

- **Unconventional participation** is relatively uncommon behavior that challenges or defies established institutions or the dominant culture (and thus is personally stressful to participants and their opponents).

Voting and writing letters to public officials are examples of conventional political participation; staging sit-down strikes in public buildings and chanting slogans outside officials' windows are examples of unconventional participation. Certainly training with a militia is unconventional; the question is whether the activity is political or not. Experts contend that group participation is often a politicizing experience, developing skills in the individual that transfer to politics.[7] Political demonstrations can be conventional (carrying signs outside an abortion clinic) or unconventional (linking arms to prevent entrance). Various forms of unconventional participation are often used by powerless groups to gain political benefits while also working within the system.[8] Militia groups, however, blatantly reject the system.

Voting and other methods of conventional participation are important to democratic government. So are unconventional forms of participation. Let us look at both kinds of political participation in the United States.

UNCONVENTIONAL PARTICIPATION

On Sunday, March 7, 1965, a group of about six hundred people attempted to march fifty miles from Selma, Alabama, to the state capitol at Montgomery. The marchers were demonstrating in favor of voting rights for blacks. (At the time, Selma had fewer than five hundred registered black voters, out of fifteen thousand who were eligible.)[9] Alabama governor George Wallace declared the march illegal and sent state troopers to stop it. The two groups met at the Edmund Pettus Bridge over the Alabama River at the edge of Selma. The peaceful marchers were disrupted and beaten by state troopers and deputy sheriffs—some on horseback—using clubs, bullwhips, and tear gas. The day became known as Bloody Sunday.

The march from Selma was a form of unconventional political participation. Marching fifty miles in a political protest is certainly not common; moreover, the march challenged the existing institutions that prevented blacks from voting. From the beginning, the marchers knew they were putting themselves in a dangerous situation, that they certainly would be taunted by whites along the way and could be physically hurt as well. But they had been prevented from participating conventionally—voting in elections—for many decades, and they chose this unconventional method to dramatize their cause.

The march ended in violence because Governor Wallace would not allow even this peaceful mode of unconventional expression. In contrast to some later demonstrations against the Vietnam War, this civil rights

● ● ● ● ● ● ● ● ● ● ● ● ●

Antiwar Protest, 1968

In August 1968, thousands of youthful antiwar protesters gathered in Chicago, where the Democrats were holding their national convention. Protests against the war had already forced president Lyndon Johnson not to seek reelection. Mayor Richard J. Daley vowed that the protest- ers would not disturb the impending nomination of Hubert Humphrey, Johnson's vice president. Daley's police kept the youths from demon- strating at the convention, but the resulting violence did not help Humphrey, who lost to Richard Nixon in an extremely close election. When the Democratic conven- tion returned to Chicago in 1996, the new Mayor Richard M. Daley (the old mayor's son) faced a different situation and hosted a relatively peaceful convention.

march posed no threat of violence. The brutal response to the marchers helped the rest of the nation understand the seriousness of the civil rights problem in the South. Unconventional participation is stressful and occa- sionally violent, but sometimes it is worth the risk.

SUPPORT FOR UNCONVENTIONAL PARTICIPATION

Unconventional political participation has a long history in the United States. The Boston Tea Party of 1773, in which American colonists dumped three cargoes of British tea into Boston Harbor, was only the first in a long line of violent protests against British rule that eventually led to revolution. The minutemen who fought at Lexington in 1775 also are part of our proud history. Yet, we know less about unconventional than con- ventional participation. The reasons are twofold: first, since it is easier to collect data on conventional practices, they are studied more frequently. Second, political scientists are simply biased toward institutionalized, or conventional, politics. In fact, some basic works on political participation explicitly exclude any behavior that is "outside the system."[10] One major study of unconventional political action asked people whether they had engaged in or approved of five types of political participation outside of voting.[11] As shown in Figure 7.1, of the five activities, only signing peti- tions was clearly regarded as conventional, in the sense that the behavior was widely practiced.

The conventionality of two other forms of behavior was questionable. Only 15 percent had ever attended a demonstration, while 41 percent said they would never demonstrate. The marchers in Selma, although peaceful, were surely demonstrating against the established order. If we measure conventionality in terms of the proportion of people who disapprove of an

figure 7.1

● What Americans Think Is Unconventional Political Behavior

A survey presented Americans with five different forms of political participation outside the electoral process and asked whether they "have done," "might do," or "never do" any of them. The respondents disapproved of two forms overwhelmingly. Only signing petitions was widely done and rarely ruled out. Even attending demonstrations (a right guaranteed in the Constitution) was disapproved of by 44 percent of the respondents. Boycotting products was less objectionable and more widely practiced. According to this test, attending demonstrations and boycotting products are only marginally conventional forms of political participation. Joining strikes and occupying buildings are clearly unconventional activities for most Americans.

Source: 1990–91 World Values Survey. Data for the United States are available from the Inter-University Consortium for Political and Social Research. The weighted sample size was 1,837.

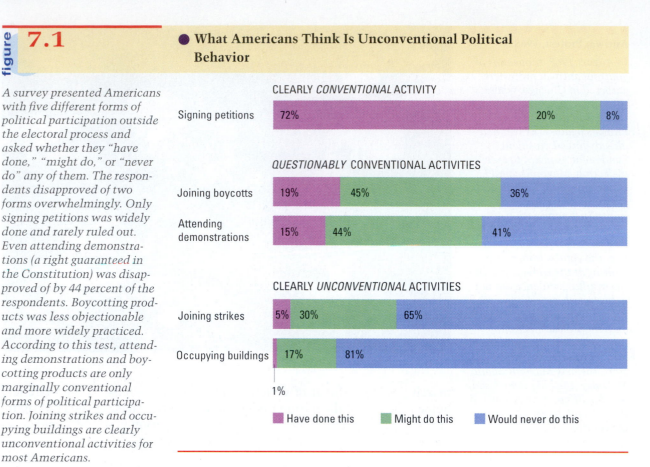

CLEARLY *CONVENTIONAL* ACTIVITY

Signing petitions 72% 20% 8%

QUESTIONABLY CONVENTIONAL ACTIVITIES

Joining boycotts 19% 45% 36%

Attending demonstrations 15% 44% 41%

CLEARLY *UNCONVENTIONAL* ACTIVITIES

Joining strikes 5% 30% 65%

Occupying buildings 17% 81% 1%

■ Have done this ■ Might do this ■ Would never do this

action, we might argue that all demonstrations border on the unconventional. The same reasoning could be applied to boycotting products—for example, refusing to buy lettuce or grapes picked by nonunion farm workers. Demonstrations and boycotts are problem cases in deciding what is and is not conventional political participation.

The other two political activities listed in Figure 7.1 are clearly unconventional. In fact, when political activities interfere with people's daily lives (occupying buildings, for example), disapproval is nearly universal. When protesters demonstrating against the Vietnam War disrupted the 1968 Democratic national convention in Chicago, they were clubbed by the city's police. Although the national television audience saw graphic footage of the confrontations and heard reporters' criticisms of the police's behavior, most viewers condemned the demonstrators, not the police.

The Effectiveness of Unconventional Participation

Vociferous antiabortion protests have discouraged many doctors from performing abortions, but they have not led to outlawing abortions. Does unconventional participation ever work (even when it provokes violence)?

Yes. Antiwar protesters helped convince President Lyndon Johnson not to seek reelection in 1968, and they heightened public concern about U.S. participation in the Vietnam War. American college students who disrupted campuses in the late 1960s and early 1970s helped end the military draft in 1973, and although it was not one of their stated goals, they sped passage of the Twenty-sixth Amendment, which lowered the voting age to eighteen.

The unconventional activities of civil rights workers also produced notable successes. Dr. Martin Luther King, Jr., led the 1955 Montgomery bus boycott (prompted by Rosa Parks's refusal to surrender her seat to a white man), which sparked the civil rights movement. He used **direct action** to challenge specific cases of discrimination, assembling crowds to confront businesses and local governments and demanding equal treatment in public accommodations and government. The civil rights movement organized more than one thousand such newsworthy demonstrations nationwide—387 in 1965 alone.[12] And like the march in Selma, many of these protests provoked violent confrontations between whites and blacks.

Denied the usual opportunities for conventional political participation, minorities used unconventional politics to pressure Congress to pass a series of civil rights laws in 1957, 1960, 1964, and 1968—each one in some way extending national protection against discrimination by reason of race, color, religion, or national origin. (The 1964 act also prohibited discrimination in employment on the basis of sex.)

In addition, the Voting Rights Act of 1965 placed some state electoral procedures under federal supervision, protecting the registration of black voters and increasing the rate of black voter turnout (especially in the South, where much of the violence occurred). Black protest activity—both violent and nonviolent—has also been credited with increased welfare support for blacks in the South.[13] The civil rights movement shows that social change can occur, even when it faces violent opposition at first. In 1995, thirty years after law enforcement officers beat civil rights marchers in Selma, some of the same marchers walked peacefully to commemorate Bloody Sunday, and they received the keys to the city from the mayor—the same mayor as in 1965. Twenty-five years after the assassination of Dr. Martin Luther King, Jr., however, racial divisions still persisted across the nation (see Politics in a Changing America 7.1).

Although direct political action and the politics of confrontation can work, using them requires a special kind of commitment. Studies show that direct action appeals most to those who both (1) distrust the political system and (2) have a strong sense of political efficacy—the feeling that they can do something to affect political decisions.[14] Whether this combination of attitudes produces behavior that challenges the system depends on the extent of organized group activity.[15] The civil rights movement involved many organized groups: King's Southern Christian Leadership Conference (SCLC); the Congress of Racial Equality (CORE), headed by James Farmer; and the Student Non-Violent Coordinating Committee (SNCC), led by Stokely Carmichael, to mention but a few.

The decision to use unconventional behavior also depends on the extent to which individuals develop a group consciousness—identification with

politics in a changing america

7.1 Race Relations Still Not Good, but Getting Better

Twenty-five years after the assassination of Dr. Martin Luther King, Jr., on April 4, 1968, the *New York Times* conducted a poll on race relations in the United States. Although most black and white respondents thought race relations were "bad" rather than "good," a clear majority of whites and a plurality of blacks felt that they were better than they had been twenty-five years before. Moreover, an overwhelming majority of both whites and blacks thought that significant progress had been made toward "Martin Luther King's dream of equality." Finally, about 40 percent of blacks and whites supported the use of nonviolent protest as "the best way" for blacks to gain their rights, which indicates the acceptability of unconventional participation in American politics.

Source: Peter Applebone, "Racial Divisions Persist 25 Years After King Killing," *New York Times*, 4 April 1993, p. 12. Copyright © 1993 The New York Times Company. Reprinted by permission.

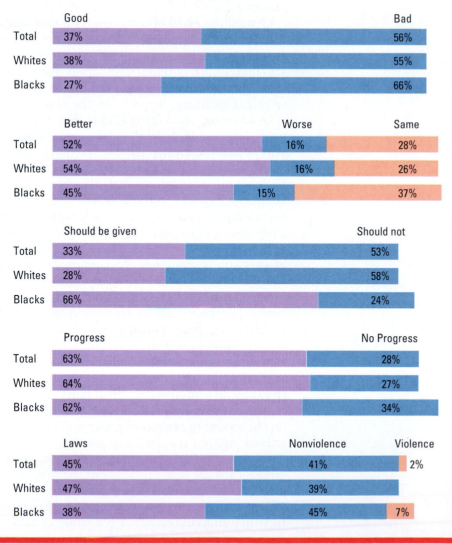

Question:
Do you think race relations in the United states are generally good or generally bad?

	Good	Bad
Total	37%	56%
Whites	38%	55%
Blacks	27%	66%

Question:
Compared to 25 years ago, do you think race relations in the United States are better now, worse, or about the same?

	Better	Worse	Same
Total	52%	16%	28%
Whites	54%	16%	26%
Blacks	45%	15%	37%

Question:
Do you believe that where there has been job discrimination in the past, preference in hiring or promotion should be given to blacks today?

	Should be given	Should not
Total	33%	53%
Whites	28%	58%
Blacks	66%	24%

Question:
Do you think there has been significant progress toward Martin Luther King's dream of equality, or don't you think so?

	Progress	No Progress
Total	63%	28%
Whites	64%	27%
Blacks	62%	34%

Question:
What's the best way for blacks to try to gain their rights — use laws and persuasion, use nonviolent protests, or be ready to use violence?

	Laws	Nonviolence	Violence
Total	45%	41%	2%
Whites	47%	39%	
Blacks	38%	45%	7%

Uncivil Service

Government employees in Washington march to protest the longest shutdown of U.S. agencies in history. About 280,000 workers were sent home for twenty-one days beginning on December 16, 1995, as the president and Congress could not agree on appropriations bills needed to fund certain agencies. Agreement was reached on January 5, 1996, on bills that allowed them to return to work. The employees' protests increased the pressure to end the shutdown.

their group and awareness of its position in society, its objectives, and its intended course of action.[16] These characteristics were present among blacks and young people in the mid-1960s and are strongly present today among blacks and to a lesser degree among women. Indeed, some researchers contend that black consciousness has heightened both African Americans' distrust of the political system and their sense of individual efficacy, generating more political participation by poor blacks than by poor whites.[17] The National Organization for Women (NOW) and other women's groups have also heightened women's group consciousness, which may have contributed to their increased participation in politics, in both conventional and unconventional ways. Today, some white Christian males find a sense of belonging in local militias.

Unconventional Participation in America

Although most Americans disapprove of using certain forms of participation to protest government policies, U.S. citizens are about as likely to take direct action in politics as citizens of European democracies. Surveys in Britain, Germany, and France in 1990 and 1991 found that Americans claim to have participated as much as or more than British, German, and French citizens in unconventional actions, such as demonstrations, boycotts, strikes, and occupying buildings.[18] Contrary to the popular view that Americans are apathetic about politics, they are more likely to engage in political protests of various sorts than citizens in other democratic countries.[19]

Is something wrong with our political system if citizens resort to unconventional—and widely disapproved of—methods of political participation? To answer this question, we must first learn how much Americans use conventional methods of participation.

CONVENTIONAL PARTICIPATION

A practical test of the democratic nature of any government is whether citizens can affect its policies by acting through its institutions—meeting with public officials, supporting candidates, voting in elections. If people must operate outside government institutions in order to influence policymaking—as civil rights workers had to do in the South—the system is not democratic. Citizens should not have to risk their life and property to participate in politics, and they should not have to take direct action to force the government to hear their views. The objective of democratic institutions is to make political participation conventional—to allow ordinary citizens to engage in relatively routine, nonthreatening behavior to get the government to heed their opinions, interests, and needs.

In a democracy, for a group to gather at a statehouse or city hall to dramatize its position on an issue—say, a tax increase—is not unusual. Such a demonstration is a form of conventional participation. The group is not powerless, and its members are not risking their personal safety by demonstrating. But violence can erupt between opposing groups demonstrating in a political setting, such as between pro-life and pro-choice groups. Circumstances, then, often determine whether organized protest is or is not conventional. In general, the less that participants anticipate a threat, the more likely it is that the protest is conventional.

Conventional political behaviors fall into two major categories: actions that show support for government policies and those that try to change or *influence* policies.

Supportive Behavior

Supportive behaviors are actions that express allegiance to country and government. When we recite the Pledge of Allegiance or fly the American flag on holidays, we are showing support for the country and, by implication, its political system. Such ceremonial activities usually require little effort, knowledge, or personal courage; that is, they demand little initiative on the part of the citizen. The simple act of turning out to vote is in itself a show of support for the political system. Other supportive behaviors—serving as an election judge in a nonpartisan election or organizing a holiday parade—demand greater initiative.

At times, people's perception of patriotism moves them to cross the line between conventional and unconventional behavior. In their eagerness to support the American system, they break up a meeting or disrupt a rally of a group they believe is radical or somehow "un-American." Radical groups may threaten the political system with wrenching change, but superpatriots pose their own threat. Their misguided excess of allegiance denies nonviolent means of dissent to others.[20]

Influencing Behavior

Citizens use **influencing behaviors** to modify or even reverse government policy to serve political interests. Some forms of influencing behavior seek particular benefits from government; other forms have broad policy objectives.

Particular Benefits.　Some citizens try to influence government to obtain benefits for themselves, their immediate families, or close friends. Two examples of attempts to influence government for personal benefit that do not require much initiative are voting to elect a relative to local office and voting against an increase in school taxes when one's own children have already left school. Serving one's self-interest through the voting process is certainly acceptable to democratic theory. Each individual has only one vote, and no single voter can wangle particular benefits from government through voting unless a majority of the voters agree.

Political actions that require considerable knowledge and initiative are another story. Individuals or small groups who influence government officials to advance their self-interest—for instance, to obtain a lucrative government contract—may secretly benefit without others knowing. Those who quietly obtain particular benefits from government pose a serious challenge to a democracy. Pluralist theory holds that groups ought to be able to make government respond to their special problems and needs. On the other hand, majoritarian theory holds that government should not do what a majority does not want it to do. A majority of citizens might very well not want the government to do what any particular person or group seeks, if it is costly to other citizens.

What might individual citizens or groups ask of their government, and how might they go about asking for it? Some citizens ask for special services from their local government. Such requests may range from contacting the city forestry department to remove a dead tree in front of a house to calling the county animal control center to deal with a vicious dog in the neighborhood. Studies of such "contacting behavior" find that it tends not to be empirically related to other forms of political activity. In other words, people who complain to city hall do not necessarily vote. Contacting behavior is related to socioeconomic status: people of higher socioeconomic status are more likely to contact public officials.[21]

Americans demand much more of their local government than of the national government. Although many people value self-reliance and individualism in national politics, most people expect local government to solve a wide range of social problems. A study of residents of Kansas City, Missouri, found that more than 90 percent thought the city had a responsibility to provide services in thirteen areas, including maintaining parks, setting standards for new home construction, demolishing vacant and unsafe buildings, ensuring that property owners clean up trash and weeds, and providing bus service. The researcher noted that "it is difficult to imagine a set of federal government activities about which there would [be] more consensus."[22] Citizens can also mobilize against a project. The 1980s saw the emergence of the "not in my back yard," or NIMBY, phenomenon, as citizens pressured local officials to stop undesired projects from being located near their homes.

Finally, contributing money to a candidate's campaign is another form of influencing behavior. Here, too, the objective can be particular or broad benefits, although determining which is which can sometimes be difficult. An example: as discussed in Chapter 9, national law limits the amount of money that an individual or organization can contribute directly to a candidate's campaign for president, but there is no limit on the

● ● ● ● ● ● ● ● ● ● ●

A Line of Argument

Tension may fill the air when citizens turn out in large numbers at local political meetings, and speaking out in such meetings requires high personal initiative. Knowledge of the issues involved helps, too. Residents attending this public transportation hearing in Austin, Texas, have come prepared to state their views. Looks like a long evening ahead.

amount that can be contributed to either of the national parties. Since tobacco companies contributed over $2.8 million to the Republican party and over $.4 million to the Democratic party in the 1996 campaign, one might suspect that they are seeking favorable treatment from the government.[23]

Several points emerge from this review of "particularized" forms of political participation. First, approaching government to serve one's particular interests is consistent with democratic theory, because it encourages participation from an active citizenry. Second, particularized contact may be a unique form of participation, not necessarily related to other forms of participation such as voting. Third, such participation tends to be used more by citizens who are advantaged in terms of knowledge and resources. Fourth, particularized participation may serve private interests to the detriment of the majority.

Broad Policy Objectives.   We come now to what many scholars have in mind when they talk about political participation: activities that influence the selection of government personnel and policies. Here, too, we find behaviors that require little initiative (such as voting) and high initiative (attending political meetings, persuading others how to vote).

Even voting intended to influence government policies is a low-initiative activity. Such "policy voting" differs from voting to show support or to gain special benefits by its broader influence on the community or society. Obviously, this distinction is not sharp: citizens vote for a number of reasons—a mix of allegiance, particularized benefits, and policy concerns. In addition to policy voting, many other low-initiative forms of conventional participation—wearing a campaign button, watching a party convention on television, posting a bumper sticker—are also connected with elections. In the next section, we focus on elections as a mechanism for participation. For now, we simply note that voting to influence policy is usually a low-initiative activity. As we discuss later, it actually requires more initiative to *register* to vote in the United States than to cast a vote on election day.

Other types of participation to affect broad policies require high initiative. Running for office requires the most (see Chapter 9). Some high-initiative activities, such as attending party meetings and working in campaigns, are associated with the electoral process; others, such as attending legislative hearings and writing letters to Congress, are not. Although many nonelectoral activities involve making personal contact, their objective is often to obtain government benefits for some group of people—farmers, the unemployed, children, oil producers. In fact, studies of citizen contacts in the United States show that about two-thirds deal with broad social issues and only one-third are for private gain.[24]

Few people realize that using the court system is a form of political participation, a way for citizens to press for their rights in a democratic society. Although most people use the courts to serve their particular interests, some also use them, as we discuss shortly, to meet broad objectives. Going to court demands high personal initiative.[25] It also requires knowledge of the law or the financial resources to afford a lawyer.

People use the courts for both personal benefit and broad policy objectives. A person or group can bring **class action suits** on behalf of other people in similar circumstances. Lawyers for the National Association for the Advancement of Colored People pioneered this form of litigation in the famous school desegregation case *Brown* v. *Board of Education* (1954).[26] They succeeded in getting the Supreme Court to outlaw segregation in public schools, not just for Linda Brown, who brought the suit in Topeka, Kansas, but for all others "similarly situated"—that is, for all other black students who wanted to attend desegregated schools. Participation through the courts is usually beyond the means of individual citizens, but it has proved effective for organized groups, especially those who have been unable to gain their objectives through Congress or the executive branch.

Individual citizens can also try to influence policies at the national level by participating directly in the legislative process. One way is to attend congressional hearings, which are open to the public and are occasionally held outside Washington. Especially since the end of World War II, the national government has sought to increase citizen involvement in creating regulations and laws by making information on government activities available to interested parties. For example, government agencies are required to publish all proposed and approved regulations in the daily *Federal Register* and to make government documents available to citizens on request.

Conventional Participation in America

You may know someone who has testified at a congressional or administrative hearing, but the odds are that you do not. Such participation is

● ● ● ● ● ● ● ● ● ● ●

Worth Waiting For

Soweto, South Africa, was for many years the center of black protests against the white minority government. Denied the right to vote in elections for all their lives, these thousands of voters in Soweto did not mind waiting several hours and longer in April 1994 to cast their first ballot in South Africa's first free multiracial elections.

high-initiative behavior. Relatively few people—only those with high stakes in the outcome of a decision—are willing to participate in this way. How often do Americans contact government officials and engage in other forms of conventional political participation, compared with citizens in other countries?

The most common political behavior reported in a study of five countries was voting for candidates (see Compared with What? 7.1). Americans are less likely to vote than citizens in the other four countries studied. On the other hand, Americans are as likely (or substantially more likely) to engage in all other forms of conventional political participation. As we have seen, the same pattern holds true for unconventional behaviors. Americans, then, are more apt to engage in nearly all forms of unconventional and conventional political participation, except voting.

Other researchers noted this paradox and wrote, "If, for example, we concentrate our attention on national elections we will find that the United States is the least participatory of [all] five nations." But looking at the other indicators, they found that "political apathy, by a wide margin, is lowest in the United States. Interestingly, the high levels of overall involvement reflect a rather balanced contribution of both . . . conventional and unconventional politics."[27] Clearly, low voter turnout in the United States constitutes a puzzle, to which we will return.

PARTICIPATING THROUGH VOTING

The heart of democratic government lies in the electoral process. Whether a country holds elections—and if so, what kind—constitutes the critical difference between democratic and nondemocratic governments. Elections institutionalize mass participation in democratic government according to the three normative principles of procedural democracy discussed in Chapter 2: electoral rules specify *who* is allowed to vote, *how much* each person's vote counts, and *how many* votes are needed to win.

Again, elections are formal procedures for making group decisions. *Voting* is the act individuals engage in when they choose among alternatives in an election. **Suffrage** and **franchise** both mean the right to vote. By formalizing political participation through rules for suffrage and for counting ballots, electoral systems allow large numbers of people, who individually have little political power, to wield great power. Electoral systems decide collectively who governs and, in some instances, what government should do.

The simple act of holding elections is less important than the specific rules and circumstances that govern voting. According to democratic theory, everyone should be able to vote. In practice, however, no nation grants universal suffrage. All countries have age requirements for voting, and all disqualify some inhabitants on various grounds: lack of citizenship, criminal record, mental incompetence, and so forth. What is the record of enfranchisement in the United States?

Expansion of Suffrage

The United States was the first country to provide for general elections of representatives through "mass" suffrage, but the franchise was far from universal. When the Constitution was framed, the idea of full adult suffrage was too radical to consider seriously. Instead, the framers left the issue of enfranchisement to the states, stipulating only that individuals who could vote for "the most numerous Branch of the State Legislature" could also vote for their representatives to the U.S. Congress (Article I, Section 2).

Initially, most states established taxpaying or property-holding requirements for voting. Virginia, for example, required ownership of twenty-five acres of settled land or five hundred acres of unsettled land. The original thirteen states began to lift such requirements after 1800. Expansion of the franchise accelerated after 1815, with the admission of new "western" states (Indiana, Illinois, Alabama), where land was more plentiful and widely owned. By the 1850s, the states had eliminated virtually all taxpaying and property-holding requirements, thus allowing the working class—at least its white male members—to vote. Extending the vote to blacks and women took longer.

The Enfranchisement of Blacks. The Fifteenth Amendment, adopted shortly after the Civil War, prohibited the states from denying the right to vote "on account of race, color, or previous condition of servitude." However, the states of the old Confederacy worked around the amendment by reestablishing old voting requirements (poll taxes, literacy tests) that worked primarily against blacks. Some southern states also cut blacks out of politics through a cunning circumvention of the amendment. Because the amendment said nothing about voting rights in private organizations, these states denied blacks the right to vote in the "private"

7.1 Conventional Political Participation

A survey of respondents in five democratic industrialized nations found that Americans are far more likely than citizens in the other countries to engage in various forms of conventional political behavior—except voting. The findings clearly contradict the idea that Americans are politically apathetic. Citizens of the United States simply do not vote as much in national elections, which says more about the nature of U.S. elections than about American citizens, who are active politically in other ways.

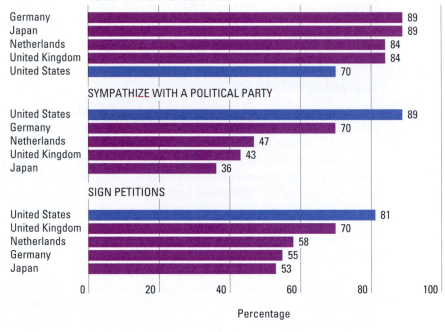

VOTED IN THE LAST ELECTION

Country	Percentage
Germany	89
Japan	89
Netherlands	84
United Kingdom	84
United States	70

SYMPATHIZE WITH A POLITICAL PARTY

Country	Percentage
United States	89
Germany	70
Netherlands	47
United Kingdom	43
Japan	36

SIGN PETITIONS

Country	Percentage
United States	81
United Kingdom	70
Netherlands	58
Germany	55
Japan	53

Percentage

Democratic *primary* elections held to choose the party's candidates for the general election. Because the Democratic party came to dominate politics in the South, the "white primary" effectively disenfranchised blacks, despite the Fifteenth Amendment. Finally, in many areas of the South, the threat of violence kept blacks from the polls.

The extension of full voting rights to blacks came in two phases, separated by twenty years. In 1944, the Supreme Court decided in *Smith* v. *Allwright* that laws preventing blacks from voting in primary elections

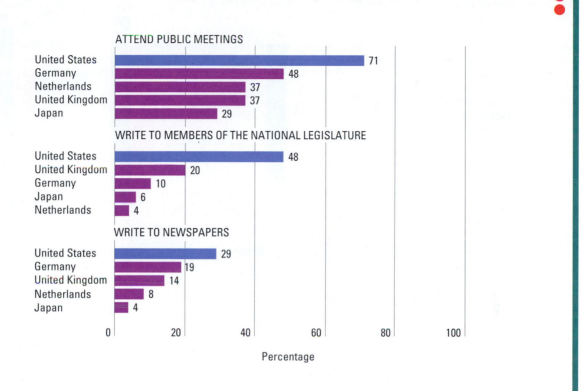

ATTEND PUBLIC MEETINGS

United States	71
Germany	48
Netherlands	37
United Kingdom	37
Japan	29

WRITE TO MEMBERS OF THE NATIONAL LEGISLATURE

United States	48
United Kingdom	20
Germany	10
Japan	6
Netherlands	4

WRITE TO NEWSPAPERS

United States	29
Germany	19
United Kingdom	14
Netherlands	8
Japan	4

Percentage

Source: International Social Justice Project, a collaborative international research effort. The data for this chart, which were kindly provided by Antal Örkény at Eötvös Loránd University (ELTE) in Hungary, came from national surveys conducted in 1991 that were supported in whole or in part by the Institute for Research, University of Michigan; the Economic and Social Research Council (United Kingdom); the Deutsche Forschungsgemeinschaft; the Institute of Social Science, Chuo University (Japan); and the Dutch Ministry of Social Affairs. (The voter turnout figures for the Netherlands came from election reports.)

were unconstitutional, holding that party primaries are part of the continuous process of electing public officials.[28] The Voting Rights Act of 1965, which followed Selma's Bloody Sunday by less than five months, suspended discriminatory voting tests against blacks. It also authorized federal registrars to register voters in seven southern states, where less than half of the voting-age population had registered to vote in the 1964 election. For good measure, in 1966 the Supreme Court ruled in *Harper* v. *Virginia State Board of Elections* that state poll taxes are unconstitutional.[29]

figure

7.2 ● Voter Registration in the South, 1960, 1980, and 1992

As a result of the Voting Rights Act of 1965 and other national actions, black voter registration in the eleven states of the old Confederacy nearly doubled between 1960 and 1980. In 1992, there was little difference between the voting registration rates of white and black voters in the deep South.

Sources: Data for 1960 and 1980 are from U.S. Bureau of the Census, *Statistical Abstract of the United States, 1982–1983* (Washington, D.C.: U.S. Government Printing Office, 1983), p. 488; data for 1992 are computed from Bureau of the Census, *Current Population Reports,* Series P20–466, *Voting and Registration in the Election of November 1992* (Washington, D.C.: U.S. Government Printing Office, 1993), pp. 10–11.

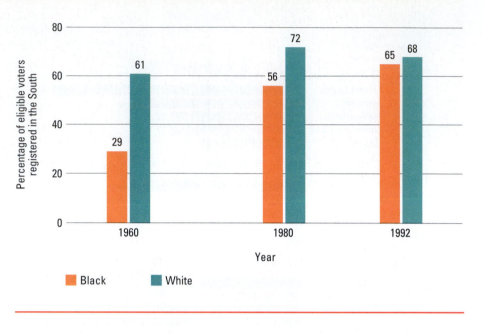

Although long in coming, these actions by the national government to enforce political equality in the states dramatically increased the registration of southern blacks (see Figure 7.2).

The Enfranchisement of Women.   The enfranchisement of women in the United States is a less sordid story but still nothing to be proud of. Women had to fight long and hard to win the right to vote. Until 1869, women could not vote anywhere in the world.[30] American women began to organize to obtain suffrage in the mid-1800s. Known then as *suffragettes,** the early feminists initially had a limited effect on politics. Their first major victory did not come until 1869, when Wyoming, while still a territory, granted women the right to vote. No state followed suit until 1893, when Colorado enfranchised women.

In the meantime, the suffragettes became more active. In 1884, they formed the Equal Rights party and nominated Belva A. Lockwood, a lawyer (who could not herself vote), as the first woman candidate for president.[31] Between 1896 and 1918, twelve other states gave women the vote. Most of these states were in the West, where pioneer women often departed from traditional women's roles. Nationally, the women's suffrage movement intensified, often resorting to unconventional political behaviors (marches, demonstrations), which occasionally invited violent attacks from men and even other women. In 1919, Congress finally passed

---

* The term *suffragist* applied to a person of either sex who advocated extending the vote to women, while *suffragette* was reserved primarily for women who did so militantly.

● ● ● ● ● ● ● ● ● ● ● ●

The Fights for Women's Suffrage . . . and Against It

Young people and minorities are not the only groups that have resorted to unconventional means of political participation. In the late 1800s and early 1900s, women marched and demonstrated for equal voting rights, sometimes encountering strong opposition. Their gatherings were occasionally disrupted by men—and other women—who opposed extending the right to vote to women.

the Nineteenth Amendment, which prohibits states from denying the right to vote "on account of sex." The amendment was ratified in 1920, in time for the November election.

Evaluating the Expansion of Suffrage in America.   The last major expansion of suffrage in the United States took place in 1971, when the Twenty-sixth Amendment lowered the voting age to eighteen. For most of its history, the United States has been far from the democratic ideal of universal suffrage. The United States initially restricted voting rights to white male taxpayers or property owners, and wealth requirements lasted until the 1850s. Through demonstrations and a constitutional amendment, women won the franchise just seventy-six years ago. Through civil war, constitutional amendments, court actions, massive demonstrations, and congressional action, blacks finally achieved full voting rights only three decades ago. Our record has more than a few blemishes.

But compared with other countries, the United States looks pretty democratic.[32] Women did not gain the vote on equal terms with men until 1921 in Norway; 1922 in the Netherlands; 1944 in France; 1946 in Italy, Japan, and Venezuela; 1948 in Belgium; and 1971 in Switzerland. Comparing the enfranchisement of minority racial groups is difficult, because most other democratic nations do not have a comparable racial makeup. We should note, however, that the indigenous Maori population in New Zealand won suffrage in 1867, but the aborigines in Australia were not fully enfranchised until 1961. And, of course, in notoriously undemocratic South Africa, blacks—who outnumber whites by more than four to one—were not allowed to vote freely in elections until 1994. With regard to voting age, nineteen of twenty-seven countries that allow free elections also have a minimum voting age of eighteen (none has a lower age), and eight have higher age requirements.

When judged against the rest of the world, the United States—which originated mass participation in government through elections—has as good a record of providing for political equality in voting rights as other democracies and a better record than many.

Voting on Policies

Disenfranchised groups have struggled to gain voting rights because of the political power that comes with suffrage. Belief in the ability of ordinary citizens to make political decisions and to control government through the power of the ballot box was strongest in the United States during the Progressive era, which began around 1900 and lasted until about 1925. **Progressivism** was a philosophy of political reform that trusted the goodness and wisdom of individual citizens and distrusted "special interests" (railroads, corporations) and political institutions (traditional political parties, legislatures). Such attitudes have resurfaced among the followers of H. Ross Perot and others who appeal to this populist outlook.

The leaders of the Progressive movement were prominent politicians (former president Theodore Roosevelt, Senator Robert La Follette of Wisconsin) and eminent scholars (historian Frederick Jackson Turner, philosopher John Dewey). Not content to vote for candidates chosen by party leaders, the Progressives championed the **direct primary**—a preliminary election, run by the state governments, in which the voters choose the party's candidates for the general election. Wanting a mechanism to remove elected candidates from office, the Progressives backed the **recall**—a special election initiated by a petition signed by a specified number of voters. Although about twenty states provide for recall elections, this device is rarely used. Only a few statewide elected officials have actually been unseated through recall.[33]

The Progressives also championed the power of the masses to propose and pass laws, approximating the citizen participation in policymaking that is the hallmark of direct democracy. They developed two voting mechanisms for policymaking that are still in use:

- A **referendum** is a direct vote by the people on either a proposed law or an amendment to a state constitution. The measures subject to popular vote are known as *propositions.* About twenty-five states permit popular referenda on laws, and all but Alabama require a referendum for a constitutional amendment. Most referenda are placed on the ballot by legislatures, not voters.

- The **initiative** is a procedure by which voters can propose a measure to be decided by the legislature or by the people in a referendum. The procedure involves gathering a specified number of signatures from registered voters (usually 5 to 10 percent of the total in the state), then submitting the petition to a designated state agency. About twenty states provide for some form of voter initiative.

Figure 7.3 shows the West's affinity for these democratic mechanisms. One scholar estimates that there have been more than 17,000 referenda since 1898 and that there were more than 2,300 between 1968 and 1978 alone.[34] Over 350 propositions have appeared on state ballots in general elections during the 1990s, although relatively few (usually fewer than fifty) got there by means of initiatives.[35] Among the 238 ballot propositions in the 1994 elections were proposals in seven states to limit the terms of U.S. senators and representatives (typically to twelve years for senators and six to twelve years for representatives). Six of the seven

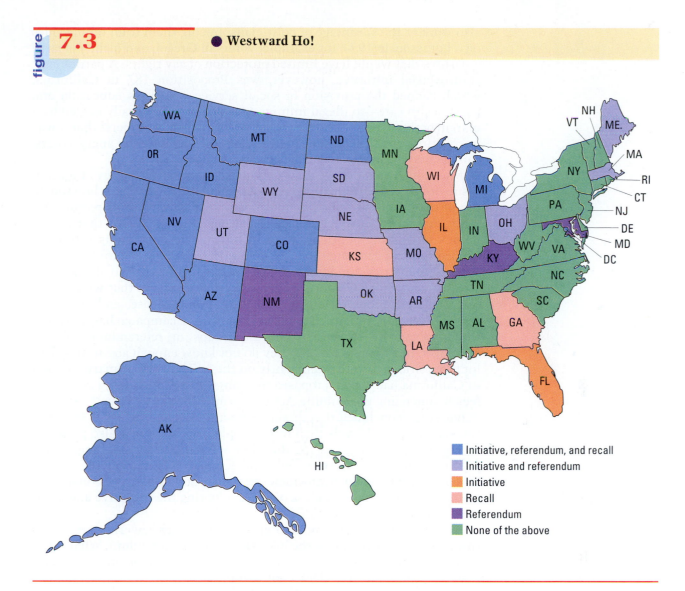

figure 7.3 ● **Westward Ho!**

■ (blue)	Initiative, referendum, and recall
■ (light purple)	Initiative and referendum
■ (orange)	Initiative
■ (pink)	Recall
■ (purple)	Referendum
■ (green)	None of the above

This map shows quite clearly the western basis of the initiative, referendum, and recall mechanisms that were intended to place government power directly in the hands of the people. Advocates of "direct legislation" sought to bypass entrenched powers in state legislatures. Established groups and parties in the East dismissed them as radicals and cranks, but they gained the support of farmers and miners in the Midwest and West. The Progressive forces usually aligned with Democrats in western state legislatures to enact their proposals, often against Republican opposition.

Source: Reprinted by permission of the publishers from *Direct Democracy: The Politics of Initiative, Referendum, and Recall* by Thomas E. Cronin (Cambridge, Mass.: Harvard University Press). Copyright © 1989 by the Twentieth Century Fund, Inc.

passed, but in 1995 the Supreme Court, in a five-to-four decision, ruled that congressional term limits were unconstitutional.[36] They were thus voided in all twenty-three states that had adopted them.

At times, many politicians oppose the initiatives that citizens propose and approve. This was true, for example, of term limits. A referendum can also work to the advantage of politicians, freeing them from taking sides on a hot issue. In 1994, for example, voters in Oregon and Idaho defeated measures that would have limited protection of gay rights. A particularly controversial initiative, however, was Proposition 187 in California, which banned the provision of social services—such as education and basic health care—to illegal immigrants. The measure easily passed by a margin of three to two, despite the belief by many legal experts that it was unconstitutional. Like other matters of policy enacted by angry voters, this awaits decision by the courts.[37]

What conclusion can we draw about the Progressives' legacy of mechanisms for direct participation in government? One scholar who studied use of the initiative and referendum paints an unimpressive picture. He notes that an expensive "industry" developed in the 1980s that makes money circulating petitions, then managing the large sums of money needed to run a campaign to approve (or defeat) a referendum.[38] In 1990, various industries conducted a $10 million campaign to defeat "Big Green," a sweeping California environmental initiative that would have imposed restrictions on offshore drilling, pesticide use, and air pollutants.[39] The money required to mount a statewide campaign has increased the involvement of special interest groups in referendum politics. Moreover, most voters confess they do not know enough about most ballot propositions to vote intelligently on them. The 1996 primary election in California had eleven propositions, ranging from regulating attorneys' fees to amending the Wildlife Act concerning mountain lions.[40] Another major study concluded that direct democracy devices "worked better at the state and local levels than most people realize," but it also proposed fourteen safeguards "to ensure that they serve the larger and longer-term public interest" at the state and local levels.[41] Noting that the United States is one of the few democracies that does not permit a national referendum, the study nevertheless opposed adopting the initiative and referendum at the national level.[42]

Clearly, citizens can exercise great power over government policy through the mechanisms of the initiative and the referendum. What is not clear is whether these forms of direct democracy improve on the policies made by representatives elected for that purpose.

Voting for Candidates

We have saved for last the most visible form of political participation: voting to choose candidates for public office. Voting for candidates serves democratic government in two ways. First, citizens can choose the candidates they think will best serve their interests. If citizens choose candidates that are "like themselves" in personal traits or party affiliation, elected officials should tend to think as their constituents do on political issues and automatically reflect the majority's views when making public policy.

Second, voting allows the people to reelect the officials they guessed right about and to kick out those they guessed wrong about. This function is very different from the first. It makes public officials accountable for their behavior through the reward-and-punishment mechanism of elections. It assumes that officeholders are motivated to respond to public opinion by the threat of electoral defeat. It also assumes that the voters (1) know what politicians are doing while they are in office and (2) participate actively in the electoral process. We look at the factors that underlie voting choice in Chapter 9. Here, we examine Americans' reliance on the electoral process.

In national politics, voters seem content to elect just two executive officers—the president and vice president—and to trust the president to appoint a cabinet to round out his administration. But at the state and local levels, voters insist on selecting all kinds of officials. Every state elects a governor (and forty-two elect a lieutenant governor). Forty elect an attorney general; thirty-five, a treasurer and a secretary of state; twenty-three, an auditor. The list goes on, down through superintendents of schools, secretaries of agriculture, controllers, boards of education, and public utilities commissioners.[43] Elected county officials commonly include commissioners, a sheriff, a treasurer, a clerk, a superintendent of schools, and a judge (often several). At the local level, voters elect all but about 600 of 15,300 school boards across the nation.[44] Instead of trusting state and local chief executives to appoint lesser administrators (as we do for more important offices at the national level), we expect voters to choose intelligently among scores of candidates they meet for the first time on a complex ballot in the polling booth.

In the American version of democracy, the laws recognize no limit to voters' ability to make informed choices among candidates and thus to control government through voting. The reasoning seems to be that elections are good; therefore, more elections are better, and the most elections are best. By this thinking, the United States clearly has the best and most democratic government in the world, because it is the undisputed champion at holding elections. The author of a study that compared elections in the United States with elections in twenty-six other democracies concluded

> No country can approach the United States in the frequency and variety of elections, and thus in the amount of electoral participation to which its citizens have a right. No other country elects its lower house as often as every two years, or its president as frequently as every four years. No other country popularly elects its state governors and town mayors; no other has as wide a variety of nonrepresentative offices (judges, sheriffs, attorneys general, city treasurers, and so on) subject to election. . . . The average American is entitled to do far more electing—probably by a factor of three or four—than the citizen of any other democracy.[45]

However, we learn from Compared with What? 7.2 that the United States ranks at the bottom of twenty-seven countries in voter turnout in national elections. How do we square low voter turnout with Americans' devotion to elections as an instrument of democratic government? To complicate matters further, how do we square low voter turnout with the findings we mentioned earlier, which establish the United States as the leader among five Western democratic nations in both conventional and unconventional political participation, except for voting? Americans seem to participate at high levels in everything except elections.

compared with what?

7.2   Voter Turnout in Democratic Nations, 1975–1995

Americans participate as much as or more than citizens of other nations in all forms of conventional political behavior except voting. Voter turnout in American presidential elections ranks at the bottom of voting rates for twenty-seven countries with competitive elections. As discussed in the text, the facts are correct, but the comparison is not as damning as it appears.

Source: Inter-Parliamentary Union, *Chronicle of Parliamentary Elections and Developments* (Geneva: Switzerland, Vols. X-XXIX (1975–1995); U.S. Bureau of the Census, Current Population Reports, P20-453 and P20-466, *Voting and Registration in the Election of 1990 [and 1992]* (Washington, D.C.: U.S. Government Printing Office, 1991 [and 1993]), pp. viii, 10. The U.S. data are for all elections from 1976 to 1992, both presidential and nonpresidential election years. (Compared with What? 7.1 shows the percent of respondents who *said* they voted, which is usually higher than the actual voting turnout in this figure.)

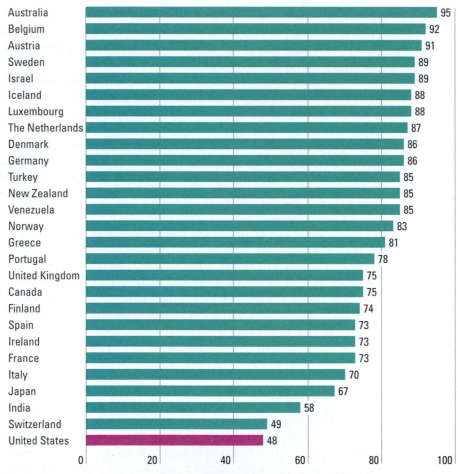

Percentage of voter turnout in democratic nations

Country	Percentage
Australia	95
Belgium	92
Austria	91
Sweden	89
Israel	89
Iceland	88
Luxembourg	88
The Netherlands	87
Denmark	86
Germany	86
Turkey	85
New Zealand	85
Venezuela	85
Norway	83
Greece	81
Portugal	78
United Kingdom	75
Canada	75
Finland	74
Spain	73
Ireland	73
France	73
Italy	70
Japan	67
India	58
Switzerland	49
United States	48

EXPLAINING
POLITICAL
PARTICIPATION

As you have seen, political participation can be unconventional or conventional, can require little or much initiative, and can serve to support the government or influence its decisions. Researchers have found that people who take part in some form of political behavior often do not take part in others. For example, citizens who contact public officials to obtain special benefits may not vote regularly, participate in campaigns, or even contact officials about broader social issues. In fact, because particularized contacting serves individual rather than public interests, it is not even considered political behavior by some people.

This section examines some factors that affect the more obvious forms of political participation, with particular emphasis on voting. The first task is to determine how much patterns of participation vary within the United States over time.

Patterns of Participation over Time

Have Americans become more politically apathetic in the 1990s than they were in the 1960s? The answer lies in Figure 7.4, which plots several measures of participation from 1952 through 1992. The graph shows a steady pattern of participation over the years (with upward spurts in 1992 because Ross Perot's candidacy added a new dimension to the presidential race). Otherwise, participation varied little across time in the percentage of citizens who worked for candidates, attended party meetings, and tried to persuade people how to vote. In fact, interest in election campaigns tended to increase even before 1992. *The only line that shows a downward trend is voting in elections.* The plot has thickened. Not only is voter turnout low in the United States compared with that in other countries, but turnout has basically declined over time. Moreover, while voting has decreased, other forms of participation have remained stable or even increased. What is going on? Who votes? Who does not? Why? And does it really matter?

The Standard Socioeconomic Explanation

Researchers have found that socioeconomic status is a good indicator of most types of conventional political participation. People with more education, higher incomes, and white-collar or professional occupations tend to be more aware of the effect of politics on their lives, to know what can be done to influence government actions, and to have the necessary resources (time and money) to take action. So they are more likely to participate in politics than are people of lower socioeconomic status. This relationship between socioeconomic status and conventional political involvement is called the **standard socioeconomic model** of participation.[46]

Unconventional political behavior is less clearly related to socioeconomic status. Studies of unconventional participation in other countries have found that protest behavior is related to low socioeconomic status and especially to youth.[47] However, scattered studies of unconventional participation in the United States have found that protesters (especially blacks) are often of higher socioeconomic status than those who do not join in protests.[48]

Obviously, socioeconomic status does not account for all the differences in the ways people choose to participate in politics, even for conventional

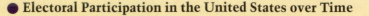

figure 7.4   ● Electoral Participation in the United States over Time

Participation patterns from five decades show that in the 1980s Americans participated in election campaigns about as much or more than they did in the 1950s on every indicator except voting. The turnout rate dropped more than ten percentage points from 1952 to 1988. The turnout for 1992 was 55 percent, a sharp rise, but the trend continued downward to only 49 percent in 1996. This general decline in voting turnout runs counter to the rise in educational level, a puzzle that is discussed in the text.

Source: Reprinted by permission of the publishers from *American National Election Studies Data Sourcebook, 1952–1978,* Warren Miller and Edward J. Schneider, eds. (Cambridge, Mass.: Harvard University Press). Copyright © 1980

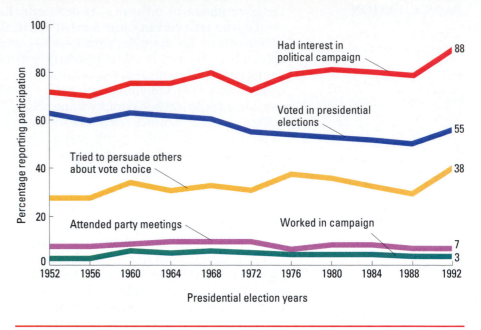

participation. Another important variable is age. As just noted, young people are more likely to take part in political protests, but they are less likely to participate in conventional politics. Voting rates tend to increase as people grow older, until about age sixty-five, when physical infirmities begin to lower rates again.[49]

Two other variables—race and gender—have been related to participation in the past, but as times have changed, so have those relationships. Blacks, who had very low participation rates in the 1950s, now participate at rates comparable to whites, when differences in socioeconomic status are taken into account.[50] Women also exhibited low participation rates in the past, but gender differences in political participation have virtually disappeared.[51] (The one exception is in attempting to persuade others how to vote, which women are less likely to do than men.[52]) Recent research on the social context of voting behavior has shown that married men and women are more likely to vote than those of either sex living without a spouse.[53]

Of all the social and economic variables, education is the strongest single factor in explaining most types of conventional political participation. A recent major study on civic participation details the impact of education:

It affects the acquisition of skills; it channels opportunities for high levels of income and occupation; it places individuals in institutional settings where they can be recruited to political activity; and it fosters psychological and cognitive engagement with politics.[54]

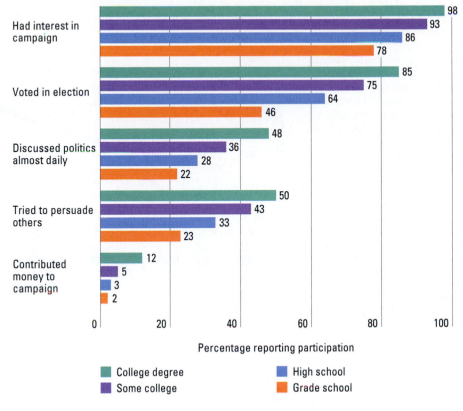

figure 7.5 ● **Effects of Education on Political Participation in 1992**

Education has a powerful effect on political participation in the United States. These data from a 1992 sample show that level of education is directly related to five different forms of conventional political participation.

Source: This analysis was based on the 1992 National Election Study done by the Center for Political Studies, University of Michigan, and distributed by the Inter-University Consortium for Political and Social Research, Ann Arbor, Michigan.

■ Use the CROSSTABS computer program that accompanies this book to analyze the effects of other variables — such as gender, race, and region — on these measures of political participation. All the variables in Figure 7.5 are contained in the "Voters" data set.

Figure 7.5 shows the striking relationship between level of formal education and various types of conventional political behavior. The strong link between education and electoral participation raises questions about low voter turnout in the United States, both over time and relative to other democracies. The fact is that the proportion of individuals with college degrees is greater in the United States than in other countries. Moreover, that proportion has been increasing steadily. Why, then, is voter turnout in elections so low? And why has it been dropping over time?

Low Voter Turnout in America

Voting is a low-initiative form of participation that can satisfy all three motives for political participation—showing allegiance to the nation, obtaining particularized benefits, and influencing broad policy. How then do we explain the decline in voter turnout in the United States?

The Decline in Voting over Time.   The graph of voter turnout in Figure 7.6 shows that the sharpest drop (five percentage points) occurred between the 1968 and 1972 elections. It was during this period (in 1971, actually) that

figure **7.6**   ● **The Decline of Voter Turnout: An Unsolved Puzzle**

Level of education is one of the strongest predictors of a person's likelihood of voting in the United States, and the percentage of citizens older than twenty-five with a high school education or more has grown steadily since the end of World War II. Nevertheless, the overall rate of voter turnout has gone down almost steadily in presidential elections since 1960, except for the spurt in 1992 inspired by Ross Perot's campaign. Alas, Perot lost the magic the second time around, and only 49 percent of a better-educated electorate voted in 1996. The phenomenon is recognized as an unsolved puzzle in American voting behavior.

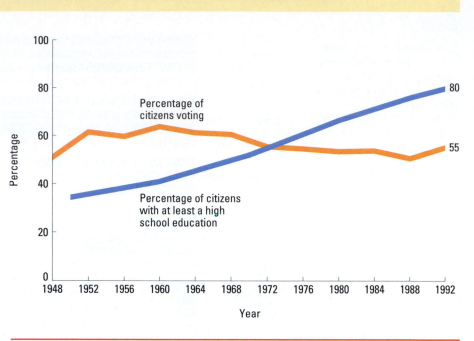

Sources: "Percentage voting" data up to 1988 come from Michael Nelson, ed., *Congressional Quarterly's Guide to the Presidency* (Washington, D.C.: Congressional Quarterly, Inc., 1989), p. 170; voter turnout for 1992 and "percentage of citizens with at least a high school education" come from U.S. Bureau of the Census, *Statistical Abstract of the United States, 1993* (Washington, D.C.: U.S. Government Printing Office, 1993), pp. 284 and 153.

Why should *you* vote? See this home page intended to increase voter turnout of eighteen- to twenty-four-year-olds.

Congress proposed and the states ratified the Twenty-sixth Amendment, which expanded the electorate by lowering the voting age from twenty-one to eighteen. Because people younger than twenty-one are much less likely to vote, their eligibility actually reduced the overall national turnout rate (the percentage of those eligible to vote who actually vote). To increase turnout of young people, an organization called "Rock the Vote" was formed in 1990 within the recording industry "to inform young Americans that their rights [to listen to racy and violent lyrics?] were in danger of being limited by a government in which they had little or no influence."[55] Some observers estimate that the enfranchisement of eighteen-year-olds accounts for about one or two percentage points in the total decline in turnout since 1952, but that still leaves more than ten percentage points to be explained.[56]

Why has voter turnout declined since 1968, while the level of education has increased? Many researchers have tried to solve this puzzle.[57] Some attribute most of the decline to changes in voters' attitudes toward politics. One major factor is the growing belief that government is not responsive to citizens and that voting does no good. One scholar refers to "a generalized withdrawal or disconnection from the political world, manifested most dramatically by declining psychological involvement in politics and a declining belief in government responsiveness."[58] Another is a change in attitude toward political parties, along with a decline in the extent and strength of party identification.[59] According to these psychological explanations, voter turnout in the United States is not likely to increase until the government does something to restore people's faith in the effectiveness of voting—with or without political parties. According to the age explanation, turnout in the United States is destined to remain a percentage point or two below its highs of the 1960s because of the lower voting rate of citizens younger than twenty-one.

U.S. Turnout Versus Turnout in Other Countries.   Scholars cite two factors to explain the low voter turnout in the United States compared with that in other countries. First are the differences in voting laws and administrative machinery.[60] In a few countries, voting is compulsory, and obviously, turnout is extremely high. But other methods can encourage voting—declaring election days to be public holidays, providing a two-day voting period, making it easy to cast absentee ballots. The United States does none of these things.

Furthermore, nearly every other democratic country places the burden of registration on the government rather than on the individual voter. This is important. Voting in the United States is a two-stage process, and the first stage (going to the proper officials to register) has required more initiative than the second stage (going to the polling booth to cast a ballot). In most American states, the registration process has been separate from the voting process in terms of both time (usually voters had to register weeks in advance of an election) and geography (often voters had to register at the county courthouse, not their polling place). One researcher who studied three states (Minnesota, Maine, and Wisconsin) that allowed citizens to register and vote on the same day estimated that such practices nationwide would alone add five points to the turnout rate.[61] Moreover, registration procedures often have been obscure, requiring potential voters to call around to find out what to do. Furthermore, people who move (and roughly one-third of the U.S. population moves between presidential elections) have had to reregister. In short, although voting requires little initiative, registration usually has required high initiative. If we compute voter turnout on the basis of those who are registered to vote, about 87 percent of Americans vote—a figure that moves the United States to the middle (but not the top) of all democratic nations.[62] We should begin to see somewhat higher voter turnout from the so-called motor-voter law, which requires states to allow citizens to register by mail (similar to renewing drivers' licenses) and at certain agencies that provide public assistance. During 1995, its first year of operation, more than 11 million voters were registered in 41 states under provisions of the motor-voter law.[63] Of course, many of these are new voters who would have registered anyway, so it will take time to assess the impact of this law. (Although Republican leaders resisted the law because they feared that it would result in more Democrats registering than Republicans, this apparently has not occurred.[64])

The second factor usually cited to explain low turnout in American elections is the lack of political parties that mobilize the vote of particular social groups, especially lower-income and less-educated people. American parties do make an effort to get out the vote, but neither party is as closely linked to specific groups as are parties in many other countries, where certain parties work hand in hand with specific ethnic, occupational, or religious groups. Research shows that strong party-group links can significantly increase turnout.[65] One important study claims that "changing mobilization patterns by parties, campaigns, and social movements accounts for at least half of the decline in electoral participation since the 1960s."[66] Other research suggests that while well-funded, vigorous campaigns mobilize citizens to vote, the effect depends on the type of citizens and the nature of the election. Highly educated, low-income citizens are more likely to be stimulated to vote than less-educated, high-income citizens, but lower-class citizens can be more mobilized to vote in presidential elections than in nonpresidential elections.[67]

To these explanations for low voter turnout in the United States—the traditional burden of registration and the lack of strong party-group links—we add another. Although the act of voting requires low initiative, the process of learning about the scores of candidates on the ballot in American elections requires a great deal of initiative. Some people undoubtedly fail to vote simply because they feel inadequate to the task of deciding among candidates for the many offices on the ballot in U.S. elections.

Teachers, newspaper columnists, and public affairs groups tend to worry a great deal about low voter turnout in the United States, suggesting that it signifies some sort of political sickness—or at least that it gives us a bad mark for democracy. Some others who study elections closely seem less concerned.[68] One scholar argues:

> Turnout rates do not indicate the amount of electing—the frequency . . . , the range of offices and decisions, the "value" of the vote—to which a country's citizens are entitled. . . . Thus, although the turnout rate in the United States is below that of most other democracies, American citizens do not necessarily do less voting than other citizens; most probably, they do more.[69]

Despite such words of assurance, the nagging thought remains that turnout ought to be higher, so various organizations mount get-out-the-vote campaigns before elections. Civic leaders often back the campaigns, because they value voting for its contribution to political order.

PARTICIPATION AND FREEDOM, EQUALITY, AND ORDER

As we have seen, Americans do participate in government in a variety of ways, and to a reasonable extent, compared with citizens of other countries. What is the relationship of political participation to the values of freedom, equality, and order?

Participation and Freedom

From the standpoint of normative theory, the relationship between participation and freedom is clear. Individuals should be free to participate in government and politics in the way they want and as much as they want. And they should be free not to participate as well. Ideally, all barriers to participation (such as restrictive voting registration and limitations on campaign expenditures) should be abolished—as should any schemes for compulsory voting. According to the normative perspective, we should

●●●●●●●●●●●●●

Million Man March

Nation of Islam minister Louis Farrakhan called for a "Million Man March" on Washington on October 16, 1995. He said the march was to show the world that black men were ready to accept their familial and community responsibilities. On that day, the crowd was perhaps the largest that had ever gathered in front of the Capitol, although estimates of its size varied widely. Using advanced techniques for crowd measurement, a team from Boston University estimated a crowd of 878,587. The team said: "With an estimated error margin of 25%, the number of participants could have been as high as 1,098,234 or as low as 658,940. These figures were acceptable to both the march organizers and the Park Service." See the Web site <www.rspac.ivv.nasa.gov/observe/exhibit/rem_sen/march/march_2.html>.

not worry about low voter turnout, because citizens should have the freedom not to vote as well as to vote.

In theory, freedom to participate also means that individuals should be able to use their wealth, connections, knowledge, organizational power (including sheer numbers in organized protests), or any other resource to influence government decisions, provided they do so legally. Of all these resources, the individual vote may be the weakest—and the least important—means of exerting political influence. Obviously, then, freedom as a value in political participation favors those with the resources to advance their own political self-interest.

Participation and Equality

The relationship between participation and equality is also clear. Each citizen's ability to influence government should be equal to that of every other citizen, so that differences in personal resources do not work against the poor or otherwise disadvantaged. Elections, then, serve the ideal of equality better than any other means of political participation. Formal rules for counting ballots—in particular, one person, one vote—cancel differences in resources among individuals.

At the same time, groups of people who have few resources individually can combine their votes to wield political power. Various European ethnic groups exercised this type of power in the late nineteenth and early twentieth centuries, when their votes won them entry to the sociopolitical system and allowed them to share in its benefits (see Chapter 5). More recently, blacks, Hispanics, homosexuals, and the disabled have used their voting power to gain political recognition. However, minorities often have had to use unconventional forms of participation to win the right to vote. As two major scholars of political participation put it, "Protest is the great equalizer, the political action that weights intensity as well as sheer numbers."[70]

Participation and Order

The relationship between participation and order is complicated. Some types of participation (pledging allegiance, voting) promote order and so are encouraged by those who value order; other types promote disorder and so are discouraged. Many citizens—men and women alike—even resisted giving women the right to vote for fear of upsetting the social order by altering the traditional roles of men and women.

Both conventional and unconventional participation can lead to the ouster of government officials, but the regime—the political system itself—is threatened more by unconventional participation. To maintain order, the government has a stake in converting unconventional participation to conventional participation whenever possible. We can easily imagine this tactic being used by authoritarian governments, but democratic governments also use it.

Think about the student unrest on college campuses during the Vietnam War. In private and public colleges alike, thousands of students stopped traffic, occupied buildings, destroyed property, struck classes, disrupted lectures, staged guerrilla theater, and behaved in other unconventional ways to protest the war, racism, capitalism, the behavior of their college presidents, the president of the United States, the military establishment, and all other institutions. (We are not exaggerating here. For example, students did all these things at Northwestern University in Evanston, Illinois, after members of the National Guard shot and killed four students at a demonstration at Kent State University in Ohio on May 4, 1970.)

Confronted by civil strife and disorder in the nation's institutions of higher learning, Congress took action. On March 23, 1971, it enacted and sent to the states the proposed Twenty-sixth Amendment, lowering the voting age to eighteen. Three-quarters of the state legislatures had to ratify the amendment before it became part of the Constitution. Astonishingly, thirty-eight states (the required number) complied by July 1, establishing a new speed record for ratification, cutting the old record nearly in half.[71] (Ironically, voting rights were not high on the list of students' demands.)

Testimony by members of Congress before the Judiciary Committee stated that the eighteen-year-old vote would "harness the energy of young people and direct it into useful and constructive channels," to keep students from becoming "more militant" and engaging "in destructive activities of a dangerous nature."[72] As one observer argued, the right to vote was extended to eighteen-year-olds not because young people demanded it but because "public officials believed suffrage expansion to be a means of institutionalizing youths' participation in politics, which would, in turn, curb disorder."[73]

PARTICIPATION AND THE MODELS OF DEMOCRACY

Ostensibly, elections are institutional mechanisms that implement democracy by allowing citizens to choose among candidates or issues. But elections also serve several other important purposes:[74]

- Elections socialize political activity. They transform what might otherwise consist of sporadic citizen-initiated acts into a routine public function. That is, the opportunity to vote for change encourages citizens to refrain from demonstrating in the streets. This helps preserve government stability by containing and channeling away potentially disruptive or dangerous forms of mass political activity.

- Elections institutionalize access to political power. They allow ordinary citizens to run for political office or to play an important role in selecting political leaders. Working to elect a candidate encourages the campaign worker to identify problems or propose solutions to the newly elected official.

- Elections bolster the state's power and authority. The opportunity to participate in elections helps convince citizens that the government is responsive to their needs and wants, which reinforces its legitimacy.

Participation and Majoritarianism

Although the majoritarian model assumes that government responsiveness to popular demands comes through mass participation in politics, majoritarianism views participation rather narrowly. It favors conventional, institutionalized behavior—primarily, voting in elections. Because majoritarianism relies on counting votes to determine what the majority wants, its bias toward equality in political participation is strong. Clearly, a class bias in voting exists because of the strong influence of socioeconomic status on turnout. Simply put, better-educated, wealthier citizens are more likely to participate in elections, and get-out-the-vote campaigns cannot counter this distinct bias.[75] Because it favors collective decisions formalized through elections, majoritarianism has little place for motivated, resourceful individuals to exercise private influence over government actions.

Majoritarianism also limits individual freedom in another way: its focus on voting as the major means of mass participation narrows the scope of conventional political behavior by defining which political actions are "orderly" and acceptable. By favoring equality and order in political participation, majoritarianism goes hand in hand with the ideological orientation of communitarianism (see Chapter 1).

Participation and Pluralism

Resourceful citizens who want the government's help with problems find a haven in the pluralist model of democracy. A decentralized and organizationally complex form of government allows many points of access and accommodates various forms of conventional participation in addition to voting. For example, wealthy people and well-funded groups can afford to hire lobbyists to press their interests in Congress. In one view of pluralist democracy, citizens are free to ply and wheedle public officials to further their own selfish visions of the public good. From another viewpoint, pluralism offers citizens the opportunity to be treated as individuals when dealing with the government, to influence policymaking in special circumstances, and to fulfill (insofar as possible in representative government) their social potential through participation in community affairs.

SUMMARY

To have "government by the people," the people must participate in politics. Conventional forms of participation—contacting officials and voting in elections—come most quickly to mind. However, citizens can also participate in politics in unconventional ways—staging sit-down strikes in public buildings, blocking traffic, and so on. Most citizens disapprove of most forms of unconventional political behavior. Yet, blacks and women used unconventional tactics to win important political and legal rights, including the right to vote.

People are motivated to participate in politics for various reasons: to show support for their country, to obtain particularized benefits for themselves or their friends, or to influence broad public policy. Their political actions may demand either little political knowledge or personal initiative, or a great deal of both.

The press often paints an unflattering picture of political participation in America. Clearly, the proportion of the electorate that votes in general elections in the United States has dropped and is far below that in other nations. When compared with other nations on a broad range of conventional and unconventional political behavior, however, the United States tends to show as much or more citizen participation in politics. Voter turnout in the United States suffers by comparison with that of other nations because of differences in voter registration requirements. We also lack institutions (especially strong political parties) that increase voter registration and help bring those of lower socioeconomic status to the polls.

People's tendency to participate in politics is strongly related to their socioeconomic status. Education, one component of socioeconomic status, is the single strongest predictor of conventional political participation in the United States. Because of the strong effect of socioeconomic status, the political system is potentially biased toward the interests of higher-status people. Pluralist democracy, which provides many avenues for resourceful citizens to influence government decisions, tends to increase this bias. Majoritarian democracy, which relies heavily on elections and the concept of one person, one vote, offers citizens without great personal resources the opportunity to influence government decisions through elections.

Elections also serve to legitimize government simply by involving the masses in government through voting. Whether voting means anything depends on the nature of voters' choices in elections. The range of choices available is a function of the nation's political parties, the topic of the next chapter.

Key Terms

political participation
conventional
  participation
unconventional
  participation

direct action
supportive behaviors
influencing behaviors
class action suit
suffrage

franchise
progressivism
direct primary
recall
referendum

initiative
standard socioeconomic
  model

Selected Readings

Conway, M. Margaret. *Political Participation in the United States*, 2d ed. Washington, D.C.: Congressional Quarterly Press, 1991. An excellent review of survey data on conventional political participation.

Craig, Stephen C. *The Malevolent Leaders: Popular Discontent in America*. Boulder, Colo.: Westview Press, 1993. This book uses in-depth interviews with citizens and members of Congress to look at the rise of popular discontent with and disengagement from politics.

Dalton, Russell J. *Citizen Politics in Western Democracies*, 2nd ed. Chatham, N.J.: Chatham House, 1996. Studies public opinion and behavior in the United States, Britain, Germany (west and east), and France. Two chapters compare conventional citizen action and protest politics in these countries.

Grofman, Bernard, and Chandler Davidson, eds.

Controversies in Minority Voting: The Voting Rights Act in Perspective. Washington, D.C.: Brookings Institution, 1992. Reviews the aims and accomplishments of the 1965 law that enforced voting rights for blacks in the South and some of its unintended consequences.

Rosenstone, Steven, and John Mark Hansen. *Mobilization, Participation, and Democracy in America*. New York: Macmillan, 1993. Explores the political meaning of citizens' declining participation in voting.

Teixeira, Ruy A. *The Disappearing American Voter*. Washington, D.C.: Brookings Institution, 1992. An empirical analysis of why many people do not vote, how that affects politics, and reflections on what can be done about it.

World Wide Web Resources

The National Political Index offers information on thirty-two means of accessing government, including contacting federal elected officials, contacting state and local officials, creating state initiatives and referenda, tracking congressional legislation, and so on.
`<www.politicalindex.com/>`

The mission statement of the Political Participation Project site, based at the Massachusetts Institute of Technology, states, "Our purpose is to understand how computer networks are affecting political participation in the United States, both traditional (campaigning and voting) and electronic (e-mail letters and online petitions)."

`<www.ai.mit.edu/people/msb/ppp/home.html>`

"The mission of the California Voter Foundation is to shape a more informed and engaged California electorate. Use our online voter resources to get substantive information on candidates and measures." More states will undoubtedly follow this model.
`<www.webcom.com/cvf/>`

Project Vote Smart is a nonpartisan, nonprofit political information system founded by former presidents Ford and Carter. It includes voting returns, candidate information, campaign finance records, and so on.
`<www.vote-smart.org>`

Political Parties

LIKE MANY OTHER CITIZENS IN EARLY 1992, H. Ross Perot was unhappy with the presidential candidates of the two major parties. Unlike most other citizens, Perot was a billionaire businessman. He could do much more than complain—and he did. In February 1992, Perot announced on national television that he was an independent candidate for president. He told CNN talk show host Larry King that he would run if his name were placed on the ballot in all fifty states. Perot's challenge struck a chord with people who were disenchanted with both President George Bush and his Democratic challenger, Bill Clinton. By mid-September, Perot's name had made the ballot in every state—thanks to the thousands of citizens who donated their time and to the millions of dollars donated by Perot.

By most estimates, Perot spent more than $65 million of his personal fortune running for president in 1992. His campaign advertised heavily on national television, and it produced impressive results. Ross Perot—a man with virtually no government experience who had never before run for public office and had no party backing—won nearly 19 percent of the popular vote. That was more than any candidate from outside the two major parties had won in a presidential election since 1912. Nevertheless, he failed to carry a single state and thus failed to win any votes in the electoral college. Although Bill Clinton won only 43 percent of the popular vote, he won the presidency by taking 370 electoral votes out of 535.

Because many analysts credited Clinton's 1992 victory to Perot's campaign attacks against President Bush, both Bill Clinton and Bob Dole—the two major candidates for president in 1996—pondered the same question: would Perot run again? Perot had already changed his strategy. In September 1995 he returned to "Larry King Live" to announce that he would create a new political party for independent voters fed up with the two-party system. With Perot's financial backing, an effort was quickly launched to get the Reform Party, as it was known, on the ballot in all fifty states for the 1996 presidential election. Although he did not name himself as the party's candidate—saying, "This is not about me running for president"—most observers assumed that Perot could be coaxed.[1] But up until July, Perot continued acting coy—until Richard Lamm, former Democratic governor of Colorado, declared that he would seek the Reform Party's nomination if Perot would not. Then Perot finally admitted that he desired the nomination of his own political party: "If anybody should do it I should do it. And I will do it, and I'm in a unique position to do it."[2]

●●●●●●●●●●●●●
Planning an Expensive Party

A volunteer working for the Reform Party in Naples, Florida, obtains a citizen's signature on a petition to place the party on the state's ballot in 1996. When Perot ran for president as an independent candidate in 1992, he was helped by thousands of volunteers who circulated petitions to get his name on the ballot. Nevertheless, he still had to pay professional petitioners to finish the job. In 1996, with public enthusiasm waning for Perot, volunteers played a smaller role, and his organization had to rely even more on paid workers to register the party on ballots across the country.

On paper, the Reform Party's chances looked good. Its creator had won almost twenty million votes in the 1992 presidential election; nearly 60 percent of a 1995 sample had agreed that "we should have a third major political party in this country in addition to the Democrats and Republicans"; and a March 1996 survey had estimated that 20 percent of registered voters would prefer some independent or third-party candidate to either Clinton or Dole.[3] Nevertheless, most political analysts predicted that the Reform Party was doomed to fail in 1996. It could only play the role of "spoiler"—as many thought Perot had done in 1992.

Political analysts discounted the Reform Party's chances because the structure and dynamics of U.S. politics work strongly *against* any third party and *for* the operation of a two-party system. Indeed, the Democratic and Republican parties have dominated national and state politics in the United States for more than 125 years. Their domination is more complete than that of any pair of parties in any other democratic government. Although all democracies have some form of multiparty politics, very few have a stable two-party system—Britain and New Zealand being the most notable exceptions (see Compared with What? 8.1). Most people take our two-party system for granted, not realizing that it is arguably the most unique feature of American government.

Why do we have any political parties? What functions do they perform? How did we become a nation of Democrats and Republicans? Do these parties truly differ in their platforms and behavior? Are parties really necessary for democratic government, or do they just get in the way of citizens and their government? In this chapter, we will answer these questions by examining political parties, perhaps the most misunderstood element of American politics.

POLITICAL PARTIES
AND THEIR
FUNCTIONS

According to democratic theory, the primary means by which citizens control their government is voting in free elections. Most Americans agree that voting is important: of those surveyed after the 1992 presidential campaign, 87 percent felt that elections make the government "pay attention to what the people think."[4] Americans are not nearly as supportive of the role played by political parties in elections, however. When asked whether Perot should run for president in 1996 as "head of a third party which would also run candidates in state and local races" or "by himself as an independent candidate," 60 percent of a national sample favored his running without a party.[5]

On the other hand, Americans are quick to condemn as "undemocratic" countries that do not regularly hold elections contested by political parties. In truth, Americans have a love-hate relationship with political parties. They believe that parties are necessary for democratic government; at the same time, they think parties are somehow obstructionist and not to be trusted. This distrust is particularly strong among younger voters. To better appreciate the role of political parties in democratic government, we must understand exactly what parties are and what they do.

What Is a Political Party?

A **political party** is an organization that sponsors candidates for political office *under the organization's name.* The italicized part of this definition is important. True political parties select individuals to run for public office through a formal **nomination** process, which designates them as the parties' official candidates. This activity distinguishes the Democratic and Republican parties from interest groups. The AFL-CIO and the National Association of Manufacturers are interest groups. They often support candidates, but they do not nominate them to run as their avowed representatives. If they did, they would be transformed into political parties. In short, the sponsoring of candidates, designated as representatives of the organization, is what defines an organization as a party.

Most democratic theorists agree that a modern nation-state cannot practice democracy without at least two political parties that regularly contest elections. In fact, the link between democracy and political parties is so firm that many people define *democratic government* in terms of competitive party politics.

Party Functions

Parties contribute to democratic government through the functions they perform for the **political system**—the set of interrelated institutions that link people with government. Four of the most important party functions are nominating candidates for election to public office, structuring the voting choice in elections, proposing alternative government programs, and coordinating the actions of government officials.

Nominating Candidates. Without political parties, voters would confront a bewildering array of self-nominated candidates, each seeking votes on the basis of personal friendships, celebrity status, or name recognition.

8.1   Only Two to Tangle

Compared with the system in other countries, the two-party system in the United States is unusual indeed. First, most democracies have multiparty systems, in which four or five parties win enough seats in the legislature to contest for government power. Even those other countries that are classified as having two-party systems, such as the United Kingdom and New Zealand, really have some minor parties that regularly gain seats and thus complicate national politics. The purity of the U.S. pattern shows clearly in these graphs of party strength over time in the U.S. House compared with the British House of Commons and the New Zealand House of Representatives.

Sources: Dick Leonard, *World Atlas of Elections* (London: The Economist Publications, 1986), pp. 102, 130. Copyright © 1986 The Economist Newspaper Group, Inc. Used by permission. Data for later elections came from Thomas T. Mackie and Richard Rose, *The International Almanac of Electoral History*, 3rd ed. (Washington, D.C.: Congressional Quarterly Press, 1991) and from The Lijphart Elections Archive at <dodgson.ucsd.edu/lij/lij Catalog.html>.

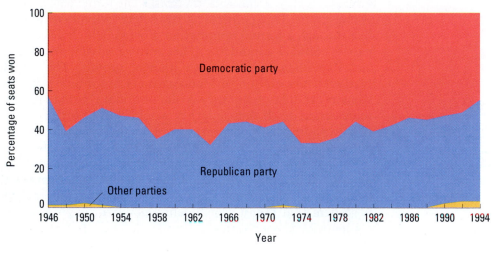

Parties can provide a form of quality control for their nominees through the process of peer review. Party insiders, the nominees' peers, usually know the strengths and faults of potential candidates much better than average voters and thus can judge their suitability for representing the party.

In nominating candidates, parties often do more than pass judgment on potential office seekers; sometimes, they go so far as to recruit talented in-

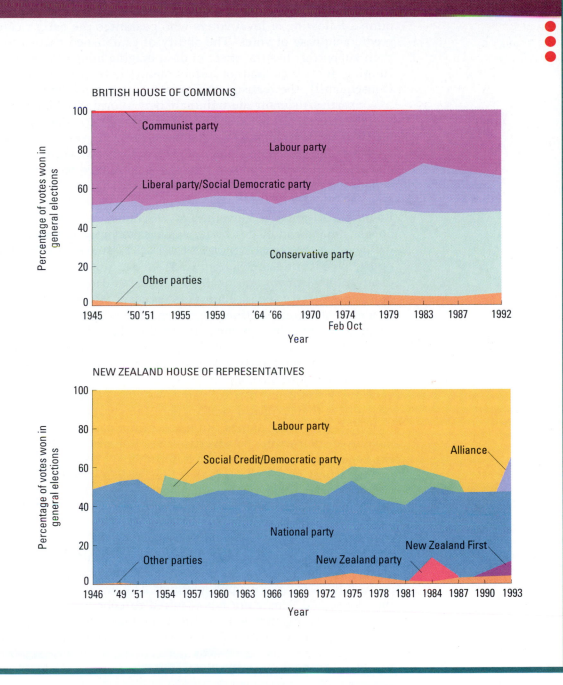

BRITISH HOUSE OF COMMONS

NEW ZEALAND HOUSE OF REPRESENTATIVES

dividuals to become candidates. In this way, parties help not only to ensure a minimum level of quality among candidates who run for office but
also to raise the quality of those candidates.

Structuring the Voting Choice.   Political parties also help democratic
government by structuring the voting choice—reducing the number of

candidates on the ballot to those who have a realistic chance of winning. Established parties—those with experience in contesting elections—acquire a following of loyal voters who guarantee the party's candidates a predictable base of votes. The ability of established parties to mobilize their supporters has the effect of discouraging nonparty candidates from running for office and of discouraging new parties from forming. Consequently, the realistic choice is between candidates offered by the major parties, reducing the amount of new information that voters need in order to make a rational decision. Contrast the voting decision in our stable two-party system (and the outcome) with the voter's task in the June 1996 Russian presidential election, where forty-five political parties were certified to run. The top two candidates combined received only 67 percent of the vote, while eight other candidates shared 30 percent.

Proposing Alternative Government Programs.   Parties also help voters choose among candidates by proposing alternative programs of government action—the general policies their candidates will pursue if they gain office. Even if voters know nothing about the qualities of the parties' candidates, they can vote rationally for the candidates of the party that has policies they favor. The specific policies advocated vary from candidate to candidate and from election to election. However, the types of policies advocated by candidates of one party tend to differ from those proposed by candidates of other parties. Although there are exceptions, candidates of the same party tend to favor policies that fit their party's underlying political philosophy, or ideology.

In many countries, parties' names—such as Conservative and Socialist—reflect their political stance. The Democrats and Republicans have ideologically neutral names, but many minor parties in the United States have used their names to advertise their policies: the Prohibition Party, the Socialist Party, and even the Reform Party. The neutrality of the two major parties' names suggests that their policies are similar. This is not true. As we shall see, they regularly adopt very different policies in their platforms.

Coordinating the Actions of Government Officials.   Finally, party organizations help coordinate the actions of public officials. A government based on the separation of powers, such as that of the United States, divides responsibilities for making public policy. The president and the leaders of the House and Senate are not required to cooperate with one another. Political party organizations are the major means for bridging the separate powers to produce coordinated policies that can govern the country effectively. Parties do this in two ways. First, candidates' and officeholders' political fortunes are linked to their party organization, which can bestow and withhold favors. Second, and perhaps more important in the United States, members of the same party in the presidency, the House, and the Senate tend to share political principles and thus often voluntarily cooperate in making policy.

So why do we have parties? One expert notes that successful politicians in the United States need electoral and governing majorities and that "no collection of ambitious politicians has long been able to think of a way to achieve their goals in this democracy save in terms of political parties."[6]

A History of U.S. Party Politics

The two major U.S. parties are among the oldest in the world. In fact, the Democratic party, founded in 1828 but with roots reaching back to the late 1700s, has a strong claim to being the oldest party in existence. Its closest rival is the British Conservative Party, formed in 1832, two decades before the Republican party was organized in 1854. Several generations of citizens have supported the Democratic and Republican parties, and they are part of American history. They have become institutionalized in our political process.

THE PREPARTY PERIOD

Today we think of party activities as normal, even essential, to American politics. It was not always so. The Constitution makes no mention of political parties, and none existed when the Constitution was written in 1787. It was common then to refer to groups pursuing some common political interest as *factions.* Although factions were seen as inevitable in politics, they were also considered dangerous. One argument for adopting the Constitution—proposed in *Federalist* No. 10 (see Chapter 3 and the Appendix)—was that its federal system would prevent factional influences from controlling the government.

Factions existed even under British rule. In colonial assemblies, supporters of the governor (and thus of the Crown) were known as *Tories* or *Loyalists*, and their opponents were called *Whigs* or *Patriots.* After independence, the arguments over whether to adopt the Constitution produced a different alignment of factions. Those who backed the Constitution were loosely known as *federalists*, their opponents as *antifederalists.* At this stage, the groups could not be called parties, because they did not sponsor candidates for election.

Elections then were vastly different from elections today. The Constitution provided for the president and vice president to be chosen by an **electoral college**—a body of electors who met in the capitals of their respective states to cast their ballots. Initially, in most states the legislatures, not the voters, chose the electors (one for each senator and representative in Congress). Presidential elections in the early years of the nation, then, actually were decided by a handful of political leaders. (See Chapter 9 for a discussion of the electoral college in modern presidential politics.) Often they met in small, secret groups, called **caucuses**, to propose candidates for public office. Often these were composed of like-minded members of state legislatures and Congress. This was the setting for George Washington's election as the first president in 1789.

We can classify Washington as a federalist, because he supported the Constitution, but he was not a factional leader and actually opposed factional politics. His immense prestige, coupled with his political neutrality, left Washington unopposed for the office of president, and he was elected unanimously by the electoral college. During Washington's administration, however, the political cleavage sharpened between those who favored a stronger national government and those who wanted a less powerful, more decentralized national government.

The first group, led by Alexander Hamilton, proclaimed themselves *Federalists.* The second group, led by Thomas Jefferson, called themselves

Republicans. (Although they used the same name, they were not Republicans as we know them today.) The Jeffersonians chose the name Republicans to distinguish themselves from the "aristocratic" tendencies of Hamilton's Federalists. The Federalists countered by calling the Republicans the *Democratic Republicans*, attempting to link Jefferson's party to the disorder (and beheadings) spawned by the "radical democrats" in France during the French Revolution of 1789.

The First Party System: Federalists and Democratic Republicans

Washington was reelected president unanimously in 1792, but his vice president, John Adams, was opposed by a candidate backed by the Democratic Republicans. This brief skirmish foreshadowed the nation's first major-party struggle over the presidency. Disheartened by the political split in his administration, Washington spoke out against "the baneful effects" of parties in his farewell address in 1796. Nonetheless, parties already existed in the political system, as Figure 8.1 shows. In the election of 1796, the Federalists supported Vice President John Adams to succeed Washington as president. The Democratic Republicans backed Thomas Jefferson for president but could not agree on a vice-presidential candidate. In the electoral college, Adams won seventy-one votes to Jefferson's sixty-eight, and both ran ahead of other candidates. At that time, the Constitution provided that the presidency would go to the candidate who won the most votes in the electoral college, with the vice presidency going to the runner-up. So Adams, a Federalist, had to accept Jefferson, a Democratic Republican, as his vice president. Obviously, the Constitution did not anticipate a presidential contest between candidates from opposing political parties.

The party function of nominating candidates emerged more clearly in the election of 1800. Both parties caucused in Congress to nominate candidates for president and vice president. The result was the first true party contest for the presidency. The Federalists nominated John Adams and Charles Pinckney; the Democratic Republicans nominated Thomas Jefferson and Aaron Burr. This time, the Democratic Republican candidates won. However, the new party organization worked too well. According to the Constitution, each elector had to vote by ballot for two persons. The Democratic Republican electors unanimously cast their two votes for Jefferson and Burr. The presidency was to go to the candidate with the most votes, but the top two candidates were tied!

Although Jefferson was the party's presidential candidate and Burr its vice-presidential candidate, the Constitution empowered the House of Representatives to choose either one of them as president. After seven days and thirty-six ballots, the House decided in favor of Jefferson.

The Twelfth Amendment, ratified in 1804, prevented a repeat of the troublesome election outcomes of 1796 and 1800. It required the electoral college to vote separately for president and vice president, implicitly recognizing that parties would nominate different candidates for the two offices.

The election of 1800 marked the beginning of the end for the Federalists, who lost the next four elections. By 1820, the Federalists were no more.

figure 8.1 ● **Two-Party Systems in American History**

Over time, the American party system has undergone a series of wrenching transformations. Since 1856, the Democrats and the Republicans have alternated irregularly in power, each party enjoying a long period of dominance.

Year		Party System	Democratic	Third Parties	Republican
1789	*Washington unanimously elected president*	PREPARTY PERIOD			
1792	*Washington unanimously reelected*				
1796	Federalist *Adams*	FIRST PARTY SYSTEM	Democratic Republican		
1800	—		*Jefferson*		
1804	—		*Jefferson*		
1808	—		*Madison*		
1812	—		*Madison*		
1816	—		*Monroe*		
1820		"ERA OF GOOD FEELING"	*Monroe*		
1824			*J.Q. Adams*		
1828		SECOND PARTY SYSTEM	Democratic *Jackson*		National Republican
1832			*Jackson*		Whig
1836			*Van Buren*		—
1840			—		*Harrison*
1844			*Polk*		
1848			—		*Taylor*
1852			*Pierce*		—
1856		THIRD PARTY SYSTEM	*Buchanan*		Republican
1860	Constitutional Union Southern Democrat		—		*Lincoln*
1864			—		*Lincoln*
1868			—		*Grant*
1872			—		*Grant*
1876			—		*Hayes*
1880			—		*Garfield*
1884		Rough Balance	*Cleveland*		—
1888			—		*Harrison*
1892			*Cleveland*		—
1896			—	Populist	*McKinley*
1900		Republican Dominance	—		*McKinley*
1904			—		*T. Roosevelt*
1908			—		*Taft*
1912			*Wilson*	Progressive	—
1916			*Wilson*		—
1920			—		*Harding*
1924			—		*Coolidge*
1928			—		*Hoover*
1932		Democratic Dominance	*F.D. Roosevelt*		—
1936			*F.D. Roosevelt*		—
1940			*F.D. Roosevelt*		—
1944			*F.D. Roosevelt*		—
1948			*Truman*	States' Rights	—
1952			—		*Eisenhower*
1956			—		*Eisenhower*
1960			*Kennedy*		—
1964			*Johnson*		—
1968			—	American Independent	*Nixon*
1972			—		*Nixon*
1976			*Carter*		—
1980			—	Independent	*Reagan*
1984			—		*Reagan*
1988			—		*Bush*
1992			*Clinton*	Independent	—
1996			*Clinton*	Reform	—

The Democratic Republican candidate, James Monroe, was reelected in the first presidential contest without party competition since Washington's time. (Monroe received all but one electoral vote, which reportedly was cast against him so that Washington would remain the only president ever elected unanimously.) Ironically, the lack of partisan competition under Monroe, in what was dubbed "the Era of Good Feelings," also fatally weakened his party, the Democratic Republicans. Lacking competition, the Democratic Republicans neglected their function of nominating candidates. In 1824, the party caucus's nominee was challenged by three other Democratic Republicans, including John Quincy Adams and Andrew Jackson, who proved to be more popular candidates among the voters in the ensuing election.

Before 1824, the parties' role in structuring the popular vote was relatively unimportant, because relatively few people were entitled to vote. But the states began to drop restrictive requirements for voting after 1800, and voting rights for white males expanded even faster after 1815 (see Chapter 7). With the expansion of suffrage, more states began to allow the voters to choose the presidential electors, rather than Congress. The 1824 election was the first in which the voters selected the presidential electors in most states. Still, the role of political parties in structuring the popular vote had not yet developed fully.

Although Jackson won a plurality of both the popular vote and the electoral vote in 1824, he did not win the necessary majority in the electoral college. The House of Representatives again had to decide the winner. It chose the second-place John Quincy Adams (from the established state of Massachusetts) over the voters' choice, Jackson (from the frontier state of Tennessee). The factionalism among the leaders of the Democratic Republican party became so intense that the party split in two.

The Second Party System: Democrats and Whigs

The Jacksonian faction of the Democratic Republican party represented the common people in the expanding South and West, and its members took pride in calling themselves simply Democrats. Jackson ran again for the presidency as a Democrat in 1828, a milestone that marked the beginning of today's Democratic party. That election was also the first "mass" election in U.S. history. Although voters had directly chosen many presidential electors in 1824, the total votes cast in that election numbered fewer than 370,000. By 1828, relaxed requirements for voting (and the use of popular elections to select presidential electors in more states) had increased the vote by more than 300 percent, to more than 1.1 million.

As the electorate expanded, the parties changed. No longer could a party rely on a few political leaders in the state legislatures to control the votes cast in the electoral college. Parties now needed to campaign for votes cast by hundreds of thousands of citizens. Recognizing this new dimension of the nation's politics, the parties responded with a new method for nominating presidential candidates. Instead of selecting candidates in a closed caucus of party representatives in Congress, the parties devised the **national convention**. At these gatherings, delegates from state parties across the nation would choose candidates for president and vice president and adopt a statement of policies called a **party platform**. The Anti-Masonic Party, which was the first "third" party in American history to challenge the two major parties for the presidency, called the first national convention in 1831. The Democrats adopted the convention idea in 1832 to nominate Jackson for a second term, as did their new opponents that year, the National Republicans.

The label *National Republicans* applied to John Quincy Adams's faction of the former Democratic Republican party. However, the National Republicans did not become today's Republican party. Adams's followers called themselves National Republicans to signify their old Federalist preference for a strong national government, but the symbolism did not appeal to the voters, and the National Republicans lost to Jackson in 1832.

Elected to another term, Jackson began to assert the power of the nation over the states (acting more like a National Republican than a Democrat). His policies drew new opponents, who started calling him "King Andrew." A coalition made up of former National Republicans, Anti-Masons, and Jackson haters formed the Whig party in 1834.[7] The name referred to the English Whigs, who opposed the powers of the British throne; the implication was that Jackson was governing like a king. For the next thirty years, Democrats and Whigs alternated in the presidency. However, the issues of slavery and sectionalism eventually destroyed the Whigs from within. Although the party had won the White House in 1848 and had taken 44 percent of the vote in 1852, the Whigs were unable to field a presidential candidate in the 1856 election.

The Current Party System: Democrats and Republicans

In the early 1850s, antislavery forces (including some Whigs and antislavery Democrats) began to organize. At meetings in Jackson, Michigan, and Ripon, Wisconsin, they recommended the formation of a new party, the Republican party, to oppose the extension of slavery into the Kansas and Nebraska territories. It is this party, founded in 1854, that continues as today's Republican party.

The Republican party entered its first presidential election in 1856. It took 33 percent of the vote, and its candidate (John Frémont) carried eleven states—all in the North. Then, in 1860, the Republicans nominated Abraham Lincoln. The Democrats were deeply divided over the slavery issue and actually split into two parties. The northern wing kept the Democratic party label and nominated Stephen Douglas. The Southern Democrats ran John Breckinridge. A fourth party, the Constitutional Union party, nominated John Bell. Lincoln took 40 percent of the popular vote and carried every northern state. Breckinridge won every southern state. But all three of Lincoln's opponents together still did not win enough electoral votes to deny him the presidency.

The election of 1860 is considered the first of three critical elections under the current party system.[8] A **critical election** is marked by a sharp change in the existing patterns of party loyalty among groups of voters. Moreover, this change in voting patterns, which is called an **electoral realignment**, does not end with the election but persists through several subsequent elections.[9] The election of 1860 divided the country politically between the northern states, whose voters mainly voted Republican, and the southern states, which were overwhelmingly Democratic. The victory of the North over the South in the Civil War cemented Democratic loyalties in the South.

For forty years, from 1880 to 1920, no Republican presidential candidate won even one of the eleven states of the former Confederacy. The South's solid Democratic record earned it the nickname "the Solid South." The Republicans did not puncture the Solid South until 1920, when Warren G. Harding carried Tennessee. The Republicans later won five southern states in 1928, when the Democrats ran the first Catholic candidate, Al Smith. Republican presidential candidates won no more southern states until 1952, when Dwight Eisenhower broke the pattern of Democratic dominance in the South—ninety years after that pattern had been set by the Civil War.

Eras of Party Dominance Since the Civil War

The critical election of 1860 established the Democratic and Republican parties as the dominant parties in our **two-party system.** In a two-party system, most voters are so loyal to one or the other of the major parties that independent candidates or candidates from a third party—which means any minor party—have little chance of winning office. Certainly that is true in presidential elections, as Perot found out in both 1992 and 1996. Third-party candidates tend to be most successful at the local or state level. Since the current two-party system was established, relatively few minor-party candidates have won election to the U.S. House, even fewer have won election to the Senate, and none have won the presidency.

The voters in a given state, county, or community are not always equally divided in their loyalties between the Republicans and the Democrats. In some areas, voters typically favor the Republicans, while voters in other areas prefer the Democrats. When one party in a two-party system *regularly* enjoys support from most voters in an area, it is called the *majority party* in that area; the other is called the *minority party*. Since the inception of the current two-party system, three periods have characterized the balance between the two major parties at the national level.

A Rough Balance: 1860–1894.   From 1860 through 1894, the Grand Old Party (or GOP, as the Republican party is sometimes called) won eight of ten presidential elections, which would seem to qualify it as the majority party. However, some of its success in presidential elections came from its practice of running Civil War heroes and from the North's domination of southern politics. Seats in the House of Representatives are a better guide to the breadth of national support. An analysis shows that the Republicans and Democrats won an equal number of congressional elections, each controlling the chamber for nine sessions between 1860 and 1894.

A Republican Majority: 1896–1930.   A second critical election, in 1896, transformed the Republican party into a true majority party. Grover Cleveland, a Democrat, occupied the White House, and the country was in a severe depression. The Republicans nominated William McKinley, gov-

● ● ● ● ● ● ● ● ● ● ● ● ● ● ●

William Jennings Bryan: When Candidates Were Orators

Today, televised images of a candidate waving his hands and shouting to an audience would look silly. But candidates once had to resort to such tactics to be effective with large crowds. One of the most commanding orators around the turn of the century was William Jennings Bryan (1860–1925), whose stirring speeches extolling the virtues of the free coinage of silver were music to the ears of thousands of westerners and southern farmers.

ernor of Ohio and a conservative, who stood for a high tariff against foreign goods and sound money tied to the value of gold. Rather than tour the country seeking votes, McKinley ran a dignified campaign from his Ohio home.

The Democrats, already in trouble because of the depression, nominated the fiery William Jennings Bryan. In stark contrast to McKinley, Bryan advocated the free and unlimited coinage of silver—which would mean cheap money and easy payment of debts through inflation. Bryan was also the nominee of the young Populist Party, an agrarian protest party that had proposed the free-silver platform Bryan adopted. Feature 8.1 explains that the book *The Wonderful Wizard of Oz*, which you probably know as a movie, was actually a Populist political fable.[10] Conservatives, especially businesspeople, were aghast at the Democrats' radical turn, and voters in the heavily populated Northeast and Midwest surged toward the Republican party, many of them permanently. McKinley carried every northern state east of the Mississippi, as Figure 8.2 shows. The Republicans also won the House, and they retained their control of it in the next six elections.

The election of 1896 helped solidify a Republican majority in industrial America and forged a link between the Republican party and business. In the subsequent electoral realignment, the Republicans emerged as a true majority party. The GOP dominated national politics—controlling the presidency, the Senate, and the House—almost continuously from 1896 until the Wall Street crash of 1929, which burst big business's bubble and launched the Great Depression.*

* *The only break in GOP domination was in 1912, when Teddy Roosevelt's Progressive Party split from the Republicans, allowing Democrat Woodrow Wilson to win the presidency and giving the Democrats control of Congress, and again in 1916, when Wilson was reelected.*

8.2 ● The Critical Election of 1896

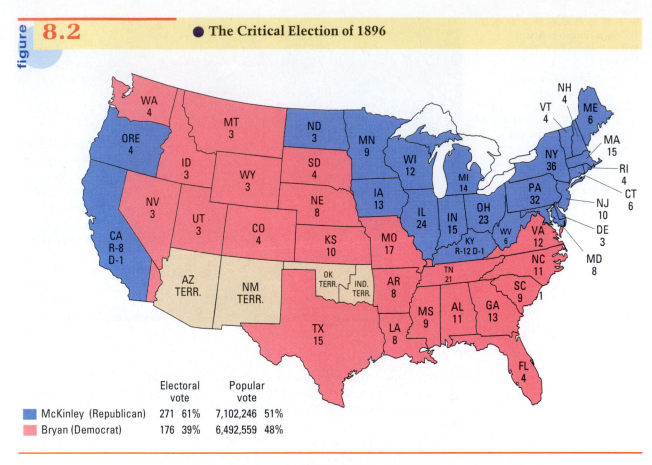

	Electoral vote		Popular vote	
■ McKinley (Republican)	271	61%	7,102,246	51%
■ Bryan (Democrat)	176	39%	6,492,559	48%

In the presidential election of 1896, voters in the populous and industrial East and Midwest elected Republican William McKinley (who was pro-business) over Democrat William Jennings Bryan (an advocate of the rural West and South). The Republicans emerged as the majority party in the national elections following this election.

A Democratic Majority: 1932 to the Present?　The Republicans' majority status ended in the critical election of 1932 between incumbent president Herbert Hoover and the Democratic challenger, Franklin Delano Roosevelt. Roosevelt promised new solutions to unemployment and the economic crisis of the Depression. His campaign appealed to labor, middle-class liberals, and new European ethnic voters. Along with Democratic voters in the Solid South, urban workers in the North, Catholics, Jews, and white ethnic minorities formed "the Roosevelt coalition." The relatively few blacks who voted at that time tended to remain loyal to the Republicans—"the party of Lincoln."

Roosevelt was swept into office in a landslide, carrying huge Democratic majorities with him into the House and Senate to enact his liberal activist programs. The electoral realignment reflected by the election of 1932 made the Democrats the majority party. Not only was Roosevelt reelected in 1936, 1940, and 1944, but Democrats held control of both Houses of Congress in most sessions from 1933 through 1994. The only exceptions were Republican control of Congress in 1947 and 1948

8.1

feature

The Wizard of Oz: A Political Fable

Most Americans are familiar with *The Wizard of Oz* through the children's books or the 1939 motion picture, but few realize that the story was written as a political fable to promote the Populist movement around the turn of the century. Next time you see or read it, try interpreting the Tin Woodsman as the industrial worker, the Scarecrow as the struggling farmer, and the Wizard as the president, who is powerful only as long as he succeeds in deceiving the people. (Sorry, but in the book Dorothy's ruby slippers were only silver shoes.)

The Wonderful Wizard of Oz was written by Lyman Frank Baum in 1900, during the collapse of the Populist movement. Through the Populist party, Midwestern farmers, in alliance with some urban workers, had challenged the banks, railroads, and other economic interests that squeezed farmers through low prices, high freight rates, and continued indebtedness.

The Populists advocated government ownership of railroad, telephone, and telegraph industries. They also wanted silver coinage. Their power grew during the 1893 depression, the worst in U.S. history until then, as farm prices sank to new lows and unemployment was widespread.

In the 1894 congressional elections, the Populist party got almost 40 percent of the vote. It looked forward to winning the presidency, and the silver standard, in 1896. But in that election, which revolved around the issue of gold versus silver, Populist Democrat William Jennings Bryan lost to Republican William McKinley by 95 electoral votes. Bryan, a congressman from Nebraska and a gifted orator, ran again in 1900, but the Populist strength was gone.

Baum viewed these events in both rural South Dakota, where he edited a local weekly, and in urban Chicago, where he wrote *Oz*. He mourned the destruction of the fragile alliance between the Midwestern farmers (the Scarecrow) and the urban industrial workers (the Tin Woodsman). Along with Bryan (the Cowardly Lion, with a roar but little else), they had been taken down the yellow brick road (the gold standard) that led nowhere. Each journeyed to Emerald City seeking favors from the Wizard of Oz (the President).

Dorothy, the symbol of Everyman, went along with them, innocent enough to see the truth before the others.

Along the way they met the Wicked Witch of the East who, Baum tells us, had kept the little Munchkin people "in bondage for many years, making them slave for her night and day." She also had put a spell on the Tin Woodsman, once an independent and hard-working man, so that each time he swung his axe, it chopped off a different part of his body. Lacking another trade, he "worked harder than ever," becoming like a machine, incapable of love, yearning for a heart. Another witch, the Wicked Witch of the West, clearly symbolizes the large industrial corporations.

The small group heads toward Emerald City, where the Wizard rules from behind a papier-mâché façade. Oz, by the way, is the abbreviation for ounce, the standard measure for gold.

Like all good politicians, the Wizard can be all things to all people. Dorothy sees him as an enormous head. The Scarecrow sees a gossamer fairy. The Woodsman sees an awful beast, the Cowardly Lion "a ball of fire so fierce and glowing he could scarcely bear to gaze upon it."

Later, however, when they confront the Wizard directly, they see he is nothing more than "a little man, with a bald head and a wrinkled face."

"I have been making believe," the Wizard confesses. "I'm just a common man." But the Scarecrow adds, "You're more than that . . . you're a humbug."

"It was a great mistake my ever letting you into the Throne Room," admits the Wizard, a former ventriloquist and circus balloonist from Omaha.

This was Baum's ultimate Populist message. The powers-that-be survive by deception. Only people's ignorance allows the powerful to manipulate and control them. Dorothy returns to Kansas with the magical help of her silver shoes (the silver issue), but when she gets to Kansas she realizes her shoes "had fallen off in her flight through the air, and were lost forever in the desert." Still, she is safe at home with Aunt Em and Uncle Henry, simple farmers.

Source: Peter Dreier, "The Wizard of Oz: A Political Fable," *Today Journal,* 14 February 1986. Copyright © 1986 Pacific News Service and the author. Used by permission.

(under President Truman); in 1953 and 1954 (under President Eisenhower); and of the Senate only in 1947 and 1948 and from 1981 to 1986 (under Reagan). In their smashing victory in the 1994 congressional elections, however, Republicans gained control of Congress for the first time in forty years. They retained control after the 1996 elections—the first time that Republicans took both houses in successive elections since Herbert Hoover's presidency in the early 1930s.

In presidential elections, however, the Democrats have not fared so well since Roosevelt. In fact, they have won only five elections (Truman, Kennedy, Johnson, Carter, and Clinton), compared with the Republicans' seven victories (Eisenhower twice, Nixon twice, Reagan twice, and Bush once). In 1996, Clinton became the first Democratic president since Roosevelt to be reelected. His feat was comparable to Republican majorities being returned to both houses of Congress in back-to-back elections in 1994 and 1996.

Signs are strong that the coalition of Democratic voters forged by Roosevelt in the 1930s has already cracked. Certainly the South is no longer solid for the Democrats. Since 1952, in fact, it has voted more consistently for Republican presidential candidates than for Democrats. The party system in the United States does not seem to be undergoing another realignment; rather, we seem to be in a period of **electoral dealignment**, in which party loyalties have become less important to voters as they cast their ballots. We examine the influence of party loyalty on voting in the next chapter, after we look at the operation of our two-party system.

THE AMERICAN TWO-PARTY SYSTEM

Our review of party history in the United States has focused on the two dominant parties. But we should not ignore the special contributions of certain minor parties, among them the Anti-Masonic Party, the Populists, and the Progressives of 1912. In this section, we study the fortunes of minor, or third, parties in American politics. We also will look at why we have only two major parties, explain how federalism helps the parties survive, and describe voters' loyalty to the two major parties today.

Minor Parties in America

Minor parties have always figured in party politics in America. Most minor parties in our political history have been one of four types:[11]

- *Bolter parties* are formed by factions that have split off from one of the major parties. Six times in the thirty-one presidential elections since the Civil War, disgruntled leaders have "bolted the ticket" and challenged their former parties. Bolter parties have occasionally won significant proportions of the vote. However, with the exception of Teddy Roosevelt's Progressive Party in 1912 and the possible exception of George Wallace's American Independent Party in 1968, bolter parties have not affected the outcome of presidential elections.

- *Farmer-labor parties* represent farmers and urban workers who believe that they, the working class, are not getting their share of society's wealth. The People's Party, founded in 1892 and nicknamed "the

Populist Party," was a prime example of a farmer-labor party. The Populists won 8.5 percent of the vote in 1892 and also became the first third party since 1860 to win any electoral votes. Flushed by success, it endorsed William Jennings Bryan, the Democratic candidate, in 1896. When he lost, the party quickly faded. Farm and labor groups revived many Populist ideas in the Progressive Party in 1924, which nominated Robert La Follette for the presidency. Although the party won 16.6 percent of the popular vote, it carried only La Follette's home state of Wisconsin. The party died in 1925.

- *Parties of ideological protest* go further than farmer-labor parties in criticizing the established system. These parties reject prevailing doctrines and propose radically different principles, often favoring more government activism. The Socialist Party has been the most successful party of ideological protest. Even at its high point in 1912, however, it garnered only 6 percent of the vote, and Socialist candidates for president have never won a single state. In recent years, the sound of ideological protest has come more from rightist parties, arguing for the radical disengagement of government from society. Such is the program of the Libertarian Party, which stresses freedom over order and equality. This party has run candidates for president in every election since 1972 and has emerged as the most active and fastest-growing minor party. Its presidential candidate for 1996, Harry Browne, an author and financial advisor living in Tennessee, was on the ballot in all fifty states. But the party never has won more than 1 percent of total votes cast.

- *Single-issue parties* are formed to promote one principle, not a general philosophy of government. The Anti-Masonic parties of the 1820s and 1830s, for example, opposed Masonic lodges and other secret societies. The Free Soil Party of the 1840s and 1850s worked to abolish slavery. The Prohibition Party, the most durable example of a single-issue party, opposed the consumption of alcoholic beverages. Prohibition candidates consistently won from 1 to 2 percent of the vote in nine presidential elections between 1884 and 1916, and the party has run candidates in every presidential election since. Its candidate in 1996 was Earl Dodge of Denver, Colorado, who appeared on the ballot only in Arkansas, California, Tennessee, and Utah.

Third parties, then, have formed primarily to express discontent with the choices offered by the major parties and to work for their own objectives within the electoral system.[12] Certainly the new Reform Party reflects discontent with existing politics, but otherwise it resists classification. It did not bolt from an existing party, it does not have a farmer-labor base, it has no clear ideological basis, and it is not devoted to any single issue. Of the nine principles presented by the Reform Party in 1996, six dealt with government reforms (such as new ethical standards, campaign reforms, and lobbying restrictions), and only three vaguely addressed substantive policies: balancing the budget, taxation, and Medicare and social security.[13] Perhaps the Reform Party foreshadows a new type of party, one created from the top by a dynamic leader through a well-funded, mass media–dependent appeal for support from citizens previously uninvolved in partisan politics.[14]

Read the philosophy of the Libertarian Party on the World Wide Web.
`<www.lp.org/lp/>`

The principles of the Reform Party are given at this address.
`<www.reformparty.org/>`

How have minor parties fared historically? As vote getters, they have not performed well. However, bolter parties have twice won more than 10 percent of the vote. More significantly, the Republican party originated in 1854 as a single-issue third party opposed to slavery in the nation's new territories; in its first election, in 1856, the party came in second, displacing the Whigs. (Undoubtedly, the Republican exception to the rule has inspired the formation of other hopeful third parties.)

As policy advocates, minor parties have a slightly better record. At times, they have had a real effect on the policies adopted by the major parties. Women's suffrage, the graduated income tax, and the direct election of senators all originated with third parties.[15] Of course, third parties may fail to win more votes because their policies lack popular support. This was a lesson the Democrats learned in 1896, when they adopted the Populists' free-silver plank in their own platform. Both their candidate and their platform went down to a defeat that hobbled the Democratic party for decades.

Most important, minor parties function as safety valves. They allow those who are unhappy with the status quo to express their discontent within the system, to contribute to the political dialogue. Surely this was the function of Perot's candidacy and of the Reform Party. If minor parties and independent candidates are indicators of discontent, what should we make of the scores of parties that have sponsored candidates in recent congressional elections or of the several minor parties (Libertarian, Reform, U.S. Taxpayers, Green, Natural Law) that held national conventions in the summer of 1996? Not much. The number of third parties that contest elections is less important than the total number of votes they receive. Despite the presence of numerous minor parties in every presidential election, the two major parties usually collect more than 99 percent of the vote. Because of Perot's candidacy, 1992 was an exception. He won 19 percent of the total vote, more than any other candidate outside the two major parties since Theodore Roosevelt ran as a Progressive in 1912. But in 1996, he took only 8.5 percent of the popular vote, and all of the other sixteen independent and minor party candidates won less than two percent. Of course, the two major parties captured all of the electoral votes.

Why a Two-Party System?

The history of party politics in the United States is essentially the story of two parties that have alternating control of the government. With relatively few exceptions, Americans conduct elections at all levels within the two-party system. This pattern is unusual in democratic countries, where multiparty systems are more common. Why does the United States have only two major parties? The two most convincing answers to this question stem from the electoral system in the United States and the process of political socialization here.

In the typical U.S. election, two or more candidates contest each office, and the winner is the single candidate who collects the most votes, whether those votes constitute a majority or not. When these two principles of *single winners* chosen by a *simple plurality* of votes govern the election of members of a legislature, the system (despite its reliance on pluralities rather than majorities) is known as **majority representation**. Think about how American states choose representatives to Congress. A state entitled to ten representatives is divided into ten congressional districts; each district elects one representative. Majority representation of voters through single-member districts is also a feature of most state legislatures.

Alternatively, a legislature might be chosen through a system of **proportional representation**, which awards legislative seats to each party in proportion to the total number of votes it wins in an election. Under this system, the state might hold a single statewide election for all ten seats, with each party presenting a rank-ordered list of ten candidates. Voters could vote for the party list they preferred, and the party's candidates would be elected from the top of each list, according to the proportion of votes won by the party. Thus, if a party got 30 percent of the vote in this example, its first three candidates would be elected.

Although this form of election may seem strange, many democratic countries (for example, the Netherlands, Israel, and Denmark) use it. Proportional representation tends to produce (or perpetuate) several parties, because each can win enough seats nationwide to wield some influence in the legislature. In contrast, our system of elections forces interest groups of all sorts to work within the two major parties, for only one candidate in each race stands a chance to be elected under plurality voting. Therefore, the system tends to produce only two parties. Moreover, the two major parties benefit from state laws that automatically list candidates on the ballot if their party won a sizeable percentage of the vote in the previous election. These laws discourage minor parties, which must petition before every election for a place on the ballot.[16]

The rules of our electoral system may explain why only two parties tend to form in specific election districts, but why do the same two parties (Democratic and Republican) operate within every state? The contest for the presidency is the key to this question. A candidate can win a presidential election only by amassing a majority of electoral votes from across the entire nation. Presidential candidates try to win votes under the same party label in each state in order to pool their electoral votes in the electoral college. The presidency is a big enough political prize to induce parties to harbor uncomfortable coalitions of voters (southern white Protestants allied with northern Jews and blacks in the Democratic party, for example) just to win the electoral vote and the presidential election.

The American electoral system may force U.S. politics into a two-party mold, but why must the same two parties reappear from election to election? In fact, they do not. The earliest two-party system pitted the Federalists against the Democratic Republicans. A later two-party system involved the Democrats and the Whigs. More than 135 years ago, the Republicans replaced the Whigs in what is our two-party system today. But with modern issues so different from the issues then, why do the Democrats and Republicans persist? This is where political socialization comes into play. The two parties persist simply because they have persisted. After more than one hundred years of political socialization, the two parties today have such a head start in structuring the vote that they

●●●●●●●●●●●●

Federalism at Work

In November 1993, Republican candidate Christine Todd Whitman was elected governor of New Jersey, defeating the Democratic incumbent, Jim Florio. Only one year earlier, New Jersey had voted for Clinton for president in 1992. Whitman's victory demonstrates the federal structure of the party system: one party may win executive office at the national level, while another party wins executive office at the state level. Before the 1994 election, approximately 60 percent of the nation's governors were Democratic; after the election, 60 percent were Republican.

discourage challenges from new parties. Of course, third parties still try to crack the two-party system from time to time, but most have had little success.

The Federal Basis of the Party System

Focusing on contests for the presidency is a convenient and informative way to study the history of American parties, but it also oversimplifies party politics to the point of distortion. By concentrating only on presidential elections, we tend to ignore electoral patterns in the states, where elections often buck national trends. Even during its darkest defeats for the presidency, a party can still claim many victories for state offices. Victories outside the arena of presidential politics give each party a base of support that keeps its machinery oiled and ready for the next contest.[17]

The 1984 election illustrates how the states can serve as a refuge for parties defeated in the contest for the presidency. Ronald Reagan swept forty-nine states in 1984—winning everywhere but the District of Columbia and Minnesota, the home of his opponent, Walter Mondale. Even in the wake of Reagan's stunning victory, however, the Democrats kept control of the House of Representatives. They also wound up with thirty-four state governorships to the Republicans' sixteen (unchanged from before the election) and the majority in 65 percent of the state legislatures. In eighteen states they controlled the governor's office, the upper house, and the lower house; the Republicans dominated only four states.[18]

Reagan's victory in 1980, his 1984 landslide, and Bush's win in 1988 might have suggested to some that the Democrats were doomed to extinction in presidential politics. Perhaps in an earlier time, when the existing parties were not so well institutionalized, that would have been so. However, the Democratic party not only remained alive but thrived in our federal system. The separation of state politics from national trends affords each party a chance to lick its wounds after a presidential election debacle and return to campaign optimistically in the next election, as the Republicans did so successfully in the 1994 congressional elections after losing the presidency in 1992.

Party Identification in America

The concept of **party identification** is one of the most important in political science. It signifies a voter's sense of psychological attachment to a party, which is not the same thing as voting for the party in any given election. Scholars measure party identification simply by asking, "Do you usually think of yourself as a Republican, a Democrat, an independent, or what?"[19] Voting is a behavior; identification is a state of mind. For example, millions of southerners voted for Eisenhower for president in 1952 and 1956 but continued to consider themselves Democrats. Across the nation, more people identify with one of the two major parties than reject a party attachment. The proportions of self-identified Republicans, Democrats, and independents (no party attachment) in the electorate since 1952 are shown in Figure 8.3. Three significant points stand out:

- The number of Republicans and Democrats combined far exceeds the independents in every year.

- The number of Democrats consistently exceeds that of Republicans.

- The number of Democrats has shrunk over time, to the benefit of both Republicans and independents, and the three groups are now almost equal in size.

Although party identification predisposes citizens to vote for their favorite party, other factors may convince them to choose the opposition candidate. If they vote against their party often enough, they may rethink their party identification and eventually switch. Apparently, this rethinking has gone on in the minds of many southern Democrats over time. In 1952, about 70 percent of white southerners thought of themselves as Democrats, and fewer than 20 percent thought of themselves as Republicans. By 1992, white southerners were only 34 percent Democratic—30 percent were Republican and 36 percent independent. Much of the nationwide growth in the proportion of Republicans and independents (and the parallel drop in the number of Democrats) stems from changes in party preferences among white southerners and from migration of northerners, which translated into substantial gains in the number of registered Republicans by 1996.[20]

Who are the self-identified Democrats and Republicans in the electorate? Figure 8.4 shows party identification by various social groups in 1992. The effects of socioeconomic factors are clear. People who have lower incomes and less education are more likely to think of themselves as Democrats than as Republicans. But the cultural factors of religion and

8.3   ● Distribution of Party Identification, 1952–1994

In every presidential election since 1952, voters across the nation have been asked, "Generally speaking, do you usually think of yourself as a Republican, a Democrat, an independent, or what?" Most voters think of themselves as either Republicans or Democrats, but the proportion of those who think of themselves as independents has increased over time. The size of the Democratic party's majority has also shrunk. Nevertheless, most Americans today still identify with one of the two major parties, and Democrats still outnumber Republicans.

Source: National Election Studies Guide to Public Opinion and Electoral Behavior, obtained at <www.umich.edu/~nes/resourcs/nesguide/toptables/tab2a_1.htm>.

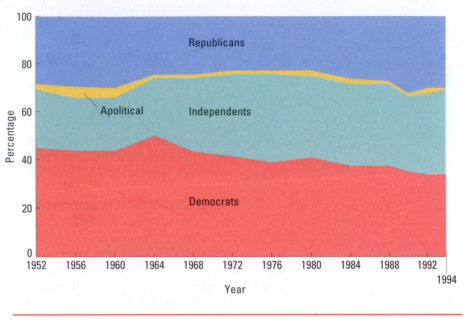

race produce even sharper differences between the parties. Jews are strongly Democratic compared with other religious groups, and African Americans are also overwhelmingly Democratic. Finally, American politics has a gender gap: women tend to be more Democratic than men.

The influence of region on party identification has changed over time. Because of the high proportion of blacks in the South, it is still the most heavily Democratic region, followed closely by the Northeast. The Midwest and West have proportionately more Republicans. Despite the erosion of Democratic strength in the South, we still see elements of Roosevelt's old Democratic coalition of different socioeconomic groups. Perhaps the major change in that coalition has been the replacement of white European ethnic groups by blacks, attracted by the Democrats' backing of civil rights legislation in the 1960s.

Studies show that about half of all Americans adopt their parents' party. But it often takes time for party identification to develop. The youngest group of voters is most likely to be independent, but they have also identified increasingly with Republicans, ever since the Reagan years (see Politics in a Changing America 8.1). The oldest group shows the greatest partisan commitment, reflecting the fact that citizens become more interested in politics as they mature. Also, the youngest age group is most evenly divided between the parties. Some analysts believe this ratio of party identification among today's young voters will persist as they age, contributing to further erosion of the Democratic majority and perhaps greater electoral dealignment.

Source: 1992 National Election Study, Center for Political Studies, University of Michigan.

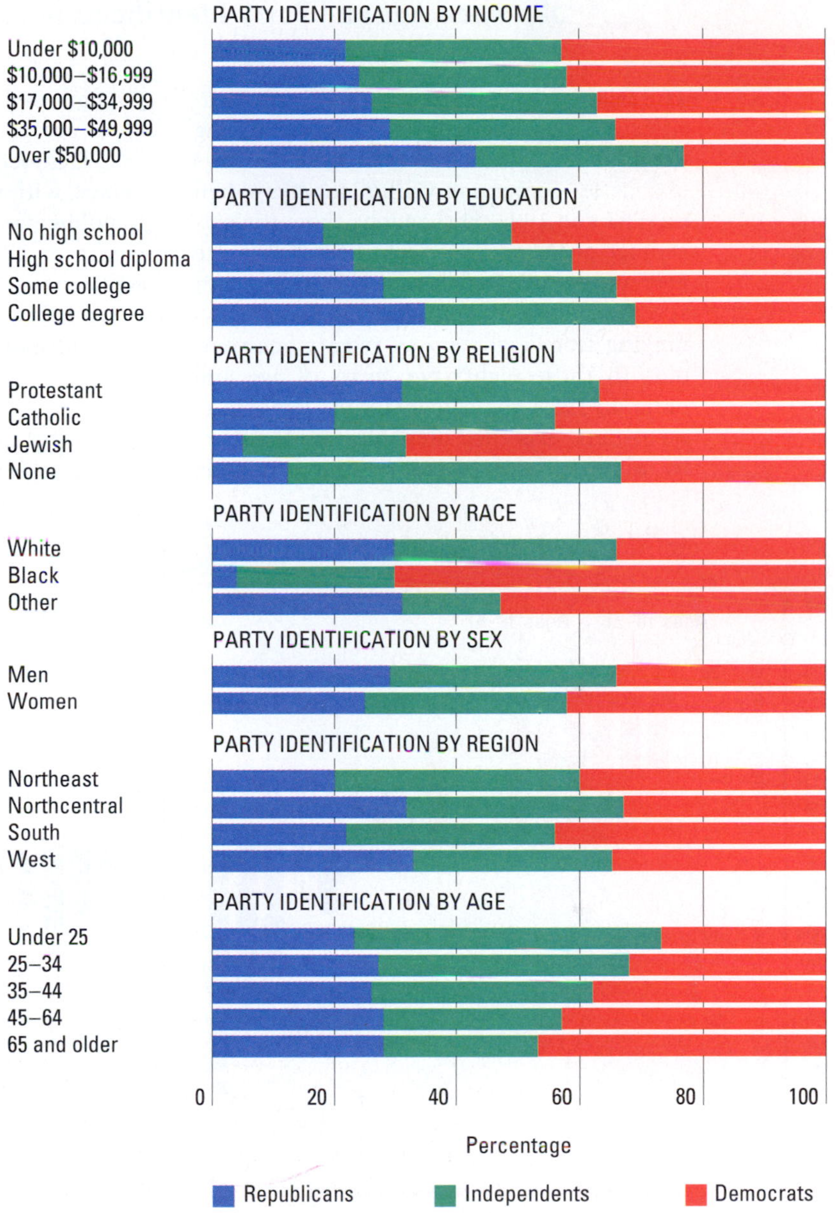

figure 8.4 ● **Party Identification by Social Groups**

Respondents to a 1992 survey were grouped by seven different socioeconomic criteria—income, education, religion, race, sex, region, and age—and analyzed according to their self-descriptions as Democrats, independents, or Republicans. Region was found to have the least effect on party identification; religion and race had the greatest effects.

Americans tend to find their political niche and stay there.[21] The enduring party loyalty of American voters tends to structure the vote even before an election is held, even before the candidates are chosen. In Chapter 9 we will examine the extent to which party identification determines voting choice. But first we will look to see whether the Democratic and Republican parties have any significant differences.

• politics in a changing america

8.1   The Changing Relationship Between Age and Party Identification

The relationship between age and party identification has changed dramatically during the past forty years. We can visualize this change by comparing Gallup surveys taken in 1952 and 1992. Both graphs show the percentage of Democratic identifiers minus the percentage of Republican identifiers for seventeen different four-year age groupings—ranging from eighteen- to twenty-one-year-olds to those eighty-two years of age and older. In 1952, the percentage of Democratic identifiers exceeded Republican identifiers by about fifteen points or more among younger and middle-aged voters, while the older age groups had far more Republicans than Democrats. By 1992, this pattern had reversed, with younger voters more likely to be Republicans and older voters (those who were young in 1952) retaining their Democratic sentiments. Note also that the overall relationship between age and party identification was substantially weaker in 1992 than in 1952.

Source: Everett Carll Ladd, "Age, Generation, and Party ID," *Public Perspective* (July–August 1992), pp. 15–16.

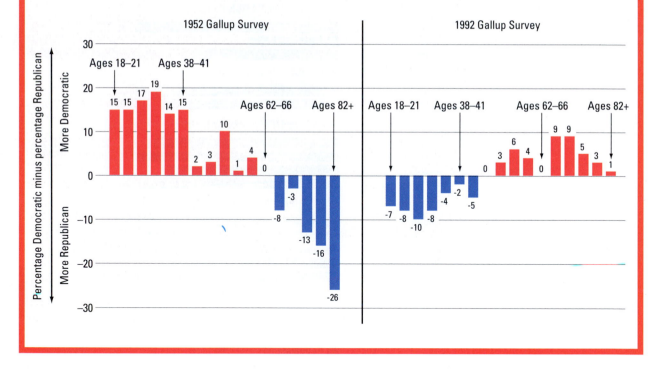

PARTY IDEOLOGY AND ORGANIZATION

George Wallace, a disgruntled Democrat who ran for president in 1968 on the American Independent Party ticket, complained that "there isn't a dime's worth of difference" between the Democrats and Republicans. Humorist Will Rogers said, "I am not a member of any organized political party—I am a Democrat." Wallace's comment was made in disgust, Rogers's in jest. Wallace was wrong; Rogers was close to being right. Here we will dispel the myth that the parties do not differ significantly on issues and explain how they are organized to coordinate the activities of party candidates and officials in government.

Differences in Party Ideology

George Wallace notwithstanding, there is more than a dime's worth of difference between the two parties. In fact, the difference amounts to many billions of dollars, the cost of the different government programs supported by each party. Democrats are more disposed to government spending to advance social welfare (and hence to promote equality) than are Republicans. And social welfare programs cost money, a lot of money. (You will see how much money in Chapters 18 and 19.) Republicans, on the other hand, are not averse to spending billions of dollars for the projects they consider important, among them national defense. Ronald Reagan portrayed the Democrats as big spenders, but the defense buildup during his first administration alone cost the country more than $1 trillion—to be more precise, $1,007,900,000,000.[22] And Reagan's Strategic Defense Initiative (the "Star Wars" space defense program), which Bush supported and the Republicans' Contract with America sought to revive in 1994, cost many billions more, even by conservative estimates. The differences in spending patterns reflect some real philosophical differences between the parties.

Voters and Activists.   One way to examine the differences is to compare party voters with party activists. As the middle portion of Figure 8.5 shows, 16 percent of a sample of registered Democratic voters in 1996 described themselves as conservatives compared with 55 percent of registered Republicans. As we discussed in Chapter 5, relatively few ordinary voters think about politics in ideological terms, but party activists often do. The ideological gap between the parties looms even larger when we focus on the party activists on the left and right sides of the figure. Only 3 percent of the delegates to the 1996 Democratic convention classified themselves as conservative, compared with 79 percent of the delegates to the Republican convention.

Platforms: Freedom, Order, and Equality.   Surveys of voters' ideological orientation may merely reflect differences in their personal self-image rather than actual differences in party ideology. For another test of party philosophy, we can look to the platforms adopted at party conventions. Although many people feel that party platforms don't matter very much, several scholars have demonstrated using different approaches that winning parties tend to carry out much of their platforms when in office.[23] One study matched the parties' platform statements from 1948 to 1985 against subsequent allocations of program funds in the federal budget. Spending priorities turned out to be quite closely linked to the platform emphases of the party that won control of Congress, especially if the party also controlled the presidency.[24]

Party platforms also matter a great deal to the parties' convention delegates—and to the interest groups that support the parties.[25] The wording of

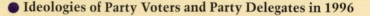

figure **8.5**   ● Ideologies of Party Voters and Party Delegates in 1996

Contrary to what many people think, the Democratic and Republican parties differ substantially in their ideological centers of gravity. When citizens were asked to classify themselves on an ideological scale, more Republicans than Democrats described themselves as conservative. When delegates to the parties' national conventions were asked to classify themselves, even greater ideological differences appeared.

Sources: The Republican data come from "Delegates, Party Voters Sometimes at Odds," *Washington Post National Weekly Edition,* 12–18 August 1996, p. A8; the Democratic data were provided by Mario Brossard of the *Washington Post* via e-mail on 21 August 1996. The *Post* surveyed 505 Republican and 508 Democratic delegates. Data for registered voters came from a national survey of approximately 1,500 respondents.

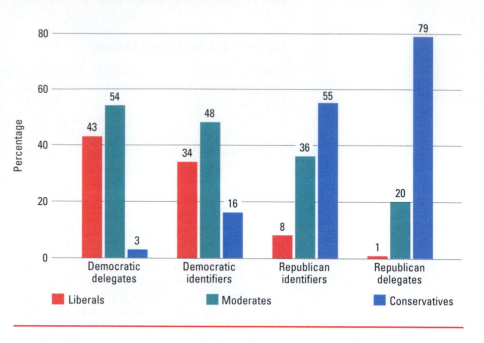

a platform plank often means the difference between victory and defeat for factions within a party. Delegates fight not only over ideas but also over words. Prior to the 1996 Republican convention, the party's pro-life and pro-choice forces clashed over whether the party should emphasize tolerance of different views in its platform. Pro-life forces proposed a plank simply stating that "the unborn child has a fundamental right to life which cannot be infringed." Pro-choice forces wanted that linked to a statement tolerating different views—a position backed by the party's nominee, Bob Dole. Despite Dole's view, the pro-life forces won, and the antiabortion plank was unencumbered by a plea for tolerance.[26]

The platforms adopted by the Democratic and Republican conventions in 1996 were strikingly different in style and substance. The Republicans, who met first, produced a long document of 27,200 words — not including a lengthy appendix that held dissenting opinions. As befits a conservative party, the 1996 Republican platform called for "moral clarity in our culture" and "free market capitalism." The Republican platform also called for several amendments to the Constitution in addition to the human life amendment. It advocated amendments that would guarantee a balanced budget, limit terms for members of Congress, deny automatic citizenship to children born in the United States to illegal immigrants, protect against defiling the flag, and ensure the rights of victims to obtain compensation from criminals.

The 1996 Democratic platform had only 16,500 words (and no appendix). It reflected Bill Clinton's move toward the political center as it echoed this proclamation about "the end of the era of big government."

Nevertheless, the Democrats proceeded to promise greater government protection of the environment, more national guidance and assistance to schools, and new initiatives for job training.

The differences between the two 1996 party platforms emerged more clearly in their specific proposals. In contrast to the Republicans, the Democrats supported "the right of every woman to choose" between birth and abortion. The Democrats favored "the assault weapons ban," whereas the Republicans defended "the constitutional right to keep and bear arms." Democrats advocated more funding for public education; Republicans proposed diverting funds to tuition subsidies for private schools. Democrats pledged "to end discrimination against gay men and lesbians"; Republicans affirmed that "homosexuality is incompatible with military service." As for medical care, the Democratic party committed itself to ensuring that "Americans have access to affordable high-quality health care, while the Republicans urged that health care providers be allowed "to respond to consumer demand through consumer choice."

These statements of values clearly distinguish the two parties on the values of freedom, order, and equality that underlie the dilemmas of government discussed in Chapter 1. According to our ideological typology, the Republicans' 1996 platform positions on abortion, homosexual rights, education, and medical care place their party firmly in the conservative category, whereas the Democrats' platform puts their party squarely into the liberal category.

The platform of the Reform Party available at the time of its convention was only 550 words (16,000 words fewer than the Democratic platform). Here is the entire statement for one of its nine planks, *Creating a New Tax System:* "The new tax system must be fair; the new tax system must be paperless; the new tax system must raise the money to pay the bills; and [it must] require that any future tax increases under the new system be approved by the people in the next federal election in order to impose discipline on spending." The main "issue" of the Reform Party was really Ross Perot.

The "Voters" data in the CROSSTABS program contain variables on "Political Orientations." Crosstabulate "Ideological Orientation" by "Party Identification" to learn how much those who identify with different parties also depart in their ideologies.

Different but Similar.   The Democrats and the Republicans have very different ideological orientations. Yet, many observers claim that the parties are really quite similar in ideology compared to the different parties of other countries. Specifically, both support capitalism; that is, both reject government ownership of the means of production (see Chapter 1). A study of Democratic and Republican positions on four economic issues—ownership of the means of production, the government's role in economic planning, redistribution of wealth, and providing for social welfare—found that Republicans consistently oppose increased government activity. Comparing these findings with data on party positions in thirteen other democracies, the researchers found about as much difference between the American parties as is usual within two-party systems. However, both American parties tend to be more conservative on economic matters than parties in other two-party systems. In most multiparty systems, the presence of strong socialist and antisocialist parties ensures a much greater range of ideological choice than we find in our system, despite genuine differences between the Democrats and Republicans.[27]

National Party Organization

Most casual observers would agree with Will Rogers's description of the Democrats as an unorganized political party. It used to apply to the Republicans, too, but this has changed since the 1970s—at least at the national level. Bear in mind the distinction between levels of party structure. American parties parallel our federal system: they have separate national and state organizations (and virtually separate local organizations, in many cases).

At the national level, each major party has four main organizational components:

- *National convention.* Every four years, each party assembles thousands of delegates from the states and U.S. territories (such as Puerto Rico and Guam) in a national convention for the purpose of nominating a candidate for president. This presidential nominating convention is also the supreme governing body of the party. It determines party policy through the platform, formulates rules to govern party operations, and designates a national committee, which is empowered to govern the party until the next convention.

- *National committee.* The **national committee,** which governs each party between conventions, is composed of party officials representing the states and territories, including the chairpersons of their party organizations. In 1996, the Republican National Committee (RNC) had about 150 members, consisting of the national committeeman, national committeewoman, and a chairperson from each state and from the District of Columbia, Guam, Puerto Rico, and the Virgin Islands. The Democratic National Committee (DNC) had approximately 400 elected and appointed members, including, in addition to the national committee members and party chairs, members representing auxiliary organizations.[28] The chairperson of each national committee is chosen by the party's presidential nominee, then duly elected by the committee. If the nominee loses the election, the national committee usually replaces the nominee's chairperson.

- *Congressional party conferences.* At the beginning of each session of Congress, the Republicans and Democrats in each chamber hold separate **party conferences** (the House Democrats call theirs a caucus) to select their party leaders and decide committee assignments. (Bernard Sanders, the lone independent member of Congress in 1991, asked to join the House Democratic Caucus but was excluded.) The party conferences deal only with congressional matters and have no structural relationship to each other and no relationship to the national committees.

- *Congressional campaign committees.* Democrats and Republicans in the House and Senate also maintain separate **congressional campaign committees,** each of which raises its own funds to support its candidates in congressional elections. The separation of these organizations from the national committee tells us that the national party structure is loose; the national committee seldom gets involved with the election

●●●●●●●●●●●

High Tech on Main Street

This is how the Republican National Committee presented itself to surfers on the Internet prior to the election of 1996. Each of these signs could be clicked to provide information about the party's history, structure, and policies. By clicking on "Gifts," moreover, you could order a GOP TV coffee mug for just $5.90, or a GOP necktie for $39.95, among other items.

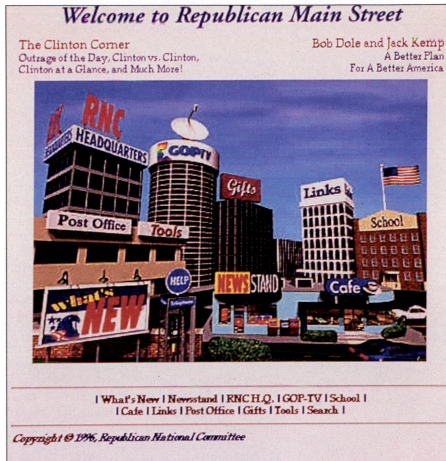

of any individual member of Congress. Moreover, even the congressional campaign organizations merely supplement the funds that senators and representatives raise on their own to win reelection.

It is tempting to think of the national party chairperson as sitting at the top of a hierarchical party organization that not only controls its members in Congress but also issues orders to the state committees and on down to the local level. Few ideas could be more wrong.[29] The national committee has virtually no voice in congressional activity, and it exercises very little direction of and even less control over state and local campaigns. In fact, the RNC and DNC do not even really direct or control presidential campaigns. Candidates hire their own campaign staffs during the party primaries to win delegates who will support them for nomination at the party conventions. Successful nominees then keep their winning staffs to contest the general election. The main role of a national committee is to support its candidate's personal campaign staff in the effort to win.

In this light, the national committees appear to be relatively useless organizations. For many years, their role was essentially limited to planning for the next party convention. The committee would select the site, invite the state parties to attend, plan the program, and so on. In the 1970s, however, the roles of the DNC and RNC began to expand—but in different ways.

In response to street rioting by Vietnam War protesters during the 1968 Democratic convention, the Democrats created a special commission to introduce party reforms. In an attempt to open the party to broader participation and to weaken local party leaders' control over the process of selecting delegates, the McGovern-Fraser Commission formulated new guidelines for the selection of delegates to the 1972 Democratic convention. Included in these guidelines was the requirement that state parties take "affirmative action"—that is, see to it that their delegates included women, minorities, and young people "in reasonable relationship to the group's presence in the population of the state."[30] Many state parties rebelled at the imposition of sex, race, and age quotas. But the DNC threatened to deny seating to any state delegation at the 1972 convention that did not comply with the guidelines.

Never before had a national party committee imposed such rules on a state party organization, but it worked. Even the powerful Illinois delegation, led by Chicago mayor Richard Daley, was denied seating at the convention for violating the guidelines. And overall, women, blacks, and young voters gained dramatically in representation at the 1972 Democratic convention. Although the party has since reduced its emphasis on quotas, the gains by women and blacks have held up fairly well. The representation of young people, however, has declined substantially (as the young activists grew older). Many "regular" Democrats feared that the political activists who had taken over the 1972 convention would cripple the party organization. But most challengers were socialized into the party within a decade and became more open to compromise and more understanding of the organization's need to combat developments within the Republican party.[31]

While the Democrats were busy with procedural reforms, the Republicans were making *organizational* reforms.[32] The RNC did little to open up its delegate selection process; Republicans were not inclined to impose quotas on state parties through their national committee. Instead, the RNC strengthened its fund-raising, research, and service roles. Republicans acquired their own building and their own computer system, and in 1976 they hired the first full-time chairperson in the history of either national party. (Until then, the chairperson had worked part-time.) As RNC chairman, William Brock (formerly a senator from Tennessee) expanded the party's staff, launched new publications, held seminars, conducted election analyses, and advised candidates—things that national party committees in other countries had been doing for years.

The vast difference between the Democratic and Republican approaches to reforming the national committees shows in the funds raised by the DNC and RNC during election campaigns. During Brock's tenure as chairman of the RNC, the Republicans raised three to four times as much money as the Democrats. Although the margin has narrowed, Republican party fund-raising efforts are still superior. From January 1, 1995, through June 30, 1996, the Republicans' national, senatorial, and congressional committees raised $180 million, compared with $102 million raised by

Get a detailed accounting of funds raised and spent by parties in the 1996 election under "Financial Information" at the URL of the Federal Election Commission.

`<www.fec.gov>`

the comparable Democratic committees.[33] Although Republicans have traditionally raised more campaign money than Democrats, they no longer rely on a relatively few wealthy contributors. In fact, the Republicans received more of their funds in small contributions (less than $100), mainly through direct-mail solicitation, than the Democrats. In short, the RNC has recently been raising far more money than the DNC, from many more citizens, as part of its long-term commitment to improving its organizational services. Its efforts have also made a difference at the state and local levels.

State and Local Party Organizations

At one time, both major parties were firmly anchored by powerful state and local party organizations. Big-city party organizations, such as the Democrats' Tammany Hall in New York City and the Cook County Central Committee in Chicago, were called *party machines*. A **party machine** was a centralized organization that dominated local politics by controlling elections—sometimes by illegal means, often by providing jobs and social services to urban workers in return for their votes. The patronage and social service functions of party machines were undercut when the government expanded unemployment compensation, aid to families with dependent children, and other social services. As a result, most local party organizations lost their ability to deliver votes and thus to determine the outcome of elections. However, machines are still strong in certain areas. In Nassau County, New York, for example, suburban Republicans have shown that they can run a machine as well as urban Democrats.[34]

The individual state and local organizations of both parties vary widely in strength, but recent research has found that "neither the Republican nor Democratic party has a distinct advantage with regard to direct campaign activities."[35] Whereas once both the RNC and the DNC were dependent for their funding on "quotas" paid by state parties, now the funds flow the other way—and state parties have benefited greatly from the transfer of funds (see Figure 8.6). In the 1993–94 election cycle, both the RNC and the DNC transferred over $13 million to nearly every state party organization.[36] In addition to money, state parties also received candidate training, poll data and research, and campaigning instruction.[37] The national committees have also taken a more active role in congressional campaigns.[38] When a poll showed in 1994 that Illinois Democrat Dan Rostenkowski, the powerful chair of the House Ways and Means Committee, had lost ground to the Republican candidate, Michael Flanagan, the RNC kicked in $50,000 for a last-minute advertising campaign, helping Flanagan score a huge upset.[39]

Decentralized but Growing Stronger

Although the national committees have gained strength over the past three decades, American political parties are still among the most decentralized parties in the world.[40] Not even the president can count on loyalty from the members (or even the officers) of his party. Consider the problem

figure

8.6 ● Changes in the Money Flow Between State and National Parties: 1950s v. 1990s

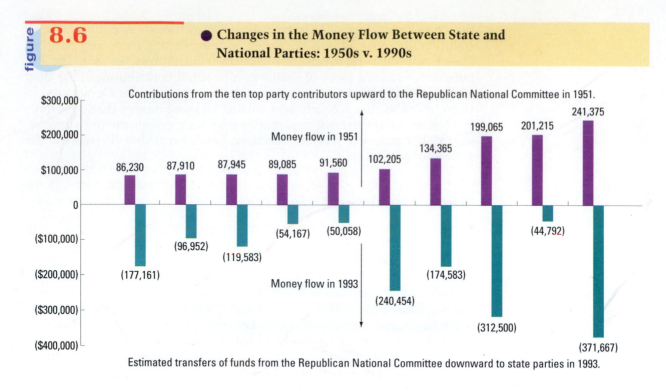

Contributions from the ten top party contributors upward to the Republican National Committee in 1951.

Money flow in 1951

Money flow in 1993

Estimated transfers of funds from the Republican National Committee downward to state parties in 1993.

Changes over time in the money flows between the state party organizations and the national party committees clearly indicate changes in their power relationships. Traditionally, the national committees were funded by voluntary contributions from state parties, set as financial "quotas." Not all states met their quotas, and the Democratic National Chairman in the 1950s, Paul Butler, praised states that did in his monthly newsletter. Beginning in the 1960s, both national committees began to raise money from party supporters through direct mail solicitations. Both parties, but especially the Republicans, began to live off their own income and soon began to transfer money back to the states. This graph shows the extent to which the Republican National Committee changed from a taker of funds from the ten top state contributors in 1951 to a giver of funds to the same states in 1993.

Sources: The 1951 data come from a typewritten "Statement of Contributions by States Received During October 1951 and to Date," so the contributions for the year were almost complete. This statement resides in the files of the Republican National Committee at the U.S. National Archives in Washington, D.C. The data for 1993 are estimated from the Federal Election Commission News Release, "FEC Reports on Political Party Activity for 1993–94," 13 April 1995, p. 12. It includes both federal and non-federal funds. All data are expressed in constant 1987 dollars. The 1951 data were divided by .20 as a deflator and the 1993 data were divided by 1.2. The FEC data for 1993–94 were also divided in half, because they were collected over two years; the 1951 data are for just one year. Thus, the 1993 data are estimates for one year based on two years of financial reporting.

that confronted President Clinton in his first term in office. Clinton was pushing hard in the House of Representatives for passage of the North American Free Trade Agreement (NAFTA), only to be opposed by both the Democratic majority leader, Richard Gephardt, and the party whip, David Bonior—whose chief job was to mobilize party votes. The House approved NAFTA in late 1993, but only because Republicans voted for it overwhelmingly. Most Democrats rejected it. President Bush experienced a similar situation in 1990, when the Republican party whip, Newt Gingrich, opposed Bush's carefully crafted budget package to deal with the deficit. Although Bush lost this key vote, Gingrich easily won reelection as party whip in 1991.

The absence of centralized power has always been the most distinguishing characteristic of American political parties. Moreover, the rise in the proportion of citizens who style themselves as independents suggests that our already weak parties are in further decline.[41] But there is evidence that our political parties, *as organizations*, are enjoying a period of resurgence. Both parties' national committees have never been better funded or more active in grassroots campaign activities.[42] And more votes in Congress are being decided along party lines—despite the Gephardt-Bonior and Gingrich mutinies. (See Chapter 11 for a discussion of the rise of party voting in Congress since the 1970s.) In fact, a specialist in congressional politics has concluded, "When compared to its predecessors of the last half-century, the current majority party leadership is more involved and more decisive in organizing the party and the chamber, setting the policy agenda, shaping legislation, and determining legislative outcomes."[43] However, the American parties have traditionally been so weak that these positive trends have not altered their basic character. American political parties are still so organizationally diffuse and decentralized that they raise questions about how well they link voters to the government.

THE MODEL OF RESPONSIBLE PARTY GOVERNMENT

According to the majoritarian model of democracy, parties are essential to making the government responsive to public opinion. In fact, the ideal role of parties in majoritarian democracy has been formalized in the four principles of **responsible party government**:[44]

1. Parties should present clear and coherent programs to voters.

2. Voters should choose candidates on the basis of party programs.

3. The winning party should carry out its program once in office.

4. Voters should hold the governing party responsible at the next election for executing its program.

How well do these principles describe American politics? You've learned that the Democratic and Republican platforms are different and that they are much more ideologically consistent than many people believe. So the first principle is being met fairly well. To a lesser extent, so is the third principle: once parties gain power, they usually try to do what they said they would do. From the standpoint of democratic theory, the real question involves principles 2 and 4: do voters really pay attention to party platforms and policies when they cast their ballots? And if so, do voters hold the governing party responsible at the next election for delivering, or failing to deliver, on its pledges? To answer these questions, we must consider in greater detail the parties' role in nominating candidates and structuring the voters' choices in elections. At the conclusion of Chapter 9, we will return to evaluating the role of political parties in democratic government.

SUMMARY

Political parties perform four important functions in a political system: nominating candidates, structuring the voting choice, proposing alternative government programs, and coordinating the activities of government officials. Political parties have been performing these functions longer in the United States than in any other country. The Democratic party, founded in 1828, is the world's oldest political party. When the Republican party emerged as a major party after the 1856 election, our present two-party system emerged—the oldest party system in the world.

America's two-party system has experienced three critical elections, each of which realigned the electorate for years and affected the party balance in government. The election of 1860 established the Republicans as the major party in the North and the Democrats as the dominant party in the South. Nationally, the two parties remained roughly balanced in Congress until the critical election of 1896. This election strengthened the link between the Republican party and business interests in the heavily populated Northeast and Midwest and produced a surge in voter support that made the Republicans the majority party nationally for more than three decades. The Great Depression produced the conditions that transformed the Democrats into the majority party in the critical election of 1932. Until the Republicans won both houses in the 1994 election, the Democrats enjoyed almost uninterrupted control of Congress for six decades.

Minor parties have not enjoyed much electoral success in America, although they have contributed ideas to the Democratic and Republican platforms. The two-party system is perpetuated in the United States by the nature of our electoral system and by the political socialization process, which results in most Americans' identifying with either the Democratic or the Republican party. The federal system of government has also helped the Democrats and Republicans survive defeats at the national level by sustaining them with electoral victories at the state level. The pattern of party identification has been changing in recent years: as more people are becoming independents and Republicans, the number of Democratic identifiers is dropping. Still, Democrats consistently outnumber Republicans, and together they both far outnumber independents.

The two major parties differ in their ideological orientations. Democratic identifiers and activists are more likely to describe themselves as liberal; Republican identifiers and activists tend to be conservative. The party platforms also reveal substantive ideological differences. The 1996 Democratic party platform showed a more liberal orientation by stressing equality over freedom; the Republican platform was more conservative, concentrating on freedom but also emphasizing the importance of restoring social order. Organizationally, the Republicans have recently become the stronger party at both the national and state levels, and both parties are showing signs of resurgence. Nevertheless, both parties are still very decentralized compared with parties in other countries.

In keeping with the model of responsible party government, American parties do tend to translate their platform positions into government policy if elected to power. But, as we examine in Chapter 9, it remains to be seen whether citizens pay much attention to parties and policies when casting their votes. If not, American parties do not fulfill the majoritarian model of democratic theory.

Key Terms

political party	party platform	proportional	congressional campaign
nomination	critical election	representation	committee
political system	electoral realignment	party identification	party machine
electoral college	two-party system	national committee	responsible
caucus	electoral dealignment	party conference	party government
national convention	majority representation		

Selected Readings

Alexander, Herbert E., and Anthony Corrado. *Financing the 1992 Election*. Armonk, N.Y.: M. E. Sharpe, 1995. The latest book in a series that analyzes spending patterns in presidential campaigns, beginning with the 1960 election.

Aldrich, John H. *Why Parties? The Origin and Transformation of Political Parties in America*. Chicago: University of Chicago Press, 1995. An original analysis of the formation of political parties that intertwines the ambitions of politicians, the problems of collective action, and the dilemmas in social choice.

Beck, Paul Allen. *Party Politics in America*, 8th ed. New York: HarperCollins, 1996. The eighth edition of a comprehensive textbook on political parties.

Schattschneider, E. E. *Party Government*. New York: Holt, 1942. A clear and powerful argument for the central role of political parties in a democracy according to the model of responsible party government; a classic book in political science.

Shea, Daniel M., and John C. Green (eds.), *The State of the Parties: The Changing Role of Contemporary American Parties*, 2nd ed. Lanham, Md.: Rowman & Littlefield, 1996. A valuable collection of empirical studies and theoretical analyses of American parties at the national and state levels. The articles document the increased activity of party organizations in election campaigns.

Wattenberg, Martin P. *The Decline of American Political Parties, 1952–1994*. Cambridge, Mass.: Harvard University Press, 1996. Argues that the American electorate has lessened its attachment to parties because people now believe that candidates, not parties, solve government problems.

World Wide Web Resources

Party Politics. This new international journal is devoted to the study of political parties, party systems, and political organizations in the United States and elsewhere. It publishes studies on the analysis of political parties, including their historical development, structure, policy programs, ideology, and electoral and campaign strategies.
`<www.polisci.nwu.edu:8000/>`

Democratic National Committee. The DNC home page describes the party's structure, bylaws, platform, and activities.
`<www.democrats.org/>`

Republican Main Street. The RNC employs a glitzy "street scene" for the entrance to its home page, which includes the same kinds of information as the Democrats offer but a bit more of everything.
`<www.rnc.org/>`

Ballot Access News. This is a nonpartisan newsletter that reports on the legal difficulties of placing candidates or new parties on the ballots across the states.
`<www.well.com/conf/liberty/ban/>`

Third Parties and the Rocky Road to the White House. Reports on political problems encountered by a variety of third parties since the 1960s.
`<www.greens.org/usa/tphist.html>`

chapter

9

Nominations, Elections, and Campaigns

● ● ● ● ● ● ● ● ● ● ●

IN THE SUMMER OF 1996, a record number of television outlets covered the nominating conventions of America's two major political parties. As has been true since 1952, all three major networks—ABC, CBS, and NBC—had their news anchors there, blow-dried and perched high above the convention floor. As in recent years, the network broadcasts were supplemented by PBS and carried on cable by C-SPAN, CNN, and CNBC. For the first time, television coverage was also offered by MSNBC, NBC and Microsoft's joint cable venture, and even MTV covered a half hour each night. Moreover, the conventions were on Univision, the Spanish TV network. The GOP convention in San Diego, August 12–15, was also carried on the Family Channel by GOPTV (the Republican party's own TV group). If the public wanted to watch the nominating conventions, they had more opportunities than ever before.[1]

And never before did the public show such colossal disinterest in the televised proceedings. Viewership of the major parties' nominating conventions has been slipping since 1968, but in 1996 it tumbled. The Nielsen ratings of the GOP's prime time audience on the convention's second night, for example, was 16 percent below that for the comparable broadcast in 1992 and 33 percent below the 1988 audience figure.[2] Were people just not at home to watch? Were citizens out that Tuesday evening, canvassing voters for the Democrats or perhaps distributing petitions for the Reform Party? No; on ABC alone, about 15 million people watched a rerun of "Home Improvement" at 9:00 P.M. EST, and 13 million absorbed a "Coach" rerun at 9:30. When ABC showed the convention at 10:00, only about 5 million stayed tuned.[3]

Journalists in Chicago who asked people about the GOP convention in San Diego reported that most hadn't watched or weren't interested. A self-described political independent found the convention a turnoff: "I flashed through the channels last night, but when I saw some of those speeches I immediately turned away. It just seems like right now, politics is all advertising." A woman said, "I flipped around, but I'm sick of it already. It's just a big hoopla."[4] Reporters in Ohio found the predominant response from shoppers in several Fishers Food Supermarkets to be, "I didn't watch it."[5]

In truth, even the networks didn't treat the conventions as seriously as in the past. Television experimented with convention coverage in 1940 and 1948, but the 1952 conventions were the first covered coast to coast.[6]

Almost 120 hours of their proceedings (about 60 hours of each party's convention) were telecast by at least one of the three networks. By 1956, when conventions on TV were no longer a novelty, the networks still telecast about 60 hours of both, providing coverage from the opening to the closing gavels. This "gavel-to-gavel" TV coverage continued for the next five conventions. But in 1980, the networks cut back to less than 50 total hours. In 1984 and 1988, they abandoned all pretext at comprehensive coverage and telecast only about 25 hours of both conventions. By 1992, they selectively offered only fifteen hours, and in 1996 they pared coverage to about twelve.[7]

The networks have cut their coverage of the parties' nominating conventions mainly because the conventions have faded as "news." In 1996, the public already knew that Bob Dole was the Republicans' nominee and Bill Clinton the Democrats'. The political director of CNN complained, "Instead of putting on a news event they hope the networks will cover, they have come to the point where they're putting on a TV program, hoping they can get much of it past TV journalists, unfiltered."[8] Indeed, the GOP convention, especially, was "tailor-made for TV"—carefully scripted with short speeches and extensive use of cameo appearances via videos.[9] What kind of TV event was this? Observers variously referred to it as a "variety show," as "part sales meeting, part high-school reunion, part Broadway tryout," and as "an awards program."[10] Ted Koppel of ABC's "Nightline" called it an "infomercial" and left after the second evening, saying that it was no longer a news event: "Nothing surprising has happened, nothing surprising is anticipated."[11] He also cancelled "Nightline's" appearance at the Democratic convention in Chicago, August 26–29, where the Democrats were destined to renominate the Clinton-Gore ticket in an equally scripted extravaganza.

In contrast to the Republicans and Democrats, the Reform Party *did* hold a genuine nominating convention, albeit in two parts. On August 11 (the day before the GOP convention began), the Reform Party met in Long Beach, California, to hear speeches from Ross Perot and Dick Lamm, both of whom had been nominated on petitions from party members. During the next week, party members voted for the nominee of their choice by mail ballot, by telephone, or over the Internet—using a verifying identification code in each instance. On August 18, the party convened again at Valley Forge, Virginia, where Ross Perot was declared the winner with 65 percent of the primary vote to Lamm's 35 percent. Most of the 49,266 votes were cast by mail (88 percent), with relatively few phoned to the 800 number or submitted over the Internet (8 and 4 percent, respectively).[12] Neither session was broadcast by network television, but they were carried by C-SPAN and CNN.

How did the nominating conventions of the major parties come to lose their function? Does the Reform Party offer the model for the future? In this chapter, we consider how election campaigns have changed over time, how candidates get nominated in the United States, what factors are important in election campaigns, and why voters choose one candidate over another. We also address these important questions: Do election campaigns function more to inform or to confuse voters? How important is money in conducting a winning election campaign? What are the roles of

The Secret Ballot v. Modern Technology

In primary elections to nominate Democratic and Republican candidates, voters cast a secret ballot. Ironically, the Reform Party abandoned secrecy in voting when nominating its 1996 candidate. Here is the front and back of the Reform Party's primary ballot. The ballot contains a Voter Identification Number (partially blanked out) to ensure that only those who requested a Reform Party ballot can vote and that they vote only once—whether by mail, by telephone, or over the Internet. To preserve the integrity of the process, the party hired the auditing and accounting firm Ernst & Young of Canada to supervise and certify the voting. Although the secret ballot had been one of our most cherished electoral reforms, the Reform Party didn't mind dropping it.

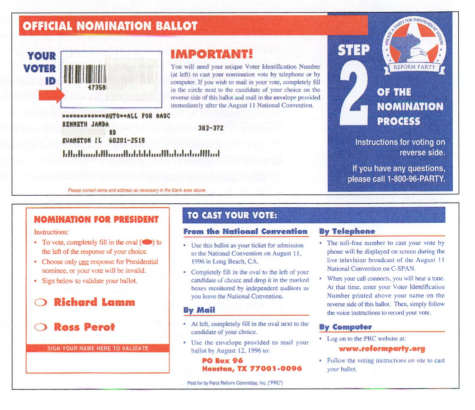

party identification, issues, and candidate attributes in influencing voters' choices and thus election outcomes? How do campaigns, elections, and parties fit into the majoritarian and pluralist models of democracy?

THE EVOLUTION OF CAMPAIGNING

Voting in free elections to choose leaders is the main way that citizens control government. As discussed in Chapter 8, political parties help structure the voting choice by reducing the number of candidates on the ballot to those who have a realistic chance of winning or who offer distinctive policies. An **election campaign** is an organized effort to persuade voters to choose one candidate over others competing for the same office. An effective campaign requires sufficient resources to acquire and analyze information about voters' interests, to develop a strategy and matching tactics for appealing to these interests, to deliver the candidate's message to the voters, and to get them to cast their ballots.[13]

In the past, political parties conducted all phases of the election campaign. As recently as the 1950s, just forty years ago, state and local party organizations "felt the pulse" of their rank-and-file members to learn what was important to the voters. They chose the candidates and then lined up leading officials to support them and to ensure big crowds at campaign rallies. They also prepared buttons, banners, and newspaper advertisements that touted their candidates, proudly named under the prominent label of the party. Finally, candidates relied heavily on the local precinct and county party organizations to contact voters before elections, to mention their names, to extol their virtues, and—most important—to make sure their supporters voted and voted correctly.

Today, candidates seldom rely much on political parties. How do candidates learn about voters' interests today? By contracting for public opinion polls, not by asking the party. How do candidates plan their campaign strategy and tactics now? By hiring political consultants to devise clever "sound bites" (brief, catchy phrases) that will catch voters' attention on television, not by consulting party headquarters. How do candidates deliver their messages to voters? By conducting media campaigns, not by counting on party regulars to canvass the neighborhoods.

Increasingly, election campaigns have evolved from being party centered to being candidate centered.[14] This is not to say that political parties no longer have a role to play in campaigns, for they do. As noted in Chapter 8, the Democratic National Committee now exercises more control over the delegate selection process than it did before 1972. Since 1976, the Republicans have greatly expanded their national organization and fundraising capacity. But whereas the parties virtually ran election campaigns in the past, now they exist mainly to support candidate-centered campaigns by providing services or funds to their candidates. Nevertheless, we will see that the party label is usually a candidate's prime attribute at election time.

Perhaps the most important change in American elections is that candidates don't campaign just to get elected anymore. It is now necessary to campaign for *nomination* as well. As we saw in Chapter 8, nominating candidates to run for office under the party label is one of the main functions of political parties. Party organizations once controlled that function. Even Abraham Lincoln served only one term in the House before the party transferred the nomination for his House seat to someone else.[15] For most important offices today, however, candidates are no longer nominated *by* the party organization but *within* the party. That is, party leaders seldom choose candidates; they merely organize and supervise the election process by which party *voters* choose the candidates. Because almost all aspiring candidates must first win a primary election to gain their party's nomination, those who would campaign for election must first campaign for nomination.

NOMINATIONS

The distinguishing feature of the nomination process in American party politics is that it usually involves an election by party voters. National party leaders do not choose their party's nominee for president or even its candidates for House and Senate seats. Virtually no other political parties in the world nominate candidates to the national legislature through party elections.[16] In more than half the world's parties, local party leaders choose legislative candidates, and their national party organization must usually approve these choices. In fact, in more than one-third of the world's parties, the national organization itself selects the candidates, as described in Compared with What? 9.1.[17]

Democrats and Republicans nominate their candidates for national and state offices in varying ways across the country, because each state is enti-

● compared with what?

9.1   Choosing Legislative Candidates

In the United States, we believe that primary elections are the normal way to nominate candidates. Compared with the practices of other countries, however, our approach is not "normal" at all. Most competitive political parties in Western democracies exercise far more control over who is allowed to represent them in elections. As this graph shows, the most common method of selection, used by thirty-two parties in nine European countries, is to have a group of party activists interview the candidates and then select among them in committees or conventions. (Some parties use a combination of methods and are thus counted twice in the tabulation.) A few parties allow all enrolled party members to hear the candidates and then vote on them in party meetings, but more parties exercise even greater control, having national executive committees choose the candidates. This is evidence of how weak our parties are compared with those elsewhere.

Source: Data are tabulated from Table 11.1 in Michael Gallagher, "Conclusion," in Michael Gallagher and Michael Marsh (eds.), *Candidate Selection in Comparative Perspective: The Secret Garden of Politics* (London: Sage, 1988), p. 237.

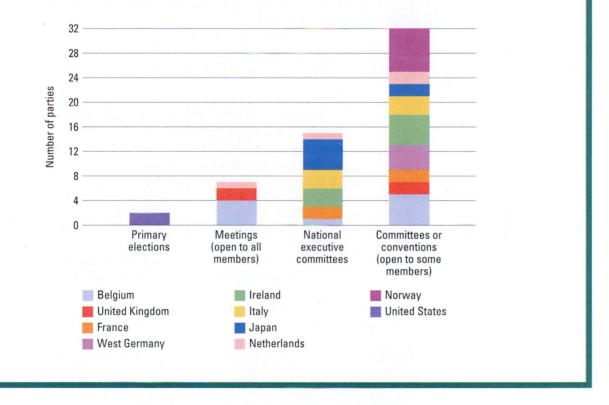

tled to make its own laws governing the nomination process. (This is significant in itself, for political parties in most other countries are largely free of laws stating how they must select their candidates.) We can classify nomination practices by the types of party elections held and the level of office sought.

Nomination for Congress and State Offices

In the United States, most aspiring candidates for major offices are nominated through a **primary election,** a preliminary election conducted within the party to select its candidates. Forty-three states use primary elections alone to nominate candidates for all state and national offices, and primaries figure in the nomination processes of all the other states.[18] The nomination process, then, is highly decentralized, resting on the decisions of thousands, perhaps millions, of the party rank and file who participate in primary elections.

In both parties, only about half of the regular party voters (about one-quarter of the voting-age population) bother to vote in a given primary, although the proportion varies greatly by state and contest.[19] Early research on primary elections concluded that Republicans who voted in their primaries were more conservative than those who did not, while Democratic primary voters were more liberal than other Democrats. This finding led to the belief that primary voters tend to nominate candidates who are more ideologically extreme than the party as a whole would prefer. But more recent research, in which primary voters were compared with those who missed the primary but voted in the general election, reported little evidence that primary voters are unrepresentative of the ideological orientation of other party voters.[20] Some studies support another interpretation: although party activists who turn out for primaries and caucuses are not representative of the average party member, they subordinate their own views to select candidates "who will fare well in the general election."[21]

States hold different types of primary elections for state and congressional offices. The most common type (used by about forty states) is the **closed primary,** in which voters must declare their party affiliation before they are given the primary ballot, which lists the party's potential nominees. A few states use the **open primary,** in which voters may choose either party's ballot, listing that party's potential nominees, to take into the polling booth. Four states use variations of the **blanket primary,** in which voters receive one or more ballots listing all parties' potential nominees for each office and can mark their ballots for any candidate, but only one for each office. The top vote-getter from each party advances to the general election. The state of Washington has used the blanket primary in this form since 1935, and Alaska adopted the same system. Under Louisiana's version of the blanket primary (devised when the state was solidly Democratic), a candidate who obtains a majority of the votes cast for that office in the primary is automatically elected without participating in the general election. (Usually the primary *was* the election.) In March 1996, California voters passed Proposition 198, which put a new twist on the blanket primary. Henceforth the candidates from all parties in a primary will appear on a single ballot *in random order* for any given office. Because California's new system even further downplays the role of parties in the nomination process, it has been called a "jungle" primary—as in "it's a jungle out there"![22]

Most scholars believe that the type of primary held in a state affects the strength of its party organizations. Open primaries (and certainly blanket primaries and the jungle primary) weaken parties more than closed primaries, for they allow voters to float between parties rather than require them to work within one. But the differences among types of primaries are much less important than the fact that our parties have primaries at all—that parties choose candidates through elections. This practice originated in the United States and largely remains peculiar to us. Placing the nomination of party candidates in the hands of voters rather than party leaders is a key factor in the decentralization of power in American parties, which contributes more to pluralist than majoritarian democracy.

Nomination for President

The decentralized nature of American parties is readily apparent in candidates' campaigns for the parties' nominations for president. Delegates attending the parties' national conventions, held the summer before the presidential election in November, nominate the presidential candidates. In the past, delegates chose their party's nominee right at the convention, sometimes after repeated balloting over several candidates who divided the vote and kept anyone from getting the majority needed to win the nomination. In 1920, for example, the Republican convention deadlocked over two leading candidates, after nine ballots. Party leaders then met in the storied "smoke-filled room" and compromised on Warren G. Harding, who won on the tenth. Harding was not among the leading candidates and had won only one primary (in his native Ohio). The last time that either party needed more than one ballot to nominate its presidential candidate was in 1952, when the Democrats took three ballots to nominate Adlai E. Stevenson. Although the Republicans took only one ballot that year to nominate Dwight Eisenhower, his nomination was contested by Senator Robert Taft, and Eisenhower won his nomination on the floor of the convention.

Although 1952 was the last year a nominating majority was constructed among delegates inside the hall, delegates to the Democratic convention in 1960 and the Republican convention in 1964 also resolved uncertain outcomes. Since 1972, both parties' nominating conventions have simply ratified the results of the complex process for selecting the convention delegates, as described in Feature 9.1. Most minor parties, like the Reform Party in 1996, still tend to use conventions to nominate their presidential candidates. Ironically, the more successful "third party" candidates—like George Wallace in 1968, John Anderson in 1980, and Perot in 1992—nominated themselves.[23]

Selecting Convention Delegates.   No national legislation specifies how the state parties must select delegates to their national conventions. Instead, state legislatures have enacted a bewildering variety of procedures, which often differ for Democrats and Republicans in the same state. The most important distinction in delegate selection is between the presidential primary and the local caucus.

A **presidential primary** is a special primary held to select delegates to attend a party's national nominating convention. In *presidential preference primaries* (used in all Democratic primaries and in thirty-five Republican primaries in 1996), party supporters vote directly for the person they favor

feature
9.1

Changes in the Presidential Nomination Process

When President Lyndon Johnson abruptly announced in late March 1968 that he would not run for reelection, the door opened for his vice president, Hubert Humphrey. Humphrey felt it was too late to campaign in primaries against other candidates already in the race; nevertheless, he commanded enough support among party leaders to win the Democratic nomination. The stormy protests outside the party's convention against the "inside politics" of his nomination led to major changes in the way both parties have nominated their presidential candidates since 1968.

Presidential Nominating Process

Until 1968

Party-Dominated
The nomination decision is largely in the hands of party leaders. Candidates win by enlisting the support of state and local party machines.

Few Primaries
Most delegates are selected by state party establishments, with little or no public participation. Some primaries are held, but their results do not necessarily determine the nominee. Primaries are used to indicate candidates' "electability."

Short Campaigns
Candidates usually begin their public campaign early in the election year.

Since 1968

Candidate-Dominated
Campaigns are independent of party establishments. Endorsements by party leaders have little effect on nomination choice.

Many Primaries
Most delegates are selected by popular primaries and caucuses. Nominations are determined largely by voters' decisions at these contests.

Long Campaigns
Candidates begin laying groundwork for campaigns three or four years before the election. Candidates who are not well organized at least eighteen months before the election may have little chance of winning.

as their party's nominee for president, and the primary candidates win delegates according to a variety of formulas. In all Democratic primaries, candidates who win at least 15 percent of the vote divide the delegates from that state in proportion to the percent they won. In almost half the Republican primaries, the winning candidate takes all the states' convention delegates. In *delegate selection primaries* (used only by Republicans in six states in 1996), party voters directly elect convention delegates, who may or may not have declared for a presidential candidate.[24]

The **local caucus** method of delegate selection has several stages. It begins with local meetings, or caucuses, of party supporters to choose delegates to attend a larger subsequent meeting, usually at the county level. Most delegates selected in the local caucuses openly back one of the presidential candidates. The county meetings, in turn, select delegates to a higher level. The process culminates in a state convention, which actually

Until 1968
Easy Money
Candidates frequently raise large amounts of money quickly by tapping a handful of wealthy contributors. No federal limits on spending by candidates.

Limited Media Coverage
Campaigns are followed by print journalists and, in later years, by television. But press coverage of campaigns is not intensive and generally does not play a major role in influencing the process.

Late Decisions
Events early in the campaign year, such as the New Hampshire primary, are not decisive. States that pick delegates late in the year, such as California, frequently are important in selecting the nominee. Many states enter the convention without making final decisions about candidates.

Open Conventions
National party conventions sometimes begin with the nomination still undecided. The outcome is determined by maneuvering and negotiations among party factions, often stretching over multiple ballots.

Since 1968
Difficult Fund Raising
Campaign contributions are limited to $1,000 per person, so candidates must work endlessly to raise money from thousands of small contributors. PAC contributions are important in primaries. Campaign spending is limited by law, both nationally and for individual states.

Media-Focused
Campaigns are covered intensively by the media, particularly television. Media treatment of candidates plays a crucial role in determining the nominee.

"Front-Loaded"
Early events, such as the Iowa caucuses and New Hampshire primary, are important. The nomination may be decided even before many major states vote. Early victories attract great media attention, which gives winners free publicity and greater fund-raising ability.

Closed Conventions
The nominee is determined before the convention, which does little more than ratify the decision made in primaries and caucuses. Convention activities focus on creating a favorable media image of the candidate for the general election campaign.

Source: Michael Nelson (ed.), *Congressional Quarterly's Guide to the Presidency* (Washington, D.C.: Congressional Quarterly Press, 1989), p. 201. Copyright © 1989 by Congressional Quarterly Press. Used by permission.

selects the delegates to the national convention. Eighteen states used the caucus process in 1996 (a few states combined caucuses with primaries), and Democrats used caucuses more than Republicans did.[25]

Primary elections (which were stimulated by the Progressive movement, discussed in Chapter 7) were first used to select delegates to nominating conventions in 1912. Heralded as a party "reform," primaries spread like wildfire. By 1916, a majority of delegates to both conventions were chosen through party elections, but presidential primaries soon dropped in popularity. From 1924 through 1960, rarely were more than 40 percent of the delegates to the national conventions chosen through primaries. Anti-war protests at the 1968 Democratic convention sparked rule changes in the national party that required more "open" procedures for selecting delegates. Voting in primaries seemed the most open procedure. By 1972, this method of selection accounted for about 60 percent of the

figure 9.1

● **Front-Loading the Delegate Selection Process**

In 1996, more delegates were selected earlier in the nominating season than ever before. This was the consequence of states' jockeying for greater candidate and media attention. In 1996, thirty states held their primaries or caucuses by March 14, and thirty-eight held them by March 31. Half of all the Republican convention delegates were selected by March 14, and 75 percent by March 31. All of these figures were increases over previous presidential election years.

Source: John Haskell, "Reforming Presidential Primaries: Three Steps for Improving the Campaign Environment," *Presidential Studies Quarterly* 26 (Spring 1996), p. 382. Permission granted by the Center for the Study of the Presidency, publisher of *Presidential Studies Quarterly.*

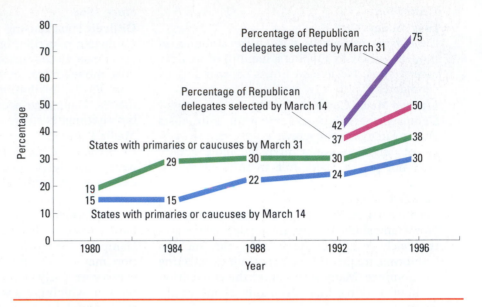

delegates at both party conventions. Now parties in about forty states rely on presidential primaries, which generate more than 80 percent of the delegates.[26] Because delegates selected in primaries are publicly committed to specific candidates, one can easily tell before the convention who is going to be nominated.

In 1996, the Democrats were certain to renominate President Clinton, so only the Republican presidential nomination was in doubt at the start of the primary season. Although nine aspirants began the race for the Republican nomination, the winner seemed destined to emerge sooner than ever due to "front-loading" of the delegate selection process, caused by states' moving their primaries and caucuses earlier in the calendar to gain attention from the media and the candidates (see Figure 9.1).

Campaigning for the Nomination.   The process of nominating party candidates for president is a complex, drawn-out affair that has no parallel in any other nation. Would-be presidents announce their candidacy and begin campaigning many months before the first convention delegates are selected. Soon after one election ends, prospective candidates quietly begin lining up political and financial support for their likely race nearly four years later. This early, silent campaign has been dubbed the *invisible primary*.[27] Indeed, the 1996 race for the Republican nomination surfaced two and a half years before the primaries actually began. In October 1993, reporters covered a parade of Republican aspirants visiting New Hampshire, including senators Robert Dole, Phil Gramm, and Richard Lugar and at least five others who were testing the political climate.[28] Indeed, in the summer of 1996, Steve Forbes, Pat Buchanan, and Lamar Alexander—all aspiring GOP candidates for the 2000 election—wooed

Pat Didn't Reach Far Enough

Eight aspirants for the 1996 Republican presidential nomination meet before a debate in New Hampshire. From the left, they are Alan Keyes, Morry Taylor, Steve Forbes, Robert Dornan, Bob Dole, Richard Lugar, Lamar Alexander, and Pat Buchanan—who couldn't move in far enough from the right to join the handshake. Phil Gramm dropped out of the race too soon to pose with the others.

delegates from the early caucus and primary states who had gathered in San Diego to nominate Bob Dole![29]

By historical accident, two small states—Iowa and New Hampshire—have become the testing ground of candidates' popularity with party voters. Accordingly, each basks in the media spotlight once every four years. Both state legislatures are now committed to leading the delegate selection process, ensuring their states' share of national publicity and their bids for political history. The Iowa caucuses and the New Hampshire primary have served different functions in the presidential nominating process.[30] The contest in Iowa has traditionally tended to winnow out candidates rejected by the party faithful. The New Hampshire primary, held one week later, tests the Iowa front-runners' appeal to ordinary party voters, which foreshadows their likely strength in the general election. Because voting takes little effort by itself, more citizens are likely to vote in primaries than to attend caucuses, which can last for hours. In 1996, about 7 percent of the voting age population participated in both parties' Iowa caucuses, whereas about 36 percent voted in both New Hampshire primaries.[31]

Presidential aspirants have sought a favorable showing in Iowa to help them win in New Hampshire. It did not work that way in 1996 for either of the two favorites, Bob Dole and Phil Gramm. Of 96,000 Iowa Republicans participating in over 2,100 caucuses, 26 percent cast straw votes for Dole, who was followed closely by political commentator Pat Buchanan (23 percent) and then former Governor Lamar Alexander (18 percent) and millionaire publisher Steve Forbes (10 percent). Gramm, a well-funded candidate widely regarded as Bob Dole's greatest threat for the nomination, ran a dismal fifth. Two days later, he withdrew from the race, and Iowa had winnowed out another presidential contender. Although Dole came in first in caucus straw votes, he won no actual delegates at that time; they were selected later, in higher-level caucuses. Dole, Buchanan, Alexander, and Forbes were considered the major candidates going into the New Hampshire primary a week later.

In thirteen of the seventeen nominating contests in both parties prior to 1996, the candidate who won New Hampshire also got the party nomination. Moreover, since 1952 no candidate had won the presidency without first winning the New Hampshire primary—until Clinton in 1992. Thus Buchanan shocked Dole by edging him in New Hampshire, 27 to 26 percent, with Alexander taking 23 percent and Forbes 12. Because New Hampshire awards delegates proportionately, Buchanan got only six, with four each going to Dole and Alexander. Moreover, Buchanan got no "bounce" coming out of New Hampshire. In the next major test, the Arizona primary, Forbes, who had campaigned on replacing the graduated income tax with a flat tax, won a surprising 33 percent of the vote, leaving behind Dole, Buchanan, and Alexander, in that order. More importantly, he took *all* of Arizona's thirty-nine delegates under that state's winner-take-all rules.

So at the end of February, the Republican race was muddled, as each major test produced a different winner. Forbes—the rich outsider—led in delegates won. Buchanan, the GOP bad boy supported by the religious right and opposed by most party leaders, was in second place in the delegate count.[32] Dole, the leaders' favorite, was only third in delegates—despite the fact that front-loading had been expected to favor his early selection.[33] Beginning with the South Carolina primary on March 2, however, Dole's funding advantage and leader support began to overwhelm his opposition. By March 12, he had won enough delegates to claim the nomination (see Figure 9.2), and only Buchanan stayed stubbornly in the race until convention time in August.

Over 35 million citizens voted in both parties' presidential primaries in 1996, and about half a million participated in party caucuses. Requiring prospective presidential candidates to campaign before many millions of party voters in primaries and hundreds of thousands of party activists in caucus states has several consequences:

- The uncertainty of the nomination process attracts a half dozen or so plausible candidates, especially when the party does not have a president seeking reelection. That accounts for the nine Republicans visiting New Hampshire in the fall of 1993.

- Candidates favored by most party identifiers usually win their party's nomination. There have been only two exceptions to this rule since 1936, when poll data first became available: Adlai E. Stevenson in 1952 and George McGovern in 1972.[34] Both were Democrats; both lost impressively in the general election.

- Candidates who win the nomination do so largely on their own and owe little or nothing to the national party organization, which usually does not promote a candidate. In fact, Jimmy Carter won the nomination in 1976 against a field of nationally prominent Democrats, although he was a party outsider with few strong connections to the national party leadership.

Go here for results of the 1996 presidential primaries, by state and party. Compiled by the Federal Election Commission. `<www.fec.gov/96fed/intro.htm>`

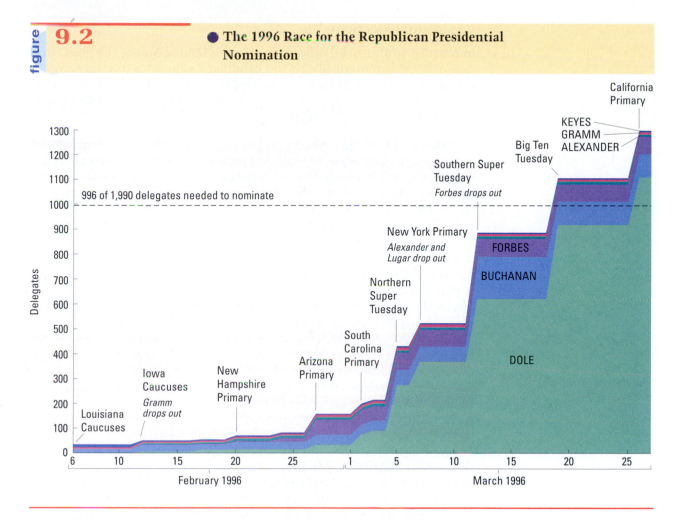

figure 9.2 ● **The 1996 Race for the Republican Presidential Nomination**

Over the first three hurdles after the starting gun, the race was close. Gramm, an early favorite, got stuck in the starting block and quit early. Dole was ahead following the straw vote in the Iowa caucuses, then Buchanan edged ahead by winning New Hampshire, and then Forbes jumped forward by taking Arizona. After that, it was all Dole. His years of service as a senior Republican leader paid off with victory in state after state. He leaped ahead with a huge block of delegates in the Southern Super Tuesday on March 12 and wrapped up the nomination after the California primary on March 26.

ELECTIONS

By national law, all seats in the House of Representatives and one-third of the seats in the Senate are filled in a **general election** held in early November in even-numbered years. Every state takes advantage of the national election to also fill some of the nearly five hundred thousand state and local offices across the country, which makes the election even more "general." When the president is chosen, every fourth year, the election is identified as a *presidential election*. The intervening elections are known as *congressional, midterm,* or *off-year elections*.

Presidential Elections

In contrast to almost all other offices in the United States, the presidency does not go automatically to the candidate who wins the most votes. Instead, a two-stage procedure specified in the Constitution decides elections for president; it requires selection of the president by a group (college) of electors representing the states.

The Electoral College.   Voters choose the president only indirectly; they actually vote for a slate of little-known electors (their names are rarely even on the ballot) pledged to one of the candidates. Occasionally, electors break their pledges when they cast their written ballots at their state capitol in December. This happened as recently as 1988, when Margaret Leach, chosen as a Democratic elector in West Virginia, abandoned Dukakis and voted for his running-mate, Senator Lloyd Bentsen.[35] But usually the electors are faithful, especially when their votes are needed to determine the winner. The fundamental principle of the electoral college is that the outcome of the popular vote determines the outcome of the electoral vote. Whether a candidate wins a state by five votes or five hundred thousand votes, he or she wins all that state's electoral votes.*

To learn more about the Electoral College, visit its home page:
`<www.nara.gov/nara/fedreg/ec/>`

In the electoral college, each state is accorded one vote for each of its senators (100 votes total) and representatives (435 votes total), adding up to 535 votes. In addition, the Twenty-third Amendment to the Constitution awarded three electoral votes to the District of Columbia, although it elects no voting members of Congress. So the total number of electoral votes is 538, and a candidate needs a majority of 270 electoral votes to win the presidency.†

These electoral votes are apportioned among the states according to their representation in Congress, which depends, in turn, on their population. Because of population changes recorded by the 1990 census, the distribution of electoral votes among the states changed between the 1988 and 1992 presidential elections. Figure 9.3 shows the distribution of electoral votes today. California, the most populous state in 1980, had grown even more by 1990 and now claims fifty-four electoral votes, corresponding to its fifty-two representatives and two senators. The greatest population growth occurred in the so-called Sunbelt states: for example, Florida and Texas picked up additional representatives at the expense of Frostbelt states such as New York, Pennsylvania, Illinois, Michigan, and Ohio.

The most troubling aspect of the electoral college is the possibility that despite winning a plurality or even a majority of popular votes, a candidate could lose the election in the electoral college. This could happen if one candidate wins certain states by very wide margins, while the other candidate wins other states by slim margins. Indeed, it has happened in three elections, the most recent in 1888, when Grover Cleveland received 48.6

---

* *The two exceptions are Maine and Nebraska, where two and three of the states' electoral votes, respectively, are awarded by congressional district. The presidential candidate who carries each district wins a single electoral vote, and the statewide winner gets two votes.*

† *If no candidate receives a majority when the electoral college votes, the election is thrown into the House of Representatives. The House votes by state, with each state casting one vote. The candidates in the House election are the top three finishers in the general election. A presidential election has gone to the House only twice in American history, in 1800 and 1824, before a stable two-party system had developed.*

9.3   ● The Political Geography of the Electoral College

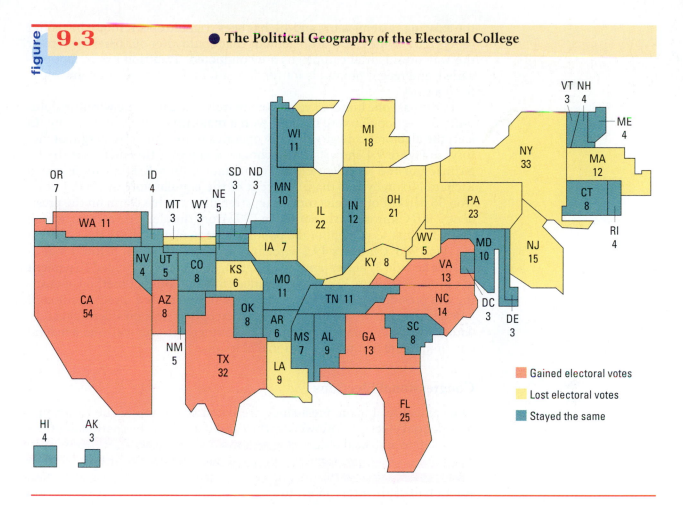

If the states were sized according to their electoral votes, the nation might resemble this map, on which the states are drawn according to their population, based on the 1990 census. Each state has as many electoral votes as its combined representation in the Senate (always two) and the House (which depends on population). Although New Jersey is much smaller in area than Montana, it has far more people and is thus bigger in terms of "electoral geography." California, with two senators and fifty-two representatives, has fifty-four electoral votes—or more than 10 percent of the total of 538. (Washington, D.C., has three electoral votes—equal to the smallest state—although it has no representation in Congress.)

Source: "The 1990 Census: The Changing Shape of the Union," *New York Times,* 27 December 1990, p. A10; and *Congressional Quarterly Weekly Report,* 23 March 1991, p. 765.

percent of the popular vote to Benjamin Harrison's 47.9 percent. Cleveland nevertheless lost to Harrison in the electoral college, 168 to 233.

Abolish the Electoral College?   About seven hundred proposals to change the electoral college scheme have been introduced in Congress since 1789.[36] Reformers argue that it is simply wrong to have a system that allows a candidate who receives the most popular votes to lose the election. They favor a purely majoritarian means of choosing the president, direct election by popular vote. Defenders of the electoral college point out that the existing system, warts and all, has been a stable one. It might be riskier to replace it with a new arrangement that could alter our party system or the way presidential campaigns are conducted. Tradition has in fact prevailed, and recent proposals for fundamental reform have not come close to adoption.

For the past one hundred years, fortunately, the candidate winning a plurality of the popular vote has also won a majority of the electoral vote. In fact, the electoral college generally operates to magnify the margin of victory, as Figure 9.4 shows. Some scholars argue that this increases the legitimacy of the president-elect. For instance, John F. Kennedy defeated Richard Nixon by less than 1 percent of the popular vote in 1960, but he won 56 percent of the electoral vote, strengthening his claim on the presidency. Bill Clinton also benefited in 1992 from the electoral college, which magnified his 43 percent of the popular vote to 69 percent of the electoral vote. In 1996, Clinton's 49.2 percent of the vote again fell below a majority, but he won 31 states (and Washington, D.C.), which yielded 70 percent of the electoral vote. In any event, since 1888 our indirect method of electing the president has produced the same outcome as a direct method of popular election would have, with the exception that presidential candidates have had to plan their campaign strategies to win states in a federal election, not just votes in a national election.[37]

Congressional Elections

The candidates for the presidency are listed at the top of the ballot in a presidential election, followed by the candidates for other national offices and for state and local offices. A voter is said to vote a **straight ticket** when she or he chooses the same party's candidates for all the offices. A voter who chooses candidates from different parties is said to vote a **split ticket.** About half of all voters admit to splitting their tickets, and the proportion of voters who chose a presidential candidate from one party and a congressional candidate from the other has increased from about 13 percent in 1952 to 25 percent in 1992.[38] A common pattern in the 1970s and 1980s was to elect a Republican as president but send mostly Democrats to Congress, producing divided government (see Chapter 12). This pattern was reversed in the 1994 election, when voters elected a Republican Congress to face a Democratic president, a situation that last confronted President Truman in 1946.

Until the historic 1994 election, Democrats for decades had a lock on congressional elections, winning a majority of House seats since 1954 and controlling the Senate for all but six years during that period. Republicans regularly complained that inequitable districts drawn by Democrat-dominated state legislatures had denied them their fair share of seats. For example, the Republicans won 46 percent of the congressional vote in 1992, but they won only 40 percent of the seats.[39] Despite the Republicans' complaint, election specialists note that this is the inevitable consequence of **first-past-the-post elections**—a British term for elections conducted in single-member districts that award victory to the candidate with the most votes. In all such elections worldwide, the party that wins the most votes tends to win more seats than projected by its percentage of the vote. (The same process operates in the electoral college, which, as discussed, gener-

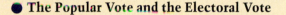

figure 9.4 ● **The Popular Vote and the Electoral Vote**

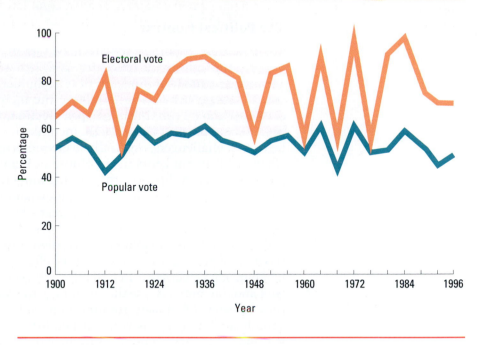

The electoral vote, not the popular vote, decides elections for president. Although a candidate could win a plurality of the popular vote but not the majority of the electoral vote needed to be elected president, this has not happened since 1888. More common is for candidates who win a plurality of the popular vote to win an even larger majority of the electoral vote. Even when Richard Nixon won only 43 percent of the vote in 1968 against Hubert Humphrey, the Democratic candidate, and George Wallace of the American Independent Party, he took 56 percent of the electoral vote. Similarly, in 1992 Bill Clinton won only 43 percent of the popular vote but took 69 percent of the electoral votes. In general, the effect of the electoral college is to magnify the winner's victory and thus increase the legitimacy of the president-elect.

Source: Harold W. Stanley and Richard G. Niemi, *Vital Statistics on American Politics,* 2d ed. (Washington, D.C.: Congressional Quarterly Press, 1990), pp. 104–106; and "Presidential Election," *Congressional Quarterly Weekly Report,* November 1992, p. 3549.

ally awards the winner a bigger majority in electoral votes than was won in popular votes.*) Thus in 1994, when Republicans got barely 50 percent of the House votes nationwide, they won 53 percent of the House seats. Gaining control of the House for the first time in forty years, they made no complaint.

The fact remains that, historically, voters have favored Democratic candidates for both the House and the Senate, even when electing Republican candidates for president. Some analysts see special significance in that voting pattern. They credit citizens for consciously voting to produce divided government, with a Republican executive pushing one way and a Democratic legislature the other.[40] If so, voters behave quite rationally in making their ballot choices, favoring a weaker, pluralist government rather than a stronger, majoritarian one. It remains to be seen whether the evidence of voting choice in general elections can support such a rational interpretation of electoral behavior.

CAMPAIGNS

As Barbara Salmore and Stephen Salmore have observed, election campaigns have been studied more through anecdotes than through systematic analysis.[41] These writers developed an analytical framework that emphasizes the political context of the campaign, the financial resources

---

* If you have trouble understanding this phenomenon, think of a basketball team that scores, on average, 51 percent of the total points in all the games it plays. Such a team usually wins more than just 51 percent of its games, for it tends to win the close ones.

available for conducting the campaign, and the strategies and tactics that underlie the dissemination of information about the candidate.

The Political Context

The two most important structural factors that face each candidate planning a campaign are the office the candidate is seeking and whether he or she is the *incumbent* (the current officeholder, running for reelection) or the *challenger* (who seeks to replace the incumbent). Alternatively, the candidate can be running in an **open election,** which lacks an incumbent because of a resignation or death. Incumbents usually enjoy great advantages over challengers, especially in elections to Congress. As explained in Chapter 11, incumbents in the House of Representatives are almost impossible to defeat, historically winning more than 95 percent of the time. However, incumbent senators are somewhat more vulnerable. An incumbent president is also difficult to defeat—but not impossible, as George Bush learned in 1992.

Every candidate organizing a campaign must also examine the characteristics of the district, including its physical size and the sociological makeup of its electorate. In general, the bigger and more populous the district and the more diverse the electorate, the more complicated and costly the campaign. Obviously, running for president means conducting a huge, complicated, and expensive campaign. After being nominated at their conventions, the parties' nominees immediately embarked on campaign trips. Bob Dole and Jack Kemp, Dole's surprising but brilliant choice for his vice-presidential running-mate, left on a three-day trip to Springfield, Illinois; Buffalo; and Pittsburgh. Bill Clinton and Al Gore took a two-day bus trip to Cape Girardeau, Missouri; Paducah, Kentucky; and Memphis.

Despite comments in the news about the decreased influence of party affiliation on voting behavior, the party preference of the electorate is an important factor in the context of a campaign. It is easier for a candidate to get elected when her or his party matches the electorate's preference, in part because raising the money needed to conduct a winning campaign is easier. Challengers for Congress, for example, get far less money from organized groups than do incumbents and must rely more on their personal funds and on raising money from individual donors.[42] So where candidates are of the minority party, they have to overcome not only a voting bias but also a funding bias. Finally, significant political issues—such as economic recession, personal scandals, and war—not only affect a campaign but can dominate it and even negate such positive factors as incumbency and the normal inclinations of the electorate. For example, the Watergate affair overshadowed the 1974 congressional elections, resulting in the loss of thirty-six seats of Republican representatives seeking reelection, mostly in Republican districts, regardless of the quality of their campaigns.

Financing

In talking about election campaigns, former House speaker Thomas ("Tip") O'Neill once said, "As it is now, there are four parts to any campaign. The candidate, the issues of the candidate, the campaign organization, and the money to run the campaign with. Without money you can forget the other three."[43] Money pays for office space, staff salaries, tele-

• • • • • • • • • • • •
Political Campaigning: The Inside Story

Actually, it's not all that exciting. Conducting a successful campaign usually involves a careful statistical analysis of voting trends and various social and economic characteristics of the electorate. The sign in Republican strategist Karl Rove's office in Austin, Texas, says a lot: these days, computers may be everything.

phone bills, postage, travel expenses, campaign literature, and, of course, advertising in the mass media. Although a successful campaign requires a good campaign organization and a good candidate, enough money will buy the best campaign managers, equipment, transportation, research, and consultants—making the quality of the organization largely a function of money.[44] Although the equation is not quite as strong, when party sources promise ample campaign funds, good candidates become available. So from a cynical but practical viewpoint, campaign resources boil down to campaign funds.

Campaign financing is now heavily regulated by the national and state governments, and regulations vary according to the level of the office—national, state, or local. Even at the national level, differences in financing laws for presidential and congressional elections are significant.

Regulating Campaign Financing. Strict campaign financing laws are relatively new to American politics. Early laws to limit campaign contributions and control campaign spending were flawed in one way or another, and none clearly provided for enforcement. In 1971, during the period of party reform, Congress enacted the Federal Election Campaign Act (FECA), which imposed stringent new rules for full reporting of campaign contributions and expenditures. The weakness of the old legislation soon became apparent. In 1968, before FECA was enacted, House and Senate candidates reported spending $8.5 million for their campaigns. In 1972, with FECA in force, the same number of candidates confessed to spending $88.9 million.[45]

FECA has been amended several times since 1971, usually to strengthen it. For example, the original law legalized political action committees, but a 1974 amendment limited the amounts they can contribute to election campaigns. (Political action committees are discussed in Chapter 10.) The 1974 amendment also created the **Federal Election Commission (FEC)** to implement the law. The FEC now enforces limits on financial contributions to national campaigns and requires full disclosure of campaign spending. The FEC also administers the public financing of presidential campaigns, which began with the 1976 election.

Financing Presidential Campaigns.   Presidential campaigns have always been expensive, and at times the legality of the methods of raising funds to support them has been open to question. In the presidential election of 1972, the last election before the FEC took over the funding of presidential campaigns and the regulating of campaign expenditures, President Richard Nixon's campaign committee spent more than $65 million, some of it obtained illegally (for which campaign officials went to jail). In 1974, a new campaign finance law made public funds available to presidential candidates under certain conditions.

Candidates for each party's nomination for president can qualify for federal funding by raising at least $5,000 (in private contributions no greater than $250 each) in each of twenty states. The FEC then matches these contributions up to one-half of a preset spending limit for the primary election campaign. Originally under the 1974 law, the FEC limited spending in presidential primary elections to $10 million. But by 1996, cost-of-living provisions had raised the limit to $30.9 million (plus $6.2 million for fund-raising activities).

The presidential nominees of the Democratic and Republican parties receive twice the primary election limit in public funds for the general election campaign ($61.8 million in 1996), provided that they spend only the public funds. Each of the two major parties also receives public funds to pay for its convention ($12.4 million in 1996). Every major candidate since 1976 has accepted public funding, holding the costs of presidential campaigns well below Nixon's record expenditures in 1972. When Ross Perot ran for president in 1992, he spent an estimated $65 million of his own money. Perot won enough votes in 1992 to qualify for $29.2 million in public funds for 1996, which he accepted and which limited him to spending only $50,000 of his own money plus whatever he might raise in contributions up to the $61.8 million limit set for Dole and Clinton.

Public funds go directly to each candidate's campaign committee, not to either party. But the FEC also limits what the national committees can spend on behalf of the nominees. In 1996, that limit was $12 million.[46] And the FEC limits the amount individuals ($1,000) and organizations ($5,000) can contribute to presidential candidates during the nomination phase and to House and Senate candidates for the primary and general elections. Individuals or organizations are not limited, however, in the amount of expenses they can incur to promote candidates of their choice. *

---

* *The distinction between contributions and expenses hinges on whether funds are spent as part of a coordinated campaign (a contribution) or spent independently of the candidate's campaign (an expense). The 1974 amendment to FECA established limits on both campaign contributions and independent expenditures by interested citizens. In* Buckley v. Valeo *(1976), the Supreme Court struck down the limits on citizens' expenditures as an infringement on freedom of speech, protected under the First Amendment.*

Public funding has had several effects on campaign financing. Obviously, it has limited campaign expenditures. Also, it has helped equalize the amounts spent by major party candidates in general elections, and it has strengthened the trend toward "personalized" presidential campaigns, because federal funds are given to the candidate, not to the party organization. Finally, public funding has forced candidates to spend a great deal of time seeking $1,000 contributions—a limit that has not changed since 1974, despite inflation that has more than doubled the FEC's spending limits. In the 1980s, however, both parties began to exploit a loophole in the law that allowed them to raise a virtually unlimited amount of "soft money," funds to be spent for the entire ticket on party mailings, voter registration, and get-out-the-vote campaigns. In the first eighteen months of the 1995–1996 campaign cycle, the Republicans raised $83.9 million and the Democrats $70.3 million—both sums were over twice what was raised for that period in the 1992 election.[47] The national committees channel soft money to state and local party committees for registration drives and other activities that are not exclusively devoted to the presidential candidates but nonetheless help them.[48] The net effect of these "coordinated campaigns" has been to enhance the role of both the national and state parties in presidential campaigns.

You might think that a party's presidential campaign would be closely coordinated with the campaigns of its candidates for Congress. But remember that campaign funds go to the presidential candidate, not to the party, and that the national party organization does not run the presidential campaign. Presidential candidates may join congressional candidates in public appearances for mutual benefit, but presidential campaigns are usually isolated—financially and otherwise—from congressional campaigns. Both parties spoke piously about rewriting campaign finance laws in the 104th Congress, but legislators could not agree on how to reform a system observers said was "in shambles" two decades after the 1974 campaign reform legislation.[49]

Strategies and Tactics

In a military campaign, strategy is the overall scheme for winning the war, whereas tactics involve the conduct of localized hostilities. In an election campaign, strategy is the broad approach used to persuade citizens to vote for the candidate, and tactics determine the content of the messages and the way they are delivered. Three basic strategies, which campaigns may blend in different mixes, are as follows:

- A party-centered strategy, which relies heavily on voters' partisan identification as well as on the party's organization to provide the resources necessary to wage the campaign

- An issue-oriented strategy, which seeks support from groups that feel strongly about various policies

- An image-oriented strategy, which depends on the candidate's perceived personal qualities, such as experience, leadership ability, integrity, independence, trustworthiness, and the like[50]

The campaign strategy must be tailored to the political context of the election. Clearly, a party-centered strategy is inappropriate in a primary, because all contenders have the same party affiliation. Research suggests that a party-centered strategy is best suited to voters with little political knowledge.[51] How do candidates learn what the electorate knows and thinks about politics, and how can they use this information? Candidates today usually turn to pollsters and political consultants, of whom there are hundreds.[52] Well-funded candidates can purchase a "polling package" that includes

- A benchmark poll that provides "campaign information about the voting preferences and issue concerns of various groups in the electorate and a detailed reading of the image voters have of the candidates in the race"

- Focus groups, consisting of ten to twenty people "chosen to represent particular target groups the campaign wants to reinforce or persuade . . . led in their discussion by persons trained in small-group dynamics," giving texture and depth to poll results

- A trend poll "to determine the success of the campaigns in altering candidate images and voting preferences"

Check this source for a running account of public approval of the president's performance.
<www.politicsnow.com/
resource/polltrak/
index.htm>

- Tracking polls that begin in early October, "conducting short nightly interviews with a small number of respondents, keyed to the variables that have assumed importance"[53]

Professional campaign managers can use information from such sources to settle on a strategy that mixes party affiliation, issues, and images in its messages. In major campaigns, the mass media disseminates these messages to voters through news coverage and advertising.[54]

Making the News. Campaigns value news coverage by the media for two reasons: the coverage is free, and it seems objective to the audience. If news stories do nothing more than report the candidate's name, that is important, for name recognition by itself often wins elections. To get favorable coverage, campaign managers cater to reporters' deadlines and needs.[55] Getting free news coverage is yet another advantage that incumbents enjoy over challengers, for incumbents can command attention simply by announcing political decisions—even if they had little to do with them. Members of Congress are so good at this, says one observer, that House members have made news organizations their "unwitting adjuncts."[56]

Campaigns vary in the effectiveness with which they transmit their messages via the news media. Effective tactics recognize the limitations of both the audience and the media. The typical voter is not deeply interested in politics and has trouble keeping track of multiple themes supported with details. By the same token, television is not willing to air lengthy statements from candidates. As a result, news coverage is often condensed to "sound bites" only a few seconds long. The media were harshly criticized during the 1988 presidential campaign for cutting the candidates' utterances to an average of only ten seconds.[57] Media leaders reacted to the criticism by pledging more substantive coverage, beginning with the 1992 election. But some critics charged that reporters then went too far in the other direction, trying to help voters "by reporting which candidates were right and which were wrong" or otherwise offering judgments in their stories.[58]

The media often use the metaphor of a horse race in covering politics in the United States. One long-time student of the media contends that reporters both enliven and simplify campaigns by describing them in terms of four basic scenarios: *bandwagons, losing ground, the front-runner,* and *the likely loser.*[59] Once the opinion polls show weakness or strength in a candidate, reporters dust off the appropriate story line. Commenting on the race for the 1996 Republican nomination, one Chicago columnist wrote

> A story that said simply "this guy beat that guy" would never cut it anymore. Instead, what you get is Dole is in the catbird seat, Dole in the toilet. Forbes on Fire, Forbes struggling for his life. . . .
>
> The same dynamic was in play after Monday's Iowa vote. Dole won, but not by an overwhelming margin so that was considered a poor showing. Pat Buchanan came in second, but the big story was Alexander, the former Tennessee governor and U.S. Education secretary whose third place bested better-funded candidates like Forbes. This is how the Associated Press characterized the Republican race going into New Hampshire:
>
> "Lamar Alexander, fresh off his strong third-place finish in Iowa, set his sights Tuesday on Bob Dole and Pat Buchanan. . . ."
>
> Strong third-place finish. By those standards, the Cubs could be considered the perennial powerhouse of the National League.[60]

Given the media's preoccupation with horse race journalism, it is not surprising that television news contains little information about the issues in the campaign. In fact, studies of recent campaigns have found that most voters get their campaign information from political ads rather than television news programs.[61]

Advertising the Candidate. In all elections, the first objective of paid advertising is name recognition. The next is to promote candidates by extolling their virtues. Finally, campaign advertising can have a negative objective—to attack one's opponent. But name recognition is usually the most important. Studies show that many voters cannot recall the names of their U.S. senators or representatives, but they can recognize their names on a list—as on a ballot. Researchers attribute the high reelection rate for members of Congress mainly to high name recognition (see Chapter 11). Name recognition is the key objective during the primary elections even in presidential campaigns, but other objectives become salient in advertising for the general election.

At one time, candidates for national office relied heavily on newspaper advertising; today, they overwhelmingly use the electronic media. Darrell West found that both George Bush and Bill Clinton spent about 60 percent of their 1992 presidential campaign budgets on radio and television ads, whereas Ross Perot devoted up to 75 percent.[62] After his nomination in 1996, Dole budgeted $45 million of his $62 million in public funds on television to overcome Clinton's lead in the polls.[63]

Political ads convey more substantive information than many people believe. West's study found that presidential campaign ads since 1984 have had more specific policy content than references to personal qualities and have had more policy content than ads in the 1950s and early 1960s.[64] However, other scholars have pointed out that the "policy content" of ads may be misleading, if not downright deceptive.[65] West also found that 1992 set a record for negative advertising. Nearly two-thirds of most prominent ads were negative.[66] And the most substantive content—on both foreign policy and domestic policy—actually appeared in negative ads. West explained, "Negative commercials are more likely to have policy-oriented content because campaigners need a clear reason to attack the opponent."[67]

The media often inflate the effect of prominent ads by reporting them as news, which means that citizens are about as likely to see controversial ads during the news as in the ads' paid time slots.[68] Although negative ads do convey information, they also breed distrust of politics—as demonstrated in a major controlled study of political advertising: "In our experiments the effect of seeing a negative as opposed to a positive advertisement is to drop intentions to vote by nearly 5 percentage points." As a result, the authors of the study say, "Negative advertising drives people away from the polls in large numbers."[69]

You want dirt on political candidates and officeholders? Poke around in the Skeleton Closet.

Using New Media. A major development in campaigning in 1992 was the strategic use of new media, including talk shows, entertainment shows, and Perot's half-hour "infomercials." Bill Clinton started the trend in January by appearing on "60 Minutes" to respond to Gennifer Flowers's claim of infidelity. In February, Ross Perot launched his campaign with an appearance on "Larry King Live." From June 2 to June 30, 1992, Clinton appeared on ten talk shows, and by the end of the month he had gained seven points in the polls and moved into first place among the candidates.[70] Most observers have concluded that these soft-format programs (watched by many people) represent an alternative form of campaigning that provide viewers with important information on candidates' character and policies.

Clinton's successful use of the new media in 1992, including a segment on MTV, guaranteed that candidates would again use it in 1996. Sure enough, even seventy-year-old Bob Dole appeared on MTV, looking cool, and Ross Perot relied on Larry King and CNN to introduce his running-mate, economist Pat Choate, to the nation a month after failing to choose a vice-presidential candidate at the August Reform Party convention. But the hottest new media in 1996 was the Internet. Not only did the major and minor parties put up their own home pages, but so did the presidential candidates—including several just seeking the Republican nomination. There were "official" sites (endorsed by the candidates) and "unofficial" ones, sometimes created by supporters—and sometimes by opponents. Both Buchanan and Dole, for example, were targeted by parody pages early in the nomination campaign.[71] During the drafting of the GOP plank on abortion, the pro-life forces mounted an e-mail campaign to hang tough going into the convention.[72] The Internet, only in its infancy, is already in politics.

EXPLAINING VOTING CHOICE

Why do people choose one candidate over another? That is not easy to determine, but there are ways to approach the question. Individual voting choices can be analyzed as products of both long-term and short-term forces. Long-term forces operate throughout a series of elections, predisposing voters to choose certain types of candidates. Short-term forces are associated with particular elections; they arise from a combination of the candidates and issues of the time. Party identification is by far the most important long-term force affecting U.S. elections. The most important short-term forces are candidates' attributes and their policy positions.

Using the "Voters" data in the CROSSTABS program, analyze when respondents decided to vote ("time of vote decision") by strength of party identification. Who decides latest?

Party Identification

Ever since the presidential election of 1952, when the University of Michigan's National Election Studies began, we have known that more than half the electorate decides how to vote before the party conventions end in the summer.[73] And voters who make an early voting decision generally vote according to their party identification. Despite frequent comments in the media about the decline of partisanship in voting behavior, party identification again had a substantial effect on the presidential vote in 1996, as Figure 9.5 shows. Nearly 85 percent of avowed Democrats voted for Clinton, and 81 percent of Republicans voted for Dole. A plurality of independents also voted for Clinton. This is a common pattern in

Sweeping Indictment

This sign of the times implies that incumbent officeholders were targets of voter discontent in the 1994 elections. But in a remarkable display of sharpshooting, the voters destroyed only Democratic targets. Every incumbent Republican governor, senator, and representative running for reelection was victorious, while voters threw out scores of prominent Democratic incumbents seeking to return to the governor's mansion or Congress. It was not a good year for Democratic officeholders.

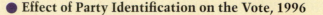

figure 9.5

● **Effect of Party Identification on the Vote, 1996**

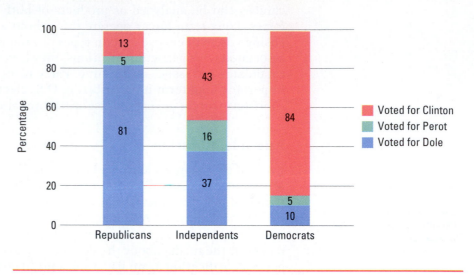

The 1996 election showed that party identification still plays a key role in voting behavior—even with an independent candidate in the contest. The chart shows the results of exit polls of thousands of voters as they left hundreds of polling places across the nation on Election Day. Voters were asked what party they identified with and how they voted for president. Those who identified with one of the two parties voted strongly for their party's candidate, whereas independent voters divided roughly evenly between Clinton and Dole and were three times more likely to vote for Perot.

Source: National Exit Poll Results for Presidential Race," distributed by *PoliticsNow* on the Internet, November 6, 1996.

presidential elections. The winner holds nearly all the voters who identify with his party. The loser holds most of his fellow Democrats or Republicans, but some percentage defects to the winner, a product of short-term forces—the candidates' attributes and the issues—surrounding the election. The winner usually gets most of the independents, who split disproportionately for him, also because of short-term forces. Perot won 30 percent of the independent vote in 1992, but only 16 percent in 1996.

Because Democrats outnumber Republicans, the Democrats should benefit. Why, then, have Republican candidates won more presidential elections since 1952 than Democrats? For one thing, Democrats do not turn out to vote as consistently as Republicans do. For another, Democrats tend to defect more readily from their party. Defections are sparked by the candidates' attributes and the issues, which have usually favored Republican presidential candidates since 1952.

In both 1992 and 1996, however, short-term forces in presidential politics clearly benefited the Democrat Clinton, first as the challenger and later as the incumbent. By winning in 1996, Clinton became the first Democratic president to be reelected to office since Franklin Delano Roosevelt in 1944. His electoral coattails, however, were not long enough or strong enough to wrest control of Congress from the Republicans.

Issues and Policies

"The economy" was seen as the major issue that won for Bill Clinton in 1992—and it probably got him reelected in 1996. Throughout 1992, his campaign exploited the public's perception of a weak economy.[74] In fact, the economy was not really performing that badly. Inflation had fallen and lower interest rates were encouraging investment. Nevertheless, Clinton attacked the issue, and independent candidate Ross Perot added economic gloom over the federal debt. A voting analysis in 1992 concluded that the budget deficit was the most important economic factor in the voter's choice: "Those who thought that the Bush and Reagan administrations were responsible for the deficit . . . overwhelmingly (80%) supported Clinton, while those who blamed the deficit on the [then] Democratic Congress . . . voted heavily for Bush (64%)."[75]

Just before the August 1996 Republican Convention (and late in the campaign), Bob Dole announced that his campaign would focus on the slow growth of the economy, which was better off by objective measures than in 1992. Nevertheless, he proposed a tax cut of 15 percent over three years for all taxpayers and promised that he could produce a balanced budget through economic growth and (unspecified) cuts in spending.[76] His proposal echoed "supply-side" economic reasoning, which argues that tax cuts will stimulate an economy to produce more revenue than they lose (see Chapter 18). Because Dole had savaged such reasoning when in the Senate, he surprised most informed observers with his change of opinion. Dole also named as his running mate former congressman Jack Kemp, a supply-side advocate. Although Dole's choice was regarded as shrewd, it too was puzzling—for the two had often exchanged sharp words.[77]

After the election, voting data showed that the voters had not taken to Dole's promised tax cut. First, most did not think that high taxes was the most important public issue. Second, many did not think that Dole would be able to reduce taxes by 15 percent and cut the deficit at the same time. Among the few who did, 84 percent voted for Dole. Among the more who didn't, 67 percent voted for Clinton.[78]

Candidates' Attributes

Candidates' attributes are especially important to voters who lack good information about a candidate's past performance and policy stands—which means most of us. Without such information, voters search for clues about the candidates to try to predict their behavior in office.[79] Some fall back on their personal beliefs about religion, gender, and race in making political judgments. Such stereotypic thinking accounts for the patterns of opposition and support met by a Catholic candidate for president (John Kennedy), a woman candidate for vice president (Geraldine Ferraro in 1984), and a black contender for a presidential nomination (Jesse Jackson in 1984 and 1988). Recently, voters have been more willing to elect candidates other than white males to public office (see Politics in a Changing America 9.1).

Evaluating the Voting Choice

Choosing among candidates according to their personal attributes might be an understandable approach, but it is not rational voting, according to democratic theory. According to that theory, citizens should vote according to the candidates' past performance and proposed policies. Voters who choose between candidates on the basis of their policies are voting on the issues, which fits the idealized conception of democratic theory. However, issues, candidates' attributes, and party identification all figure in the voting decision.

Unfortunately for democratic theory, most studies of presidential elections show that issues are less important than either party identification or the candidates' attributes when people cast their ballots. Only in 1972,

politics in a changing america

9.1   Growth in Hispanic Elected and Appointed Officials, 1983 to 1994

In the late 1980s and early 1990s, Hispanics were elected or appointed to government office far less than might have been expected according to their representation in the population. In 1992, Hispanics constituted 9.2 percent of the adult population of the United States but held only 1.2 percent of all local elected offices. They have shown their greatest gains among county and municipal offices and in education-related offices, such as school board seats. All of the indicators show a steady increase, however, and the proportions of Hispanic women in public office have increased in every category.

Source: Robert Brischetto, "Women Lead the Modest Jump in Hispanic Political Representation," *Hispanic Business,* October 1995, p. 98. Reprinted by permission of Hispanic Business, Inc., 360 S. Hope Ave., Suite 300C, Santa Barbara, CA 93105.

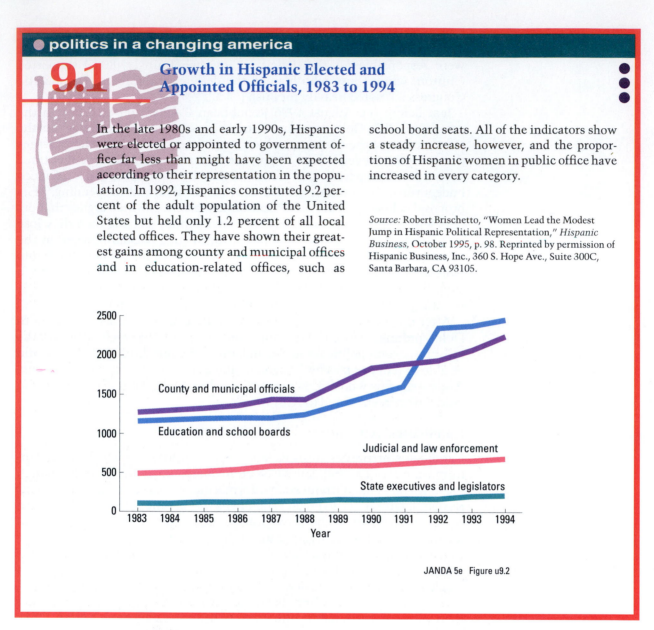

JANDA 5e   Figure u9.2

when voters perceived George McGovern as too liberal for their tastes, did issue voting exceed party identification in importance.[80] Even that year, issues were less important than the candidate's image. According to polls taken at the time, voters saw McGovern as weak and uncertain, and Nixon as strong and (ironically) highly principled.[81]

Although party voting has declined somewhat since the 1950s, the relationship between voters' positions on the issues and their party identification is clearer and more consistent today. For example, Democratic party identifiers are now more likely than Republican identifiers to describe themselves as liberal, and they are more likely than Republican identifiers to favor government spending for social welfare and abortions. The more closely party identification is aligned with ideological orientation, the more sense it makes to vote by party. In the absence of detailed information about candidates' positions on the issues, party labels are a handy indicator of those positions.[82]

Campaign Effects

If party identification is the most important factor in the voting decision and is also resistant to short-term changes, there are definite limits to the capacity of a campaign to influence the outcome of elections.[83] In a close election, however, just changing a few votes means the difference between victory and defeat, so a campaign can be decisive even if it has little overall effect.

The Television Campaign.   It is not surprising that campaigns are most effective when one side has weapons that the other side lacks, which sometimes happens in races for lower offices. In presidential elections, however, the capacity of image makers and campaign consultants to influence the outcome is minimized, because they regularly offset one another by working on both sides. In 1996, both major presidential candidates hired professional campaign consultants and advertising firms. Although Perot hired an experienced advertising firm, he again managed his own campaign. But the novelty of Perot's appeal was gone in 1996, and his half-hour chart-laden "infomercials" failed to attract large audiences of viewers. Perot was not much of a factor in the advertising battle.

The Clinton and Dole campaigns differed starkly in how they advertised and how the public perceived their efforts. Clinton, who had been spared a primary fight for the nomination, had far more money to spend. He began spending it in 1995, mostly on negative television ads against the Republicans and Newt Gingrich, and later against Dole. Of thirty-one different Clinton-Gore commercials broadcast between the summer of 1995 and October 1996, only five were entirely positive. In contrast, the Dole campaign ran out of funds during the primary season and could not begin television advertising until mid-August, when Dole became the official nominee of the Republican Party and could receive public funds from the Federal Election Commission. For the next two months Dole spent more than $20 million on negative ads and only $6.5 million on positive ones.[84]

Although the Clinton forces had run more negative ads during the campaign than the Dole team, the voters didn't see it that way. In a poll at the height of the campaign, 50 percent of the respondents said that Dole was spending more time attacking Clinton, while only 19 percent thought that Clinton was concentrating on attacking Dole.[85] Frustrated, Dole urged voters to "rise up" in "outrage" against the liberal media, saying "Don't read that stuff! Don't watch television! You make up your own mind!"[86]

The Presidential Debates.   In 1960, John F. Kennedy and Richard Nixon held the first televised presidential debate (thought to benefit Kennedy), but debates were not used again until 1976. Since then, candidate debates in some form have been a regular feature of presidential elections. Sitting presidents have been reluctant to debate except on their own terms. Clinton wanted two debates of 90 minutes each (thought to favor his age and talkative nature), whereas Dole pushed for three one-hour debates. Mostly, Dole wanted to exclude Ross Perot, fearing he would compete for votes needed to defeat Clinton. So Clinton did not insist on including Perot, and he got his debate format.

The two debates were held ten days apart in early October, between which there was a 90-minute vice-presidential debate between Al Gore and Jack Kemp. All major polls showed that the Democratic side "won" each debate. Most notably, neither the debates nor the campaign itself had much impact on voters' preferences, which favored Clinton throughout. After all, he was an incumbent president with a secure economy at a time of peace.[87] Such presidents usually get reelected.[88]

CAMPAIGNS, ELECTIONS, AND PARTIES

Election campaigns today tend to be highly personalized, candidate centered, and conducted outside the control of party organizations. The increased use of electronic media, especially television, has encouraged candidates to personalize their campaign messages; at the same time, the decline of party identification has decreased the power of party-related appeals. Although the party affiliations of the candidates and the party identifications of the voters jointly explain a good deal of electoral behavior, party organizations are not central to elections in America, and this has implications for democratic government.

Parties and the Majoritarian Model

According to the majoritarian model of democracy, parties link people with their government by making government responsive to public opinion. Chapter 8 outlined the model of responsible party government in a majoritarian democracy. This model holds that parties should present clear and coherent programs to voters, that voters should choose candidates according to the party programs, that the winning party should carry out its programs once in office, and that voters should hold the governing party responsible at the next election for executing its program. As noted in Chapter 8, the Republican and Democratic parties do follow the model in that they formulate different platforms and tend to pursue their announced policies when in office. The weak links in this model of responsible party government are those that connect candidates to voters through campaigns and elections.

You have not read much about the role of the party platform in nominating candidates, in conducting campaigns, or in explaining voters' choices. In nominating presidential candidates, basic party principles (as captured in the party platform) do interact with the presidential primary process, and the candidate who wins enough convention delegates through the primaries will surely be comfortable with any platform that her or his delegates adopt. But House and Senate nominations are rarely fought over the party platform. And usually, thoughts about party platforms are virtually absent from campaigning and from voters' minds when they cast their ballots.

The Republicans' "Contract with America" was an exception to the rule that party platforms do not matter in elections and in governing. On September 27, 1994, more than three hundred Republican candidates for the House of Representatives gathered in front of the Capitol to unveil the Contract, which consisted of ten major proposals that they promised to bring to a vote if the voters elected them to power in the November elections. Given that the Republicans had not controlled the House for forty years, it seemed like an act of bravado.

At first, House Republicans got little publicity for their audacity. By October 7, less than a quarter of the respondents in a national survey had heard of the Contract with America.[89] Yet the Contract with America became a significant factor in the 1994 election campaign and an even larger part of the Republicans' legislative agenda in the 104th Congress, for they not only won control of the House but also control of the Senate in what was called the "Republican Revolution."

The Republicans took the Contract seriously when Congress began in January. Speaker Newt Gingrich stated the party's "absolute obligation" to deliver on its promises.[90] Indeed it did deliver, bringing all ten proposals to a vote in the House within one hundred days. By then, about half the public had heard of the Contract, and most of those looked at it favorably.[91] As detailed in Chapter 11 (especially Table 11.1), several points in the Contract even became law. In early 1995, it appeared that the Republicans were following the script of responsible party government, and—accordingly—that they would run on the Contract with America in the 1996 election.

But later in the 104th Congress, some Republicans (especially in the Senate) failed to follow parts of the script, as the public turned against some of their proposals. Before the year ended, Gingrich was viewed negatively in the polls, and Republicans stopped talking about the Contract with America. In fact, when Gingrich addressed the GOP convention in August 1996, he did not mention it once, thus seemingly ending this short experiment with responsible party government.[92]

Parties and the Pluralist Model

The way parties in the United States operate is more in keeping with the pluralist model of democracy than the majoritarian model. Our parties are not the basic mechanism through which citizens control their government; instead, they function as two giant interest groups. The parties' interests lie in electing and reelecting their candidates, in enjoying the benefits of public office. Except in extreme cases, the parties care little about the positions or ideologies favored by their candidates for Congress or state offices. One exception that proves the rule is the Republican party's rejection of David E. Duke, the former Ku Klux Klan leader who in 1990 emerged as the party's nominee for senator in Louisiana. In a highly unusual move, national party leaders disowned Duke, and he lost the election. Otherwise, the parties are grateful for victories by almost any candidate running under their banner. In turn, individual candidates operate as entrepreneurs, running their own campaigns as they like, without party interference.

Some scholars believe that stronger parties would strengthen democratic government, even if they could not meet all the requirements of the responsible party model. Our parties already perform valuable functions in structuring the vote along partisan lines and in proposing alternative government policies, but stronger parties might also be able to play a more important role in coordinating government policies after elections. At present, the decentralized nature of the nominating process and of campaigning for office offers many opportunities for organized groups outside the parties to identify and back candidates who favor their interests. Although this is in keeping with pluralist theory, it is certain to frustrate majority interests on occasion.

SUMMARY

Campaigning has evolved from a party-centered to a candidate-centered process. The successful candidate for public office usually must campaign first to win the party nomination, then to win the general election. A major factor in the decentralization of American parties is their reliance on primary elections to nominate candidates. Democratic and Republican nominations for president are no longer actually decided in the parties' national conventions but are determined in advance through the complex process of selecting delegates pledged to particular candidates. Although candidates cannot win the nomination unless they have broad support within the party, the winners can legitimately say that they captured the nomination through their own efforts and that they owe little to the party organization.

The need to win a majority of votes in the electoral college structures presidential elections. Although a candidate can win a majority of the popular vote but lose in the electoral college, that has not happened in more than one hundred years. In fact, the electoral college typically magnifies the victory margin of the winning candidate. Since World War II, Republicans have usually won the presidency, whereas Democrats have usually controlled Congress; such divided government has interfered with party control of government.

In the general election, candidates usually retain the same staff that helped them win the nomination. The dynamics of campaign financing force candidates to rely mainly on their own resources or—in the case of presidential elections—on public funds. Party organizations now often contribute money to congressional candidates, but the candidates must still raise most of the money themselves. Money is essential in running a modern campaign for major office—for conducting polls and advertising the candidate's name, qualifications, and issue positions through the media. Candidates seek free news coverage whenever possible, but most must rely on paid advertising to get their message across. Ironically, voters also get most of their campaign information from advertisements. The trend in recent years has been toward negative advertising, which seems to work, although it contributes to voters' distaste for politics.

Voting choice can be analyzed in terms of party identification, candidates' attributes, and policy positions. Party identification is still the most important long-term factor in shaping the voting decision, but few candidates rely on it in their campaigns. Most candidates today run personalized campaigns that stress their attributes and policies.

The way that nominations, campaigns, and elections are conducted in America is out of keeping with the ideals of responsible party government that fit the majoritarian model of democracy. In particular, campaigns and elections do not function to link parties strongly to voters, as the model posits. The Republicans' Contract with America, however, fulfilled some features of the responsible party model. American parties are better suited to the pluralist model of democracy, which sees them as major interest groups competing with lesser groups to further their own interests. At least political parties aspire to the noble goal of representing the needs and wants of most people. As we see in the next chapter, interest groups do not even pretend as much.

Key Terms

election campaign
primary election
closed primary
open primary

blanket primary
presidential primary
local caucus
general election

straight ticket
split ticket
first-past-the-post
  election

open election
Federal Election
  Commission (FEC)

Selected Readings

Ansolabehere, Stephen, and Shanto Iyengar. *Going Negative: How Political Advertisements Shrink and Polarize the Electorate*. New York: Free Press, 1995. The subtitle describes the book's thesis, but the book also contends that political advertising also conveys useful information to citizens about politics.

Mayer, William G., ed. *In Pursuit of the White House: How We Choose Our Presidential Nominees*. Chatham, N.J.: Chatham House, 1996. A valuable set of studies, with plenty of data, on the nomination process, including the problems facing third-party candidates.

Patterson, Thomas E. *Out of Order*. New York: Knopf, 1993. This study of mass media's influence in presidential elections from 1960 to 1992 argues that the media, and particularly television, have replaced parties in choosing presidential candidates, with woeful results.

Pomper, Gerald M., F. Christopher Arterton, Ross K. Baker, Walter Dean Burnham, Kathleen A. Frankovic, Marjorie Randon Hershey, and Wilson Carey McWilliams. *The Election of 1992*. Chatham, N.J.: Chatham House, 1993. A group of experts thoroughly analyzes the presidential nomination and election campaigns and the congressional elections.

Simpson, Dick. *Winning Elections: A Handbook of Modern Participatory Politics*. New York: Harper-Collins, 1996. Based on personal experience, this is a manual for practical politics, written by a former Chicago alderman, campaign manager, and college professor.

Thurber, James A., and Candice J. Nelson, eds. *Campaigns and Elections: American Style*. Boulder, Colo.: Westview Press, 1995. Written by academics and campaign practitioners, these studies treat campaign strategy, the use of money and media, opinion polls, and—even—ethics.

West, Darrell M. *Air Wars: Television Advertising in Election Campaigns, 1952–1992*. Washington, D.C.: Congressional Quarterly Press, 1993. A wide-ranging analysis that concludes that, yes, television ads are becoming more negative, but voters still learn much about policy from ads, even negative ads.

World Wide Web Resources

Emily's List. Identifies viable pro-choice Democratic women candidates for key federal and statewide offices and supports their campaigns, financially and organizationally. "Emily" is an acronym for "Early Money is Like Yeast." Why yeast? "It makes the dough rise," so "early money" in a campaign brings later money.
`<www.emilyslist.org/>`

PoliticsNow. A service of ABC News, the *National Journal*, the *Washington Post*, the *Los Angeles Times*, and *Newsweek*, PoliticsNow covers politics as comprehensively as any Web site, and its poll tracking graphs are particularly valuable.
`<www.politicsnow.com>`

Campaigns & Elections Online. This is the site for the magazine *Campaigns & Elections*, which reports on current campaigns and campaign strategy, methods, products, and so on.
`<www.camelect.com/>`

AllPolitics. Time and CNN (both owned by Time Warner) join forces to cover issues, polls, elections, Congress, and virtually everything else in national politics.
`<www.allpolitics.com/>`

Interest Groups

ITS DEATH WAS SLOW AND PAINFUL. The cause: a thousand cuts followed by a hemorrhage. Sadly, when the BTU tax was finally buried, no one would claim to be the parent of the proposal. Just about everyone wanted to take credit for the murder, though.

The BTU proposal—a tax levied on the amount of heat in an energy source, as measured by British thermal units (BTUs)—was part of President Bill Clinton's deficit reduction package introduced at the beginning of his administration in the winter of 1993. Deficit reduction had been an issue in the fall campaign, pushed especially hard by the independent presidential candidate, Ross Perot. Shortly after the election, when Clinton assembled business leaders to talk about repairing the stagnant American economy, they strongly urged him to attack the deficit. And he did. Using a combination of spending cuts and tax increases, the deficit reduction proposal was designed to cut the deficit in half within five years.

A broad-based energy tax does not affect everyone the same way. Industries that use a lot of energy are going to pay more. People who live in some areas of the country are going to be affected more because of their dependence on a particular fuel. Interest groups seized on the inequities they saw in the BTU tax and pressed Congress to exempt them. Congress cooperated.

The bill was first taken up in the House, and the farm lobby was fast off the mark in getting the House to reduce the tax on diesel fuel used by tractors. The steel industry got an exemption for metallurgical coal, used in great quantities in their mills. Aluminum producers and chlorine producers argued that because their manufacturing processes use so much energy, they needed a reduction in their BTU tax, too. The administration agreed, and more exemptions went into the bill. Firms that made products for the export market were upset, because an energy tax would make their goods more expensive on the world market. The administration mollified these lobbies by promising a rebate on the tax for energy-intensive export products, such as chemicals. The oil lobby got an exemption for fuel used by ships and jets. The farm lobby went back for a double scoop, asking that ethanol, a fuel made from corn, be exempted. Here, the House Ways and Means Committee, which is responsible for initially writing tax legislation, finally drew the line and said no. Not to worry—leading senators promised to put an ethanol exemption in when they got the bill.

By the time the legislation passed the House, interest groups had won so many exemptions that it was hard for most people to understand what the

BTU tax still covered. The *New York Times* described the bill as "one of the most exemption-loaded, head-scratchingly complicated, brow-furrowing revenue raisers in history."[1] What was left of the tax came under immediate attack in the Senate. Energy producers, especially oil companies, asked their senators to try to block the tax. With a narrow majority in the Senate, the administration could not afford many defections, because all the Republicans were promising to vote against the bill, no matter what was in it. With the BTU proposal already so badly shredded by all the exemptions, it was hardly worth fighting for. The Clinton administration quickly threw in the towel, promising to introduce another tax instead.[2] The bill that finally passed Congress included a modest increase in the tax on gasoline.

Although Americans tell pollsters that they believe strongly in deficit reduction, the BTU tax was a clear example of pluralism triumphing over majoritarianism. The majority wants the deficit reduced, but no majority favors any particular method of paring it down. People may grudgingly accept the need for new taxes in any deficit reduction package, but they are not going to demand that their representatives and senators vote for a tax when a specific deficit reduction plan comes before Congress. At the same time, interest groups push hard for exemptions, because their members are intensely upset about some aspect of the plan.

In this chapter, we look at the central dynamic of pluralist democracy: the interaction of interest groups and government. In analyzing the process by which interest groups and lobbyists come to speak on behalf of different groups, we focus on a number of questions. How do interest groups form? Who do they represent? What tactics do they use to convince policymakers that their views are best for the nation? Is the interest group system biased in favor of certain types of people? If so, what are the consequences?

INTEREST GROUPS AND THE AMERICAN POLITICAL TRADITION

An **interest group** is an organized body of individuals who share some political goals and try to influence public policy decisions. Among the most prominent interest groups in the United States are the AFL-CIO (representing labor union members), the American Farm Bureau Federation (representing farmers), the Business Roundtable (representing big business), and Common Cause (representing citizens concerned with reforming government). Interest groups are also called **lobbies,** and their representatives are referred to as **lobbyists.**

Interest Groups: Good or Evil?

A recurring debate in American politics concerns the role of interest groups in a democratic society. Are interest groups a threat to the well-being of the political system, or do they contribute to its proper functioning? A favorable early evaluation of interest groups can be found in the writings of Alexis de Tocqueville, a French visitor to the United States in the early nineteenth century. During his travels, Tocqueville marveled at the array of organizations he found, and he later wrote that "Americans of all ages, all conditions, and all dispositions, constantly form associations."[3] Tocqueville was suggesting that the ease with which we form organizations reflects a strong democratic culture.

Yet, other early observers were concerned about the consequences of interest group politics. Writing in the *Federalist* papers, James Madison warned of the dangers of "factions," the major divisions in American society. In *Federalist* No. 10, written in 1787, Madison said it was inevitable that substantial differences would develop between factions. It was only natural for farmers to oppose merchants, tenants to oppose landlords, and so on. Madison further reasoned that each faction would do what it could to prevail over other factions, that each basic interest in society would try to persuade government to adopt policies that favored it at the expense of others. He noted that the fundamental causes of faction were "sown in the nature of man."[4]

But Madison argued against trying to suppress factions. He concluded that factions can be eliminated only by removing our freedoms, because "Liberty is to faction what air is to fire."[5] Instead, Madison suggested that relief from the self-interested advocacy of factions should come only through controlling the effects of that advocacy. The relief would be provided by a democratic republic in which government would mediate between opposing factions. The size and diversity of the nation as well as the structure of government would ensure that even a majority faction could never come to suppress the rights of others.[6]

How we judge interest groups—as "good" or "evil"—may depend on how strongly we are committed to freedom or equality (see Chapter 1). People dislike interest groups in general because they do not offer equal representation to all—some sectors of society are better represented than others. A survey of the American public showed that almost two-thirds of those polled regarded lobbying as a threat to American democracy.[7] Yet, as we'll demonstrate later, in recent years interest groups have enjoyed unparalleled growth; many new groups have formed, and old ones have expanded. Apparently we distrust interest groups as a whole, but we like those that represent our views. Stated more bluntly, we hate lobbies—except those that speak on our behalf.

The Roles of Interest Groups

The "evil" side of interest group politics is all too apparent. Each group pushes its own selfish interests, which, despite the group's claims to the contrary, are not always in the best interest of other Americans. The "good" side of interest group advocacy may not be so clear. How do the actions of interest groups benefit our political system?[8]

Representation. Interest groups represent people before their government. Just as a member of Congress represents a particular constituency, so does a lobbyist. A lobbyist for the National Association of Broadcasters, for example, speaks for the interests of radio and television broadcasters when Congress or a government agency is considering a relevant policy decision.

Whatever the political interest—the cement industry, social security, endangered species—it helps to have an active lobby operating in

● politics in a changing america

10.1   A Political Voice for Christians

New political movements organized in recent years represent diverse interests and constituencies. What their members have in common, however, is a feeling of being marginalized by our political system. Members share a belief that unless they are highly mobilized and aggressive in pursuing their political objectives, policymakers will ignore their concerns. This is certainly the attitude of fundamentalists—Christians whose religious beliefs are based on a literal interpretation of the Bible.

Fundamentalist Christians believe that modern society has turned away from basic moral principles, leading to serious social problems. In their eyes, liberal and moderate politicians have mistakenly tried to solve these problems with expensive, wasteful, and counterproductive social programs. Christian fundamentalists feel that what is needed instead is a return to strong family values.

Many groups claim to represent fundamentalists in the political arena, but the Christian Coalition plays a central leadership role. Based in Virginia, this conservative group is closely allied with the Reverend Pat Robertson. Robertson, who ran unsuccessfully for the Republican presidential nomination

in 1988, is probably best known for his TV show, "The 700 Club," which is shown around the country on the Christian Broadcasting Network. The Christian Coalition has roughly 1.6 million members and an annual budget in excess of $25 million.

Over the years the issues that have most animated the Christian Coalition include abortion, homosexuality, prayer in school, and the decline of the nuclear family. In the past few years, however, Christian Coalition strategist Ralph Reed has led the group in a more secular direction. After the Republicans captured the Congress in the 1994 elections, Reed was in an excellent position to bargain with the House and Senate leadership over the GOP's legislative priorities. Christian Coalition volunteers had fueled many of the newly elected Republicans' campaigns, including distributing 33 million voter guides at churches on the Sunday prior to the election.

Despite the GOP's debt to the Christian Coalition, Reed opted to make the group's highest legislative priority the passage of the House Republicans' "Contract with America." The Christian Coalition spent $1 million on direct mail, ads, and phone calls on behalf of the Contract with America, an ex-

Washington. Members of Congress represent a multitude of interests, some of them conflicting, from their own districts and states. Government administrators, too, are pulled in different directions and have their own policy preferences. Interest groups articulate their members' concerns, presenting them directly and forcefully in the political process (see Politics in a Changing America 10.1).

Participation.   Interest groups are also vehicles for political participation. They provide a means by which like-minded citizens can pool their resources and channel their energies into collective political action. People band together because they know it is much easier to get government to listen to a group than to an individual. One farmer fighting against a new pesticide proposal in Congress probably will not get very far, but thousands of farmers united in an organization stand a much better chance of getting policymakers to consider their needs.

traordinary contribution by any standards. Reed said of all the Contract proposals, the Christian Coalition was most interested in enactment of the $500-per-child tax credit. Although the tax credit has no obvious connection to Christian theology, the Christian Coalition's leadership views it as a critical step in supporting the American family. Reed's strategy seemed oriented toward making the organization appear more mainstream and having the Republicans in Congress regard it as a team player. Still, one wonders if Reed sold the Christian Coalition a bit short. After the House disposed of all the items of the Contract with America, Reed unveiled the Christian Coalition's "Contract with the American Family." This ten-point program was a one-day story; this second contract quickly sank from sight. All in all, the Christian Coalition didn't get much legislative return on its campaign investment.

Many liberals are antagonistic to the Christian Coalition and other such groups, not simply because they hold competing political views but also because they believe that the Christian right is trying to impose its particular brand of religion on the rest of the country. Yet, in America political activism can also be found in black churches, synagogues, mainline Protestant congregations, and Catholic parishes. Nevertheless, it is the Christian conservatives that are the best organized of all the religious sects in the United States. Also, churches embracing the beliefs of the Christian right are the most rapidly growing denominations in the country. Pentecostals, an evangelical denomination whose followers are generally sympathetic to Christian conservatism, grew in membership from about 1.9 million in 1960 to 9.9 million in 1990, an increase of 423 percent.

What is especially impressive about the Christian Coalition and other groups associated with the religious right is their success in involving rank-and-file citizens in politics and government. Former Senator Nancy Kassebaum of Kansas says of the religious right, "It's a voice that in many ways comes from people who feel that they've never been part of the process." As many Christians who dislike the religious right point out, the Christian Coalition does not speak for all Christians. But for those Christians it does represent, the Christian Coalition is a powerful and passionate advocate.

In CROSSTABS, the variables "AFL-CIO" and "Chamber of Commerce" are ratings of all members of Congress by these two opposing interest groups. How does the Congress score on their scales?

Education. As part of their efforts to lobby government and to increase their membership, interest groups help educate their members, the public at large, and government officials. After the Republican-controlled Congress proposed significant cutbacks in research money for universities in 1995, the schools and their Washington lobbies swung into action. When Charles Vest, president of the Massachusetts Institute of Technology (MIT), went to Washington to lobby on behalf of research universities, he repeatedly told members of Congress about a study done by the Bank of Boston that demonstrated that three hundred thousand people in Massachusetts were employed by companies utilizing technology and other resources developed by MIT researchers. The point was clear: cut research funding, and you will damage your local economy's chance to grow.[9] To gain the attention of the policymakers they are trying to educate, interest groups need to provide them with information that is not easily obtained from other sources.[10]

figure

10.1   ● Pay Attention!

Women's interest groups have played a crucial role in gaining the public's attention on issues that were once ignored. In comparison with the executive branch and Congress, the women's movement initiates many more events that get coverage by the New York Times *(used here as a barometer of national press coverage). The news stories measured in this figure include such "events" as demonstrations, action on legislation in Congress, and lawsuits.*

Source: Anne N. Costain, *Inviting Women's Rebellion.* Baltimore/ London: The Johns Hopkins University Press, 1992, p. 101. Reprinted with permission.

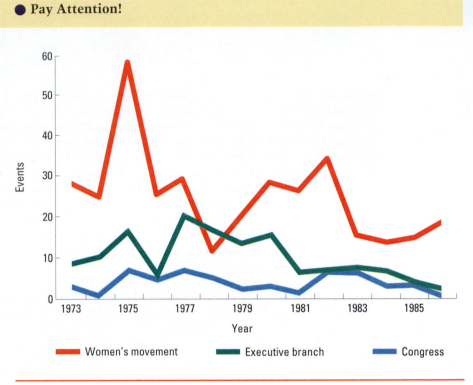

Agenda Building.   In a related role, interest groups bring new issues into the political limelight through a process called **agenda building.** American society has many problem areas, but public officials are not addressing all of them. Through their advocacy, interest groups make the government aware of problems and then try to see to it that something is done to solve them. Women's groups have played a critical role in gaining attention for problems—such as unequal pay for women doing similar jobs as men— that were being systematically ignored. As Figure 10.1 shows, the women's movement (especially women's interest groups) generated the most news coverage of issues of concern to women.[11]

Program Monitoring.   Finally, interest groups engage in **program monitoring.** Lobbies follow government programs that are important to their constituents, keeping abreast of developments in Washington and in the communities where the policies are implemented. When a program is not operating as it should, concerned interest groups push administrators to change them in ways that promote the group's goals. They draw attention to agency officials' transgressions and even file suit to stop actions they consider unlawful. When the United Auto Workers felt that the Occupational Safety and Health Administration (OSHA) was not doing enough to protect workers when they cleaned dangerous machinery, the group took the agency to court. The union documented some gruesome deaths, but the court found no violations of OSHA program guidelines.

Interest groups do, then, play some positive roles in their pursuit of self-interest. But we should not assume that the positive side of interest groups neatly balances the negative. Questions remain about the overall influence of interest groups on public policymaking. Most important, are the effects of interest group advocacy being controlled, as Madison believed they should be?

HOW INTEREST GROUPS FORM

Do some people form interest groups more easily than others? Are some factions represented while others are not? Pluralists assume that when a political issue arises, interest groups with relevant policy concerns begin to lobby. Policy conflicts are ultimately resolved through bargaining and negotiation between the involved organizations and the government. Unlike Madison, who dwelled on the potential for harm by factions, pluralists believe interest groups are a good thing, that they further democracy by broadening representation within the system.

An important part of pluralism is the belief that new interest groups form as a matter of course when the need arises. David Truman outlines this idea in his classic work, *The Governmental Process.*[12] He says that when individuals are threatened by change, they band together in an interest group. For example, if government threatens to regulate a particular industry, the firms that compose that industry will start a trade association to protect their financial well-being. Truman sees a direct cause-and-effect relationship in all of this: existing groups stand in equilibrium until some type of disturbance (such as falling wages or declining farm prices) forces new groups to form.

Truman's thinking on the way interest groups form is like the "invisible hand" notion of laissez-faire economics: self-correcting market forces will remedy imbalances in the marketplace. But in politics, no invisible hand, no force, automatically causes interest groups to develop. Truman's disturbance theory paints an idealized portrait of interest group politics in America. In real life, people do not automatically organize when they are adversely affected by some disturbance. A good example of "nonorganization" can be found in Herbert Gans's book *The Urban Villagers.*[13] Gans, a sociologist, moved into the West End, a low-income neighborhood in Boston, during the late 1950s. The neighborhood had been targeted for urban redevelopment; the city was planning to replace old buildings with modern ones. This meant that the people living there—primarily poor Italian Americans who very much liked their neighborhood—would have to move.

Being evicted is a highly traumatic experience, so the situation in the West End certainly qualified as a bona fide disturbance according to Truman's scheme of interest group formation. Yet, the people of the West End barely put up a fight to save their neighborhood. They started an organization, but it attracted little support. Residents remained unorganized; soon they were moved, and buildings were demolished.

Disturbance theory clearly fails to explain what happened (or didn't happen) in Boston's West End. An adverse condition or change does not automatically mean that an interest group will form. What, then, is the missing ingredient? Political scientist Robert Salisbury says that the quality of interest group leadership may be the crucial factor.[14]

●●●●●●●●●●●●
There Goes the Neighborhood

When the city of Boston tar-geted its West End for urban renewal, residents did not organize to fight the decision. Wrecking balls soon demol-ished the neighborhood, clear-ing the way for various redevelopment projects, in-cluding high-rise housing.

Interest Group Entrepreneurs

Salisbury likens the role of an interest group leader to that of an entrepre-neur in the business world. An entrepreneur is someone who starts new enterprises, usually at considerable personal financial risk. Salisbury says that an **interest group entrepreneur,** or organizer, succeeds or fails for many of the same reasons a business entrepreneur succeeds or fails. The interest group entrepreneur must have something attractive to "market" in order to convince people to join.[15] Potential members must be per-suaded that the benefits of joining outweigh the costs. Someone starting a new union, for example, must convince workers that the union can win them wages high enough to offset their membership dues. The organizer of an ideological group must convince potential members that the group can effectively lobby the government to achieve their particular goals. (In democracies with different kinds of electoral systems, advocacy organiza-tions that are first formed as interest groups sometimes evolve into politi-cal parties. See Compared with What? 10.1.)

The development of the United Farm Workers Union shows the impor-tance of leadership in the formation of an interest group. The union is made up of men and women who pick crops in California and other parts of the country. The work is backbreaking, performed in the hot growing season. The pickers are predominantly poor, uneducated Mexican Americans.

Their chronically low wages and deplorable living conditions made the farm workers prime candidates for organization into a labor union. And throughout the twentieth century, various unions tried to organize the pickers. Yet, for many reasons, including distrust of union organizers, in-timidation by employers, and lack of money to pay union dues, all failed. Then, in 1962, the late Cesar Chavez, a poor Mexican American, began to crisscross the central valley of California, talking to workers and planting the idea of a union. Chavez had been a farm worker himself (he first

compared with what?

10.1   Interest Parties in Israeli Politics

In the United States there is a clear distinction between political parties and interest groups: parties run candidates for office; interest groups stand outside government and try to influence those in office. In Israel, however, the boundaries are less clear.

Over the years, a number of Israeli lobbies have decided that the major parties have ignored their interests in the Knesset (the Israeli parliament) and that they need direct representation in the legislative process. These "interest parties" most commonly represent different ethnic groups in Israeli society. (Israeli Jews have immigrated from all over the world, and these ethnic bonds remain part of their identity.) The Black Panthers, for example, are an interest group started in 1971 by young Moroccan immigrants to Israel to protest discrimination against darker-skinned Jews. When the government appeared to be unresponsive to their demands, the Black Panthers ran some candidates for the Knesset on a platform calling for equitable educational and housing opportunities. Other lobbies representing women, the disabled, and senior citizens have also run candidates for the Knesset. These interest parties typically coalesce with one of the major parties and are sometimes part of the ruling coalition running the country.

The primary reason why interest parties can gain office in Israel but don't exist at all in the United States is that Israel's electoral system, unlike the U.S. system, uses proportional representation. Each party that runs a slate of candidates for the Knesset and receives some measurable support among the electorate wins seats in proportion to the percentage of the popular vote its slate receives nationwide. Thus a party winning 5 percent of the vote in Israel will win roughly 5 percent of the seats in the Knesset. In the United States, where elections are held district by district, with a plurality required to win, a party whose candidates for the House win 5 percent of the nationwide vote would likely win no seats. If the United States had the same kind of proportional representation as Israel, a party winning 5 percent of the House vote nationwide would win 22 seats.

Israel is not the only country where proportional representation encourages interest groups to become political parties as well. In a number of European countries, lobbies trying to protect the environment have formed "Green" parties and have been successful in winning some representation in national legislatures. In Israel, however, it is much easier for an interest party to win representation in the Knesset, because the seats are allocated to any slate that wins a minimum of just 1 percent of the vote nationwide. The threshold for representation in other parliamentary democracies tends to be significantly higher. It is no wonder that when election time rolls around in Israel, twenty-five to thirty parties compete for votes. When the ballots are all counted, it's usually the case that four or five interest parties have won seats in the Knesset.

Source: Information on Israeli interest parties can be found in Yael Yishai, *Land of Paradoxes* (Albany: State University Press of New York, 1991), pp. 121–127.

worked as a picker at the age of ten), and he was well aware of the difficulties that lay ahead for his newly organized union.

After a strike against grape growers failed in 1965, Chavez changed his tactic of trying to build a stronger union merely by recruiting a larger membership. Copying the civil rights movement, Chavez and his followers marched 250 miles to the state capitol in Sacramento to demand help

● ● ● ● ● ● ● ● ● ● ●
Lobbying to the Extreme

Some interest groups feel that policymakers are generally opposed or indifferent to their cause and that there is little to be gained from conventional lobbying. Instead, they use unusual and even extreme tactics to draw media attention to their side of an issue. On the left, the Reverend Rob Schenk of Operation Rescue holds up an aborted fetus outside a Buffalo, New York, abortion clinic. Members of Operation Rescue believe that abortion is murder and that they must do whatever they can to shut down abortion clinics. On the right is a casket carrying the body of AIDS victim Tim Bailey. Bailey told friends in Act Up, an AIDS protest group, that he wanted a political funeral in Washington, D.C. Activists from the organization tried to take the coffin out of this van to carry it into the Capitol, but Capitol police kept shoving it back in. Finally, the protesters gave up and took Bailey's body back home with them to New York.

from the governor. The march and other nonviolent tactics began to draw sympathy from people who had no direct involvement in farming. Seeing the movement as a way to help poor members of the church, the Catholic clergy was a major source of support. This support, in turn, gave the charismatic Chavez greater credibility, and his followers cast him in the role of spiritual as well as political leader. At one point, he fasted for twenty-five days to show his commitment to nonviolence. Democratic senator Robert Kennedy of New York, one of the most popular politicians of the day, joined Chavez when he broke his fast at a mass conducted on the back of a flatbed truck in Delano, California.[16]

Chavez subsequently called for a boycott, and a small but significant number of Americans stopped buying grapes. The growers, who had bitterly fought the union, were finally hurt economically. Under this and other economic pressures, they eventually agreed to recognize and bargain with the United Farm Workers. The union then helped its members with the wage and benefit agreements it was able to negotiate.

Who Is Being Organized?

Cesar Chavez is a good example of the importance of leadership in the formation of a new interest group. Despite many years of adverse conditions, efforts to organize the farm workers had failed. The dynamic leadership of Cesar Chavez is what seems to have made the difference.

But another important element is at work in the formation of interest groups. The residents of Boston's West End and the farm workers in California were poor, uneducated or undereducated, and politically inexperienced—factors that made it extremely difficult to organize them into interest groups. If they had been well-to-do, educated, and politically experienced, they probably would have banded together immediately. People who have money, are educated, and know how the system operates are more confident that their actions can make a difference. Together, these attributes give people more incentive to devote their time and ample resources to organizing and supporting interest groups (see Figure 10.2).

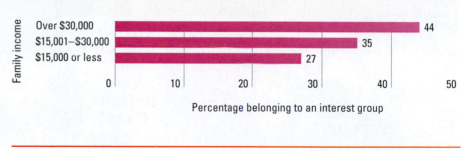

Source: Based on Jeffrey M. Berry, Kent E. Portney, and Ken Thomson, *The Rebirth of Urban Democracy* (Washington, D.C.: Brookings Institution, 1993). Used with permission.

figure 10.2 ● Social Class and Interest Group Membership

Membership in interest groups is clearly linked to social class. The higher their total family income, the more likely it is that individuals will belong to at least one political interest group. The data here come from a survey of citizens in five American cities (Birmingham, Alabama; Dayton, Ohio; Portland, Oregon; St. Paul, Minnesota; and San Antonio, Texas).

Every existing interest group has its own history, but the three variables just discussed can help explain why groups may or may not become fully organized. First, an adverse change or disturbance can contribute to people's awareness that they need political representation. However, this alone does not ensure that an organization will form, and organizations have formed in the absence of a disturbance. Second, the quality of leadership is critical in the organization of interest groups. Some interest group entrepreneurs are more skilled than others at convincing people to join their organizations. Finally, the higher the socioeconomic level of potential members, the more likely they are to know the value of interest groups and to participate in politics by joining them.

Because wealthy and better-educated Americans are more likely to form and join lobbies, they seem to have an important advantage in the political process. Nevertheless, as the United Farm Workers' case shows, poor and uneducated people are also capable of forming interest groups. The question that remains, then, is not *whether* various opposing interests are represented but *how well* they are represented. Or, in terms of Madison's premise in *Federalist* No. 10, are the effects of faction—in this case, the advantages of the wealthy and well educated—being controlled? Before we can answer this question about how interest groups affect the level of political equality in our society, we need to turn our attention to the resources available to interest groups.

INTEREST GROUP RESOURCES

The strengths, capabilities, and influence of an interest group depend in large part on its resources. A group's most significant resources are its members, lobbyists, and money, including funds that can be contributed to political candidates. The sheer quantity of a group's resources is important, and so is the wisdom with which its resources are used.

Members

One of the most valuable resources an interest group can have is a large, politically active membership. If a lobbyist is trying to convince a legislator to support a particular bill, having a large group of members who live in the legislator's home district or state is tremendously helpful. A legislator who has not already taken a firm position on a bill might be swayed by

Diagnosis: GOP Plan Terminal

After defeating the Clinton health care reform bill in the 103d Congress, the Republicans found themselves on the defensive in the 104th. Here, nurses have gathered together at the Capitol to protest a GOP managed care proposal. This rally draws on a favorite tactic of interest groups. Instead of putting their lobbyists out front, the group instead displays rank-and-file members, in this case nurses wearing their uniforms so their identity is unmistakable. Not only does this make for more compelling pictures for the newspaper and television cameras, but rank-and-file constituents come across as more credible and remind legislators that the folks back home are watching the way they vote.

the knowledge that voters back home are kept informed by interest groups of his or her votes on key issues.

Members give an organization not only the political muscle to influence policy but also financial resources. The more money an organization can collect through dues and contributions, the more people it can hire to lobby government officials and monitor the policymaking process. The American Medical Association has considerable resources, because its members—physicians—have high incomes and can pay expensive dues. The organization's wealth helped to make it a major player when President Clinton put comprehensive health care reform at the top of his agenda.

Greater resources also allow an organization to communicate with its members more and to inform them better. And funding helps a group maintain its membership and attract new members.

Maintaining Membership.   To keep the members it already has, an organization must persuade them that it is doing a good job in its advocacy. Most lobbies use a newsletter to keep members apprised of developments in government that relate to issues of concern to them. However, newsletters are more than a means of communicating news to members. Interest groups use them as a public relations tool to try to keep members believing that their lobby is playing a critical role in protecting their interests. Thus, the role the organization is playing in trying to influence government always receives prominent coverage in its newsletters.

Business, professional, and labor associations generally have an easier time holding on to members than do citizen groups, whose basis of organization is a concern for issues not directly related to their members' jobs. In many companies, corporate membership in a trade group constitutes only a minor business expense. Big individual corporations have no memberships as such, but they often open their own lobbying offices in Washington. They have the advantage of being able to use institutional financial resources to support their lobbying; they do not have to rely on voluntary contributions. Labor unions are helped in states that require workers to affiliate with the union that is the bargaining agent with their employer. On the other hand, citizen groups base their appeal on members' ideological sentiments. These groups face a difficult challenge: issues can blow hot and cold, and a particularly hot issue one year may not hold the same interest to citizens the next.

Attracting New Members. All membership groups are constantly looking for new adherents to expand their resources and clout. Groups that rely on ideological appeals have a special problem, because the competition in most policy areas is intense. People concerned about the environment, for example, can join a seemingly infinite number of local, state, and national groups. The National Wildlife Federation, Environmental Action, the Environmental Defense Fund, the Natural Resources Defense Council, Friends of the Earth, the Wilderness Society, the Sierra Club, and the Environmental Policy Center are just some of the national organizations that lobby on environmental issues. Groups try to distinguish themselves from competitors by concentrating on a few key issues and developing a reputation as the most involved and knowledgeable about them.[17] The Sierra Club, one of the oldest environmental groups, has long had a focus on protecting national parks. The names of newer groups, such as Clean Water Action and the National Toxics Campaign, reveal their substantive focus (and marketing strategy). Still, organizations in a crowded policy area must go beyond such differentiation and aggressively market themselves to potential contributors. Indeed, these groups are like businesses—their "profits" (their members and income) depend on their management's wisdom in allocating resources and in choosing which issues to work on.[18]

One common method of attracting new members is *direct mail*—letters sent to a selected audience to promote the organization and appeal for contributions. The key to direct mail is a carefully targeted audience. An organization can purchase a list of people who are likely to be sympathetic to its cause, or it can trade lists with a similar organization. A group trying to fight abortion, for instance, might use the subscription list from the conservative magazine *National Review,* while a pro-choice lobby might use that of the more liberal *New Republic.* The main drawbacks to direct mail are its expense and low rate of return. A response rate of 2 percent of those newly solicited is considered good. Groups usually lose money when prospecting for members from a mailing list they have rented from a direct mail broker, but they hope to recoup the money as the new members contribute again and again over time. Still, they have no assurance of this. To maximize the chances of a good return, care and thought are given to the design and content of letters. Letters often try to play on the reader's emotions, to create the feeling that the reader should be personally involved in the struggle.[19]

The Free-Rider Problem. The need for aggressive marketing by interest groups suggests that getting people who sympathize with a group's goals actually to join and support it with their contributions is difficult.

Economists call this difficulty the **free-rider problem,** but we might call it, more colloquially, the "let-George-do-it problem."[20] Funding for public television stations illustrates the dilemma. Almost all agree that public television, which survives in large part through viewers' contributions, is of great value. But only a fraction of those who watch public television contribute on a regular basis. Why? Because people can watch the programs whether they contribute or not. The free rider has the same access to public television as the contributor.

The same problem crops up for interest groups. When a lobbying group wins benefits, those benefits are not restricted to the members of the organization. For instance, if the American Business Conference wins a tax concession from Congress for capital expenditures, all businesses that fall within the provisions of the law can take advantage of the tax break. Thus, many business executives might not support their firm's joining the American Business Conference, even though they might benefit from the group's efforts; they prefer instead to let others shoulder the financial burden.

The free-rider problem increases the difficulty of attracting paying members, but it certainly does not make the task impossible. Many people realize that if everyone decides to let George do it, the job simply will not get done. Millions of Americans contribute to interest groups because they are concerned about an issue or feel a responsibility to help organizations that work on their behalf. Also, many organizations offer membership benefits that have nothing to do with politics or lobbying. Business trade associations, for example, are a source of information about industry trends and effective management practices; they organize conventions at which members can learn, socialize, and occasionally find new customers or suppliers. An individual firm in the electronics industry may not care that much about the lobbying done by the Electronics Industries Association, but it may have a vital interest in the information about marketing and manufacturing that the organization provides. Successful interest groups are adept at supplying the right mix of benefits to their target constituency.[21]

Lobbyists

Part of the money raised by interest groups is used to pay lobbyists, who represent the organizations before the government. Lobbyists make sure that people in government know what their members want and that their organizations know what the government is doing. For example, when an administrative agency issues new regulations, lobbyists are right there to interpret the content and implications of the regulations for rank-and-file members. The Washington representative of an oil trade association was reading the *Federal Register* (a daily compendium of all new regulations issued by the government) as part of his daily routine when he noticed that the Federal Aviation Administration planned to issue new regulations requiring detailed flight plans by noncommercial aircraft. The policy would make rescue efforts for noncommercial planes easier, but the lobbyist realized that it could compromise the confidentiality surrounding the flights of company planes for aerial exploration for oil and gas. Anyone could obtain the filed flight plans. He notified the member companies, and

The Son Also Rises

It is no surprise that Tommy Boggs has built a career in the political world. His father, Hale Boggs, was a Democratic member of the House of Representatives and served as majority leader. After the senior Boggs died in a plane crash, his wife, Lindy, succeeded him in the House. Tommy Boggs turned away from electoral politics, however, and pursued a career as a lawyer-lobbyist in Washington. Enormously skillful and highly intelligent, Boggs has attracted many corporate clients to Patton, Boggs, and Blow, a law firm known for its lobbying prowess. Although he's done well no matter who has been in office, his family's close identification with the Democrats made Bill Clinton's election especially sweet for Boggs. Shortly before the 1992 election, a Washington-based magazine, the National Journal, *embarrassed Boggs by putting his picture on its cover with the caption "Ready to Cash in on Clinton."*

their lobbying prevented the implementation of the regulations, precluding the possibility of competitors' getting hold of such secret data.[22]

Lobbyists can be full-time employees of their organization or employees of public relations or law firms who are hired on retainer. When hiring a lobbyist, an interest group looks for someone who knows her or his way around Washington. Lobbyists are valued for their experience and their knowledge of how government operates. Often, they are people who have served in the legislative or executive branches, people who have firsthand experience with government. For example, when they left Congress in 1992, former Democratic representatives Beryl Anthony of Arkansas and Dennis Eckart of Ohio joined the law firm of Winston and Strawn to work as lobbyists. Their lucrative list of clients includes the American Hospital Association, the American Insurance Association, and the Walt Disney Company.[23] (When legislators and staffers leave Capitol Hill, there is a one-year "cooling off" period before they can directly lobby their former colleagues. Nothing stops them from directing others in their firms in what to do or who to call, however.)

Anthony and Eckart are far from exceptions. More than half of all lobbyists have some experience in government. The value of experience in the legislative or executive branch includes knowledge of the policymaking process, expertise in particular issues, and contacts with those still in government.[24] Contacts with former colleagues can be invaluable. As one lobbyist said of her former associates on Capitol Hill, "They know you, and they return your phone calls."[25] Lobbying is a lucrative profession, and

figure

10.3

● **A City of Lawyers**

In Washington, the practice of law is largely lobbying work. Law firms are hired by corporations and other clients to interpret what is going on and to press for policies that will work to their clients' advantage. Although the demand for lawyers has slowed across the country, Washington seems to have a never-ending need for more and more attorneys to fight on behalf of more and more interest groups.

Source: Jeffrey M. Berry, *The Interest Group Society* (New York: Longman, 1997), p. 25.

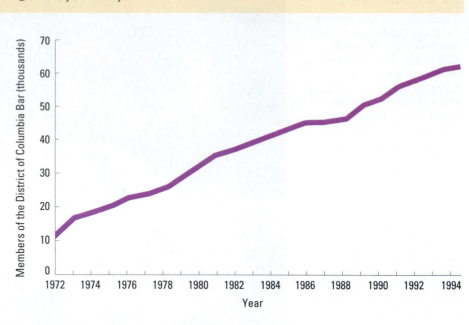

good people with experience can easily make over $100,000 a year. The very best make considerably more.

Many lobbyists have law degrees and find their legal backgrounds useful in bargaining and negotiating over laws and regulations. Because of their location, many Washington law firms are drawn into lobbying. As Figure 10.3 suggests, expanding interest group advocacy has created a boom for Washington law firms. Corporations without their own Washington office rely heavily on law firms to lobby for them before the national government. For example, NEC, the big Japanese electronics firm, has a vital interest in trade issues. It has the Washington office of Manatt, Phelps & Phillips on retainer to represent it on trade matters.

Some lobbyists and firms are known for their connections to one of the two major political parties. Manatt, Phelps & Phillips benefited when Bill Clinton was elected president, because one of its partners, Charles Manatt, is a former national chairman of the Democratic party. Another partner, Mickey Kantor, was a high-ranking official in the Clinton campaign and resigned from the firm when the new president appointed him to the post of special trade representative.[26] Often, a firm that becomes identified closely with one party will go out of its way to hire a prominent member of the other party so that it will be seen as having clout regardless of who is in the White House.

The most common image of a lobbyist is that of an arm twister, someone who spends most of his or her time trying to convince a legislator or administrator to back a certain policy. The stereotype of lobbyists also portrays them as people of dubious ethics, because they trade on their connections and may hand out campaign donations to candidates for office. The campaign donations that interest groups make to congressional candidates justifiably create an unsavory image for lobbyists. Yet, lobbying is

● ● ● ● ● ● ● ● ● ● ● ●

Ford Salesman

Ford Motor Company Vice President Elliott Hall is the chief lobbyist for the car company and heads a Washington staff of twenty-six, including fourteen lobbyists and engineers. This staff monitors developments in Congress, administrative agencies, and the White House. By training, Hall is a lawyer who worked many years at a Detroit law firm before being recruited by Ford. Among recent efforts, Hall successfully led Ford and other car makers in defeating a proposal backed by environmental groups to increase minimum fuel economy standards for new cars. Using the Washington office's computerized database, he mobilized thousands of Ford managers and dealers who, in turn, told members of Congress that the bill would hurt the company and lead to layoffs.

a much maligned profession. The lobbyist's primary job is not to trade on favors or campaign contributions but to pass information on to policymakers. Lobbyists provide government officials and their staffs with a constant flow of data that support their organizations' policy goals. Lobbyists also try to build a compelling case for their goals, showing that the "facts" dictate that a particular change be made or avoided. What lobbyists are really trying to do, of course, is to convince policymakers that their data deserve more attention and are more accurate than those presented by other lobbyists.

Political Action Committees

Follow the PAC money.
`<www.fec.gov>`

One of the organizational resources that can make a lobbyist's job easier is a **political action committee (PAC).** PACs pool campaign contributions from group members and donate the money to candidates for political office. Under federal law, a PAC can give as much as $5,000 to a candidate for Congress for each separate election. A change in campaign finance law in 1974 led to a rapid increase in the number of PACs, and nearly four thousand PACs were active in the 1994 election.[27] The greatest growth came from corporations, most of which had been prohibited from operating PACs. There was also rapid growth in the number of nonconnected PACs, largely ideological groups that have no parent lobbying organization and are formed solely for the purpose of raising and channeling campaign funds. (Thus, a PAC can be the campaign-wing affiliate of an existing interest group or a wholly independent, unaffiliated group.) Most PACs are rather small, and most give less than $50,000 in total contributions during a two-year election cycle. Some, however, are enormous. The largest contributor in the 1994 election was the United Parcel Service PAC, which gave $2.6 million to congressional candidates. Overall, PACs contributed $189 million to candidates during 1993–1994, and corporate PACs were the biggest contributors (see Figure 10.4).[28]

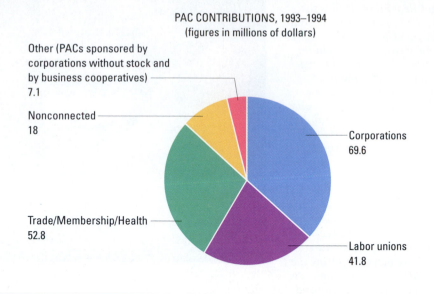

figure

10.4   ● **PACs Americana**

Most PAC money comes from corporations, business trade groups, and professional associations. Labor unions contribute significantly as well. A much smaller proportion of all PAC contributions comes from citizen PACs, who form the bulk of the "nonconnected" category. Americans at the lower end of the economic spectrum are left out entirely. As Bob Dole once put it, "There aren't any Poor PACs or Food Stamp PACs or Nutrition PACs or Medicare PACs."

Source: "PAC Activity in 1994 Elections Remains at 1992 Levels," *Federal Election Commission*, March 31, 1995, p. 3.

PAC CONTRIBUTIONS, 1993–1994
(figures in millions of dollars)

Other (PACs sponsored by corporations without stock and by business cooperatives)
7.1

Nonconnected
18

Corporations
69.6

Trade/Membership/Health
52.8

Labor unions
41.8

Why do interest groups form PACs? The chief executive officer of one manufacturing company said his corporation had a PAC because "the PAC gives you access. It makes you a player."[29] Lobbyists believe that campaign contributions help significantly when they are trying to gain an audience with a member of Congress. Members of Congress and their staffers generally are eager to meet with representatives of their constituencies, but their time is limited. However, a member of Congress or staffer would find it difficult to turn down a lobbyist's request for a meeting if the PAC of the lobbyist's organization had made a significant campaign contribution in the last election.

Typically, PACs, like most other interest groups, are highly pragmatic organizations; pushing a particular political philosophy takes second place to achieving immediate policy goals. Although many corporate executives strongly believe in a free-market economy, for example, their company PACs tend to hold congressional candidates to a much more practical standard. As a group, corporate PACs gave 76.4 percent of their contributions to incumbent members of Congress—many of them liberal and moderate Democrats—during the 1993–1994 election cycle.[30] After the Republicans' capture of Congress in 1994, corporations and other business PACs could target more of their money to conservative Republicans. This in turn helped many vulnerable Republican freshmen in the House fight off labor-supported Democrats in 1996, and the GOP maintained control of both houses of Congress.

The role of PACs in financing congressional campaigns has become the most controversial aspect of interest group politics. Critics charge that members of Congress cannot help but be influenced by the PAC contributions they receive. For example, during the 1994 elections PACs representing accountants made $3.6 million in contributions to members of Congress, an increase of 71 percent over 1992. The accountants wanted legislation limiting their liability in securities-fraud lawsuits. After the election, the Republican-controlled Congress responded with legislation designed to do just that. Many believe that the accountants purchased the legislation through their contributions. On the other hand, Representative Jack Fields (R.-Texas), a key committee chair who shepherded the legislation through the House and received $28,500 in contributions from accounting PACs, emphatically rejects this view: "I haven't changed my philosophy in the 15 years I've been in Congress. My philosophy has always been free enterprise. . . . Those who want to contribute to me are free to do so."[31]

Political scientists have not been able to document any consistent link between campaign donations and the way members of Congress vote on the floor of the House and Senate.[32] The case of Representative Fields points out the problem: do PAC contributions influence votes in Congress, or are they really just rewards for legislators who would vote for the PACs' interests anyway, because of their long-standing ideology? How do we determine the answer to this question? Simply looking for the influence of PACs in the voting patterns of members of Congress may be shortsighted; influence can also be felt before bills get to the floor of the full House or Senate for a vote. Some recent, sophisticated research shows that PAC donations do seem to influence what goes on in congressional committees. As will be discussed in Chapter 11, committees are where the bulk of the work on legislation takes place. Lobbies with PACs have an advantage in the committee process and appear to gain influence because of the additional access they receive.[33]

Whatever the research shows, it is clear that the American public is suspicious of PACs and regards them as a problem in our political system. PACs are seen as a means of securing privileges for those sectors of society with the resources to purchase additional access to Congress. But in a democracy, influence should not be a function of money; some citizens have little to give, yet their interests need to be protected. From this perspective, the issue is political equality—the freedom to give should not outweigh the need for equal political access for all sectors of society.

Strong arguments can also be made for retaining PACs. They offer a means for people to participate in the political system. They allow small givers to pool their resources and fight the feeling that one person cannot make a difference. Finally, PAC defenders also point out that prohibiting PACs would amount to a restriction on the freedom of political expression. (We take up the question of PACs and potential reforms at the end of this chapter.)

LOBBYING TACTICS

When an interest group decides to try to influence the government on an issue, its staff and officers must develop a strategy, which may include a number of tactics aimed at various officials or offices. Together, these tactics should use the group's resources as effectively as possible.

Keep in mind that lobbying extends beyond the legislative branch. Groups can seek help from the courts and administrative agencies as well as from Congress. Moreover, interest groups may have to shift their focus from one branch of government to another. After a bill becomes a law, for

Friendly Skies, Friendly Senator

Lobbyists rely heavily on key representatives and senators who are willing to work hard on issues of particular concern to them. Here two lobbyists representing commercial aviation interests—Nancy Van Duyne of Continental Airlines and Peter Pike of the Air Transport Association of America—meet with Senator Slade Gorton (R.-Wash.). Gorton wants to do what he can to promote commercial aviation, because Boeing is located in his state. When the airlines are doing well, Boeing does well.

example, a group that lobbied for the legislation will probably try to influence the administrative agency responsible for implementing the new law. Some policy decisions are left unresolved by legislation and are settled through regulations. Lobbies want to make sure regulatory decisions are as close to their group's preferences as possible.

We discuss three types of lobbying tactics here: those aimed at policymakers and implemented by interest group representatives (direct lobbying), those that involve group members (grassroots lobbying), and those directed at the public (information campaigns). We also examine the use of new high-tech lobbying tactics as well as cooperative efforts of interest groups to influence government through coalitions.

Direct Lobbying

Direct lobbying relies on personal contact with policymakers. One survey of Washington lobbyists showed that 98 percent use direct contact with government officials to express their group's views.[34] This interaction occurs when a lobbyist meets with a member of Congress, an agency official, or a staff member. In their meetings, lobbyists usually convey their arguments by providing data about a specific issue. If a lobbyist from, for example, a chamber of commerce meets with a member of Congress about a bill the chamber backs, the lobbyist does not say (or even suggest), "Vote for this bill, or our people in the district will vote against you in the next election." Instead, the lobbyist might say, "If this bill is passed, we're going to see hundreds of new jobs created back home." The representative has no trouble at all figuring out that a vote for the bill can help in the next election.

Personal lobbying is a day-in, day-out process. It is not enough simply to meet with policymakers just before a vote or a regulatory decision. Lobbyists must maintain contact with congressional and agency staffers, constantly providing them with pertinent data. One lobbyist described his strategy in personal meetings with policymakers as rather simple and straightforward: "Providing information is the most effective tool. People begin to rely on you." Another lobbyist gave this advice: "You'd better bring good ideas and some facts, and they'd better be accurate."[35]

A tactic related to direct lobbying is testifying at committee hearings when a bill is before Congress. This tactic allows the interest group to put its views on record and to make them widely known when the hearing testimony is published. Although testifying is one of the most visible parts of lobbying, it is generally considered window dressing. Most lobbyists believe that such testimony usually does little by itself to persuade members of Congress.

Another direct but somewhat different approach is legal advocacy. Using this tactic, a group tries to achieve its policy goals through litigation. Claiming some violation of law, a group will file a lawsuit and ask that a judge make a ruling that will benefit the organization. After the Food and Drug Administration (FDA) proposed regulations aimed at reducing smoking by minors, cigarette manufacturers counterattacked with a lawsuit filed in federal court. The tobacco industry believed the FDA had exceeded its authority, and it was concerned that if the regulations went unchallenged, the agency would take further steps to restrict smoking.[36]

Grassroots Lobbying

Grassroots lobbying involves an interest group's rank-and-file members and may include people outside the organization who sympathize with its goals. Grassroots tactics, such as letter-writing campaigns and protests, are often used in conjunction with direct lobbying by Washington representatives. Letters, telegrams, e-mail, faxes, and telephone calls from a group's members to their representatives in Congress or to agency administrators add to a lobbyist's credibility in talks with these officials. Policymakers are more concerned about what a lobbyist says when they know that constituents are really watching their decisions.

Group members—especially influential members (corporation presidents, local civic leaders)—occasionally go to Washington to lobby. But the most common grassroots tactic is letter writing. "Write your member of Congress" is not just a slogan for a civics test. Legislators are highly sensitive to the content of their mail. Interest groups often launch letter-writing campaigns through their regular publications or special alerts. They may even provide sample letters and the names and addresses of specific policymakers.

If people in government seem unresponsive to conventional lobbying tactics, a group might resort to some form of political protest. A protest or demonstration, such as picketing or marching, is designed to attract media attention to an issue. Protesters hope that television and newspaper coverage will help change public opinion and make policymakers more receptive to their group's demands. In one protest near the Capitol, an antiabortion group created a mock "cemetery of the innocents," with 4,400 white crosses stuck in the ground to symbolize the number of abortions performed each day in the United States.[37] The goal was to create a striking visual image that would attract media attention; if reporters

An Image That Angered a Nation

Demonstrations by blacks during the early 1960s played a critical role in pushing Congress to pass civil rights legislation. This photo of vicious police dogs attacking demonstrators in Birmingham, Alabama, is typical of scenes shown on network news broadcasts and in newspapers that helped build public support for civil rights legislation.

covered the protest, people around the country would be exposed to the abortion opponents' belief that an abortion is the death of a living human being.

The main drawback to protesting is that policymaking is a long-term, incremental process, and a demonstration is only short-lived. It is difficult to sustain anger and activism among group supporters—to keep large numbers of people involved in protest after protest. A notable exception was the civil rights demonstrations of the 1960s, which were sustained over a long period. National attention focused not only on the widespread demonstrations but also on the sometimes violent confrontations between protesters and white law enforcement officers. For example, the use of police dogs and high-power fire hoses against blacks marching in Alabama in the early 1960s angered millions of Americans who saw films of the confrontations on television. The protests were a major factor in stirring public opinion, which in turn hastened the passage of the Civil Rights Act of 1964 and the Voting Rights Act of 1965.

Information Campaigns

As the strategy of the civil rights movement shows, interest groups generally feel that public backing adds strength to their lobbying efforts. And because all interest groups believe they are absolutely right in their policy orientation, they believe that they will get that backing if they can only make the public aware of their position and the evidence supporting it. To this end, interest groups launch **information campaigns,** organized efforts to gain public backing by bringing their views to the public's attention. The underlying assumption is that public ignorance and apathy are as

much a problem as the views of competing interest groups. Various means
are used to combat apathy. Some are directed at the larger public; others
are directed at smaller audiences with long-standing interest in an issue.

Public relations is one information-campaign tactic. A public relations
campaign might involve sending speakers to meetings in various parts of
the country, producing pamphlets and handouts, or taking out newspaper
and magazine advertising. During the fight over the Clinton administration's health care reform proposal during 1993 and 1994, the Health
Insurance Association of America (HIAA) launched a television ad campaign designed to turn public opinion against the plan. These ads featured
a fictional couple named Harry and Louise, who in a series of spots talked
conversationally about the plan and pointed out its critical flaws. The ads
were ubiquitous, and many felt they played a major role in defeating the
plan. Yet surveys showed that the $14 million ad campaign had little im-
pact on public opinion.[38] Given the costs of televised advertising and the
difficulty of truly swaying public opinion through them, it's not surprising
that few groups rely on paid TV advertising as their primary weapon in advocacy campaigns.

Sponsoring research is another way interest groups press their cases.
When a group believes that evidence has not been fully developed in a certain area, it may commission research on the subject. When the
Environmental Working Group wanted to try to reduce agriculture-related
pollution, it initiated tests of water quality in twenty-nine cities located
near concentrations of corn farms. The study published by the liberal advocacy group documented the presence of herbicides in all twenty-nine
cities, and levels that exceeded federal safety standards in eighteen of
them. The study received a modest amount of press coverage.[39]

High-Tech Lobbying

In recent years, Washington lobbies have added many high-tech tactics to
their arsenals. Using such resources as direct mail, e-mail, faxes, polling,
and the World Wide Web, lobbies have tried to find ways to expand their
reach and increase their impact. The most conspicuous effect of high-tech
lobbying is that it speeds up the political process. Using electronic communication, groups can quickly mobilize their constituents, who will in
turn quickly contact policymakers about pending decisions. When the
Clinton administration proposed that computer manufacturers be required to install a "clipper chip" in all the machines they sell, it set off
alarms in the computer industry and among civil libertarians. (The chip
would facilitate government access to encoded computerized communications, which are scrambled for security reasons.) Worrying that the clipper chip would lead to government spying, Computer Professionals for
Social Responsibility and the Electronic Frontier Foundation used the
Internet to build opposition to the proposal. Before the administration had
a chance to make its case, fifty-five thousand e-mail messages had been
sent to Washington asking that the proposal be dropped. The administration did just that.[40]

Impressive as this case sounds, it is important to recognize that electronic lobbying isn't all that different from old-fashioned lobbying. Before
the computer, interest groups used to telephone their activists and ask

Electronic Frontier
Foundation's Action Alerts.
`<www.eff.org/pub/Alerts/>`

them to write letters to policymakers. That approach may have been a little slower, but it still let those in Washington know what their constituents back home wanted. Moreover, since the use of technology is widespread, it is likely that most sides in a policy dispute will take advantage of it to try to influence the government.

Although high-tech lobbying tactics facilitate direct communication between citizens and policymakers, which is to be applauded, there is a down side as well. Technology is expensive, so the introduction of such tactics favors groups that are wealthy and can best utilize them and citizens who own personal computers or have access to them at work. In short, high-tech tactics work to the advantage of those who are already well represented in the political process.[41]

Coalition Building

A final aspect of lobbying strategy is **coalition building**, in which several organizations band together for the purpose of lobbying. Such joint efforts conserve or make more effective use of the resources of groups with similar views. Most coalitions are informal, ad hoc arrangements that exist only for the purpose of lobbying on a single issue. Coalitions most often form among groups that work in the same policy area and have similar constituencies, such as environmental groups or feminist groups. When an issue arises that several such groups agree on, they are likely to develop a coalition.

Yet, coalitions often extend beyond organizations with similar constituencies and similar outlooks. Environmental groups and business groups are often thought of as dire enemies. But some businesses support the same goals as environmental lobbies, because it is in their self-interest. For example, companies in the business of cleaning up toxic waste sites have worked with environmental groups to strengthen the Superfund program, the government's primary weapon for dealing with dangerous waste dumps.[42] Lobbyists see an advantage in having a diverse coalition. In the words of one health and education lobbyist, "If you have three hundred associations on a list, that's a pretty strong message."[43]

IS THE SYSTEM BIASED?

As we noted in Chapter 2, our political system is more pluralist than majoritarian. Policymaking is determined more by the interaction of groups with the government than by elections. The great advantage of majoritarianism is that it is built around the most elemental notion of fairness: what the government does is determined by what most of the people want.

How, then, do we justify the policy decisions made under a pluralist system? How do we determine whether they are fair? There is no precisely agreed-upon formula, but most people would agree with the following two simple notions. First, all significant interests in the population should be adequately represented by lobbying groups. That is, if a significant number of people with similar views have a stake in the outcome of policy decisions in a particular area, they should have a lobby to speak for them. If government makes policy that affects farmers who grow wheat, for example, then wheat farmers should have a lobby.

Second, government should listen to the views of all major interests as it develops policy. Lobbies are of little value unless policymakers are willing to listen to them. We should not require policymakers to perfectly balance all competing interests, however, because some interests are diametrically opposed. Moreover, elections inject some of the benefits of majoritarianism into our system, because the party that wins an election will have more say in the making of public policy than its opponent.

Membership Patterns

Public opinion surveys of Americans and surveys of interest groups in Washington can be used to determine who is represented in the interest group system. A clear pattern is evident: some sectors of society are much better represented than others. As noted in the earlier discussions of the Boston West Enders and the United Farm Workers, who it is that is being organized makes a big difference. Those who work in business or in a profession, those with a high level of education, and those with high incomes (recall Figure 10.2) are the most likely to belong to interest groups. Even middle-income people are much more likely to join interest groups than those who are poor.

For example, one-third of those receiving veterans' benefits belong to an organization that works to protect and enhance veterans' benefits. A quarter of social security recipients are members of a group that works to protect that program. By contrast, less than 1 percent of food stamp recipients belong to a group that represents their interests in this program. Only about 2 percent of recipients of Aid to Families with Dependent Children (AFDC) are members of welfare rights groups.[44] Clearly, a **membership bias** is part of the pattern of who belongs to interest groups: certain types of people are much more likely to belong to interest groups than others.

The Public Interest Movement

Because the bias in interest group membership is unmistakable, should we conclude that the interest group system is biased? Before reaching that conclusion, we should examine another set of data. The actual population of interest groups in Washington surely reflects a class bias in interest group membership, but that bias may be modified in an important way. Some interest groups derive support from sources other than their membership. Thus, although they have no food stamp recipients as members, the Washington-based Food Research and Action Committee and the Community Nutrition Institute have been effective long-term advocates of the food stamp program. The Center for Budget and Policy Priorities and the Children's Defense Fund have no welfare recipients among their members, but they are highly respected Washington lobbies working on the problems of poor people. Poverty groups gain their financial support from philanthropic foundations, government grants, corporations, and wealthy individuals.

Groups such as these have played an important role in influencing policy on poor people's programs. Given the large numbers of Americans who are on such programs as food stamps and AFDC, poor people's lobbies are not numerous enough.[45] Nevertheless, the poor are represented by these

Learn more about the Children's Defense Fund. <www.tmn.com/cdf/>

and other organizations (such as labor unions and health lobbies) that regard the poor as part of the constituency they must protect. In short, some bias exists in the representation of the poor, but it is not nearly so bad as interest group membership patterns suggest.

Another part of the problem of membership bias has to do with free riders. The interests that are most affected by free riders are broad societal problems, such as the environment and consumer protection, in which literally everyone can be considered as having a stake in the outcome. We are all consumers, and we all care about the environment. But the greater the number of potential members of a group, the more likely it is that individuals will decide to be free riders, because they believe that plenty of others can offer financial support to the organization. As noted earlier, business trade associations and professional associations do not have the same problem, because they can offer many benefits that cannot be obtained without paying for membership.

Environmental and consumer interests have been chronically underrepresented in the Washington interest group community. In the 1960s, however, a strong public interest movement emerged. **Public interest groups are citizen groups that have no economic self-interest in the policies they pursue.**[46] For example, the members of environmental groups fighting for stricter pollution control requirements receive no financial gain from the enactment of environmental protection policies. The benefits to its members are largely ideological and esthetic. In contrast, a corporation fighting the same stringent standards is trying to protect its economic interests. A law that requires a corporation to install expensive antipollution devices can reduce stockholders' dividends, depress salaries, and postpone expansion. Although both the environmental group and the corporation have valid reasons for their stands, their motives are different. The environmental lobby is a public interest group; the corporation is not.

Today, many public interest groups are important players in Washington politics. Most are environmental and consumer groups, but other public interest groups work on corporate accountability, good government, and, as discussed previously, poverty and nutrition. Many conservative public interest groups exist as well, working in areas such as abortion and family values. The Center for Law and Religious Freedom, for example, lobbies on behalf of those who want religion to play a more central role in American life. It wants to counteract the influence of liberal groups like the American Civil Liberties Union, which argues for a strict separation of church and state. Overall, the public interest movement has broadened interest group representation in national politics and made the pluralist system more democratic.

Business Mobilization

Because a strong public interest movement has become an integral part of Washington politics, an easy assumption is that the bias in interest group representation in favor of business has been largely overcome. What must be factored in is that business has become increasingly mobilized as well.[47] The 1970s and 1980s saw a vast increase in the number of business lobbies in Washington. Many corporations opened up Washington lobby-

● ● ● ● ● ● ● ● ● ● ●

Well-Fed Lobbyists

At first glance, the restaurant business may not seem to be an industry with serious political problems. Yet government regulation and taxation policies can significantly affect restaurant operations and profits. The National Restaurant Association, which employs these five lobbyists, is the trade association that represents restaurant owners, food and equipment manufacturers, and distributors. Headquartered in Washington with a staff of 115 and a budget of $16 million, it is just one of the thousands of trade groups working to influence public policy in Washington.

ing offices, and many trade associations headquartered elsewhere either moved to Washington or opened up branch offices there.

This mobilization was partly a reaction to the success of the liberal public interest movement, which business tended to view as hostile to the free-enterprise system. The reaction of business also reflected the expanded scope of the national government. As the Environmental Protection Agency, the Consumer Product Safety Commission, OSHA, and other regulatory agencies were created, many more companies found they were affected by federal regulations. And many corporations found that they were frequently reacting to policies that were already made rather than participating in their making. They saw representation in Washington—where the policymakers are—as critical if they were to obtain information on pending government actions soon enough to act on it. Finally, the competitive nature of business lobbying fueled the increase in business advocacy in Washington. This competition exists because legislation and regulatory decisions never seem to apply uniformly to all businesses; rather, they affect one type of business or one industry more than others.

The health care industry is a case in point. Government regulation has become an increasingly important factor in determining health care profits. Through reimbursement formulas for Medicare, Medicaid, and other health care programs funded by Washington, the national government limits what providers can charge. As this regulatory influence grew, more and more health care trade associations (like the American Hospital Association) and professional associations (like the American Nurses Association) came to view Washington lobbying as increasingly significant to the well-being of their members. As Figure 10.5 indicates, in recent

figure **10.5**

● **One Part of the Health Care System That Isn't Ailing: Lobbies**

As the national government has become more involved in regulating the health care industry, the number of health care lobbies in Washington has risen sharply. Between 1984 and 1991, the number of health groups more than doubled. When the government proposes regulatory changes, it often pits one segment of the industry against another, thus intensifying the lobbying competition between them.

Source: Jonathan Rauch, *Demosclerosis* (New York: Times Books, 1994), p. 91. Copyright © 1994 by Jonathan Rauch. Reprinted by permission of Random House, Inc.

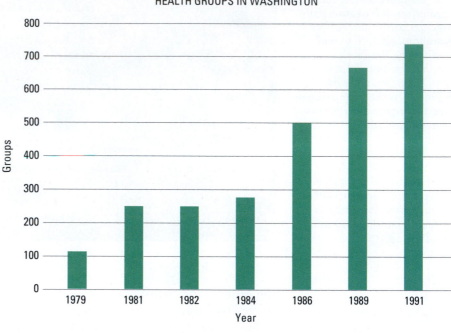

HEALTH GROUPS IN WASHINGTON

years an increasing number of health groups have opened up offices in Washington so that they can make more of an effort to influence the government.

The number of organizations is far from a perfect indicator of interest group strength, however. The AFL-CIO, which represents millions of union members, is more influential than a two-person corporate listening post in Washington; nevertheless, as a rough indicator of interest group influence, the data show that business has an advantage in this country's interest group system.

Access

At the outset of this discussion of interest group bias, we noted the importance of finding out not only which types of constituencies are represented by interest groups but also whether those in government listen to the various groups that approach them. The existence of an interest group makes little difference if the government systematically ignores it. Evidence shows that any particular policymaker or office of government can be highly selective in granting access to interest groups. The Reagan White House, for example, worked directly with only a small proportion of interest groups, and wealthy, conservative groups had much more access than others.[48]

The ideological compatibility between any given interest group and the policymaker it approaches certainly affects the likelihood that the policymaker will grant the group access and listen to what its lobbyists have to say. However, pluralists are convincing when they argue that the national government has many points of access, and virtually all lobbying organizations can find some part of that government that will listen to them. If liberal poverty lobbies are shut out of a conservative White House, liberal members of Congress will work with them. All forms of access are not of equal importance, and some organizations have wider access than others. Nevertheless, American government is generally characterized by the broad access it grants to interest groups.

Reform

If the interest group system is biased, should the advantages of some groups somehow be eliminated or reduced? This is hard to do. In an economic system marked by great differences in income, great differences in the degree to which people are organized are inevitable. Moreover, as Madison foresaw, limiting interest group activity is difficult without limiting fundamental freedoms. The First Amendment guarantees Americans the right to petition their government, and lobbying, at its most basic level, is a form of organized petitioning.

Still, some sectors of the interest group community may enjoy advantages that are unacceptable. If it is felt that the advantages of some groups are so great that they affect the equality of people's opportunity to be heard in the political system, then restrictions on interest group behavior can be justified on the grounds that the disadvantaged must be protected. Pluralist democracy is justified on exactly these grounds: all constituencies must have the opportunity to organize, and competition between groups as they press their case before policymakers must be fair.

Some critics charge that a system of campaign finance that relies so heavily on PACs undermines our democratic system. They claim that access to policymakers is purchased through the wealth of some constituencies. In the 1994 election, thirty PACs contributed at least $1 million in campaign funds to congressional candidates.[49] Over 65 percent of PAC contributions come from corporations, business trade associations, and professional associations (recall Figure 10.4).[50] It is not merely a matter of wealthy interest groups showering incumbents with donations; members of Congress aggressively solicit donations from PACs. Indeed, members of Congress are so aggressive in seeking PAC funds that their behavior sometimes borders on extortion. A month before the 1994 congressional election, Newt Gingrich met with PAC directors and warned them that unless they contributed to Republican candidates, they could expect the "two coldest years in Washington."[51] Although observers disagree on whether PAC money actually influences policy outcomes, agreement is widespread that PAC donations give donors better access to members of Congress.

The government has placed some restrictions on interest group campaign donations, however. During the 1970s, Congress put some important reforms into effect. Strong disclosure requirements now exist—the source of all significant contributions to candidates for national office is a matter of public record. Legislation also provides for public financing of presidential campaigns; taxpayer money goes in equal amounts to the presidential nominees of the major parties. In 1995 Congress passed some modest reforms outside of the campaign finance area. Lobbyists are now subject to a strict registration requirement and must file reports every six months listing all their clients, the amount they spent on lobbying activities, and how much they were paid.[52] Another reform banned all gifts from lobbyists to legislators (with the exception of gifts of trivial value).[53]

Reformers have called for public financing of congressional elections to reduce the presumed influence of PACs on Congress. Public financing would restrict people's freedom to give to whom they want; the tradeoff is that it also would reduce political inequality. Other proposed approaches include reducing the amount individual PACs can give; limiting the overall amount of money any one candidate can accept from PACs; reducing the costs of campaigning by subsidizing the costs of commercials, printing, and postage; and giving tax incentives to individuals to contribute to candidates. However, incumbents usually find it easier to raise money from PACs than do challengers, so the incentive to leave the status quo intact is strong. And Republicans and Democrats have sharp, partisan differences over campaign finance reform, because each party believes that the other is trying to fashion a system that will somehow handicap the opposing party.

SUMMARY

Interest groups play many important roles in our political process. They are a means by which citizens can participate in politics, and they communicate their members' views to those in government. Interest groups differ greatly in the resources at their disposal and in the tactics they use to influence government. The number of interest groups has grown sharply in recent years.[54]

Despite the growth and change in the nature of interest groups, the fundamental problem identified by Madison more than two hundred years ago endures. In a free and open society, groups form to pursue policies that favor them at the expense of the broader national interest. Madison hoped that the solution to the problem would come from the diversity of the population and the structure of our government.

To a certain extent, Madison's expectations have been borne out. The natural differences between groups have prevented a tyranny of any one faction. Yet, the interest group system remains unbalanced, with some segments of society (particularly business, the wealthy, and the educated) considerably better organized than others. The growth of citizen groups has reduced the disparity somewhat, but significant inequalities remain in how well different interests are represented in Washington.

The inequities point to flaws in pluralist theory. There is no mechanism to automatically ensure that interest groups will form to speak for those who need representation. Likewise, when an issue arises and policymakers meet with interest groups that have a stake in the outcome, those groups may not equally represent all the constituencies that the policy changes will affect. The interest group system clearly compromises the principle of political equality stated in the maxim "one person, one vote." Formal political equality is certainly more likely to occur outside interest group politics, in elections between candidates from competing political parties—which better fits the majoritarian model of democracy.

Despite the inequities of the interest group system, little direct effort has been made to restrict interest group activity. Madison's dictum to avoid suppressing political freedoms, even at the expense of permitting interest group activity that promotes the selfish interests of narrow segments of the population, has generally guided public policy. Yet, as the problem of PACs demonstrates, government has had to set some restrictions on interest groups. Permitting PACs to give unlimited amounts to political candidates would undermine confidence in the system. Where to draw the line on PAC activity remains a thorny issue, because there is little consensus on how to balance the conflicting needs of our society. Congress is one institution that must try to balance our diverse country's conflicting interests. In the next chapter, we will see how difficult this part of Congress's job is.

Key Terms

interest group
lobby
lobbyist
agenda building
program monitoring

interest group
 entrepreneur
free-rider problem
trade association

political action
 committee (PAC)
direct lobbying
grassroots lobbying

information campaign
coalition building
membership bias
public interest group

Selected Readings

Berry, Jeffrey M. *The Interest Group Society*, 3d ed. New York: Longman, 1997. An analysis of the growth of interest group politics.

Cigler, Allan J., and Burdett A. Loomis, eds. *Interest Group Politics*, 4th ed. Washington, D.C.: Congressional Quarterly Press, 1995. This reader includes eighteen essays on lobbying groups.

Costain, Anne N. *Inviting Women's Rebellion*. Baltimore: Johns Hopkins University Press, 1992. A careful and original examination of the origins of the women's movement and its development into a political force.

Heinz, John P., Edward O. Laumann, Robert L. Nelson, and Robert H. Salisbury. *The Hollow Core*. Cambridge, Mass.: Harvard University Press, 1993. The best study available of large-scale issue networks in national politics.

Woliver, Laura. *From Outrage to Action*. Urbana: University of Illinois Press, 1993. Four incisive case studies of ad hoc grassroots advocacy groups.

Wright, John R. *Interest Groups and Congress*. Boston: Allyn & Bacon, 1996. An overview of how lobbies and PACs try to influence Congress.

World Wide Web Resources

U. S. Chamber of Commerce. Find out how interest groups function and the services they provide to their membership. The site lists management training information, a video library, and seminars for business—those in business, and those seeking to start a business. `<www.uschamber.org/chamber/chb.text.htm>`
AFL-CIO. Read the organization's policy statements, press releases, and its "Boycott List." Find information on how to organize a union. A dominant feature of this Web site is information about the AFL-CIO's "Standup Campaign"—a campaign to lobby for good jobs, good wages, and worker protection. `<www.aflcio.org/>`

The Sierra Club. Find out how public interest groups work. Visitors to this Web page can read the Sierra Club's magazine as well as *The Planet*, a newsletter for environmental activists. Get information on Sierra Club chapters, politics, and the environment. Follow links to other environmental sites on the Internet. `<www.sierraclub.org/>`

Voters Telecommunications Watch. Track telecommunications policy from a voter/citizen perspective. Find out why voters should be interested in telecommunications policy (regulatory policy, legislation, and so forth). Find out more information on free speech issues and issues of universal access. Use the "Citizen's Guide to the Internet." Help pave the information superhighway. `<www.vtw.org/>`

part

IV

Institutions of Government

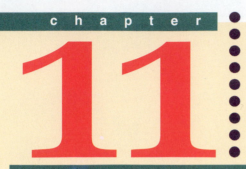

Congress

NEWT GINGRICH THREW DOWN THE GAUNTLET. "So long as I'm Speaker we're going to spend every day working on decisions that get us to a balanced budget by 2002, period."[1] True to his word, the 104th Congress did work obsessively toward passing a balanced budget amendment to the Constitution. After promising in the 1994 campaign that the Republicans would deliver one if the GOP won control of Congress, Gingrich moved quickly after the new Congress came into session the following January. With joyful exuberance, virtually all the Republicans and a minority of Democrats marched into the House of Representatives and passed the amendment by a vote of 300–132.

In the Senate, however, the amendment ran into trouble. Although all the Republican senators but one voted for the amendment, it failed by a single vote to garner the two-thirds majority required of constitutional amendments before they can be sent on to the states. Most Democrats opposed the amendment, and President Clinton worked against its passage. Yet this "defeat" seemed a clear tactical victory for the Republicans. Since the public had expressed support for the amendment by a margin of four to one, the Democrats would shoulder the blame for defeating this popular proposal. Moreover, the Republicans articulated their arguments for the balanced budget in general terms, never detailing how they would cut $1.2 *trillion* over seven years to pull the budget out of red ink. The program cuts would have been staggering. As House Majority Leader Dick Armey (R.-Texas) acknowledged early in the fight, "The fact of the matter is, once members of Congress know exactly, chapter and verse, the pain that the government must live with in order to get a balanced [budget], their knees will buckle."[2] It seemed to be the best of both worlds for the Republicans: not only had they won the public relations battle on the balanced budget, but since the Democrats had sunk the amendment, protecting popular programs from being slashed, GOP legislators wouldn't have to incur the wrath of the people back home.

Yet this moral victory for the Republicans wasn't enough. They pressed on, trying to achieve their goal of a balanced budget by passing appropriations bills that made the necessary spending cuts. (Congress can balance the budget without a constitutional mandate; it simply has to appropriate government spending at a lower rate than the government's income until the deficit is paid off and income equals outflow.) With this strategy, however, came the necessity of specifying which programs to curb. The huge Medicare program, which provides health care to the elderly, was one of the Republicans' targets. Low- and middle-income seniors are a crucial Democratic party constituency, and President Clinton and his congressional allies relentlessly attacked the Republicans for trying to cut medical services to the elderly. Republicans responded that they were merely cutting the *rate of increase* of future Medicare spending. The Democrats had the upper hand, though, because polls demonstrated that two-thirds of the public preferred keeping Medicare from being cut significantly over balancing the federal budget.[3]

Republican congressional leaders entered into negotiations with President Clinton to see if they could come to an agreement for the entire budget. As they became increasingly frustrated with the Democrats because the party wouldn't accede to a balanced budget, the GOP refused on more than one occasion to pass short-term spending bills to keep the whole government running. The public blamed the Republicans for the resulting partial government shutdowns, however, so eventually short-term appropriations bills were passed. Finally, put on the defensive by a public that didn't seem so committed to a balanced budget after all, the Republicans threw in the towel. In the spring of 1996, a spending bill funding the government for the rest of the fiscal year was passed. Gingrich mused, "It may just be that we need one more election."[4]

Although the fight was over a highly partisan issue that highlights the different values of the two congressional parties, it also illustrates the continuing tension in American politics between majoritarianism and pluralism. The Republicans certainly believed they had a mandate from a majority of Americans to balance the nation's budget. The Democrats pulled together a coalition of different interests, not only senior citizens but also environmentalists, educators, students, minorities, and others who would be hurt by budget cuts. The defeat of both balanced budget strategies pursued by the Republicans may seem a victory of pluralism over majoritarianism. But what was the true majoritarian position? One majority said it wanted a balanced budget, but another majority said it preferred to protect Medicare.

In this chapter and throughout Part IV of this book, we emphasize the tension between pluralist and majoritarian visions of democracy. In the pages that follow, we'll examine more closely the relationship between members of Congress and their constituents, as well as the forces (such as political parties) that push legislators toward majoritarianism. We'll also focus on Congress's relations with the executive branch and analyze how the legislative process affects public policy. A starting point is to ask how the framers envisioned Congress.

THE ORIGIN AND POWERS OF CONGRESS

The framers of the Constitution wanted to keep power from being concentrated in the hands of a few, but they were also concerned with creating a union strong enough to overcome the weaknesses of the government that had operated under the Articles of Confederation. They argued passionately about the structure of the new government. In the end, they produced a legislative body that was as much of an experiment as the new nation's democracy.

● ● ● ● ● ● ● ● ● ● ● ●

The Capitol

The Capitol sits on a site city planner Pierre L'Enfant called "a pedestal waiting for a monument." This is what the building looked like from 1825 to 1856.

The Great Compromise

The U.S. Congress has two separate and powerful chambers: the House of Representatives and the Senate. A bill cannot become law unless it is passed in identical form by both chambers. When drafting the Constitution during the summer of 1787, "the fiercest struggle for power" centered on representation in the legislature.[5] The small states wanted all the states to have equal representation. The more populous states wanted representation based on population; they did not want their power diluted. The Great Compromise broke the deadlock: the small states would receive equal representation in the Senate, but the number of each state's representatives in the House would be based on population, and the House would have the sole right to originate revenue-related legislation.

As the Constitution specifies, each state has two senators, and senators serve six-year terms of office. Terms are staggered, so that one-third of the Senate is elected every two years. When it was ratified, the Constitution directed that senators be chosen by the state legislatures. However, the Seventeenth Amendment, adopted in 1913, provided for the direct election of senators by popular vote. From the beginning, the people have directly elected members of the House of Representatives. They serve two-year terms, and all House seats are up for election at the same time.

There are 435 members of the House of Representatives. Because each state's representation in the House is in proportion to its population, the Constitution provides for a national census every ten years; population shifts are handled by the **reapportionment** (redistribution) of seats among the states after each census is taken. Since recent population growth has been centered in the Sunbelt, California, Texas, and Florida have gained seats while the Northeast and Midwest states have lost them. Each representative is elected from a particular congressional district within his or her state, and each district elects only one representative. The districts within a state must be roughly equal in population.

Duties of the House and Senate

Although the Great Compromise provided for considerably different schemes of representation for the House and Senate, the Constitution gives them essentially similar legislative tasks. They share many important powers, among them the powers to declare war, raise an army and navy, borrow and coin money, regulate interstate commerce, create federal courts, establish rules for the naturalization of immigrants, and "make all Laws which shall be necessary and proper for carrying into Execution the foregoing Powers."

Of course, the constitutional duties of the two chambers are different in at least a few important ways. As noted earlier, the House alone has the right to originate revenue bills, a right that apparently was coveted at the Constitutional Convention. In practice, this power is of limited consequence because both the House and Senate must approve all bills—including revenue bills. The House also has the power of **impeachment,** the power formally to charge the president, vice president, or other "civil Officers" of the national government with "Treason, Bribery, or other high Crimes and Misdemeanors." The Senate is empowered to act as a court to try impeachments; a two-thirds majority vote of the senators present is necessary for conviction. Only one president—Andrew Johnson—has ever been impeached, and in 1868 the Senate came within a single vote of finding him guilty. More recently, the House Judiciary Committee voted to impeach President Richard Nixon for his role in the Watergate cover-up, but he resigned (in August 1974) before the full House could vote. A small number of federal judges, however, have been impeached, convicted, and removed from the bench.

The Constitution gives the Senate the power to approve major presidential appointments (such as to federal judgeships, ambassadorships, and cabinet posts) and treaties with foreign nations. The president is empowered to make treaties, but he must submit them to the Senate for approval by a two-thirds majority. Because of this requirement, the executive branch generally considers the Senate's sentiments when it negotiates a treaty.[6] At times, a president must try to convince a doubting Senate of the worth of a particular treaty. Shortly after World War I, President Woodrow Wilson submitted to the Senate the Treaty of Versailles, which contained the charter for the proposed League of Nations. Wilson had attempted to convince the Senate that the treaty deserved its support; when the Senate refused to approve the treaty, Wilson suffered a severe setback.

Despite the long list of congressional powers in the Constitution, the question of what powers are appropriate for Congress has generated substantial controversy. For example, although the Constitution gives Congress the sole power to declare war, many presidents have initiated military action on their own. And at times, the courts have found that congressional actions have usurped the rights of the states.

ELECTING CONGRESS   If Americans are not happy with the job Congress is doing, they can use their votes to say so. With a congressional election every two years, the voters have frequent opportunities to express themselves.

figure
11.1   ● Incumbents: Life Is Good

Despite the public's dissatisfaction with Congress in general, incumbent representatives win reelection at an exceptional rate. Incumbent senators aren't quite as successful but still do well in reelection races. Voters seem to believe that their own representatives and senators don't share the same foibles that they attribute to the other members of Congress.

Source: Norman J. Ornstein, Thomas E. Mann, and Michael J. Malbin, *Vital Statistics on Congress, 1995–1996* (Washington, D.C.: Congressional Quarterly Press, 1996), pp. 60–61.

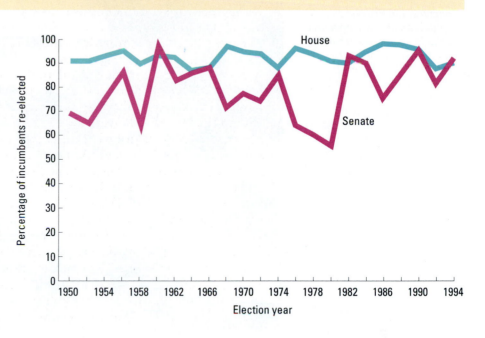

The Incumbency Effect

Congressional elections offer voters a chance to show their approval of Congress's performance by reelecting **incumbents** or to demonstrate their disapproval by "throwing the rascals out." The voters do more reelecting than rascal throwing. The reelection rate is astonishingly high; in the majority of elections since 1950, more than 90 percent of all House incumbents have held on to their seats (see Figure 11.1). In some years, as few as a half-dozen incumbents have been defeated in the general election. Most House elections aren't even close; in recent elections, most House incumbents have won at least 60 percent of the vote. Senate elections are more competitive, but incumbents still have a high reelection rate.[7]

These findings may seem surprising, since the public does not hold Congress as a whole in particularly high esteem. Two-thirds of the American public tell pollsters that they disapprove of the job Congress is doing.[8] Close to 60 percent of Americans believe that at least half of all members of Congress are personally corrupt, a harsh indictment of the institution.[9] Americans strongly support term limits for members of Congress, to limit the number of years a legislator can serve in the House or Senate.[10] Although term limits have been imposed in many states, in 1995 the House voted against a Constitutional amendment for term limits on members of Congress. Although Americans feel disdain for Congress, they tend to distinguish the institution as a whole from their own members of Congress. Only 15 percent believe that their own representative is financially corrupt.[11] It is not entirely clear why Americans hate Congress so much despite their satisfaction with their own members

● ● ● ● ● ● ● ● ● ● ● ●

Bad Hair Day?

Congressman Jim Nussle, Republican of Iowa, appeared on the House floor with a bag over his head because he wanted to show voters back home how embarrassed he was by a scandal involving House members who overdrew their accounts at the House bank without having any penalty or interest assessed. (Nussle was not guilty of any overdrafts.) Nussle's juvenile antics are a little unusual, but it is common for members of the House and Senate to tell their constituents how awful Congress is. They do this because voters are cynical about Congress, and incumbents don't want to appear to be defending the institution.

of the House and Senate. Tough economic times and various scandals have surely influenced public attitudes. Campaign finance practices, especially the central role of political action committee (PAC) contributions, are another problem. Finally, American culture has traditionally held politicians in low esteem: we don't expect much from politicians, and we react sharply to their failings.

Redistricting.   One explanation for the incumbency effect centers on redistricting, the way House districts are redrawn by state legislatures after a census-based reapportionment. It is entirely possible for them to draw the new districts to benefit the incumbents of one or both parties. Altering district lines for partisan advantage is commonly called **gerrymandering.**

But redistricting does not explain the incumbency effect in the House as a whole.[12] Redistricting may be very helpful for some incumbents, but it does not explain why more than 90 percent of House incumbents are routinely reelected. Nevertheless, politicians regard gerrymandering as an important factor in elections, and the political parties put considerable effort into trying to make sure that new boundaries are drawn in the most advantageous way.

Name Recognition.   Holding office brings with it some important advantages. First, incumbents develop significant name recognition among voters simply by being members of Congress. Congressional press secretaries help the name recognition advantage along through their efforts to get publicity for the activities and speeches of their bosses. The primary focus of such publicity seeking is on the local media back in the district—that's where the votes are.[13] The local press, in turn, is eager to cover what local members of Congress are saying about the issues.

Another resource available to members of Congress is the *franking privilege*—the right to send mail free of charge. Mailings work to make constituents aware of their legislators' names, activities, and accomplishments. Periodic newsletters, for example, almost always highlight legislators' success at securing funds and projects for their district, such as money to construct a highway or a new federal building. Newsletters also "advertise for business," encouraging voters to phone or visit their legislators' district offices if they need help with a problem. When members of Congress visit their districts and states, making appearances in public, on TV, or on the radio, they also encourage people to contact their offices for any help they may need. Democratic senator Barbara Boxer goes back to California frequently and always tells people to write to her with their opinions or problems. Boxer receives ten thousand letters a day from her constituents.[14]

Much of the work performed by the large staffs of members of Congress is **casework**—such services for constituents as tracking down a social security check or directing the owner of a small business to the appropriate federal agency. Constituents who are helped in this way usually remember who assisted them.

Campaign Financing.   It should be clear that anyone who wants to challenge an incumbent needs solid financial backing. Challengers must spend large sums of money to run a strong campaign with an emphasis on advertising—an expensive but effective way to bring their name and record to the voters' attention. But here, too, the incumbent has the advantage. Challengers find raising campaign funds difficult because they have to overcome contributors' doubts about whether they can win. In the 1994 elections, incumbents raised about 53 percent of all money contributed to campaigns for election to the House. Only 24 percent went to challengers. (Those running for open seats received the rest.) Challengers to Senate incumbents did better than their House counterparts, which is usually the case.[15]

PACs show a strong preference for incumbents (see Chapter 10). They tend not to want to risk offending an incumbent by giving money to a long-shot challenger. The attitude of the American Medical Association's PAC is fairly typical. "We have a friendly incumbent policy," says its director. "We always stick with the incumbent if we agree with both candidates."[16] But along with their pragmatism, PACs also have an ideological side. Although corporate PACs, which tend to favor conservative economic policies, will not hesitate to give to liberal Democratic incumbents to whom they need access, they decidedly favor Republican candidates in contests in which no incumbent is running.[17]

Successful Challengers.   Clearly, the deck is stacked against challengers to incumbents. As one analyst put it, "The typical House challenger is in a position similar to that of a novice athlete pitted against a world-class sprinter."[18] Yet some challengers do beat incumbents. How? The opposing party and unsympathetic PACs may target incumbents who seem vulnerable because of age, lack of seniority, a scandal, or unfavorable redistricting. Some incumbents appear vulnerable because they were elected by a

Torricelli to the Senate

One of the new senators elected in 1996 is Democrat Robert Torricelli of New Jersey. He defeated Republican Richard Zimmer who, like Torricelli, was a member of the House of Representatives. In a year of extensive negative campaigning, the New Jersey senate race stood out as one of the worst in the nation. Torricelli's and Zimmer's ceaseless accusations and nasty television commercials focused attention on the lack of civility in American politics.

narrow margin, or the ideological and partisan composition of their district does not favor their holding the seat. Vulnerable incumbents also bring out higher-quality challengers—individuals who have held elective office and are capable of raising adequate campaign funds. Such experienced challengers are more likely to defeat incumbents than are amateurs with little background in politics.[19] The reason Senate challengers have a higher success rate than House challengers is that they are generally higher-quality candidates. Often they are governors or members of the House, who enjoy high name recognition and can attract significant campaign funds because they are regarded as credible candidates.[20]

The broad sweep of national opinion also influences the outcome of House elections. The president's party almost always loses seats in the midterm elections, as voters take out their disappointments with the president on the House candidates of his party. In the 1994 election, voters dealt the Democrats a stunning defeat. Negative feelings about government in general and President Clinton in particular fueled a Republican takeover of both the House and the Senate. Thirty-four Democratic House incumbents were defeated, and the Republicans gained fifty-two seats overall to become the majority in the House for the first time since 1952. The incumbents who lost tended to come from districts that were not as strongly Democratic as those where Democratic incumbents survived. Those Democrats who were loyal to President Clinton in their voting on the House floor were also more vulnerable to Republican challengers.[21] (Yet even in this volatile year, 90 percent of all incumbent members of the House who were running won reelection.[22])

With Speaker Gingrich's unpopularity and President Clinton headed toward a decisive reelection victory, Democrats hoped that they could regain control of the House of Representatives in 1996. Democrats and their allies in the labor movement targeted many of the freshmen Republicans who had loyally supported Gingrich and his Contract with America. Like most congressional elections, however, 1996 was a very good year for incumbents of both political parties. There were around twenty House incumbents who lost, but only a dozen of the seventy Republican House freshmen running for reelection went down to defeat. With some recounts pending, the Democrats picked up around ten seats, which left them roughly ten seats shy of a majority. With a narrower GOP margin, however, House Republican moderates should have more leverage with Gingrich in the 105th Congress. Only a single incumbent senator lost, and the Republicans gained two seats and maintained control of that chamber as well.

Whom Do We Elect?

Use your ZIP code to identify your representative.
`<www.voxpop.org/zipper/>`

The people we elect (then reelect) to Congress are not a cross section of American society. Most members of Congress are professionals—primarily lawyers, businesspeople, and educators.[23] Although nearly a third of the American labor force works in blue-collar jobs, someone currently employed as a blue-collar worker rarely wins a congressional nomination.

Women and minorities have long been underrepresented in elective office, although both groups have recently increased their representation in Congress significantly (see Politics in a Changing America 11.1). Other members of Congress don't necessarily ignore the concerns of women and minorities—there are many white men, for example, who have championed equal rights. Yet, many women and minorities believe that only members of their own group—people who have experienced what they have experienced—can truly represent their interests. This is a belief in **descriptive representation,** the view that a legislature should resemble the demographic characteristics of the population it represents.[24]

During the 1980s, both Congress and the Supreme Court provided support for the principle of descriptive representation for blacks and Hispanic Americans. When Congress amended the Voting Rights Act in 1982, it encouraged the states to draw districts that concentrated minorities together, so blacks and Hispanic Americans would have a better chance of being elected to office. Supreme Court decisions also pushed the states to concentrate minorities in House districts.[25] After the 1990 census, states redrew House boundaries with the intent of creating districts with majority or near-majority minority populations. Some districts were very oddly shaped, snaking through their state to pick up black neighborhoods in various cities but leaving adjacent white neighborhoods to other districts. This effort led to a roughly 50 percent increase in the number of blacks elected to the House. Hispanic representation in the House also increased, from ten to seventeen members, after redistricting created new districts with large concentrations of Hispanic American voters.

In a decision that surprised many, the Supreme Court ruled in 1993 that states' efforts to increase minority representation through **racial gerrymandering** could violate the rights of whites. In *Shaw* v. *Reno*, the majority ruled in a split decision that a North Carolina district that meandered

● politics in a changing america

11.1   If Congress Looks Different, Will It Act Different?

African Americans were first elected to Congress during the Reconstruction era after the Civil War. After the military occupation of the South ended, the number of African Americans in Congress dwindled to a single representative by the end of the nineteenth century. (Blacks were systematically disenfranchised by southern whites after they resumed control of their state governments.) George White, the last African American legislator of this period, stood on the floor of the House in 1901 and prophesied of the black man in Congress, "Phoenix-like he will rise up some day and come again."

The phoenix has indeed risen. In the wake of the redistricting after the 1990 census, which created many new districts with a majority of minorities, thirty-nine African Americans won election to the House. The same number won election in the 1994 elections. This is a substantial number of legislators, but does it make any difference? Does descriptive representation bring about more effective representation for a particular sector of society?

Because the sharp increase in African American representation is so recent, there is no definitive answer. Still, early indications are that the Congressional Black Caucus— the organization of African Americans in the House—is gaining leverage in the legislative process. The leader of the Black Caucus, Donald Payne, a Democrat from New Jersey, can bargain with a considerable number of votes when he negotiates with the House leadership. (All but one of the blacks in the House are Democrats.) On issues directly affecting African Americans, the Black Caucus is influential with Democratic presidents, too. President Clinton wanted to nominate John Payton, a District of Columbia government lawyer, as head of the civil rights division of the Justice Department. Members of the Black Caucus objected privately, because Payton refused to commit himself to the racial gerrymandering that has brought more blacks into Congress. Clinton bowed to the Black Caucus's wishes and did not go forward with the nomination.

African Americans have also enhanced their clout by moving up the seniority ladder. Before the Republicans took control of the House in 1994, three blacks chaired House committees and thirteen chaired subcommittees. John Lewis of Georgia serves as chief deputy whip, an important position in the congressional party hierarchy. This leadership cohort of African Americans is in a strong position to initiate policy and advance the interests of their constituents.

The same questions about descriptive representation can be asked about women representatives, who also increased sharply in number in the House. (Progress is also being made in the Senate. When members of the 104th Congress took their seats in 1995, there were eight women senators, up from two in 1991.) Although research on women in Congress has been hampered by their low numbers, interesting studies have been done on women in state legislatures.

160 miles from Durham to Charlotte was an example of "political apartheid" (see Figure 11.2). (In some places, the Twelfth District is no wider than Interstate 85.) In effect, the Court ruled that racial gerrymandering segregated blacks from whites instead of creating districts built around contiguous communities. The ruling sent the case back to a North Carolina court to reconsider the district's legality in light of the Court's decision.[26] In a 1995 case, *Miller* v. *Johnson,* the Supreme Court went even

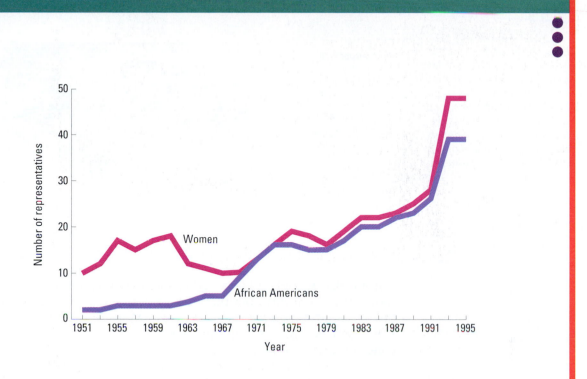

In many respects, female state legislators act very similarly to male legislators of the same party. In some areas, however, women do operate differently. They are more likely than their male counterparts to introduce bills on issues pertaining to women, children, and the family. They are also likely to make such bills their priorities—the ones they work hardest to get passed. Men and women state legislators are equally successful in getting their priority bills passed, but women's emphasis on these issues means that more such legislation gets passed and signed into law.

Simply put, women bring different concerns to a legislature. Their presence influences the mix of issues on the table and brings new perspectives on how problems may be solved. As one scholar puts it, "Leaving any group out of policy formulation and legitimation necessarily means that the range of ideas is artificially limited."

Source: Data for the figure come from Norman J. Ornstein, Thomas E. Mann, and Michael J. Malbin, *Vital Statistics on Congress, 1995–1996* (Washington, D.C.: Congressional Quarterly Press, pp. 38–39.

further in restricting the force of the Voting Rights Act. The Court's majority said that states should not draw district boundaries where race is the "predominant factor."[27] Thus, it is not merely the shape of the district that is suspect, but the very intent to draw districts to favor an ethnic or racial group. If equality requires descriptive representation, then the Court's direction to states to move away from racial gerrymandering is a retreat from equality in Congress.

figure 11.2 ● **"Political Apartheid" or Racial Equality?**

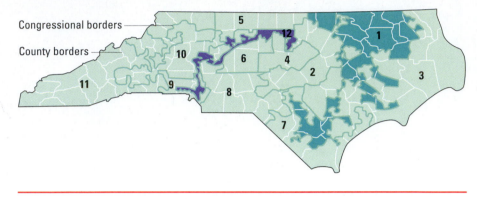

To create districts in which African American candidates were likely to win, the boundaries of two North Carolina congressional districts, 1 and 12, had to weave across the state to incorporate enough neighborhoods with concentrated minority populations. Justice Sandra Day O'Connor called these districts examples of "political apartheid." The Shaw v. Reno *and* Miller v. Johnson *cases are forcing states to redraw the boundaries of some of these oddly shaped districts designed to enhance the representation of minorities in the House of Representatives.*

Source: Shaw v. Reno 509 U.S. 630 (1993).

Ironically, spreading black and Hispanic voters around more districts, rather than concentrating them in a relatively small number of them, might actually increase their influence. More representatives will have significant numbers of minority voters in their district and will have to consider their views as they contemplate their stand on the issues. Likewise, the Court decisions will probably have a small, but negative, effect on Republican electoral fortunes in the House. The GOP has benefited from having black and Hispanic voters, who are overwhelmingly Democratic, concentrated in districts designed to elect minority representatives. This left the remaining districts not merely "whiter" but also more Republican than they would have otherwise been.[28]

HOW ISSUES GET ON THE CONGRESSIONAL AGENDA

The formal legislative process begins when a member of Congress introduces a *bill*, a proposal for a new law. In the House, members drop new bills in the "hopper," a mahogany box near the rostrum where the Speaker presides. Senators give their bills to a Senate clerk or introduce them from the floor.[29] But before a bill can be introduced to solve a problem, someone must perceive that a problem exists or that an issue needs to be resolved. In other words, the problem or issue somehow must find its way onto the congressional agenda. *Agenda* actually has two meanings in the vocabulary of political scientists. The first is that of a narrow, formal agenda, such as a calendar of bills to be voted on. The second meaning refers to the broad, imprecise, and unwritten agenda that consists of all the issues an institution is considering. Here we use the term in the second, broader sense.

Many issues Congress is working on at any given time seem to have been around forever. Foreign aid, the national debt, and social security have come up in just about every recent session of Congress. Yet, all issues begin at some point in time. There has always been violence on TV, for example, but for years it was seen as a matter best left to the private sector to

Congress Smokes Tobacco Execs

Congressional hearings are often structured like dramas, staged to portray villains at the witness table whose evil doings are uncovered by the crusading heroes on the committee. The villains in this bit of congressional theater are the chief executive officers of the nation's largest tobacco companies. They defended the cigarette industry and refused to acknowledge that smoking causes cancer. The prop at the right was set there by congressional staffers so that television pictures and still photographs of the executives together would include this easel. The placards on the easel were periodically changed from charts with statistics documenting the health risks of tobacco to gruesome photos of oral cancer.

solve. Eventually, though, people began to see the problem as a *political* issue. In 1996, Congress passed legislation requiring that new televisions be equipped with a "V chip," an electronic device that will allow parents to lock out all programs they deem unsuitable for their children.

New issues reach the congressional agenda in many ways. Sometimes a highly visible event focuses national attention on a problem. An explosion in a West Virginia mine in 1968 killed seventy-eight miners; Congress promptly went to work on laws to promote miners' safety.[30] Presidential support can also move an issue onto the agenda quickly. The media attention paid to the president gives him enormous opportunity to draw the nation's attention to problems he believes need some form of government action.

Within Congress, party leaders and committee chairs have the opportunity to move issues onto the agenda, but they rarely act capriciously, seizing upon issues without rhyme or reason. They often bide their time, waiting for other members of Congress to learn about an issue as they attempt to gauge the level of support for some kind of action. At times, the efforts of an interest group spark support for action, or at least awareness of an issue. When congressional leaders—or, for that matter, rank-and-file members—sense that the time is ripe for action on a new issue, they often are spurred on by the knowledge that sponsoring an important bill can enhance their own image. In the words of one observer, "Congress exists to do things. There isn't much mileage in doing nothing."[31]

THE DANCE OF LEGISLATION: AN OVERVIEW

The process of writing bills and getting them enacted is relatively simple, in the sense that it follows a series of specific steps. What complicates the process is the many different ways legislation can be treated at each step.

Here, we examine the straightforward process by which laws are made. In the next few sections, we discuss some of the complexities of that process.

After a bill is introduced in either house, it is assigned to the committee with jurisdiction over that policy area (see Figure 11.3). A banking bill, for example, would be assigned to the Banking and Financial Services Committee in the House or to the Banking, Housing, and Urban Affairs Committee in the Senate. When a committee actively considers a piece of legislation assigned to it, the bill is usually referred to a specialized subcommittee. The subcommittee may hold hearings, and legislative staffers may do research on the bill. The original bill usually is modified or revised; if passed in some form, it is sent to the full committee. A bill approved by the full committee is reported (that is, sent) to the entire membership of the chamber, where it may be debated, amended, and either passed or defeated.

Bills coming out of House committees go to the Rules Committee before going before the full House membership. The Rules Committee attaches a rule to the bill that governs the coming floor debate, typically specifying the length of the debate and the types of amendments House members can offer. On major legislation, most rules are complex and quite restrictive in terms of any amendments that can be offered.[32] The Senate does not have a comparable committee, although restrictions on the length of floor debate can be reached through unanimous consent agreements (see the "Rules of Procedure" section later in the chapter).

Even if both houses of Congress pass a bill on the same subject, the Senate and House versions are typically different from each other. In that case, a conference committee, composed of legislators from both houses, works out the differences and develops a compromise version. This version goes back to both houses for another floor vote. If both chambers approve the bill, it goes to the president for his signature or veto.

When the president signs a bill, it becomes law. If the president **vetoes** (disapproves) the bill, he sends it back to Congress with his reasons for rejecting it. The bill becomes law only if Congress overrides the president's veto by a two-thirds vote in each house. If the president neither signs nor vetoes the bill within ten days (Sundays excepted) of receiving it, the bill becomes law. There is an exception here: if Congress adjourns within the ten days, the president can let the bill die through a **pocket veto,** by not signing it.

In 1996, Congress gave presidents a new tool, the **line item veto**. This gives presidents the authority to strike out different sections of a bill, invalidating particular items but allowing the rest of the bill to become law. Thus, if a president thinks three different projects in an appropriations bill are wasteful "pork barrel," he can now cross out the lines in the legislation carrying those projects, vetoing the spending for those parts of the bill only. This new law faces a constitutional challenge and will eventually end up before the Supreme Court. Many scholars believe it is unconstitutional because the Constitution specifies what a president must do with a bill before him (sign, veto, do neither, or pocket veto it); it says nothing about a president altering bills to make them more to his liking. Supporters claim that the line item veto is just another form of legislative delegation of authority to the executive branch and that there are many such

figure

11.3 ● The Legislative Process

The process by which a bill becomes law is subject to much variation. This diagram depicts the typical process a bill might follow. It is important to remember that a bill can fail at any stage because of lack of support.

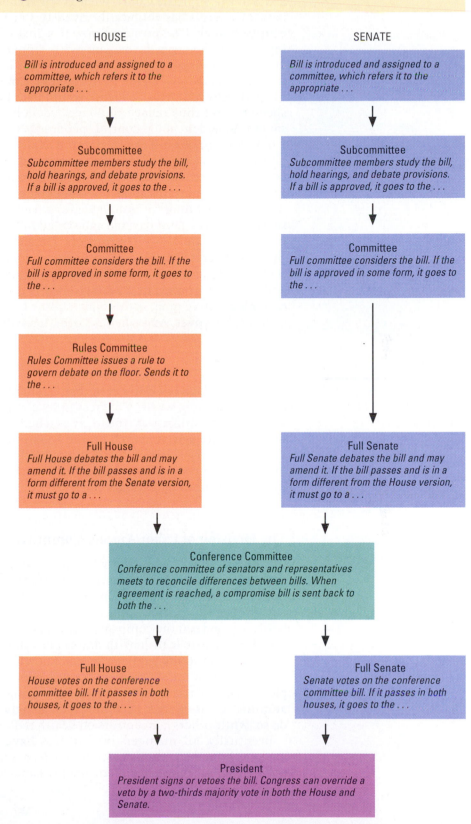

HOUSE

Bill is introduced and assigned to a committee, which refers it to the appropriate . . .

Subcommittee
Subcommittee members study the bill, hold hearings, and debate provisions. If a bill is approved, it goes to the . . .

Committee
Full committee considers the bill. If the bill is approved in some form, it goes to the . . .

Rules Committee
Rules Committee issues a rule to govern debate on the floor. Sends it to the . . .

Full House
Full House debates the bill and may amend it. If the bill passes and is in a form different from the Senate version, it must go to a . . .

SENATE

Bill is introduced and assigned to a committee, which refers it to the appropriate . . .

Subcommittee
Subcommittee members study the bill, hold hearings, and debate provisions. If a bill is approved, it goes to the . . .

Committee
Full committee considers the bill. If the bill is approved in some form, it goes to the . . .

Full Senate
Full Senate debates the bill and may amend it. If the bill passes and is in a form different from the House version, it must go to a . . .

Conference Committee
Conference committee of senators and representatives meets to reconcile differences between bills. When agreement is reached, a compromise bill is sent back to both the . . .

Full House
House votes on the conference committee bill. If it passes in both houses, it goes to the . . .

Full Senate
Senate votes on the conference committee bill. If it passes in both houses, it goes to the . . .

President
President signs or vetoes the bill. Congress can override a veto by a two-thirds majority vote in both the House and Senate.

perfectly legal delegations already in practice. Whatever the eventual outcome in the Supreme Court, what is remarkable about the line item veto is that Congress has voluntarily given away considerable power to the executive branch. The president now has greater authority to direct spending, greater leverage to bargain with Congress, and greater ability to punish uncooperative members of Congress by deleting the projects that legislators care most about. Nevertheless, Congress passed the statute because it believed that presidents would use the line item veto to control spending and thus reduce the budget deficit. The Congress, in essence, said the president could control spending better than it could.[33]

The content of a bill can be changed at any stage of the process in either house. Lawmaking (and thus policymaking) in Congress has many access points for those who want to influence legislation. This openness tends to fit within the pluralist model of democracy. As a bill moves through the dance of legislation,[34] it is amended again and again, in a search for a consensus that will get it enacted and signed into law. The process can be tortuously slow, and it is often fruitless. Derailing legislation is much easier than enacting it. The process gives groups frequent opportunities to voice their preferences and, if necessary, thwart their opponents. One foreign ambassador stationed in Washington aptly described the twists and turns of our legislative process this way: "In the Congress of the U.S., it's never over until it's over. And when it's over, it's still not over."[35]

COMMITTEES: THE WORKHORSES OF CONGRESS

Woodrow Wilson once observed that "Congress in session is Congress on public exhibition, whilst Congress in its committee-rooms is Congress at work."[36] His words are as true today as when he wrote them more than one hundred years ago. A speech on the Senate floor, for example, may convince the average citizen, but it is less likely to influence other senators. Indeed, few of them may even hear it. The real nuts and bolts of lawmaking go on in the congressional committees.

The Division of Labor Among Committees

The House and Senate are divided into committees for the same reason that other large organizations are broken into departments or divisions—to develop and use expertise in specific areas. At IBM, for example, different groups of people design computers, write software, assemble hardware, and sell the company's products. Each task requires an expertise that may have little to do with the others. Likewise, in Congress, decisions on weapons systems require a special knowledge that is of little relevance to decisions on reimbursement formulas for health insurance, for example. It makes sense for some members of Congress to spend more time examining defense issues, becoming increasingly expert on the topic as they do so, while others concentrate on health matters.

Eventually, all members of Congress have to vote on each bill that emerges from the committees. Those who are not on a particular committee depend on committee members to examine the issues thoroughly, to make compromises as necessary, and to bring forward a sound piece of legislation that has a good chance of being passed. Each member decides individually on the bill's merits. But once it reaches the House or Senate floor, members may get to vote on only a handful of amendments (if any at all) before they must cast their yea or nay for the entire bill.

Standing Committees.   There are several different kinds of congressional committees, but the **standing committee** is predominant. Standing committees are permanent committees that specialize in a particular area of legislation—for example, the House Judiciary Committee or the Senate Environment and Public Works Committee. Most of the day-to-day work of drafting legislation takes place in the eighteen standing Senate committees and twenty standing House committees. Typically, sixteen to twenty senators serve on each standing Senate committee, and an average of forty-two members serve on each standing committee in the House. The proportions of Democrats and Republicans on a standing committee generally reflect party proportions in the full Senate or House.

With a few exceptions, standing committees are further broken down into subcommittees. The House Agriculture Committee, for example, has five subcommittees, among them one on specialty crops and another on livestock, dairy, and poultry. Subcommittees exist for the same reason parent committees exist: members acquire expertise by continually working within the same fairly narrow policy area. Typically, members of the subcommittee are the dominant force in the shaping of the content of a bill.[37]

Other Congressional Committees.   Members of Congress can also serve on joint, select, and conference committees. **Joint committees** are made up of members of both the House and the Senate. Like standing committees, the small number of joint committees are concerned with particular policy areas. The Joint Economic Committee, for instance, analyzes the country's economic policies. Joint committees are much weaker than standing committees because they are almost always restricted from reporting bills to the House or Senate. Thus, their role is usually that of fact-finding and publicizing problems and policy issues that fall within their jurisdiction.

A **select committee** is a temporary committee created for a specific purpose. Congress establishes select committees to deal with special circumstances or with issues that either overlap or fall outside the areas of expertise of standing committees. The Senate committee that investigated the Watergate scandal was a select committee, created for that purpose only.

A **conference committee** is also a temporary committee, created to work out differences between the House and Senate versions of a specific piece of legislation. Its members are appointed from the standing committees or subcommittees, from each house, that originally handled and reported the legislation. Depending on the nature of the differences and the importance of the legislation, a conference committee may meet for hours or for weeks on end. The conference committee for a complex defense bill had to resolve 2,003 separate differences between the two versions.[38] When the conference committee reaches a compromise, it reports the bill to both

Republican Future?

The strong tilt toward the right in the Republican platform damaged the party's standing with women. More-moderate Republicans, like Susan Molinari, a representative from Staten Island, New York, are clearly outnumbered in the Congress. Molinari was a featured speaker at the Republican national convention in 1996, however, because candidate Bob Dole recognized that he needed to moderate the party's image and, in particular, to reach out to women.

houses, which must then either approve or disapprove the compromise; they cannot amend or change it in any way. Only about 15 to 25 percent of all bills that eventually pass Congress go to a conference committee (although virtually all important or controversial bills do).[39] Committee or subcommittee leaders of both houses reconcile differences in other bills through informal negotiation.

Congressional Expertise and Seniority

Once appointed to a committee, a representative or senator has great incentive to remain on it and to gain expertise over the years. Influence in Congress increases with a member's expertise. Influence also grows in a more formal way, with **seniority,** or years of consecutive service, on a committee. In their quest for expertise and seniority, members tend to stay on the same committees. However, sometimes they switch places when they are offered the opportunity to move to one of the high-prestige committees (such as Ways and Means in the House or Finance in the Senate) or to a committee that handles legislation of vital importance to their constituents.

Within each committee, the senior member of the majority party usually becomes the committee chair. (The majority party in each house controls committee leadership.) Other senior members of the majority party become subcommittee chairs, whereas their counterparts from the minority party gain influence as ranking minority members. In the House and Senate combined, there are over 150 subcommittees, offering multiple opportunities for power and status. Unlike seniority, expertise does not follow simply from length of service. Ability and effort are critical factors, too. Senator Daniel Moynihan (D.-N.Y.) began studying welfare policy as a young academic out of graduate school. He also worked for President Nixon as a domestic policy adviser, concentrating on social welfare issues. After being elected to the Senate, he spent a good deal of time on welfare issues, and members of both parties soon looked to him for leadership in this area.

After the Republicans gained control of the House in 1994, Speaker of the House Newt Gingrich made a major break with the seniority system by rejecting three Republicans who were in line to become committee chairs. Gingrich passed over the three to choose committee members whom he thought would be more conservative and more aggressive in promoting the Republican program. Speakers have not appointed House committee chairs in this fashion since the first part of this century, when "Uncle Joe" Cannon ruled the chamber with an iron fist.[40] Gingrich also instituted term limits for committee and subcommittee chairs, restricting their tenure to six years.

The way in which committees and subcommittees are led and organized within Congress is significant, because much public policy decision making takes place there. The first step in drafting legislation is to collect information on the issue. Committee staffers research the problem, and committees hold hearings to take testimony from witnesses who have some special knowledge of the subject.

At times, committee hearings are more theatrical than informational, to draw public attention to them. When the House Judiciary Sub-

● ● ● ● ● ● ● ● ● ● ●
Republican Future?

Senator Rick Santorum, a Republican of Pennsylvania, is one of the many recently-elected members of Congress who have tried to pull their party toward a strict, unbending adherence to conservative principles. He describes himself as "aggressive . . . the Energizer Bunny conservative." He has not hesitated to ruffle feathers when he felt being outspoken was warranted. In a floor debate over an abortion bill in 1996, he screamed at some of the Democrats who made pro-choice arguments.

committee on Administrative Law held hearings on alleged malpractice in military hospitals, for example, it did not restrict its list of witnesses to experts who had done relevant research. Instead, it called witnesses such as Dawn Lambert, a former member of the navy, who sobbed as she told the subcommittee that she had been left sterile by a misdiagnosis and a botched operation that had left a sponge and a green marker inside her. It was an irresistible story for the evening news, and it brought the malpractice problem in the military to light.[41]

The meetings at which subcommittees and committees actually debate and amend legislation are called *markup sessions*. The process by which committees reach decisions varies. Many committees have a strong tradition of decision by consensus. The chair, the ranking minority member, and others in these committees work hard, in formal committee sessions and in informal negotiations, to find a middle ground on issues that divide committee members. In other committees, members exhibit strong ideological and partisan sentiments. However, committee and subcommittee leaders prefer to find ways to overcome inherent ideological and partisan divisions so that they can build compromise solutions that will appeal to the broader membership of their house. The skill of committee leaders in assembling coalitions that produce legislation that can pass on the floor of their house is critically important. When committees are mired in disagreement, they lose power. Since jurisdictions overlap, other committees may take more initiative in their common policy area. Committee disagreements also enhance the power of the executive branch, especially in foreign and defense policy, where the president has considerable latitude.[42]

Oversight: Following Through on Legislation

It is often said in Washington that knowledge is power. For Congress to retain its influence over the programs it creates, it must be aware of how the agencies responsible for them are administering them. To that end, legislators and their committees engage in **oversight,** the process of reviewing agencies' operations to determine whether they are carrying out policies as Congress intended.

As the executive branch has grown and policies and programs have become increasingly complex, oversight has become more difficult. The sheer magnitude of executive branch operations is staggering. On a typical weekday, for example, agencies issue more than a hundred pages of new regulations. Even with the division of labor in the committee system, determining how good a job an agency is doing in implementing a program is no easy task.

Congress performs its oversight function in a number of different ways. The most visible is the hearing. Hearings may be part of a routine review or the by-product of information that reveals a major problem with a program or with an agency's administrative practices. Another way Congress keeps track of what departments and agencies are doing is by requesting reports on specific agency practices and operations. When President Clinton requested funds to help pay for reconstruction of Bosnia, the chair of the Appropriations Subcommittee on Foreign Operations was willing to grant the money only if a key condition was subsequently met by the administration. Disturbed that Iranian soldiers who had come to fight on behalf of the Muslim population of Bosnia were still there after the peace accord was in place, the subcommittee chair insisted that the appropriations bill be amended to pressure the administration to take action. President Clinton was to report back to the committee and the Senate to certify that the Iranians had left. No money could be spent on Bosnian reconstruction until the committee received the certification.[43]

Also, a good deal of congressional oversight takes place informally. There are ongoing contacts between committee and subcommittee leaders and agency administrators and between committee staffers and top agency staffers. Despite their partisan differences, the Clinton administration's treasury secretary, Robert Rubin, is always ready to talk to Republican House Ways and Means Chairman Bill Archer. Archer is not only powerful but also highly knowledgeable about economic affairs, and Rubin knows that cooperation is essential if the administration is going to get the type of legislation it wants out of the committee.

Congressional oversight of the executive branch has increased sharply since the early 1970s.[44] A primary reason for this increase was that Congress gave itself the staff necessary to watch over the growing federal government.[45] In addition to significantly expanding the staffs of individual legislators and of House and Senate committees, Congress enhanced its analytical capabilities by creating the Congressional Budget Office and by strengthening the Government Accounting Office (GAO) and the Congressional Research Service of the Library of Congress.

Oversight is often stereotyped as a process in which angry legislators bring some administrators before the hot lights and TV cameras at a hearing and proceed to dress them down for some recent scandal or mistake. Some of this does go on, but the pluralist side of Congress makes it likely that at least some members of a committee are advocates of the programs they oversee, because those programs serve their constituents back home. Members of the House and Senate Agriculture Committees, for example, both Democrats and Republicans, want farm programs to succeed. Thus, most oversight is aimed at trying to find ways to improve programs and is not directed at efforts to discredit them.[46]

Majoritarian and Pluralist Views of Committees

Government by committee vests a tremendous amount of power in the committees and subcommittees of Congress—and especially their leaders. This is particularly true of the House, which has more decentralized patterns of influence than the Senate and is more restrictive about letting members amend legislation on the floor. Committee members can bury a bill by not reporting it to the full House or Senate. The influence of committee members extends even further, to the floor debate. Many of them also make up the conference committees charged with developing compromise versions of bills.

In some ways, the committee system enhances the force of pluralism in American politics. Representatives and senators are elected by the voters in particular districts and states, and they tend to seek membership on the committees that make the decisions most important to their constituents. Members from farm areas, for example, want membership on the House and Senate Agriculture Committees. Westerners like to serve on the committees that deal with public lands and water rights. Urban liberals like the committees that handle social programs. As a result, committees with members who represent constituencies with an unusually strong interest in their policy area are predisposed to write legislation favorable to those constituencies.

The committees have a majoritarian aspect as well. Although some committees have an imbalance of legislators from particular kinds of districts or states, the memberships of most committees tend to resemble the general ideological profiles of the two parties' congressional contingents. For example, Republicans on individual House committees tend to vote like all Republicans in the House. Moreover, even if a committee's views are not in line with those of the full membership, it is constrained in the legislation it writes because bills cannot become law unless they are passed by the parent chamber and by the other house. Consequently, in formulating legislation, committees anticipate what other representatives and senators will accept. The parties within each chamber also have means of rewarding members who are the most loyal to party priorities. Party committees and the party leadership within each chamber make committee assignments and respond to requests for transfers from less prestigious to more prestigious committees. Those whose voting is the most in line with the party get better assignments.[47]

In the Gingrich-led House of Representatives, committee-based pluralism has been reduced. First, by violating the seniority norm in selecting chairs, Gingrich served notice on all chairs that they served at his pleasure. Second, on occasion Gingrich would publicly side with other members of a committee when the chair pursued policy goals he opposed. When Commerce Committee chair Thomas Bliley (R.-Va.) brought forth a telecommunications reform bill that Gingrich judged to be too friendly to AT&T and not friendly enough to the regional Bell phone companies, he was invited to the Speaker's office, where he found other members of his committee who stood with Gingrich on the issue. The rebuke to Bliley was not lost on other committee chairs.[48]

LEADERS AND FOLLOWERS IN CONGRESS

Above the committee chairs is another layer of authority in the organization of the House and Senate. The Democratic and Republican leaders in each house work to maximize the influence of their own party while trying to keep their chamber functioning smoothly and efficiently. The operation of the two houses is also influenced by the rules and norms that each chamber has developed over the years.

The Leadership Task

Each of the two parties elects leaders in each of the two houses. In the House of Representatives, the majority party's leader is the **Speaker of the**

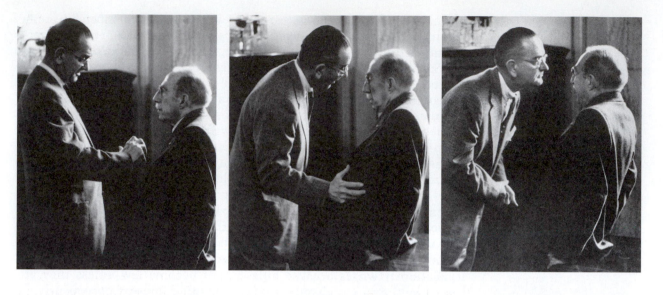

●●●●●●●●●●
The Johnson Treatment

When he was Senate majority leader in the 1950s, Lyndon Johnson was well known for his style of interaction with other members. In this unusual set of photographs, we see him applying the "Johnson treatment" to Democrat Theodore Francis Green of Rhode Island. Washington journalists Rowland Evans and Robert Novak offered the following description of the treatment: "Its tone could be supplication, accusation, cajolery, exuberance, scorn, tears, complaint, the hint of threat. It was all of these together. It ran the gamut of human emotions. Its velocity was breathtaking and it was all in one direction. Interjections from the target were rare. Johnson anticipated them before they could be spoken. He moved in close, his face a scant millimeter from his target, his eyes widening and narrowing, his eyebrows rising and falling. From his pockets poured clippings, memos, statistics. Mimicry, humor, and the genius of analogy made The Treatment an almost hypnotic experience and rendered the target stunned and helpless" (Rowland Evans and Robert Novak, Lyndon B. Johnson: The Exercise of Power. New York: New American Library, 1966, p. 104).

House, who, gavel in hand, chairs sessions from the ornate rostrum at the front of the chamber. The Speaker's counterpart in the opposing party is the minority leader. The Speaker is a constitutional officer, but the Constitution does not list the Speaker's duties. The minority leader is not mentioned in the Constitution, but that post has evolved into an important party position in the House.

The Constitution makes the vice president of the United States the president of the Senate. But in practice the vice president rarely visits the Senate chamber, unless there is a possibility of a tie vote, in which case he can break the tie. The *president pro tempore* (president "for the time"), elected by the majority party, is supposed to chair the Senate in the vice president's absence, but by custom this constitutional position is entirely honorary.

The real power in the Senate resides in the **majority leader.** As in the House, the top position in the opposing party is that of minority leader. Technically, the majority leader does not preside over Senate sessions (members rotate in the president pro tempore's chair), but he or she does schedule legislation, in consultation with the minority leader. More broadly, party leaders play a critical role in getting bills through Congress. The most significant function that leaders play is steering the bargaining and negotiating over the content of legislation. When an issue divides their party, their house, the two houses, or their house and the White House, the leaders must take the initiative to work out a compromise.

Day in, day out, much of what leaders do is to meet with other members of their house to try to strike deals that will yield a majority on the floor. It is often a matter of finding out whether one faction is willing to give up a policy preference in exchange for another concession. Beyond trying to engineer tradeoffs that will win votes, the party leaders must persuade others (often powerful committee chairs) that theirs is the best deal possible. After serving his first years as Senate majority leader, Bob Dole said he thought "majority pleader" was a more apt title.[49]

As recently as the 1950s, strong leaders dominated the legislative process. When he was Senate majority leader, Lyndon Johnson made full use of his intelligence, parliamentary skills, and forceful personality to direct the Senate. When he approached individual senators for one-on-one persuasion, "no one subjected to the 'Johnson treatment' ever forgot it."[50] In the contemporary Congress, however, it has been difficult for leaders to control rank-and-file members because they have independent electoral bases in their districts and states and receive the vast bulk of their campaign funds from nonparty sources. Contemporary party leaders are coalition builders, not autocrats. Newt Gingrich, however, is a throwback to the Johnson style of leadership. Gingrich won the fierce loyalty and support of rank-and-file Republicans by his hard work for the party, recruiting attractive Republican candidates for office, raising campaign money for them, and campaigning around the country for GOP hopefuls. His dynamic vision for the Republican platform in the 1994 congressional campaign, the "Contract with America," attracted support from others in the party for its daring, its strategic possibilities, and its commitment to principle. While Gingrich was successful in getting almost all of the Contract's provisions through the House, gaining acclaim as the most effective Speaker in recent history, he has not fared so well with the American people. As the public became more familiar with the Republican program in Congress, they became more critical of Gingrich and the party in general. Gingrich's personality grates on many, and his unyielding partisanship led some Americans to believe that he was contributing to gridlock in Washington. After a little over a year as Speaker, polls showed that Americans were overwhelmingly negative in their opinion of him.[51]

Rules of Procedure

The operations of the House and Senate are structured by both formal rules and informal norms of behavior. Rules in each chamber are mostly matters of parliamentary procedure. For example, they govern the scheduling of legislation, outlining when and how certain types of legislation can be brought to the floor. Rules also govern the introduction of floor amendments. In the House, amendments must be directly germane (relevant) to the bill at hand; in the Senate, except in certain, specified instances, amendments that are not germane to the bill at hand can be proposed.

As noted earlier, an important difference between the two chambers is the House's use of its Rules Committee to govern floor debate. Lacking a similar committee to act as a "traffic cop" for legislation approaching the floor, the Senate relies on unanimous consent agreements to set the starting time and length of debate. If one senator objects to such an agreement, it does not take effect. Senators do not routinely object to unanimous consent agreements, however, because they will need them when bills of their own await scheduling by the leadership. The rules facilitate cooperation among the competing interests and parties in each house so that legislation can be voted on. However, the rules are not neutral: they are a tool of the majority party and help it control the legislative process.[52]

If a senator wants to stop a bill badly enough, she or he may start a **filibuster** and try to talk the bill to death. By historical tradition, the Senate gives its members the right of unlimited debate. During a 1947 debate, Idaho Democrat Glen Taylor "spoke for $8\frac{1}{2}$ hours on fishing, baptism, Wall Street, and his children." The record for holding the floor belongs to Republican Senator Strom Thurmond of South Carolina, however, for a twenty-four-hour, eighteen-minute marathon.[53] In the House, no member is allowed to speak for more than an hour without unanimous consent.

After a 1917 filibuster by a small group of senators killed President Wilson's bill to arm merchant ships—a bill favored by a majority of senators—the Senate finally adopted **cloture,** a means of limiting debate. A petition signed by sixteen senators initiates a cloture vote. It now takes the votes of sixty senators to invoke cloture. Senators successfully invoked cloture when a filibuster by southern senators threatened passage of the far-reaching Civil Rights Act of 1964. There is considerable criticism of the filibuster, not simply because it can frustrate the majority in the Senate but also because it is often used against relatively minor legislation and gives a small group of committed senators far too much leverage on any single issue. Yet there is no significant movement within the Senate to reform the rules of debate.

Norms of Behavior

Both houses have codes of behavior that help keep them running. These codes are largely unwritten norms, although some have been formally adopted as rules. Members of Congress recognize that they must eliminate (or minimize) personal conflict, lest Congress dissolve into bickering factions unable to work together. One of the most celebrated norms is that members show respect for their colleagues in public deliberations. During floor debate, bitter opponents still refer to one another in such terms as "my good friend, the senior senator from . . ." or "my distinguished colleague."

Members of Congress are only human, of course, and tempers occasionally flare. For example, when Democrat Barney Frank of Massachusetts was angered by what he thought were unusually harsh charges against the Democratic party from Republican Robert Walker of Pennsylvania, Frank rose to ask the presiding officer if it was permissible to refer to Walker as a "crybaby." When he was informed that it was not, Frank sat down, having made his point without technically violating the House's code of behavior.[54] There are no firm measures of civility in Congress, but it seems to have declined in recent years.

Probably the most important norm of behavior in Congress is that individual members should be willing to bargain with one another. Policymaking is a process of give and take; it demands compromise. And the cost of not compromising is high. When President Bush nominated Clarence Thomas to the Supreme Court, Senator Warren Rudman (R.-N.H.), like many other senators, had serious reservations about Thomas's qualifications and character. When it was clear that the Thomas confirmation vote was going to be close, Rudman cut a deal: he'd vote for Thomas, but three of his long-time friends would be given federal judgeships.[55]

It is important to point out that members of Congress are not expected to violate their conscience on policy issues simply to strike a deal. They are expected, however, to listen to what others have to say and to make every effort to reach a reasonable compromise. Obviously, if they all stick rigidly to their own view, they will never agree on anything. Moreover, few policy matters are so clear-cut that compromise destroys one's position.

Some important norms have changed in recent years, most notably the notion that junior members of the House and Senate should serve apprenticeships and defer to their party and committee elders during their first couple of years in Congress. Aggressive, impatient, and ambitious junior legislators of both parties chafed at this norm, and it has weakened considerably in the past few decades. When seventy-three new Republicans entered the House after the GOP sweep in the 1994 elections, these freshmen served notice that they would use their size to change the way things were done in Congress. Said one GOP freshman, "We came here to be different and we are not going to be housebroken."[56]

These Republican freshmen did have an impact, most notably in pushing Speaker Gingrich to hold fast on principle in his negotiations with President Clinton. The freshmen thought that there is too much compromise in American politics and that political parties should stand firmly for what they believe in. Their strident, unbending conservatism sometimes pulled the GOP too far to the right, especially in battles over the budget and the environment. Over time, the freshmen legislators began to look a little bit more like all the other legislators, searching for projects for their home districts and denying that it was pork barrel. George Nethercutt (R.-Wash.) won election in 1994 by promising to put an end to politics as usual. Before his first year was out, he was trying to land a $400,000 wheat research facility for his district.[57] Still, these freshmen destroyed whatever was left of the apprenticeship norm. These days, rookie legislators are heard as well as seen.[58]

THE LEGISLATIVE ENVIRONMENT

After legislation emerges from committee, it is scheduled for floor debate. How do legislators make up their minds on how to vote? In this section, we examine the broader legislative environment that affects decision making in Congress. More specifically, we look at the influence on legislators of political parties, the president, constituents, and interest groups. The first two influences, parties and the president, push Congress toward majoritarian democracy. The other two, constituents and interest groups, are pluralist influences on congressional policymaking.

Political Parties

The national political parties might appear to have limited resources at their disposal to influence lawmakers. They do not control the nominations of House and Senate candidates. Candidates receive the bulk of their funds from individual contributors and political action committees, not from the national parties. Nevertheless, the parties are strong forces in the legislative process. The party leaders and various party committees within each house can help or hinder the efforts of rank-and-file legislators to get on the right committees, get their bills and amendments considered, and climb on the leadership ladder themselves. Moreover, as we saw earlier, the Democrats and Republicans on a given committee tend to reflect the views of the entire party membership in the chamber. Thus, party members on a committee tend to act as agents of their party as they search for solutions to policy problems.[59]

● ● ● ● ● ● ● ● ● ● ●

Rivals for Power

Democrats tried to make the 1996 congressional elections a referendum on the unpopular Speaker of the House, Newt Gingrich. The Democrats gained seats, but fell short of a majority, leaving Gingrich in power and Dick Gephardt as the Democrats' minority leader. Gingrich's strategy for the 105th Congress is to appear as cooperating with President Clinton to solve the nation's problems, while at the same time defining differences between the two parties that will work to the Republicans' advantage.

The most significant reason that the parties are important in Congress is, of course, that Democrats and Republicans have different ideological views. Both parties have diversity, but as Figure 11.4 illustrates, Democrats increasingly tend to vote one way and Republicans the other. The primary reason why partisanship has been rising is that the parties are becoming more homogeneous.[60] The liberal wing of the Republican party has practically disappeared, and the party is unified around a conservative agenda for America. Likewise, the conservative wing of the Democratic party has declined. The changes for the Democrats had their origins in the civil rights movement. When the national Democratic party embraced the civil rights movement in the 1960s, white southern conservatives began to gravitate to the Republicans. Southern Democratic legislators did their best to disassociate themselves from the national party and were generally able to retain their seats.[61] Over time, however, more and more southern House seats moved from the Democrats to the Republicans. As the parties have sorted themselves out, their ideological wingspans have shrunk.

Some applaud this rising partisanship, because it is a manifestation of majoritarianism. When congressional parties are more unified, it gives voters a stronger means of influencing public policy choices through their selection of representatives and senators. Others are skeptical of majoritarianism, believing that Congress is more productive and responsible when it relies on bipartisanship. In their view, parties that cooperate in searching for consensus will serve the nation better.

figure 11.4 ● **Rising Partisanship**

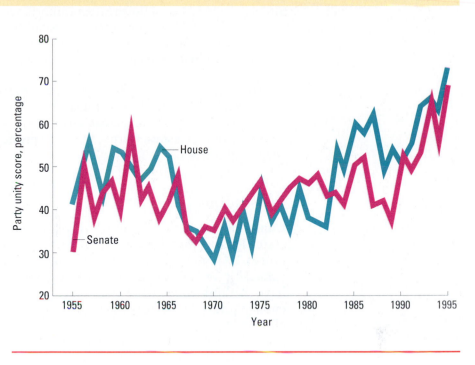

The lines in this graph show the percentages of representatives and senators who voted with their party on party unity votes. (Party unity votes are those in which a majority of one party votes one way and a majority of the other party votes the opposite way.) The rising percentage of party unity votes indicates that congressional parties are more frequently at odds with each other. In a true majoritarian system, parties vote against each other on all key issues.

Sources: Norman J. Ornstein, Thomas E. Mann, and Michael J. Malbin (eds.), *Vital Statistics on Congress, 1995–1996* (Washington, D.C.: Congressional Quarterly Press, 1994), p. 208; and Dan Carney, "As Hostilities Rage on the Hill, Partisan-Vote Rate Soars," *Congressional Quarterly Weekly Report*, 27 January 1996, p. 199.

The President

Unlike members of Congress, the president is elected by voters across the entire nation. The president has a better claim, then, to representing the nation than does any single member of Congress. But it can also be argued that Congress as a whole has a better claim than the president to representing the majority of voters. In fact, when Congress and the president differ, opinion surveys sometimes show that Congress's position on a given bill more closely resembles the majority view; at other times, these surveys show that the president's position accords with the majority. Nevertheless, presidents capitalize on their popular election and usually act as though they are speaking for the majority.

During the twentieth century, the public's expectations of what the president can accomplish in office have grown enormously. We now expect the president to be our chief legislator: to introduce legislation on major issues and to use his influence to push bills through Congress.[62] This is much different from our early history, when presidents felt constrained by the constitutional doctrine of separation of powers and had to have members of Congress work confidentially for them during legislative sessions.[63]

Today, the White House is openly involved not only in the writing of bills but also in their development as they wind their way through the legislative process. If the White House does not like a bill, it tries to work out a compromise with key legislators in order to have the legislation amended. On issues of the greatest importance, the president himself may meet with individual legislators to persuade them to vote a certain way. To monitor daily congressional activities and lobby for the administration's policies, hundreds of legislative liaison personnel work for the executive branch.

Although members of Congress grant presidents a leadership role in proposing legislation, they jealously guard the power of Congress to debate, shape, and pass or defeat any legislation the president proposes. Congress often clashes sharply with the president when his proposals are seen as ill-advised.

Constituents

Constituents are the people who live and vote in a legislator's district or state. Their opinions are a crucial part of the legislative decision-making process. As much as members of Congress want to please their party's leadership or the president by going along with their preferences, they have to think about what the voters back home want. If they displease enough people by the way they vote, they might lose their seat in the next election.

Constituents' influence contributes to pluralism, because the diversity of America is mirrored by the geographical basis of representation in the House and Senate. A representative from Los Angeles, for instance, may need to be sensitive to issues of particular concern to constituents whose backgrounds are Korean, Vietnamese, Hispanic, African American, or Jewish. A representative from Montana will have few such constituents but must pay particular attention to issues involving minerals and mining. A senator from Nebraska will give higher priority to agricultural issues than to urban issues. Conversely, a senator from New York will be hypersensitive to issues involving the cities. All these constituencies, enthusiastically represented by legislators who want to do a good job for the people back home, push and pull Congress in many different directions.

At all stages of the legislative process, the interests of the voters are on the minds of members of Congress. As they decide what to spend time on and how to vote, they weigh how different courses of action will affect their constituents' views of them.[64]

Interest Groups

As we pointed out in Chapter 10, interest groups are one way constituents influence Congress. Because they represent a vast array of vocational, regional, and ideological groupings within our population, interest groups exemplify pluralist politics. Interest groups press members of Congress to take a particular course of action, believing sincerely that what they prefer is also best for the country. Legislators, in turn, are attentive to interest groups, not because of an abstract commitment to pluralist politics but because these organizations represent citizens, some of whom live back home in their district or state. Lobbies are also sources of useful informa-

Senator Boxer and Staffers

The Congress of the United States is, in and of itself, a huge bureaucracy. There are just 535 members of the House and Senate, but there are over 17,000 staffers who work for them. Another 6,000 staffers work for the General Accounting Office and other congressional support agencies. Here, Senator Barbara Boxer (D.-Calif.) goes over some instructions with some of the many staffers who work for her.

tion and potentially of political support (and, in some instances, campaign contributions) for members of Congress.

Because the four external sources of influence on Congress—parties, the president, constituents, and interest groups—push legislators in both majoritarian and pluralist directions, Congress exhibits aspects of both pluralism and majoritarianism in its operations. We'll return to the conflict between pluralism and majoritarianism at the end of this chapter.

THE DILEMMA OF REPRESENTATION

When candidates for the House and Senate campaign for office, they routinely promise to work hard for their district's or state's interests. When they get to Washington, though, they all face a troubling dilemma: what their constituents want may not be what the people across the nation want.

Presidents and Shopping Bags

In doing the research for his book *Home Style,* political scientist Richard Fenno accompanied several representatives as they worked and interacted with constituents in their home district. On one of Fenno's trips, he was in an airport with a congressional aide, waiting for the representative's plane from Washington to land. When the representative arrived, he said, "I spent fifteen minutes on the telephone with the president this afternoon. He had a plaintive tone in his voice and he pleaded with me." His side of the issue had prevailed over the president's, and he was elated by the victory. When the three men reached the aide's car, the representative saw the back seat piled high with campaign paraphernalia: shopping bags printed with his name and picture. "Back to this again," he sighed.[65]

Every member of Congress lives in two worlds: the world of presidents and the world of personalized shopping bags. A typical week in the life of a representative means working in Washington, then boarding a plane and flying back to the home district. There the representative spends time meeting with individual constituents and talking to civic groups, church gatherings, business associations, labor unions, and the like. A survey of House members during a nonelection year showed that each made an average of thirty-five trips back to her or his district, spending an average of 138 days there.[66]

Members of Congress are often criticized for being out of touch with the people they are supposed to represent. This charge does not seem justified. Legislators work extraordinarily hard at keeping in touch with voters, at finding out what is on their constituents' minds. The problem is how to act on that knowledge.

Compare your views with those of your representatives in Congress.
`<pnl.politicsnow.com/interact/ctr/>`

Trustees or Delegates?

Are members of Congress bound to vote the way their constituents want them to vote, even if it means voting against their conscience? Some say no. They argue that legislators must be free to vote in line with what they think is best. This view has long been associated with the eighteenth-century English political philosopher Edmund Burke (1729–1797). Burke, who served in Parliament, told his constituents in Bristol that "you choose a member, indeed; but when you have chosen him, he is not a member of Bristol, but he is a member of *Parliament.*"[67] Burke reasoned that representatives are sent by their constituents to vote as they think best. As **trustees,** representatives are obligated to consider the views of their constituents, but they are not obligated to vote according to those views if they think they are misguided.

Others hold that legislators are duty-bound to represent the majority view of their constituents, that they are **delegates** with instructions from the people at home on how to vote on critical issues. And delegates, unlike trustees, must be prepared to vote against their own policy preferences. When the Senate considered a constitutional amendment to outlaw desecration of the American flag, Senator Bob Kerrey knew that most of his Nebraska constituents favored the amendment. Kerrey chose not to act as a delegate, though, and instead voted his conscience. He regarded the First Amendment's freedom of expression as paramount and told his Senate colleagues that flag burning "is not, in my judgment, a great threat to this country."[68]

Members of Congress are subject to two opposing forces, then. While the interests of their districts encourage them to act as delegates, their interpretation of the larger national interest calls on them to be trustees. Given these conflicting role definitions, it is not surprising that Congress is not clearly either a body of delegates or one of trustees. Research has shown, however, that members of Congress are more apt to take the delegate role on issues that are of great concern to their constituents.[69] But much of the time, what constituents really want is not clear. Many issues are not highly visible back home, they may cut across the constituency to affect it in different ways, or constituents only partially understand them. For such issues, no delegate position is obvious.

Ardent Advocate

The Congressional Black Caucus began in its earliest form in 1969 when nine African-American members banded together in an effort to influence the Democratic leadership in the House. Over the years it has been a tireless advocate on issues affecting African Americans. Donald Payne (D.-N.J.) ran twice unsuccessfully for the House before he was elected to Congress in 1988. He became chairman of the Congressional Black Caucus in 1994 and has worked especially hard with his colleagues to protect the government's affirmative action programs.

PLURALISM, MAJORITARIANISM, AND DEMOCRACY

The dilemma that individual members of Congress face in adopting the role of either delegate or trustee has broad implications for the way our country is governed. If legislators tend to act as delegates, congressional policymaking is more pluralistic, and policies reflect the bargaining that goes on among lawmakers who speak for different constituencies. If, instead, legislators tend to act as trustees and vote their consciences, policymaking becomes less tied to the narrower interests of districts and states. But even here there is no guarantee that congressional decision making reflects majority interests. True majoritarian legislatures require a paramount role for political parties.

We end this chapter with a short discussion of pluralism versus majoritarianism in Congress. But first, to establish a frame of reference, we need to take a quick look at a more majoritarian type of legislature—the parliament.

Parliamentary Government

In our system of government, the executive and legislative functions are divided between a president and a congress, each elected separately. Most other democracies—for example, Britain and Japan—have parliamentary governments. In a **parliamentary system,** the chief executive is the legislative leader whose party holds the most seats in the legislature after an election or whose party forms a major part of the ruling coalition. For instance, in Great Britain, voters do not cast a ballot for prime minister. They vote only for their member of Parliament and thus must influence the choice of prime minister indirectly, by voting for the party they favor in the local district election. Parties are unified, and in Parliament legislators vote for their party's position, giving voters a strong and direct means of influencing public policy.

The British Parliament on the WWW.

In a parliamentary system, government power is highly concentrated in the legislature, because the leader of the majority party is also the head of the government. Moreover, parliamentary legislatures are usually composed of only one house or have a second chamber that is much weaker than the other. (In the British Parliament, the House of Commons makes the decisions of government; the other chamber, the House of Lords, is largely an honorary debating club for distinguished members of society.) And parliamentary governments usually do not have a court that can invalidate acts of the parliament. Under such a system, the government is in the hands of the party that controls the parliament. With no separation of government powers, checks on government action are few. Parliamentary systems can differ in many respects, as described in Compared with What? 11.1, but overall these governments fit the majoritarian model of democracy to a much greater extent than a separation-of-powers system.

Pluralism Versus Majoritarianism in Congress

The U.S. Congress is often criticized for being too pluralist and not majoritarian enough. The federal budget deficit, discussed at the beginning of this chapter, provides a case in point. Americans are deeply concerned about the big deficits that have plagued our national budgets in recent years. And both Democrats and Republicans in Congress repeatedly call for reductions in those deficits. But when spending bills come before Congress, legislators' concern turns to what the bills will or will not do for their district or state. Appropriations bills usually include pork barrel projects that benefit specific districts or states and further add to the deficit. In a recent transportation bill, Democrat Nita Lowey got a $4.5 million bus facility for Westchester County in New York. Her Republican colleague from New York, James Walsh, got $7 million for buses and transportation projects for Syracuse. One legislator defended the money earmarked for his district by declaring, "This project is not pork. This project is a vital infrastructure necessity."[70]

Projects such as these get into the budget through bargaining among members; as we saw earlier in this chapter, congressional norms encourage it. Members of Congress try to win projects and programs that will benefit their constituents and thus help them at election time. To win approval of such projects, members must be willing to vote for other legislators' projects in turn. Such a system obviously promotes pluralism (and spending).

Although legislators have taken significant steps to reduce the national deficit, critics contend that Congress will have to largely abandon pluralism if it is ever to balance the budget. Members will have to forgo bus subsidies and the like for their districts if the country is going to continue making progress against the deficit. Indeed, a primary motivation for the line item veto was to give the president a tool to strip such projects out of the budget. A psychologist might say it was a congressional scream for help: "Stop us before we fund bus projects again!" Yet, those who favor pluralism are quick to point out Congress's merits. Many different constituencies are well served by an appropriations process that allows for

● **compared with what?**

11.1 Women in Legislatures

The percentage of women in the national legislature differs considerably from one country to another. Among the Western democracies, some countries have the highest percentage of women of all legislatures, but there is substantial variation here, too. While Sweden has over 40 percent women in its legislature, the United States has only 11 percent and Japan less than 3 percent. The number of women does not seem to be a function of the structure of the legislature or the party system in these countries. Countries that are not democracies vary considerably as well. Clearly, each society's cultural expectations about the role of women are of paramount importance. The Scandinavian countries appear to be the most open to the full participation of women in politics.

Source: Women in Parliaments, 1945–1995 (Geneva, Switzerland: Inter-Parliamentary Union, 1995), pp. 41–44.

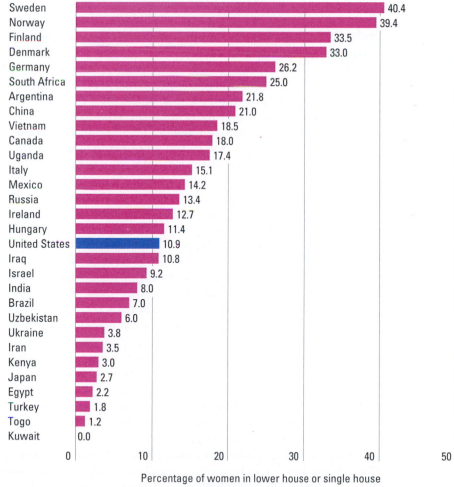

Percentage of women in lower house or single house
Selected countries, 1995

pluralism. For the low-income residents of Syracuse and Westchester County, bus service is vital to their livelihood. Middle-class people drive their cars to work and couldn't care less about their local bus system. But dishwashers, maids, and janitors pay taxes to fund the government, too, and they have a right to expect the government to care about the problems they have in getting to work.

Proponents of pluralism also argue that the makeup of Congress generally reflects that of the nation, that different members of Congress represent farm areas, oil and gas areas, low-income inner cities, industrial areas, and so on. They point out that America itself is pluralistic, with a rich diversity of economic, social, religious, and racial groups, and that even if our own representatives and senators don't represent our particular viewpoint, it's likely that someone in Congress does.[71]

The House Republicans' push to enact the Contract with America represented a concerted effort to move the national government toward a more majoritarian system. By presenting the voters in 1994 with a platform of policies they promised to pass, GOP House candidates were emulating candidates running for Parliament in a responsible party system (recall Chapter 8). Majoritarian parties and legislatures give voters more direct control over public policy by allowing citizens a clear means of expressing their preference and of mandating that the majority legislators carry out their platform.

With the 104th Congress (1995–1996) now over, how might this bold experiment be evaluated? What was most impressive was the exceptional unity of House Republicans in voting for the bills that were part of the Contract with America. Almost all of the bills passed with relatively few defections in the Republican ranks. The Republican House candidates kept the promise they made in the 1994 campaign that they would pass the Contract if they won a majority. Yet a good portion of the Contract, including some of its most visible provisions—a balanced budget amendment, term limits for members of Congress, and a $500-per-child tax credit and capital gains tax cut—never became law (see Table 11.1). Although Republicans could blame Democrat Bill Clinton for vetoing some important parts of the Contract, one of the problems was the Republican majority in the Senate. A number of GOP senators were only nominally committed to the Contract, which was developed by Newt Gingrich, and voted against some of the bills when they reached the Senate. Although they gave the Republicans a landslide victory in 1994, voters were not of one mind on the Contract. As noted in Chapter 9, most voters did not actually hear of the Contract during the election campaign. On some items the public actually turned against the Contract (on regulatory reform, for example, because the proposed legislation would have weakened environmental protections).

While they seemingly embraced majoritarianism with the Contract with America, the Republicans of the 104th Congress did not completely abandon pluralism. Business groups had extraordinary access to GOP leaders and committee chairs, and many bills were put forward to benefit various industries.[72] Majoritarian political systems do not eliminate all traces of interest group politics from the legislative process; nevertheless, interest groups played far too important a role in the 104th Congress for it to be judged an example of majoritarian democracy. Although the Contract

table
11.1 🍎 A Contract Fulfilled?

The Republicans' Contract with America "was born on a snowy weekend in February 1994. . . . At a conference of House Republicans in Salisbury, Maryland, a direction was set for making sure citizens could clearly understand what the Republican party stood for and meant to deliver if ever given a chance to control the federal legislative process."* House Republicans delivered on their promise, but many of the Contract's proposals never became law.

Policy Proposal	Outcome
Apply labor laws to Congress	Passed and signed into law
Prohibit unfunded mandates	Passed and signed into law
Balanced Budget Amendment	Passed House but failed by a single vote in the Senate
Line item veto	Passed and signed into law
Violent crime	
Truth in sentencing	Passed House, died in the Senate; also added to an appropriations bill that was vetoed
Relax exclusionary rule	Passed House but died in the Senate
Welfare reform	Passed and signed into law
Tax reform	
$500-a-child tax credit	Did not become law
Capital gains tax cut	Did not become law
Family Reinforcement Act	
Tax credits for adoption, senior care	Passed and signed into law
National defense	
Restrict U.S. troops under U.N. flag	Passed House but died in the Senate
Increase defense spending	Passed and signed into law
Reduce Soc. Sec. earnings limit	Passed and signed into law
Roll back regulations	Efforts to weaken Superfund and Clean Water Act failed to pass
Legal reform	
Securities litigation	Clinton veto overturned by Congress
Product liability	Passed by Congress but vetoed by Clinton
Term limits	Defeated in the House

**Contract with America* (New York: Times Books, 1994), p. 4.

with America was an important step in that direction, a true majoritarian democracy would require that both parties put forward platforms they are committed to carrying out, that voters understand what the parties have pledged to do and then vote on that basis, and that the influence of interest groups on policy formulation in Congress be modest. Although increased party unity in legislators' voting and the Contract with America have both enhanced majoritarianism in Congress, the House and the Senate still remain more pluralistic than majoritarian in nature.

SUMMARY

Congress writes the laws of the land and attempts to oversee their implementation. It helps to educate us about new issues as they appear on the political agenda. Most important, members of Congress represent us, working to see to it that interests from home and from around the country are heard throughout the policymaking process.

We count on Congress to do so much that criticism about how well it does some things is inevitable. However, certain strengths are clear. The committee system fosters expertise; representatives and senators who know the most about particular issues have the most influence over them. And the structure of our electoral system keeps legislators in close touch with their constituents.

Bargaining and compromise play important roles in the congressional policymaking process. Some find this disquieting. They want less deal making and more adherence to principle. This thinking is in line with the desire for a more majoritarian democracy. Others defend the current system, arguing that the United States is a large, complex nation, and the policies that govern it should be developed through bargaining among various interests.

There is no clear-cut answer to whether a majoritarian or a pluralist legislative system provides better representation for voters. Our system is a mix of pluralism and majoritarianism. It serves minority interests that might otherwise be neglected or even harmed by an unthinking or uncaring majority. At the same time, congressional parties work to represent the broader interests of the American people.

Key Terms

reapportionment	racial gerrymandering	select committee	filibuster
impeachment	veto	conference committee	cloture
incumbent	pocket veto	seniority	constituents
gerrymandering	line item veto	oversight	trustee
casework	standing committee	Speaker of the House	delegate
descriptive representation	joint committee	majority leader	parliamentary system

Selected Readings

Fenno, Richard F., Jr. *Home Style*. Boston: Little, Brown, 1978. A classic analysis of how House members interact with constituents during visits to their home districts.

Glaser, James. *Race, Campaign Politics, and the Realignment in the South*. New Haven, Conn.: Yale University Press, 1996. This examination of congressional races in the South looks at how Democratic candidates try to build biracial coalitions.

Herrnson, Paul S. *Congressional Elections*. Washington, D.C.: Congressional Quarterly Press, 1995. Herrnson's study is a comprehensive look at congressional candidates and the electorate.

Lindsay, James M. *Congress and the Politics of U.S. Foreign Policy*. Baltimore: Johns Hopkins University Press, 1994. A careful, measured assessment of the influence of Congress in foreign policymaking.

Swain, Carol M. *Black Faces, Black Interests*. Cambridge, Mass.: Harvard University Press, 1993. Swain looks at a variety of districts that have elected African American representatives and outlines a strategy for electing more that goes beyond racial gerrymandering.

Thomas, Sue. *How Women Legislate*. New York: Oxford University Press, 1994. Using surveys of state legislators, the author details how women are different from men in the way they do their jobs.

World Wide Web Resources

Project VoteSmart's Congressional Information Center. Keep track of your member of Congress. See how members voted on bills, get biographical information, access the Congressional Record, and follow links to other congressional information services. Also find the status of current legislation and see how members are evaluated by interest groups. Use the "zipper" to find your member of Congress by zip code and to send "netgrams."
`<www.vote-smart.org/congress/congress.html>`

Library of Congress. View current library exhibitions and retrieve current news and events. A highlight of this home page is the "American Memory," which contains historical collections (viewable on the net) for the "National Digital Library."
`<www.loc.gov>`

Thomas. The congressional service of the Library of Congress. Read historical documents such as the *Federalist* papers and 274 other documents relating to the work of Congress and the drafting and ratification of the Constitution. Many of these documents date back to 1774. Track congressional floor activity and retrieve committee information.
`<www.thomas.loc.gov>`

House of Representatives. Retrieve information on current and recent legislation and information on members, committees, and other congressional organizations.
`<www.house.gov>`

Senate. Visitors can get information from and about Senate members, search the member directory, read about Senate history, and search a glossary of Senate terms.
`<www.senate.gov>`

The Presidency

BILL CLINTON PROMISED to hit the ground running when he came to Washington. He had ambitious plans to reorient the country's priorities—"putting people first," as he had stressed in his campaign. His strategy for reviving the lagging economy was to create an investment program that would improve the nation's infrastructure, increase educational opportunities, and enhance training for those whose skills were not adequate for the demands of today's job market.

Clinton's first step was a modest $16.3 billion economic stimulus package, introduced less than a month after he took office. The legislation was intended to give a jump start to an economy that had performed poorly for the previous three years. The increased spending was not concentrated in any one area but had additional money for a variety of programs, including summer youth employment, AIDS care, child immunization, highway construction, Pell grants for college students, water projects, and Head Start. The biggest component of the package was simply a continuation of unemployment compensation.

Republicans in Congress were hostile to the plan. They wondered why Clinton was proposing more spending when he was about to introduce a deficit reduction package. Less partisan critics suggested that, given the aggregate size of our economy, $16.3 billion wasn't enough to get the economy moving. Democrats countered that the bill would directly create 200,000 jobs and that another 150,000 jobs would result from the increased economic activity generated by the new spending. For the unemployed, this proposal hardly represented frivolous spending. Moreover, the Democrats, with their traditional commitment to equality and social justice, felt that they needed to begin reversing the twelve years of Reagan-Bush cutbacks in social programs.

The big Democratic majority in the House easily approved the bill in mid-March. In the Senate, Appropriations Committee chair Robert Byrd, a Democrat, was so eager to demonstrate his support to the president that he devised a complicated legislative strategy to get the bill through without any Republican amendments. Byrd's actions incensed the Republicans, who began a filibuster. The Democrats needed three Republican votes to break the filibuster, but the Republicans held firm in their unanimous opposition to the bill. Although polls showed that Americans supported the stimulus package, this public sentiment did not appear to be intensely held, and the Republicans weren't worried about an adverse public reaction to their efforts to scuttle the bill. Clinton resisted compromise at first,

Bridge for Sale

When he gave his acceptance speech at the 1996 Democratic convention, President Bill Clinton gave an optimistic assessment of the nation's health, but was generally cautious in outlining plans for a second term. Using an evocative phrase, he said repeatedly that his goal was to "build a bridge to the twenty-first century." Clinton wanted to position the Democrats as the party of the future, while drawing a subtle contrast between himself and a seventy-three-year-old opponent whom he wanted to portray as the candidate of a generation whose time had passed.

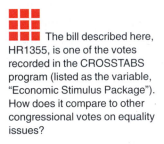

The bill described here, HR1355, is one of the votes recorded in the CROSSTABS program (listed as the variable, "Economic Stimulus Package"). How does it compare to other congressional votes on equality issues?

and by the time he reluctantly realized that the bill could not get through without concessions to the Republicans, Senate minority leader Bob Dole knew that his party had beaten the president. At the end of April, Clinton finally gave up on the economic stimulus package; Congress later enacted a narrowly focused bill extending unemployment benefits.

The new president had gone eyeball to eyeball with Bob Dole and suffered a humiliating defeat. It was not merely that Clinton had been sabotaged by Byrd, who had been too eager to help; Clinton himself bore much of the responsibility for the bill's failure. He never convinced the American people that the bill was vital. (The economy did, in fact, sharply improve in the months to come, despite the lack of a stimulus package.) The Republicans had made Clinton understand that without bipartisan support, he wouldn't be able to get much through Congress. It was a cruel lesson for the new president. Rather than hitting the ground running, Bill Clinton had simply hit the ground.[1]

As we analyze the various facets of the presidency, bear in mind one recurring question: is the presidency primarily an instrument of pluralist democracy, serving small but vocal constituencies, or does the office promote majoritarian democracy by responding primarily to public opinion? In the case we have just discussed, President Clinton thought that both pluralist and majoritarian politics would work in his favor. In fact, neither did. That is, he thought the public would back him, but it was apathetic, and he thought that interest groups benefiting from the bill would help him get the legislation through, but these organizations had little influence with the Republicans. In addition to examining the majoritarian and pluralist sides of presidential politics, we focus in this chapter on a number of other important questions. What are the powers of the presidency?

How is the president's advisory system organized? How does the separation of powers between the executive and legislative branches affect public policymaking? Finally, what are the particular issues and problems that presidents face in foreign affairs?

THE CONSTITUTIONAL BASIS OF PRESIDENTIAL POWER

When the presidency was created, the colonies had just fought a war of independence; their reaction to British domination had focused on the autocratic rule of King George III. Thus, the delegates to the Constitutional Convention were extremely wary of unchecked power and were determined not to create an all-powerful, dictatorial presidency.

The delegates' fear of a powerful presidency was counterbalanced by their desire for strong leadership. The Articles of Confederation—which did not provide for a single head of state—had failed to bind the states together into a unified nation (see Chapter 3). In addition, the governors of the individual states had generally proved to be inadequate leaders, because they had few formal powers. The new nation was conspicuously weak; its congress had no power to compel the states to obey its legislation. The delegates knew they had to create some type of effective executive office. Their task was to provide for national leadership without allowing opportunity for tyranny.

A history of the presidency. <www.grolier.com/ presidents/preshome.html>

Initial Conceptions of the Presidency

Debates about the nature of the office began. Should there be one president or a presidential council or committee? Should the president be chosen by Congress and remain largely subservient to that body? The delegates gave initial approval to a plan that called for a single executive, chosen by Congress for a seven-year term and ineligible for reelection.[2] But some delegates continued to argue for a strong president who would be elected independent of the legislative branch.

The final structure of the presidency reflected the "checks and balances" philosophy that had shaped the entire Constitution. In the minds of the delegates, they had imposed important limits on the presidency through the powers specifically delegated to Congress and the courts. Those counterbalancing powers would act as checks, or controls, on presidents who might try to expand the office beyond its proper bounds.

The Powers of the President

The requirements for the presidency are set forth in Article II of the Constitution: the president must be a U.S.-born citizen, at least thirty-five years old, who has lived in the United States for a minimum of fourteen years. Article II also sets forth the responsibilities of presidents. In view of the importance of the office, the constitutional description of the president's duties is surprisingly brief and vague. This vagueness has led to repeated conflict about the limits of presidential power.

The delegates undoubtedly had many reasons for the lack of precision in Article II. One likely explanation was the difficulty of providing and at the same time limiting presidential power. Furthermore, the framers of the

● ● ● ● ● ● ● ● ● ●

We've Come to Praise Nixon and to Bury Him

Richard Nixon, who served as president between 1969 and 1974, died on April 22, 1994, and was buried a few days later with all living former presidents and their spouses in attendance. President Clinton, who had secretly consulted with Nixon after taking office, gave a generous eulogy and, in an allusion to Watergate, spoke to Nixon's place in history by suggesting that "the day of judging President Nixon on anything less than his entire life and career come to a close." Speaking with great emotion in his eulogy, Senator Robert Dole summed up Nixon this way: "Strong, brave, unafraid of controversy, unyielding in his convictions, living every day of his life to the hilt, the largest figure of our time—that was Richard Nixon."

Constitution had no model—no existing presidency—on which to base their description of the office. And, ironically, their description of the presidency might have been more precise if they had had less confidence in George Washington, the obvious choice for the first president. According to one account of the Constitutional Convention, "when Dr. Franklin predicted on June 4 that 'the first man put at the helm will be a good one,' every delegate knew perfectly well who that first good man would be."[3] The delegates had great trust in Washington; they did not fear that he would try to misuse the office.

The major duties and powers that the delegates listed for Washington and his successors can be summarized as follows:

- *Serve as administrative head of the nation.* The Constitution gives little guidance on the president's administrative duties. It states merely that "the executive Power shall be vested in a President of the United States of America" and that "he shall take Care that the Laws be faithfully executed." These imprecise directives have been interpreted to mean that the president is to supervise and offer leadership to various departments, agencies, and programs created by Congress. In practice, a chief executive spends much more time making policy decisions for his cabinet departments and agencies than enforcing existing policies.

- *Act as commander in chief of the military.* In essence, the Constitution names the president as the highest-ranking officer in the armed forces. But it gives Congress the power to declare war. The framers no doubt intended Congress to control the president's military power; nevertheless, presidents have initiated military action without the approval of Congress.[4] The entire Vietnam War was fought without a congressional declaration of war.

- *Convene Congress.* The president can call Congress into special session on "extraordinary Occasions," although this has rarely been done. He must also periodically inform Congress of "the State of the Union."

- *Veto legislation.* The president can **veto** (disapprove) any bill or resolution enacted by Congress, with the exception of joint resolutions that propose constitutional amendments. Congress can override a presidential veto with a two-thirds vote in each house.

- *Appoint various officials.* The president has the authority to appoint federal court judges, ambassadors, cabinet members, other key policymakers, and many lesser officials. Many appointments are subject to Senate confirmation.

- *Make treaties.* With the "Advice and Consent" of at least two-thirds of those senators voting at the time, the president can make treaties with foreign powers. The president is also to "receive Ambassadors," a phrase that presidents have interpreted to mean the right to formally recognize other nations.

- *Grant pardons.* The president can grant pardons to individuals who have committed "Offenses against the United States, except in Cases of Impeachment."

THE EXPANSION OF PRESIDENTIAL POWER

The framers' limited conception of the president's role has given way to a considerably more powerful interpretation. In this section, we look beyond the presidential responsibilities explicitly listed in the Constitution and examine the additional sources of power that presidents have used to expand the authority of the office. First, we look at the claims that presidents make about "inherent" powers implicit in the Constitution. Second, we turn to congressional grants of power to the executive branch. Third, we discuss the influence that comes from a president's political skills. Finally, we analyze how a president's popular support affects his political power.

The Inherent Powers

Several presidents have expanded the power of the office by taking actions that exceeded commonly held notions of the president's proper authority. These men justified what they had done by saying that their actions fell within the **inherent powers** of the presidency. From this broad perspective, presidential power derives not only from those duties clearly outlined in Article II but also from inferences that may be drawn from the Constitution.

When a president claims a power that has not been considered part of the chief executive's authority, he forces Congress and the courts to either acquiesce to his claim or restrict it. When presidents succeed in claiming a new power, they leave to their successors the legacy of a permanent expansion of presidential authority. Claims of inherent powers often come at critical points in the nation's history. During the Civil War, for example, Abraham Lincoln issued a number of orders that exceeded the accepted limits of presidential authority. One order increased the size of the armed forces well beyond the congressionally mandated ceiling, although the Constitution gives only Congress the power "to raise and support Armies." And because military expenditures would then have exceeded military appropriations, Lincoln clearly also acted to usurp the taxing and spending powers constitutionally conferred on Congress. In another order, Lincoln instituted a blockade of Southern ports, thereby committing acts of war against the Confederacy without the approval of Congress.

Lincoln said the urgent nature of the South's challenge to the Union forced him to act without waiting for congressional approval. His rationale was simple: "Was it possible to lose the nation and yet preserve the Constitution?"[5] In other words, Lincoln circumvented the Constitution in order to save the nation. Subsequently, Congress and the Supreme Court approved Lincoln's actions. That approval gave added legitimacy to the theory of inherent powers—a theory that over time has transformed the presidency.

Any president who lays claim to new authority runs the risk of being rebuffed by Congress or the courts and suffering political damage. After Andrew Jackson vetoed a bill reauthorizing a national bank, for example, he ordered William Duane, his secretary of the treasury, to withdraw all federal deposits and place them in state banks. Duane refused, claiming that he was under the supervision of both Congress and the executive branch; Jackson responded by firing him. The president's action angered many members of Congress, who believed that Jackson had overstepped his constitutional bounds; the Constitution does not actually state that a president may remove his cabinet secretaries. Although that prerogative is now taken for granted, Jackson's presidency was weakened by the controversy. His censure by the Senate was a slap in the face, and he was denounced even by members of his own party. It took many years for the president's right to remove cabinet officers to become widely accepted.[6]

Congressional Delegation of Power

Presidential power grows when presidents successfully challenge Congress, but in many instances Congress willingly delegates power to the executive branch. As the American public pressures the national government to solve various problems, Congress, through a process called **delegation of powers,** gives the executive branch more responsibility to administer programs that address those problems. One example of delegation of congressional power occurred in the 1930s, during the Great Depression, when Congress gave Franklin Roosevelt's administration wide latitude to do what it thought was necessary to solve the nation's economic ills.

When Congress concludes that the government needs flexibility in its approach to a problem, the president is often given great freedom in how or when to implement policies. Richard Nixon was given discretionary authority to impose a freeze on wages and prices in an effort to combat escalating inflation. If Congress had been forced to debate the timing of the freeze, merchants and manufacturers would surely have raised their prices in anticipation of the event. Instead, Nixon was able to act suddenly, imposing the freeze without warning. (We discuss congressional delegation of authority to the executive branch in more detail in Chapter 13.)

However, at other times Congress believes that too much power has accumulated in the executive branch, and it enacts legislation to reassert congressional authority. During the 1970s, many representatives and senators agreed that Congress's role in the American political system was declining, that presidents were exercising power that rightfully belonged to the legislative branch. The most notable reaction was the enactment of the War Powers Resolution (1973), which was directed at ending the president's ability to pursue armed conflict without explicit congressional approval.

The President's Power to Persuade

A president's influence in office comes not only from his assigned responsibilities but also from his political skills and from how effectively he uses the resources of his office. A classic analysis of the use of presidential resources is offered by Richard Neustadt in his book *Presidential Power.* Neustadt develops a model of how presidents gain, lose, or maintain their influence. His initial premise is simple enough: "Presidential power is the power to persuade."[7] Presidents, for all their resources—a skilled staff, extensive media coverage of presidential actions, the great respect the country holds for the office—must depend on others' cooperation to get things done. Harry Truman echoed Neustadt's premise when he said, "I sit here all day trying to persuade people to do the things they ought to have sense enough to do without my persuading them. . . . That's all the powers of the President amount to."[8]

Ability in bargaining, dealing with adversaries, and choosing priorities, according to Neustadt, separates above-average presidents from mediocre ones. A president must make wise choices about which policies to push and which to put aside until he can find more support. He must decide when to accept compromise and when to stand on principle. He must know when to go public and when to work behind the scenes.

Often, a president faces a dilemma in which all the alternatives carry some risk. After Dwight Eisenhower took office in 1953, he had to decide how to deal with Joseph McCarthy, the Republican senator from Wisconsin who had been largely responsible for creating national hysteria over allegations about communists in government. McCarthy had made many wild, reckless charges, damaging a number of innocent people's careers by accusing them of communist sympathies. Many people expected Eisenhower to control McCarthy—not only because he was president but also because he was a fellow Republican. Yet Eisenhower, worrying about his own popularity, chose not to confront him. He used a "hidden hand" strategy, working behind the scenes to weaken McCarthy. Politically, Eisenhower seems to have made the right choice; McCarthy soon discredited himself.[9] However, Eisenhower's performance can be criticized as weak moral leadership. If he had publicly denounced the senator, he might have ended the McCarthy witch hunt sooner.

A president's political skills can be important in affecting outcomes in Congress. The chief executive cannot intervene in every legislative struggle. He must choose his battles carefully, then try to use the force of his personality and the prestige of his office to forge an agreement among differing factions. In terms of getting members to vote a certain way, presidential influence is best described as taking place "at the margins." That is, presidents do not have the power to consistently move large numbers of votes one way or the other. They can, however, affect some votes—perhaps enough to affect the outcome of a closely fought piece of legislation.[10]

Neustadt stresses that a president's influence is related to his professional reputation and prestige. When a president pushes hard for a bill that Congress eventually defeats or emasculates, the president's reputation is hurt. The public perceives him as weak or as showing poor judgment, and Congress becomes even less likely to cooperate with him in the future. President Clinton was clearly damaged by his failure to gain passage of his ambitious plan to reform the nation's health care system. Yet presidents cannot easily avoid controversial bills, especially those meant to deliver on campaign promises. Clinton took risks with his strong backing for controversial issues such as the North American Free Trade Agreement and handgun control legislation, and he gained considerable respect for his efforts when these bills were enacted. One scholar describes the dilemma facing presidents this way: "If they risk big, they may gain big, but they are more likely to fail big. If they choose safe strategies, there is no doubt that they will be criticized for not seeking greater yields."[11]

The President and the Public

Track presidential popularity.
`<www.gallup.com>`

Neustadt's analysis suggests that a popular president is more persuasive than an unpopular one. A popular president has more power to persuade, because he can use his public support as a resource in the bargaining process.[12] Members of Congress who know that the president is highly popular back home have more incentive to cooperate with the administration. If the president and his aides know that a member of Congress does not want to be seen as hostile to the president, they can apply more leverage to achieve a favorable compromise in a legislative struggle.

A familiar aspect of the modern presidency is the effort presidents devote to mobilizing public support for their programs. A president uses televised addresses (and the media coverage surrounding them), remarks to reporters, and public appearances to speak directly to the American people and convince them of the wisdom of his policies.

In recent years, presidents have increased their direct communication with the American people; as Figure 12.1 illustrates, the number of public presidential appearances has grown sharply since World War II. Obviously, modern technology has contributed to this growth. Nonetheless, the increase in public appearances and speeches represents something more than increased visibility for the president and his views. The power of the presidency also has changed fundamentally. The decline of party and congressional leadership has hastened the rise of the public president; at the same time, the president's direct communication with the American people has made it more difficult for political parties and Congress to reinvigorate themselves.[13]

Presidential popularity is typically at its highest during a president's first year in office. This "honeymoon period" affords the president a particularly good opportunity to use public support to get some of his programs through Congress.[14] When Ronald Reagan made a televised appeal for support for a legislative proposal during his first year in office, some members of Congress received calls and letters running ten to one in favor of the president. At the beginning of his second term, however, congressional offices typically received an equal number of negative and positive responses after a Reagan appeal.[15] Perhaps the positions he advocated were

figure

12.1   ● **Going Public**

This graph depicts the average number of public appearances made in a year by presidents from 1929 to 1990. ⃰ *The increase in presidential public appearances is driven in large part by the efforts of presidents to rally public support for their proposals and policies.*

⃰ *Only the first three years of their first terms were examined; the fourth year was not tabulated in order to exclude appearances arranged with an eye toward an upcoming election. Gerald Ford's term is also excluded for this reason. The Bush figures are for his first two years only.*

Source: Samuel Kernell, *Going Public,* 2nd ed. (Washington, D.C.: Congressional Quarterly Press, 1993), p. 102. Copyright © 1993 by Congressional Quarterly Press. Used with permission.

less attractive, but it was also clear that the public viewed Reagan with a more skeptical eye than it had four years earlier.

Several factors generally explain the rise and fall in presidential popularity. First, public approval of the job done by a president is affected by economic conditions, such as inflation and unemployment, as Figure 12.2 shows. Voters hold presidents responsible for the state of the economy, although much of what happens in the economy is beyond presidents' control. Second, a president is affected by unanticipated events of all types that occur during his administration.[16] When American embassy personnel were taken hostage in Teheran by militant anti-American Iranians, Jimmy Carter's popularity soared. This "rally 'round the flag" support for the president eventually gave way to frustration with his inability to gain the hostages' release, and Carter's popularity plummeted. The third factor

figure

12.2

● **Bad Economy, Bad Poll Ratings**

As the public's perception of economic conditions declined during the Bush years, people's confidence in the president's handling of the economy declined in tandem. Notice that confidence in Congress's performance took a similar tumble. Yet in the 1992 elections, most congressional incumbents were re-elected, although President Bush was voted out of office. As we discussed in Chapter 11, people judge the Congress as a whole much differently than they judge their own members of the House and Senate.

Source: Gary C. Jacobson, "Congress: Unusual Year, Unusual Election," in *The Elections of 1992*, Michael Nelson, ed. (Washington, D.C.: Congressional Quarterly Press, 1993), p. 163. Copyright © 1993 by Congressional Quarterly Press. Used with permission.

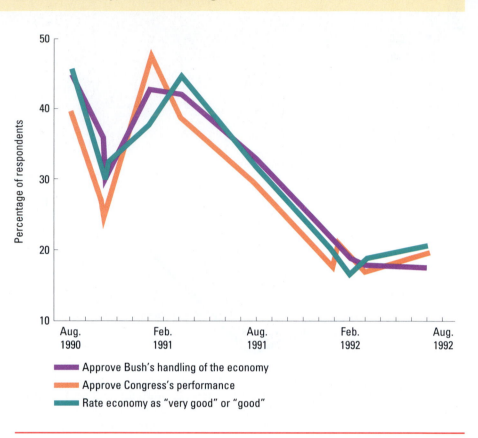

that affects presidential popularity is American involvement in a war. Lyndon Johnson, for example, suffered a loss of popularity during his escalation of the American effort in Vietnam.[17]

Presidents closely monitor their popularity, because it is widely regarded as a basic report card on how well they are performing their duties. First-term presidents are especially concerned about their popularity, because they are worried about their reelection prospects. Carter, Ford, and Bush, all unpopular at the time of the election, were defeated in their efforts to win another term. A president's popularity can change dramatically during the course of a term. In the aftermath of the Gulf War, roughly nine in ten Americans approved of President Bush's performance in office. A month before the 1992 election, however, fewer than four in ten Americans approved of Bush.

The strategy of leading by courting public opinion has considerable risks. It is not easy to move public opinion, and presidents who plan to use it as leverage in dealing with Congress are left highly vulnerable if public support for their position does not materialize. When Bill Clinton came into office, he was strongly predisposed toward governing by leading public opinion. His strategy worked poorly, though, as he was frequently unsuccessful in rallying the public to his side on issues crucial to his

● ● ● ● ● ● ● ● ● ● ●

Time Runs Out on the Bush Presidency

During the second straight debate of 1992 in which he performed poorly, the TV camera caught George Bush looking at his watch. The scene poignantly evoked the end of the Bush presidency, as the three presidential debates did little to turn around Bush's faltering campaign.

administration, such as the economic stimulus package described earlier. After his first two years in office, he told an interviewer that the problems bedeviling his presidency were due to a failure to communicate: "what I've got to do is to spend more time communicating with the American people about what we've done and where we're going."[18] Communicating with the public is crucial to a modern president's success, but so too is an ability to form bipartisan coalitions in Congress and broad interest group coalitions. Clinton's administration suffered from shortcomings in these areas as well during its rocky first years.

Presidents' obsessive concern with public opinion can be defended as a means of furthering majoritarian democracy: the president tries to gauge what the people want so that he can offer policies that reflect popular preferences. Some believe that presidents are too concerned about their popularity and are unwilling to champion unpopular causes or take principled stands that may affect their poll ratings. Commenting on the presidential polls that first became widely used during his term, Harry Truman said, "I wonder how far Moses would have gone if he'd taken a poll in Egypt?"[19]

THE ELECTORAL CONNECTION

In his farewell address to the nation, Jimmy Carter lashed out at the interest groups that had plagued his presidency. Interest groups, he said, "distort our purposes because the national interest is not always the sum of all our single or special interests." Carter noted the president's singular responsibility: "The president is the only elected official charged with representing all the people."[20] Like all other presidents, Carter quickly recognized the dilemma of majoritarianism versus pluralism after he took office. The president must try to please countless separate constituencies while trying to do what is best for the whole country.

It is easy to stand on the sidelines and say that presidents should always try to follow a majoritarian path, pursuing policies that reflect the preferences of most citizens. However, simply by running for office, candidates align themselves with particular segments of the population. As a result of their electoral strategy, their identification with activists in their party, and their own political views, candidates come into office with an interest in pleasing some constituencies more than others.

Each candidate attempts to put together an electoral coalition that will provide at least the minimum 270 (out of 538) electoral votes needed for election. As the campaign proceeds, each candidate tries to win votes from different groups of voters through his stand on various issues. He promises that once he is in office, he will take certain actions that appeal to people holding a particular view on an issue. Just as each presidential candidate attracts voters with his stand on particular issues, he offends others who are committed to the opposite side of those issues. In 1992, George Bush emphasized that environmental protection can cost jobs, surely making the Republican ticket more attractive to many businesspeople and workers in industries in which environmental regulation is an issue. On the other hand, Bush's stand gave environmentalists more reason to vote for Clinton.

Because issue stances can cut both ways—attracting some voters but driving others away—candidates may try to finesse an issue by being deliberately vague. Candidates sometimes hope that voters will put their own interpretations on ambiguous stances. If the tactic works, the candidate will attract some voters without offending others. During the 1968 campaign, Nixon said he was committed to ending the war in Vietnam but gave few details about how he would accomplish that end. He wanted to appeal not only to those who were in favor of military pressure against the North Vietnamese but also to those who wanted quick military disengagement.[21]

But candidates cannot be deliberately vague about all issues. A candidate who is noncommittal on too many issues appears wishy-washy. And future presidents do not build their political careers without working strongly for and becoming associated with important issues and constituencies. Moreover, after the election is over, the winning candidate wants to claim that he has been given a **mandate**, or endorsement, by the voters to carry out the policies he campaigned on. Newly chosen presidents make a majoritarian interpretation of the electoral process, claiming that their election-day victory is an expression of the direct will of the people. For such a claim to be credible, the candidate must have emphasized some specific issues during the campaign and offered some distinctive solutions.

Mandates tend to be more rhetorical than real.[22] Although presidents claim that the votes they receive at the polls are expressions of support for their policy proposals, more dispassionate observers usually find it difficult to document concrete evidence of broad public support for the range of specific policies a winning candidate wants to pursue. As Feature 12.1 suggests, the "mandate" that came out of the 1996 presidential election is muddled at best.

President Bill Clinton's easy victory over Bob Dole came as no surprise—the polls had been predicting it throughout the campaign. What was surprising, however, was that only a year earlier it had looked as though it would be the *Republican* candidate who would roll to an easy victory.

Although fortune appeared to turn quickly on the Republicans, viewing the election within a broader historical context suggests that 1996 strongly favored the Democratic candidate. The country was at peace and the nation's economy had been performing strongly since the beginning of the Clinton administration. In postwar America, the party controlling the White House has usually been successful in winning reelection when there was both peace and prosperity. What beat Bob Dole was not the mistakes he made in strategy or that he wasn't more telegenic. What beat him was four years of a steady, growing economy. Although the economy wasn't the only issue in the 1996 campaign, pocketbook issues were central to the public's decision to give four more years to Bill Clinton.

Still, if a Clinton victory seemed foreordained in 1996, why had Clinton looked so weak for the first three years of his term? The public certainly had doubts about Clinton and, indeed, his popularity ratings were unimpressive during his first three years. His first two years in office disappointed even his most ardent followers. His ill-fated economic stimulus package, a budget deficit reduction bill that included some tax increases on upper-income Americans, and the defeat of his health care reform bill, his most important legislative priority, all contributed to a widely held perception of presidential failure. Compounding Clinton's problems was the fact that he came across to the public as wavering and unsteady, as if he wasn't quite sure what he believed in.

The congressional election in 1994 was a disaster for Clinton. Not only had the Republicans won a huge and unexpected victory, taking over both houses of Congress, but by just about everyone's account the election was a referendum on Clinton's first two years in office. As Newt Gingrich led a blitzkrieg through the House with his Contract with America, the Democrats seemed stunned by the tidal wave that hit them.

Fortunately for Clinton, the Republicans overplayed their hand—they saw a mandate to sharply reduce the size and scope of government. Americans do want a small government, but they also want extensive government services. Although this is contradictory, public opinion is not subject to logic tests. When Clinton refused to go along with their extensive budget cuts, the Republicans refused to appropriate money to keep large segments of the government running. Clinton stood fast and parts of the government shut down. But the public sided with Clinton and it was Newt Gingrich who was on the defensive.

After the shattering repudiation of his administration in 1994, Clinton critically reassessed his performance and began talking with Dick Morris, a political consultant who had advised Clinton during his years in Arkansas. Morris pushed Clinton to move toward the moderate middle of the political spectrum, and he convinced the president that he needed to shed his image as a big-spending liberal. Especially noteworthy was Clinton's support for a welfare reform bill denounced by liberals in his own party. In the 1992 campaign Clinton had promised to "end welfare as we know it," and his signature on the legislation in 1996 sent a loud signal to the American people that he was a different kind of Democrat. At the same time, he remained steadfast in his support for education, the environment, and gun control—all issues popular with the American people and all issues on which the Republicans do poorly.

As Clinton skillfully and strategically positioned his party in line with public opinion on a wide range of issues, the public's perception of the economy grew more generous. There was clearly a lag as the public remained unconvinced for some time that the recession of the Bush years had fully ended and that the recovery was significant and enduring. When Bill Clinton faced the voters in the 1996 campaign, he could claim credit for an economy that had produced 10.5 million jobs during his term, had steadily expanded, and had low unemployment and low inflation. At the same time, the budget deficit had been reduced by more than half and the country was at peace. For Bill Clinton, it was the best of times.

table 12.1 ● Unified and Divided Party Control of Government, 1901–1996

Divided government exists when one party controls the White House and the other party controls one or both houses of Congress. Earlier in this century, divided government was rare. In recent years, however, it has become common.

Source: James A. Thurber, "An Introduction to Presidential-Congressional Rivalry," in *Rivals of Power*, ed. James A. Thurber (Washington, D.C.: Congressional Quarterly Press, 1996), pp. 8–9. Copyright © 1996 by Congressional Quarterly Press. Used with permission.

Year	President	Senate	House
1901–1903	R	R	R
1903–1905	R	R	R
1905–1907	R	R	R
1907–1909	R	R	R
1909–1911	R	R	R
1911–1913	R	R	D
1913–1915	D	D	D
1915–1917	D	D	D
1917–1919	D	D	D
1919–1921	D	R	R
1921–1923	R	R	R
1923–1925	R	R	R
1925–1927	R	R	R
1927–1929	R	R	R
1929–1931	R	R	R
1931–1933	R	R	D
1933–1935	D	D	D
1935–1937	D	D	D
1937–1939	D	D	D
1939–1941	D	D	D
1941–1943	D	D	D
1943–1945	D	D	D
1945–1947	D	D	D
1947–1949	D	R	R
1949–1951	D	D	D
1951–1953	D	D	D
1953–1955	R	R	R

A central reason why it is difficult to read the president's political tea leaves from election results is that the president is elected independently of Congress. Often this leads to **divided government,** with one party controlling the White House and the other party controlling at least one house of Congress. President Bush, for example, had to work with a Democratic-controlled House and Senate throughout all four years of his term. This may seem politically schizophrenic, with the electorate saying one thing by electing a president and another by electing a majority in Congress that opposes his policies. This does not appear to bother the American people, however: polls often show that the public feels it is desirable for control of the government to be divided between Republicans and Democrats.[23] One study estimates that as much as 8 percent of the public deliberately chooses presidential and congressional candidates from different parties to increase the likelihood of split control of government.[24] As Table 12.1 shows, divided government has become more and more frequent.

Voters appear to use quite different criteria when choosing a president than they do when choosing congressional representatives. As one scholar

Year	President	Senate	House
1955–1957	R	D	D
1957–1959	R	D	D
1959–1961	R	D	D
1961–1963	D	D	D
1963–1965	D	D	D
1965–1967	D	D	D
1967–1969	D	D	D
1969–1971	R	D	D
1971–1973	R	D	D
1973–1975	R	D	D
1975–1977	R	D	D
1977–1979	D	D	D
1979–1981	D	D	D
1981–1983	R	R	D
1983–1985	R	R	D
1985–1987	R	R	D
1987–1989	R	D	D
1989–1991	R	D	D
1991–1993	R	D	D
1993–1995	D	D	D
1995–1996	D	R	R

☐ Unified party control of government

☐ Divided party control of government

Source: "Political Party Affiliations in Congress and the Presidency, 1789–1991," *Congressional Quarterly's Guide to Congress,* 4th ed. (Washington, D.C.: Congressional Quarterly Press, 1991), 93-A and 94-A.

has noted, "Presidential candidates are evaluated according to their views on national issues and their competence in dealing with national problems. Congressional candidates are evaluated on their personal character and experience and on their devotion to district services and local issues."[25]

Congressional independence is at the heart of why contemporary presidents work so hard to gain public support for their policies.[26] Without a strong base of representatives and senators who feel their election was tied to his, a president often feels that he needs to win in the court of public opinion. Favorable public opinion can help a president build consensus in a highly independent legislative branch. Scholars are divided as to the impact of divided government. One study showed that just as much significant legislation gets passed and signed into law when there is divided government as when one party controls both the White House and Congress.[27] Using different approaches, other scholars have shown that divided governments are in fact less productive than unified ones.[28] Despite these differences in the scholarly literature, political scientists generally

12.1   The World's Largest Democracy Elects a Prime Minister

Since India's independence, the Congress Party has dominated the country's politics. Going into the May 1996 national election, the party had controlled the government for forty-four of forty-eight years. This time, however, the Congress Party was in trouble. Scandals had weakened the party, and despite its market reforms, which had spurred economic growth, there was widespread dissatisfaction with the Congress Party and with Prime Minister P. V. Narasimha Rao.

When the returns came in, the party did even worse than expected. Its candidates for Parliament won only 32 percent of the vote, and it lost half of the seats it had held. Yet while the 300 million voters in this nation of 930 million were clear in their rejection of the incumbent government, they didn't speak with a clear voice as to who they wanted to replace the Congress Party. Two other parties—more accurately, coalitions of parties—were both far from a majority in the 545-seat parliament. The more controversial of the two, the Bharatiya Janata Party (BJP), was a Hindu nationalist party that was hostile to the nation's Muslim minority.

India is a mosaic of different regions; different religious, ethnic, and linguistic groups; and different classes, including the rigidly defined Hindu castes. This delicate social fabric was clearly threatened by the emergence of the BJP. In 1992, Hindu extremists destroyed the oldest Muslim shrine in India, setting off the worst rioting since the partition of India and concomitant birth of Pakistan in 1947.

The deaths of three thousand in the ensuing conflict scarred India and shocked the world. Although the BJP officially preached moderation, it frightened many in India who feared more unrest if the party took over the government. The other party coalition, however, the National Front–Left Front, won fewer seats than Congress or the BJP and was initially unable to agree on a leader to stake its claim to the reins of government.

Consequently, the BJP was given the first opportunity to form a government. Its leader, Atal Bihari Vajpayee, was sworn in as prime minister and given two weeks to find more coalition partners to give him a working majority in Parliament. With 194 seats, Vajpayee needed 79 more members of Parliament, which in effect meant he needed the Congress Party's support to put him over the top. The Congress Party, ever sensitive to its history and its central role in developing a secular Indian democracy, refused to go along. The BJP lasted in office just thirteen days.

With the collapse of one government, it was now the turn of the National Front–Left Front (newly renamed the United Front) to form a majority coalition in Parliament. The United Front, which finally chose H. D. Deve Gowda as its leader, is a collection of thirteen different centrist and left-leaning political parties. The common thread among all these parties is their strong support of the interests of working-class and lower-caste Indians. Badly beaten and discredited, the Congress Party could not credibly try to form its own govern-

don't believe that divided government produces **gridlock**, a situation where government is incapable of acting on important policy issues.[29] There is a strong tradition of bipartisan policymaking in Congress, which facilitates cooperation when the government is divided. The rising partisanship in Congress (recall Figure 11.4) may, however, make divided government more of a problem. During 1995 and 1996, when the Republicans controlled both houses of Congress and Bill Clinton the White House, the

H. D. Deve Gowda

ment, and consequently it threw its support behind the United Front. Almost a month after the election, India finally had a government in office.

Yet the United Front hardly has a secure future. After the Congress Party licks its wounds and decides the time is right, it can withdraw its support and bring down the government. If and when that happens, a new election would be called to try to sort out the public's preferences in the world's largest democracy. Parliamentary governments are not inherently unstable, but a broad coalition without a majority of its own faces many risks.

traditional spirit of compromise was usually overwhelmed by sharp, partisan conflict.[30]

A parliamentary system, where the legislative and executive branches are united, might seem the logical solution to the problem of divided government. In parliamentary systems, however, the ruling government is sometimes internally divided because it is composed of a coalition of various political parties (see Compared with What? 12.1).

THE EXECUTIVE BRANCH ESTABLISHMENT

As the president tries to maintain the support of his electoral coalition for the policies he pursues, he draws on the extensive resources of the executive branch of government. The president has a White House staff that helps him formulate policy. The vice president is another resource; his duties within the administration vary according to his relationship with the president. The president's cabinet secretaries—the heads of the major departments of the national government—play a number of roles, including the critical function of administering the programs that fall within their jurisdictions. Effective presidents think strategically about how best to use the resources available. Each must find ways to organize structures and processes that best suit his management style.[31]

The Executive Office of the President

The president depends heavily on key aides. They advise him on crucial political choices, devise the general strategies the administration will follow in pursuing congressional and public support, and control access to the president to ensure that he has enough time for his most important tasks. Consequently, he needs to trust and respect these top staffers; many in a president's inner circle of assistants are long-time associates. The president's personal staff constitutes the White House Office.

Presidents typically have a chief of staff, who may be a first among equals or, in some administrations, the unquestioned leader of the staff. H. R. Haldeman, Richard Nixon's chief of staff, played the stronger role. He ran a highly disciplined operation, frequently prodding staff members to work harder and faster. Haldeman also felt that part of his role was to take the heat for the president by assuming responsibility for many of the administration's unpopular decisions: "Every president needs a son of a bitch, and I'm Nixon's."[32] Hamilton Jordan, President Carter's chief of staff, was at the other end of the spectrum: Carter did not give him the authority to administer the White House with a strong hand.

Presidents also have a national security adviser to provide daily briefings on foreign and military affairs and longer-range analyses of issues confronting the administration. The Council of Economic Advisers is also located in the White House. Senior domestic policy advisers help determine the administration's basic approach to such areas as health, education, and social services.

Below these top aides are the large staffs that serve them and the president. These staffs are organized around certain specialties. Some staff members work on political matters, such as liaison with interest groups, relations with ethnic and religious minorities, and party affairs. One staff deals exclusively with the media, and a legislative liaison staff lobbies the Congress for the administration. The large Office of Management and Budget (OMB) analyzes budget requests, is involved in the policymaking process, and examines agency management practices. This extended White House executive establishment, including the White House Office, is known as the **Executive Office of the President.** The Executive Office employs close to 1,600 individuals and has an annual budget of nearly $200 million.[33]

No one agrees about a "right way" for a president to organize his White House staff. Dwight Eisenhower, for example, a former general, wanted

New Chief

A few days after his reelection, President Clinton appointed North Carolina businessman Erskine Bowles to be his new chief of staff. Bowles succeeded Leon Panetta (left), who had resigned the position. Panetta was brought into the White House to replace Clinton's first chief of staff, Mack McLarty, a long-time friend of the President. Panetta was widely credited with improving White House management and instituting more-disciplined policymaking procedures.

clear lines of authority and a hierarchical structure that mirrored a military command. One factor that influences how a president uses his senior staff is the degree to which he delegates authority to them. Carter immersed himself in the policymaking process to ensure that he made all the significant decisions himself. Early in his administration, he told his staff, "Unless there's a holocaust, I'll take care of everything the same day it comes in."[34]

When Bill Clinton took over the White House, he instituted a loose staff structure that gave many top staffers direct access to him. (The president's wife, Hillary Rodham Clinton, was a key adviser from the beginning of the administration, which we discuss in Politics in a Changing America 12.1.) Clinton made a surprising (and questionable) choice for his chief of staff, Mack McLarty. McLarty, a friend of Clinton's since childhood and a successful Arkansas businessman, had no Washington experience. This appointment seemed to suggest that Clinton really wanted to be his own chief of staff, deeply involved in the nuts and bolts of White House policymaking. Indeed, as the White House planned the president's program during the first year, "Clinton found no detail too small for his attention."[35] The president's own undisciplined style and his tendency to take too much on led to considerable criticism of White House operations.[36] Clinton's open, freewheeling style had the advantage of ensuring that he heard different viewpoints on major issues and engaged in active debates over policy. Nevertheless, Clinton recognized that his staff structure was too inefficient and undisciplined. In June 1994, McLarty was moved aside to become a senior adviser to Clinton, and Leon Panetta, the president's budget director, became the new chief of staff. Panetta had served in Congress for many years, and he made clear improvements in White House operations.

● politics in a changing america

12.1   A Different Kind of First Lady

Hillary Rodham Clinton is not the first first lady to play a prominent political role in her husband's administration. Edith Wilson was said to have made decisions for her husband Woodrow after he was debilitated by a stroke. Eleanor Roosevelt was a visible and tireless advocate for causes she believed in. (Republicans were critical of her, some calling the liberal first lady "Lenin in skirts.") But just as Rosie the Riveter returned to the kitchen after World War II, the first ladies who followed Mrs. Roosevelt—Bess Truman and Mamie Eisenhower—were content to stand in the background and play the role of dutiful wife and mother.

A significant change in the role of the first lady came with "Lady Bird" Johnson. Her predecessor, the youthful Jackie Kennedy, had captivated the American public with her beauty, charm, and elegance. Lady Bird Johnson shrewdly staked out her own territory, choosing an issue with which to identify herself (the beautification of America) and playing a visible role in working for relevant policy changes. Since that time, most first ladies have also selected an uncontroversial issue to work on. Nancy Reagan's "Just Say No" antidrug campaign was typical.

Despite these important historical antecedents, there's never been a first lady quite like Hillary Rodham Clinton. She is the first woman of her generation to occupy the White House, and the change from the grandmotherly Barbara Bush was startling. She grew up in suburban Chicago and attended Wellesley

College, where she was president of the student body. After Wellesley came Yale Law School (where she met Bill Clinton) and work as a congressional staffer, law professor, and corporate lawyer for the most prestigious law firm in Little Rock, Arkansas. While working as an attorney, she did volunteer work—notably, chairing the Children's Defense Fund, a Washington-based advocacy group, and spearheading an educational reform drive in Arkansas.

When the Clintons arrived in Washington, the president announced that his wife would be in charge of developing a plan to restructure the nation's health care system. The new president had made health care a central issue in the campaign, promising to reform the system so that it would provide insurance for the uninsured and to reduce the sharply rising health care expenditures of all Americans. Never had a first lady been given such a controversial and visible leadership position. The American public initially reacted positively to Hillary Clinton as a person, but the reaction to this role was cautious. A poll at the beginning of the administration showed that 74 percent believed she was "a positive role model for American women," but only 47 percent said it was appropriate for her "to be involved in the development of major policy positions." Forty-five percent said she shouldn't be involved.

The first lady's initial efforts on health care were successful, and members of Congress were highly impressed with her comprehen-

The Vice President

The vice president's primary function is to serve as standby equipment. Only a heartbeat from the presidency itself, vice presidents must be ready and able to take over the presidency if anything happens to the president during his term in office. Traditionally, vice presidents have not been used in any important advisory capacity. Instead, presidents tend to give them political chores—campaigning, fund raising, and "stroking" the party faithful. This is often the case because vice presidential candidates are

sive grasp of the intricacies of this complex issue. Her successive appearances before five congressional committees were, in the words of one journalist, "widely perceived as virtuoso."

Yet not all has gone well for Hillary Clinton in the White House. The plan she and her task force devised for restructuring the health care system fared poorly, failing to get out of Congress—a highly devastating defeat for the Clintons. Many attribute to her the Clintons' initial resistance to a special prosecutor to investigate the Whitewater matter. Politically, it would have been much wiser to have accepted early on what became inevitable. The Clintons' opposition looked to many like a cover-up. The first lady's finances also became an embarrassment when it was revealed that in 1979 she turned a $1,000 investment into $100,000 in a short time by trading cattle futures and other commodities. Commodities are an extremely risky investment, and it is unlikely that a novice could do so well the first time out. She subsequently acknowledged that a leading Arkansas businessman had made many of the trades for her, and there were allegations that her broker had manipulated the trades to enhance her earnings. By 1995, she was deliberately keeping a lower profile and was no longer acting as a spokesperson for the administration on any top issue.

chosen for reasons that have more to do with the political campaign than with governing the nation. Richard Nixon chose the little-known governor of Maryland, Spiro Agnew, to be his vice-presidential candidate and assigned Agnew to play the same role Nixon had under Dwight Eisenhower—that of a political hatchet man who went after the Democrats.

President Carter broke the usual pattern of relegating the vice president to political chores; he relied heavily on his vice president, Walter Mondale.

Off and Running

After the reelection of the Clinton-Gore team in 1996, Vice President Al Gore became the early favorite to capture the Democratic nomination for president in 2000. Gore is popular with the party faithful, though unpredictable things happen in electoral politics and there is no assurance that he will win the nomination. Jack Kemp's selection as Bob Dole's running mate met with widespread approval by Republicans, and Kemp could be a formidable candidate if, as expected, he seeks his party's nomination for president.

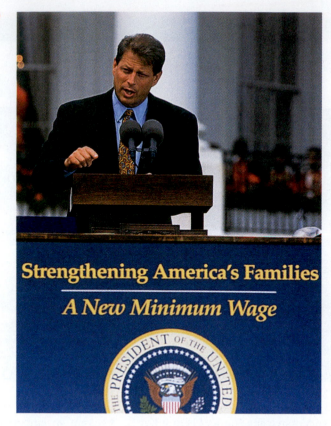

Strengthening America's Families

A New Minimum Wage

Carter was wise enough to recognize that Mondale's experience in the Senate could be of great value to him, especially because Carter had never served in Congress. Although neither Ronald Reagan's vice president, George Bush, nor George Bush's vice president, Dan Quayle, played as central a role as Mondale, their positions were enhanced because of the Mondale example. Al Gore, Clinton's vice president, has been given considerable responsibility.

The Cabinet

Locate all cabinet departments here.
`<www.whitehouse.gov/ WH/Cabinet/html/ cabinet_links.html>`

The president's **cabinet** is composed of the heads of the departments of the executive branch and a small number of other key officials, such as the head of the Office of Management and Budget and the ambassador to the United Nations. The cabinet has expanded greatly since George Washington formed his first cabinet, which included an attorney general and the secretaries of state, treasury, and war. Clearly, the growth of the cabinet to fourteen departments reflects the growth of government responsibility and intervention in areas such as energy, housing, and transportation.

In theory, the members of the cabinet constitute an advisory body that meets with the president to debate major policy decisions. In practice, however, cabinet meetings have been described as "vapid non-events in which there has been a deliberate non-exchange of information as part of a process of mutual nonconsultation."[37] One Carter cabinet member called the meetings "adult Show-and-Tell."[38] Why is this so? First, the cabinet has become rather large. Counting department heads, other officials of cabinet rank, and presidential aides, it is a body of at least twenty people—a size that many presidents find unwieldy for the give-and-take of political decision making. Second, most cabinet members have limited areas of expertise and simply cannot contribute much to deliberations in policy areas they know little about. The secretary of defense, for example, would probably be a poor choice to help decide important issues of agricultural policy. Third, although cabinet members have impressive backgrounds, they may not be personally close to the president or easy for him to work with. Cabinet choices are not necessarily made on the basis of personal relationships. The president often chooses cabinet members because of their reputations, or he may be guided by a need to give his cabinet some racial, ethnic, geographic, sexual, or religious balance.

Finally, modern presidents do not rely on the cabinet to make policy because they have such large White House staffs, which offer most of the advisory support they need.[39] And in contrast to cabinet secretaries, who may be pulled in different directions by the wishes of the president and those of their clientele groups, staffers in the White House Office are likely to see themselves as being responsible to the president alone. Thus, despite periodic calls for the cabinet to be a collective decision-making body, cabinet meetings seem doomed to be little more than academic exercises. In practice, presidents prefer the flexibility of ad hoc groups, specialized White House staffs, and the advisers and cabinet secretaries with whom they feel most comfortable.

More broadly, presidents use their personal staff and the large Executive Office of the President to centralize control over the entire executive branch. The vast size of the executive branch and the number and complexity of decisions that must be made each day pose a challenge for the White House. Each president must be careful to appoint people to top administration positions who are not merely competent but also passionate about the president's goals and skillful enough to lead others in the executive branch to fight for the president's program instead of their own agendas.[40] Ronald Reagan was especially good at communicating to his top appointees clear ideological principles that they were to follow in shaping administration policy. To fulfill more of their political goals and policy preferences, modern presidents have given their various staffs more responsibility for overseeing decision making throughout the executive branch.[41]

THE PRESIDENT AS NATIONAL LEADER

With an election behind him and the resources of his office at hand, a president is ready to lead the nation. Each president enters office with a general vision of how government should approach policy issues. During his term, a president spends much of his time trying to get Congress to enact legislation that reflects his general philosophy and specific policy preferences.

From Political Values . . .

Presidents differ greatly in their views of the role of government. Lyndon Johnson had a strong liberal ideology concerning domestic affairs. He

● ● ● ● ● ● ● ● ● ●
Maybe Some Day You'll Grow Up to Be President

A seminal event in young Bill Clinton's life was when he shook hands with his idol, President John F. Kennedy, in the White House's Rose Garden. When Clinton became president, he traveled to Russia, and in one of his public appearances there he held a televised town meeting. A precocious young Muscovite, Alexander Fyodorov, asked Clinton about the time he got to shake Kennedy's hand. Fyodorov was rewarded with more than an answer—he was invited up on the stage, where Clinton shook his hand for posterity. Maybe some day Fyodorov will grow up and . . . who knows?

believed that government has a responsibility to help disadvantaged Americans. Johnson described his vision of justice in his inaugural address:

> Justice was the promise that all who made the journey would share in the fruits of the land.
>
> In a land of wealth, families must not live in hopeless poverty. In a land rich in harvest, children just must not go hungry. In a land of healing miracles, neighbors must not suffer and die untended. In a great land of learning and scholars, young people must be taught to read and write.
>
> For [the] more than thirty years that I have served this nation, I have believed that this injustice to our people, this waste of our resources, was our real enemy. For thirty years or more, with the resources I have had, I have vigilantly fought against it.[42]

Johnson used *justice* and *injustice* as code for *equality* and *inequality*. He used them six times in his speech; he used *freedom* only twice. Johnson used his popularity, his skills, and the resources of his office to press for a "just" America—a "Great Society."

To achieve his Great Society, Johnson sent Congress an unprecedented package of liberal legislation. He launched such projects as the Job Corps (which created centers and camps offering vocational training and work experience to youths aged sixteen to twenty-one), Medicare (which provided medical care for the elderly), and the National Teacher Corps (which paid teachers to work in impoverished neighborhoods). Supported by huge Democratic majorities in Congress during 1965 and 1966, he had tremendous success getting his proposals through. Liberalism was in full swing.

In 1985, exactly twenty years after Johnson's inaugural speech, Ronald Reagan took his oath of office for the second time. Addressing the nation, Reagan reasserted his conservative philosophy. He emphasized freedom, using the term fourteen times, and failed to mention justice or equality once. In the following excerpts, we have italicized the term *freedom* for easy reference:

> By 1980, we knew it was time to renew our faith, to strive with all our strength toward the ultimate in individual *freedom* consistent with an orderly society. . . . We will not rest until every American enjoys the fullness of *freedom*, dignity, and opportunity as our birthright. . . . Americans . . . turned the tide of history away from totalitarian darkness and into the warm sunlight of human *freedom*. . . . Let history say of us, these were golden years—when the American Revolution was reborn, when *freedom* gained new life, when America reached for her best. . . . *Freedom* and incentives unleash the drive and entrepreneurial genius that are at the core of human progress. . . . From new *freedom* will spring new opportunities for growth. . . . Yet history has shown that peace does not come, nor will our *freedom* be preserved by good will alone. There are those in the world who scorn our vision of human dignity and *freedom*. . . . Human *freedom* is on the march, and nowhere more so than in our own hemisphere. *Freedom* is one of the deepest and noblest aspirations of the human spirit. . . . America must remain *freedom's* staunchest friend, for *freedom* is our best ally. . . . Every victory for human *freedom* will be a victory for world peace. . . . One people under God, dedicated to the dream of *freedom* that He has placed in the human heart.[43]

Reagan turned Johnson's philosophy on its head, declaring that "government is not the solution to our problem. Government *is* the problem." During his presidency, Reagan worked to undo many welfare and social service programs and cut funding for such programs as the Job Corps and food stamps. By the end of his term, there had been a fundamental shift in federal spending, with sharp increases in defense spending and "decreases in federal social programs [which] served to defund Democratic interests and constituencies."[44]

Although Johnson and Reagan had well-defined political philosophies and communicated a clear vision of where they wanted to lead the country, not all presidents bring such ideological passion to their position. George Bush was much more comfortable as the "faithful son" of Reaganism, trying to uphold and improve upon its programs rather than articulate a vision of his own.[45] Indeed, Bush derided what he called "the vision thing." In the end, his administration's timid domestic initiatives helped create an impression among the public of a president comfortable with the status quo. Recognizing Bush's vulnerability on this score, his two opponents, Clinton and Perot, preached change during the 1992 campaign. Looking back, one Bush aide concluded that "the absence of ideology coming from the Oval Office signaled an Administration lacking in direction."[46]

... To Policy Agenda

The roots of particular policy proposals, then, can be traced to the more general political ideology of the president. Presidential candidates outline that philosophy of government during their campaign for the White

12.3 ● Group Appeals

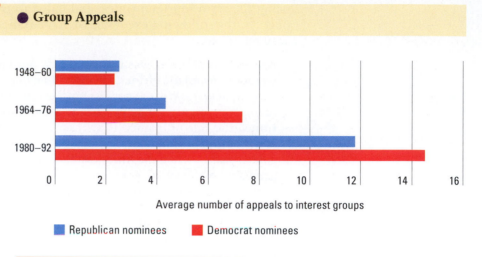

Average number of appeals to interest groups

■ Republican nominees   ■ Democrat nominees

This graph shows the results of an analysis of the acceptance speeches of both Republican and Democratic presidential nominees from 1948 to 1992 at their national party conventions. It was noted each time the nominee appealed to an interest group constituency in this widely followed speech, and a summary count was produced. When Dwight Eisenhower accepted the Republican nomination in 1952, he made not a single appeal for the support of an identifiable interest group constituency. When George Bush made his acceptance speech in 1992, he appealed to interest groups a total of fifteen times, including four separate references affirming his support for the Christian right. Interest group appeals are up sharply for both of the parties.

Source: Jeffrey M. Berry with Deborah Schildkraut, "Citizen Groups, Political Parties, and the Decline of the Democrats," paper delivered at the annual meeting of the American Political Science Association, Chicago, September 1995, p. 16a.

House. As Figure 12.3 illustrates, when presidential candidates give their acceptance speech at their nominating convention, they are increasingly likely to discuss their policy goals in terms of appeals to different interest groups. Over time, presidential candidates have been increasingly likely to make appeals for support that reflect a pluralist view of American politics.

When the hot rhetoric of the presidential campaign meets the cold reality of what is possible in Washington, the newly elected president must make some hard choices about what to push for during the coming term. These choices are reflected in the bills the president submits to Congress, as well as in the degree to which he works for their passage. The president's bills, introduced by his allies in the House and Senate, always receive a good deal of initial attention. In the words of one Washington lobbyist, "When a president sends up a bill, it takes first place in the queue. All other bills take second place."[47]

The president's role in legislative leadership is largely a twentieth-century phenomenon. Not until the Budget and Accounting Act of 1921 did executive branch departments and agencies have to clear their proposed budget bills with the White House. Before this, the president did not even coordinate proposals for how much the executive branch would spend on all the programs it administered. Later, Franklin D. Roosevelt required that all major legislative proposals by an agency or department be cleared by the White House. No longer could a department submit a bill without White House support.[48]

Roosevelt's influence on the relationship between the president and Congress went far beyond this new administrative arrangement. With the nation in the midst of the Great Depression, Roosevelt began his first term in 1933 with an ambitious array of legislative proposals. During the first hundred days Congress was in session, it enacted fifteen significant laws, including the Agricultural Adjustment Act, the act creating the Civilian Conservation Corps, and the National Industrial Recovery Act. Never had a president demanded—and received—so much from Congress. Roosevelt's legacy was that the president would henceforth provide aggressive leadership of Congress through his own legislative program.

figure 12.4 ● **Legislative Success**

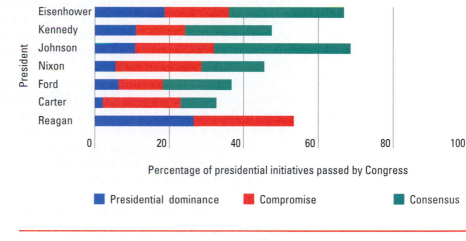

Percentage of presidential initiatives passed by Congress

■ Presidential dominance   ■ Compromise   ■ Consensus

Presidents vary considerably in their ability to convince Congress to enact the legislation that they send to Capitol Hill. Eisenhower and Johnson got about two-thirds of their proposals enacted, whereas Jimmy Carter was successful only one-third of the time. There is also substantial variation in the degree to which presidents have had to compromise to get their bills enacted. The category "presidential dominance" refers to presidential initiatives that were opposed in Congress but that opponents failed to defeat or alter. "Compromise" represents initiatives that Congress changed significantly before enacting. "Consensus" refers to initiatives for which there was no real opposition in Congress. All remaining legislation for each president failed to pass Congress.

Source: Adapted and reprinted by permission of the publishers from Mark A. Peterson, *Legislating Together: The White House and Capitol Hill from Eisenhower to Reagan* (Cambridge, Mass.: Harvard University Press, 1990). Copyright © 1990 by the President and Fellows of Harvard College.

Chief Lobbyist

When Franklin D. Roosevelt and Harry Truman first became heavily involved in preparing legislative packages, political scientists typically described the process as one in which "the president proposes and Congress disposes." In other words, once the president sends his legislation to Capitol Hill, Congress decides what to do with it. Over time, though, presidents have become increasingly active in all stages of the legislative process. The president is expected not only to propose legislation but also to make sure that it passes (see Figure 12.4).

The president's efforts to influence Congress are reinforced by the work of his legislative liaison staff. All departments and major agencies have legislative specialists as well. These department and agency people work with the White House liaison staff to coordinate the administration's lobbying on major issues.

The **legislative liaison staff** is the communications link between the White House and Congress. As a bill slowly makes its way through Congress, liaison staffers advise the president or a cabinet secretary on the problems that emerge. They specify what parts of a bill are in trouble and may have to be modified or dropped. They tell their boss what amendments are likely to be offered, which members of Congress need to be lobbied, and what the bill's chances for passage are with or without certain provisions. Decisions on how the administration will respond to such developments must then be reached. For example, when the Reagan White House realized that it was still a few votes short of victory on a budget bill in the House, it reversed its opposition to a sugar price-support bill. This attracted the votes of representatives from Louisiana and Florida, two sugar-growing states, for the budget bill. The White House would not call what happened a deal, but it noted that "adjustments and considerations" had been made.[49]

A certain amount of the president's job consists of stereotypical arm twisting—pushing reluctant legislators to vote a certain way. Yet most day-in, day-out interactions between the White House and Congress tend to be more subtle, with the liaison staff trying to build consensus by working cooperatively with legislators. When a congressional committee is working on a bill, liaison people talk to committee members individually to see what concerns they have and to help fashion a compromise if some differ with the president's position.

The White House also works directly with interest groups in its efforts to build support for legislation. Presidential aides hope key lobbyists will activate the most effective lobbyists of all: the voters back home. Interest groups can quickly reach the constituents who are most concerned about a bill, using their communications network to quickly mobilize members to write, call, or e-mail their members of Congress. There are so many interest groups in our pluralist political system that they could easily overload the White House with their demands. Consequently, except for those groups most important to the president, lobbies tend to be granted access only when the White House needs them to activate public opinion.[50]

Although much of the liaison staff's work with Congress is done in a cooperative spirit, agreement cannot always be reached. When Congress passes a bill the president opposes, he may veto it and send it back to Congress; as we noted earlier, Congress can override a veto with a two-thirds majority of those voting in each house. Presidents use their veto power sparingly, but the threat that a president will veto an unacceptable bill increases his bargaining leverage with members of Congress. We have also seen that a president's leverage with Congress is related to his standing with the American people. The ability of the president and his liaison staff to bargain with members of Congress is enhanced when he is riding high in the public opinion polls and hindered when the public is critical of his performance.[51]

Party Leader

Part of the president's job is to lead his party. This is very much an informal duty, with no prescribed tasks. In this respect, American presidents are considerably different from European prime ministers, who are the formal leader of their party in the national legislature as well as the head of their government. Because political parties in Europe tend to have strong national organizations, prime ministers have more reason to lead the party organization. In the United States, national party committees play a relatively minor role in national politics, although they are active in raising money for their congressional candidates (see Chapter 8).

The simple fact is that presidents can operate effectively without the help of a national party apparatus. Lyndon Johnson was contemptuous of the Democratic National Committee. He saw to it that the committee's budget was cut and refused some advisers' request that he replace its ineffectual head. Johnson thought a weak national committee would allow him to control party affairs from the White House. Like other modern presidents, Johnson believed he would be most effective communicating directly with the American people and did not see the need for national, state, or local party officials to be intermediaries in the process of coalition building.[52]

Working with the party may be more important for gaining the presidency than for actually governing. During the 1996 campaign, Vice President Al Gore campaigned tirelessly for Democratic candidates at all levels and did his best to raise money for the party. Regardless of whether the Clinton-Gore ticket won reelection, he wanted to position himself to make a likely run for the presidency in 2000. Working to shore up support among party activists was seen by Gore as a critical step toward gaining the nomination.[53] Yet such party work is not absolutely essential. In 1976, Carter not only won the nomination without much of a record of party work—he campaigned as an outsider, claiming that he would be a better president for not having ties to those who had long been in power.

THE PRESIDENT AS WORLD LEADER

The president's leadership responsibilities extend beyond Congress and the nation to the international arena. Each administration tries to further what it sees as the country's best interests in its relations with allies, adversaries, and the developing countries of the world. In this role, the president must be ready to act as diplomat and crisis manager.

Foreign Relations

From the end of World War II to the beginning of the Bush administration, presidents were preoccupied with containing communist expansion around the globe. Truman and Korea, Kennedy and Cuba, Johnson and Nixon and Vietnam, and Reagan and Nicaragua are just some examples of presidents and the communist crosses they had to bear. Presidents not only used overt and covert military means to fight communism but also tried to reduce tensions through negotiations. President Nixon made particularly important strides in this regard, completing an important arms control agreement with the Soviet Union and beginning negotiations with the Chinese, with whom the United States had had no formal diplomatic relations.

With the collapse of communism in the Soviet Union and Eastern Europe, American presidents have entered a new era in international relations. The new presidential job description places much more emphasis on managing economic relations with the rest of the world. Trade relations are an especially difficult problem, because presidents must balance the conflicting interests of foreign countries (many of them our allies), the interests of particular American industries, the overall needs of the American economy, and the demands of the legislative branch. President Clinton walked a difficult tightrope when China failed to carry out an agreement to crack down on companies there that counterfeit American computer software, compact discs, and videotapes. Clinton needed to make a credible threat to impose sanctions on China to demonstrate U.S. resolve, but at the same time he wanted to make sure he didn't ignite a trade war that would damage American companies trying to gain a

Our American Friend

As a young politician, Richard Nixon was notorious for his staunch anticommunism. As president, however, he achieved a stunning reversal of U.S. policy toward the People's Republic of China. His trip there in 1972 signaled an end to the Cold War hostility between the United States and the communist regime.

foothold in the huge Chinese market. In June of 1996 a new agreement was reached incorporating additional anti-counterfeiting measures on the part of the Chinese.

The decline of communism has not enabled the president to ignore security issues. The world remains a dangerous place, and regional conflicts can still embroil the United States. When Iraq invaded and quickly conquered Kuwait in August 1990, President Bush felt he had no choice but to respond firmly to protect our economic interests and to stand beside our Arab allies in the area. Bush worked the phones hard to get both Western and Arab leaders to join the United States in a coordinated military buildup in the area surrounding Kuwait. He had laid the groundwork for such cooperation with the heavy emphasis he had placed in the early months of his administration on building personal relationships with many important heads of state. It was, said one journalist, a "dazzling performance. In roughly four days, Bush organized the world against Saddam Hussein."[54]

Bush's impressive leadership of the twenty-eight-nation coalition continued in the months that followed. The coalition remained unified even through the difficult decision to go to war in January, when the air campaign began. Bush played a key role in convincing the Israelis, who were not part of the coalition, to refrain from retaliating against Iraq after Israel came under attack from Scud missiles. (Iraq had hoped that by drawing Israel into the war, the United States' Arab allies would withdraw their support for the war because of their opposition to the Jewish state.) The successful ground war against Iraqi forces was a capstone to a remarkable foreign policy achievement.

Crisis Management

Periodically, the president faces a grave situation in which conflict is imminent or a small conflict threatens to explode into a larger war. Handling such episodes is a critical part of the president's job. Thus voters may make the candidates' personal judgment and intelligence primary considerations in how they cast their ballots. A major reason for Barry Goldwater's crushing defeat in the 1964 election was his warlike image. His bellicose rhetoric scared many Americans. Fearing that Goldwater would be too quick to resort to nuclear weapons, they voted for Lyndon Johnson instead.

A president must be able to exercise good judgment and remain cool in crisis situations. John Kennedy's behavior during the Cuban missile crisis of 1962 has become a model of effective crisis management. When the United States learned that the Soviet Union had placed missiles containing nuclear warheads in Cuba, U.S. government leaders saw those missiles as an unacceptable threat to this country's security. Kennedy asked a group of senior aides, including top people from the Pentagon, to advise him on feasible military and diplomatic responses. An armed invasion of Cuba and air strikes against the missiles were two options considered. In the end, Kennedy decided on a less dangerous response: a naval blockade of Cuba. The Soviet Union thought better of prolonging its challenge to the United States and soon agreed to remove its missiles. For a short time, though, the world held its breath over the very real possibility of a nuclear war.

Are there guidelines for what a president should do in times of crisis or at other important decision-making junctures? Drawing on a range of advisers and opinions is certainly one.[55] Not acting in unnecessary haste is another. A third is having a well-designed, formal review process that promotes thorough analysis and open debate.[56] A fourth guideline is rigorously examining the chain of reasoning that has led to the option chosen, to ensure that presumptions have not been subconsciously equated with what is actually known to be true. When Kennedy decided to back a CIA plan to sponsor a rebel invasion of Cuba by expatriates hostile to Fidel Castro, he never really understood that its chances for success were based on unfounded assumptions of immediate uprisings by the Cuban population.[57]

Still, these are rather general rules, and they provide no assurance that mistakes will not be made. Almost by definition, each crisis is a unique event. Sometimes all alternatives carry substantial risks. And almost always, time is of the essence. This was the situation when Cambodia captured the American merchant ship *Mayaguez* off its coast in 1975. Not wanting to wait until the Cambodian government moved the sailors inland, where there would be little chance of rescuing them, President Gerald Ford immediately sent in the Marines. Unfortunately, forty-one American soldiers were killed in the fighting, "all in vain because the American captives had shortly before the attack been released and sent across the border into Thailand."[58] Even so, Ford can be defended for making the decision he did; he did not know what the Cambodians would do. World events are unpredictable, and in the end presidents must rely on their own judgment in crisis situations.

PRESIDENTIAL CHARACTER

How does the public assess which presidential candidate has the best judgment and whether a candidate's character is suitable to the office? Americans must make a broad evaluation of the candidates' personalities and leadership styles. The character issue emerged in 1992 when the Bush campaign harshly attacked Bill Clinton for evasiveness about how he had avoided the Vietnam draft.[59] Questions about Clinton's marital fidelity had materialized earlier in the year, during the primaries, and many interpreted his acknowledgment on "60 Minutes" that he was responsible for "causing pain in my marriage" as an indirect admission of infidelity.[60] The economy seemed to weigh more heavily on the voters' minds, however, and Clinton won despite the harsh attacks on his character by the Bush campaign.

The character issue continued to dog Clinton in the White House. Questions were raised about an investment that he and Hillary Rodham Clinton had made in the Whitewater land development project. In the 1996 campaign, it was "like déjà vu all over again." With the economy strong and his own campaign off to a slow start, Dole tried to make character one of the defining issues of the presidential race. Partially disabled from a serious injury he suffered in World War II, Dole offered a striking contrast to an incumbent president who had done his best to get out of serving in Vietnam. Early in the campaign, only 30 percent of the public believed that Clinton had more honesty and integrity than most people in public life. Dole's integrity ratings, however, were only modestly higher.[61]

A president's character is clearly relevant to his performance in office. His actions in office reflect something more than ideology and politics; they also reflect the moral, ethical, and psychological forces that compose his character. Much of any person's character is formed in childhood, and many individual traits can be traced to early experiences. Lyndon Johnson had a troubled relationship with his father, who questioned his son's masculinity. Johnson recalled that when he ran away from home after wrecking his father's car, his father phoned him and said that people in town were calling Lyndon "yellow" and a coward.[62] Johnson biographer Robert Caro notes another crucial episode in young Lyndon's life—a humiliating

● ● ● ● ● ● ● ● ● ● ● ● ●

The Race Ends

Bob Dole's concession speech on election night, 1996, was a poignant moment, as his life in public service came to a formal close. (After the primaries he had resigned from the Senate and his position as majority leader to devote full time to his race for the presidency.) Dole found some humor in the disappointment that night, telling his supporters that on the elevator on his way down to give his concession speech, he realized that he "didn't have anything to do tomorrow."

beating at the hands of a dance partner's jealous boyfriend. In front of family and friends, "blood was pouring out of Lyndon's nose and mouth, running down his face and onto the crepe-de-chine shirt."[63]

Was Johnson overly concerned about his masculinity? Did this psychological problem make it difficult for him to extricate the United States from the Vietnam War? Another Johnson biographer, Doris Kearns, argues that Johnson wanted to make sure he "was not forced to see himself as a coward, running away from Vietnam."[64] Nonetheless, it is almost impossible to establish the precise roots of Johnson's behavior as president, and some might find connections between his childhood humiliations and his presidential policy decisions rather speculative.

Whatever their roots, the personality characteristics of presidents clearly have an important effect on their success or failure in office. Richard Nixon had such an exaggerated fear of what his "enemies" might try to do to him that he created a climate in the White House that nurtured the Watergate break-in and subsequent cover-up. Franklin D. Roosevelt, on the other hand, was certainly aided in office by his relaxed manner and self-confidence.[65]

SUMMARY

When the delegates to the Constitutional Convention met to design the government of their new nation, they had trouble shaping the office of the president. They struggled to find a balance—an office that was powerful enough to provide unified leadership but not so strong that presidents could use their powers to become tyrants or dictators. The initial conceptions of the presidency have slowly been transformed over time, as presidents have adapted the office to meet the nation's changing needs. The trend has been to expand presidential power. Some expansion has come from presidential actions taken under claims of inherent powers. Congress has also delegated a great deal of power to the executive branch, further expanding the role of the president.

Because the president is elected by the entire nation, he can claim to represent all citizens when proposing policy; this broad electoral base equips the presidency to be an institution of majoritarian democracy. Whether the presidency actually operates in a majoritarian manner depends on several factors—the individual president's perception of public opinion on specific issues, the relationship between public opinion and the president's political ideology, and the extent to which the president is committed to pursuing his values through his office.

The executive branch establishment has grown rapidly, and the White House has become a sizable bureaucracy. New responsibilities of the twentieth-century presidency are particularly noticeable in the area of legislative leadership. Now a president is expected to be a policy initiator for Congress, as well as a lobbyist who guides his bills through the legislative process.

The presidential "job description" for foreign policy has also changed considerably. Post–World War II presidents had been preoccupied with containing the spread of communism, but with the collapse of communism in the Soviet Union and Eastern Europe, international economic relations now loom largest as a priority for presidents. However, national security issues remain, because regional conflicts can directly involve the interests of the United States.

Key Terms

veto	mandate	Executive Office of the	legislative liaison staff
inherent powers	divided government	President	
delegation of powers	gridlock	cabinet	

Selected Readings

Campbell, Colin, and Bert A. Rockman, eds., *The Clinton Presidency*. Chatham, N.J.: Chatham House, 1996. A first effort by political scientists to evaluate Bill Clinton's presidency.

Jones, Charles O. *The Presidency in a Separated System*. Washington, D.C.: Brookings Institution, 1994. Jones argues that ours is not a presidency-centered system and that policy initiation in Congress is more independent of the executive branch than most scholars realize.

Neustadt, Richard E. *Presidential Power*, rev. ed. New York: Wiley, 1980. Neustadt's classic work examines the president's power to persuade.

Skowronek, Stephen. *The Politics Presidents Make*. Cambridge, Mass.: Harvard University Press, 1993. A sweeping, magisterial analysis of the cycles of presidential history.

Thurber, James A. *Rivals for Power*. Washington, D.C.: Congressional Quarterly Press, 1996. An excellent collection of essays reviewing the major issues in executive-legislative relations.

Walcott, Charles E., and Karen M. Hult. *Governing the White House*. Lawrence: University Press of Kansas, 1995. An organizational perspective on change in the White House during the modern presidency.

World Wide Web Resources

The White House. The highlight of this White House home page is the "interactive citizen handbook," a guide to how to be a good citizen on the internet. Also available are White House tours and entry into White House "briefing rooms." Enter the briefing rooms to get current information on White House speeches, statements, and press releases as well as current government statistics.
`<www.whitehouse.gov.>`

Presidential Address. This page is sponsored by the University of Oklahoma Law Center. It allows the visitor to retrieve all state of the union and inaugural addresses dating back to George Washington. Other historically significant presidential speeches are also available.
`<www.law.uoknor.edu/ushist.html>`

Office of Management and Budget. Find out what it is, what it does, and how it is organized. You can search OMB documents via the "OMB locator."
`<www.whitehouse.gov/WH/EOP.omb>`

13

The Bureaucracy

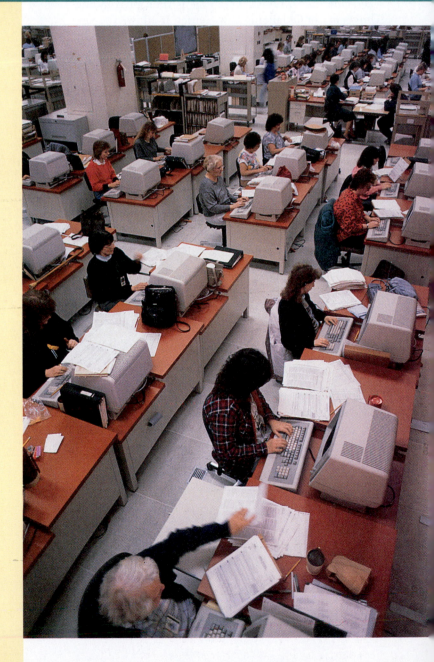

ON MAY 11, 1996, VALUJET FLIGHT 592 TOOK OFF from the Miami airport and headed north. A few minutes later smoke began to fill the cabin, and the pilot turned the plane around to return to Miami. Before it could reach the airport, however, the plane lost power and nose-dived into an alligator-infested swamp in the Everglades. None of the 109 on board survived.

Plane crashes are shocking, not just because of the carnage but because commercial airline crashes are so rare. Travel on the major air carriers is commonly thought to be the safest form of transportation. Even more shocking than the crash was the revelation that the Federal Aviation Administration (FAA), the regulatory agency charged with setting, monitoring, and enforcing airline safety standards, had previously documented a poor maintenance record by ValuJet. Yet the agency had done little to force ValuJet to improve its repair and record-keeping practices. After the crash, a high-ranking Department of Transportation official said she had stopped flying ValuJet some time ago "because of its many mishaps."[1]

The cause of the crash appears to have been some used oxygen canisters, which can heat up to 430 degrees in flight and must be packed according to strict safety standards. ValuJet was not authorized to carry such cargo, and the canisters were loaded by mistake. Why weren't correct procedures followed? Beyond the individual errors in judgment are the financial pressures brought on the airlines by deregulation. Until the late 1970s, airline pricing was oligopolistic, with common fares approved by the government. Today, airlines compete vigorously, and many cut-rate start-ups like ValuJet have taken market share away from major carriers like United, American, and Delta.

Many of the new low-cost carriers save money by buying or leasing used aircraft with considerable mileage on them. Another cost-cutting measure is to farm out maintenance work to subcontractors who can do the work more cheaply. Indeed, it was a subcontractor who loaded the fatal canisters onto flight 592. This has made the FAA's work more difficult, as its work force has not expanded to match the increasing number of companies running or servicing commercial airlines.[2]

But why is this so? Why doesn't the FAA just add inspectors and write more regulations to improve its monitoring of carriers and subcontractors? Americans surely want commercial airliners to be as safe as possible. Yet, at the same time that Americans want government to reduce the risks of everyday life, there is also great pressure to cut the budget, reduce the deficit, and shrink the size of government. Less than four months before

● ● ● ● ● ● ● ● ● ● ● ●

Flight to Oblivion

After ValuJet flight #592 crashed into the Everglades, the FAA was roundly criticized for failing to do a better job of monitoring airline maintenance and safety standards. After reviewing its own performance the FAA announced that it was taking steps to improve its supervision of maintenance subcontractors, such as Sabretech, the company that worked for ValuJet at the time of the crash. In September of 1996 ValuJet began flying again on a limited basis.

the ValuJet crash, President Clinton declared in his State of the Union address that "the era of big government is over."[3] As we'll explore in this chapter, Americans don't want big government, but they want the services big government provides. The controversy over the bureaucracy's role is not just a function of majoritarian opinion that is contradictory; it is also due to the fact that majoritarianism is often pitted against pluralism. One reason the FAA didn't take more concerted action against ValuJet prior to the crash is that any government rebuke of the carrier would have jeopardized the company's future. (After the crash, the FAA did force the company to suspend its service.) More broadly, one of the FAA's responsibilities is to promote the airline industry, and it is thus lobbied heavily on both business and safety issues by large and small carriers alike. Beyond our focus on pluralist and majoritarian dynamics in bureaucratic politics, we'll also look closely at why it is that Americans dislike government so much. Many people believe that bureaucracies are unresponsive to what the public wants. Finally, we will discuss reforms that might make government work better.

ORGANIZATION MATTERS

A nation's laws and policies are administered, or put into effect, by a variety of departments, agencies, bureaus, offices, and other government units, which together are known as its *bureaucracy*. **Bureaucracy** actually means any large, complex organization in which employees have specific job responsibilities and work within a hierarchy of authority. The employees of these government units, who are quite knowledgeable within their narrow areas, have become known somewhat derisively as **bureaucrats.**

We study bureaucracies because they play a central role in the governments of modern societies. In fact, organizations are a crucial part of any

Bureaucrats, Planners, Auctioneers

The Federal Communications Commission plays a central role in overseeing the nation's telecommunications industry. These FCC bureaucrats did the planning that led to the 1994 sale of airwave licenses for paging and data transmission services. The successful auction yielded $617 million for the federal government.

society, no matter how elementary. For example, a preindustrial tribe is an organization. It has a clearly defined leader (a chief), senior policymakers (elders), a fixed division of labor (some hunt, some cook, some make tools), an organizational culture (religious practices, initiation rituals), and rules of governance (what kind of property belongs to families and what belongs to the tribe). How that tribe is organized is not merely a quaint aspect of its evolution but is critical to the survival of its members in a hostile environment.

The organization of modern government bureaucracies also reflects their need to survive. The environment of modern bureaucracies, filled with conflicting political demands and the ever-present threat of budget cuts, can be no less hostile than that of preindustrial tribes. The way a given government bureaucracy is organized also reflects the particular needs of its clients. The bottom line, however, is that the manner in which any bureaucracy is organized affects how well it is able to accomplish its tasks.

A recent study of America's schools vividly demonstrates the importance of organization. After studying a large number of high schools around the country, two political scientists tried to determine what makes some better than others. They used the test scores of students to measure the achievement level of each school. Because some high schools' students are much better prepared to begin with than others, the authors compared similar schools. In other words, schools in low-income neighborhoods where entering students had average or below-average reading scores were compared with similar schools, not with schools in wealthy suburban neighborhoods where entering students had above-average reading scores. When similar schools were compared in terms of improvements in student performance, it was evident that the students in some schools achieved more than the students in other schools. Why?

The authors' statistical tests led them to conclude that the differences in student performance were a result of the way the schools were organized. The biggest influence on the effectiveness of a school's organization was its level of autonomy. Schools that had more control over hiring, curriculum, and discipline did better in terms of student achievement. This freedom seemed to allow for strong leadership, which helped the schools develop coherent goals and build staffs strongly supportive of those goals.[4]

Clearly, organization matters. The ways in which bureaucracies are structured to perform their work directly affect their ability to accomplish their tasks. Unfortunately, "if organization matters, it is also the case that there is no one best way of organizing."[5] Although greater autonomy may improve the performance of public schools, it may not improve other kinds of organizations. If a primary goal of a state social welfare agency, for example, is to treat its clients equally, to provide the same benefits to people with the same needs and circumstances, then giving local offices a lot of individual autonomy is not a good approach. The study of bureaucracy, then, centers around finding solutions to the many different kinds of problems faced by large government organizations.

THE DEVELOPMENT OF THE BUREAUCRATIC STATE

A common complaint voiced by Americans is that the national bureaucracy is too big and tries to accomplish too much. To the average citizen, the national government may seem like an octopus—its long arms reach just about everywhere. Ironically, compared to other Western democracies, the size of the United States government is proportionally smaller (see Compared with What? 13.1).

The Growth of the Bureaucratic State

American government seems to have grown unchecked during this century. As one observer noted wryly, "The assistant administrator for water and hazardous materials of the Environmental Protection Agency [presides] over a staff larger than Washington's entire first administration."[6] Yet, even during George Washington's time, bureaucracies were necessary. No one argued then about the need for a postal service to deliver mail or a treasury department to maintain a system of currency.

However, government at all levels (national, state, and local) has grown enormously in the twentieth century.[7] There are a number of major reasons for this. A principal cause of government expansion is the increasing complexity of society. George Washington did not have an assistant administrator for water and hazardous materials because he had no need for one. The National Aeronautics and Space Administration (NASA) was not necessary until rockets were invented.

Another reason government has grown is that the public's attitude toward business has changed. Throughout most of the nineteenth century, there was little or no government regulation of business. Business was generally autonomous, and any government intervention in the economy that might limit that autonomy was considered inappropriate. This attitude began to change toward the end of the nineteenth century, as more Americans became aware that the end product of a laissez-faire approach

● compared with what?

13.1 Not So Big by Comparison

When the United States is viewed against the other Western democracies, our government turns out to be relatively small. Measuring the size of government is difficult, but one way is to calculate government outlays as a percentage of a nation's entire economic output (gross domestic product, or GDP).

The primary reason why European governments spend so much in comparison to the United States is that they offer a much more extensive array of welfare and social service benefits to their citizens. These countries tend to have generous pension, health, and unemployment benefits. These benefits do not come cheaply, however; residents of the other advanced industrialized countries tend to pay much higher taxes than do Americans. There's no free lunch. In recent years, budget pressures have forced European governments to try to trim their spending.

Source: Terrence Roth, "Europeans Are Moving to Overhaul Welfare," *Wall Street Journal,* 3 June 1996, p. A1.

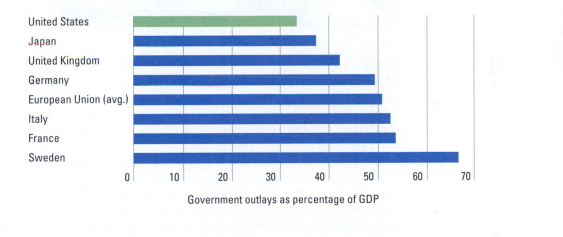

Government outlays as percentage of GDP

was not always highly competitive markets that benefited consumers. Instead, businesses sometimes formed oligopolies, such as the infamous "sugar trust," a small group of companies that controlled virtually the entire sugar market.

Gradually, government intervention came to be accepted as necessary to protect the integrity of markets. And if government was to police unfair business practices effectively, it needed administrative agencies. During the twentieth century, new bureaucracies were organized to regulate specific industries. Among them are the Securities and Exchange Commission (SEC), which oversees securities trading, and the Food and Drug Administration (FDA), which tries to protect consumers from unsafe food, drugs, and cosmetics. Through bureaucracies such as these, government has become a referee in the marketplace, developing standards of fair trade, setting rates, and licensing individual businesses for operation. As new problem areas have emerged, government has added new agencies,

● ● ● ● ● ● ● ● ●

Activist Bureaucrat

Dr. David Kessler, head of the Food and Drug Administration, is popular among liberals for his activist bent and his aggressive efforts to promote safety and honesty in the business markets regulated by his agency. He is very unpopular with business, which sees him as unsympathetic to its needs and unconcerned about the lengthy review process that their products are subjected to by FDA rules and regulations. Tobacco companies are particularly hostile toward Kessler and have donated money to think tanks publicly critical of the FDA.

further expanding the scope of its activities. During the 1960s, for instance, Ralph Nader made the public aware that certain design flaws in automobiles made them unnecessarily dangerous. For example, sharp, protruding dashboard knobs caused a car's interior to be dangerous on impact. Congress responded to public demands for change by creating the National Highway Traffic Safety Administration in 1966.

General attitudes about government's responsibilities in the area of social welfare have changed, too. An enduring part of American culture is the belief in self-reliance. People are expected to overcome adversity on their own, to succeed on the basis of their own skills and efforts. Yet, certain segments of our population are believed to deserve government support, either because we particularly value their contribution to society or have come to believe that they cannot realistically be expected to overcome adversity on their own.[8]

This belief goes as far back as the nineteenth century. The government provided pensions to Civil War veterans, because they were judged to deserve financial support. Later, programs to help mothers and children were developed.[9] Further steps toward income security came in the wake of the Great Depression, when the Social Security Act became law, creating a fund that workers pay into and then collect income from during old age. In the 1960s, the government created programs designed to help minorities. As the government made these new commitments, it also made new bureaucracies or expanded existing ones.

Finally, government has grown because ambitious, entrepreneurial agency officials have expanded their organizations and staffs to take on added responsibilities.[10] Each new program leads to new authority. Larger budgets and staffs, in turn, are necessary to support that authority. In the wake of the collapse of communism, the budgets of the Defense Department and various security agencies came under pressure from those

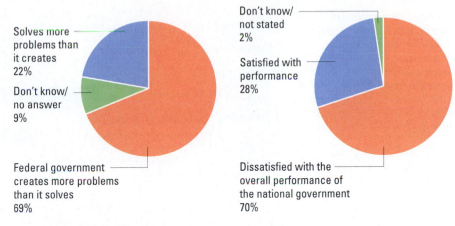

figure 13.1 ● We Hate Government (in General)

Americans demonstrate little confidence in government when asked about its general capabilities. Poll results show that citizens believe government creates more problems than it solves and are dissatisfied with its performance.

Source: American Enterprise, March-April 1993, p. 89.

Solves more problems than it creates 22%

Don't know/ no answer 9%

Federal government creates more problems than it solves 69%

Don't know/ not stated 2%

Satisfied with performance 28%

Dissatisfied with the overall performance of the national government 70%

---

who believed those parts of the government could shrink a little. To bolster itself against the budget cutters, the CIA volunteered its spy satellites to monitor environmental quality around the world.[11] Agency administrators saw expanding the agency's mission as a key to survival in a time of government austerity.

Can We Reduce the Size of Government?

When candidates for Congress and the presidency campaign, they typically "run against the government"—even if they are incumbents. Government is unpopular: Americans have little confidence in its capabilities and feel that it wastes money and is out of touch with the people (see Figure 13.1). Americans want a smaller government that costs less and performs better.

Most of the national government is composed of large bureaucracies, so if government is to become smaller, bureaucracies will have to be eliminated or reduced in size. Everyone wants to believe that government can be shrunk just by eliminating unnecessary bureaucrats. Although efficiencies can be found, serious budget cuts also require serious reductions in programs. Not surprisingly, presidents and members of Congress face a tough job when they try to cut specific programs. Each government bureaucracy performs a service of value to some sector of society. For example, even though bankers as a group favor laissez-faire capitalism, the principles of a free market, and minimal government intervention, few bankers voiced such preferences when the savings and loan industry collapsed in the late 1980s. A noninterventionist government could have stood by and done nothing, but inaction would have had a disastrous effect on the U.S. financial system—in this case, free-market corrections to the problem looked like a very unattractive option. Bankers became more concerned about order than freedom and were happy to see the government

Learn how to influence the bureaucracy.
`<www.2020vision.org/ admin.html>`

figure **13.2**   ● We Like Government (in Particular)

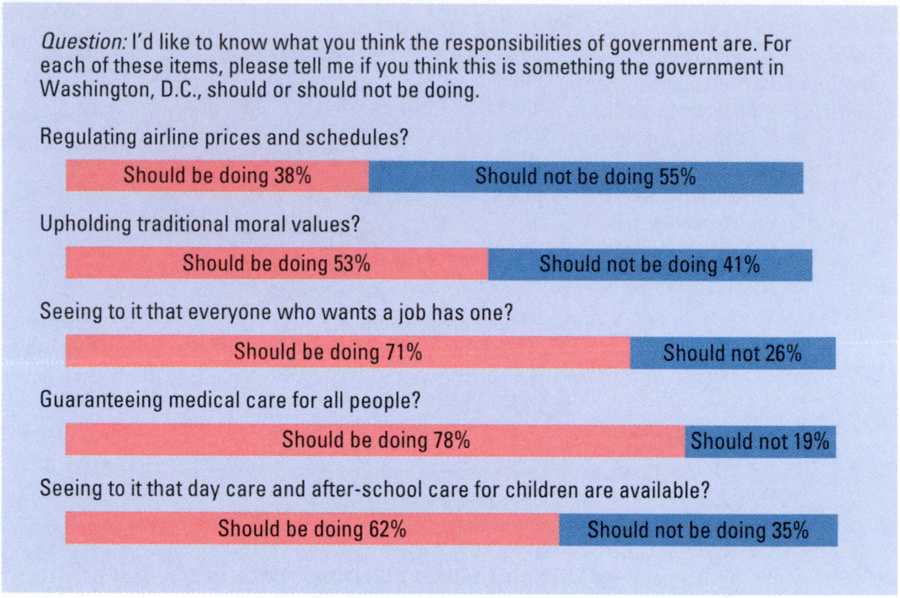

Americans are critical of government, believing that it tries to do too much, has become too powerful, and wastes a lot of money. When asked about specific programs, however, they tend to be much more supportive of what the government is doing.

Source: Adapted from a November 1987 *New York Times*/CBS News poll. Berman, Larry, ed. *Looking Back on the Reagan Presidency.* Baltimore, Md.: The Johns Hopkins University Press, 1990, p. 307. Reprinted with permission.

Question: I'd like to know what you think the responsibilities of government are. For each of these items, please tell me if you think this is something the government in Washington, D.C., should or should not be doing.

Regulating airline prices and schedules?
Should be doing 38% | Should not be doing 55%

Upholding traditional moral values?
Should be doing 53% | Should not be doing 41%

Seeing to it that everyone who wants a job has one?
Should be doing 71% | Should not 26%

Guaranteeing medical care for all people?
Should be doing 78% | Should not 19%

Seeing to it that day care and after-school care for children are available?
Should be doing 62% | Should not be doing 35%

mount a rescue effort. A new bureaucracy, the Resolution Trust Corporation, was created to administer the medicine to the sick patient. Big government got even bigger.

Bankers are far from the only group that wants to be protected by the national government. Farmers want the price supports of the U.S. Department of Agriculture. Builders profit from programs offered by the U.S. Department of Housing and Urban Development. And labor unions want a vigorous Occupational Safety and Health Administration. Interest groups that have a stake in an agency almost always resist efforts to cut back its scope.

As for the public, people's attitudes toward government in general tell only part of the story.[12] When asked about specific programs or functions of government, citizens tend to be highly supportive. As Figure 13.2 shows, public support for expensive government endeavors (including guaranteeing a job for all who want one, which would be a significant expansion of government's reach into the economy) is considerable.

Given interest group and public support, it is rare for the government to abolish a department or agency. But agencies are not immune to change. Major reorganizations, in which programs are consolidated and the size and scope of activities are reduced, are not uncommon.

In recent years, most change has come from budget cuts. In 1995 the Republican-controlled Congress cut the budget for the Environmental Protection Agency (EPA), reducing programs designed to identify sources of pollution at factories. Republicans said there wasn't enough money to tackle all the country's environmental problems. EPA defenders said these programs were vital to protecting the nation's health. Opinions may differ as to the value of the EPA, but these budget cuts did make the bureaucracy smaller by restricting its antipollution inspection programs.[13]

The tendency for big government to endure reflects the tension between majoritarianism and pluralism. Even when the public as a whole wants a smaller national government, that sentiment can be undermined by the strong desire of different segments of society for government to continue performing some valuable function for them. Lobbies that represent these segments work strenuously to convince Congress and the administration that certain agencies' funding is vital and that any cuts ought to come out of other agencies' budgets. At the same time, those other agencies are also working to protect themselves and to garner support. In the case of the EPA's budget cuts, the publicity surrounding the cuts and other efforts by the GOP to shrink the agency led to a public backlash against the Republicans. Stung by the criticism that they were against the environment, congressional Republicans pulled back from their attempts to make the EPA smaller.

BUREAUS AND BUREAUCRATS

We often think of the bureaucracy as a monolith. In reality, the bureaucracy in Washington is a disjointed collection of departments, agencies, bureaus, offices, and commissions—each a bureaucracy in its own right.

The Organization of Government

By examining the basic types of government organizations, we can better understand how the executive branch operates. In our discussion, we pay particular attention to the relative degree of independence of these organizations and to their relationship with the White House.

Departments. **Departments** are the biggest units of the executive branch, covering broad areas of government responsibility. As noted in Chapter 12, the secretaries (heads) of the departments, along with a few other key officials, form the president's cabinet. The current cabinet departments are State, Treasury, Defense, Interior, Agriculture, Justice, Commerce, Labor, Health and Human Services, Housing and Urban Development, Transportation, Energy, Education, and Veterans Affairs. Each of these massive organizations is broken down into subsidiary agencies, bureaus, offices, and services.

Independent Agencies.   Within the executive branch there are also many **independent agencies** that are not part of any cabinet department. Instead, they stand alone and are controlled to varying degrees by the president. Some, among them the CIA, are directly under the president's control. Others, such as the Federal Communications Commission, are structured as **regulatory commissions.** Each commission is run by a small number of commissioners (usually an odd number, to prevent tied votes) appointed to fixed terms by the president. Some commissions were formed to guard against unfair business practices. Others were formed to protect the public from unsafe products. Although presidents don't have direct control over these regulatory commissions, they can strongly influence their direction through their appointments of new commissioners.

Government Corporations.   Finally, Congress has also created a small number of **government corporations.** The services these executive branch agencies perform theoretically could be provided by the private sector, but Congress has decided that the public is better served by these organizations' having some link with the government. For example, the national government maintains the postal service as a government corporation because it feels that Americans need low-cost, door-to-door service for all kinds of mail, not just for profitable routes or special services. In some instances, the private sector does not have enough financial incentive to provide an essential service. This is the case with the financially troubled Amtrak train line.[14]

The Civil Service

The national bureaucracy is staffed by about three million civilian employees, who account for about 2.4 percent of the U.S. work force.[15] Americans have a tendency to stereotype all government workers as faceless paper pushers, but the public work force is actually quite diverse. Government workers include forest rangers, FBI agents, typists, foreign service officers, computer programmers, policy analysts, public relations specialists, security guards, librarians, administrators, engineers, plumbers, and people from literally hundreds of other occupations.

An important feature of the national bureaucracy is that most of its workers are hired under the requirements of the **civil service.** The civil service was created after the assassination of President James Garfield, who was killed by an unbalanced and dejected job seeker. Congress responded by passing the Pendleton Act (1883), which established the Civil Service Commission (now the Office of Personnel Management). The objective of the act was to reduce patronage—the practice of filling government positions with the president's political allies or cronies. The civil service fills jobs on the basis of merit and sees to it that workers are not fired for political reasons. Over the years, job qualifications and selection procedures have been developed for most government positions.

The vast majority of the national government's workers are employed outside Washington. One reason for this decentralization is to make government offices accessible to the people they serve. The Social Security Administration, for example, has to have offices within a reasonable distance of most Americans, so that its many clients have somewhere to take their questions, problems, and paperwork. Decentralization is also a way to distribute jobs and income across the country. The headquarters of the Centers for Disease Control could easily have been located in Washington, but it is in Atlanta. Likewise, NASA's headquarters for space flights is located in Houston. Members of Congress, of course, are only too happy to place some of the "pork" back home, so that their constituents will credit them with the jobs and money that government installations create.

Given the enormous variety of government jobs, employees come from all walks of life. Like most large organizations, the federal government has taken steps to try to make its work force mirror the larger population in

● ● ● ● ● ● ● ● ●
Anybody Home?

Census workers called enumerators try to find people who did not receive a census questionnaire through the mail. During the 1990 census, big city mayors pressured the Census Bureau to locate and count the homeless. Because funding for many national grants-in-aid programs is based on per capita formulas, an undercount of a city's homeless population could lessen the amount of federal aid the city receives.

terms of race and gender (on gender, see Politics in a Changing America 13.1). Minorities have substantial representation within the federal government's work force, but at the highest level of the civil service, minorities are underrepresented.[16]

Presidential Control over the Bureaucracy

Civil service and other reforms have effectively insulated the vast majority of government workers from party politics. An incoming president can appoint only about three thousand people to jobs in his administration—fewer than 1 percent of all executive branch employees.[17] Still, presidential appointees fill the top policymaking positions in government. Each new president, then, establishes an extensive personnel review process to find appointees who are both politically compatible and qualified in their field. Although the president selects some people from his campaign staff, most political appointees have not been campaign workers. Instead, cabinet secretaries, assistant secretaries, agency heads, and the like tend to be drawn directly from business, universities, and government itself.

Because so few of their own appointees are in each department and agency, presidents often believe that they do not have enough control over the bureaucracy. Republican presidents have also worried that the civil service would be hostile to their objectives, because they assume that career bureaucrats have a liberal Democratic bias.

Recent presidents have tried repeatedly to centralize power by tightening the reins on the rest of the executive branch. During his two terms in office, Ronald Reagan and his White House staff were effective at gaining control over the bureaucracy. Through two key strategies, the Reagan White House was able to infuse the bureaucracy with greater ideological direction. First, the administration required that all major regulations formulated by executive branch departments and agencies be approved by the Office of Management and Budget (OMB), which is part of the Executive

politics in a changing america

13.1   Does Gender Make a Difference?

When the U.S. Forest Service was sued for discriminating against women employees, it signed a consent decree pledging to hire enough women at each level of the organization so that its employment mix would be similar to the gender composition of the rest of the American work force. It moved quickly to hire more women in all types of jobs.

It is easy to applaud the Forest Service for tackling discrimination within its ranks in order to create more opportunities for women. Clearly, it makes a difference for women, who can now compete more fairly for better jobs with increased responsibility and better pay. But does it make a difference in how the Forest Service operates? Does employing more women have an impact on the Forest Service's policy decisions? After all, the primary job of the Forest Service is to manage publicly owned forests—is there a distinctly "feminine" approach to managing trees?

Recent research demonstrates that men and women in the Forest Service are different in important ways. A survey of those working for the agency shows that women are decidedly more concerned about environmental protection. Women in the Forest Service are more likely to believe that there are limits to the number of people the earth can sup-

port, that the balance of nature is easily upset, that economic growth should be "steady-state," and that humans are abusing the environment.

The Forest Service must balance the needs of consumers for wood products with the desire of Americans to have our forests preserved for generations to come. But if a larger percentage of employees entering the Forest Service believes we need to do more to protect the environment, then the existing balance between development and preservation is likely to be challenged.

The influx of women into the agency is too recent to measure whether these attitudes have carried over into new policies. Furthermore, basic policy is set by Congress and by the president's appointees who run the agency. Inevitably, though, the different mix of men and women within the Forest Service is going to affect policy, just as adding a lot more liberals or conservatives to an agency would change it. The National Forest Products Association, a trade group of businesses that develop or use public-forest resources, has warned its members that "the sharp changes in the demographic characteristics of Forest Service employees will lead to further deemphasis on commodity production and

Office of the President. OMB used its authority to push the bureaucracy to develop policies more in line with the president's strong conservative principles. Second, the Reagan administration also made a concerted effort to ensure that its top appointees were steadfast in their support of the president's program. Reagan's appointments were far more partisan in nature than those of either of his immediate Republican predecessors, Richard Nixon and Gerald Ford.[18]

When George Bush became president, he placed less emphasis on appointing "true believers" than Ronald Reagan had, and he selected many Republican moderates who lacked the ideological zeal of those in the previous administration. Bush's head of the National Endowment for the Arts (NEA), John Frohnmayer, had not even voted for Bush for president, and he repeatedly clashed with conservative Republicans in Congress who be-to increasing emphasis accorded to non-timber resource values." In other words, more women in the agency means a different outlook on how to manage the nation's forests.

Source: Greg Brown and Charles C. Harris, "The Implications of Work Force Diversification in the U.S. Forest Service," *Administration and Society* 25 (May 1993), pp. 85–113.

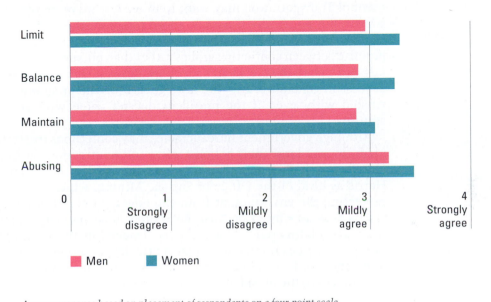

Average response based on placement of respondents on a four-point scale.
Limit = We are approaching the limit of the number of people the earth can support.
Balance = The balance of nature is very delicate and easily upset.
Maintain = To maintain a healthy economy we will have to develop a "steady-state" economy, where industrial growth is controlled.
Abusing = Humankind is severely abusing the environment.

lieved the NEA was funding artists whose work was obscene. The NEA had given grants to performance artist Karen Finley, for example, who as part of her art would sometimes symbolically defile her partially nude body by smearing chocolate over it. Frohnmayer was far more concerned about protecting artistic freedom than rooting out obscenity in the art world, and he resisted efforts in Congress to legislate antiobscenity guidelines for projects funded with taxpayer dollars. In his eyes, artistic freedom was much more important than the order Congress wanted to impose. Frohnmayer became such a political liability that he was fired.[19]

Bush was slow to learn that presidents must be aggressive in taking control of the executive branch. The scope of what it does is staggering, and presidents must be strategic in marshaling their resources to get the bureaucracy moving in the direction they want. Appointing loyal people and developing mechanisms for White House control of agencies are means by which presidents try to get the individual parts of the executive branch to be responsive to their goals. His frustrations with the bureaucracy finally led Bush to use the resources of the White House to exert control over the executive branch.[20] In his first years in office, Bill Clinton behaved more like Bush than Reagan when it came to appointments and White House control. His appointees were certainly left of center, but they were also pragmatists and generally avoided sharply ideological initiatives.[21]

Presidents find that the bureaucracy is not always as responsive as they might like, for a number of reasons. Principally, pluralism can pull agencies in a direction other than that favored by the president. The Department of Transportation may want to move toward more support for mass transit, but politically it cannot afford to ignore the preferences of highway builders. An agency administrator must often try to broker a compromise between conflicting groups rather than pursue a position that holds fast and true to the president's ideology. Bureaucracies must also follow—at least in general terms—the laws governing the programs they are entrusted with, even if the president doesn't agree with some of those statutes.

Although government bureaucracies may sometimes frustrate the president, by and large their policies move in the direction set by the White House. When President Reagan came into office, he appointed James Harris as head of the Office of Surface Mining, which is responsible for protecting the environment from the effects of coal mining operations. Harris was appointed because he shared Reagan's belief that business needed regulatory relief. Under Harris's leadership, the agency reduced the number of mines it cited for violating the law and issued fewer cessation of business orders.[22] Bureaucracies are strongly influenced by the policy preferences of the president.

ADMINISTRATIVE POLICYMAKING: THE FORMAL PROCESSES

Many Americans wonder why agencies sometimes actually make policy rather than merely carry it out. Administrative agencies are, in fact, authoritative policymaking bodies, and their decisions on substantive issues are legally binding on the citizens of this country.

Administrative Discretion

What are executive agencies set up to do? To begin with, cabinet departments, independent agencies, and government corporations are creatures of Congress. Congress creates a new department or agency by enacting a law that describes the organization's mandate, or mission. As part of that mandate, Congress grants the agency the authority to make certain policy decisions. Congress long ago recognized that it has neither the time nor the technical expertise to make all policy decisions. Ideally, it sets general guidelines for policy and expects agencies to act within those guidelines. The latitude that Congress gives agencies to make policy in the spirit of their legislative mandate is called **administrative discretion.** When this discretion is granted to agencies, it is also indirectly granted to the White House, because it is the president who appoints agency heads.

●●●●●●●●●●●●●●
Goring the Bureaucracy

Under the direction of Vice President Gore, the Clinton administration promised to "reinvent government" by streamlining administrative procedures, reducing the number of bureaucrats, and delivering better service to the public. After the first year of this effort, the Brookings Institution, a respected Washington think tank, gave the Gore initiative mixed grades. It criticized the reform program for focusing too much on short-term savings rather than long-term management issues. On the other hand, it praised the campaign for cutting red tape, simplifying rules, and improving procurement practices.

In 1988, the Department of Health and Human Services (HHS) finalized regulations that forbade family planning clinics that receive federal money to provide "counseling concerning the use of abortion as a method of family planning" or even to provide referrals to clinics that would discuss abortion as a method of family planning. Antiabortion Republicans at both the White House and HHS believed they had the authority to issue such regulations, because Congress had given HHS the administrative discretion to write regulations governing the dispersal of grants under Title X of the Public Health Services Act.[23] When the Clinton administration came into office, the new HHS secretary, Donna Shalala, in turn used her administrative discretion to rescind the so-called gag rule that prohibited discussion of the abortion option at federally funded family planning clinics. At both points in time, HHS was acting under the same law; different administrations interpreted that law in different ways.[24]

Critics of the bureaucracy frequently complain that agencies are granted too much discretion. In his book *The End of Liberalism*, Theodore Lowi argues that Congress commonly gives vague directives in its initial enabling legislation instead of truly setting guidelines.[25] Congress charges agencies with protecting "the public interest" but leaves them to determine on their own what policies best serve the public. Lowi and other critics believe that members of Congress delegate too much of their responsibility for difficult policy choices to appointed administrators.

Congress often is vague about its intent when setting up a new agency or program. At times, a problem is clear cut, but the solution is not; yet Congress is under pressure to act. So it creates an agency or program to show that it is concerned and responsive, but it leaves it to administrators to develop specific solutions. For example, the 1934 legislation that established the FCC recognized a need for regulation in the burgeoning radio industry. The growing number of stations and overlapping frequencies would soon have made it impossible to listen to the radio. But Congress avoided tackling several sticky issues by giving the FCC the ambiguous directive that broadcasters should "serve the public interest, convenience, and necessity."[26] In other cases, a number of obvious solutions to a problem may be available, but lawmakers cannot agree on which is best. Compromise wording is often ambiguous, papering over differences and ensuring conflict over administrative regulations as agencies try to settle lingering policy disputes.

The wide latitude Congress gives administrative agencies often leads to charges that the bureaucracy is out of control, a power unto itself. But such claims are frequently exaggerated. Administrative discretion is not a fixed commodity. Congress has the power to express its displeasure by reining in agencies with additional legislation. If Congress is unhappy with an agency's actions, it can pass laws invalidating specific policies. This method of control may seem cumbersome, but Congress does have periodic opportunities to amend the original legislation that created an agency or program. Over time, Congress makes increasingly detailed policy decisions, often affirming or modifying agency decisions.[27] A second, powerful tool is Congress's control over the budget. Congress can influence an agency because it has the power to cut budgets and to reorder agency priorities through its detailed appropriations legislation.

In general, then, the bureaucracy is not out of control. But Congress has chosen to limit its own oversight in one area—domestic and international security. Both the FBI and the CIA have enjoyed a great deal of freedom from formal and informal congressional constraints because of the legitimate need for secrecy in their operations. During the years that the legendary J. Edgar Hoover ran the FBI (1924–1972), it was something of a rogue elephant, independent of both Congress and the president. Politicians were afraid of Hoover, who was not above keeping files on them and using those files to increase his power. At Hoover's direction, the FBI spied on Martin Luther King, Jr., and once sent King a tape recording with embarrassing revelations gathered by bugging his hotel rooms. The anonymous letter accompanying the tape suggested that King save himself further embarrassment by committing suicide.[28]

Rule Making

Agencies exercise their policymaking discretion through formal administrative procedures, usually rule making. **Rule making** is the administrative process that results in the issuance of regulations. **Regulations** are rules that govern the operation of government programs. When an agency issues regulations, it is using the discretionary authority granted to it by Congress to implement a program or policy enacted into law.

Because they are authorized by congressional statutes, regulations have the effect of law. The policy content of regulations is supposed to follow from the intent of enabling legislation. After Congress enacted the Nutrition Labeling and Education Act, for example, the FDA drew up regulations to implement the policy guidelines set forth in the law. One part of the law says that producers of foods and food supplements can make health claims for their products only when "significant scientific agreement" exists to support those claims. Following that principle, the FDA proposed regulations requiring manufacturers of vitamins and dietary supplements to substantiate the health claims they make for their products on their labels. Clearly, the FDA was following the intent of a law enacted by Congress.

Regulations are first published as proposals, to give all interested parties an opportunity to comment on them and to try to persuade the agency to adopt, alter, or withdraw them. When the FDA issued its proposed regulations on vitamins and health supplements, the industry fought them vigorously. Aware that many of their health claims could not be substantiated and that it would be expensive to finance scientific studies to try to prove their assertions, the manufacturers asked Congress for relief. Although it was responsible for the legislation authorizing the regulations, Congress passed a one-year moratorium on the proposed rules. Congress seemed to want to have it both ways, ensuring the integrity of food and drugs while protecting the business interests of industry constituents. When the moratorium expired, however, the FDA announced plans to reissue the regulations.[29]

The regulatory process is controversial because regulations often require individuals and corporations to act against their own self-interest. In this case, the producers of vitamins and dietary supplements resented the implication that they were making false claims and reminded policymakers that they employ many people to make products that consumers want. The FDA must, however, balance its desire not to put people out of work through overregulation with its concern that people not be misled or harmed by false labeling.

Food safety: all you wanted to know.
`<vm.cfsan.fda.gov/list.html>`

ADMINISTRATIVE POLICYMAKING: INFORMAL POLITICS

When an agency is considering a new regulation and all the evidence and arguments have been presented, how does an administrator reach a decision? Because policy decisions typically address complex problems that lack a single satisfactory solution, they rarely exhibit mathematical precision and efficiency.

The Science of Muddling Through

In his classic analysis of policymaking, "The Science of Muddling Through," Charles Lindblom compared the way policy might be made in the ideal world with the way it is formulated in the real world.[30] The ideal, rational decision-making process, according to Lindblom, begins with an administrator tackling a problem by ranking values and objectives. After the objectives are clarified, the administrator thoroughly considers all possible solutions to the problem. The administrator comprehensively analyzes alternative solutions, taking all relevant factors into account. Finally, the administrator chooses the alternative that is seen as the most effective means of achieving the desired goal and solving the problem.

Lindblom claims that this "rational-comprehensive" model is unrealistic. To begin with, policymakers have great difficulty defining precise values and goals. Administrators at the U.S. Department of Energy, for example, want to be sure that supplies of home heating oil are sufficient

●●●●●●●●●●●●●

Out of Gas?

In the wake of gas lines and energy shortages, Congress created a new Department of Energy in August 1977. (President Jimmy Carter is shown here signing the legislation authorizing the new cabinet department.) Over time, however, public concern over energy has waned as supplies have remained plentiful and many see the department as a symbol of a bloated, over-expansive bureaucracy. Some politicians have proposed shutting down the Department of Energy and, while this has been resisted, it has been subjected to budgetary cuts.

each winter. At the same time, they want to reduce dependence on foreign oil. Obviously, the two goals are not fully compatible. How do administrators decide which is more important? And how do they relate them to the other goals of the nation's energy policy?

Real-world decision making parts company with the ideal in another way: the policy selected cannot always be the most effective means to the desired end. Even if a tax at the pump is the most effective way to reduce gasoline consumption during a shortage, motorists' anger would make this theoretically "right" decision politically difficult. So the "best" policy is often the one on which most people can agree. However, political compromise may mean that the government is able to solve only part of a problem.

Finally, critics of the rational-comprehensive model point out that policymaking can never be based on truly comprehensive analyses. A secretary of energy cannot possibly find the time to read a comprehensive study of all alternative energy sources and relevant policy considerations for the future. A truly thorough investigation of the subject would produce thousands of pages of text. Instead, administrators usually rely on short staff memos that outline a limited range of feasible solutions to immediate problems. Time is of the essence, and problems are often too pressing to wait for a complete study.

In short, policymaking tends to be characterized by **incrementalism**, with policies and programs changing bit by bit, step by step.[31] Decision makers are constrained by competing policy objectives, opposing political forces, incomplete information, and the pressures of time. They choose from a limited number of feasible options that are almost always modifications of existing policies rather than wholesale departures from them.

Because policymaking proceeds by means of small modifications of existing policies, it is easy to assume that incrementalism describes a process that is intrinsically conservative, sticking close to the status quo. Yet even if policymaking moves in small steps, those steps may all be in the same direction. Over time, a series of incremental changes can significantly alter a program.[32]

The Culture of Bureaucracy

How an agency makes decisions and performs its tasks is greatly affected by the people who work there—the bureaucrats. Americans often find their interactions with bureaucrats frustrating, because bureaucrats are inflexible (they go by the book) or lack the authority to get things done. Top administrators, too, can become frustrated with the bureaucrats who work for them.

Why do people act bureaucratically? Individuals who work for large organizations cannot help but be affected by the culture of bureaucracy. Modern bureaucracies develop explicit rules and standards in order to make their operations more efficient and guarantee fair treatment for their clients. But within each organization, **norms** (informal, unwritten rules of behavior) also develop and influence the way people act on the job. At the CIA, for example, not only do rules mandate secrecy for sensitive intelligence activities but a norm enshrines secrecy for virtually everything that the employees do. In the wake of the collapse of the Cold War, a 1992 internal assessment at the CIA concluded that excessive secrecy has fed public misunderstanding of what the agency does and a lack of appreciation for what it has accomplished. The report found that the passion for secrecy meant that documents analyzing troop movements at the beginning of World War I were still classified for national security reasons.[33]

Bureaucracies are often influenced in their selection of policy options by the prevailing customs, attitudes, and expectations of the people working within them. Departments and agencies commonly develop a sense of mission, where a particular objective or a means for achieving it is emphasized. The Army Corps of Engineers, for example, is dominated by engineers who define the agency's objective as protecting citizens from floods by building dams. There could be other objectives, and there are certainly other methods of achieving this one, but the engineers promote the solutions that fit their conception of what the agency should be doing. As one study concluded, "When asked to generate policy proposals for review by their political superiors, bureaucrats are tempted to bias the search for alternatives so that their superiors wind up selecting the kind of program the agency wants to pursue."[34]

Despite budget cutbacks, adverse public opinion, and other constraints that make their job difficult, most bureaucrats work hard and try to serve the public as best they can. Those agencies with a clear sense of mission are likely to have a strong esprit de corps that adds to the bureaucrats' motivation. Bureaucrats' caution and close adherence to agency rules offer a measure of consistency. It would be unsettling if government employees interpreted rules as they pleased. Simply put, bureaucrats "go by the book" because "the book" consists of the laws and regulations of this country as well as the internal rules and norms of a particular agency. Americans expect to be treated equally before the law, and bureaucrats work with that expectation in mind.

● ● ● ● ● ● ● ● ● ● ● ●
Gagged with a Regulation

When the White House cannot get Congress to pass what it wants, it may try to accomplish certain of its goals through the administrative powers of a relevant agency. The Reagan administration, sympathetic to the aims of the pro-life movement, instituted the so-called gag rule to stop federally funded clinics from discussing abortion with clients. The rule was rescinded by the Clinton administration.

PROBLEMS IN IMPLEMENTING POLICY

One of the questions in the IDEAlog program that accompanies this book deals with the issue of pornography. How did you answer that question in the self-test?

The development of policy in Washington is the end of one phase of the policymaking cycle and the beginning of another. After policies have been developed, they must be implemented. **Implementation** is the process of putting specific policies into operation. Ultimately, bureaucrats must convert policies on paper into policies in action. It is important to study implementation because policies do not always do what they were designed to do.

Implementation may be difficult because the policy to be carried out is not clearly stated. Policy directives to bureaucrats sometimes lack clarity and leave them with too much discretion. We noted earlier that when John Frohnmayer headed the NEA, he fought legislation intended to prohibit federal funding for "obscene" art. After a bitter fight in Congress, a compromise required that NEA grants be restricted to works that fall within "general standards of decency." But what exactly is a "general standard of decency"? It was left to the NEA—with an administrator hostile to the very idea of a decency standard—to figure it out.[35]

Implementation can also be problematic because of the sheer complexity of some government endeavors. Take, for example, the government's Superfund program to clean up toxic waste sites. When the EPA cleans up a site itself, the cleanup takes an average of eight years to complete. Yet, this is not a program that works badly because of malfeasance by administrators. Superfund cleanups pose complex engineering, political, and financial problems. Inevitably, regional EPA offices and key actors on the local level must engage in considerable negotiations at each stage of the process.[36] The more organizations and levels of government involved, the more difficult it is to coordinate implementation.

Policymakers can create implementation difficulties by ignoring the administrative capabilities of an agency they have chosen to carry out a program. This happened in 1981 when the Reagan administration and Congress instructed the Social Security Administration to expand its review of those citizens receiving disability insurance benefits. The disability program had grown during the 1970s when eligibility requirements were broadened to take in younger people and those with shorter-term disabilities.

The increased costs associated with the changes made the program a target of the Reagan administration's effort to cut domestic spending. Eligibility reviews were increased dramatically as a means of assessing whether people were still disabled and merited continued benefits. The state agencies that carried out the reviews had been doing 20,000 to 30,000 cases a quarter. The same agencies were ordered to review 100,000 to 150,000 cases a quarter. As the number of people terminated increased, so did the legal appeals to reverse the terminations, and the backlog of unresolved cases grew sharply. With tens of thousands of individuals believing they had been unfairly removed from the disability rolls and the administrative system inundated with more cases than it could handle, the problems with the program reached crisis proportions.

The lesson of this episode was that policymakers were so eager to cut costs that they made wholly unrealistic assumptions about the administrative capacities of the state agencies implementing the program. Because those agencies were given a huge increase in work without a significant increase in resources to hire additional people, they inevitably buckled under the expanded case load.[37]

Ironically, although one of the central criticisms of the bureaucracy is that agencies are given too much discretion in developing policies under the laws they are given to administer, another common criticism is that there is not enough discretion available to lower-level bureaucrats. Often the agency officials doing the actual implementing in schools, hospitals, and other local settings find that their agency's programs have become "encrusted with rules."[38] Some see this as causing inflexibility, with local bureaucrats unable to fashion solutions most appropriate to the specific context.[39] For example, using the discretionary authority granted them by Congress, Clinton administration officials in the U.S. Department of Agriculture (USDA) decided to issue new dietary guidelines for school lunches. The new regulations limited fat in the lunches for any given week to 30 percent of total calories. School chefs implemented these guidelines in different ways, but then the USDA decided that it wanted the chefs to reach the 30 percent level by using specified amounts of particular foods. As school system employees, the chefs in this instance were the front-line bureaucrats, but they couldn't implement a simple policy in the way they saw fit. The chefs believed they knew best what kids are most likely to eat.[40]

Obstacles to effective implementation can create the impression that nothing the government does succeeds, but programs can and do work. Problems in implementation demonstrate why patience and continual analysis are necessary ingredients of successful policymaking. To return to a term we used earlier, implementation is by its nature an *incremental* process, in which trial and error eventually lead to policies that work.

REFORMING THE BUREAUCRACY: MORE CONTROL OR LESS?

As we saw at the beginning of this chapter, organization matters. How bureaucracies are designed directly affects how effective they are in accomplishing their tasks.[41] People in government constantly tinker with the structure of bureaucracies, trying to find ways to improve their performance. Administrative reforms have taken many different approaches in recent years as criticism of government has mounted.[42] Like those before it, the Clinton administration has proposed many management changes to save the taxpayers money and streamline the bureaucracy. Led by Vice President Al Gore, the Reinventing Government initiative put forth eight hundred proposals, "ranging from a top-to-bottom overhaul of the civil-service system to elimination of the subsidy for mohair."[43]

Reinventing government.
<www.npr.gov>

A central question that surrounds much of the debate over bureaucratic reform is whether we need to establish more control over the bureaucracy or less. There is no magic bullet that will work for every type of bureaucracy: less control may be best for public schools, but the NEA may need more direction by Congress if it is to retain the public's confidence. Those who advocate less government control extol the virtues of letting consumer preferences and popular opinion play more of a role in the workings of government and the economy. Those who believe that the problem is to reform government without reducing its role look for a way to enhance government performance by improving management. We will look at both broad approaches.

Deregulation

Many people believe that government is too involved in **regulation,** intervening in the natural working of business markets to promote some social goal. For example, government might regulate a market to ensure that products pose no danger to consumers. Through **deregulation,** the government reduces its role and lets the natural market forces of supply and demand take over. Conservatives have championed deregulation because they see freedom in the marketplace as the best route to an efficient and growing economy. Indeed, nothing is more central to capitalist philosophy than the belief that the free market will efficiently promote the balance of supply and demand. Considerable deregulation took place in the 1970s and 1980s, notably in the airline, trucking, financial services, and telecommunications industries.

In telecommunications, for example, consumers had no choice in choosing a long-distance vendor—one could call on the Bell system or not call at all. After an out-of-court settlement broke up the Bell system in 1982, AT&T was awarded the right to sell the long-distance services that had previously been provided by that system, but it now had to face competition from other long-distance carriers, like MCI and Sprint. Consumers have benefited from the competition, and more recently, competition has opened up for local phone service as well.

● ● ● ● ● ● ● ● ● ● ● ● ●
No Longer Banking on Their Savings and Loan

Deregulation of the nation's savings and loans illustrates the tradeoffs between the desire to reduce government and the desire to have government protect citizens from unfair or fraudulent business practices. Among the many reasons for the collapse of so many S&L's during the 1980s was that after deregulation there were too few government auditors to monitor the risky investments and shady business dealings that came to characterize the industry. However, depositors (like these outside their New York S&L), got all their money back as the government reimbursed deposits in full, including those in excess of the insurance limit. This bailout of the S&L's cost the taxpayers hundreds of billions of dollars.

Deciding on an appropriate level of deregulation is particularly difficult for health and safety issues. Companies within a particular industry may legitimately claim that health and safety regulations are burdensome, making it difficult for them to earn sufficient profits or compete effectively with foreign manufacturers. But the drug-licensing procedures used by the FDA illustrate the potential danger of deregulating such policy areas. The thorough and lengthy process the FDA uses to evaluate drugs has as its ultimate validation the thalidomide case. The William S. Merrill Company purchased the license to market this sedative, already available in Europe, and filed an application with the FDA in 1960. The company then began a protracted fight with an FDA bureaucrat, Dr. Frances Kelsey, who was assigned to evaluate the thalidomide application. She demanded that the company abide by all FDA drug-testing requirements, despite the fact that the drug was already in use in other countries. She and her superiors resisted pressure from the company to bend the rules a little and expedite approval. Before Merrill had conducted all the FDA tests, news came pouring in from Europe that some women who had taken thalidomide during pregnancy were giving birth to babies without arms, legs, or ears. Strict adherence to government regulation protected Americans from the same tragic consequences.

Nevertheless, the pharmaceutical industry has been highly critical of the FDA, claiming that its licensing procedures are so complex that drugs of great benefit are kept from the marketplace for years, with people suffering from diseases denied access to new treatments.[44] Manufacturers claim that there is a "drug lag" and point to the fact that many more new medicines are introduced in Great Britain than in the United States. They have encouraged the FDA to adopt faster procedures to save the industry substantial research and development costs and to speed valuable drugs into the hands of seriously ill Americans. The FDA has resisted doing anything that would compromise what it sees as necessary precautions.

In recent years, however, the AIDS epidemic has brought about some concessions from the FDA. Although AIDS is incurable, drugs have been found to help patients deal with various symptoms of the disease and to lengthen their lives. The FDA has issued new rules expediting the availability of experimental drugs, and more generally, the FDA has adopted a somewhat speedier timetable for clinical tests of new drugs.[45]

The conflict over how far to take deregulation reflects the traditional dilemma of choosing between freedom and order. A strong case can be made for deregulated business markets, in which free and unfettered competition benefits consumers and promotes productivity. The strength of capitalist economies comes from the ability of individuals and firms to compete freely in the marketplace, and the regulatory state places restrictions on this freedom. But without regulation, nothing ensures that marketplace participants will act responsibly.

Monitoring, Accountability, and Responsiveness

Bureaucracies must also strive to be responsive to the public, to provide services in an efficient and accessible manner. In the past few years, a management reform program known as **total quality management (TQM)** has increasingly gotten attention. Although initially directed at improving the quality of manufacturing, it is now being adapted to organizations (such as government bureaucracies) that provide services as their "product." The principles of TQM include listening to the customer, relying on teamwork, focusing on continually improving quality, breaking down barriers between parts of organizations, and engaging in participatory management.[46]

Most Americans believe that government has a long way to go toward treating its clients like "customers." As one manual on TQM in government asked, "When was the last time you felt like a 'valued customer' when you encountered a government bureaucracy?"[47] Government, of course, does not have to treat people as customers, because its customers cannot go to the competition—government has a monopoly over most everything it does.

Yet in an era when people are highly antagonistic toward government and budgets are tight, government bureaucrats know they need to do better. TQM has shown some promise. After hearing a lecture on TQM, Mayor Joseph Sensenbrenner of Madison, Wisconsin, thought about the long delays the city was experiencing in getting its motor vehicles repaired. Squad cars, dump trucks, garbage trucks, and road scrapers were often unavailable while the city garage waited for a part. Because TQM preaches that managers need to break down barriers to solve problems, the mayor went to the garage himself. He talked to the parts manager and found out that the city owned 440 different models of motor vehicles, with a total fleet of only 765. It was impossible to stock parts for such a large array, so repairs had to await the arrival of parts ordered as they were needed.

The mayor asked why the city owned so many different kinds of cars and trucks. The parts manager told him the city had a policy designed to save money by requiring the purchase of whatever appropriate vehicle had the lowest sticker price on the day it was ordered. When Sensenbrenner asked the city's central purchasing office whether the policy could be changed, the purchaser replied that the city comptroller would not allow it. The mayor went to see the comptroller, but he could not approve such a change, because the city attorney would not allow it. Sensenbrenner went to see the city attorney, who told him, "Why, of course you can do that" and told him how to make the simple changes. Once instituted, the new purchasing policy reduced the average turnaround time for car and truck repairs from nine days to three.[48]

The compelling philosophy behind TQM led the Clinton administration to launch its "reinventing government" initiative, aimed at improving the management of the national government. It has had some short-term successes, but there is no shortage of problems with TQM.[49] The single most important rule of TQM is to listen to your customers in an effort to serve them better. But for a government agency, who is the customer? Are the Department of Agriculture's customers the farmers who want the agency to spend a lot of money providing them with services and subsidies, or are they the taxpayers who want the agency to minimize the amount of money spent by government? TQM does not solve this basic conflict between pluralism and majoritarianism. More broadly, evidence suggests that following public opinion may lead bureaucracies to make poor choices in setting priorities. A study of the EPA shows that it favors spending money on problems characterized by high public concern rather than on those that pose the greatest risks to public health (see Figure 13.3).

SUMMARY

As the scope of government activity has grown during the twentieth century, so too has the bureaucracy. The executive branch has evolved into a complex set of departments, independent agencies, and government corporations. The way in which the various bureaucracies are organized matters a great deal, because their structure affects their ability to carry out their tasks.

Through the administrative discretion granted them by Congress, these bodies make policy decisions by making rules that have the force of law. In making policy choices, agency decision makers are influenced by their external environment, especially the White House, Congress, and interest groups. Internal norms and the need to work cooperatively with others both inside and outside their agencies also influence decision makers.

The most serious charge facing the bureaucracy is that it is unresponsive to the will of the people. In fact, the White House, Congress, interest groups, and public opinion act as substantial controls on the bureaucracy. Still, to many Americans, the bureaucracy seems too big, too costly, and too intrusive. Reducing the size and scope of bureaucratic activity is difficult, because pluralism characterizes our political system. The entire executive branch may appear too large, and each of us can point to agencies that we believe should be reduced or eliminated. Yet each bureaucracy has its supporters. The Department of Agriculture performs vital services for farmers. Unions care a great deal about the Department of Labor. Scholars want the National Science Foundation protected. And home builders do not want Housing and Urban Development programs cut back. Bureaucracies survive because they provide important services to groups of

figure

13.3   ● Should Government Listen to Its Customers?

When a Washington-based think tank analyzed the allocation of resources within the Environmental Protection Agency, it found that EPA spends only about 20 percent of its funds on the pollution problems that present the most serious risks to either public health or the environment. The study concluded that EPA spending was driven by the public's perception of what was important. (Hazardous waste management was not ranked according to actual risk.)

Source: Jeff Bailey and Timothy Noah, "EPA Spending Is Off Target, Study Says," *Wall Street Journal,* 24 May 1993, p. B1. Reprinted by permission of The Wall Street Journal, © 1993 by Dow Jones & Company, Inc. All Rights Reserved Worldwide.

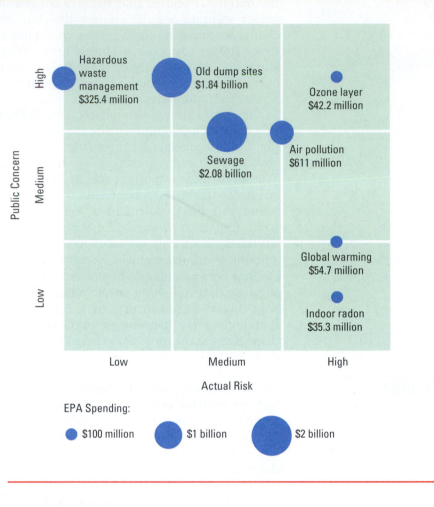

people, and those people—no matter how strong their commitment to shrinking the government—are not willing to sacrifice their own benefits.

Plans for reforming the bureaucracy to make it work better are not in short supply. Proponents of deregulation believe our economy would be more productive if we freed the marketplace from the heavy hand of government supervision. Opponents believe that deregulation involves considerable risk and that we ought to be careful in determining which markets and business practices can be subjected to less government supervision. To prevent disasters such as the thalidomide episode and the savings and loan scandal, government bureaucracies must be able to monitor the behavior of people inside and outside government and supervise business practices in a wide range of industries. However, most people continue to believe that the overall management of bureaucracies is poor and that government needs to be more customer-driven.

Key Terms

bureaucracy	government corporation	incrementalism	total quality management
bureaucrat	civil service	norms	(TQM)
department	administrative discretion	implementation	
independent agency	rule making	regulation	
regulatory commission	regulations	deregulation	

Selected Readings

Eisner, Marc Allen. *Regulatory Politics in Transition.* Baltimore: Johns Hopkins University Press, 1993. Eisner offers an overview of regulation in different periods of American history.

Harris, Richard A., and Sidney M. Milkis. *The Politics of Regulatory Change*, 2nd ed. New York: Oxford University Press, 1996. A study of how the regulatory regime of the Reagan years affected policymaking at the Federal Trade Commission and the Environmental Protection Agency.

Howard, Philip K. *The Death of Common Sense.* New York: Warner Books, 1994. A sharp attack on government bureaucracies for being too inflexible and for not giving agency officials more discretion in solving problems.

Kerwin, Cornelius M. *Rulemaking: How Government Agencies Write Law and Make Policy.* Washington, D.C.: Congressional Quarterly Press, 1994. An inside look at how agencies write regulations to carry out the laws they must administer.

Osborne, David, and Ted Gaebler. *Reinventing Government.* New York: Plume Books, 1993. Although it makes the process of administrative reform seem too simple, this is a valuable guide to making government more entrepreneurial and customer-driven.

World Wide Web Resources

Fedworld. This site is operated by the National Technical Information Service (of the Department of Commerce). A "central access point" for U.S. government information on-line, it allows you to "locate, order, and have government information delivered to you." It also contains information on federal employment opportunities, abstracts of recent government reports (from all agencies), links to departments for which Fedworld provides home pages (Federal Energy Regulatory Commission, IRS, Treasury), and the World-News Connection (access to non-U.S. media sources).
`<www.fedworld.gov/>`

Federal Bureau of Investigation. The FBI home page contains information on investigations, programs, law enforcement services, bureau accomplishments, and bureau history. In addition to the text of the FBI director's speeches and crime statistics, visitors can also find descriptions of the "ten most wanted fugitives" and information on "headline" cases such as the Unabomber case.
`<www.fbi.gov/>`

Federal Communications Commission. This home page provides access to the FCC's Daily Digest, policy agenda, agendas of open meetings, consumer information, a link to the text of the 1996 Telecommunications Act (which includes internet policy) and the FCC's implementation schedule, and speeches made by commissioners.
`<www.fcc.gov/>`

chapter 14

The Courts

"WE'RE GOING TO KILL HIM POLITICALLY—THIS LITTLE CREEP. Where did he come from?" asked feminist activist Florence Kennedy[1]. Her target was Judge Clarence Thomas, who had just been nominated by President George Bush for a seat on the nation's highest court, the Supreme Court of the United States. Thomas was a staunch conservative. His 1991 appointment, to replace the retiring liberal Justice Thurgood Marshall, would put many liberal decisions at risk.

Thomas endured a determined effort by a range of liberal organizations, including the American Civil Liberties Union and the National Organization for Women, to scuttle his confirmation by the U.S. Senate (a constitutional requirement). He weathered days of questioning from the Senate Judiciary Committee, declining to express his opinions about policies and approaches to constitutional interpretation and thus stymieing his opponents. Thomas's nomination seemed assured until a last-minute witness, Professor Anita Hill, came forward with charges that Thomas had made unwanted advances when she had worked for him ten years earlier. Thomas categorically denied the charges and characterized the process as "a high-tech lynching."[2]

Suddenly, the hearing galvanized the press and the public. A transfixed nation watched the riveting testimony of Hill, Thomas, and a parade of corroborating witnesses. The coverage pre-empted soap operas and competed for World Series viewers. Thomas's critics heaved charges of sexism; his champions leveled charges of racism. The committee failed to unearth convincing proof of Hill's allegations. (National polls at the time showed Americans believed Thomas over Hill by a margin of two to one.) In the end, the Senate voted by a slim margin—fifty-two to forty-eight—to confirm Thomas's nomination.

Anita Hill: feminist hero.
`<www.now.org/now/issues/`
`harass/anitahil.html>`

Clarence Thomas: a defense.
`<www.counterattack.com/`
`thom.htm>`

Thomas joined the ranks of the judicial elite, the youngest member of the nation's highest court and its sole African American. Upon taking the oaths of office, he withdrew into his work, secure in the knowledge that the Constitution now placed him above his detractors. For her part, Anita Hill became a much-sought-after celebrity for liberal and feminist causes. For his part, Thomas has the consolation of serving on the nation's highest court for the rest of his life. "They can say what they want about me," Thomas later remarked to a friend, "but I'm going to be making law for a long time."[3]

The Supreme Court is like a cloister: outsiders find it very difficult to know what transpires inside. This is especially true of the events that take

"She Said. He Said."

President George Bush nominated forty-three-year-old Clarence Thomas to the nation's highest court in 1991. As Thomas was on the verge of confirmation, Anita Hill, a former Thomas assistant, stepped forward to assert that Thomas had made unwanted advances years earlier. Her charges nearly scuttled Thomas's nomination.

place in the conference room where the justices gather twice weekly to cast tentative decisions on cases that have recently been argued. Surprisingly, the conference room is not a cauldron of powerful advocacy or intellectual debate. The justices tend to keep their emotions in check.

After hearing arguments in two important 1995 cases related to issues of race, Thomas spoke fervently in the conference room of his own struggles with racial segregation and bigotry. (The justices reported these events to their assistants, who spoke without attribution to a reporter.) As Thomas saw it, race-based solutions (such as forcing whites and blacks to attend the same schools or giving African Americans special advantages in securing contracts or employment) are misdirected and harmful because they rest on the patronizing belief that blacks are inherently inferior. The solution, Thomas averred, is to ensure equality of opportunity and to remove government from the business of racial classifications. The Constitution, Thomas declared, should be color-blind.[4] He cast his votes accordingly.

A single vote can make a difference. In both cases, the justices split five to four, with Thomas in the majority. As a result, the Court curtailed the government's power to fashion remedies to racial discrimination in the name of equality and allowed more room for freedom to flourish.[5] These cases and others have signaled a conservative shift in the Court's ideological center—a shift that is largely unaffected by representative institutions or majority rule.

Judges confront conflicting values in the cases brought before them; and in crafting their decisions, judges—especially Supreme Court justices—make policy. Their decisions become the precedents other judges use to rule in similar cases. A judge makes public policy to the extent that she or he influences decisions in other courts.

The power of the courts to shape policy creates a difficult problem for democratic theory. According to that theory, the power to make law resides only in the people or their elected representatives. When judges undo the work of elected majorities, they risk depriving the people of the right to make the laws to govern themselves.

Court rulings—especially Supreme Court rulings—extend far beyond any particular case. Judges are students of the law, but they remain human beings. They have their own opinions about the values of freedom, order, and equality. And although all judges are constrained by statutes and precedents from expressing their personal beliefs in their decisions, some judges are more prone than others to interpret laws in light of those beliefs.

America's courts are deeply involved in the life of the country and its people. Some courts, such as the Supreme Court, make fundamental policy decisions vital to the preservation of freedom, order, and equality. Through checks and balances, the elected branches link the courts to democracy, and the courts link the elected branches to the Constitution. But does it work? Can the courts exercise political power within the pluralist model? Or are judges simply sovereigns in black robes, making decisions independent of popular control? In this chapter, we try to answer these questions by exploring the role of the judiciary in American political life.

NATIONAL JUDICIAL SUPREMACY

Section 1 of Article III of the Constitution creates "one supreme Court." The founders were divided on the need for other national courts, so they deferred to Congress the decision to create a national court system. Those who opposed the creation of national courts believed that such a system would usurp the authority of state courts.[6] Congress considered the issue in its first session and, in the Judiciary Act of 1789, gave life to a system of federal (that is, national) courts that would coexist with the courts in each state but be independent of them. Federal judges would also be independent of popular influences, because the Constitution provided for their virtual lifetime appointment.

In the early years of the republic, the federal judiciary was not a particularly powerful branch of government. It was especially difficult to recruit and keep Supreme Court justices. They spent much of their time as individual traveling judges ("riding circuit"); disease and poor transportation were everyday hazards. The justices met as the Supreme Court only for a few weeks in February and August.[7] John Jay, the first chief justice, refused to resume his duties in 1801 because he concluded that the Court could not muster the "energy, weight, and dignity" to contribute to national affairs.[8] Several distinguished statesmen refused appointments to the Court, and several others, including Oliver Ellsworth, the third chief justice, resigned. But a period of profound change began in 1801 when President John Adams appointed his secretary of state, John Marshall, to the position of chief justice.

Judicial Review of the Other Branches

Shortly after Marshall's appointment, the Supreme Court confronted a question of fundamental importance to the future of the new republic: if a law enacted by Congress conflicts with the Constitution, which should prevail? The question arose in the case of *Marbury* v. *Madison* (1803), which involved a controversial series of last-minute political appointments.

The case began in 1801, when an obscure Federalist, William Marbury, was designated a justice of the peace in the District of Columbia. Marbury and several others were appointed to government posts created by Congress in the last days of John Adams's presidency, but the appointments were never completed. The newly arrived Jefferson administration had little interest in delivering the required documents; qualified Jeffersonians would welcome the jobs.

To secure their jobs, Marbury and the other disgruntled appointees invoked an act of Congress to obtain the papers. The act authorized the Supreme Court to issue orders against government officials. Marbury and the others sought such an order in the Supreme Court against the new secretary of state, James Madison, who held the crucial documents.

Marshall observed that the act of Congress invoked by Marbury to sue in the Supreme Court conflicted with Article III, which did not authorize such suits. In February 1803, the Court delivered its opinion.*

---

* *Courts publish their opinions in volumes called reporters. Today, the* United States Reports *is the official reporter for the U.S. Supreme Court. For example, the Court's opinion in the case of* Brown v. Board of Education *is cited as 347 U.S. 483 (1954). This means that the opinion in* Brown *begins on page 483 of Volume 347 in* United States Reports. *The citation includes the year of the decision, in this case 1954.*

Before 1875, the official reports of the Supreme Court were published under the names of private compilers. For example, the case of Marbury v. Madison *is cited as 1 Cranch 137 (1803). This means that the case is found in Volume 1, compiled by reporter William Cranch, starting on page 137, and that it was decided in 1803.*

● ● ● ● ● ● ● ● ● ● ● ●
Chief Justice John Marshall

John Marshall (1755–1835) clearly ranks as the Babe Ruth of the Supreme Court. Both Marshall and the Bambino transformed their respective games and became symbols of their institutions. Scholars now recognize both men as originators—Marshall of judicial review, and Ruth of the modern age of baseball.

Must the Court follow the law or the Constitution? The High Court held, in Marshall's forceful argument, that the Constitution was "the fundamental and paramount law of the nation" and that "an act of the legislature, repugnant to the constitution, is void." In other words, when an act of the legislature conflicts with the Constitution—the nation's highest law—that act is invalid. Marshall's argument vested in the judiciary the power to weigh the validity of congressional acts:

> It is emphatically the province and duty of the judicial department to say what the law is. Those who apply the rule to particular cases, must of necessity expound and interpret that rule. . . . So if a law be in opposition to the constitution; if both the law and the constitution apply to a particular case, so that the court must either decide that case conformably to the law, disregarding the constitution; or conformably to the constitution, disregarding the law; the court must determine which of these conflicting rules governs the case. This is of the very essence of judicial duty.[9]

The decision in *Marbury* v. *Madison* established the Supreme Court's power of **judicial review**—the power to declare congressional acts invalid if they violate the Constitution.* Subsequent cases extended the power to cover presidential acts as well.[10]

Marshall expanded the potential power of the Supreme Court to equal or exceed the power of the other branches of government. Should a congressional act (or, by implication, a presidential act) conflict with the Constitution, the Supreme Court claimed the power to declare the act void. The judiciary would be a check on the legislative and executive branches, consistent with the principle of checks and balances embedded in the Constitution. Although Congress and the president may sometimes wrestle with the constitutionality of their actions, judicial review gave the Supreme Court the final word on the meaning of the Constitution.

The exercise of judicial review—an appointed branch's checking of an elected branch in the name of the Constitution—appears to run counter to democratic theory. But in nearly two hundred years of practice, the Supreme Court has invalidated fewer than 150 provisions of national law. Only a small number have had great significance for the political system.[11] (The Court did produce a bumper crop of four invalidations in 1995, but only one—involving handgun possession near a school—merited broad media and scholarly attention.) Moreover, there are mechanisms to override judicial review (constitutional amendments) and to control the excesses of the justices (impeachment). In addition, the Court can respond to the continuing struggle among competing interests (a struggle that is consistent with the pluralist model) by reversing itself.

Judicial Review of State Government

The establishment of judicial review of national laws made the Supreme Court the umpire of the national government. When acts of the national government conflict with the Constitution, the Supreme Court can de-

---

* *The Supreme Court had earlier upheld an act of Congress in* Hylton v. United States *(3 Dallas 171 [1796]).* Marbury v. Madison *was the first exercise of the power of a court to invalidate an act of Congress.*

clare those acts invalid. But suppose state laws conflict with the Constitution, national laws, or federal treaties. Can the U.S. Supreme Court invalidate them as well?

The Court answered in the affirmative in 1796. The case involved a British creditor who was trying to collect a debt from the state of Virginia.[12] Virginia law canceled debts owed to British subjects, yet the Treaty of Paris (1783), in which Britain formally acknowledged the independence of the colonies, guaranteed that creditors could collect such debts. The Court ruled that the Constitution's supremacy clause (Article VI), which embraces national laws and treaties, nullified the state law.

The states continued to resist the yoke of national supremacy. Advocates of strong states' rights conceded that the supremacy clause obligates state judges to follow the Constitution when state law conflicts with it; however, they maintained that the states were bound only by their own interpretation of the Constitution. The Supreme Court said no, ruling that it had the authority to review state court decisions that called for the interpretation of national law.[13] National supremacy required the Supreme Court to impose uniformity on national law; otherwise, the Constitution's meaning would vary from state to state. The people, not the states, had ordained the Constitution, and the people had subordinated state power in order to establish a viable national government. In time, the Supreme Court would use its judicial review power in nearly 1,200 instances to invalidate state and local laws, on issues as diverse as abortion, the death penalty, the rights of the accused, and reapportionment.[14]

The Exercise of Judicial Review

These early cases, coupled with other historic decisions, established the components of judicial review:

- The power of the courts to declare national, state, and local laws invalid if they violate the Constitution

- The supremacy of national laws or treaties when they conflict with state and local laws

- The role of the Supreme Court as the final authority on the meaning of the Constitution

This political might—the power to undo decisions of the representative branches of the national and state governments—lay in the hands of appointed judges, people who were not accountable to the electorate. Did judicial review square with democratic government?

Alexander Hamilton had foreseen and tackled the problem in *Federalist* No. 78. Writing during the ratification debates surrounding the adoption of the Constitution (see Chapter 3), Hamilton maintained that despite the power of judicial review, the judiciary would be the weakest of the three branches of government, because it lacked "the strength of the sword or the purse." The judiciary, wrote Hamilton, had "neither FORCE nor WILL, but only judgment."

Although Hamilton was defending legislative supremacy, he argued that judicial review was an essential barrier to legislative oppression.[15] He recognized that the power to declare government acts void implied the

● compared with what?

14.1   Judicial Review

The U.S. Constitution does not explicitly give the Supreme Court the power of judicial review. In a controversial interpretation, the Court inferred this power from the text and structure of the Constitution. Other countries, trying to avoid political controversy over the power of their courts to review legislation, explicitly define that power in their constitutions. For example, Japan's constitution, inspired by the American model, went beyond it in providing that "the Supreme Court is the court of last resort with power to determine the constitutionality of any law, order, regulation, or official act."

The basic objection to the American form of judicial review is an unwillingness to place federal judges, who are usually appointed for life, above representatives elected by the people. Some constitutions explicitly deny judicial review. For example, Article 84 of the recently revised Belgian constitution (1994) firmly asserts that "the authoritative interpretation of laws is solely the prerogative of the Legislative authority."

The logical basis of judicial review—that government is responsible to a higher authority—can take interesting forms in other countries. In some, judges can invoke an authority higher than the constitution—God, an ideology, or a code of ethics. For example,

both Iran and Pakistan provide for an Islamic review of all legislation. (Pakistan also has the American form of judicial review.)

By 1992, about seventy countries—most in Western Europe, Latin America, Africa, and the Far East—had adopted some form of judicial review. Australia, Brazil, Canada, India, Japan, and Pakistan give their courts a full measure of judicial review power. Australia and Canada come closest to the American model of judicial review, but the fit is never exact. And wherever courts exercise judicial review, undoing it requires extraordinary effort. For example, in Australia the federal parliament has no recourse after a law is declared unconstitutional by the high court but to redraft the offending act in a manner prescribed by the court. In the United States, overruling judicial review by the Supreme Court would require a constitutional amendment.

Governments with a tradition of judicial review share some common characteristics: stability, competitive political parties, distribution of power (akin to separation of powers), a tradition of judicial independence, and a high degree of political freedom. Is judicial review the cause or the consequence of these characteristics? More likely than not, judicial review contributes to stability, judicial independence, and political freedom. And separa-

superiority of the courts over the other branches. But this power, he contended, simply reflects the will of the people, declared in the Constitution, as opposed to the will of the legislature, expressed in its statutes. Judicial independence, guaranteed by lifetime tenure and protected salaries, frees judges from executive and legislative control, minimizing the risk of their deviating from the law established in the Constitution. If judges make a mistake, the people or their elected representatives have the means to correct the error, through constitutional amendments and impeachment.

Their lifetime tenure does free judges from the direct influence of the president and Congress. And although mechanisms to check judicial

tion of powers, judicial independence, and political freedom contribute to the effectiveness of judicial review.

Some constitutional courts possess extraordinary power compared with the American model. The German constitutional court, for example, has the power to rectify the failure of the nation's lawmakers to act. In 1975, for example, the German constitutional court nullified the legalization of abortion and declared that the government had a duty to protect unborn human life against all threats. The court concluded that the German constitution required the legislature to enact legislation protecting the fetus.

Some judges take their power at face value. South Africa created a constitutional court in 1995 and gave it powers on a par with the legislative and executive branches. In its first major decision, the court's eleven appointed justices abolished the death penalty, a decades-old practice that placed South Africa among the nations with the highest rate of capital punishment. "Everyone, including the most abominable of human beings, has a right to life, and capital punishment is therefore unconstitutional," declared the court's president.

The Supreme Court of India offers an extreme example of judicial review. In 1967, the court held that the Indian parliament could not change the fundamental rights sections of the country's constitution, even by constitutional amendment. The parliament then amended the constitution to secure its power to amend the constitution. The Supreme Court upheld the amendment but declared that any amendments that attacked the "basic structure" of the constitution would be invalid. In India, the Supreme Court is truly supreme.

Switzerland's Supreme Federal Tribunal is limited by the country's constitution to ruling on the constitutionality of cantonal laws (the Swiss equivalent of our state laws). It lacks the power to nullify laws passed by the national assembly. Through a constitutional initiative or a popular referendum, the Swiss people may exercise the sovereign right to determine the constitutionality of federal law. In Switzerland, the people are truly supreme.

Sources: Henry J. Abraham, *The Judicial Process*, 6th ed. (New York: Oxford University Press, 1993), pp. 270–310; Chester J. Antineau, *Adjudicating Constitutional Issues* (London: Oceana, 1985), pp. 1–6; Jerold L. Waltman and Kenneth M. Holland, *The Political Role of Law Courts in Modern Democracies* (New York: St. Martin's Press, 1988), pp. 46, 99–100; Robert L. Hardgrave, Jr., and Stanley A. Kochanek, *India: Government and Politics in a Developing Nation*, 4th ed. (New York: Harcourt Brace Jovanovich, 1986), p. 93; Howard W. French, "South Africa's Supreme Court Abolishes Death Penalty," *New York Times*, 7 June 1995, p. A3.

power are in place, these mechanisms require extraordinary majorities and are rarely used. When they exercise the power of judicial review, then, judges can and occasionally do operate counter to majoritarian rule by invalidating the actions of the people's elected representatives (see Compared with What? 14.1 for a discussion of the nature of judicial review in other governments, democratic and nondemocratic). Are the courts out of line with majority sentiment in such cases? Or are they simply responding to pluralist demands—the competing demands of interest groups that turn to the courts to make public policy? We will return to these questions later in this chapter.

THE ORGANIZATION OF COURTS

The American court system is complex, partly as a result of our federal system of government. Each state runs its own court system, and no two states' courts are identical. In addition, we have a system of courts for the national government. The national, or federal, courts coexist with the state courts (see Figure 14.1). Individuals fall under the jurisdiction of both court systems. They can sue or be sued in either system, depending mostly on what their case is about. Litigants file nearly all cases (99 percent) in state courts.[16]

Some Court Fundamentals

Courts are full of mystery to citizens uninitiated in their activities. Lawyers, judges, and seasoned observers understand the language, procedures, and norms associated with legal institutions. Let's start with some fundamentals.

Criminal and Civil Cases.   A crime is a violation of a law that forbids or commands an activity. Criminal laws are defined in each state's penal code, as are punishments for violations. Some crimes—murder, rape, arson—are on the books of every state. Others—sodomy between consenting adults is one example—are considered crimes in certain states but not all. Because crime is a violation of public order, the government prosecutes **criminal cases.** Maintaining public order through the criminal law is largely a state and local function. Criminal cases brought by the national government represent only a small fraction of all criminal cases prosecuted in the United States. In theory, the national penal code is limited by the principle of federalism. The code is aimed at activities that fall under the delegated and implied powers of the national government, enabling the government, for example, to criminalize tax fraud or counterfeit money.

The definition of crime rests with the legislative branch. And the definition is dynamic; that is, it is subject to change. For example, desktop publishing technology has given a big boost to the counterfeiting of stock certificates, bank checks, purchase orders, even college transcripts. As a result, the national government has made it illegal to use computers and laser printers for counterfeiting purposes.

Fighting crime is popular, and politicians sometimes outbid one another in their efforts. National crime-fighting measures have begun to usurp areas long viewed to be under state authority. Since 1975, Congress has added hundreds of new federal criminal provisions across a wide range of activities once thought to be within the states' domain. This includes carjacking, willful failure to pay child support, and crossing state lines to engage in gang-related street crime.[17]

Courts decide both criminal and civil cases. **Civil cases** stem from disputed claims to something of value. Disputes arise from accidents, contractual obligations, and divorce, for example. Often, the parties disagree over tangible issues (possession of property, custody of children), but civil cases can involve more abstract issues, too (the right to equal accommodations,

14.1 • The Federal and State Court Systems, 1995

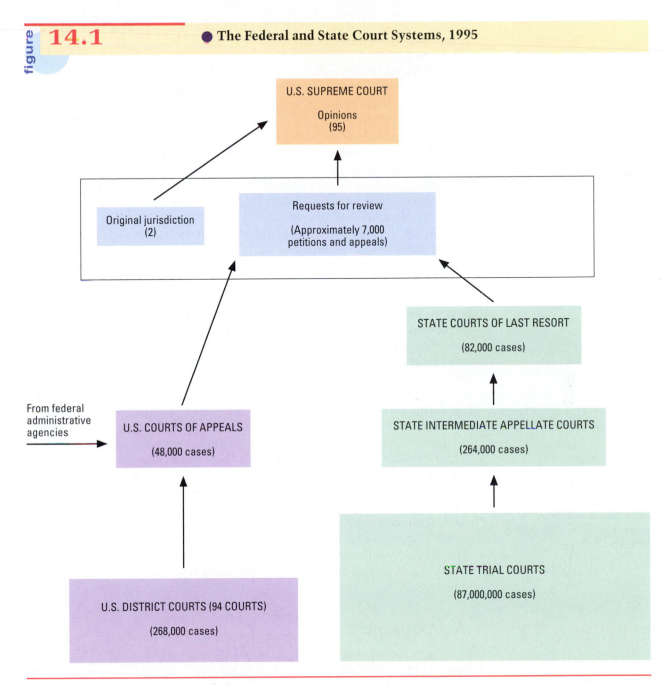

The federal courts have three tiers: district courts, courts of appeals, and the Supreme Court. The Supreme Court was created by the Constitution; all other federal courts were created by Congress. Most litigation occurs in state courts. The structure of state courts varies from state to state; usually, there are minor trial courts for less serious cases, major trial courts for more serious cases, intermediate appellate courts, and supreme courts. State courts were created by state constitutions.

Sources: National Center for State Courts, "State Court Caseload Statistics," *Annual Report, 1994* (Williamsburg, Va.: National Center for State Courts, 1996); Administrative Office of the United States Courts, Statistics Division, Analysis and Reports Branch; Clerk's Office, Supreme Court of the United States; "Foreword," 109 *Harvard Law Review* 344 (1995).

damages for pain and suffering). The government can be a party to civil disputes, called on to defend its actions or to allege wrongdoing.

Procedures and Policymaking.   Most civil and criminal cases never go to trial. In a criminal case, a defendant's lawyer and the prosecutor might plea-bargain, which means they negotiate the severity and number of charges; the defendant pleads guilty in return for a reduction in the more serious charges or a promise to seek less severe punishment. In a civil case, one side may be using a lawsuit as a threat to exact a concession from the other. Often, the parties settle their dispute. Less frequently, cases end with *adjudication*, a court judgment resolving the parties' claims and ultimately enforced by the government. When trial judges adjudicate cases, they may offer written reasons to support their decisions. When the issues or circumstances of cases are novel, judges may publish *opinions*, explanations justifying their rulings.

Judges make policy in two different ways. Occasionally, in the absence of legislation, they use rules from prior decisions. We call this body of rules the **common, or judge-made, law.** The roots of the common law lie in the English legal system. Contracts, property, and torts (an injury or wrong to the person or property of another) are common-law domains. The second area of judicial lawmaking involves the application of statutes enacted by legislatures. The judicial interpretation of legislative acts is called *statutory construction.* The application of a statute is not always clear from its wording. To determine how a statute should be applied, judges look for the legislature's intent, reading reports of committee hearings and debates. If these sources do not clarify the statute's meaning, the court does so. With or without legislation to guide them, judges look to the relevant opinions of higher courts for authority to decide the issues before them.

The federal courts are organized in three tiers, as a pyramid. At the bottom of the pyramid are the **U.S. district courts,** where litigation begins. In the middle are the **U.S. courts of appeals.** At the top is the Supreme Court of the United States. To *appeal* means to take a case to a higher court. The courts of appeals and the Supreme Court are appellate courts; with few exceptions, they only review cases that have already been decided in lower courts. Most federal courts hear and decide a wide array of civil and criminal cases.

Understanding the federal courts, including flow charts and pictures.
`<www.uscourts.gov/ understanding_courts/ 899_toc.htm>`

The U.S. District Courts

There are ninety-four federal district courts in the United States. Each state has at least one district court, and no district straddles more than one state.[18] In 1995, there were 649 full-time federal district judges, and they received almost 268,000 new criminal and civil cases.[19]

The district courts are the entry point for the federal court system. When trials occur in the federal system, they take place in the federal district courts. Here is where witnesses testify, lawyers conduct cross-examinations, and judges and juries decide the fate of litigants. More than one judge may sit in each district court, but each case is tried by a single judge, sitting alone. Federal magistrates assist district judges, but they lack independent judicial authority. In 1996, there were 416 full-time magistrates.

● ● ● ● ● ● ● ● ● ● ●

A Great Justice

Oliver Wendell Holmes, Jr. (1841–1935), is a towering figure in American law. Born to a prominent Boston family, Holmes became a fervent abolitionist and served courageously with the Twentieth Massachusetts Volunteers in the Civil War. Holmes was seriously wounded three times. He was a distinguished scholar, a state judge, and a Supreme Court justice. His considerable ability hardly dimmed with age, though he served on the High Court until he was ninety-one. Holmes's opinions were remarkable for their poetic metaphors, their brevity, and their freedom from legal jargon. Holmes was said to employ a simple rule of thumb when judging the constitutionality of legislation: "Does it make you puke?"

Sources of Litigation. Today, the authority of U.S. district courts extends to

- federal criminal cases, as defined by national law (for example, robbery of a nationally insured bank or interstate transportation of stolen securities);

- civil cases brought by individuals, groups, or government, alleging violation of national law (for example, failure of a municipality to implement pollution-control regulations required by a national agency);

- civil cases brought against the national government (for example, a vehicle manufacturer sues the motor pool of a government agency for its failure to take delivery of a fleet of new cars); and

- civil cases between citizens of different states, when the amount in controversy exceeds $50,000 (for example, when a citizen of New York sues a citizen of Alabama in a U.S. district court in Alabama for damages stemming from an auto accident that occurred in Alabama).

The U.S. Courts of Appeals

All cases resolved in a U.S. district court and all decisions of federal administrative agencies can be appealed to one of the thirteen U.S. courts of appeals. These courts, with a corps of 167 full-time judges, received forty-eight thousand new cases in 1995.[20] Each appeals court hears cases from a geographic area known as a *circuit*. The U.S. Court of Appeals for the Seventh Circuit, for example, is located in Chicago; it hears appeals from the U.S. district courts in Illinois, Wisconsin, and Indiana. The United States is divided into twelve circuits.*

Appellate Court Proceedings. Appellate court proceedings are public, but they usually lack courtroom drama. There are no jurors, witnesses, or cross-examinations; these are features only of the trial courts. Appeals are based strictly on the rulings made and procedures followed in the trial courts. Suppose, for example, that in the course of a criminal trial, a U.S. district judge allows the introduction of evidence that convicts a defendant but was obtained under questionable circumstances. The defendant can appeal on the ground that the evidence was obtained in the absence of a valid search warrant and so was inadmissible. The issue on appeal is the admissibility of the evidence, not the defendant's guilt or innocence. If the appellate court agrees with the trial judge's decision to admit the evidence, the conviction stands. If the appellate court disagrees with the trial judge and rules that the evidence is inadmissible, the defendant must be retried without the incriminating evidence or be released.

It is common for litigants to try to settle their dispute while it is on appeal. For example, when Pennzoil won an $11 billion state court judgment against Texaco Oil Company in 1985 (the dispute was over Texaco's questionable purchase of another company), settlement discussions began immediately. Texaco settled with Pennzoil in 1988 for $3 billion. Occasionally, litigants abandon their appeals for want of resources or resolve. Most of the time, however, appellate courts adjudicate the cases.

The courts of appeals are regional courts. They usually convene in panels of three judges to render judgments. The judges receive written arguments known as briefs (which are also sometimes submitted in trial courts). Often, the judges hear oral arguments and question the lawyers to probe their arguments.

Precedents and Making Decisions. Following review of the briefs and, in many appeals, oral arguments, the three-judge panel will meet to reach a judgment. One judge attempts to summarize the panel's views, although each judge remains free to disagree with the judgment or the reasons for it. When an appellate opinion is published, its influence can reach well beyond the immediate case. For example, a lawsuit turning on the meaning of the Constitution produces a ruling, which then serves as a **precedent** for subsequent cases; that is, the decision becomes a basis for deciding similar cases in the same way. Although district judges sometimes publish their

---

* *The thirteenth court, the U.S. Court of Appeals for the Federal Circuit, is not a regional court; it specializes in appeals involving patents, contract claims against the national government, and federal employment cases.*

opinions, it is the exception rather than the rule. At the appellate level, however, precedent requires that opinions be written.

Making decisions according to precedent is central to the operation of our legal system, providing continuity and predictability. The bias in favor of existing decisions is captured by the Latin expression **stare decisis,** which means "let the decision stand." But the use of precedent and the principle of *stare decisis* do not make lower-court judges cogs in a judicial machine. "If precedent clearly governed," remarked one federal judge, "a case would never get as far as the Court of Appeals: the parties would settle."[21]

Judges on the courts of appeals direct their energies to correcting errors in district court proceedings and interpreting the law (in the course of writing opinions). When judges interpret the law, they often modify existing laws. In effect, they are making policy. Judges are politicians in the sense that they exercise political power, but the black robes that distinguish judges from other politicians signal constraints on their exercise of power.

Uniformity of Law. Decisions by the courts of appeals ensure a measure of uniformity in the application of national law. For example, when similar issues are dealt with in the decisions of different district judges, the decisions may be inconsistent. The courts of appeals harmonize the decisions within their region so that laws are applied uniformly.

The regional character of the courts of appeals undermines uniformity somewhat, because the courts are not bound by the decisions of other circuits. A law may be interpreted differently in different courts of appeals. For example, the Internal Revenue Code imposes identical tax burdens on similar individuals. But thanks to the regional character of the courts of appeals, national tax laws may be applied differently throughout the United States. The percolation of cases up through the federal system of courts virtually guarantees that, at some point, two or more courts of appeals, working with similar sets of facts, are going to interpret the same law differently. However, the problem of conflicting decisions in the intermediate appellate courts can be corrected by review in the Supreme Court, where policymaking, not error correction, is the paramount goal.

THE SUPREME COURT Above the west portico of the Supreme Court building are inscribed the words EQUAL JUSTICE UNDER LAW. At the opposite end of the building, above the east portico, are the words JUSTICE THE GUARDIAN OF LIBERTY. The mottos reflect the Court's difficult task: achieving a just balance among the values of freedom, order, and equality. Consider how these values came into conflict in two controversial issues the Court has faced in recent years.

Flag burning as a form of political protest pits the value of order, or the government's interest in maintaining a peaceful society, against the value of freedom, including the individual's right to vigorous and unbounded political expression. In two flag-burning cases, the Supreme Court affirmed constitutional protection for unbridled political expression, including the emotionally charged act of desecrating a national symbol.[22]

School desegregation pits the value of equality (in this case, equal educational opportunities for minorities) against the value of freedom (the right of parents to send their children to neighborhood schools). In *Brown* v. *Board of Education,* the Supreme Court carried the banner of racial equality by striking down state-mandated segregation in public schools. The decision helped launch a revolution in race relations in the United States. The justices recognized the disorder their decision would create in a society accustomed to racial bias, but in this case, equality clearly outweighed freedom. Twenty-four years later, the Court was still embroiled in controversy over equality when it ruled that race could be a factor in university admissions (to diversify the student body), in the *Bakke* case.[23] Having secured equality for blacks, the Court then had to confront the charge that it was denying whites the freedom to compete for admission. The controversy continued in 1995 as a new majority of conservative justices limited race-based preferences in government policies.[24]

The Supreme Court makes national policy. Because its decisions have far-reaching effects on all of us, it is vital that we understand how it reaches those decisions. With this understanding, we can better evaluate how the Court fits within our model of democracy.

Access to the Court

There are rules of access that must be followed to bring a case to the Supreme Court. Also important is a sensitivity to the justices' policy and ideological preferences. The notion that anyone can take a case all the way to the Supreme Court is true only in theory, not fact.

Rules of the Supreme Court of the United States.
`<www.law.cornell.edu/ rules/supct/overview.html>`

The Supreme Court's cases come from two sources. A few (two cases in 1995) arrive under the Court's **original jurisdiction,** conferred by Article III, Section 2, of the Constitution, which gives the Court the power to hear and decide "all Cases affecting Ambassadors, other public Ministers and Consuls, and those in which a State shall be Party." Cases falling under the Court's original jurisdiction are tried and decided in the Court itself; the cases begin and end there. For example, the Court is the first and only forum in which legal disputes between states are resolved. The Court hears few original jurisdiction cases today, however, usually referring them to a special master, often a retired judge, who reviews the parties' contentions and recommends a resolution that the justices are free to accept or reject.

Most cases enter the Supreme Court from the U.S. courts of appeals or the state courts of last resort. This is the Court's **appellate jurisdiction.** These cases have been tried, decided, and reexamined as far as the law permits in other federal or state courts. The Court exercises judicial power under its appellate jurisdiction only because Congress gives it the authority to do so. Congress may change (and, perhaps, eliminate) the Court's appellate jurisdiction. This is a powerful but rarely used weapon in the congressional arsenal of checks and balances.

Litigants in state cases who invoke the Court's appellate jurisdiction must satisfy two conditions: first, the case must reach the end of the line in the state court system. Litigants cannot jump at will from state to national arenas of justice. Second, the case must raise a **federal question,** an issue covered under the Constitution, federal laws, or national treaties.

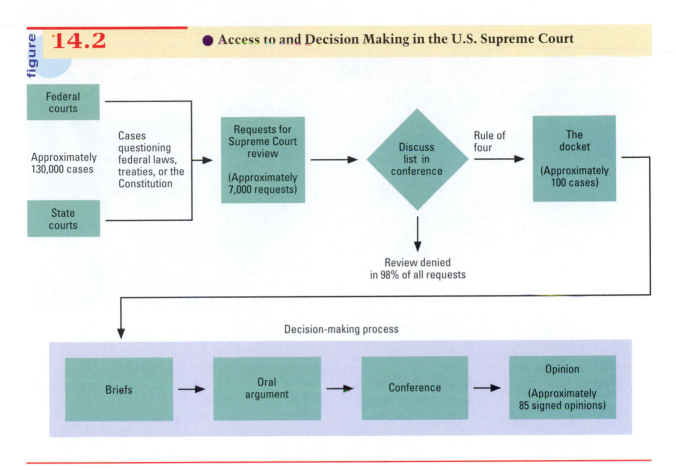

figure 14.2 ● **Access to and Decision Making in the U.S. Supreme Court**

State and national appeals courts churn out thousands of decisions each year. Only a fraction end up on the Supreme Court's docket. This chart sketches the several stages leading to a decision from the High Court.

Sources: Administrative Office of the United States Courts, Statistics Division, Analysis and Reports Branch; "Foreword," 109 *Harvard Law Review* 344 (1995).

However, even most cases that meet these conditions do not reach the High Court.

Since 1925, the Court has exercised substantial (today, nearly complete) control over its **docket,** or agenda (see Figure 14.2). The Court selects a handful of cases (less than one hundred) for consideration from the seven thousand or more requests filed each year. These requests take the form of petitions for *certiorari*, in which a litigant seeking review asks the Court "to become informed" of the lower-court proceeding. For the vast majority of cases, the Court denies the petition for *certiorari*, leaving the decision of the lower court undisturbed. No explanations accompany cases that are denied review, so they have little or no value as court rulings.

The Court grants a review only when four or more justices agree that a case warrants full consideration. This unwritten rule is known as the **rule of four.** With advance preparation by their law clerks, who screen petitions and prepare summaries, all nine justices make these judgments at secret conferences held twice a week.[25] During the conferences, justices vote on

The Supreme Court, 1996 Term: The Starting Lineup

The justices of the Supreme Court of the United States, pictured from left to right: Clarence Thomas, Antonin Scalia, Sandra Day O'Connor, Anthony Kennedy, David Souter, Stephen Breyer, John Paul Stevens, Chief Justice William Rehnquist, Ruth Bader Ginsburg.

previously argued cases and consider which new cases to add to the docket. The chief justice circulates a "discuss list" of worthy petitions. Cases on the list are then subject to the rule of four. Though it takes only four votes to place a case on the docket, it may ultimately take an enormous leap to garner a fifth and deciding vote on the merits of the appeal. This is especially true if the Court is sharply split ideologically. Thus, a minority of justices in favor of an appeal may oppose review if they are not confident the outcome will be to their satisfaction.[26]

The Solicitor General

Why does the Court decide to hear certain cases but not others? The best evidence scholars have adduced suggests that agenda setting depends on the individual justices, who vary in their decision-making criteria, and on the issues raised by the cases. Occasionally, justices will weigh the ultimate outcome of a case when granting or denying review. At other times, justices will grant or deny review based on disagreement among the lower courts or because delay in resolving the issues would impose alarming economic or social costs.[27] The solicitor general plays a vital role in the Court's agenda setting.

The **solicitor general** represents the national government before the Supreme Court. Appointed by the president, the solicitor general is the third-ranking official in the U.S. Department of Justice (after the attorney general and the deputy attorney general). President Bill Clinton's current choice for the position is Walter Dellinger, a Duke law school professor. Dellinger replaced Drew S. Days III, who stepped down in 1996. The solicitor general's duties include determining whether the government should appeal lower-court decisions; reviewing and modifying, when necessary, the briefs filed in government appeals; and deciding whether the government should file an **amicus curiae brief*** in any appellate court.[28] The objective is to create a cohesive program for the executive branch in the federal courts.

Solicitors general play two different, occasionally conflicting, roles. First, they are advocates for the president's policy preferences; second, as officers of the Court, they traditionally defend the institutional interests of the national government.

Solicitors general usually act with considerable restraint in recommending to the Court that a case be granted or denied review. By recommending only cases of general importance, they increase their credibility and their influence. Rex E. Lee, who was solicitor general from 1981 to 1985, acknowledged in an unusually candid interview that he had refused to make arguments that members of the Reagan administration had urged on him: "I'm not the pamphleteer general; I'm the solicitor general. My audience is not 100 million people; my audience is nine people.... Credibility is the most important asset that any solicitor general has."[29]

By contrast, President Bush's solicitor general, Kenneth Starr, reluctantly but vigorously argued that the justices should uphold an act of Congress designed to curb flag burning, although the Court had struck down a similar Texas law the year before. "There was no doubt at all in my mind that the constitutionality of the statute could appropriately be defended," recalled Starr. "Once Congress passes a law, our duty is to defend it. That is perhaps the most fundamental duty of this office."[30] Starr lost— the Court struck down the prohibition.

By carefully selecting the cases it presses, the solicitor general's office usually maintains a very impressive record of wins in the Supreme Court. But 1995 was not such a year: the office won only 64 percent of its cases, down from its average of 80 percent or more. One defender cleverly remarked, "The solicitor general's job is not to guess where the Court will be and then get on that side."[31]

Solicitors general are a "formidable force" in the process of setting the Supreme Court's agenda.[32] Their influence in bringing cases to the Court and arguing them there has earned them the informal title of "the tenth justice."

Decision Making

Once the Court grants review, attorneys submit written arguments (briefs). Oral arguments, limited to thirty minutes for each side, usually follow. From October through April, the justices spend four hours a day, five or six days a month, hearing arguments. Experience seems to help. Like the solicitor general, seasoned advocates enjoy a greater success rate regardless of the party they represent.[33] The justices like crisp, concise, conversational presentations; they disapprove of attorneys who read from a prepared text. Some justices are aggressive, relentless questioners who frequently interrupt the lawyers; others are more subdued. In a recent free speech case, an attorney who offered an impassioned plea on the facts of the case was soon "awash in a sea of judicial impatience that at times

---

* *Amicus curiae is Latin for "friend of the court." Amicus briefs can be filed with the consent of all the parties or with the permission of the Court. They allow groups and individuals who are not parties to the litigation but have an interest in it to influence the Court's thinking and, perhaps, its decision.*

seemed to border on anger. . . . 'We didn't take this case to determine who said what in the cafeteria,' " snapped one justice.[34]

Court protocol prohibits the justices from addressing one another directly during oral arguments, but they often debate obliquely through the questions they pose to the attorneys. The justices reach no collective decision at the time of oral arguments. They reach a tentative decision only after they have met in conference.

Our knowledge of the dynamics of decision making on the Supreme Court is all secondhand. Only the justices attend the Court's Wednesday and Friday conferences. By tradition, the justices first shake hands, a gesture of harmony. The chief justice then begins the presentation of each case with a combined discussion and vote, followed by the discussion and vote of the other justices in order of their seniority on the Court. Justice Antonin Scalia, who joined the Court in 1986, remarked that "not much conferencing goes on." By *conferencing*, Scalia meant efforts to persuade others to change their view by debating points of disagreement. "To call our discussion of a case a conference," he said, "is really something of a misnomer. It's much more a statement of the views of each of the nine Justices, after which the totals are added and the case is assigned" for an opinion.[35]

Judicial Restraint and Judicial Activism.   How do the justices decide how to vote on a case? According to some scholars, legal doctrines and previous decisions explain their votes. This explanation, which is consistent with the majoritarian model, anchors the justices closely to the law and minimizes the contribution of their personal values. This view is embodied in the concept of **judicial restraint,** which maintains that legislators, not judges, should make the laws. Judges are said to exercise judicial restraint when they hew closely to statutes and previous cases in reaching their decisions. Other scholars contend that the value preferences and resulting ideologies of the justices provide a more powerful interpretation of their voting.[36] This view is embodied in the concept of **judicial activism,** which maintains that judges should interpret laws loosely, using their power to promote their preferred social and political goals. Judges are said to exercise judicial activism when they are apt to interpret existing laws and rulings with little regard to precedent and to interject their own values into court decisions.

The terms *judicial restraint* and *judicial activism* describe the relative assertiveness of judicial power. Judges acting according to an extreme model of judicial restraint would never question the validity of duly enacted laws, deferring to the superiority of other government institutions in construing the laws. Judges acting according to an extreme model of judicial activism would be an intrusive and ever-present force that would dominate other government institutions. Actual judicial behavior lies somewhere in between these two extremes.

In recent history, many activist judges have tended to opt for equality over freedom in their decisions, a tendency that has linked the concept of judicial activism to liberalism. However, there is no necessary connection between judicial activism and liberalism. Judges who interpret statutes and precedents loosely to favor order over freedom are also activists—conservative activists.

A Power Player . . .

Antonin Scalia, the 103d justice appointed to the Supreme Court, began his tenure in 1986 after four years as a federal appellate court judge. The confirmation hearings and subsequent Senate vote on his appointment were remarkably unanimous for this most conservative justice. Scalia has lived up to his reputation as a brilliant scholar, using his personal computer to write incisive, and occasionally scornful, opinions.

Judicial activism, which is consistent with the pluralist model, sees the justices as actively promoting their value preferences. In a recent study of the legal versus the ideological approach to judicial voting, the legal model required tempering by political forces, and the ideological approach required legal constraints. These shortcomings suggest an integrated model of decision making that takes into account both law and politics to explain judicial decisions.[37]

Judgment and Argument.   The voting outcome is the **judgment,** the decision on who wins and who loses. The justices often disagree, not only on winners and losers but also on the reasons for their judgment. This should not be surprising, given nine independent minds and issues that can be approached in several ways. Voting in the conference does not end the work or resolve the disagreements. Votes remain tentative until the Court issues an opinion announcing its judgment.

After voting, the justices in the majority must draft an opinion setting out the reasons for their decision. The **argument** is the kernel of the opinion—its logical content, as distinct from facts, rhetoric, and procedures. If all justices agree with the judgment and the reasons supporting it, the opinion is unanimous. Agreement with a judgment, but for different reasons than those set forth in the majority opinion, is called a **concurrence.** Or a justice can **dissent** if she or he disagrees with a judgment. Both concurring and dissenting opinions may be drafted in addition to the majority opinion.

The Opinion.   After the conference, the chief justice writes the majority opinion or assigns that responsibility to another justice in the majority. If the chief justice is not in the majority, the writing or assignment of responsibility rests with the most senior associate justice in the majority.

...And a Junior Member of His Team

Supreme Court justices use recent law school graduates as short-term clerks. Here, Larry Lessig, one of Scalia's four clerks, divides his time between one of the thousands of petitions for review that arrive at the Court each year and the final draft of a dissent by Scalia concerning the length of time a person can be held in custody without a hearing. The Court majority established a forty-eight-hour limit; Scalia argued that the limit should be set at twenty-four hours (County of Riverside v. McLaughlin [1991]).

The assigning justice may consider several factors in allocating the crucial opinion-writing task: workload, expertise, public opinion, and, above all, the author's ability to hold the majority together. (Remember, at this point the votes are only tentative.) If the drafting justice holds an extreme view on the issues in a case and is not able to incorporate the views of more moderate colleagues, those justices may withdraw their votes. On the other hand, assigning a more moderate justice to draft an opinion could weaken the argument on which the opinion rests. Opinion-writing assignments can also be punitive. Justice Harry Blackmun once commented, "If one's in the doghouse with the Chief [former Chief Justice Warren Burger], he gets the crud."[38]

Opinion writing is the justices' most critical function. It is not surprising, then, that they spend much of their time drafting opinions. The justices usually call on their law clerks—top graduates of the nation's elite law schools—to help them prepare opinions and carry out other tasks. The commitment can be daunting. According to one close Court observer, the clerks shoulder much of the writing responsibility for most of the justices.[39]

On the occasion of his eightieth birthday, after more than thirty years of service on the Court, Justice William J. Brennan, Jr., offered a rare account of the process of preparing and exchanging memoranda and drafts that leads to a final opinion: "It's startling to me every time I read these darned things to see how much I've had in the way of exchanges and how the exchanges have resulted in changes of view, both of my own and of colleagues. And all of a sudden at the end of the road, we come up with an agreement on an opinion of the Court."[40]

The writing justice distributes a draft opinion to all the justices; the other justices read it, then circulate criticisms and suggestions. An opinion may have to be rewritten several times to accommodate colleagues who remain unpersuaded by the draft. Justice Felix Frankfurter was a perfectionist; some of his opinions went through thirty or more drafts. Justices can change their votes, and perhaps alter the judgment, up until the decision is officially announced. And the justices announce their decisions only when they are ready. Often, the most controversial cases pile up as coalitions on the Court vie for support or sharpen their criticisms. When the Court announces a decision, the justices who wrote the opinion read or summarize their views in the courtroom. Printed and electronic copies of the opinion, known as *slip opinions,* are then distributed to interested parties and the press. (See World Wide Web Resources at the end of this chapter.)

Justices in the majority frequently try to muffle or stifle dissent in order to encourage institutional cohesion. Since the mid-1940s, however, unity has been more difficult to obtain.[41] Gaining agreement from the justices today is akin to negotiating with nine separate law firms. It may be more surprising that the justices ever agree. Nevertheless, the justices must be keenly aware of the slender foundation of their authority, which rests largely on public respect. That respect is tested whenever the Court ventures into areas of controversy. Banking, slavery, and Reconstruction policies embroiled the Court in controversy in the nineteenth century. Freedom of speech and religion, racial equality, and the right to privacy have led the Court into controversy in this century.

Strategies on the Court

The Court is more than the sum of its formal processes. The justices exercise real political power. If we start with the assumption that the justices attempt to stamp their own policy views on the cases they review, we should expect typical political behavior from them. Cases that reach the Supreme Court's docket pose difficult choices. Because the justices are grappling with conflict on a daily basis, they probably have well-defined ideologies that reflect their values. Scholars and journalists have attempted to pierce the veil of secrecy that shrouds the Court from public view and analyze the justices' ideologies.[42]

The beliefs of most justices can be located on the two-dimensional model of political values discussed in Chapter 1 (see Figure 1.2). Liberal justices, such as John Paul Stevens and Ruth Bader Ginsburg, choose freedom over order and equality over freedom. Conservative justices—Antonin Scalia and Clarence Thomas, for example—choose order over freedom and freedom over equality. These choices translate into policy preferences as the justices struggle to win votes and retain coalitions.

As in any group of people, the justices also vary in intellectual ability, advocacy skills, social graces, temperament, and the like. For example, Chief Justice Charles Evans Hughes (1930–1941) had a photographic memory and came to each conference armed with well-marked copies of Supreme Court opinions. Few justices could keep up with him in debates. Then, as now, justices argue for the support of their colleagues, offering information in the form of drafts and memoranda to explain the advantages and disadvantages of voting for or against an issue. And justices make

Choosing Sides

Justices Ruth Bader Ginsburg (left) and Sandra Day O'Connor (right) are occasional allies on issues of abortion and gender equality. But O'Connor parts company with Ginsburg and tends to side with Chief Justice William Rehnquist (center) on matters dealing with racial equality and federalism. The justices are pictured here in the conference room of the Supreme Court building.

occasional, if not regular, use of friendship, ridicule, and appeals to patriotism to mold their colleagues' views.

A justice might adopt a long-term strategy of encouraging the appointment of like-minded colleagues in order to marshal additional strength on the Court. Chief Justice (and former president) William Howard Taft, for example, bombarded President Warren G. Harding with recommendations and suggestions whenever a Court vacancy was announced. Taft was especially determined to block the appointment of anyone who might side with the "dangerous twosome," Justices Oliver Wendell Holmes and Louis D. Brandeis. Taft said he "must stay on the Court in order to prevent the Bolsheviki from getting control."[43]

The Chief Justice

The chief justice is only one of nine justices, but he has several important functions based on his authority. Apart from his role in forming the docket and directing the Court's conferences, the chief justice can also be a social leader, generating solidarity within the group. Sometimes, a chief justice can embody intellectual leadership. Finally, the chief justice can provide policy leadership, directing the Court toward a general policy position. Perhaps only John Marshall could lay claim to possessing social, intellectual, and policy leadership. Warren E. Burger, who resigned as chief justice in 1986, was reputed to be a lackluster leader in all three areas.[44]

When presiding at the conference, the chief justice can control the discussion of issues, although independent-minded justices are not likely to acquiesce to his views. Moreover, justices today rarely engage in a debate of the issues in the conference. Rather, they use their law clerks as ambassadors between justices' chambers and, in effect, "run the Court without talking to one another."[45]

JUDICIAL RECRUITMENT

Neither the Constitution nor national law imposes formal requirements for appointment to the federal courts. Once appointed, district and appeals judges must reside in the district or circuit to which they are appointed.

The president appoints judges to the federal courts, and all nominees must be confirmed by majority vote in the Senate. Congress sets, but cannot lower, a judge's compensation. In 1996, salaries were as follows:

Chief justice of the Supreme Court	$171,500
Associate Supreme Court justices	164,100
Courts of appeals judges	141,700
District judges	133,600
Magistrates	122,912

State courts operate somewhat similarly. Governors appoint judges in more than half the states, often in consultation with judicial nominating commissions. In many of these states, voters decide whether judges should be retained in office. Other states select their judges by partisan, nonpartisan, or (rarely) legislative election.[46] In some states, nominees must be confirmed by the state legislature. Contested elections for judgeships are unusual. In Chicago, where judges are elected, even highly publicized and widespread criminal corruption in the courts in the 1980s failed to unseat incumbents. Most voters paid no attention whatsoever.

The Appointment of Federal Judges

The Constitution states that federal judges shall hold their commission "during good Behaviour," which in practice means for life.* A president's judicial appointments, then, are likely to survive his administration, providing a kind of political legacy. The appointment power assumes that the president is free to identify candidates and appoint judges who favor his policies. President Franklin D. Roosevelt had appointed nearly 75 percent of all sitting federal judges by the end of his twelve years in office. In contrast, President Ford appointed fewer than 13 percent in his three years in office. Presidents Reagan and Bush together appointed more than 60 percent of all federal judges. In the first three years of his administration, President Clinton has appointed about 22 percent of the 846 federal judges at all levels.

Judicial vacancies occur when sitting judges resign, retire, or die. Vacancies also arise when Congress creates new judgeships to handle increasing case loads. In both cases, the president nominates a candidate, who must be confirmed by the Senate. The president has the help of the Justice Department, which screens candidates before the formal nomination, subjecting serious contenders to FBI investigation. The department and the Senate vie for control in the appointment of district and appeals judges.

Only twelve federal judges have been impeached. Of these, seven were convicted in the Senate and removed from office. Three judges were impeached by the Senate in the 1980s. In 1992, Alcee Hastings became the first such judge to serve in Congress.

From the age of four, Bertina Lampkin accompanied her father, a criminal defense attorney, to court. Today, she is a judge in Cook County, Illinois, assigned to the criminal court. "I don't think there is a better job. I love to hear the arguments. If the lawyers come prepared and give good arguments, it is the best day I can have" (Anne Keegan, "Women on the Bench," *Chicago Tribune Magazine*, 12 May 1991, p. 11).

The "Advice and Consent" of the Senate.   For district and appeals vacancies, the appointment process hinges on the nominee's acceptability to the senior senator in the president's party from the state in which the vacancy arises. The senator's influence is greater for appointments to district court than for appointments to the courts of appeals.

This practice, called **senatorial courtesy,** forces presidents to share the nomination power with members of the Senate. The Senate will not confirm a nominee who is opposed by the senior senator from the nominee's state if that senator is a member of the president's party. The Senate does not actually reject the candidate. Instead, the chairman of the Senate Judiciary Committee, which reviews all judicial nominees, will not schedule a confirmation hearing, effectively killing the nomination.

Although the Justice Department is still sensitive to senatorial prerogatives, senators can no longer submit a single name to fill a vacancy. The department searches for acceptable candidates and polls the appropriate senator for her or his reaction to them. President Bush asked Republican senators to seek more qualified female and minority recommendations. Bush made progress in developing a more diverse bench of judges, and President Clinton is accelerating the change.[47]

The Senate Judiciary Committee conducts a hearing for each judicial nominee. The chairman exercises a measure of control in the appointment process that goes beyond senatorial courtesy. If a nominee is objectionable to the chairman, he or she can delay a hearing or hold up other appointments until the president and the Justice Department find an alternative. Such behavior does not win a politician much influence in the long run, however. So committee chairmen are usually loathe to place obstacles in a president's path, especially when they may want presidential support for their own policies and constituencies.

The American Bar Association. The American Bar Association (ABA), the biggest organization of lawyers in the United States, has been involved in screening candidates for the federal bench since 1946.[48] Its role is defined by custom, not law. At the president's behest, the ABA's Standing Committee on the Federal Judiciary routinely rates prospective appointees, using a three-value scale: "well qualified," "qualified," and "not qualified."

Presidents do not always agree with the committee's judgment, in part because its objections can be motivated by disagreements with a candidate's political views. Occasionally, a candidate deemed "not qualified" is nominated and even appointed, but the overwhelming majority of appointees to the federal bench since 1946 have had the ABA's blessing.

Recent Presidents and the Federal Judiciary

President Jimmy Carter had two objectives in his judicial appointments. First, Carter wanted to base judicial appointments on merit, to appoint judges of higher quality than his predecessors had done. Carter's second objective was to make the judiciary more representative of the general population. He appointed substantially more blacks, women, and Hispanics to the federal bench than did any of his predecessors or his immediate successors. (Nearly all Carter judges were Democrats.)

Early in his administration, it was clear that President Reagan did not share Carter's second objective. Although Reagan generally heeded senatorial recommendations for the district courts and, like Carter, held a firm rein on appointments to the appeals courts, the differences were strong. Only 2 percent of Reagan's appointments were blacks and only 8 percent were women; in contrast, 14 percent of Carter's appointments were blacks and 16 percent were women (see Figure 14.3). Four percent of Reagan judges were Hispanics, compared to 6 percent of Carter judges. Bush's record on women and minority appointments was better than Reagan's.

President Clinton's appointments stand in stark contrast to his conservative predecessors. For the first time in history, more than half of a president's judicial appointments have been women or minorities. Clinton's chief judge selector, Assistant Attorney General Eleanor Acheson, is following through on Clinton's campaign pledge to make his appointees "look like America."

The racial and ethnic composition of the parties themselves helps to explain much of the variation between the appointments of presidents of different parties. It seems clear that political ideology, not demographics, lies at the heart of judicial appointments. Reagan and Bush sought nominees with particular policy preferences in order to leave their stamp on the judiciary well into the twenty-first century. Clinton is animated by the same goal. The Reagan-Bush legacy is considerable. They appointed more than half of all judges sitting today.[49] When it comes to ideological preferences as revealed by judicial choices, Carter's judges take the cake. A review of more than twenty-five thousand federal court decisions from 1968 to 1995 concluded that Carter-appointed judges were the most liberal, whereas

figure

14.3

● Diversity on the Federal Courts

To what extent should the courts reflect the diverse character of the population? President Jimmy Carter sought to make the federal courts more representative of the population by appointing more blacks, Hispanics, and women. Ronald Reagan's appointments reflected neither the lawyer population nor the population at large. Bush's appointments were somewhat more representative than Reagan's on race and gender criteria. Clinton's nominees represent a dramatic departure in appointments, especially in terms of race and gender.

Sources: Sheldon Goldman, "Judicial Selection Under Clinton: A Midterm Examination," *Judicature* 78, pp. 276–291 (1995) with additional data kindly provided by Professor Goldman; U.S. Bureau of the Census, *Statistical Abstract of the United States, 1993* (Washington, D.C.: U.S. Government Printing Office, 1993), Table No. 644.

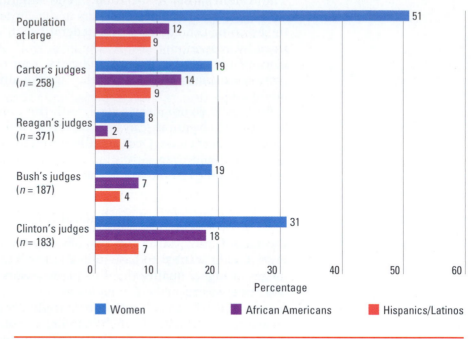

Reagan- and Bush-appointed judges were the least liberal. Clinton-appointed judges are less liberal than Carter's but decidedly more liberal than the legacy of Nixon, Ford, Reagan, or Bush.[50] On another criterion, personal wealth, nearly one-third of Clinton's judges possessed millionaire status, trailing behind Bush's judges (35 percent). Whatever their candidates' experience or wealth, presidents are likely to appoint men and women who share similar value preferences.

Appointment to the Supreme Court

The announcement of a vacancy on the High Court usually causes quite a stir. Campaigns for Supreme Court seats are commonplace, although the public rarely sees them. Hopefuls contact friends in the administration and urge influential associates to do the same on their behalf. Some candidates never give up hope. Judge John J. Parker, whose nomination to the Court was defeated in 1930, tried in vain to rekindle interest in his appointment until he was well past the age—usually the early sixties—that appointments are made.[51]

The president is not shackled by senatorial courtesy when it comes to nominating a Supreme Court justice. However, appointments to the Court attract more intense public scrutiny than do lower-level appointments, effectively narrowing the president's options and focusing attention on the Senate's advice and consent.

Of the 146 men and 2 women nominated to the Court, 28—or about 1 in 5—have failed to receive Senate confirmation. Only five such fumbles occurred in this century, the last one during the Reagan administration. The most important factor in the rejection of a nominee is partisan politics. Thirteen candidates lost their bids for appointment because the presidents who nominated them were considered likely to become lame ducks: the party in control of the Senate anticipated victory for its candidate in an upcoming presidential race and sought to deny the incumbent president an important political appointment.[52] The most recent nominee to be rejected on partisan and ideological grounds was Judge Robert H. Bork.

Sixteen of the twenty-two successful Supreme Court nominees since 1950 have had prior judicial experience in federal or state courts. This tendency toward "promotion" from within the judiciary may be based on the idea that a judge's previous opinions are good predictors of his or her future opinions on the High Court. After all, a president is handing out a powerful lifetime appointment; it makes sense to want an individual who is sympathetic to his views. Federal or state court judges holding lifetime appointments are likely to state their views frankly in their opinions. In contrast, the policy preferences of High Court candidates who have been in legal practice or in political office must be based on the conjecture of professional associates or on the text of speeches to the local Rotary Club, on the floor of a legislature, and the like.

The resignation of Chief Justice Warren Burger in 1986 gave Reagan the chance to elevate Associate Justice William H. Rehnquist to the position of chief justice. Elevation within the Court to the chief justice position is not routine. Sixteen chief justices have served, but only three were elevated from positions as sitting associate justices. Rehnquist faced stern questioning from critics during his Senate confirmation hearings. (Testimony from Supreme Court nominees is a relatively recent phenomenon; it began in 1925 when Harlan Fiske Stone was nominated to the High Court.) Reagan then nominated Antonin Scalia, a judge in a federal court of appeals, as Rehnquist's replacement. Rehnquist and Scalia did not try to defend their judicial records; they argued that judicial independence meant that they could not be called to account for their decisions before the Senate. Both judges also ducked discussing issues that might come to the Court, for fear of compromising their impartiality. Rehnquist's opponents were unable to stop his confirmation. The Republican-controlled Senate voted to confirm, 65–33. The same day, the Senate confirmed Scalia unanimously, 98–0.[53]

In 1987, when Justice Lewis F. Powell, Jr., resigned, Reagan had an opportunity to shift the ideological balance on the Court toward a more conservative consensus. He nominated Bork, a conservative, to fill the vacancy. Although Bork advocated judicial restraint, some of Bork's critics maintained that he was really a judicial activist draped in the robes of judicial restraint. Bork's critics charged that his true purpose, spelled out in his prodigious writings, was to advance his conservative ideology from the High Court.

The hearings concluded after several days of televised testimony from Judge Bork and a parade of witnesses. Liberals formed a temporary anti-Bork coalition of feminist, labor, environmental, senior citizen, abortion rights, and civil rights groups. They put aside their disagreements and mounted a massive campaign to defeat the nomination, overwhelming conservative efforts to buttress Bork. At first, the public was undecided on Bork's confirmation; by the time the televised hearings ended, public opinion had shifted against him. (This gave rise to a new verb, *to bork*, meaning to mount an organized effort by interest groups to disqualify a nominee for high office by creating an extremist image to alarm constituents and build pressure on public officials.) Although his defeat was a certainty, Bork insisted that the Senate vote on his nomination, hoping for a sober discussion of his record. But the rancor never abated. Bork was defeated by a vote of 42–58, the biggest vote margin by which the Senate has ever rejected a Supreme Court nominee.

Reagan's choice for the seat finally went to Anthony M. Kennedy, a federal appeals judge from California. By 1996, Kennedy had emerged as the Court's pivot point. In nearly all the close cases in the past three years (those decided by a single vote), Kennedy has been on the winning side across a range of important issues. Kennedy holds to the view that government may not classify people by group attributes (for example, race or sexual preference), making him a "conservative" on affirmative action and a "liberal" on gay rights. On many vital issues, Kennedy seems to prefer freedom to either order or equality.

The rules of the game for appointment to the High Court appeared to have changed in 1990 when President Bush plucked David H. Souter from relative obscurity to replace liberal justice William J. Brennan, Jr., who retired because of failing health. Souter fit the model of other nominees: he had extensive judicial experience as a justice on the New Hampshire Supreme Court and had recently been appointed to the federal court of appeals. But there was one significant difference: Souter was a "stealth" candidate. His views on provocative topics were undetectable, because he had written little and spoken less on privacy, abortion, religious liberty, and equal protection. To elicit his views, some members of the Senate Judiciary Committee tried sparring with Souter at his confirmation hearings; he successfully avoided or deflected the most controversial topics. Souter was confirmed by the Senate, 90–9.

Souter has proved a disappointment of sorts for conservatives. He has eschewed the rock-ribbed conservatism of his native New Hampshire. In his very first year on the Court, Souter resisted a conservative effort to roll back abortion rights. Since then, he has dissented in many blockbuster conservative victories. Some Court watchers see these dissents as the seeds for reversals years hence.

Recall from the beginning of this chapter that George Bush left an additional stamp on the Supreme Court in 1991 when he nominated a conservative black judge, Clarence Thomas, to replace ailing liberal justice Thurgood Marshall.[54] Thomas has proved a strong ally for other conservatives on the Court, tipping close decisions away from the liberal precedents of an earlier day.

The fallout from Thomas's confirmation hearings has marked government and politics. Led by Anita Hill's example, women have increasingly stepped forward to level charges of *sexual harassment*—unwanted and offensive sexual advances or sexually derogatory or discriminatory remarks—in the workplace. Sexual harassment complaints to the Equal Employment Opportunity Commission jumped 150 percent in the year

Clarence Thomas: Liberals' Target

Supreme Court nominee Clarence Thomas proved a substantial target for criticism from liberals frustrated by successive conservative judicial appointments during the Reagan and Bush presidencies. Thomas continues to generate liberal ire.

Resumes of current Supreme Court justices hyperlinked to their important opinions.
`<www.law.cornell.edu/supct/justices/fullcourt.html>`

following the hearing. Charges of sexual misconduct drove Senator Brock Adams (D.-Wash.) to retire in 1992 and forced Senator Bob Packwood (R.-Oreg.) to resign in 1995.

President Clinton made his mark on the Court in 1993 when Associate Justice Byron R. White announced his retirement. Clinton chose Ruth Bader Ginsburg for the vacancy; she had been an active civil rights litigator, a law professor, and a federal judge. Some Court watchers described her as the Thurgood Marshall of women's rights because of her tireless efforts to alter the legal status of women. In the 1970s, she argued several key cases before the Supreme Court. Ginsburg's Senate confirmation hearing revealed little of her constitutional philosophy beyond her public record. Some Republican senators tried to coax greater specificity from her broad affirmations of constitutional principles. Ginsburg declined their implicit invitation to reveal her constitutional value preferences. She cruised through to a 96–3 confirmation vote in the Senate.

Justice Harry Blackmun's resignation in 1994 gave Clinton a second opportunity to leave his imprint on the Court. After six weeks of deliberation, Clinton chose federal appeals judge Stephen G. Breyer for the coveted appointment. Breyer's moderate pragmatic views made him a consensus candidate. He sailed through tame confirmation hearings to take his place as the 108th justice.

Ginsburg and Breyer have tended to avoid ideological extremes. In close cases decided in 1995 and 1996, they remained part of a moderate-to-liberal minority. But that minority may soon find itself cast into the dominant majority. In President Clinton's second term, he is likely to have one or more additional opportunities to appoint Democrats to the nation's highest court. You can bet that the fight for the Court's ideological future will be as intense as any confirmation contests in recent memory.

THE CONSEQUENCES OF JUDICIAL DECISIONS

Lawsuits are the tip of the iceberg of legal disputes; most never surface in the courts. Of all the lawsuits begun in the United States, the overwhelming majority end without a court judgment. Many civil cases are settled, or the parties give up, or the courts dismiss the suits because they are beyond the legitimate bounds of judicial resolution. Most criminal cases end with a **plea bargain,** the defendant's admission of guilt in exchange for a less severe punishment. Only about 10 percent of criminal cases in the federal district courts are tried; an equally small percentage of civil cases are adjudicated.

Furthermore, the fact that a judge sentences a criminal defendant to ten years in prison or a court holds a company liable for $11 billion in damages does not guarantee that the defendant will lose his or her freedom or the company will give up any assets. In the case of the criminal defendant, the road of seeking an appeal following trial and conviction is well traveled and, if nothing else, serves to delay the day when no alternative to prison remains. In civil cases, the immediate consequence of a judgment may also be an appeal, which delays the day of reckoning.

Supreme Court Rulings: Implementation and Impact

When the Supreme Court makes a decision, it relies on others to implement it, to translate policy into action. How a judgment is implemented rests in good measure on how it was crafted. Remember that the justices, in preparing their opinions, must work to hold their majorities together, to gain greater, if not unanimous, support for their arguments. This forces them to compromise in their opinions, to moderate their arguments, which introduces ambiguity into many of the policies they articulate. Ambiguous opinions affect the implementation of policy. For example, when the Supreme Court issued its order in 1955 to desegregate public school facilities "with all deliberate speed,"[55] judges who opposed the Court's policy dragged their feet in implementing it. In the early 1960s, the Supreme Court prohibited prayers and Bible reading in public schools. Yet, state court judges and attorneys general reinterpreted the High Court's decision to mean that only compulsory prayer or Bible reading was unconstitutional, that state-sponsored voluntary prayer or Bible reading was acceptable.[56]

Because the Supreme Court confronts issues freighted with deeply felt social values or fundamental political beliefs, its decisions have influence beyond the immediate parties in a dispute. The Court's decision in *Roe* v. *Wade,* legalizing abortion, generated heated public reaction. The justices were barraged with thousands of angry letters. Groups opposing abortion vowed to overturn the decision; groups favoring the freedom to obtain an abortion moved to protect the right they had won. Within eight months of the decision, more than two dozen constitutional amendments had been introduced in Congress, although none managed to carry the extraordinary majority required for passage. Still, the antiabortion faction achieved a modest victory with the passage of a provision forbidding the use of national government funds for abortions except when the woman's life is in jeopardy. Since 1993, the exception has also included victims of rape or incest.

Opponents of abortion have also directed their efforts at state legislatures, hoping to load abortion laws with enough conditions to discourage women from terminating their pregnancies. For example, one state required that women receive detailed information about abortions, then wait at least twenty-four hours before consenting to the procedure. The information listed every imaginable danger associated with abortion and included a declaration that fathers are liable to support their children financially. A legal challenge to these new restrictions reached the Supreme Court, and in 1989, it abandoned its strong defense of abortion rights.[57] The Court continued to support a woman's right to abortion but in yet another legal challenge in 1992, it recognized the government's power to further limit the exercise of that right.[58]

Public Opinion and the Supreme Court

Democratic theorists have a difficult time reconciling a commitment to representative democracy with a judiciary that is not accountable to the electorate yet has the power to undo legislative and executive acts. The difficulty may simply be a problem for theorists, however. The policies coming from the Supreme Court, although lagging years behind public opinion, rarely seem out of line with the public's ideological choices.[59] Surveys in several controversial areas reveal that an ideologically balanced Court seldom departs from majority sentiment or trends (see Figure 14.4).[60]

The evidence supports the view that the Supreme Court reflects public opinion at least as often as other elected institutions. In a comprehensive study matching 146 Supreme Court rulings with nationwide opinion polls from the mid-1930s through the mid-1980s, the Court reflected public opinion majorities or pluralities in more than 60 percent of its rulings.[61] The fit is not perfect, however. The Court parted company with public opinion in a third of its rulings. For example, the Court has clearly defied the wishes of the majority for decades on the issue of school prayer. Most Americans today do not agree with the Court's position. And so long as the public continues to want prayer in schools, the controversy will continue.

There are at least three explanations for the Court's reflecting majority sentiment. First, the modern Court has shown deference to national laws and policies, which typically echo national public opinion. Second, the Court moves closer to public opinion during periods of crisis. And third, rulings that reflect the public view are subject to fewer changes than rulings that depart from public opinion.

Finally, the evidence also supports the view that the Court seldom influences public opinion. Americans have little factual knowledge of the Court. According to a recent survey, more than half of all Americans can't name a single justice, although two-thirds can correctly identify the Three Stooges.[62] It is not surprising that the Court enjoys only moderate popularity and that its decisions are not much noticed by the public. With few exceptions, there is no evidence of shifting public opinion before and after a Supreme Court ruling.[63]

figure

14.4

● **Public and Supreme Court Support for Rights Claims**

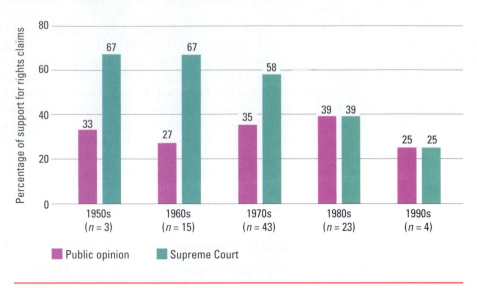

The bar graph compares national public opinion to specific Supreme Court decisions. Each pair of bars represents an assertion of a civil liberties or civil rights claim before the Supreme Court. Public support for these rights claims has hovered between 25 and 39 percent. The Supreme Court's support for these rights claims has declined steadily since the 1950s.

Source: Thomas R. Marshall and Joseph Ignagni, "Supreme Court and Public Support for Rights Claims," *Judicature* 78 (Nov.–Dec. 1994), pp. 146–151, with additional data kindly provided by Professors Marshall and Ignagni.

THE COURTS AND MODELS OF DEMOCRACY

How far should judges stray from existing statutes and precedents? Supporters of the majoritarian model would argue that the courts should adhere to the letter of the law, that judges must refrain from injecting their own values into their decisions. If the law places too much (or not enough) emphasis on equality or order, the elected legislature, not the courts, can change the law. In contrast, those who support the pluralist model maintain that the courts are a policymaking branch of government. It is thus legitimate for the individual values and interests of judges to mirror group interests and preferences and for judges to consciously attempt to advance group interests as they see fit. However, when, where, and how to proceed are difficult questions for judges at all levels (see Politics in a Changing America 14.1).

The argument that our judicial system fits the pluralist model gains support from a legal procedure called a **class action.** A class action is a device for assembling the claims or defenses of similarly situated individuals so that they can be tried in a single lawsuit. A class action makes it possible for people with small individual claims and limited financial resources to aggregate their claims and resources in order to make a lawsuit viable. The class action also permits the case to be tried by representative parties, with the judgment binding on all. Decisions in class action suits can have broader impact than decisions in other types of cases. Since the 1940s, class action suits have been the vehicles through which groups have asserted claims involving civil rights, legislative apportionment, and environmental problems. For example, schoolchildren have sued (through their parents) under the banner of class action to rectify claimed racial discrimination on the part of school authorities, as in *Brown* v. *Board of Education.*

politics in a changing america

14.1   Is This the Right Issue at the Right Time in the Right Case with the Right Theory?

Two recent federal appeals court decisions from opposite ends of the continent raise two critical questions concerning the creation of a constitutional right to assisted suicide. Will the justices put their stamp on such a right, and if so, which path will they take into this brave new world? The Supreme Court has managed to dodge the right-to-suicide argument before, but now the Court appears ready to act.

In March 1996, the United States Court of Appeals for the Ninth Circuit (which covers California, Oregon, Washington, Arizona, Idaho, Nevada, Montana, Alaska, Hawaii, Northern Mariana Islands, and Guam) struck down a Washington State law against aiding or abetting suicide. In April, the United States Court of Appeals for the Second Circuit (which covers New York, Connecticut, and Vermont) held that a similar New York State law was unconstitutional.

A panel of three Second Circuit judges found the New York law wanting under the equal protection clause of the Constitution. The law banned physician assistance to terminally ill patients seeking to self-administer lethal doses of prescription drugs, but other terminally ill patients could legally hasten their deaths by ordering the removal of life-support systems. The Constitution's equal protection clause stood at the core of the opinion:

> New York does not treat similarly circumstanced persons alike: those in the final stages of terminal illness who are on life-support systems are allowed to

hasten their deaths by directing the removal of such systems . . . [while others] are not allowed to hasten death by self-administering prescribed drugs.

In contrast, the Ninth Circuit relied on a liberty argument to strike down Washington's law. The majority of eight judges found authority in the Supreme Court's 1992 decision in *Planned Parenthood* v. *Casey*, which declared, "At the heart of liberty is the right to define one's own concept of existence, of meaning, of the universe, and of the mystery of human life." The circuit court stressed "the compelling similarities between right-to-die cases and abortion cases." The right of a woman to choose abortion stems from the same concept of liberty that now justifies a competent adult's right to physician-assisted suicide.

The losing parties in both cases petitioned the Supreme Court for review. Recall that the justices have near-total control of their docket. Their decision depends on the likely benefits and risks attending controversial cases and the issues that such cases and others are likely to raise. The justices granted review in both cases. The ensuing debate will hinge on three core values: freedom, order, and equality. A decision is expected by June 1997.

Sources: Compassion in Dying v. *State of Washington*, 79 F.3d 790 (9th Cir.)(March 6, 1996); *Quill* v. *Vacco*, 80 F.3d 716 (2d Cir.)(April 2, 1996); *Planned Parenthood* v. *Casey*, 505 U.S. ____ (1992). David J. Garrow, "The Justices' Life-or-Death Choices," *New York Times*, 7 April 1996, Sect. 4, p. 6.

Abetting the class action is the resurgence of state supreme courts' fashioning policies consistent with group preferences. Informed Americans often look to the U.S. Supreme Court for protection of their rights and liberties. In many circumstances, that expectation is correct. But state courts may serve as the staging areas for legal campaigns to change the law in the nation's highest court. They also exercise substantial influence over the

Courtly Demeanor

The New York Court of Appeals is the highest court in the state. Although it is bound by the decisions of the U.S. Supreme Court when defining and limiting national constitutional rights, it may rely on provisions of the state constitution to extend protections to individuals beyond those granted by the Supreme Court. For example, the New York court requires police to follow stricter procedures during car searches than those required by the U.S. Supreme Court.

policies that affect citizens daily, including the rights and liberties enshrined in state constitutions, statutes, and common law.[64]

Furthermore, state judges need not look to the U.S. Supreme Court for guidance on the meaning of certain state rights and liberties. If a state court chooses to rely solely on national law in deciding a case, that case is reviewable by the U.S. Supreme Court. But a state court can avoid review by the U.S. Supreme Court by basing its decision solely on state law or by plainly stating that its decision rests on both state and federal law. If the U.S. Supreme Court is likely to render a restrictive view of a constitutional right and the judges of a state court are inclined toward a more expansive view, the state judges can use the state ground to avoid Supreme Court review. In a period when the nation's highest court is moving in a decidedly conservative direction, some state courts have become safe havens for liberal values. And individuals and groups know where to moor their policies.

Turnabout in state politics is also fair play. Though only four states allow governors the sole authority to appoint judges to their highest courts, the surge in Republican control of state government nevertheless augurs more conservative judges and policies. For example, California governor Pete Wilson (R) has the rare opportunity to appoint a majority of justices to the seven-member California Supreme Court. His choices are likely to reflect law-and-order interests. Although New York governor George Pataki (R) selects judges from a list recommended by a nonpartisan commission, he's likely to aim for conservative candidates to fill the state's high bench.

The New Jersey Supreme Court has been more aggressive than most state supreme courts in following its own liberal constitutional path. It has gone further than the U.S. Supreme Court in promoting equality at the expense of freedom by prohibiting discrimination against women by private employers and by striking down the state's public school financing system, which had perpetuated vast disparities in public education within the state. The court has also preferred freedom over order in protecting the right to terminate life-support systems and in protecting free speech against infringement.[65] The New Jersey judges have charted their own path, despite the similarity in language between sections of the New Jersey Constitution and the U.S. Constitution. And the New Jersey judges have parted company with their national "cousins" even when the constitutional provisions at issue were identical.

For example, the U.S. Supreme Court ruled in 1988 that warrantless searches of curbside garbage are constitutionally permissible. Both the New Jersey Constitution and the U.S. Constitution bar unreasonable searches and seizures. Yet, in a 1990 decision expanding constitutional protections, the New Jersey court ruled that police officers need a search warrant before they can rummage through a person's trash. The court claimed that the New Jersey Constitution offers a greater degree of privacy than the U.S. Constitution. Because the decision rested on an interpretation of the state constitution, the existence of a similar right in the national charter had no bearing. The New Jersey court cannot act in a more restrictive manner than the U.S. Supreme Court allows, but it can be—and is—less restrictive.[66]

When judges reach decisions, they pay attention to the views of other courts—and not just those above them in the judicial hierarchy. State and federal court opinions are the legal storehouse from which judges regularly draw their ideas. Often the issues that affect individual lives—property, family, contracts—are grist for state courts, not federal courts. For example, when a state court faces a novel issue in a contract dispute, it will look at how other state courts have dealt with the problem. (Contract disputes are not a staple of the federal courts.) And if courts in several states have addressed an issue and the direction of the opinion is largely one-sided, the weight and authority of those opinions may move the court in that direction.[67] Courts that confront new issues with cogency and clarity are likely to become leaders of legal innovation.

State courts have become renewed arenas for political conflict, with litigants—individually or in groups—vying for their preferred policies. The multiplicity of the nation's court system, with overlapping state and national responsibilities, provides alternative points of access for individuals and groups to present and argue their claims. This description of the courts fits the pluralist model of government.

SUMMARY

The power of judicial review, claimed by the Supreme Court in 1803, placed the judiciary on an equal footing with Congress and the president. The principle of checks and balances can restrain judicial power through several means, such as constitutional amendments and impeachment. But restrictions on that power have been infrequent, leaving the federal courts to exercise considerable influence through judicial review and statutory construction.

The federal court system has three tiers. At the bottom are the district courts, where litigation begins and most disputes end. In the middle are the courts of appeals. At the top is the Supreme Court. The ability of judges to make policy increases as they move up the pyramid from trial courts to appellate courts to the Supreme Court.

The Supreme Court, free to draft its agenda through the discretionary control of its docket, harmonizes conflicting interpretations of national law and articulates constitutional rights. It is helped at this crucial stage by the solicitor general, who represents the executive branch of government before the High Court. The solicitor general's influence with the justices affects their choice of cases to review.

Political allegiance and complementary values are necessary conditions for appointment by the president to the coveted position of judge. The president and senators from the same party share the power of appointment of federal district and appellate judges. The president has more leeway in the nomination of Supreme Court justices, although all nominees must be confirmed by the Senate.

Courts inevitably fashion policy for each of the states and for the nation. They provide multiple points of access for individuals to pursue their preferences and so fit the pluralist model of democracy. Furthermore, the class action enables people with small individual claims and limited financial resources to pursue their goals in court, reinforcing the pluralist model.

Judges confront both the original and the modern dilemmas of government. The impact of their decisions can extend well beyond a single case. Some democratic theorists are troubled by the expansion of judicial power. But today's courts fit within the pluralist model and usually are in step with what the public wants.

As the U.S. Supreme Court heads in a more moderate direction, some state supreme courts have become safe havens for more liberal policies on civil rights and civil liberties. The state court systems have overlapping state and national responsibilities, offering groups and individuals many access points to present and argue their claims.

Key Terms

judicial review	precedent	rule of four	argument
criminal case	*stare decisis*	solicitor general	concurrence
civil case	original jurisdiction	*amicus curiae* brief	dissent
common (judge-made) law	appellate jurisdiction	judicial restraint	senatorial courtesy
	federal question	judicial activism	plea bargain
U.S. district courts	docket	judgment	class action
U.S. courts of appeals			

Selected Readings

Baum, Lawrence. *American Courts: Process and Policy,* 3d ed. Boston: Houghton Mifflin, 1994. A comprehensive review of trial and appellate courts in the United States that addresses their activities, describes their procedures, and explores the processes that affect them.

Coffin, Frank M. *On Appeal: Court, Lawyering, and Judging.* New York: Norton, 1994. A close look at the workings of a federal appellate court and the ways in which its chief judge reaches decisions.

Friedman, Lawrence M. *American Law: An Introduction.* New York: Norton, 1984. A clear, highly readable introduction to the bewildering complexity of the law. Explains how law is made and administered.

O'Brien, David M. *Storm Center: The Supreme Court*

in American Politics, 4th ed. New York: Norton, 1996. A primer on the Supreme Court, its procedures, personalities, and political influence.

Salokar, Rebecca Mae. *The Solicitor General: The Politics of Law.* Philadelphia: Temple University Press, 1992. A timely and well-researched empirical assessment of one of the least known but most important offices in the national government.

World Wide Web Resources

OYEZ. The U.S. Supreme Court has recorded its public proceedings from 1955 to the present. "Oyez. Oyez. Oyez."—a Web site developed at Northwestern University—contains an archive of the most important arguments and decisions. Download and install the free player from RealAudio <www.realaudio.com>, navigate to the OYEZ site, and the audio files will stream in real time to your desktop.
`<oyez.at.nwu.edu/oyez.html>`

The Legal Information Institute, Cornell University. The institute maintains a megasite of law-related materials including a searchable database of Supreme Court opinions since 1990.
`<www.law.cornell.edu/>`

The Virtual Law Library, Indiana University School of Law. Provides access to hundreds of law-related documents and resources. Includes alphabetical listings of U.S. law schools and law firms, U.S. government servers, and international law sites.
`<www.law.indiana.edu/law/v-lib/lawindex.html>`

part

Civil Liberties
and Civil Rights

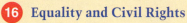

chapter

15

Order and Civil Liberties

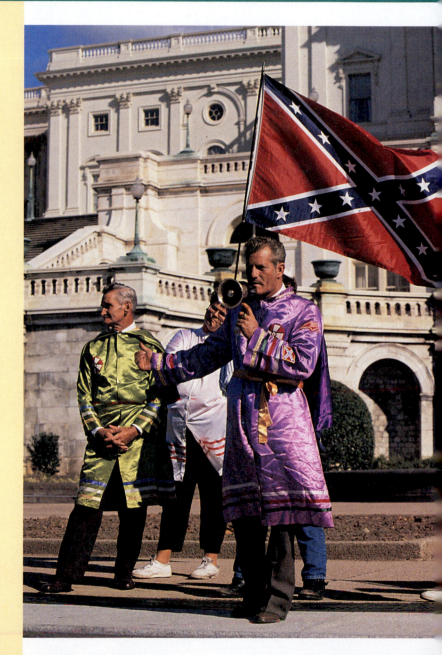

JAKE BAKER, A NINETEEN-YEAR-OLD LINGUISTICS STUDENT at the University of Michigan, posted shockingly explicit sex stories to an electronic bulletin board, one of the thousands of newsgroups that form the worldwide collection of networked information called Usenet. Baker wrote fictional fantasies that frequently included rape and violence to women and girls. In one story in which Baker graphically described the torture, rape, and murder of a woman, he gave the victim the name of a classmate at the University of Michigan.[1] Baker's stories could be read by millions of people every day. Some read them and moved on. Others were appalled and complained.

A computer operator in Washington, D.C., thought it was the grossest thing he had ever read on-line. He e-mailed University of Michigan officials that one of their students might be dangerous. Five thousand miles away, a sixteen-year-old girl in Russia read one of Baker's stories and showed it to her father. He in turn alerted an American attorney and Michigan alumnus who was working in Moscow, who thought that Baker's stories had gone beyond bad taste. He also contacted university officials. Media attention soon followed.

When the clamor rose, university officials acted. They visited Baker in his dorm room. He admitted writing the stories, waived his right to an attorney, and provided his e-mail password so officials could read his electronic mail. Shortly thereafter, the university president suspended Baker without a hearing. He was told to pack his bags and leave the university immediately.[2]

The Federal Bureau of Investigation and the Justice Department contemplated a criminal prosecution. Had Baker committed a crime? If so, what was it? Writing fiction is not a crime, even when it describes harmful acts. However, after reading his private e-mail, prosecutors decided to charge Baker with making threats to kill or kidnap in electronic messages transmitted via the Internet to a correspondent in Canada. U.S. commerce law prohibits the interstate or international transmission of threats to injure or kidnap a victim. Baker became the first person charged with making e-mail threats via the Internet. The law carries a penalty of up to five years of imprisonment. Baker was detained in jail for twenty-nine days while a federal judge contemplated releasing him on bail.

The government prosecuted Baker to maintain order—that is, to ensure the peace and safety of the community. The government viewed Baker's private correspondence as evidence of a threat of imminent harm. Baker's

● ● ● ● ● ● ● ● ● ● ●

Freedom's Embrace

Jake Baker, a college under-graduate, stood accused of criminal conduct in 1995 after he posted messages about his shockingly explicit fantasies on the Internet. Baker was embraced by his mother when he was released on bail after spending twenty-nine days in jail.

This is the address for Judge Cohn's opinion in the Jake Baker case.

`<ic.net/~sberaha/baker.html>`

attorney, joined by the American Civil Liberties Union, urged dismissal of the government's case. They maintained that the free speech clause of the First Amendment protected Baker from government action. A federal judge, Avern Cohn, sat at the center of the controversy, holding in the balance Baker's freedom and the community's demand for order. (We will examine the outcome of the case later in this chapter.)

How well do the courts respond to clashes that pit freedom against order in some cases and freedom against equality in others? Are freedom, order, or equality ever unconditional? In this chapter, we explore some value conflicts that the judiciary has resolved. You will be able to judge from the decisions in these cases whether American government has met the challenge of democracy by finding the appropriate balance between freedom and order and between freedom and equality.

The value conflicts described in this chapter revolve around claims or entitlements that rest on law. Although we concentrate here on conflicts over constitutional issues, the Constitution is not the only source of people's rights. Government at all levels can—and does—create rights through laws written by legislatures and regulations issued by bureaucracies.

We begin this chapter with the Bill of Rights and the freedoms it protects. Then we take a closer look at the role of the First Amendment in the original conflict between freedom and order. Next we turn to the Fourteenth Amendment and the limits it places on the states. Then we examine the Ninth Amendment and its relationship to issues of personal autonomy. Finally, we examine the threat to the democratic process when judges transform policy issues into constitutional issues. In Chapter 16, we will look at the Fourteenth Amendment's promise of equal protection, which sets the stage for the modern dilemma of government: the struggle between freedom and equality.

THE BILL OF RIGHTS

You may remember from Chapter 3 that at first the framers of the Constitution did not include a list of individual liberties—a bill of rights—in the national charter. They believed that a bill of rights was not necessary, because the Constitution spelled out the extent of the national government's power. But during the ratification debates, it became clear that the omission of a bill of rights was the most important obstacle to the adoption of the Constitution by the states. Eventually, the First Congress approved twelve amendments and sent them to the states for ratification. In 1791, the states ratified ten of the twelve amendments, and the nation had a bill of rights.

The Bill of Rights imposed limits on the national government but not on the state governments.* During the next seventy-seven years, litigants pressed the Supreme Court to extend the amendments' restraints to the states, but the Court refused until well after the adoption of the Fourteenth Amendment in 1868. Before then, protection from repressive state government had to come from state bills of rights.

The U.S. Constitution guarantees Americans numerous liberties and rights. In this chapter we explore a number of them. We will define and distinguish civil liberties and civil rights. (On some occasions, we will use the terms interchangeably.) **Civil liberties** are freedoms that are guaranteed to the individual. The guarantees take the form of restraints on government. For example, the First Amendment declares that "Congress shall make no law . . . abridging the freedom of speech." Civil liberties declare what the government cannot do.

In contrast, civil rights declare what the government must do or provide. **Civil rights** are powers and privileges that are guaranteed to the individual and protected against arbitrary removal at the hands of the government or other individuals. The right to vote and the right to a jury trial in criminal cases are civil rights embedded in the Constitution. Today, civil rights also embrace laws that further certain values. The Civil Rights Act of 1964, for example, furthered the value of equality by establishing the right to nondiscrimination in public accommodations and the right to equal employment opportunity. Civil liberties are the subject of this chapter; we discuss civil rights and their ramifications in Chapter 16.

The Bill of Rights lists both civil liberties and civil rights. When we refer to the rights and liberties of the Constitution, we mean the protections that are enshrined in the Bill of Rights and in the first section of the Fourteenth Amendment.[3] The list includes freedom of religion, freedom of speech and of the press, the rights to assemble peaceably and to petition

---

* *Congress considered more than one hundred amendments in its first session. One that was not approved would have limited the power of the states to infringe on the rights of conscience, speech, press, and jury trial in criminal cases. James Madison thought this amendment was the "most valuable" of the list, but it failed to muster a two-thirds vote in the Senate.*

the government, the right to bear arms, the rights of the criminally accused, the requirement of due process, and the equal protection of the laws.

FREEDOM OF RELIGION

Congress shall make no law respecting an establishment of religion, or prohibiting the free exercise thereof.

Religious freedom was important to the colonies and later to the states. That importance is reflected in its position among the ratified amendments that we know as the Bill of Rights: first, in the very first amendment. The First Amendment guarantees freedom of religion in two clauses: the **establishment clause** prohibits laws establishing religion; the **free-exercise clause** prevents the government from interfering with the exercise of religion. Together, they ensure that the government can neither promote nor inhibit religious beliefs or practices.

At the time of the Constitutional Convention, many Americans, especially in New England, maintained that government could and should foster religion, specifically Protestantism. However, many more Americans agreed that this was an issue for state governments, that the national government had no authority to meddle in religious affairs. The religion clauses were drafted in this spirit.[4]

The Supreme Court has refused to interpret the religion clauses definitively. The result is an amalgam of rulings, the cumulative effect of which is that freedom to believe is unlimited, but freedom to practice a belief can be limited. Religion cannot benefit directly from government actions (for example, government cannot make contributions to churches or synagogues), but it can benefit indirectly from those actions (for example, government can supply books on secular subjects for use in all schools—public, private, and parochial).

America is the most religious nation in the developed world.[5] Most Americans identify with a particular religious faith, and 40 percent attend church in a typical week. The vast majority believe in God, a judgment day, and life after death. Majoritarians might argue, then, that government should support religion. They would agree that the establishment clause bars government support of a single faith, but they might maintain that government should support all faiths. Such support would be consistent with what the majority wants and true to the language of the Constitution. In its decisions, the Supreme Court has rejected this interpretation of the establishment clause, leaving itself open to charges of undermining democracy. Those charges may be true with regard to majoritarian democracy, but the Court can justify its protection in terms of the basic values of democratic government.

The Establishment Clause

The provision that "Congress shall make no law respecting an establishment of religion" bars government sponsorship or support of religious activity. The Supreme Court has consistently held that the establishment clause requires government to maintain a position of neutrality toward religions and to maintain that position in cases that involve choices be-

Sacrificing Rights

Animal sacrifice is a central ritual in the Afro-Caribbean–based religion of Santeria. The Miami suburb of Hialeah banned such sacrifices, and a Santeria church in Hialeah challenged the local law. In a 1993 ruling, the Supreme Court sided with the church. Animal sacrifice for religious purposes is protected by the First Amendment free-exercise clause.

tween religion and nonreligion. However, the Court never has interpreted the clause as barring all assistance that incidentally aids religious institutions.

Government Support of Religion.   In 1879, the Supreme Court contended, quoting Thomas Jefferson's words, that the establishment clause erected "a wall of separation between church and State."[6] That wall was breached somewhat in 1947, when the justices upheld a local government program that provided free transportation to parochial school students.[7] The breach seemed to widen in 1968, when the Court held constitutional a government program in which parochial school students borrowed state-purchased textbooks.[8] The objective of the program, reasoned the majority, was to further educational opportunity. The students, not the schools, borrowed the books, and the parents, not the church, realized the benefits.

But in 1971, in ***Lemon v. Kurtzman,*** the Court struck down a state program that would have helped pay the salaries of teachers hired by parochial schools to give instruction in secular subjects.[9] The justices proposed a three-pronged test for determining the constitutionality of government programs and laws under the establishment clause:

- They must have a secular purpose (such as lending books to parochial school students).

- Their primary effect must not be to advance or inhibit religion.

- They must not entangle the government excessively with religion.

A program or law missing any prong would be unconstitutional.

The program at issue in *Lemon* failed on the last ground: to be certain that they did not include religious instruction in their lessons, the government would have to constantly monitor the secular teachers. For example, the government would be required to monitor mathematics lessons to ensure that the instruction did not reinforce religious dogma. Such supervision would entangle the government in religious activity, violating the Constitution's prohibition.

Does the display of religious artifacts on public property violate the establishment clause? In *Lynch* v. *Donnelly* (1984), the Court said no, by a vote of 5–4.[10] At issue was a publicly funded nativity scene on public property, surrounded by commercial symbols of the Christmas season such as Santa and his sleigh. While conceding that a crèche has religious significance, Chief Justice Warren E. Burger, writing for the majority, maintained that the display had a legitimate secular purpose: the celebration of a national holiday. Second, the display did not have the primary effect of benefiting religion; the religious benefits were "indirect, remote and incidental." And third, the display led to no excessive entanglement of religion and government. The justices hinted at a relaxation of the establishment clause by asserting their "unwillingness to be confined to any single test or criterion in this sensitive area." The upshot of *Lynch* was an "acknowledgment" of the religious heritage of the majority of Americans, although the Christmas holiday is a vivid reminder to religious minorities and the nonreligious of their separateness from the dominant Christian culture.

The *Lynch* decision led to a proliferation of cases testing the limits of government-sponsored religious displays. In 1989, a divided Court approved the display of a menorah while rejecting the display of a crèche.[11] The menorah appeared on the steps of the main entrance to a government building, alongside a Christmas tree and a sign reading "Salute to Liberty." The crèche appeared in a courthouse during the Christmas season. A majority found that the crèche display violated the second prong of the *Lemon* test but could not agree on the reasons for validating the menorah display. In such circumstances, the justices become vulnerable to the charge that they serve as constitutional "interior designers," imposing their own value preferences when they cannot fully explain why one religious image passes muster but another does not.

In the latest test of the establishment clause, the Court in 1994 struck down a New York law that created a public school district for the benefit of a village of Orthodox Jews. The district's sole purpose was to provide special education in a sheltered environment for children of the Satmar Hasidim. The parents had refused to send their children to the nearby public school program for fear that their Yiddish-speaking children, with their unusual deportment, would become targets of ridicule.

Justice David H. Souter wrote the majority opinion for a sharply divided bench in *Board of Education* v. *Grumet*.[12] The existence of the new district violated the principle at the heart of the establishment clause, declared Souter: "Government should not prefer one religion to another, or religion to irreligion."

Interestingly, the Court avoided its own *Lemon* test, neither endorsing nor repudiating it. A majority of the justices have expressed doubt about the test's utility, but they evidently have not agreed on an appropriate replacement.

• • • • • • • • • • • • •

Contested Rights

In 1993, students at Wingfield High School in Jackson, Mississippi, with the approval of the principal, read short nondenominational prayers over the school intercom. The school superintendent fired the principal, citing a 1962 Supreme Court ruling that banned school prayer. Hundreds of students and parents staged protests and vigils (pictured here). The principal was reinstated six months later.

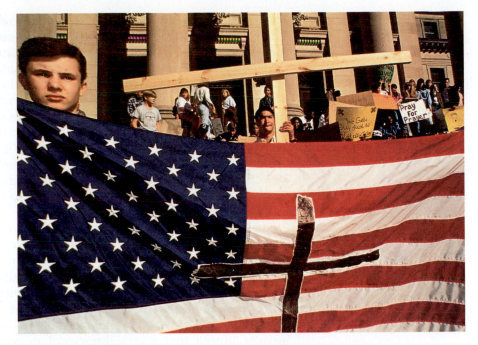

The cautious but fragmented approach employed by the majority suggested a new avenue for the New York State legislature. Within two weeks of the Court's decision, the legislature enacted a slightly different law to accomplish the same objective. A state court struck down this new approach as an indirect means of circumventing the Supreme Court's decision.[13]

School Prayer.   The Supreme Court has consistently equated prayer in public schools with government support of religion. In 1962, it struck down the daily reading of this twenty-two-word nondenominational prayer in New York's public schools: "Almighty God, we acknowledge our dependence upon Thee, and we beg Thy blessings upon us, our parents, our teachers and our country." Justice Hugo L. Black, writing for a 6–1 majority, held that official state approval of prayer was an unconstitutional attempt on the part of the state to establish a religion. This decision, in *Engle* v. *Vitale,* drew a storm of protest that has yet to subside.[14]

The following year, the Court struck down a state law calling for daily Bible reading and recitation of the Lord's Prayer in Pennsylvania's public schools.[15] The school district defended the reading and recitation on the grounds that they taught literature, perpetuated traditional institutions, and inculcated moral virtues. But the Court held that the state's involvement violated the government's constitutionally imposed neutrality in matters of religion.

A new school prayer issue arose in 1992 when the Court struck down the offering of nonsectarian prayers at official public school graduations. In a 5–4 decision, the Court held that government involvement creates "a state-sponsored and state-directed religious exercise in a public school."[16] The justices said that the establishment clause means that government may not conduct a religious exercise in the context of a school event.

School prayer persists despite Court opinions to the contrary. In 1996, a federal judge ordered the public schools in rural Pontotoc County, Mississippi, to stop allowing student-led prayers over the intercom, classroom prayers before lunch, and Bible classes taught by instructors chosen and paid by local churches. A single family—transplants from Wisconsin—endured years of harassment and ostracism resulting from its objections to the long-standing policy of allowing prayer in the schools. In 1996, federal judge Neal Biggers, Jr., ordered the school district to end the practices. "The Bill of Rights was created to protect the minority from tyranny by the majority," Biggers declared.[17]

The Constitution bars school prayer. Does it also bar silent meditation in school? In *Wallace* v. *Jaffree* (1985), the Court struck down a series of Alabama statutes requiring a moment of silence for meditation or voluntary prayer in elementary schools.[18] In a 6–3 decision, the Court renewed its use of the *Lemon* test and reaffirmed the principle of government neutrality between religion and nonreligion. The Court found that the purpose of the statute was to endorse religion; however, a majority of the justices hinted that a straightforward moment-of-silence statute that steered clear of religious endorsements might pass constitutional muster.

In yet another response to the school prayer controversy, Congress enacted the Equal Access Act in 1984. The act declares that no public secondary school receiving federal funds may bar after-school meetings on school property by student religious or political groups if it extends the same privileges to other extracurricular activities. In an 8–1 decision in 1990, the Court upheld the validity of the act, opening the door to the Bible Society as well as the Chess Club, and making room for the Witches' Coven, too.[19]

The establishment clause creates a problem for government. Support for all religions at the expense of nonreligion seems to pose the least risk to social order. Tolerance of the dominant religion at the expense of other religions risks minority discontent, but support for no religion (neutrality between religion and nonreligion) risks majority discontent, as illustrated in Politics in a Changing America 15.1.

The Free-Exercise Clause

The free-exercise clause of the First Amendment states that "Congress shall make no law . . . prohibiting the free exercise [of religion]." The Supreme Court has struggled to avoid absolute interpretations of this restriction so as not to violate its complement, the establishment clause. An example: suppose Congress grants exemptions from military service to individuals who have religious scruples against war. These exemptions could be construed as a violation of the establishment clause, because they favor some religious groups over others. But if Congress forced conscientious objectors to fight—to violate their religious beliefs—the government would run afoul of the free-exercise clause. In fact, Congress has granted military draftees such exemptions. But the Supreme Court has avoided a conflict between the establishment and free-exercise clauses by equating religious objection to war with any deeply held humanistic opposition to it. This solution leaves unanswered a central question: does the free-exercise clause require government to grant exemptions from legal duties that conflict with religious obligations, or does it guarantee only that the law will be applicable to religious believers without discrimination or preference?[20]

In the free-exercise cases, the justices have distinguished religious beliefs from actions based on those beliefs. Beliefs are inviolate, beyond the reach of government control. But the First Amendment does not protect antisocial actions. Consider conflicting values about saluting the flag, working on the Sabbath, and using drugs as religious sacraments.

Saluting the Flag. The values of order and religious freedom clashed in 1940, when the Court considered the first of two cases involving compulsory flag saluting in the public schools. In *Minersville School District* v. *Gobitis*, a group of Jehovah's Witnesses challenged the law on the ground that the action forced them to worship graven images, which their faith forbids.[21] Order won, in an 8–1 decision. "The mere possession of religious convictions," wrote Justice Felix Frankfurter, "which contradict the relevant concerns of a political society does not relieve the citizen from the discharge of political responsibilities." The reaction in Minersville and elsewhere was brutal and swift: people jeered the Gobitises on the streets, schoolmates beat up one of the children, and local churches led a boycott of the family business. In other communities, Jehovah's Witnesses were forced to swallow castor oil when they refused to salute the flag; others were tarred, feathered, and even castrated for following the dictates of their faith.[22]

Three years later, the Court reversed itself in **West Virginia State Board of Education v. Barnette.** This time, the Court saw a larger issue: can an individual be forced to salute the flag against his or her will? The Court had decided *Gobitis* on the narrower issue of religious belief versus saluting the flag. In *Barnette,* the justices chose to focus instead on the broader issue of freedom of expression. In stirring language, Justice Robert H. Jackson argued in the majority opinion that no one could be compelled by the government to declare any belief:

> If there is any fixed star in our constitutional constellation, it is that no official, high or petty, can prescribe what shall be orthodox in politics, nationalism, religion, or other matters of opinion or force citizens to confess by word or act their faith therein. If there are any circumstances which permit an exception, they do not now occur to us.[23]

Working on the Sabbath. The modern era of free-exercise thinking began with **Sherbert v. Verner** (1963). Adeil Sherbert, a Seventh-Day Adventist, lost her mill job because she refused to work on Saturday, her Sabbath. She filed for unemployment compensation and was referred to a job, which she declined, because it also required Saturday work. Because she declined the job, the state disqualified her from receiving unemployment benefits. In a

● politics in a changing america

15.1   Freedom Versus Order: When Christmas Conflicts with Diversity

Forget about peace and joy. December heralds a season of chaos and conflict as public school systems, parents, and children thrash out an intensifying annual debate: what winter holidays to celebrate, and how? Christmas, it seems, is clashing with diversity.

"The public school system is a battleground this time of year," says Rabbi A. James Rudin, director of interreligious affairs for the American Jewish Committee. "I am very fearful that this December dilemma will become even tougher as America becomes more multiracial, multiethnic, and multireligious."

In Chicago, the principal of the Walt Disney Magnet School saw his attempt at holiday harmony backfire. This elementary school has a mix of students, including black, Asian, Muslim, Hispanic, Yugoslavian, Romanian, and Jewish children, so the principal tried to tone down Christmas by issuing a ban on Santa Claus and any other symbols or activities associated with "a specific religious tradition." Teachers protested—one gave the principal a copy of *How the Grinch Stole Christmas*—and the head of the school board overturned the ban. With Christmas parties, decorations, and carols in full swing throughout the school, Essam Ammar, a Muslim parent, asked, "How am I going to raise my children as proud Muslims with all this going on?"

Passions are intensifying as school boards in increasingly diverse communities try to be sensitive to everyone. Some parents are demanding that a wide variety of other religious and ethnic holidays, including the Hindu Diwali festival, Hanukkah, and Kwanzaa, get equal time with Christmas. Others protest any diminution of Christmas traditions, such as bans on trees and Santa Claus in some communities.

Paradoxically, public school holiday observances, which now seem to be pulling school boards and parents apart, were first devised at the turn of the century as a way to bring people together. Holidays were a way of creating Americanizing rituals for new immigrants. Now, however, at the end of the century, legal decisions about holidays have conflicted with parental sensibilities in an increasingly multiethnic society.

The Supreme Court ruled in 1989 that Christmas trees and menorahs are secular symbols of the holiday season and that their public display does not violate the First Amendment. In December 1995, a federal judge in Newark, New Jersey, ruled that the Nativity scene and menorah in front of Jersey City's City Hall should be joined by a Santa Claus and a snowman to make the display more secular and therefore constitutional. Nonetheless, in 1994 the school board in Scarsdale, New York, banned menorahs, trees, and garlands and wreaths, along with holiday celebrations that had a religious connotation and no educational purpose, in the schools. Therefore, classroom parties had no holiday theme: one celebrated the winter solstice; another, birds.

After an outcry, the stringent guidelines were moderated. But in practice, things are much the same as before: there are no Christmas trees or Santa Claus decorations, parties celebrate the coming winter vacation instead of the holidays, and decorations consist largely of snowflakes and snowmen.

The main change in Scarsdale is a new four-holiday "Festival of Lights" curriculum for children in kindergarten and first and second grades. The community's new buzzwords are "educate, don't celebrate." The children are learning about Christmas, Hanukkah, Kwanzaa, and Diwali. Parents are invited to talk to classes about their families' customs and to bring in holiday foods. There is no holiday curriculum for older children.

In Cherry Hill, New Jersey, good will reigns with the school board's new policy requiring

In Cherry Hill, N.J., the Bret Harte Elementary School displays a Christmas tree, a Kwanzaa candleholder, a menorah, and Buddha during the December holiday season.

all holiday displays to include four elements: a Christmas tree, a menorah, a Kwanzaa kinara candleholder, and a gold laminated picture of Buddha in celebration of Bodhi Day, the day of Buddha's enlightenment.

The town leaves little to chance in its attempt to be all-inclusive. "Christmas vacation" is now called "winter recess." A high school's traditional December concert now takes place early in the month so it doesn't coincide with any particular holiday observance. But the two traditional closing numbers have not changed: the "Hallelujah Chorus" and the Hebrew song "Sholom, Chaverim" ("Goodbye, Friends").

In all Cherry Hill schools, children cannot sing Christmas carols with a religious message, like "Silent Night," explains Laurie Zellnik, a public information officer for the school district, but they are allowed to sing songs such as "Santa Claus Is Coming to Town" and "I Have a Little Dreidel." Buddhist and Kwanzaa songs are not part of the celebration. "Nobody knows any," she says.

It seems that few Christians are happy with these attempts to be all-inclusive. Kathleen McCreary, a lawyer who lives in Scarsdale and who successfully sued the village a few years ago to permit the display of a crèche on public property, says, "You should not dumb-down a holiday to the point where it is unrecognizable."

Sources: Carol Lawson, "The Debate on Holiday Diversity," *New York Times,* 21 December 1995, p. A18. Copyright © 1995 by The New York Times Company. Reprinted by permission. Eric L. Schmidt, *Consumer Rites: The Buying and Selling of American Holidays* (Princeton, N.J.: Princeton University Press, 1995).

7–2 decision, the Supreme Court ruled that the disqualification imposed an impermissible burden on Sherbert's free exercise of religion. The First Amendment, declared the majority, protects observance as well as belief. A neutral law that burdens the free exercise of religion is subject to **strict scrutiny.** This means that the law may be upheld only if the government can demonstrate that the law is justified by a "compelling governmental interest" and is the least restrictive means for achieving that interest.[24] And only rarely can government muster enough evidence to demonstrate a compelling interest.

The *Sherbert* decision prompted religious groups and individual believers to challenge laws that conflict with their faith. We have seen how conflicts arise from the imposition of penalties for refusing to engage in religiously prohibited conduct. But conflicts may also arise from laws that impose penalties for engaging in religiously motivated conduct.[25]

Using Drugs as Sacraments.   Partaking of illegal substances as part of a religious sacrament forces believers to violate the law. For example, the Rastafarians and members of the Ethiopian Zion Coptic church smoke marijuana in the belief that it is the body and blood of Christ. Obviously, taking to an extreme the freedom to practice religion can result in a license to engage in illegal conduct. And even when such conduct stems from deeply held convictions, government resistance to it is understandable. The inevitable result is a clash between religious freedom and social order.

The courts used the compelling-government-interest test for many years, and on that basis invalidated most laws restricting free exercise. But in 1990 the Supreme Court abruptly and unexpectedly rejected its long-standing rule, tipping the balance in favor of social order. In *Employment Division* v. *Smith,* two members of the Native American Church sought an exemption from an Oregon law that made the possession or use of peyote a crime.[26] (Peyote is a cactus that contains the hallucinogen mescaline. Native Americans have used it for centuries in their religious ceremonies.) Oregon did not prosecute the two church members for their use or possession of peyote. Rather, the state rejected their applications for unemployment benefits after they were dismissed from their drug-counseling jobs for using peyote. Oregon believed it had a compelling interest in proscribing the use of certain drugs according to its own drug laws.

Justice Antonin Scalia, writing for the 6–3 majority, examined the conflict between freedom and order through the lens of majoritarian democratic thought. He observed that the Court has never held that an individual's religious beliefs excuse him or her from compliance with an otherwise valid law prohibiting conduct that government is free to regulate. Allowing exceptions to every state law or regulation affecting religion "would open the prospect of constitutionally required exemptions from civic obligations of almost every conceivable kind." Scalia cited as examples compulsory military service, payment of taxes, vaccination requirements, and child-neglect laws. Laws that indirectly restrict religious practices are acceptable; only laws aimed at religious groups are constitutionally prohibited.

The decision brought in its wake scores of government actions infringing on religious exercise. One such case involved unauthorized autopsy.

Several religions proscribe the mutilation of the human body; they view autopsy as a form of mutilation. Many Jews, Navajo Indians, and the Hmong, an immigrant group from Laos, hold this belief. For the Hmong, an autopsy means that the deceased's spirit will never be free. Yet, Rhode Island performed an autopsy on a Hmong without regard to the family's religious beliefs. Because the autopsy rule did not target a religious group, the family had no recourse against the shame of government mutilation of their loved one. The demands of social order triumphed over the spirit of religious freedom.

The political response to *Employment Division* v. *Smith* was an example of pluralism in action. An unusual coalition of religious and nonreligious groups (including the National Association of Evangelicals, the American Civil Liberties Union, the National Islamic Prison Foundation, and B'nai B'rith) organized to restore the more restrictive strict scrutiny test. At first the coalition failed to rouse much public interest in a case involving the use of hallucinogenic drugs. But as government infringements on religious practice mounted, public interest and legislative reaction soon meshed.

Spanning the theological and ideological spectrum, the alliance established in Congress what it had lost in the Supreme Court. In 1993, President Bill Clinton signed into law the Religious Freedom Restoration Act. The law once again requires government to satisfy the strict scrutiny standard before it can institute measures that interfere with religious practices. Voicing wonder at this alliance of groups so often at odds over religion and ideology, Clinton observed, "The power of God is such that even in the legislative process miracles can happen."[27]

FREEDOM OF EXPRESSION

Congress shall make no law . . . abridging the freedom of speech, or of the press; or the right of the people peaceably to assemble, and to petition the Government for a redress of grievances.

James Madison introduced the original versions of the speech clause and the press clause of the First Amendment in the House of Representatives in June 1789. One early proposal provided that "the people shall not be deprived of their right to speak, to write, or to publish their sentiments, and the freedom of the press, as one of the great bulwarks of liberty, shall be inviolable." That version was rewritten several times, then merged with the religion and peaceable assembly clauses to yield the First Amendment.

The original House debates on the proposed speech and press clauses are not informative. There is no record of debate in the Senate or in the states during ratification. But careful analysis of other records supports the view that the press clause prohibited only the imposition of **prior restraint**—censorship before publication. Publishers could not claim protection from punishment if works they had already published were later deemed improper, mischievous, or illegal.

The spare language of the First Amendment seems perfectly clear: "Congress shall make no law . . . abridging the freedom of speech, or of the press." Yet, a majority of the Supreme Court has never agreed that this "most majestic guarantee" is absolutely inviolable.[28] Historians have long debated the framers' intentions regarding these **free-expression clauses,** the press and speech clauses of the First Amendment. The dominant view is that the clauses confer the right to unrestricted discussion of public affairs.[29] Other scholars, examining much the same evidence, conclude that few, if any, of the framers clearly understood the clause; moreover, they insist that the First Amendment does not rule out prosecution for seditious statements (statements inciting insurrection).[30]

The license to speak freely does not move multitudes of Americans to speak out on controversial issues. Americans have woven subtle restrictions into the fabric of our society: the risk of criticism or ostracism by family, peers, or employers tends to reduce the number of people who test the limits of free speech to individuals ready to bear the burdens. As Mark Twain once remarked, "It is by the goodness of God that in our country we have three unspeakably precious things: freedom of speech, freedom of conscience, and the prudence never to practice either of them."[31]

Today, the clauses are deemed to bar most forms of prior restraint (consistent with the framers' understanding) as well as after-the-fact prosecution for political and other discourse. The Supreme Court has evolved two approaches to the resolution of claims based on the free-expression clauses. First, government can regulate or punish the advocacy of ideas, but only if it can prove an intent to promote lawless action and demonstrate that a high probability exists that such action will occur. Second, government may impose reasonable restrictions on the means for communicating ideas, restrictions that can incidentally discourage free expression.

Suppose, for example, that a political party advocates nonpayment of personal income taxes. Government cannot regulate or punish that party for advocating tax nonpayment, because the standards of proof—that the act be directed at inciting or producing imminent lawless action and that the act be likely to produce such action—do not apply. But government can impose restrictions on the way the party's candidates communicate what they are advocating. Government can bar them from blaring messages from loudspeakers in residential neighborhoods at 3 A.M.

Freedom of Speech

The starting point for any modern analysis of free speech is the **clear and present danger test,** formulated by Justice Oliver Wendell Holmes in the Supreme Court's unanimous decision in *Schenck* v. *United States* (1919). Charles T. Schenck and his fellow defendants were convicted under a federal criminal statute for attempting to disrupt World War I military recruitment by distributing leaflets claiming that conscription was unconstitutional. The government believed this behavior threatened the public order. At the core of the Court's opinion, as Holmes wrote, was the view that

> the character of every act depends upon the circumstances in which it is done.... The most stringent protection of free speech would not protect a man in falsely shouting fire in a theatre, and causing a panic.... The ques-

tion in every case is whether the words used are used in such circumstances and are of such a nature as to create *a clear and present danger*
that they will bring about the substantive evils that Congress has a right
to prevent. It is a question of proximity and degree. When a nation is at
war many things that might be said in time of peace are such a hindrance
to its effort that their utterance will not be endured so long as men fight,
and that no court could regard them as protected by any constitutional
right [emphasis added].[32]

Because the actions of the defendants in *Schenck* were deemed to create
a clear and present danger to the United States at that time, the Supreme
Court upheld the defendants' convictions. The clear and present danger
test helps to distinguish the advocacy of ideas, which is protected, from incitement, which is not. However, Holmes later frequently disagreed with
a majority of his colleagues in applying the test.

In an often-quoted dissent in *Abrams* v. *United States* (1919), Holmes
revealed his deeply rooted resistance to the suppression of ideas. The majority had upheld Jacob Abrams's criminal conviction for distributing
leaflets that denounced the war and U.S. opposition to the Russian
Revolution. Holmes wrote,

When men have realized that time has upset many fighting faiths, they
may come to believe … that the ultimate good desired is better reached by
free trade in ideas—that the best test of truth is the power of the thought
to get itself accepted in the competition of the market, and that truth is
the only ground upon which their wishes safely can be carried out. That
at any rate is the theory of our Constitution.[33]

In 1925, the Court issued a landmark decision in *Gitlow* v. *New York*.[34]
Benjamin Gitlow was arrested for distributing copies of a "left-wing manifesto" that called for the establishment of socialism through strikes and
working-class uprisings of any form. Gitlow was convicted under a state
criminal anarchy law; Schenck and Abrams had been convicted under a
federal law. For the first time, the Court assumed that the First
Amendment speech and press provisions applied to the states through the
due process clause of the Fourteenth Amendment. Still, a majority of the
justices affirmed Gitlow's conviction. Justices Holmes and Louis D.
Brandeis argued in dissent that Gitlow's ideas did not pose a clear and present danger. "Eloquence may set fire to reason," conceded the dissenters.
"But whatever may be thought of the redundant discourse before us, it had
no chance of starting a present conflagration."

The protection of advocacy faced yet another challenge in 1948, when
eleven members of the Communist Party were charged with violating the
Smith Act, a federal law making the advocacy of force or violence against
the United States a criminal offense. The leaders were convicted, although
the government introduced no evidence that they had actually urged people to commit specific violent acts. The Supreme Court mustered a majority for its decision to uphold the convictions under the act, but it could
not get a majority to agree on the reasons in support of that decision. The
biggest bloc, of four justices, announced the plurality opinion in 1951,

arguing that the government's interest was substantial enough to warrant criminal penalties.[35] The justices interpreted the threat to the government to be the gravity of the advocated action, "discounted by its improbability." In other words, a single soap-box orator advocating revolution stands little chance of success. But a well-organized, highly disciplined political movement advocating revolution in the tinderbox of unstable political conditions stands a greater chance of success. In broadening the meaning of "clear and present danger," the Court held that the government was justified in acting preventively rather than waiting until revolution is about to occur.

By 1969, the pendulum had swung back in the other direction: the justices began to put more emphasis on freedom. That year, in ***Brandenburg v. Ohio***, a unanimous decision extended the freedom of speech to new limits.[36] Clarence Brandenburg, the leader of the Ohio Ku Klux Klan, had been convicted under a state law for advocating racial strife at a Klan rally. His comments, which had been filmed by a television crew, included threats against government officials.

The Court reversed Brandenburg's conviction because the government had failed to prove that the danger was real. The Court went even further and declared that threatening speech is protected by the First Amendment unless the government can prove that such advocacy is "directed to inciting or producing imminent lawless action and is likely to incite or produce such action." The ruling offered wider latitude for the expression of political ideas than ever before in the nation's history.

Symbolic Expression.   Symbolic expression, or nonverbal communication, generally receives less protection than pure speech. But the courts have upheld certain types of symbolic expression. ***Tinker v. Des Moines Independent County School District*** (1969) involved three public school students who wore black arm bands to school to protest the Vietnam War. Principals in their school district had prohibited the wearing of arm bands on the ground that such conduct would provoke a disturbance; the district suspended the students. The Supreme Court overturned the suspensions. Justice Abe Fortas declared for the majority that the principals had failed to show that the forbidden conduct would substantially interfere with appropriate school discipline:

> Undifferentiated fear or apprehension of disturbance is not enough to overcome the right to freedom of expression. Any departure from absolute regimentation may cause trouble. Any variation from the majority's opinion may inspire fear. Any word spoken, in class, in the lunchroom, or on the campus, that deviates from the views of another person may start an argument or cause a disturbance. But our Constitution says we must take this risk.[37]

The flag is an object of deep veneration in our society, yet its desecration is also a form of symbolic expression protected by the First Amendment. In 1989, a divided Supreme Court struck down a Texas law that barred the desecration of venerated objects. Congress then enacted the Flag Protection Act of 1989 in an attempt to overcome the constitutional flaws of the Texas decision. Gregory Johnson, whose 1984 flag burning in Texas led to the Court's 1989 decision, joined other protesters and burned an American flag on the steps of the Capitol in October 1989, in a test of the new national law.

The Supreme Court nullified the federal flag-burning statute in *United States* v. *Eichman* (1990). The Court was unpersuaded that the new law was distinguishable from its Texas cousin. By a vote of 5–4, the justices reaffirmed First Amendment protection for all expressions of political ideas. The vote was identical to the Texas case, with conservative justices Anthony M. Kennedy and Scalia joining with the liberal wing to forge an unusual majority. The majority placed the same emphasis on freedom that it had in the Texas case, including a quotation from its earlier opinion: " 'If there is a bedrock principle underlying the First Amendment, it is that the Government may not prohibit the expression of an idea simply because society finds the idea itself offensive or disagreeable.' Punishing desecration of the flag dilutes the very freedom that makes this emblem so revered, and worth revering."[38]

In this opinion, the Court majority relied on the substantive conception of democratic theory, which embodies the principle of freedom of speech.

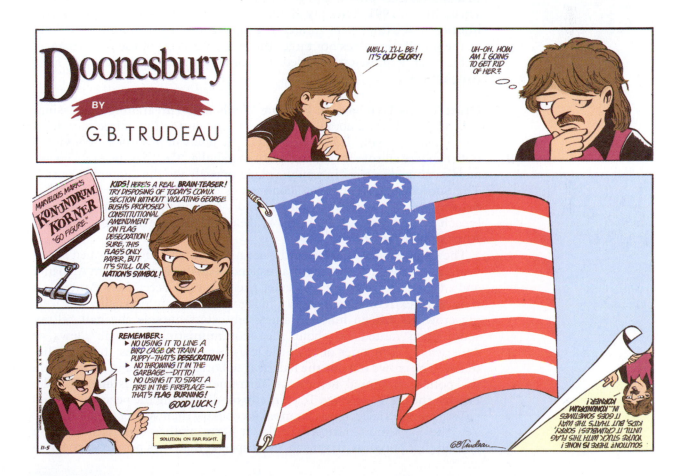

Yet, a May 1990 poll revealed that most people wanted to outlaw flag burning as a means of political expression and that a clear majority favored a constitutional amendment to that end.[39] (Such an amendment won Senate approval in 1990, but it fell thirty-four votes shy of the required two-thirds majority in the House.) The procedural interpretation of democratic theory holds that government should do what the people want. In the case of flag burning, the people are apparently willing to abandon the principle of freedom of speech embodied in the substantive view of democracy.

Although offensive to the vast majority of Americans, flag burning is a form of political expression. But suppose the conduct in question does not embody a political idea. May government ever legitimately ban that conduct? Consider the case of three nude dancers in JR's Kitty Kat Lounge, a South Bend, Indiana, strip joint, who sought to block the enforcement of an Indiana law that bans all public nudity. If nude dancing is merely conduct, government has the latitude to control or even ban it. But if nude dancing is expression, government action to prohibit it runs afoul of the First Amendment.

The distinction between conduct and expression masks underlying value conflicts. Control advocates who sought to promote social order argued that the statute attempted to promote public decency and morality. Expression advocates who sought to promote a form of freedom argued that the dancers provided entertainment, communicating eroticism and sensuality. In 1991, a sharply divided Supreme Court upheld the state prohibition in the interest of "protecting societal order and morality," so long as the prohibition does not target the erotic message of the performance, a form of expression entitled to some protection under the First Amendment.[40]

Order Versus Free Speech: Fighting Words and Threatening Expression. Fighting words are a notable exception to the protection of free speech. In *Chaplinsky* v. *New Hampshire* (1942), a Jehovah's Witness, convicted under a state statute for calling a city marshal a "God-damned racketeer" and "a damned fascist" in a public place, appealed to the Supreme Court.[41] The Supreme Court upheld Chaplinsky's conviction on the theory that **fighting words**—words that "inflict injury or tend to incite an immediate breach of the peace"—do not convey ideas and thus are not subject to First Amendment protection.

The Court sharply narrowed the definition of *fighting words* just seven years later. Arthur Terminiello, a suspended Catholic priest from Alabama and a vicious anti-Semite, addressed the Christian Veterans of America, a right-wing extremist group, in a Chicago hall. Terminiello called the jeering crowd of fifteen hundred angry protesters outside the hall "slimy scum" and ranted on about the "communistic, Zionistic" Jews of America, evoking cries of "kill the Jews" and "dirty kikes" from his listeners. The crowd outside the hall heaved bottles, bricks, and rocks, while the police attempted to protect Terminiello and his listeners inside. Finally, the police arrested Terminiello for disturbing the peace.

Terminiello's speech was far more incendiary than Walter Chaplinsky's. Yet, the Supreme Court struck down Terminiello's conviction on the ground that provocative speech, even speech that stirs people to anger, is protected by the First Amendment. "Freedom of speech," wrote Justice William O. Douglas in the majority opinion, "though not absolute . . . is nevertheless protected against censorship or punishment, unless shown likely to produce a clear and present danger of a serious substantive evil that rises far above public inconvenience, annoyance, or unrest."

This broad view of protection brought a stiff rebuke in Justice Jackson's dissenting opinion:

> The choice is not between order and liberty. It is between liberty with order and anarchy without either. There is danger that, if the Court does not temper its doctrinaire logic with a little practical wisdom, it will convert the constitutional Bill of Rights into a suicide pact.[42]

Navigate to this site to listen to the arguments in *Cohen* v. *California.* Be sure to install the RealAudio Player on your system.

`<oyez.at.nwu.edu/cases/71-299>`

The times seem to have caught up with the idealism that Jackson criticized in his colleagues. In **Cohen v. California** (1971), a nineteen-year-old department store worker expressed his opposition to the Vietnam War by wearing a jacket in the hallway of a Los Angeles county courthouse emblazoned with the words FUCK THE DRAFT. STOP THE WAR. The young man, Paul Cohen, was charged in 1968 under a California statute that prohibits "maliciously and willfully disturb[ing] the peace and quiet of any neighborhood or person [by] offensive conduct." He was found guilty and sentenced to thirty days in jail. On appeal, the U.S. Supreme Court reversed Cohen's conviction.

The Court reasoned that the expletive he used, while provocative, was not directed at anyone in particular; besides, the state presented no evidence that the words on Cohen's jacket would provoke people in "substantial numbers" to take some kind of physical action. In recognizing that "one man's vulgarity is another's lyric," the Supreme Court protected two elements of speech: the emotive (the expression of emotion) and the cognitive (the expression of ideas).[43]

University campuses are new sources of speech restrictions. Public and private campuses have established rules barring racial or ethnic slurs on the ground that such language is a form of harassment or discrimination. But such restrictions, though authorized by the government, may go too far, according to a 1992 case that raised a similar fundamental issue in the context of a crime rooted in racial bias.

When a teenager burned a cross on a black family's lawn, police officials charged him with the bias-motivated crime of "arousing anger, alarm, or resentment in others on the basis of race, color, creed, religion or gender." (They could have charged him with arson, terrorism, or trespass.) In a unanimous 1992 decision, the justices struck down the bias-motivated criminal statute on free speech grounds.[44] The justices observed that the law punished some expression (odious racial epithets) but not others (odious homophobic epithets). Such distinctions regarding expression were out of bounds. Government has no authority "to license one side of a debate to fight freestyle," wrote Justice Scalia, "while requiring the other to follow the Marquis of Queensberry Rules."

Recall the government's prosecution of Jake Baker for transmitting threats to injure or kidnap in e-mail transmitted over the Internet. Baker's prosecution involved pure speech, so it is subject to First Amendment limits. The task involved distinguishing true threats, which are punishable, from constitutionally protected speech, which is not punishable. True threats must be unequivocal, unconditional, immediate, and specific as to the person threatened.

Judge Cohn threw out the indictment before the case reached a trial. The charges against Baker failed to meet the "true threat" standard. "Discussion of desires, alone," reasoned Cohn, "is not tantamount to threatening to act on those desires." In the absence of a threat to act, Baker's communications were protected by the First Amendment.[45]

Though Jake Baker has his freedom, the demand for social order on the Internet has significant support. In 1996, Congress passed the Communications Decency Act, which made it a crime for a person knowingly to circulate "patently offensive" sexual material to Internet sites accessible to those under eighteen years old. Is this an acceptable way to protect children from offensive material (perhaps like Baker's stories), or is it a muzzle on free speech? A federal court quickly declared the act unconstitutional. In an opinion of over two hundred pages, the court observed that "just as the strength of the Internet is chaos, so the strength of our liberty depends on the chaos and cacophony of the unfettered speech the First Amendment protects."[46] The Supreme Court will likely provide a final answer, as the government plans a special appeal to the High Court.

This site contains a copy of the decision voiding the Communications Decency Act. <www.eff.org/Alerts/HTML/ 960612_aclu_v_reno_ decision.html>

Free Speech Versus Order: Obscenity.   The Supreme Court has always viewed obscene material—whether in words, music, books, magazines, or films—as outside the bounds of constitutional protection, which means that states may regulate or even ban obscenity. However, difficulties arise in determining what is obscene and what is not. In *Roth* v. *United States* (1957), Justice William J. Brennan, Jr., outlined a test for judging a work as obscene: "Whether to the average person, applying contemporary community standards, the dominant theme of the material taken as a whole appeals to prurient interest."[47] (*Prurient* means having a tendency to incite lustful thoughts.) Yet, a definition of obscenity has proved elusive; no objective test seems adequate. Justice Potter Stewart will long be remembered for his solution to the problem of identifying obscene materials. He declared that he could not define it. "But," he added, "I know it when I see it."[48]

In *Miller v. California* (1973), its most recent major attempt to clarify constitutional standards governing obscenity, the Court declared that a work—a play, film, or book—is obscene and may be regulated by government if (1) the work taken as a whole appeals to the prurient interest; (2) the work portrays sexual conduct in a patently offensive way; and (3) the work taken as a whole lacks serious literary, artistic, political, or scientific value.[49] Local community standards govern application of the first and second prongs of the *Miller* test.

Feminism, Free Expression, and Equality.   Historically, civil liberties have conflicted with demands for social order. However, civil liberties can also conflict with demands for equality. In the 1980s, city officials in Indianapolis, Indiana—influenced by feminist theorists—invoked Fourteenth Amendment equality principles to justify legislation restrict-

Rappin' Rights

Luther Campbell and the rap group 2 Live Crew recorded the album Nasty As They Wanna Be. *A federal trial judge found the album's lyrics obscene in an attempt to ban its sale and distribution in Florida. An appellate court overturned the ruling in 1993. The court held that artistic expression was protected by the First Amendment. The group returned for an encore in 1994, when the Supreme Court ruled that the group's parody of Roy Orbison's "Pretty Woman" did not violate copyright law.*

ing freedom of expression. Specifically, they argued that pornography is sex discrimination.[50]

The ordinance focused on pornography and its effect on women's status and treatment. It defined pornography as the graphic, sexually explicit subordination of women in words or pictures that present women as "sexual objects who experience pleasure in being raped" or as "sexual objects of domination, conquest, violation, exploitation, possession, or use, or [in] postures or positions of servility or submission or display." The ordinance rested on three findings:

- That pornography is a form of discrimination that denies equal opportunities in society.

- That pornography is central in creating and maintaining gender as a category of discrimination.

- That pornography is a systematic practice of exploitation and subordination based on sex, imposing differential harms on women.

The ordinance then banned pornographic material according to the following argument: government interest in equality outweighs any First Amendment interest in communication; pornography affects thoughts; it works by socializing, by establishing the expected and permissible; depictions of subordination tend to perpetuate subordination, and this leads to affronts to women and to the continuation of lower pay at work, insult and injury at home, and battery and rape in the streets. Since pornography conditions society to subordinate women, an ordinance regulating pornographic expression will also regulate and control the underlying unacceptable conduct.

According to the ordinance, works depicting sexual encounters premised on equality are lawful no matter how sexually explicit. And works that treat women in the disapproved way—as sexually submissive or as enjoying humiliation—are unlawful no matter how significant the literary, artistic, or political qualities of the work. U.S. District Judge Sarah Evans Barker declared the ordinance unconstitutional, stating that it went beyond the categories of unprotected expression (such as child pornography) to suppress otherwise protected expression.

Judge Barker thus confronted the trade-off between equality and freedom in a pluralist democracy. Interest groups that use the democratic process to carve exceptions to the First Amendment benefit at the expense of everyone's rights. Although efforts to restrict behavior that leads to the humiliation and degradation of women may be necessary and desirable, "free speech, rather than being the enemy," wrote Judge Barker, "is a long-tested and worthy ally. To deny free speech in order to engineer social change in the name of accomplishing a greater good for one sector of our society erodes the freedom of all."[51]

This novel effort to recast an issue of freedom versus order as one of freedom versus equality remains a theory. Barker's decision protected freedom. Her judgment was affirmed by the U.S. Court of Appeals in 1985 and affirmed without argument by the Supreme Court in 1986. In 1988, the citizens of Bellingham, Washington, approved by referendum an ordinance similar to the one in Indianapolis, but a federal district judge invalidated it in 1989. The Massachusetts legislature introduced a narrower version in 1992. In the next confrontation—and, in a pluralist democracy, there will surely be others—equality may prove the victor.

Freedom of the Press

The First Amendment guarantees that government "shall make no law … abridging the freedom … of the press." Although the free press guarantee was originally adopted as a restriction on the national government, since 1931 the Supreme Court has held that it applies to state and local governments as well.

The ability to collect and report information without government interference was (and still is) thought to be essential to a free society. The print media continue to use and defend the freedom conferred on them by the framers. However, the electronic media have had to accept some government regulation stemming from the scarcity of broadcast frequencies (see Chapter 6).

Defamation of Character.   Libel is the written defamation of character.[*] A person who believes his or her name and character have been harmed by false statements in a publication can institute a lawsuit against the publication and seek monetary compensation for the damage. Such a lawsuit can impose limits on freedom of expression; at the same time, false statements impinge on the rights of individuals. In a landmark decision in *New*

---

[*] *Slander is the oral defamation of character. The durability of the written word usually means that libel is a more serious accusation than slander.*

York Times **v.** *Sullivan* (1964), the Supreme Court declared that freedom of the press takes precedence—at least when the defamed individual is a public official.[52] The Court unanimously agreed that the First Amendment protects the publication of all statements—even false ones—about the conduct of public officials, except statements made with actual malice (with knowledge that they are false or in reckless disregard for their truth or falsity). Citing John Stuart Mill's 1859 treatise *On Liberty*, the Court declared that "even a false statement may be deemed to make a valuable contribution to public debate, since it brings about the 'clearer perception and livelier impression of truth, produced by its collision with error.'"

Three years later, the Court extended this protection to apply to suits brought by any public figure, whether a government official or not. **Public figures** are people who assume roles of prominence in society or who thrust themselves to the forefront of public controversy—including officials, actors, writers, television personalities, and others. These people must show actual malice on the part of the publication that prints false statements about them. Because the burden of proof is so great, few plaintiffs prevail. And freedom of the press is the beneficiary.

What if the damage inflicted is not to one's reputation but to one's emotional state? Government seeks to maintain the prevailing social order, which prescribes proper modes of behavior. Does the First Amendment restrict the government in protecting citizens from behavior that intentionally inflicts emotional distress? This issue arose in a parody of a public figure in *Hustler* magazine. The target was the Reverend Jerry Falwell, a Baptist televangelist who founded the Moral Majority and organized conservative Christians into a political force. The parody had Falwell—in an interview—discussing a drunken, incestuous rendezvous with his mother in an outhouse, saying, "I always get sloshed before I go out to the pulpit." Falwell won a $200,000 award for "emotional distress." The magazine appealed, and the Supreme Court confronted the issue of social order versus free speech in 1988.[53]

In a unanimous decision, the Court overturned the award. In his sweeping opinion for the Court, Chief Justice William H. Rehnquist gave wide latitude to the First Amendment's protection of free speech. He observed that "graphic depictions and satirical cartoons have played a prominent role in public and political debate" throughout the nation's history and that the First Amendment protects even "vehement, caustic, and sometimes unpleasantly sharp attacks." Free speech protects criticism of public figures, even if the criticism is outrageous and offensive.

Prior Restraint and the Press.   As discussed above, in the United States, freedom of the press has primarily meant protection from prior restraint, or censorship. The Supreme Court's first encounter with a law imposing prior restraint on a newspaper was in *Near* v. *Minnesota* (1931).[54] In Minneapolis, Jay Near published a scandal sheet in which he attacked local officials, charging that they were in league with gangsters.[55] Minnesota officials obtained an injunction to prevent Near from publishing his newspaper under a state law that allowed such action against periodicals deemed "malicious, scandalous, and defamatory."

The Supreme Court struck down the law, declaring that prior restraint is a special burden on a free press. Chief Justice Charles Evans Hughes forcefully articulated the need for a vigilant, unrestrained press: "The fact that the liberty of the press may be abused by miscreant purveyors of scandal does not make any the less necessary the immunity of the press from previous restraint in dealing with official misconduct." Although the Court acknowledged that prior restraint may be permissible in exceptional circumstances, it did not specify those circumstances, nor has it yet done so.

Consider another case, which occurred during a war, a time when the tension between government-imposed order and individual freedom is often at a peak. In 1971, Daniel Ellsberg, a special assistant in the Pentagon's Office of International Security Affairs, delivered portions of a classified U.S. Department of Defense study to the *New York Times* and the *Washington Post.* By making the documents public, he hoped to discredit the Vietnam War and thereby end it. The U.S. Department of Justice sought to restrain the *Times* and the *Post* from publishing the documents, contending that publication would prolong the war and embarrass the government. The case was quickly brought before the Supreme Court, which delayed its summer adjournment to hear oral arguments.

Three days later, in a 6–3 decision in **New York Times v. United States** (1971), the Court concluded that the government had not met the heavy burden of proving that immediate, inevitable, and irreparable harm would follow publication.[56] The majority expressed its view in a brief, unsigned opinion; individual and collective concurring and dissenting views added nine opinions to the decision. Two justices maintained that the First Amendment offers absolute protection against government censorship, no matter what the situation. But the other justices left the door ajar for the imposition of prior restraint in the most extreme and compelling of circumstances. The result was hardly a ringing endorsement of freedom of the press, nor was it a full affirmation of the public's right to all the information that is vital to the debate of public issues.

Freedom of Expression Versus Maintaining Order.   The courts have consistently held that freedom of the press does not override the requirements of law enforcement. A grand jury called a Louisville, Kentucky, reporter who had researched and written an article about drug-related activities to identify people he had seen in possession of marijuana or in the act of processing it. The reporter refused to testify, maintaining that freedom of the press shielded him from inquiry. In a closely divided decision, the Supreme Court in 1972 rejected this position.[57] The Court declared that no exception, even a limited one, is permissible to the rule that all citizens have a duty to give their government whatever testimony they are capable of giving.

A divided Supreme Court reiterated in 1978 that journalists are not protected from the demands of law enforcement. The Court upheld a lower court's warrant to search a Stanford University campus newspaper office for photographs of a violent demonstration. The investigation of criminal conduct seems to be a special area—one in which the Court is not willing to provide the press with extraordinary protection of its freedom.[58]

The Supreme Court again confronted the conflict between free expression and order in 1988.[59] The principal of a St. Louis high school had deleted articles on divorce and teenage pregnancy from the school's newspaper on the ground that the articles invaded the privacy of the students and families who were the focus of the stories. Three student editors filed suit in federal court, claiming that the principal had violated their First Amendment rights. They argued that the principal's censorship interfered with the newspaper's function as a public forum, a role protected by the First Amendment. The principal maintained that the newspaper was just an extension of classroom instruction and was thus not protected by the First Amendment.

In a 5–3 decision, the Court upheld the principal's actions in sweeping terms. Educators may limit speech within the confines of the school curriculum and speech that might seem to bear the approval of the school, provided their actions serve any "valid educational purpose." The majority justices maintained that "students in public school do not 'shed their constitutional rights to freedom of expression at the schoolhouse gate,'" but recent Court decisions suggest that students do lose certain rights—including elements of free expression—when they pass through the public school portals.

The Rights to Assemble Peaceably and to Petition the Government

The final clause of the First Amendment states that "Congress shall make no law . . . abridging . . . the right of the people peaceably to assemble, and to petition the Government for a redress of grievances." The roots of the right of petition can be traced to the Magna Carta, the charter of English political and civil liberties granted by King John at Runnymede in 1215. The right of peaceable assembly arose much later. The framers meant that the people have the right to assemble peaceably *in order to* petition the government. Today, however, the right to assemble peaceably is equated with the right to free speech and a free press, independent of whether or not the government is petitioned. Precedent has merged these rights and made them indivisible.[60] Government cannot prohibit peaceful political meetings and cannot brand as criminals those who organize, lead, and attend such meetings.[61]

The clash of interests in cases involving these rights illustrates the continuing nature of the effort to define and apply fundamental principles. The need for order and stability has tempered the concept of freedom. And when freedom and order conflict, the justices of the Supreme Court, who are responsible only to their consciences, strike the balance. Such clashes are certain to occur again and again. Freedom and order conflict when public libraries become targets of community censors, when religious devotion interferes with military service, when individuals and groups express views or hold beliefs at odds with majority sentiment. Conflicts between freedom and order, and between minority and majority viewpoints, are part and parcel of politics and government, here and abroad. How do other nations rank on the degree of civil liberties they guarantee their citizens?

● compared with what?

15.1   Freedom in Retreat

Each year, Freedom House researchers analyze the state of freedom around the world. Using a seven-point scale, they rank nations from 1 (the greatest degree of freedom) to 7 (the least degree of freedom). In countries rated 1, the press is a free outlet for the expression of political opinions, especially when the intent of that expression is to affect the political process legitimately. In addition, in these countries no major medium serves as a simple conduit for government propaganda. The courts protect the individual; people cannot be punished for their opinions; there is respect for private rights and wants in people's education, occupation, religion, and residence; and law-abiding citizens do not fear for their lives because of their political activities.

Moving down the scale from 2 to 7, we see a steady loss of civil freedoms. Compared with those in nations rated 1, the police and courts in nations rated 2 have more authoritarian traditions or a less institutionalized or secure set of liberties. Nations rated 3 or higher may have political prisoners and varying forms of censorship. Often, their security services torture prisoners. States rated 6 almost always have political prisoners. Here the mainstream media are usually completely under government supervision; there is no right to assembly; and often, there are narrow restrictions on travel, on where people may live, and on the occupations they may pursue. However, at level 6 there may still be relative freedom within private conversations, especially in homes; demonstrations against the government can or do occur; and underground literature circulates. At 7 on the scale, there is pervasive fear; there is little independent expression, even in private; and there is almost no public expression of opposition to the government. Imprisonment and execution are swift and sure.

In 1996, a country is considered free if it scores between 1 and 2.5 ($n = 76$), partly free if it scores between 3 and 5.5 ($n = 62$), and not free if it scores between 5.5 and 7 ($n = 53$). The number of people denied basic freedoms fell by almost twenty-three million from 1995 to 1996, with a corresponding increase in the number of people living under partly free conditions. The proportion of people who are free today stands at 19.6 percent, slightly above the lowest level of 19.0 percent recorded in 1994.

Source: Adrian Karatnycky, "The Comparative Survey of Freedom: 1994," 1 *Freedom Review* 27, 1996, pp. 1–16. Published by Freedom House, New York.

Is freedom increasing or declining worldwide? For some answers, see Compared with What? 15.1.

THE RIGHT TO BEAR ARMS

The Second Amendment declares

> A well-regulated militia being necessary to the security of a free State, the right of the people to keep and bear arms shall not be infringed.

This amendment has created a hornet's nest of problems for gun-control advocates and their opponents. Gun-control advocates assert that the

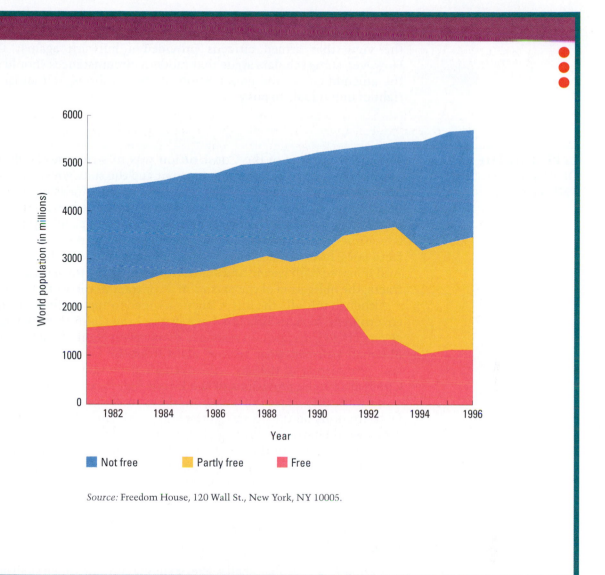

Source: Freedom House, 120 Wall St., New York, NY 10005.

amendment protects the right of the states to maintain *collective* militias. Gun-use advocates assert that the amendment protects the right of *individuals* to own and use guns. There are good arguments on both sides.

Federal firearms regulations did not come into being until Prohibition, so the Supreme Court had little to say on the matter. In 1939, however, a unanimous Court upheld a 1934 federal law requiring the taxation and registration of machine guns and sawed-off shotguns. The Court held that the Second Amendment protects a citizen's right to own ordinary militia weapons; sawed-off shotguns did not qualify for protection.[62]

Restrictions on gun ownership (for example, registration and licensing) have passed constitutional muster. However, outright prohibitions on gun ownership (for example, a ban on handguns) might run afoul of the amendment. After all, Madison and others supported the amendment based on the view that armed citizens provided a bulwark against tyranny. However, some scholars argue that modern circumstances should confine the amendment to the preservation of state militias, relinquishing the right of individuals to possess modern lethal weapons.[63]

APPLYING THE BILL OF RIGHTS TO THE STATES

The major purpose of the Constitution was to structure the division of power between the national government and the state governments. Even before it was amended, the Constitution set some limits on both the nation and the states with regard to citizens' rights. It barred both governments from passing **bills of attainder,** laws that make an individual guilty of a crime without a trial. It also prohibited them from enacting **ex post facto laws,** laws that declare an action a crime after it has been performed. And it barred both nation and states from impairing the **obligation of contracts,** the obligation of the parties in a contract to carry out its terms.

Although initially the Bill of Rights seemed to apply only to the national government, various litigants have pressed the claim that its guarantees also apply to the states. In response to one such claim, Chief Justice John Marshall affirmed what seemed plain from the Constitution's language and "the history of the day" (the events surrounding the Constitutional Convention): the provisions of the Bill of Rights served only to limit national authority. "Had the framers of these amendments intended them to be limitations on the powers of the state governments," wrote Marshall, "they would have ... expressed that intention."[64]

Change came with the Fourteenth Amendment, which was adopted in 1868. The due process clause of that amendment is the linchpin that holds the states to the provisions of the Bill of Rights.

The Fourteenth Amendment: Due Process of Law

> *Section 1.* . . . No State shall make or enforce any law which shall abridge the privileges or immunities of citizens of the United States; nor shall any State deprive any person of life, liberty, or property, without due process of law. . . .

Most freedoms protected in the Bill of Rights today function as limitations on the states. And many of the standards that limit the national government serve equally to limit state governments. The changes have been achieved through the Supreme Court's interpretation of the due process clause of the Fourteenth Amendment: "nor shall any State deprive any person of life, liberty, or property, without due process of law." The clause has two central meanings. First, it requires the government to adhere to appropriate procedures. For example, in a criminal trial, the government must establish the defendant's guilt beyond a reasonable doubt. Second, it forbids unreasonable government action. For example, at the turn of the century, the Supreme Court struck down a state law that forbade bakers from working more than sixty hours a week. The justices held the law unreasonable under the due process clause.

The Supreme Court has used the first meaning of the due process clause as a sponge, absorbing or incorporating the procedural specifics of the Bill of Rights and spreading or applying them to the states. The history of due process cases reveals that unlikely litigants often champion constitutional guarantees and that freedom is not always the victor.

The Fundamental Freedoms

In 1897, the Supreme Court declared that the states are subject to the Fifth Amendment's prohibition against taking private property without providing just compensation.[65] The Court reached that decision by absorbing the prohibition into the due process clause of the Fourteenth Amendment, which explicitly applies to the states. Thus, one Bill of Rights protection—but only that one—applied to both the states and the national government, as illustrated in Figure 15.1. In 1925, the Court assumed that the due process clause protected the First Amendment speech and press liberties from impairment by the states.[66]

The inclusion of other Bill of Rights guarantees within the due process clause faced a critical test in ***Palko v. Connecticut*** (1937).[67] Frank Palko had been charged with homicide in the first degree. He was convicted of second-degree murder, however, and sentenced to life imprisonment. The state of Connecticut appealed and won a new trial; this time, Palko was found guilty of first-degree murder and sentenced to death. Palko appealed the second conviction on the ground that it violated the protection against double jeopardy guaranteed to him by the Fifth Amendment. This protection applied to the states, he contended, because of the Fourteenth Amendment's due process clause.

The Supreme Court upheld Palko's second conviction. In his opinion for the majority, Justice Benjamin N. Cardozo formulated principles that were to guide the Court's actions for the next three decades. He reasoned that some Bill of Rights guarantees—such as freedom of thought and speech—are fundamental and that these fundamental rights are absorbed by the Fourteenth Amendment's due process clause and are therefore applicable to the states. These rights are essential, argued Cardozo, because "neither liberty nor justice would exist if they were sacrificed." Trial by jury and other rights, although valuable and important, are not essential to liberty and justice and therefore are not absorbed by the due process clause. "Few would be so narrow or provincial," Cardozo claimed, "as to maintain that a fair and enlightened system of justice would be impossible" without these other rights. In other words, only certain provisions of the Bill of Rights—the "fundamental" provisions—were absorbed into the due process clause and made applicable to the states. Because protection against double jeopardy was not one of them, Palko died in Connecticut's gas chamber in 1938.

The next thirty years saw slow but perceptible change in the standard for determining whether a Bill of Rights guarantee was fundamental. The reference point changed from the idealized "fair and enlightened system of justice" in *Palko* to the more realistic "American scheme of justice" thirty

15.1   ● The Incorporation of the Bill of Rights

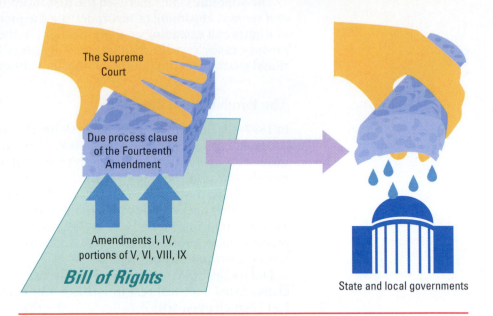

The Supreme Court has used the due process clause of the Fourteenth Amendment as a sponge, absorbing most—but not all—of the provisions in the Bill of Rights and applying them to state and local governments. All provisions in the Bill of Rights apply to the national government.

The Supreme Court

Due process clause of the Fourteenth Amendment

Amendments I, IV, portions of V, VI, VIII, IX

Bill of Rights

State and local governments

years later.[68] Case after case tested various guarantees that the Court found to be fundamental. By 1969, when *Palko* was finally overturned, the Court had found most of the Bill of Rights applicable to the states.

Criminal Procedure: The Meaning of Constitutional Guarantees

"The history of liberty," remarked Justice Frankfurter, "has largely been the history of observance of procedural safeguards."[69] The safeguards embodied in the Fourth through Eighth Amendments to the Constitution specify how government must behave in criminal proceedings. Their application to the states has reshaped American criminal justice in the past thirty years, in two steps. The first step is the judgment that a guarantee asserted in the Bill of Rights also applies to the states. The second step requires that the judiciary give specific meaning to the guarantee. The courts cannot allow the states to define guarantees themselves without risking different definitions from state to state—and thus differences among citizens' rights. If rights are fundamental, their meaning cannot vary. But life is not quite so simple under the U.S. Constitution. The concept of federalism is sewn into the constitutional fabric, and the Supreme Court recognizes that there may be more than one way to prosecute the accused while heeding fundamental rights.

Consider, for example, the right to a jury trial in criminal cases, which is guaranteed by the Sixth Amendment. This right was made obligatory for the states in *Duncan* v. *Louisiana* (1968). The Supreme Court later held that the right applied to all nonpetty criminal cases, those in which the penalty for conviction was more than six months' imprisonment.[70] But the Court did not require that state juries have twelve members, the number required for federal criminal proceedings. The Court permits jury size to vary from state to state, although it has set the minimum number at six. Furthermore, it has not imposed on the states the federal requirement of a unanimous jury verdict. As a result, even today many states do not require unanimous verdicts for criminal convictions. Some observers question whether criminal defendants in these states enjoy the same rights as defendants in unanimous-verdict states.

In contrast, the Court left no room for variation in its definition of the fundamental right to an attorney, also guaranteed by the Sixth Amendment. Clarence Earl Gideon was a penniless vagrant accused of breaking into and robbing a pool hall. (The "loot" he was charged with taking was mainly change from vending machines.) Because Gideon could not afford a lawyer, he asked the state to provide him with legal counsel for his trial. The state refused and subsequently convicted Gideon and sentenced him to five years in the Florida State Penitentiary. From his cell, Gideon appealed to the U.S. Supreme Court, claiming that his conviction should be struck down because the state had denied him his Sixth Amendment right to counsel. (Gideon was also without counsel in this appeal; he filed a handwritten "pauper's petition" with the Court after studying law texts in the prison library. When the Court agreed to consider his case, he was assigned a prominent Washington attorney, Abe Fortas, who later became a Supreme Court justice.)[71]

In its landmark decision in **Gideon v. Wainwright** (1963), the Court set aside Gideon's conviction and extended to defendants in state courts the Sixth Amendment right to counsel.[72] The state retried Gideon, who this time had the assistance of a lawyer, and the court found him not guilty.

In subsequent rulings that stretched over more than a decade, the Court specified at which points in the course of criminal proceedings a defendant is entitled to a lawyer (from arrest to trial, appeal, and beyond). These pronouncements are binding on all states. In state as well as federal proceedings, the government must furnish legal assistance to those who do not have the means to hire their own attorney.

During this period the Court also came to grips with another procedural issue: informing suspects of their constitutional rights. Without this knowledge, procedural safeguards are meaningless. Ernesto Miranda was arrested in Arizona in connection with the kidnapping and rape of an eighteen-year-old woman. After the police questioned him for two hours and the woman identified him, Miranda confessed to the crime. An Arizona court convicted him on the basis of that confession—although he was never told that he had the right to counsel and the right not to incriminate himself. Miranda appealed his conviction, which was overturned by the Supreme Court in 1966.[73]

The Court based its decision in *Miranda* v. *Arizona* on the Fifth Amendment privilege against self-incrimination. According to the Court, the police had forced Miranda to confess during in-custody questioning, not with physical force but with the coercion inherent in custodial interrogation without counsel. The Court said that warnings are necessary to

● ● ● ● ● ● ● ● ● ●

A Pauper's Plea

Clarence Earl Gideon, penniless and without a lawyer, was convicted and sent to prison for breaking into and robbing a pool hall. At his trial, Gideon pleaded with the judge: "Your Honor, the U.S. Constitution says I am entitled to be represented by counsel." The judge was required by state law to deny Gideon's request. Undaunted, Gideon continued his quest for recognition of his Sixth Amendment right to counsel. On the basis of his penciled petition, the Supreme Court agreed to consider his case, ultimately granting Gideon the right he advocated with such conviction.

DIVISION OF CORRECTIONS
CORRESPONDENCE REGULATIONS
MAIL WILL NOT BE DELIVERED WHICH DOES NOT CONFORM WITH THESE RULES

No. 1 -- Only 2 letters each week, not to exceed 2 sheets letter-size 8 1/2 x 11" and written *on one side only,* and if ruled paper, do not write between lines. *Your complete name* must be signed at the close of your letter. *Clippings, stamps, letters* from other people, *stationery* or *cash* must not be enclosed in your letters.
No. 2 -- All *letters* must be addressed in the *complete prison name* of the inmate. *Cell number,* where applicable, and *prison number* must be placed in lower left corner of envelope, with your complete name and address in the upper left corner.
No. 3 -- *Do not send any packages without a Package Permit.* Unauthorized *packages* will be destroyed.
No. 4 -- *Letters* must be written in English only.
No. 5 -- *Books, magazines, pamphlets,* and *newspapers* of reputable character will be delivered only *if* mailed direct from the publisher.
No. 6 -- *Money* must be sent in the form of *Postal Money Orders* only, in the inmate's complete prison name and prison number.

INSTITUTION _____   CELL NUMBER _____

NAME _____   NUMBER _____

In The Supreme Court of The United States
Washington D.C.
Clarence Earl Gideon }
Petitioner } *Petition for a writ*
vs. } *of Certiorari directed*
H.G. Cochran, Jr., as } *to The Supreme Court*
Director, Divisions } *State of Florida.*
of corrections state } *No. 890 Misc.*
of Florida } *OCT. TERM 1961*
U.S. Supreme Court

To. The Honorable Earl Warren, Chief
Justice of the United States
Comes now The petitioner, Clarence
Earl Gideon, a citizen of The United States
of America, in proper person, and appearing
as his own counsel. Who petitions this
Honorable Court for a Writ of Certiorari
directed to The Supreme Court of The State
of Florida. To review the order and Judgement
of the court below denying The
petitioner a writ of Habeus Corpus.
Petitioner submits That The Supreme
Court of The United States has The authority
and jurisdiction to review The final Judgement
of The Supreme Court of The State
of Florida The highest court of The State
Under sec. 344 (B) Title 28 U.S.C.A. and
Because the "Due process clause" of the

dispel that coercion. The Court does not require warnings if a person is only in custody without questioning or subject to questioning without arrest. But in *Miranda,* the Court found the combination of custody and interrogation sufficiently intimidating to require warnings before questioning. These statements are known today as the **Miranda warnings:**

● You have the right to remain silent.

● Anything you say can be used against you in court.

● You have the right to talk to a lawyer of your own choice before questioning.

● If you cannot afford to hire a lawyer, a lawyer will be provided without charge.

In each area of criminal procedure, the justices have had to grapple with two steps in the application of constitutional guarantees to criminal defendants: the extension of a right to the states and the definition of that right. In *Duncan*, the issue was the right to jury trial, and the Court allowed variation from state to state. In *Gideon*, the Court applied the right to counsel uniformly from state to state. Finally, in *Miranda*, the Court declared that all governments—national, state, and local—have a duty to inform suspects of the full measure of their constitutional rights.

The problems in balancing freedom and order can be formidable. A primary function of government is to maintain order. What happens when the government infringes upon individuals' freedom for the sake of order? Consider the guarantee in the Fourth Amendment: "The right of the people to be secure in their persons, houses, papers, and effects, against unreasonable searches and seizures, shall not be violated." The Court made this right applicable to the states in *Wolf* v. *Colorado* (1949).[74] Following the reasoning in *Palko*, the Court found that the core of the amendment—security against arbitrary police intrusion—is a fundamental right and that citizens must be protected from illegal searches by state and local governments. But how? The federal courts had long followed the **exclusionary rule,** which holds that evidence obtained from an illegal search and seizure cannot be used in a trial. And of course, if that evidence is critical to the prosecution, the case dissolves. But the Court refused to apply the exclusionary rule to the state courts. Instead, it allowed the states to decide on their own how to handle the fruits of an illegal search. The decision in *Wolf* stated that obtaining evidence illegally violated the Constitution and that states could fashion their own rules of evidence to give effect to this constitutional decree. The states were not bound by the exclusionary rule.

The justices considered the exclusionary rule again twelve years later, in *Mapp* v. *Ohio*.[75] An Ohio court had found Dolree Mapp guilty of possessing obscene materials after an admittedly illegal search of her home for a fugitive. The Ohio Supreme Court affirmed her conviction, and she appealed to the U.S. Supreme Court. Mapp's attorneys argued for a reversal based primarily on freedom of expression, contending that the First Amendment protected the confiscated materials. However, the Court elected to use the decision in *Mapp* to give meaning to the constitutional guarantee against unreasonable search and seizure. In a 6–3 decision, the justices declared that "all evidence obtained by searches and seizures in violation of the Constitution is, by [the Fourth Amendment], inadmissible in a state court." Ohio had convicted Mapp illegally; the evidence should have been excluded.

The decision was historic. It placed the exclusionary rule under the umbrella of the Fourth Amendment and required all levels of government to operate according to the provisions of that amendment. Failure to do so could result in the dismissal of criminal charges against guilty defendants.

Mapp launched a divided Supreme Court on a troubled course of determining how and when to apply the exclusionary rule. For example, the Court has continued to struggle with police use of sophisticated electronic eavesdropping devices and searches of movable vehicles. In each case, the justices have confronted a rule that appears to handicap the police and to offer freedom to people whose guilt has been established by the illegal evidence. In the Court's most recent pronouncements, order has triumphed over freedom.

The struggle over the exclusionary rule took a new turn in 1984, when the Court reviewed *United States* v. *Leon.*[76] In this case, the police obtained a search warrant from a judge on the basis of a tip from an informant of unproved reliability. The judge issued a warrant without firmly establishing probable cause to believe the tip. The police, relying on the warrant, found large quantities of illegal drugs. The Court, by a vote of 6–3, established the **good faith exception** to the exclusionary rule. The justices held that the state could introduce at trial evidence seized on the basis of a mistakenly issued search warrant. The exclusionary rule, argued the majority, is not a right but a remedy justified by its ability to deter illegal police conduct. The rule is costly to society. It excludes pertinent valid evidence, allowing guilty people to go unpunished and generating disrespect for the law. These costs are justifiable only if the exclusionary rule deters police misconduct. Such a deterrent effect was not a factor in *Leon:* the police acted in good faith. Hence, the Court decided, there is a need for an exception to the rule.

In 1988, the justices ruled 6–2 that police may search through garbage bags and other containers that people leave outside their houses. The case resulted from an investigation of a man police suspected of narcotics trafficking. The police obtained his trash bags from the local garbage collector; the bags contained evidence of narcotics, which then served as the basis for obtaining a search warrant for his house. That search revealed quantities of cocaine and hashish and led to criminal charges. The lower courts dismissed the drug charges on the ground that the warrant was based on an unconstitutional search. By overturning that ruling, the Supreme Court further eroded the Fourth Amendment's protection of individual privacy.[77]

The exclusionary rule continues to divide the Supreme Court. In 1990, the justices again reaffirmed the rule, but only by a bare 5–4 majority.[78] The current Supreme Court line-up has a more conservative bent, which suggests that the battle over the exclusionary rule has not ended.

Mapp and all the cases that followed it forced the Court to confront the classic dilemma of democracy: the choice between freedom and order. If the justices tip the scale too far toward freedom, guilty parties might go free and perhaps break the law again. If they choose excessive order, however, they might give official sanction to police conduct that violates the Constitution.

THE NINTH AMENDMENT AND PERSONAL AUTONOMY

The enumeration in the Constitution, of certain rights, shall not be construed to deny or disparage others retained by the people.

The wording and history of the Ninth Amendment remain an enigma; the evidence supports two different views. The amendment may protect rights that are not enumerated, or it may simply protect state governments against the assumption of power by the national government.[79] The meaning of the amendment was not an issue until 1965, when the Supreme Court used it to protect privacy, a right that is not enumerated in the Constitution.

● ● ● ● ● ● ● ● ● ● ● ● ●

Anguished Voices; Angry Voices

Every year on January 22, demonstrators gather on the plaza outside the United States Supreme Court building to protest the Court's 1973 abortion decision, Roe v. Wade. The justices and the public remain divided on abortion. In 1992, the Court upheld a woman's right to choose abortion but it also upheld new restrictions on the exercise of that right.

Controversy: From Privacy to Abortion

In ***Griswold v. Connecticut*** (1965), the Court struck down, by a vote of 7–2, a seldom-enforced Connecticut statute that made the use of birth control devices a crime.[80] Justice Douglas, writing for the majority, asserted that the "specific guarantees in the Bill of Rights have penumbras [partially illuminated regions surrounding fully lit areas]" that give "life and substance" to broad, unspecified protections in the Bill of Rights. Several specific guarantees in the First, Third, Fourth, and Fifth Amendments create a zone of privacy, Douglas argued, and this zone is protected by the Ninth Amendment and is applicable to the states by the due process clause of the Fourteenth Amendment.

Three justices gave further emphasis to the relevance of the Ninth Amendment, which, they contended, protects fundamental rights derived from those specifically enumerated in the first eight amendments. This view contrasted sharply with the position expressed by the two dissenters, Justices Black and Stewart. In the absence of some specific prohibition, they argued, the Bill of Rights and the Fourteenth Amendment do not allow judicial annulment of state legislative policies, even if those policies are abhorrent to a judge or justice.

Griswold established the principle that the Bill of Rights as a whole creates a right to make certain intimate, personal choices, including the right of married people to engage in sexual intercourse for reproduction or pleasure. This zone of personal autonomy, protected by the Constitution, was the basis of a 1973 case that sought to invalidate state antiabortion laws.

If you have installed the RealAudio Player, you can point your browser to this location to listen to the arguments in *Roe* v. *Wade.*

`<oyez.at.nwu.edu/cases/70-18>`

But rights are not absolute, and in weighing the interests of the individual against the interests of the government, the Supreme Court found itself caught up in a flood of controversy that has yet to subside.

In **Roe v. Wade** (1973), the Court in a 7–2 decision declared unconstitutional a Texas law making it a crime to obtain an abortion except for the purpose of saving the woman's life.[81]

Justice Harry A. Blackmun, who wrote the majority opinion, could not point to a specific constitutional guarantee to justify the Court's ruling. Instead, he based the decision on the right to privacy protected by the due process clause of the Fourteenth Amendment. In effect, state abortion laws were unreasonable and hence unconstitutional. The Court declared that in the first three months of pregnancy, the abortion decision must be left to the woman and her physician. In the interest of protecting the woman's health, states may restrict but not prohibit abortions in the second three months of pregnancy. Finally, in the last three months of pregnancy, states may regulate or even prohibit abortions to protect the life of the fetus, except when medical judgment determines that an abortion is necessary to save the woman's life. In all, the Court's ruling affected the laws of forty-six states.

The dissenters—Justices Byron R. White and Rehnquist—were quick to assert what critics have frequently repeated since the decision: the Court's judgment was directed by its own dislikes, not by any constitutional compass. In the absence of guiding principles, they asserted, the majority justices simply substituted their views for the views of the state legislatures whose abortion regulations they invalidated.[82] In a 1993 television interview, Blackmun insisted that "*Roe* versus *Wade* was decided . . . on constitutional grounds."[83] It was as if Blackmun were trying, by sheer force of will, to turn back twenty years' worth of stinging objections to the opinion he had crafted.

The composition of the Court shifted under President Ronald Reagan. His elevation of Rehnquist to chief justice in 1986 and his appointment of Scalia in 1986 and Kennedy in 1988 raised new hope among abortion foes and old fears among advocates of choice.

A perceptible shift away from abortion rights materialized in *Webster* v. *Reproductive Health Services* (1989). The case was a blockbuster, attracting voluminous media coverage. *Webster* also set a record for the number of amicus briefs submitted on behalf of individuals and organizations with an interest in the outcome. (The number of briefs—seventy-eight—surpassed the old record of fifty-eight set in the landmark affirmative action case *Regents of the State of California* v. *Bakke* in 1978.)

In *Webster,* the Supreme Court upheld the constitutionality of a Missouri law that denied the use of public employees or publicly funded facilities in the performance of an abortion unless the woman's life was in danger.[84] Furthermore, the law required doctors to perform tests to determine whether fetuses twenty weeks and older could survive outside the womb. This was the first time that the Court upheld significant government restrictions on abortion.

The justices issued five opinions, but no single opinion captured a majority. Four justices (Blackmun, Brennan, Thurgood Marshall, and John Paul Stevens) voted to strike down the Missouri law and hold fast to *Roe.*

Four justices (Kennedy, Rehnquist, Scalia, and White) wanted to overturn *Roe* and return to the states the power to regulate abortion. The remaining justice—Sandra Day O'Connor—avoided both camps. Her position was that state abortion restrictions are permissible provided they are not "unduly burdensome." She voted with the conservative plurality to uphold the restrictive Missouri statute on the ground that it did not place an undue burden on women's rights. But she declined to reconsider (and overturn) *Roe.*

The Court has since moved cautiously down the road toward greater government control of abortion. In 1990, the justices split on two state parental notification laws. The Court struck down a state requirement that compelled unwed minors to notify both parents before having an abortion. In another case, however, the Court upheld a state requirement that a physician notify one parent of a pregnant minor of her intent to have an abortion. In both cases, the justices voiced widely divergent opinions, revealing a continuing division over abortion.[85]

The abortion issue pits freedom against order. The decision to bear or beget children should be free from government control. Yet, government has a legitimate interest in protecting and preserving life, including fetal life, as part of its responsibility to maintain an orderly society. Rather than choose between freedom and order, the majority on the Court has loosened constitutional protection on abortion rights and cast the politically divisive issue into the state legislative process, where elected representatives can thrash out the conflict.

Many groups defending or opposing abortion have now turned to state legislative politics to advance their policies. This approach will force candidates for state office to debate the abortion issue and then translate electoral outcomes into legislation that restricts or protects abortion. If the abortion issue is deeply felt by Americans, pluralist theory would predict that the strongest voices for or against abortion will mobilize the greatest support in the political arena.

With a clear conservative majority, the Court seemed poised to reverse *Roe* in 1992. But a new coalition—forged by Reagan and Bush appointees O'Connor, Souter, and Kennedy—has reaffirmed *Roe* yet tolerates additional restrictions on abortions. In *Planned Parenthood* v. *Casey,* a bitterly divided bench opted for the O'Connor "undue burden" test. The Court apparently remains deeply divided on abortion.[86]

Presidential values, as reflected in the appointment of Supreme Court justices, have left an imprint on the abortion controversy. Justices appointed by presidents Reagan and Bush weakened abortion as a constitutional right. But President Clinton's High Court appointments of Ruth Bader Ginsburg and Stephen G. Breyer in 1993 and 1994 added two liberal votes to a conservative Court and made good on a Clinton campaign promise to protect women's access to abortion from further assault. (Ginsburg replaced White, who had opposed *Roe* v. *Wade* from its inception. Breyer replaced Blackmun, the principal author of the *Roe* opinion.)

Although Ginsburg ducked most questions at her confirmation hearings, she was forthright in her judgment that the Constitution protects a woman's right to choose. But Ginsburg offered objections of her own to the Court's reasoning on abortion. She seemed unpersuaded by the "right to privacy" roots of *Roe*. Instead, she saw a woman's right to abortion as rooted in the equal protection clause of the Fourteenth Amendment.[87]

Breyer, a self-described pragmatist, made clear his view that a woman's right to an abortion is now settled law. Interestingly, Breyer's research as a Supreme Court law clerk in 1965 contributed to the right-to-privacy decision in *Griswold* v. *Connecticut*.

Personal Autonomy and Sexual Orientation

The right-to-privacy cases may have opened a Pandora's box of divisive social issues. Does the right to privacy embrace private homosexual acts between consenting adults? Consider the case of Michael Hardwick, who was arrested in 1982 in his Atlanta bedroom while having sex with another man. In a standard approach to prosecuting homosexuals, Georgia charged him under a state criminal statute with the crime of sodomy, which means oral or anal intercourse. The police said that they had gone to his home to arrest him for failing to pay a fine for drinking in public. Although the prosecutor dropped the charges, Hardwick sued to challenge the law's constitutionality. He won in the lower courts, but the state pursued the case.

The conflict between freedom and order lies at the core of the case. "Our legal history and our social traditions have condemned this conduct uniformly for hundreds and hundreds of years," argued Georgia's attorney. Constitutional law, he continued, "must not become an instrument for a change in the social order." Hardwick's attorney, a noted constitutional scholar, said that government must have a more important reason than "majority morality to justify regulation of sexual intimacies in the privacy of the home." He maintained that the case involved two precious freedoms: the right to engage in private sexual relations and the right to be free from government intrusion in one's home.[88]

More than half the states have eliminated criminal penalties for private homosexual acts between consenting adults. The rest still outlaw homosexual sodomy, and many outlaw heterosexual sodomy as well. As a result, homosexual rights groups and some civil liberties groups followed Hardwick's case closely. Fundamentalist Christian groups and defenders of traditional morality expressed deep interest in the outcome, too.

In a bitterly divided ruling in 1986, the Court held in *Bowers* v. *Hardwick* that the Constitution does not protect homosexual relations between consenting adults, even in the privacy of their own homes.[89] The logic of the findings in the privacy cases involving contraception and abortion would seem to have compelled a finding of a right to personal autonomy—a right to make personal choices unconstrained by government—in this case as well. But the 5–4 majority maintained that only heterosexual choices—whether and whom to marry, whether to conceive a child, whether to have an abortion—fall within the zone of privacy established by the Court in its earlier rulings. "The Judiciary necessarily takes to itself further authority to govern the country without express constitutional authority" when it expands the list of fundamental rights not rooted in the language or design of the Constitution, wrote Justice White, the author of the majority opinion.

What's in a Name?

A generation of young homosexuals has adopted with pride the term queer, which was once regarded a degrading slur. Despite a new militancy on the part of gay and lesbian activists, the quest for national constitutional protection of homosexual rights halted with the Supreme Court's 1986 decision upholding state laws against sodomy. In response, many activists have shifted their efforts from the national level to state and local arenas.

The arguments on both sides of the privacy issue are compelling. This makes the choice between freedom and order excruciating for ordinary citizens and Supreme Court justices alike. At the conference to decide the merits of the *Hardwick* case, Justice Lewis Powell cast his vote to extend privacy rights to homosexual conduct. Later, he joined with his conservative colleagues, fashioning a new majority. Four years after the *Hardwick* decision, Powell revealed another change of mind: "I probably made a mistake," he declared, speaking of his decision to vote with the conservative majority.[90]

The appointment of conservatives to replace liberals on the Court casts freedom-preferring policies such as gay rights in continued jeopardy. Powell, who was ambivalent on the issue of homosexual rights, retired in 1987; Reagan appointed moderate conservative Anthony Kennedy as Powell's replacement. Liberal justice William J. Brennan, Jr., stepped down in 1990; President Bush appointed a conservative unknown, David Souter, as a replacement. And when liberal stalwart Thurgood Marshall resigned in poor health in 1991, Bush turned to conservative judge Clarence Thomas to ensure a new conservative majority on the High Court. But the conservative juggernaut appears over for now. Clinton's appointing Ginsburg and Breyer signals a move toward a more liberal bench: Ginsburg, for example, did not evade or hedge during her confirmation hearings on her support for the constitutional rights of homosexuals.

That the Court will soon reverse course on matters of personal autonomy is unlikely. It will take several more liberal Court appointments—and the right cases—to create the conditions for a change in direction. The conservative justices are among the youngest on the bench, and today they command a clear majority. As the sexual orientation issues percolate up the court system, other personal autonomy issues loom on the horizon.

Finding the right case to extend constitutional liberties requires timing and skill, as we saw in Politics in a Changing America 14.1.

Issues around sexual orientation have shifted toward the states, where various groups continue to assert their political power. For example, the Hawaii Supreme Court opened the door to same-sex marriages when it ruled in 1993 that the state's ban on such marriages shall be presumed to violate the state's constitution unless the state government can show that compelling government interests justify the ban.[91] All fifty states ban same-sex marriages. Should the Hawaii decision stand, every state would have to recognize same-sex marriages performed in Hawaii, unless the states or Congress acted affirmatively to bar the effects of Hawaii's policy. (The Constitution's full faith and credit clause imposes a duty on all the states to enforce the legal acts of every other state.) In an affirmation of majoritarian values, Congress passed, and President Clinton signed, the Defense of Marriage Act in September 1996. The law defines marriage as a union between people of opposite sexes and declares that states are not obliged to recognize gay marriages elsewhere. The law does not ban such unions; it only protects states against having to recognize homosexual marriage sanctioned by other states.

The pluralist model provides one solution for groups dissatisfied with rulings from the nation's highest court. State courts and state legislatures have demonstrated their receptivity to positions that are probably untenable in the federal courts. However, state-by-state decisions offer little comfort to Americans who believe the U.S. Constitution protects them in their most intimate decisions and actions, regardless of where they reside.

CONSTITUTIONAL-IZING PUBLIC POLICIES

The issues embedded in *Griswold* and *Roe* are more fundamental and disturbing for democracy than the surface issues of privacy and personal autonomy. By enveloping a policy in the protection of the Constitution, the courts remove that policy from the legislative arena, where the people's will can be expressed through the democratic process.

As the abortion controversy demonstrates, the courts can place under the cloak of the Constitution a host of public policies that the democratic process once debated and resolved. By giving a policy constitutional protection (as the Court did with abortion), judges assume responsibilities that have traditionally been left to the elected branches to resolve. If we trust appointed judges to serve as guardians of democracy, we have no reason to fear for the democratic process. But if we believe that democratic solutions are necessary to resolve such questions, our fears may well be grounded. The controversy will continue as the justices wrestle among themselves and with their critics over whether the Constitution authorizes them to fill the due process clause with fundamental values that cannot easily be traced to constitutional text, history, or structure.

Although the courts may be "the chief guardians of the liberties of the people," they ought not have the last word, argued the great jurist Learned Hand, because

> a society so riven that the spirit of moderation is gone, no court can save;
> ... a society where that spirit flourishes, no court need save; ... in a soci-

ety which evades its responsibilities by thrusting upon the courts the nurture of that spirit, that spirit in the end will perish.[92]

SUMMARY

Using the "Voters" data in the CROSSTABS program, analyze issue variables (e.g., abortion, school prayer, death penalty) by ideological orientation. Do value preferences match policy positions?

When they established the new government of the United States, the states and the people compelled the framers, through the Bill of Rights, to protect their freedoms. In their interpretation of these ten amendments, the courts, especially the Supreme Court, have taken on the task of balancing freedom and order.

The First Amendment protects several freedoms: freedom of religion, freedom of speech and of the press, and the freedom to assemble peaceably and petition the government. The establishment clause demands government neutrality toward religions and between the religious and the nonreligious. According to judicial interpretations of the free-exercise clause, religious beliefs are inviolable, but the Constitution does not protect antisocial actions in the name of religion. Extreme interpretations of the religion clauses could bring the clauses into conflict with each other.

Freedom of expression encompasses freedom of speech, freedom of the press, and the right to assemble peaceably and petition the government. Freedom of speech and freedom of the press have never been held to be absolute, but the courts have ruled that the Bill of Rights gives them far greater protection than other freedoms. Exceptions to free speech protections include some forms of symbolic expression, fighting words, and obscenity. Press freedom has enjoyed broad constitutional protection, because a free society depends on the ability to collect and report information without government interference. The rights to assemble peaceably and to petition the government stem from the guarantees of freedom of speech and of the press. Each freedom is equally fundamental, but the right to exercise them is not absolute.

The adoption of the Fourteenth Amendment in 1868 extended the guarantees of the Bill of Rights to the states. The due process clause became the vehicle for applying specific provisions of the Bill of Rights—one at a time, case after case—to the states. The designation of a right as fundamental also called for a definition of that right. The Supreme Court has tolerated some variation from state to state in the meaning of certain constitutional rights. The Court has also imposed a duty on governments to inform citizens of their rights so that they are equipped to exercise them.

As it has fashioned new fundamental rights from the Constitution, the Supreme Court has become embroiled in controversy. The right to privacy served as the basis for the right of women to terminate a pregnancy, which in turn suggested a right to personal autonomy. The abortion controversy is still raging, and the justices appear to have called a halt to the extension of personal privacy in the name of the Constitution.

In the meantime, judicial decisions raise a basic issue. By offering constitutional protection to certain public policies, the courts may be threatening the democratic process, the process that gives the people a say in government through their elected representatives. One thing is certain: the challenge of democracy requires the constant balancing of freedom and order.

Key Terms

civil liberties	prior restraint	public figures	Miranda warnings
civil rights	free-expression clauses	bill of attainder	exclusionary rule
establishment clause	clear and present danger	ex post facto law	good faith exception
free-exercise clause	test	obligation of contracts	
strict scrutiny	fighting words		

Key Cases

Lemon v. *Kurtzman*
West Virginia State Board
 of Education v. *Barnette*
Sherbert v. *Verner*
Brandenburg v. *Ohio*

Tinker v. *Des Moines*
 Independent County
 School District
Cohen v. *California*
Miller v. *California*

New York Times v.
 Sullivan
New York Times v.
 United States
Palko v. *Connecticut*

Gideon v. *Wainwright*
Griswold v. *Connecticut*
Roe v. *Wade*
Bowers v. *Hardwick*

Selected Readings

Carter, Stephen L. *The Culture of Disbelief: How American Law and Politics Trivialize Religious Devotion.* New York: Basic Books, 1993. In this wide-ranging, thoughtful work, Carter argues that Americans can simultaneously preserve separation of church and state, embrace American spirituality, and avoid treating believers with disdain.

Downs, Donald Alexander. *The New Politics of Pornography.* Chicago: University of Chicago Press, 1990. An exploration of the controversial modern anti-pornography movement. Downs analyzes similar ordinances, in Minneapolis and Indianapolis, rooted in the radical feminist thought of Catharine MacKinnon and Andrea Dworkin.

Garrow, David. *Liberty & Sexuality: The Right to Privacy and the Making of* Roe v. Wade. New York: Macmillan, 1994. This is a comprehensive, historical narrative of the fundamental right to sexual privacy.

Levy, Leonard W. *The Establishment Clause: Religion and the First Amendment.* New York: Macmillan, 1986. This searching study of the establish-ment clause claims that the view that government can assist all religions is historically groundless. Levy argues that it is unconstitutional for government to provide aid to any religion.

Lewis, Anthony. *Make No Law: The Sullivan Case and the First Amendment.* New York: Random House, 1991. This is an enlightening study of a great constitutional decision. Lewis illuminates the history and evolution of the First Amendment guarantees of free expression and free press.

Polenberg, Richard. *Fighting Faiths.* New York: Alfred A. Knopf, 1987. By focusing on the famous case of *Abrams* v. *United States,* a noted historian examines anarchism, government surveillance, freedom of speech, and the impact of the Russian Revolution on American liberals.

Smolla, Rodney A. *Free Speech in an Open Society.* New York: Alfred A. Knopf, 1993. A lucid examination covering a wide range of contemporary problems in free speech, such as flag burning, hate speech, and new technologies.

World Wide Web Resources

Oyez. Oyez. Oyez.: A Supreme Court WWW Resource. You can listen to the oral arguments in the great constitutional cases mentioned in this chapter and decided after 1955. Just point your browser to "Oyez. Oyez. Oyez." Be sure to download and install the RealAudio Player for your system first.

`<www.realaudio.com>`

`<oyez.at.nwu.edu/oyez.html>`

The American Civil Liberties Union Freedom Network. Check out this site to get up-to-the-minute reports on the state of civil liberties around the nation.
`<www.aclu.org>`

The Freedom Forum First Amendment Center. The Freedom Forum First Amendment Center at Vanderbilt University was founded December 15, 1991, the two hundredth anniversary of the ratification of the Bill of Rights to the U.S. Constitution. The Center serves as a forum for dialogue, discussion, and debate on free-expression and freedom-of-information issues. The Center was created by the Freedom Forum, a financially

independent, nonpartisan, international organization dedicated to a free press, free speech, and a free spirit.
`<www.fac.org>`

Justice on Campus. The Justice on Campus Project's mission is to preserve free expression and due process rights at universities. You will find a Jake Baker link here as well as other university-inspired restrictions on free expression.
`<joc.mit.edu>`

Flag Burning As Protest. Some protesters have employed the WWW to make the case for flag burning as political expression.
`<www.indirect.com/user/warren/flag.html>`

Save Old Glory From Flames Home Page. The above site spawned this one, protesting flag desecration.
`<www.pic.net/flameout/oldglory/>`

chapter
16

Equality and Civil Rights

LOW BID WINS. This is an axiom of everyday life, whether you are repairing a car or remodeling a home. Provided the items or services bid are identical, free competition usually means the lowest bidder gets the job. This is especially so when government is the buyer and taxpayers are footing the bill. Picking the lowest bidder keeps government costs down and provides an incentive for competitors to keep costs down in the future.

Like millions of sellers, Randy Pech believed this axiom when his company, Adarand Constructors, bid for work installing highway guardrails in Colorado. Five companies construct and maintain the state's guardrails. Adarand Constructors is the only one owned by a white man. Each of the other four companies has been designated a "Disadvantaged Business Enterprise," or DBE. National-government regulations presume that designated minorities (blacks, Spanish-speaking groups, Native Americans, Asian Pacific Islanders) and women are socially or economically disadvantaged.

The government's objective in designating some businesses as DBEs is to promote affirmative action. **Affirmative action** is a commitment by a business, employer, school, or other public or private institution to expand opportunities for women, blacks, Hispanic Americans, and members of other minority groups. Affirmative action embraces a wide range of policies, from special recruitment efforts to numerical goals and quotas.

In 1987, Congress passed a law requiring the U.S. Department of Transportation to set aside at least 10 percent of its highway construction funds for businesses owned by women or members of designated racial minorities. In addition, general contractors—who are responsible for the entire task of highway construction, from demolition through landscaping, and who hire people like Pech as subcontractors—receive a 1.5 percent bonus when they hire DBEs, even when there are few white competitors.

The government's set-aside policy restricts free competition in order to give DBEs business. This meant that in Colorado, a DBE did not have to submit the lowest bid to win the guardrail contract, provided Pech's company was the lowest bidder. If Adarand did not bid on the contract—and the other four firms did—the lowest-bid rule would have determined the outcome. And whenever Pech was the lowest bidder, he lost the contract. In 1989, Pech submitted the lowest bid for a guardrail job, but the general contractor awarded the work to Gonzales Construction, a DBE, solely on the basis of the bonus payment. Pech challenged the law, claiming that it unconstitutionally discriminated on the basis of race.[1]

● ● ● ● ● ● ● ● ● ● ●
Randy Pech: Low Bid Loser

"Low bid wins" is an every-day axiom. In 1989, Randy Pech's company—Adarand Constructors—submitted the lowest bid for a government-sponsored project to build guardrails on Colorado highways. The contract went to a higher bidder solely on the ground that the contractor was a member of a designated minority group. Pech fought the decision all the way to the Supreme Court. The Court rendered its judgment in 1995.

Pech believed that the government's actions violated his constitutional right to equal protection. The Fourteenth Amendment declares that no *state* shall deny any person equal protection. While there is no equivalent constitutional provision compelling the national government to treat persons equally, the Supreme Court has held that the Fifth Amendment's due process guarantee embraces the equal protection principle. Was the national government's affirmative action policy consistent with the Supreme Court's conception of equal protection? (We will explore the Court's answer later in this chapter.)

Laws and policies that promote equality inevitably come into conflict with demands for freedom. In this case, the government's policy to advance minority- and women-owned businesses disrupted the free competition of the marketplace and thereby imposed an unequal burden on Randy Pech. The conflict intensifies when we recognize that Americans advocate competing conceptions of equality.

TWO CONCEPTIONS OF EQUALITY

Americans want equality, at least in principle. Public support for the principle of equal treatment has increased dramatically from the 1940s to the 1980s. Today, more than nine in ten Americans espouse equal treatment for all in schools, public accommodations, housing, employment, and public transportation. However, Americans are far less united in their approach to implementing this principle.[2]

Most Americans support **equality of opportunity,** the idea that people should have an equal chance to develop their talents and that effort and

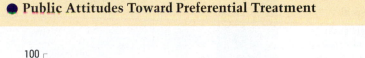

figure 16.1

● **Public Attitudes Toward Preferential Treatment**

Polls since the 1970s have revealed low levels of support for preferential policies aiding minorities and women in employment and college admissions. More than 80 percent of Americans consistently favor using ability as the only criterion for hiring and college entrance decisions. Depending on how poll questions are worded, the level of support for race- and gender-based preferences appears to now be somewhat higher than it was in the seventies, though it has declined again somewhat in the last few years. QUESTION 1: Some people say that to make up for past discrimination, women and members of minority groups should be given preferential treatment in getting jobs and places in college. Others say that ability, as determined by test scores, should be the main consideration. Which point of view comes closer to how you feel on the subject? (Gallup) QUESTION 2: Do you believe that where there has been job discrimination against blacks (women) in the past, preference in hiring and promotion should be given to blacks (women) today? (CBS/NYT) QUESTION 3: Some people say that because of past discrimination, blacks should be given preference in hiring and promotion. Others say that such a preference in hiring and promotion of blacks is wrong because it gives blacks advantages they haven't earned. What about your opinion—are you for or against preferential hiring and promotion of blacks? (NES)

Source: Charlotte Steeh and Maria Krysan, "Affirmative Action and the Public, 1970–1995," *Public Opinion Quarterly* 60, 1996, 128–158.

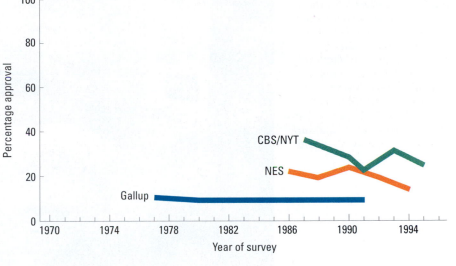

ability should be rewarded equitably. This form of equality offers all individuals the same chance to get ahead; it glorifies personal achievement and free competition and allows everyone to play on a level field where the same rules apply to all. Special recruitment efforts aimed at identifying qualified minority or female job applicants, for example, ensure that everyone has the same chance starting out. Low-bid contracting illustrates equality of opportunity, because every bidder has the same chance to compete for work.

Americans are far less committed to **equality of outcome,** which means greater uniformity in social, economic, and political power among different social groups. For example, schools and businesses aim at equality of outcome when they allocate admissions or jobs on the basis of race, gender, or disability, which are unrelated to ability. (Some observers refer to these allocations as *quotas*, while others call them *goals*. The difference is subtle. A quota *requires* that a specified, proportional share of some benefit go to a favored group. A goal *aims* for proportional allocation of benefits, without requiring it.) The government seeks equality of outcome when it adjusts the rules to handicap some bidders and favor others. The vast majority of Americans, however, consistently favor low-bid contracting and merit-based admissions and employment over preferential treatment.[3] Quota- or goal-based policies muster only modest support (see Figure 16.1).[4]

Some people believe that equality of outcome can occur in today's society only if we restrict the free competition that is the basis of equality of opportunity. One such restriction takes the form of a barrier to personal achievement. Preferential treatment in contracting is an apt example. The government-mandated preference for DBEs prevented Randy Pech from

Separate and Unequal

The Supreme Court gave constitutional protection to racial separation on the theory that states could provide "separate but equal" facilities for blacks. But racial separation meant unequal facilities, as these two water fountains dramatically illustrate. The Supreme Court struck a fatal blow against the separate-but-equal doctrine in its landmark 1954 ruling in Brown v. Board of Education.

competing on a level playing field. He submitted the lowest bid, but he still lost to a higher (DBE) bidder.

Quota policies generate the most opposition because they confine competition. Quotas limit advancement for some individuals and ensure advancement for others. They alter the results by taking into account factors unrelated to ability. Equal outcomes policies that benefit minorities, women, or the disabled at the expense of whites, men, or the able-bodied create strong opposition, because quotas seem to be at odds with individual initiative. In other words, equality clashes with freedom. To understand the ways government resolves this conflict, we have to understand the development of civil rights in this country.

The history of civil rights in the United States is primarily the story of a search for social and economic equality. This search has persisted for more than a century and is still going on today. It began with the battle for civil rights for black citizens, whose prior subjugation as slaves had roused the passions of the nation and brought about its bloodiest conflict, the Civil War. The struggle of blacks has been a beacon lighting the way for Native Americans, Hispanic Americans, women, and the disabled. Each of these groups has confronted **invidious discrimination.** Discrimination is simply the act of making or recognizing distinctions. When making distinctions among people, discrimination may be benign (that is, harmless) or invidious (harmful). Sometimes this harm has been subtle, sometimes it has been overt, and sometimes it has come from other minorities. Each group has achieved a measure of success by pressing its interests on government, even challenging it. These challenges and the government's responses to them have helped shape our democracy.

Remember that **civil rights** are powers or privileges guaranteed to the individual and protected from arbitrary removal at the hands of the government or other individuals. (Rights need not be confined to humans. Some advocates claim that animals have rights, too.) In this chapter, we will concentrate on the rights guaranteed by the constitutional amendments adopted after the Civil War and by laws passed to enforce those guarantees. Prominent among them is the right to equal protection of the laws. This right remained a promise rather than a reality well into the twentieth century.

THE CIVIL WAR AMENDMENTS

The Civil War amendments were adopted to provide freedom and equality to black Americans. The Thirteenth Amendment, ratified in 1865, provided that

> neither slavery nor involuntary servitude . . . shall exist within the United States, or any place subject to their jurisdiction.

The Fourteenth Amendment was adopted three years later. It provides first that freed slaves are citizens:

> All persons born or naturalized in the United States, and subject to the jurisdiction thereof, are citizens of the United States and of the State wherein they reside.

As we saw in Chapter 15, it also prohibits the states from abridging the "privileges or immunities of citizens of the United States" or depriving "any person of life, liberty, or property, without due process of law." The amendment then goes on to protect equality under the law, declaring that no state shall

> deny to any person within its jurisdiction the equal protection of the laws.

The Fifteenth Amendment, adopted in 1870, added a measure of political equality:

> The right of citizens of the United States to vote shall not be denied or abridged by the United States or by any State on account of race, color, or previous condition of servitude.

American blacks were thus free and politically equal—at least according to the Constitution. But for many years, the courts sometimes thwarted the efforts of the other branches to protect these constitutional rights.

Congress and the Supreme Court: Lawmaking Versus Law Interpreting

In the years after the Civil War, Congress went to work to protect the rights of black citizens. In 1866, lawmakers passed a civil rights act that gave the national government some authority over the treatment of blacks by state courts. This legislation was a response to the **black codes,** laws enacted by the former slave states to restrict the freedom of blacks. For example, vagrancy and apprenticeship laws forced blacks to work and denied them a free choice of employers. One section of the 1866 act that still applies today grants all citizens the right to make and enforce contracts, the right to sue others in court (and the corresponding ability to be sued), the duty and ability to give evidence in court, and the right to inherit, purchase, lease, sell, hold, or convey property. Later, in the Civil Rights Act of 1875, Congress attempted to guarantee blacks equal access to public accommodations (streetcars, inns, parks, theaters, and the like).

While Congress was enacting laws to protect the civil rights of black citizens, the Supreme Court weakened some of those rights. In 1873, the Court ruled that the Civil War amendments had not changed the relationship between the state and national governments.[5] State citizenship and national citizenship remained separate and distinct. According to the Court, the Fourteenth Amendment did not obligate the states to honor the rights guaranteed by U.S. citizenship. In effect, the Court stripped the amendment of its power to secure for black citizens the freedoms guaranteed by the Bill of Rights.

In subsequent years, the Court's decisions narrowed some constitutional protections for blacks. In 1876, the justices limited congressional attempts to protect the rights of blacks.[6] A group of Louisiana whites had used violence and fraud to prevent blacks from exercising their basic constitutional rights, including the right of peaceable assembly. The justices held that the rights allegedly infringed on were not nationally protected rights and that therefore Congress was powerless to punish those who violated them. On the very same day, the Court ruled that the Fifteenth Amendment did not guarantee all citizens the right to vote; it simply listed grounds that could not be used to deny that right.[7] And in 1883, the Court struck down the public accommodations section of the Civil Rights Act of 1875.[8] The justices declared that the national government could prohibit only government action that discriminated against blacks; private acts of discrimination or acts of omission by a state were beyond the reach of the national government. For example, a state law excluding blacks from jury service was an unlawful abridgment of individual rights. However, a person who refused to serve blacks in a private club was outside the control of the national government, because the discrimination was a private—not a governmental—act. The Court refused to see racial discrimination as an act that the national government could prohibit. In many cases the justices tolerated racial discrimination. In the process they abetted **racism,** the belief that there are inherent differences among the races that determine people's achievement and that one's own race is superior to and thus has a right to dominate others.

The Court's decisions gave the states ample room to maneuver around civil rights laws. In the matter of voting rights, for example, states that wanted to bar black men from the polls simply used nonracial means to do so. One popular tool was the **poll tax,** first imposed by Georgia in 1877. This was a tax of $1 or $2 on every citizen who wanted to vote. The tax was not a burden for most whites. But many blacks were tenant farmers, deeply in debt to white merchants and landowners; they just did not have any extra money for voting. Other bars to black suffrage included literacy tests, minimum education requirements, and a grandfather clause that restricted suffrage to men who could establish that their grandfathers were eligible to vote before 1867 (three years before the Fifteenth Amendment declared that race could not be used to deny individuals the right to vote).[9] White southerners also used intimidation and violence to keep blacks from the polls.

The Roots of Racial Segregation

Well before the Civil War, **racial segregation** was a way of life in the South: blacks lived and worked separately from whites. After the war, southern states began to enact Jim Crow laws that enforced segregation. (*Jim Crow* was a derogatory term for a black person.) Once the Supreme Court took the teeth out of the Civil Rights Act of 1875, such laws proliferated. They required blacks to live in separate (generally inferior) areas and restricted them to separate sections of hospitals, separate cemeteries, separate drinking and toilet facilities, separate schools, and separate sections of streetcars, trains, jails, and parks. Each day, in countless ways, they were reminded of the inferior status accorded them by white society.

In 1892, Homer Adolph Plessy—who was seven-eighths Caucasian—took a seat in a "whites-only" car of a Louisiana train. He refused to move to the car reserved for blacks and was arrested. Plessy argued that Louisiana's law mandating racial segregation on its trains was an unconstitutional infringement on both the privileges and immunities guaranteed by the Fourteenth Amendment and its equal protection clause. The Supreme Court disagreed. The majority in ***Plessy* v. *Ferguson*** (1896) upheld state-imposed racial segregation.[10] They based their decision on what came to be known as the **separate-but-equal doctrine,** which held that separate facilities for blacks and whites satisfied the Fourteenth Amendment so long as they were equal. The lone dissenter was John Marshall Harlan (the first of two distinguished justices with the same name). Harlan, who envisioned a "color-blind Constitution," wrote this in his dissenting opinion:

> We boast of the freedom enjoyed by our people above all other peoples. But it is difficult to reconcile that boast with a state of the law which, practically, puts the brand of servitude and degradation upon a large class of our fellow citizens, our equals before the law. The thin disguise of "equal" accommodations for passengers in railroad coaches will not mislead anyone, or atone for the wrong this day done.[11]

Three years later, the Supreme Court extended the separate-but-equal doctrine to the schools.[12] The justices ignored the fact that black educational facilities (and most other "colored-only" facilities) were far from equal to those reserved for whites.

By the end of the nineteenth century, racial segregation was firmly and legally entrenched in the American South. Although constitutional amendments and national laws to protect equality under the law were in place, the Supreme Court's interpretation of those amendments and laws rendered them ineffective. Several decades would pass before any change was discernible.

THE DISMANTLING OF SCHOOL SEGREGATION

Denied the right to vote and be represented in the government, blacks sought access to power through other parts of the political system. The National Association for the Advancement of Colored People (NAACP), founded in 1909 by W. E. B. Du Bois and others, both black and white, with the goal of ending racial discrimination and segregation, took the lead in the campaign for black civil rights. The plan was to launch a two-pronged legal and lobbying attack on the separate-but-equal doctrine: first by pressing for fully equal facilities for blacks, then by proving the unconstitutionality of segregation. The process would be a slow one, but the strategies involved did not require a large organization or heavy financial backing; at the time, the NAACP had neither.*

Pressure for Equality . . .

By the 1920s, the separate-but-equal doctrine was so deeply ingrained in American law that no Supreme Court justice would dissent from its continued application to racial segregation. But a few Court decisions offered hope that change would come. In 1935, Lloyd Gaines graduated from Lincoln University, a black college in Missouri, and applied to the state law school. The law school rejected him because he was black. Missouri refused to admit blacks to its all-white law school; instead, the state's policy was to pay the costs of blacks admitted to out-of-state law schools. With the support of the NAACP, Gaines appealed to the courts for admission to the University of Missouri Law School. In 1938, the U.S. Supreme Court ruled that he must be admitted.[13] Under the *Plessy* ruling, Missouri could not shift to other states its responsibility to provide an equal education for blacks.

Two later cases helped reinforce the requirement that segregated facilities must be equal in all major respects. One was brought by Heman Sweatt, again with the help of the NAACP. The all-white University of Texas Law School had denied Sweatt entrance because of his race. A federal court ordered the state to provide a black law school for him; the state responded by renting a few rooms in an office building and hiring two black lawyers as teachers. Sweatt refused to attend the school and took his case to the Supreme Court.[14]

The second case raised a related issue. A doctoral program in education at the all-white University of Oklahoma had refused George McLaurin admission because he was black. The state had no equivalent program for blacks. McLaurin sought a federal court order for admission, and under pressure from the decision in *Gaines*, the university amended its procedures and admitted McLaurin "on a segregated basis." It restricted the sixty-eight-year-old McLaurin to hastily designated "colored-only" sections of a few rooms. With the help of the NAACP, McLaurin appealed this obvious lack of equal facilities to the Supreme Court.[15]

The Court ruled on *Sweatt* and *McLaurin* in 1950. The justices unanimously found that the facilities in each case were inadequate: the separate "law school" provided for Sweatt did not approach the quality of the white state law school, and the restrictions placed on McLaurin's interactions

---

* In 1939, the NAACP established an offshoot, the NAACP Legal Defense and Education Fund, to work on legal challenges while the parent organization concentrated on lobbying.

with other students would result in an inferior education. Their respective state universities had to give both Sweatt and McLaurin full student status. But the Court avoided reexamining the separate-but-equal doctrine.

. . . And Pressure for Desegregation

These decisions—especially *McLaurin*—suggested to the NAACP that the time was right for an attack on segregation itself. In addition, public attitudes toward race relations were slowly changing from the predominant racism of the nineteenth and early twentieth centuries. Black groups had fought with honor—albeit in segregated military units—in World War II. Blacks and whites were working together in unions and in service and religious organizations. Social change and court decisions suggested that government-imposed segregation was vulnerable.

President Harry S Truman risked his political future with his strong support of blacks' civil rights. In 1947, he established the President's Committee on Civil Rights. The committee's report, issued later that year, became the agenda for the civil rights movement during the next two decades. It called for national laws prohibiting racially motivated poll taxes, segregation, and brutality against minorities and for guarantees of voting rights and equal employment opportunity. In 1948, Truman ordered the **desegregation** (the dismantling of authorized racial segregation) of the armed forces.

In 1947, the U.S. Department of Justice had begun to submit briefs to the courts in support of civil rights. The department's most important intervention probably came in ***Brown v. Board of Education.***[16] This case was the culmination of twenty years of planning and litigation on the part of the NAACP to invalidate racial segregation in public schools.

Linda Brown was a black child whose father tried to enroll her in a white public school in Topeka, Kansas. The white school was close to Linda's home; the walk to the black school meant that she had to cross a dangerous set of railroad tracks. Brown's request was refused because of Linda's race. A federal district court found that the black public school was, in all major respects, equal in quality to the white school; therefore, according to the *Plessy* doctrine, Linda was required to go to the black public school. Brown appealed the decision.

Brown v. *Board of Education* reached the Supreme Court in late 1951. The justices delayed argument on the sensitive case until after the 1952 national election. *Brown* was merged with four similar cases into a class action, a device for combining the claims or defenses of similar individuals so that they can be tried in a single lawsuit (see Chapter 14). The class action was supported by the NAACP and coordinated by Thurgood Marshall, who would later become the first black justice to sit on the Supreme Court. The five cases squarely challenged the separate-but-equal doctrine. By all tangible measures (standards for teacher licensing, teacher-pupil ratios, library facilities), the two school systems in each case—one white, the other black—were equal. The issue was legal separation of the races.

On May 17, 1954, Chief Justice Earl Warren, who had only recently joined the Court, delivered a single opinion covering four of the cases. Warren spoke for a unanimous Court when he declared that "in the field of public

Anger Erupts in Little Rock

In 1957, the school board in Little Rock, Arkansas, attempted to implement court-ordered desegregation. The first step called for admitting nine blacks to Central High School on September 3, but the governor sent in the national guard to bar their attendance. On September 23, when the black students again attempted entry, police escorts could not control the mob that gathered at the school. Two days later, under the protection of federal troops ordered by President Eisenhower, the students were finally admitted. Although hostility and violence led the school board to seek a postponement of the desegregation plan, the Supreme Court, meeting in special session, affirmed the Brown *decision and ordered the plan to proceed.*

education the doctrine of 'separate but equal' has no place. Separate educational facilities are inherently unequal,"[17] depriving the plaintiffs of the equal protection of the laws. Segregated facilities generate in black children "a feeling of inferiority . . . that may affect their hearts and minds in a way unlikely ever to be undone."[18] In short, the nation's highest court found that state-imposed public school segregation violated the equal protection clause of the Fourteenth Amendment.

A companion case to *Brown* challenged the segregation of public schools in Washington, D.C.[19] Segregation there was imposed by Congress. The equal protection clause protected citizens only against state violations; no equal protection clause restrained the national government. It was unthinkable for the Constitution to impose a lesser duty on the national government than on the states. In this case, the Court unanimously decided that the racial segregation requirement was an arbitrary deprivation of liberty without due process of law, a violation of the Fifth Amendment. In short, the concept of liberty encompassed the idea of equality. (Forty years later, Randy Pech would rely on this understanding of liberty when he challenged the U.S. Department of Transportation's preferential contracting policy.)

The Court deferred implementation of the school desegregation decisions until 1955. Then, in **Brown v. Board of Education II,** it ruled that school systems must desegregate "with all deliberate speed" and assigned the task of supervising desegregation to the lower federal courts.[20]

Some states quietly complied with the *Brown* decree. Others did little to desegregate their schools. And many communities in the South defied the Court, sometimes violently. Some white business and professional people formed "white citizens' councils." The councils put economic pressure on blacks who asserted their rights, by foreclosing on their mortgages and denying them credit at local stores. Georgia and North Carolina resisted desegregation by paying tuition for white students attending private schools. Virginia and other states ordered that desegregated schools be closed.

This resistance, along with the Supreme Court's "all deliberate speed" order, placed a heavy burden on federal judges to dismantle what was the fundamental social order in many communities.[21] Gradual desegregation under *Brown* was in some cases no desegregation at all. In 1969, a unanimous Supreme Court ordered that the operation of segregated school systems must stop "at once."[22]

Two years later, the Court approved several remedies to achieve integration, including busing, racial quotas, and the pairing or grouping of noncontiguous school zones. In *Swann* v. *Charlotte-Mecklenburg County Schools*, the Supreme Court affirmed the right of lower courts to order the busing of children to ensure school desegregation.[23] But these remedies applied only to **de jure** **segregation,** government-imposed segregation (for example, government assignment of whites to one school and blacks to another within the same community). Court-imposed remedies did not apply to **de facto** **segregation,** segregation that is not the result of government action (for example, racial segregation resulting from residential patterns).

The busing of schoolchildren came under heavy attack in both the North and the South. Desegregation advocates saw busing as a potential remedy in many northern cities, where schools had become segregated as white families left the cities for the suburbs. This "white flight" had left inner-city schools predominantly black and suburban schools almost all white. Public opinion strongly opposed the busing approach, and Congress sought to impose limits on busing as a remedy. In 1974, a closely divided Court ruled that lower courts could not order busing across school district boundaries, unless each district had practiced racial discrimination or unless school district lines had been deliberately drawn to achieve racial segregation.[24] This ruling meant an end to large-scale school desegregation in metropolitan areas.

THE CIVIL RIGHTS MOVEMENT

Although the NAACP concentrated on school desegregation, it also made headway in other areas. The Supreme Court responded to NAACP efforts in the late 1940s by outlawing whites-only primary elections in the South, declaring them to be in violation of the Fifteenth Amendment. The Court also declared segregation on interstate bus routes to be unconstitutional and desegregated restaurants and hotels in the District of Columbia. Despite these and other decisions that chipped away at existing barriers to equality, states still were denying black citizens political power, and segregation remained a fact of daily life.

Dwight D. Eisenhower, who became president in 1953, was not as concerned about civil rights as his predecessor had been. He chose to stand above the battle between the Supreme Court and those who resisted the Court's decisions. He even refused to reveal whether he agreed with the Court's decision in *Brown* v. *Board of Education.* "It makes no difference,"

Dishonoring Old Glory

The struggle for racial equality in Boston in the 1970s divided the city and generated hatred and resentment between blacks and whites. Federal court orders mandating school desegregation touched off particularly violent reactions. In 1976, a white protester marching toward the federal courthouse tried to impale a black passerby with a flagstaff. This photograph captures the ugliness of the city's conflicts more powerfully than words can.

Eisenhower declared, because "the Constitution is as the Supreme Court interprets it."[25]

Eisenhower did enforce school desegregation when the safety of schoolchildren was involved, but he appeared unwilling to do much more to advance racial equality. That goal seemed to require the political mobilization of the people—black and white—in what is now known as the **civil rights movement.**

Black churches served as the crucible of the movement. More than places of worship, they served hundreds of other functions. In black communities, the church was "a bulletin board to a people who owned no organs of communication, a credit union to those without banks, and even a kind of people's court."[26] Some of its preachers were motivated by fortune, others by saintliness. One would prove to be a modern-day Moses.

Civil Disobedience

Rosa Parks, a black woman living in Montgomery, Alabama, sounded the first call to action. That city's Jim Crow ordinances were tougher than those in other southern cities, where blacks were required to sit in the back of the bus while whites sat in the front, both races converging as the bus filled with passengers. In Montgomery, however, bus drivers had the power to define and redefine the floating line separating blacks and whites: drivers could order blacks to vacate an entire row to make room for one white or order blacks to stand even when some seats were vacant. Blacks could not walk through the white section to their seats in the back; they had to leave the bus after paying their fare and reenter through the rear.[27] In December 1955, Parks boarded a city bus on her way home from work and took an available seat in the front of the bus; she refused to give up her seat when the driver asked her to do so and was arrested and fined $10 for violating the city ordinance.

Montgomery's black community responded to Parks's arrest with a boycott of the city's bus system. A **boycott** is a refusal to do business with a company or individual as an expression of disapproval or a means of coercion. Blacks walked or car-pooled or made no trips that were not absolutely necessary. As the bus company moved close to bankruptcy and downtown merchants suffered from the loss of black business, city officials began to harass blacks, hoping to frighten them into ending the boycott. But Montgomery's black citizens now had a leader—a charismatic twenty-six-year-old Baptist minister named Martin Luther King, Jr.

King urged the people to hold out, and they did. A year after the boycott began, a federal court ruled that segregated transportation systems violated the equal protection clause of the Constitution. The boycott had proved to be an effective weapon.

In 1957, King helped organize the Southern Christian Leadership Conference (SCLC) to coordinate civil rights activities. King was totally committed to nonviolent action to bring racial issues into the light. To that end, he advocated **civil disobedience,** the willful but nonviolent breach of unjust laws.

One nonviolent tactic was the sit-in. On February 1, 1960, four black freshmen from North Carolina Agricultural and Technical College in Greensboro sat down at a whites-only lunch counter. They were refused service by the black waitress, who said, "Fellows like you make our race look bad." The freshmen stayed all day and promised to return the next morning to continue what they called a "sit-down protest." Other students soon joined in, rotating shifts so that no one missed classes. Within two days, eighty-five students had flocked to the lunch counter. Although abused verbally and physically, the students would not move. Finally, they were arrested. Soon people held similar sit-in demonstrations throughout the South and then in the North.[28] The Supreme Court upheld the actions of the demonstrators, although the unanimity that had characterized its earlier decisions was gone. (In this decision, three justices argued that even bigots had the right to call on the government to protect their property interests.)[29]

The Civil Rights Act of 1964

In 1961, a new administration, headed by President John F. Kennedy, came to power. At first Kennedy did not seem to be committed to civil rights. His stance changed as the movement gained momentum and as more and more whites became aware of the abuse being heaped on sit-in demonstrators, freedom riders (who tested unlawful segregation on interstate bus routes), and those who were trying to help blacks register to vote in southern states. Volunteers were being jailed, beaten, and killed for advocating activities among blacks that whites took for granted.

A Modern-Day Moses

Martin Luther King, Jr., was a Baptist minister who believed in the principles of nonviolent protest practiced by India's Mohandas ("Mahatma") Gandhi. This photograph, taken in 1963 in Baltimore, captures the crowd's affection for King, the man many thought would lead them to a new Canaan of racial equality. King, who won the Nobel Peace Prize in 1964, was assassinated in 1968 in Memphis, Tennessee.

For a Web site devoted to the life and work of Dr. Martin Luther King, Jr., navigate to `<www.seattletimes.com/mlk/>`

In late 1962, President Kennedy ordered federal troops to ensure the safety of James Meredith, the first black to attend the University of Mississippi. In early 1963, Kennedy enforced the desegregation of the University of Alabama. In April 1963, television viewers were shocked to see civil rights marchers in Birmingham, Alabama, attacked with dogs, fire hoses, and cattle prods. (The idea of the Birmingham march was to provoke confrontations with white officials in an effort to compel the national government to intervene on behalf of blacks.) Finally, in June 1963, Kennedy asked Congress for legislation that would outlaw segregation in public accommodations.

Two months later, Martin Luther King, Jr., joined in a march on Washington, D.C. The organizers called the protest "A March for Jobs and Freedom," signaling the economic goals of black America. More than 250,000 people, black and white, gathered peaceably at the Lincoln Memorial to hear King speak. "I have a dream," the great preacher extemporized, "that my little children will one day live in a nation where they will not be judged by the color of their skin but by the content of their character."[30]

Congress had not yet enacted Kennedy's public accommodations bill when he was assassinated on November 22, 1963. His successor, Lyndon B. Johnson, considered civil rights his top legislative priority. Within months, Congress enacted the Civil Rights Act of 1964, which included a vital provision barring segregation in most public accommodations. This congressional action was, in part, a reaction to Kennedy's death. But it was also almost certainly a response to the brutal treatment of blacks throughout the South.

Congress had enacted civil rights laws in 1957 and 1960, but they dealt primarily with voting rights. The 1964 act was the most comprehensive legislative attempt ever to erase racial discrimination in the United States. Congress acted after the longest debate in Senate history and only after the first successful use of cloture, a procedure used to end a filibuster.

Among its many provisions, the act

- Entitled all persons to "the full and equal enjoyment" of goods, services, and privileges in places of public accommodation, without discrimination on the grounds of race, color, religion, or national origin

- Established the right to equality in employment opportunities

- Strengthened voting rights legislation

- Created the Equal Employment Opportunity Commission (EEOC) and charged it with hearing and investigating complaints of job discrimination*

- Provided that funds could be withheld from federally assisted programs administered in a discriminatory manner

The last of these provisions had a powerful effect on school desegregation when Congress enacted the Elementary and Secondary Education Act in 1965. That act provided for billions of federal dollars for the nation's schools; the threat of losing that money spurred local school boards to formulate and implement new plans for desegregation.

The 1964 act faced an immediate constitutional challenge. Its opponents argued that the Constitution does not forbid acts of private discrimination—the position the Supreme Court itself had taken in the late nineteenth century. But this time, a unanimous Court upheld the law, declaring that acts of discrimination impose substantial burdens on interstate commerce and thus are subject to congressional control.[31] In a companion case, Ollie McClung, the owner of a small restaurant, had refused to serve blacks. McClung maintained that he had the freedom to serve whomever he wanted in his own restaurant. The justices, however, upheld the government's prohibition of McClung's racial discrimination on the ground that a substantial portion of the food served in his restaurant had moved in interstate commerce.[32] Thus, the Supreme Court vindicated the Civil Rights Act of 1964 by reason of the congressional power to regulate interstate commerce rather than on the basis of the Fourteenth Amendment. Since 1937, the Court had approved ever-widening authority to regulate state and local activities under the commerce clause. It was the most powerful basis for the exercise of congressional power in the Constitution.

President Johnson's goal was a "great society." Soon a constitutional amendment and a series of civil rights laws were in place to help him meet his goal:

- The Twenty-fourth Amendment, ratified in 1964, banned poll taxes in primary and general elections for national office.

---

* *Since 1972, the EEOC has had the power to institute legal proceedings on behalf of employees who allege that they have been victims of illegal discrimination.*

- The Economic Opportunity Act of 1964 provided education and training to combat poverty.

- The Voting Rights Act of 1965 empowered the attorney general to send voter registration supervisors to areas in which fewer than half the eligible minority voters had been registered. This act has been credited with doubling black voter registration in the South in only five years.[33]

- The Fair Housing Act of 1968 banned discrimination in the rental and sale of most housing.

The Continuing Struggle over Civil Rights

However, civil rights laws on the books do not ensure civil rights in action. This was the case in 1984, when the Supreme Court was called on to interpret a law forbidding sex discrimination in schools and colleges receiving financial assistance from the national government. Must the entire institution comply with the regulations, or only those portions of it that receive assistance?

In *Grove City College* v. *Bell,* the Court ruled that government educational grants to students implicate the institution as a recipient of government funds; therefore, it must comply with government nondiscrimination provisions. However, only the specific department or program receiving the funds (in Grove City's case, the financial aid program), not the whole institution, was barred from discriminating.[34] Athletic departments rarely receive such government funds, so colleges had no obligation to provide equal opportunity for women in their sports programs.

The *Grove City* decision had widespread effects, because three other important civil rights laws were worded similarly. The implication was that any law barring discrimination on the basis of race, sex, age, or disability would be applicable only to programs receiving federal funds, not to the entire institution. So a university laboratory that received federal research grants could not discriminate, but other departments that did not receive federal money could. The effect of *Grove City* was to frustrate enforcement of civil rights laws. In keeping with pluralist theory, civil rights and women's groups shifted their efforts to the legislative branch.

Congress reacted immediately, exercising its lawmaking power to check the law-interpreting power of the judiciary. Congress can revise national laws to counter judicial decisions; in this political chess game, the Court's move is hardly the last one. Legislators protested that the Court had misinterpreted the intent of the antidiscrimination laws, and they forged a bipartisan effort to make that intent crystal clear: if any part of an institution gets federal money, no part of it can discriminate. Their work led to the Civil Rights Restoration Act, which became law in 1988 despite a presidential veto by Ronald Reagan.

While Congress tried to restore and expand civil rights enforcement, the Supreme Court weakened it again. The Court restricted minority contractor set-asides of state public works funds, an arrangement it had approved in 1980. (Recall that a set-aside is a purchasing or contracting provision that reserves a certain percentage of funds for minority-owned contractors.) The five-person majority held that past societal discrimination alone cannot serve as the basis for rigid quotas.[35]

Buttressed by Republican appointees, the Supreme Court continued to narrow the scope of national civil rights protections in a string of decisions that suggested the ascendancy of a new conservative majority more concerned with freedom than equality.[36] To counter the Court's changing interpretations of civil rights laws, liberals turned to Congress to restore and enlarge earlier Court decisions by writing them into law. The result was a comprehensive new civil rights bill. President George Bush vetoed a 1990 version, asserting that it would impose quotas in hiring and promotion. But a year later, after months of debate, Bush signed a similar measure. The Civil Rights Act of 1991 reversed or altered twelve Court decisions that had narrowed civil rights protections. The new law clarified and expanded earlier legislation and increased the costs to employers for intentional, illegal discrimination. Continued resentment generated by equal outcomes policies would move the battle back to the courts, however.

Racial Violence and Black Nationalism

Increased violence on the part of those who demanded their civil rights and those who refused to honor them marked the middle and late 1960s. Violence against civil rights workers was confined primarily to the South, where volunteers continued to work for desegregation and to register black voters. Among the atrocities that incensed even complacent whites were the bombing of dozens of black churches; the slaying of three young civil rights workers in Philadelphia, Mississippi, in 1964 by a group of whites, among them deputy sheriffs; police violence against demonstrators marching peacefully from Selma, Alabama, to Montgomery in 1965; and the assassination of Martin Luther King, Jr., in Memphis in 1968.

Black violence took the form of rioting in northern inner cities. Civil rights gains had come mainly in the South. Northern blacks had the vote and were not subject to Jim Crow laws, yet most lived in poverty. Unemployment was high, work opportunities at skilled jobs were limited, and earnings were low. The segregation of blacks into the inner cities, although not sanctioned by law, was nevertheless real; their voting power was minimal, because they constituted a small minority of the northern population. The solid gains made by southern blacks added to their frustration. Beginning in 1964, northern blacks took to the streets, burning and looting. Riots in 168 cities and towns followed King's assassination in 1968, and many were met with violent responses from urban police forces and the National Guard.

The lack of progress toward equality for northern blacks was an important factor in the rise of the black nationalist movement in the 1960s. The Nation of Islam, or Black Muslims, called for separation from whites rather than integration and for violence in return for violence; Malcolm X was their leading voice, until he distanced himself from the Muslims shortly before his assassination by fellow Muslims in 1965. The militant Black Panther Party generated fear with its denunciation of the values of white America. In 1966, Stokely Carmichael, then chairman of the Student Nonviolent Coordinating Committee (SNCC), called on blacks to assert "We want black power" in their struggle for civil rights. Organizations that had espoused integration and nonviolence now argued that blacks needed power more than white friendship.

The movement had several positive effects. Black nationalism instilled and promoted pride in black history and black culture. By the end of the decade, U.S. colleges and universities were beginning to institute black studies programs. More black citizens were voting than ever before, and their voting power was evident: increasing numbers of blacks were winning election to public office. In 1967, Cleveland's voters elected Carl Stokes, the first black mayor of a major American city. And by 1969, black representatives were able to form the Congressional Black Caucus. These achievements were incentives for other groups that also faced barriers to equality.

CIVIL RIGHTS FOR OTHER MINORITIES

Recent civil rights laws and court decisions protect members of all minority groups. The Supreme Court underscored the breadth of this protection in an important decision in 1987.[37] The justices ruled unanimously that the Civil Rights Act of 1866 (known today as Section 1981) offers broad protection against discrimination to all minorities. Previously, members of white ethnic groups could not invoke the law in bias suits. Under the 1987 decision, members of any ethnic group—Italian, Iranian, Chinese, Norwegian, or Vietnamese, for example—can recover money damages if they prove they have been denied a job, excluded from rental housing, or subjected to another form of discrimination prohibited by the law. The 1964 Civil Rights Act offers similar protections but specifies strict procedures for filing suits that tend to discourage litigation. Moreover, the remedies in most cases are limited. In job discrimination, for example, back pay and reinstatement are the only remedies. Section 1981 has fewer hurdles and allows litigants to seek punitive damages (damages awarded by a court as additional punishment for a serious wrong). In some respects, then, the older law is a more potent weapon than the newer one in fighting discrimination.

Clearly, the civil rights movement has had an effect on all minorities. However, the United States has granted equality most slowly to nonwhite minorities. Here we examine the civil rights struggles of three groups—Native Americans, Hispanic Americans, and the disabled.

Native Americans

During the eighteenth and nineteenth centuries, the U.S. government took Indian lands, isolated Native Americans on reservations, and denied them political and social rights. The government's dealings with the Indians were often marked by violence and broken promises. The agencies responsible for administering Indian reservations kept Native Americans poor and dependent on the national government.

The national government switched policies at the turn of the century, promoting assimilation instead of separation. The government banned the

Righting a Wrong

During World War II, Congress authorized the quarantine of Japanese residents in the western United States. The Supreme Court upheld the congressional action in 1944. More than 110,000 men, women, and children—including native-born U.S. citizens—were incarcerated simply because they were of Japanese ancestry. The men pictured here were confined to the Japanese Evacuation Colony at Manzanar, California. In 1988, Congress passed legislation that offered apologies and a $20,000 tax-free reparation to each surviving internee. The cost to the government: $1.25 billion.

use of native languages and religious rituals; it sent Indian children to boarding schools and gave them non-Indian names. In 1924, Indians received U.S. citizenship. Until that time, they were considered members of tribal nations whose relations with the U.S. government were determined by treaties. The Native American population suffered badly during the Depression, primarily because the poorest Americans were affected most but also because of the inept administration of Indian reservations. (Today, Indians make up less than 1 percent of the population.) Poverty persisted on the reservations well after the Depression was over, and Indian land holdings continued to shrink through the 1950s and into the 1960s—despite signed treaties and the religious significance of portions of the lands they lost. In the 1960s, for example, a part of the Hopi Sacred Circle, which is considered the source of all life in the Hopi tribal religion, was strip-mined for coal.

Anger bred of poverty, unemployment, and frustration with an uncaring government exploded in militant action in late 1969, when several American Indians seized Alcatraz Island, an abandoned island in San Francisco Bay. The group cited an 1868 Sioux treaty that entitled them to unused federal lands; they remained on the island for a year and a half. In 1973, armed members of the American Indian Movement seized eleven hostages at Wounded Knee, South Dakota, the site of an 1890 massacre of two hundred Sioux (Lakota) by U.S. cavalry troops. They remained there, occasionally exchanging gunfire with federal marshals, for seventy-one days, until the government agreed to examine the treaty rights of the Oglala Sioux.[38]

In 1946, Congress enacted legislation establishing an Indian claims commission to compensate Native Americans for land that had been

●●●●●●●●●●●
Bury My Heart

Native American mourners gathered at Wounded Knee, South Dakota, on December 29, 1990, to remember a tragedy. On that site a hundred years earlier, Seventh Cavalry soldiers massacred two hundred Sioux—including women and children. Descendants of the survivors traveled by foot and horseback to mark the anniversary and to honor their heritage.

taken from them. In the 1970s, the Native American Rights Fund and other groups used that legislation to win important victories in the courts. The tribes won the return of lands in the Midwest and in the states of Oklahoma, New Mexico, and Washington. In 1980, the Supreme Court ordered the national government to pay the Sioux $117 million plus interest for the Black Hills of South Dakota, which had been stolen from them a century before. Other cases, involving land from coast to coast, are still pending.

The fight for lost lands and for the survival of ancient native cultures continues. However, the preservation of Native American culture and the exercise of Native American rights sometimes create conflict with the interests of the majority. For example, the Chippewa in northern Wisconsin engage in an annual battle with local anglers on the shores of Lake Minocqua. The Indians wish to exercise their acknowledged right to spearfish for walleyed pike. Anglers fear that the Indians will deplete the stock and drive sport fishing away. The Chippewa voluntarily limit their annual catch, but they are offended that their ancestral rights are envied as government concessions.

In other instances, economic necessity may overwhelm ancient ways. One Alaskan tribe desperate for funds has been forced into unsettling choices: sign away logging rights, permit oil drilling in a wildlife area, or allow the construction of an airfield in a vast habitat for Kodiak bears. Some tribes have allowed the use of their reservations for dumps and waste disposal, only to face land and water contamination as a consequence.

The special status accorded Indian tribes in the Constitution has proved attractive to a new breed of Indian leaders. As we discussed in Chapter 4, some of the 557 recognized tribes have successfully instituted casino gambling on their reservations, even in the face of state opposition to their plans. The tribes pay no taxes on their profits, transforming gambling into a powerful engine of economic growth and giving a once impoverished people undreamed-of riches and responsibilities. Congress has allowed these developments provided that the tribes spend their profits on Indian assistance programs.

It is important to remember that throughout American history, Native Americans have been coerced physically and pressured economically to assimilate into the mainstream of white society. The destiny of Native Americans as viable groups with separate identities depends in no small measure on curbing their dependence on the national government.[39] The wealth created by casino gambling and other ventures funded with gambling profits may prove to be Native Americans' most effective weapon for retaining and regaining their heritage.

Hispanic Americans

Many Hispanic Americans have a rich and deep-rooted heritage in America, but until the 1920s that heritage was largely confined to the southwestern states, particularly California. Then, unprecedented numbers of Mexican and Puerto Rican immigrants came to the United States in search of employment and a better life. Businesspeople who saw in them a source of cheap labor welcomed them. Many Mexicans became farm workers, but both groups settled mainly in crowded, low-rent, inner-city districts: the Mexicans in the Southwest, the Puerto Ricans primarily in New York City. Both groups formed their own barrios, or neighborhoods, within the cities, where they maintained the customs and values of their homelands.

Like blacks who had migrated to northern cities, most new Latino immigrants found poverty and discrimination. And, like poor blacks and Native Americans, the Depression hit them hard. About one-third of the Mexican American population (mainly those who had been migratory farm workers) returned to Mexico during the 1930s.

World War II gave rise to another influx of Mexicans, this time primarily courted to work farms in California. But by the late 1950s, most farm workers—blacks, whites, and Hispanics—were living in poverty. Those Hispanic Americans who lived in cities fared little better. Yet, millions of Mexicans continued to cross the border into the United States, both legally and illegally. The effect was to depress wages for farm labor in California and the Southwest.

In 1965, Cesar Chávez led a strike of the United Farm Workers union against growers in California. The strike lasted several years and eventually, in combination with a national boycott, resulted in somewhat better pay, working conditions, and housing for workers.

In the 1970s and 1980s, the Hispanic American population continued to grow. The 20 million Hispanics living in the United States in the 1970s were still mainly Puerto Rican and Mexican American, but they were joined by immigrants from the Dominican Republic, Colombia, Cuba, and Ecuador. Although civil rights legislation helped them to an extent, they were among the poorest and least-educated groups in the United States.

Their problems were similar to those faced by other nonwhites, but most also had to overcome the further difficulty of learning and using a new language.

One effect of the language barrier is that voter registration and voter turnout among Latinos are lower than among other groups. The creation of nine Hispanic-majority congressional districts ensured a measure of representation. These majority minority districts are now in jeopardy as a result of Supreme Court decisions prohibiting race-based districting. Also, voter turnout depends on effective political advertising, and Hispanics are not targeted as often as other groups with political messages that they can understand. But despite these stumbling blocks, Latinos have started to exercise a measure of political power.

Hispanics occupy positions of power in national and local arenas. Hispanics or Latinos constitute 9 percent of the population and 4 percent of Congress. The 104th Congress (1995 to 1997) convened with a diverse group of eighteen Hispanic House members (fifteen Democrats and three Republicans). They form the Congressional Hispanic Caucus, an informal bipartisan group dedicated to voicing and advancing issues affecting Hispanic Americans. The National Hispanic Caucus of State Legislators, which has 250 members, has a similar mission, targeted to state and local concerns. The group's president, Ephraín González, Jr. (D.-N.Y.), has observed that "We're coming together [in Washington, D.C.] to work in a more united fashion. We've got 435 representatives, 100 senators and more than 3,000 staff members we have to educate about our communities' needs."[40]

Latinos have won the mayoralties of San Antonio, San Diego, Denver, and Miami. President Clinton appointed two Hispanics to his cabinet: Henry G. Cisneros, secretary of the Department of Housing and Urban Development, and Frederico F. Peña, secretary of Transportation. Cuban Americans look with pride as two of their own serve in Congress. Hispanics have also increased their access to political power; in 1996, two Hispanic Americans served on the powerful House Appropriations Committee.[41]

Disabled Americans

Minority status is not confined to race or ethnicity. After more than two decades of struggle, 43 million disabled Americans gained recognition in 1990 as a protected minority with the enactment of the Americans with Disabilities Act (ADA).

The law extends the protections embodied in the Civil Rights Act of 1964 to people with physical or mental disabilities, including people with AIDS, recovering alcoholics, and drug abusers. It guarantees them access to employment, transportation, public accommodations, and communication services.

The roots of the disabled rights movement stem from the period after World War II. Thousands of disabled veterans returned to a country and a society that were inhospitable to their needs. Institutionalization seemed the best way to care for the disabled, but this approach came under increasing fire as the disabled and their families sought care at home.

Advocates for the disabled found a ready model in the existing civil rights laws. Opponents argued that the changes mandated by the 1990 law (such as access for those confined to wheelchairs) could cost billions of dollars, but supporters replied that the costs would be offset by an equal or greater reduction in federal aid to disabled people, who would rather be working.

The law's enactment set off an avalanche of job discrimination complaints filed with the national government's watchdog agency, the EEOC. By 1995, the EEOC had received more than fifty-four thousand ADA-related complaints. Curiously, most complaints came from already-employed people, both previously and recently disabled. They charged that their employers failed to provide reasonable accommodations as required by the new law. The disabilities cited most frequently were back problems, mental illness, heart trouble, neurological disorders, and substance abuse.

A deceptively simple question lies at the heart of many ADA suits: what is the meaning of *disability*? The deliberately vague language of the statute has thrust the courts into the role of providing needed specificity, a path that politicians have feared to tread.[42]

A change in the law, no matter how welcome, does not ensure a change in people's attitudes. Laws that end racial discrimination do not extinguish racism, and laws that ban biased treatment of the disabled cannot mandate their acceptance. But civil rights advocates predict that bias against the disabled, like similar biases against other minorities, will wither as they become full participants in society.

GENDER AND EQUAL RIGHTS: THE WOMEN'S MOVEMENT

Together with such unconventional political activities as protests and sit-ins, conventional political tools such as the ballot box and the lawsuit have brought minorities in America a measure of equality. The Supreme Court—once responsible for perpetuating inequality for blacks—has expanded the array of legal weapons available to all minorities to help them achieve social equality. Women, too, have benefited from this change.

Protectionism

Until the early 1970s, laws that affected the civil rights of women were based on traditional views of the relationship between men and women. At the heart of these laws was **protectionism**—the notion that women must be sheltered from life's harsh realities. Thomas Jefferson, author of the Declaration of Independence, believed that "were our state a pure democracy there would still be excluded from our deliberations women, who, to prevent deprivation of morals and ambiguity of issues, should not mix promiscuously in gatherings of men."[43] And "protected" they were, through laws that discriminated against them in employment and other areas. With few exceptions, women were also "protected" from voting until early in the twentieth century.

The demand for women's rights arose from the abolition movement and later was based primarily on the Fourteenth Amendment's prohibition of laws that "abridge the privileges or immunities of citizens of the United States." However, the courts consistently rebuffed challenges to protectionist state laws. In 1873, the Supreme Court upheld an Illinois statute that prohibited women from practicing law. The justices maintained that the Fourteenth Amendment had no bearing on a state's authority to regulate admission of members to the bar. In a concurring opinion, Justice Joseph P. Bradley articulated the common protectionist belief that women were unfit for certain occupations: "Man is, or should be, woman's protector and defender. The natural and proper timidity and delicacy which belongs to the female sex evidently unfits it for many of the occupations of civil life."[44]

Protectionism reached a peak in 1908, when the Court upheld an Oregon law limiting the number of hours women could work.[45] The decision was rife with assumptions about the nature and role of women, and it gave wide latitude to laws that "protected" the "weaker sex." It also led to protectionist legislation that barred women from working more than forty-eight hours a week and from working at jobs that required them to lift more than thirty-five pounds. (The average work week for men was sixty hours or longer.) In effect, women were locked out of jobs that called for substantial overtime (and overtime pay); instead, they were shunted to jobs that men believed suited their abilities.

Protectionism can take many forms. Some employers hesitate to place women at risk in the workplace. Some have excluded women capable of bearing children from jobs that involve exposure to toxic substances that could harm a developing fetus. Usually, such jobs offer more pay to compensate for their higher risk. Although they face similar reproductive risks, men have faced no such exclusions.

In 1991, the Supreme Court struck down a company's fetal protection policy in strong terms. The Court relied on amendments to the 1964 Civil Rights Act that provide for very few, narrow exceptions to the principle that unless some workers differ from others in their ability to work, they must be treated the same as other employees. "In other words," declared the majority, "women as capable of doing their jobs as their male counterparts may not be forced to choose between having a child and having a job."[46]

Political Equality for Women

With a few exceptions, women were not allowed to vote in this country until 1920. In 1869, Francis and Virginia Minor sued a St. Louis, Missouri, registrar for not allowing Virginia Minor to vote. In 1875, the Supreme Court held that the Fourteenth Amendment's privileges and immunities clause did not confer the right to vote on all citizens or require that the states allow women to vote.[47]

The decision clearly slowed the movement toward women's suffrage, but it did not stop it. In 1878, Susan B. Anthony, a women's rights activist, convinced a U.S. senator from California to introduce a constitutional amendment requiring that "the right of citizens of the United States to vote shall not be denied or abridged by the United States or by any State on account of sex." The amendment was introduced and voted down a number of times over the next twenty years. Meanwhile, as noted in Chapter 7, a number of states—primarily in the Midwest and West—did grant limited suffrage to women.

The movement for women's suffrage became a political battle to amend the Constitution. In 1917, police arrested 218 women from twenty-six states when they picketed the White House demanding the right to vote. Nearly one hundred went to jail, some for days, others for months. Hunger strikes and force feedings followed. The movement culminated in the adoption in 1920 of the **Nineteenth Amendment,** which gave women the right to vote. Its wording was that first suggested by Anthony.

Meanwhile, the Supreme Court continued to act as the benevolent protector of women. Women entered the work force in significant numbers during World War I and did so again during World War II, but they received lower wages than the men they replaced. Again, the justification was the "proper" role of women as mothers and homemakers. Because society expected men to be the principal providers, it followed that women's earnings were less important to the family's support. This thinking perpetuated inequalities in the workplace. Economic equality was closely tied to social attitudes. Because society expected women to stay at home, the assumption was that they needed less education than men. Therefore, they tended to qualify only for low-paying, low-skilled jobs with little chance for advancement.

Prohibiting Sex-Based Discrimination

The movement to provide equal rights to women advanced a step with the passage of the Equal Pay Act of 1963. That act requires equal pay for men and women doing similar work. However, state protectionist laws still had the effect of restricting women to jobs that men usually did not want. Where employment was stratified by sex, equal pay was an empty promise. To remove the restrictions of protectionism, women needed equal opportunity for employment. They got it in the Civil Rights Act of 1964 and later legislation.

The objective of the Civil Rights Act of 1964 was to eliminate racial discrimination in America. The original wording of Title VII of the act prohibited employment discrimination based on race, color, religion, and national origin—but not gender. In an effort to scuttle the provision during House debate, Democrat Howard W. Smith of Virginia proposed an amendment barring job discrimination based on sex. Smith's intention was to make the law unacceptable; his effort to ridicule the law brought gales of laughter to the debate. But Democrat Martha W. Griffiths of Michigan used Smith's strategy against him. With her support, Smith's amendment carried, as did the act.[48] Congress extended the jurisdiction of the EEOC to cover cases of invidious sex discrimination, or **sexism.**

Presidential authority also played a crucial role in the effort to eliminate sexism. In 1965, President Johnson issued an executive order that required federal contractors to take affirmative action in hiring and employment and to practice nondiscrimination with regard to race, color, religion, and national origin. Three years later, he amended the order to include gender as well. The result was new opportunity for women.

Subsequent women's rights legislation was motivated by the pressure for civil rights, as well as by a resurgence of the women's movement, which had subsided in 1920 after the adoption of the Nineteenth Amendment. One particularly important law was Title IX of the Education Amendments of 1972, which prohibited sex discrimination in federally aided education programs. Another boost to women came from the Revenue Act of 1972, which provided tax credits for child care expenses. In effect, the act subsidized parents with young children so that women could enter or remain in the work force. However, the high-water mark in the effort to secure women's rights was the Equal Rights Amendment, as we shall explain shortly.

Stereotypes Under Scrutiny

After nearly a century of protectionism, the Supreme Court began to take a closer look at gender-based distinctions. In 1971, it struck down a state law that gave men preference over women in administering the estate of a person who died without naming an administrator.[49] The state maintained that the law reduced court workloads and avoided family battles; however, the Court dismissed those objections, because they were not important enough to justify making gender-based distinctions between individuals. Two years later, the justices declared that paternalism operated to "put women not on a pedestal, but in a cage."[50] They then proceeded to strike down several gender-based laws that either prevented or discouraged departures from "proper" sex roles. In 1976, the Court finally developed a workable standard for reviewing such laws: gender-based distinctions are justifiable only if they serve some important government purpose.[51]

The objective of the standard is to dismantle laws based on sexual stereotypes while fashioning public policies that acknowledge relevant differences between men and women. Perhaps the most controversial issue is the idea of "comparable worth," which would require employers to pay comparable wages for different jobs, filled predominantly by one sex or the other, that are of about the same worth to the employer. Absent new legislation, the courts remain reluctant and ineffective vehicles for ending wage discrimination.[52]

The courts have not been reluctant to extend to women the *constitutional* guarantees won by blacks. In 1994, the Supreme Court extended the Constitution's equal protection guarantee by forbidding the exclusion of potential jurors on the basis of their sex. In a 6–3 decision, the justices held that gender, like race, is an unconstitutional proxy for juror competence and impartiality. "Discrimination in jury selection," wrote Justice Harry A. Blackmun for the majority, "whether based on race or on gender, causes harm to the litigants, the community, and the individual jurors who are wrongfully excluded from participation in the judicial process."[53] The 1994 decision completed a constitutional revolution in jury selection that began in 1986 with a bar against juror exclusions based on race.

In 1996, the Court spoke with uncommon clarity when it declared that the men-only admissions policy of the Virginia Military Institute (VMI), a state-supported military college, violated the equal protection clause of the Fourteenth Amendment. Virginia defended the school's policy on the ground that it was preserving diversity among America's educational institutions.

VMI employs a unique approach. All freshmen are "rats"; they receive miserable treatment for the first seven months of their college experience. Thereafter, their treatment changes in a highly structured class system. Eventually they enter the first or senior class, at which point they achieve the status of "dykes" and mentor rats. All rats are subject to minute regulation of their individual behavior, frequent punishments, and intense physical training comparable to Marine boot camp in its physical demands and mental stresses.

The lifestyle at VMI is special. All VMI cadets are subject to strict egalitarianism in dress and deportment. They live in barracks where privacy of any sort does not exist. The windows have no shades or curtains; all the doors have windows; no doors have locks. On the fourth (rat) floor, the group toilets and showers are observable by everyone and any floor. No other institution, including the military academies, places such emphasis on barracks life.

In an effort to meet women's demands to enter VMI—and to stave off continued legal challenges—Virginia established a separate-but-equal institution called the Virginia Women's Institute for Leadership (VWIL). The program was housed at Mary Baldwin College, a private liberal arts college for women.

Though Virginia agreed to pay for women enrolled in VWIL to the same degree it supports men enrolled in VMI, the two programs were decidedly unequal. In contrast to the "adversative" method used at VMI, VWIL depends on a cooperative method designed to reinforce students' self-esteem. VWIL students do not live together, take meals together, or wear uniforms.

The presence of women at VMI would require substantial changes in the physical environment and the traditional close scrutiny of the students. Moreover, the presence of women would, in itself, alter the manner in which "rats" and other cadets interacted socially. Is the uniqueness of VMI worth preserving at the expense of women who could otherwise meet the academic, physical, and psychological stress imposed by the VMI approach?

For a plain-text or formatted version of the opinion in *United States* v. *Virginia* (docket number 94-1941, decided 26 June 1996), go to `<www.law.cornell.edu/supct/supct.june.1996.html>`

In a 7–1 decision, the High Court voted no. Writing for a six-member majority in **United States v. Virginia**, Justice Ruth Bader Ginsburg applied a demanding test she labeled "skeptical scrutiny" to official acts that deny individuals rights or responsibilities based on their sex. "Parties who seek to defend gender-based government action," she wrote, "must demonstrate an 'exceedingly persuasive justification' for that action." Ginsburg declared that "women seeking and fit for a VMI-quality education cannot be offered anything less, under the State's obligation to afford them genuinely equal protection." Ginsburg went on to note that the VWIL program offered no cure for the "opportunities and advantages withheld from women who want a VMI education and can make the grade."[54] The upshot is that distinctions based on sex are almost as suspect as distinctions based on race.

Three months after the Court's decision, VMI's board of directors finally voted 9–8 to admit women. This ended VMI's distinction as the last government-supported single-sex school. However, school officials plan to make few allowances for women. Buzz haircuts and fitness requirements will remain the standard for all students. "It would be demeaning to women to cut them slack," declared VMI's superintendent.[55]

The Equal Rights Amendment

Policies protecting women, based largely on sexual stereotypes, have been woven into the legal fabric of American life. This protectionism has limited the freedom of women to compete with men socially and economically on an equal footing. However, the Supreme Court has been hesitant to extend the principles of the Fourteenth Amendment beyond issues of race. If constitutional interpretation imposes such a limit, then only a constitutional amendment can overcome it.

The National Women's Party, one of the few women's groups that did not disband after the Nineteenth Amendment was enacted, first introduced the proposed **Equal Rights Amendment (ERA)** in 1923. The ERA declared that "equality of rights under the law shall not be denied or abridged by the United States or any State on account of sex." It remained bottled up in committee in every Congress until 1970, when Representative Martha Griffiths filed a discharge petition to bring it to the House floor for a vote. The House passed the ERA, but the Senate scuttled it by attaching a section calling for prayer in the public schools.

A national coalition of women's rights advocates generated enough support to get the ERA through Congress in 1972. Its proponents then had seven years in which to get the amendment ratified by thirty-eight state legislatures, as required by the Constitution. By 1977, they were three states short of that goal, and three states had rescinded earlier ratification. Then, in an unprecedented action, Congress extended the ratification deadline. It didn't help. The ERA died in 1982, still three states short of adoption.

Why did the ERA fail? There are several explanations. Its proponents mounted a national campaign to generate approval, while its opponents organized state-based anti-ERA campaigns. ERA proponents hurt their cause by exaggerating the amendment's effects; such claims only gave ammunition to the amendment's opponents. For example, the puffed-up claim that the amendment would make wife and husband equally responsible for their family's financial support caused alarm among the undecided. As the opposition grew stronger, especially from women who wanted to maintain their traditional role, state legislators began to realize that supporting the amendment involved risk. Given the exaggerations and counterexaggerations, lawmakers ducked. It takes an extraordinary majority to amend the Constitution, which is equivalent to saying that it takes only a committed minority to thwart the majority's will.

Despite its failure, the movement to ratify the ERA produced real benefits. It raised the consciousness of women about their social position, it spurred the formation of the National Organization for Women (NOW) and other large organizations, it contributed to women's participation in politics, and it generated important legislation affecting women.[56]

The failure to ratify the ERA stands in stark contrast to the quick enactment of many laws that now protect women's rights. Such legislation had little audible opposition. If years of racial discrimination called for government redress, then so did years of gender-based discrimination. Furthermore, laws protecting women's rights required only the amending of civil rights bills or the enactment of similar bills.

Some scholars argue that, for practical purposes, the Supreme Court has implemented the equivalent of the ERA through its decisions. It has struck down distinctions based on sex and held that stereotyped generalizations about sexual differences must fall.[57] In recent rulings, the Court has held that states may require employers to guarantee job reinstatement to women taking a maternity leave, that sexual harassment in the workplace is illegal, and that a hostile work environment will be judged by a reasonable perception of abuse rather than a demonstration of psychological injury.[58]

But the Supreme Court can reverse its decisions, and legislators can repeal statutes. Without an equal rights amendment, argue some feminists, the Constitution will continue to bear the sexist imprint of a document written by men for men. Until the ERA becomes part of the Constitution, said veteran feminist Betty Friedan, "We are at the mercy of a Supreme Court that will interpret equality as it sees fit."[59]

AFFIRMATIVE ACTION: EQUAL OPPORTUNITY OR EQUAL OUTCOME?

In his vision of a Great Society, President Johnson linked economic rights with civil rights and equality of outcome with equality of opportunity. "Equal opportunity is essential, but not enough," he declared. "We seek not just legal equity but human ability. Not just equality as a right and a theory but equality as a fact and equality as a result."[60] This commitment led to affirmative action programs to expand opportunities for women, minorities, and the disabled.

Affirmative action, as we have seen, aims to overcome the effects of present and past discrimination. It embraces a range of public and private programs, policies, and procedures, including special recruitment, preferential treatment, and quotas in job training and professional education, employment, and the awarding of government contracts. The point of these programs is to move beyond equality of opportunity to equality of outcome.

Establishing numerical goals (such as designating a specific number of places in a law school for minority candidates or specifying that 10 percent of the work on a government contract must be subcontracted to minority-owned companies) is the most aggressive form of affirmative action, and it generates more debate and opposition than any other aspect of the civil rights movement. Advocates claim that such goal setting for college admissions, training programs, employment, and contracts will move minorities, women, and the disabled out of their second-class status. President Johnson explained why aggressive affirmative action was necessary:

You do not take a person who for years has been hobbled by chains, liberate him, bring him up to the starting line of a race, and then say, "You are free to compete with all the others," and still justly believe that you have been completely fair. Thus, it is not enough just to open the gates of opportunity; all our citizens must have the ability to walk through those gates.[61]

Arguments for affirmative action programs (from increased recruitment efforts to quotas) tend to use the following reasoning: certain groups have historically suffered invidious discrimination, denying them educational and economic opportunities. To eliminate the lasting effects of such discrimination, the public and private sectors must take steps to provide access to good education and jobs. If the majority once discriminated to hold groups back, discriminating to benefit those groups is fair. Therefore, quotas are a legitimate means to provide a place on the ladder to success.[62]

Affirmative action opponents maintain that quotas for designated groups necessarily create invidious discrimination (in the form of reverse discrimination) against individuals who are themselves blameless. Moreover, they say, quotas lead to admission, hiring, or promotion of the less qualified at the expense of the well qualified. In the name of equality, such policies thwart individuals' freedom to succeed.

Government-mandated preferential policies probably began in 1965 with the creation of the Office of Federal Contract Compliance. Its purpose was to ensure that all private enterprises doing business with the federal government complied with nondiscrimination guidelines. Because so many companies do business with the federal government, a large portion of the American economy became subject to these guidelines. In 1968, the guidelines required "goals and timetables for the prompt achievement of full and equal employment opportunity." By 1971, they called for employers to eliminate "underutilization" of minorities and women, which meant that employers had to hire minorities and women in proportion to the government's assessment of their availability.[63]

Preferential policies are seldom explicitly legislated. More often, such policies are the result of administrative regulations, judicial rulings, and initiatives in the private sector to provide a remedial response to specific discrimination or new legal standards of proof. Quotas or goals enable administrators to assess changes in hiring, promotion, and admissions policies. Racial quotas are an economic fact of life today. Employers engage in race-conscious preferential treatment to avoid litigation. Cast in value terms, equality trumps freedom. Do preferential policies in other nations offer lessons for us? See Compared with What? 16.1 to learn the answer.

Reverse Discrimination

The Supreme Court confronted an affirmative action quota program for the first time in ***Regents of the University of California*** v. ***Bakke.***[64] Allan Bakke, a thirty-five-year-old white man, had twice applied for admission to the University of California Medical School at Davis. He was rejected both times. The school had reserved sixteen places in each entering class of one hundred for qualified minority applicants, as part of the university's affirmative action program, in an effort to redress long-standing and unfair exclusion of minorities from the medical profession. Bakke's qualifica-

● ● ● ● ● ● ● ● ● ● ● ● ●
Affirmative Action Baby

Dr. Patrick Chavis is an obstetrician-gynecologist serving the poor in the Los Angeles suburb of Compton. Chavis was the beneficiary of a special minorities-only affirmative action program at the University of California Medical School at Davis. Chavis and four other African-Americans were admitted to the program in 1973. Allan Bakke, a white applicant with better grades and test scores, was not admitted. He sued the medical school for discriminating against him on the basis of his race. To some people, racial preferences are a great injustice. To others, racial preferences are an opening to a world of opportunity otherwise foreclosed on account of race.

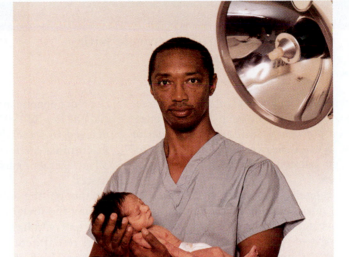

Listen to the announcement of the judgment and opinions in the *Bakke* case.

`<oyez.at.nwu.edu/cases/76-811>`

tions (college grade point average and test scores) exceeded those of all of the minority students admitted in the two years his applications were rejected. Bakke contended, first in the California courts, then in the Supreme Court, that he was excluded from admission solely on the basis of race. He argued that the equal protection clause of the Fourteenth Amendment and the Civil Rights Act of 1964 prohibited this reverse discrimination.

The Court's decision in *Bakke* contained six opinions and spanned 154 pages. But even after careful analysis of the decision, discerning what the Court had decided was difficult: no opinion had a majority. One bloc of four justices opposed the medical school's plan, contending that any racial quota system endorsed by the government violated the Civil Rights Act of 1964. A second bloc of four justices supported the plan, arguing that the government may use a racial classification scheme, provided it does not demean or insult any racial group and only to remedy the disadvantages imposed on minorities by racial prejudice. Justice Lewis F. Powell, Jr., agreed with parts of both arguments. With the first bloc, he argued that the school's rigid use of racial quotas violated the equal protection clause of the Fourteenth Amendment. With the second bloc, he contended that the use of race was permissible as one of several admissions criteria. Powell cast the deciding vote ordering the medical school to admit Bakke. Despite the confusing multiple opinions, the Court signaled its approval of affirmative action programs in education that use race as a *plus* factor (one of

16.1   How Other Nations Struggle with Affirmative Action

Americans are not alone in their disagreements over affirmative action. Controversies, and even bloodshed, have been the order of the day in countries where certain groups receive government-sanctioned preferences over others.

India, Sri Lanka, Malaysia, Nigeria, Australia, and Canada are among the nations with affirmative action policies of their own. The phraseology of these policies may differ somewhat from the American model. Although Australia and Canada use the American label *affirmative action*, India refers to its policy as *positive discrimination*. Nigeria's preferential policy is designed to "reflect the federal character of the country." In Malaysia, the constitution recognizes the "special position" of the Malays (the dominant group) and reserves a share of public benefits (including government jobs, educational scholarships, and land) for them.

The particular problems created by the affirmative action policy in India recently claimed international attention. The untouchables, a pariah group, have long been the chief beneficiary of the nation's preferential policies. In 1990, the government of India decided to strengthen its policy of positive discrimination by reserving more than half of all government jobs for members of the lower castes.

Although the job quotas proved popular among the lower castes, who make up well over half of India's population, they generated deep resentment among the higher castes. Students from the higher castes have traditionally viewed government jobs as a way to secure their middle-class expectations. The new ruling made government jobs much more difficult for them to obtain. Regardless of their academic success, many high-caste students will be passed over for government jobs. In a singularly gruesome form of protest, scores of young upper-caste men and women have set themselves ablaze. And when the Indian courts issued a temporary injunction that halted the government's affirmative action plan, terrorists who supported the plan protested by bombing a train, killing dozens of people. Tension is likely to remain high in

many such factors) but not as *the* factor (one that alone determines the outcome). Thus, the Court managed to minimize white opposition to the goal of equality (by finding for Bakke) while extending gains for racial minorities through affirmative action.

Although the Court sent a mixed message, *Bakke* may have achieved tangible benefits. The number of minority physicians in the United States doubled in the decade after the decision. Moreover, minority physicians tended to relocate to areas that had critical health care shortages. They also tended to serve significantly larger proportions of poor patients, regardless of race or ethnicity.[65]

Other cases followed. In 1979, the Court upheld a voluntary affirmative action plan that gave preferences to blacks in an employee training program.[66] Five years later, however, the Court held that affirmative action did not exempt minorities (typically the most recently hired employees) from traditional work rules, which generally specify that the last hired are

Indian society, given the country's ancient caste hierarchy and an economy that is not expanding rapidly enough to satisfy every interest.

One recent study of preferential policies has aimed to generalize from the experiences of many nations. The cultures, politics, and economies of nations with preferential policies vary enormously. The groups benefiting from these policies also vary; they may be locally or nationally dominant, or they may be poor and relatively powerless politically.

Despite these variables, nations with affirmative action policies seem to share some common patterns. First, although often defined as temporary, preferential policies tend to persist and even expand to embrace more individuals and groups. Second, benefits tend to flow disproportionately to members of recipient groups who are already more fortunate. Third, antagonism among groups tends to increase in the wake of the implementation of preferential policies. The reactions of groups that do not benefit from such policies range from a change in voting behavior to violence, even civil war. And fourth, false claims of membership in designated beneficiary groups increase.

These observations have implications for majoritarian and pluralist models of democracy. All governments broker conflict in varying degrees. Under a majoritarian model, group demands could lead quickly to conflict and instability, because majority rule leaves little room for compromise. A pluralist model allows different groups to get a piece of the pie. By parceling out benefits, pluralism mitigates disorder in the short term. But in the long term, repeated demands for increased benefits can spark instability. A vigorous pluralist system should provide acceptable mechanisms (legislative, executive, bureaucratic, judicial) to vent such frustrations and yield a new allocation of benefits.

Sources: Donald L. Horowitz, *Ethnic Groups in Conflict* (Berkeley: University of California Press, 1985); *Facts on File*, 19 October 1990, pp. 784–785; Edward W. Desmond, "Fatal Fires of Protest," *Time*, 15 October 1990, p. 63; and Thomas Sowell, *Race and Culture: A World View* (New York: Basic Books, 1994).

the first fired. Layoffs must proceed by seniority, declared the Court, unless minority employees can demonstrate that they are actually victims of discrimination.[67]

Sexism can cut both ways, against both women and men. Overcoming sexism may inadvertently create invidious discrimination against men. In 1974, the transportation agency of Santa Clara, California, promoted Diane Joyce to the position of road dispatcher over Paul Johnson. Both candidates were qualified for the job. The agency took into account the sex of the applicants in making the promotion decision. Because none of the employees at the level of dispatcher were women, the agency decided to give the job to Joyce. Johnson claimed that the agency impermissibly took into account the sex of the applicants, in violation of Title VII of the Civil Rights Act of 1964, which declares that employers cannot "limit, segregate or classify" workers so as to deprive "any individual of employment opportunities."

Go to this site to hear the Supreme Court oral argument in the *Adarand* case.
`<oyez.at.nwu.edu/cases/93-1841>`

● ● ● ● ● ● ● ● ● ● ●

Right Remedied

Cheryl Hopwood and others challenged preferential admissions policies at the University of Texas Law School. Hopwood's victory cast doubt on the viability of other government-sponsored preference policies.

In a 6–3 vote, the Supreme Court affirmed the promotion procedures in 1987. Writing for the majority in **Johnson v. Transportation Agency, Santa Clara County,** Justice William J. Brennan, Jr., argued that in light of *Bakke* it was not unreasonable to consider sex as one factor among many in making promotion decisions. Moreover, the agency's actions did not create an absolute barrier to the advancement of men.[68]

The most crippling jolt to some forms of affirmative action came in 1995. The Supreme Court struck a sharp blow to the legal foundations of government policies that award benefits on the basis of race, signaling an end to equal outcomes policies. Recall Randy Pech's lawsuit challenging a government set-aside program for minority contractors. Writing for a 5–4 majority in **Adarand Constructors v. Peña,** Justice Sandra Day O'Connor declared that such programs must be subject to the most searching judicial inquiry (what the Court calls "strict scrutiny") and must be "narrowly tailored" to achieve a "compelling government interest."[69] Few, if any, programs can satisfy the Court's stringent requirements for constitutionality. (The Court sent the case back to the trial court so that it could evaluate the facts in light of the "strict scrutiny" approach.) The decision casts doubt on more than $14 billion in government contracts earmarked for minority- or women-owned firms.[70]

Quota policies are now under serious threat from several quarters. In 1996, a federal appeals court, relying on the *Adarand* case, rejected the use of race or ethnicity as the determining factor in law school admissions. (In the absence of race-based criteria, few minorities would have been admitted.) Although the ruling addressed the admissions policy at the University of Texas Law School, it stunned universities nationwide that had similar programs.[71] Texas appealed the adverse decision to the Supreme Court, but the Court declined to grant review. For Texas, and for other schools in the region, minority-based admissions policies are over. Other educational institutions will remain perplexed regarding the limits of preferential policies based on race, national origin, and sex until the Supreme Court speaks with a clearer voice.[72]

Meanwhile, the governing board of the University of California has voted to scrap its race-based admissions policy. And legislative movements in more than a dozen states aim to curtail or eliminate racial preferences in educational admissions and financial aid. Colorado, for example, has begun to offer college scholarships on the basis of need rather than race.[73]

The biggest showdown to date regarding the future of affirmative action occurred during the 1996 elections. California voters were asked to approve or reject a ballot initiative to amend the state constitution as follows:

> Neither the State of California, nor any of its political subdivisions or agents, shall use race, sex, color, ethnicity or national origin as a criterion for either discriminating against, or granting preferential treatment to, any individual or group in the operation of the State's system of public employment, public education or public contracting.

The initiative had implications for the 1996 presidential race as well. President Clinton continued to support race- and gender-based preferences in hiring and admissions policies ("Mend them, don't end them," he averred). Clinton's opposition to the initiative did not jeopardize his popularity, however. He carried the state with 51 percent of the vote, while the initiative passed with 54 percent of the vote. Initiative opponents seem undeterred, vowing to take the matter to court.

The Politics of Affirmative Action

A comprehensive review of nationwide surveys conducted over the past twenty years reveals an unsurprising truth: that blacks favor affirmative action programs and whites do not. Women and men do not differ on this issue. The gulf between the races was wider in the 1970s than it is today, but the moderation results from shifts among blacks, not whites. Perhaps the most important finding is that "whites' views have remained essentially unchanged over 20 years."[74]

How do we account for the persistence of equal outcomes policies? A majority of Americans have consistently rejected explicit race or gender preferences for the awarding of contracts, employment decisions, and college admissions, regardless of the groups such preferences benefit. Nevertheless, preference policies have survived and thrived under both Democrats and Republicans, because they are attractive. They encourage unprotected groups to strive for inclusion. The list of protected groups has expanded beyond African Americans to include Hispanic Americans, Native Americans, Asian Pacific Americans, Subcontinental Asian Americans, and women. Politicians have a powerful motive—votes—to expand the number of protected groups and the benefits such policies provide.

Recall that affirmative action programs began as temporary measures, ensuring a "jump start" for minorities shackled by decades or centuries of invidious discrimination. For example, forty years ago minority racial identity was a fatal flaw on a medical or law school application. Today it is viewed as an advantage and sometimes a sure bet, encouraging applicants to think in minority-group terms. Thinking in group terms and conferring benefits on such ground generates hostility from the majority, who see the deck stacked against them for no other reason than their race. It is not surprising that affirmative action has become controversial, since many Americans view it as a violation of their individual freedom.

Recall Lyndon Johnson's justification for equal outcomes policies. Though free to compete, a person once hobbled by chains cannot run a fair race. Americans are willing to do more than remove the chains. They will support special training and financial assistance for those who were previously shackled. The hope is that such efforts will enable once-shackled runners to catch up with those who have forged ahead. But Americans stop short at endorsing equal outcomes policies, because they predetermine the results of the race.[75]

The conflict between freedom and equality will continue as other individuals and groups press their demands through litigation and legislation. The choice the country makes will depend on whether and to what extent Americans are prepared to change their minds on these thorny issues, questions we explore in Politics in a Changing America 16.1.

● politics in a changing america

16.1   Do Americans Change Their Minds on Racial Equality?

Many Americans express only a qualified or conflicted commitment to racial equality. This is not surprising, given the cluster of values and concerns raised by race-related issues, from affirmative action to welfare dependency. Yet it is not customary to think of white Americans as pliable when it comes to racial issues.

Social scientists Paul Sniderman and Thomas Piazza have examined the extent to which white Americans' beliefs about race are conditional or contingent. To test their commitment or opposition to racial equality, Sniderman and Piazza developed an ingenious strategy to measure *pliability:* the degree to which people can be dislodged from positions they have taken by directly calling their attention to a counterargument.

In a 1986 random telephone poll of adults in the San Francisco Bay area, Sniderman and Piazza obtained data on support for various racial policies before and after they introduced counterarguments in an attempt to change their respondents' minds.

The four pairs of pie charts contrast two situations: the left side shows responses when no pressure on either side of the issue was exerted, and the right side shows responses when arguments on both sides of the issue were presented. In the unpressured condition, three of the four policies generated liberal majorities; only one policy drew a conservative majority. After presenting arguments for and against each policy, some majorities shifted, while others remained the same.

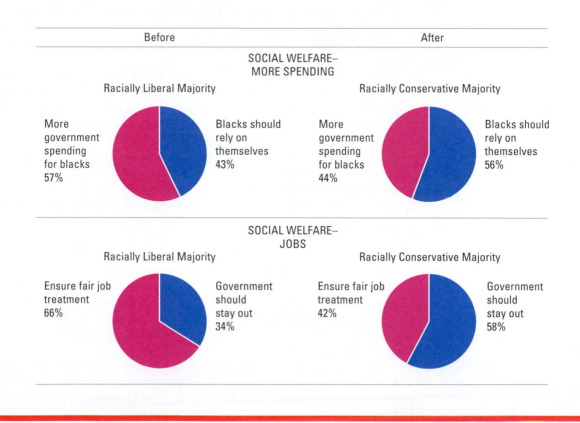

Before	After

SOCIAL WELFARE—MORE SPENDING

Racially Liberal Majority — More government spending for blacks 57% / Blacks should rely on themselves 43%

Racially Conservative Majority — More government spending for blacks 44% / Blacks should rely on themselves 56%

SOCIAL WELFARE—JOBS

Racially Liberal Majority — Ensure fair job treatment 66% / Government should stay out 34%

Racially Conservative Majority — Ensure fair job treatment 42% / Government should stay out 58%

- On the issues of more government spending for blacks and government assurance of fair treatment in employment for blacks, racially liberal majorities switched to racially conservative majorities following the introduction of arguments to persuade respondents on both sides of the issue.

- In contrast, an initial liberal majority on fair housing was unmoved by counterarguments on both sides. And an initial conservative majority opposed to racial quotas in college admissions remained a majority (though somewhat smaller) when confronted with counterarguments on both sides.

The results suggest that a current liberal majority favoring government activism to assist blacks harbors within it a countermajority that is more likely to emerge as advocates articulate strong arguments both for and against social welfare assistance and fair job treatment for blacks. When equality and freedom conflict in these areas, freedom-preferring arguments appear more persuasive than equality-preferring arguments.

Source: Paul M. Sniderman and Thomas Piazza, *The Scar of Race* (Cambridge, Mass.: Harvard University Press, 1993). Copyright © 1993 by the president and fellows of Harvard College. Reprinted by permission of the publisher.

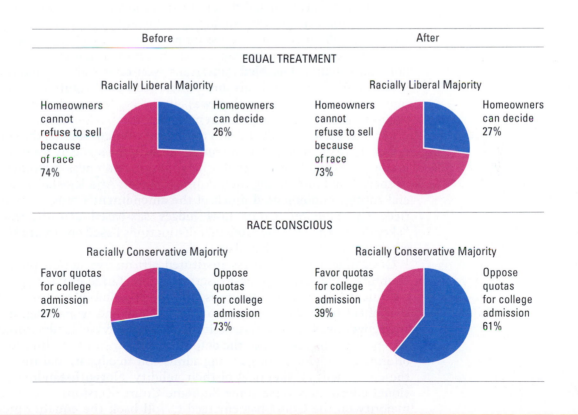

Before	After

EQUAL TREATMENT

Racially Liberal Majority

Homeowners cannot refuse to sell because of race 74% — Homeowners can decide 26%

Racially Liberal Majority

Homeowners cannot refuse to sell because of race 73% — Homeowners can decide 27%

RACE CONSCIOUS

Racially Conservative Majority

Favor quotas for college admission 27% — Oppose quotas for college admission 73%

Racially Conservative Majority

Favor quotas for college admission 39% — Oppose quotas for college admission 61%

SUMMARY

Using the "Voters" data in the CROSSTABS program, analyze issue variables (e.g., affirmative action, women's role, equal rights) by ideological orientation. Do value preferences match policy positions?

Americans want equality, but they disagree on the extent to which government should guarantee it. At the heart of this conflict is the distinction between equal opportunities and equal outcomes.

Congress enacted the Civil War amendments—the Thirteenth, Fourteenth, and Fifteenth Amendments—to provide full civil rights to black Americans. In the late nineteenth century, however, the Supreme Court interpreted the amendments very narrowly, declaring that they did not restrain individuals from denying civil rights to blacks and that they did not apply to powers reserved for the states. The Court's rulings had the effect of denying the vote to most blacks and of institutionalizing racism, making racial segregation a fact of daily life.

Through a series of court cases spanning two decades, the Court slowly dismantled segregation in the schools. The battle for desegregation culminated in the *Brown* cases in 1954 and 1955, in which a now-supportive Supreme Court declared segregated schools to be inherently unequal and therefore unconstitutional. The Court also ordered the desegregation of all schools and upheld the use of busing to do so.

Gains in other spheres of civil rights came more slowly. The motivating force was the civil rights movement, led by Martin Luther King, Jr., until his assassination in 1968. King believed strongly in civil disobedience and nonviolence, strategies that helped secure for blacks equality in voting rights, public accommodations, higher education, housing, and employment opportunity.

Civil rights activism and the civil rights movement worked to the benefit of all minority groups—in fact, they benefited all Americans. Native Americans obtained some redress for past injustices. Hispanic Americans came to recognize the importance of group action to achieve economic and political equality. Disabled Americans won civil rights protections enjoyed by African Americans and others. And civil rights legislation removed the protectionism that was, in effect, legalized discrimination against women in education and employment.

Despite legislative advances in the area of women's rights, the states did not ratify the Equal Rights Amendment. Still, the struggle for ratification produced several positive results, heightening awareness of women's roles in society and mobilizing their political power. And legislation and judicial rulings implemented much of the amendment's provisions in practice. The Supreme Court now judges sex-based classification with "skeptical scrutiny," meaning that distinctions based on sex are almost as suspect as distinctions based on race.

Government and business instituted affirmative action programs to counteract the results of past discrimination. These provide preferential treatment for women, minorities, and the disabled in a number of areas that affect individuals' economic opportunity and well-being. In effect, such government programs discriminate to remedy earlier discrimination. When programs make race the determining factor in awarding contracts, offering employment, or granting admission to educational institutions, the courts will be skeptical of their validity. Notwithstanding congressional efforts to reverse some Supreme Court decisions, a conservative majority on the Court has emerged to roll back the equality-preferring policies of the more liberal bench that held sway through the 1980s.

We can guarantee equal outcomes only if we restrict the free competition that is an integral part of equal opportunity. Many Americans object to policies that restrict individual freedom, such as quotas and set-asides that arbitrarily change the outcome of the race. The challenge of pluralist democracy is to balance the need for freedom with demands for equality.

Key Terms

affirmative action	racism	*de jure* segregation	Nineteenth Amendment
equality of opportunity	poll tax	*de facto* segregation	sexism
equality of outcome	racial segregation	civil rights movement	Equal Rights Amendment
invidious discrimination	separate-but-equal	boycott	(ERA)
civil rights	doctrine	civil disobedience	
black codes	desegregation	protectionism	

Key Cases

Plessy v. *Ferguson*
Brown v. *Board of Education*
Brown v. *Board of Education II*

United States v. *Virginia*
Regents of the University of California v. *Bakke*

Johnson v. *Transportation Agency, Santa Clara County*

Adarand Constructors v. *Peña*

Selected Readings

Berger, Raoul. *Government by Judiciary: The Transformation of the Fourteenth Amendment.* Cambridge, Mass.: Harvard University Press, 1977. This provocative work argues that the framers of the Fourteenth Amendment had narrow aims and that the Supreme Court, especially since 1954, has disregarded this historical legacy in its promotion of freedom and equality.

Branch, Taylor. *Parting the Waters: America in the King Years, 1954–1963.* New York: Simon & Schuster, 1988. A riveting, Pulitzer Prize–winning narrative history and biography of the King years.

Browning, Rufus P., Dale Rogers Marshall, and David H. Tabb. *Racial Politics in American Cities.* New York: Longman, 1990. This collection of essays documents the continuing struggle for minority access to political power in cities across the United States.

Lyons, Oren, et al. *Exiled in the Land of the Free: Democracy, Indian Nations, and the U.S. Constitution.* Santa Fe, N.M.: Clear Light, 1992. A collection of essays exploring the relationship of Indians to the Consti-

tution, how Indian traditions influenced the Constitution's creation, and how constitutional interpretation has affected Indian lives.

Mansbridge, Jane J. *Why We Lost the ERA.* Chicago: University of Chicago Press, 1986. A valuable study of organizations pitted for and against the Equal Rights Amendment in Illinois.

Sniderman, Paul M., and Thomas Piazza. *The Scar of Race.* Cambridge, Mass.: Belknap Press of Harvard University Press, 1993. The authors of this insightful study argue that the problems of race cannot be reduced to racism. On many racial issues, white Americans are open to argument and persuasion, even though they disagree on racial policies.

Verba, Sidney, and Gary R. Orren. *Equality in America: The View From the Top.* Cambridge, Mass.: Harvard University Press, 1985. Two political scientists isolate different meanings of equality, then analyze the opinions of American leaders on the application of equality of opportunity and equality of outcome across a range of policy areas.

World Wide Web Resources

Americans with Disabilities Act (ADA) Document Center. Everything you might wish to know about the ADA and its application to a long list of issues.

`<janweb.icdi.wvu.edu/kinder/>`

Native American Resources. A wealth of links to issues related to native peoples.

`<www.cowboy.net/native/>`

Latinoweb. A fine source for content links addressing the concerns of Spanish-speaking people.

`<www.latinoweb.com/favision/resource.htm>`

Asian American Resources. A good source for links to other relevant sites.

`<www.mit.edu:8001/afs/athena.mit.edu/user/i/r/irie/www/aar.html>`

Universal Black Pages. This site is a comprehensive source of information related to the black experience.

`<www.gatech.edu/bgsa/blackpages.html>`

The National Organization for Women (NOW) Home Page. A very useful home page that provides access to NOW policy statements, press releases, and research, as well as links to women's resources on the Internet.

`<www.now.org/>`

part

VI

Making Public Policy

17

Policymaking

KIMBER REYNOLDS RETURNED HOME to Fresno, California, from her fashion design college to take part in a friend's wedding. She was walking out of a trendy restaurant after meeting a friend for dessert when two men on motorcycles stopped her on the way to her car. One man grabbed her purse; Reynolds grabbed it back. The man put a .357 Magnum in her ear and shot her to death.

The Fresno police quickly identified two suspects. The gunman, Joe Davis, died in a shoot-out when the police tried to apprehend him. The other, Doug Walker, was captured and pleaded guilty as an accessory to the crime. He was sentenced to nine years in prison.

Both Davis and Walker had recently been paroled from prison. When Reynolds's father, Mike, a wedding photographer, found out that with "good behavior" Walker could again be paroled after serving less than half of his sentence, he knew he had to do something.

After meeting with some judges and attorneys he knew, Mike Reynolds launched a campaign to put a "three strikes and you're out" initiative on the state ballot. The measure required that anyone convicted of a third serious crime be sentenced to a minimum of twenty-five years in prison. Fed up with violent crime, Californians responded enthusiastically to Reynolds's crusade. "Three strikes" has a gut-level appeal to people, because its intent is to take career criminals off the street and put them in prison until they die or become too old to be much of a threat.

Caught off guard by an issue that seemed to have sprung from nowhere, state legislators rushed to introduce legislation that would accomplish much the same goals as Reynolds's initiative. In March 1994, a three strikes bill passed the California legislature and was signed into law. Reynolds pressed on with the ballot initiative, however, because in his mind he had made a promise to his deceased daughter to see the ballot fight through. That November, 72 percent of California voters cast ballots in favor of the referendum, giving the state its second three strikes law. "I think this is a promise kept," Reynolds told the press after the vote.[1]

Three strikes won overwhelming support despite the fact that many judges, district attorneys, and criminologists thought such a law was a bad idea. Their concerns were that it would overwhelm prison capacity and reduce repeat offenders' incentive to plea bargain, thus increasing the need for time-consuming and expensive trials. Their concerns were well founded: a year after three strikes was passed, for the first time in its history, the state of California budgeted more for its prisons than for its

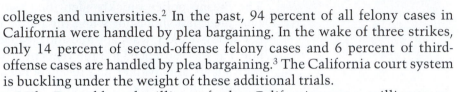

● ● ● ● ● ● ● ● ● ●

A Death, Then Outrage

After Kimber Reynolds (left) was brutally murdered, her father was grief-stricken. Reminiscing about her childhood, Mike Reynolds described her as his "little buddy." His grief turned to political advocacy, however, and "three strikes and you're out" is now law in California. Ironically, three strikes would not necessarily have kept Kimber's murderer, Joe Davis (middle), off the streets prior to his assault on her. Davis had only two prior felonies before he shot her to death. Doug Walker (right) was convicted as an accessory and sentenced to nine years in prison.

California's Legislative Analyst's Office monitors the effects of the state's "three strikes" law.
`<www.lao.ca.gov/3strikes.html>`

colleges and universities.[2] In the past, 94 percent of all felony cases in California were handled by plea bargaining. In the wake of three strikes, only 14 percent of second-offense felony cases and 6 percent of third-offense cases are handled by plea bargaining.[3] The California court system is buckling under the weight of these additional trials.

Mike Reynolds and millions of other Californians were willing to endure these additional costs and problems because they were sick of revolving-door justice, in which violent criminals are paroled after they have served only part of their sentences. Before three strikes, nearly 60 percent of California parolees were back in prison within just two years. A year after three strikes, crime was down in California, though the reasons are surely more complex than just the mandatory sentencing under the new law. After a year of three strikes, five thousand second-strike defendants were convicted and sentenced to terms twice as long as they would likely have served before. One hundred and fifty third-strike defendants were convicted and received sentences of twenty-five years to life.[4]

Mike Reynolds and the volunteers he attracted to this cause put the issue of repeat offenders and revolving-door justice on California's political agenda. In turn, California's size and visibility worked to put three strikes on the national agenda. Other states took up the issue, and President Clinton endorsed three strikes as part of a national crime package enacted in 1994. (However, most violent crimes are prosecuted under state, not federal, law.)

In this case, an issue arose because of a gruesome homicide and because a political activist effectively capitalized on the anger of other citizens. But how do issues usually reach the political agenda? And what happens to them once they are there? Previous chapters have focused on individual institutions of government. Here we focus on government more broadly and ask how policymaking takes place across institutions. We first identify different types of public policies and then analyze the stages in the policymaking process. Because different institutions and different levels of government (national, state, and local) frequently work on the same issues, policymaking is often fragmented. How can better coordination be achieved? We then turn from the general to the specific by focusing on one policy area: telecommunications. In particular, we will examine how policy is made when many competing interest groups are trying to influence the outcome and how the relationships between those groups, and between such groups and different parts of government, structure the policymaking process.

GOVERNMENT PURPOSES AND PUBLIC POLICIES

In Chapter 1, we noted that virtually all citizens are willing to accept limitations on their personal freedom in return for various benefits of government. We defined the major purposes of government as maintaining order, providing public benefits, and promoting equality. Different governments place different values on each broad purpose, and those differences are reflected in their public policies. A **public policy** is a general plan of action adopted by a government to solve a social problem, counter a threat, or pursue an objective.

At times, governments choose not to adopt a new policy to deal with a troublesome situation; instead, they just "muddle through," hoping the problem will go away or diminish in importance. This, too, is a policy decision, because it amounts to choosing to maintain the status quo. Sometimes government policies are carefully developed and effective. Sometimes they are hastily drawn and ineffective, even counterproductive. But careful planning is no predictor of success. Well-constructed policies may result in total disaster, and quick fixes may work just fine.

Whatever their form and effectiveness, however, all policies have this in common: they are the means by which government pursues certain goals in specific situations. People disagree about public policies because they disagree about one or more of the following elements: the goals government should have, the means it should use to meet them, and how the situation at hand should be perceived.

How do policymakers attempt to achieve their goals? As a starting point, we will divide all government approaches to solving problems into four broad types: we can analyze public policies according to whether they prohibit, protect, promote, or provide.

Some policies are intended to prohibit behaviors that endanger society. All governments outlaw murder, robbery, and rape. Governments that emphasize order tend to favor policies of prohibition, which instruct people in what they must not do (drink liquor, have abortions, use illegal drugs).

Government policies can also protect certain activities, business markets, or special groups of citizens. For example, taxes were once levied on colored margarine (a butter substitute) to reduce its sales and protect the dairy industry from competition. Regulations concerning the testing of new drugs are intended to protect citizens from harmful side effects; government rules about safety in the workplace are enacted to protect workers. Although governments argue that these kinds of regulations serve the public good, some people believe that most protective legislation is unwarranted government interference.

Policies can also promote social activities that are important to the government. One way that government promotes is by persuasion. For instance, our government has used advertising to urge people to buy bonds or to join the army. When policymakers really want to accomplish a goal they have set, they can be quite generous. To promote railroad construction in the 1860s, Congress granted railroad companies huge tracts of public land as rights-of-way through western states.

Citizens for Tax Justice
identifies tax expenditures.
<www.ctj.org/hid_ent/
contents/content.htm>

The government also promotes activities through favorable treatment within the tax structure. Because it amounts to a loss of government revenue, the technical term for this form of government promotion is *tax expenditure.* For example, the government encourages people to buy their own home by allowing them to deduct the interest they pay on their mortgage from their taxable income. In 1995, this tax expenditure cost the national government nearly $51 billion.[5] And of course, churches and private educational institutions typically pay no property taxes to state and local governments.

Finally, public policies can provide benefits directly to citizens, either collectively or selectively. Collective benefits are facilities or services that all residents share (mail service, roads, schools, street lighting, libraries, parks). Selective benefits go to certain groups of citizens (poor people, farmers, veterans, college students). Collective benefits can be difficult to deliver, because they require either the construction of facilities (roads, dams, sewer systems) or the creation of organizations (transportation agencies, power companies, sanitation departments) to provide them. Many selective benefits are simply payments to individuals in the form of food stamps, subsidies, pensions, and loans. The payments are made because the recipients are particularly needy or powerful, or both.

In sum, the notion of policy is a many-splendored thing. Government has many different means at its disposal for pursuing particular goals. Those means and goals, in turn, are shaped by the specific situations that surround a problem at the time. Policies aimed at specific problems are not static; means, goals, and situations change.

THE POLICYMAKING PROCESS

We distinguish government policies according to their approach not simply to create an inventory of problem-solving methods but also to emphasize the relationship between policy and process. By *process* we mean the configuration of participants involved, the procedures used for decision making, and the degree of cooperation or conflict usually present. The premise is simple: different kinds of policies affect the political process in different ways.

The Effect of Policy

One basic reason for the various policymaking processes is that different approaches to public policy affect people in different ways. If a policy proposal affects a well-organized constituency adversely, that constituency will fight it aggressively. When Secretary of the Interior Bruce Babbitt proposed legislation to raise fees on the use of federal land for grazing, western ranchers who wanted to maintain the relatively low rates they were paying resisted bitterly. (Ostensibly, the existing policy was a tax expenditure aimed at promoting the beef industry. However, in Babbitt's eyes, the industry did not need promotion and the policy was little more than a way to provide direct benefits to ranchers.) The ranchers' anger led sympathetic senators to successfully filibuster the proposal, but Babbitt announced plans to put it into effect anyway, through his administrative powers.[6]

Other policies pit well-organized groups against one another. Action for Children's Television and other organizations promoting children's educational programming have long pressured the Federal Communications Commission (FCC) to require broadcasters to air more high-quality shows for young viewers. The National Association for Broadcasters, representing 1,400 local TV stations, fought against such rules. The broadcasters wanted the freedom to put on the kind of programming that they feel works best for their individual stations. It was a protracted fight, but after the Clinton White House pressured the broadcasters, a compromise was reached that requires each TV station to show three hours of regularly scheduled children's programming each week.[7]

Whether a policy is intended to prohibit, protect, promote, or provide does not fully predict the level of public involvement it will generate, the degree to which it will mobilize affected constituencies, or the degree of competition it will spark between organizations working on different sides of the same issue. But by being aware of the kind of approach the government proposes to take on an issue, we can begin to understand which factors are going to influence policymaking. If a well-entrenched set of interest groups is ready to fight a policy that would prohibit one activity, a solution emphasizing promotion of another, countervailing activity might be more feasible politically.

A government may use more than one approach to a problem, not only because some alternatives engender less opposition than others but also because public policy problems can be quite complex. One approach will not always ameliorate all manifestations of a problem. Let us return to the subject of career criminals. Even the most ardent backers of three strikes laws do not pretend that they will completely stop paroled convicts from committing additional crimes. Shouldn't we have counseling and job training for those convicted of a single crime? How about youthful offenders who might be saved by combining education with punishment? Boot camps might work for them. But why wait for a first crime to be committed? At-risk populations must receive needed support from social service agencies if we are to minimize the problems associated with broken homes and poverty. And can any progress really be made against repeat offenders when so much crime is associated with drugs? Getting people off drugs and into treatment programs has to be part of any serious effort to reduce the crime problem in America. Different communities and states vary widely in how they have approached crime, and sharp differences are evident among nations as well (see Compared with What? 17.1).

When officials have a choice in how to address a problem, they consider how each approach would affect policymaking. Is the best approach one that is likely to generate a lot of conflict between opposing groups? If so, will it be possible to enact a new policy, or is the conflict likely to scuttle new proposals, leaving the status quo intact? In short, when policymakers weigh new policy options, they carefully consider the effect of each approach on those most directly affected.

More controversial than three strikes is the death penalty. How did your position compare to that of the American population in the IDEAlog program?

compared with what?

17.1   Japan: Shame on Crime

There may be crime everywhere, but there's certainly not the same amount of crime everywhere. Comparative statistics on incarceration shows vast differences between countries. Particularly striking is Japan, which has an extremely low crime rate and has only thirty-seven people in prison per one hundred thousand residents. Analysts cite a number of reasons. Japan bans handguns, and in a recent, typical year there were only thirty-eight murders nationwide. More people are shot each *day* in the United States. Japanese prisons are particularly odious. The cells are tiny cubicles, and many prisoners are forbidden to speak. The Japanese police force is unusually effective and solves 37 percent of

crimes, compared to just 20 percent in the United States.

Probably the most important factor, though, is the shame associated with crime. In Japan, a convicted criminal is subject to severe ostracism. Someone who commits a serious crime, such as murder, is likely to be disowned by his family, who may refuse to see him even after his release from prison. Japan is a society that clearly values order, and those who violate the strong taboo against criminal activity are judged harshly and isolated.

Source: Nicholas Kristof, "Japanese Say No to Crime: Tough Methods at a Price," *New York Times,* 14 May 1995, p. 1.

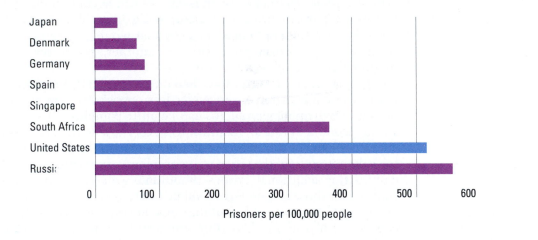

Prisoners per 100,000 people

A Policymaking Model

Clearly, different approaches to solving policy problems affect the policymaking process, but common patterns do underlie most processes. Political scientists have produced many models of the policymaking process to distinguish the different types of policy, such as our framework of policies that prohibit, protect, promote, or provide. They also distinguish different stages of the policymaking process and try to identify patterns in the way people attempt to influence decisions and in the way decisions are reached.

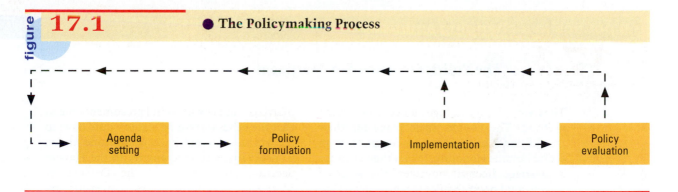

figure 17.1 ● **The Policymaking Process**

This model, one of many possible ways to depict the policymaking process, shows four policymaking stages. Feedback on program operations and performance from the last two stages stimulates new cycles of the process.

We can separate the policymaking process into four stages: agenda setting, policy formulation, implementation, and policy evaluation.[8] Figure 17.1 shows the four stages in sequence. Note, however, that the process does not end with policy evaluation. As you will see, policymaking is a circular process; the end of one phase is really the beginning of another.

Agenda Setting.   **Agenda setting** is the part of the process when problems are defined as political issues. Many problems confront Americans in their daily lives, but government is not actively working to solve them all. Today, for example, social security seems a hardy perennial of American politics, but the old-age insurance program was not created until the New Deal. The problem of poverty among the elderly did not suddenly arise during the 1930s—there have always been poor people of all ages—but that is when inadequate income for the elderly was defined as a political problem. (See Politics in a Changing America 17.1 for a discussion of how another political issue emerged.) During this time people began arguing that it was government's responsibility to create a system of income security for the aged rather than leaving old people to fend for themselves.

When the government begins to consider acting on an issue it has previously ignored, we say that the issue has become part of the political agenda. Usually when we use *agenda* in this context, we are simply referring to the entire set of issues before all the institutions of government. (There is no formal list of issues for the entire political system; the concept of an agenda for the system is merely a useful abstraction.[9])

Why does an existing social problem become redefined as a political problem? There is no single reason; many different factors can stimulate new thinking about a problem. Sometimes, highly visible events or developments push issues onto the agenda. Examples include great calamities (such as a terrible oil spill, showing a need for safer tankers), technological changes (such as the pollution that comes from automobiles), or irrational human behavior (such as airline hijackings, pointing to the need for greater airport security).[10] The probability that a certain problem will move onto the agenda is also affected by who controls the government and by broad ideological shifts. After President Bush went on television to announce a War on Drugs campaign, the proportion of Americans who said

17.1   The Politics of Same-Sex Marriages

They were "crazy in love" and decided to get married. The couple made plans for their wedding and for a sumptuous reception at an estate outside Honolulu. When they went for a marriage license, however, the state of Hawaii said no: it didn't recognize gay or lesbian marriages as legal. Ninia Baher and Genora Dancel decided to sue, as did two other homosexual couples who had recently been denied a marriage license. In May 1993, that state's Supreme Court found that the denial of a marriage license to the couples could be unconstitutional. The court reasoned that banning same-sex marriage is a form of gender discrimination—if a man can marry a woman, then it is discriminatory not to allow a woman to marry a woman, or a man to marry a man. The state Supreme Court sent the case back to the trial court, where Hawaii's attorney general will have to argue that the state has a "compelling interest" in such a ban. If the state is unable to make a convincing argument, same-sex marriage may soon be legal—at least in Hawaii.

The Hawaii ruling drew attention from the rest of the country. Since Article IV of the U.S. Constitution provides that "Full Faith and Credit shall be given in each State to the public Acts, Records, and judicial Proceedings of every other State," legalization of gay marriages in Hawaii would presumably mean that the other forty-nine states would have to recognize such marriages performed there. Conservatives reacted angrily to the Hawaii decision and introduced the Defense of Marriage Act into Congress, a measure excluding homosexual marriages from the full faith and credit clause. Congress passed the legislation in 1996 and President Clinton signed it into law. States can still decide on their own to permit same-sex marriages, but they are not required to recognize the legality of same-sex marriages performed in states where they may be legal.

Though the immediate factor propelling the issue onto the national agenda was a state court ruling, the same-sex marriage movement has grown out of a general trend toward recognition of "domestic partnerships." Such domestic partnership arrangements are indicative of broader socioeconomic trends, particularly changing sexual mores, the rising number of single parents, and changing attitudes toward homosexuality. In addition, as a group, gays and lesbians are much more open about their sexual orientation than in the past and have mobilized to lobby policymakers. Civil and legal domestic partnership arrangements have become more common in recent years, as employers and some local

in surveys that drugs were the nation's most important problem more than doubled. As the administration's interest in the issue waned, the public went back to viewing drugs as it had before Bush's speech.[11]

Issues may also be placed on the agenda through the efforts of scholars and activists, to get more people to pay attention to a condition of which the public is generally unaware. The problem of child abuse was long hidden in America. It goes on behind closed doors, and it is difficult for the victims to ask for assistance. However, in 1962 a group of pediatricians who were studying child abuse published an article in a medical journal on the "battered child syndrome." This article stimulated popular treatments of the subject that ran in widely circulated magazines such as *Time*

governments have responded to demands that they extend the rights of married heterosexuals to nontraditional families—that is, unmarried couples, both heterosexual and homosexual, who live together and have a profound emotional and financial commitment to each other. Thus Apple Computer, the government of New York City, Disney, TicketMaster, Xerox, and other employers now recognize domestic partnerships. Benefits sought, and won, by advocates of domestic partnership arrangements include inheritance rights, the right to make medical decisions and funeral arrangements, and the right to spousal benefits (including health and pension plans) for employees.

Americans are of two minds on this issue. While nearly two-thirds of Americans believe that homosexual partners should receive some spousal benefits, nearly the same proportion believe that gay people should not be allowed to marry. To those on both sides of the debate, it is a matter of values. Specifically, it is a battle over freedom, order, and equality.

In its search for equality, the gay community argues that marriage is primarily about love and commitment and that homosexuals should have the same opportunity as heterosexuals to have their love legally recognized through the civil and religious symbol of marriage. Gay and lesbian rights groups regard limiting them to just domestic partnership arrangements as inherently unequal. In an era in which the American family is in decline, these organizations argue that allowing homosexuals to marry would be a conservatizing force.

Social conservatives and much of the religious community see the issue as one of maintaining the national moral order. They argue that diluting the value of marriage by extending its sanctification to gay couples would be dangerous to the nation's social fabric and would further hasten the decline of the family. Marriage, they believe, is chiefly for the purpose of procreation. Since homosexual couples can't procreate, they should not be allowed to marry.

Conservative activists believe that states must now stand firm and resist the pressure from gay rights organizations pressing for legislation legalizing same-sex marriages. Gay and lesbian groups feel just as strongly that their right to be treated equally before the law is being abridged by the religious right and conservative citizen groups. This fundamental conflict over same-sex marriages makes it likely that the issue will be around for many years to come.

and the *Saturday Evening Post,* articles that played a major role "in creating a sense of an urgent national problem."[12]

Agenda building consists not only of bringing new issues to the attention of government but also of redefining old issues so that people look at them in different ways.[13] For years, the nuclear power industry convinced Congress that the primary issue concerning nuclear power was America's growing demand for energy. Beginning in the mid-1960s, some activists began to charge that nuclear power plants were unsafe. Over time, more and more people began to take the charge seriously, and Congress responded with more hearings, which were largely critical of the safety practices within the industry.[14] Criticism of the industry peaked after a

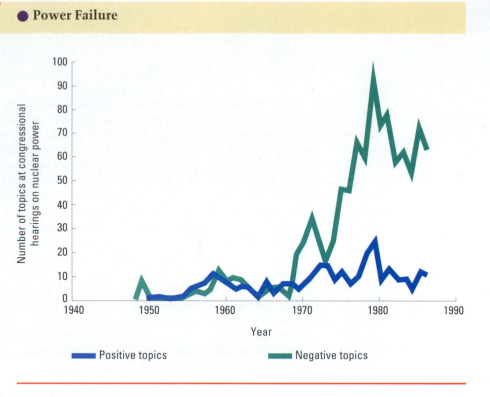

figure 17.2

● **Power Failure**

The change in tone over time at congressional hearings held to discuss nuclear power vividly illustrates the appearance of nuclear safety on the political agenda. Hearings that were generally supportive of the industry were roughly equal in number to those negative in tone until the late 1960s. Since then, congressional hearings on the topic have sharply increased in number and have been largely critical of safety practices in the industry.

Source: Frank R. Baumgartner and Bryan D. Jones, *Agendas and Instability in American Politics* (Chicago: University of Chicago Press, 1993), p. 75. Reprinted with permission of the publisher.

dangerous accident at the Three Mile Island nuclear facility in Pennsylvania in 1979 (see Figure 17.2).

Policy Formulation.   **Policy formulation** is that stage of the policymaking process in which formal policy proposals are developed and officials decide whether to adopt them. The most obvious kind of policy formulation is the proposal of a measure by the president or the development of legislation by Congress. Administrative agencies also formulate policy through the regulatory process. Courts formulate policy, too, when their decisions establish new interpretations of the law. We usually think of policy formulation as a formal process with a published document (a statute, regulation, or court opinion) as the final outcome. In some instances, however, policy decisions are not published or otherwise made explicit. Presidents and secretaries of state may not always fully articulate their foreign policy decisions, for example, because they want some wiggle room for adapting policy to changing conditions.

Although policy formulation is depicted in Figure 17.1 as one stage, it can actually take place over a number of separate stages. For example, the Americans with Disabilities Act of 1990 was enacted by Congress to protect the civil rights of those who are blind, deaf, wheelchair-bound, otherwise physically disabled, or mentally ill. In 1991, the Architectural and Transportation Barriers Compliance Board issued administrative regulations that set some highly specific standards. For instance, at least 5 percent of the tables in a restaurant must be accessible to those with disabilities, and at least half the drinking fountains on every floor in an of-

●●●●●●●●●●●●●

A Winning Team

The Supreme Court's power to formulate policy has never been illustrated more dramatically than when it declared in 1954 that segregation in public schools is unconstitutional. The team of litigators that won this momentous case was (left to right) George E. C. Hayes, Thurgood Marshall, and James Nabrit, Jr.

fice building must be accessible to those in wheelchairs.[15] And the Justice Department has issued guidelines for those who want to bring legal complaints against the government for failing to properly implement the act.[16]

Keep in mind that policy formulation is only the development of proposals designed to solve a problem. Some issues reach the agenda and stimulate new proposals but then fail to win enactment because political opposition mobilizes. In the early 1980s, for example, a movement arose to freeze the development of nuclear weapons. Although a freeze resolution gained significant support in Congress, it never gained enough votes to pass. The nuclear freeze movement quickly withered away and disappeared from sight. Thus, the move from proposal to policy requires the approval of some authoritative, policymaking body.

Implementation.   Policies are not self-executing; **implementation** is the process by which they are carried out. When regulations are issued by agencies in Washington, some government bodies must then put those policies into effect. This may involve notifying the intended targets of agency actions that program regulations have changed. In the case of the 1990 Americans with Disabilities Act, for example, the owners of office buildings would probably not have repositioned their water fountains simply because Washington published new regulations. Administrative bodies at the regional, state, or local level had to inform them of the rule, give them a timetable for compliance, communicate the penalties for noncompliance, be available to answer questions that emerged, and report to Washington on how well the regulations were working.

As pointed out in Chapter 13, one of the biggest problems at the implementation stage of policymaking is coordination. After officials in Washington enact a law and write the subsequent regulations, people outside Washington typically are designated to implement the policy. The agents may be local officials, state administrators, or federal bureaucrats headquartered in regional offices around the country. Those who implement programs are often given considerable discretion as to how to apply general policies to specific, local situations. The discretion can give agents flexibility to tailor situations to local conditions, but it can also mean that people affected by the programs are treated differently depending on where they live. Some polluters, for example, may be treated more leniently than others, depending on which regional office of the Environmental Protection Agency (EPA) is handling their case.[17]

Often, officials implementing a policy are faced with problems no one anticipated, and short of money and time, they must scramble to try to solve them. As discussed at the opening of this chapter, opponents of three strikes laws predicted that there would be many more trials because defendants facing mandatory sentences would have little to lose by going to trial. (In fact, the three strikes law is specifically designed to stop defendants from plea bargaining to lesser charges and shorter sentences.) When this came true, another problem, which hadn't been predicted, emerged: some counties started to run out of qualified jurors. Los Angeles County found itself spending money to make jury duty more attractive, money that was desperately needed elsewhere in the court system.[18]

Although it may sound highly technical, implementation is very much a political process. It involves a great deal of bargaining and negotiation among different groups of people in and out of government. The difficulty of implementing complex policies in a federal system, with multiple layers of government, and in a pluralistic system, with multiple competing interests, seems daunting. Yet, there are incentives for cooperation, not the least of which is to avoid blame if a policy fails. (We will discuss coordination in more detail later in the chapter.)

Policy Evaluation.   How does the government know whether a policy is working? In some cases, success or failure may be obvious, but at other times experts in a specific field must tell government officials how well a policy is working. **Policy evaluation** is the analysis of public policy. Although there is no one method of evaluating policy, evaluation tends to draw heavily on approaches used by academics, including cost-effectiveness analysis and various statistical methods designed to provide concrete measurements of program outcomes. Although technical, the studies can be quite influential in decisions on whether to continue, expand, alter, reduce, or eliminate programs. The continuing stream of negative evaluations of programs designed to bring jobs to the unemployed has clearly reduced political support for such policies.[19]

Evaluating public policy is extremely difficult. The most pertinent data are not always available, predicting trends may require making problematic assumptions, and policy analysts may have biases that influence their research. Sometimes, the data are unclear and subject to differing interpretations. One interesting case involves weaponry used in the Persian Gulf War. For the first time, the United States made extensive use of "smart bombs"—bombs that are electronically guided to their targets instead of being dropped the old-fashioned way with visual sighting of targets. During the war the Pentagon touted the effectiveness of these weapons, showing the American public dramatic videotapes of smart bombs hitting targets in Iraq. One tape showed a smart bomb aimed so ac-

Not So Smart After All

During the Gulf War the Pentagon extolled the effectiveness and precision of "smart" bombs, which were electronically guided to their destinations (like this Baghdad target). Five years after the war, however, a thorough and sophisticated analysis concluded that the Pentagon's claims about smart bombs were "overstated, misleading, inconsistent with the best available data, or unverifiable."

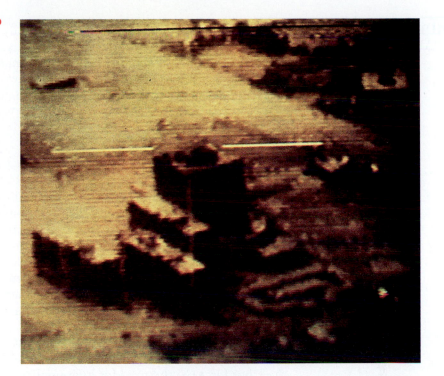

curately that it went down the air shaft of a Baghdad building. Some early independent assessments at the end of the war were positive, and one study concluded that "The criticism that America's weapons were too complex and fragile to work in war was dispelled."[20] Later, a thorough and dispassionate study by Congress's General Accounting Office demonstrated that those tapes showed the exceptions and not the rule. Its systematic comparison of smart bombs and "dumb bombs" showed no difference in their accuracy. This was a critically important finding because smart bombs are much more expensive. Although smart bombs accounted for only 8 percent of the ordnance used in the Gulf War, they consumed 84 percent of the money spent on munitions.[21] This is the kind of policy evaluation that is most useful: directly comparing different ways of achieving the same goal, and determining the relative effectiveness and efficiency of each approach.

Evaluation is part of the policymaking process, because it helps to identify problems and issues that arise from current policy. In other words, evaluation studies provide **feedback** to policymakers on program performance. (The dotted line in Figure 17.1 represents a feedback loop. Problems that emerge during the implementation stage also provide feedback to policymakers.) By drawing attention to emerging problems, policy evaluation influences the political agenda. For instance, you may recall our discussion of oversight in Chapter 11. When congressional committees perform oversight duties, they are evaluating policy with an eye toward identifying issues they will have to deal with in subsequent legislation. Thus, we have come full circle. The end of the process—evaluating whether the policy is being implemented as it was envisioned when it was formulated—is the beginning of a new cycle of public policymaking.

A MULTIPLICITY OF PARTICIPANTS

The policymaking process encompasses many different stages and many different participants at each stage. Here we examine some forces that pull the government in different directions and make problem solving less coherent than it might otherwise be. In the next section, we look at some structural elements of American government that work to coordinate competing and sometimes conflicting approaches to the same problem.

Multiplicity and Fragmentation

A single policy problem may be attacked in different and sometimes competing ways by government for many reasons. At the heart of this **fragmentation** of policymaking is the fundamental nature of government in America. Separation of powers divides authority among the branches of the national government; federalism divides authority among the national, state, and local levels of government. The multiple centers of power are, of course, a primary component of pluralist democracy. Different groups try to influence different parts of the government; no one entity completely controls policymaking.

The fragmentation of policymaking is illustrated by policymaking concerning day care. Sixty percent of women with children under six are in the labor force, so the need for high-quality, affordable day care is acute. It's easy for politicians to agree with such homilies as "children are our future," but one would never know they feel that way from the government's approach to the care of its youngest citizens. The national government plays only a modest role in the area of day care, and communities and states vary widely in the degree to which they regulate day care, if they regulate it at all. In the United States there are approximately 80,000 day care centers and close to 670,000 homes providing family day care.[22] Some of this care is clearly substandard, and there is no coherent approach for ensuring that children receive care that is safe and stimulating. Studies show that day care that is regulated is of clearly higher quality, but there is little prospect in the near future that the state and national governments will institute greater coherence and coordination in day care policy.[23]

Fragmentation exists not only because of a lack of coordination between branches and levels of government, but also because of conflict between them. Despite the furor over drug abuse in America, the executive branch of the national government has been beset by chronic infighting among the more than thirty agencies involved in one way or another in combating drugs. In the area of drug enforcement alone, nineteen agencies share responsibility. The Customs Service and the Drug Enforcement Administration (DEA) regard each other with suspicion, although they ostensibly are working toward the same goal. Neither wants the other to encroach on what it regards as its territory. One consequence of these attitudes is that the DEA will not give the Customs Service direct access to DEA intelligence files.[24]

Congress is characterized by the same diffusion of authority. Seventy-five separate House and Senate committees and subcommittees claim some jurisdiction over drug legislation, and the committees jealously guard their prerogatives.[25]

● ● ● ● ● ● ● ● ● ● ● ●

It Takes a Village to Raise a Child

The growing percentage of women with young children in the labor force has sharply increased the demand for day care. The majority of providers offer care in their homes. Some of this care, such as that pictured here, is of high quality, but much of it is unregulated and is not subject to any kind of outside review. One study estimates that two-thirds of all home day care providers are operating illegally by not informing licensing agencies that they have a home day care business.

The multiplicity of institutional participants is partly the product of the complexity of public policy issues. Controlling illegal drugs is not one problem but a number of different, interrelated problems. Drug treatment questions, for example, have little in common with questions related to the smuggling of drugs into the country. Still, the responsibilities of agencies and committees do overlap. Why are responsibilities not parceled out more precisely to clarify jurisdictions and eliminate overlap? Such reorganizations create winners and losers, and agencies fearing the loss of jurisdiction over an issue become highly protective of their turf.

The Pursuit of Coordination

How does the government overcome fragmentation so that it can make its public policies more coherent? Coordination of different elements of government is not impossible, and fragmentation often creates a productive pressure to rethink jurisdictions.

One common response to the problem of coordination is the formation of interagency task forces within the executive branch. Their common goal is to develop a broad policy response that all relevant agencies will endorse. Such task forces include representatives of all agencies claiming responsibility for a particular issue. They attempt to forge good policy as well as good will among competing agencies. Because of its frustration with the lack of progress in the development of drugs to combat AIDS, the

Clinton administration formed a task force. A primary goal of the Task Force on AIDS Drug Development is to make sure that red tape does not delay approval of promising AIDS drugs.[26]

Sometimes, the executive branch attempts to reassign jurisdictions among its agencies, although certain players may resist the loss of their turf. Reorganization of jurisdictions is more common within than across agencies. A shift across agencies is likely to require White House involvement. Nevertheless, the president and his aides sometimes orchestrate such restructurings, which may involve creating a new agency to assume control over other, existing agencies or programs. With congressional approval, President Richard Nixon created the Environmental Protection Agency in 1970 to better coordinate fifteen programs administered by five other parts of the executive branch.[27]

The Office of Management and Budget (OMB) also fosters coordination in the executive branch. The OMB can do much more than review budgets and look for ways to improve management practices. The Reagan administration used OMB to clear regulations before they were proposed publicly by the administrative agencies. It initiated OMB's regulatory review role to centralize control of the executive branch. The Bush administration used the President's Council on Competitiveness in a comparable way to review regulations before agencies implemented them. Under Vice President Dan Quayle, the council rejected regulations that it regarded as detrimental to the economy.[28] The virtue of centralized control by the White House through such instruments as OMB and the Council on Competitiveness is that the administration can ensure that its objectives are carried out and not compromised by agencies eager to please interest groups that give them political support. Critics say that such White House control excludes many relevant groups from the policymaking process.

Congress has moved in some limited ways toward greater coherence and coordination in its policymaking. After the Republicans captured the House in the 1994 elections, Speaker Newt Gingrich was successful in rationalizing at least some committee jurisdictions. Most notably, he trimmed the jurisdiction of the Committee on Energy and Commerce—which had at least partial control over 40 percent of the legislation in the House—making it the Committee on Commerce.[29] Other committee jurisdictions were expanded, however, and it's not clear if any long-term reduction of overlapping jurisdictions has been achieved.[30]

Finally, the policy fragmentation created by federalism may be solved when an industry asks the national government to develop a single regulatory policy. Often, the alternative is for that industry to try to accommodate the different regulatory approaches used in various states. Although an industry may prefer no regulation at all, it generally prefers one master to fifty.

The effect of pluralism on the problem of coordination is all too evident. In a decentralized, federal system of government with large numbers of interest groups, fragmentation is inevitable. Beyond the structural factors is the natural tendency of people and organizations to defend their base of power. Government officials understand, however, that mechanisms of coordination are necessary so that fragmentation does not overwhelm policymaking. Such mechanisms as interagency task forces, reorganizations, and White House review can bring some coherence to policymaking.

ISSUE NETWORKS

So far, we have emphasized how different kinds of issues can affect the policymaking process in different ways and how government officials cope with the problems of fragmentation and coordination. We want to extend these themes by focusing more closely on interest groups. Within any issue area, a number—often a very large number—of interest groups try to influence policy decisions. Representatives from these organizations interact with each other and with government officials on a recurring basis. The ongoing interaction produces both conflict and cooperation.

Government by Policy Area

We noted earlier that policy formulation takes place across different institutions. Participants from these institutions do not patiently wait their turn as policymaking proceeds from one institution to the next. Rather, they try to influence policy at whatever stage they can. Suppose that Congress is considering amendments to the Clean Air Act. Because Congress does not function in a vacuum, the other parts of government that will be affected by the legislation participate in the process, too. The EPA has an interest in the outcome because it will have to administer the law. The White House is concerned about any legislation that affects such vital sectors of the economy as the steel and coal industries. As a result, officials from both the EPA and the White House work with members of Congress and the appropriate committee staffs to try to ensure that their interests are protected. At the same time, lobbyists representing corporations, trade associations, and environmental groups do their best to influence Congress, agency officials, and White House aides. Trade associations might hire public relations firms to sway public opinion toward their industry's point of view. Experts from think tanks and universities might be asked to testify at hearings or to serve in an informal advisory capacity in regard to the technical, economic, and social effects of the proposed amendments.

The various individuals and organizations that work in a particular policy area form a loosely knit community. More specifically, those "who share expertise in a policy domain and who frequently interact constitute an issue network."[31] The boundaries and membership of an **issue network** are hardly precise, but in general terms networks include members of Congress, committee staffers, agency officials, lawyers, lobbyists, consultants, scholars, and public relations specialists. This makes for a large number of participants—in a broad policy area, the number of interest group organizations alone is usually in the dozens, if not hundreds.[32]

Not all of the participants in an issue network have a working relationship with all the others. Indeed, some may be chronic antagonists. Others tend to be allies. For example, environmental groups will coalesce in trying to influence a clean air bill but are likely to be in opposition to business groups. The common denominator for friends and foes in an issue network is technical mastery of a particular policy area.

Political scientists have long analyzed policymaking by issue area. However, the issue network framework is a relatively new tool. In the 1950s, policy communities were typically much smaller, with a few key committee or subcommittee chairs, a top agency official, and a couple of lobbyists from the principal trade groups negotiating behind the scenes to settle important policy questions. Political scientists used to call such small, tightly knit policy communities *iron triangles*. Iron triangles were thought to be relatively autonomous and to operate by consensus. The explosion in the number of interest groups and the growth of government and overlapping jurisdictions put an end to iron triangles. Today, policy communities are much more open and much more conflictual.

The Case of Telecommunications

The telecommunications industry provides a useful illustration of the changing nature of politics in Washington. Once a harmonious iron triangle, telecommunications is today a large issue network filled with conflict.

Until fairly recently, the telecommunications industry was dominated by American Telephone & Telegraph (AT&T), which, with its affiliated Bell System telephone companies around the country, constituted a monopoly.[33] Customers had no choice but to use the phone lines and phone equipment of "Ma Bell." It was easy for AT&T executives to defend their company's control of the industry. The United States had an impressive system, with low-cost, reliable service to residential customers. Moreover, the AT&T network was a mainstay of our defense communications system. Within the telecommunications iron triangle—a policymaking community made up of some key members of Congress, the Federal Communications Commission, and AT&T—policymaking was usually consensual and uncontroversial.

At one time, AT&T was the world's biggest corporation, and it seemed invulnerable. But in 1968, the Federal Communications Commission (FCC) ruled that other companies could compete against AT&T in the "terminal" equipment market. This meant that a customer could buy a telephone (or more complex telephone equipment) from a company other than AT&T and attach it to AT&T phone lines. This jolt of competition was followed a year later by a second blow to AT&T, when the FCC ruled that MCI, a small start-up company marketing microwave technology, could sell a limited form of long-distance service to business clients.

As significant as these changes were, the greatest challenge to AT&T lay ahead. In 1974, the U.S. Department of Justice brought a lawsuit against the corporation, charging it with illegal monopolistic behavior in the telecommunications industry. The eventual outcome of the suit was an out-of-court settlement that required AT&T to give up control over local operating service. The Bell System was broken up into seven independent regional telephone companies (the "Baby Bells"). AT&T was allowed to retain its long-distance service, but it would have to compete against other long-distance carriers. (AT&T did win the right to enter the computer industry, which was one of its major goals.) All in all, AT&T lost three-quarters of its assets.[34] The giant telephone company had fallen victim to a growing belief among academics and policymakers that government regulation was hampering the economy by restricting competition and lessening incentives for innovation, as well as limiting the price and product choices available to consumers. Thus, telecommunications was deregulated by the changes that introduced more business competition.[35]

● ● ● ● ● ● ● ● ● ● ● ● ●

Toll Taker on the Information Superhighway

John Malone, the chief executive officer of TCI, is a shrewd business visionary and one of the most influential leaders in the telecommunications industry. He built the Denver-based TCI into the largest operator of cable television franchises around the country and created strategic business alliances with a number of important telecommunications companies.

Today, policymaking in telecommunications bears no resemblance to an iron triangle. After the AT&T divestiture, competition among businesses selling various communications services and equipment became even more intense. Many new companies emerged to join the highly fractious issue network. Much of the political conflict that ensued had its origins in the consent agreement, which tried to define major markets (such as local telephone service) and specify who could participate. Various companies made repeated attempts to get the government to change the rules of the consent agreement so that they could compete in more markets. Thus, in the aftermath of the breakup, typical policy conflicts involved fights between the Baby Bells and long-distance carriers, each side wanting to expand into new markets while protecting their current markets from encroachment by would-be competitors.

Over time, the consent agreement proved incapable of regulating the rapidly changing telecommunications industry. Three important developments in telecommunications forced the government to abandon this regulatory framework, which had tried to determine which kinds of firms could engage in which kinds of business. First were various technological innovations that were either not anticipated by the consent decree or excluded from it, because commercial markets for the technology had not yet matured. One example is cellular phones and other forms of wireless communication. Second was the pivotal convergence of various technologies. One of the more significant examples is that telephone lines became critically important to computer users as the electronic transmission of data and digital communications became more feasible. As technologies converged, new business opportunities beckoned in reconfigured markets.

Third was the fact that entrepreneurs began to see the future as one in which the strongest companies—or at least those that survived the tumultuous changes in the marketplace—would be those that were alliances of many different businesses with expertise in individual products. Such alliances could offer an array of services to customers through the use of integrated technology. For example, John Malone of TCI (Tele-Communications, Inc.), the nation's biggest operator of cable TV services, is one business visionary who sees the future of cable TV as a five-hundred-channel center of home life.[36] People will be able to order movies on demand, purchase airline tickets, watch the sporting events of their choice, take part in interactive programming with a hand-held console, and do countless other things—all over their phone line. These developments forced the government to move toward a truly deregulated market with legislation passed in 1996. Telecommunications firms can now enter virtually any business they wish. For example, telephone companies can go into the cable TV business and package these services together. Local phone companies can offer long-distance services, and vice versa.[37]

As Figure 17.3 shows, the changes in the industry have led to an issue network characterized not so much by political alliances as by business alliances. Mergers, acquisitions, joint ventures, and cross-ownership arrangements have created many firms with far-reaching interests.[38] (The figure depicts the industry in the spring of 1994, and the changes have accelerated since then.) Generally, though, issue network politics is characterized by rapidly changing coalitions, as partners on one issue become opponents on the next. Conflict within the telecommunications

figure

17.3   ● The Telecommunications Issue Network

There is no one way to draw an issue network. This graphic illustrates the different types of relationships among the different private sector groups involved in the telecommunications industry. Recent trends in the industry are toward more and more mergers and acquisitions as companies try to expand into integrated, large-scale entities that can provide a range of services that will be popular in the future. The congressional committees and units of the executive branch specified in this figure are those with primary responsibility for telecommunications policymaking.

Source: Jeffrey M. Berry, "The Dynamic Qualities of Issue Networks," paper delivered at the annual meeting of the American Political Science Association, New York City, September 1994. Used with permission.

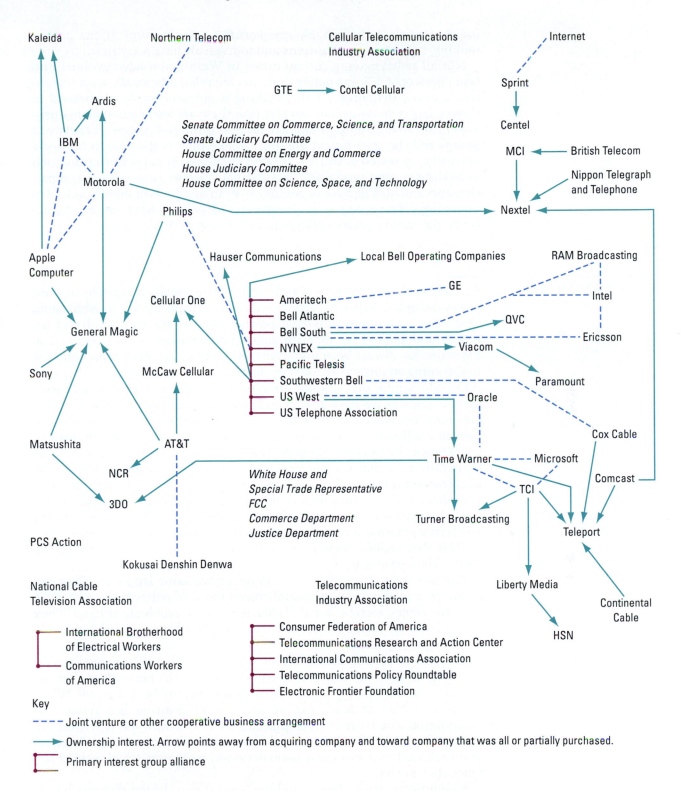

issue network is chronic. No one controls telecommunications policy-making, but many organizations and individuals have a say in it.

Not all policymaking communities in Washington have evolved into issue networks.[39] Some policy domains are relatively small, with few interest group participants. Policymaking is not necessarily consensual in these smaller domains, but the fact that there are fewer participants usually means that patterns of interaction among interest groups and between groups and the government are more stable than is the case in big issue networks, in which coalitions are ever changing. Broad policy areas, such as health care and agriculture, are distinguished by large numbers of participants and high degrees of conflict.[40] With hundreds of lobbies active in many important policy areas, issue network politics has come to characterize the contemporary policymaking process in Washington.

POLICY EXPERTISE

Although issue networks are fluid communities, easily entered by new interest group participants, there is still a significant barrier to admission. One must have the necessary expertise to enter the community of activists and politicians that influence policymaking in an issue area. Expertise has always been important, but "more than ever, policymaking is becoming an intramural activity among expert issue watchers."[41]

Oil companies, for example, are crucial to our economy, and lobbyists for the major firms have always had easy access to policymakers in government. Yet, there are lots of oil lobbyists in Washington, and not all have the same influence. They compete for the attention and respect of those in government by offering solutions that are technically feasible as well as politically palatable. Consider the issues addressed during a period of expanding regulation of the domestic oil industry. Seemingly obscure and complicated policy questions were unending. How were "original costs" to be distinguished from "reproduction costs"? Was it fair for "secondary and tertiary production" to be exempted from "base-period volumes"? Did drilling that yielded "new pays" or "extensions" qualify as "new" oil or "old" oil for pricing purposes?[42]

The members of an issue network speak the same language. They can participate in the negotiation and compromise of policymaking because they can offer concrete, detailed solutions to the problems at hand. They understand the substance of policy, the way Washington works, and one another's viewpoints.

One reason participants in an issue network have such a good understanding of the needs and problems of others in the network is that job switches within policy communities continue to be common. When someone wants to leave her or his current position but remain in Washington, the most obvious place to look for a new job is within the same policy field. For these **in-and-outers,** knowledge and experience remain relevant to a particular issue network, no matter which side of the fence they are on.

A common pattern of job switching—one that is the focus of much criticism—is to work in government for a number of years, build up knowledge of a policy area, and then take a lobbying job (see Figure 17.4). Law firms, consulting firms, public relations firms, and trade associations gen-

figure

17.4   ● **Government Service: A Useful Credential**

Individuals who have held high-level government jobs become very attractive to the private sector. This survey of political appointees to top executive branch positions shows that only a little more than one-fourth came to those jobs directly from business or law. When they left their appointed positions, however, nearly two-thirds took jobs with corporations or law firms.

Source: Linda L. Fisher, "Fifty Years of Presidential Appointments," in G. Calvin Mackenzie, ed., *The In-and-Outers* (Baltimore: The Johns Hopkins University Press, 1987), p. 27. Used with permission.

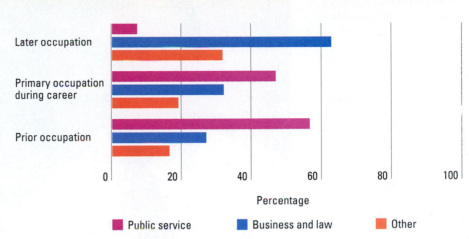

erally pay much higher salaries than the government. And they pay not just for experience and know-how but also for connections with government.[43] Alan Wm. Wolff gained valuable experience working for the Office of the Special Trade Representative in the executive branch. He worked on various foreign trade conflicts and then parlayed his valuable government experience into a lucrative job with the Washington office of Dewey, Ballantine, a nationally known law firm. There he represents clients such as Kodak and the American Iron and Steel Institute, trying to get his former employer to take action against foreign companies allegedly engaging in illegal trade practices. For his valuable time, clients are charged $450 an hour.[44]

In short, experience in government not only gives individuals expertise in an issue area, it also gives them contacts with those who remain in the executive or legislative branches and retain authority over policy. Although not everyone who leaves government for the private sector will command Wolff's half a million dollars or more a year in salary, it is very common for high-ranking officials to leave government for jobs that pay considerably higher than what they were earning. Indeed, people who take high-level government jobs often do so at some cost to their income. One survey of political appointees to top government jobs showed that 55 percent said they had made a financial sacrifice to move into government. Yet, roughly 50 percent indicated that government service enhanced their subsequent earning power.[45]

One constraint on in-and-outers is the Ethics in Government Act of 1978, which specifies that senior executive branch officials cannot lobby their former agency for a year after leaving the government. Critics have complained, however, that in-and-outers have not found this requirement much of an inhibition and that some former executive branch officials have had little trouble getting around it. To counter this problem, Bill Clinton issued a new, seemingly tougher standard of ethics for those joining his administration. At the outset of his administration, eleven

hundred top appointees were required to sign a pledge not to lobby their former agencies for five years after they leave government and to promise to never lobby on behalf of foreign clients.[46] Clinton announced that the new rules would "stop the revolving door from public service to private enrichment."[47]

Within a year, the Clinton administration's ethics rules proved to be embarrassingly ineffective. The president's congressional liaison chief, Howard Paster, resigned from the administration to take a job as head of Hill and Knowlton, a public relations and lobbying firm, at a reported salary of $1 million a year. Roy Neel, deputy chief of staff at the White House, resigned to take a job as president of the United States Telephone Association, a lobbying arm of the Baby Bells (see Figure 17.3). Neel's salary is estimated at $500,000, quadruple his White House salary. Both Paster and Neel told the press that they would not lobby the White House in their new jobs.[48] Yet, nothing prevents them from directing other lobbyists or from using their knowledge of how the White House operates to their firm's advantage.

ISSUE NETWORKS AND DEMOCRACY

Are issue networks making the government too fragmented? Are some issue networks beyond popular control? Has the increasing complexity of public policy given technical experts too much policymaking authority?

These questions relate to the broad issues raised in Chapter 2. For many years, political scientists have described American democracy as a system in which different constituencies work energetically to influence policies of concern to them. Policymaking is seen as a response to these groups rather than to majority will. This is a considerably different conception of democracy than the more traditional perspective, that policies reflect what most people want. It is a pluralist, not a majoritarian, view of American government.

In a number of ways, issue networks promote pluralist democracy. They are open systems, populated by a wide range of interest groups. Decision making is not centralized in the hands of a few key players; policies are formulated in a participatory fashion. But there is still no guarantee that all relevant interests are represented, and those with greater financial resources have an advantage. Nevertheless, issue networks provide access to government for a diverse set of competing interests and thus further the pluralist ideal.[49]

For those who prefer majoritarian democracy, however, issue networks are an obstacle to achieving their vision of how government should operate. The technical complexity of contemporary issues makes it especially difficult for the public at large to exert control over policy outcomes. When we think of the complexity of such issues as nuclear power, toxic wastes, air pollution, poverty, drug abuse, and so on, it is easy to understand why majoritarian democracy is so difficult to achieve. The more complex the issue, the more elected officials must depend on a technocratic elite for policy guidance. And technical expertise, of course, is a chief characteristic of participants in issue networks.

At first glance, having technical experts play a key role in policymaking may seem highly desirable. After all, who but the experts should be making decisions about toxic wastes? This works to the advantage of government bureaucracies, which are full of people hired for their technical expertise. But governmental dependence on technocrats also helps interest groups, which use policy experts to maximize their influence with government. Seen in this light, issue networks become less appealing. Interest groups—at least those with which we do not personally identify—are seen as selfish. They pursue policies that favor their constituents rather than the national interest.

Although expertise is an important factor in bringing interest groups into the decision-making process, it is not the only one. Americans have a fundamental belief that government should be open and accessible to "the people." If some constituency has a problem, they reason, government ought to listen to it. However, the practical consequence of this view is a government that is open to interest groups.

Finally, although issue networks promote pluralism, keep in mind that majoritarian influences on policymaking are still significant. The broad contours of public opinion can be a dominant force on highly visible issues. Policymaking on civil rights, for example, has been sensitive to shifts in public opinion. Elections, too, send messages to policymakers about the most widely discussed campaign issues. What issue networks have done, however, is facilitate pluralist politics in policy areas in which majoritarian influences are weak.

SUMMARY

Government tries to solve problems through a variety of approaches. Some public policies prohibit, some protect, some promote, and some provide. The approach chosen can significantly affect the policymaking process.

Although there is much variation in the policymaking process, we can conceive of it as consisting of four stages. The first stage is agenda setting, the process by which problems become defined as political issues worthy of government attention. Once people in government feel that they should be doing something about a problem, an attempt at policy formulation will follow. All three branches of the national government formulate policy. Once policies have been formulated and ratified, administrative units of government must implement them. Finally, once policies are being carried out, they need to be evaluated. Implementation and program evaluation influence agenda building, because program shortcomings become evident during these stages. Thus, the process is really circular, with the end often marking the beginning of a new round of policymaking.

Our policymaking system is also characterized by forces that push it toward fragmentation and by institutional structures intended to bring some element of coordination to government. The multiplicity of participants in policymaking, the diffusion of authority within both Congress and the executive branch, the separation of powers, and federalism are chief causes of conflict and fragmentation in policymaking.

Policymaking in many areas can be viewed as an ongoing process of interaction within issue networks composed of actors inside and outside government. Each network is a way to communicate and exchange information and ideas about a particular policy area. In a network, lobbying coalitions form easily and dissolve rapidly as new issues arise. Issue networks place a high premium on expertise as public policy problems grow ever more complex.

Political scientists view issue networks with some concern. The networks unquestionably facilitate the representation of many interests in the policymaking process, but they do so at a price. They allow well-organized, aggressive constituencies to prevail over the broader interests of the nation. Once again, the majoritarian and pluralist models of democracy conflict. It is easy to say that the majority should rule. But in the real world, the majority tends to be far less interested in many issues than are the constituencies most directly affected by them. It is also easy to say that those most affected by issues should have the most influence. But experience teaches us that such influence leads to policies that favor the well represented at the expense of those who should be at the bargaining table but are not.

Key Terms

public policy
agenda setting
policy formulation
implementation
policy evaluation
feedback
fragmentation
issue network
in-and-outer

Selected Readings

Anderson, James E. *Public Policymaking*, 2nd ed. Boston: Houghton Mifflin, 1994. A brief overview of the policymaking system.

Baumgartner, Frank R., and Bryan D. Jones. *Agendas and Instability in American Politics*. Chicago: University of Chicago Press, 1993. A systematic analysis of how issues arise and how they fall off the national agenda.

Church, Thomas W., and Robert T. Nakamura. *Cleaning Up the Mess.* Washington, D.C.: Brookings Institution, 1993. The authors focus on different strategies for implementing the Superfund program for cleaning up hazardous waste sites.

Gormley, William T. *Everybody's Children.* Washington, D.C.: Brookings Institution, 1995. A comprehensive evaluation of U.S. day care policy—or the lack thereof.

Mackenzie, G. Calvin, ed. *The In-and-Outers.* Baltimore: Johns Hopkins University Press, 1987. A collection of essays examining the problems associated with the movement of people between the private sector and the executive branch.

Pierson, Paul. *Dismantling the Welfare State.* New York: Cambridge University Press, 1994. The decline of support for welfare in the United States and Britain during the 1980s is viewed through a comparative lens.

World Wide Web Resources

General Accounting Office. This is the home page for the General Accounting office, the investigative arm of Congress. In addition to information about, and the history of, the GAO, this site provides access to GAO reports and testimony, the decisions and opinions of the comptroller general, and "policy and guidance" materials.

`<www.gao.gov/>`

Bureau of Labor Statistics. The home page of the Bureau of Labor Statistics of the Department of Commerce, this page provides the user with access to large amounts of data, broken down by function, region, etc. Bureau publications are also available.

`<stats.bls.gov/>`

Bureau of the Census. This is the home page of the Bureau of the Census. It provides the current U.S. population count, as well as current economic indicators. The Bureau's press releases can be accessed in the "newsroom." In addition, visitors can have access to Bureau publications.

`<www.census.gov/>`

The Heritage Foundation. This is the home page for this conservative public policy think tank. In addition to "this week's top ten facts," visitors interested in public policy jobs can access the foundation's job bank. This page also provides its "Candidate Education Guide," the latest news on current issues (such as tax reform) and various foundation publications, including current and back issues of the foundation's magazine, *Policy Review: Journal of American Citizenship.*

`<www.heritage.org/>`

Progressive Policy Institute. This is the home page of the Progressive Policy Institute of the Democratic Leadership Council. In addition to accessing information on the organization's history and ideology, visitors can access the institute's library, read current news articles about the DLC, and read current and back issues of the institute's "flagship magazine," *The New Democrat.*

`<www.dlcppi.org/>`

Economic Policy

THE STORY WAS IN THE HEADLINES.   On July 6, 1996, the *New York Times* ran this good news as its main headline: "U.S. JOBLESS RATE FOR JUNE AT 5.3%; LOWEST IN 6 YEARS." But its secondary headline carried this bad news: "STOCKS AND BONDS DROP."[1] These headlines reflect a recent pattern in the American media—good news about the economy means bad news for investors.

How good was the good news? First, the decline in unemployment represented 239,000 new jobs since May. The 5.3% unemployment rate contrasted favorably with the 7.8% unemployed in June 1992, when George Bush was running for reelection.[2] Second, the average hourly wage jumped to $11.82, nearly 9 cents an hour more than the previous month's—and the largest one-month increase since 1983.[3] In short, more Americans were making higher wages. To trumpet the good news, President Clinton hastily called a news conference, where he proclaimed, "We have the most solid American economy in a generation."[4]

How bad was the bad news? The Dow Jones Industrial Average—the thirty stocks that make up the most widely known stock market index— dropped 115 points on July 5, the day that Clinton praised the economy, and the sell-off did not stop then. On July 11, the Dow Jones average fell another 83 points; on July 15, the index plunged 161 points; and on July 16, it plummeted 167 points in the early afternoon before recovering to close with a 9-point gain.[5] Clearly, investors were worried that month, and memories of the record stock market crash of October 1987 produced a queasy feeling.[6]

Why should good economic news for the president translate into bad economic news for Wall Street? Simply put, investors feared that the economy was doing *too* well, that low unemployment would produce pressure for higher wages, leading to price inflation. Although inflation might occur in the long run, why should the market act so abruptly? In truth, they were not reacting to the long run but to the short run. They feared that the government would soon raise interest rates in an effort to head off inflation before it occurred.[7] Higher interest rates would make investing more costly, thus slowing down economic growth.

Since President Clinton, the head of the government, stood to benefit in the November 1996 election from continued economic growth, why were investors worried that "the government" would raise interest rates that summer? The answer is that the Federal Reserve Board, not the president, controls interest rates, and by law the Fed, as it is called, is independent of

607

● ● ● ● ● ● ● ● ● ● ● ●
Fed Head

As Fed chairman, Alan Greenspan heads the central banking operation of the United States. He was appointed by Reagan in 1987 and reappointed by Bush. Prior to his reelection campaign, Clinton benefited from the Fed not raising interest rates, and he reappointed Greenspan to a third term.

presidential control. Historically, the Fed has adjusted interest rates to combat inflation rather than to stimulate economic growth.[8] A former Fed chairman once described its task as being "to remove the punch bowl when the party gets going."[9] Accordingly, Alan Greenspan, the chairman of the Fed in 1996, was giving "heightened surveillance" to signs of inflation in the summer. By fall, the market climbed to record highs.[10]

Although the presidency is formally responsible for the state of the economy and although voters hold the president accountable for the economy, that exalted office neither determines interest rates (the Fed does) nor controls spending (Congress does). In this respect, President Clinton suffered the same restrictions as his twentieth-century predecessors. All have had to work with a Fed that was made independent of both the president and Congress, and all have had to deal with the fact that Congress ultimately controls spending. These restrictions on presidential authority are consistent with the pluralist model of democracy, but a president responsible for the economy may not appreciate that theoretical argument.

How much control can government really exercise over the economy through the judicious use of economic theory? How is the national budget formulated, and why has the deficit grown so large and proved so difficult to control? What effects do government taxing and spending policies have on the economy and on economic equality? We grapple with these and other questions in this chapter on the economics of public policy.

THEORIES OF ECONOMIC POLICY

Government control of the economy relies on theories about how the economy responds to government taxing and spending policies. How policymakers tax and spend depends on their beliefs about (1) how the economy functions and (2) the proper role of government in the economy. The American economy is so complex that no policymaker knows exactly how it works. Policymakers rely on economic theories to explain its functioning, and there are nearly as many theories as economists. Unfortunately, different theories (and economists) often predict different outcomes. One source of differing predictions is the assumptions that underlie every economic theory, for these differ from theory to theory. Another problem is the difference between an abstract theory and the real world. Still, despite the disagreement among economists, a knowledge of basic economics is necessary to understand how government approaches public policy.

We are concerned here with economic policy in a market economy—one in which the prices of goods and services are determined through the interaction of sellers and buyers (that is, through supply and demand). This kind of economy is typical of the consumer-dominated societies of Western Europe and the United States. A nonmarket economy relies on government planners to determine both the prices of goods and the amounts that are produced. The old Soviet economy is a perfect example. In a nonmarket economy, the government owns and operates the major means of production.

Market economies are loosely called *capitalist economies:* they allow private individuals to own property; to sell goods for profit in free, or open, markets; and to accumulate wealth, called *capital.* Market economies

Economists Getting Data for Predictions

The forecast you get depends on which economist is yours.

THE ECONOMISTS

often exhibit a mix of government and private ownership. For example, Britain has had considerably more government-owned enterprises (railroads, broadcasting, and housing) than the United States. The competing theories about market economies differ largely on how free the markets should be—in other words, on government's role in directing the economy.

Laissez-Faire Economics

The French term *laissez faire,* introduced in Chapter 1 and discussed again in Chapter 13, describes the absence of government control. The economic doctrine of laissez faire likens the operation of a free market to the process of natural selection. Economic competition weeds out the weak and preserves the strong. In the process, the economy prospers and everyone eventually benefits.

Advocates of laissez-faire economics are fond of quoting Adam Smith's *The Wealth of Nations.* In this 1776 treatise, Smith argued that each individual, pursuing his own selfish interests in a competitive market, was "led by an invisible hand to promote an end which was no part of his intention." Smith's "invisible hand" has been used for two centuries to justify the belief that the narrow pursuit of profits serves the broad interests of society. Strict advocates of laissez faire maintain that government interference with business tampers with the laws of nature, obstructing the workings of the free market.

Keynesian Theory

One problem with laissez-faire economics is its insistence that government should do little about **economic depressions** (periods of high unemployment and business failures) or raging **inflation** (price increases that decrease the value of currency). Inflation is ordinarily measured by the Consumer Price Index (CPI), which Feature 18.1 explains. Since the beginning of the Industrial Revolution, capitalist economies have suffered through many cyclical fluctuations. The United States has experienced more than fifteen of these **business cycles**—expansions and contractions

●●●●●●●●●●●
We Make Money the Old-Fashioned Way: We Print It

The U.S. Mint stamps out coins, but paper money is produced by the Bureau of Engraving and Printing, which also prints Treasury notes and other U.S. securities. Imagine how frustrating it might be to work among these sheets of money.

of business activity, the first stage accompanied by inflation and the second stage by unemployment. No one had a theory that really explained these cycles until the Great Depression of the 1930s.

That was when John Maynard Keynes, a British economist, theorized that business cycles stem from imbalances between aggregate demand and productive capacity. **Aggregate demand** is the income available to consumers, business, and government to spend on goods and services. **Productive capacity** is the total value of goods and services that can be produced when the economy is working at full capacity. The value of the goods and services actually produced is called the **gross domestic product (GDP).** When demand exceeds productive capacity, people are willing to pay more for available goods, which leads to price inflation. When productive capacity exceeds demand, producers cut back on their output of goods, which leads to unemployment. When many people are unemployed for an extended period, the economy is in a depression. Keynes theorized that government could stabilize the economy (and smooth out or eliminate business cycles) by controlling the level of aggregate demand.

Keynesian theory holds that aggregate demand can be adjusted through a combination of fiscal and monetary policies. **Fiscal policies,** which are enacted by the president and Congress, involve changes in government spending and taxing. When demand is too low, according to Keynes, government should either spend more itself, hiring people and thus giving them money, or cut taxes, giving people more of their own money to spend. When demand is too great, the government should either spend less or raise taxes, giving people less money to spend. **Monetary policies,** which are largely determined by the Federal Reserve Board, involve changes in the money supply and operate less directly on the economy. Increasing the amount of money in circulation increases aggregate demand and thus increases price inflation. Decreasing the money supply decreases aggregate demand and inflationary pressures.

feature 18.1

The Consumer Price Index

Inflation in the United States is usually measured in terms of the Consumer Price Index, which is calculated by the U.S. Bureau of Labor Statistics. The CPI is based on prices paid for food, clothing, shelter, transportation, medical services, and other items necessary for daily living. Data are collected from eighty-five areas across the country, from nearly sixty thousand homes and almost twenty thousand businesses.

The CPI is not a perfect yardstick. One problem is that it does not differentiate between inflationary price increases and other price increases. A Ford sedan bought in 1987, for instance, is not the same as a Ford sedan bought in 1997. To some extent, the price difference reflects improvements in quality as well as a decrease in the value of the dollar. The CPI is also slow to reflect changes in purchasing habits. Wash-and-wear clothes were tumbling in the dryer for several years before the government agreed to include them as an item in the index.

These are minor issues compared with the weight given over time to the cost of housing. Until 1983, twenty-six percent of the CPI was attributed to the cost of purchasing and financing a home. This formula neglected the realities that many people rent and that few people buy a home every year. A better measure of the cost of shelter is the cost of renting equivalent housing. Using this method of calculating the cost of shelter, the weight given to housing in the CPI dropped from 26 percent to 14 percent.

The government uses the CPI to make cost-of-living adjustments in civil service and military pension payments, social security benefits, and food stamp allowances. Moreover, many union wage contracts with private businesses are indexed (tied) to the CPI. Because the CPI tends to rise each year, so do payments that are tied to it. In a way, indexing payments to the CPI promotes both the growth of government spending and inflation itself. The United States is one of the few nations that also ties its tax brackets to a price index, which reduces government revenues by eliminating the effect of inflation on taxpayer incomes.

The last overhaul of the CPI was in 1987, and a revision was planned for 1996. The Bureau of Labor Statistics estimates that the current measure overestimates the true amount of inflation by about one-fourth. Thus, people whose incomes are tied to the index, such as retirees on social security, may actually be enjoying an increasing standard of living. Although few politicians would attempt to tell that to voters older than sixty-five, both Democrats and Republicans are considering paring .5 percent off the CPI, a move calculated to save over $30 billion over seven years.

Despite its faults, the CPI is at least a consistent measure of prices, and it is likely to continue as the basis for adjustments to wages, benefits, and payments affecting millions of people.

Source: Adapted from David S. Moore, *Statistics: Concepts and Controversies*, 2d ed. (New York: Freeman, 1985), pp. 238–241. Used by permission of W. H. Freeman. Also see U.S. Bureau of the Census, U.S. Department of Commerce, *Statistical Abstract of the United States, 1990* (Washington, D.C.: U.S. Government Printing Office, 1990), pp. 465–466; Robert D. Hershey, Jr., "An Inflation Index Is Said to Overstate the Case," *New York Times*, 11 January 1994, C1–C2; and David Wessel, "Why the CPI Fix Looks So Likely," *Wall Street Journal*, 11 December 1995, p. 1.

Despite some problems with the assumptions of Keynesian theory, capitalist countries have widely adopted it in some form.[11] At one time or another, virtually all have used the Keynesian technique of **deficit financing**—spending in excess of tax revenues—to combat an economic slump. The objective of deficit financing is to inject extra money into the economy to stimulate aggregate demand. Most deficits are financed with funds borrowed through the issuing of government bonds, notes, or other securities. The theory holds that deficits can be paid off with budget surpluses after the economy recovers.

Because Keynesian theory requires government to play an active role in controlling the economy, it runs counter to laissez-faire economics. Before Keynes, no administration in Washington would shoulder responsibility for maintaining a healthy economy. In 1946, the year Keynes died, Congress passed an employment act establishing "the continuing responsibility of the national government to . . . promote maximum employment, production and purchasing power." It also created the **Council of Economic Advisers (CEA)** within the Executive Office of the President to advise the president on maintaining a stable economy. The CEA normally consists of three economists (usually university professors) appointed by the president with Senate approval. Aided by a staff of about twenty-five people (mostly economists), the CEA helps the president prepare his annual economic report, also a provision of the 1946 act. The chair of the CEA is usually a prominent spokesperson for the administration's economic policy. Clinton's first chair, Laura D'Andrea Tyson, (formerly a professor of economics at the University of California at Berkeley), was succeeded by Joseph Stiglitz (on leave from Stanford).

The Employment Act of 1946, which reflected Keynesian theory, had a tremendous effect on government economic policy. Many people believe it was the primary source of "big government" in America. Even Richard Nixon, a conservative president, admitted that "we are all Keynesians now," by accepting government responsibility for the economy.

Monetary Policy

Although most economists accept Keynesian theory in its broad outlines, they depreciate its political utility. Some especially question the value of fiscal policies in controlling inflation and unemployment. They argue that government spending programs take too long to enact in Congress and to implement through the bureaucracy. As a result, jobs are created not when they are needed but years later, when the crisis may have passed and government spending needs to be reduced.

Also, government spending is easier to start than to stop, because the groups that benefit from spending programs tend to defend them even when they are no longer needed. A similar criticism applies to tax policies. Politically, it is much easier to cut taxes than to raise them. In other words, Keynesian theory requires that governments be able to begin and end spending quickly and to cut and raise taxes quickly. But in the real world, these fiscal tools are easier to use in one direction than the other. Ronald Reagan gained popularity by cutting taxes, whereas George Bush may have lost the 1992 election by raising them after having said, "Read my lips—no new taxes." As for cutting spending, the Republican Congress elected in 1994 found that cuts were more popular in the abstract than in reality.

Recognizing these limitations of fiscal policies, **monetarists** argue that government can control the economy's performance effectively only by controlling the nation's money supply. Monetarists favor a long-range policy of small but steady growth in the amount of money in circulation rather than frequent manipulation of monetary policies.

Monetary policies in the United States are under the control of the **Federal Reserve System,** which acts as the country's central bank. Established in 1914, the Fed is not a single bank but a system of banks. At the top of the system is the board of governors, seven members appointed by the president for staggered terms of fourteen years. The president designates one member of the board to be its chairperson, serving a four-year term that extends beyond the president's term of office. This complex arrangement was intended to make the board independent of the president and even of Congress. An independent board, the reasoning went, would be able to make financial decisions for the nation without regard to their political implications.

The Fed controls the money supply, which affects inflation, in three ways. It can change the *reserve requirement,* which is the amount of cash that member banks must keep on deposit in their regional Federal Reserve bank. An increase in the reserve requirement reduces the amount of money banks have available to lend. The Fed can also change its *discount rate,* the interest rate that member banks have to pay to borrow money from a Federal Reserve bank. A lower rate encourages member banks to borrow and lend more freely. Finally, the Fed can *buy and sell government securities* (such as U.S. Treasury notes and bonds) on the open market. When it buys securities, it pays out money, putting more money into circulation; when it sells securities, the process works in reverse. These transactions influence the federal funds rate, which banks charge one another for overnight loans. Again, a lower federal funds rate encourages borrowing and lending money.

The Fed's activities are essential parts of the government's overall economic policy, but they lie outside the direct control of the president. This can create problems in coordinating economic policy. For example, the president might want the Fed to lower interest rates to stimulate the economy, but the Fed might resist for fear of inflation. Such policy clashes can pit the chair of the Federal Reserve Board directly against the president. This happened early in 1991, when President Bush publicly criticized the Fed for not taking action to lower interest rates. When the Fed finally did cut its discount rate to encourage banks to lower interest rates in the spring of 1991, some analysts felt that the cut came partly in response to Bush's criticisms.[12] Clinton carefully courted the same Fed chairman, Alan Greenspan, even inviting him to sit next to Hillary Rodham Clinton when the president announced his economic plan to Congress in a televised address.[13] Clinton had good reason for courting Greenspan, for the Fed's low interest rates were credited in 1993 with pulling the economy out of its depression, underscoring the importance of monetary policy.[14] In 1996, Clinton reappointed Greenspan for a third term.

Although the Fed's economic policies are not perfectly insulated from political concerns, they are sufficiently independent that the president is not able to control monetary policy without the Fed's cooperation. This means that the president cannot be held completely responsible for the state of the economy—despite the Employment Act of 1946. Moreover, economic theories that predict the outcome of various moves by the Fed are sometimes proved incorrect. For example, when the Fed attempted to raise interest rates slightly in February 1994, the market did not respond as predicted: short-term rates moved less than the Fed wanted, and long-term rates moved more. As one analyst said, "None of this was forecast, either

Ticking Time Bomb

Say, buddy, can you tell me the debt? If you were in downtown New York on one day in the summer of 1996, you would have seen that your family's share of the national debt was nearly $70,000 then. And, minute by minute, it continues to increase.

by the Fed or by most private economists."[15] Of course, academic theories interact with investor psychology, and according to one Nobel Prize–winning economist, "The markets just aren't sophisticated about economics."[16] Nor, perhaps, are politicians.

Supply-Side Economics

When Reagan came to office in 1981, he embraced a school of thought called **supply-side economics** to deal with the double-digit inflation that the nation was experiencing. Keynesian theory argues that inflation results when consumers, businesses, and governments have more money to spend than there are goods and services to buy. The standard Keynesian solution is to reduce demand (for example, by increasing taxes). Supply-siders argue that inflation can be lowered more effectively by increasing the supply of goods. (That is, they stress the supply side of the economic equation.) Specifically, they favor tax cuts to stimulate investment (which, in turn, leads to the production of more goods) and less government regulation of business (again, to increase productivity—which they hold will yield more, not less, government revenue).

To support their theory, supply-side economists point to a 1964 tax cut initiated by President Kennedy. It stimulated investment and raised the total national income. As a result, the government took in as much tax revenue after the tax cut as it had before. Supply-siders also argue that the rich should receive larger tax cuts than the poor, because the rich have more money to invest. The benefits of increased investment will then "trickle down" to working people in the form of additional jobs and income.

In a sense, supply-side economics resembles laissez-faire economics in that it prefers less government regulation and less taxation. Supply-siders believe that government interferes too much with the efforts of individuals to work, save, and invest. Inspired by supply-side theory, Reagan proposed (and got) massive tax cuts in the Economic Recovery Tax Act of 1981. The bill's major legislative architect in the House was Representative Jack Kemp, whom Bob Dole chose as his vice-presidential running mate in 1996. It reduced individual tax rates by 23 percent over a three-year period and cut the marginal tax rate for the highest income group from 70 to 50 percent. Reagan also launched a program to deregulate business. According to supply-side theory, these actions would generate extra government revenue, making spending cuts unnecessary. Nevertheless, Reagan also cut funding for some domestic programs, including Aid to Families with Dependent Children and the food stamp program (see Chapter 19). Contrary to supply-side theory, he also proposed hefty increases in military spending. This blend of tax cuts, deregulation, cuts in spending for social programs, and increases in spending for defense became known, somewhat disparagingly, as *Reaganomics*.

How well did Reaganomics work? Although it reduced inflation and unemployment (aided by a sharp decline in oil prices) and worked largely as expected in the area of industry deregulation, Reaganomics failed massively to reduce the budget deficit. Contrary to supply-side theory, the 1981 tax cut was accompanied by a massive drop in tax revenues. Shortly after taking office, Reagan promised that his economic policies would balance the national budget by 1984, but lower tax revenues and higher defense spending produced the largest budget deficits ever, as shown in Figure 18.1.[17]

Although as Senate majority leader Bob Dole worked to implement Reagan's economic policies in 1981, he remained skeptical of supply-side theory. Nevertheless, when he needed to make a dramatic appeal to the voters in his 1996 presidential campaign, Dole succumbed to his supply-side advisers and announced an economic plan that featured a 15 percent across-the-board tax cut, declaring that cutting taxes and balancing the budget at the same time are "just a matter of presidential will."[18] Even the *Wall Street Journal* inquired whether "Dole's math adds up."[19]

PUBLIC POLICY AND THE BUDGET

To most people—college students included—the national budget is B-O-R-I-N-G. To national politicians, it is an exciting script for high drama. The numbers, categories, and percentages that numb normal minds cause politicians' nostrils to flare and their hearts to pound. The budget is a battlefield on which politicians wage war over the programs they support.

Control of the budget is important to members of Congress because they are politicians, and politicians want to wield power, not watch someone else wield it. Also, the Constitution established Congress, not the president, as the "first branch" of government and the people's representatives. Unfortunately for Congress, the president has emerged as the leader in shaping the budget. Although Congress often disagrees with presidential spending priorities, it has been unable to mount a serious challenge to presidential authority by presenting a coherent alternative budget.

Today, the president prepares the budget, and Congress approves it. This was not always the case. Before 1921, Congress prepared the budget under its constitutional authority to raise taxes and appropriate funds. The budget was formed piecemeal by enacting a series of laws that originated in

figure 18.1   ● **Budget Deficits over Time**

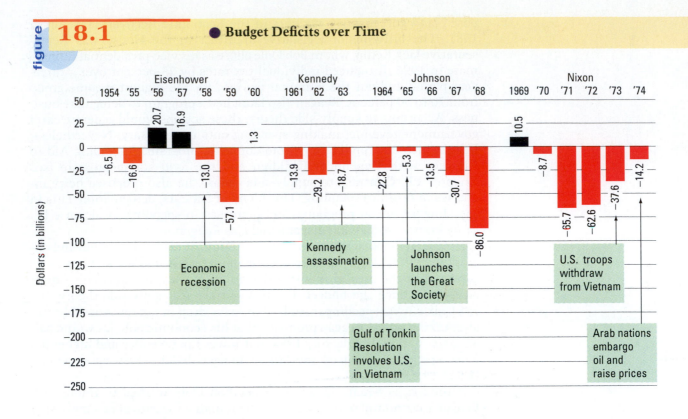

In his first inaugural address, President Reagan said, "You and I, as individuals, can, by borrowing, live beyond our means, but only for a limited period of time. Why, then, should we think that collectively, as a nation, we're not bound by that same limitation?" But borrow he did. Reagan's critics charged that the budget deficits under his administration— more than $1.3 trillion—exceeded the total deficits of all previous presidents. But this charge does not take inflation into account. A billion dollars in the 1990s is worth much less than it was a century ago or even ten years ago.

the many committees involved in the highly decentralized process of raising revenue, authorizing expenditures, and appropriating funds. Executive agencies even submitted their budgetary requests directly to Congress, not to the president. No one was responsible for the big picture—the budget as a whole. The president's role was essentially limited to approving revenue and appropriations bills, just as he approved other pieces of legislation.

Congressional budgeting (such as it was) worked well enough for a nation of farmers, but not for an industrialized nation with a growing population and an increasingly active government. Soon after World War I, Congress realized that the budget-making process needed to be centralized. With the Budgeting and Accounting Act of 1921, it thrust the responsibility for preparing the budget onto the president. The act established the Bureau of the Budget to help the president write "his" bud-

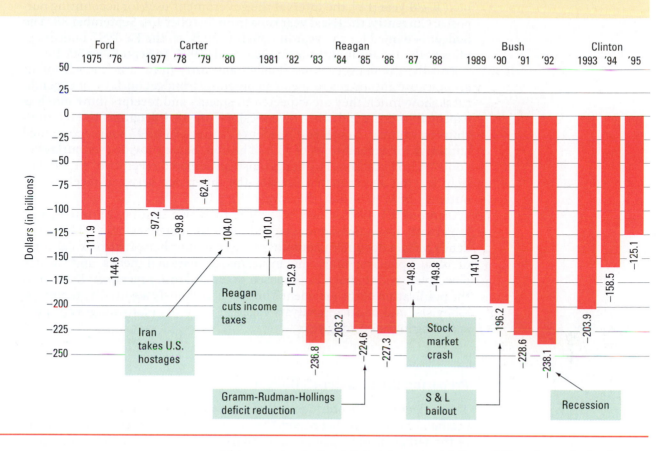

A fairer way to calculate deficits is in constant dollars—dollars whose value has been standardized to a given year. This chart shows the actual deficits in 1987 dollars incurred under presidential administrations from Eisenhower to Clinton. Even computed this way, Reagan's deficits were enormous—especially for a president who claimed to oppose government borrowing. The deficit grew to be as large under Bush before being reduced under Clinton.

Source: Executive Office of the President, *Budget of the United States Government, Fiscal Year 1997: Historical Tables* (Washington, D.C.: U.S. Government Printing Office, 1996), p. 17.

get, which had to be submitted to Congress each January. Congress retained its constitutional authority to raise and spend funds, but now Congress would begin its work with the president's budget as its starting point. And all executive agencies' budget requests had to be funneled for review through the Bureau of the Budget (which became the Office of Management and Budget in 1970); those consistent with the president's overall economic and legislative program were incorporated into the president's budget.

The Nature of the Budget

The national budget is complex. But its basic elements are not beyond understanding. We begin with some definitions. The *Budget of the United States Government* is the annual financial plan that the president is required to submit to Congress at the start of each year. It applies to the next **fiscal year (FY),** the interval the government uses for accounting purposes. Currently, the fiscal year runs from October 1 to September 30. The budget is named for the year in which it *ends,* so the FY 1997 budget applies to the twelve months from October 1, 1996, to September 30, 1997.

Broadly, the budget defines **budget authority** (how much government agencies are authorized to spend on programs); **budget outlays,** or expenditures (how much they are expected to spend); and **receipts** (how much is expected in taxes and other revenues). Figure 18.2 diagrams the relationship of authority to outlays. President Clinton's FY 1997 budget contained authority for expenditures of $1,638 billion, but it provided for outlays of "only" $1,635 billion. His budget also anticipated receipts of $1,495 billion, leaving an estimated deficit—the difference between receipts and outlays—of $140 billion, the lowest since 1987.

Clinton's FY 1997 budget was more than two thousand printed pages long (with appendices) and weighed more than eight pounds. (The president's budget document contains more than numbers. It also explains individual spending programs in terms of national needs and agency objectives, and it analyzes proposed taxes and other receipts.) Each year, the publication of the president's budget is anxiously awaited by reporters, lobbyists, and political analysts eager to learn his plans for government spending in the coming year.

Preparing the President's Budget

The budget that the president submits to Congress each winter is the end product of a process that begins the previous spring under the supervision of the **Office of Management and Budget (OMB).** OMB is located within the Executive Office of the President and is headed by a director appointed by the president with the approval of the Senate. The OMB, with a staff of more than five hundred, is the most powerful domestic agency in the bureaucracy, and its director, who attends meetings of the president's cabinet, is one of the most powerful figures in government. In 1996, Franklin Raines was nominated as director of OMB to succeed Alice Rivlin, whom Clinton named to be vice-chairman of the Federal Reserve Board.

The OMB initiates the budget process each spring by meeting with the president to discuss the economic situation and his budgetary priorities. It then sends broad budgeting guidelines to every government agency and requests their initial projection of how much money they will need for the next fiscal year. The OMB assembles this information and makes recommendations to the president, who then develops more precise guidelines describing how much each is likely to get. By summer, the agencies are asked to prepare budgets based on the new guidelines. By fall, they submit their formal budgets to the OMB, where budget analysts scrutinize agency requests, considering both their costs and their consistency with the president's legislative program. A lot of politicking goes on at this stage, as agency heads try to circumvent the OMB by pleading for their pet projects with presidential advisers and perhaps even the president himself. Unlike presidents Reagan and Bush, who basically delegated economic policy to others in their administrations, Clinton has been more involved in the

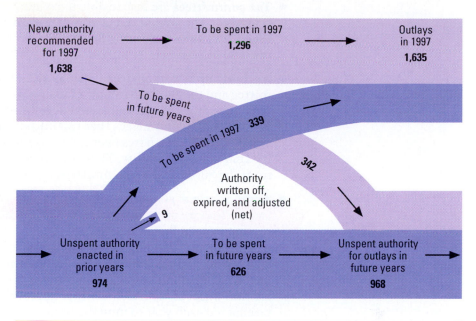

figure 18.2 ● **Relationship of Budget Authority to Budget Outlays**

The national budget is a complicated document. One source of confusion for people studying the budget for the first time is the relationship of budget authority to budget outlays. These two amounts differ because of sums that are carried over from previous years and to future years. The diagram helps explain the relationship (all amounts are in billions of dollars).

Source: Executive Office of the President, *Budget of the United States Government, Fiscal Year 1997: Analytical Perspectives* (Washington, D.C.: U.S. Government Printing Office, 1996), p. 282.

process and makes more of the big decisions himself. Although often criticized for his lack of understanding of foreign policy, Clinton appears to have a genuine grasp of economic policy. According to his chief assistant on economic matters, Robert E. Rubin, "He understands this, he really does. I don't mean he just read a paper on some topic or other. He has a feel for these economic issues."[20] The voters seemed to buy his view in 1996.

Political negotiations over the budget may extend into the early winter—often until it goes to the printer. The voluminous document looks very much like a finished product, but the figures it contains are not final. In giving the president the responsibility for preparing the budget in 1921, Congress simply provided itself with a starting point for its own work. Even then, Congress has had a hard time disciplining itself to produce a coherent, balanced budget.

Passing the Congressional Budget

The president's budget must be approved by Congress. Its process for doing so is a creaky conglomeration of traditional procedures overlaid with structural reforms from the 1970s, external constraints from the 1980s, and changes introduced by the 1990 Budget Enforcement Act. The cumbersome process has had difficulty producing a budget according to Congress's own timetable.

The Traditional Procedure: The Committee Structure. Traditionally, the tasks of budget making were divided among a number of committees—a process that has been retained. Three types of committees are involved in budgeting:

- **Tax committees** are responsible for raising the revenues to run the government. The Ways and Means Committee in the House and the Finance Committee in the Senate consider all proposals for taxes, tariffs, and other receipts contained in the president's budget.

- **Authorization committees** (such as the House Armed Services Committee and the Senate Banking, Housing, and Urban Affairs Committee) have jurisdiction over particular legislative subjects. The House has about twenty committees that can authorize spending, and the Senate about fifteen. Each pores over the portions of the budget that pertain to its area of responsibility. However, in recent years power has shifted from the authorization committees to the appropriations committees.

- **Appropriations committees** decide which of the programs approved by the authorization committees will actually be funded (that is, given money to spend). For example, the House Armed Services Committee might propose building a new line of tanks for the army, and it might succeed in getting this proposal enacted into law. But the tanks will never be built unless the appropriations committees appropriate funds for that purpose. Thirteen distinct appropriations bills are supposed to be enacted each year to fund the nation's spending.

Two serious problems are inherent in a budgeting process that involves three distinct kinds of congressional committees. First, the two-step spending process (first authorization, then appropriation) is complex; it offers wonderful opportunities for interest groups to get into the budgeting act in the spirit of pluralist democracy. Second, because one group of legislators in each house plans for revenues and many other groups plan for spending, no one is responsible for the budget as a whole. In the 1970s, Congress added a new committee structure that combats the pluralist politics inherent in the old procedures and allows budget choices to be made in a more majoritarian manner, by votes in both chambers. In the 1980s, Congress tried to force itself to balance the budget by setting targets. In 1990, Congress tried again to patch the leaks in the budget boat with additional reforms. When the Republicans gained control of Congress in 1995, they gave a willing president an additional budgetary weapon: the line item veto. Here is a brief account of these developments.

Reforms of the 1970s: The Budget Committee Structure.   Congress surrendered considerable authority in 1921 when it gave the president the responsibility of preparing the budget. During the next fifty years, attempts by Congress to regain control of the budgeting process failed because of jurisdictional squabbles between the revenue and appropriations committees. The Budget and Impoundment Control Act of 1974 fashioned a typically political solution to the problems of wounded egos and competing jurisdictions, which had frustrated previous attempts to change the budget-making process. All the tax and appropriations committees (and chairpersons) were retained, but new House and Senate budget committees were superimposed over the old committee structure. The **budget committees** supervise a comprehensive budget review process, aided by the Congressional Budget Office. The **Congressional Budget Office (CBO)**, with a staff of more than two hundred, acquired a budgetary expertise equal to that of the president's OMB, so it can prepare credible alternative budgets for Congress.

At the heart of the 1974 reforms was a timetable for the congressional budgeting process. The budget committees are supposed to propose an initial budget resolution that sets overall revenue and spending levels, broken down into twenty-one different "budget functions," such as national defense, agriculture, and health. By April 15, both houses are supposed to have agreed on a single budget resolution to guide their work on the budget during the summer. The appropriations committees are supposed to begin drafting the thirteen appropriations bills by May 15 and complete them by June 30. Throughout, the levels of spending set by majority vote in the budget resolution are supposed to constrain pressures by special interests to increase spending.

Congress implemented this process (or one very much like it) in 1975, and it worked reasonably well for the first few years. Congress was able to work on and structure the budget as a whole rather than in pieces. But the process broke down during the Reagan administration, when the president submitted annual budgets with huge deficits. The Democratic Congress adjusted Reagan's spending priorities away from the military and toward social programs, but it refused to propose a tax increase to reduce the deficit without the president's cooperation. At loggerheads with the president, Congress encountered increasing difficulty in enacting its budget resolutions according to its own timetable.

External Constraints of the 1980s: Gramm-Rudman.   Alarmed by the huge deficits in Reagan's budgets, frustrated by his refusal to raise taxes, and stymied by their own inability to cut the deficit, members of Congress were ready to try almost anything. Republican senators Phil Gramm of Texas and Warren Rudman of New Hampshire were joined by Democrat Ernest Hollings of South Carolina in a drastic proposal to force a balanced budget by gradually eliminating the deficit. Officially titled the Balanced Budget and Emergency Deficit Control Act (1985), their bill became known simply as Gramm-Rudman-Hollings, or **Gramm-Rudman**.

In its original form, Gramm-Rudman mandated that the budget deficit be lowered to a specified level each year until the budget was balanced by FY 1991. If Congress did not meet the mandated deficit level in any year, across-the-board budget cuts were to be made automatically. In 1986, the very first year under Gramm-Rudman, Congress failed to meet its deficit target. The president and Congress saw 4.3 percent sliced from every domestic and defense program (except for those specifically exempted, such as social security), regardless of their importance. In 1987, again unable to make the deficit meet the mandated level, Congress and the president simply changed the law to match the deficit. The Gramm-Rudman law will be remembered for demonstrating that Congress once tried to balance the budget by progressively decreasing the deficit on a year-by-year basis, but it failed for lack of will.

Reforms of 1990: The Budget Enforcement Act.   When the 1990 recession threatened another huge deficit in FY 1991, Congress and the president agreed on a new package of reforms and deficit targets in the Budget

No Dough, No Show

Twice in late 1995, impasses between the president and Congress over the national budget created a shortage of operating funds that shut down most of the government. Not only did many agencies cease operating, but prime Washington attractions—such as the National Gallery of Art, the Washington Monument, and the White House—were closed to the public. The public blamed both sides for the shutdown, but Congress took the most criticism.

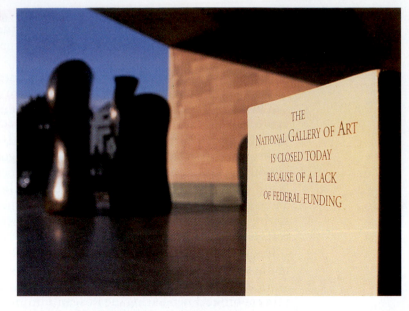

Try your hand at cutting the national budget by playing this game.
`<garnet.berkeley.edu:3333`
`/budget/budget-1.html>`

Enforcement Act. This law divided government spending into two types and imposed certain restrictions on both. It defined **mandatory spending** as expenditures required by legal commitments. For example, spending is mandatory for **entitlement** programs (such as social security and veterans' programs) that provide benefits to individuals legally entitled to them (see Chapter 19). For the first time, the law established **pay-as-you-go** restrictions on mandatory spending. Under "paygo," any domestic (defense) spending increase must be matched by a domestic (defense) savings, or a tax increase. Similarly, any tax cut must be offset by a tax increase elsewhere or by savings.[21] That drastically altered the significance of the latest deficit targets. The law defined **discretionary spending** as authorized expenditures from annual appropriations (such as the personnel budget for the military). For the first time, the law imposed limits, or "caps," on discretionary (but not mandatory) spending.

Significantly, the 1990 law, with its caps on spending and its paygo requirements, removed most of the pressure to reduce the deficit to meet the Gramm-Rudman targets. Under earlier rules, any economic downturn that caused the government to spend more or resulted in less revenue than expected might cause the deficit to exceed the Gramm-Rudman target and thus trigger across-the-board cuts. But now these unexpected external events (including war and the massive costs of the S&L bailout) are—like acts of God—regarded as "outside" the budgetary agreement, which requires only that everyone keep their part of the bargain on spending caps and pay-as-you-go restrictions.

A failure to limit discretionary spending in any category to its cap in any year or a violation of pay-as-you-go restrictions by Congress will trigger a **sequestration**—an across-the-board spending cut in the overspent category or in nonexempt entitlement programs. These cuts would occur automatically fifteen days after Congress adjourns. In evaluating the reforms of the 1990s, one budgetary scholar concluded that they ensured that the president and the Congress "would battle over domestic discretionary spending in a controlled zero-sum budget game."[22] But following the sweeping electoral victory in 1994 that gave their party control of Congress, Republicans deployed new forces in an all-out campaign for a balanced budget.

Reforms of 1996: The Balanced Budget Amendment and the Line Item Veto.   Recalling Congress's failed attempts since the 1980s to balance the budget, Representative Tim Hutchinson (Republican from Arkansas) said on the House floor, "If this body is ever going to face fiscal responsibility, balancing the budget must be a requirement made by the supreme law of the land. Laws control men, but only the Constitution can control Government."[23] The idea of a constitutional amendment requiring a balanced budget dates back to 1787, and it was the first item mentioned in the Republicans' Contract with America.[24] Republicans introduced a proposed balanced budget amendment immediately upon taking control of Congress in 1995. The resolution passed the House but failed in the Senate by only one vote, so it was never submitted to the states for ratification. Although this venerable idea was submerged once again, the balanced budget amendment resurfaced in the 1996 Republican party platform.

The second item mentioned in the Contract with America was the line item veto, a power that President Reagan had requested in his 1984 State of the Union address. As governor of California—like most other governors—he had enjoyed the power to approve parts of bills he liked and reject other parts. Under the Constitution, however, the president can only veto entire bills, not just parts of them. In 1995, Republicans introduced legislation to permit the president to reject individual items in annual appropriations bills. Such cuts must stand unless Congress passes a specific bill to overturn them. Although this measure was passed in 1996, the Republican Congress could not bear to surrender this power to Bill Clinton during an election year, so the law was written to take effect on January 1, 1997.

Giving this power to the president was deemed a "historic concession" that "potentially shifted enormous power from Congress to the president."[25] Republican Senator Dan Coats of Indiana, who backed the bill, admitted, "It's Congress's way of saying, 'We've lost control of the spending process.'"[26] Once again, Congress had surrendered some of its power to the president—as it did in 1921 by giving the president the duty (and the power) to submit an annual budget to Congress. The constitutionality of the line item veto is in doubt, however, because Congress provided the president with additional authority by statute, not by constitutional amendment. Scholarly opinions differ about the legality of this approach, and the Supreme Court will ultimately decide the issue after January 1, 1997.

TAX POLICIES

So far, we have been concerned mainly with the spending side of the budget, for which appropriations must be enacted each year. The revenue side of the budget is governed by overall tax policy, which is designed to provide a continuous flow of income without annual legislation. A major text on government finance says that tax policy is sometimes changed to accomplish one or more of several objectives:

- To adjust overall revenue to meet budget outlays

- To make the tax burden more equitable for taxpayers

- To help control the economy by raising taxes (thus decreasing aggregate demand) or by lowering taxes (thus increasing demand)[27]

The Reagan administration engineered a significant change in the nation's tax policies in the 1980s. In Reagan's first three years, personal income taxes were lowered by 23 percent, resulting in a total revenue loss of $500 billion over the next five years.[28] According to supply-side economic theory, that massive tax cut should have stimulated the economy and yielded even more revenue than was lost—if not in the first year, then soon afterward. It didn't happen. Revenues lagged badly behind spending, and the deficit grew.

Although the Reagan administration enacted various tax increases in 1982 and 1984 to offset the lost revenue, few politicians in the 1980s dared mention a hike in income tax rates. Democratic presidential candidate Walter Mondale tried it in the 1984 election and was beaten badly. The Democratic leadership in Congress and many leading Republicans believed that taxes had to be raised to cut the deficit, but no one was willing to propose an increase. Reagan went even further in 1986. He urged Congress to enact sweeping tax reform that would (1) lower still further the rate for those in the highest income tax bracket, (2) reduce the number of tax brackets, (3) eliminate virtually all the tax loopholes through which many wealthy people and corporations avoided paying taxes, and (4) be revenue neutral, in the sense that it would bring in no more and no less revenue than existing tax policy.

Tax Reform

Tax reform proposals are usually so heavily influenced by interest groups looking for special benefits that they end up working against their original purpose. However, Reagan's proposals met with relatively few major changes, and in 1986 Congress passed one of the most sweeping tax reform laws in history. The new policy reclaimed a great deal of revenue by eliminating many deductions for corporations and wealthy citizens. That revenue was supposed to pay for a general reduction in tax rates for individual citizens. By eliminating many tax brackets, the new tax policy approached the idea of a flat tax—one that requires everyone to pay at the same rate. Steve Forbes, a millionaire publisher who had never run for office, campaigned for the 1996 Republican presidential nomination on instituting a flat tax of 17 percent on wages (but not on investment income). His bold and controversial plan attracted enough attention to give him the lead in convention delegates by the end of February, before he was overwhelmed by Bob Dole later in the primaries. Even many conservative economists did not think Forbes's flat tax would produce enough revenue to eliminate deficits, however.[29]

A flat tax has the appeal of simplicity, but it violates the principle of **progressive taxation,** under which the rich pay proportionately higher taxes than the poor. The ability to pay has long been a standard of fair taxation, and surveys show that citizens favor this idea in the abstract.[30] In practice, however, they have different opinions, as we will see. Nevertheless, governments rely on progressive taxation to redistribute wealth and thus promote economic equality.

Representation Without Taxation!

Across the nation, citizens are up in arms about high taxes, although the United States has one of the lowest tax burdens in the world. Taxes are not perceived as high at just the national level. This demonstration against state taxes is for the benefit of the Texas legislature.

In general, the greater the number of tax brackets, the more progressive a tax can be. Before Reagan proposed his tax reforms in 1986, there were fourteen tax brackets, ranging from 11 percent to 50 percent. After the law took effect in 1988, there were only two rates—15 and 28 percent. In 1990, Bush was forced to violate his pledge of "no new taxes" by creating a third tax rate, 31 percent, for those with the highest incomes. Clinton created a fourth level, 40 percent, in 1993, moving toward a more progressive tax structure, although still less progressive than before 1986.

Comparing Tax Burdens

No one likes to pay taxes, so it is politically popular to attack taxation. Bob Dole resorted to this strategy late in his 1996 presidential campaign, announcing a fifteen percent across-the-board cut in personal income tax, to begin in 1997 and to be spread over three years, and by selecting Jack Kemp, the prominent tax cutter and supply-side advocate, as his vice-presidential running mate.[31] Is the tax burden too heavy on American citizens? One way to compare tax burdens is to examine taxes over time in the same country; another is to compare taxes in different countries at the same time. By comparing taxes over time in the United States, we find that the total tax burden on U.S. citizens has indeed been growing. For the average family, the percentage of income that went to all national, state, and local taxes doubled, to 23 percent, between 1953 and 1993.[32]

However, neither the national government nor the national income tax accounts for the bulk of that increase. First, national taxes as a percentage of the gross national product have changed very little during the last thirty years; it is the state and local tax burden that has doubled in size.[33] Second, the income tax has not been the main culprit in the increasing tax bite at the national level; the proportion of national budget receipts contributed by income taxes has remained fairly constant since the end of World War II. The largest increases have come in social security taxes, which have

compared with what?

18.1 Tax Burdens in Twenty-Two Countries

All nations tax their citizens, but some nations impose a heavier tax burden than others. This graph compares tax burdens in 1992 as a percentage of gross domestic product (GDP), which is the market value of goods produced inside the country by workers, businesses, and government. The percentages include national, state, and local taxes and social security contributions. By this measure, the U.S. government extracts less in taxes from its citizens than the governments of virtually all democratic nations. First on the list is Sweden, well known as a state that provides heavily for social welfare, which consumes about 50 percent of its GDP in taxes.

Source: U.S. Bureau of the Census, U.S. Department of Commerce, *Statistical Abstract of the United States, 1995* (Washington, D.C.: U.S. Government Printing Office, 1995), p. 860.

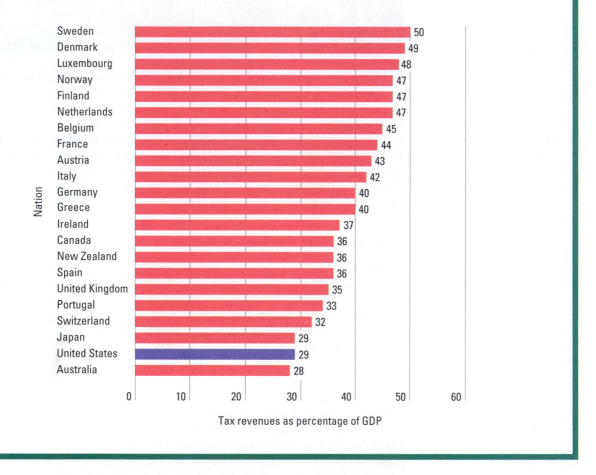

risen steadily to pay for the government's single largest social welfare program, aid to the elderly (see Chapter 19).

Another way to compare tax burdens is to examine tax rates in different countries. Despite complaints about high taxes, the U.S. tax burden is not large compared with that of other democratic nations. As shown in Compared with What? 18.1, Americans' taxes are quite low in general

Angry about taxes? Search the U.S. Taxpayers Party Web site for sympathy.
`<www.ustaxpayers.org/usearch.html>`

compared with those in twenty-one other democratic nations. Primarily because they provide their citizens with more generous social benefits (such as health care and unemployment compensation), every nation except Australia ranked equal to or above the United States.

SPENDING POLICIES

The national government spends hundreds of billions of dollars every year. Where does the money go? Figure 18.3 shows the $1.7 trillion in outlays in President Clinton's FY 1997 budget, broken down according to eighteen major budgetary functions. The largest amount (22 percent of the total budget) was earmarked for social security. Until FY 1993, the largest spending category was national defense, but military spending dropped into second place after the collapse of communism. The third-largest outlay was interest on the accumulated national debt, which alone accounts for about 15 percent of all government spending. The fourth-largest category, income security, encompasses a variety of programs that provide a "social safety net": unemployment compensation, food for low-income parents and children, aid to families with dependent children, help for the blind and disabled, and assistance for the homeless. Medicare and health, the next largest categories, together account for more than 18 percent of all budgetary outlays, which underscores the importance of controlling the costs of health care.

To understand current expenditures, it is a good idea to examine national expenditures over time, as in Figure 18.4. The effect of World War II is clear: spending for national defense rose sharply after 1940, peaked at about 90 percent of the budget in 1945, and fell to about 30 percent in peacetime. The percentage allocated to defense rose again in the early 1950s, reflecting rearmament during the Cold War with the Soviet Union. Thereafter, the share of the budget devoted to defense decreased steadily (except for the bump during the Vietnam War in the late 1960s), until the trend was reversed by the Carter administration in the 1970s and shot upwards during the Reagan presidency. Defense spending significantly decreased under Bush, and continued to go down under Clinton.

Government payments to individuals (social security checks) consistently consumed less of the budget than national defense until 1971. Since then, payments to individuals have accounted for the largest portion of the national budget, and they have been increasing. Net interest payments have also increased substantially in recent years, reflecting the rapidly growing national debt. Pressure from payments for national defense, individuals, and interest on the national debt has squeezed all other government outlays.

One might expect government expenditures to increase steadily, roughly matching the rate of price inflation; however, national spending has far outstripped inflation. Figure 18.5 graphs government receipts and outlays as a percentage of gross domestic product (GDP), which eliminates the effect of inflation. It shows that national spending has increased from about 15 percent of GDP soon after World War II to over 20 percent, most recently at the price of a growing national deficit. There are two major explanations for this steady increase in government spending. One is bureaucratic, the other political.

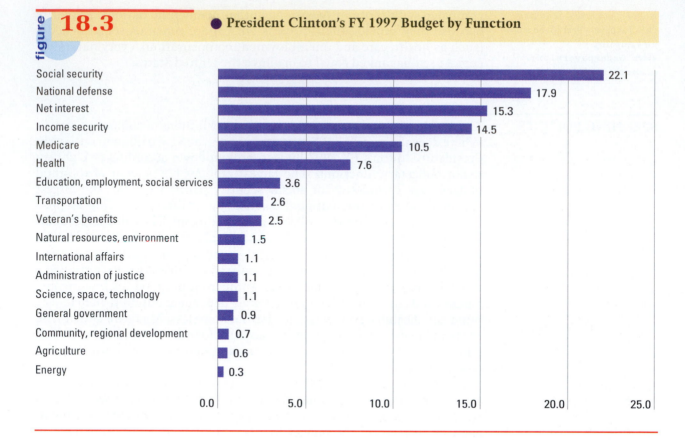

figure 18.3   ● President Clinton's FY 1997 Budget by Function

Function	Value
Social security	22.1
National defense	17.9
Net interest	15.3
Income security	14.5
Medicare	10.5
Health	7.6
Education, employment, social services	3.6
Transportation	2.6
Veteran's benefits	2.5
Natural resources, environment	1.5
International affairs	1.1
Administration of justice	1.1
Science, space, technology	1.1
General government	0.9
Community, regional development	0.7
Agriculture	0.6
Energy	0.3

Federal budget authorities and outlays are organized into about twenty categories, some of which exist mainly for bookkeeping purposes. This graph shows expected outlays for each of seventeen substantive functions in Clinton's FY 1997 budget. The final budget differed somewhat from this distribution, because Congress amended some of the president's spending proposals, but the proportions remained nearly the same. The graph makes clear the huge differences between spending categories. Nearly 40 percent of government outlays are for social security and income security—that is, payments to individuals. Health costs (including Medicare) account for nearly 20 percent more, slightly more than national defense, and net interest consumes about 15 percent. This leaves relatively little for transportation, agriculture, justice, science, and energy—matters often regarded as the object of government activity but which fall under the heading of "discretionary spending."

Source: Congressional Quarterly Weekly Report, 23 March 1996, pp. 774–775. Copyright © 1996 by Congressional Quarterly. Used with permission.

Incremental Budgeting . . .

The bureaucratic explanation for spending increases involves **incremental budgeting:** bureaucrats, in compiling their funding requests for the following year, traditionally ask for the amount they got in the current year plus some incremental increase to fund new projects. Because Congress has already approved the agency's budget for the current year, it pays little attention to the agency's current size (the largest part of its budget) and focuses instead on the extra money (the increment) requested for the next

18.4 ● National Government Outlays over Time

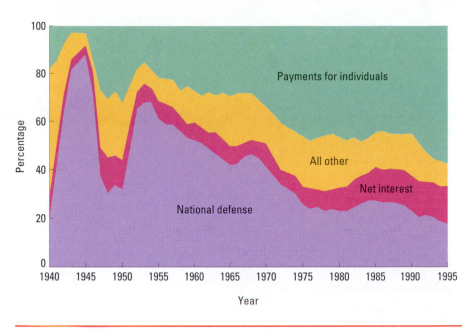

This chart plots the percentage of the annual budget devoted to four major expense categories over time. It shows that significant changes have occurred in national spending since 1940. During World War II, defense spending consumed more than 80 percent of the national budget. Defense again accounted for most national expenditures during the Cold War of the 1950s. Since then, the military's share of expenditures has declined, while payments to individuals (mostly in the form of social security benefits) have increased dramatically. Also, as the graph shows, the proportion of the budget paid in interest on the national debt has increased substantially since the 1970s.

Source: Executive Office of the President, *Budget of the United States Government, Fiscal Year 1997: Historical Tables* (Washington, D.C.: U.S. Government Printing Office, 1996), pp. 23–24.

year. As a result, few agencies are ever cut back, and spending continually goes up.

Incremental budgeting produces a sort of bureaucratic momentum that continually pushes up spending. Once an agency is established, it attracts a clientele that defends its existence and supports the agency's requests for extra funds to do more year after year. Because budgeting is a two-step process, agencies that get cut back in the authorizing committees sometimes manage (assisted by their interest group clientele) to get funds restored in the appropriations committees—and if not in the House, then perhaps in the Senate. So incremental budgeting and the congressional budget-making process itself are ideally suited to pluralist politics. However, recent political reactions to the huge budget deficit have substantially checked the practice of incremental budgeting.

When the Republicans took over control of Congress in 1995, they largely disregarded Clinton's FY 1996 budget and proceeded to slash government programs under discretionary spending. Ten of the thirteen appropriations bills Congress sent to the president provided *less* money than was appropriated for 1995.[34] Together, these cuts resulted in a more than $15 billion decrease from the previous year's spending levels—hardly an example of incremental budgeting. Only after Clinton vetoed five of these appropriations bills and the government experienced two historic shutdowns did the president and Congress compromise on spending.[35] Nevertheless, the final spending bill for FY 1996 was judged by an outside expert to be "one of the most significant reversals in the course of government since World War II."[36] Many agencies had to deal with less money than they had spent in FY 1995. For example, the National Park Service

figure 18.5 ● Government Outlays and Receipts as a Percentage of GDP

We can see the growth of national government spending—and the rising national debt—by plotting budget outlays and receipts against each other over time. In this graph, outlays and receipts are each expressed as a percentage of GDP, to control for inflation and to demonstrate that both government spending and taxes have represented a progressively larger share of the nation's productive output. The deficit for 1995 was only 2.3 percent of GDP, close to the average of 2 percent.

Source: Executive Office of the President, *Budget of the United States Government, Fiscal Year 1997: Historical Tables* (Washington, D.C.: U.S. Government Printing Office, 1996), p. 24.

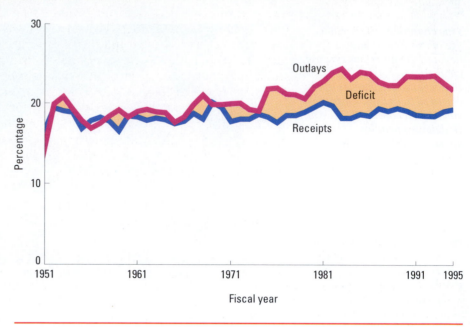

got $67 million less, NASA lost $473 million, the State Department got $490 million less, and so on.[37] Despite all this cutting, Congress only nibbled at the margins of government spending, for it failed to make significant cuts in the major domestic portions of the budget, the so-called "uncontrollable" spending.

… And Uncontrollable Spending

Certain government programs are effectively immune to budget reductions, because they have been enacted into law and are enshrined in politics. For example, social security legislation guarantees certain benefits to program participants when they retire. Medicare and veterans' benefits also entitle citizens to certain payments. Because these payments have to be made under existing law, they represent **uncontrollable outlays.** In Clinton's FY 1997 budget, nearly two-thirds of all budget outlays were uncontrollable or relatively uncontrollable—mainly payments to individuals under social security, Medicare, and public assistance; interest on the national debt; and farm price supports. About half of the rest went for defense, leaving about 17 percent in domestic discretionary spending for balancing the budget.

To be sure, Congress could change the laws to abolish entitlement payments, and it does modify them through the budgeting process. But politics argues against large-scale reductions. The Republicans in Congress drew public criticism for "reducing" spending on health care, even though they took pains to explain that their program actually allowed for increased spending; they were only "cutting the rate of increase."[38]

■■■
■■■
■■■ The "Voters" data in the
CROSSTABS program contains
responses to questions asked
about increasing or decreasing
government spending in twelve
different areas. Analyze the responses according to the voters'
"Personal Traits" to see who
favors what programs.

What spending cuts would be acceptable to or even popular with the public? At the most general level, voters favor cutting government spending, but they tend to favor maintaining "government programs that help needy people and deal with important national problems."[39] Substantial majorities favor spending the same or even more on social security, Medicare, education, job training, programs for poor children, and the military. There is not even a majority for cutting spending on food stamps or welfare.[40] One of the few areas of spending that generates a strong and settled majority for decreased spending is foreign aid, which about 70 percent would like to see cut. But because less than one percent of the budget goes to foreign aid, this area does not offer much savings.

In truth, a perplexed Congress, trying to reduce the budget deficit, faces a public that favors funding programs at even higher levels than those favored by most lawmakers.[41] Moreover, spending for the most expensive of these programs—social security and Medicare—is uncontrollable. Americans have grown accustomed to certain government benefits, but they do not like the idea of raising taxes to pay for them.

TAXING, SPENDING, AND ECONOMIC EQUALITY

As we noted in Chapter 1, the most controversial purpose of government is to promote equality, especially economic equality. Economic equality comes about only at the expense of economic freedom, for it requires government action to redistribute wealth from the rich to the poor. One means of redistribution is government tax policy, especially the progressive income tax. The other instrument for reducing inequalities is government spending through welfare programs. The goal in both cases is not to produce equality of outcome; it is to reduce inequalities by helping the poor.

The national government introduced an income tax in 1862 to help finance the Civil War. That tax was repealed in 1871, and a new tax imposed in 1893 was declared unconstitutional by the Supreme Court. The Sixteenth Amendment (1913) gave the government the power to levy a tax on individual incomes, and it has done so every year since 1914.[42] From 1964 to 1981, people who reported taxable incomes of $100,000 or more paid a top marginal tax rate of 70 percent (except during the Vietnam War), whereas those with lower incomes paid taxes at progressively lower rates, as set forth in Figure 18.6. About the same time, the government launched the War on Poverty as part of President Johnson's Great Society initiative. His programs and their successors are discussed at length in Chapter 19. For now, let us look at the overall effect of government spending and tax policies on economic equality in America.

Government Effects on Economic Equality

We begin by asking whether government spending policies have any measurable effect on income inequality. Economists refer to government payments to individuals through social security, unemployment insurance, food stamps, and other programs, such as agricultural subsidies, as **transfer payments.** Transfer payments need not always go to the poor. In fact, one problem with the farm program is that the wealthiest farmers have

●●●●●●●●●●●●●
**But You MUST Have a
Computer Number!**

*Government programs that
deal with the needs of millions of citizens are inherently
bureaucratic. As this unemployment office shows, people
of all types sometimes lose
their job and need help in
finding a new one.*

often received the largest subsidies.[43] Nevertheless, most researchers have
determined that transfer payments have had a definite effect in reducing
income inequality.

A study of government policies from 1966 to 1985 found that families in
the lowest tenth of the population in terms of income paid 33 percent of
their income in national, state, and local taxes but also received payments
from all levels of government that almost equaled their earned income.[44]
So the lowest-income group enjoyed a net benefit from government because of transfer payments. Another study, covering 1979 to 1988, found
that transfer payments nearly cut in half the percentage of families with
children that were below the official poverty line.[45] Both studies found
that tax policies had little effect on the redistribution of income. From
1966 to 1985, ironically, families in the top 1 percent of income paid proportionately less of their income in taxes (about 28 percent) than did people in the lowest-income group.[46] The tax burden has grown even greater
for younger generations of Americans (see Politics in a Changing America
18.1).

How can people in the lowest-income group pay a higher percentage of
their income in taxes than those in the very highest group? The answer has
to do with the combination of national, state, and local tax policies. Only
the national income tax is progressive, with rates rising as income rises.
The national payroll tax, which funds social security and Medicare, is
highly regressive: its effective rate decreases as income increases beyond a
certain point. Everyone pays social security at the same rate (6.2 percent in
1996), but this tax is levied only up to a maximum wage ($62,700 annually
in 1996). There is no social security tax at all on wages over that amount.
So the effective rate of the social security tax is higher for lower-income
groups than for the very top group.

18.6 ● The Ups and Downs of National Tax Rates

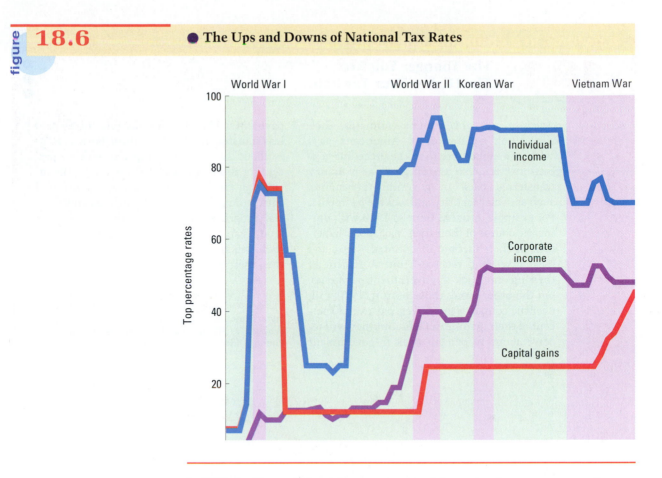

In 1913, the Sixteenth Amendment empowered the national government to collect taxes on income. Since then, the government has levied taxes on individual and corporate income and on capital gains realized by individuals and corporations from the sale of assets, such as stocks or real estate. This chart of the top marginal tax rates shows that they have fluctuated wildly over time, from less than 10 percent to more than 90 percent. (They tend to be highest during periods of war.) During the Reagan administration, the maximum individual income tax rate fell to the lowest level since the Coolidge and Hoover administrations in the late 1920s and 1930s. The top rate increased slightly for 1991, to 31 percent, as a result of a law enacted in 1990, and it jumped to 39.6 percent for 1994 under Clinton's 1993 budget package.

Sources: *Wall Street Journal*, 18 August 1986, p. 10. Reprinted by permission of the Wall Street Journal, Dow Jones & Company, Inc., 1986. All rights reserved worldwide. Additional data from *Congressional Quarterly Weekly Report*, 3 November 1990, pp. 3714–3715; and Tax Law Update, published by Merrill Lynch, 1993.

Most state and local sales taxes are equally regressive. Poor and rich usually pay the same flat rate on their purchases. But the poor spend almost everything they earn on purchases, which are taxed, whereas the rich are able to save. A study showed that the effective sales tax rate for the lowest-income group was thus about 7 percent, whereas that for the top 1 percent was only 1 percent.[47]

In general, the nation's tax policies at all levels have historically favored not only the wealthy but also those who draw their income from capital

politics in a changing america

18.1   The Younger You Are, The Higher Your Tax Rate

According to government estimates, each succeeding generation of Americans pays taxes at a higher rate than the preceding generation, but it also gets a higher rate of money transferred back in government benefits, such as social security and welfare payments. For example, citizens born in 1920 will, during the course of their lives, pay about 36 percent of their income in national, state, and local taxes and receive about 7 percent of their income back in government payments. On the other hand, those born in 1970 will, over the course of their lives, pay over 50 percent of their income in taxes, but they will receive about 14 percent back in government payments. Thus the net tax rate (taxes paid less transfers received) for those born in 1920 is about 29 percent, compared with 36 percent for those born in 1970. So despite the increasing rate at which taxes are transferred back from government through expanded social programs, students in the 1990s, as a group, can expect to pay a good deal more of their income in taxes during their lifetime than their grandparents or even their parents.

Source: These data are adapted from Tables 3–1 and 3–3 in Executive Office of the President, *Budget of the United States Government, Fiscal Year 1995: Analytical Perspectives* (Washington, D.C.: U.S. Government Printing Office, 1994), pp. 23 and 25.

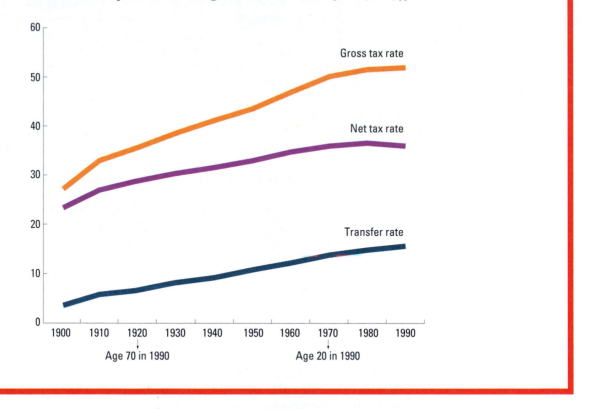

(wealth) rather than labor.[48] For example:

- The tax on income from the sale of real estate or stocks (called *capital gains*) has typically been lower than the highest tax on income from salaries.

- The tax on earned income (salaries and wages) is withheld from pay-checks by employers under national law; the tax on unearned income (interest and dividends) is not.

- There is no national tax at all on investments in certain securities, including municipal bonds (issued by local governments for construction projects).

Effects of Taxing and Spending Policies over Time

In 1966, at the beginning of President Johnson's Great Society programs, the poorest fifth of American families received 4 percent of the nation's income after taxes and transfer payments, whereas the richest fifth held 46 percent. In 1993, after many billions of dollars had been spent on social programs, the poorest fifth had no more of the nation's income, whereas the richest fifth had slightly more, as illustrated in Figure 18.7.[49] In short, little change had occurred in the distribution of income. (Moreover, many households in the lowest category had about one-third more earners, mainly women, going to work.)[50]

The economic policies of the Reagan administration had more effect on the truly rich than on the rest of the top 20 percent, and some analysts say this is due to tax policy. This is the conclusion of Kevin Phillips, a former Republican election strategist. According to Phillips, in his book *The Politics of Rich and Poor:* "Most of the Reagan decade, to put it mildly, was a heyday for unearned income as rents, dividends, capital gains and interest gained relative to wages and salaries as a source of wealth and increasing economic inequality."[51] Still, many economists believe that the main cause of the growth of income inequality in the 1980s was declining wages at the bottom of the income scale and stagnating salaries in the middle.[52]

In a capitalist system, some degree of inequality is inevitable. Is there some mechanism that limits how much economic equality can be achieved and prevents government policies from further equalizing income, no matter what is tried? To find out, we can look to other democracies to see how much equality they have been able to sustain. A 1991 study of sixteen Western democracies found that the gap in after-tax income between the rich (those at the 90th percentile of the income scale) and the poor (those at the 10th percentile) was greater in the United States than in any other country.[53] The comparison suggests that our society has measurably more economic inequality than others. The question is, why?

Democracy and Equality

Although the United States is a democracy that prizes political equality for its citizens, its record in promoting economic equality is not as good. In fact, its distribution of wealth—which includes not only income but also ownership of savings, housing, automobiles, stocks, and so on—is strikingly unequal. According to the Federal Reserve, the wealthiest 1 percent of American families control almost 40 percent of the nation's household wealth.[54] Moreover, the distribution of wealth among ethnic groups is alarming. The typical white family—whose annual income is more than

figure

18.7 ● **Distribution of Family Income over Time**

During the past three decades, the 20 percent of U.S. families with the highest incomes received over 45 percent of all income. This distribution of income is one of the most unequal among Western nations. At the bottom end of the scale, the poorest 20 percent of families received less than 5 percent of total family income.

Sources: For the 1966 data, Joseph A. Pechman, *Who Paid the Taxes, 1966–1985?* (Washington, D.C.: Brookings Institution, 1985), p. 74; for the 1993 data, U.S. Bureau of the Census, U.S. Department of Commerce, *Statistical Abstract of the United States, 1995* (Washington, D.C.: U.S. Government Printing Office, 1995), p. 475.

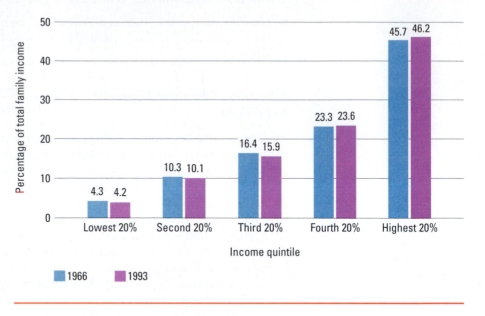

1.7 times that of blacks and 1.5 times that of Hispanics—has more than ten times the accumulated wealth of black families and nearly eight times the wealth of Hispanic families.[55] If democracy means government "by the people," why aren't the people sharing more equally in the nation's wealth? If one of the supposed purposes of government is to promote equality, why are government policies not working that way?

One scholar theorizes that interest group activity in a pluralist democracy distorts government's efforts to promote equality. His analysis of pluralism sees "corporations and organized groups with an upper-income slant as exerting political power over and above the formal one-man-one-vote standard of democracy."[56] As you learned in Chapters 10 and 17, the pluralist model of democracy rewards those groups that are well organized and well funded.

What would happen if national tax policy were determined according to principles of majoritarian rather than pluralist democracy? Perhaps not much, if public opinion is any guide. The people of the United States are not eager to redistribute wealth by increasing the only major progressive tax, the income tax. If national taxes must be raised, Americans strongly favor a national sales tax over increased income taxes.[57] But a sales tax is a flat tax, paid by rich and poor at the same rate, and it would have a regressive effect on income distribution, promoting inequality. The public also prefers a weekly $10 million national lottery to an increase in the income tax.[58] Because the poor are willing to chance more of their income on winning a fortune through lotteries than are rich people, lotteries (run by thirty-six states) also contribute to wealth inequality.[59]

Although most citizens tend to favor the idea that the rich should pay more, which is inherent in the concept of progressive taxation, they respond differently when asked specific questions about what amount of taxation "would be fair" for people of different incomes. In a 1995 survey, the average respondent thought that it would be fair to pay no more than 19 percent of *his or her own* income in all taxes combined—local, state, and national. When asked what would be the highest fair rate for a family making $200,000 a year, the median response was only 25 percent. Moreover, this was the median rate *regardless* of the respondents' income level, race, age, or party![60] The professor conducting the survey describes this remarkable consensus on a tax rate "ceiling" as "the most extraordinary finding in the history of domestic-policy polling in the United States."[61] Ironically, people making $200,000 already pay about 39 percent in total taxes—far more than most people think just. One wonders whether most citizens realize that their own taxes would increase for the same services if the rich did not pay progressively more than what the public thinks is just. For example, Clinton's 1993 tax increase, which raised the rate for people with incomes beginning at $115,000 from 31 to 36 percent and also created a new 39.6 percent bracket for incomes above $250,000, produced $31 billion in additional revenue over the 1992 rates.[62] This additional revenue helped reduce the budget deficit.

Majoritarians might argue that most Americans fail to understand the inequities of the national tax system, which hides regressiveness in sales taxes and social security taxes. However, majoritarians cannot argue that the public demands "fairer" tax rates that take from richer citizens to help poorer ones. If the public did, the lowest-income families might receive a greater share of the national income than they do. Instead, economic policy is determined mainly through a complex process of pluralist politics that returns nearly half the national income into the hands of only 20 percent of the nation's families.

SUMMARY

There are conflicting theories about how market economies work best. Laissez-faire economics holds that the government should keep its hands off the economy. Keynesian theory holds that government should take an active role in dealing with inflation and unemployment, using fiscal and monetary policies to produce desired levels of aggregate demand. Monetarists believe fiscal policies are unreliable; they opt instead to use the money supply to affect aggregate demand. Supply-side economists, who had an enormous influence on economic policy during the Reagan administration and also advised Bob Dole on his economic plan during the 1996 presidential campaign, focus on controlling the supply of goods and services rather than the demand for them.

Congress alone prepared the budget until 1921, when it thrust the responsibility onto the president. After World War II, Congress tried unsuccessfully to regain control of the process. Later, Congress managed to restructure the process under the House and Senate budget committees. The new process worked well until it confronted the huge budget deficits of the 1980s. Because so much of the budget involves military spending and uncontrollable payments to individuals, it is virtually impossible to balance the budget by reducing what remains—mainly spending for nonentitlement domestic programs. Unwilling to accept responsibility for passing a tax increase, Congress passed the Gramm-Rudman deficit-reduction law in 1985. Under that law, deficits were to be reduced in stages, through automatic across-the-board cuts if necessary, until the budget was balanced by FY 1991. The deficit problem proved so intractable, however, that Congress had to amend the law in 1987 to extend the deadline to 1993—and the budget still wasn't balanced. When the Republicans gained control of Congress in 1995, they abandoned the informal policy of incremental budgeting and drastically cut spending on discretionary programs. While they failed in their attempt to produce a definite path to a balanced budget and were unable to pass a constitutional amendment for a balanced budget, they did succeed in passing a law giving the president a line item veto over appropriations bills. The constitutionality of this provision remains to be tested in court, however.

Although President Bush promised "no new taxes" when he was campaigning for office in 1988, he had to acknowledge the need for revenue increases to cut the deficit and was forced to accept the Budget Enforcement Act of 1990, which raised the income tax. This act modified the budgeting procedure and made it easier to meet the Gramm-Rudman targets, but Bush suffered in his reelection campaign for breaking his pledge. The act also amended the sweeping tax reform bill of 1986, which had eliminated tax loopholes and drastically reduced the number of tax brackets. The new law added a third bracket, at 31 percent, which was much lower than the top rate before 1986. In an effort to reduce the deficit, President Clinton formulated a budget that created a fourth bracket, set at 40 percent. Nevertheless, current U.S. tax rates are lower than taxes in most other major countries and lower than they have been in the United States since the Depression. But even the heavily progressive tax rates of the past did little to redistribute income. Government transfer payments to individuals have helped reduce income inequalities. Nevertheless, the distribution of income is less equal in the United States than in most major Western nations.

Pluralist democracy as practiced in the United States has allowed well-organized, well-financed interest groups to manipulate tax and spending policies to their benefit. The result is that a larger and poorer segment of society is paying the price. Taxing and spending policies in the United States are tipped in the direction of freedom rather than equality.

Key Terms

economic depression	deficit financing	Office of Management and Budget (OMB)	Gramm-Rudman
inflation	Council of Economic Advisers (CEA)	tax committees	mandatory spending
business cycle	monetarists	authorization committees	entitlement
aggregate demand	Federal Reserve System	appropriations committees	pay-as-you-go
productive capacity	supply-side economics	budget committees	discretionary spending
gross domestic product (GDP)	fiscal year (FY)	Congressional Budget Office (CBO)	sequestration
Keynesian theory	budget authority		progressive taxation
fiscal policies	budget outlays		incremental budgeting
monetary policies	receipts		uncontrollable outlays
			transfer payment

Selected Readings

Axelrod, Donald. *Budgeting for Modern Government*, 2nd ed. New York: St. Martin's Press, 1995. A thorough explanation of the process of public budgeting, from agency requests to the finished budget. Excellent in evaluating criticisms and proposing reforms.

Penny, Timothy J., and Steven E. Schier. *Payment Due: A Nation in Debt, A Generation in Trouble*. Boulder, Colo: Westview Press, 1996. A former member of Congress (Penny) and a scholar collaborate in analyzing the problems in reducing the deficit and the consequences for America if we do not.

Peters, B. Guy. *The Politics of Taxation: A Comparative Approach*. Cambridge, Mass.: Basil Blackwell, 1991. A worldwide survey of how governments raise revenue; contains many informative tables about sources of revenue, spending policies, and attitudes toward taxation.

Phillips, Kevin. *The Politics of Rich and Poor: Wealth and the American Electorate in the Reagan Aftermath*. New York: Random House, 1990. A serious indictment of the economic policies of the Reagan administration from an unlikely source, a conservative Republican who outlined the victorious "southern strategy" for Richard Nixon in 1968.

Stein, Herbert. *On the Other Hand . . . Reflections on Economics, Economists, and Politics*. Washington, D.C.: American Enterprise Institute, 1995. The chairman of President Nixon's Council of Economic Advisers, Herbert Stein, examines controversies over economic growth, employment, taxes, and deficits, and the ideas of economists whose theories have influenced economic practice.

Steuerle, C. Eugene. *The Tax Decade*. Washington, D.C.: Urban Institute Press, 1992. Written by a top tax official in the Reagan administration, this book not only describes the important tax laws enacted during the 1980s but also explains them in the context of previous and later administrations.

World Wide Web Resources

Federal Reserve Board. In addition to explaining the structure and functions of the Federal Reserve Board, this site contains the famous "Beige Book" that reports on economic conditions in the nation eight times a year. It is an easy-to-read executive summary of business, manufacturing, and commercial activities in each of the system's twelve regional Federal Reserve banks.
`<www.bog.frb.fed.us/>`

Office of Management and Budget. The place to go to get recent versions of the federal budget. The site provides data as well as graphs and text.
`<www.whitehouse.gov/WH/EOP/omb>`

Economic Policy Institute. This site offers analysis and commentary about economic issues from the left side of the ideological spectrum.
`<epinet.org/>`

CATO Institute. "CATO" is derived from *Cato's Letters*, "libertarian pamphlets that helped lay the philosophical foundation for the American Revolution." This site offers analysis and commentary about economic issues from the right side of the ideological spectrum.
`<www.cato.org/>`

Domestic Policy

HE WAS JUST A CHILD, and yet at times he seemed to bear the weight of the world on his shoulders. Nine-year-old Michael Moran had already faced more than his share of low points in his brief lifetime. Poverty and a disrupted family life (his father disappeared when Michael was two) dovetailed with new surroundings to produce a truly vulnerable child.[1]

Having just moved with his mother and younger brother from a poor, working-class Massachusetts neighborhood to a mostly middle-class Boston suburb, Michael struggled to fit in. Bright but introverted and awkward, Michael had a hard time interacting with his teachers and schoolmates. This problem was exacerbated by a learning disability that at first had been diagnosed as hyperactivity. Although employed, Michael's mother struggled to make ends meet, using welfare checks to supplement her inadequate wages.

The teasing began. Michael was called a "welly" (other students' derogatory term for someone on welfare), and his tormentors threatened him with physical harm. They punished him for his cheap, out-of-fashion clothes and his poverty. Feeling out of control and rapidly approaching the breaking point, Michael sometimes spoke to his mother about wanting to end his life. Although she was terribly concerned, Michael's mother felt powerless to change the conditions that placed her family in such a predicament. One day, she had a telephone call from Michael's teacher, who informed her that Michael was under a desk, his hands covering his ears, screaming "Go away!" It was too much for one small boy to handle.

Michael's cries for help were the result of many contributing factors: poverty, hunger, his stage of psychological and physiological development, and mistreatment by his peers. His story is suggestive of ways to undercut common presumptions about the disadvantaged. Although poor, Michael and his mother did not passively accept their circumstances, as stereotypical views of those in poverty often suggest. Instead, they tried as hard as they could to get by and to make things better. Even so, employment alone did not lift Michael's family from poverty. A poor single parent faces tremendous hardships in providing for child care while holding down a job. Michael's mother performed admirably at doing both. This was not a tale of abuse or neglect. Michael and his family were impoverished, and they struggled to cope with the difficulties of a system that did not readily provide a way for them to reach for the American dream.

Somehow, in a land of promise and opportunity, countless Americans live without the benefits that most of us take for granted: good housing,

● ● ● ● ● ● ● ● ● ●
Public Assistance: Begin Here

Public assistance (or "welfare") can take many forms: cash subsidies for housing and clothing, food stamps, and health care. For more than sixty years, the national government set the standards for such assistance and conditioned its support to the states on compliance. But in 1996, the Republicans in Congress and President Bill Clinton reached agreement that the welfare system required radical reform. Now in many welfare-related areas, the national government no longer calls the tune. States possess much more leeway to revise their own welfare programs.

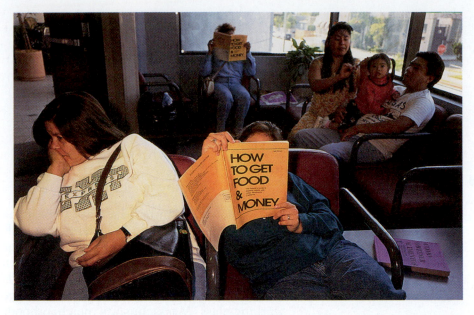

good nutrition, safe neighborhoods, good schools.[2] Although America is one of the freest and richest countries in the world, people like Michael Moran and his family can take little comfort in its liberties and its wealth. Government action helped generate this contradiction, and government action aims to correct it. We call this kind of government action **public policy**: a general plan of action adopted by government to solve a social problem, counter a threat, or pursue an objective.

In Chapter 17 we examined the policymaking process in general; in this chapter we look at specific domestic public policies, government action targeting concerns internal to the United States. We begin our inquiry with policies that provide social insurance and public assistance. These are among the most enduring and costly programs that the government has launched on behalf of its citizens. (We discussed policies that promote disadvantaged groups through affirmative action programs in Chapter 16.) Four key questions guide our inquiry: What are the origins and politics of specific domestic policies? What are the effects of those policies once they are implemented? Why do some policies succeed and others fail? Finally, are disagreements about policy really disagreements about values?

Public policies sometimes seem as numerous as fast-food restaurants, offering something for every appetite and budget. With such a wide range of policies worth exploring, you may be wondering why we plan to spend much of this chapter discussing social insurance and public assistance. These policies deserve special consideration for three reasons. First, government expenditures in these areas represent more than half the national budget and one-tenth of our gross domestic product (the total market value of all goods and services produced in this country during a year). In 1995, of every dollar spent by the national government, 58 cents went to direct payments to individuals.[3] All citizens ought to know how their resources are allocated and why. Regrettably, the public has limited and distorted knowledge about national government spending. For example, only one in four Americans knows that the government spends more for social security than for national defense.[4] Second, one goal of social insurance and public assistance policies is to alleviate some consequences of economic inequality. Nevertheless, poverty remains a fixture of American life, and we must try to understand why. Third, these policies pose some vexing questions involving the conflict between freedom and order, and freedom and equality.

This chapter concentrates on policies based on the authority of the national government to tax and spend for the general welfare. But it is important to recognize that state and local governments play a vital role in shaping and directing the policies that emanate from Washington. For example, in 1996 the national government largely abandoned setting standards for the allocation of welfare benefits. Now states may impose their own standards for recipients.[5]

GOVERNMENT POLICIES AND INDIVIDUAL WELFARE

The most controversial purpose of government is to promote social and economic equality. To do so may conflict with the freedom of some citizens, for it requires government action to redistribute income from rich to poor. This choice between freedom and equality constitutes the modern dilemma of government; it has been at the center of many conflicts in U.S. public policy since World War II. On one hand, most Americans believe that government should help the needy. On the other hand, they do not want to sacrifice their own standard of living to provide government handouts to those whom they may perceive as shiftless and lazy.

The Growth of the American Welfare State

Using the "Voters" data in the CROSSTABS program, analyze issue variables (e.g., government services, give everyone a job, health insurance) by trust in government. Does trust in government tend to go hand-in-hand with some issues but not others?

At one time, governments confined their activities to the minimal protection of people and property—to ensuring security and order. Now, however, almost every modern nation may be characterized as a **welfare state,** serving as the provider and protector of individual well-being through economic and social programs. **Social welfare programs** are government programs designed to provide the minimum living conditions necessary for all citizens. Income for the elderly, health care, subsidized housing, and nutrition are among the concerns addressed by government social welfare programs.

The recent history of U.S. government spending in support of social welfare policies is illustrated in Figure 18.4. In 1960, twenty-six percent of the national budget went to payments for individuals. In 1970, thirty-three percent of the budget went to payments for individuals. And in 1980, more than forty percent went to individuals. By 1985, spending for individuals had fallen off by a few percentage points. The latest data, for 1995, show that well over half of national spending goes to direct payments to individuals or grants in support of individuals. The elderly have been the principal beneficiaries. By 2000, such outlays will likely account for more than 60 percent of national spending. The national government clearly remains a provider of social welfare, despite changes in administrations.

The origins of social welfare policy go back to the Industrial Revolution, when the mechanization of production resulted in a shift away from home manufacturing to large-scale factory production. As more and more people switched to working for wages, many more were subjected to the dreadful consequences of a loss of employment because of sickness, injury, old age, or economic conditions. The sick, the disabled, and the aged were tended, for the most part, by their families and by private charities. Communities confined the destitute to poorhouses or almshouses, which were little more than warehouses for the impoverished. In the eighteenth and nineteenth centuries, poverty was viewed as a disgrace. Poor people were seen as lazy and incompetent. (Indeed, many Americans still hold this view.) Relief was made disagreeable to discourage dependence on outside assistance.

America today is far from being a welfare state on the order of Germany or Great Britain; those nations provide many more medical, educational, and unemployment benefits to their citizens. However, the United States does have several social welfare functions. To understand social welfare policies in the United States, you must first understand the significance of a major event in U.S. history—the Great Depression—and the two presidential plans that extended the scope of the government, the New Deal and the Great Society.

The Great Depression.   Throughout its history, the U.S. economy has experienced alternating good times and hard times, generally referred to as business cycles (see Chapter 18). The **Great Depression** was, by far, the longest and deepest setback that the American economy has ever experienced. It began with the stock market crash of 1929 (on October 29, a day known as Black Tuesday) and did not end until the start of World War II. By 1932, one out of every four U.S. workers was unemployed, and millions more were underemployed. No other event has had a greater effect on the thinking and the institutions of government in the twentieth century.

In the 1930s, the forces that had stemmed earlier business declines were no longer operating. There were no more frontiers, no growth in export markets, no new technologies to boost employment. Unchecked, unemployment spread like an epidemic. And the crisis fueled itself. Workers who lost their source of income could no longer buy the food, goods, and services that kept the economy going. Thus, private industry and commercial farmers tended to produce more than they could sell profitably. Closed factories, surplus crops, and idle workers were the consequences.

The Great Depression generated powerful ironies. Seeking to restore profits, producers trimmed costs by replacing workers with machines, which only increased unemployment. Unemployed workers could not afford to buy goods, which drove down profits. People went hungry, because so much food had been produced that it could not be sold profitably; dumping it was cheaper than taking it to market.

The industrialized nations of Europe were also hit hard. The value of U.S. exports fell, and the value of imports increased; this led Congress to impose high tariffs, which strangled trade and fueled the Depression. From 1929 to 1932, more than 44 percent of the nation's banks failed when unpaid loans exceeded the value of bank assets. Farm prices fell by more than half in the same period. Marginal farmers lost their land, and tenant farmers succumbed to mechanization. The uprooted—tens of thousands of dispossessed farm families—headed West with their possessions atop their cars and trucks in a hopeless quest for opportunity.

● ● ● ● ● ● ● ● ● ●

A Human Tragedy

The Great Depression made able-bodied Americans idle. By 1933, when President Herbert Hoover left office, about one-fourth of the labor force was out of work. Private charities were swamped with the burden of feeding the destitute. The hopeless men pictured here await a handout from a wealthy San Francisco matron known as the "White Angel" who provided resources for a bread line.

The New Deal.   In his speech accepting the presidential nomination at the 1932 Democratic National Convention, Franklin Delano Roosevelt (then governor of New York) made a promise: "I pledge you, I pledge myself to a new deal for the American people." Roosevelt did not specify what his **New Deal** would consist of, but the term was later applied to measures undertaken by the Roosevelt administration to stem the Depression. Some scholars regard these measures as the most imaginative burst of domestic policy in the nation's history. Others see them as the source of massive government growth without matching benefits.

President Roosevelt's New Deal was composed of two phases. The first, which ended in 1935, was aimed at boosting prices and lowering unemployment. The second phase, which ended in 1938, was aimed at aiding the forgotten people: the poor, the aged, unorganized working men and women, and farmers.

The New Deal programs were opportunistic; they were not guided by, or based on, a single political or economic theory. They aimed at relief for the needy, recovery for the nation, and long-range reform for the economy. Many New Deal programs were rooted in the concept of short-term relief to get people back on their feet without continuous dependence on government assistance. (For example, the Civilian Conservation Corps Reconstruction Relief Act of 1933 provided short-term jobs for young men.) Administering these programs called for government growth; funding them required higher taxes. Government could no longer rely on either the decentralized political structure of federalism or the market forces of laissez-faire capitalism to bring the country out of its decline. The New

Deal embodied the belief that a complex economy required centralized government control. (One of the New Deal's lasting legacies is the social security system, which we will examine in detail later in this chapter.)

The Supreme Court stymied Roosevelt's first-phase reform efforts by declaring major New Deal legislation unconstitutional, beginning in 1935. A majority of the justices maintained that in its legislation, Congress had exceeded its constitutional authority to regulate interstate commerce.

The Democrats won overwhelming popular support for their efforts at relief and recovery. The voters returned Roosevelt to office in a landslide election in 1936. But the Supreme Court continued its opposition to New Deal legislation. This prompted Roosevelt to advocate an increase in the number of justices on the Court; his goal was to appoint justices sympathetic to the legislation he endorsed. However, Roosevelt's attack on the Court, coupled with increasing labor violence, alarmed conservatives and put the New Deal on the defensive. Still, within a few months of the 1936 election, the Supreme Court began to adopt an interpretation of the Constitution that permitted expanded power for the national government. In an abrupt about-face, the Court upheld the New Deal policies that composed the second phase. (It was, said one wag, "the switch in time that saved nine.")

Poverty and unemployment persisted, however, despite the best efforts of the Democrats. By 1939, seventeen percent of the work force (more than 9 million people) were still unemployed. Only World War II was able to provide the economic surge needed to yield lower unemployment and higher prices, the elusive goals of the New Deal.

Roosevelt's overwhelming popularity did not translate into irresistibly popular policy or genuine popularity for government. Public opinion polls revealed that Americans were divided over New Deal policies through the early 1940s. Eventually, the New Deal became the status quo, and Americans grew satisfied with it. But Americans remained wary of additional growth in the power of the national government.[6]

Economists still debate whether the actual economic benefits of the New Deal reforms outweighed their costs. It is clear, however, that New Deal policies initiated a long-range trend toward government expansion. And another torrent of domestic policymaking burst forth three decades later.

The Great Society. John F. Kennedy's election in 1960 brought to Washington public servants sensitive to persistent poverty and the needs of minorities. This raised expectations that national government policies would benefit the poor and minorities. But Kennedy's razor-thin margin of victory was far from a mandate to improve the plight of the poor and dispossessed. At first, Kennedy proposed technical and financial aid for depressed areas and programs for upgrading the skills of workers in marginal jobs. But Kennedy and influential members of his administration were motivated by politics as well as poverty; in 1962, with the economy faltering again, the Kennedy administration proposed substantial tax breaks for middle- and upper-income groups. Fixing the economy took precedence over the needs of the less fortunate. Many low-income Americans remained untouched by the administration's programs.

Kennedy's assassination in November 1963 provided the backdrop and generated needed support for new policies founded on equality, proposed by his successor, Lyndon Baines Johnson. In his 1965 State of the Union address, President Johnson offered his own version of the New Deal; his vision of the **Great Society** included a broad array of programs designed to redress political, social, and economic inequality. In contrast to the New Deal, few if any of Johnson's programs were aimed at short-term relief; most were targeted at chronic ills requiring a long-term commitment by the national government. Some programs had already been enacted when Johnson articulated his vision, whereas others were still in the planning stage. The Civil Rights Act of 1964 was aimed at erasing racial discrimination from most areas of American life. The Voting Rights Act of 1965 had as its goal the elimination of voting restrictions that discriminated against blacks and other minorities. Both statutes prohibited conduct that was inconsistent with political and social equality (see Chapter 16).

Another part of Johnson's Great Society plan was based on the traditional American belief that social and economic equality could be attained through equality of educational opportunity. The Elementary and Secondary Education Act of 1965 provided, for the first time, direct national government aid to local school districts, based on the number of low-income families in each district. Later, the national government was able to use the threat of withholding school aid (under the 1964 Civil Rights Act) to dramatically increase the pace of school integration in the South.

Still another vital element of the Great Society was the **War on Poverty.** The major weapon in this war was the Economic Opportunity Act (1964); its proponents promised that it would eradicate poverty in ten years. The act encouraged a variety of local community programs to educate and train people for employment. Among them were college work-study programs, summer employment for high school and college students, loans to small businesses, a domestic version of the Peace Corps (called VISTA, for Volunteers in Service to America), educational enrichment for preschoolers, and legal services for the poor. It offered opportunity: a hand up, rather than a handout.

The act also established the Office for Economic Opportunity (OEO), which was the administrative center of the War on Poverty. Its basic strategy was to involve the poor themselves in administering antipoverty programs, in the hope that they would know which programs would best serve their needs. The national government channeled money directly to local community action programs. This approach avoided the vested interests of state and local government bureaucrats and political machines. But it also led to new local controversies by shifting the control of government funds from local politicians to other groups. (In one notorious example, the Blackstone Rangers, a Chicago street gang, received funds for a job-training program.)

In 1967, the Johnson administration responded to pressure from established local politicians by requiring that poverty funds be distributed through certified state and local agencies. In addition, all sectors of the community (including business, labor, and local leaders) would now be represented, along with the poor, in administering community action programs.

The War on Poverty eventually faded as funding was diverted to the Vietnam War. Although it had achieved little in the way of income redistribution, it did lead to one significant change: it made the poor aware of their political power. Some candidates representing the poor ran for political office, and officeholders paid increased attention to the poor. The poor also found that they could use the legal system to their benefit. For example, with legal assistance from the OEO, low-income litigants were successful in striking down state laws requiring a minimum period of residency before people could receive public assistance.[7]

Some War on Poverty programs remain as established features of U.S. government. (Among these is the work-study program that enables many college students to finance their education.) Yet poverty remains, and the evidence suggests that it may once again be on the rise. However, public attitudes toward poverty have changed since the Great Depression. When Americans were polled in 1990 on the reasons for poverty, they cited in approximately equal measure circumstances beyond the control of the poor and lack of effort. Many Americans believe that the persistence of poverty results from flawed programs that encourage dependence on government assistance.[8]

The Cyber Herald offers weekly views on poverty in America. `<www2.ari.net/home/poverty/news.html>`

Social welfare policy is based on the premise that society has an obligation to provide for the basic needs of its members. In an unusual national survey targeting the poor and nonpoor, both sectors agreed that government should protect its citizens against risks they are powerless to combat. Americans expressed a clear conviction that money and wealth ought to be more evenly shared.[9] The term *welfare state* describes this protective role of government.

By meeting people's minimum needs, government welfare policies attempt to promote equality. New Deal policies were aimed at meeting the needs of the poor by redistributing income: people paid progressively higher taxes as their incomes rose—in effect, the wealthy paid to alleviate poverty. Today's liberals tend to follow the New Deal path. They are willing to curtail economic freedom somewhat to promote economic equality. As a result, their policies aim at providing direct income subsidies and government jobs. Today's conservatives avoid this government-as-provider approach, preferring economic freedom to government intervention. Their policies aim at curbing inflation and reducing government spending, on the theory that the rising tide of a growing economy lifts all boats.

The evidence from the 1980s, however, offers reassurance to both conservatives and liberals. Both before-tax and after-tax income grew in absolute terms; inequality also grew in the same period (see Chapter 18). Changes in families and household composition suggest several plausible explanations for this increased gulf between the haves and the have-nots. The rising number of double-worker households may explain income growth. Growth in the number of elderly people—who have substantially lower incomes—tends to increase income inequality. Growth in the number of persons living alone (or with nonrelatives)—who typically have much lower incomes than households composed of families—also increases income inequality. In addition, the growth in the number of female-headed households contributes to income inequality. About half of such households are in the lowest income group, as described in Politics in a Changing America 19.1. Researchers have labeled this trend toward

• politics in a changing america

19.1   The Feminization of Poverty

When we examine the composition of poor families, especially over the past twenty-five years, we observe a dramatic and disturbing trend. One in every two poor Americans resides in a family in which a woman is the sole householder, or head of the household (see graph). Thirty years ago, only one in every four poor people lived in such a family. What accounts for this dramatic upward shift in the proportion of female-headed poor families?

This century bears witness to extraordinary changes for women. Women won the right to vote and to own property. Women also gained a measure of legal and social equality (see Chapter 16). But increases in the rates of divorce, marital separation, and adolescent pregnancy have cast more and more women in the head-of-household role. Caring for children competes with women's ability to work. Affordable child care is out of reach for many single parents. In the absence of a national child care policy, single women with young children face limited employment opportunities and lower wages in comparison to full-time workers. These factors and others contribute to the **feminization of poverty,** the fact that a growing percentage of all poor Americans are women or the dependents of women.

Sources: Barbara Ehrenreich and Frances Fox Piven, "The Feminization of Poverty," *Dissent* (Spring 1984), 162–170; Harrell R. Rodgers, Jr., *Poor Women, Poor Families: The Economic Plight of America's Female-Headed Households*, 2d ed. (Armonk, N.Y.: M. E. Sharpe, 1990).

Source for data: U.S. Bureau of the Census, U.S. Department of Commerce, *Poverty in the United States, 1992,* Current Population Reports, Series P-60, No. 185 (Washington, D.C.: U.S. Government Printing Office, 1993).

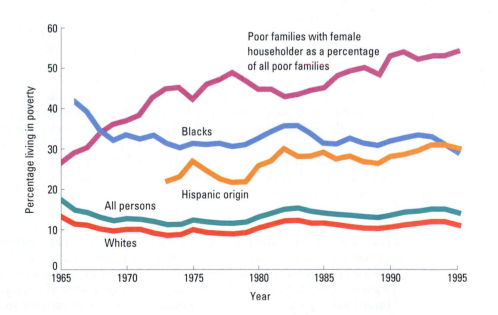

greater poverty among women the **feminization of poverty,** as a growing percentage of all poor Americans are women or dependents of women.[10]

The Reduction of the Welfare State

A spirit of equality—equality of opportunity—motivated the reforms of the 1960s, many of which carried over to the 1970s. But Ronald Reagan's overwhelming election in 1980 and his landslide reelection in 1984 forced a reexamination of social welfare policy.

In a dramatic departure from his predecessors (Republicans as well as Democrats), Reagan shifted emphasis from economic equality to economic freedom. He questioned whether government alone should continue to be responsible for guaranteeing the economic and social well-being of less fortunate citizens. And, to the extent that government should bear this responsibility, he maintained that state and local governments could do so more efficiently than the national government. Ironically, when Reagan attempted to act on his rhetoric about limited government, his political support started to evaporate. Two political scientists articulated the lesson for all post–Great Society presidents, including Reagan: "A powerful central government is here to stay, and its beneficiaries, many of whom approved of Reagan, want it that way."[11]

Reagan professed support for the "truly needy" and for preservation of a "reliable safety net of social programs," by which he meant the core programs begun in the New Deal. Nevertheless, his administration abolished a number of social welfare programs and redirected others. Reagan proposed sharp cutbacks in housing assistance, welfare, the food stamp program, and education and job-training programs. Reagan and Congress also trimmed the most basic of American social welfare programs—social security—although cuts here were less severe than in other areas.[12]

Congress blocked some of the president's proposed cutbacks, and many Great Society programs remained in force, although with less funding. Overall spending on social welfare programs (as a proportion of the gross national product) fell to about mid-1970s levels. But the dramatic growth in the promotion of social welfare that began with the New Deal ended with the Reagan administration. It remained in repose during the Bush administration. And the national budget deficit—a deficit that ballooned during the Reagan and Bush administrations—has served to dampen efforts to expand the government's social welfare role. The enormous government debt has forced Congress to avoid new and costly social welfare programs until income and expenditures approach coming into balance.

SOCIAL INSURANCE   Insurance is a device for protecting against loss. Since the late nineteenth century, there has been a growing tendency for governments to offer **social insurance**, which is government-backed protection against loss by individuals, regardless of need. The most common forms of social insurance offer health protection and guard against losses from worker sickness, injury, and disability; old age; and unemployment. The first example of social insurance in the United States was workers' compensation. Beginning early in this century, most states created systems of insurance that compensated workers who lost income because they were injured in the workplace.

Social insurance benefits are distributed to recipients without regard to their economic status. Old-age benefits, for example, are paid to workers—rich or poor—provided that they have enough covered work experience and they have reached the required age. In most social insurance programs, employees and employers contribute to a fund from which employees later receive payments.*

Social insurance programs are examples of **entitlements**—benefits to which every eligible person has a legal right and that government cannot deny. National entitlement programs consume about half of every dollar of government spending; the largest entitlement program is social security.

Social Security

Social security is social insurance that provides economic assistance to people faced with unemployment, disability, or old age; it is financed by taxes on employers and employees. Initially, social security benefits were distributed only to the aged, the unemployed, and surviving spouses—most of whom were widows—with dependent children. Today, social security also provides medical care for the elderly and income support for the disabled.

Origins of Social Security. The idea of social security came late to the United States. As early as 1883, Germany enacted legislation to protect workers against the hazards of industrial life. Most European nations adopted old-age insurance after World War I; many provided income support for the disabled and income protection for families after the death of the principal wage earner. In the United States, however, the needs of the elderly and the unemployed were left largely to private organizations and individuals. Although twenty-eight states had old-age assistance programs by 1934, neither private charities nor state and local governments—nor both together—could cope with the prolonged unemployment and distress that resulted from the Great Depression. It became clear that a national policy was necessary to deal with a national crisis.

The first important step came on August 14, 1935, when President Franklin Roosevelt signed the **Social Security Act;** that act is the cornerstone of the modern American welfare state. The act's framers developed three approaches to the problem of dependence. The first provided social insurance in the form of old-age and surviving-spouse benefits and cooperative state-national unemployment assistance. To ensure that the elderly did not retire into poverty, it created a program to provide income to retired workers. Its purpose was to guarantee that the elderly had a reliable base income after they stopped working. (Most Americans equate social security with this program.) An unemployment insurance program, financed by employers, was also created to provide payments for a limited

---

* *Examine your next paycheck stub. It should indicate your contribution to Social Security Tax (SST) and Medicare Tax (MT). SST supports disability, survivors', and retirement benefits. In 1996, it was 6.2 percent of the first $62,700 earned. MT pays for Medicare benefits. In 1996, it was 1.45 percent of all wages. Employers provide matching contributions to SST and MT.*

The reason Congress doesn't touch Social Security....

GRANBO

Mike Luckovich
Times-Picayune

time to workers who were laid off or dismissed for reasons beyond their control.

The second approach provided aid to the destitute in the form of grants-in-aid to the states. The act represented the first permanent national commitment to provide financial assistance to the needy aged, needy families with dependent children, the blind, and (since the 1950s) the permanently and totally disabled. By the 1990s, the disabled category grew to include the learning-disabled and the drug- and alcohol-dependent.

The third approach provided health and welfare services through federal aid to the states. Included were health and family services for disabled children and orphans and vocational rehabilitation for the disabled.

How Social Security Works.   Old-age retirement revenue goes into its own *trust fund* (each social security program has a separate fund). The fund is administered by the Social Security Administration, which became an independent government agency in 1995. Trust fund revenue can be spent only for the old-age benefits program. Benefits, in the form of monthly payments, begin when an employee reaches retirement age, which today is sixty-five. (People can retire as early as age sixty-two but with reduced benefits.) The age at which full benefits are paid will increase to sixty-seven after the year 2000.

Many Americans believe that each person's social security contributions are set aside specifically for his or her retirement, like a savings account.[13] But social security doesn't operate quite like that. Instead, the social security taxes collected today pay the benefits of today's retirees. Thus, social security (and social insurance in general) is not a form of savings; it is a pay-as-you-go tax system. Today's workers support today's elderly.

When the social security program began, it had many contributors and few beneficiaries. The program could thus provide relatively large benefits

19.1   ● **Day of Reckoning**

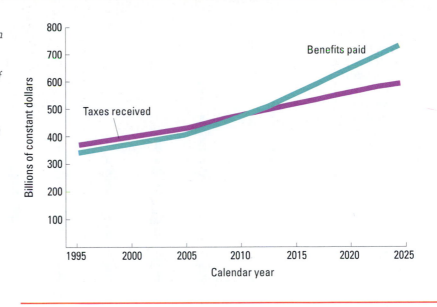

For all the words exchanged in the 104th Congress, the one debate that has yet to occur may be the most significant of them all: the future of the social security system. Social security taxes now exceed benefits paid out. But by 2010 or so, benefits will exceed receipts. With bankruptcy of the system looming so predictably, the debate over change boils down to two questions that politicians politely decline to answer: How soon does the national government change the current system, and how much does it change it?

Source: 1995 annual report of Social Security trustees.

with low taxes. In 1937, for example, the tax rate was 1 percent, and the social security taxes of nine workers supported each beneficiary. As the program matured and more people retired, the ratio of workers to recipients decreased. In 1994, the social security system paid benefits to 42.9 million people and collected tax revenues from 139 million, a ratio of only three workers for every beneficiary.[14]

The solvency of the social security program will soon be tested. As the baby boomer generation retires, beginning about 2010, politicians will face an inevitable dilemma: lower benefits and generate the ire of retirees or raise taxes and generate the ire of taxpayers (see Figure 19.1).

At one time, federal workers, members of Congress, judges, even the president were omitted from the social security system. Today there are few exceptions. Universal participation is essential for the system to operate, because it is a tax program, not a savings program. If participation were not compulsory, there would not be enough revenue to provide benefits to current retirees. Government—the only institution that can coerce—requires all employees and their employers to contribute, thereby imposing restrictions on freedom.

Those people who currently pay into the system will receive retirement benefits financed by future participants. As with a pyramid scheme or a chain letter, success depends on the growth of the base. If the birthrate remains steady or grows, future wage earners will be able to support today's contributors when they retire. If the economy expands, there will be more jobs, more income, and a growing wage base to tax for increased benefits to retirees. But suppose the birthrate falls, or unemployment rises and the economy falters? Then contributions could decline to the point at which benefits exceed revenues. The pyramidal character of social security is its Achilles' heel, as Figure 19.2 shows.

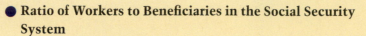

19.2   ● Ratio of Workers to Beneficiaries in the Social Security System

figure

Demographers predict a steady decline in the ratio of workers to social security beneficiaries, starting in the year 2000. By 2030, there will be only two workers for every beneficiary. If current trends continue, it is a sure bet that social security taxes will increase or benefits will de-crease as the worker-bene-ficiary ratio falls.

Source: Social Security Administration Board of Trustees, "Federal Old-Age and Survivors Insurance and Disability Insurance Trust Funds," 1995 Annual Report, p. 123.

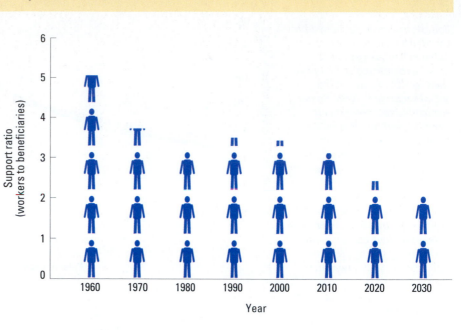

Who Pays? Who Benefits?   "Who pays?" and "Who benefits?" are always important questions in government policymaking, and they continue to shape social security policy. In 1968, the Republican party platform called for automatic increases in social security payments as the cost of living rose. The theory was simple: as the cost of living rises, so should retire-ment benefits; otherwise, benefits are paid in "shrinking dollars" that buy less and less. Cost-of-living adjustments (COLAs) became a political foot-ball in 1969 as Democrats and Republicans tried to outdo each other by suggesting larger increases for retirees. The result was a significant expan-sion in benefits, far in excess of the cost of living. The beneficiaries were the retired, who were beginning to flex their political muscle. Politicians knew that alienating this constituency could lose an election.[15]

In 1972, Congress adopted automatic adjustments in benefits and in the dollar amount of contributors' wages subject to tax, so that revenue would expand as benefits grew. This approach set social security on automatic pilot. When inflation exceeds 3 percent, the automatic adjustment goes into effect. (Politicians sometimes fear retribution at the polls if there is no annual adjustment: although it appeared that inflation would fall below 3 percent in 1986, Congress authorized an adjustment for that year.) When most economists criticized the COLA as overly generous, Congress tem-pered it.

Calculating COLAs.
`<www.ssa.gov/OACT/`
`95COLA/FR.sum.html>`

Then, when stagflation (high unemployment coupled with high infla-tion) took hold in the 1970s, it jeopardized the entire social security sys-tem. Stagflation gripped the social security system in an economic vise:

●●●●●●●●●●●●
Life Begins at Sixty-five

Old age and impoverishment used to go hand in hand but not any more. Because of social security, people aged sixty-five and older are the second-richest age group in the United States. Only Americans aged fifty-five to sixty-four are better off. One political economist recently estimated that the government spends about $350 billion on the aged, more than on national defense. Today's elderly remain vulnerable to impoverishment only if they need long-term nursing home care.

unemployment meant a reduction in revenue; high inflation meant automatically growing benefits. This one-two punch drained social security trust fund reserves to critically low levels in the late 1970s and early 1980s. Meanwhile, other troubling factors were becoming clear. A lower birthrate meant that in the future, fewer workers would be available to support the pool of retirees. And the number of retirees would grow, as average life spans lengthened and the baby-boom generation retired. Higher taxes—an unpopular political move—loomed as one alternative. Another was to pay for social security out of general revenues—that is, income taxes. Social security would then become a public assistance program, similar to welfare. In 1983, shortly before existing social security benefit funds would have become exhausted, Congress and President Reagan agreed to a solution that called for two painful adjustments: increased taxes and reduced benefits.

The changes enacted in 1983 may have saved the social security system. However, future economic conditions will determine its success or failure. Despite various revenue-generating plans, higher taxes or lower benefits may be the only means for ensuring the viability of social security.[16]

Today, few argue against the need for social security. But debate surrounds the extent of coverage and the level of benefits. "The [Social Security] Act is the most successful program of the modern state," declared Nobel Prize laureate Paul Samuelson. Yet Milton Friedman, another Nobel laureate and social security opponent, labeled the act "a sacred cow that no politician can criticize." How can two renowned economists maintain such dramatically different views? Samuelson is a liberal in the Keynesian tradition; he favors equality over freedom. According to his view, social security lifted the elderly from destitution by redistributing income from workers (who have growing incomes) to the elderly (who have little or no income). Friedman is a libertarian and a monetarist; he favors freedom over equality. Because social security limits freedom in order to provide economic equality, Friedman would no doubt prefer that the program be scaled back or even eliminated. However, the political risks associated with social security cutbacks are too great for most politicians to bear.

As a group, older Americans exercise enormous political power. People at or near retirement age now make up almost 30 percent of the potential electorate, and voter turnout among older Americans is reported to be about twice that of younger people.[17] These facts help explain the stability of social security and the expansion of health care for the elderly.

Medicare

In 1962, the Senate considered extending social security benefits to provide hospitalization and medical care for the elderly. In opposing the extension, Democratic senator Russell Long of Louisiana declared, "We are not staring at a sweet old lady in bed with her kimono and nightcap. We are looking into the eyes of the wolf that ate Red Riding Hood's grandma."[18] Long was concerned that costs would soar without limit. Other opponents echoed the fears of the American Medical Association (AMA), which saw virtually any form of government-provided medical care as a step toward government control of medicine. Long and his compatriots won the battle that day. Three years later, however, the Social Security Act was amended to provide **Medicare,** health care for all people aged sixty-five and older.

Origins of Medicare.   As early as 1945, public opinion clearly supported some form of national health insurance. However, that idea became entangled in Cold War politics—the growing crusade against communism in America.[19] The AMA, representing the nation's physicians, mounted and financed an all-out campaign to link national health insurance (so-called socialized medicine) with socialism; the campaign was so successful that the prospect of a national health care policy vanished.

Both proponents and opponents of national health insurance tried to link their positions to deeply rooted American values: advocates emphasized equality and fairness; opponents stressed individual freedom. In the absence of a clear mandate on the kind of insurance (publicly funded or private) the public wanted, the AMA was able to exert its political influence to prevent any national insurance at all.[20]

By 1960, however, the terms of the debate had changed. It no longer focused on the clash between freedom and equality. Now the issue of health insurance was cast in terms of providing assistance to the aged, and a ground swell of support forced it onto the national agenda.[21]

The Democratic victory in 1964 and the advent of President Johnson's Great Society made some form of national health care policy almost inevitable. On July 30, 1965, Johnson signed a bill that provided a number of health benefits to the elderly and the poor. Fearful of the AMA's power to punish its opponents, the Democrats had confined their efforts to a compulsory hospitalization insurance plan for the elderly. (This is known today as Part A of Medicare.) In addition, the bill contained a version of an

Medicare for Mummies

Senator Tom Harkin (D.–Iowa) (pictured on the left) went ballistic in 1995 when he learned from the Government Accounting Office (the government's watchdog agency) that Medicare paid $2.32 for surgical gauze that could be bought wholesale for 19 cents. To dramatize his criticism of Medicare payment practices, Harkin had his aide, Pete Selfridge (on the right), dress himself in surgical gauze.

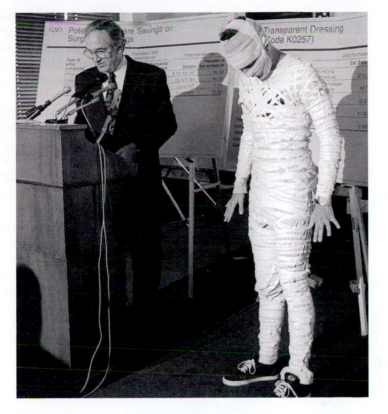

alternative Republican plan, which called for voluntary government-subsidized insurance to cover physician's fees. (This is known today as Part B of Medicare.) A third program, added a year later, is called *Medicaid*; it provides medical aid to the poor through federally assisted state health programs. Medicaid is a need-based comprehensive medical and hospitalization program: if you are poor, you qualify. Medicaid today covers 35.1 million people, at a cost that exceeded $135 billion in 1994.[22]

For a table of current Medicare benefits, go to:

`<www.ssa.gov/medicare. html>`

Medicare Today.   Part A of Medicare is compulsory insurance that covers certain hospital services for people aged sixty-five and older. Workers pay a tax; retirees pay premiums deducted from their social security payments. Payments for necessary services are made by the national government directly to participating hospitals and other qualifying facilities. In 1994, more than 36 million people were enrolled in Part A, and the government paid more than $103 billion in benefits.[23]

Part B of Medicare is a voluntary program of medical insurance for people aged sixty-five and older who pay the premiums. The insurance covers the services of physicians and other qualifying providers. In 1994, thirty-five million people were enrolled; the government spent more than $58 billion for Part B benefits, of which about $15 billion came from enrollees. The difference of $43 billion comes from general tax revenue. In 1996, the monthly premium for this insurance was $42.50.[24]

The fears that Senator Long voiced in 1962 approached reality in the 1980s: Medicare costs soared out of control. By 1986, Medicare costs exceeded $75 billion, representing a fourfold increase in ten years. For the moment, Medicare is solvent, thanks to modest payroll tax increases and low unemployment, but the program lacks a financial cushion. Spending reductions (through curtailed benefits) or income increases (through raised taxes) are still viable, although politically unpalatable, alternatives.[25]

Medicare costs continue to increase at rates in excess of the cost of living. Consequently, government has sought to contain those costs. One attempt at cost containment makes use of economic incentives in the hospital treatment of Medicare patients. The plan seems to have had the desired economic benefits, but it raises questions about possibly endangering the health of elderly patients. Previously, Medicare payments to hospitals were based on the length of a patient's stay: the longer the stay, the more revenue the hospital earned. This approach encouraged longer, more expensive hospital stays, because the government was paying the bill. In 1985, however, the government switched to a new payment system, under which hospitals are paid a fixed fee based on the patient's diagnosis. If the patient's stay costs more than the fee schedule allows, the hospital pays the difference. On the other hand, if the hospital treats a patient for less than the fixed fee, the hospital reaps a profit. This new system provides an incentive for hospitals to discharge patients sooner, perhaps in some cases before they are completely well.

Health Care for Everyone

Medicare provides health care for the elderly. Medicaid provides health care for the poor. Yet the United States is the only major industrialized nation without a universal health care system. Nearly everyone maintains that the U.S. health care system needs fixing. Let's consider the two main problems.

First, many Americans have no health insurance. In 1992, thirty-seven million Americans—that's about 15 percent of the nonelderly population—were uninsured on any given day. They are uninsured because either their employers do not provide health insurance or the cost of health insurance is prohibitive for them. In 1993, the average annual family premium for employer-based group health insurance was $5,200, which was more than double the average premium in 1988. Compounding the problem is the fact that a job change or job loss often entails losing one's health insurance coverage.

Second, the cost of health care is rising faster than the cost of living. The United States spends far more money on health than any other nation. Today, we spend more than $800 billion a year on health care, or 14 percent of the gross domestic product. Without some cost containment, U.S. health care costs will exceed 18 percent of GDP by the year 2000. The benefits of high spending may be elusive, according to Compared with What? 19.1.

The American public remains divided on the remedy. The Clinton administration has held firm to its objective of universal coverage, but none of the proposed approaches to this end has gained the support of a majority of Americans. Moreover, there is no clear sense of how to pay for the increased cost that any plan will entail. Half the public is prepared to pay higher taxes to ensure universal coverage, but the only taxes that generate strong support are "sin" taxes on alcohol and cigarettes. Yet these taxes are insufficient to pay for the comprehensive coverage Americans want. In summarizing the array of data on health care reform, a commentator remarked, "We want the government to reform our health care system, but we lack a shared vision of what that system should be or how to achieve it."[26]

The two central problems of health care give rise to two key goals and a familiar dilemma. First, any reform should democratize health care—that is, it should make health care available to everyone. But by providing broad access to medical care, we will increase the amount we spend on such care. Second, any reform must control the ballooning cost of health care. But controlling costs requires restricting the range of procedures and providers available to patients. Thus, the health care issue goes to the heart of the modern dilemma of government: we must weigh greater equality in terms of universal coverage and cost controls against a loss of freedom in markets for health care and in choosing a doctor.

The Clinton administration's effort at health care reform started boldly in September 1993 with a plan for a total overhaul of the system. Hundreds of experts under the direction of Hillary Rodham Clinton conceived the plan. It weighed in at a hefty 1,300 pages. Their version called for universal coverage and cost controls. But universal coverage necessarily meant more taxes, and cost controls implied limits on consumer behavior. In short, reforming health care was no free lunch. It became an easy target for critics, and criticism there was aplenty.

The plan proved appealing to big business, strong labor unions, and corporate medical practices, who stood to gain from its adoption. But the plan also proved appalling to small businesses, the insurance industry, and the doctors, who stood to lose from many of its provisions. There was something in it for each of them to support and to oppose. By August 1994—just one year following its introduction—the administration's proposal was dead, a victim of the old adage that "it is easier to stop what you're against than to achieve what you are for."

President Clinton claimed a small victory in August 1996 when he signed a bill to expand access to health insurance for twenty five million Americans. The new law—enacted with bipartisan support—allows workers to maintain health insurance coverage if they change or lose their jobs and it effectively bars insurance companies from denying coverage to people who have preexisting medical conditions. Two years earlier, Clinton had declared that incremental changes in health care would do more harm than good. He threatened then to veto any bill that fell short of universal health care coverage.

Congress enacted two additional health care changes in September 1996. One change grants most working Americans the same level of coverage for mental health that they now enjoy for medical and surgical services. The second change guarantees forty-eight-hour hospital stays for new mothers and their infants. These changes are popular with voters. With national elections less than six weeks away, politicians of all stripes joined the bandwagon.

19.1   Health Spending and Its Possible Effects

In 1993, the United States spent more than 14 percent of its gross domestic product (the total market value of all goods and services produced in this country during the year) on health care. This was substantially more than any other large-population nation. Most of American health care spending was in the private sector. *Public health* spending is far less, both as a proportion of the GDP and in comparison to other nations.

What does health spending achieve? Measures of health spending outcomes are too nu-

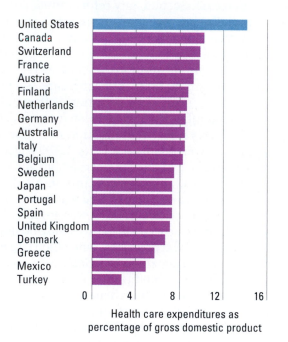

United States
Canada
Switzerland
France
Austria
Finland
Netherlands
Germany
Australia
Italy
Belgium
Sweden
Japan
Portugal
Spain
United Kingdom
Denmark
Greece
Mexico
Turkey

0   4   8   12   16

Health care expenditures as
percentage of gross domestic product

Health Expenditures by Country, 1993

Total health care expenditures as a percentage of the gross domestic product.

Source: *1995 Statistical Abstract of the United States*, p. 853.

PUBLIC ASSISTANCE

Public assistance is what most people mean when they use the terms *welfare* or *welfare payments*; it is government aid to individuals who can demonstrate a need for that aid. Although much public assistance is directed toward those who lack the ability or the resources to provide for themselves or their families, the poor are not the only recipients of wel-

merous for inclusion here. Let's focus on just one: longevity. With only one exception (Spain), life expectancy in large-population nations reveals very little variation. Babies born in Turkey in 1995 can expect to live on average to 72. Babies born in Japan in 1995 can expect to live on average to nearly 80. Despite the fact that Americans outspend other nations on health care, the payoff in life expectancy has not yet been realized.

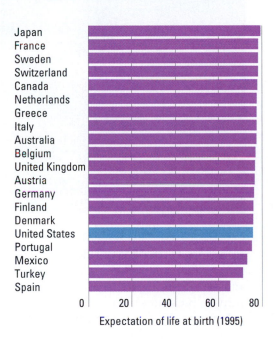

Life Expectancy in 1995

The United States spends more of its wealth, as a percentage of its gross domestic product, on health-related expenditures than any other country. This spending has not bought a high return, at least in life expectancy. With one exception, children born in 1995 in the countries listed above can expect to live between 70 and 80 years. Though the differences between countries are small, the United States ranks toward the bottom of the list.

Source: *1995 Statistical Abstract of the United States*, pp. 849–850. Excludes countries with populations less than 5 million in 1995.

A featured series in the *Boston Globe* on "corporate welfare." `<www.boston.com/globe/nat /corporate.htm>`

fare. Corporations, farmers, and college students are among the many recipients of government aid in the form of tax breaks, subsidized loans, and other benefits.

Public assistance programs instituted under the Social Security Act are known today as *categorical assistance programs*. They include (1) old-age

Boxed In, Boxed Out

Most observers agree that homelessness is increasing, but there is little reliable information about the scope and causes of the problem. Some advocates for the homeless attribute the increase to the national economy and the lack of affordable housing; others cite the deinstitutionalization of the mentally ill. With nowhere to go, the homeless are always in sight.

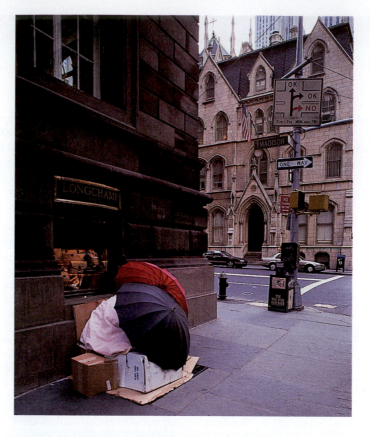

assistance for the needy elderly not covered by old-age pension benefits, (2) aid to the needy blind, (3) aid to needy families with dependent children, and (4) aid to the totally and permanently disabled. Adopted initially as stopgap measures during the Depression, these programs have become entitlements. They are administered by the states, but the bulk of the funding comes from the national government's general tax revenues. Because the states also contribute to the funding of their public assistance programs, the benefits vary widely from state to state.

Poverty and Public Assistance

Until 1996, the national government imposed national standards on state welfare programs. It distributed funds to each state based on the proportion of its population living in poverty. That proportion is determined on the basis of a federally defined **poverty level,** or poverty threshold, which is the minimum cash income that will provide for a family's basic needs. The poverty level varies by family size and is calculated as three times the cost of a minimally nutritious diet for a given number of people over a given time period. (The threshold is computed in this way because research suggests that poor families of three or more persons spend approximately one-third of their income on food.*)

---

*Although it has been the source of endless debate, today's definition of poverty retains remarkable similarity to its precursors. As early as 1795, a group of English magistrates "decided that a minimum income should be the cost of a gallon loaf of bread, multiplied by three, plus an allowance for each dependent." See Alvin L. Schorr, "Redefining Poverty Levels," New York Times, 9 May 1984, p. 27.

The poverty level is fairly simple to apply, but it is only a rough measure for distinguishing the poor from the nonpoor. Using it is like using a wrench as a hammer: it works, but not very well. We attach importance to the poverty level figure, despite its inaccuracies, because measuring poverty is a means of measuring how the American promise of equality stands up against the performance of our public policies. In 1995, the government calculated that more than 36 million people, or 13.8 percent of the population, were living in poverty in the United States.[27]

The poverty level is adjusted each year to reflect changes in consumer prices. In 1995, the poverty threshold for a family of four was a cash income below $15,150.[28] This is income *before* taxes. If the poverty threshold were defined as disposable income (income *after* taxes), the proportion of the population categorized as living in poverty would increase.

Some critics believe that factors other than income should be considered in computing the poverty level. Assets (home, cars, possessions), for example, are excluded from the definition. Also, the computation fails to take into account such noncash benefits as food stamps, health benefits (Medicaid), and subsidized housing. Presumably, the inclusion of these noncash benefits as income would reduce the number of individuals seen as living below the poverty level.

The graphic in Politics in a Changing America 19.1 shows that the poverty rate in the United States has declined since the mid-1960s. It rose again slightly in the 1980s, then declined slightly, and now is just below 14 percent. In 1995, the poverty rate for blacks fell below 30 percent, the lowest level since the government started to record poverty data in the 1960s. Still, poverty retains a hold on the American population. The food stamp program and cash payments for the poor (what most people call welfare) are aimed at addressing the problems of poverty.

Assistance to the Needy: Food Stamps

The national government's **food stamp program** aims to improve the diets of low-income households by supplementing their food-purchasing power. The nationally funded program is administered through local agencies, which distribute the stamps to needy individuals and families. The stamps are actually coupons that can be used to purchase food. Some states are experimenting with electronic distribution of food stamps and other forms of aid to the poor.

Food stamps and the safety net. `<www.urban.org/welfare/chap13.htm>`

Food stamp benefits are set nationally and do not vary from state to state. Food stamps remain a federal entitlement despite legislative efforts in 1996 to give states greater autonomy concerning eligibility criteria and benefit levels. In 1994, the food stamp program cost the government nearly $24 billion. More than 27 million participants (about one in ten Americans) received an average of $69 a month in food stamps.[29] Projected spending will be cut by several billion dollars by denying food stamps to illegal aliens and legal non-immigrants—such as travelers and students—and by limiting the amounts given to people who are not raising children.

Poverty was once a condition of old age. Social security changed that. Today, poverty is still related to age, but in the opposite direction: it is largely a predicament of the young. Twenty-two percent of persons younger than eighteen live in poverty.[30]

It is relatively easy to draw a portrait of the poor. It is much more difficult to craft policies that move them out of destitution. Critics of social welfare spending, led by Charles Murray, argue that antipoverty policies have made poverty more attractive by removing incentives to work. They believe that policies aimed at providing for the poor have actually promoted poverty.

Another explanation, proposed by William Julius Wilson, maintains that the failure of government policies to reduce poverty rests on changes in racial attitudes. In the 1960s, racial barriers kept the black middle class in the same urban neighborhoods as poor blacks. Their presence provided social stability, role models, and strong community institutions and businesses. Then the decline of racial barriers allowed middle-class blacks to move out of the inner cities. As a result, the inner cities became increasingly poor and increasingly dependent on welfare.[31] In the 1992 and 1994 elections, candidates for all offices turned up the rhetoric regarding the future of public assistance to the poor. In 1996, the Republican-led Congress sought a fundamental revision of the welfare system and managed to enlist the president in their cause (see Figure 19.3).

Work versus welfare: a libertarian view.
`<www.cato.org/pubs/pas/pa-240.html>`

Welfare Reform: Major Changes, Uncertain Consequences

Although candidate Bill Clinton had promised to "end welfare as we know it," he was hard-pressed in 1996 to accept the welfare reform proposals served up by the Republican-led Congress. President Clinton vetoed two attempts at welfare reform. On the Republicans' third try, however, Clinton signed a compromise welfare reform bill into law.

The bill President Clinton signed into law on August 22, 1996, eliminated a federal guarantee of cash assistance that had, over its sixty-one-year-history, kept millions of citizens afloat during difficult times. Critics maintained that, for some recipients, floating had become a way of life, that government payments discouraged them from swimming on their own. The new measure impacted nearly all of the 12.8 million people on welfare and the 27 million receiving food stamps. It abolished the biggest public assistance program, **Aid to Families with Dependent Children (AFDC)**, affecting more than one-fifth of the families in America with children—some nine million children and four million parents.[32] In addition, most immigrants who arrived after the bill was signed would not be eligible for the majority of federal benefits and services.

Under the plan, individual adult recipients of welfare payments will have to become employed within two years. The law will place the burden of job creation on the states. Families can receive no more than a total of five years' of benefits in a lifetime, and states can set a minimum limit much lower than that. However, even before signing the bill, Clinton already was granting waivers permitting states to offer extensions beyond the five-year limit, as long as recipients continue to look for work. Republicans countered that such provisions effectively undermined the law.[33] In practice, however, there are no mechanisms for monitoring current welfare recipients at the national level. Until such a system is implemented, recipients can skirt the work requirements by moving from state to state.

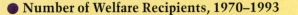

19.3 ● Number of Welfare Recipients, 1970–1993

Until 1996, Aid to Families with Dependent Children (AFDC) was the cornerstone of the nation's welfare policy. In 1993, benefits of more than $23 billion went to more than 14 million people monthly, of which nearly 10 million were children.

Source: Social Security Bulletin, Annual Statistical Supplement, 1995, p. 17.

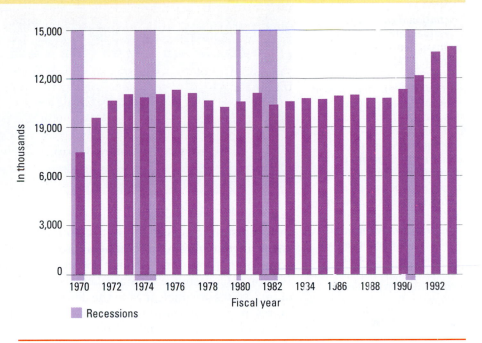

The reform phase-in was set to occur in stages. From August 1996 to July 1997, states would alter their welfare programs to meet new federal guidelines for cash assistance under block grants. At the same time, most noncitizens receiving food stamps and Supplemental Security Income would become ineligible for benefits. At the start of fiscal year 1997, "no individual or family shall be entitled to any benefits or services" under AFDC.[34] Food stamp benefits were set to decrease over the course of three months, from October 1996 to January 1997, and as of the new year, states would be allowed, but not required, to cut off all cash assistance and social services to noncitizens. And by July 1997, states would be required to submit a new welfare plan to the Department of Health and Human Services, although some federal waivers might be granted.[35]

Under the old entitlement system, benefits varied dramatically from state to state. The basic monthly benefit for a family varied from a low of $187 in Mississippi to a high of $655 in Vermont.[36] Nonetheless, for the 328 House members and 74 senators who voted for the bill (Republicans heavily in favor, Democrats split), devolving power to the states proved a prime force in the reform effort. President Clinton's own desire to permit states to act as laboratories for welfare reform provided ample ammunition for advocates of change. When the bill was signed into law, some forty-five states had already begun experimenting with their welfare system.[37] Clinton and others had heaped praise on such experiments as Wisconsin's "W-2" plan ("Wisconsin Works"), which Republican governor Tommy Thompson expected to put into effect by the fall of 1997. Its pilot program had seen some success in dropping the state's welfare case load.

How will the states be affected by the welfare reform bill of 1996? As envisioned, there will be fifty new welfare systems under the plan of block,

The Welfare Card: American Distress

The national government is experimenting with a new means of distributing welfare benefits: ATM cards. Independence Card holders use their cards in machines at banks and grocery stores to obtain cash or draw against a food stamp account. Officials hope the new system will reduce administrative costs and recipient fraud. The stigma and inconvenience traditionally associated with welfare may also be reduced; some critics view the latter result as a disadvantage, believing that stigma and inconvenience serve a purpose by helping keep people off welfare.

or lump-sum, grants to the states. Some state officials were concerned by the stringent work requirements imposed by the new law and confused by some of its provisions. As Jack Tweedie, a welfare policy specialist at the National Conference of State Legislatures, put it, "The word is confusion." States are unclear as to the definition of "work." For example, some states regard job-training as work, but the aim of the legislation is to achieve employment. In addition, states will be forced to make difficult decisions in allocating the yearly total of $16.4 billion in block grants, a figure that will remain unchanged until 2002, with no adjustments for inflation or population shifts.[38]

What will be the effect on those people who will feel the greatest impact of the changes? Although estimates vary widely, according to LaDonna Pavetti of the Urban Institute, a policy-oriented think tank, if the five-year limit were immediately put into effect (rather than phased in over a period of approximately two years, as will be the case), some 2 million adults and 4.5 million children would find themselves without a safety net. Government estimates indicate that up to 1 million children may be put into poverty. Impoverished individuals (often single mothers), many of whom are underskilled, with limited education and few resources (such as jobs) to draw upon in their rural and inner-city environments, may be hard pressed to keep their heads above water. In some areas, the jobs simply may not be there. In Chicago's primarily black North Lawndale neighborhood, for example, two large factories that provided the majority of area employment have vacated the neighborhood, taking with them some fifty-seven thousand jobs.[39] As some critics of the new plan's work requirement have asked, without adequate numbers and types of jobs, what are people to do?

Many policymakers were concerned with the dramatic nature of the changes. As Senator Carol Moseley-Braun (D.-Ill.) said, "I believe that the Senate will rue the day that we passed this legislation. This day, in the name of reform, the Senate will do actual violence to poor children, putting millions of them into poverty who were not in poverty before."[40] Longtime civil rights activist and House member John Lewis (D.-Ga.) asked his fellow representatives, "Where is the compassion? Where is the sense of decency? Where is the heart of Congress?" For many Democratic party loyalists, the president had taken his position of "New Democrat" too far. But Clinton stated that "the nature of the poverty population is so different now that I am convinced we have got to be willing to experiment, to try to work to find ways to break the cycle of dependency." And, rare in the age of partisanship, many Republicans agreed. As Representative John Kasich (R.-Ohio), the House Budget Committee chairman, stated, "People are not entitled to anything but opportunity."[41] It remains to be seen what shape that opportunity takes.

In effect, these reforms move away from promoting equal outcomes. For many impoverished people, the decline of national entitlement policies and the beginning of state experimentation will determine the course of their lives, and their children's lives, for years to come. Will they be able to keep their heads above water?

BENEFITS AND FAIRNESS

Ronald Reagan once observed, "In the war on poverty, poverty won." Americans tend to agree. About half of all Americans believe the liberal welfare policies of the 1960s made things "somewhat better" for the poor; only 10 percent maintain that those policies made the poor much better off.[42] But more than 90 percent of Americans seem convinced that poverty will remain a persistent problem, partly because, more than 70 percent believe, the government doesn't know enough about how to eliminate poverty.[43]

The national government provides many Americans with benefits. There are two kinds of benefits: cash, such as a retiree's social security check, and noncash, such as food stamps. Some benefits are conditional. **Means-tested benefits** impose an income test to qualify. For example, free or low-cost school lunch programs and Pell college grants are available to households that have an income that falls below a designated threshold. **Non-means-tested benefits** impose no such income test; benefits such as Medicare and social security are available to all, regardless of income.

Some Americans question the fairness of non-means-tested benefits. After all, benefits are subsidies, and some people need them more than others. If the size of the benefit pie remains fixed because of large budget deficits, imposing means tests on more benefits has real allure. For example, all elderly people now receive the same Medicare benefits, regardless of their income. Fairness advocates maintain that the affluent elderly should shoulder a higher share of Medicare costs, shifting more benefits to the low-income elderly. If the idea of shifting benefits gains support in the future, debate will focus on the income level below which a program will apply.

In the long run, understanding the consequences of public policy will help reduce poverty in America. For the moment, however, debates among scholars and policymakers offer no comfort to Michael Moran and his brother and mother, who daily confront the struggle to overcome shame and dependence because they are poor.

SUMMARY

In this chapter, we have examined domestic policy, a general plan of action adopted by the government to solve a social problem, counter a threat, or pursue an objective within the country's own borders. Often, disagreements about public policy are disagreements about values. Some of the oldest and most costly domestic policies, such as social security and Medicare, pose choices between freedom and equality.

Many domestic policies that provide benefits to individuals and promote economic equality were instituted during the Great Depression. Today, the government plays an active role in providing benefits to the poor, the elderly, and the disabled. The object of these domestic policies is to alleviate conditions that individuals are powerless to prevent. This is the social welfare function of the modern state. The call for health care reform is a reflection of the modern dilemma of democracy: universal coverage and cost controls versus a loss of freedom in health care choices. Incremental reforms in 1996 broadened coverage but fell far short of quality health care for all Americans.

Government confers benefits on individuals through social insurance and public assistance. Social insurance is not based on need; public assistance (welfare) hinges on proof of need. In one form of social insurance—old-age benefits—a tax on current workers pays retired workers' benefits. Aid for the poor, by contrast, comes from the government's general tax revenues. Although the current welfare system has few defenders, clear solutions to the problem of welfare dependence have yet to emerge. In contrast, the food stamp program has proved successful by improving the diet of low-income Americans.

Programs to aid the elderly and the poor have been gradually transformed into entitlements, or rights that accrue to eligible persons. These government programs have reduced poverty among some groups, especially the elderly. However, poverty retains a grip on certain segments of the population. Social and demographic changes have feminized poverty, and there is little prospect of reversing that trend anytime soon.

Bill Clinton and the Republican-led Congress have reformed the welfare system. The biggest entitlement program (AFDC) is gone, and individual state programs will substitute for a single national policy. Food stamps remain a federal entitlement, but new restrictions will limit the program's reach. Work requirements and time limits on welfare may break the cycle of dependency, but the reforms run the risk of endangering the neediest among us. Time and experience will likely tell whether this grand experiment will produce better outcomes.

Some government subsidy programs provide means-tested benefits, wherein eligibility hinges on income. Non-means-tested benefits are available to all, regardless of income. As the demand for such benefits exceeds available resources, policymakers have come to question their fairness. Subsidies for rich and poor alike are the basis for a broad national consensus. A departure from that consensus in the name of fairness may very well be the next challenge of democracy.

Key Terms

public policy	Great Society	Social Security Act	Aid to Families with
welfare state	War on Poverty	Medicare	Dependent Children
social welfare programs	"feminization of poverty"	public assistance	(AFDC)
Great Depression	social insurance	poverty level	means-tested benefits
New Deal	entitlements	food stamp program	non-means-tested
	social security		benefits

Selected Readings

Bennett, Linda L. M., and Stephen Earl Bennett. *Living with Leviathan: Americans Coming to Terms with Big Government.* Lawrence: University Press of Kansas, 1990. An analysis of public opinion about the powers and responsibilities of national government, from Franklin Roosevelt to Ronald Reagan.

Ellwood, David T. *Poor Support: Poverty in the American Family.* New York: Basic Books, 1988. Ellwood agrees with Murray's analysis (see below) but argues for incentives to break the grip of poverty. Ellwood's ideas have been part of the Clinton's administration's effort to "end welfare as we know it."

Goldberg, Gertrude Schaffner, and Eleanor Kremen, eds. *The Feminization of Poverty: Only in America?* New York: Greenwood, 1990. This comparative study of poverty among females in seven capitalist and socialist countries argues that the feminization of poverty is not unique to the United States.

Katz, Michael B. *The Undeserving Poor: From the War on Poverty to the War on Welfare.* New York: Pantheon, 1989. A historical overview of the ideas and assumptions that shaped policies toward the poor from the 1960s through the 1980s.

Murray, Charles. *Losing Ground.* New York: Basic Books, 1985. An assessment of American social policy from 1950 to 1980. Murray argues that by attempting to remove the barriers to the good life for the poor, policymakers have created a poverty trap. Controversial in its day, Murray's analysis is taken as received wisdom today.

Wilson, William Julius. *The Truly Disadvantaged: The Inner City, the Underclass, and Public Policy.* Chicago: University of Chicago Press, 1987. Wilson argues that the decay of the inner city cannot be explained by racism alone and targets the class structure of ghetto neighborhoods as the most important factor in a complex web of reasons.

World Wide Web Resources

Electronic Policy Network. A rich treasure trove of timely materials on politics and public policy.
`<epn.org>`

The Social Security Administration Home Page. Everything you always wanted to know about social security but were afraid to ask. (Check out PEBES for a personal earnings and benefit estimate statement.)
`<www.ssa.gov>`

Medicare and Medicaid Explained. Everything you could ever want to know about Medicare and Medicaid.
`<www.hcfa.gov>`

The Urban Institute's Welfare Reform Overview. A detailed analysis of welfare reform issues, prepared by the Urban Institute, an independent Washington think tank.
`<www.urban.org/welfare/overview.htm>`

Global Policy

IN UKRAINE, THE MISSILE SILOS ARE GONE. Sunflowers have taken their place. In June 1996, to mark the completion of Ukraine's nuclear disarmament, the defense ministers of Russia and Ukraine and the U.S. secretary of defense planted sunflowers on ground once occupied by Soviet S-19 missiles. Ukraine's disarmament, which has helped reduce the worldwide nuclear threat, was one of the positive results of the end of the Cold War.

The **Cold War,** an intense rivalry between the U.S.-led Western alliance and the former Soviet Union with its Eastern European satellites, had shaped global politics for over four decades. Its end came into view late in 1988, when Soviet president Mikhail Gorbachev, squeezed by economic troubles, began military cutbacks. Soviet control over Eastern Europe soon disintegrated. One after another, the peoples of Poland, Hungary, Czechoslovakia, East Germany, and Romania ousted their communist governments and proclaimed their commitment to freedom and democracy. The menacing Berlin Wall, for thirty years the most prominent symbol of East-West confrontation, came down late in 1989. Soon after, East and West Germany reunified. These events were cause for jubilation—the greatest threat to global security in the late twentieth century seemed to have passed. The U.S. president, George Bush, called for a "New World Order."

But the end of the Cold War did not bring worldwide peace and stability. By the end of 1990, the United States and twenty-seven other nations were gearing up for war against Iraq in the Persian Gulf. Although that conflict resulted in the swift defeat of Iraqi forces, some twenty-nine other major armed conflicts were still going on around the world.[1] In the years after the fall of communism, United Nations forces became involved in fourteen peacekeeping missions—as many as the U.N. had undertaken in the previous forty-three years.[2] In the Middle East, as leaders moved toward peace, terrorists tried to short-circuit their efforts. U.S. troops headed off to far-flung trouble spots, including Somalia, Bosnia, and Haiti. In short, the post–Cold War world seemed anything but orderly.

Although the end of the Cold War did not bring world peace, it did bring about fundamental changes in the context of international politics. The approaches to foreign policy crafted during the Cold War no longer fit, and policymakers often appeared to be floundering as they tried to redefine America's goals in the arena of world politics. New issues came into prominence. During the Cold War, issues of war, peace, and military security (sometimes called **high politics**) dominated the nation's foreign policy

671

Against All Odds

Though Israeli prime minister Yitzhak Rabin and PLO leader Yassir Arafat signed a Middle East peace agreement, forces on both sides have seemed bent on torpedoing the peace process. On the Palestinian side, organizations such as Hamas and Hezbollah have engaged in terrorist attacks on Israelis. In Israel, Prime Minister Rabin was assassinated by an Israeli who opposed the peace settlement.

agenda. In the post–Cold War world, global economic and environmental problems (or **low politics**) received more attention than before.

The handling of foreign policy in a democracy has long been a subject of debate. Many have argued that foreign policy, which concerns dealings with nations and peoples outside the United States, requires a degree of unity rarely found in domestic politics. People disagree about foreign policies because they differ about the goals government should adopt, the means to reach them, and the nature of any given situation. Although vigorous discussion is usually thought to show vitality in a democracy, some people think it can lead to problems in foreign policy. Because foreign policy often involves high stakes—matters concerning national security and defending the nation from outside threats—some argue that "politics should stop at the water's edge." As far back as 1837, Alexis de Tocqueville, a French political thinker and observer of the American scene, noted that certain features inherent in democracies could cause problems in the area of foreign policy:

> Foreign politics demand scarcely any of those qualities which are peculiar to a democracy; they require, on the contrary, the perfect use of almost all those in which it is deficient. . . . A democracy can only with great difficulty regulate the details of an important undertaking, persevere in a fixed design, and work out its execution in spite of severe obstacles. It cannot combine its measures with secrecy or await their consequences with patience.[3]

As Tocqueville predicted, the workings of foreign policy have challenged American democracy. During the Cold War, especially, some observers insisted that foreign policy should be free from the democratic wrangling that characterizes domestic policymaking. In the aftermath of World War II, faced with a communist threat spearheaded by the Soviet Union, the United States forged a foreign policy consensus built on bipartisanship and strong presidential leadership. That consensus broke down during the Vietnam era amid doubts about the nature of the threat and the means appropriate to counter it. Divided government and power struggles between the president and Congress intensified the breakdown. In the post–Cold War era, signs have already appeared that future U.S. foreign policy may be highly politicized and that the new configurations of opinion will not always fall along party lines. Also, as issues of low politics are increasing in importance, it is harder to draw clear distinctions between domestic and foreign policy. The North American Free Trade Agreement (NAFTA), for instance, pertains to international relations with Mexico and Canada, but it also involves American jobs. More and more, foreign policy issues are likely to be **"intermestic"**—a blend of international and domestic concerns—as discussed in Politics in a Changing America 20.1.

Does more democracy make for bad foreign policy? Is it possible for a democracy to achieve its goals around the globe without compromising its domestic political process? Specifically, can America pursue freedom, order, and equality abroad without undermining these values at home? This chapter examines these questions. We focus on new challenges to U.S. foreign policy in the realms of high and low politics. We consider the process of making foreign policy in America and the strains it places on democratic government. Finally, we discuss the division of responsibility for foreign policy among the branches of government and the effect this division has on the process of making and implementing policy.

U.S. VALUES AND INTERESTS: THE HISTORICAL CONTEXT

Above all else, the goal of American foreign policy is to preserve our national interests. The most important of these interests is national security. The difficulty in making foreign policy comes in deciding just what "national interests" and "national security" mean and exactly what to do to preserve them. For the decades of the Cold War, Americans defined national security in terms of preventing communist expansion. Now that the Cold War is over, other goals, such as promoting economic prosperity and preserving environmental quality, receive increased attention as important components of our national interest.

From Isolationism to Regionalism to Globalism

Americans have not always viewed national security interests in global terms. For most of the nineteenth century, the limits of American interests were those staked out by the Monroe Doctrine of 1823, in which the United States rejected European intervention in the Western hemisphere and agreed not to involve itself in European politics. Americans generally practiced a policy of isolationism or withdrawal from the political entanglements of Europe. American isolationism was never total, however. As the nineteenth century wore on, the United States continued its expansion from coast to coast and also became a regional power, increasingly involved in the affairs of nations in the Pacific and Latin America. Still, America's defense establishment and foreign policy commitments remained limited.

20.1   Immigration Policy and Foreign Policy— Who Comes in the Golden Door?

When Bill Clinton campaigned for the presidency in 1992, he criticized as cruel the Bush administration's policy of returning Haitian boat people to Haiti rather than allowing them to seek political asylum in the United States. As president, however, Clinton continued the Bush policy. He refused to end the ban on Haitian immigration until mid-1994, when, pressured by the hunger strike of political activist Randall Robinson, he relented and ordered U.S. vessels to screen Haitian refugees and not repatriate those who had a well-founded fear of political reprisals.

Clinton's vacillation on the Haitian issue points up the fact that although the United States is a nation of immigrants, immigration policy has often been a political hot potato. Recently, those interested in "getting tough" on immigrants have offered a variety of proposals. Some have called for a moratorium on all immigration. Welfare reforms passed in 1996 denied welfare benefits to legal immigrants. The 1996 Republican party platform called for ending the 128-year-old guarantee of citizenship for all children born within U.S. borders.

Immigration also presents a classic domestic-versus-foreign-policy issue. The question of whom to let inside the "golden door" is important for both domestic and global politics. Should our support for human rights lead us to open the door wide for those fleeing political oppression? What about those fleeing poverty? What about our own citizens who fear that immigrants may take their jobs?

Until 1882, immigration was virtually unrestricted. The nation welcomed newcomers, who helped make continental expansion a reality; approximately one out of every seven people living in the United States was for-

eign-born. In 1882, Congress enacted the first immigration law, which, among other things, excluded Chinese immigrants. In 1921, a new law established quotas on immigration from overseas. (There was no quota on immigrants from other nations in the Western Hemisphere.) By setting the limit for each country at 3 percent of the number of that nationality already living in the United States, the quota act had the effect of limiting ethnic and cultural diversity. The formula heavily favored Northern and Western Europeans; it penalized Eastern and Southern Europeans; it virtually excluded Asians and Africans. This system was not changed until the 1960s.

After the United States moved to limit the number of immigrants admitted, it established a special category, outside the regular immigration quotas, for those fleeing political oppression. After World War II, under the Displaced Persons Act, the United States admitted hundreds of thousands of European refugees who fell outside the allotted quotas. As part of America's Cold War strategy, people fleeing communist countries could jump the quota queue and seek political asylum; among these were many Hungarians in the 1950s, Cubans in the 1960s, and Vietnamese in the 1970s.

Still, the percentage of foreign-born people living in the United States decreased. By 1970, only about one in every twenty residents had been born outside the country. But in the 1970s and 1980s, immigration—legal and illegal—increased. In 1990, Congress responded with the Immigration Reform and Control Act, which provided amnesty for illegal immigrants already in the United States, eased legal immigration, and cracked down on employers who hired illegals. Today, one

World War I was the United States' first serious foray into European politics. The rhetoric that surrounded our entry into the war in 1917—"to make the world safe for democracy"—gave an idealistic tone to America's effort to advance its own interest in freedom of the seas. Such moralism has often characterized America's approach to international politics. At

in every twelve U.S. residents is foreign-born. Nearly 1 million immigrants and refugees enter the country legally each year.

Who are today's immigrants? Until the 1950s, some two-thirds of legal immigrants came from Canada and Europe. But by the 1980s, that had changed. The percentage of immigrants from Europe shrank to 14 percent, whereas Asians climbed to 44 percent and Latin Americans to 40 percent of new arrivals admitted legally. In addition to those arriving legally, many hundreds of thousands of immigrants arrive illegally—as many as 3 million each year across the Mexican border. Yet, most of them do not expect to stay permanently. Tales of Mexicans streaming across the border and Haitians and Asians trying to sneak in by boat have captured media attention, but as much as 40 percent of the two hundred thousand to three hundred thousand illegal immigrants who take up permanent residence in the United States each year enter the country legally as visitors, then overstay their visas. Many are Europeans, who are more difficult to track and deport than Mexicans caught at the border.

The overall pattern of new immigration is increasing America's cultural diversity. Many Americans think the new arrivals make the country better. Still, immigration is controversial. Some of the opposition is no doubt a reaction to changes in "American identity," as America becomes more Asian, more African, more Latino, and less European. Particularly in times of high unemployment, many people worry about immigrants' taking jobs from native-born Americans. A high number of complaints about immigration come from a few states, such as California, New York, Florida, and Texas, that have been the major destinations of new immigrants. Politicians in these states have complained that social services for immigrants have increased state and local government costs. They have begun to call for the national government to restrict the flow of immigrants or to take over some of these costs. There are widespread feelings that America does not have control of its borders and needs stronger police measures to keep illegal entrants out. Still others have called for drastic limitations, such as a three-year moratorium on all immigration. Such a strategy might not prove effective, however. Previous crackdowns on legal immigration usually have led to more illegal entries. Political oppression and lack of economic opportunity around the world tend to fuel immigration to the United States. So foreign policy may also become a tool for reducing immigration. European immigration to America declined as prosperity and stability took hold in Europe. Measures such as NAFTA, geared to increase Mexican prosperity, might also help stem the tide of immigration. Experts estimate that if Mexico's wage rate were to climb to one-quarter of America's, the number of Mexicans seeking work in the United States would decline drastically. Similarly, working to end political oppression or restore democracy in countries such as Haiti and Guatemala may also help reduce the numbers of those seeking asylum in the United States.

Sources: Dick Kirschten, "Catch-Up Ball," *National Journal,* 7 August 1993, pp. 1976–1979; Rodman D. Griffen, "Illegal Immigration," *CQ Researcher,* 24 April 1992, pp. 361–363; Mary H. Cooper, "Immigration Reform," *CQ Researcher,* 24 September 1993.

the Versailles Peace Conference in 1919, for instance, President Woodrow Wilson championed the League of Nations as a device for preventing future wars. When the Senate failed to ratify the Treaty of Versailles in a form acceptable to Wilson, America's brief moment of internationalism ended. Until the Second World War, America continued to define its security interests narrowly and needed only a small military establishment to defend them.

World War II dramatically changed America's orientation toward the world. The United States emerged from the war a superpower, and its national security interests became global in scope. The country did not withdraw into isolationism again, but instead confronted a new rival—its wartime ally, the Soviet Union. In the fight against Hitler, the Soviets overran much of Eastern Europe. In the aftermath of the war, the Soviets solidified their control over these lands. Their communist ideology was spreading. To Americans, Soviet communism appeared to destroy freedom, and the possibility of continued Soviet expansion in Europe threatened international order. European conflicts had drawn the United States into war twice in twenty-five years. American foreign policy experts believed that the Soviets, if left unchecked, might soon do it again.

Cold War and Containment

To frustrate Soviet expansionist designs, Americans prepared to wage a new kind of war: not an actual shooting war, or "hot war," but a cold one, in which the relationship between the superpowers would be characterized by suspicion, rivalry, mutual ideological revulsion, and a military buildup on both sides—but no direct hostilities. To wage cold war, U.S. policymakers fashioned a foreign policy consensus around the idea of **containment,** or holding Soviet power in check as if it were in a container.[4]

Holding Soviet power in check had domestic consequences.
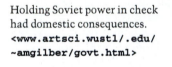

The policy of containment had military, economic, and political dimensions. Militarily, the United States committed itself to high defense expenditures, including maintaining a large fighting force with troops stationed around the world. Economically, the United States backed the

●●●●●●●●●●●●●
The Same in Any Language

These three World War I posters (from Germany, Great Britain, and the United States) were used to persuade men to join the army. Interestingly, they all employed the same psychological technique—pointing at viewers to make each individual feel the appeal personally.

establishment of an international economic system, known as the GATT-Bretton Woods system, that relied on free trade, fixed currency exchange rates, and America's ability to act as banker for the world. This system, plus an aid program to rebuild Europe (the Marshall Plan), fueled recovery and reduced the economic appeal of communism. Politically, the United States forged numerous alliances against Soviet aggression. The first treaty of alliance (1949) created the **North Atlantic Treaty Organization (NATO),** dedicated to the defense of member countries in Europe and North America. In addition, the United States tried to use international institutions such as the United Nations as instruments of containment. Because the Soviets had veto power in the U.N. Security Council, the United States was rarely able to use the U.N. as anything more than a sounding board to express anti-Soviet feelings. A major exception to this occurred in 1950, when the United States took advantage of the Soviets' absence from the Security Council to win support for a collective response to North Korea's invasion of South Korea. (The Soviets were absent in protest of Communist China's exclusion from the Security Council.)

In the first decades of the Cold War, the United States relied heavily on its superiority in nuclear weapons. American policy emphasized nuclear **deterrence.** It discouraged Soviet expansion by threatening to use nuclear weapons to retaliate against Soviet advances. The Soviets countered with their own nuclear program. By the late 1960s, both nations' nuclear technology had reached the level where they could totally destroy each other. From this came the policy of **mutual assured destruction (MAD)**—a first strike from either nation would result in the complete annihilation of both sides. Faced with this possibility, the two nations began to seek out new strategies. During the Kennedy administration in the early 1960s, the United States adopted a defense policy of **"flexible response,"** under which

Polishing the Coneheads

War often stimulates social change. During World War II, more than 6 million women entered the labor force, many doing jobs—such as making tailgunner cones for bombers —that had previously been done only by men.

America would develop its conventional (nonnuclear) military forces. In the event of Soviet provocation, the United States would have multiple options available short of nuclear war.

Also in the 1950s and 1960s, many countries in the developing world were gaining independence from colonial control imposed by Western nations. By the late 1950s, the Soviets were paying close attention to these developing nations. They offered to help forces involved in what they called wars of national liberation—that is, wars fought to end colonialism. The Soviets expected that the forces they supported would be pro-Soviet when and if they came to power. Americans were particularly distressed when Fidel Castro, who swept to power in Cuba in 1959, embraced Soviet-style communism in a nation only ninety miles from U.S. shores. To counter the Soviets, the United States followed policies aimed at **nation building.** These measures were designed to strengthen the opponents of communism in newly emerging nations by promoting democratic reforms and shoring up their economies. While U.S. rhetoric in promoting these policies often emphasized freedom, sometimes freedom took a back seat to America's desire for order. Speaking about different potential regimes in the Dominican Republic, President Kennedy made U.S. priorities clear: "There are three possibilities in descending order of preference: a decent democratic regime, a continuation of the Trujillo regime [a right-wing dictatorship], or a Castro [communist] regime. We ought to aim at the first, but we really can't renounce the second until we are sure that we can avoid the third."[5]

Vietnam and the Challenge to the Cold War Consensus

One place where Soviet support for a war of national liberation came into conflict with American nation building was in Vietnam. There, the United States tried to strengthen noncommunist institutions in South

At the Vietnam Memorial in Washington, D.C., visitors leave flowers, medals, photos, and other poignant reminders of their loved ones. Not only were fifty-eight thousand lives lost in the conflict, but the Cold War foreign policy consensus also became a casualty of war.

Vietnam in order to prevent a takeover by Soviet-backed forces from North Vietnam and their communist allies in the South, the Viet Cong. In Vietnam, the Cold War turned hot by the mid-1960s. Over fifty-eight thousand American lives were lost during the protracted fighting, until the United States withdrew in 1973. This was not the first major conflict of the Cold War era. Nearly as many Americans had been killed in the conflict in Korea between the communist North and the noncommunist South in 1950–1953. But the Vietnam War badly damaged the Cold War consensus on containment. Critics of the American presence in Vietnam came in many varieties. Some complained that America lacked the will to use enough military force to win the war. Others argued that America relied too much on military force to solve what were really political problems. Still others objected that America was intervening in a civil war rather than blocking Soviet expansion. In short, Americans disagreed passionately on what to do in Vietnam and how to do it. Eventually, after signing a peace agreement in 1973, the United States pulled its forces out of Vietnam, and in 1975, North and South were forcibly united under a communist regime.

Not only did the Vietnam War call into question both the military and the political dimensions of America's foreign policy consensus, it also undermined its economic basis. The cost of the war was an important factor contributing to balance-of-payments deficits that weakened the dollar, increased inflation, and forced an end to the system of currency exchange fashioned at Bretton Woods.

Even as the war in Vietnam wore on, President Nixon and his chief foreign policy adviser (and later secretary of state), Henry Kissinger, over-

This site offers a wealth of information about the Vietnam War, as well as about Vietnam today.
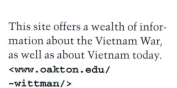
`<www.oakton.edu/`
`~wittman/>`

hauled American foreign policy. Under the **Nixon Doctrine,** an attempt to scale back America's overseas commitments, America would no longer "undertake all the defense of the free nations of the world." Instead, the United States would intervene only where "it makes a real difference and is considered in our interest."[6] Kissinger had long been a student of nineteenth-century diplomatic history. He believed that peace had prevailed then because the great nations of Europe maintained a balance of power among themselves. Nixon and Kissinger sought to create a similar framework for peace among the world's most powerful nations in the late twentieth century. To this end, they pursued better relations (détente) with the Soviet Union and ended decades of U.S. hostility toward the communist People's Republic of China. The theory of **détente** emphasized the value of order—order based not only on military might but also on recognition of mutual interests among the superpowers. Kissinger believed that if the Soviets and the Chinese were treated as legitimate participants in the international system, they would then have a vested interest in supporting world order. Specifically, they would have less incentive to promote revolutionary challenges to international stability. The brief period of détente saw the conclusion of a major arms agreement, the Strategic Arms Limitation Treaty (SALT I), in 1972. This pact limited the growth of strategic nuclear weapons. The thaw in the Cold War also witnessed greater cooperation between the United States and the U.S.S.R. in other spheres, including a joint space mission.

Critics have noted that détente, with its attention to U.S.-Soviet relations, did not bring about a successful end to the Vietnam War. Nor did it solve other problems, such as the 1973 oil embargo, a decision by Arab nations at war with Israel to cut oil supplies to the United States because of U.S. military support for Israel. In fact, while Kissinger concentrated on East-West politics—relations between Eastern-bloc communist nations and Western capitalist nations—other issues were increasing in importance. These often pitted the richer, more developed nations of the north against the poorer, less developed nations of the south. Others have suggested that the Nixon-Kissinger approach to foreign policy was too cynical, paid too much attention to power and interests, and deemphasized basic American values such as human rights.

Initially, President Jimmy Carter's stance on foreign policy differed substantially from that of his predecessors. From 1977 to 1979, he tended to downplay the importance of the Soviet threat. He saw revolutions in Nicaragua and Iran as products of internal forces rather than of Soviet involvement. Nonetheless, Carter did attempt to articulate U.S. national interests—in particular, America's stake in the Persian Gulf region. The United States had depended on the Shah of Iran as a bulwark of support for American policies in the Gulf. But the Shah was deposed and ultimately succeeded by an Islamic fundamentalist regime. In December 1979, a few months after the Shah's ouster, the Soviets marched into Afghanistan, a country bordered by the Soviet Union and Iran. Fearing that the Soviets might see the Iranian Revolution as an opportunity, the president set forth the **Carter Doctrine,** warning that attempts by outside forces to take control of the Persian Gulf region would be seen as "an assault on the vital interests of the United States of America" and would be repelled by military force if necessary.[7] Carter also initiated a major defense buildup in response to a series of Soviet thrusts, from Angola and Ethiopia to Afghanistan.

In contrast to Nixon and Kissinger, Carter was sometimes criticized as being overly idealistic. He emphasized human rights, leveling criticism—and sometimes even sanctions—at both friends and enemies with poor human rights records. He usually leaned toward open (rather than secret) diplomacy. Nonetheless, his greatest foreign policy achievement, the Camp David accords, which brought about peace between Egypt and Israel, resulted from closed negotiations he arranged between Egyptian president Anwar Sadat and Israeli premier Menachem Begin.

In many ways, Carter's foreign policy reflected the influence of the "Vietnam syndrome," a crisis of confidence that resulted from America's failure in Vietnam and the breakdown of the Cold War consensus about America's role in the world. For example, his administration deemphasized the use of military force but could offer no effective alternatives when Iranians took American diplomats hostage and when the Soviets invaded Afghanistan.

Reagan and Cold War II

Carter's successor, Ronald Reagan, came to the Oval Office untroubled by the Vietnam syndrome. He believed that the Soviets were responsible for most of the evil in the world. Attributing instability in Central America, Africa, and Afghanistan to Soviet meddling, he argued that the best way to combat the Soviet threat was to renew and demonstrate American military strength.

The Reagan years witnessed a new willingness to use American military muscle—in Libya and Grenada, for example. Defense spending was further increased and was focused on major new weapons systems, such as the **Strategic Defense Initiative** (or "Star Wars" program), a new space-based missile defense system. The Reagan administration argued that its massive military buildup was both a deterrent and a bargaining chip to use in talks with the Soviets. During this period, the Cold War climate grew even chillier.

But things changed when Mikhail Gorbachev came to power in the Soviet Union in 1985. Gorbachev wished to reduce his nation's commitments abroad in order to concentrate its resources on needed domestic reforms. By the end of Reagan's second term, the United States and the Soviet Union had concluded agreements outlawing intermediate-range nuclear forces (the INF Treaty) and providing for a Soviet military pullout from Afghanistan.[8]

The Reagan administration also took a hard line at the United Nations. Until the mid-1960s, votes in the U.N. General Assembly had usually supported U.S. positions. Later, however, as the U.N. expanded its membership to include many newly independent states, the United States and its Western European allies frequently found themselves outvoted. Under Reagan, the United States reduced its commitment to international institutions such as the U.N. and the World Court when they acted in ways that ran counter to American interests. For example, the United States began to drag its feet on paying its U.N. assessments, briefly withdrew from the International Labor Organization, and rejected the jurisdiction of the World Court in cases involving U.S. activities in Nicaragua.

As noted at the outset of this chapter, the Cold War ended not long after Reagan left office. The conventional view is that the Cold War ended and America won.[9] How? Because of Reagan's "peace through strength" policies, some believed. Others insisted that the appeal of Western affluence, Gorbachev's own new thinking, and a shared interest in overcoming the nuclear threat led to the end of the Cold War.[10] Still others argued that both superpowers had lost by spending trillions of dollars on defense while neglecting other sectors of their economies.[11] A weak economy can make a nation more vulnerable to outside pressures. Historian Paul Kennedy argued that America risked "imperial overstretch" by assuming too large a world military role. For example, although in 1988 the United States had a 46 percent share of the GNP of the five most advanced industrial nations, it picked up the tab for 70 percent of their combined defense expenditures. Compared to Japan and Germany, the United States invested far more on defense research and far less on research in high-tech commercial areas. As Kennedy pointed out, a similar pattern of overspending on defense combined with underspending on other areas had characterized the decline of former great powers such as Spain, the Netherlands, and Great Britain. These issues will be debated for a long time. But, for now, a more important question for our purposes is this: what will be the direction of U.S. foreign policy in the future? For over forty years, the main goal of American foreign policy had been to contain the Soviet threat. With that goal apparently achieved, what will shape American foreign policy?

What New World Order? Foreign Policy under Bush and Clinton

The Bush and Clinton administrations have struggled to articulate firm answers to these questions. President Bush came to the White House with an excellent foreign policy résumé. He had served as U.N. ambassador, director of the CIA, and ambassador to China, as well as vice president. Often described as a "consummate cold warrior," he was faulted for a lack of vision in seeking out new directions for American foreign policy in the post–Cold War world.[12]

When Iraq's invasion of Kuwait threatened U.S. interests in the Persian Gulf (interests clearly set forth years earlier under the Carter Doctrine), Bush responded skillfully. He emphasized multilateral action and the use of international organizations like the U.N. U.S. diplomats, led by Secretary of State James Baker, carefully built a coalition of nations that included America's Western allies, the Soviet Union, Eastern European states, many Arab states, and other developing countries to oppose Saddam Hussein. The United States also won U.N. Security Council approval for a series of actions against Iraq. During the Cold War, the Security Council usually proved ineffective in major crises, because most crises pitted U.S.-backed nations against states supported by the Soviet Union. As a result, one or the other superpower could usually be counted on for a veto. However, in this post–Cold War crisis, the two superpowers cooperated against Saddam.

●●●●●●●●●●●●
Most Favored Nation?

As the Clinton administration was considering whether or not to support China's application for favorable trade treatment, the Chinese were conducting war maneuvers near the coast of Taiwan. Despite strong economic and political differences with the People's Republic, the administration continued its support, at least partly for domestic reasons—namely, concern about losing trade and jobs.

The Gulf War showed the United States continuing to act as world leader. But when the international political agenda shifted toward such issues as economic competition, the environment, human rights, and emerging democracy in Europe and elsewhere, American leadership was less evident. For example, recession and federal fiscal problems made Washington slow to help underwrite Eastern Europe's development of democratic and market-oriented institutions, and America offered little beyond rhetoric in response to Serbian atrocities in the former Yugoslavia. At the Earth Summit on the environment in Rio in 1992, the United States served more as an obstructionist than as a leader.

Under Bill Clinton, too, the White House has struggled to provide clear, coherent foreign policy leadership. Clinton came to the presidency with virtually no foreign policy experience. His presidential campaign emphasized domestic concerns, but he soon found that crises in Somalia, Bosnia, and Haiti absorbed a good deal of his time. In place of containment, the Clinton administration opted for a national security strategy of "engagement and enlargement." In pursuing "enlargement," the United States would seek to increase the number of democracies with market economies and also add to the membership of NATO. A policy of "engagement" meant rejection of isolationism, but critics worried that beyond that the policy did not provide adequate guidelines about when, where, and why the United States should be engaged.[13] Instead, they charged, defining the national interest had become "a process of trial and error."[14] Others argued that the administration needed to retain flexibility in a chaotic global era. As Representative David Obey (D.-Wis.) put it, "I'm often asked, 'Does [the Clinton] administration have a coherent, well-planned and clearly articulated foreign policy?' And my response to that question has been that if they do, they ought to be locked up."[15]

The difficulties both Bush and Clinton have had may reflect the nature of post–Cold War problems rather than personal failures. In analyzing the situation in Somalia, for example, General Merrill A. McPeak, air force chief of staff, remarked, "This is really a typical post–cold war security problem. It's messy, it's ambiguous, and there's not a common agreement on goals or threats."[16] Still, the inability of presidents to supply a clear rationale for foreign policy and the increased blurring of domestic and foreign affairs issues may encourage Congress to be more assertive in the foreign policy process.

FOREIGN POLICY ISSUE AREAS

During the Cold War, U.S. foreign policy was preoccupied with the communist threat to American national security. In the post–Cold War era, the foreign policy problems the United States faces have changed. While issues of high politics such as national security and defense remain important, low politics issues have increased in importance. At the same time, foreign and domestic policy issues have become increasingly intermingled. In this section we examine a few of these issues.

National Security and Defense

The United States remains concerned with promoting peace and stability in Europe and with preventing nuclear proliferation. Aware that democracies seldom go to war with other democracies, U.S. policymakers have tried to promote democracy in Eastern Europe and the Soviet successor states, as well as elsewhere, by providing economic aid and technical assistance. The changes in Europe have also brought about a need to rethink NATO, America's oldest alliance. During the Cold War era, the United States relied on NATO to deter Soviet expansion into Western Europe. Lately, Eastern European states, fearing a revival of Russian expansionism, have asked to join NATO. Reluctant to cause alarm in Russia, the NATO nations, with U.S. prodding, created the "Partnership for Peace," a special status short of full NATO membership, for Eastern European nations. Soon the Russians, too, applied for membership in the "Partnership for Peace."

The United States has also worked to reduce the continued threat of nuclear weapons by negotiating with Soviet successor states such as Ukraine and Belarus to get them to dismantle their nuclear arsenals and by attempting to prevent "renegade" states such as Iraq and North Korea from acquiring nuclear capability.

To protect its national interests, the United States will continue to need an adequate defense. Few disagree with that statement, but beyond that point, agreement breaks down.[17] Now that the Cold War is over, against whom are we defending ourselves? What constitutes an adequate defense? To what extent should defense spending take priority over other kinds of spending?

During the late Carter and early Reagan years, the Soviet threat was used to justify America's enormous defense buildup. As Soviet power declined, many Americans anticipated large defense cuts, a "peace dividend." Policymakers debated how far and how fast the defense budget could be reduced. This discussion slowed with the outbreak of war in the Persian Gulf, but subsequently both the Bush and Clinton administrations made significant cuts in defense spending. Nonetheless, the fact that the United States had found itself involved in a full-scale war against a nation other than the Soviet Union raised new questions about future U.S. defense policy. In the new world order, would the United States need to continue high levels of defense spending in order to be a global police officer?

With the end of the Cold War, U.S. armed forces have been scaled back in size. Policymakers have also begun to envision different tasks for the military services—such as providing humanitarian relief to Kurds and Somalis, fighting natural disasters, combating the drug trade, and even fighting violent crime in Washington, D.C. Not all of these roles have been or are likely to be adopted, but the fact that they have been entertained suggests a shift in the way America thinks about its military.

Defense policy also requires decisions about how to use defense dollars. Should they be used to pay for a volunteer military force, or should the United States require service by its citizens? Who should serve? Should homosexuals be permitted to serve? What about women? (Women's roles in the military are discussed in Compared with What? 20.1.) Other issues concern the kinds of weapons systems to build and the pace at which to build them. One recent question concerned funding for an anti-missile defense system. Many observers believed that as the threat from Russian missiles waned, so did the need for a missile defense system. But in 1996, Congress debated funding a ballistic missile defense system to protect the United States against threats from potential nuclear adversaries such as North Korea, Iraq, and China. Presidential candidates Clinton and Dole differed on the issue. Clinton favored continuing research and development, while Dole sought a commitment to build and deploy the weapons within a decade. The issue has considerable international ramifications— for example, many analysts have argued that deployment of a missile defense system would violate the Anti-Ballistic Missile Treaty the United States signed in 1972. It has important domestic consequences, too. Building a missile defense system would channel billions of dollars to defense contractors; it would also add billions to the nation's defense bill and, possibly, to the federal deficit as well.

Critics of defense spending worry that levels of spending contribute to budget deficits that endanger the overall performance of the U.S. economy. Thus, while a strong defense may be important to foreign policy, it is not the only factor to consider. Not every foreign policy objective can be achieved by applying military force. Military might helped the United States push Iraq out of Kuwait, but it isn't very useful, for example, in solving the Mexican debt crisis or slowing global warming.

Investment and Trade

Nowadays, some of the greatest problems the United States faces around the globe are not military but are economic and environmental. American policymakers, used to the high politics of the Cold War, have been challenged to formulate consistent, coherent policies to deal with the increased importance of issues of low politics.

During the Cold War, the economically dominant United States often used its foreign economic policy as a weapon. For example, to shore up anti-Soviet forces in Western Europe and Japan, the United States lowered trade barriers for those countries, without receiving equal access to their markets. Meanwhile, the United States forbade the export to communist

● compared with what?

20.1   Women in Combat

During the last two decades, women in America's all-volunteer military have found more and more job classifications open to them. Some thirty-five thousand of the more than half-million Americans who served in the Persian Gulf War were women. Women served in dangerous spots, but they were officially banned from jobs actually defined as combat positions. After the Gulf War, the Pentagon reexamined its stance on women in combat, and in 1993 the Secretary of Defense ordered the military to allow women to serve in combat roles in fighter planes, bombers, and armed helicopters. In allowing women to take up combat assignments, the United States followed a path already taken by some other nations, including some of our NATO allies. Below, we summarize the policies concerning women's participation in the military and look at the percentage of women in the military forces of several states.

Britain: Women may serve in combat roles in the navy and air force as well as in all positions with the ground forces, except the armored and infantry divisions.

Canada: Women serve in all combat jobs, except submarine duty. New submarines will have separate women's quarters.

Denmark: Women are eligible for every job, except combat aircraft.

Germany: Women are allowed only in medical jobs and military bands.

Israel: Women are drafted but barred from serving in combat positions.

Netherlands: Women serve in all combat jobs, except submarine duty.

Norway: Women are eligible for every job in the military.

Russia: Women are allowed in combat support and noncombat roles.

United States: Women are allowed in aerial combat jobs; the military has been ordered to seek repeal of legislation barring women from serving on warships.

Source: Adapted from "Women in Combat: How Other Nations Rank," *New York Times*, 2 May 1993, p. 4.

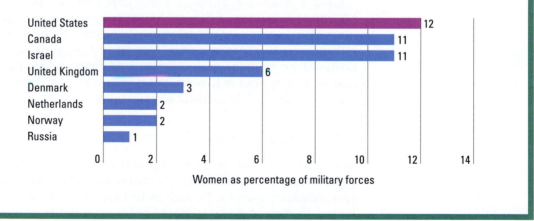

Women as percentage of military forces

countries of products with possible military uses.[18] These policies were thought to produce security gains that outweighed their economic costs. Now that both the Cold War and the era of absolute American economic ascendance are over, American policymakers find themselves challenged to think of international economic policy in different terms.

One fact about the American economy that policymakers face is its increasing interdependence, that is, its closer ties to the economies of other nations. This interdependence, exemplified both in investment and in trade, carries with it new vulnerability as well as new opportunities.

At the end of World War II, the United States dominated the world's economy. Half of all international trade involved the United States. The dollar played a key role in underwriting economic recovery in Europe and Asia. While America could not expect to retain forever the economic dominance it enjoyed in the late 1940s and 1950s, even through the 1970s the United States was able to invest heavily abroad, prompting European concern that both profits and control of European-based firms would drain away to America. In the 1980s, however, the situation began to reverse itself. A combination of tax cuts and defense spending increases created gaping deficits in the federal budget. These gaps were partly financed by selling U.S. Treasury obligations to foreigners at high rates of interest. As investors from abroad bought up American government debt, the value of the dollar soared. This made American goods very expensive on the world market and foreign goods relatively cheap for Americans. The result was a shift in our balance of trade—the United States began to import more than it exported. And we continued to borrow heavily. In 1985, an agreement among the industrialized nations resulted in a devaluation of the dollar against the currencies of other nations. As the dollar fell in value, American corporations and real estate became attractive investments for foreign investors. By 1988, foreigners held bonds totaling approximately $272 billion of the $1.7 trillion used to finance the national debt. They also owned $1.6 trillion in real property in America.[19] With the recession and declining interest rates in the 1990s, foreign firms became less interested in investing in the United States. As the flow of foreign capital into the United States slowed, American economic problems deepened. These developments illustrate that the United States is now an interdependent part of a global web of international finance.

International trade also ties the American economy to other countries. In 1970, the value of U.S. foreign trade came to 13 percent of the nation's GDP; by 1995 it had reached 30 percent.[20] As foreign trade becomes more important to the American economy, policymakers face a number of alternative approaches to handling it. Among them are free trade, fair trade, managed trade, and protectionism.

For the past half century or so, the United States has generally favored a liberal international trade regime. (In this case, *liberal* is used in its classic sense, meaning "free." A liberal trade regime would allow for the unfettered operation of the free market—nations would not impose tariffs or other barriers to keep foreign goods from being sold in their countries.) All trading partners would benefit under free trade, which would allow the principle of **comparative advantage** to work unhindered. According to this principle, all trading nations gain when each produces goods it can make comparatively cheaply and then trades them to obtain funds for the things it can produce only at a comparatively higher cost (see Feature 20.1).

Though free trade may seem a simple idea, it is not one that is easily put into practice. Americans critical of free trade policies complain that for the United States, free trade has too often been a one-way street. Indeed, as we have noted, during the Cold War, America was willing to grant many

feature **20.1**

Comparative Advantage: Trade Makes Everybody Richer

According to the principle of comparative advantage, international trade allows nations to use their resources more efficiently, increases productivity, and makes everyone richer. How does it work? Consider these two examples.

Example 1. Imagine a case involving the United States and Mexico. Suppose an American worker can make either 4 units of microchips or 8 units of potato chips in an hour. By comparison, suppose a Mexican worker can make either 2 units of microchips or 10 units of potato chips in an hour. Here the Mexican worker is better at making potato chips than the U.S. worker, while the U.S. worker leads the Mexican in the production of microchips. Suppose each worker produced potato chips for an hour and then made microchips for an hour. At the end of two hours, there would be a total of 6 units of microchips and 18 units of potato chips. What would happen

if each worker concentrated on his strength? What if the American made only microchips and the Mexican made only potato chips? At the end of two hours, there would be 20 units of potato chips and 8 units of microchips.

The American could trade an hour's microchip production (4 units) for an hour of the Mexican's potato chip production (10 units). In the end, each would wind up with 4 units of microchips and 10 units of potato chips. Through trade, the American would gain 2 units of potato chips and the Mexican 2 units of microchips.

In this example, trade makes sense because Americans are better at producing one good while Mexicans are better at producing another. What if American workers were more productive than Mexican workers in both microchips and potato chips? Would trade make sense? Under the principle of comparative advantage, the answer is still yes, as the following example illustrates.

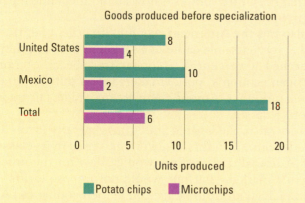

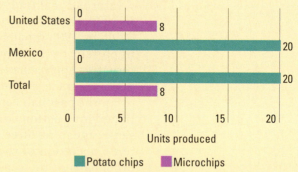

Example 2. Imagine that America and Mexico each had one hundred workers making microchips and one hundred workers making potato chips. Suppose that the American microchip makers could produce 400 units in an

hour, while the potato chip workers could make 800 units of potato chips. Suppose that in Mexico, microchip workers could make 200 units, while those making potato chips could produce 600 units. In this example, the Americans have a bigger advantage over Mexico in making microchips (4:2) than in making potato chips (8:6 = 4:3). According to the principle of comparative advantage, Americans should put more of their productive effort into making microchips, and the Mexicans should specialize more in making potato chips, where they are at a lesser disadvantage. Then, through trade, both would be better off, even though the Americans were more productive in both areas. If ten American potato chip makers made microchips instead, the Americans would end up with 440 units of microchips and 720 units of potato chips. If the Mexicans moved 15 microchip makers into potato chips, they would have 170 units of microchips and 690 units of potato chips. If the Americans trade 30 units of microchips for 80 units of Mexican potato chips, they will end up with 800 units of potato chips as before, as well as 410 units of microchips—a gain of 10 units of microchips. The Mexicans will have 200 units of microchips, as before, and 610 units of potato chips, an increase of 10 units of potato chips. The result, a net increase in goods on both sides, means an increase in the standard of living in each country.

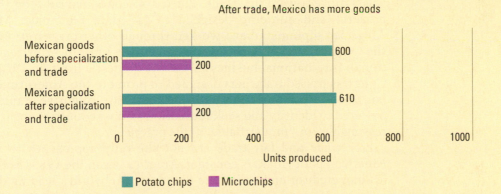

After trade, Mexico has more goods

Mexican goods before specialization and trade: Potato chips 600, Microchips 200

Mexican goods after specialization and trade: Potato chips 610, Microchips 200

Units produced

Potato chips   Microchips

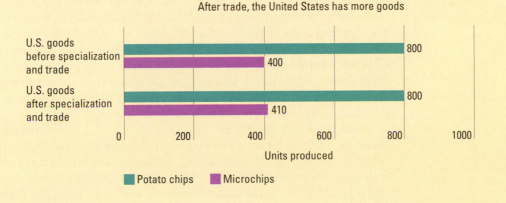

After trade, the United States has more goods

U.S. goods before specialization and trade: Potato chips 800, Microchips 400

U.S. goods after specialization and trade: Potato chips 800, Microchips 410

Units produced

Potato chips   Microchips

friendly nations access to our market without demanding similar access to their markets. America's trading partners could sell their goods in the United States while restricting their own markets through an array of tariffs and non-tariff barriers. **Non-tariff barriers (NTBs)** are regulations that make importation of foreign goods difficult or impossible by outlining exacting specifications that an imported product must meet in order to be offered for sale. The Japanese, for example, have been criticized for excessive use of NTBs. In one instance, American-made baby bottles were barred from the Japanese market because the bottles provided level marks in ounces as well as centiliters.[21]

Although the United States has sought to make trade freer by reducing tariff and non-tariff barriers, Americans do not want only freedom in the world market. They want order, too. Policymakers committed to the idea of "fair trade" have worked to create order by obtaining international agreements outlawing what they see as unfair business practices. These practices include bribery; pirating intellectual property such as software, CDs, and films; and "dumping," a practice in which a country sells its goods below cost in order to capture the market for its products in another country. In 1993, after years of negotiating, the United States signed the latest round (called the "Uruguay Round") of the General Agreement on Tariffs and Trade (GATT), an agreement among 123 countries to reform international trade. GATT reduced tariffs and other barriers to trade, so it was a move toward free trade. But it also contained rules on intellectual property and dumping designed to facilitate fair trade. Meanwhile, American diplomats have worked through other organizations, such as the Organization of American States (OAS), to limit bribery and corruption in international business.[22] On the domestic front, in 1974 and 1988 Congress passed trade acts designed to promote the American concept of fair trade. Under Section 301 of these acts, the executive branch was empowered to identify and seek retaliation against countries engaged in "unreasonable" or "unjustifiable" trade practices.

Free trade and fair trade are not the only approaches to trade that American policymakers consider. America began the 1980s as the world's leading creditor and ended the decade as the world's leading debtor. For years the nation has run up huge balance-of-payments deficits with other nations. By far the largest of these deficits has been with Japan. The trade acts just mentioned are one way the United States has tried to redress trade imbalances. Another method is **managed trade,** in which the government intervenes in trade policy in order to achieve a specific result—a clear departure from a free trade system. Under the Reagan, Bush, and Clinton administrations, the United States negotiated agreements with Japan that established guarantees or numerical benchmarks to give American firms a larger share of the Japanese market for various products, including semiconductors and auto parts.

Trade policy is clearly an "intermestic" issue, and domestic political pressure often bears on trade issues. Although free traders claim that the principle of comparative advantage ensures that eliminating trade barriers will make everyone better off in the long run, their opponents argue that imports threaten American industries and cost jobs. To guard against these hazards, **protectionists** want to retain barriers to free trade. For example, most unions and many small manufacturers opposed NAFTA.

They believed that if tariffs were removed, Mexico, with its low labor costs, would be able to undersell American producers and thus run them out of business or force them to move their operations to Mexico. Either alternative threatened American jobs. At the same time, many Americans were eager to take advantage of new opportunities in a growing Mexican market for goods and services. They realized that protectionism can be a double-edged sword. Countries whose products are kept out of the United States retaliate by refusing to import American goods. And protectionism enormously complicates the process of making foreign policy. It is a distinctly unfriendly move to make toward nations that may be our allies.

Still, some analysts have worried that an overemphasis on free enterprise may put the United States at a disadvantage in competition with, among others, the Germans and the Japanese, who have adopted national industrial policies—that is, government-sponsored, coordinated plans for promoting economic expansion.[23] When Japanese makers of semiconductors threatened to drive American microchip producers out of business, the U.S. government responded by helping to fund Sematech, a consortium of semiconductor manufacturers whose goal was to rescue the American microchip industry and recapture its lost share of the world market. The industry revived, and as a result, other businesses, such as automakers and aerospace firms, have sought government backing to create similar consortia within their industries.[24]

Many in the Clinton administration contend that, free trade and the principle of comparative advantage notwithstanding, in the twenty-first century it will be better to design microchips than to manufacture potato chips. Before becoming Clinton's secretary of labor, Robert Reich wrote that those engaged in producing high-value-added goods and services—which requires problem identification, problem solving, and the management of ideas—will do far better in the future than "routine producers" or those engaged in "in-person" service. Though Reich warns against "economic nationalism," as secretary of labor he has also argued for the need to develop an American work force capable of delivering high-value-added goods and services.[25]

Trade, Aid, and Human Rights

As trade policy becomes more important, so does the need to square it with other foreign policy objectives, such as America's commitment to human rights. Rhetorically, America has long championed democracy and human rights—from President Wilson's call to "make the world safe for democracy" to President Carter's claim that "human rights is the soul of our foreign policy," President Reagan's pledge to "foster the infrastructure of democracy," and Bill Clinton's call for the United States to back democratic change and thus draw a "new map of freedom" around the world.

To an extent, support for moral ideals such as freedom, democracy, and human rights fits in well with U.S. interests. It is enormously useful to the United States to have other nations adopt elements of the liberal political ideology that suffuses our political culture. But the relationship between America's human rights policy goals and its economic policy goals has often been problematic.

● ● ● ● ● ● ● ● ● ● ● ● ●

Business, Not Bullets

Believing that economic stability and political stability are linked, U.S. Commerce Secretary Ron Brown led American executives on a mission to Bosnia. There they explored ways that business could aid in the recovery and development of the war-ravaged area. Shortly after this photo was taken, the secretary's plane crashed, killing all on board.

This is the Commerce Department's web site devoted to big emerging markets. `<www.stat-usa.gov/ itabems.html>`

For example, in studying the potential for growth in exports, the Clinton administration identified ten rapidly growing markets that seemed especially promising for the United States. These **big emerging markets (BEMs)** include the "Chinese economic area" (the People's Republic of China, Taiwan, and Hong Kong), Indonesia, India, South Korea, Mexico, Brazil, Argentina, South Africa, Turkey, and Poland. These nations have large areas and populations. They are growing rapidly, are influential in their region, and buy the types of goods and services America has to sell. The Commerce Department has taken the lead in helping American businesses win contracts in these nations.[26] But engagement with these countries raises questions that go beyond America's economic interests. Some of the BEMs have dubious records in the areas of human rights, worker's rights, and child labor. Some are lax about environmental standards, intellectual property protection, or nuclear nonproliferation. To what extent should development of commercial ties to these nations override other policy objectives? The People's Republic of China offers a case in point. It has engaged in a variety of acts the United States has opposed. Militarily, it has attempted to intimidate neighboring Taiwan by conducting war exercises and firing missiles near Taiwan's borders. Economically, the Chinese have been lax about protecting American software, CDs, and videos from piracy within China's borders. Politically, the country has a poor human rights record. Despite these problems, President Clinton has continued to support China's application for most-favored nation (MFN) status (a trading category that gives a nation access to the American market on favorable terms). Some analysts note that the strategy of economic engagement with China is partly based on domestic considerations, namely the American jobs that would be lost if trade with China were cut.[27] More important, others would argue, is that continued engagement with China gives the United States its only chance of influencing a nation that is potentially among the most powerful on earth.

In addition to granting nations favorable trade terms, the United States has other economic tools available to help pursue its policy objectives. These include development aid, debt forgiveness, and loans with favorable credit terms. Assistance to developing countries also takes the form of donations of American goods, which directly benefits the American businesses who supply the products.

Inequality between rich nations and poor nations is growing. Figures show an increasing gap in income between the industrialized states of the north and the nonindustrialized states of the south.[28] This gap is a cause of concern for several reasons. Many people believe it is unjust for the developed world to enjoy great wealth while people in the Global South or Third World (the world's less developed states) are deprived. Sheer self-interest may also motivate policymakers to address this problem. Great disparities in wealth between the developed and developing worlds may lead to political instability and disorder and thus threaten the interests of the industrially developed democracies (the First World). Recently, Russia and the countries of Eastern Europe (sometimes called the Second World during the communist era) have begun to compete with the Third World for development dollars. As they have, American lawmakers have taken into account the need to ensure political stability and bring about a successful transition to democracy in the former communist states. As a result, between 1991 and 1995, some $15 billion in aid and credits were supplied to Russia and other newly independent states.[29]

Although foreign aid serves both humanitarian and political ends, in times of fiscal austerity it is an easy target for budget cutters. Foreign aid tends to be unpopular, partly because foreign aid recipients do not vote in American elections and also because American citizens overestimate what the nation spends on aid. A 1995 poll showed that half of those surveyed thought that at least 15 percent of the federal budget went to foreign aid. Half thought it would be appropriate to devote 5 percent of the budget to aid and that 3 percent would be too little. In actuality, less than 1 percent of the federal budget goes to foreign aid.[30] See Figure 20.1, which shows how America's aid to developing countries stacks up against the contributions of other developed nations.

The Environment

Monitor international progress on achieving the goals of the Earth Summit.
`<www.intr.net/esw/>`

The 1992 United Nations Conference on Environment and Development, popularly known as the "Earth Summit," signaled a growing worldwide acknowledgment of a new and vital group of issues in global politics. Nations have become more aware that various human activities threaten to degrade or destroy the earth's environment. But reaching international agreement on how to deal with these challenges and crafting national policies to meet them has proved difficult. The Earth Summit considered a wide range of environmental problems. Two of the most critical were the decrease in biodiversity and global warming.

figure 20.1   ● **Aid to Developing Countries**

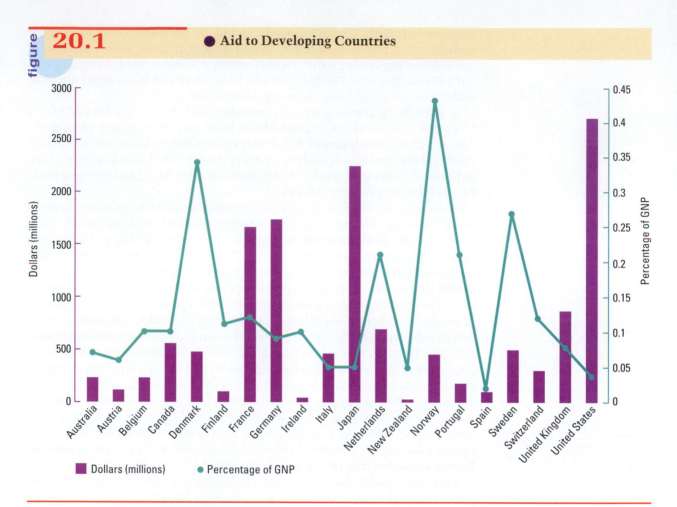

This figure compares U.S. aid to developing countries with the aid given by other developed countries. The chart shows the absolute dollar amount of aid as well as the proportion of a country's GDP that goes for foreign aid. In 1994 the United States was at the top in absolute dollars, but compared to other nations, gave a very small proportion of its GDP to help the developing world.

Source: Organization for Economic Cooperation and Development.
<www.oecd.org:80/dac/htm/table39.htm/>

Biodiversity.   Humans have become increasingly dependent on a limited number of species, for food and other needs. Some 80 percent of our food comes from fewer than two dozen species. In 1992, some one hundred to two hundred species became extinct, according to some environmental scientists.[31] If disease or climatic change ever threatened these species, the food supply could be seriously threatened. Furthermore, many species yet unknown could offer opportunities for new advances in agriculture, medicine, or other fields—unless they are driven into extinction before they and their benefits are even discovered.

Global Warming.   A buildup of gases such as carbon dioxide and methane emitted by automobiles, industry, and agriculture act as a barrier that prevents heat from escaping earth's atmosphere, creating a "greenhouse effect." The result, many scientists believe, will be a gradual increase in global surface temperatures, causing the polar ice caps to melt. This would submerge vast areas in low-lying countries. In addition, increased global temperatures could render presently valuable agricultural land less productive.

Although environmental problems were becoming clearer to the world at Rio, the steps put forth there to solve them were not acceptable to the United States. Nations that agreed to the biodiversity treaty offered there committed themselves to preserving animal habitats. Other treaty provisions called for developed nations to pay less developed states for the right to extract biological products from rare species in protected habitats. President Bush feared that the treaty placed too many limits on U.S. patent rights in biotechnology and failed to protect U.S. intellectual property rights. Consequently, he refused to sign the biodiversity treaty. Nor did the United States agree to a timetable designed to slow global warming. In the view of the Bush administration, the measures proposed at Rio would threaten the U.S. economy. When the Clinton administration came to office, the president promised to reverse his predecessor's stand on these issues. But he, too, avoided asking for tough actions to crack down on major sources of carbon dioxide emissions, such as automobiles and coal-burning utilities, again demonstrating that global environmental issues are likely to take a back seat to domestic politics.

MAKING FOREIGN POLICY: THE CONSTITUTIONAL CONTEXT

The president is the dominant actor in American foreign policy. The Constitution gives the president significant foreign policy powers, but the framers also included checks and balances to prevent the president from conducting foreign policy without substantial congressional cooperation. Still, presidents have found ways to sidestep these provisions when they have felt it important to do so. Congress, for its part, sometimes seeks to rein in presidential power over foreign policy, but it has had a mixed record of success in this regard.

The Formal Division of Power

The Constitution gives the president four significant powers related to making foreign policy:

- The president is commander in chief of the armed forces.

- The president has the power to make treaties (subject to the consent of the Senate).

- The president appoints U.S. ambassadors and the heads of executive departments (also with the advice and consent of the Senate).

- The president receives (and may refuse to receive) ambassadors from other countries.

The Constitution also gives Congress several specific powers in the foreign policy arena:

- Congress alone may declare war.

Lonely at the Top

Being commander in chief of the armed forces is an awesome responsibility. Stunned by a resurgence of enemy activity during the Vietnam War in early 1968, President Lyndon Johnson decided not to seek reelection. Here, in July 1968, the president listens to a tape-recorded message from his son-in-law, who was serving in Vietnam.

- Congress has the legislative power.

- Congress controls the nation's purse strings.

- Congress is charged with raising, supporting, and maintaining the army and navy.

- Congress may call out the state militias to repel invasions.

- Congress may regulate commerce with foreign nations.

- Congress may define and punish piracy on the high seas and offenses against the law of nations.

The most important foreign policy power the Constitution gives Congress is the power to declare war, a power it has used only five times. Congress has become involved in foreign policy in other ways, however. Using its legislative power, it may create programs of international scope, such as the SEED (Support for East European Democracy) Act of 1989, a program to improve trade relationships with Poland and Hungary. Congress may also use its legislative power to impose legal limits on the actions of the executive branch, as it did when it restricted arms transfers under the Arms Control Export Act (1988). Probably most important, Congress has used its power of the purse to provide funds for activities it supports and to prohibit funds for those it opposes. Finally, there are some foreign policy functions that belong to the Senate alone:

- The Senate consents to treaties.

- The Senate gives its advice and consent concerning the appointment of ambassadors and various other public officials involved in foreign policy.

The Senate has not been shy about using these powers. We have already mentioned its refusal to ratify the Versailles treaty submitted by President Wilson after World War I. More recently, the U.S.-Soviet SALT II treaty, an arms limitation agreement negotiated by the Carter administration, was introduced into the Senate but never brought to a vote because its supporters feared defeat.

Sidestepping the Constitution

Although the Constitution gives the chief executive enormous power in the foreign policy area, it also places limits on that power. Presidents and their advisers have often found ingenious ways around these constitutional limitations, however. Among the innovative devices they have used are executive agreements, discretionary funds, transfer authority and reprogramming, undeclared wars, and special envoys. Since the Vietnam War and the breakdown of the Cold War foreign policy consensus, however, Congress has attempted to assert control over the use of these presidential tools.

An **executive agreement** is a pact between the heads of two countries. Initially, such agreements were used to work out the tedious details of day-to-day international affairs. The Supreme Court has ruled that executive agreements are within the inherent powers of the president and have the legal status of treaties.[32] Executive agreements have become an enormously powerful tool. Like treaties, they have the force of law; but unlike treaties, they do not require Senate approval. Until 1972 the texts of these agreements did not even have to be reported to Congress. Legislation passed that year required the president to send copies to the House and Senate Foreign Relations Committees.

This requirement has not seriously affected the use of executive agreements, which has escalated dramatically. From 1933 to 1960, executive agreements outnumbered treaties by about ten to one. From 1961 to 1974, the ratio increased to sixteen to one. Between 1975 and 1992, it shot up to twenty-two to one.[33] And presidents have used these agreements to make substantive foreign policy. In fact, senators have complained that the treaties now submitted for Senate approval deal with petty, unimportant matters, whereas serious issues are handled by executive agreements.

Moreover, executive agreements are subject to very few limits. One observer noted that "the principal limitation on their use is political in nature—the degree to which it is wise to exclude the Senate from [its] constitutional foreign policy role."[34]

Presidents have also used several devices to circumvent congressional control over the nation's finances. For one, the chief executive is provided with discretionary funds—large sums of cash that may be spent on unforeseen needs to further the national interest. Kennedy used discretionary funds to run the Peace Corps in its first year. In 1965 and 1966, President Johnson used $1.5 billion in discretionary funds to pursue the war in Southeast Asia.[35] In 1994 the Treasury Department relied on discretionary funds to extend a $9 billion credit line to shore up the Mexican economy.

The president's transfer authority or the reprogramming of funds allows him to take money that Congress has approved for one purpose and to spend it on something else. In 1989, the Bush administration made an unsuccessful effort to shift $777 million from other defense accounts in order to avoid making personnel cuts.[36] The executive branch has control over the disposal of excess government stocks, including surplus or infrequently used equipment. The Central Intelligence Agency (CIA) has been an important beneficiary of excess stock disposal.

The Constitution makes the president the commander in chief of the armed forces. In this role, several presidents have exercised the right to involve the United States in undeclared wars by committing American troops in emergency situations. America's undeclared wars, police actions, and similar interventions have outnumbered its formal, congressionally declared wars by about forty to one. Since the last declared war ended in 1945, over one hundred thousand American servicemen and servicewomen have died in locations ranging from Korea and Vietnam to Grenada, Somalia, and the Persian Gulf.

During the Vietnam War, congressional opponents of that conflict passed the **War Powers Resolution** to restrict the president's ability to wage undeclared wars. Under this resolution, a president must "consult" with Congress in "every possible instance" before involving U.S. troops in hostilities. In addition, the president is required to notify Congress within forty-eight hours of committing troops to a foreign intervention. Once troops have been deployed, they may not remain there for more than sixty days without congressional approval (although the president may take up to thirty days more to remove troops "safely"). President Nixon vetoed the War Powers Resolution as an unwarranted restriction on the president's constitutional authority, but it was approved over his veto. Critics charged that the legislation, far from restricting presidential power, gives the president a free hand to wage war for up to sixty days.[37] By the end of that period, Congress might find it difficult to force the president to bring the troops home. The actual impact of the War Powers Resolution is probably quite minimal. Nixon's successors in the White House have all questioned its constitutionality, and no president has ever been "punished" for violating its provisions. At the time of the Persian Gulf crisis, Congress passed a resolution authorizing the use of force and avoided a showdown between the branches over this thorny issue.

Although the Senate rarely rejects a presidential personnel choice, senators have used confirmation hearings as opportunities to investigate the president's foreign policy activities. For example, when Robert Gates was nominated to head the CIA, his confirmation hearings provided members of Congress with an opportunity to ask hard questions about foreign policy during the Reagan era. More recently, Jesse Helms (R.-N.C.) delayed confirmation of diplomatic appointees in an effort to force reorganization of executive agencies concerned with making foreign policy.

One way presidents get around the Senate's power over appointments is to rely heavily on the White House staff, which is accountable to no one but the president, or to use special envoys or "personal representatives," who may perform a wide variety of foreign policy tasks. For example, President Clinton appointed William Gray, a former member of Congress, as his special envoy to Haiti.

MAKING FOREIGN POLICY: THE ADMINISTRATIVE MACHINERY

Although American foreign policy is developed and administered by the executive branch, it requires approval and funding from Congress and is subject to congressional oversight. When America assumed a larger role in world affairs following World War II, the old foreign policy machinery proved inadequate to the demands of America's superpower status. In 1947 Congress overhauled the system, enacting the National Security Act, which established three new organizations with important foreign policy roles: the Department of Defense, the National Security Council, and the CIA. These organizations joined the existing executive branch department with major foreign policy power and responsibility, the Department of State.

The Department of State

The department most responsible for the overall conduct of foreign affairs is the Department of State. It helps to formulate American foreign policy and then executes and monitors it throughout the world. The department's head, the secretary of state, is the highest-ranking official in the cabinet; he is also, in theory at least, the president's most important foreign policy adviser. However, some chief executives, like John Kennedy, preferred to act as their own secretary of state and have thus appointed relatively weak figures to the post. Others, such as Dwight Eisenhower, appointed stronger individuals to the post (John Foster Dulles). Presidents often come to the Oval Office promising to rely on the State Department and its head to play a leading role in formulating and carrying out foreign policy. The reality that emerges is usually somewhat different and prompts analysts to bemoan the chronic weakness of the department.[38] During his first term, Richard Nixon planned to control foreign policy from the White House. He appointed William Rogers as secretary of state but relied far more heavily on Henry Kissinger, his national security adviser, whose office was located in the White House. More recently, President George Bush named one of his closest advisers, James Baker, to head the State Department (when Bush's reelection effort began to run into trouble, he pulled his trusted lieutenant out of the State Department and used him instead to help with the campaign).

Like other executive departments, the State Department is staffed by political appointees and permanent employees selected under the civil service merit system. The former include deputy secretaries and under-secretaries of state and some—but not all—ambassadors; the latter include approximately 3,500 foreign service officers, home and abroad, who staff and service U.S. embassies and consulates throughout the world. They have primary responsibility for representing America to the world and caring for American citizens and interests abroad. Although the foreign service is highly selective (fewer than two hundred of the fifteen thousand candidates who take the annual examination are appointed), the State Department is often charged with lacking initiative and creativity. Critics claim that bright young foreign service officers quickly realize that conformity is the best path to career advancement.[39] As one observer put it, "There are old foreign service officers; and there are bold foreign service officers; but, there are no old, bold foreign service officers."[40] Some presidents have complained that the department's foreign policy machinery is too slow and unwieldy. As President Kennedy remarked, "Bundy [Kennedy's national security adviser] and I get more done in one day in the White House than they do in six months in the State Department. . . . They never have any ideas over there, never come up with anything new."[41]

A serious problem facing the State Department is its lack of a strong domestic constituency to exert pressure in support of its policies. The Department of Agriculture, by contrast, can mobilize farmers to support its activities; the Department of Defense can count on help from defense industries and veterans' groups. In a pluralist democracy, the lack of a natural constituency is a serious drawback for an agency or department. Exacerbating this problem is the changing character of global political issues. As foreign policy issues have become more "intermestic," executive agencies with pertinent domestic policy expertise have become more involved in shaping foreign policy.

The Department of Defense

The Department of Defense replaced two cabinet-level departments: the War Department and the Department of the Navy. It was created in 1947 to provide the modern bureaucratic structure needed to manage America's greatly expanded peacetime military and to promote unity and coordination among the armed forces. In keeping with the U.S. tradition of civilian control of the military, the new department was given a civilian head—the secretary of defense—a cabinet member with authority over the military. Later reorganizations of the department (in 1949 and 1958) have given the secretary greater budgetary powers, control of defense research, and the authority to transfer, abolish, reassign, and consolidate functions among the military services.

The power wielded by the defense secretary often depends on the individual secretary's own vision of the job and willingness to use the tools available. Strong secretaries of defense, including Robert McNamara (under Kennedy and Johnson), Melvin Laird (under Nixon), James Schlesinger (under Nixon and Ford), and Caspar Weinberger (under Reagan) have wielded significant power.

Below the secretary are the civilian secretaries of the army, navy, and air force; below them are the military commanders of the individual branches of the armed forces. These military leaders make up the Joint Chiefs of Staff. The Joint Chiefs meet to coordinate military policy among the different branches; they also serve as the primary military advisers to the president, the secretary of defense, and the National Security Council, helping to shape policy positions on such matters as alliances, plans for nuclear and conventional war, and arms control and disarmament.

The CIA and the Intelligence Community

Before World War II, the United States had no permanent agency specifically charged with gathering intelligence (that is, information) about the actions and intentions of foreign powers. In 1941, poor American intelligence procedures contributed to the success of the Japanese surprise attack on Pearl Harbor. After the war, when America began to play a much greater international role and the ice of the Cold War had begun to harden, Congress created the Central Intelligence Agency to collect such information. The Departments of Defense, State, Energy, and the Treasury also possess intelligence-related agencies, which together with the CIA make up the "intelligence community."

The CIA's charter charges it with collecting, analyzing, evaluating, and circulating intelligence relating to national security matters. Most of these activities are relatively uncontroversial. By far the bulk of material obtained by the CIA comes from readily available sources: statistical abstracts, books, and newspapers. The agency's Intelligence Directorate is responsible for these overt (open) information-processing activities.

The charter also empowers the CIA "to perform such other functions and duties related to intelligence affecting the national security as the National Security Council shall direct." This vague clause has been used by the agency as its legal justification for the covert (secret) activities undertaken by its Operations Directorate. These activities have included espionage, coups, assassination plots, wiretaps, interception of mail, and infiltration of protest groups.

Critics sometimes point out that the CIA's intelligence gathering has not eliminated unpleasant foreign policy "surprises" for the United States. As Senator Ernest Hollings (D.-S.C.) put it, "We've flunked Iran; we've flunked Angola . . . Ethiopia . . . Iraq . . . Kuwait. We've flunked the fall of the Berlin wall."[42] Some of these gaffes have been the result of faulty intelligence, but others were more the result of policymakers' failure to accept analyses or to interpret them properly. The usual congressional response to intelligence failures is to investigate and then propose structural changes in institutions, but at least one analyst claims that "intelligence failure is political and psychological more often than it is institutional."[43] Even the best-designed intelligence network could not prevent the United States from being caught by surprise some of the time— at most, it might minimize the frequency or intensity of such surprises.

A key dilemma posed by the CIA and the intelligence community concerns the role of covert activities. Covert operations raise both moral and legal questions for a democracy. Allen Dulles, President Eisenhower's CIA director, once called these operations "an essential part of the free world's struggle against communism." But are they equally important in a post–Cold War world? Can they be reconciled with America's stated commitment to open, democratic government, free elections, and self-determination, at home and abroad? Abroad, covert activities may undermine the opportunity for citizens of other nations to choose their own leaders, as has happened when the CIA secretly tried to engineer election results favorable to U.S. interests.

It is also difficult to reconcile such activities with the basic operating principles of the American government, such as the principle of checks and balances. Obviously, when the government engages in clandestine actions that the public knows nothing about, the people are not able to hold their government accountable for its actions.

Is the intelligence community needed at all in the post–Cold War world? One analyst argues that "the Cold War may be over, but the U.S. need for accurate information about the world remains acute."[44] Such commentators see a new role for the intelligence community, addressing issues such as terrorism, drug trafficking, nuclear proliferation, and possibly even U.S. economic security.

The National Security Council

The National Security Council (NSC) is made up of a group of advisers created to help the president mold a coherent approach to foreign policy by integrating and coordinating details of domestic, foreign, and military affairs that relate to national security. The statutory members of the NSC include the president, the vice president, and the secretaries of state and defense. At the pleasure of the president, these are advised by others, including the chairman of the Joint Chiefs of Staff, the director of the CIA, the director of the United States Information Agency, the director of the Arms Control and Disarmament Agency, and others. NSC discussions can cover a wide range of issues, such as how to deal with changes in Eastern Europe or what U.S. policy in the Middle East should be. In theory, at least, NSC discussions offer the president an opportunity to solicit advice and allow key participants in the foreign policy–making process to keep abreast of the policies and capabilities of other departments.

In practice, the role played by the NSC has varied considerably under different presidents. Truman and Kennedy seldom met with the NSC; Eisenhower and Nixon brought it into much greater prominence. During the Nixon administration, the NSC was critically important in making foreign policy. Much of this importance derived from Nixon's reliance on Henry Kissinger, his assistant for national security affairs (the title of the head of the NSC staff). Under Nixon and Kissinger, the NSC staff ballooned to over one hundred people—in effect, a little State Department in the White House. Kissinger also used this staff for direct diplomacy and covert operations, as did the Reagan administration. By using the NSC, which has been almost completely exempt from outside scrutiny, staffers hoped to preserve secrecy and, more importantly, to prevent Congress from prohibiting operations they wished to undertake.

Practitioners of international relations have traditionally valued secrecy, but democratic theory requires that citizens know what their leaders are doing. As we have seen, Tocqueville believed that democracies' weakness in foreign affairs stemmed in part from the difficulty of combining the secrecy necessary for foreign policy with the openness needed for democratic government. This dilemma continues to cause problems for American policymakers.

Other Parts of the Foreign Policy Bureaucracy

The last few decades have witnessed a proliferation in the number of players in the foreign policy game. Many departments and agencies other than those described above now find themselves involved in shaping foreign policy. For some, foreign affairs constitute their chief concern. The Agency for International Development (AID) oversees aid programs to nations around the globe. In doing so, AID works with a full range of other departments and agencies, including the Defense Department, the CIA, the Peace Corps, and the Department of Agriculture. The United States Information Agency, which has over two hundred offices in some 120 countries, provides educational and cultural materials about the United States. An array of government corporations, independent agencies, and quasi-governmental organizations also participate in the foreign policy arena. These include the National Endowment for Democracy, an independent, quasi-governmental organization established to promote democracy in other countries; the Export-Import Bank, a government corporation that subsidizes the export of American products; and the Overseas Private Investment Corporation, an independent agency that helps American companies invest abroad.

Other departments and agencies primarily concerned with domestic issues have become more active in the foreign policy arena. For example, the Department of Agriculture provides agricultural assistance to other countries and promotes American farm products abroad. Likewise, the Department of Commerce tries to expand overseas markets for nonagricultural U.S. goods. In addition, Commerce administers export control laws to prevent other nations from gaining access to American technologies connected with national security (such as computers and military equipment). As trade has become a more important aspect of foreign policy, the role of the Commerce Department in promoting American business abroad has also grown. The Department of Energy monitors nuclear weapons programs internationally and works with foreign governments and international agencies such as the International Atomic Energy Agency to coordinate international energy programs. Recently it also has supported American energy companies trying to do business abroad.

This list of bureaucratic entities with foreign policy interests is by no means exhaustive, but it does suggest the complexity of the foreign policy–making machinery. Furthermore, as issues of low politics become more prominent on the foreign policy agenda, we can expect an increase in the involvement of agencies not traditionally preoccupied with foreign policy. Finally, states and localities have also begun to pay attention to international matters. Most state governments now have separate offices, bureaus, or divisions to promote export of state goods and to attract

overseas investment into their state.[45] All this suggests that the line between domestic and foreign policy will become even more blurred, offering more opportunities for the practice of pluralist politics.

**THE PUBLIC, THE
MEDIA, AND
FOREIGN POLICY**

Another foreign affairs difficulty Tocqueville predicted for democracies
stems from the changeable views of a mass electorate. He believed that
foreign relations require patience and persistence in the pursuit of long-
term goals. But the public can be fickle, unwilling to set aside short-term
gains for long-term security, and unable to wait long enough for a policy to
bear fruit. In response to domestic pressures, leaders can be forced to act in
ways that are harmful to global interests. Was Tocqueville right? What do
the data on public opinion suggest?

The Public and the Majoritarian Model

When foreign policy practitioner George Kennan worried about the "erratic and subjective nature of public reaction," he echoed Tocqueville's
fears.[46] For many years, political scientists played down such concerns,
not because they took a more flattering view of the public, but because
they believed that the public had little impact on foreign policy. They observed that, in general, the public was uninformed about foreign affairs
and uninterested in the subject. Furthermore, although public opinion
about foreign policy issues tended to be volatile, the issues themselves
were not very important to voters. As a result, foreign policy remained essentially an elite preserve where the general public had little impact and
tended to "follow the leader."[47] During much of the Cold War, this simply
reinforced the consensus on containment.

   The picture became more complicated during the Vietnam era, when
America's foreign policy elite split and three new groups emerged: conservative interventionists, liberal interventionists, and noninterventionists.[48] Conservative interventionists focused on the East-West split; they
emphasized the threat posed by Soviet communism and the need to keep
America strong to oppose it. In contrast, liberal interventionists emphasized the complexity of world politics and the interdependence of nations.
They stressed the importance of U.S. relations with other developed, capitalist countries and with the less developed countries of the south.
Finally, noninterventionists argued for the United States to scale back its
international commitments and concentrate more on domestic problems.
Researchers initially found this three-way division among the elite, but
further research suggested that it mirrored the attitudes of the mass public
as well. Thus there seemed little need to reevaluate the overall view of the
public in the foreign policy area.[49]

   More recently, however, some political scientists have questioned these
long-held beliefs about the public's role in foreign policy. Some researchers
have shown that the public's attitudes concerning foreign policy are actually more stable than those of the elite.[50] Examining responses to questions asked repeatedly in public opinion polls over the years, researchers
have found no significant change in the public's response on more than
half the questions asked about foreign policy. Only a small minority of

questions (15 percent) saw shifts of 20 percent or more. Although public opinion did change more frequently on foreign policy issues than on domestic ones, these analysts argue that the public's underlying attitudes about foreign policy have remained remarkably stable.[51] And even when abrupt opinion shifts do occur, they are not necessarily erratic but may well represent a rational response to new information or changed circumstances.[52] For example, from 1986 to 1990, the public's attitude toward the Soviet Union "warmed" from 32° to 59° as measured by a "feelings thermometer" (respondents were asked to express their feelings toward other nations in terms of degrees of warmth on a thermometer).[53] This was a huge swing, but arguably it was an appropriate reaction to the momentous political changes that occurred in the Soviet Union during those years.

Finally, newer research on public opinion suggests that foreign policy issues are important to voters and that the public can indeed have an impact on the policymaking process. For one thing, researchers note that presidential candidates often give considerable attention to foreign policy issues—a strange thing to do if these issues are irrelevant to winning elections![54] They conclude that candidates who make foreign policy appeals to voters are acting rationally, because "voters do in fact respond to their appeals" on foreign policy matters.[55] Very often, though, such appeals really consist of an effort to ride the wave of preexisting mass attitudes, not to chart new directions in foreign policy.[56]

Furthermore, although public opinion can be influential, foreign policy formulation and implementation do not, as Thomas Graham notes, take place in "a world of majority rule."[57] Public opinion may be influential, but usually it must reach consensus levels (say, in the vicinity of 60 percent) in order to overcome the inertia of policymakers and their innate suspicion of the general public.[58] While recent research lends more credibility to the majoritarian model, it does not fully describe the policymaking process in the United States.

Interest Groups and the Pluralist Model

Many people take an interest in foreign policy issues when they believe those issues affect them directly. Autoworkers and automakers may favor import restrictions on Japanese cars. Jewish citizens may pay close attention to America's relations with Israel. These individuals often join organizations that present their positions to policymakers.

The most prominent lobbies concerned with foreign policy include businesses and unions, which often seek trade protections, and ethnic groups attempting to influence U.S. foreign policy toward "the old country." Some members of Congress have found ethnic interest groups a rich source of campaign funds. For example, the Sikhs, an ethnic minority from India, have become key contributors to Representative Dan Burton (R.-Ind.). Although Burton has fewer than 120 Sikhs in his district, he received over $61,000 in 1991–1992 for his reelection war chest from 146 Sikhs around the country.[59] Over his career the congressman has emerged as an advocate for Sikh causes, supporting over twenty legislative initiatives on behalf of the Sikhs and other ethnic minorities in India, often despite State Department opposition.

Using the "Voters" data in the CROSSTABS program, analyze issue variable (U.S. role in the world) or spending variable (money for former USSR) by political party identification. Does party preference matter when it comes to America's role in the world or spending for the former USSR?

In keeping with the current lobbying boom in Washington, foreign firms, groups, and governments have also hired high-powered Washington lobbying firms to represent their interests before the U.S. government. In 1996 the Palestinian Liberation Organization opened up an office on Washington's K Street, where vast numbers of lobbying groups are located. Among other groups in their neighborhood are Sinn Fein, the Ulster Unionists, the Liberal Democratic Party of Russia, the Bahrain Freedom Movement, the Kashmir American Council, and the National Council of Resistance of Iran.[60]

The influence of these groups varies, depending on the issue. In general, however, lobbying seems to be more effective when it takes place behind the scenes and when it deals with noncrisis issues of little importance to the public at large. Interest groups are more effective at maintaining support for the status quo than at bringing about policy changes.[61]

As is true in regard to domestic issues, there is a tendency for foreign policy interest groups to counterbalance one another. The Turkish lobby may try to offset the Greek lobby; the Arms Control Association or the Federation of American Scientists may oppose the American Legion or the Veterans of Foreign Wars on issues of détente and military spending. The result is often that "foreign policy making resembles a taffy-pull: every group attempts to pull policy in its own direction while resisting the pulls of others, with the result that policy fails to move in any discernible direction. The process encourages solutions tending toward the middle of the road and maintenance of the status quo."[62]

The Media and Foreign Policy

Do the media shape foreign policy? Or do policymakers manage the media's coverage of foreign affairs? Television coverage of the Vietnam War is often credited, or blamed, for the shift in public opinion against that war. Fearing a repetition of this phenomenon, the Pentagon restricted press coverage of Operation Desert Storm in the Persian Gulf.

The media do help to set the foreign policy agenda (see Chapter 6). By giving coverage to a particular issue, policy, or crisis, the media are able to focus public opinion on it. Media attention to starvation in Somalia helped pave the way for U.S. intervention there. As in domestic affairs, the media may not tell people what to think, but they help tell them what to think about.[63] Some issues lend themselves more to media coverage than do others, however. Pictures of malnourished children make better television than do technical negotiations over import quotas for agricultural products.

The relationship between policymakers and the media may often appear adversarial, but it is also highly symbiotic (that is, interdependent). Official Washington sometimes learns about breaking stories from worldwide television news networks such as CNN and ITN. Yet despite dramatic video footage from Somalia, Bosnia, or Baghdad, news gathering in the foreign policy arena still depends heavily on official sources. Reporters make the rounds of the White House, State Department, Defense Department, and Capitol Hill. They tend to be most dependent on these sources where national security issues are involved, and they tend to discount the qualifications and reliability of activist groups in this arena. If conflict or controversy breaks out within the executive branch or between the executive branch and Congress, the media will increase their coverage and may also turn to grassroots groups for new angles. When an official consensus prevails, however, news coverage tends to fade.

As foreign policy matters become more "intermestic," news coverage may increasingly resemble that accorded to domestic political issues, with more open debate and greater reliance on a wide variety of sources. Simultaneously, the government may attempt to "mass-market" its foreign policy decisions by using the media to influence public opinion. The struggle over the NAFTA agreement involved considerable efforts to sway public opinion through political advertising, and a debate on "Larry King Live" between Vice President Al Gore and NAFTA opponent H. Ross Perot was widely credited with helping to turn the tide of public opinion in favor of NAFTA.

THE FOREIGN POLICY–MAKING PROCESS

Having explained the historical context of American foreign policy and the participants in developing it, let us examine the policymaking process itself. How is foreign policy made?

Sources of Information for the Executive Branch

By virtue of his constitutional position and practical control of resources, the president is the leading figure in the foreign policy–making process. A president comes to the job with a world view that helps him interpret and evaluate international events. And, as chief executive, he commands vast foreign policy resources, including information and personnel. The Pentagon, the State Department, and the CIA are among his main sources of information about the outside world, and their staffs advise him on foreign policy and its implementation. And the president's sources of foreign policy advice are not limited to executive branch officials. Members of Congress can try to pressure the White House into a particular course of action. And foreign governments can also attempt to move an administration in a certain direction. The availability of so many sources of information and pressure can create a dilemma, however. Presidential advisers often present conflicting information and provide different, even contradictory, advice. Advisers may compete for a president's ear or bargain among themselves to shape administration policy. As a result of these competing pressures, the president's most important task in the foreign policy–making process is figuring out whom to believe—those who agree with his policy predispositions or those who challenge them. The wrong choice can be extremely costly. Some observers argue that President Lyndon Johnson's tendency to surround himself with yes men kept him from hearing critical analyses of the Vietnam situation.

Congress and the President

A president may carry out a policy without congressional approval if he has a clear constitutional mandate (for example, when he recognizes a government or puts troops on alert). He may ask Congress for the funds or authority to carry out a policy. When his legal authority is shaky or congressional approval appears unlikely, he may use the techniques described earlier in this chapter.

The president's command of information and personnel gives him an advantage over Congress. Legislators have ample access to independent sources of information on domestic issues, but their sources on foreign affairs are more limited (though they have improved significantly in recent years).[64] Members of Congress may go on fact-finding tours or get information from lobbyists, but they still lack the president's sources of information and thus must rely on the executive branch, particularly where matters of high politics are involved.

The president may use his informational advantage to swing votes. During the 1991 congressional debate over the use of force in Iraq, CIA director William Webster sent a letter to members of Congress providing data on the sanctions policy, along with his department's conclusion that an embargo alone would not force Saddam Hussein to leave Kuwait. The White House also fed information to Les Aspin, then the chair of the House Armed Services Committee, designed to convince him that American casualties would be very low in a military action against Iraq.

The chief executive's personnel resources give him considerable ability to influence events. Many analysts argue, for example, that President Johnson used the incidents that sparked the Gulf of Tonkin Resolution as pretexts to expand American involvement in Vietnam.

Another disadvantage Congress faces in the foreign policy process is its fragmented authority over international issues. Each house has its own committees with authority over the armed services, foreign relations, intelligence oversight, foreign trade, and development assistance. There is no congressional equivalent of the National Security Council to coordinate congressional foreign policy–making activities. Granted, disagreements occur within the executive branch and can even spill over into the congressional arena. For example, a Pentagon official might quietly appeal to friendly members of the Armed Services Committees to restore a defense appropriations cut requested by the president. Disaffected executive-branch officials do leak information. But, by and large, the executive branch is still better equipped to mold a unified approach to foreign policy.

Faced with these disadvantages in information, personnel, and organization, the general tendency is for Congress to accede to the president's foreign policy programs, especially when the president has popular support.

Lobbies and the "Lobbyist in Chief"

Lobbies participate in the foreign policy–making process in many ways. When during the Persian Gulf crisis the Bush administration floated the possibility of putting together a $21 billion arms package for Saudi Arabia, lobbyists from the American Israeli Public Affairs Committee, fearing future Saudi aggression, immediately began to mobilize their congressional allies; soon the administration retreated and offered only $7 billion. As fighting began in the Gulf, a variety of newly organized groups geared up to express opinions on all sides of the issue. Among them were the Coalition

to Stop U.S. Intervention in the Middle East, Churches for a Middle East Peace, Citizens for a Free Kuwait, and the Coalition for America at Risk.

More recently, the NAFTA agreement brought out lobbyists in droves. Opposition to NAFTA ranged from the AFL-CIO to the Doris Day Animal League; a variety of environmental, family farm, and consumer groups; and Ross Perot's organization, United We Stand. NAFTA supporters, including trade associations, business coalitions, and corporations, put together an umbrella group called USA*NAFTA. In addition to direct contact with legislators, both sides spent considerable sums on advertising to generate grassroots support for their position.

The single most effective "lobbyist" on an issue, though, is often not a lobbyist at all, but the president, as both Presidents Bush and Clinton have demonstrated in recent years. When Congress began its new session on January 3, 1991, few would have guessed that only nine days later it would, in effect, vote to authorize a war. Since Republicans were in a minority in Congress, President Bush knew he had to win substantial support among Democrats for his Persian Gulf policy. He courted Dante Fascell, the Florida Democrat who chaired the House Foreign Affairs Committee, as well as several liberal members of Congress known for their long-standing support of Israel. He invited one hundred members to the White House for breakfast to hear his side of things. In the end, presidential arm-twisting paid off, and Congress passed a resolution supporting Bush's policy.

Because his party, the Democratic party, controlled both houses of Congress, President Clinton might have expected an easy time securing passage of the NAFTA agreement. Yet, only days before the vote, NAFTA opponents confidently predicted that the measure would be defeated. Powerful interest groups aligned with the Democrats strongly opposed the pact, as did some of the party's congressional leadership. As a result, President Clinton had to work hard to forge a coalition that included more Republicans than Democrats. To woo recalcitrant lawmakers, Clinton promised an array of concessions and spent hours breakfasting, lunching, and golfing with fence sitters. To win over Representative Harold Ford of Tennessee, a Democrat and a minister, the president prayed with him at the Olivet Baptist Church in his Memphis home district. When the results were tallied, the president scored a major victory—NAFTA passed with votes to spare.

Policy Implementation

A president may decide on a course of action, and Congress may authorize it, but the policy must still then be carried out. The question of who should carry out a particular policy is not always easy to answer. The functions of certain departments and agencies overlap, and they sometimes squabble over which should perform a particular mission. In 1962, for example, when the Soviets precipitated a crisis by building missiles in Cuba, the CIA and the military squabbled over who should fly reconnaissance flights over Cuba. Coordination among competing bureaucracies can also be a problem. Rivalries among the various branches of the military were blamed for logistical and communications breakdowns when the United States invaded Grenada in 1983. The army and navy used different communications frequencies. One officer on the ground in Grenada, stymied by his inability to contact the navy on his army communications equipment, resorted to using a long-distance calling card to telephone the Pentagon and ask to have his message relayed to the navy.[65]

Congress is responsible for overseeing the implementation of programs. That means, among other things, monitoring the correct use of funds and evaluating the effectiveness of programs (see Chapter 11). It may mean designing new legislation to deal with shortcomings. For example, in the 1980s, Congress heard a great deal about military failures (such as the calling-card case in Grenada) as well as about wasteful defense spending. In a famous case, Congress learned that the Pentagon had paid $500 for a hammer. To address these problems, Congress passed the Defense Reorganization Act of 1986 (the Goldwater-Nichols Act), which gave more power to the chairman of the Joint Chiefs of Staff and reduced the power of the individual services.

SUMMARY

America emerged as a superpower following World War II and soon developed a consensus on foreign policy: communism was the threat, and the goal was to contain Soviet expansion. The Vietnam War challenged that consensus. In the post–Cold War era, international issues and domestic concerns have become more closely entwined, so today it seems less meaningful to suggest that "politics should stop at the water's edge." With shared responsibility among Congress, the executive branch, and various agencies and no clear consensus, foreign policy can become a political football. These contests are frequently played before a mass audience on live television. It was exactly the potential for this kind of conflict that led Alexis de Tocqueville to predict that democracies would not be very good at foreign policy. Increasingly, the pluralism characteristic of the rest of the political system of the United States characterizes the foreign policy arena as well.

Key Terms

Cold War
high politics
low politics
intermestic
containment
North Atlantic Treaty
  Organization (NATO)

deterrence
mutual assured
  destruction (MAD)
flexible response
nation building
Nixon Doctrine
détente

Carter Doctrine
Strategic Defense
  Initiative
comparative advantage
non-tariff barriers (NTBs)
managed trade
protectionist

big emerging markets
  (BEMs)
executive agreement
War Powers Resolution

Selected Readings

Crabb, Cecil V., and Pat M. Holt. *An Invitation to Struggle.* Washington, D.C.: Congressional Quarterly Press, 1980. This work describes the interplay between Congress and the executive on foreign policy issues.

Deese, David, ed. *The New Politics of American Foreign Policy.* New York: St. Martin's Press, 1994. A good collection of articles focusing on the reasons for the increased politicization of the foreign policy process.

Kennedy, Paul. *The Rise and Fall of the Great Powers.* New York: Random House, 1988. Discusses the reasons why various nations have gained and lost power in the modern world and concludes with a section titled "The United States: The Problem of Number One in Relative Decline."

Nathan, James, and James Oliver. *United States Foreign Policy and World Order*, 4th ed. Boston: Little, Brown, 1989. An excellent general history of American foreign policy since World War II.

Snow, Donald, and Eugene Brown. *Puzzle Palace and Foggy Bottom: U.S. Foreign and Defense Policy Making in the 1990s.* New York: St. Martin's Press, 1994. A study of key foreign policy institutions as they try to cope with the challenges of the post–Cold War world.

World Wide Web Resources

The State Department. This site contains extensive information about foreign service careers, as well as information on current policies concerning specific issues and countries.
`<www.state.gov/>`

The Central Intelligence Agency. This site provides information about the agency as well as access to *The World Factbook*, a collection of data about other countries.
`<www.odci.gov/cia/>`

The Center for Defense Information. A private, non-governmental research organization that serves as an independent monitor of the military.
`<www.cdi.org/>`

The Human Rights Home Page. Provides legal documents about human rights, information about human rights emergencies, and information on opportunities for active participation to further the cause of human rights.
`<www.traveller.com/~hrweb/hrweb.html>`

The International Affairs Network Home Page. This site, maintained by the University of Pittsburgh, provides an excellent jumping-off point for all kinds of information about foreign affairs.
`<www.pitt.edu:81/~ian/ianframe.htm>`

Appendices

The Declaration of Independence
July 4, 1776

The unanimous Declaration of the thirteen United States of America

When in the course of human events, it becomes necessary for one people to dissolve the political bands which have connected them with another, and to assume, among the powers of the earth the separate and equal station to which the Laws of Nature and of Nature's God entitle them, a decent respect to the opinions of mankind requires that they should declare the causes which impel them to the separation.

We hold these truths to be self-evident, that all men are created equal, that they are endowed by their Creator with certain unalienable rights, that among these are life, liberty, and the pursuit of happiness. That to secure these rights, governments are instituted among men, deriving their just powers from the consent of the governed. That whenever any form of government becomes destructive of these ends, it is the right of the people to alter or to abolish it, and to institute new government, laying its foundation on such principles, and organizing its power in such form, as to them shall seem most likely to effect their safety and happiness. Prudence, indeed, will dictate that governments long established should not be changed for light and transient causes; and accordingly all experience hath shown, that mankind are more disposed to suffer, while evils are sufferable, than to right themselves by abolishing the forms to which they are accustomed. But when a long train of abuses and usurpations, pursuing invariably the same object evinces a design to reduce them under absolute despotism, it is their right, it is their duty, to throw off such government, and to provide new guards for their future security. Such has been the patient sufferance of these Colonies; and such is now the necessity which constrains them to alter their former systems of government. The history of the present King of Great Britain is a history of repeated injuries and usurpations, all having in direct object the establishment of an absolute tyranny over these States. To prove this, let facts be submitted to a candid world.

He has refused his assent to laws, the most wholesome and necessary for the public good.

He has forbidden his governors to pass laws of immediate and pressing importance, unless suspended in their operation till his assent should be obtained; and, when so suspended, he has utterly neglected to attend to them.

He has refused to pass other laws for the accommodation of large districts of people, unless those people would relinquish the right of representation in the legislature, a right inestimable to them, and formidable to tyrants only.

He has called together legislative bodies at places unusual, uncomfortable, and distant from the depository of their public records, for the sole purpose of fatiguing them into compliance with his measures.

He has dissolved representative houses repeatedly, for opposing, with manly firmness, his invasions on the rights of the people.

He has refused for a long time, after such dissolutions, to cause others to be elected; whereby the legislative powers, incapable of annihilation, have returned to the people at large for their exercise; the State remaining, in the meantime exposed to all the dangers of invasions from without and convulsions within.

He has endeavored to prevent the population of these States; for that purpose obstructing the laws for naturalization of foreigners; refusing to pass others to encourage their migration hither, and raising the conditions of new appropriations of lands.

He has obstructed the administration of justice, by refusing his assent to laws for establishing judiciary powers.

He has made judges dependent on his will alone, for the tenure of their offices, and the amount and payment of their salaries.

He has erected a multitude of new offices, and sent hither swarms of officers to harass our people, and eat out their substance.

He has kept among us, in times of peace, standing armies, without the consent of our legislatures.

He has affected to render the military independent of and superior to the civil power.

He has combined with others to subject us to a jurisdiction foreign to our constitution, and unacknowledged by our laws; giving his assent to their acts of pretended legislation:

For quartering large bodies of armed troops among us:

For protecting them, by a mock trial, from punishment for any murders which they should commit on the inhabitants of these states:

For cutting off our trade with all parts of the world:

For imposing taxes on us without our consent:

For depriving us, in many cases, of the benefits of trial by jury:

For transporting us beyond seas, to be tried for pretended offenses:

For abolishing the free system of English laws in a neighboring province, establishing therein an arbitrary government, and enlarging its boundaries, so as to render it at once an example and fit instrument for introducing the same absolute rule into these Colonies:

For taking away our Charters, abolishing our most valuable laws, and altering fundamentally the forms of our governments:

For suspending our own Legislatures, and declaring themselves invested with power to legislate for us in all cases whatsoever.

He has abdicated government here, by declaring us out of his protection and waging war against us.

He has plundered our seas, ravaged our coasts, burned our towns, and destroyed the lives of our people.

He is at this time transporting large armies of foreign mercenaries to complete the works of death, desolation, and tyranny, already begun with circumstances of cruelty and perfidy scarcely paralleled in the most barbarous ages, and totally unworthy the head of a civilized nation.

He has constrained our fellow-citizens taken captive on the high seas to bear arms against their country, to become the executioners of their friends and brethren, or to fall themselves by their hands.

He has excited domestic insurrection among us, and has endeavored to bring on the inhabitants of our frontiers the merciless Indian savages, whose known rule of warfare is an undistinguished destruction of all ages, sexes, and conditions.

In every stage of these oppressions we have petitioned for redress in the most humble terms: our repeated petitions have been answered only by repeated injury. A prince whose character is thus marked by every act which may define a tyrant, is unfit to be the ruler of a free people.

Nor have we been wanting in our attentions to our British brethren. We have warned them, from time to time, of attempts by their Legislature to extend an unwarrantable jurisdiction over us. We have reminded them of the circumstances of our emigration and settlement here. We have appealed to their native justice and magnanimity, and we have conjured them by the ties of our common kindred to disavow these usurpations, which would inevitably interrupt our connections and correspondence. They too have been deaf to the voice of justice and of consanguinity. We must, therefore, acquiesce in the necessity, which denounces our separation, and hold them, as we hold the rest of mankind, enemies in war, in peace friends.

We, therefore, the Representatives of the United States of America, in General Congress assembled, appealing to the Supreme Judge of the world for the rectitude of our intentions, do, in the name, and by the authority of the good people of these Colonies, solemnly publish and declare, That these United Colonies are, and of right ought to be, FREE AND INDEPENDENT STATES; that they are absolved from all allegiance to the British Crown, and that all political connection between them and the State of Great Britain is, and ought to be, totally dissolved; and that, as Free and Independent States they have full power to levy war, conclude peace, contract alliances, establish commerce, and do all other acts and things which independent States may of right do. And for the support of this declaration, with a firm reliance on the protection of Divine Providence, we mutually pledge to each other our lives, our fortunes and our sacred honor.

JOHN HANCOCK
and fifty-five others

Articles of Confederation

Whereas the Delegates of the United States of America in Congress assembled did on the fifteenth day of November in the Year of our Lord One Thousand Seven Hundred and Seventy seven, and in the Second Year of the Independence of America agree to certain articles of Confederation and perpetual Union between the States of Newhampshire, Massachusetts-Bay, Rhode Island and Providence Plantations, Connecticut, New York, New Jersey, Pennsylvania, Delaware, Maryland, Virginia, North-Carolina, South-Carolina and Georgia in the Words following, viz. "Articles of Confederation and perpetual Union between the states of Newhampshire, Massachusetts-Bay, Rhode Island and Providence Plantations, Connecticut, New-York, New-Jersey, Pennsylvania, Delaware, Maryland, Virginia, North-Carolina, South-Carolina and Georgia."

Article I   The Stile of this confederacy shall be "The United States of America."

Article II   Each state retains its sovereignty, freedom and independence, and every power, jurisdiction and right, which is not by this Confederation expressly delegated to the United States, in Congress assembled.

Article III   The said states hereby severally enter into a firm league of friendship with each other, for their common defence, the security of their liberties, and their mutual and general welfare, binding themselves to assist each other, against all force offered to, or attacks made upon them, or any of them, on account of religion, sovereignty, trade, or any other pretence whatever.

Article IV   The better to secure and perpetuate mutual friendship and intercourse among the people of the different states in this union, the free inhabitants of each of these states, paupers, vagabonds and fugitives from justice excepted, shall be entitled to all privileges and immunities of free citizens in the several states; and the people of each state shall have free ingress and regress to and from any other state, and shall enjoy therein all the privileges of trade and commerce, subject to the same duties, impositions and restrictions as the inhabitants thereof respectively, provided that such restriction shall not extend so far as to prevent the removal of property imported into any state, to any other state of which the owner is an inhabitant; provided also that no imposition, duties or restriction shall be laid by any state, on the property of the united states, or either of them.

If any person guilty of, or charged with treason, felony, or other high misdemeanor in any State, shall flee from justice, and be found in any of the United States, he shall upon demand of the Governor or executive power, of the State from which he fled, be delivered up and removed to the state having jurisdiction of his offence.

Full faith and credit shall be given in each of these States to the records, acts and judicial proceedings of the courts and magistrates of every other State.

Article V   For the more convenient management of the general interests of the United States, delegates shall be annually appointed in such manner as the legislature of each State shall direct, to meet in Congress on the first Monday in November, in every year, with a power reserved to each State, to recall its delegates, or any of them, at any time within the year, and to send others in their stead, for the remainder of the year.

No State shall be represented in Congress by less than two, nor by more than seven members; and no person shall be capable of being a delegate for more than three years in any term of six years; nor shall any person, being a delegate, be capable of holding any office under the United States, for which he, or another for his benefit receives any salary, fees or emolument of any kind.

Each State shall maintain its own delegates in a meeting of the States, and while they act as members of the committee of the States.

In determining questions in the United States, in Congress assembled, each State shall have one vote.

Freedom of speech and debate in Congress shall not be impeached or questioned in any court, or place out of Congress, and the members of Congress shall be protected in their persons from arrests and imprisonments, during the time of their going to and from, and attendance on Congress, except for treason, felony, or breach of the peace.

Article VI   No State without the consent of the United States in Congress assembled, shall send any embassy to, or receive any embassy from, or enter into any conference, agreement, or alliance or treaty with any king, prince or state; nor shall any person holding any office of profit or trust under the United States, or any of them, accept of any present, emolument, office or title of any kind whatever from any king, prince or foreign state; nor shall the United States in Congress assembled, or any of them, grant any title of nobility.

No two or more states shall enter into any treaty, confederation or alliance whatever between them, without the consent of the United States in Congress assembled, specifying accurately the purposes for which the same is to be entered into, and how long it shall continue.

No State shall lay any imposts or duties, which may interfere with any stipulations in treaties, entered into by the United States in Congress assembled, with any king, prince or state, in pursuance of any treaties already proposed by Congress, to the courts of France and Spain.

No vessels of war shall be kept up in time of peace by any State, except such number only, as shall be deemed necessary by the United States in Congress assembled, for the defence of such State or its trade; nor shall any body of forces be kept up by any State, in time of peace, except such number only, as in the judgment of the United States in Congress assembled, shall be deemed requisite to garrison the forts necessary for the defence of such State; but every State shall always keep up a well regulated and disciplined militia, sufficiently armed and accoutred, and shall provide and constantly have ready for use, in public stores, a due number of field-pieces and tents, and a proper quantity of arms, ammunition and camp equipage.

No State shall engage in any war without the consent of the United States in Congress assembled, unless such State be actually invaded by enemies, or shall have received certain advice of a resolution being formed by some nation of Indians to invade such State, and the danger is so imminent as not to admit of a delay, till the United States in Congress assembled can be consulted: nor shall any State grant commissions to any ships or vessels of war, nor letters of marque or reprisal, except it be after a declaration of war by the United States in Congress assembled, and then only against the kingdom or state and the subjects thereof, against which war has been so declared, and under such regulations as shall be established by the United States in Congress assembled, unless such State be infested by pirates, in which case vessels of war may be fitted out for that occasion, and kept so long as the danger shall continue, or until the United States in Congress assembled shall determine otherwise.

Article VII   When land forces are raised by any state for the common defence, all officers of or under the rank of colonel shall be appointed by the legislature of each State respectively by whom such forces shall be raised, or in such manner as such State shall direct; and all vacancies shall be filled up by the State which first made the appointment.

Article VIII   All charges of war and all other expences that shall be incurred for the common defence or general welfare, and allowed by the United States in Congress assembled, shall be defrayed out of a common treasury, which shall be supplied by the several States, in proportion to the value of all land within each State, granted to or surveyed for any person, as such land and the buildings and improvements thereon shall be estimated according to such mode as the United States in Congress assembled, shall from time to time direct and appoint.

The taxes for paying that proportion shall be laid and levied by the authority and direction of the legislatures of the several States within the time agreed upon by the United States in Congress assembled.

Article IX The United States in Congress assembled, shall have the sole and exclusive right and power of determining on peace and war, except in the cases mentioned in the sixth article—of sending and receiving ambassadors—entering into treaties and alliances, provided that no treaty of commerce shall be made whereby the legislative power of the respective States shall be restrained from imposing such imposts and duties on foreigners, as their own people are subjected to, or from prohibiting the exportation or importation of any species of goods or commodities whatsoever—of establishing rules for deciding in all cases, what captures on land or water shall be legal, and in what manner prizes taken by land or naval forces in the service of the United States shall be divided or appropriated—of granting letters of marque and reprisal in times of peace—appointing courts for the trial of piracies and felonies committed on the high seas and establishing courts for receiving and determining finally appeals in all cases of captures, provided that no member of Congress shall be appointed a judge of any of the said courts.

The United States in Congress assembled shall also be the last resort on appeal in all disputes and differences now subsisting or that hereafter may arise between two or more States concerning boundary, jurisdiction or any other cause whatever; which authority shall always be exercised in the manner following:—Whenever the legislative or executive authority or lawful agent of any State in controversy with another shall present a petition to Congress, stating the matter in question and praying for a hearing, notice thereof shall be given by order of Congress to the legislative or executive authority of the other State in controversy, and a day assigned for the appearance of the parties by their lawful agents, who shall then be directed to appoint by joint consent, commissioners or judges to constitute a court for hearing and determining the matter in question: but if they cannot agree, Congress shall name three persons out of each of the United States, and from the list of such persons each party shall alternately strike out one, the petitioners beginning, until the number shall be reduced to thirteen; and from that number not less than seven, nor more than nine names as Congress shall direct, shall in the presence of Congress be drawn out by lot, and the persons whose names shall

be so drawn or any five of them, shall be commissioners or judges, to hear and finally determine the controversy, so always as a major part of the judges who shall hear the cause shall agree in the determination: and if either party shall neglect to attend at the day appointed, without showing reasons, which Congress shall judge sufficient, or being present shall refuse to strike, the Congress shall proceed to nominate three persons out of each State, and the Secretary of Congress shall strike in behalf of such party absent or refusing; and the judgment and sentence of the court to be appointed, in the manner before prescribed, shall be final and conclusive; and if any of the parties shall refuse to submit to the authority of such court, or to appear to defend their claim or cause, the court shall nevertheless proceed to pronounce sentence or judgment, which shall in like manner be final and decisive, the judgment or sentence and other proceedings being in either case transmitted to Congress, and lodged among the acts of Congress for the security of the parties concerned: provided that every commissioner, before he sits in judgment, shall take an oath to be administered by one of the judges of the Supreme or Superior Court of the State, where the cause shall be tried, *"well and truly to hear and determine the matter in question, according to the best of his judgment, without favour, affection or hope of reward,"* provided also that no State shall be deprived of territory for the benefit of the United States.

All controversies concerning the private right of soil claimed under different grants of two or more States, whose jurisdictions as they may respect such lands, and the States which passed such grants are adjusted, the said grants or either of them being at the same time claimed to have originated antecedent to such settlement of jurisdiction, shall on the petition of either party to the Congress of the United States, be finally determined as near as may be in the same manner as is before prescribed for deciding disputes respecting territorial jurisdiction between different States.

The United States in Congress assembled shall also have the sole and exclusive right and power of regulating the alloy and value of coin struck by their own authority, or by that of the respective States—fixing the standard of weights and measures throughout the United States—regulating the trade and managing all affairs with the Indians, not members of any of the States, provided that the legislative right of any State within its own limits be not infringed or violated—establishing and regulating post-offices from one State to another, throughout all the United States, and exacting such postage on the papers passing through the same as may be requisite to defray the expences of the said office—appointing all officers of the land forces, in the service of the United States, excepting regimental officers—appointing all the officers of the naval forces, and commissioning all officers whatever in the service of the United States—making rules for the government and regulation of the said land and naval forces, and directing their operations.

The United States in Congress assembled shall have authority to appoint a committee, to sit in the recess of

Congress, to be denominated "A Committee of the States," and to consist of one delegate from each State; to appoint such other committees and civil officers as may be necessary for managing the general affairs of the United States under their direction; and to appoint one of their number to preside, provided that no person be allowed to serve in the office of president more than one year in any term of three years—to ascertain the necessary sums of money to be raised for the service of the United States, and to appropriate and apply the same for defraying the public expences—to borrow money, or emit bills on the credit of the United States, transmitting every half-year to the respective States an account of the sums of money so borrowed or emitted—to build and equip a navy—to agree upon the number of land forces, and to make requisitions from each State for its quota, in proportion to the number of white inhabitants in such State; which requisition shall be binding, and thereupon the legislature of each State shall appoint the regimental officers, raise the men and clothe, arm and equip them in a soldier-like manner, at the expence of the United States, and the officers and men so clothed, armed and equipped shall march to the place appointed, and within the time agreed on by the United States in Congress assembled; but if the United States in Congress assembled shall, on consideration of circumstances, judge proper that any State should not raise men, or should raise a smaller number than its quota, and that any other State should raise a greater number of men than the quota thereof, such extra number shall be raised, officered, clothed, armed and equipped in the same manner as the quota of such State, unless the legislature of such State shall judge that such extra number cannot be safely spared out of the same, in which case they shall raise, officer, clothe, arm and equip as many of such extra number as they judge can be safely spared: and the officers and men so clothed, armed and equipped, shall march to the place appointed, and within the time agreed on by the United States in Congress assembled.

The United States in Congress assembled shall never engage in a war, nor grant letters of marque and reprisal in time of peace, nor enter into any treaties or alliances, nor coin money, nor regulate the value thereof, nor ascertain the sums and expences necessary for the defence and welfare of the United States, or any of them, nor emit bills, nor borrow money on the credit of the United States, nor appropriate money, nor agree upon the number of vessels of war, to be built or purchased, or the number of land or sea forces to be raised, nor appoint a commander-in-chief of the army or navy, unless nine States assent to the same; nor shall a question on any other point, except for adjourning from day to day be determined, unless by the votes of a majority of the United States in Congress assembled.

The Congress of the United States shall have power to adjourn to any time within the year, and to any place within the United States, so that no period of adjournment be for a longer duration than the space of six months, and shall publish the journal of their proceedings monthly, except such parts thereof relating to treaties, alliances or military operations as in their judgment require secrecy; and the yeas and nays of the delegates of each State on any question shall be entered on the journal, when it is desired by any delegate; and the delegates of a State, or any of them, at his or their request shall be furnished with a transcript of the said journal, except such parts as are above excepted, to lay before the legislatures of the several States.

Article X The Committee of the States, or any nine of them, shall be authorized to execute, in the recess of Congress, such of the powers of Congress as the United States in Congress assembled, by the consent of nine States, shall from time to time think expedient to vest them with; provided that no power be delegated to the said Committee, for the exercise of which, by the Articles of Confederation, the voice of nine States in the Congress of the United States assembled is requisite.

Article XI Canada, acceding to this Confederation, and joining in the measures of the United States, shall be admitted into, and entitled to all the advantages of this union; but no other colony shall be admitted into the same, unless such admission be agreed to by nine States.

Article XII All bills of credit emitted, monies borrowed and debts contracted by, or under the authority of Congress, before the assembling of the United States, in pursuance of the present Confederation, shall be deemed and considered as a charge against the United States, for payment and satisfaction whereof the said United States, and the public faith are hereby solemnly pledged.

Article XIII Every State shall abide by the determinations of the United States in Congress assembled, on all questions which by this Confederation are submitted to them. And the Articles of this Confederation shall be inviolably observed by every State, and the Union shall be perpetual; nor shall any alteration at any time hereafter be made in any of them; unless such alteration be agreed to in a Congress of the United States, and be afterwards confirmed by the legislatures of every State.

AND WHEREAS it hath pleased the Great Governor of the World to incline the hearts of legislatures we respectively represent in Congress to approve of and to authorize us to ratify the said Articles of Confederation and perpetual Union. KNOW YE that we the under-signed delegates, by virtue of the power and authority to us given for that purpose, do by these presents, in the name and in behalf of our respective constituents, fully and entirely ratify and confirm each and every of the said Articles of Confederation and perpetual Union, and all and singular the matters and things therein contained: and we do further solemnly plight and engage the faith of our respective constituents that they shall abide by the determinations of the United States in Congress assembled, on all questions which by the said Confederation are submitted to them. And that the Articles thereof shall be inviolably observed by the States we respectively represent, and that the Union shall be perpetual. In Witness whereof we have hereunto set our hands in Congress. Done at Philadelphia in the state of Pennsylvania the ninth day of July, in the year of our Lord one Thousand seven Hundred and Seventy-eight, and in the third year of the independence of America.

The Constitution of the United States of America*

(Preamble: outlines goals and effect)

We the people of the United States, in order to form a more perfect Union, establish Justice, insure domestic Tranquility, provide for the common defence, promote the general Welfare, and secure the Blessings of Liberty to ourselves and our Posterity, do ordain and establish this Constitution for the United States of America.

Article I   (The legislative branch)

(Powers vested)

Section 1   All legislative Powers herein granted shall be vested in a Congress of the United States, which shall consist of a Senate and a House of Representatives.

(House of Representatives: selection, term, qualifications, apportionment of seats, census requirement, exclusive power to impeach)

Section 2   The House of Representatives shall be composed of Members chosen every second Year by the people of the several States, and the Electors in each State shall have the Qualifications requisite for Electors of the most numerous Branch of the State Legislature.

No person shall be a Representative who shall not have attained to the Age of twenty five Years, and been seven Years a Citizen of the United States, and who shall not, when elected, be an Inhabitant of that State in which he shall be chosen.

Representatives and direct Taxes shall be apportioned among the several States which may be included within this Union, according to their respective numbers, *which shall be determined by adding to the whole Number of free Persons, including those bound to Service for a Term of Years and excluding Indians not taxed, three-fifths of all other Persons.* The actual Enumeration shall be made within three Years after the first Meeting of the Congress of the United States, and within every subsequent Term of ten Years, in such Manner as they shall by Law direct. The number of Representatives shall not exceed one for every thirty Thousand, but each State shall have at Least one Representative; *and until such enumeration shall be made, the State of New Hampshire shall be entitled to choose three, Massachusetts eight, Rhode Island and Providence Plantations one, Connecticut five, New York six, New Jersey four, Pennsylvania eight, Delaware one, Maryland six, Virginia ten, North Carolina five, South Carolina five, and Georgia three.*

When vacancies happen in the Representation from any State, the Executive Authority thereof shall issue Writs of Election to fill such Vacancies.

The House of Representatives shall chuse their Speaker and other Officers; and shall have the sole Power of Impeachment.

(Senate: selection, term, qualifications, exclusive power to try impeachments)

Section 3   The Senate of the United States shall be composed of two Senators from each State, *chosen by the Legislature thereof,* for six years; and each Senator shall have one Vote.

Immediately after they shall be assembled in Consequence of the first Election, they shall be divided as equally as may be into three Classes. The Seats of the Senators of the first Class shall be vacated at the Expiration of the second Year, of the second Class at the expiration of the fourth Year, and of the third Class at the expiration of the sixth Year, so that one-third may be chosen every second Year; *and if Vacancies happen by Resignation or otherwise, during the Recess of the Legislature of any State, the Executive thereof may make temporary Appointments until the next meeting of the legislature, which shall then fill such Vacancies.*

No person shall be a Senator who shall not have attained to the Age of thirty Years, and been nine Years a Citizen of the United States, and who shall not, when elected, be an Inhabitant of that State for which he shall be chosen.

The Vice-President of the United States shall be President of the Senate, but shall have no Vote, unless they be equally divided.

The Senate shall choose their other officers, and also a President pro tempore, in the absence of the Vice-President, or when he shall exercise the Office of President of the United States.

The Senate shall have the sole Power to try all impeachments. When sitting for that purpose, they shall be on Oath or Affirmation. When the President of the United States is tried, the Chief Justice shall preside: and no Person shall be convicted without the Concurrence of two-thirds of the members Present.

Judgment in Cases of Impeachment shall not extend further than to removal from the Office, and disqualification to hold and enjoy any Office of honor, Trust or Profit under the United States: but the Party convicted shall nevertheless be liable and subject to Indictment, Trial, Judgment and Punishment, according to Law.

---

*Passages no longer in effect are printed in italic type.

(Elections)

Section 4 The Times, Places and Manner of holding Elections for Senators and Representatives shall be prescribed in each State by the Legislature thereof; but the Congress may at any time by Law make or alter such regulations, except as to the Places of chusing Senators.

The Congress shall assemble at least once in every Year, and such meeting *shall be on the first Monday in December, unless they shall by Law appoint a different Day.*

(Powers and duties of the two chambers: rules of procedure, power over members)

Section 5 Each House shall be the Judge of the Elections, Returns and Qualifications of its own Members, and a Majority of each shall constitute a Quorum to do Business; but a smaller Number may adjourn from day to day, and may be authorized to compel the Attendance of absent Members, in such Manner, and under such Penalties as each House may provide.

Each House may determine the Rules of its proceedings, punish its Members for disorderly behaviour, and with the Concurrence of two thirds, expel a Member.

Each House shall keep a Journal of its Proceedings, and from time to time publish the same, excepting such Parts as may in their Judgment require Secrecy; and the Yeas and Nays of the Members of either House on any question shall, at the Desire of one fifth of those Present, be entered on the Journal.

Neither House, during the Session of Congress, shall, without the Consent of the other, adjourn for more than three days, nor to any other Place than that in which the two Houses shall be sitting.

(Compensation, privilege from arrest, privilege of speech, disabilities of members)

Section 6 The Senators and Representatives shall receive a Compensation for their services, to be ascertained by Law, and paid out of the Treasury of the United States. They shall in all Cases, except Treason, Felony and Breach of the Peace, be privileged from Arrest during their Attendance at the Session of their respective Houses, and in going to and returning from the same; and for any Speech or Debate in either House, they shall not be questioned in any other Place.

No Senator or Representative shall, during the Time for which he was elected, be appointed to any civil office under the Authority of the United States, which shall have been created, or the Emoluments whereof shall have been increased, during such time; and no Person holding any Office under the United States, shall be a Member of either House during his Continuance in Office.

(Legislative process: revenue bills, approval or veto power of president)

Section 7 All bills for raising Revenue shall originate in the House of Representatives; but the Senate may propose or concur with Amendments as on other Bills.

Every Bill which shall have passed the House of Representatives and the Senate, shall, before it become a Law, be presented to the President of the United States; if he approve he shall sign it, but if not he shall return it with Objections to that House in which it originated, who shall enter the Objections at large on their journal, and proceed to reconsider it. If after such Reconsideration two thirds of that House shall agree to pass the Bill, it shall be sent, together with the Objections, to the other House, by which it shall likewise be reconsidered, and, if approved by two thirds of that house, it shall become a Law. But in all such Cases the Votes of both Houses shall be determined by yeas and Nays, and the Names of the Persons voting for and against the Bill shall be entered on the journal of each House respectively. If any Bill shall not be returned by the President within ten Days (Sundays excepted) after it shall have been presented to him, the Same shall be a Law, in like Manner as if he had signed it, unless the Congress by their Adjournment prevent its Return, in which Case it shall not be a Law.

Every Order, Resolution, or Vote to which the Concurrence of the Senate and House of Representatives may be necessary (except on a question of Adjournment) shall be presented to the President of the United States; and before the Same shall take Effect, shall be approved by him, or being disapproved by him, shall be repassed by two thirds of the Senate and House of Representatives, according to the Rules and Limitations prescribed in the Case of a Bill.

(Powers of Congress enumerated)

Section 8 The Congress shall have Power

To lay and collect Taxes, Duties, Imposts, and Excises, to pay the Debts and provide for the common Defence and general Welfare of the United States; but all Duties, Imposts and Excises shall be uniform throughout the United States;

To borrow Money on the credit of the United States;

To regulate Commerce with foreign Nations, and among the several States, and with the Indian tribes;

To establish an uniform Rule of Naturalization, and uniform Laws on the subject of Bankruptcies throughout the United States;

To coin Money, regulate the Value thereof, and of foreign Coin, and fix the Standard of Weights and Measures;

To provide for the Punishment of counterfeiting the Securities and current Coin of the United States;

To establish Post Offices and post Roads;

To promote the Progress of Science and useful Arts by securing for limited Times to Authors and Inventors the exclusive Right to their respective Writings and Discoveries;

To constitute Tribunals inferior to the supreme Court;

To define and punish Piracies and Felonies committed on the high Seas, and offenses against the Law of Nations;

To declare War, grant Letters of Marque and Reprisal, and make Rules concerning Captures on Land and Water;

To raise and support Armies, but no Appropriation of Money to that Use shall be for a longer Term than two Years;

To provide and maintain a Navy;

To make rules for the Government and Regulation of the land and naval Forces;

To provide for calling forth the Militia to execute the Laws of the Union, suppress Insurrections, and repel Invasions;

To provide for organizing, arming, and disciplining the Militia, and for governing such Part of them as may be employed in the Service of the United States, reserving to the States respectively the Appointment of the Officers, and the Authority of training the Militia according to the discipline prescribed by Congress;

To exercise exclusive Legislation in all Cases whatsoever, over such District (not exceeding ten Miles square) as may, by cession of particular States, and the Acceptance of Congress, become the Seat of Government of the United States, and to exercise like Authority over all places purchased by the Consent of the Legislature of the State in which the Same shall be, for Erection of Forts, Magazines, Arsenals, dock-Yards, and other needful Buildings;—And

(Elastic clause)

To make all Laws which shall be necessary and proper for carrying into Execution the foregoing Powers, and all other powers vested by this Constitution in the Government of the United States, or in any Department or Officer thereof.

(Powers denied Congress)

Section 9 *The Migration or Importation of such persons as any of the States now existing shall think proper to admit, shall not be prohibited by the Congress prior to the Year 1808; but a Tax or duty may be imposed on such Importation, not exceeding $10 for each Person.*

The Privilege of the Writ of Habeas Corpus shall not be suspended, unless when in Cases of Rebellion or Invasion the public Safety may require it.

No Bill of Attainder or ex post facto Law shall be passed.

No Capitation, or other direct, Tax shall be laid, unless in Proportion to the Census or Enumeration herein before directed to be taken.

No Tax or Duty shall be laid on Articles exported from any State.

No Preference shall be given by any Regulation of Commerce or Revenue to the Ports of one State over those of another; nor shall Vessels bound to, or from, one State, be obliged to enter, clear, or pay Duties in another.

No Money shall be drawn from the Treasury, but in Consequence of Appropriations made by Law; and a regular Statement and Account of the receipts and Expenditures of all public Money shall be published from time to time.

No Title of Nobility shall be granted by the United States: And no Person holding any Office or Profit or trust under them, shall, without the Consent of the Congress, accept of any present, Emolument, Office, or Title, of any kind whatever, from any King, Prince, or foreign State.

(Powers denied the states)

Section 10 No State shall enter into any Treaty, Alliance, or Confederation; grant Letters of Marque and Reprisal; coin Money; emit Bills of Credit; make any Thing but gold and silver Coin a Tender in Payment of Debts; pass any Bill of Attainder, ex post facto law, or Law impairing the obligation of Contracts, or grant any Title of Nobility.

No State shall, without the Consent of Congress, lay any Imposts or Duties on Imports or Exports, except what may be absolutely necessary for executing its inspection Laws: and the net Produce of all duties and imposts, laid by any State on Imports or Exports, shall be for the Use of the Treasury of the United States; and all such Laws shall be subject to the Revision and Controul of the Congress.

No State shall, without the consent of Congress, lay any Duty of Tonnage, keep Troops or Ships of War in time of Peace, enter into any Agreement or Compact with another State, or with a foreign Power, or engage in War, unless actually invaded, or in such imminent Danger as will not admit of delay.

Article II   (The executive branch)

(The president: power vested, term, electoral college, qualifications, presidential succession, compensation, oath of office)

Section 1   The executive Power shall be vested in a President of the United States of America. He shall hold his office during the Term of four Years, and, together with the Vice President, chosen for the same Term, be elected as follows:

Each State shall appoint, in such Manner as the Legislature thereof may direct, a Number of Electors, equal to the whole Number of Senators and Representatives to which the State may be entitled in the Congress; but no Senator or Representative, or Person holding an Office of Trust or Profit under the United States, shall be appointed an Elector.

The Electors shall meet in their respective States, and vote by Ballot for two Persons, of whom one at least shall not be an inhabitant of the same State with themselves. And they shall make a List of all the Persons voted for, and of the Number of Votes for each: which List they shall sign and certify, and transmit sealed to the Seat of Government of the United States, directed to the President of the Senate. The President of the Senate shall, in the presence of the Senate and House of Representatives, open all the Certificates, and the Votes shall then be counted. The Person having the greatest Number of Votes shall be the President, if such Number be a Majority of the whole number of Electors appointed; and if there be more than one who have such Majority, and have an equal Number of Votes, then the House of Representatives shall immediately chuse by Ballot one of them for President; and if no Person have a Majority, then from the five highest on the List said House shall in like Manner chuse the President. But in chusing the President the Votes shall be taken by States, the Representation from each State having one Vote; a quorum for this purpose shall consist of a Member or Members from two thirds of the States, and a Majority of all the States shall be necessary to a Choice. In every Case, after the Choice of the President, the person having the greatest Number of Votes of the Electors shall be the Vice President. But if there should remain two or more who have equal Votes, the Senate shall chuse from them by Ballot the Vice President.

The Congress may determine the Time of chusing the Electors and the Day on which they shall give their Votes; which Day shall be the same throughout the United States.

No person except a natural born Citizen, or a Citizen of the United States at the time of the Adoption of this Constitution, shall be eligible to the Office of President; neither shall any Person be eligible to that Office who shall not have attained to the age of thirty-five Years, and been fourteen Years a Resident within the United States.

In cases of the Removal of the President from Office or of his Death, Resignation, or Inability to discharge the Powers and Duties of the said Office, the same shall devolve on the Vice President, and the Congress may by law provide for the case of Removal, Death, Resignation, or inability, both of the President and Vice President, declaring what Officer shall then act as President, and such Officer shall act accordingly, until the Disability be removed, or a President shall be elected.

The President shall, at stated Times, receive for his Services, a Compensation, which shall neither be increased nor diminished during the Period for which he shall have been elected, and he shall not receive within that Period any other emolument from the United States, or any of them.

Before he enter on the Execution of his Office, he shall take the following Oath or Affirmation:—"I do solemnly swear (or affirm) that I will faithfully execute the Office of the President of the United States, and will to the best of my Ability preserve, protect and defend the Constitution of the United States."

(Powers and duties: as commander in chief, over advisers, to pardon, to make treaties and appoint officers)

Section 2   The President shall be Commander in Chief of the Army and Navy of the United States, and of the Militia of the several States, when called into the actual service of the United States; he may require the Opinion, in writing, of the principal Officer in each of the executive Departments, upon any Subject relating to the Duties of their respective Offices, and he shall have Power to grant Reprieves and Pardons for Offences against the United States, except in Cases of Impeachment.

He shall have Power, by and with the Advice and Consent of the Senate, to make Treaties, provided two-thirds of the Senators present concur; and he shall nominate, and by and with the Advice and Consent of the Senate, shall appoint Ambassadors, other public Ministers and Consuls, Judges of the supreme Court, and all other Officers of the United States, whose Appointments are not herein otherwise provided for, and which shall be established by Law: but Congress may by Law vest the Appointment of such inferior Officers, as they think proper, in the President alone, in the courts of Law, or in the Heads of Departments.

The President shall have Power to fill up all Vacancies that may happen during the Recess of the Senate, by granting Commissions which shall expire at the end of their next Session.

(Legislative, diplomatic, and law-enforcement duties)

Section 3   He shall from time to time give to the Congress Information of the State of the Union, and recommend to their Consideration such Measures as he shall judge necessary and expedient; he may, on extraordinary Occasions, convene both Houses, or either of them, and in Case of Disagreement between them, with Respect to the Time of Adjournment, he may adjourn them to such Time as he shall think proper; he shall receive Ambassadors and other public Ministers; he shall take Care that the Laws be faithfully executed, and shall Commission all the Officers of the United States.

(Impeachment)

Section 4   The President, Vice President and all civil Officers of the United States shall be removed from Office on Impeachment for, and on Conviction of, Treason, Bribery, or other high Crimes and Misdemeanors.

Article III   (The judicial branch)

(Power vested; Supreme Court; lower courts; judges)

Section 1   The judicial Power of the United States shall be vested in one supreme Court, and in such inferior Courts as the Congress may from time to time ordain and establish. The Judges, both of the supreme and inferior Courts, shall hold their Offices during good Behaviour, and shall, at stated Times, receive for their Services a Compensation which shall not be diminished during their Continuance in Office.

(Jurisdiction; trial by jury)

Section 2 The judicial Power shall extend to all Cases, in Law and Equity, arising under this Constitution, the Laws of the United States, and Treaties made, or which shall be made, under their Authority;—to all Cases affecting Ambassadors, other public Ministers and Consuls;—to all Cases of admiralty and maritime Jurisdiction;—to Controversies to which the United States shall be a Party;—to controversies between two or more States;—*between a State and Citizens of another State;*—between Citizens of different States—between Citizens of the same State claiming Lands under grants of different States, and between a State, or the Citizens thereof, and foreign States, Citizens or Subjects.

In all cases affecting Ambassadors, other public Ministers and Consuls, and those in which a State shall be Party, the supreme Court shall have original Jurisdiction. In all the other Cases before mentioned, the supreme Court shall have appellate Jurisdiction, both as to Law and Fact, with such Exceptions, and under such Regulations, as the Congress shall make.

The Trial of all Crimes, except in cases of Impeachment, shall be by Jury; and such Trial shall be held in the State where said Crimes shall have been committed; but when not committed within any State, the Trial shall be at such Place or Places as the Congress may by Law have directed.

(Treason: definition, punishment)

Section 3 Treason against the United States shall consist only in levying War against them, or in adhering to their Enemies, giving them Aid and Comfort. No Person shall be convicted of Treason unless on the Testimony of two Witnesses to the same overt Act, or on confession in open Court.

The Congress shall have power to declare the Punishment of Treason, but no Attainder of Treason shall work Corruption of Blood, or Forfeiture except during the Life of the Person attainted.

Article IV (States' relations)

(Full faith and credit)

Section 1 Full Faith and Credit shall be given in each State to the public Acts, Records, and judicial Proceedings of every other State. And the Congress may by general laws prescribe the Manner in which such Acts, Records, and Proceedings shall be proved, and the Effect thereof.

(Interstate comity, rendition)

Section 2 The Citizens of each State shall be entitled to all Privileges and Immunities of Citizens in the several States.

A Person charged in any State with Treason, Felony,

or other Crime, who shall flee from Justice, and be found in another State, shall on Demand of the executive Authority of the State from which he fled, be delivered up, to be removed to the State having Jurisdiction of the Crime.

No person held to Service or Labor in one State, under the Laws thereof, escaping into another, shall, in consequence of any Law or Regulation therein, be discharged from such Service or Labor, but shall be delivered up on Claim of the Party to whom such Service or Labor may be due.

(New states)

Section 3 New States may be admitted by the Congress into this Union; but no new State shall be formed or erected within the Jurisdiction of any other State; nor any State be formed by the Junction of two or more States, or parts of States, without the Consent of the Legislatures of the States concerned as well as of the Congress.

The Congress shall have Power to dispose of and make all needful Rules and Regulations respecting the Territory or other Property belonging to the United States; and nothing in this Constitution shall be so construed as to Prejudice any Claims of the United States, or of any particular State.

(Obligations of the United States to the states)

Section 4 The United States shall guarantee to every State in this Union a Republican Form of Government, and shall protect each of them against Invasion; and on Application of the Legislature, or of the Executive (when the Legislature cannot be convened), against domestic Violence.

Article V (Mode of amendment)

The Congress, whenever two-thirds of both Houses shall deem it necessary, shall propose Amendments to this Constitution, or, on the Application of the Legislatures of two-thirds of the several States, shall call a Convention for proposing Amendments, which, in either Case, shall be valid to all Intents and Purposes, as part of this Constitution, when ratified by the legislatures of three-fourths of the several States, or by Conventions in three-fourths thereof, as the one or the other Mode of Ratification may be proposed by the Congress; Provided *that no Amendment which may be made prior to the Year One thousand eight hundred and eight shall in any Manner affect the first and fourth clauses in the Ninth Section of the first Article;* and that no State, without its Consent, shall be deprived of its equal suffrage in the Senate.

Article VI (Prior debts; supremacy of Constitution; oaths of office)

All Debts contracted and Engagements entered into, before the Adoption of this Constitution, shall be as valid against the United States under this Constitution, as under the Confederation.

This Constitution, and the Laws of the United States which shall be made in Pursuance thereof; and all Treaties made, or which shall be made, under the Authority of the United States, shall be the supreme Law of the Land; and the judges in every State shall be bound thereby, anything in the Constitution or Laws of any State to the Contrary notwithstanding.

The Senators and Representatives before mentioned, and the Members of the several State Legislatures, and all executive and judicial Officers, both of the United States and of the several States, shall be bound by Oath or Affirmation to support this Constitution; but no religious test shall ever be required as a Qualification to any Office or public Trust under the United States.

Article VII   (Ratification)

The ratification of the Conventions of nine States shall be sufficient for the Establishment of this Constitution between the States so ratifying the Same.

Done in Convention by the Unanimous Consent of the States present, the seventeenth day of September in the Year of our Lord one thousand seven hundred and eighty-seven and of the Independence of the United States of America the twelfth. In WITNESS whereof We have hereunto subscribed our Names.

GEORGE WASHINGTON
and thirty-seven others

Amendments to the Constitution

(The first ten amendments—the Bill of Rights—were adopted in 1791.)

Amendment I   (Freedom of religion, speech, press, assembly)

Congress shall make no law respecting an establishment of religion, or prohibiting the free exercise thereof; or abridging the freedom of speech, or of the press; or the right of the people peaceably to assemble, and to petition the Government for a redress of grievances.

Amendment II   (Right to bear arms)

A well-regulated militia being necessary to the security of a free State, the right of the people to keep and bear arms shall not be infringed.

Amendment III   (Quartering of soldiers)

No Soldier shall, in time of peace, be quartered in any house without the consent of the Owner, nor in time of war, but in a manner to be prescribed by law.

Amendment IV   (Searches and seizures)

The right of the people to be secure in their persons, houses, papers, and effects, against unreasonable searches and seizures, shall not be violated, and no Warrants shall issue but upon probable cause, supported by Oath or affirmation, and particularly describing the place to be searched, and the persons or things to be seized.

Amendment V   (Rights of persons: grand juries; double jeopardy; self-incrimination; due process; eminent domain)

No person shall be held to answer for a capital, or otherwise infamous crime, unless on a presentment or indictment of a Grand Jury, except in cases arising in the land or naval forces, or in the Militia, when in actual service in time of War or public danger; nor shall any person be subject for the same offense to be twice put in jeopardy of life or limb; nor shall be compelled in any criminal case to be a witness against himself, nor be deprived of life, liberty, or property, without due process of law; nor shall private property be taken for public use without just compensation.

Amendment VI   (Rights of accused in criminal prosecutions)

In all criminal prosecutions, the accused shall enjoy the right to a speedy and public trial, by an impartial jury of the State and district wherein the crime shall have been committed, which district shall have been previously ascertained by law, and to be informed of the nature and cause of the accusation; to be confronted with the witnesses against him; to have compulsory process for obtaining Witnesses in his favor, and to have the assistance of counsel for his defence.

Amendment VII   (Civil trials)

In Suits at common law, where the value in controversy shall exceed twenty dollars, the right of trial by jury shall be preserved, and no fact tried by a jury shall be otherwise reexamined in any Court of the United States, than according to the rules of the common law.

Amendment VIII   (Punishment for crime)

Excessive bail shall not be required, nor excessive fines imposed, nor cruel and unusual punishments inflicted.

Amendment IX   (Rights retained by the people)

The enumeration in the Constitution, of certain rights, shall not be construed to deny or disparage others retained by the people.

Amendment X   (Rights reserved to the states)

The powers not delegated to the United States by the Constitution, nor prohibited by it to the States, are reserved to the States respectively, or to the people.

Amendment XI (Suits against the states; adopted 1798)

The Judicial power of the United States shall not be construed to extend to any suit in law or equity, commenced or prosecuted against one of the United States by Citizens of another state, or by Citizens or Subjects of any Foreign State.

Amendment XII (Election of the president; adopted 1804)

The electors shall meet in their respective States, and vote by ballot for President and Vice-President, one of whom, at least, shall not be an inhabitant of the same state with themselves; they shall name in their ballots the person voted for as President, and in distinct ballots the person voted for as Vice-President, and they shall make distinct lists of all persons voted for as President, and of all persons voted for as Vice-President, and of the number of votes for each, which lists they shall sign and certify, and transmit sealed to the seat of government of the United States, directed to the President of the Senate;—the President of the Senate shall, in the presence of the Senate and House of Representatives, open all the certificates and the votes shall then be counted;—the person having the greatest number of votes for President shall be the President, if such number be a majority of the whole number of electors appointed; and if no person have such majority, then from the persons having the highest numbers not exceeding three on the list of those voted for as President, the House of Representatives shall choose immediately, by ballot, the President. But in choosing the President, the votes shall be taken by States, the representation from each State having one vote; a quorum for this purpose shall consist of a member or members from two-thirds of the States, and a majority of all the States shall be necessary to a choice. And if the House of Representatives shall not choose a President whenever the right of choice shall devolve upon them, before *the fourth day of March* next following, then the Vice-President shall act as President, as in the case of the death or other constitutional disability of the President.—The person having the greatest number of votes as Vice-President shall be the Vice-President, if such number be a majority of the whole number of electors appointed; and if no person have a majority, then from the two highest numbers on the list the Senate shall choose the Vice-President; a quorum for the purpose shall consist of two-thirds of the whole number of Senators, and a majority of the whole number shall be necessary to a choice. But no person constitutionally ineligible to the office of President shall be eligible to that of Vice-President of the United States.

Amendment XIII (Abolition of slavery; adopted 1865)

Section 1 Neither slavery nor involuntary servitude, except as a punishment for crime whereof the party shall have been duly convicted, shall exist within the United States, or any place subject to their jurisdiction.

Section 2 Congress shall have power to enforce this article by appropriate legislation.

Amendment XIV (Adopted 1868)

(Citizenship rights; privileges and immunities; due process; equal protection)

Section 1 All persons born or naturalized in the United States, and subject to the jurisdiction thereof, are citizens of the United States and of the State wherein they reside. No State shall make or enforce any law which shall abridge the privileges or immunities of citizens of the United States; nor shall any State deprive any person of life, liberty, or property, without due process of law; nor deny to any person within its jurisdiction the equal protection of the laws.

(Apportionment of representation)

Section 2 Representatives shall be apportioned among the several States according to their respective numbers, counting the whole number of persons in each State, excluding Indians not taxed. But when the right to vote at any election for the choice of Electors for President and Vice-President of the United States, Representatives in Congress, the Executive and Judicial officers of a State, or the members of the Legislature thereof, is denied to any of the male inhabitants of such State, being twenty-one years of age and citizens of the United States, or in any way abridged, except for participation in rebellion, or other crime, the basis of representation therein shall be reduced in the proportion which the number of such male citizens shall bear to the whole number of male citizens twenty-one years of age in such State.

(Disqualification of Confederate officials)

Section 3 No person shall be a Senator or Representative in Congress, or Elector of President and Vice-President, or hold any office, civil or military, under the United States, or under any State, who, having previously taken an oath, as a member of Congress, or as an officer of the United States, or as a member of any State legislature, or as an executive or judicial officer of any State, to support the Constitution of the United States, shall have engaged in insurrection or rebellion against the same, or given aid or comfort to the enemies thereof. Congress may, by a vote of two-thirds of each house, remove such disability.

(Public debts)

Section 4 The validity of the public debt of the United States, authorized by law, including debts incurred for payment of pensions and bounties for services in suppressing insurrection or rebellion, shall not be questioned. But neither the United States nor any State shall assume or pay any debt or obligation incurred in aid of insurrection or rebellion against the United States, or any claim for the loss of emancipation of any slave; but all such debts, obligations, and claims shall be held illegal and void.

(Enforcement)

Section 5 The Congress shall have power to enforce, by appropriate legislation, the provisions of this article.

Amendment XV (Extension of right to vote; adopted 1870)

Section 1 The right of citizens of the United States to vote shall not be denied or abridged by the United States or by any State on account of race, color, or previous condition of servitude.

Section 2 The Congress shall have power to enforce this article by appropriate legislation.

Amendment XVI (Income tax; adopted 1913)

The Congress shall have power to lay and collect taxes on incomes, from whatever source derived, without apportionment among the several States, and without regard to any census or enumeration.

Amendment XVII (Popular election of senators; adopted 1913)

Section 1 The Senate of the United States shall be composed of two Senators from each State, elected by the people thereof, for six years; and each Senator shall have one vote. The electors in each State shall have the qualifications requisite for electors of the most numerous branch of the State legislatures.

Section 2 When vacancies happen in the representation of any State in the Senate, the executive authority of such State shall issue writs of election to fill such vacancies: Provided, that the Legislature of any State may empower the executive thereof to make temporary appointments until the people fill the vacancies by election as the Legislature may direct.

Section 3 This amendment shall not be so construed as to affect the election or term of any Senator chosen before it becomes valid as part of the Constitution.

Amendment XVIII (Prohibition of intoxicating liquors; adopted 1919, repealed 1933)

Section 1 After one year from the ratification of this article the manufacture, sale or transportation of intoxicating liquors within, the importation thereof into, or the exportation thereof from the United States and all territory subject to the jurisdiction thereof, for beverage purposes, is hereby prohibited.

Section 2 The Congress and the several States shall have concurrent power to enforce this article by appropriate legislation.

Section 3 This article shall be inoperative unless it shall have been ratified as an amendment to the Constitution by the legislatures of the several States, as provided by the Constitution, within seven years from the date of the submission thereof to the States by the Congress.

Amendment XIX (Right of women to vote; adopted 1920)

Section 1 The right of citizens of the United States to vote shall not be denied or abridged by the United States or by any State on account of sex.

Section 2 The Congress shall have power to enforce this article by appropriate legislation.

Amendment XX (Commencement of terms of office; adopted 1933)

Section 1 The terms of the President and Vice-President shall end at noon on the 20th day of January, and the terms of Senators and Representatives at noon on the 3d day of January, of the years in which such terms would have ended if this article had not been ratified; and the terms of their successors shall then begin.

Section 2 The Congress shall assemble at least once in every year, and such meetings shall begin at noon on the 3d day of January, unless they shall by law appoint a different day.

(Extension of presidential succession)

Section 3 If, at the time fixed for the beginning of the term of the President, the President-elect shall have died, the Vice-President-elect shall become President. If a President shall not have been chosen before the time fixed for the beginning of his term, or if the President-elect shall have failed to qualify, then the Vice-President-elect shall act as President until a President shall have qualified; and the Congress may by law provide for the case wherein neither a President-elect nor a Vice-President-elect shall have qualified, declaring who shall then act as President, or the manner in which one who is to act shall be selected, and such persons shall act accordingly until a President or Vice-President shall have qualified.

Section 4   The Congress may by law provide for the case of the death of any of the persons from whom the House of Representatives may choose a President whenever the right of choice shall have devolved upon them, and for the case of the death of any of the persons from whom the Senate may choose a Vice-President whenever the right of choice shall have devolved upon them.

Section 5   Sections 1 and 2 shall take effect on the 15th day of October following the ratification of this article.

Section 6   This article shall be inoperative unless it shall have been ratified as an amendment to the Constitution by the Legislatures of three-fourths of the several States within seven years from the date of its submission.

Amendment XXI   (Repeal of Eighteenth Amendment; adopted 1933)

Section 1   The eighteenth article of amendment to the Constitution of the United States is hereby repealed.

Section 2   The transportation or importation into any State, Territory, or Possession of the United States for delivery or use therein of intoxicating liquors, in violation of the laws thereof, is hereby prohibited.

Section 3   This article shall be inoperative unless it shall have been ratified as an amendment to the Constitution by conventions in the several States, as provided in the Constitution, within seven years from the date of submission thereof to the States by the Congress.

Amendment XXII   (Limit on presidential tenure; adopted 1951)

Section 1   No person shall be elected to the office of President more than twice, and no person who has held the office of President, or acted as President, for more than two years of a term to which some other person was elected President shall be elected to the office of President more than once. But this article shall not apply to any person holding the office of President when this article was proposed by the Congress, and shall not prevent any person who may be holding the office of President, or acting as President, during the term within which this article becomes operative from holding the office of President or acting as President during the remainder of such term.

Section 2   This article shall be inoperative unless it shall have been ratified as an amendment to the Constitution by the legislatures of three-fourths of the several States within seven years from the date of its submission to the States by the Congress.

Amendment XXIII   (Presidential electors for the District of Columbia; adopted 1961)

Section 1   The District constituting the seat of Government of the United States shall appoint in such manner as the Congress may direct:
A number of electors of President and Vice President equal to the whole number of Senators and Representatives in Congress to which the District would be entitled if it were a State, but in no event more than the least populous State; they shall be in addition to those appointed by the States, but they shall be considered for the purposes of the election of President and Vice President, to be electors appointed by a State; and they shall meet in the District and perform such duties as provided by the twelfth article of amendment.

Section 2   The Congress shall have the power to enforce this article by appropriate legislation.

Amendment XXIV   (Poll tax outlawed in national elections; adopted 1964)

Section 1   The right of citizens of the United States to vote in any primary or other election for President or Vice President, for electors for President or Vice President, or for Senator or Representative in Congress, shall not be denied or abridged by the United States or any State by reason of failure to pay any poll tax or other tax.

Section 2   The Congress shall have the power to enforce this article by appropriate legislation.

Amendment XXV   (Presidential succession; adopted 1967)

Section 1   In case of the removal of the President from office or of his death or resignation, the Vice President shall become President.

(Vice presidential vacancy)

Section 2 Whenever there is a vacancy in the office of the Vice President, the President shall nominate a Vice President who shall take office upon confirmation by a majority vote of both Houses of Congress.

Section 3 Whenever the President transmits to the President pro tempore of the Senate and the Speaker of the House of Representatives his written declaration that he is unable to discharge the powers and duties of his office, and until he transmits to them a written declaration to the contrary, such powers and duties shall be discharged by the Vice President as Acting President.

(Presidential disability)

Section 4 Whenever the Vice President and a majority of either the principal officers of the executive departments or of such other body as Congress may by law provide, transmit to the President pro tempore of the Senate and the Speaker of the House of Representatives their written declaration that the President is unable to discharge the powers and duties of his office, the Vice President shall immediately assume the powers and duties of the office as Acting President.

Thereafter, when the President transmits to the President pro tempore of the Senate and the Speaker of the House of Representatives his written declaration that no inability exists, he shall resume the powers and duties of his office unless the Vice President and a majority of either the principal officers of the executive department(s) or of such other body as Congress may by law provide, transmit within four days to the President pro tempore of the Senate and the Speaker of the House of Representatives their written declaration that the President is unable to discharge the powers and duties of his office. Thereupon Congress shall decide the issue, assembling within forty-eight hours for that purpose if not in session. If the Congress, within twenty-one days after receipt of the latter written declaration, or, if Congress is not in session, within twenty-one days after Congress is required to assemble, determines by two-thirds vote of both Houses that the President is unable to discharge the powers and duties of his office, the Vice President shall continue to discharge the same as Acting President; otherwise, the President shall resume the powers and duties of his office.

Amendment XXVI (Right of eighteen-year-olds to vote; adopted 1971)

Section 1 The right of citizens of the United States, who are eighteen years of age or older, to vote shall not be denied or abridged by the United States or by any State on account of age.

Section 2 The Congress shall have power to enforce this article by appropriate legislation.

Amendment XXVII (Congressional pay raises; adopted 1992)

No law, varying the compensation for the services of the Senators and Representatives shall take effect, until an election of Representatives shall have intervened.

Federalist No. 10   1787

To the People of the State of New York: Among the numerous advantages promised by a well-constructed Union, none deserves to be more accurately developed than its tendency to break and control the violence of faction. The friend of popular governments never finds himself so much alarmed for their character and fate, as when he contemplates their propensity to this dangerous vice. He will not fail, therefore, to set a due value on any plan which, without violating the principles to which he is attached, provides a proper cure for it. The instability, injustice, and confusion introduced into the public councils, have, in truth, been the mortal diseases under which popular governments have everywhere perished; as they continue to be the favourite and fruitful topics from which the adversaries to liberty derive their most specious declamations. The valuable improvements made by the American constitutions on the popular models, both ancient and modern, cannot certainly be too much admired; but it would be an unwarrantable partiality, to contend that they have as effectually obviated the danger on this side, as was wished and expected. Complaints are everywhere heard from our most considerate and virtuous citizens, equally the friends of public and private faith, and of public and personal liberty, that our governments are too unstable; that the public good is disregarded in the conflicts of rival parties; and that measures are too often decided, not according to the rules of justice, and the rights of the minor party, but by the superior force of an interested and overbearing majority. However anxiously we may wish that these complaints had no foundation, the evidence of known facts will not permit us to deny that they are in some degree true. It will be found, indeed, on a candid review of our situation, that some of the distresses under which we labor have been erroneously charged on the operation of our governments; but it will be found, at the same time, that other causes will not alone account for many of our heaviest misfortunes; and, particularly, for that prevailing and increasing distrust of public engagements, and alarm for private rights, which are echoed from one end of the continent to the other. These must be chiefly, if not wholly, effects of the unsteadiness and injustice, with which a factious spirit has tainted our public administrations.

By a faction, I understand a number of citizens, whether amounting to a majority or minority of the whole, who are united and actuated by some common impulse of passion, or of interest, adverse to the rights of other citizens, or to the permanent and aggregate interests of the community.

There are two methods of curing the mischiefs of faction: The one, by removing its causes; the other, by controlling its effects.

There are again two methods of removing the causes of faction: The one, by destroying the liberty which is essential to its existence; the other, by giving to every citizen the same opinions, the same passions, and the same interests.

It could never be more truly said, than of the first remedy, that it was worse than the disease. Liberty is to faction what air is to fire, an ailment without which it instantly expires. But it could not be a less folly to abolish liberty, which is essential to political life, because it nourishes faction, than it would be to wish the annihilation of air, which is essential to animal life, because it imparts to fire its destructive agency.

The second expedient is as impracticable, as the first would be unwise. As long as the reason of man continues fallible, and he is at liberty to exercise it, different opinions will be formed. As long as the connection subsists between his reason and his self-love, his opinions and his passions will have a reciprocal influence on each other; and the former will be objects to which the latter will attach themselves. The diversity in the faculties of men, from which the rights of property originate, is not less an insuperable obstacle to an uniformity of interests. The protection of these faculties is the first object of government. From the protection of different and unequal faculties of acquiring property, the possession of different degrees and kinds of property immediately results; and from the influence of these on the sentiments and views of the respective proprietors, ensues a division of the society into different interests and parties.

The latent causes of faction are thus sown in the nature of man; and we see them everywhere brought into different degrees of activity, according to the different circumstances of civil society. A zeal for different opinions concerning religion, concerning government, and many other points, as well as of speculation as of practice; an attachment to different leaders ambitiously contending for preeminence and power; or to persons of other descriptions whose fortunes have been interesting to the human passions, have, in turn, divided mankind into parties, inflamed them with mutual animosity, and rendered them much more disposed to vex and oppress each other, than to cooperate for their common good. So strong is this propensity of mankind, to fall into mutual animosities, that where no substantial occasion presents itself, the most frivolous and fanciful distinctions have been sufficient to kindle their unfriendly passions and excite their most violent conflicts. But the most common and durable source of factions has been the various and unequal distribution of property. Those who hold and those who are without property have ever formed distinct interests in society. Those who are creditors, and those who are debtors, fall under alike discrimination. A landed interest, a manufacturing interest, a mercantile interest, a moneyed interest, with many lesser interests, grow up of necessity in civilized nations, and divide them into different classes, actuated by different sentiments and views. The regulation of these various and interfering interests forms the principal task of modern legislation, and involves the spirit of the party and faction in the necessary and ordinary operations of the government.

No man is allowed to be a judge in his own cause; because his interest will certainly bias his judgment, and, not improbably, corrupt his integrity. With equal, nay with greater reason, a body of men are unfit to be both judges and parties at the same time; yet what are many of the most important acts of legislation, but so many judicial determinations, not indeed concerning the right of single persons, but concerning the rights of large bodies of citizens? And what are the different classes of legislators, but advocates and parties to the causes which they determine? Is a law proposed concerning private debts? It is a question to which the creditors are parties on one side, and the debtors on the other. Justice ought to hold the balance between them. Yet the parties are, and must be, themselves the judges; and the most numerous party, or, in other words, the most powerful faction, must be expected to prevail. Shall domestic manufactures be encouraged, and in what degree, by restrictions on foreign manufactures? are questions which would be differently decided by the landed and the manufacturing classes; and probably by neither with a sole regard to justice and the public good. The apportionment of taxes, on the various descriptions of property, is an act which seems to require the most exact impartiality; yet there is, perhaps, no legislative act, in which greater opportunity and temptation are given to a predominant party to trample on the rules of justice. Every shilling, with which they overburden the inferior number, is a shilling saved to their own pockets.

It is in vain to say, that enlightened statesmen will be able to adjust these clashing interests, and render them all subservient to the public good. Enlightened statesmen will not always be at the helm: nor, in many cases, can such an adjustment be made at all, without taking into view indirect and remote considerations, which will rarely prevail over the immediate interest which one party may find in disregarding the rights of another, or the good of the whole.

The inference to which we are brought is, that the *causes* of faction cannot be removed; and that relief is only to be sought in the means of controlling its *effects*.

If a faction consists of less than a majority, relief is supplied by the republican principle, which enables the majority to defeat its sinister views, by regular vote. It may clog the administration, it may convulse the society; but it will be unable to execute and mask its violence under the forms of the constitution. When a majority is included in a faction, the form of popular government, on the other hand, enables it to sacrifice to its ruling passion or interest, both the public good and the rights of other citizens. To secure the public good, and private rights, against the danger of such a faction, and at the same time to preserve the spirit and the form of popular government, is then the great object to which our inquiries are directed. Let me add, that it is the great desideratum by which alone this form of government can be rescued from the opprobrium under which it has so long labored, and be recommended to the esteem and adoption of mankind.

By what means is this object attainable? Evidently by one of two only. Either the existence of the same passion or interest in a majority, at the same time, must be prevented; or the majority, having such coexistent passion or interest, must be rendered, by their number and local situation, unable to concert and carry into effect schemes of oppression. If the impulse and the opportunity be suffered to coincide, we well know that neither moral nor religious motives can be relied on as an adequate control. They are not found to be such on the injustice and violence of individuals, and lose their efficacy in proportion to the number combined together; that is, in proportion as their efficacy becomes needful.

From this view of the subject, it may be concluded, that a pure democracy, by which I mean a society consisting of a small number of citizens, who assemble and administer the government in person, can admit of no cure for the mischiefs of faction. A common passion or interest will, in almost every case, be felt by a majority of the whole; a communication and concert, results from the form of government itself; and there is nothing to check the inducements to sacrifice the weaker party, or an obnoxious individual. Hence, it is, that such democracies have ever been spectacles of turbulence and contention; have ever been found incompatible with personal security, or the rights of property; and have in general been as short in their lives, as they have been violent in their deaths. Theoretic politicians, who have patronized this species of government, have erroneously supposed, that by reducing mankind to a perfect equality in their political rights, they would, at the same time, be perfectly equalized and assimilated in their possessions, their opinions, and their passions.

A republic, by which I mean a government in which the scheme of representation takes place, opens a different prospect, and promises the cure for which we are seeking. Let us examine the points in which it varies from pure democracy, and we shall comprehend both the nature of the cure and the efficacy which it must derive from the union.

The two great points of difference, between a democracy and a republic, are: first, the delegation of the government, in the latter, to a small number of citizens, elected by the rest; secondly, the greatest number of citizens, and greater sphere of country, over which the latter may be extended.

The effect of the first difference is, on the one hand, to refine and enlarge the public views, by passing them through the medium of a chosen body of citizens, whose wisdom may best discern the true interest of their country, and whose patriotism and love of justice, will be least likely to sacrifice it to temporary or partial considerations. Under such a regulation, it may well happen, that the public voice, pronounced by the representatives of the people, will be more consonant to the public good, than if pronounced by the people themselves, convened for the purpose. On the other hand, the effect may be inverted. Men of factious tempers, of local preju-

dices, or of sinister designs, may by intrigue, by corruption, or by other means, first obtain the suffrages, and then betray the interest of the people. The question resulting is, whether small or extensive republics are most favourable to the election of proper guardians of the public weal; and it is clearly decided in favour of the latter by two obvious considerations.

In the first place, it is to be remarked that, however small the republic may be, the representatives must be raised to a certain number, in order to guard against the cabals of a few; and that however large it may be, they must be limited to a certain number, in order to guard against the confusion of a multitude. Hence, the number of representatives in the two cases not being in proportion to that of the constituents, and being proportionally greatest in the small republic, it follows, that if the proportion of fit characters be not less in the large than in the small republic, the former will present a greater option, and consequently a greater probability of a fit choice.

In the next place, as each representative will be chosen by a greater number of citizens in the large than in the small republic, it will be more difficult for unworthy candidates to practise with success the vicious arts, by which elections are too often carried; and the suffrages of the people being more free, will be more likely to centre in men who possess the most attractive merit, and the most diffusive and established characters.

It must be confessed that in this, as in most other cases, there is a mean, on both sides of which inconveniences will be found to lie. By enlarging too much the number of electors, you render the representatives too little acquainted with all their local circumstances and lesser interests; as by reducing it too much, you render him unduly attached to these, and too little fit to comprehend and pursue great and national objects. The federal Constitution forms a happy combination being referred to the national, the local and particular to the state legislatures.

The other point of difference is, the greater number of citizens, and extent of territory, which may be brought within the compass of republican, than of democratic government; and it is this circumstance principally which renders factious combinations less to be dreaded in the former, than in the latter. The smaller the society, the fewer probably will be the distinct parties and interests composing it; the fewer the distinct parties and interests, the more frequently will a majority be found of the same party; and the smaller the number of individuals composing a majority, and the smaller the compass within which they are placed, the more easily will they concert and execute their plans of oppression. Extend the sphere and you take in a greater variety of parties and interests; you make it less probable that a majority of the whole will have a common motive to invade the rights of other citizens; or if such a common motive exists, it will be more difficult for all who feel it to discover their own strength, and to act in unison with each other. Besides other impediments, it may be remarked, that where there is a consciousness of unjust or dishonourable purposes, communication is always checked by distrust, in proportion to the number whose concurrence is necessary.

Hence, it clearly appears, that the same advantage, which a republic has over a democracy, in controlling the effects of faction, is enjoyed by a large over a small republic,—is enjoyed by the Union over the States composing it. Does this advantage consist in the substitution of representatives whose enlightened views and virtuous sentiments render them superior to local prejudices, and to schemes of injustice? It will not be denied that the representation of the Union will be most likely to possess these requisite endowments. Does it consist in the greater security afforded by a greater variety of parties, against the event of any one party being able to outnumber and oppress the rest? In an equal degree does the increased variety of parties, comprised within the Union, increase the security? Does it, in fine, consist in the greater obstacles opposed to the concert and accomplishment of the secret wishes of an unjust and interested majority? Here, again, the extent of the Union gives it the most palpable advantage.

The influence of factious leaders may kindle a flame within their particular States, but will be unable to spread a general conflagration through the other States. A religious sect may degenerate into a political faction in a part of the confederacy; but the variety of sects dispersed over the entire face of it, must secure the national councils against any danger from that source. A rage for paper money, for an abolition of debts, for an equal division of property, or for any other improper or wicked project, will be less apt to pervade the whole body of the Union than a particular member of it; in the same proportion as such a malady is more likely to taint a particular county or district, than an entire State.

In the extent and proper structure of the Union, therefore, we behold a republican remedy for the diseases most incident to republican government. And according to the degree of pleasure and pride we feel in being republicans, ought to be our zeal in cherishing the spirit, and supporting the character of Federalists.

JAMES MADISON

Federalist No. 51   1788

To the People of the State of New York: To what expedient, then, shall we finally resort for maintaining in practice the necessary partition of power among the several departments, as laid down in the Constitution? The only answer that can be given is, that as all these exterior provisions are found to be inadequate, the defect must be supplied, by so contriving the interior structure of the government, as that its several constituent parts may, by their mutual relations, be the means of keeping each other in their proper places. Without presuming to undertake a full development of this important idea, I will hazard a few general observations, which may perhaps place it in a clearer light, and enable us to form a more correct judgment of the principles and structure of the government planned by the convention.

In order to lay a due foundation for that separate and distinct exercise of the different powers of government, which to a certain extent, is admitted on all hands to be essential to the preservation of liberty, it is evident that each department should have a will of its own; and consequently should be so constituted, that the members of each should have as little agency as possible in the appointment of the members of the others. Were this principle rigorously adhered to, it would require that all the appointments for the supreme executive, legislative, and judiciary magistracies, should be drawn from the same fountain of authority, the people, through channels, having no communication whatever with one another. Perhaps such a plan of constructing the several departments would be less difficult in practice than it may in contemplation appear. Some difficulties, however, and some additional expense would attend the execution of it. Some deviations, therefore, from the principle must be admitted. In the constitution of the judiciary department in particular, it might be inexpedient to insist rigorously on the principle; first, because peculiar qualifications being essential in the members, the primary consideration ought to be to select that mode of choice, which best secures these qualifications; secondly, because the permanent tenure by which the appointments are held in that department, must soon destroy all sense of dependence on the authority conferring them.

It is equally evident that the members of each department should be as little dependent as possible on those of the others, for the emoluments annexed to their offices. Were the executive magistrate, or the judges, not independent of the legislature in this particular, their independence in every other would be merely nominal.

But the great security against a gradual concentration of the several powers in the same department, consists in giving to those who administer each department, the necessary constitutional means, and personal motives, to resist encroachments of the others. The provision for defense must in this, as in all other cases, be made commensurate to the danger of attack. Ambition must be made to counteract ambition. The interest of the man must be connected with the constitutional rights of the place. It may be a reflection on human nature, that such devices should be necessary to control the abuses of government. But what is government itself, but the greatest of all reflections on human nature? If men were angels, no government would be necessary. If angels were to govern men, neither external nor internal controls on government would be necessary. In framing a government which is to be administered by men over men, the great difficulty lies in this: you must first enable the government to control the governed; and in the next place, oblige it to control itself. A dependence on the people is, no doubt, the primary control on the government; but experience has taught mankind the necessity of auxiliary precautions.

This policy of supplying by opposite and rival interests, the defect of better motives, might be traced through the whole system of human affairs, private as well as public. We see it particularly displayed in all the subordinate distributions of power, where the constant aim is to divide and arrange the several offices in such a manner as that each may be a check on the other—that the private interest of every individual, may be a sentinel over the public rights. These inventions of prudence cannot be less requisite in the distribution of the supreme powers of the State.

But it is not possible to give to each department an equal power of self-defense. In republican government, the legislative authority necessarily predominates. The remedy for this inconveniency is to divide the legislature into different branches; and to render them by different modes of election, and different principles of action, as little connected with each other, as the nature of their common functions, and their common dependence on the society, will admit. It may even be necessary to guard against dangerous encroachments by still further precautions. As the weight of the legislative authority requires that it should be thus divided, the weakness of the executive may require, on the other hand, that it should be fortified. An absolute negative, on the legislature, appears, at first view, to be the natural defence with which the executive magistrate should be armed. But perhaps it would be neither altogether safe nor alone sufficient. On ordinary occasions, it might not be exerted with the requisite firmness, and on extraordinary occasions it might be perfidiously abused. May not this defect of an absolute negative be supplied by some qualified connection between this weaker department, and the weaker branch of the stronger department, by which the latter may be led to support the constitutional rights of the former, without being too much detached from the rights of its own department?

If the principles on which these observations are founded be just, as I persuade myself they are, and they be applied as a criterion, to the several State constitutions, and to the federal Constitution, it will be found, that if the latter does not perfectly correspond with them, the former are infinitely less able to bear such a test.

There are, moreover, two considerations particularly applicable to the federal system of America, which place that system in a very interesting point of view.

First. In a single republic, all the power surrendered by the people is submitted to the administration of a single government; and usurpations are guarded against by a division of the government into distinct and separate departments. In the compound republic of America, the power surrendered by the people, is first divided between two distinct governments, and then the portion allotted to each, subdivided among distinct and separate departments. Hence a double security arises to the rights of the people. The different governments will control each other, at the same time that each will be controlled by itself.

Second. It is of great importance in a republic, not only to guard the society against the oppression of its rulers; but to guard one part of the society against the injustice of the other part. Different interests necessarily exist in different classes of citizens. If a majority be united by a common interest, the rights of the minority will be insecure. There are but two methods of providing against this evil: The one by creating a will in the community independent of the majority—that is, of the society itself; the other, by comprehending in the society so many separate descriptions of citizens as will render an unjust combination of a majority of the whole very improbable, if not impracticable. The first method prevails in all governments possessing an hereditary or self-appointed authority. This at best is but a precarious security; because a power independent of the society may as well espouse the unjust views of the major, as the rightful interests of the minor party, and may possibly be turned against both parties. The second method will be exemplified in the federal republic of the United States. Whilst all authority in it will be derived from and dependent on the society, the society itself will be broken into so many parts, interests and classes of citizens, that the rights of individuals or of the minority, will be in little danger from interested combinations of the majority. In a free government, the security for civil rights must be the same as for religious rights. It consists in the one case in the multiplicity of interests, and in the other in the multiplicity of sects. The degree of security in both cases will depend on the number of interests and sects; and this may be presumed to depend on the extent of country and number of people comprehended under the same government. This view of the subject must particularly recommend a proper federal system to all the sincere and considerate friends of republican government, since it shows that in exact proportion as the territory of the Union may be formed into more circumscribed Confederacies, or States, oppressive combinations of a majority will be facilitated; the best security under the republican forms, for the rights of every class of citizens, will be diminished; and consequently, the stability and independence of some member of the government, the only other security, must be proportionally increased. Justice is the end of government. It is the end of civil society. It ever has been, and ever will be pursued, until it be obtained, or until liberty be lost in the pursuit. In a society under the forms of which the stronger faction can readily unite and oppress the weaker, anarchy may as truly be said to reign, as in a state of nature where the weaker individual is not secured against the violence of the stronger; and as, in the latter state, even the stronger individuals are prompted, by the uncertainty of their condition, to submit to a government which may protect the weak as well as themselves, so in the former state, will the more powerful factions or parties be gradually induced, by a like motive, to wish for a government which will protect all parties, the weaker as well as the more powerful. It can be little doubted, that if the State of Rhode Island was separated from the Confederacy and left to itself, the insecurity of rights under the popular form of government within such narrow limits would be displayed by such reiterated oppressions of factious majorities that some power altogether independent of the people would soon be called for by the voice of the very factions whose misrule had proved the necessity of it. In the extended republic of the United States, and among the great variety of interests, parties and sects which it embraces, a coalition of a majority of the whole society could seldom take place on any other principles than those of justice and the general good; whilst there being thus less danger to a minor from the will of the major party, there must be less pretext, also, to provide for the security of the former, by introducing into the government a will not dependent on the latter, or, in other words, a will independent of the society itself. It is no less certain than it is important, notwithstanding the contrary opinions which have been entertained, that the larger the society, provided it lie within a practicable sphere, the more duly capable it will be of self-government. And happily for the *republican cause,* the practicable sphere may be carried to a very great extent, by a judicious modification and mixture of the *federal principle.*

JAMES MADISON

Presidents of the United States

President	Party	Term
1. George Washington (1732–1799)	Federalist	1789–1797
2. John Adams (1734–1826)	Federalist	1797–1801
3. Thomas Jefferson (1743–1826)	Democratic-Republican	1801–1809
4. James Madison (1751–1836)	Democratic-Republican	1809–1817
5. James Monroe (1758–1831)	Democratic-Republican	1817–1825
6. John Quincy Adams (1767–1848)	Democratic-Republican	1825–1829
7. Andrew Jackson (1767–1845)	Democratic	1829–1837
8. Martin Van Buren (1782–1862)	Democratic	1837–1841
9. William Henry Harrison (1773–1841)	Whig	1841
10. John Tyler (1790–1862)	Whig	1841–1845
11. James K. Polk (1795–1849)	Democratic	1845–1849
12. Zachary Taylor (1784–1850)	Whig	1849–1850
13. Millard Fillmore (1800–1874)	Whig	1850–1853
14. Franklin Pierce (1804–1869)	Democratic	1853–1857
15. James Buchanan (1791–1868)	Democratic	1857–1861
16. Abraham Lincoln (1809–1865)	Republican	1861–1865
17. Andrew Johnson (1808–1875)	Union	1865–1869
18. Ulysses S. Grant (1822–1885)	Republican	1869–1877
19. Rutherford B. Hayes (1822–1893)	Republican	1877–1881
20. James A. Garfield (1831–1881)	Republican	1881
21. Chester A. Arthur (1830–1886)	Republican	1881–1885
22. Grover Cleveland (1837–1908)	Democratic	1885–1889
23. Benjamin Harrison (1833–1901)	Republican	1889–1893
24. Grover Cleveland (1837–1908)	Democratic	1893–1897
25. William McKinley (1843–1901)	Republican	1897–1901
26. Theodore Roosevelt (1858–1919)	Republican	1901–1909
27. William Howard Taft (1857–1930)	Republican	1909–1913
28. Woodrow Wilson (1856–1924)	Democratic	1913–1921
29. Warren G. Harding (1865–1923)	Republican	1921–1923
30. Calvin Coolidge (1871–1933)	Republican	1923–1929
31. Herbert Hoover (1874–1964)	Republican	1929–1933
32. Franklin Delano Roosevelt (1882–1945)	Democratic	1933–1945
33. Harry S Truman (1884–1972)	Democratic	1945–1953
34. Dwight D. Eisenhower (1890–1969)	Republican	1953–1961
35. John F. Kennedy (1917–1963)	Democratic	1961–1963
36. Lyndon B. Johnson (1908–1973)	Democratic	1963–1969
37. Richard M. Nixon (1913–1994)	Republican	1969–1974
38. Gerald R. Ford (b. 1913)	Republican	1974–1977
39. Jimmy Carter (b. 1924)	Democratic	1977–1981
40. Ronald Reagan (b. 1911)	Republican	1981–1989
41. George Bush (b. 1924)	Republican	1989–1993
42. Bill Clinton (b. 1946)	Democratic	1993–

Twentieth-Century Justices of the Supreme Court

Justice*	Term of Service	Years of Service	Life Span	Justice*	Term of Service	Years of Service	Life Span
Oliver W. Holmes	1902–1932	30	1841–1935	Wiley B. Rutledge	1943–1949	6	1894–1949
William R. Day	1903–1922	19	1849–1923	Harold H. Burton	1945–1958	13	1888–1964
William H. Moody	1906–1910	3	1853–1917	*Fred M. Vinson*	1946–1953	7	1890–1953
Horace H. Lurton	1910–1914	4	1844–1914	Tom C. Clark	1949–1967	18	1899–1977
Charles E. Hughes	1910–1916	5	1862–1948	Sherman Minton	1949–1956	7	1890–1965
Willis Van Devanter	1911–1937	26	1859–1941	*Earl Warren*	1953–1969	16	1891–1974
Joseph R. Lamar	1911–1916	5	1857–1916	John Marshall Harlan	1955–1971	16	1899–1971
Edward D. White	1910–1921	11	1845–1921	William J. Brennan, Jr.	1956–1990	34	1906–
Mahlon Pitney	1912–1922	10	1858–1924	Charles E. Whittaker	1957–1962	5	1901–1973
James C. McReynolds	1914–1941	26	1862–1946	Potter Stewart	1958–1981	23	1915–1985
Louis D. Brandeis	1916–1939	22	1856–1941	Byron R. White	1962–1993	31	1917–
John H. Clarke	1916–1922	6	1857–1930	Arthur J. Goldberg	1962–1965	3	1908–1990
William H. Taft	1921–1930	8	1857–1945	Abe Fortas	1965–1969	4	1910–1982
George Sutherland	1922–1938	15	1862–1942	Thurgood Marshall	1967–1991	24	1908–1993
Pierce Butler	1922–1939	16	1866–1939	*Warren E. Burger*	1969–1986	17	1907–1995
Edward T. Sandford	1923–1930	7	1865–1930	Harry A. Blackmun	1970–1994	24	1908–
Harlan F. Stone	1925–1941	16	1872–1946	Lewis F. Powell, Jr.	1972–1987	15	1907–
Charles E. Hughes	1930–1941	11	1862–1948	William H. Rehnquist	1972–1986	14	1924–
Owen J. Roberts	1930–1945	15	1875–1955	John P. Stevens	1975–	—	1920–
Benjamin N. Cardozo	1932–1938	6	1870–1938	Sandra Day O'Connor	1981–	—	1930–
Hugo L. Black	1937–1971	34	1886–1971	*William H. Rehnquist*	1986–	—	1924–
Stanley F. Reed	1938–1957	19	1884–1980	Antonin Scalia	1986–	—	1936–
Felix Frankfurter	1939–1962	23	1882–1965	Anthony M. Kennedy	1988–	—	1936–
William O. Douglas	1939–1975	36	1898–1980	David H. Souter	1990–	—	1939–
Frank Murphy	1940–1949	9	1890–1949	Clarence Thomas	1991–	—	1948–
Harlan F. Stone	1941–1946	5	1872–1946	Ruth Bader Ginsburg	1993–	—	1933–
James F. Byrnes	1941–1942	1	1879–1972	Stephen G. Breyer	1994–	—	1938–
Robert H. Jackson	1941–1954	13	1892–1954				

* The names of chief justices are printed in italic type.

Party Control of the Presidency, Senate, and House of Representatives 1901–1997

Congress	Years	President	Senate D	R	Other*	House D	R	Other*
57th	1901–1903	McKinley T. Roosevelt	31	55	4	151	197	9
58th	1903–1905	T. Roosevelt	33	57	—	178	208	—
59th	1905–1907	T. Roosevelt	33	57	—	136	250	—
60th	1907–1909	T. Roosevelt	31	61	—	164	222	—
61st	1909–1911	Taft	32	61	—	172	219	—
62d	1911–1913	Taft	41	51	—	228	161	1
63d	1913–1915	Wilson	51	44	1	291	127	17
64th	1915–1917	Wilson	56	40	—	230	196	9
65th	1917–1919	Wilson	53	42	—	216	10	6
66th	1919–1921	Wilson	47	49	—	190	240	3
67th	1921–1923	Harding	37	59	—	131	301	1
68th	1923–1925	Coolidge	43	51	2	205	225	5
69th	1925–1927	Coolidge	39	56	1	183	247	4
70th	1927–1929	Coolidge	46	49	1	195	237	3
71st	1929–1931	Hoover	39	56	1	167	267	1
72d	1931–1933	Hoover	47	48	1	220	214	1
73d	1933–1935	F. Roosevelt	60	35	1	319	117	5
74th	1935–1937	F. Roosevelt	69	25	2	319	103	10
75th	1937–1939	F. Roosevelt	76	16	4	331	89	13
76th	1939–1941	F. Roosevelt	69	23	4	261	164	4
77th	1941–1943	F. Roosevelt	66	28	2	268	162	5
78th	1943–1945	F. Roosevelt	58	37	1	218	208	4
79th	1945–1947	Truman	56	38	1	242	190	2
80th	1947–1949	Truman	45	51	—	188	245	1
81st	1949–1951	Truman	54	42	—	263	171	1
82d	1951–1953	Truman	49	47	—	234	199	1
83d	1953–1955	Eisenhower	47	48	1	211	221	—
84th	1955–1957	Eisenhower	48	47	1	232	203	—
85th	1957–1959	Eisenhower	49	47	—	233	200	—
86th**	1959–1961	Eisenhower	65	35	—	284	153	—
87th**	1961–1963	Kennedy	65	35	—	263	174	—
88th	1963–1965	Kennedy Johnson	67	33	—	258	177	—

Sources: Department of Commerce, Bureau of the Census, *Statistical Abstract of the United States* (Washington, D.C.: U.S. Government Printing Office, 1980), p. 509, and *Members of Congress Since 1789*, 2d ed. (Washington, D.C.: Congressional Quarterly Press, 1981), pp. 176–177. Adapted from Barbara Hinckley, *Congressional Elections* (Washington, D.C.: Congressional Quarterly Press, 1981), pp. 144–145.

* Excludes vacancies at beginning of each session.

** The 437 members of the House in the 86th and 87th Congresses is attributable to the at-large representative given to both Alaska (January 3, 1959) and Hawaii (August 2, 1959) prior to redistricting in 1962.

**Party Control of the Presidency, Senate, and
House of Representatives　1901–1997 *(continued)***

Congress	Years	President	Senate			House		
			D	R	Other*	D	R	Other*
89th	1965–1967	Johnson	68	32	—	295	140	—
90th	1967–1969	Johnson	64	36	—	247	187	—
91st	1969–1971	Nixon	57	43	—	243	192	—
92d	1971–1973	Nixon	54	44	2	254	180	—
93d	1973–1975	Nixon Ford	56	42	2	239	192	1
94th	1975–1977	Ford	60	37	2	291	144	—
95th	1977–1979	Carter	61	38	1	292	143	—
96th	1979–1981	Carter	58	41	1	276	157	—
97th	1981–1983	Reagan	46	53	1	243	192	—
98th	1983–1985	Reagan	45	55	—	267	168	—
99th	1985–1987	Reagan	47	53	—	252	183	—
100th	1987–1989	Reagan	54	46	—	257	178	—
101st	1989–1991	Bush	55	45	—	262	173	—
102d	1991–1993	Bush	56	44	—	276	167	—
103d	1993–1995	Clinton	56	44	—	256	178	1
104th	1995–1997	Clinton	47	53	—	204	230	1
105th[†]	1997–	Clinton	45	55	—	206	228	—

[†] House seats subject to revision due to special redistricting elections in Texas.

Glossary

administrative discretion   The latitude that Congress gives agencies to make policy in the spirit of their legislative mandate. (13)

affirmative action   Any of a wide range of programs, from special recruitment efforts to numerical quotas, aimed at expanding opportunities for women and minority groups. (16)

agenda building   The process by which new issues are brought into the political limelight. (10)

agenda setting   The stage of the policymaking process during which problems get defined as political issues. (17)

aggregate demand   The money available to be spent for goods and services by consumers, businesses, and government. (18)

Aid to Families with Dependent Children (AFDC)   A federal public assistance program that provides cash to low-income families with children. (19)

amicus curiae brief   A brief filed (with the permission of the court) by an individual or group that is not a party to a legal action but has an interest in it. (14)

anarchism   A political philosophy that opposes government in any form. (1)

appellate jurisdiction   The authority of a court to hear cases that have been tried, decided, or reexamined in other courts. (14)

appropriations committees   Committees of Congress that decide which of the programs passed by the authorization committees will actually be funded. (18)

argument   The heart of a judicial opinion; its logical content separated from facts, rhetoric, and procedure. (14)

Articles of Confederation   The compact among the thirteen original states that established the first government of the United States. (3)

attentive policy elites   Leaders who follow news in specific policy areas. (6)

authorization committees   Committees of Congress that can authorize spending in their particular areas of responsibility. (18)

autocracy   A system of government in which the power to govern is concentrated in the hands of one individual. Also called *monarchy*. (2)

big emerging markets (BEMs)   Rapidly growing international markets that are especially promising for the United States. (20)

bill of attainder   A law that pronounces an individual guilty of a crime without a trial. (15)

Bill of Rights   The first ten amendments to the Constitution. They prevent the national government from tampering with fundamental rights and civil liberties, and emphasize the limited character of national power. (3)

bimodal distribution   A distribution (of opinions) that shows two responses being chosen about as frequently as each other. (5)

black codes   Legislation enacted by former slave states to restrict the freedom of blacks. (16)

blanket primary   A primary election in which voters receive a ballot containing both parties' potential nominees and can help nominate candidates for all offices for both parties. (9)

block grant   A grant-in-aid awarded for general purposes, allowing the recipient great discretion in spending the grant money. (4)

boycott   A refusal to do business with a firm, individual, or nation as an expression of disapproval or as a means of coercion. (16)

budget authority   The amounts that government agencies are authorized to spend for their programs. (18)

budget committees   One committee in each house of Congress that supervises a comprehensive budget review process. (18)

budget outlays   The amounts that government agencies are expected to spend in the fiscal year. (18)

bureaucracy   A large, complex organization in which employees have specific job responsibilities and work within a hierarchy of authority. (13)

bureaucrat   An employee of a bureaucracy, usually meaning a government bureaucracy. (13)

business cycle   Expansions and contractions of business activity, the first accompanied by inflation and the second by unemployment. (18)

cabinet   A group of presidential advisers; the heads of the executive departments and other key officials. (12)

capitalism   The system of government that favors free enterprise (privately owned businesses operating without government regulation). (1)

Carter Doctrine   A statement asserting that attempts "by any outside force to gain control of the Persian Gulf region" would be seen "as an assault on the vital interests of the United States." (20)

casework   Solving problems for constituents, especially problems involving government agencies. (11)

categorical grant   A grant-in-aid targeted for a specific purpose. (4)

caucus   A closed meeting of the members of a political party to decide upon questions of policy and the selection of candidates for office. (8)

checks and balances   A government structure that gives each branch some scrutiny and control over the other branches. (3)

civil case   A court case that involves a private dispute arising from such matters as accidents, contractual obligations, and divorce. (14)

civil disobedience   The willful but nonviolent violation of laws that are regarded as unjust. (16)

civil liberties   Freedoms guaranteed to individuals. (15)

civil rights   Powers or privileges guaranteed to individuals and protected from arbitrary removal at the hands of government or individuals. (15, 16)

civil rights movement   The mass mobilization during the 1960s that sought to gain equality of rights and opportunities for blacks in the South and to a lesser extent in the North, mainly through nonviolent unconventional means of participation. Martin Luther King, Jr., was the leading figure and symbol of the civil rights movement, but it was powered by the commitment of great numbers of people, black and white, of all sorts and stations in life. (16)

civil service   The system by which most appointments to the federal bureaucracy are made, to ensure that government jobs are filled on the basis of merit and that employees are not fired for political reasons. (13)

class-action suit   A legal action brought by a person or group on behalf of a number of people in similar circumstances. (7, 14)

clear and present danger test   A means by which the Supreme Court has distinguished between speech as the advocacy of ideas, which is protected by the First Amendment, and speech as incitement, which is not protected. (15)

closed primary   A primary election in which voters must declare their party affiliation before they are given the primary ballot containing that party's potential nominees. (9)

cloture   The mechanism by which a filibuster is cut off in the Senate. (11)

coalition building   The banding together of several interest groups for the purpose of lobbying. (10)

Cold War   A prolonged period of adversarial relations between the two superpowers, the United States and the Soviet Union. During the Cold War, which lasted from the late 1940s to the late 1980s, many crises and confrontations brought the superpowers to the brink of war, but they avoided direct military conflict with each other. (20)

commerce clause   The third clause of Article I, Section 8, of the Constitution, which gives Congress the power to regulate commerce among the states. (4)

common (judge-made) law   Legal precedents derived from previous judicial decisions. (14)

communism   A political system in which, in theory, ownership of all land and productive facilities is in the hands of the people, and all goods are equally shared. The production and distribution of goods are controlled by an authoritarian government. (1)

communitarians   Those who adhere to a viewpoint that affirms the individual's responsibility to the community and assigns to government, as agent of the community, the role of guaranteeing equality and moral order. In particular, communitarians are those who belong to, or are sympathetic with, a newly-formed movement called the Communitarian Network. (1)

comparative advantage   A principle of international trade that states that all nations will benefit when each nation specializes in those goods that it can produce most efficiently. (20)

concurrence   The agreement of a judge with the court's majority decision, for a reason other than the majority reason. (14)

confederation   A loose association of independent states that agree to cooperate on specified matters. (3)

conference committee   A temporary committee created to work out differences between the House and Senate versions of a specific piece of legislation. (11)

Congressional Budget Office (CBO)   The budgeting arm of Congress, which prepares alternative budgets to those prepared by the president's OMB. (18)

congressional campaign committee   An organization maintained by a political party to raise funds to support its own candidates in congressional elections. (8)

conservatives   Generally, those people whose political ideology favors a narrow scope for government. Also, those who value freedom more than equality but would restrict freedom to preserve social order. (1)

constituents   People who live and vote in a government official's district or state. (11)

containment   The basic U.S. policy toward the Soviet Union during the Cold War, according to which the Soviets were to be contained within existing boundaries by military, diplomatic, and economic means, in the expectation that the Soviet system would decay and disintegrate. (20)

conventional participation   Relatively routine political behavior that uses institutional channels and is acceptable to the dominant culture. (7)

cooperative federalism   A view that holds that the Constitution is an agreement among people who are citizens of both state and nation, so there is little distinction between state powers and national powers. (4)

Council of Economic Advisers (CEA) A group that works within the executive branch to provide advice on maintaining a stable economy. (18)

county government The government unit that administers a county. (4)

criminal case A court case involving a crime, or violation of public order. (14)

critical election An election that produces a sharp change in the existing pattern of party loyalties among groups of voters. (8)

Declaration of Independence Drafted by Thomas Jefferson, the document that proclaimed the right of the colonies to separate from Great Britain. (3)

de facto segregation Segregation that is not the result of government influence. (16)

deficit financing The Keynesian technique of spending beyond government income to combat an economic slump. Its purpose is to inject extra money into the economy to stimulate aggregate demand. (18)

de jure segregation Government-imposed segregation. (16)

delegate A legislator whose primary responsibility is to represent the majority view of his or her constituents, regardless of his or her own view. (11)

delegation of powers The process by which Congress gives the executive branch the additional authority needed to address new problems. (12)

deliberative democracy That model of democracy in which citizens and their elected representatives exercise reasoned and full debate on questions of public policy. (2)

democracy A system of government in which, in theory, the people rule, either directly or indirectly. (2)

democratic socialism A socialist form of government that guarantees civil liberties such as freedom of speech and religion. Citizens determine the extent of government activity through free elections and competitive political parties. (1)

democratization A process of transition as a country attempts to move from an authoritarian form of government to a democratic one. (2)

department The biggest unit of the executive branch, covering a broad area of government responsibility. The heads of the departments, or secretaries, form the president's cabinet. (13)

deregulation A bureaucratic reform by which the government reduces its role as a regulator of business. (13)

descriptive representation A belief that constituents are most effectively represented by legislators who are similar to them in such key demographic characteristics as race, ethnicity, religion, or gender. (11)

desegregation The ending of authorized segregation, or separation by race. (16)

detente A reduction of tensions. This term is particularly used to refer to a reduction of tensions between the United States and the Soviet Union in the early 1970s during the Nixon administration. (20)

deterrence The defense policy of American strategists during the Eisenhower administration, who believed the Soviets would not take aggressive action knowing they risked nuclear annihilation. (20)

direct action Unconventional participation that involves assembling crowds to confront businesses and local governments to demand a hearing. (7)

direct lobbying Attempts to influence a legislator's vote through personal contact with the legislator. (10)

direct primary A preliminary election, run by the state government, in which the voters choose each party's candidates for the general election. (7)

discretionary spending In the Budget Enforcement Act of 1990, authorized expenditures from annual appropriations. (18)

dissent The disagreement of a judge with a majority decision. (14)

divided government The situation in which one party controls the White House and the other controls the Congress. (12)

docket A court's agenda. (14)

dual federalism A view that holds the Constitution is a compact among sovereign states, so that the powers of the national government are fixed and limited. (4)

economic depression A period of high unemployment and business failures; a severe, long-lasting downturn in a business cycle. (18)

elastic clause See *necessary and proper clause.*

election campaign An organized effort to persuade voters to choose one candidate over others competing for the same office. (9)

electoral college A body of electors chosen by voters to cast ballots for president and vice president. (8)

electoral dealignment A lessening of the importance of party loyalties in voting decisions. (8)

electoral realignment The change in voting patterns that occurs after a critical election. (8)

elite theory The view that a small group of people actually makes most of the important government decisions. (2)

entitlement A benefit to which every eligible person has a legal right and that the government cannot deny. (18, 19)

enumerated powers The powers explicitly granted to Congress by the Constitution. (3)

equality of opportunity The idea that each person is guaranteed the same chance to succeed in life. (1, 16)

equality of outcome   The concept that society must ensure that people are equal, and governments must design policies to redistribute wealth and status so that economic and social equality is actually achieved. (1, 16)

equal opportunities rule   Under the Federal Communications Act of 1934, the requirement that if a broadcast station gives or sells time to a candidate for any public office, it must make available an equal amount of time under the same conditions to all other candidates for that office. (6)

Equal Rights Amendment (ERA)   A failed constitutional amendment first introduced by the National Women's party in 1923, declaring that "equality of rights under the law shall not be denied or abridged by the United States or any State on account of sex." (16)

establishment clause   The first clause in the First Amendment, which forbids the establishment of a national religion. (15)

exclusionary rule   The judicial rule that states that evidence obtained in an illegal search and seizure cannot be used in trial. (15)

executive agreement   A pact between the heads of two countries. (20)

executive branch   The law-enforcing branch of government. (3)

Executive Office of the President   The president's executive aides and their staffs; the extended White House executive establishment. (12)

ex post facto law   A law that declares an action to be criminal *after* it has been performed. (15)

extraordinary majorities   Majorities greater than that required by majority rule, that is, greater than 50 percent plus one. (3)

Federal Communications Commission (FCC)   An independent federal agency that regulates interstate and international communication by radio, television, telephone, telegraph, cable, and satellite. (6)

Federal Election Commission (FEC)   A federal agency that oversees the financing of national election campaigns. (9)

federalism   The division of power between a central government and regional governments. (3, 4)

federal question   An issue covered by the constitution, national laws, or U.S. treaties. (14)

Federal Reserve System   The system of banks that acts as the central bank of the United States and controls major monetary policies. (18)

feedback   Information received by policymakers about the effectiveness of public policy. (17)

feminization of poverty   The term applied to the fact that a growing percentage of all poor Americans are women or the dependents of women. (19)

fighting words   Speech that is not protected by the First Amendment because it inflicts injury or tends to incite an immediate disturbance of the peace. (15)

filibuster   A delaying tactic, used in the Senate, that involves speechmaking to prevent action on a piece of legislation. (11)

first-past-the-post election   A British term for elections conducted in single-member districts that award victory to the candidate with the most votes. (9)

fiscal policies   Economic policies that involve government spending and taxing. (18)

fiscal year (FY)   The twelve-month period from October 1 to September 30 used by the government for accounting purposes. A fiscal-year budget is named for the year in which it ends. (18)

flexible response   The basic defense policy of the Kennedy administration, involving the ability to wage both nuclear and conventional war. (20)

food stamp program   A federally funded program that increases the purchasing power of needy families by providing them with coupons they can use to purchase food. (19)

formula grant   A grant-in-aid distributed according to a particular formula, which specifies who is eligible for the grants and how much each eligible applicant will receive. (4)

fragmentation   In policymaking, the phenomenon of attacking a single problem in different and sometimes competing ways. (17)

franchise   The right to vote. Also called *suffrage*. (7)

freedom from   Immunity, as in *freedom from want*. (1)

freedom of   An absence of constraints on behavior, as in *freedom of speech*, or *freedom of religion*. (1)

free-exercise clause   The second clause in the First Amendment, which prevents the government from interfering with the exercise of religion. (15)

free-expression clauses   The press and speech clauses of the First Amendment. (15)

free-rider problem   The situation in which people benefit from the activities of an organization (such as an interest group) but do not contribute to those activities. (10)

gatekeepers   Media executives, news editors, and prominent reporters who direct the flow of news. (6)

general election   A national election held by law in November of every even-numbered year. (9)

gerrymandering   Redrawing a congressional district to intentionally benefit one political party. (11)

good faith exception   An exception to the Supreme Court exclusionary rule, holding that evidence seized on the basis of a mistakenly issued search warrant can be introduced at trial if the mistake was made in good faith, that is, if all the parties involved had reason at the time to believe that the warrant was proper. (15)

government The legitimate use of force to control human behavior; also, the organization or agency authorized to exercise that force. (1)

government corporation A government agency that performs services that might be provided by the private sector but that involve either insufficient financial incentive or are better provided when they are somehow linked with government. (13)

Gramm-Rudman Popular name for an act passed by Congress in 1985 that, in its original form, sought to lower the national deficit to a specified level each year, culminating in a balanced budget in FY 1991. New reforms and deficit targets were agreed on in 1990. (18)

grant-in-aid Money provided by one level of government to another, to be spent for a specific purpose. (4)

grassroots lobbying Lobbying activities performed by rank-and-file interest group members and would-be members. (10)

Great Compromise Submitted by the Connecticut delegation to the Constitutional Convention of 1787, and thus also known as the *Connecticut Compromise,* a plan calling for a bicameral legislature in which the House of Representatives would be apportioned according to population and the states would be represented equally in the Senate. (3)

Great Depression The longest and deepest setback the American economy has ever experienced. It began with the stock market crash on October 12, 1929, and did not end until the start of World War II. (19)

Great Society President Lyndon Johnson's broad array of programs designed to redress political, social, and economic inequality. (19)

gridlock A situation in which government is incapable of acting on important issues, usually because of divided government. (12)

gross domestic product (GDP) The total value of the goods and services produced by a country during a year. (18)

group media Communications technologies, such as the fax and the Internet, used primarily within groups of people of common interests. (6)

high politics A term used to describe strategic and security issues in global politics. Traditionally, policymakers involved in global politics were expected to give greater priority to these issues than to issues of low politics such as socioeconomic or welfare issues . (20)

home rule The right to enact and enforce legislation locally. (4)

horse race journalism Election coverage by the mass media that focuses on which candidate is ahead, rather than on national issues. (6)

impeachment The formal charging of a government official with "Treason, Bribery, or other High Crimes and Misdemeanors." (11)

implementation The process of putting specific policies into operation. (13, 17)

implied powers Those powers that Congress requires in order to execute its enumerated powers. (3, 4)

in-and-outer A participant in an issue network who has a good understanding of the needs and problems of others in the network and can easily switch jobs within the network. (17)

incremental budgeting A method of budget making that involves adding new funds (an increment) onto the amount previously budgeted (in last year's budget). (18)

incrementalism The situation in which policies or programs change slowly and gradually, step by step. (13)

incumbent A current officeholder. (11)

independent agency An executive agency that is not part of a cabinet department. (13)

inflation An economic condition characterized by price increases linked to a decrease in the value of the currency. (18)

influencing behavior Behavior that seeks to modify or reverse government policy to serve political interests. (7)

information campaign An organized effort to gain public backing by bringing a group's views to public attention. (10)

infotainment The practice of mixing journalism with theater, employed by some news programs. (6)

inherent powers Authority claimed by the president that is not clearly specified in the Constitution. Typically, these powers are inferred from the Constitution. (12)

initiative A procedure by which voters can propose an issue to be decided by the legislature or by the people in a referendum. It requires gathering a specified number of signatures and submitting a petition to a designated agency. (7)

interest group An organized group of individuals that seeks to influence public policy. Also called a *lobby.* (2, 10)

interest group entrepreneur An interest group organizer or leader. (10)

intermestic issues Issues in which international and domestic concerns are mixed. (20)

invidious discrimination Discrimination against persons or groups that works to their harm and is based on animosity. (16)

issue network A shared-knowledge group consisting of representatives of various interests involved in some particular aspect of public policy. (17)

joint committee A committee made up of members of both the House and the Senate. (11)

judgment The judicial decision in a court case. (14)

judicial activism   A judicial philosophy whereby judges interpret existing laws and precedents loosely and interject their own values in court decisions. (14)

judicial branch   The branch of government that interprets laws. (3)

judicial restraint   A judicial philosophy whereby judges adhere closely to statutes and precedents in reaching their decisions. (14)

judicial review   The power to declare congressional (and presidential) acts invalid because they violate the Constitution. (3, 14)

Keynesian theory   An economic theory stating that the government can stabilize the economy—i.e., can smooth business cycles—by controlling the level of aggregate demand, and that the level of aggregate demand can be controlled by means of fiscal and monetary policies. (18)

laissez faire   An economic doctrine that opposes any form of government intervention in business. (1)

legislative branch   The lawmaking branch of government. (3)

legislative liaison staff   Those people who comprise the communications link between the White House and Congress, advising the president or cabinet secretaries on the status of pending legislation. (12)

liberals   Generally, those people whose political ideology favors a broad scope for government; those who value freedom more than order but not more than equality. (1)

libertarianism   A political ideology that is opposed to all government action except as necessary to protect life and property. (1)

libertarians   Those who advocate minimal government action; those who subscribe to libertarianism. (1)

line item veto   A presidential veto applied to particular sections or particular line items of a bill. (11)

lobby   See *interest group.*

lobbyist   A representative of an interest group. (10)

local caucus   A method used to select delegates to attend a party's national convention. Generally, a local meeting selects delegates for a county-level meeting, which in turn selects delegates for a higher-level meeting; the process culminates in a state convention that actually selects the national convention delegates. (9)

low politics   A term used to describe socioeconomic or welfare issues. Traditionally, policymakers involved in global politics were expected to place less emphasis on these issues than on issues of high politics such as strategic and security issues. (20)

majoritarian model of democracy   The classical theory of democracy in which government by the people is interpreted as government by the majority of the people. (2)

majority leader   The head of the majority party in the Senate; the second highest ranking member of the majority party in the House. (11)

majority representation   The system by which one office, contested by two or more candidates, is won by the single candidate who collects the most votes. (8)

majority rule   The principle—basic to procedural democratic theory—that the decision of a group must reflect the preference of more than half of those participating; a simple majority. (2)

managed trade   Government intervention in trade policy in order to achieve a specific result. (20)

mandate   An endorsement by voters. Presidents sometimes argue they have been given a mandate to carry out policy proposals. (4, 12)

mandatory spending   In the Budget Enforcement Act of 1990, expenditures required by previous commitments. (18)

mass media   The means employed in mass communication, often divided into print media and broadcast media. (6)

means-tested benefits   Conditional benefits provided by government to individuals whose income falls below a designated threshold. (19)

media event   A situation that is so "newsworthy" that the mass media are compelled to cover it; candidates in elections often create such situations to garner media attention. (6)

Medicare   A health-insurance program for all persons older than sixty-five. (19)

membership bias   The tendency of some sectors of society—especially the wealthy, the highly educated, professionals, and those in business—to organize more readily into interest groups. (10)

minority rights   The benefits of government that cannot be denied to any citizens by majority decisions. (2)

Miranda warnings   Statements concerning rights that police are required to make to a person before he or she is subjected to in-custody questioning. (15)

monetarists   Those who argue that government can effectively control the performance of an economy only by controlling the supply of money. (18)

monetary policies   Economic policies that involve control of, and changes in, the supply of money. (18)

municipal government   The government unit that administers a city or town. (4)

mutual assured destruction (MAD)   The capability of the two great superpowers—the United States and the Soviet Union—to destroy each other, ensuring no winner of a nuclear war. (20)

national committee   A committee of a political party composed of party chairpersons and party officials from every state. (8)

national convention A gathering of delegates of a single political party from across the country to choose candidates for president and vice president and to adopt a party platform. (8)

nation-building policy A policy once intended to shore up Third World countries economically and democratically, thereby making them less attractive targets for Soviet opportunism. (20)

necessary and proper clause The last clause in Section 8 of Article I of the Constitution, which gives Congress the means to execute its enumerated powers. This clause is the basis for Congress's implied powers. Also called the *elastic clause*. (3, 4)

New Deal The measures advocated by the Roosevelt administration to alleviate the Depression. (19)

"new" ethnicity A newer outlook on the people comprising America's "melting pot," with focus on race. (5)

New Jersey Plan Submitted by the head of the New Jersey delegation to the Constitutional Convention of 1787, a set of nine resolutions that would have, in effect, preserved the Articles of Confederation by amending rather than replacing them. (3)

newsworthiness The degree to which a news story is important enough to be covered in the mass media. (6)

Nineteenth Amendment The amendment to the Constitution, adopted in 1920, that assures women of the right to vote. (16)

Nixon Doctrine An attempt to reduce America's foreign involvement by calling for U.S. intervention only where it made a "real difference" and was considered to be in our interest. (20)

nomination Designation as an official candidate of a political party. (8)

non-means-tested benefits Benefits provided by government to all citizens, regardless of income; Medicare and social security are examples. (19)

nontariff barrier (NTB) A regulation that outlines the exact specifications an imported product must meet in order to be offered for sale. (20)

norm An organization's informal, unwritten rules that guide individual behavior. (13)

normal distribution A symmetrical bell-shaped distribution (of opinions) centered on a single mode, or most frequent response. (5)

North Atlantic Treaty Organization (NATO) An organization including nations of Western Europe, the United States, and Canada, created in 1949 to defend against Soviet expansionism. With the Soviet threat in Western Europe diminished or eliminated, the purposes and membership of NATO are under examination. (20)

nullification The declaration by a state that a particular action of the national government is not applicable to that state. (4)

obligation of contracts The obligation of the parties to a contract to carry out its terms. (15)

Office of Management and Budget (OMB) The budgeting arm of the Executive Office; prepares the president's budget. (18)

"old" ethnicity An older outlook on the people comprising America's "melting pot," with focus on religion and country of origin. (5)

oligarchy A system of government in which power is concentrated in the hands of a few people. (2)

open election An election that lacks an incumbent. (9)

open primary A primary election in which voters need not declare their party affiliation but must choose one party's primary ballot to take into the voting booth. (9)

opinion schema A network of organized knowledge and beliefs that guides a person's processing of information regarding a particular subject. (5)

order The rule of law to preserve life and protect property. Maintaining order is the oldest purpose of government. (1)

original jurisdiction The authority of a court to hear a case before any other court does. (14)

oversight The process of reviewing the operations of an agency to determine whether it is carrying out policies as Congress intended. (11)

parliamentary system A system of government in which the chief executive is the leader whose party holds the most seats in the legislature after an election or whose party forms a major part of the ruling coalition. (11)

participatory democracy A system of government where rank-and-file citizens rule themselves rather than electing representatives to govern on their behalf. (2)

party conference A meeting to select party leaders and decide committee assignments, held at the beginning of a session of Congress by Republicans or Democrats in each chamber. (8)

party identification A voter's sense of psychological attachment to a party. (8)

party machine A centralized party organization that dominates local politics by controlling elections. (8)

party platform The statement of policies of a national political party. (8)

pay-as-you-go (PAYGO) In the Budget Enforcement Act of 1990, the requirement that any tax cut or expansion of an entitlement program must be offset by a tax increase or other savings. (18)

plea bargain A defendant's admission of guilt in exchange for a less severe punishment. (14)

pluralist model of democracy An interpretation of democracy in which government by the people is taken to mean government by people operating through competing interest groups. (2)

pocket veto   A means of killing a bill that has been passed by both houses of Congress, in which the president does not sign the bill within ten days of Congress's adjournment. (11)

policy evaluation   Analysis of a public policy so as to determine how well it is working. (17)

policy formulation   The stage of the policymaking process during which formal proposals are developed and adopted. (17)

political action committee (PAC)   An organization that pools campaign contributions from group members and donates those funds to candidates for political office. (10)

political agenda   A list of issues that need government attention. (6)

political equality   Equality in political decision making: one vote per person, with all votes counted equally. (1, 2)

political participation   Actions of private citizens by which they seek to influence or support government and politics. (7)

political party   An organization that sponsors candidates for political office under the organization's name. (8)

political socialization   The complex process by which people acquire their political values. (5)

political system   A set of interrelated institutions that links people with government. (8)

poll tax   A tax of $1 or $2 on every citizen who wished to vote, first instituted in Georgia in 1877. Although it was no burden on white citizens, it effectively disenfranchised blacks. (16)

poverty level   The minimum cash income that will provide for a family's basic needs; calculated as three times the cost of a market basket of food that provides a minimally nutritious diet. (19)

precedent   A judicial ruling that serves as the basis for the ruling in a subsequent case. (14)

preemption   The power of Congress to enact laws by which the national government assumes total or partial responsibility for a state government function. (4)

presidential primary   A special primary election used to select delegates to attend the party's national convention, which in turn nominates the presidential candidate. (9)

primary election   A preliminary election conducted within a political party to select candidates who will run for public office in a subsequent election. (9)

prior restraint   Censorship before publication. (15)

procedural democratic theory   A view of democracy as being embodied in a decision-making process that involves universal participation, political equality, majority rule, and responsiveness. (2)

productive capacity   The total value of goods and services that can be produced when the economy works at full capacity. (18)

program monitoring   Keeping track of government programs, usually by interest groups. (10)

progressive taxation   A system of taxation whereby the rich pay proportionately higher taxes than the poor; used by governments to redistribute wealth and thus promote equality. (18)

progressivism   A philosophy of political reform based upon the goodness and wisdom of the individual citizen as opposed to special interests and political institutions. (7)

project grant   A grant-in-aid awarded on the basis of competitive applications submitted by prospective recipients. (4)

proportional representation   The system by which legislative seats are awarded to a party in proportion to the vote that party wins in an election. (8)

protectionism   The notion that women must be protected from life's cruelties; until the 1970s, the basis for laws affecting women's civil rights. (16)

protectionists (trade)   Those who wish to prevent imports from entering the country and therefore oppose free trade. (20)

public assistance   Government aid to individuals who can demonstrate a need for that aid. (19)

public figures   People who assume roles of prominence in society or thrust themselves to the forefront of public controversy. (15)

public goods   Benefits and services, such as parks and sanitation, that benefit all citizens but are not likely to be produced voluntarily by individuals. (1)

public interest group   A citizen group that generally is considered to have no economic self-interest in the policies it pursues. (10)

public opinion   The collected attitudes of citizens concerning a given issue or question. (5)

public policy   A general plan of action adopted by the government to solve a social problem, counter a threat, or pursue an objective. (17, 19)

racial gerrymandering   The drawing of a legislative district to maximize the chances that a minority candidate will win election. (11)

racial segregation   Separation from society because of race. (16)

racism   A belief that human races have distinct characteristics such that one's own race is superior to, and has a right to rule, others. (16)

reapportionment   Redistribution of representatives among the states, based on population movement. Congress is reapportioned after each census. (11)

reasonable access rule   An FCC rule that requires broadcast stations to make their facilities available for the expression of conflicting views or issues by all responsible elements in the community. (6)

recall   The process for removing an elected official from office. (7)

receipts   For a government, the amount expected or obtained in taxes and other revenues. (18)

referendum   An election on a policy issue. (7)

regulation   Government intervention in the workings of business to promote some socially desired goal. (13)

regulations   Administrative rules that guide the operation of a government program. (13)

regulatory commission   An agency of the executive branch of government that controls or directs some aspect of the economy. (13)

representative democracy   A system of government where citizens elect public officials to govern on their behalf. (2)

republic   A government without a monarch; a government rooted in the consent of the governed, whose power is exercised by elected representatives responsible to the governed. (3)

republicanism   A form of government in which power resides in the people and is exercised by their elected representatives. (3)

responsible party government   A set of principles formalizing the ideal role of parties in a majoritarian democracy. (8)

responsiveness   A decision-making principle, necessitated by representative government, that implies that elected representatives should do what the majority of people wants. (2)

restraint   A requirement laid down by act of Congress, prohibiting a state or local government from exercising a certain power. (4)

rights   The benefits of government to which every citizen is entitled. (1)

rule making   The administrative process that results in the issuance of regulations by government agencies. (13)

rule of four   An unwritten rule that requires at least four justices to agree that a case warrants consideration before it is reviewed by the Supreme Court. (14)

school district   An area for which a local government unit administers elementary and secondary school programs. (4)

select committee   A temporary congressional committee created for a specific purpose and disbanded after that purpose is fulfilled. (11)

self-interest principle   The implication that people choose what benefits them personally. (5)

senatorial courtesy   A practice whereby the Senate will not confirm for a lower federal court judgeship a nominee who is opposed by the senior senator in the president's party in the nominee's state. (14)

seniority   Years of consecutive service on a particular congressional committee. (11)

separate-but-equal doctrine   The concept that providing separate but equivalent facilities for blacks and whites satisfies the equal protection clauses of the Fourteenth Amendment. (16)

separation of powers   The assignment of law-making, law-enforcing, and law-interpreting functions to separate branches of government. (3)

sequestration   In the Budget Enforcement Act of 1990, an automatic across-the-board spending cut in an overspent category or in nonexempt entitlement programs. (18)

sexism   Sex discrimination. (16)

skewed distribution   An asymmetrical but generally bell-shaped distribution (of opinions); its mode, or most frequent response, lies off to one side. (5)

social contract theory   The belief that the people agree to set up rulers for certain purposes and thus have the right to resist or remove rulers who act against those purposes. (3)

social equality   Equality in wealth, education, and status. (1)

social insurance   A government-backed guarantee against loss by individuals without regard to need. (19)

socialism   A form of rule in which the central government plays a strong role in regulating existing private industry and directing the economy, although it does allow some private ownership of productive capacity. (1)

social security   Social insurance that provides economic assistance to persons faced with unemployment, disability, or old age. It is financed by taxes on employers and employees. (19)

Social Security Act   The law that provided for social security and is the basis of modern American social welfare. (19)

social welfare   Government programs that provide the minimum living standards necessary for all citizens. (19)

socioeconomic status   Position in society, based on a combination of education, occupational status, and income. (5)

solicitor general   The third highest ranking official of the U.S. Department of Justice, and the one who represents the national government before the Supreme Court. (14)

Speaker of the House   The presiding officer of the House of Representatives. (11)

special district   A government unit created to perform particular functions, especially when those functions are best performed across jurisdictional boundaries. (4)

split ticket   In voting, candidates from different parties for different offices. (9)

stable distribution   A distribution (of opinions) that shows little change over time. (5)

standard socioeconomic model   A relationship between socioeconomic status and conventional political involvement: People with higher status and more education are more likely to participate than those with lower status. (7)

standing committee A permanent congressional committee that specializes in a particular legislative area. (11)

stare decisis Literally, let the decision stand; decision making according to precedent. (14)

states' rights The idea that all rights not specifically conferred on the national government by the Constitution are reserved to the states. (4)

straight ticket In voting, a single party's candidates for all the offices. (9)

Strategic Defense Initiative (SDI) A large-scale research and development effort to build a system that will defend the United States against Soviet missiles. Also called "Star Wars." (20)

strict scrutiny A standard used by the Supreme Court in deciding whether a law or policy is to be adjudged Constitutional or not. To pass strict scrutiny, the law or policy must be justified by a "compelling governmental interest" as well as being the least restrictive means for achieving that interest. (15)

substantive democratic theory The view that democracy is embodied in the substance of government policies rather than in the policymaking procedure. (2)

suffrage The right to vote. Also called the *franchise*. (7)

supply-side economics Economic policies aimed at increasing the supply of goods (as opposed to increasing demand), consisting mainly of tax cuts for possible investors and less regulation of business. (18)

supportive behavior Actions that express allegiance to government and country. (7)

supremacy clause The clause in Article VI of the Constitution that asserts that national laws take precedence over state and local laws when they conflict. (3)

tax committees The two committees of Congress responsible for raising the revenue with which to run the government. (18)

television hypothesis The belief that television is to blame for the low level of citizens' knowledge about public affairs. (6)

totalitarianism A political philosophy that advocates unlimited power for the government to enable it to control all sectors of society. (1)

total quality management (TQM) A management philosophy emphasizing listening closely to customers, breaking down barriers between parts of an organization, and continually improving quality. (13)

trade association An organization that represents firms within a particular industry. (10)

transfer payment A payment by government to an individual, mainly through social security or unemployment insurance. (18)

trustee A representative who is obligated to consider the views of constituents but is not obligated to vote according to those views if he or she believes they are misguided. (11)

two-party system A political system in which two major political parties compete for control of the government. Candidates from a third party have little chance of winning office. (8)

two-step flow of communication The process in which a few policy elites gather information and then inform their more numerous followers, mobilizing them to apply pressure to government. (6)

uncontrollable outlay A payment that government must make by law. (18)

unconventional participation Relatively uncommon political behavior that challenges or defies established institutions and dominant norms. (7)

universal participation The concept that everyone in a democracy should participate in governmental decision making. (2)

U.S. Court of Appeals A court within the second tier of the three-tiered federal court system, to which decisions of the district courts and federal agencies may be appealed for review. (14)

U.S. district court A court within the lowest tier of the three-tiered federal court system; a court where litigation begins. (14)

veto The president's disapproval of a bill that has been passed by both houses of Congress. Congress can override a veto with a two-thirds vote in each house. (11, 12)

Virginia Plan A set of proposals for a new government, submitted to the Constitutional Convention of 1787; included separation of the government into three branches, division of the legislature into two houses, and proportional representation in the legislature. (3)

War on Poverty A part of President Lyndon Johnson's Great Society program, intended to eradicate poverty within ten years. (19)

War Powers Resolution An act of Congress that limits the president's ability to wage undeclared war. (20)

welfare state A nation in which the government assumes responsibility for the welfare of its citizens, redistributing income to reduce social inequality. (19)

References

Chapter 1 / Freedom, Order, or Equality? / pp. 1–29

1. "Kevorkian Attends Another Michigan Death," *New York Times*, 30 January 1996, p. A8.
2. Jack Lessenberry, "In Tactical Change, Kevorkian Promises To Halt Suicide Aid," *New York Times*, 26 December 1993, p. 1.
3. Center for Political Studies of the Institute for Social Research, *Election Study 1992* (Ann Arbor, Mich., University of Michigan).
4. 1977 Constitution of the Union of Soviet Socialist Republics, Article 11, in *Constitutions of Countries of the World*, ed. A. P. Blaustein and G. H. Flanz (Dobbs Ferry, N.Y.: Oceana, 1971).
5. Karl Marx and Friedrich Engels, *Critique of the Gotha Programme* (New York: International Publishers, 1938), p. 10. Originally written in 1875 but published in 1891.
6. See the argument in Amy Gutman, *Liberal Equality* (Cambridge, England: Cambridge University Press, 1980), pp. 9–10.
7. See John H. Schaar, "Equality of Opportunity and Beyond," in *Equality*, NOMOS IX, eds. J. Roland Pennock and John W. Chapman (New York: Atherton Press, 1967), pp. 228–249.
8. Jean Jacques Rousseau, *The Social Contract and Discourses*, trans. G. D. H. Cole (New York: Dutton, 1950), p. 5.
9. Sam Vincent Meddis, "Crime's No Worse, But USA's Fear Grows," *USA Today* (International Edition), 28 October 1993, p. 1. See also Wesley G. Skogan, *Disorder and Decline: Crime and the Spiral of Decay in American Neighborhoods* (New York: Free Press, 1990), Chap. 2.
10. "Public Opinion and Demographic Report," *Public Perspective* (November-December 1993), p. 79.
11. Linnet Myers, "Crime Wave Washes over East Europe," *Chicago Tribune*, 20 December 1995, pp. 1 and 24.
12. "MN Express Poll," *Moscow News*, No. 7, February 1993, p. 1.
13. *Morbidity and Mortality Weekly Report*, 44 (24 November 1995), p. 849.
14. Craig R. Whitney, "Moscow a Year Later: Rutted Streets and Despair," *New York Times*, 19 February 1990, p. A6.
15. Alessandra Stanley, "Russian TV, Freed of Communism, Gilds It," *New York Times*, 30 December 1995, p. 1.
16. Milton Friedman, *Capitalism and Freedom* (Chicago: University of Chicago Press, 1962).
17. Lewis MacAdams, "A Gathering of the Tribes," *Rolling Stone*, 23 December 1993, p. 118; Doreen Carvajal, "After an Anarchist Melee, Neighbors Reclaim a Park," *New York Times*, 4 September 1995, p. 23.
18. Various interpretations of what "populist" really means could be seen in the spirited debate that occurred on H-POL (the Internet daily discussion group on American political history) in the spring and summer of 1995. For a discussion of definitions in print, see Michael Kazin, *The Populist Persuasion: An American History* (New York: Basic Books, 1995).
19. The communitarian movement was founded by a group of ethicists and social scientists who met in Washington, D.C., in 1990 at the invitation of sociologist Amitai Etzioni and political theorist William Galston to discuss the declining state of morality and values in the United States. Etzioni became the leading spokesperson for the movement. See his *Rights and the Common Good: The Communitarian Perspective* (New York: St. Martin's Press, 1995), pp. iii–iv. The communitarian political movement should be distinguished from communitarian thought in political philosophy, which is associated with theorists such as Alasdair MacIntyre, Michael Sandel, and Charles Taylor, who wrote in the late 1970s and early 1980s. In essence, communitarian theorists criticized liberalism, which stressed freedom and individualism, as excessively individualistic. Their fundamental critique was that liberalism slights the values of community life. See Allen E. Buchanan, "Assessing the Communitarian Critique of Liberalism," *Ethics*, 99 (July 1989), pp. 852–882, and Patrick Neal and David Paris, "Liberalism and the Communitarian Critique: A Guide for the Perplexed," *Canadian Journal of Political Science*, 23 (September 1990), pp. 419–439. Communitarian philosophers attacked liberalism over the inviolability of civil liberties. In our framework, such issues involve the tradeoff between freedom and order. Communitarian and liberal theorists differ less concerning the tradeoff between freedom and equality. See William R. Lund, "Communitarian Politics and the Problem of Equality," *Political Research Quarterly*, 46 (September 1993), pp. 577–600. But see also Susan Hekman, "The Embodiment of the Subject: Feminism and the Communitarian Critique of Liberalism," *Journal of Politics*, 54 (November 1992), pp. 1098–1119.
20. Etzioni, *Rights and the Common Good*, p. iv, and Etzioni, "Communitarian Solutions/What Communitarians Think," *The Journal of State Government*, 65 (January-March), pp. 9–11. For a critical review of the communitarian program, see Jeremiah Creedon, "Communitarian Manifesto," *Utne*

Reader (July-August 1992), pp. 38–40.

21. Etzioni, "Communitarian Solutions/What Communitarians Think," p. 10. See also Lester Thurow, "Communitarian vs. Individualistic Capitalism," in Etzioni, *Rights and the Common Good*, pp. 277–282. Note, however, that government's role in dealing with issues of social and economic inequality is far less developed in communitarian writings than is its role in dealing with issues of order. In the same volume, an article by David Osborne, "Beyond Left and Right: A New Political Paradigm" (pp. 283–290), downplays the role of government in guaranteeing entitlements.

22. Etzioni, *Rights and the Common Good*, p. 17.

23. *Ibid.*, p. 22.

Chapter 2 / Majoritarian or Pluralist Democracy? / pp. 30–56

1. Francis X. Clines, "Echo of Gunshots Past as House Votes," *New York Times*, 23 March 1996, p. 10.

2. Joe Davidson, "Effort to Lift Ban on Assault Weapons Faces an Uphill Struggle in the Senate," *Wall Street Journal*, 25 March 1996, p. C24.

3. Adam Clymer, "House Approves Repeal of the Ban on Assault Weapons," *New York Times*, 23 March 1996, p. 1.

4. Alan Greenblatt, "Repeal of Assault Weapons Ban Unlikely to Go Beyond House," *Congressional Quarterly Weekly Report*, 23 March 1996, p. 803.

5. Kenneth Janda, "What's in a Name? Party Labels Across the World," in *The CONTA Conference: Proceedings of the Conference of Conceptual and Terminological Analysis of the Social Sciences*, ed. F. W. Riggs (Frankfurt: Indeks Verlage, 1982), pp. 46–62.

6. Richard F. Fenno, Jr., *The President's Cabinet* (New York: Vintage, 1959), p. 29.

7. Robert A. Dahl, *Democracy and Its Critics* (New Haven: Yale University Press, 1989), pp. 13–23.

8. Jeffrey M. Berry, Kent E. Portney, and Ken Thomson, *The Rebirth of Urban Democracy* (Washington, D.C.: Brookings Institution, 1993).

9. Isabel Wilkerson, "Chicago On Brink of New School System," *New York Times*, 11 October 1989, p. A18.

10. Jean Jacques Rousseau, *The Social Contract*, 1762. Reprint (Hammondsworth, England: Penguin, 1968), p. 141.

11. Berry, Portney, and Thomson, *Rebirth*, p. 77.

12. See James A. Stimson, Michael B. MacKuen, and Robert S. Erikson, "Dynamic Representation," *American Political Science Review*, 89 (September 1995), pp. 543–565.

13. See C. B. Macpherson, *The Real World of Democracy* (New York: Oxford University Press, 1975), pp. 58–59.

14. Thomas E. Cronin, *Direct Democracy* (Cambridge, Mass.: Harvard University Press, 1989), p. 47.

15. James F. Clarity, "Ireland's Anti-Divorce Camp Gears Up for Court Challenge," *New York Times*, 27 November 1995, p. A3.

16. Jack Citrin, "Who's the Boss? Direct Democracy and Popular Control of Government," in *Broken Contract?* ed. Stephen C. Craig (Boulder, Colo.: Westview, 1996), p. 271.

17. Lawrence K. Grossman, *The Electronic Republic* (New York: Viking, 1995).

18. M. Margaret Conway, *Political Participation in the United States*, 2nd ed. (Washington, D.C.: Congressional Quarterly, 1991), p. 44.

19. Joseph M. Bessette, *The Mild Voice of Reason: Deliberative Democracy and American National Government* (Chicago: University of Chicago Press, 1994).

20. Benjamin I. Page and Robert Y. Shapiro, *The Rational Public* (Chicago: University of Chicago Press, 1992), p. 387.

21. See *Citizens and Politics* (Dayton, Ohio: Kettering Foundation, 1991).

22. See Robert A. Dahl, *Dilemmas of Pluralist Democracy* (New Haven, Conn.: Yale University Press, 1982), p. 5.

23. Robert A. Dahl, *Pluralist Democracy in the United States* (Chicago: Rand McNally, 1967), p. 24.

24. The classic statement on elite theory is C. Wright Mills, *The Power Elite* (New York: Oxford University Press, 1956).

25. Michael Useem, *The Inner Circle* (New York: Oxford University Press, 1984). On a broader level, see Charles Lindblom, *Politics and Markets* (New York: Basic Books, 1977).

26. Thomas R. Dye, *Who's Running America?* 5th ed. (Englewood Cliffs, N. J.: Prentice-Hall, 1990), p. 12.

27. Robert A. Dahl, *Who Governs?* (New Haven, Conn.: Yale University Press, 1961).

28. Clarence N. Stone, *Regime Politics* (Lawrence: University of Kansas Press, 1989).

29. John P. Heinz, Edward O. Laumann, Robert L. Nelson, and Robert H. Salisbury, *The Hollow Core* (Cambridge, Mass.: Harvard University Press, 1993).

30. Peter Bachrach and Morton S. Baratz, "Two Faces of Power," *American Political Science Review*, 56 (December 1962), pp. 947–952; and John Gaventa, *Power and Powerlessness* (Urbana: University of Illinois Press, 1980).

31. See, for example, Dan Clawson, Alan Neustatdl, and Denise Scott, *Money Talks* (New York: Basic Books, 1992).

32. Kay Lehman Schlozman and John T. Tierney, *Organized Interests and American Politics* (New York: Harper & Row, 1986).

33. Jeffrey M. Berry, "The Rise of Postmaterialism in American Politics," paper delivered at the annual meeting of the American Political Science Association, San Francisco, 1 September 1996.

34. Jeffrey M. Berry, *The Interest Group Society*, 3d ed. (New York: Longman, 1997).

35. Jonathan Rauch, *Demosclerosis* (New York: Times Books, 1994).

36. Arend Lijphart, *Democracies* (New Haven, Conn.: Yale University Press, 1984).

37. *Africa Demos*, 3 (February 1993), pp. 1 and 19; and Michael Bratton and Nicholas van de Walle, "Popular Protest and Political Reform in Africa," *Comparative Politics*, 24 (July 1992), pp. 419–442.

38. See generally, Samuel P. Huntington, *The Third Wave* (Norman: University of Oklahoma Press, 1991).

39. Alessandra Stanley, "Communists Lead the Ruling Party By 2 to 1 in

Russia," *New York Times*, 19 December 1995, p. A1.

40. The classic treatment of the conflict between freedom and order in democratizing countries is Samuel P. Huntington, *Political Order in Changing Societies* (New Haven, Conn.: Yale University Press, 1968).

41. Benjamin R. Barber, "Jihad vs. McWorld," *Atlantic Monthly*, March 1992, p. 53.

42. Rita Jalai and Seymour Martin Lipset, "Racial and Ethnic Conflicts: A Global Perspective," *Political Science Quarterly*, 107 (Winter 1992–93), p. 588.

43. E. E. Schattschneider, *The Semi-Sovereign People* (New York: Holt, Rinehart, & Winston, 1960), p. 35.

44. Citrin, "Who's the Boss?" pp. 286–287.

Chapter 3 / The Constitution / pp. 57–99

1. Carl Bernstein and Bob Woodward, *All the President's Men* (New York: Warner, 1975); Stanley I. Kutler, *The Wars of Watergate* (New York: Alfred A. Knopf, 1990).

2. Bernstein and Woodward, *All the President's Men*, p. 30.

3. *The Encyclopedia of American Facts and Dates* (New York: Crowell, 1979), p. 946.

4. Richard B. Morris, ed., *Encyclopedia of American History* (New York: Harper & Row, 1976), p. 544.

5. Seymour M. Hersh, "A Reporter at Large; Nixon's Last Cover-up: The Tapes He Wants the Archives To Suppress," *The New Yorker*, 14 December 1992, p. 76.

6. Gallup Organization, *Gallup Poll Monthly*, June 1992, pp. 2–3.

7. Samuel Eliot Morison, *Oxford History of the American People* (New York: Oxford University Press, 1965), p. 182.

8. *Ibid.*, p. 172.

9. Richard Walsh, *Charleston's Sons of Liberty: A Study of the Artisans, 1763–1789* (Columbia: University of South Carolina Press, 1959).

10. Mary Beth Norton, *Liberty's Daughters* (Boston: Little, Brown, 1980), pp. 155–157.

11. Morison, *Oxford History*, p. 204.

12. John Plamentz (rev. ed. by M. E. Plamentz and Robert Wokler), *Man and Society*, Vol. 1: From the Middle Ages to Locke (New York: Longman, 1992), pp. 216–218.

13. Charles H. Metzger, S. J., *Catholics and the American Revolution: A Study in Religious Climate* (Chicago: Loyola University Press, 1962).

14. Extrapolated from U.S. Department of Defense, *Selected Manpower Statistics, FY 1982* (Washington, D.C.: U.S. Government Printing Office, 1983), Table 2-30, p. 130; and U.S. Bureau of the Census, *1985 Statistical Abstract of the United States* (Washington, D.C.: U.S. Government Printing Office, 1985), Tables 1 and 2, p. 6.

15. Joseph T. Keenan, *The Constitution of the United States* (Homewood, Ill.: Dow-Jones-Irwin, 1975).

16. David P. Szatmary, *Shays' Rebellion: The Making of an Agrarian Insurrection* (Amherst: University of Massachusetts Press, 1980), pp. 82–102.

17. As cited in Morison, *Oxford History*, p. 304.

18. "The Call for the Federal Constitutional Convention, Feb. 21, 1787" in Edward M. Earle (ed.), *The Federalist* (New York: Modern Library), p. 577.

19. Robert H. Jackson, *The Struggle for Judicial Supremacy* (New York: Alfred A. Knopf, 1941), p. 8.

20. John Dickinson of Delaware, as quoted in Morison, *Oxford History*, p. 270.

21. Catherine Drinker Bowen, *Miracle at Philadelphia* (Boston: Little, Brown, 1966), p. 122.

22. Forrest McDonald, *Novus Ordo Seclorum: The Intellectual Origins of the Constitution* (Lawrence: University Press of Kansas, 1985), pp. 205–209.

23. Donald S. Lutz, "The Preamble to the Constitution of the United States," *This Constitution*, 1 (September 1983), pp. 23–30.

24. Richard E. Neustadt, *Presidential Power: The Politics of Leadership* (New York: Wiley, 1960), p. 33.

25. Charles A. Beard, *An Economic Interpretation of the Constitution of the United States* (New York: Macmillan, 1913).

26. Leonard W. Levy, *Constitutional Opinions* (New York: Oxford University Press, 1986), p. 101.

27. Robert E. Brown, *Charles Beard and the Constitution* (Princeton, N.J.: Princeton University Press, 1956); Levy, *Constitutional Opinions*, pp. 103–104; and Forrest McDonald, *We the People: Economic Origins of the Constitution* (Chicago: University of Chicago Press, 1958).

28. Compare Eugene D. Genovese, *The Political Economy of Slavery: Studies in the Economics and Society of the Slave South* (Middletown, Conn.: Wesleyan University Press, 1989); and Robert William Fogel, *Without Contract or Consent: The Rise and Fall of American Slavery* (New York: W. W. Norton, 1989).

29. Robert A. Goldwin, Letter to the Editor, *Wall Street Journal*, 30 August 1993, p. A11.

30. Bernard Bailyn, *Faces of Revolution: Personalities and Themes in the Struggle for American Independence* (New York: Alfred A. Knopf, 1990), pp. 221–222.

31. Walter Berns, *The First Amendment and the Future of Democracy* (New York: Basic Books, 1976), p. 2.

32. Herbert J. Storing, ed., *The Complete Anti-Federalist*, 7 vols. (Chicago: University of Chicago Press, 1981).

33. Alexis de Tocqueville, *Democracy in America*, 1835–1839, Reprint, eds. J. P. Mayer and Max Lerner (New York: Harper & Row, 1966), p. 102.

34. Russell L. Caplan, *Constitutional Brinkmanship: Amending the Constitution by National Convention* (New York: Oxford University Press, 1988), p. 162.

35. Richard L. Berke, "1789 Amendment Is Ratified but Now the Debate Begins," *New York Times*, 8 May 1992, p. A1.

36. The interpretation debate is fully explored in John H. Garvey and T. Alexander Aleinikoff, *Modern Constitutional Theory: A Reader*, 2d ed. (Minneapolis, Minn.: West Publishing Co., 1991).

37. Jerold L. Waltman, *Political Origins of the U.S. Income Tax* (Jackson: University Press of Mississippi, 1985), p. 10.

Chapter 4 / Federalism / pp. 100–134

1. Rick Bragg, "Louisiana Stands Alone on Drinking at 18," *New York Times*, 23 March 1996, p. 1; "Louisiana Court Upholds Drinking

Age of 21," *New York Times*, 3 July 1996, p. A17.

2. Ronald Reagan, "National Minimum Drinking Age: Remarks on Signing HR4616 into Law (17 July 1984)," *Weekly Compilation of Presidential Documents*, 23 July 1984, p. 1036.

3. *South Dakota* v. *Dole*, 483 U.S. 203 (1987).

4. *Budget of the United States Government*, FY 1997, Table 16-3, p. 266 (Washington, D.C.: U.S. Government Printing Office, 1996).

5. *Manuel* v. *State*, 1996 La. LEXIS 597 (March 8, 1996), revised in *Manuel* v. *State*, 1996 LEXIS 1693 (July 2, 1996).

6. Joe Gyan, Jr., and Doug Myers, "Drinking Age Revived," *The Advocate*, 3 July 1996, p. 1A.

7. Taylor Branch, *Parting the Waters: America in the King Years, 1954–63* (New York: Simon & Schuster, 1988), Chap. 17.

8. Daniel J. Elazar, "Opening the Third Century of American Federalism: Issues and Prospects," *Annals of the American Academy of Political and Social Sciences*, 509 (May 1990), p. 14.

9. William H. Stewart, *Concepts of Federalism* (Lanham, Md.: University Press of America, 1984).

10. Edward Corwin, *The Passing of Dual Federalism*, 36 *University of Virginia Law Review* 4 (1950).

11. See Daniel J. Elazar, *The American Partnership* (Chicago: *University of Chicago Press*, 1962); and Morton Grodzins, *The American System* (Chicago: Rand McNally, 1966).

12. Sam Howe Verhovek, "States Are Already Providing Glimpse at Welfare's Future," *New York Times*, 21 September 1995, p. A1.

13. Martha Derthick, "The Enduring Features of American Federalism," *The Brookings Review*, Summer 1989, p. 35.

14. *South Carolina* v. *Katzenbach*, 383 U.S. 301 (1966).

15. *Miranda* v. *Arizona*, 384 U.S. 436 (1966).

16. *Baker* v. *Carr*, 369 U.S. 186 (1962); *Wesberry* v. *Sanders*, 376 U.S. 1 (1964); and *Reynolds* v. *Sims*, 377 U.S. 533 (1964).

17. Raoul Berger, *Federalism: The Founders' Design* (Norman:

University of Oklahoma Press, 1987), pp. 61–62.

18. *United States* v. *Lopez*, ____ U.S. ____ (1995).

19. *Seminole Tribe of Florida* v. *Florida*, ____ U.S. ____ (1996).

20. Advisory Commission on Intergovernmental Relations, *Characteristics of Federal Grant-in-Aid Programs to State and Local Governments: Grants Funded FY 1993* (Washington, D.C.: U.S. Government Printing Office, 1994), Table 2.

21. *Ibid.*, Table 2, p. 5.

22. *McCulloch* v. *Maryland*, 4 Wheat. 316 (1819).

23. *Dred Scott* v. *Sandford*, 19 How. 393, 426 (1857).

24. James T. Patterson, *The New Deal and the States: Federalism in Transition* (Princeton, N.J.: Princeton University Press, 1969).

25. *United States* v. *Darby*, 312 U.S. 100 (1941).

26. *Brown* v. *Board of Education of Topeka*, 347 U.S. 483 (1954).

27. Aaron Wildavsky, "Bare Bones: Putting Flesh on the Skeleton of American Federalism," in Advisory Commission on Intergovernmental Relations, *The Future of Federalism in the 1980s* (Washington, D.C.: U.S. Government Printing Office, 1981), p. 80.

28. Advisory Commission on Intergovernmental Relations, *The Federal Role in the Federal System: The Dynamics of Growth* (A-86) (Washington, D.C.: U.S. Government Printing Office, 1981), p. 101.

29. Ronald Reagan, "Statement on Signing Executive Order Establishing the Presidential Advisory Committee on Federalism," 1981 Pub. Papers 341, 8 April 1981.

30. *Budget of the United States Government*, FY 1997 Historical Tables (Washington, D.C.: U.S. Government Printing Office, 1996), p. 257.

31. Joseph F. Zimmerman, *Contemporary American Federalism: The Growth of National Power* (New York: Praeger, 1992), Chap. 4.

32. Council of State Governments, *The Book of the States, 1994–95*, Vol. 30 (Lexington, Ky: Council of State Governments, 1994), pp. 580–581.

33. John Abell, "Clinton Says Bush Not Credible on Jobs Creation," *Reuter Library Report* (31 August 1992), NEXIS.

34. "Unfunded Federal Mandates," *Congressional Digest*, March 1995, p. 68.

35. Albert Hunt, "Federalism Debate Is as Much About Power as About Principle," *Wall Street Journal*, 19 January 1995, p. A17.

36. David Rogers, "Republicans' Move to Curb 'Unfunded Mandates' For States, Localities Has Its Own Complications," *Wall Street Journal*, 10 January 1995, p. A22.

37. U.S. Bureau of the Census, *Statistical Abstract of the United States: 1993* (Washington, D.C.: U.S. Government Printing Office, 1993), Table 466, p. 291.

38. Dirk Johnson, "Wisconsin Acts to End Welfare Entirely," *New York Times*, 25 April 1996, p. A26.

39. *Book of the States, 1992–93*, p. 246; *Book of the States, 1994–95*, p. 356.

40. Alice Rivlin, *Reviving the American Dream: The Economy, the States, and the Federal Government* (Washington, D.C.: Brookings Institution, 1992).

41. Michael A. Pagano and Ann O'M. Bowman, "The State of American Federalism, 1992–93" *Publius* 23 (Summer 1993), pp. 1–22.

Chapter 5 / Public Opinion and Political Socialization / pp. 135–171

1. Gallup Organization, *Gallup Poll Monthly*, June 1995, p. 23.

2. Gallup Organization, *Gallup Report*, 280 (January 1989), 27.

3. Warren Weaver, Jr., "Death Penalty a 300-Year Issue in America," *New York Times*, 3 July 1976.

4. *Furman* v. *Georgia*, 408 U.S. 238 (1972).

5. *Gregg* v. *Georgia*, 248 U.S. 153 (1976).

6. "56 Executions This Year Were the Most Since 1957," *New York Times*, 30 December 1995, p. 10.

7. Gallup Organization, *Gallup Monthly Poll* (June 1991), p. 41.

8. *Ibid.*, p. 42.

9. E. Wayne Carp, "If Pollsters Had Been Around During the American Revolution" (letter to the editor), *New York Times*, 17 July 1993, p. 10.

10. Sidney Verba, "The Citizen as

Respondent: Sample Surveys and American Democracy," *American Political Science Review*, 90 (March 1996), p. 3.

11. Nine national surveys taken from 1971 through 1988 found that an average of 61 percent of Americans disapproved of the ruling in *Abington School District* v. *Schempp*, 374 U.S. 203 (1963). See Richard Niemi, John Mueller, and Tom Smith, *Trends in Public Opinion: A Compendium of Survey Data* (New York: Greenwood Press, 1989), p. 263.

12. Jeffrey Schmalz, "Poll Finds an Even Split on Homosexuality's Cause," *New York Times*, 5 March 1993, p. A11.

13. Warren E. Miller and Santa A. Traugott, *American National Election Studies Sourcebook, 1952–1986* (Cambridge, Mass.: Harvard University Press, 1989), pp. 94–95. See Niemi, Mueller, and Smith, *Trends*, p. 19, for later years.

14. Tom W. Smith and Paul B. Sheatsley, "American Attitudes Toward Race Relations," *Public Opinion* 7 (October/November 1984), p. 15.

15. *Ibid.*, p. 83.

16. Steven A. Peterson, *Political Behavior: Patterns in Everyday Life* (Newbury Park, Calif.: Sage, 1990), pp. 28–29. For the importance of early learning for political attitudes, see also Jon A. Krosnick and Duane F. Alwin, "Aging and Susceptibility to Attitude Change," *Journal of Personality and Social Psychology*, 57 (1989), 416–423.

17. Paul Allen Beck, "The Role of Agents in Political Socialization," in *Handbook of Political Socialization Theory and Research*, ed. Stanley Allen Renshon (New York: Free Press, 1977), pp. 117–118.

18. W. Russell Neuman, *The Paradox of Mass Politics: Knowledge and Opinion in the American Electorate* (Cambridge, Mass.: Harvard University Press, 1986), pp. 113–114. See also Richard G. Niemi and Jane Junn, "Civics Courses and the Political Knowledge of High School Seniors," paper prepared for presentation at the annual meeting of the American Political Science Association, Washington, D.C., September 1993. They found that a favorable home environment (for example, having reading and reference material at home) related significantly to factual knowledge in a high school civics test.

19. M. Kent Jennings and Richard G. Niemi, *The Political Character of Adolescence: The Influence of Families and Schools* (Princeton, N.J.: Princeton University Press, 1974), p. 39. See also Stephen E. Frantzich, *Political Parties in the Technological Age* (New York: Longman, 1989), p. 152. Frantzich presents a table showing that more than 60 percent of children in homes in which both parents have the same party preference will adopt that preference. When parents are divided, the children tend to be divided among Democrats, Republicans, and independents.

20. In a panel study of parents and high school seniors in 1965 and in 1973, some years after their graduation, Jennings and Niemi found that 57 percent of children shared their parents' party identification in 1965, but only 47 percent did by 1973. See Jennings and Niemi, *Political Character*, pp. 90–91. See also Robert C. Luskin, John P. McIver, and Edward G. Carmines, "Issues and the Transmission of Partisanship," *American Journal of Political Science* 33 (May 1989), pp. 440–458. They found that children are more likely to shift between partisanship and independence than to "convert" to the other party. When conversion occurs, it is more likely to be based on economic issues than on social issues.

21. Robert D. Hess and Judith V. Torney, *The Development of Political Attitudes in Children* (Chicago: Aldine, 1967). But other researchers disagree. See Jerry L. Yeric and John R. Todd, *Public Opinion: The Visible Politics* (Itasca, Ill.: F. E. Peacock, 1989), pp. 45–47, for a summary of the issues. For a critical evaluation of the early literature on political socialization, see Pamela Johnston Conover, "Political Socialization: Where's the Politics?" in *Political Science: Looking to the Future*, Volume 3: *Political Behavior*, ed. William Crotty (Evanston, Ill.: Northwestern University Press, 1991), pp. 125–152.

22. David Easton and Jack Dennis, *Children in the Political System* (New York: McGraw-Hill, 1969).

23. Jarol B. Manheim, *The Politics Within* (New York: Longman, 1982), pp. 83, 125–151.

24. Richard Niemi and Jane Y. Junn, "Civics Courses and the Political Knowledge of High School Seniors," paper prepared for presentation at the annual meeting of the American Political Science Association, Washington, D.C., September 1993.

25. Edith J. Barrett, "The Political Socialization of Inner-City Adolescents," paper prepared for presentation at the annual meeting of the American Political Science Association, Washington, D.C., September 1993.

26. Janie S. Steckenrider and Neal E. Cutler, "Aging and Adult Political Socialization: The Importance of Roles and Transitions," in *Political Learning in Adulthood: A Sourcebook of Theory and Research*, ed. Roberta S. Sigel (Chicago: University of Chicago Press, 1989), pp. 56–88.

27. See Robert Huckfeldt and John Sprague, "Networks in Context: The Social Flow of Information," *American Political Science Review* 81 (December 1987), 1197–1216. The authors' study of voting in neighborhoods in South Bend, Indiana, found that residents who favored the minority party were acutely aware of their minority status.

28. Theodore M. Newcomb et al., *Persistence and Social Change: Bennington College and Its Students After Twenty-Five Years* (New York: Wiley, 1967); and Duane F. Alwin, Ronald L. Cohen, and Theodore M. Newcomb, *Political Attitudes over the Life Span: The Bennington Women after Fifty Years* (Madison: University of Wisconsin Press, 1991).

29. M. Kent Jennings and Gregory Marcus, "Yuppie Politics," *Institute of Social Research Newsletter*, August 1986.

30. See Roberta S. Sigel, ed., *Political Learning in Adulthood: A Sourcebook of Theory and Research* (Chicago: University of Chicago Press, 1989).

31. Times Mirror Center for the People

& the Press, *The New Political Landscape* (Washington, D.C.: 1994), p. 144; The Pew Center for The People & The Press, News Release, 29 February 1996, p. 28.

32. The wording of this question is criticized by R. Michael Alvarez and John Brehm in "When Core Beliefs Collide: Conflict, Complexity, or Just Plain Confusion?" a paper prepared for delivery at the annual meeting of the American Political Science Association, Washington, D.C., September 1993, p. 9. They argue that using the phrase "personal choice" (which they call a core value) triggers the psychological effect of reactance, or the feeling that a freedom has been removed. But this core value is precisely our focus in this analysis. Alvarez and Brehm favor using instead the battery of six questions on abortion that have been used in the General Social Survey. Those six questions are also used in Elizabeth Adell Cook, Ted G. Jelen, and Clyde Wilcox, *Between Two Absolutes: Public Opinion and the Politics of Abortion* (Boulder, Colo.: Westview, 1992). Those interested primarily in analyzing various attitudes toward abortion probably should use data from the General Social Survey.

33. Although some people view the politics of abortion as "single issue" politics, the issue has broader political significance. In their book on the subject, Cook, Jelen, and Wilcox say, "Although embryonic life is one important value in the abortion debate, it is not the only value at stake." They contend that the politics is tied to alternative sexual relationships and traditional roles of women in the home, which are "social order" issues. See *Between Two Absolutes*, pp. 8–9.

34. *Ibid.*, p. 50.

35. The increasing wealth in industrialized societies may or may not be replacing class conflict with conflict over values. See the exchange between Ronald Inglehart and Scott C. Flanagan, "Value Change in Industrial Societies," *American Political Science Review* 81 (December 1987), pp. 1289–1319.

36. Nathan Glazer, "The Structure of Ethnicity," *Public Opinion* 7 (October/November 1984), p. 4.

37. For a review of these studies, see Robert S. Erikson, Norman R. Luttbeg, and Kent L. Tedin, *American Public Opinion*, 3d ed. (New York: Macmillan, 1988).

38. Felicity Barringer, "Census Shows Profound Change in Racial Makeup of the Nation," *New York Times*, 11 March 1991, pp. 1, 12. See also Steven A. Holmes, "Census Sees a Profound Ethnic Shift in U.S.," *New York Times*, 14 March 1996, p. A8.

39. Glazer, "Structure of Ethnicity," p. 5.

40. National Election Study for 1994, an election survey conducted by the Center for Political Studies at the University of Michigan.

41. See David C. Leege and Lyman A. Kellstedt, eds., *Rediscovering the Religious Factor in American Politics* (Armonk, N.Y.: M. E. Sharpe, 1993) for a comprehensive examination of religion in political life that goes far beyond the analysis here.

42. "The Diminishing Divide . . . American Churches, American Politics," news release, 25 June 1996 (Washington, D.C.: Pew Research Center for the People & the Press), pp. 1 and 12. See also Lyman A. Kellstedt, "Religion, the Neglected Variable: An Agenda for Future Research on Religion and Political Behavior," in Leege and Kellstedt, *Rediscovering the Religious Factor*, p. 273.

43. John Robinson, "The Ups and Downs and Ins and Outs of Ideology," *Public Opinion* 7 (February/March 1984), p. 12.

44. For a more positive interpretation of ideological attitudes within the public, see William G. Jacoby, "The Structure of Ideological Thinking in the American Electorate," paper presented at the Annual Meeting of the American Political Science Association, Washington, D.C., September 1993. Jacoby applies a new method to survey data for the 1984 and 1988 elections and concludes "that there is a systematic, cumulative structure underlying liberal-conservative thinking in the American public" (p. 1).

45. Angus Campbell, Philip E. Converse, Warren E. Miller, and Donald E. Stokes, *The American Voter* (New York: Wiley, 1960), Chap. 10.

46. Neuman, *Paradox*, pp. 19–20.

47. Arthur Sanders, "Ideological Symbols," *American Politics Quarterly* 17 (July 1989), p. 235.

48. See Norman H. Nie, Sidney Verba, and John R. Petrocik, *The Changing American Voter*, 2d ed. (Cambridge, Mass.: Harvard University Press, 1979), Chap. 7.

49. Some scholars believe that the methods previously used for classifying respondents as ideologues were too generous. See Robert C. Luskin, "Measuring Political Sophistication," *American Journal of Political Science* 31 (November 1987), pp. 878, 887–888. For a comprehensive critique, see Eric R. A. N. Smith, *The Unchanging American Voter* (Berkeley: University of California Press, 1989), especially Chap. 1.

50. See William G. Jacoby, "Levels of Conceptualization and Reliance on the Liberal-Conservative Continuum," *Journal of Politics* 48 (May 1986), pp. 423–432. We also know that certain political actors, such as delegates to national party conventions, hold far more consistent and durable beliefs than the public. See M. Kent Jennings, "Ideological Thinking Among Mass Publics and Political Elites," *Public Opinion Quarterly* 56 (Winter 1992), pp. 419–441.

51. National Election Study, 1992.

52. However, citizens can have ideologically consistent attitudes toward candidates and perceptions about domestic issues without thinking about politics in explicitly liberal and conservative terms. See William G. Jacoby, "The Structure of Liberal-Conservative Thinking in the American Public," paper prepared for presentation at the annual meeting of the Midwest Political Science Association, 1990.

53. Pamela Johnston Conover, "The Origins and Meaning of Liberal-Conservative Self-identifications," *American Journal of Political Science* 25 (November 1981), pp. 621–622, 643.

54. A relationship between liberalism and political tolerance was found by John L. Sullivan et al., "The Sources of Political Tolerance: A Multivariate Analysis," *American Political Science Review* 75 (March

1981), p. 102. See also Robinson, "Ups and Downs," pp. 13–15.

55. Herbert Asher, *Presidential Elections and American Politics* (Homewood, Ill.: Dorsey, 1980), pp. 14–20. Asher also constructs a two-dimensional framework, distinguishing between "traditional New Deal" issues and "new lifestyle" issues.

56. John E. Jackson, "The Systematic Beliefs of the Mass Public: Estimating Policy Preferences with Survey Data," *Journal of Politics* 45 (November 1983), pp. 840–865.

57. Milton Rokeach also proposed a two-dimensional model of political ideology grounded in the terminal values of freedom and equality. See *The Nature of Human Values* (New York: Free Press, 1973), especially Chap. 6. Rokeach found that positive and negative references to the two values permeate the writings of socialists, communists, fascists, and conservatives and clearly differentiate the four bodies of writing from one another (pp. 173–174). However, Rokeach built his two-dimensional model around only the values of freedom and equality; he did not deal with the question of freedom versus order.

58. William S. Maddox and Stuart A. Lilie, *Beyond Liberal and Conservative: Reassessing the Political Spectrum* (Washington, D.C.: Cato Institute, 1984), p. 68. From 1993 to 1996, the Gallup Organization, in conjunction with CNN and *USA Today*, has asked national samples two questions: (1) whether individuals or government should solve our country's problems, and (2) whether the government should promote traditional values. Gallup constructed a similar ideological typology from responses to these questions and found a similar distribution of the population into four groups. See Gallup's "Final Top Line" for 12–15 January 1996, pp. 30–31.

59. See Neuman, *Paradox*, p. 81. See also Aaron Wildavsky, "Choosing Preferences by Constructing Institutions: A Cultural Theory of Preference Formation," *American Political Science Review* 81 (March 1987), p. 13.

60. The same conclusion was reached in a major study of British voting behavior. See Hilde T. Himmelweit, et al., *How Voters Decide* (New York: Academic Press, 1981), pp. 138–141. See also Wildavsky, "Choosing Preferences," p. 13.

61. In our framework, opposition to abortion is classified as a communitarian position. However, the Communitarian movement led by Amitai Etzioni adopted no position on abortion. (Personal communication from Vanessa Hoffman by e-mail, in reply to my query of 5 February 1996.)

62. But a significant literature is developing on the limitations of self-interest in explaining political life. See Jane J. Mansbridge, ed., *Beyond Self-interest* (Chicago: University of Chicago Press, 1990).

63. Wildavsky, "Choosing Preferences," pp. 3–21.

64. David O. Sears and Carolyn L. Funk, "Self-interest in Americans' Political Opinions," in Mansbridge, *Beyond Self-interest*, pp. 147–170.

65. Two researchers who compared the public's knowledge on various topics in 1989 with its knowledge of the same topics in the 1940s and 1950s found similar levels of knowledge across the years. They point out, however, "That knowledge has been stable during a period of rapid changes in education, communication, and the public role of women seems paradoxical." They suspect, but cannot demonstrate, that the expected increase in knowledge did not materialize because of a decline in the public's interest in politics over time. See Michael X. Delli Carpini and Scott Keeter, "Stability and Change in the U.S. Public's Knowledge of Politics," *Public Opinion Quarterly* 55 (Winter 1991), p. 607.

66. Richard Morin, "Who's in Control? Many Don't Know or Care," *Washington Post*, 29 January 1996, p. A6.

67. Benjamin I. Page and Robert Y. Shapiro, *The Rational Public* (Chicago: University of Chicago Press, 1992).

68. *Ibid.*, p. 45.

69. *Ibid.*, p. 385. The argument for a rational quality in public opinion by Page and Shapiro was supported by Stimson's massive analysis of swings in the liberal-conservative attitudes of the U.S. public from 1956 to 1990. Analyzing more than one thousand attitude items, he found that the public mood had already swung away from liberalism when Ronald Reagan appeared on the scene to campaign for president as a conservative. See James A. Stimson, *Public Opinion in America: Moods, Cycles, & Swings* (Boulder, Colo.: Westview, 1992).

70. See R. Michael Alvarez and John Brehm, "When Core Beliefs Collide"; and Scott L. Althaus, "Opinion Polls, Information Effects, and Political Equality: Exploring Ideological Biases in Collective Opinion," *Political Communication*, 13 (January-March 1996), pp. 3–21.

71. Michael X. Delli Carpini and Scott Keeter, *What Americans Know About Politics and Why It Matters* (New Haven, Conn.: Yale University Press, 1996).

72. *Ibid.*, p. 269.

73. *Ibid.*, p. 271.

74. There is evidence that the educational system and parental practices hamper the ability of women to develop their political knowledge. See Linda L. M. Bennett and Stephen Earl Bennett, "Enduring Gender Differences in Political Interests," *American Politics Quarterly* 17 (January 1989), pp. 105–122.

75. Neuman, *Paradox*, p. 81.

76. Pamela Johnston Conover and Stanley Feldman, "How People Organize the Political World: A Schematic Model," *American Journal of Political Science* 28 (February 1984), p. 96. For an excellent review of schema structures in contemporary psychology—especially as they relate to political science—see Reid Hastic, "A Primer of Information-Processing Theory for the Political Scientist," in *Political Cognition*, ed. Richard R. Lau and David O. Sears (Hillsdale, N.J.: Erlbaum, 1986), pp. 11–39.

77. John Hurwitz and Mark Peffley, "How Are Foreign Policy Attitudes Structured? A Hierarchical Model," *American Political Science Review* 81 (December 1987), pp. 1099–1220.

78. Richard L. Allen, Michael C. Dawson, and Ronald E. Brown, "A Schema-Based Approach to Modeling an African-American

Racial Belief System," *American Political Science Review* 83 (June 1989), pp. 421–441.

79. See Milton Lodge and Ruth Hamill, "A Partisan Schema for Political Information Processing," *American Political Science Review* 80 (June 1986), pp. 505–519.

80. Arthur Sanders, *Making Sense Out of Politics* (Ames: Iowa State University Press, 1990).

81. Lee Sigelman, "Disarming the Opposition: The President, the Public, and the INF Treaty," *Public Opinion Quarterly* 54 (Spring 1990), p. 46.

82. Benjamin I. Page, Robert Y. Shapiro, and Glenn R. Dempsey, "What Moves Public Opinion?" *American Political Science Review* 81 (March 1987), pp. 23–43.

83. Michael Margolis and Gary A. Mauser, *Manipulating Public Opinion: Essays on Public Opinion as a Dependent Variable* (Pacific Grove, Calif.: Brooks/Cole, 1989).

Chapter 6 / The Media / pp. 172–209

1. Michael Elliott, "The Making of a Fiasco," *Newsweek*, 18 October 1993, p. 34.

2. Lee Michael Katz, "Graphic Photos from Somalia Gave 'Urgency,'" *USA Today* (International), 14 October 1993, p. 7a.

3. Chris Hedges, "Iranians, Marking 1979 Crisis, Denounce U.S.," *New York Times*, 5 November 1993, p. A4.

4. Kenneth Janda was able to watch all these programs when he was in Budapest as a Fulbright scholar in 1993 and 1994.

5. A man who shot a state trooper in Austin, Texas, in 1992 blamed his action on antipolice rap music from a Shakur album he was listening to before he was stopped by the trooper. See "Rap Music Blamed in Trooper's Killing," *Chicago Tribune*, 3 June 1993, p. 13.

6. S. N. D. North, *The Newspaper and Periodical Press* (Washington, D.C.: U.S. Government Printing Office, 1884), p. 27. This source provides much of the information reported here about newspapers and magazines before 1880.

7. John Schmeltzer, "Iowa Towns Deliver Twice the News," *Chicago Tribune*, 1 April 1993, Section 3, p. 1.

8. In 1950, a total of 1,772 daily papers had a circulation of 53.8 million; in 1993, a total of 1,556 papers had a circulation of 59.8 million. The number of newspapers per capita was 0.35 in 1950 and 0.23 in 1993. See Harold W. Stanley and Richard G. Niemi (eds.), *Vital Statistics on American Politics*, 5th ed. (Washington, D.C.: Congressional Quarterly Press, 1995), p. 50.

9. Tim Jones, "Newspaper Circulation Maintains Downward Trend," *Chicago Tribune*, 30 April 1996, Section 3, p. 1.

10. Benjamin I. Page, *Who Deliberates?: Mass Media in Modern Democracy* (Chicago: University of Chicago Press, 1996), p. 106.

11. Douglas Kellner, *Television and the Crisis of Democracy* (Boulder, Colo.: Westview Press, 1990), pp. 225–248.

12. Howard Kurtz, *Hot Air: All Talk, All the Time* (New York: Times Books, 1996). See also Michael Traugott, et al., "The Impact of Talk Radio on Its Audience," paper prepared for presentation at the annual meeting of the Midwest Political Science Association, Chicago, 1996. This study demonstrates that listening to talk radio increases people's attention to political news.

13. Dana R. Ulloth, Peter L. Klinge, and Sandra Eells, *Mass Media: Past, Present, Future* (St. Paul, Minn.: West, 1983), p. 278.

14. Daily fax assaults against the Clinton campaign in the 1992 election season are discussed in Jacob Weisberg, "True Fax: Mary Matalin, Vindicated," *New Republic*, 5 June 1993, pp. 11–12.

15. Robin Wright, "Hyper Democracy: Washington Isn't Dangerously Disconnected from the People; the Trouble May Be It's Too Plugged In," *Time*, 23 January 1995, pp. 14–31.

16. Rich Lowry, "Fax Populi: Armed with Computers and Fax Machines, Grass-Roots Organizations Are Shaking Up the Liberal Establishment," *National Review*, 7 November 1994, pp. 50–54. *Fax Congress Now* is a computer program designed to facilitate faxing government officials; see *Macworld*, May 1995, p. 48. The percentage of homes with fax machines comes from Steve Lohr, "The Great

Unplugged Masses Confront the Future," *New York Times*, 21 January 1996, Section 4, p. 1.

17. Fittingly, this history of the Internet came from the Discovery Channel Online Web site at <www.discovery.com/DCO/doc/1012/world/technology/internet/inet1.5.html>.

18. John December, Neil Randall, and Wes Tatters, *Discover the World Wide Web with Your Sportster* (Indianapolis, Ind.: Sams.net Publishing, 1995), pp. 11–12.

19. Bill Mann, *Politics on the Net* (Indianapolis, Ind.: Que Corporation, 1995).

20. Pew Research Center for The People & The Press, "TV News Viewership Declines," press release, 13 May 1996. National survey of 1,751 adults during 19–25 April 1996.

21. Steve Lohr, "European TV's Vast Growth: Cultural Effect Stirs Concern," *New York Times*, 16 March 1989, p. 1.

22. Roper Organization, *Trends in Attitudes Toward Television and Other Media* (New York: Television Information Office, 1983), p. 8.

23. U.S. Bureau of the Census, *Statistical Abstract of the United States, 1982–1983* (Washington, D.C.: U.S. Government Printing Office, 1984), p. 562.

24. Doris A. Graber, *Mass Media and American Politics* (Washington, D.C.: Congressional Quarterly Press, 1984), pp. 78–79. See also W. Lance Bennett, *News: The Politics of Illusion*, 3d ed. (White Plains, N.Y.: Longman, 1996), Chap. 2.

25. Kenneth R. Clark, "Network Audience Share at Record Low," *Chicago Tribune*, 30 November 1990, section 3, p. 1.

26. *Editor & Publisher International Yearbook* (New York: Editor & Publisher Company, 1996).

27. Christopher H. Sterling, *Electronic Media: A Guide to Trends in Broadcasting and Newer Technologies, 1920–1983* (New York: Praeger, 1984), p. 22.

28. Steven Lipin and Elizabeth Jensen, "Westinghouse, Infinity Deal Sets Stage For Other Radio Groups Seeking Mergers," *Wall Street Journal*, 21 June 1996, p. A3.

29. Joseph Turow, *Media Industries: The Production of News and Entertainment* (New York:

Longman, 1984), p. 18. Our discussion of government regulation draws heavily on this source.

30. Rep. Edward J. Markey (D.-Mass.), quoted in Dan Carney, "Congress Fires Its First Shot in Information Revolution," *CQ Weekly Report*, 3 February 1996, p. 289.

31. "Likely Mergers Herald an Era of Megacarriers," *Wall Street Journal*, 2 February 1996, p. B1.

32. *Ibid.*

33. Mark Crispin Miller, "Free the Media," *The Nation*, 3 June 1996, pp. 9–15.

34. Jared Sandberg, "Federal Judges Block Censorship on the Internet," *Wall Street Journal*, 13 June 1996, p. B1.

35. Graber, *Mass Media*, p. 110.

36. Robert Entman, *Democracy Without Citizens: Media and the Decay of American Politics* (New York: Oxford University Press, 1989), pp. 103–108.

37. S. Robert Lichter and Richard E. Noyes, *Good Intentions Make Bad News* (Lanham, Md.: Rowman & Littlefield, 1995), p. 26, note 9.

38. Michael Nelson (ed.), *Guide to the Presidency* (Washington, D.C.: Congressional Quarterly Press, 1989), p. 729.

39. *Ibid.*, p. 735.

40. Graber, *Mass Media*, p. 241.

41. Warren Weaver, "C-Span on the Hill: 10 Years of Gavel to Gavel," *New York Times*, 28 March 1989, p. 10; and Francis X. Clines, "C-Span Inventor Offers More Politics Up Close," *New York Times*, 31 March 1996, p. 11.

42. Bennett, *News: The Politics of Illusion*, p. 26.

43. Austin Ranney, *Channels of Power: The Impact of Television on American Politics* (New York: Basic Books, 1983), p. 46.

44. Doris A. Graber, *Mass Media and American Politics*, 3d ed. (Washington, D.C.: Congressional Quarterly Press, 1989), p. 237. See also Janet Hook, "Most of Us Don't Have a Clue About How Congress Works," *Chicago Tribune*, 10 June 1993, section 1, p. 17.

45. Gregory Katz, "Issues Distant Second to 'Horse-Race' Stories," *USA Today*, 22 April 1988, p. 6A.

46. Twentieth Century Fund, *1–800 PRESIDENT: The Report of the Twentieth Century Fund Task Force on Television and the Campaign of 1992* (New York: Twentieth Century Fund Press, 1993), p. 5.

47. "America's Watching: Public Attitudes Toward Television," pamphlet published in New York by the Network Television Association and the National Association of Broadcasters, 1995, pp. 17–18.

48. Pew Research Center for the People and the Press, "TV News Viewership Declines," press release, 13 May 1996, p. 1.

49. Times-Mirror Center for the People and the Press, "The American Media," 15 July 1990.

50. This fits with findings by Stephen Earl Bennett in "Trends in Americans' Political Information, 1967–1987," *American Politics Quarterly* 17 (October 1989), pp. 422–435. Bennett found that race was significantly related to level of political information in a 1967 survey but not in a 1987 survey.

51. Linda L. M. Bennett and Stephen Earl Bennett, "Enduring Gender Differences in Political Interests," *American Politics Quarterly* 17 (January 1989), pp. 105–122, especially pp. 116–117.

52. Times-Mirror Center for the People and the Press, press release, "The Generations Divide," 8 July 1992, p. 80.

53. One seasoned journalist argues instead that the technology of mini-cams and satellites has set back the quality of news coverage. Now a television crew can fly to the scene of a crisis and immediately televise information without knowing much about the local politics or culture, which was not true of the old foreign correspondents. See David R. Gergen, "Diplomacy in a Television Age: The Dangers of Teledemocracy," in *The Media and Foreign Policy*, ed. Simon Serfaty (New York: St. Martin's Press, 1990), p. 51.

54. Bennett, "Trends in Americans' Political Information." Bennett's findings are supported by a national poll in 1990 that found only 40 percent of the sample had read a newspaper "yesterday," compared with 71 percent in 1965. Times-Mirror Center for the People and the Press, "The American Media," p. 100. Two researchers who compared the public's level of knowledge in 1989 with answers to the same questions in the 1940s and 1950s found similar levels of knowledge across the years but added, "That knowledge has been stable during a period of rapid changes in education, communication, and the public role of women seems paradoxical." They suspect, but cannot demonstrate, that the lack of expected increase is because of a decline in political interest over time. See Michael X. Delli Carpini and Scott Keeter, "Stability and Change in the U.S. Public's Knowledge of Politics," *Public Opinion Quarterly* 55 (Winter 1991), pp. 583–612.

55. W. Russell Neuman, Marion R. Just, and Ann N. Crigler, *Common Knowledge: News and the Construction of Political Meaning* (Chicago: University of Chicago Press, 1992), p. 10.

56. Doris A. Graber, *Processing the News: How People Tame the Information Tide*, 2d ed. (New York: Longman, 1988), pp. 166–169.

57. Neuman, Just, and Crigler, *News and the Contruction of Political Meaning.*

58. *Ibid.*, pp. 86–87.

59. *Ibid.*, pp. 106–107.

60. *Ibid.*, p. 113.

61. Laurence Parisot, "Attitudes About the Media: A Five-Country Comparison," *Public Opinion* 10 (January/February 1988), p. 60.

62. The statistical difficulties in determining media effects owing to measurement error are discussed in Larry M. Bartels, "Messages Received: The Political Impact of Media Exposure," paper prepared for delivery at the annual meeting of the American Political Science Association, Washington, D.C., September 1993. According to Bartels, "More direct and convincing demonstrations of significant opinion changes due to media exposure will require data collections spanning considerably longer periods of time" (p. 27).

63. A poll of 357 viewers reported in *USA Today*, 10 November 1993.

64. Benjamin I. Page, Robert Y. Shapiro, and Glenn R. Dempsey, "What Moves Public Opinion?" *American Political Science Review* 81 (March 1987), p. 31.

65. Donald L. Jordan, "Newspaper Effects on Policy Preferences," *Public Opinion Quarterly* 57 (Summer 1993), pp. 191–204. Interestingly, Bartels's study of media effects in the 1980 presidential election, which used very different methodology, found that "the average impact of newspaper exposure across a wide range of candidate and issue perceptions was only about half as large as the corresponding impact of television news exposure" (Bartels, "Messages Received," p. 26).

66. Shanto Iyengar and Donald R. Kinder, *News That Matters: Television and American Opinion* (Chicago: University of Chicago Press, 1987), p. 33.

67. *Ibid.*, p. 60.

68. Herbert Jacob, *The Frustration of Policy: Responses to Crime by American Cities* (Boston: Little, Brown, 1984), pp. 47–50.

69. Sam Vincent Meddis, "Crime's No Worse, But USA's Fear Grows," *USA Today International*, 28 October 1993, p. 1. See also Jeffrey D. Alderman, "Leading the Public: The Media's Focus on Crime Shaped Sentiment," *Public Perspective* 5 (March/April 1994), pp. 26–27.

70. W. Russell Neuman, "The Threshold of Public Attention," *Public Opinion Quarterly* 54 (Summer 1990), pp. 159–176.

71. David E. Harrington, "Economic News on Television: The Determinants of Coverage," *Public Opinion Quarterly* 53 (Spring 1989), pp. 17–40.

72. Entman, *Democracy Without Citizens*, p. 86.

73. *Ibid.*, pp. 47–48.

74. A panel study of ten- to seventeen-year-olds during the 1988 presidential campaign found that the campaign helped these young people crystallize their party identifications and their attitudes toward the candidates but had little effect on their political ideology and views on central campaign issues. See David O. Sears, Nicholas A. Valentino, and Rick Kosterman, "Domain Specificity in the Effects of Political Events on Preadult Socialization," paper prepared for delivery at the annual meeting of the American Political Science Association, Washington, D.C., September 1993.

75. Richard Zoglin, "Is TV Ruining Our Children?" *Time*, 5 October 1990, p. 75. Moreover, much of what children see are advertisements. See "Study: Almost 20% of Kid TV Is Ad-Related," *Chicago Tribune*, 22 April 1991, p. 11.

76. John J. O'Connor, "Soothing Bromides? Not on TV," *New York Times*, 28 October 1990, Arts & Leisure section, pp. 1, 35.

77. Douglas Kellner, *Television and the Crisis of Democracy* (Boulder, Colo.: Westview Press, 1990), p. 17.

78. James Fallows, *Breaking the News: How the Media Undermine American Democracy* (New York: Pantheon Books, 1996).

79. For analysis of elections from 1964 to 1976, see S. Robert Lichter and Stanley Rothman, "Media and Business Elites," *Public Opinion* 5 (October/November 1981), pp. 42–46. For a study of the 1980 election, see L. Brent Bozell II and Brent H. Baker (eds.), *And That's the Way It Isn't* (Alexandria, Va.: Media Research Center, 1990), p. 32.

80. "Journalism Heavy with Democrats," *Chicago Tribune*, 18 November 1992, section 1, p. 14.

81. Elizabeth Kolbert, "For Bush, More TV News Is Also Good News," *New York Times*, 22 September 1992, p. 1.

82. Elizabeth Kolbert, "Maybe the Media DID Treat Bush a Bit Harshly," *New York Times*, 22 November 1992, p. 3E.

83. "Press Coverage of the 1992 Campaign," *American Enterprise* (May/June 1993), p. 95. Thomas E. Patterson found that European journalists were more likely to be partisan in their work than American journalists. See his "New Decisions: Journalists as Partisan Actors," paper prepared for delivery at the 1995 annual meeting of the Midwest Political Science Association, p. 19.

84. *The People, The Press, & Their Leaders* (Washington, D.C.: Times-Mirror Center for the People and the Press, 1995).

85. Stanley and Niemi, *Vital Statistics on American Politics*, p. 73.

86. *Editor & Publisher*, 24 October 1992, and 7 November 1992.

87. Michael Robinson and Margaret Sheehan, *Over the Wire and on TV: CBS and UPI in Campaign '80* (New York: Russell Sage Foundation, 1983).

88. Michael J. Robinson, "The Media in Campaign '84: Part II; Wingless, Toothless, and Hopeless," *Public Opinion* 8 (February/March 1985), p. 48.

89. Maura Clancey and Michael J. Robinson, "General Election Coverage: Part I," *Public Opinion* 7 (December/January 1985), p. 54.

90. Lichter and Noyes, *Good Intentions Make Bad News*, p. 214.

91. *The People, The Press, & Their Leaders*, p. 12.

92. Stanley Rothman and S. Robert Lichter, "Elite Ideology and Risk Perception in Nuclear Energy Policy," *American Political Science Review* 81 (June 1987), p. 393.

93. For a historical account of efforts to determine voters' preferences before modern polling, see Tom W. Smith, "The First Straw? A Study of the Origin of Election Polls," *Public Opinion Polling* 54 (Spring 1990), pp. 21–36. See also Chapter 4 in Susan Herbst, *Numbered Voices: How Opinion Polling Has Shaped American Politics* (Chicago: University of Chicago Press, 1993).

94. Philip Meyer, "The Media Reformation: Giving the Agenda Back to the People," in *The Elections of 1992*, ed. Michael Nelson (Washington, D.C.: Congressional Quarterly Press, 1993), p. 102.

95. Michael W. Traugott, "Public Attitudes About News Organizations, Campaign Coverage, and Polls," in *Polling and Presidential Election Coverage*, p. 135.

96. Schneider and Lewis, "Views on the News," p. 11. For similar findings from a 1994 study, see Times-Mirror Center for the People and the Press, "Mixed Message about Press Freedom on Both Sides of the Atlantic," press release of 16 March 1994, p. 65. See also Patterson, "News Decisions," p. 21.

97. Times-Mirror Center for the People & the Press, "The People, the Press and the War in the Gulf," 31 January 1991, p. 1.

98. Times-Mirror Center for the People & the Press, "Mixed Message," p. 65.

99. "7 Arrested for Lying About Objects in Pepsi's," *Chicago Tribune,* 18 June 1993, p. 3; and Charles M. Madigan, "Canned Hoax: The Media and the Pepsi Scare," *Chicago Tribune,* 20 June 1993, section 4, p. 1.

Chapter 7 / Participation and Voting / pp. 210–245

1. V. Dion Haynes, "'Normal' Folks Held in Arizona Militia Plot," *Chicago Tribune,* 4 July 1996, p. 1.
2. Patricia King, "'Vipers' in the 'Burbs," *Newsweek,* 15 July 1996, p. 23.
3. Haynes, p. 1.
4. This information is taken from the Link section of "The Militia Watchdog" at <www.greyware. com/authors/pitman/militia.htm>, updated June 16, 1996.
5. Cited in "Minuteman Press Online," obtained at <www.afn.org/ ~mpress/page1.html> on July 6, 1996. The "Restoring America" militia site can be found at <www.techmgmt.com/restore/ restore.html>.
6. Lester W. Milbrath and M. L. Goel, *Political Participation* (Chicago: Rand McNally, 1977), p. 2.
7. See Sidney Verba, Kay Lehman Scholozman, and Henry E. Brady, *Voice and Equality: Civic Voluntarism in American Politics* (Cambridge, Mass.: Harvard University Press, 1995), pp. 40–42. In a highly publicized article, Robert D. Putnam argued that participation in politics in the United States has suffered because our nation is losing the "social capital" that is based on active participation in community life. For example, Americans are "bowling alone"—that is, they are still bowling, but not in organized leagues. See his "Bowling Alone: America's Declining Social Capital," *Journal of Democracy,* 6 (January 1995), pp. 65–78. Putnam's analysis inspired related critical observations on contemporary society, but it also sparked criticism of his data and his argument. For an empirical rebuttal, see Everett C. Ladd, "The Data Just Don't Show Erosion of America's 'Social Capital,' " *Public Perspective,* 7 (June–July 1996), pp. 1, 5–22.
8. Michael Lipsky, "Protest as a Political Resource," *American Political Science Review* 62 (December 1968), p. 1145.
9. William E. Schmidt, "Selma Marchers Mark 1965 Clash," *New York Times,* 4 March 1985.
10. See Sidney Verba and Norman H. Nie, *Participation in America: Political Democracy and Social Equality* (New York: Harper & Row, 1972), p. 3.
11. Russell J. Dalton, *Citizen Politics,* 2d ed. (Chatham, N.J.: Chatham House, 1996).
12. Jonathan D. Casper, *Politics of Civil Liberties* (New York: Harper & Row, 1972), p. 90.
13. David C. Colby, "A Test of the Relative Efficacy of Political Tactics," *American Journal of Political Science* 26 (November 1982), pp. 741–753. See also Frances Fox Piven and Richard Cloward, *Poor People's Movements* (New York: Vintage, 1979).
14. Stephen C. Craig and Michael A. Magiotto, "Political Discontent and Political Action," *Journal of Politics* 43 (May 1981), pp. 514–522. But see Mitchell A. Seligson, "Trust Efficacy and Modes of Political Participation: A Study of Costa Rican Peasants," *British Journal of Political Science* 10 (January 1980), pp. 75–98, for a review of studies that came to different conclusions.
15. Philip H. Pollock III, "Organizations as Agents of Mobilization: How Does Group Activity Affect Political Participation?" *American Journal of Political Science* 26 (August 1982), pp. 485–503. Also see Jan E. Leighley, "Social Interaction and Contextual Influence on Political Participation," *American Politics Quarterly* 18 (October 1990), pp. 459–475.
16. Arthur H. Miller et al., "Group Consciousness and Political Participation," *American Journal of Political Science* 25 (August 1981), p. 495. See also Susan J. Carroll, "Gender Politics and the Socializing Impact of the Women's Movement," in *Political Learning in Adulthood: A Sourcebook of Theory and Research,* ed. Roberta S. Sigel (Chicago: University of Chicago Press, 1989), p. 307.
17. Richard D. Shingles, "Black Consciousness and Political Participation: The Missing Link," *American Political Science Review* 75 (March 1981), pp. 76–91. See also Lawrence Bobo and Franklin D. Gilliam, Jr., "Race, Sociopolitical Participation, and Black Empowerment," *American Political Science Review* 84 (June 1990), pp. 377–393; and Jan Leighley, "Group Membership and the Mobilization of Political Participation," *Journal of Politics,* 58 (May 1996), pp. 447–463.
18. Dalton, *Citizen Politics,* p. 65.
19. M. Kent Jennings, Jan W. van Deth, et al., *Continuities in Political Action: A Longitudinal Study of Political Orientations in Three Western Democracies* (New York: Walter de Gruyter, 1990).
20. See James L. Gibson, "The Policy Consequences of Political Intolerance: Political Repression During the Vietnam War Era," *Journal of Politics* 51 (February 1989), pp. 13–35. Gibson found that individual state legislatures reacted quite differently in response to antiwar demonstrations on college campuses, but the laws passed to discourage dissent were not related directly to public opinion within the state.
21. See Verba and Nie, *Participation in America,* p. 69. Also see John Clayton Thomas, "Citizen-Initiated Contacts with Government Agencies: A Test of Three Theories," *American Journal of Political Science* 26 (August 1982), pp. 504–522; and Elaine B. Sharp, "Citizen-Initiated Contacting of Government Officials and Socioeconomic Status: Determining the Relationship and Accounting for It," *American Political Science Review* 76 (March 1982), pp. 109–115.
22. Elaine B. Sharp, "Citizen Demand Making in the Urban Context," *American Journal of Political Science* 28 (November 1984), pp. 654–670, especially pp. 654 and 665.
23. Jane Fritsch, "Democrats as Well as G.O.P. Profit from Tobacco," *New York Times,* 6 July 1996, p. 1.
24. Verba and Nie, *Participation in America,* p. 67; and Sharp, "Citizen Demand Making," p. 660.
25. See Joel B. Grossman et al., "Dimensions of Institutional Participation: Who Uses the Courts and How?" *Journal of Politics* 44 (February 1982), pp. 86–114; and

Frances Kahn Zemans, "Legal Mobilization: The Neglected Role of the Law in the Political System," *American Political Science Review* 77 (September 1983), pp. 690–703.

26. *Brown* v. *Board of Education*, 347 U.S. 483 (1954).

27. Max Kaase and Alan Marsh, "Political Action: A Theoretical Perspective," in Samuel H. Barnes and Max Kaase (eds.), *Political Action: Mass Participation in Five Western Democracies* (Beverly Hills, Calif.: Sage Publications, 1979), p. 168.

28. *Smith* v. *Allwright*, 321 U.S. 649 (1944).

29. *Harper* v. *Virginia State Board of Elections*, 383 U.S. 663 (1966).

30. Everett Carll Ladd, *The American Polity* (New York: W. W. Norton, 1985), p. 392.

31. Gorton Carruth and associates, eds., *The Encyclopedia of American Facts and Dates* (New York: Crowell, 1979), p. 330. For an eye-opening account of women's contribution to politics before gaining the vote, see Robert J. Dinkin, *Before Equal Suffrage: Women in Partisan Politics from Colonial Times to 1920* (Westport, Conn.: Greenwood Press, 1995).

32. Ivor Crewe, "Electoral Participation," in *Democracy at the Polls: A Comparative Study of Competitive National Elections*, ed. David Butler, Howard R. Penniman, and Austin Ranney (Washington, D.C.: American Enterprise Institute, 1981), pp. 219–223.

33. Thomas E. Cronin, *Direct Democracy: The Politics of Initiative, Referendum, and Recall* (Cambridge, Mass.: Harvard University Press, 1989), p. 127.

34. David B. Magleby, *Direct Legislation: Voting on Ballot Propositions in the United States* (Baltimore: Johns Hopkins University Press, 1984), p. 70.

35. Cronin, *Direct Democracy*, p. 197. David B. Magleby, "Direct Legislation in the American States," in David Butler and Austin Ranney, eds., *Referendums around the World* (Washington, D.C.: American Enterprise Press, 1994), p. 232.

36. Hugh Dellios, "Angry Voters Have Their Say on Crime, Taxes, and More," *Chicago Tribune*, 10

November 1994, p. 10; and Linda Greenhouse, "High Court Blocks Term Limits for Congress in a 5–4 Decision," *New York Times*, 23 May 1995, p. 1.

37. B. Drummond Ayers, Jr., "Californians Pass Measure on Aliens; Courts Bar It," *New York Times*, 10 November 1994, p. B7.

38. Magleby, *Direct Legislation*, p. 59. See also Ernest Tollerson, "In 90's Ritual, Hired Hands Carry Democracy's Petitions," *New York Times*, 9 July 1996, p. 1.

39. "Fears on Economy Doom Environment Issues, Tax Cuts," *Chicago Tribune*, 8 November 1990, Section 1, p. 22.

40. Robert Reinhold, "Complicated Ballot Is Becoming Burden to California Voters," *New York Times*, 24 September 1990, p. 1. Data for 1996 from <www.lao.ca.gov/ prop197.html> found on July 12, 1996.

41. Cronin, *Direct Democracy*, p. x.

42. Cronin, *Direct Democracy*, p. 251.

43. *The Book of the States 1996–97*, vol. 28 (Lexington, Ky.: Council of State Governments, 1996), p. 150.

44. *Chicago Tribune*, 10 March 1985.

45. Crewe, "Electoral Participation," p. 232. Several scholars have successfully explained variations in voting turnout across nations with only a few institutional and contextual variables. (See G. Bingham Powell, Jr., "American Voter Turnout in Comparative Perspective," *American Political Science Review* 80 (March 1986), pp. 17–43; and Robert W. Jackman, "Political Institutions and Voter Turnout in the Industrial Democracies," *American Political Science Review* 81 (June 1987), pp. 405–423.) However, this work has been criticized on methodological grounds and also for failing to successfully explain two deviant cases, the United States and Switzerland, both of which have low voter turnout. (See Wolfgang Hirczy, "Comparative Turnout: Beyond Cross-National Regression Models," paper prepared for presentation at the annual meeting of the American Political Science Association, Chicago, September 1992.)

46. Verba and Nie, *Participation in America*, p. 13.

47. Max Kaase and Alan Marsh, "Distribution of Political Action," in *Political Action*, p. 186. Dalton, *Citizen Politics*, p. 80.

48. Milbrath and Goel, *Political Participation*, pp. 95–96. Dalton, *Citizen Politics*, p. 80.

49. Verba and Nie, *Participation in America*, p. 148. For a concise summary of the effect of age on voting turnout, see Michael M. Gant and Norman R. Luttbeg, *American Electoral Behavior* (Itasca, Ill.: F. E. Peacock, 1991), pp. 103–104.

50. Richard Murray and Arnold Vedlitz, "Race, Socioeconomic Status, and Voting Participation in Large Southern Cities," *Journal of Politics* 39 (November 1977), pp. 1064–1072; and Verba and Nie, *Participation in America*, p. 157. See also Bobo and Gilliam, "Race, Sociopolitical Participation, and Black Empowerment." Their study of 1987 national survey data with a black oversample found that African Americans participated more than whites of comparable socioeconomic status in cities in which the mayor's office was held by an African American.

51. William H. Flanigan and Nancy H. Zingale, *Political Behavior of the American Electorate, 8th ed.* (Washington, D.C.: Congressional Quarterly Press, 1994), pp. 41–43.

52. Ronald B. Rapoport, "The Sex Gap in Political Persuading: Where the 'Structuring Principle' Works," *American Journal of Political Science* 25 (February 1981), pp. 32–48.

53. Bruce C. Straits, "The Social Context of Voter Turnout," *Public Opinion Quarterly* 54 (Spring 1990), pp. 64–73.

54. Sidney Verba, Kay Lehman Scholzman, and Henry E. Brady, *Voice and Equality: Civic Voluntarism in American Politics* (Cambridge, Mass.: Harvard University Press, 1995), p. 433.

55. Obtained on July 11, 1996 from "Rock the Vote" home page at <www.rockthevote.org/and/Rock Vote/INSIDERTV/155/15_5_1.html>.

56. Stephen D. Shaffer, "A Multivariate Explanation of Decreasing Turnout in Presidential Elections, 1960–1976," *American Journal of Political Science* 25 (February 1981),

pp. 68–95; and Paul R. Abramson and John H. Aldrich, "The Decline of Electoral Participation in America," *American Political Science Review* 76 (September 1981), pp. 603–620. However, one scholar argues that this research suffers because it looks only at voters and nonvoters in a single election. When the focus shifts to people who vote sometimes but not at other times, the models do not fit so well. See M. Margaret Conway and John E. Hughes, "Political Mobilization and Patterns of Voter Turnout," paper prepared for delivery at the annual meeting of the American Political Science Association, Washington, D.C., September 1993.

57. Apparently, Richard A. Brody was the first scholar to pose this problem as a puzzle. See his "The Puzzle of Political Participation in America," in Anthony King, ed., *The New American Political System* (Washington, D.C.: American Enterprise Institute, 1978), pp. 287–324. Since then, a sizable literature has attempted to explain the decline in voter turnout in the United States. Some authors have claimed to account for the decline with just a few variables, but their work has been criticized for being too simplistic. See Carol A. Cassel and Robert C. Luskin, "Simple Explanations of Turnout Decline," *American Political Science Review* 82 (December 1988), pp. 1321–1330. They contend that most of the post–1960 decline is still unexplained. If it is any comfort, voter turnout in Western European elections has seen a somewhat milder decline, and scholars have not been very successful at explaining it, either. See Richard S. Flickinger and Donley T. Studlar, "The Disappearing Voters? Exploring Declining Turnout in Western European Elections," *West European Politics* 15 (April 1992), pp. 1–16.

58. Ruy A. Teixeira, *The Disappearing American Voter* (Washington, D.C.: Brookings Institution, 1992), p. 57.

59. Abramson and Aldrich, "Decline of Electoral Participation," p. 519; and Shaffer, "Multivariate Explanation," pp. 78, 90.

60. The negative effect of registration laws on voter turnout is argued in Frances Fox Piven and Richard Cloward, "Government Statistics and Conflicting Explanations of Nonvoting," *PS: Political Science and Politics* 22 (September 1989), pp. 580–588. Their analysis was hotly contested in Stephen Earl Bennett, "The Uses and Abuses of Registration and Turnout Data: An Analysis of Piven and Cloward's Studies of Nonvoting in America," *PS: Political Science and Politics* 23 (June 1990), pp. 166–171. Bennett showed that turnout declined 10 to 13 percent after 1960, despite efforts to remove or lower legal hurdles to registration. For their reply, see Frances Fox Piven and Richard Cloward, "A Reply to Bennett," *PS: Political Science and Politics* 23 (June 1990), pp. 172–173. You can see that reasonable people can disagree on this matter.

61. Mark J. Fenster, "The Impact of Allowing Day of Registration Voting on Turnout in U.S. Elections from 1960 to 1992: A Research Note," *American Politics Quarterly* 22 (January 1994), pp. 74–87.

62. David Glass, Peverill Squire, and Raymond Wolfinger, "Voter Turnout: An International Comparison," *Public Opinion* 6 (December/January 1984), p. 52. Wolfinger says that because of the strong effect of registration on turnout, most rational choice analyses of voting would be better suited to analyzing turnout of only registered voters. See Raymond E. Wolfinger, "The Rational Citizen Faces Election Day," *Public Affairs Report* 6 (November 1992), p. 12.

63. Data from a League of Women Voters Study published on the NBC News Web site at <www.decision96.msn.com/vote/motor.htm> and dated 16 May 96.

64. John Harwood, "In a Surprise for Everyone, Motor-Voter Law Is Providing a Boost for GOP, Not Democrats," *Wall Street Journal*, 11 June 1996, p. A16.

65. Recent research finds that "party contact is clearly a statistically and substantively important factor in predicting and explaining political behavior." See Peter W. Wielhouwer and Brad Lockerbie, "Party Contacting and Political Participation, 1952–1990," paper prepared for delivery at the annual meeting of the American Political Science Association, Chicago, 1992, p. 14. Of course, parties strategically target the groups that they want to see vote in elections. See Peter W. Wielhouwer, "Strategic Canvassing by Political Parties, 1952–1990," *American Review of Politics*, 16 (Fall 1995), pp. 213–238.

66. Steven J. Rosenstone and John Mark Hansen, *Mobilization, Participation, and Democracy in America* (New York: Macmillan Publishing Company, 1993), p. 213.

67. See Robert A. Jackson, "Voter Mobilization in the 1986 Midterm Election," *Journal of Politics* 55 (November 1993), pp. 1081–1099; and Kim Quaile Hill and Jan E. Leighley, "Political Parties and Class Mobilization in Contemporary United States Elections," *American Journal of Political Science*, 40 (August 1996), pp. 787–804.

68. See Charles Krauthammer, "In Praise of Low Voter Turnout," *Time*, 21 May 1990, p. 88. Krauthammer says, "Low voter turnout means that people see politics as quite marginal to their lives, as neither salvation nor ruin. . . . Low voter turnout is a leading indicator of contentment." A major study in 1996 that compared 1,000 likely *non*-voters with 2,300 likely voters found that 24 percent of the non-voters said they "hardly ever" followed public affairs, versus 5 percent of likely voters. See Dwight Morris, "No-Show '96: Americans Who Don't Vote," Summary Report to the Medill News Service and WTTW Television, Northwestern University School of Journalism, 1996.

69. Crewe, "Electoral Participation," p. 262.

70. Samuel H. Barnes and Max Kaase, *Political Action*, p. 532.

71. *1971 Congressional Quarterly Almanac* (Washington, D.C.: Congressional Quarterly Press, 1972), p. 475.

72. Benjamin Ginsberg, *The Consequences of Consent: Elections, Citizen Control, and Popular Acquiescence* (Reading, Mass.: Addison-Wesley, 1982), p. 13.

73. Ginsberg, *Consequences of Consent*, pp. 13–14.

74. Ginsberg, *Consequences of Consent*, pp. 6–7.

75. Some people have argued that the decline in voter turnout during the 1980s served to increase the class bias in the electorate, because people of lower socioeconomic status stayed home. But recent research has concluded that "class bias has not increased since 1964" (p. 734, Jan E. Leighley and Jonathan Nagler, "Socioeconomic Class Bias in Turnout, 1964–1988: The Voters Remain the Same," *American Political Science Review* 86 [September 1992], pp. 725–736). Nevertheless, Rosenstone and Hansen say, "the economic inequalities in political participation that prevail in the United States today are as large as the racial disparities in political participation that prevailed in the 1950s. America's leaders today face few incentives to attend to the needs of the disadvantaged," in *Mobilization, Participation, and Democracy in America*, p. 248.

Chapter 8 / Political Parties / pp. 246–281

1. Michael Tackett, "Perot Invites Voters to 3rd Party," *Chicago Tribune*, 26 September 1995, p. 1. See also Sam Howe Verhovek, "Perot, Back on the Stump Again, Still Dances Around the Question," *New York Times*, 31 March 1996, p. 1.

2. Richard L. Berke, "Perot Declares He Will Seek His Party's Presidential Nod," *New York Times*, 12 July 1996, p. 1.

3. "Voter Anxiety Dividing GOP; Energized Democrats Backing Clinton," news release, 14 November 1995 (Washington, D.C.: Times-Mirror Center for the People & the Press), p. 101; and "Democratic Congressional Prospects Improve," news release, 5 April 1996 (Washington, D.C.: Pew Research Center for the People & the Press), p. 32.

4. Center for Political Studies of the Institute for Social Research, *American National Election Study 1992* (Ann Arbor: University of Michigan, 1993, p. 997).

5. David W. Moore, "Perot Supporters: For the Man, Not a Third Party," Gallup Organization Newsletter Archive, 60, August 17, 1995; the Gallup Organization's Web page at <www.gallup.com/newsletter/aug95/>.

6. John H. Aldrich, *Why Parties? The Origin and Transformation of Political Parties in America* (Chicago: University of Chicago Press, 1995), p. 296.

7. Richard B. Morris (ed.), *Encyclopedia of American History* (New York: Harper & Row, 1976), p. 209.

8. See Jerome M. Clubb, William H. Flanigan, and Nancy H. Zingale, *Partisan Realignment: Voters, Parties, and Government in American History*, vol. 108 (Beverly Hills, Calif.: Sage, 1980), p. 163.

9. See Gerald M. Pomper, "Classification of Presidential Elections," *Journal of Politics* 29 (August 1967), pp. 535–566.

10. For a more extensive treatment, see Henry M. Littlefield, "The Wizard of Oz: Parable on Populism," *American Quarterly* 16 (Spring 1964), pp. 47–58.

11. The discussion that follows draws heavily on Austin Ranney and Willmoore Kendall, *Democracy and the American Party System* (New York: Harcourt, Brace, 1956), Chaps. 18 and 19.

12. See Steven J. Rosenstone, Roy L. Behr, and Edward H. Lazarus, *Third Parties in America: Citizen Response to Major Party Failure* (Princeton, N.J.: Princeton University Press, 1984), pp. 5–6.

13. Of these topics, reducing the deficit seems to be the most popular with American voters (although it attracts the attention of only about 50 percent of the electorate). See David W. Moore and Lydia Saad, "Americans Still Favor Independent and Third-party Candidates," *Gallup Organization Newsletter Archive*, 60, 7 July 1995; see also the Gallup Organization's Web page at <www.gallup.com/newsletter/july 95/>.

14. Perot activists were mainly well-off, highly educated white males, mostly self-styled independents. See Randall W. Partin, Lori M. Weber, Ronald B. Rapoport, and Walter J. Stone, "Sources of Activism in the 1992 Perot Campaign," in Daniel M. Shea and John C. Green (eds.), *The State of the Parties* (Lanham, Md.: Rowman and Littlefield, 1994), pp. 147–162.

15. Rosenstone, Behr, and Lazarus, *Third Parties in America*, p. 8.

16. State laws and court decisions may systematically support the major parties, but the U.S. Supreme Court seems to hold a more neutral position toward major and minor parties. See Lee Epstein and Charles D. Hadley, "On the Treatment of Political Parties in the U.S. Supreme Court, 1900–1986," *Journal of Politics* 52 (May 1990), pp. 413–432.

17. See James Gimpel, *National Elections and the Autonomy of American State Party Systems* (Pittsburgh, Pa.: University of Pittsburgh Press, 1996).

18. *Public Opinion* 7 (December-January 1985), p. 26.

19. Measuring the concept of party identification has had its problems. For recent insights into the issues, see R. Michael Alvarez, "The Puzzle of Party Identification," *American Politics Quarterly* 18 (October 1990), pp. 476–491; and Donald Philip Green and Bradley Palmquist, "Of Artifacts and Partisan Instability," *American Journal of Political Science* 34 (August 1990), pp. 872–902.

20. Rhodes Cook, "GOP Shows Dramatic Growth, Especially in the South," *Congressional Quarterly Weekly Report*, 13 January 1996, pp. 97–100.

21. There is some dispute over how stable party identification really is, when the same respondents are asked about their party identification over a period of several months during an election campaign. The research literature is reviewed in Brad Lockerbie, "Change in Party Identification: The Role of Prospective Economic Evaluations," *American Politics Quarterly* 17 (July 1989), pp. 291–311. Lockerbie argues that respondents change their party identification according to whether they think a party will help them personally in the future. But also see Green and Palmquist, "Of Artifacts and Partisan Instability."

22. Bill Keller, "As Arms Buildup Eases, U.S. Tries to Take Stock," *New York*

Times, 14 May 1985; Ed Gillespie and Bob Schellhas, *Contract with America* (New York: Times Books, 1994), p. 107.

23. See, for example, Gerald M. Pomper, *Elections in America* (New York: Dodd, Mead, 1968); Benjamin Ginsberg, "Election and Public Policy," *American Political Science Review* 70 (March 1976), pp. 41–50; and Jeff Fishel, *Presidents and Promises* (Washington, D.C.: Congressional Quarterly Press, 1985).

24. Ian Budge and Richard I. Hofferbert, "Mandates and Policy Outputs: U.S. Party Platforms and Federal Expenditures," *American Political Science Review* 84 (March 1990), pp. 111–131.

25. See Terri Susan Fine, "Economic Interests and the Framing of the 1988 and 1992 Democratic and Republican Party Platforms," *The American Review of Politics*, 16 (Spring 1995), 79–93.

26. Katharine Q. Seelye, "Under Pressure, Dole Reconsiders Abortion Plank," *New York Times*, 13 July 1996, p. 1.

27. Robert Harmel and Kenneth Janda, *Parties and Their Environments: Limits to Reform?* (New York: Longman, 1982), pp. 27–29. See also John Huber and Ronald Inglehart, "Expert Interpretations of Party Space and Party Locations in 42 Societies," *Party Politics* 1 (January 1995), pp. 73–111; and Alan Ware, *Political Parties and Party Systems* (New York: Oxford University Press, 1996), Chap. 1.

28. Personal communication with DNC and RNC staff, 24 January 1994, and information updated from the national committees' home pages on the Web (see World Wide Web Resources for this chapter).

29. See Ralph M. Goldman, *The National Party Chairmen and Committees: Factionalism at the Top* (Armonk, N.Y.: M. E. Sharpe, 1990). The subtitle is revealing.

30. William Crotty and John S. Jackson III, *Presidential Primaries and Nominations* (Washington, D.C.: Congressional Quarterly Press, 1985), p. 33.

31. Debra L. Dodson, "Socialization of Party Activists: National Convention Delegates, 1972–1981,"

American Journal of Political Science 34 (November 1990), pp. 1119–1141.

32. Phillip A. Klinkner, "Party Culture and Party Behavior," in Shea and Green, *The State of the Parties*, pp. 275–287; and Philip A. Klinkner, *The Losing Parties: Out-Party National Committees, 1956–1993* (New Haven: Yale University Press, 1994).

33. The Federal Election Commission, "FEC Releases 18-Month Report on Political Party Finances," press release of 7 August 1996, p. 1.

34. Dan Barry, "Republicans on Long Island Master Science of Politics," *New York Times*, 8 March 1996, p. A15.

35. John Frendreis, Alan R. Gitelson, Gregory Flemming, and Anne Layzell, "Local Political Parties and Legislative Races in 1992," in Shea and Green, *The State of the Parties*, p. 139.

36. Federal Election Commission, "FEC Reports on Political Party Activity for 1993–94," press release of 13 April 1995, pp. 12–13.

37. Robert Biersack, "Hard Facts and Soft Money: State Party Finance in the 1992 Federal Elections," in Shea and Green, *The State of the Parties*, p. 114.

38. Paul S. Herrnson, "Party Strategy and Campaign Activities in the 1992 Congressional Elections, *ibid.*, pp. 83–106.

39. Philip D. Duncan and Christine C. Lawrence, *Politics in America 1996* (Washington, D.C.: Congressional Quarterly Press, 1995), p. 406.

40. See the evidence presented in Harmel and Janda, *Parties and Their Environments*, Chap. 5.

41. Martin P. Wattenberg, *The Decline of American Political Parties, 1952–1994* (Cambridge, Mass.: Harvard University Press, 1996).

42. In 1996, the Democratic National Committee mounted an unprecedented drive to organize up to sixty thousand precinct captains in twenty states, while the new Republican candidate for U.S. Senator from Illinois, Al Salvi, fired his own campaign manager and replaced him with someone from the National Republican Senatorial Campaign Committee. See Sue Ellen Christian, "Democrats Will

Focus on Precincts," *Chicago Tribune*, 29 June 1996, p. 5; and Michael Dizon, "Salvi Fires Top Senate Race Aides," *Chicago Tribune*, 24 May 1996, Section 2, p. 3.

43. Barbara Sinclair, "The Congressional Party: Evolving Organizational, Agenda-Setting, and Policy Roles," in *Parties Respond*, p. 227.

44. The model is articulated most clearly in a report by the American Political Science Association, "Toward a More Responsible Two-Party System," *American Political Science Review* 44 (September 1950), Part II. See also Gerald M. Pomper, "Toward a More Responsible Party System? What, Again?" *Journal of Politics* 33 (November 1971), pp. 916–940. See also the seven essays in the symposium, "Divided Government and the Politics of Constitutional Reform," *PS: Political Science & Politics*, 24 (December 1991), pp. 634–657.

Chapter 9 / Nominations, Elections, and Campaigns / pp. 282–315

1. "Today's Schedule," *New York Times*, 15 August 1996, p. A14.

2. Associated Press, "Ratings Erode for Convention Coverage," <politicsnow.com/news/Aug96/14/ap0814 ratings/>.

3. James Bennet, "'Nightline' Pulls the Plug on Convention Coverage," *New York Times*, 15 August 1996, p. A11.

4. Bob Secter and Pamela Cytrynbaum, "The People Ask: What Else Is on?" *Chicago Tribune*, 14 August 1996, p. 16.

5. Michael Winerip, "One Town Left the G.O.P. Alone During the Convention Spectacle," *New York Times*, 17 August 1996, p. 1.

6. Michael Nelson (ed.), *Guide to the Presidency* (Washington, D.C.: Congressional Quarterly Press, 1989), p. 230.

7. Harold W. Stanley and Richard G. Niemi, *Vital Statistics on American Politics*, 5th ed. (Washington, D.C.: Congressional Quarterly Press, 1995), p. 69, for the data on coverage from 1952 through 1992; "Less Air Time for Conventions," *New York Times*, 14 August 1996, p. A12, for the data on 1996 coverage.

8. James Bennet, "G.O.P. Convention to Be a TV Variety Show," *New York Times*, 8 August 1996, p. 1.

9. James M. Perry and John Harwood, "An Old Reagan Hand Will Try to Add Spark to GOP Convention," *Wall Street Journal*, 9 August 1996, p. 1.

10. Bennet, "G.O.P. Convention to Be a TV Variety Show"; Perry and Harwood; and Steve Johnson, "TV Extravaganza Trots Out New Talent to Mixed Results," *Chicago Tribune*, 14 August 1996, p. 16. See also James Bennet, "Media Seeks the Elusive: The Moments Off the Script," *New York Times*, 16 August 1996, p. A14.

11. Bennet, "'Nightline' Pulls the Plug on Convention Coverage."

12. Rogers Worthington, "Reform Party Selects Perot in Low Turnout," *Chicago Tribune*, 18 August 1996, p. 14.

13. This is essentially the framework for studying campaigns set forth in Barbara G. Salmore and Stephen A. Salmore, *Candidates, Parties, and Campaigns: Electoral Politics in America*, 2d ed. (Washington, D.C.: Congressional Quarterly Press, 1989).

14. Martin P. Wattenberg, *The Rise of Candidate-Centered Politics: Presidential Elections of the 1980s* (Cambridge, Mass.: Harvard University Press, 1991).

15. Stephen E. Frantzich, *Political Parties in the Technological Age* (New York: Longman, 1989), p. 105.

16. Michael Gallagher, "Conclusion," in Michael Gallagher and Michael Marsh (eds.), *Candidate Selection in Comparative Perspective: The Secret Garden of Politics* (London: Sage, 1988), p. 238.

17. Kenneth Janda, *Political Parties: A Cross-National Survey* (New York: Free Press, 1980), p. 112.

18. *The Book of the States*, 1996–97, vol. 31 (Lexington, Ky.: Council of State Governments, 1996), pp. 157–158.

19. Malcolm E. Jewell and David M. Olson, *Political Parties and Elections in American States*, 3d ed. (Chicago: Dorsey Press, 1988), pp. 108–112. For data on turnout in the Republican primaries and caucuses in 1996, see "Guide to the 1996 Republican National Convention," *Congressional Quarterly Supplement to Weekly Report Number 31*, 3 August 1996, pp. 62–63.

20. See John G. Geer, "Assessing the Representativeness of Electorates in Presidential Elections," *American Journal of Political Science* 32 (November 1988), pp. 929–945; and Barbara Norrander, "Ideological Representativeness of Presidential Primary Voters," *American Journal of Political Science* 33 (August 1989), pp. 570–587.

21. James A. McCann, "Presidential Nomination Activists and Political Representation: A View from the Active Minority Studies," in William G. Mayer (ed.), *In Pursuit of the White House: How We Choose Our Presidential Nominees* (Chatham, N.J.: Chatham House, 1996), p. 99.

22. Benjamin Sheffner, "California Votes to Join the 'Jungle' with New Primary Election Setup," *Roll Call*, 1 April 1996. Obtained on 17 August 1996 from <www.electionline.com/HTEL/npre033196rccalif/page1.cgi/317d5e92ba2beb0c>.

23. Emmet T. Flood and William G, Mayer, "Third-Party and Independent Candidates: How They Get on the Ballot, How They Get Nominated," in Mayer, *In Pursuit of the White House*, pp. 311–313.

24. Rhodes Cook, "Earlier Voting in 1996 Forecasts Fast and Furious Campaigns," *Congressional Quarterly Weekly Report*, 19 August 1995, p. 2485.

25. Ibid., pp. 2485–2487. For a description of how caucuses operate and how differently they work in the two parties, see William G. Mayer, "Caucuses: How They Work, What Difference They Make," in Mayer, *In Pursuit of the White House*, pp. 105–157.

26. Stanley and Niemi, *Vital Statistics on American Politics*, p. 138.

27. Arthur T. Hadley, *The Invisible Primary* (Englewood Cliffs, N.J.: Prentice-Hall, 1976). For a recent test of some of Hadley's assertions, see Emmett H. Buell, Jr., "The Invisible Primary," in Mayer, *In Pursuit of the White House*, pp. 1–43.

28. Richard L. Berke, "In New Hampshire, It's Already 1996," *International Herald Tribune*, 26 October 1993, p. 3.

29. Lisa Anderson, "2000 Next: Wooing of New Hampshire," *Chicago Tribune*, 18 August 1996, p. 13.

30. Gary R. Orren and Nelson W. Polsby (eds.), *Media and Momentum: The New Hampshire Primary and Nomination Politics* (Chatham, N.J.: Chatham House, 1987), p. 23.

31. Rod Boshart, "Iowans Celebrate 'Great Success' of 1996 Caucus," *The Gazette*, 14 February 1996; and Federal Election Commission, Primary Election Results. Data on voting age population in each state came from Philip D. Duncan and Christine C. Lawrence, *Politics in America 1996* (Washington, D.C.: Congressional Quarterly Press, 1995).

32. See Steve Daley, "GOP Leaders Angling to Slow Buchanan," *Chicago Tribune*, 22 February 1996, p. 1; R. W. Apple, "Why the Party Can't Stop Buchanan," *New York Times*, 25 February 1996, Section 4, p. 1; and George Melloan, "Buchanan Is the Worst Possible GOP Choice," in *Wall Street Journal*, 26 February 1996, p. A13.

33. Michael Tackett, "No Quick Pick for GOP," *Chicago Tribune*, 29 February 1996, p. 1.

34. See James R. Beniger, "Winning the Presidential Nomination: National Polls and State Primary Elections, 1936–1972," *Public Opinion Quarterly* 40 (Spring 1976), pp. 22–38.

35. Michael Nelson (ed.), *Congressional Quarterly Guide to the Presidency* (Washington, D.C.: Congressional Quarterly Press, 1989), p. 1427. You can find the other exceptions there, too.

36. Shlomo Slonim, "The Electoral College at Philadelphia: The Evolution of an Ad Hoc Congress for the Selection of a President," *Journal of American History*, 73 (June 1986), p. 35. For a recent critique and proposal for reform, see David W. Abbott and James P. Levine, *Wrong Winner: The Coming Debacle in the Electoral College* (New York: Praeger, 1991).

37. The framers had great difficulty deciding how to allow both the people and the states to participate in selecting the president. This matter was debated on 21 different days before they compromised on the electoral college, which Slonim says, "in the eyes of its admirers . . .

represented a brilliant scheme for successfully blending national and federal elements in the selection of the nation's chief executive," p. 58.

38. Harold W. Stanley and Richard G. Niemi, *Vital Statistics on American Politics*, 2d ed. (Washington, D.C.: Congressional Quarterly Press, 1990), p. 132; and the 1992 National Election Study, Center for Political Studies, University of Michigan.

39. Rhodes Cook, "House Republicans Scored a Quiet Victory in '92," *Congressional Quarterly Weekly Report*, 17 April 1993, p. 966.

40. Everett Carll Ladd, "The 1988 Elections: Continuation of the Post–New Deal System," *Political Science Quarterly* 104 (1989), pp. 1–18; and Seymour Martin Lipset, "A Reaffirming Election: 1988," *International Journal of Public Opinion Research* 1 (January 1989).

41. Salmore and Salmore, *Candidates, Parties, and Campaigns*, p. 1.

42. "PACs Give $90.8 Million to Candidates in First 15 Months of '96 Election Cycle," *Federal Election Commission Record*, 22 (August 1996), pp. 5–6.

43. Quoted in E. J. Dionne, Jr., "On the Trail of Corporation Donations," *New York Times*, 6 October 1980.

44. Salmore and Salmore, *Candidates, Parties, and Campaigns*, p. 11. See also David Himes, "Strategy and Tactics for Campaign Fund-Raising," in James A. Thurber and Candice J. Nelson (eds.), *Campaigns and Elections: American Style* (Boulder, Colo.: Westview Press, 1995), pp. 62–77.

45. Federal Election Commission, "The First Ten Years: 1975–1985" (Washington, D.C.: Federal Election Commission), 14 April 1985, p. 1.

46. "FEC Announces 1996 Presidential Spending Limits," Federal Election Commission press release of 15 March 1996.

47. "FEC Releases 18-Month Report on Political Party Finances," Federal Election Commission press release of 7 August 1996, p. 1.

48. Paul S. Herrnson, "Party Strategies and Campaign Activities in the 1992 Congressional Elections," in Daniel M. Shea and John C. Green (eds.), *The State of the Parties: The Changing Role of Contemporary American Parties* (Lanham, Md.: Rowman & Littlefield, 1994), pp.

83–106; and Robert Biersack, "Hard Facts and Soft Money: State Party Finance in the 1992 Federal Elections," in Shea and Green, pp. 107–132.

49. Adam Clymer, "System to Limit Election Spending Found in Shambles," *New York Times*, 16 June 1996, p. 1.

50. Salmore and Salmore, *Candidates, Parties, and Campaigns*, p. 11.

51. David Moon, "What You Use Depends on What You Have: Information Effects on the Determinants of Electoral Choice," *American Politics Quarterly* 18 (January 1990), pp. 3–24.

52. See the "Marketplace" section in monthly issues of the magazine, *Campaigns & Elections*, which contains more than a hundred names, addresses, and telephone numbers of people who supply "political products and services"— from "campaign schools" to "voter files and mailing lists."

53. Salmore and Salmore, *Candidates, Parties, and Campaigns*, pp. 115–116.

54. Stephen Ansolabehere, Roy L. Behr, and Shanto Iyengar, "Mass Media and Elections: An Overview," *American Politics Quarterly* 19 (January 1991), pp. 109–139.

55. James Warren, "Politicians Learn Value of Sundays—Too Well," *Chicago Tribune*, 22 October 1990, p. 1.

56. Timothy E. Cook, *Making Laws and Making News: Media Strategies in the U.S. House of Representatives* (Washington, D.C.: Brookings Institution, 1989). Recent research into media effects on Senate and House elections finds that in low-information elections, which characterize House more than Senate elections, the media coverage gives an advantage to incumbents, particularly among independent voters. See Robert Kirby Goidel, Todd G. Shields, and Barry Tadlock, "The Effects of the Media in United States Senate and House Elections: A Comparative Analysis," paper presented at the annual meeting of the American Political Science Association, Washington, D.C., September 1993.

57. Kiku Adatto, "The Incredible Shrinking Sound Bite," *New Republic*, 28 May 1990, p. 20.

58. S. Robert Lichter and Richard E. Noyes, *Good Intentions Make Bad News* (Lanham, Md.: Rowman & Littlefield, 1995), p. 268.

59. Ann N. Crigler, Marion R. Just, and Timothy E. Cook, "Local News, Network News and the 1992 Presidential Campaign," paper presented at the annual meeting of the American Political Science Association, Washington, D.C., September 1993, p. 9.

60. Bob Specter, "In Political Reporting, the Misses Just Keep Coming," *Chicago Tribune*, 18 February 1996, Section 2, p. 1.

61. Montague Kern, *30-Second Politics: Political Advertising in the Eighties* (New York: Praeger, 1989), p. 57; and Stephen Ansolabehere and Shanto Iyengar, *Going Negative: How Political Advertisements Shrink and Polarize the Electorate* (New York: Free Press, 1995), p. 145.

62. Darrell M. West, *Air Wards: Television Advertising in Election Campaigns, 1952–1992* (Washington, D.C.: Congressional Quarterly Press, 1993), p. 7.

63. Phil Kuntz, "Dole Is Lifted by the Selection of Kemp, Convention That Avoided Divisiveness," *Wall Street Journal*, 19 August 1996, p. A14.

64. West, *Air Wards*, p. 40.

65. This theme runs throughout Kathleen Hall Jamieson's *Dirty Politics: Deception, Distraction, and Democracy* (New York: Oxford University Press, 1992). See also John Boiney, "You Can Fool All of the People . . . Evidence on the Capacity of Political Advertising to Mislead," paper presented at the annual meeting of the American Political Science Association, Washington, D.C., September 1993.

66. West, *Air Wards*, p. 50. West's figures are roughly comparable to data reported by L. Patrick Devlin, "Contrasts in Presidential Campaign Commercials," who says that both Clinton and Bush had a 50:50 positive-to-negative ad-buying ratio and cites this as a "new high" in negative advertising, p. 287.

67. West, *Air Wards*, p. 52.

68. *Ibid.*, p. 58.

69. Ansolabehere and Iyengar, *Going Negative*, p. 112.

70. Christine F. Ridout, "News Coverage and Talk Shows in the 1992 Presidential Campaign," *PS:*

Political Science & Politics 26 (December 1993), pp. 712–716.

71. Edmund L. Andrews, "The '96 Race on the Internet: Surfer Beware," *New York Times*, 23 October 1995, p. 1.

72. James Coates, "Internet Is the Latest Player in Campaign Politics," *Chicago Tribune*, 18 August 1996, Section 4, p. 5.

73. See the web site for the National Election Studies at <www.umich.edu/~nes/resourcs/nesguide/gd-index.htm>.

74. Gerald M. Pomper, *The Presidential Election of 1992*, ed. Gerald M. Pomper, et al. (Chatham: N.J.: Chatham House, 1993), p. 145.

75. Arthur H. Miller, "Economic, Character, and Social Issues in the 1992 Presidential Election," *American Behavioral Scientist* 37 (November 1993), p. 319.

76. Alissa J. Rubin, "Dole 'Bets the Country' on Tax Cut Package," *Congressional Quarterly Weekly Report* (10 August 1996), p. 2245.

77. Quotations of Mr. Dole criticizing Mr. Kemp and his policies during the 1988 campaign for the Republican Presidential Nomination, *New York Times*, 11 August 1996.

78. National Exit Poll Data reported on the *PoliticsNow* web site, November 5, 1996.

79. Pamela Johnston Conover and Stanley Feldman, "Candidate Perception in an Ambiguous World: Campaigns, Cues, and Inference Processes," *American Journal of Political Science* 33 (November 1989), pp. 912–940.

80. Michael M. Gant and Norman R. Luttbeg, *American Electoral Behavior* (Itasca, Ill.: Peacock, 1991), pp. 63–64. The literature on the joint effects of party, issues, and candidates is quite involved. See also David W. Romero, "The Changing American Voter Revisited: Candidate Evaluations in Presidential Elections, 1952–1984," *American Politics Quarterly* 17 (October 1989), pp. 409–421. Romero contends that research that finds a "new" American voter who votes according to issues is incorrectly looking at standardized rather than unstandardized regression coefficients.

81. Herbert Asher, *Presidential Elec-*

tions and American Politics (Homewood, Ill.: Dorsey, 1980), p. 196.

82. Conover and Feldman, "Candidate Perception," p. 938.

83. Party identification has been assumed to be relatively resistant to short-term campaign effects, but see Dee Allsop and Herbert F. Weisberg, "Measuring Change in Party Identification in an Election Campaign," *American Journal of Political Science* 32 (November 1988), pp. 996–1017. They conclude that partisanship is more volatile than we have thought.

84. James Bennet, "Clinton Makes Use of Negative Ads," *New York Times*, 22 October 1996, p. A12.

85. Richard L. Berke, "Should Dole Risk Tough Image? Poll Says He Already Has One," *New York Times*, 16 October 1996, p. 1.

86. Katharine Q. Seelye, "Dole Is Imploring Voters to 'Rise up' Against the Press," 26 October, 1996, p. 1.

87. New York Times/CBS News Poll, "Trial Heats Throughout the Campaign," *New York Times*, 4 November 1996, p. A12.

88. See Allan J. Lichtman, *The Keys to the White House: A Surefire Guide to Predicting the Next President* (Lanham, Md: Madison Books, 1996). Argues that presidential elections are referenda on the administration in power and that campaigns have little effect on their outcomes.

89. Gallup/CNN/*USA Today* poll, 7–9 October 1994.

90. "Gingrich Address," *Congressional Quarterly Weekly Report*, 7 January 1995, p. 119.

91. *New York Times*/CBS News survey, 22–25 February 1995.

92. For an analysis of the Republicans' problem, see Russell L. Riley, "Party Government and the Contract With America," *PS: Political Science and Politics*, 28 (December 1995), pp. 703–707.

Chapter 10 / Interest Groups / pp. 316–348

1. Michael Wines, "Congress's Twists and Turns Reshape Bill on Energy," *New York Times*, 6 June 1993, p. A1.

2. John Harwood and David Wessel, "White House Gives Ground on

Energy Tax," *Wall Street Journal*, 27 May 1993, p. A3; Steven Greenhouse, "Energy Plan To Be Scaled Back, Moynihan Reports," *New York Times*, 30 May 1993, p. 1; Wines, "Congress's Twists and Turns"; Timothy Noah, "BTU Tax Is Dying Death of a Thousand Cuts as Lobbyists Seem Able to Write Their Own Exemptions," *Wall Street Journal*, 8 June 1993, p. A18.

3. Alexis de Tocqueville, *Democracy in America, 1835–1839*, Reprint, ed. Richard D. Heffner (New York: Mentor Books, 1956), p. 79.

4. *The Federalist Papers* (New York: Mentor Books, 1961), p. 79.

5. *Ibid.*, p. 78.

6. See Robert A. Dahl, *A Preface to Democratic Theory* (Chicago: University of Chicago Press, 1956), pp. 4–33.

7. Alan Rosenthal, *The Third House* (Washington, D.C.: Congressional Quarterly, 1993), p. 7.

8. This discussion follows from Jeffrey M. Berry, *The Interest Group Society* (New York: Longman, 1997), pp. 6–8.

9. William H. Honan, "With Money Threatened, Colleges Are Moving on All Lobbying Fronts," *New York Times*, 28 June 1995, p. B7.

10. John Mark Hansen, *Gaining Access* (Chicago: University of Chicago Press, 1991), pp. 11–17.

11. Anne N. Costain, *Inviting Women's Rebellion* (Baltimore: Johns Hopkins University Press, 1992).

12. David B. Truman, *The Governmental Process* (New York: Alfred A. Knopf, 1951).

13. Herbert Gans, *The Urban Villagers* (New York: Free Press, 1962).

14. Robert H. Salisbury, "An Exchange Theory of Interest Groups," *Midwest Journal of Political Science* 13 (February 1969), pp. 1–32.

15. See Mancur Olson, Jr., *The Logic of Collective Action* (New York: Schocken, 1968).

16. Peter Matthiessen, *Sal Si Puedes* (New York: Random House, 1969); and John G. Dunne, *Delano*, rev. ed. (New York: Farrar, Strauss & Giroux, 1971).

17. William P. Browne, "Organized Interests and Their Issue Niches: A Search for Pluralism in a Policy Domain," *Journal of Politics* 52 (May 1990), pp. 477–509.

18. Christopher Boerner and Jennifer

Chilton Kallery, *Restructuring Environmental Big Business*, Occasional Paper No. 146, Center for the Study of American Business, Washington University, St. Louis, Mo., December 1994; and Christopher J. Bosso, "The Color of Money: Environmental Groups and the Pathologies of Fund Raising," in *Interest Group Politics*, 4th ed., ed. Allan J. Cigler and Burdett A. Loomis (Washington, D.C.: Congressional Quarterly, 1995), pp. 101–130.

19. R. Kenneth Godwin, *One Billion Dollars of Influence* (Chatham, N.J.: Chatham House, 1988), pp. 1–34.

20. See Olson, *Logic*.

21. David C. King and Jack L. Walker, "The Provision of Benefits by Interest Groups in the United States," *Journal of Politics* 54 (May 1992), pp. 394–426.

22. Edward O. Laumann and David Knoke, *The Organizational State* (Madison: University of Wisconsin Press, 1987), p. 3. Cited in Robert H. Salisbury, "The Paradox of Interest Groups in Washington—More Groups, Less Clout," in *The New American Political System*, 2d ed., ed. Anthony King (Washington, D.C.: American Enterprise Institute, 1990), p. 226.

23. Jackie Calmes, "Revolving Door Between Congress and Lobbyists Spins on Despite Yearlong Cooling-Off Period," *Wall Street Journal*, 24 January 1994, p. A14.

24. John P. Heinz, Edward O. Laumann, Robert L. Nelson, and Robert H. Salisbury, *The Hollow Core* (Cambridge, Mass.: Harvard University Press, 1993), pp. 105–155.

25. Jeffrey H. Birnbaum, *The Lobbyists* (New York: Times Books, 1992), pp. 128–129.

26. Jill Abramson, "Influence of Lobbyist Groups Likely Won't Diminish," *Wall Street Journal*, 5 November 1992, p. A12; and Richard B. Schmitt, "Ties to Clinton Aid Law Firms in Washington," *Wall Street Journal*, 12 March 1993, p. B1.

27. "FEC Releases Semi-Annual Federal PAC Count," Federal Election Commission, 23 January 1996, p. 2.

28. "PAC Activity in 1994 Remains at 1992 Levels," Federal Election Commission, 31 March 1995, pp. 2–3.

29. Dan Clawson, Alan Neustadl, and Denise Scott, *Money Talks* (New York: Basic Books, 1992), p. 1.

30. "PAC Activity in 1994," p. 5.

31. Jeffrey Taylor, "Accountants' Campaign Contributions Are About To Pay Off in Legislation on Lawsuit Protection," *Wall Street Journal*, 8 March 1995, p. A22.

32. See John R. Wright, *Interest Groups and Congress* (Boston: Allyn & Bacon, 1996), pp. 136–145.

33. John R. Wright, "Contributions, Lobbying, and Committee Voting in the U.S. House of Representatives," *American Political Science Review* 84 (June 1990), pp. 417–438; and Richard L. Hall and Frank W. Wayman, "Buying Time: Money Interests and the Mobilization of Bias in Congressional Committees," *American Political Science Review*, 84 (September 1990), pp. 797–820.

34. Kay Lehman Schlozman and John T. Tierney, *Organized Interests and American Democracy* (New York: Harper & Row, 1986), p. 150.

35. Berry, *The Interest Group Society*, p. 166

36. Yumiko Ono, "Tobacco Firms Rush to Counterattack Despite Signs of Dissension in Ranks," *Wall Street Journal*, 14 August 1995, p. A3.

37. Barbara Hinkson Craig and David M. O'Brien, *Abortion and American Politics* (Chatham, N.J.: Chatham House, 1993), p. 67.

38. Darrell M. West, Diane J. Heith, and Chris Goodwin, "Harry and Louise Go to Washington," *Journal of Health Policy, Politics and Law* 21 (Spring 1996), pp. 35–68.

39. Dirk Johnson, "Weed Killers in Tap Water in Corn Belt," *New York Times*, 18 August 1995, p. A10.

40. Graeme Browning, "Zapping the Capitol," *National Journal*, 22 November 1994, p. 2449.

41. Berry, *The Interest Group Society*, pp. 135–137.

42. Marc K. Landy and Mary Hague, "Private Interests and Superfund," *Public Interest* 108 (Summer 1992), pp. 97–115.

43. Kevin Hula, "Rounding Up the Usual Suspects: Forging Interest Group Coalitions in Washington," paper delivered at the annual meeting of the Midwest Political Science Association, Chicago, April 1993, p. 29.

44. Sidney Verba, Kay Lehman Schlozman, Henry Brady, and Norman H. Nie, "Citizen Activity: Who Participates? What Do They Say?" *American Political Science Review* 87 (June 1993), p. 311.

45. Douglas R. Imig, *Poverty and Power: The Political Representation of Poor Americans* (Lincoln: University of Nebraska Press, 1996).

46. Jeffrey M. Berry, *Lobbying for the People* (Princeton, N.J.: Princeton University Press, 1977), pp. 6–10.

47. Schlozman and Tierney, *Organized Interests*, pp. 58–87.

48. Mark A. Peterson, "The Presidency and Organized Interests: White House Patterns of Interest Group Liaison," *American Political Science Review* 86 (September 1992), pp. 612–625.

49. "PAC Activity in 1994 Elections," p. 20.

50. "PAC Activity in 1994 Elections," p. 3.

51. Jennifer Babson and Kelly St. John, "Momentum Helps GOP Collect Record Amounts from PACs," *Congressional Quarterly Weekly Report*, 3 December 1994, p. 3457.

52. Adam Clymer, "Congress Passes Bill to Disclose Lobbyists' Roles," *New York Times*, 30 November 1995, p. A1.

53. Eric Schmitt, "Order for Lobbyists: Hold the Gravy," *New York Times*, 11 February 1996, p. 30.

54. See Jonathan Rauch, *Demosclerosis* (New York: Times Books, 1994).

Chapter 11 / Congress / pp. 349–387

1. David S. Cloud, "GOP's Balancing Act Gets Tricky as Budget Amendment Sinks," *Congressional Quarterly Weekly Report*, 4 March 1995, p. 671.

2. Andrew Taylor, "Amendment Remains a Gamble Despite Its Popularity," *Congressional Quarterly Weekly Report*, 14 January 1995, p. 141.

3. Adam Clymer, "Americans Reject Big Medicare Cuts, a New Poll Finds," *New York Times*, 26 October 1995, p. A1.

4. Alissa Rubin and George Hager, "Chances of a Budget Deal Now Anyone's Guess," *Congressional Quarterly Weekly Report*, 13 January 1996, p. 89.

5. Clinton Rossiter, *1787: The Grand Convention* (New York: Mentor, 1968), p. 158.

6. James M. Lindsay and Randall B. Ripley, "How Congress Influences Foreign and Defense Policy," in *Congress Resurgent*, eds. Randall B. Ripley and James M. Lindsay (Ann Arbor: University of Michigan Press, 1993), pp. 25–28.

7. Norman J. Ornstein, Thomas E. Mann, and Michael J. Malbin, *Vital Statistics on Congress, 1995–1996* (Washington, D.C.: Congressional Quarterly Press, 1996), pp. 56–58.

8. Albert R. Hunt, "In Congress, Some Things Never Change," *Wall Street Journal*, 28 March 1996, p. A15.

9. "The Critique of Congress," *American Enterprise* 3 (May-June 1992), p. 101.

10. Karlyn Bowman and Everett Carll Ladd, "Public Opinion Toward Congress: A Historical Look," in *Congress, the Press, and the Public*, ed. Thomas E. Mann and Norman J. Ornstein (Washington, D.C.: American Enterprise Institute and the Brookings Institution, 1994), p. 55.

11. "Ethics," *American Enterprise* 3 (November-December 1992), p. 84.

12. John A. Ferejohn, "On the Decline of Competition in Congressional Elections," *American Political Science Review* 71 (March 1977), pp. 166–176.

13. Timothy E. Cook, *Making Laws and Making News* (Washington, D.C.: Brookings Institution, 1989), p. 83.

14. Barbara Boxer, "'Write Me,' Senator Says, and the People Take Heed," *New York Times*, 25 October 1993, p. A15.

15. "1994 Congressional Fundraising Climbs to New High," Federal Election Commission, 28 April 1995, p. 4.

16. Larry Sabato, *PAC Power* (New York: Norton, 1984), p. 72.

17. Frank J. Sorauf, *Inside Campaign Finance* (New Haven, Conn.: Yale University Press, 1992), p. 84.

18. Paul S. Herrnson, *Congressional Elections* (Washington, D.C.: Congressional Quarterly Press, 1995), p. 211.

19. Gary C. Jacobson and Samuel Kernell, *Strategy and Choice in Congressional Elections* (New Haven, Conn.: Yale University Press, 1983). See also L. Sandy Maisel et al., "Re-Exploring the Weak-Challenger Hypothesis: The 1994 Candidate Pools," in *Midterm: Elections of 1994 in Context*, ed. Philip A. Klinkner (Boulder, Colo.: Westview Press, 1996), pp. 137–155.

20. Jonathan S. Krasno, *Challengers, Competition, and Reelection* (New Haven, Conn.: Yale University Press, 1994).

21. Gary C. Jacobson, "The 1994 Elections in Perspective," paper delivered at the annual conference of the Midwest Political Science Association, Chicago, April 1995.

22. Ornstein, Mann, and Malbin, *Vital Statistics*, p. 60.

23. Ornstein, Mann, and Malbin, *Vital Statistics*, pp. 22–23, 28–29.

24. Hanna Fenichel Ptikin, *The Concept of Representation* (Berkeley: University of California Press, 1967), pp. 60–91.

25. Carol M. Swain, *Black Faces, Black Interests* (Cambridge, Mass.: Harvard University Press, 1993), p. 197.

26. *Shaw* v. *Reno*, 509 U.S. 630 (1993).

27. *Miller* v. *Johnson*, 115 S.Ct. 2475 (1995).

28. Kevin A. Hill, "Does the Creation of Majority Black Districts Aid Republicans?" *Journal of Politics* 57 (May 1995), pp. 384–401.

29. Walter J. Oleszek, *Congressional Procedures and the Policy Process* (Washington, D.C.: Congressional Quarterly Press, 1996), p. 91.

30. Roger W. Cobb and Charles D. Elder, *Participation in American Politics*, 2d ed. (Baltimore: Johns Hopkins University Press, 1983), pp. 64–65.

31. John W. Kingdon, *Agendas, Alternatives, and Public Policies* (Boston: Little, Brown, 1984), p. 41.

32. Barbara Sinclair, "Change and Continuity in the Legislative Process," paper delivered at the annual meeting of the American Political Science Association, Chicago, September 1995.

33. Andrew Taylor, "Congress Hands President a Budgetary Scalpel," *Congressional Quarterly Weekly Report*, 30 March 1996, pp. 864–867.

34. It was Woodrow Wilson who described the legislative process as the "dance of legislation." Eric Redman used the phrase for the title of his case study, *The Dance of Legislation* (New York: Touchstone, 1973).

35. David Shribman, "Canada's Top Envoy to Washington Cuts Unusually Wide Swath," *Wall Street Journal*, 29 July 1985, p. 1.

36. Woodrow Wilson, *Congressional Government* (Boston: Houghton Mifflin, 1885), p. 79.

37. Richard L. Hall and C. Lawrence Evans, "The Power of Subcommittees," *Journal of Politics* 52 (May 1990), p. 342.

38. Lawrence D. Longley and Walter J. Oleszek, *Bicameral Politics* (New Haven, Conn.: Yale University Press, 1989), p. 10.

39. *Ibid.*, p. 4.

40. Karen Foerstal, "Gingrich Flexes His Power in Picking Panel Chiefs," *Congressional Quarterly Weekly Report*, 7 January 1995, p. 3326.

41. Philip M. Boffey, "Lawmakers Vow a Legal Recourse for Military Malpractice Victims," *New York Times*, 9 July 1985, p. A14.

42. James M. Lindsay, *Congress and the Politics of U.S. Foreign Policy* (Baltimore: Johns Hopkins University Press, 1994), pp. 53–75.

43. Carroll J. Doherty and Pat Towell, "Senate Restricts Bosnia Aid Until Iranians Leave," *Congressional Quarterly Weekly Report*, 16 March 1996, p. 713.

44. Joel D. Aberbach, *Keeping a Watchful Eye* (Washington, D.C.: Brookings Institution, 1990), p. 44.

45. Ornstein, Mann, and Malbin, *Vital Statistics*, pp. 131–137.

46. Aberbach, *Keeping a Watchful Eye*, pp. 162–183.

47. Gary W. Cox and Mathew D. McCubbins, *Legislative Leviathan* (Berkeley: University of California Press, 1993); and Keith Krehbiel, *Information and Legislative Organization* (Ann Arbor: University of Michigan Press, 1992).

48. David Rogers, "GOP's Rare Year Owes Much to How Gingrich Disciplined the House," *Wall Street Journal*, 18 December 1995, p. A1.

49. Andy Plattner, "Dole on the Job," *Congressional Quarterly Weekly Report*, 29 June 1985, p. 1270.

50. Roger H. Davidson, "Senate Leaders: Janitors for an Untidy Chamber?" in *Congress Reconsidered*, 3d ed., ed. Lawrence C. Dodd and Bruce Oppenheimer (Washington, D.C.: Congressional Quarterly Press, 1985), p. 228.

51. "Gingrich's Popularity Has Faded Sharply As 33% Have a 'Very Negative' View," *Wall Street Journal*, 8 March 1995, p. R6.

52. Cox and McCubbins, *Legislative Leviathan*; and Sinclair, "Change and Continuity in the Legislative Process."

53. Charles O. Jones, *The United States Congress* (Homewood, Ill.: Dorsey Press, 1982), p. 322.

54. Deborah Baldwin, "Pulling Punches," *Common Cause* (May-June 1985), p. 22.

55. John Milne, "Memoir: Rudman Had Doubt About Thomas," *Boston Globe*, 12 April 1996, p. 29.

56. Jackie Koszczuk, "Freshmen: New, Powerful Voice," *Congressional Quarterly Weekly Report*, 28 October 1995, p. 3254.

57. *Ibid.*

58. See Jerry Gray, "Freshman Challenge G.O.P. Elders," *New York Times*, 21 October 1995, p. 1; and Jackie Calmes, "Militancy of GOP Freshmen May Leave Gingrich Little Room to Compromise," *Wall Street Journal*, 22 December 1995, p. A3.

59. Cox and McCubbins, *Legislative Leviathan*; D. Roderick Kiewiet and Mathew D. McCubbins, *The Logic of Delegation* (Chicago: University of Chicago Press, 1991); and Krehbiel, *Information and Legislative Organization*.

60. Dan Carney, "As Hostilities Rage on the Hill, Partisan-Vote Rate Soars," *Congressional Quarterly Weekly Report*, 27 January 1996, pp. 199–201; and Martin P. Wattenberg, *The Decline of American Political Parties, 1994* (Cambridge, Mass.: Harvard University Press, 1996), Chap. 11.

61. See James Glaser, *Race, Campaign Politics, and the Realignment in the South* (New Haven, Conn.: Yale University Press, 1996).

62. See Mark A. Peterson, *Legislating Together* (Cambridge, Mass.: Harvard University Press, 1990).

63. James Sterling Young, *The Washington Community* (New York: Harcourt, Brace, 1964).

64. R. Douglas Arnold, *The Logic of Congressional Action* (New Haven, Conn.: Yale University Press, 1990).

65. Richard F. Fenno, Jr., *Home Style* (Boston: Little, Brown, 1978), p. xii.

66. *Ibid.*, p. 32.

67. Louis I. Bredvold and Ralph G. Ross (eds.), *The Philosophy of Edmund Burke* (Ann Arbor: University of Michigan Press, 1960), p. 148.

68. Robin Toner, "Flag-Burning Amendment Fails in Senate, but Margin Narrows," *New York Times*, 13 December 1995, p. A1.

69. Warren E. Miller and Donald E. Stokes, "Constituency Influence in Congress," *American Political Science Review* 57 (March 1963), pp. 45–57. On minority legislators, see James B. Johnson and Philip E. Secret, "Focus and Style: Representational Roles of Congressional Black and Hispanic Caucus Members, *Journal of Black Studies*, 26 (January 1996), pp. 245–273.

70. Michael Wines, "Watch Out With That Budget Ax. My District NEEDS That Dam," *New York Times*, 30 July 1995, section 4, p. 7.

71. Robert Weissberg, "Collective vs. Dyadic Representation in Congress," *American Political Science Review* 72 (June 1978), pp. 535–547.

72. Jeffrey M. Berry, *The Interest Group Society*, 3d ed. (New York: Longman, 1997).

Chapter 12 / The Presidency / pp. 388–423

1. Jon Healey, "Spending Increases Come First in Rush to Pass Package," *Congressional Quarterly Weekly Report*, 20 February 1993, pp. 365–369; Jon Healey, "Republicans Slam the Brakes on Economic Stimulus Package," *Congressional Quarterly Weekly Report*, 3 April 1993, pp. 817–819; Gwen Ifill, "White House Trying to Trim Blocked Jobs Bill, Aides Say," *New York Times*, 8 April 1993, p. D20; Ann Devroy and David S. Broder, "Missteps Mired Clinton Package," *Washington Post*, 11 April 1993, p. A1; Jeffrey H. Birnbaum and David Rogers, "GOP Filibuster Defeats Clinton Stimulus Package," *Wall Street Journal*, 22 April 1993, p. A2; and Bob Woodward, *The Agenda* (New York: Simon & Schuster, 1994).

2. Clinton Rossiter, *1787: The Grand Convention* (New York: Mentor, 1968), p. 148.

3. *Ibid.*, pp. 190–191.

4. See Louis Fisher, *Presidential War Power* (Lawrence: University Press of Kansas, 1995).

5. Wilfred E. Binkley, *President and Congress*, 3rd ed. (New York: Vintage, 1962), p. 155.

6. Richard M. Pious, *The American Presidency* (New York: Basic Books, 1979), pp. 60–63.

7. Richard E. Neustadt, *Presidential Power* (New York: John Wiley, 1980), p. 10.

8. *Ibid.*, p. 9.

9. Fred I. Greenstein, *The Hidden-Hand Presidency* (New York: Basic Books, 1982), pp. 155–227.

10. George C. Edwards III, *At the Margins* (New Haven, Conn.: Yale University Press, 1989). See also Jon R. Bond and Richard Fleisher, *The President in the Legislative Arena* (Chicago: University of Chicago Press, 1990).

11. Bert Rockman, "Leadership Style and the Clinton Presidency," in *The Clinton Presidency: First Appraisals*, ed. Colin Campbell and Bert A. Rockman (Chatham, N.J.: Chatham House, 1996), p. 328.

12. See Edwards, *At the Margins*, pp. 101–125.

13. Theodore J. Lowi, *The Personal President* (Ithaca, N.Y.: Cornell University Press, 1985).

14. Richard A. Brody, *Assessing the President* (Stanford, Calif.: Stanford University Press, 1991), pp. 27–44.

15. Darrell M. West, *Congress and Economic Policymaking* (Pittsburgh: University of Pittsburgh Press, 1987), p. 33.

16. Paul Brace and Barbara Hinckley, *Follow the Leader* (New York: Basic Books, 1992).

17. Charles W. Ostrom and Dennis M. Simon, "Promise and Performance: A Dynamic Model of Presidential Popularity," *American Political Science Review* 79 (June 1985), pp. 334–358.

18. George C. Edwards III, "Frustration and Folly: Bill Clinton and the Public Presidency," in *The Clinton Presidency*, p. 255.

19. Brace and Hinckley, *Follow the Leader*, p. 19.

20. "Prepared Text of Carter's Farewell Address," *New York Times*, 15 January 1981, p. B10.

21. Benjamin I. Page, *Choices and Echoes in Presidential Elections* (Chicago: University of Chicago Press, 1978).

22. Robert A. Dahl, "Myth of the Presidential Mandate," *Political Science Quarterly* 105 (Fall 1990), pp. 355–372.

23. "Two Cheers for United Government," *American Enterprise* 4 (January-February 1993), pp. 107–108.

24. Morris Fiorina, *Divided Government*, 2d ed. (Needham Heights, Mass.: Allyn & Bacon, 1996), p. 153.

25. Gary C. Jacobson, "Meager Patrimony: The Reagan Era and Republican Representation in Congress," in *Looking Back at the Reagan Presidency*, ed. Larry Berman (Baltimore: Johns Hopkins University Press, 1990), p. 300.

26. See generally, Charles O. Jones, *The Presidency in a Separated System* (Washington, D.C.: Brookings Institution, 1994).

27. David R. Mayhew, *Divided We Govern* (New Haven: Yale University Press, 1991); and David R. Mayhew, "The Return to Unified Government Under Clinton: How Much of a Difference in Lawmaking," in *The New American Politics*, ed. Bryan D. Jones (Boulder, Colo.: Westview Press, 1995), pp. 111–121.

28. See Sean Kelley, "Divided We Govern: A Reassessment," *Polity* 25 (Spring 1993), pp. 475–484; and George Edwards, Andrew Barrett, and Jeffrey Peake, "The Legislative Impact of Divided Government: What *Failed* to Pass in Congress," n.d., Center for Presidential Studies, Texas A&M University.

29. For an overview of the gridlock argument, see James L. Sundquist, ed., *Back to Gridlock?* (Washington, D.C.: Brookings Institution, 1995).

30. Dan Carney, "As Hostilities Rage on the Hill, Partisan-Vote Rate Soars," *Congressional Quarterly Weekly Report*, 27 January 1996, pp. 199–201.

31. See Charles E. Walcott and Karen M. Hult, *Governing the White House* (Lawrence: University of Kansas Press, 1995).

32. Jeb Stuart Magruder, *An American Life* (New York: Atheneum, 1974), p. 58, quoted in Benjamin I. Page and Mark Petracca, *The American Presidency* (New York: McGraw-Hill, 1983), p. 171.

33. U.S. Bureau of the Census, U.S. Department of Commerce, *Statistical Abstract of the United States, 1995* (Washington, D.C.: U.S. Government Printing Office, 1995), p. 350; and U.S. Office of Management and Budget, *Budget of the United States Government, Fiscal Year 1995* (Washington, D.C.: 1994), p. 237.

34. Paul J. Quirk, "Presidential Competence," in *The Presidency and the Political System*, 4th ed., ed. Michael Nelson (Washington, D.C.: Congressional Quarterly Press, 1995), p. 174.

35. Bob Woodward, *The Agenda* (New York: Simon & Schuster, 1994), p. 127.

36. Jeffrey H. Birnbaum, *Madhouse: The Private Turmoil of Working for the President* (New York: Times Books, 1996).

37. Edward Weisband and Thomas M. Franck, *Resignation in Protest* (New York: Penguin, 1975), p. 139, quoted in Thomas E. Cronin, *The State of the Presidency*, 2d ed. (Boston: Little, Brown, 1980), p. 253.

38. Griffin B. Bell with Ronald J. Ostrow, *Taking Care of the Law* (New York: Morrow, 1982), p. 45.

39. See Shirley Anne Warshaw, *Powersharing* (Albany: State University Press of New York, 1995).

40. See Richard W. Waterman, "Combining Political Resources: The Internalization of the President's Appointment Power," in *The Presidency Reconsidered*, ed. Richard W. Waterman (Itasca, Ill.: Peacock, 1993), pp. 172–210.

41. Terry M. Moe, "The Politicized Presidency," in *The New Direction in American Politics*, ed. John E. Chubb and Paul E. Peterson (Washington, D.C.: Brookings Institution, 1985), pp. 235–271.

42. *Public Papers of the President, Lyndon B. Johnson, 1965*, vol. 1 (Washington, D.C.: Government Printing Office, 1966), p. 72.

43. "Transcript of Second Inaugural Address by Reagan," *New York Times*, 22 January 1985, p. 72.

44. Kevin Phillips, *The Politics of Rich and Poor* (New York: Random House, 1990), p. 88.

45. Stephen Skowronek, *The Politics Presidents Make* (Cambridge, Mass.:

Harvard University Press, 1993), pp. 429–441.

46. Charles Kolb, *White House Daze* (New York: Free Press, 1994), p. 9.

47. John W. Kingdon, *Agendas, Alternatives, and Public Policies* (Boston: Little, Brown, 1984), p. 25.

48. Richard E. Neustadt, "Presidency and Legislation: The Growth of Central Clearance," *American Political Science Review* 48 (September 1954), pp. 641–671.

49. Seth King, "Reagan, in Bid for Budget Votes, Reported to Yield on Sugar Prices," *New York Times*, 27 June 1981, p. A1.

50. Jeffrey M. Berry and Kent E. Portney, "Centralizing Regulatory Control and Interest Group Access: The Quayle Council on Competitiveness," in *Interest Group Politics*, 4th ed., ed. Allan J. Cigler and Burdett A. Loomis (Washington, D.C.: Congressional Quarterly Press, 1994), pp. 319–347.

51. The extent to which popularity affects presidential influence in Congress is difficult to determine with any precision. For an overview of this issue, see Jon R. Bond, Richard Fleisher, and Glen S. Katz, "An Overview of the Empirical Findings on Presidential-Congressional Relations," in *Rivals for Power*, ed. James A. Thurber (Washington, D.C.: Congressional Quarterly Press, 1996), pp. 103–139.

52. Sidney M. Milkis, *The President and the Parties* (New York: Oxford University Press, 1993), pp. 189–191.

53. John Aloysius Farrell, "A Loyal Standard Bearer," *Boston Globe*, 7 June 1996, p. A1.

54. Fred Barnes, "Hour of Power," *New Republic*, 3 September 1990, p. 12.

55. Alexander George, "The Case for Multiple Advocacy in Foreign Policy," *American Political Science Review* (September 1972), pp. 751–782.

56. John P. Burke and Fred I. Greenstein, *How Presidents Test Reality* (New York: Russell Sage Foundation, 1989).

57. Richard E. Neustadt and Earnest R. May, *Thinking in Time* (New York: Free Press, 1986), p. 143.

58. Lowi, *Personal President*, p. 185.

59. On the development of Clinton's character, see David Maraniss, *First in His Class* (New York: Simon & Schuster, 1995).

60. Dan Balz, "Clinton Concedes

Marital Wrongdoing," *Washington Post,* 27 January 1992, p. A1.

61. Richard L. Berke, "Voter Ratings for President Change Little," *New York Times,* 5 June 1996, p. A1.

62. Robert A. Caro, *The Path to Power* (New York: Alfred A. Knopf, 1982), p. 131.

63. *Ibid.,* p. 135.

64. Doris Kearns, *Lyndon Johnson and the American Dream* (New York: Signet, 1977), p. 363.

65. See generally, James David Barber, *The Presidential Character,* 4th ed. (Englewood Cliffs, N.J.: Prentice-Hall, 1992).

Chapter 13 / The Bureaucracy / pp. 424–451

1. Adam Bryant, "Crash Stirs Up Safety Debate in U.S. Agency," *New York Times,* 15 May 1996, p. A1.

2. Adam Bryant, "F.A.A. Struggles as Airlines Turn to Subcontracts," *New York Times,* 2 June 1996, p. 1.

3. Alison Mitchell, "Clinton Offers Challenge to Nation, Declaring, 'Era of Big Government is Over,'" *New York Times,* 24 January 1996, p. A1.

4. John E. Chubb and Terry M. Moe, *Politics, Markets, and America's Schools* (Washington, D.C.: Brookings Institution, 1990).

5. James Q. Wilson, *Bureaucracy* (New York: Basic Books, 1989), p. 25.

6. Bruce D. Porter, "Parkinson's Law Revisited: War and the Growth of American Government," *Public Interest* 60 (Summer 1980), p. 50.

7. See generally, Ballard C. Campbell, *The Growth of American Government* (Bloomington: Indiana University Press, 1995).

8. See Anne Schneider and Helen Ingram, "Social Construction of Target Populations: Implications for Politics and Policy," *American Political Science Review* 87 (June 1993), pp. 334–347.

9. Theda Skocpol, *Protecting Soldiers and Mothers: The Political Origins of Social Policy in the United States* (Cambridge, Mass.: Harvard University Press, 1992).

10. Paul C. Light, *Thickening Government* (Washington, D.C.: Brookings Institution, 1995).

11. William J. Broad, "U.S. Will Deploy Its Spy Satellites on Nature Mission," *New York Times,* 27 November 1995, p. A1.

12. Linda L. M. Bennett and Stephen Earl Bennett, "Looking at Leviathan: Dimensions of Opinion About Big Government," in *Broken Contract,* ed. Stephen C. Craig (Boulder, Colo.: Westview Press, 1996), pp. 23–45.

13. John H. Cushman, Jr., "E.P.A. Is Canceling Pollution Testing Across the Nation," *New York Times,* 25 November 1995, p. 1.

14. John T. Tierney, "Government Corporations and Managing the Public's Business," *Political Science Quarterly* 99 (Spring 1984), pp. 73–92.

15. U.S. Bureau of the Census, *Statistical Abstract of the United States, 1995* (Washington, D.C.: U.S. Governmental Printing Office, 1995), pp. 351, 400.

16. U.S. Bureau of the Census, *Statistical Abstract of the United States, 1992* (Washington, D.C.: U.S. Government Printing Office, 1992), pp. 332–333.

17. Patricia Wallace Ingraham, *The Foundation of Merit* (Baltimore: Johns Hopkins University Press, 1995), p. 9.

18. Joel D. Aberbach and Bert A. Rockman, with Robert M. Copeland, "From Nixon's Problem to Reagan's Achievement," in *Looking Back on the Reagan Presidency,* ed. Larry Berman (Baltimore: Johns Hopkins University Press, 1990), p. 180.

19. John Frohnmeyer, *Leaving Town Alive* (Boston: Houghton Mifflin, 1993).

20. Jeffrey M. Berry and Kent E. Portney, "Centralizing Regulatory Control and Interest Group Access: The Quayle Council on Competitiveness," in *Interest Group Politics,* 4th ed., ed. Allan J. Cigler and Burdett A. Loomis (Washington, D.C.: Congressional Quarterly Press, 1995), pp. 319–347.

21. Joel Aberbach, "The Federal Executive under Clinton," in *The Clinton Presidency,* ed. Colin Campbell and Bert A. Rockman (Chatham, N.J.: Chatham House, 1996), pp. 163–187.

22. B. Dan Wood and Richard W. Waterman, *Bureaucratic Dynamics* (Boulder, Colo.: Westview, 1994), pp. 62–67.

23. Barbara Hinkson Craig and David M. O'Brien, *Abortion and American Politics* (Chatham, N.J.: Chatham House, 1993), pp. 188–189.

24. See generally, Michael W. Spicer and Larry D. Terry, "Administrative Interpretation of Statutes," *Public Administration Review* 56 (January-February 1996), pp. 38–47.

25. Theodore J. Lowi, Jr., *The End of Liberalism,* 2d ed. (New York: Norton, 1979).

26. Doris A. Graber, *Mass Media and American Politics,* 3rd ed. (Washington, D.C.: Congressional Quarterly Press, 1989), p. 51.

27. Jeffrey M. Berry, *Feeding Hungry People* (New Brunswick, N.J.: Rutgers University Press, 1984).

28. David J. Garrow, *Bearing the Cross* (New York: Morrow, 1986), pp. 373–374.

29. Marian Burros, "F.D.A. Is Again Proposing To Regulate Vitamins and Supplements," *New York Times,* 15 June 1993, p. A25.

30. Charles E. Lindblom, "The Science of Muddling Through," *Public Administration Review* 19 (Spring 1959), pp. 79–88.

31. See Michael T. Hayes, *Incrementalism and Public Policy* (White Plains, N.Y.: Longman, 1992).

32. Andrew Weiss and Edward Woodhouse, "Reframing Incrementalism: A Constructive Response to the Critics," *Policy Sciences* 25 (August 1992), pp. 255–273.

33. Elaine Sciolino, "Panel from C.I.A. Urges Curtailing of Agency Secrecy," *New York Times,* 12 January 1992, p. A1.

34. Jonathan Bendor, Serge Taylor, and Roland Van Gaalar, "Stacking the Deck: Bureaucratic Mission and Policy Design," *American Political Science Review* 81 (Spring 1987), p. 874.

35. Frohnmayer, *Leaving Town Alive,* pp. 213 and 262.

36. Thomas W. Church and Robert T. Nakamura, *Cleaning Up the Mess* (Washington, D.C.: Brookings Institution, 1993).

37. Martha Derthick, *Agency Under Stress* (Washington, D.C.: Brookings Institution, 1990), pp. 33–48.

38. Gerald Garvey, *Facing the Bureaucracy: Living and Dying in a Public Agency* (San Francisco: Jossey-Bass, 1993), p. 190.

39. See Philip K. Howard, *The Death of*

Common Sense (New York: Warner Books, 1994).

40. Eric Schmitt, "Agriculture Dept. Rebuffed on School Lunches," *New York Times*, 15 May 1996, p. A17.

41. See generally, Terry M. Moe, "The Politics of Bureaucratic Structure," in *Can the Government Govern?* ed. John E. Chubb and Paul E. Peterson (Washington, D.C.: Brookings Institution, 1989), pp. 267–329.

42. See generally, John J. DiIulio, Jr., Gerald Garvey, and Donald F. Kettl, *Improving Government Performance: An Owner's Manual* (Washington, D.C.: Brookings Institution, 1993).

43. Jeffrey H. Birnbaum and Paulette Thomas, "Clinton Moves to Streamline Government," *Wall Street Journal*, 8 September 1993, p. A2.

44. Peter H. Stone, "Ganging Up on the FDA," *National Journal*, 18 February 1995, pp. 410–414.

45. David Vogel, "AIDS and the Politics of Drug Lag," *Public Interest* 96 (Summer 1989), pp. 73–85.

46. A good, short introduction to TQM in government is James E. Swiss, "Adapting Total Quality Management to Government," *Public Administration Review* 52 (July-August 1992), pp. 356–362.

47. David Osborne and Ted Gaebler, *Reinventing Government* (New York: Plume Books, 1993), p. 166.

48. Joseph Sensenbrenner, "Quality Comes to City Hall," *Harvard Business Review* 69 (March-April 1991), pp. 64–75.

49. See Donald F. Kettl and John J. DiIulio, Jr., eds., *Inside the Reinvention Machine* (Washington, D.C.: Brookings Institution, 1995); and Ronald Moe, "The 'Reinventing Government' Exercise: Misinterpreting the Problem, Misjudging the Consequences," *Public Administration Review* 54 (March-April 1994), pp. 111–122.

Chapter 14 / The Courts / pp. 452–490

1. Keith White, "Danforth Says Court Nominee Is Making His Own Case," Gannett News Service, 19 July 1991 (LEXIS).

2. David Brock, *The Real Anita Hill* (New York: Free Press, 1992), p. 61; Jane Mayer and Jill Abramson, *Strange Justice: The Selling of Clarence Thomas* (Boston: Houghton Mifflin, 1994).

3. Jeffrey Rosen, "Annals of Law: Moving On," *The New Yorker*, 29 April and 6 May 1996, p. 73.

4. *Ibid.*, pp. 66–67.

5. *Missouri* v. *Jenkins*, 515 U.S. ____ (1995); *Adarand* v. *Peña*, 515 U.S. ____ (1995).

6. Felix Frankfurter and James M. Landis, *The Business of the Supreme Court* (New York: Macmillan, 1928), pp. 5–14; and Julius Goebel, Jr., *Antecedents and Beginnings to 1801*, vol. 1 of *The History of the Supreme Court of the United States* (New York: Macmillan, 1971).

7. Maeva Marcus, ed., *The Justices on Circuit, 1795–1800*, vol. 3 of *The Documentary History of the Supreme Court of the United States, 1789–1800* (New York: Columbia University Press, 1990).

8. Robert G. McCloskey, *The United States Supreme Court* (Chicago: University of Chicago Press, 1960), p. 31.

9. *Marbury* v. *Madison*, 1 Cranch 137 at 177, 178 (1803).

10. Interestingly, the term *judicial review* dates only to 1910; it was apparently unknown to Marshall and his contemporaries. Robert Lowry Clinton, *Marbury* v. *Madison and Judicial Review* (Lawrence: University Press of Kansas, 1989), p. 7.

11. Henry J. Abraham, *The Judicial Process*, 6th ed. (New York: Oxford University Press, 1993), pp. 274–279. Lee Epstein et al., *The Supreme Court Compendium* (Washington, D.C.: Congressional Quarterly Press, 1994), Table 2-12.

12. *Ware* v. *Hylton*, 3 Dallas 199 (1796).

13. *Martin* v. *Hunter's Lessee*, 1 Wheat. 304 (1816).

14. *Constitution of the United States of America: Annotated and Interpreted* (Washington, D.C.: U.S. Government Printing Office, 1987) and supplements.

15. Garry Wills, *Explaining America: The Federalist* (Garden City, N.Y.: Doubleday, 1981), pp. 127–136.

16. *State Justice Institute News*, 4 (Spring 1993), p. 1.

17. William P. Marshall, "Federalization: A Critical Overview," 44 *DePaul Law Review* 719 (1995), 722–723.

18. Charles Alan Wright, *Handbook on the Law of Federal Courts*, 3d ed. (St. Paul, Minn.: West, 1976), p. 7.

19. Federal Court Management Statistics, October 1995, Administrative Office of the United States Courts, Statistics Division, Analysis and Reports Branch.

20. *Ibid.*

21. Linda Greenhouse, "Precedent for Lower Courts: Tyrant or Teacher?" *New York Times*, 29 January 1988, p. B7.

22. *Texas* v. *Johnson*, 491 U.S. 397 (1989); *United States* v. *Eichman*, 496 U.S. 310 (1990).

23. *Regents of the University of California* v. *Bakke*, 438 U.S. 265 (1978).

24. *Adarand Constructors* v. *Peña*, 515 U.S. ____ (1995); *Miller* v. *Johnson*, ____ U.S. ____ (1995).

25. "Reading Petitions Is for Clerks Only at High Court Now," *Wall Street Journal*, 11 October 1990, p. B7.

26. H. W. Perry, Jr., *Deciding to Decide: Agenda Setting in the United States Supreme Court* (Cambridge, Mass.: Harvard University Press, 1991); Linda Greenhouse, "Justice Delayed; Agreeing Not to Agree," *New York Times*, 17 March 1996, Sect. 4, p. 1.

27. Perry, *Deciding to Decide*; Gregory A. Caldiera and John R. Wright, "The Discuss List: Agenda Building in the Supreme Court," 24 *Law & Society Review* 807 (1990).

28. Doris M. Provine, *Case Selection in the United States Supreme Court* (Chicago: University of Chicago Press, 1980), pp. 74–102.

29. Elder Witt, *A Different Justice: Reagan and the Supreme Court* (Washington, D.C.: Congressional Quarterly Press, 1986), p. 133.

30. Neil A. Lewis, "Solicitor General's Career Advances at Intersection of Law and Politics," *New York Times*, 1 June 1990, p. A11.

31. Tony Mauro, "Courtside: High Court High Jinks," *American Lawyer*, 8 January 1996, p. 17.

32. Perry, *Deciding to Decide*, p. 286.

33. Kevin T. McGuire, "Repeat Players in the Supreme Court: The Role of Experienced Lawyers in Litigation Success," *Journal of Politics* 57 (1995), pp. 187–196.

34. Michael Kirkland, *Court Hears "Subordinate" Speech Debate*, UPI, 1 December 1993, available in

NEWSNET News Bulletin Board. The oral argument in the case, *Waters* v. *Churchill*, can be found at <oyez.at.nwu.edu/cases/92–1450/>.

35. "Rising Fixed Opinions," *New York Times*, 22 February 1988, p. 14. See also Linda Greenhouse, "At the Bar," *New York Times*, 28 July 1989, p. 21.

36. Jeffrey A. Segal and Harold J. Spaeth, *The Supreme Court and the Attitudinal Model* (Cambridge, England: Cambridge University Press, 1993).

37. Jeffrey A. Segal and Albert D. Cover, "Ideological Values and the Votes of U.S. Supreme Court Justices," *American Political Science Review* 83 (1989), pp. 557–565; Tracy E. George and Lee Epstein, "The Nature of Supreme Court Decision Making," *American Political Science Review* 86 (1992), pp. 323–337.

38. Stuart Taylor, Jr., "Lifting of Secrecy Reveals Earthy Side of Justices," *New York Times*, 22 February 1988, p. A16.

39. Glen Elasser, "Courting Justice," *Chicago Tribune*, 6 June 1990, Tempo, p. 1.

40. Stuart Taylor, Jr., "Brennan: 30 Years and the Thrill Is Not Gone," *New York Times*, 16 April 1986, p. B8.

41. Thomas G. Walker, Lee Epstein, and William J. Dixon, "On the Mysterious Demise of Consensual Norms in the United States Supreme Court," *Journal of Politics* 50 (1988), pp. 361–389.

42. See, for example, Walter F. Murphy, *Elements of Judicial Strategy* (Chicago: University of Chicago Press, 1964), and Bob Woodward and Scott Armstrong, *The Brethren* (New York: Simon & Schuster, 1979).

43. Henry J. Abraham, *Justices and Presidents: A Political History of Appointments to the Supreme Court*, 2d ed. (New York: Oxford University Press, 1985), pp. 183–185.

44. Stephen L. Wasby, *The Supreme Court in the Federal Judicial System*, 3d ed. (Chicago: Nelson-Hall, 1988), p. 241.

45. Linda Greenhouse, "At the Bar," *New York Times*, 28 July 1989, p. 21.

46. Lawrence Baum, *American Courts: Process and Policy*, 3d ed. (Boston: Houghton Mifflin, 1994), pp. 114–129.

47. Paul Barrett, "More Minorities, Women Named to U.S. Courts," *Wall Street Journal*, 23 December 1993, p. B1.

48. Wasby, *Supreme Court*, pp. 107–110.

49. Sheldon Goldman, "Judicial Selection Under Clinton: A Midterm Examination," 78 *Judicature* 276 (1995). Professor Goldman kindly provided additional data from the 104th Congress.

50. Ronald Stidham, Robert A. Carp, and Donald R. Songer, "The Voting Behavior of Judges Appointed by President Clinton," paper presented at the annual meeting of the Southwestern Political Science Association, Houston, Texas, March 1996.

51. Peter G. Fish, "John J. Parker," in *Dictionary of American Biography*, supp. 6, 1956–1980 (New York: Scribner's, 1980), p. 494.

52. *Congressional Quarterly's Guide to the U.S. Supreme Court*, 2d ed. (Washington, D.C.: Congressional Quarterly Press, 1990), pp. 655–656.

53. Ibid., pp. 878–890.

54. Maureen Dowd, "The Supreme Court: Conservative Black Judge, Clarence Thomas, Named to Marshall's Court Seat," *New York Times*, 2 July 1991, pp. A1, A16.

55. *Brown* v. *Board of Education II*, 349 U.S. 294 (1955).

56. Charles A. Johnson and Bradley C. Canon, *Judicial Policies: Implementation and Impact* (Washington, D.C.: Congressional Quarterly Press, 1984).

57. *Webster* v. *Reproductive Health Services*, 492 U.S. 490 (1989).

58. *Planned Parenthood* v. *Casey*, 505 U.S. ___ (1992).

59. Alexander M. Bickel, *The Least Dangerous Branch* (Indianapolis: Bobbs-Merrill, 1962); and Robert A. Dahl, "Decision-Making in a Democracy: The Supreme Court as a National Policy-Maker," 6 *Journal of Public Law* 279 (1962).

60. William Mishler and Reginal S. Sheehan, "The Supreme Court as a Countermajoritarian Institution? The Impact of Public Opinion on Supreme Court Decisions," *American Political Science Review* 87 (1993), pp. 87–101.

61. Thomas R. Marshall, *Public Opinion and the Supreme Court* (Boston: Unwin Hyman, 1989).

62. Richard Morin, "Unconventional Wisdom," *Washington Post*, 8 October 1995, p. C5.

63. Marshall, *Public Opinion and the Supreme Court*, pp. 192–193; Gerald N. Rosenberg, *The Hollow Hope: Can Courts Bring About Social Change?* (Chicago: University of Chicago Press, 1991).

64. William J. Brennan, Jr., "State Supreme Court Judge Versus United States Supreme Court Justice: A Change in Function and Perspective," 19 *University of Florida Law Review* 225 (1966).

65. G. Alan Tarr and M. C. Porter, *State Supreme Courts in State and Nation* (New Haven, Conn.: Yale University Press, 1988), pp. 206–209.

66. Dennis Hevesi, "New Jersey Court Protects Trash from Police Searches," *New York Times*, 19 July 1990, p. A9.

67. Baum, *American Courts*, pp. 319–347.

Chapter 15 / Order and Civil Liberties / pp. 491–535

1. *United States* v. *Baker and Gonda*, 890 F. Supp. 1375 (1995).

2. Charles Platt, *Anarchy Online* (New York: HarperCollins, forthcoming).

3. Learned Hand, *The Bill of Rights* (Boston: Atheneum, 1958), p. 1.

4. Leonard W. Levy, *The Establishment Clause: Religion and the First Amendment* (New York: Macmillan, 1986); Leo Pfeffer, *Church, State, and Freedom* (Boston: Beacon, 1953); and Leonard W. Levy, "The Original Meaning of the Establishment Clause of the First Amendment," in *Religion and the State*, ed. James E. Wood, Jr. (Waco, Texas: Baylor University Press, 1985), pp. 43–83.

5. Garry Wills, *Under God: Religion and American Politics* (New York: Simon & Schuster, 1990); Barry A. Kosmin and Seymour P. Lachman, *One Nation Under God: Religion in Contemporary American Society* (New York: Harmony Books, 1993).

6. *Reynolds* v. *United States*, 98 U.S. 145 (1879).

7. *Everson* v. *Board of Education*, 330 U.S. 1 (1947).

8. *Board of Education* v. *Allen*, 392 U.S. 236 (1968).

9. *Lemon* v. *Kurtzman*, 403 U.S. 602 (1971).

10. *Lynch* v. *Donnelly*, 465 U.S. 668 (1984).

11. *County of Allegheny* v. *ACLU Greater Pittsburgh Chapter*, 492 U.S. 573 (1989).
12. 515 U.S. ____ (1994).
13. "Bill Signed to Keep Hasidic School Open," *New York Times*, 9 July 1994, p. 16; "Hasidic School District Illegal in New York State," *Wall Street Journal*, 27 August 1996, p. B5.
14. *Engle* v. *Vitale*, 370 U.S. 421 (1962).
15. *Abington School District* v. *Schempp*, 374 U.S. 203 (1963).
16. *Lee* v. *Weisman*, 505 U.S. (1992).
17. *Herdahl* v. *Pontotoc County School District, No. 3*, 1996 U.S. Dist. LEXIS 7671 (N.D. Miss. W.D.) (3 June 1996).
18. *Wallace* v. *Jaffree*, 472 U.S. 38 (1985).
19. *Board of Education* v. *Mergens*, 496 U.S. 226 (1990).
20. Michael W. McConnell, "The Origins and Historical Understanding of the Free Exercise of Religion," 103 *Harvard Law Review* 1409, 1990.
21. *Minersville School District* v. *Gobitis*, 310 U.S. 586 (1940).
22. David Margolick, "Pledge Dispute Evokes Bitter Memories," *New York Times*, 11 September 1988, p. A1.
23. *West Virginia State Board of Education* v. *Barnette*, 319 U.S. 624 at 642 (1943).
24. *Sherbert* v. *Verner*, 374 U.S. 398 (1963).
25. McConnell, *Origins and Historical Understanding*.
26. *Employment Division* v. *Smith*, 494 U.S. 872 (1990).
27. Peter Steinfels, "Clinton Signs Law Protecting Religious Practices," 16 November 1993, *New York Times*, p. A18.
28. Laurence Tribe, *Treatise on American Constitutional Law*, 2d ed. (St. Paul, Minn.: West, 1988), p. 566.
29. Zechariah Chafee, *Free Speech in the United States* (Cambridge, Mass.: Harvard University Press, 1941).
30. Leonard W. Levy, *The Emergence of a Free Press* (New York: Oxford University Press, 1985).
31. Mark Twain, *Following the Equator* (Hartford, Conn.: American Publishing, 1897).
32. *Schenck* v. *United States*, 249 U.S. 47 (1919).
33. *Abrams* v. *United States*, 250 U.S. 616 (1919).
34. *Gitlow* v. *New York*, 268 U.S. 652 (1925).
35. *Dennis* v. *United States*, 341 U.S. 494 (1951).
36. *Brandenburg* v. *Ohio*, 395 U.S. 444 (1969).
37. *Tinker* v. *Des Moines Independent County School District*, 393 U.S. 503 at 508 (1969) ____.
38. *United States* v. *Eichman*, 496 U.S. 310 (1990).
39. Linda Greenhouse, "Supreme Court Voids Flag Law," *New York Times*, 12 June 1990, p. A1.
40. *Barnes* v. *Glen Theatre*, 501 U.S. 560 (1991).
41. *Chaplinsky* v. *New Hampshire*, 315 U.S. 568 (1942).
42. *Terminiello* v. *Chicago*, 337 U.S. 1.
43. *Cohen* v. *California*, 403 U.S. 15 (1971).
44. *R.A.V.* v. *City of St. Paul*, 504 U.S. ____ (1992).
45. *United States* v. *Baker and Gonda*, 890 F. Supp. 1375 (1995).
46. *ACLU* v. *Reno* (1996 U.S. Dist. LEXIS) (June 12, 1996).
47. *Roth* v. *United States*, 354 U.S. 476 (1957).
48. *Jacobellis* v. *Ohio*, 378 U.S. 184 (1964).
49. *Miller* v. *California*, 413 U.S. 15 (1973).
50. Donald Alexander Downs, *The New Politics of Pornography* (Chicago: University of Chicago Press, 1989), pp. 95–143.
51. *American Booksellers Ass'n* v. *Hudnut*, 598 F. Supp. 1316 (1984).
52. *New York Times* v. *Sullivan*, 376 U.S. 254 (1964).
53. *Hustler Magazine* v. *Falwell*, 485 U.S. 46 (1988).
54. *Near* v. *Minnesota*, 283 U.S. 697 (1931).
55. For a detailed account of *Near*, see Fred W. Friendly, *Minnesota Rag* (New York: Random House, 1981).
56. *New York Times* v. *United States*, 403 U.S. 713 (1971).
57. *Branzburg* v. *Hayes*, 408 U.S. 665 (1972).
58. *Zurcher* v. *Stanford Daily*, 436 U.S. 547 (1978).
59. *Hazelwood School District* v. *Kuhlmeier*, 484 U.S. 260 (1988).
60. *United States* v. *Cruikshank*, 92 U.S. 542 (1876); *Constitution of the United States of America: Annotated and Interpreted* (Washington, D.C.: U.S. Government Printing Office, 1973), p. 1031.
61. *DeJonge* v. *Oregon*, 299 U.S. 353 (1937).
62. *United States* v. *Miller*, 307 U.S. 174 (1939).
63. Laurence H. Tribe and Michael C. Dorf, *On Reading the Constitution* (Cambridge, Mass.: Harvard University Press, 1991), p. 10.
64. *Barron* v. *Baltimore*, 32 U.S. (7 Pet.) 243 (1833).
65. *Chicago B. & Q. R.* v. *Chicago*, 166 U.S. 226 (1897).
66. *Gitlow* v. *New York*, 268 U.S. at 666 (1925).
67. *Palko* v. *Connecticut*, 302 U.S. 319 (1937).
68. *Duncan* v. *Louisiana*, 391 U.S. 145 (1968).
69. *McNabb* v. *United States*, 318 U.S. 332 (1943).
70. *Baldwin* v. *New York*, 399 U.S. 66 (1970).
71. Anthony Lewis, *Gideon's Trumpet* (New York: Random House, 1964).
72. *Gideon* v. *Wainright*, 372 U.S. 335 (1963).
73. *Miranda* v. *Arizona*, 384 U.S. 436 (1966).
74. *Wolf* v. *Colorado*, 338 U.S. 25 (1949).
75. *Mapp* v. *Ohio*, 367 U.S. 643 (1961).
76. *United States* v. *Leon*, 468 U.S. 897 (1984).
77. *California* v. *Greenwood*, 486 U.S. 35 (1988).
78. *James* v. *Illinois*, 493 U.S. 307 (1990).
79. Paul Brest, *Processes of Constitutional Decision-making* (Boston: Little, Brown, 1975), p. 708.
80. *Griswold* v. *Connecticut*, 381 U.S. 479 (1965).
81. *Roe* v. *Wade*, 410 U.S. 113 (1973).
82. See John Hart Ely, "The Wages of Crying Wolf: A Comment on *Roe* v. *Wade*," 82 *Yale Law Journal* 920 (1973).
83. Interview with Justice Harry Blackmun, ABC's "Nightline," 2 December 1993.
84. *Webster* v. *Reproductive Health Services*, 492 U.S. 490 (1989).
85. *Hodgson* v. *Minnesota*, 497 U.S. 417 (1990); *Ohio* v. *Akron Center for Reproductive Health*, 497 U.S. 502 (1990).
86. *Planned Parenthood* v. *Casey*, 505 U.S. ____ (1992).
87. Ruth Bader Ginsburg, "Some Thoughts on Autonomy and Equality in Relation to *Roe* v.

Wade," 63 *North Carolina Law Review* 375 (1985).

88. Stuart Taylor, "Supreme Court Hears Case on Homosexual Rights," *New York Times,* 1 April 1986, p. A-24.

89. *Bowers* v. *Hardwick,* 478 U.S. 186 (1986).

90. Linda Greenhouse, "Washington Talk: When Second Thoughts Come Too Late," *New York Times,* 5 November 1990, p. A9.

91. *Baehr* v. *Lewin,* 852 P. 2d 44 (1993).

92. Learned Hand, "The Contribution of an Independent Judiciary to Civilization," in *The Spirit of Liberty: Papers and Addresses of Learned Hand,* ed. Irving Dilliard, 3d ed. (New York: Alfred A. Knopf, 1960), p. 164.

Chapter 16 / Equality and Civil Rights / pp. 536–576

1. *Adarand Constructors, Inc.* v. *Peña,* 518 U.S. ___ (1995); Seth Mydans, "Challenging the Concept of 'Disadvantaged,'" *New York Times,* 18 June 1995, Section 1, p. 8.

2. Howard Schuman, Charlotte Steeh, and Lawrence Bobo, *Racial Attitudes in America: Trends and Interpretations* (Cambridge, Mass.: Harvard University Press, 1985); Sidney Verba and Gary R. Orren, *Equality in America: The View from the Top* (Cambridge, Mass.: Harvard University Press, 1985), especially pp. 1–51; Jack Citrin, "Affirmative Action in the People's Court," *The Public Interest* 122, 1996, pp. 39–48.

3. *The Gallup Poll Monthly,* August 1991, p. 56; Paul M. Sniderman and Thomas Piazza, *The Scar of Race* (Cambridge, Mass.: Belknap Press of Harvard University Press, 1993), pp. 133–134; Citrin, pp. 40–41.

4. David W. Moore, "Americans Today Are Dubious About Affirmative Action," *The Gallup Poll Monthly,* March 1995, pp. 36–38.

5. *The Slaughterhouse Cases,* 83 U.S. 36 (1873).

6. *United States* v. *Cruikshank,* 92 U.S. 542 (1876).

7. *United States* v. *Reese,* 92 U.S. 214 (1876).

8. *Civil Rights Cases,* 109 U.S. 3 (1883).

9. Mary Beth Norton et al., *A People and a Nation: A History of the*

United States, 3d ed. (Boston: Houghton Mifflin, 1990), p. 490.

10. *Plessy* v. *Ferguson,* 163 U.S. 537 (1896).

11. *Plessy,* 163 U.S. at 562 (Harlan, J., dissenting).

12. *Cummings* v. *County Board of Education,* 175 U.S. 528 (1899).

13. *Missouri ex rel. Gaines* v. *Canada,* 305 U.S. 337 (1938).

14. *Sweatt* v. *Painter,* 339 U.S. 629 (1950).

15. *McLaurin* v. *Oklahoma State Regents,* 339 U.S. 637 (1950).

16. *Brown* v. *Board of Education,* 347 U.S. 483 (1954).

17. *Brown* v. *Board of Education,* 347 U.S. 483, 495 (1954).

18. *Brown* v. *Board of Education,* 347 U.S. 483, 494 (1954).

19. *Bolling* v. *Sharpe,* 347 U.S. 497 (1954).

20. *Brown* v. *Board of Education II,* 349 U.S. 294 (1955).

21. Jack W. Peltason, *Fifty-Eight Lonely Men,* rev. ed. (Urbana: University of Illinois Press, 1971).

22. *Alexander* v. *Holmes County Board of Education,* 396 U.S. 19 (1969).

23. *Swann* v. *Charlotte-Mecklenburg County Schools,* 402 U.S. 1 (1971).

24. *Milliken* v. *Bradley,* 418 U.S. 717 (1974).

25. Richard Kluger, *Simple Justice* (New York: Alfred A. Knopf, 1976), p. 753.

26. Taylor Branch, *Parting the Waters: America in the King Years, 1955–1963* (New York: Simon & Schuster, 1988), p. 3.

27. Ibid., p. 14.

28. Ibid., p. 271.

29. *Bell* v. *Maryland,* 378 U.S. 226 (1964).

30. Norton et al., *People and a Nation,* p. 943.

31. *Heart of Atlanta Motel* v. *United States,* 379 U.S. 241 (1964).

32. *Katzenbach* v. *McClung,* 379 U.S. 294 (1964).

33. But see Abigail M. Thernstrom, *Whose Vote Counts? Affirmative Action and Minority Voting Rights* (Cambridge, Mass.: Harvard University Press, 1987).

34. *Grove City College* v. *Bell,* 465 U.S. 555 (1984).

35. *Richmond* v. *J.A. Croson Co.,* 488 U.S. 469 (1989).

36. *Martin* v. *Wilks,* 490 U.S. 755 (1989); *Wards Cove Packing Co.* v. *Atonio,* 490 U.S. 642 (1989); *Patterson* v.

McLean Credit Union, 491 U.S. 164 (1989); *Price Waterhouse* v. *Hopkins,* 490 U.S. 228 (1989); *Lorance* v. *AT&T Technologies,* 490 U.S. 900 (1989); and *EEOC* v. *Arabian American Oil Co.,* 499 U.S. 244 (1991).

37. *Saint Francis College* v. *Al-Khazraji,* 481 U.S. 604 (1987).

38. Dee Brown, *Bury My Heart at Wounded Knee: An Indian History of the American West* (New York: Holt, Rinehart & Winston, 1971).

39. Francis Paul Prucha, *The Great Father: The United States Government and the American Indian,* vol. 2 (Lincoln: University of Nebraska Press, 1984).

40. Jonathan J. Higuera, "Block Grants Worry Latino Legislators," <www.latinolink.com/hisbl16e. html> (1995).

41. Rufus P. Browning, Dale Rogers Marshall, and David H. Tabb, *Protest Is Not Enough* (Berkeley: University of California Press, 1984); Congressional Hispanic Caucus, <www.hispanic.org/hcc. htm>.

42. Lisa J. Stansky, "Opening Doors," *ABA Journal,* 1996, pp. 66–69.

43. Cited in Martin Gruberg, *Women in American Politics* (Oshkosh, Wisc.: Academic Press, 1968), p. 4.

44. *Bradwell* v. *Illinois,* 83 U.S. 130 (1873).

45. *Muller* v. *Oregon,* 208 U.S. 412 (1908).

46. *International Union, United Automobile, Aerospace and Agricultural Implement Workers of America* v. *Johnson Controls, Inc.,* 499 U.S. 187 (1991).

47. *Minor* v. *Happersett,* 88 U.S. 162 (1875).

48. John H. Aldrich et al., *American Government: People, Institutions, and Policies* (Boston: Houghton Mifflin, 1986), p. 618.

49. *Reed* v. *Reed,* 404 U.S. 71 (1971).

50. *Frontiero* v. *Richardson,* 411 U.S. 677 (1973).

51. *Craig* v. *Boren,* 429 U.S. 190 (1976).

52. Paul Weiler, "The Wages of Sex: The Uses and Limits of Comparable Worth," 99 *Harvard Law Review* 1728, 1986; Paula England, *Comparable Worth: Theories and Evidence* (New York: Aldine de Gruyter, 1992).

53. *J.E.B.* v. *Alabama ex rel. T.B.*, 508 U.S. ___ (1994).
54. *United States* v. *Virginia*, slip op. 94–1941 & 94–2107 (decided June 26, 1996).
55. Mike Allen, "Defiant V.M.I. to Admit Women But Will Not Ease Rules for Them," *New York Times*, 22 September 1996, Section 1, p.1.
56. Jane J. Mansbridge, *Why We Lost the ERA* (Chicago: University of Chicago Press, 1986).
57. Melvin I. Urofsky, *A March of Liberty* (New York: Alfred A. Knopf, 1988), p. 902.
58. *Harris* v. *Forklift Systems*, 510 U.S. ___ (1993).
59. *Time*, 6 July 1987, p. 91.
60. *Facts on File* 206B2 (4 June 1965).
61. As quoted in Melvin I. Urofsky, *A Conflict of Rights: The Supreme Court and Affirmative Action* (New York: Scribner's, 1991), p. 17.
62. *Ibid.*, p. 29.
63. Thomas Sowell, *Preferential Policies: An International Perspective* (New York: Morrow, 1990), pp. 103–105.
64. *Regents of the University of California* v. *Bakke*, 438 U.S. 265 (1978).
65. Steven N. Keith, Robert M. Bell, and Albert P. Williams, *Assessing the Outcome of Affirmative Action in Medical Schools* (Santa Monica, Calif.: Rand, 1987).
66. *United Steelworkers of America, AFL-CIO* v. *Weber*, 443 U.S. 193 (1979).
67. *Firefighters* v. *Stotts*, 467 U.S. 561 (1984).
68. *Johnson* v. *Transportation Agency, Santa Clara County*, 480 U.S. 616 (1987).
69. *Adarand Constructors, Inc.* v. *Peña*, 518 U.S. ___ (1995).
70. "Death by Judges? Affirmative Action," *The Economist*, 17 June 1995, p. 28.
71. *Hopwood* v. *Texas*, 78 F. 3d 932 (1996).
72. *Texas* v. *Hopwood*, 1996 U.S. LEXIS 4267.
73. William H. Honan, "Moves to End Affirmative Action Gain Support Nationwide," *New York Times*, 31 March 1996, p. 30; James Brooke, "Colorado Bases College Aid on Need Rather Than Race," *New York Times*, 16 January 1996, p. A8.
74. Stephen Earl Bennett et al., *Americans' Opinions About Affirmative Action* (Cincinnati: University of Cincinnati, Institute for Policy Research, 1995), p. 4.
75. Seymour Martin Lipset, "Two Americas, Two Systems: Whites, Blacks, and the Debate Over Affirmative Action," *The New Democrat*, May-June 1995.

Chapter 17 / Policymaking / pp. 577–605

1. Dan Morain and Virginia Ellis, "California Elections/Propositions," *Los Angeles Times*, 9 November 1994, p. 3.
2. Fox Butterfield, "Prison-Building Binge in California Casts Shadow on Higher Education," *New York Times*, 12 April 1996, p. A14.
3. Fox Butterfield, "3 Strikes Law in California is Clogging Courts and Jails," *New York Times*, 23 March 1995, p. A1.
4. "The Serious Wrinkles Still in 'Three Strikes,'" *Los Angeles Times*, 10 April 1995, p. B4; and Sandra Ann Harris, "California's 'Three Strikes Law' Burdens Courts," United Press International wire story, 9 April 1996.
5. U.S. Bureau of the Census, *Statistical Abstract of the United States, 1995* (Washington, D.C.: Government Printing Office, 1995), p. 339.
6. Catalina Camia, "As Interior Filibuster Continues, Risks for Westerners Grow," *Congressional Quarterly Weekly Report*, 30 October 1993, pp. 2957–2959.
7. Lawrie Mifflin, "TV Broadcasters Agree to 3 Hours of Children's Educational Programs a Week," *New York Times*, 30 July 1996, p. A8.
8. The policymaking process can be depicted in many ways. Another approach, a bit more elaborate than this, is described in James E. Anderson, *Public Policymaking*, 2d ed. (Boston: Houghton Mifflin, 1994), p. 37.
9. Roger W. Cobb and Charles D. Elder, *Participation in American Politics*, 2d ed. (Baltimore: Johns Hopkins University Press, 1983), p. 14.
10. *Ibid.*, p. 84.
11. Bryan D. Jones, *Reconceiving Decision-Making in Democratic Politics* (Chicago: University of Chicago Press, 1994), pp. 107–108.
12. Barbara J. Nelson, *Making an Issue Out of Child Abuse* (Chicago: University of Chicago Press, 1984), p. 13.
13. See Christopher J. Bosso, "The Contextual Bases of Problem Definition," in *The Politics of Problem Definition*, eds., David A. Rochefort and Roger W. Cobb (Lawrence: University Press of Kansas, 1994), pp. 182–203.
14. Frank D. Baumgartner and Bryan D. Jones, *Agendas and Instability in American Politics* (Chicago: University of Chicago Press, 1993), pp. 59–82.
15. Robert Pear, "U.S. Proposes Rules To Bar Obstacles for the Disabled," *New York Times*, 22 January 1991, p. A1.
16. Peter C. Bishop and Augustus J. Jones, Jr., "Implementing the Americans with Disability Act: Assessing the Variables of Success," *Public Administration Review* 53 (March-April 1993), p. 126.
17. Thomas W. Church and Robert T. Nakamura, *Cleaning Up the Mess* (Washington, D.C.: Brookings Institution, 1993).
18. Arlene Jacobius, "California Three-Strikes Law Gobbling Up Jurors," *ABA Journal* 81 (December 1995).
19. Margaret Weir, *Politics and Jobs* (Princeton, N.J.: Princeton University Press, 1992).
20. Michael R. Gordon and Bernard E. Trainor, *The Generals' War* (Boston: Little, Brown, 1995), p. 475.
21. Tim Weiner, "'Smart' Weapons Were Overrated, Study Concludes," *New York Times*, 9 July 1996, p. A1.
22. William T. Gormley, *Everybody's Children* (Washington, D.C.: Brookings Institution, 1995), pp. 3–5.
23. *Ibid*, p. 81.
24. John E. Yang and Paul M. Barrett, "Drug Issue Triggers Washington Habit: Turf Wars in Congress, Administration," *Wall Street Journal*, August 11, 1989, p. A5.
25. *Ibid.*
26. Philip J. Hilts, "Panel Is Created To Speed Effort on AIDS Drugs," *New York Times*, 1 December 1993, p. A18.
27. Alfred Marcus, "Environmental Protection Agency," in *The Politics of Regulation*, ed., James Q. Wilson (New York: Basic Books, 1980), p. 267.

28. Jeffrey M. Berry and Kent E. Portney, "Centralizing Regulatory Control and Interest Group Access: The Quayle Council on Competitiveness," in *Interest Group Politics*, 4th ed., eds. Allan J. Cigler and Burdett A. Loomis (Washington, D.C.: Congressional Quarterly Press, 1995), pp. 319–347.

29. Clyde Wilcox, *The Latest American Revolution* (New York: St. Martin's Press, 1995), p. 39.

30. On fragmentation in the Congress and some of its possible benefits, see Paul J. Quirk, "Policy Making in the Contemporary Congress: Three Dimensions of Performance," in *The New Politics of Public Policy*, ed. Marc K. Landy and Martin A. Levin (Baltimore: Johns Hopkins University Press, 1995), pp. 228–245.

31. Jeffrey M. Berry, *The Interest Group Society*, 3d ed. (New York: Longman, 1997), p. 187.

32. John P. Heinz, Edward O. Laumann, Robert L. Nelson, and Robert H. Salisbury, *The Hollow Core* (Cambridge, Mass.: Harvard University Press, 1993).

33. For a brief overview of the evolution of AT&T and government regulation, see Robert W. Crandell, *After the Breakup* (Washington, D.C.: Brookings Institution, 1991), pp. 16–42.

34. This account is based on Steven Coll, *The Deal of the Century* (New York: Atheneum, 1986); and Peter Temin with Louis Galambos, *The Fall of the Bell System* (New York: Cambridge University Press, 1987).

35. See Martha Derthick and Paul J. Quirk, *The Politics of Deregulation* (Washington, D.C.: Brookings Institution, 1985); and Robert Britt Horowitz, *The Irony of Regulatory Reform* (New York: Oxford University Press, 1989).

36. Allan R. Meyerson, "A Corporate Man and a Cable King," *New York Times*, 14 October 1993, p. B6.

37. Edmund L. Andrews, "Congress Votes To Reshape Communications Industry, Ending a 4-Year Struggle," *New York Times*, 2 February 1996, p. A1.

38. Jeffrey M. Berry, "The Dynamic Qualities of Issue Networks," paper delivered at the annual meeting of the American Political Science Association, New York, September 1994.

39. For an alternative perspective, see James A. Thurber, "Dynamics of Policy Subsystems in American Politics," in *Interest Group Politics*, 3d ed., eds. Allan J. Cigler and Burdett A. Loomis (Washington, D.C.: Congressional Quarterly Press, 1991), pp. 319–343.

40. Heinz, Laumann, Nelson, and Salisbury, *The Hollow Core*.

41. Hugh Heclo, "Issue Networks and the Executive Establishment," in *The New American Political System*, ed. Anthony King (Washington, D.C.: American Enterprise Institute, 1978), p. 105.

42. John M. Blair, *The Control of Oil* (New York: Pantheon, 1976), pp. 354–370.

43. Robert H. Salisbury and Paul Johnson, "Who You Know Versus What You Know," *American Journal of Political Science* 33 (February 1989), pp. 175–195.

44. Ben Wildavsky, "Wolff at the Door," *National Journal*, 5 August 1995, pp. 1994–1997.

45. Carl Brauer, "Tenure, Turnover, and Postgovernment Employment Trends of Presidential Appointees," in *The In-and-Outers*, ed. G. Calvin MacKenzie (Baltimore: Johns Hopkins University Press, 1993), p. 62.

46. "Clinton Announces New Ethics Standards," *Congressional Quarterly Almanac, 1992* (Washington, D.C.: Congressional Quarterly Press, 1993), p. 62.

47. "Many Will Escape Ethics Restriction," *New York Times*, 9 December 1993, p. A1.

48. Douglas Jehl, "Lobbying Rules for Ex-Officials at Issue Again," *New York Times*, 8 December 1993, p. A1.

49. Jeffrey M. Berry, "Subgovernments, Issue Networks, and Political Conflict," in *Remaking American Politics*, ed. Richard A. Harris and Sidney M. Milkis (Boulder, Colo.: Westview Press, 1989), pp. 239–260.

Chapter 18 / Economic Policy / pp. 606–639

1. Robert D. Hershey, Jr., "U.S. Jobless Rate for June at 5.3%; Lowest in 6 Years," *New York Times*, 6 July 1996, p. 1.

2. *Ibid.*, p. 30.

3. Louis Uchitelle, "Hourly Wage Jumps for 2nd Straight Month," *New York Times*, 6 July 1996, p. 17.

4. Hershey, p. 1.

5. Suzanne Woolley, "Thirteen Days That Shook the Market, *Business Week*, 29 July 1996, p. 28.

6. Jack Egan, "A Wild and Wounded Bull," *U.S. News & World Report*, 29 July 1996, p. 54.

7. James C. Cooper and Kathleen Madigan, "Wages: Why the Fed Has Its Pistol Cocked," *Business Week*, 22 July 1996, pp. 31–32.

8. Lawrence Malkin, "In Financial Markets, All Eyes Are on the Fed," *International Herald Tribune*, 17 May 1994, pp. 1 and 4.

9. David Wessel, "Common Interest: The President and Fed Appear to Be in Step on Latest Rate Rise," *Wall Street Journal*, 7 February 1994, p. A1. See also Lawrence Malkin, "Markets Satisfied as U.S. Rates Rise," *International Herald Tribune*, 18 May 1994, pp. 1 and 6, and "Fed Chief Tries to Ease Fears in Senate on Rates," *International Herald Tribune*, 28–29 May 1994, p. 11.

10. James C. Cooper and Kathleen Madigan, "Will Greenspan See Inflation Clouds Gathering?" *Business Week*, 5 August 1996, p. 21.

11. N. Gregory Mankiw, "Symposium on Keynesian Economics Today," *Journal of Economic Perspectives*, 7 (Winter 1993), pp. 3–4. In his preface to four articles in the symposium, Mankiw says, "The literature that bears the label 'Keynesian' is broad, and it does not offer a single vision of how the economy behaves."

12. Louis Uchitelle, "Federal Reserve Trims Loan Costs to Spur Economy," *New York Times*, 1 May 1991, p. A1.

13. Wessel, "Common Interest," p. A5. See also David E. Rosenbaum, "Clinton Economic Team: An Island in a Sea of Troubles," *International Herald Tribune*, 28–29 May 1994, pp. 1 and 4.

14. Sylvia Nasar, "Economy's Happy Landing: No-Inflation Growth," *New York Times*, 27 January 1994, pp. A1 and C5.

15. Floyd Norris, "The Case of the Misbehaving Yield Curve," *International Herald Tribune*, 25 April 1994, p. 11.

16. Peter Passell, "Dollar Off, Growth Up—Go Figure: Inflation Is Unlikely," *International Herald Tribune*, 14–15 May 1994, p. 11. See also Peter Passell, "Why Economic Forecasting Became a Sideshow," *New York Times*, 1 February 1996, p. C1.

17. Jonathan Rauch, Lawrence J. Haas, and Bruce Stokes, "Payment Deferred," *National Journal*, 14 May 1988, p. 1256.

18. Gerald F. Seib and Jackie Calmes, "Dole Launches His Economic Proposal," *Wall Street Journal*, 6 August 1996, p. A2.

19. John R. Wilke and Christina Duff, "Experts Wonder if Dole's Math Adds Up," *Wall Street Journal*, 6 August 1996, pp. A2 and A16. See also "Smart Move or 'Hogwash'? Debating Dole's Plan," *Wall Street Journal*, 6 August 1996, pp. B1 and B12.

20. Rosenbaum, "Clinton Economic Team," p. 4.

21. For a concise discussion of the 1990 budget reforms, see James A. Thurber, "Congressional-Presidential Battles to Balance the Budget," in James A. Thurber (ed.), *Rivals for Power: Presidential-Congressional Relations* (Washington, D.C.: Congressional Quarterly Press, 1996), pp. 196–202.

22. *Ibid.*, p. 200.

23. *Congressional Record*, 16 March 1993, p. H1238. The quotation was obtained from the House of Representatives' Web site at <rs9.loc.gov/home/thomas.html>.

24. Sondra J. Nixon, "Budget Amendments: An Idea That Never Goes Out of Style," *Congressional Quarterly Weekly Report*, 14 January 1995, pp. 142–143.

25. Andrew Taylor, "Congress Hands President a Budgetary Scalpel," *Congressional Quarterly Weekly Report*, 30 March 1996, p. 864.

26. Christopher Georges, "Senate Approves, 69–31, Line-Item Veto Aimed at Curbing Government Spending," *Wall Street Journal*, 28 March 1996, p. A3.

27. Richard A. Musgrave and Peggy B. Musgrave, *Public Finance in Theory and Practice*, 2d ed. (New York: McGraw-Hill, 1976), p. 42.

28. Kevin Phillips, *The Politics of Rich and Poor: Wealth and the American Electorate in the Reagan Aftermath* (New York: Random House, 1990), p. 78.

29. Albert R. Hunt, "The Flat-Tax Snow Job," *Wall Street Journal*, 11 January 1996, p. A15; Gerald F. Seib, "Forbes Forces a Real Debate of GOP Priorities," *Wall Street Journal*, 7 February 1996, p. A16; and Herbert Stein, "We Can't Afford Voodoo 2," *New York Times*, 7 February 1996, p. A15. But also see this editorial: "An 'Untested' Flat Tax?" *Wall Street Journal*, 9 February 1996, p. A12.

30. Michael L. Roberts, Peggy A. Hite, and Cassie F. Bradley, "Understanding Attitudes Toward Progressive Taxation," *Public Opinion Quarterly*, 58 (Summer 1994), pp. 167–168. See also David W. Moore and Frank Newport, "Public Lukewarm on Flat Tax," *The Gallup Poll Monthly*, January 1996, pp. 18–20.

31. John Harwood and Jackie Calmes, "Dole's Economic Plan Calls for a 15% Cut in Personal Income Tax," *Wall Street Journal*, 5 August 1996, p. A1; and David E. Rosenbaum, "A Passion for Ideas: Jack French Kemp," *New York Times*, 11 August 1996, pp. 1 and 13.

32. Advisory Commission on Intergovernmental Relations, *Significant Features of Fiscal Federalism, 1981–1982* (Washington, D.C., 1983), p. 54; and David E. Rosenbaum, "A New Heave in Tax Tug-of-War," *New York Times*, 8 December 1992, p. C1.

33. Lawrence Mishel and David M. Frankel, *The State of Working America*, 1990–91 ed. (Washington, D.C.: Economic Policy Institute, 1990), p. 62. In 1994, however, many states enacted tax reductions, both to improve their tax climate to attract business and in reaction to the improving national economy. See Tom Redburn, "Many States Moving to Ease Property Tax Burdens," *New York Times*, 17 March 1994, p. A9.

34. Donna Cassata, "GOP Scores Partial Success in Effort to Cut Spending," *Congressional Quarterly Weekly Report*, 9 December 1995, p. 3727.

35. Mark T. Kehoe, "Clinton Veto Tally: Up to 11," *Congressional Quarterly Weekly Report*, 6 January 1996, p. 10.

36. George Hager, "Congress, Clinton Yield Enough to Close the Book on Fiscal '96," *Congressional Quarterly Weekly Report*, 27 April 1996, p. 1155.

37. Amounts reported in Congressional *Quarterly Weekly Report*, 27 April 1996, pp. 1159, 1160, and 1162.

38. Elizabeth Kolbert, "Public Opinion Polls Swerve with the Turns of a Phrase," *New York Times*, 5 June 1995, p. 1; and Adam Clymer, "Of Touching Third Rails and Tackling Medicare," *New York Times*, 27 October 1995, p. A11.

39. Times-Mirror Center for the People & the Press, "Voter Anxiety Dividing GOP: Energized Democrats Backing Clinton," press release of 14 November 1995, p. 88.

40. Supporting data for these comments came from various survey questions retrieved through the Dialog File 468 (POLL) from the Roper Center for Public Opinion Research. The surveys included Yankelovich Partners' polls of 25–26 January 1995, 8–9 May 1996, and 10–11 July 1996 for CNN and CBS News/*New York Times* polls of 15–17 February 1994, 6–9 December 1994, and 3–4 August 1996.

41. Fay Lomax Cook et al., *Convergent Perspectives on Social Welfare Policy: The Views from the General Public, Members of Congress, and AFDC Recipients* (Evanston, Ill.: Center for Urban Affairs and Policy Research, Northwestern University, 1988), Table 4-1.

42. B. Guy Peters, *The Politics of Taxation: A Comparative Perspective* (Cambridge, Mass.: Basil Blackwell, 1991), p. 228.

43. David S. Cloud, "Farm Bloc on the Defensive as Bills Move to Floor," *Congressional Quarterly Weekly Report*, 14 July 1990, pp. 2209–2212.

44. Joseph A. Pechman, *Who Paid the Taxes, 1966–1985?* (Washington, D.C.: Brookings Institution, 1985).

45. Mishel and Frankel, *State of Working America*, pp. 178–179. The proportion of people living below the poverty line is also less if one uses the consumption of commodities as the measure of well-being instead of before-tax income. See Daniel T. Slesnick, "Gaining Ground: Poverty in the Postwar United States," *Journal of Political Economy* 101 (1993), pp. 1–38.

46. But the rich received only 1 percent of their income in transfer payments, suffering a net loss from government. See Pechman, *Who Paid the Taxes?* p. 53. Families in the top 1 percent of income actually had their effective national tax rate drop from 31.7 percent in 1980 to 24.9 percent in 1985, before they were raised to 28.8 percent in 1992 after the 1990 tax increase. See Sylvia Nasar, "One Group Saw Relief: Richest 1%," *New York Times*, 1 October 1992, p. C2.

47. Pechman, *Who Paid the Taxes?* p. 80.

48. *Ibid.*, p. 73.

49. *Ibid.*, p. 74. See also Steven A. Holmes, "Income Disparity between Poorest and Richest Rises," *New York Times*, 20 June 1996, p. 1.

50. Mishel and Frankel, *State of Working America*, pp. 37–39. See also Gary Burtless, ed., *A Future of Lousy Jobs? The Changing Structure of U.S. Wages* (Washington, D.C.: Brookings Institution, 1990), for discussions of the rise in women's earnings and the decline in lower-scale men's earnings. Other researchers have found that women's earnings have also accounted for increases in "the rich." See Sheldon Danziger, Peter Gottschalk, and Eugene Smolensky, "How the Rich Have Fared, 1973–87," *American Economic Association, Papers and Proceedings* 79 (May 1989), pp. 310–314.

51. Phillips, *The Politics of Rich and Poor*, p. 11. The share of after-tax income going to the superrich rose greatly in the 1980s but stalled in the early 1990s. Those whose incomes were in the top 1 percent ($438,000 in 1996) received 7.3 percent of total after-tax income in 1977 but a startling 12.4 percent in 1989. By 1992, their share of the national income had virtually stabilized to 12.1 percent. See Christina Duff, "Superrich's Share of After-Tax Income Stopped Rising in Early '90s, Data Show," *Wall Street Journal*, 22 November 1995, p. A2.

52. Sylvia Nasar, "After Tax Changes of 80's, Burden Is No Lighter," *New York Times*, 1 October 1992, p. C1. See also R. C. Longworth, "Job Fears Haunt Growing Economy," *Chicago Tribune*, 2 January 1994, pp. A1, A10.

53. Keith Bradsher, "Widest Gap in Incomes? Research Points to U.S.," *New York Times*, 27 October 1995, p. C2.

54. Keith Bradsher, "Gap in Wealth in U.S. Called Widest in West," *New York Times*, 17 April 1995, p. 1; Keith Bradsher, "Rich Control More of U.S. Wealth, Study Says, as Debts Grow for Poor," *New York Times*, 22 June 1996, p. 17.

55. "Nation Top-Heavy with Wealth," *Chicago Tribune*, 19 July 1986, p. A1; and U.S. Bureau of the Census, U.S. Department of Commerce, *Statistical Abstract of the United States, 1993* (Washington, D.C.: U.S. Government Printing Office, 1993), p. 462. See also Bureau of the Census, "Household Wealth and Asset Ownership: 1988," *Current Population Reports*, Series P–70, No. 22, December 1990.

56. Benjamin I. Page, *Who Gets What from Government?* (Berkeley: University of California Press, 1983), p. 213.

57. Peters, *The Politics of Taxation*, p. 168, reporting data from a 1987 survey.

58. *Public Opinion* 8 (February-March 1985), p. 27.

59. James Sterngold, "Muting the Lotteries' Perfect Pitch," *New York Times*, national edition, 14 July 1996, Section 4, p. 1.

60. "Taxes: What's Fair?" *Public Perspective*, 7 (April-May 1996), pp. 40–41. Similar findings were found in experiments involving undergraduate students in advanced tax classes at two public universities; see Roberts, Hite, and Bradley, "Understanding Attitudes Toward Progressive Taxation."

61. Rachel Wildavsky, "How Fair Are Our Taxes?" *Wall Street Journal*, 10 January 1996, p. A10.

62. Associated Press, "Well-to-Do Paid 16% More in Taxes in '93, Study Says," *New York Times*, 17 April 1995, p. C4.

Chapter 19 / Domestic Policy / pp. 640–669

1. Richard Weissbourd, *The Vulnerable Child: What Really Hurts America's Children and What We Can Do About It* (Reading, Mass.: Addison Wesley Longman, 1996), pp. 3–6, 125–128.

2. Karl Zinsmeister, "Growing Up Scared," *Atlantic Monthly*, June 1990, p. 49.

3. U.S. Social Security Administration, *Social Security Bulletin, Annual Statistical Supplement*, 1993, Table 3.A.1, p. 128; *Budget of the United States Government, FY 1995*, Historical Table 3.1, p. 42.

4. "The People, Press & Economics," in *A Times Mirror Multi-National Study of Attitudes Toward U.S. Economic Issues* (The Gallup Organization, May 1989).

5. Thomas J. Anton, *American Federalism and Public Policy* (Philadelphia: Temple University Press, 1989).

6. Linda L. M. Bennett and Stephen Earl Bennett, *Living with Leviathan: Americans Coming to Terms with Big Government* (Lawrence: University Press of Kansas, 1990), pp. 21–24.

7. *Shapiro* v. *Thompson*, 394 U.S. 618 (1969).

8. George Gallup, Jr., *The Gallup Poll, Public Opinion 1989* (Wilmington, Del.: Scholarly Resources, 1990), pp. 183–185.

9. I. A. Lewis and William Schneider, "Hard Times: The Public on Poverty," *Public Opinion* 8 (June-July 1985), p. 2.

10. U.S. Bureau of the Census, U.S. Department of Commerce, *Current Population Reports: Money Income and Poverty Status in the United States, 1989*, Series P–60, No. 168, pp. 5–7 (1990); Bureau of the Census, Poverty in the United States, 1992 Series P–60, No. 185, p. xvii (1993).

11. Bennett and Bennett, *Living with Leviathan*, p. 142.

12. D. Lee Bawden and John L. Palmer, "Social Policy: Challenging the Welfare State," in *The Reagan Record: An Assessment of America's Changing Domestic Priorities*, ed. John L. Palmer and Isabel V. Sawhill (Cambridge, Mass.: Ballinger, 1984), pp. 177–215.

13. Paul C. Light, *Artful Work: The Politics of Social Security Reform* (New York: Random House, 1985), p. 63.

14. *Social Security Bulletin, Annual Statistical Supplement*, 1995, p. 14.

15. Martha Derthick, *Policymaking for Social Security* (Washington, D.C.: Brookings Institution, 1979), pp. 346–347.

16. Julie Kosterlitz, "Who Will Pay?" *National Journal*, 8 March 1985, pp. 570–574.
17. U.S. Bureau of the Census, U.S. Department of Commerce, *Statistical Abstract of the United States, 1995* (Washington, D.C.: U.S. Government Printing Office, 1995), p. 289.
18. Derthick, *Policymaking*, p. 335.
19. Paul Starr, *The Social Transformation of American Medicine* (New York: Basic Books, 1982), pp. 279–280.
20. *Ibid.*, p 287.
21. Theodore Marmor, *The Politics of Medicare* (Chicago: Aldine, 1973).
22. *Social Security Bulletin*, p. 16.
23. *Ibid.*
24. *Ibid.*, Table 2.C.1, p. 87.
25. Lawrence J. Haas, "Big-Ticket Restrictions," *National Journal*, 26 September 1987, p. 2413.
26. Bob Blendon, "The Gridlock Is Us," *New York Times*, 12 June 1994, Sect. 4, p. 3.
27. U.S. Bureau of the Census, U.S. Department of Commerce, *Income, Poverty, and Valuation of Noncash Income Benefits: 1993*, Series P-60, No. 188, Table C.
28. *Social Security Bulletin*, Table 3.E.8, p. 167.
29. *Social Security Bulletin, Annual Statistical Supplement, 1994*, Table 9.H.1, p. 360.
30. *Statistical Abstract of the United States, 1995*, p. 480.
31. William Julius Wilson, *The Truly Disadvantaged: The Inner City, the Underclass, and Public Policy* (Chicago: University of Chicago Press, 1987).
32. Robert Pear, "The Welfare Bill: The Overview," *New York Times*, 1 August 1996, p. Al; Jason DeParle, "Get a Job: The New Contract with America's Poor," *New York Times*, 28 July 1996, p. E1.
33. Francis X. Clines, "Clinton Signs Bill Cutting Welfare," *New York Times*, 23 August 1996, p. A1.
34. Robert Pear, "Overhauling Welfare: A Look at the Year Ahead," *New York Times*, 7 August 1996, p. A7.
35. *Ibid.*
36. George J. Church, "Ripping Up Welfare," *Time*, 12 August 1996, p. 21.
37. Peter T. Kilborn, "With Welfare Overhaul Now Law, States Grapple with the Consequences," *New York Times*, 23 August 1996, p. A10.
38. *Ibid.*
39. William Julius Wilson, "Work," *New York Times Magazine*, 18 August 1996, pp. 28–29.
40. Robert Pear, "Senate Approves Sweeping Change in Welfare Policy," *New York Times*, 24 July 1996, p. A1.
41. Christopher Ogden, "Bye-Bye, American Pie," *Time*, 12 August 1996, p. 17.
42. Lewis and Schneider, "Hard Times," pp. 3–7.
43. Gallup, *Gallup Poll*, pp. 183–185 (1990).

**Chapter 20 / Global Policy /
pp. 670–711**

1. Birger Heldt et al., eds., *Stockholm International Peace Research Institute (SIPRI) Yearbook 1992* (New York: Oxford University Press, 1992), pp. 424–456.
2. Stephen John Stedman, "The New Interventionists," *Foreign Affairs America and the World*, 72 (February 1993), p. 7.
3. Alexis de Tocqueville, *Democracy in America* (Oxford: Oxford University Press, 1946), p. 161.
4. "X" [George F. Kennan], "The Sources of Soviet Conduct," *Foreign Affairs* 25 (July 1947), 575.
5. Quoted in Arthur M. Schlesinger, Jr., *A Thousand Days* (Boston: Houghton Mifflin, 1965), pp. 704–705.
6. Richard M. Nixon, *U.S. Foreign Policy for the 1970s: A New Strategy for Peace* (Washington, D.C.: U.S. Government Printing Office, 1970), p. 2.
7. Jimmy Carter, "State of the Union," January 23, 1980, *Public Papers of the Presidents of the United States* (Washington, D.C.: U.S. Government Printing Office, 1981), p. 197.
8. Thomas Halverson, *The Last Great Nuclear Debate: NATO and Short-Range Nuclear Weapons in the 1980s* (New York: St. Martin's Press, 1995).
9. See, for example, Francis Fukuyama, *The End of History and the Last Man* (New York: Free Press, 1992).
10. Daniel Deudney and G. John Ikenberry, "Who Won the Cold War?" *Foreign Policy* 87 (Summer 1992), 128–138.
11. See, for example, Paul Kennedy, *Preparing for the Twenty-First Century* (New York: Random House, 1993), especially Chap. 13.
12. Thomas Omestad, "Why Bush Lost," *Foreign Policy* 89 (Winter 1992/93), 70–81.
13. Richard H. Ullman, "A Late Recovery," *Foreign Policy* 101 (Winter 1996), 76–79; James M. McCormick, "Assessing Clinton's Foreign Policy at Midterm," *Current History* (November 1995), 370–374; Michael Mandelbaum, "Foreign Policy as Social Work," *Foreign Affairs* (January-February 1996), 16–32.
14. Carroll J. Doherty, "Defining the National Interest: A Process of Trial and Error," *Congressional Quarterly*, 26 March 1994, pp. 750–754.
15. *Ibid.*, p. 754.
16. Quoted in Eric Schmitt, "Somalia Role: Why? U.S. Seeks Clear Rationale for Mission," *New York Times*, 27 August 1993, p. A10.
17. James Kitfield, "Fit to Fight?" *National Journal*, 16 March 1996, pp. 582–586.
18. Michael Mastanduno, "Trade Policy," in Robert J. Art and Seyom Brown, eds., *U.S. Foreign Policy: The Search for a New Role* (New York: Macmillan, 1993), p. 142.
19. Daniel S. Papp, *Contemporary International Relations*, 4th ed. (New York: Macmillan, 1994), p. 420.
20. Joan Spero, "Promoting U.S. Economic Interests and the FY97 International Affairs Budget Request," prepared statement before the House Appropriations Committee's Subcommittee on Commerce, Judiciary, 8 May 1996 (available at <www.state.gov/www/about_state/may96_economic_interests.html>.
21. "Hills, in Japan, Stirs a Baby-Bottle Dispute," *New York Times*, 14 October 1989, p. 35.
22. Kirk Victor, "Dirty Dealing," *National Journal*, 20 April 1996, p. 870.
23. See commentary by A. M. Rosenthal in *New York Times*, 31 March 1989, p. 35; also see Kevin Kearns,

"Economic Orthodoxies Offered U.S. Students Won't Prepare Them to Work in World Markets," *The Chronicle of Higher Education* 27 (March 1991), B3.

24. Katie Hafner, "Does Industrial Policy Work? Lessons from Sematech," *New York Times*, 7 November 1993, p. F5.

25. Robert Reich, *The Work of Nations* (New York: Alfred A. Knopf, 1991).

26. John Stremlau, "Clinton's Dollar Diplomacy," *Foreign Policy*, 97 (Winter 1995), pp. 18–35.

27. Douglas Jehl, "No Wish to Jeopardize Billions in Trade and Many Jobs in U.S.," *New York Times*, 27 May 1994, p. A1.

28. Papp, *Contemporary International Relations*, p. 194.

29. Steven Erlanger, "For U.S. Russia-Watchers, Bipartisan Fear over Future," *New York Times*, 17 June 1996, p. A7.

30. Steven Kull, "What the Public Knows That Washington Doesn't," *Foreign Policy* 101 (Winter 1995–96), pp. 102–115.

31. Papp, *Contemporary International Relations*, pp. 557–558.

32. *U.S.* v. *Curtiss—Wright Export Corporation*, 299 U.S. 304 (1936); *U.S.* v. *Belmont*, 301 U.S. 324 (1937).

33. Mary H. Cooper, "Treaty Ratification,"*Editorial Research Reports*, 29 January 1988; Committee on Foreign Relations, United States Senate, *Treaties and Other International Agreements: The Role of the United States Senate* (Washington, D.C.: U.S. Government Printing Office, 1993).

34. C. Herman Pritchett, "The President's Constitutional Position," in Rexford Tugwell and Thomas Cronin, eds. *Presidency Reappraised* (New York: Praeger, 1977), p. 23.

35. James Nathan and James Oliver, *Foreign Policy Making* (Boston: Little, Brown, 1983), p. 125.

36. "Duels over Dollars Shuffle," *Congressional Quarterly Weekly Report* (February 1990), p. 606.

37. These critics included both conservative Republican senator Barry Goldwater of Arizona and liberal Democratic senator Thomas Eagleton of Missouri. The latter's feelings were succinctly summa-

rized in the title of his book *War and Presidential Power: A Chronicle of Congressional Surrender* (New York: Liveright, 1974).

38. Duncan Clarke, "Why State Can't Lead," *Foreign Policy* 66 (Spring 1987), pp. 128–142.

39. Harry Crosby (pseudonym), "Too At Home Abroad: Swilling Beer, Licking Boots and Ignoring the Natives with One of Jim Baker's Finest," *The Washington Monthly* (September 1991), pp. 16–20.

40. James A. Nathan and James K. Oliver, *Foreign Policy Making and the American Political System*, 2d ed. (Boston: Little, Brown, 1987), p. 44.

41. Quoted in Schlesinger, *A Thousand Days*, p. 406.

42. Quoted in Rodney D. Griffin,"The New CIA," *CQ Researcher*, 11 December 1992, p. 1084.

43. Richard K. Betts, "Analysis, War and Decision Making: Why Intelligence Failures Are Inevitable," *World Politics* (October 1978), p. 61.

44. Loch K. Johnson, "Now that the Cold War Is Over, Do We Need the CIA?" in Charles Kegley and Eugene Wittkopf, eds., *The Future of American Foreign Policy* (New York: St. Martin's Press, 1992), p. 306.

45. *State Administrative Officials Classified by Function, 1991–1992* (Lexington, Ky.: Council of State Governments), pp. 160–161.

46. Quoted in Robert Y. Shapiro and Benjamin I. Page, "Foreign Policy and Public Opinion," in David Deese, ed., *The New Politics of American Foreign Policy* (New York: St. Martin's Press, 1993), p. 216.

47. Thomas W. Graham, "Public Opinion and U.S. Foreign Policy Decision Making," in Deese, *The New Politics of American Foreign Policy*, pp. 190–191.

48. William Schneider, "Peace and Strength: American Public Opinion on National Security," in Gregory Flynn and Hans Rattinger, eds., *The Public and Atlantic Defense* (Totowa, N.J.: Rowman and Allanheld, 1985). Ole Holsti and James Rosenau identify similar phenomena, but use alternate terminology, in "The Structure of Foreign Policy Attitudes Among American

Leaders," *Journal of Politics* 52 (February 1990), pp. 94–125, as well as in their earlier book, *American Leadership in World Affairs: Vietnam and the Breakdown of Consensus* (Boston: Allen and Unwin, 1984).

49. Graham, "Public Opinion and U.S. Foreign Policy Decision Making," p. 192.

50. *Ibid.*, p. 194; William Gamson and Andre Modigliani, "Knowledge and Foreign Policy Options: Some Models for Consideration," *Public Opinion Quarterly*, 30 (Summer 1966), 187–199; William Gamson and Andre Modigliani, *Untangling the Cold War* (Boston: Little, Brown, 1971).

51. Shapiro and Page, "Foreign Policy and Public Opinion," p. 222.

52. *Ibid.*, pp. 223–229.

53. John E. Rielly, "Public Opinion: The Pulse of the '90s," *Foreign Policy* 82 (Spring 1991), pp. 79–96.

54. John L. Aldrich, John L. Sullivan, and Eugene Borgida, "Foreign Affairs and Issue Voting: Do Presidential Candidates Waltz Before a Blind Audience?" *American Political Science Review* 83 (March 1989), pp. 123–141.

55. *Ibid.*, p. 136.

56. Graham, "Public Opinion and U.S. Foreign Policy Decision Making," p. 199.

57. *Ibid.*, p. 196.

58. *Ibid.*, p. 196.

59. George Stuteville, "By Aiding Sikhs, Burton Builds Coffers, 2nd Constituency and Political Scorn," *Indianapolis Star*, 14 November 1993, p. 1.

60. "From the K-Street Corridor," *National Journal*, 9 March 1996, p. 540.

61. Charles Kegley and Eugene Wittkopf, *American Foreign Policy: Pattern and Process*, 4th ed. (New York: St. Martin's Press, 1991), pp. 272–273; Lester Milbrath, "Interest Groups and Foreign Policy," in James Rosenau, ed., *Domestic Sources of Foreign Policy* (New York: Free Press, 1967), pp. 231–252.

62. Kegley and Wittkopf, *American Foreign Policy*, p. 276.

63. *Ibid.*, p. 310.

64. Robert F. Hahn, "The Congressional Defense Department: Competitive Strategy Making in the Post–Cold

War World," *Air Power Journal* (Special Edition 1995), pp. 62–76. Available on-line at <www.cdsar.af. mil/se95.html>.

65. Donald Snow and Eugene Brown, *Puzzle Palace and Foggy Bottom: U.S. Foreign and Defense Policy Making in the 1990s* (New York: St. Martin's Press, 1994), p. 170.

Index of References

Credits

Index